State Electoral Votes in 2008

The map of the United States shown here is distorted to show the relative weight of the states in terms of the electoral votes in 2000, following the changes required by the 2000 census. A candidate must win 270 electoral votes to be elected president.

2

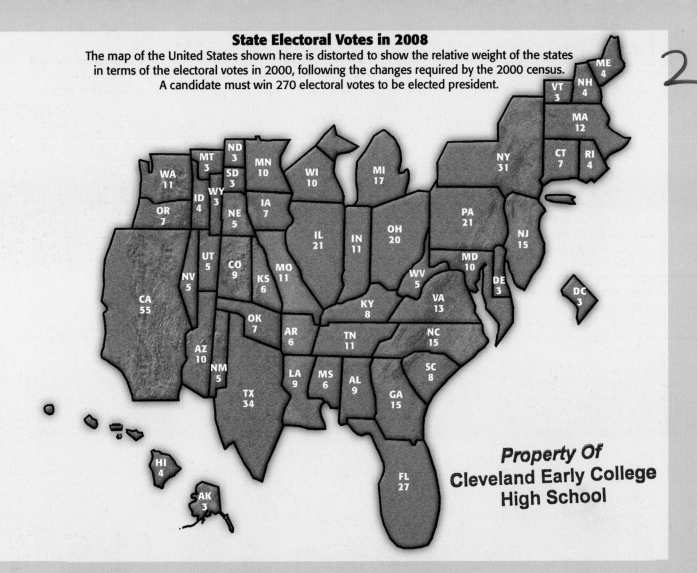

Property Of
Cleveland Early College
High School

2008 Presidential Election Results

Barack ~~~~ ~~~~~~ electoral votes

John McCain won 173 electoral votes

D1402525

American Government and Politics Today

THE ESSENTIALS
2009–2010 Edition

Barbara A. Bardes
University of Cincinnati

Mack C. Shelley II
Iowa State University

Steffen W. Schmidt
Iowa State University

WADSWORTH
CENGAGE Learning™

Australia • Brazil • Japan • Korea • Mexico • Singapore • Spain • United Kingdom • United States

WADSWORTH
CENGAGE Learning™

American Government and Politics Today
THE ESSENTIALS 2009–2010 Edition
Bardes • Shelley • Schmidt

Publisher: Suzanne Jeans

Executive Editor: Carolyn Merrill

Developmental Editor: Suzy Spivey

Assistant Editor: Katherine Hayes

Editorial Assistant: Nathan Gamache

Associate Development Project Manager: Caitlin Holroyd

Senior Marketing Manager: Amy Whitaker

Marketing Communications Manager: Heather Baxley

Senior Content Production Manager: Ann Borman

Print Buyer: Judy Inouye

Photo Research: Ann Hoffman, Anne Sheroff

Copy Editor: Mary Berry

Proofreader: Judy Kiviat

Indexer: Deborah Patton

Art Director: Linda Helcher

Interior Design: IRDG

Cover Design: Rokusek Design

Compositor: Parkwood Composition Service

For product information and technology assistance, contact us at **Cengage Learning Academic Resource Center, 1-800-423-0563**. For permission to use material from this text or product, submit all requests online at **www.cengage.com/permissions**. Further permissions questions can be emailed to **permissionrequest@cengage.com**.

Library of Congress Control Number: 2005933014

Student Edition ISBN-13: 978-0-495-57170-4
Student Edition ISBN-10: 0-495-57170-9

Instructor's Edition ISBN-13: 978-0-495-57237-4
Instructor's Edition ISBN-10: 0-495-57237-3

Wadsworth Political Science
25 Thomson Place
Boston, MA 02210

Cengage Learning products are represented in Canada by Nelson Education, Ltd.

For your course and learning solutions, visit **academic.cengage.com**. Purchase any of our products at your local college store or at our preferred online store at **www.ichapters.com**.

Printed in the United States of America

3 4 5 6 7 11 10

ContentsinBrief

Contents

(AP Photo/Chuck Burton)

v

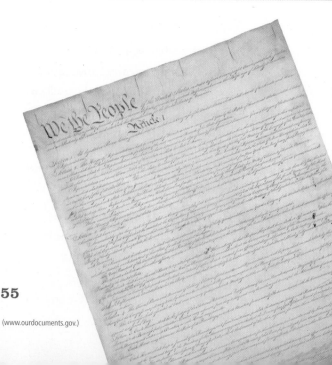

(www.ourdocuments.gov.)

Chapter 3 Features

(Richard Cummins/Corbis)

(AP Photo/Carlos Osorio)

CHAPTER 5: Civil Rights 146

(AP Photo/Greg Smith)

Chapter 5 Features

(Realistic Reflections, Getty)

Part III: People and Politics

CHAPTER 6: Public Opinion and Political Socialization 190

Chapter 6 Features

Chapter 7 Features

(AP Photo/Jose Luis Magana)

CHAPTER 8: Political Parties 250

Chapter 8 Features

(© Corbis. All Rights Reserved.)

CHAPTER 9: Campaigns, Elections, and the Media 286

(AP Photo/Matt Sayles)

(Photo by Joe Raedle/Getty Images)

Part IV: Political Institutions

CHAPTER 10: The Congress 338

Chapter 10 Features

Discussion and Analysis • Key Terms •
Chapter Summary • Selected Print and Media Resources

(NICHOLAS KAMM/AFP/Getty Images)

CHAPTER 11: The President 374

Chapter 11 Features

Discussion and Analysis • Key Terms •
Chapter Summary • Selected Print and Media Resources

(AP Photo/Chris Carlson)

CHAPTER 12:
The Bureaucracy 408

Chapter 12 Features

Politics and . . .
The Cyber Sphere
Moving Government Online 412

Politics and . . .
The Bureaucracy
Big Government Just Keeps Getting
Bigger 416

Which Side Are You On?
Is Too Much Government Work Being
Contracted Out? 428

Beyond Our Borders
India, the Land of Bureaucratic
Paperwork, Goes Online (at Least in
One State) 430

Why Should You Care about
The Bureaucracy? 436

E-mocracy
The Presidency and the Internet 439

(Jeff Kubina/Creative Commons)

(AP Photo/Jennifer Graylock)

(Mark Wilson/Getty Images)

CHAPTER 15: Foreign Policy 514

Chapter 15 Features

The Major Foreign Policy Themes 540

Discussion and Analysis • Key Terms • Chapter Summary • Selected Print and Media Resources

(AP Photo/Rahmatullah Naikzad)

PREFACE

As with previous editions, the 2009–2010 Edition of *American Government and Politics Today: The Essentials* contains thoroughgoing revisions to make it as up to date as possible. We have included the latest statistics, and we have made major revisions based on the most recent research and pedagogical approaches.

Many of these changes respond to the unprecedented events of the 2008 presidential campaigns. In the extraordinarily hard-fought and protracted Democratic primary elections, voters in that party were able to choose between two history-making alternatives: to nominate either the first African American or the first woman as a major-party candidate. While the Republican primary contests were not as dramatic, each of the major Republican contenders offered the party's voters something new and unusual.

In the presidential election campaigns of 2008, two senators, Democrat Barack Obama and Republican John McCain, faced a series of crucial questions. How should America manage the war in Iraq, and how soon should U.S. forces be withdrawn? How should the world respond to Iran's nuclear ambitions? At home, how should the nation deal with an economy in serious difficulties after the collapse of the housing and financial markets? What should be done in response to skyrocketing fuel prices? What about health-care reform? What steps should be taken to protect civil liberties after their erosion during the George W. Bush administration? The election of Barack Obama and increased Democratic majorities in the House and Senate ensured that the Democratic Party would take the lead in answering these questions.

2008 ELECTION RESULTS INCLUDED AND ANALYZED

Because we have learned that students respond to up-to-date information about political events, we have included results of the November 2008 elections. We have updated all of the text to reflect these results and have analyzed how the results will affect political processes at all levels of government. In addition, for the first time in the *Essentials* edition, we have inserted special *Elections 2008* features, which appear in many of the chapters.

THE INTERACTIVE FOCUS OF THIS TEXT

Whether the topic is voter participation, terrorism, or the problems that face the president, we constantly strive to involve the student in the analysis. We make sure that the student comes to understand that politics is not an abstract process but a very human enterprise. We emphasize how different outcomes can affect students' civil rights and liberties, employment opportunities, and economic welfare.

EMPHASIS ON CRITICAL THINKING

Throughout the text, we encourage the student to think critically. Almost all of the features end with questions designed to engage the student's critical-thinking and analytical skills. A feature titled *Which Side Are You On?* challenges the student to find a connection between controversial issues facing the nation and the student's personal positions on these issues.

NEW QUESTIONS FOR DISCUSSION AND ANALYSIS

New to this edition is a section titled "Questions for Discussion and Analysis," which appears at the end of each chapter. This section consists of a series of five questions, each of which asks the student to explore a particular issue relating to a topic covered in the chapter. The first of these questions always refers back to the chapter's *Which Side Are You On?* feature and asks the student to take a position on that controversy.

OTHER INTERACTIVE FEATURES

We further encourage interaction with the political system by ending each chapter with a feature titled *Why Should You Care?,* which shows students not only what they can do to become politically involved but also why they should care enough to do so. Online exercises (found on the companion Web site) for each chapter show students how to access and analyze political information.

SPECIAL PEDAGOGY AND FEATURES

The 2009–2010 Edition of *American Government and Politics Today: The Essentials* contains many pedagogical aids and high-interest features to assist both students and instructors. The following list summarizes the special elements that can be found in each chapter:

- *Politics and the Cyber Sphere*—A feature that examines the profound impact of the Internet and telecommunications in general on American politics and government.
- *What If . . .*—A chapter-opening feature that discusses a hypothetical situation concerning a topic covered in the chapter.
- *Margin Definitions*—For all important terms.
- *Did You Know . . . ?*—Margin features presenting various facts and figures that add interest to the learning process.
- *Which Side Are You On?*—A feature designed to challenge students to take a stand on controversial issues.
- *Politics and . . .*—A feature that examines the influence of politics on a variety of issues. Topics range from *Politics and Ideology,* to *Politics and Diversity,* to *Politics and the Presidency.*
- *Beyond Our Borders*—A feature that provides a context for American institutions by looking at the experiences of other countries.
- *Why Should You Care?*—A chapter-ending feature that gives the student some specific reasons why he or she should care about the topics covered in the chapter and provides ways in which she or he can become actively involved in American politics.
- *Questions for Discussion and Analysis*—A series of questions at the end of each chapter that are designed to promote in-class discussions.
- *Key Terms*—A chapter-ending list, with page numbers, of all terms in the chapter that are **boldfaced** in the text and defined in the margins.
- *Chapter Summary*—A point-by-point summary of the chapter text.
- *Selected Print and Media Resources*—An annotated list of suggested scholarly readings as well as popular books, films, and documentaries relevant to chapter topics.
- *E-mocracy*—A feature that discusses politics and the Internet and that offers Web sites and Internet activities related to the chapter's topics.

APPENDICES

Because we know that this book serves as a reference, we have included important documents for the student of American government to have close at hand. A fully annotated copy of the U.S. Constitution appears at the end of Chapter 2, as an appendix to that chapter. In addition, we have included the following appendices:

- The Declaration of Independence.
- How to Read Case Citations and Find Court Decisions.
- *Federalist Papers* Nos. 10, 51, and 78.

■ Justices of the United States Supreme Court since 1900.
■ Party Control of Congress since 1900.
■ Spanish Equivalents for Important Terms in American Government.

Useful material is also located immediately inside the front and back covers of this text. Inside the front cover, you will find a pictorial diagram of the Capitol of the United States. Inside the back cover, you will find a cartogram that distorts the size of the various states to indicate their relative weight in the Electoral College.

A COMPREHENSIVE SUPPLEMENTS PACKAGE

We are proud to be the authors of a text that has the most comprehensive, accessible, and fully integrated supplements package on the market. Together, the text and the supplements listed below constitute a total learning/teaching package for you and your students. For further information on any of these supplements, contact your Wadsworth Higher Education sales representative.

SUPPLEMENTS FOR INSTRUCTORS

■ **PowerLecture DVD with JoinIn™ for** *American Government and Politics Today: The Essentials*

- **Interactive PowerPoint® lectures**—This one-stop lecture and class preparation tool makes it easy for you to assemble, edit, publish, and present custom lectures for your course. The interactive PowerPoint lectures bring together text-specific outlines; audio and video clips from historic to current-day events (including 2008 ABC video); new animated learning modules illustrating key concepts; and tables, statistical charts and graphs, and photos from the book, as well as outside sources. In addition, you can add your own materials—culminating in a powerful, personalized, media-enhanced presentation.

- *Test Bank* **in Microsoft Word® and ExamView® computerized testing**—Instructors will find a large array of well-crafted multiple-choice and essay questions, along with their answers and page references.

- *Instructor's Manual*—This includes learning objectives; chapter outlines; discussion questions; suggestions for stimulating class activities and projects; tips on integrating media into your class, including step-by-step instructions on how to create your own podcasts; suggested readings and Web resources; and a section specially designed to help teaching assistants and adjunct instructors.

- *Resource Integration Guide*—This guide outlines the rich collection of resources available to instructors and students within the chapter-by-chapter framework of the book, suggesting how and when each supplement can be used to optimize learning.

- **JoinIn book-specific "clicker" questions**—These questions test and track student comprehension of key concepts. Political Polling questions simulate voting, engage the classroom, foster dialogue on group behaviors and values, and add personal relevance. Results can be compared with national data, leading to lively discussions. Visual Literacy questions tied to images from the book add useful pedagogical tools and high-interest feedback during your lecture. Save the data from your students' responses all semester—track their progress and show them how political science works by incorporating this exciting new tool into your classroom. ***Contact your Wadsworth representative for more information about JoinIn on TurningPoint and our exclusive infrared or radio frequency hardware solutions.***

- **The Resource Center for *American Government and Politics Today: The Essentials*—**The Resource Center for *American Government and Politics Today: The Essentials* offers a variety of rich online learning resources designed to enhance the student experience. These resources include podcasts, quizzes, sixteen new simulations, animated learning modules, Internet activities, self-assessments, videos, an Associated Press newsfeed, and links to Election 2008 information and analysis. All resources are correlated with key chapter learning concepts, and users can browse or search for content in a variety of ways. More than a collection of ancillary learning materials, however, the *American Government and Politics Today: The Essentials* Resource Center also features important content and community tools that extend the education experience, including tools for instructors to author their own content, content-sharing features, blogs (online journals) available for each registered user, and a built-in messaging center for class communications. We provide separate options for the delivery of an e-book.

- **WebTutor™—**Rich with content for your American government course, this Web-based teaching and learning tool includes course management, study/mastery, and communication tools. Use WebTutor to provide virtual office hours, post your syllabus, and track student progress with WebTutor's quizzing material. For students, WebTutor offers real-time access to interactive online tutorials and simulations, practice quizzes, and Web links—all correlated to *American Government and Politics Today: The Essentials.* Available on WebCT and Blackboard.

- **Political Theatre DVD 2.0—**This DVD offers a comprehensive, rich collection of video and audio clips drawn from key political events from the last seventy-five years: presidential speeches, campaign ads, debates, news reports, national convention coverage, demonstrations, speeches by civil rights leaders, and more. New critical-thinking questions follow each clip to help engage your students in the content.

- **JoinIn on TurningPoint for Political Theatre 2.0—**For even more interaction, combine **Political Theatre 2.0** with the innovative teaching tool of a classroom response system through JoinIn. Poll your students with questions we have created for you or create your own. Built within the Microsoft PowerPoint software, it's easy to integrate into your current lectures, in conjunction with the "clicker" hardware of your choice.

- **ABC News Videos for American Government 2010 DVD—**This collection of three- to six-minute video clips on relevant political issues serves as great lecture or discussion launchers. These clips, which have been updated to include coverage of the Democratic and Republican conventions, are available on DVD.

- **Building Democracy: Readings in American Government—**This extraordinary collection provides access to more than five hundred historical documents and scholarly readings to create the ideal supplement for any American Government course. Cengage Learning Custom Solutions' intuitive **TextChoice** Web site at **www.textchoice.com/democracy** allows you to quickly browse the collection, preview selections, arrange your table of contents, and create a custom cover that will include your own course information. Or if you prefer, your local Wadsworth representative will be happy to guide you through the process.

CONSIDER THESE AVAILABLE SUPPLEMENTS FOR STUDENTS—PACKAGED WITH THE BOOK

- *Study Guide*—This guide includes a Chapter Summary, Key Terms, and a Practice Exam for every chapter of the book.
- **Companion Web site for *American Government and Politics Today: The Essentials*—**At **www.cengage.com/politicalscience/bardes/agandptessentials15e**, students will find free and open access to Learning Objectives, Quizzes, Chapter Glossaries, Flashcards, Crossword Puzzles, and Internet activities, all correlated by chapter.
- *The Handbook of Selected Court Cases*—This handbook includes case summaries

and analyses for more than thirty United States Supreme Court cases.

■ ***The Handbook of Selected Legislation and Other Documents***—This handbook features excerpts from twelve laws passed by the U.S. Congress that have had a significant impact on American politics.

■ ***Election 2008: An American Government Supplement***—The use of real examples in this election booklet, which addresses the 2008 presidential, congressional, and gubernatorial races, makes the concepts covered in the textbook come alive for students.

FOR USERS OF THE PREVIOUS EDITION

We thank you for your past support of our work. We have made numerous changes to this volume for the 2009–2010 Edition, many of which we list below. We have rewritten the text as necessary, added many new features, and updated the book to reflect the results of the 2008 elections.

■ **Chapter 1 (The Democratic Republic)**—We devote more attention to dictatorship as an alternative to democracy, in the text as well as in two new features: *What If . . . We Elected a Dictator?* and *Beyond Our Borders: Greasing the Wheels of Autocracy.* The second of these features looks at the relationship between oil wealth and dictatorship. America's concern with big government receives a completely new—and longer—treatment. A final section discusses the paradox of declining trust in government at the very time that the government has grown stronger.

■ **Chapter 2 (The Constitution)**—Gun rights have recently been a major constitutional issue, and the feature *What If . . . Guns Were Allowed on Campus?* looks at one aspect of the controversy. Another new feature is *Politics and . . . the Constitution: Why Didn't the Founders Think a Bill of Rights Was Necessary?*

■ **Chapter 3 (Federalism)**—The statistical analysis of national and state spending has been improved and updated. While interference of the central government in the affairs of the states is an ongoing theme, two of the newly added features—*Which Side Are You On? Should We Lower the Flag for Every Fallen Soldier?* and *Politics and Immigration: State and Local Governments Take Action*—also look at how states address issues that are supposedly national.

■ **Chapter 4 (Civil Liberties)**—We have added material on intelligent design and warrantless wiretaps, and the section on student speech has been rewritten. The chapter's many new features include *Which Side Are You On? Should Muslims' Religious Needs Be Accommodated on Campus?* This discusses the footbaths that have been installed on a number of campuses. *Politics and the Cyber Sphere: Some Unintended Consequences of the Patriot Act* tells how a Patriot Act investigation forced New York governor Eliot Spitzer to resign in a prostitution scandal.

■ **Chapter 5 (Civil Rights)**—We describe recent attempts to reduce socioeconomic inequality, as opposed to racial inequality. The section on immigration has been completely rewritten and much expanded. It now discusses the demographics of immigration, America's changing racial composition, and the civil rights of immigrants (or lack thereof). Immigration reform, however, is discussed in Chapter 14. A feature titled *Politics and Diversity: The Zero-Sum Political Struggle between Latinos and African Americans* is relevant to these issues. The section on older Americans now includes up-to-date demographic data.

■ **Chapter 6 (Public Opinion and Political Socialization)**—The discussion of religion has been improved, and we have added a new section on the Hispanic vote. We have also added material on how polls can go wrong. Gambling operations that set odds on the outcome of elections are sometimes more accurate than public opinion polls, as we explain in the feature *Politics and Campaigns: Opinion Polling Faces Competi-*

tion.

- **Chapter 7 (Interest Groups)**—Alterations to this chapter reflect changes in lobbying laws and practices over the last two years. Have these new laws really accomplished anything? We look at that question in the feature *Politics and Ethics: Lobbying Rules—The More They Change, the More They Stay the Same.* We cover another recent controversy in the feature *Which Side Are You On? Should Foreign Interests Be Allowed to Lobby Congress?*

- **Chapter 8 (Political Parties)**—The story of how partisan trends have affected the two major parties is carried forward to the elections of November 2008. A *Which Side Are You On?* feature looks at the question of whether partisanship is good for America. We provide new discussions of cultural tensions within the Democratic and Republican parties. Another new feature of interest is *Politics and Terminology: What Is the Difference between a* Liberal *and a* Progressive?

- **Chapter 9 (Campaigns, Elections, and the Media)**—This chapter has been reworked extensively. Major changes to the sections on campaign financing look at current laws and practices. The section on presidential primaries and caucuses is completely new and reflects changes that have taken place since the last presidential campaign cycle, and caucuses now receive greater coverage. We have added more material on cable television news, the Web, and bias in the media. New features include *Which Side Are You On? Are Stiff Voter ID Laws a Good Thing?* and *Politics and Voting: Are Voter Choices Rational?*

- **Chapter 10 (The Congress)**—The cost of legislative earmarks, or pork barrel spending, has grown rapidly in recent years. The chapter-opening feature *(What If . . . Pork Were Banned?)* addresses this issue. Congressional resistance to the online world is described in a new *Politics and the Cyber Sphere* feature.

- **Chapter 11 (The President)**—We have added more detail about the president's war powers and the State of the Union address. We look at one way the president tries to manage the news in *Politics and the Cyber Sphere: Scrubbing the White House Web Site Squeaky Clean.* We explain how parliamentary governments differ from the American system in *Beyond Our Borders: Heads of Government Are Not Always Directly Elected.*

- **Chapter 12 (The Bureaucracy)**—The presentation of statistics on government employment has been improved. We provide more detail on the Freedom of Information Act and on whistleblowing. Two features address bringing the bureaucracy online: *Politics and the Cyber Sphere: Moving Government Online* and *Beyond Our Borders: India, the Land of Bureaucratic Paperwork, Goes Online (At Least in One State).*

- **Chapter 13 (The Courts)**—We have added detail about the common law and civil law traditions. We discuss the record of the Roberts Court, including an analysis of its decisions during the 2007–2008 term. A feature discusses a major controversy at the state level—*Politics and the States: Judicial Elections.* A new *Which Side Are You On?* feature looks at the question of whether the number of Supreme Court justices should be increased.

- **Chapter 14 (Domestic and Economic Policy)**—This chapter has also received a major facelift. We now define various types of domestic policy. The section on the policymaking process has been revised and uses a more current example. We have expanded the health-care section considerably and now discuss the issue of universal coverage in depth. The section on immigration policy has been completely rewritten and much expanded. We have added material on deficit spending and how the Fed regulates banks. Almost all of the features are new. They include *Which Side Are You On? Do We Treat Immigrants Too Harshly?* and *Politics and Taxes: Who Pays the Lion's Share of Taxes?*

- **Chapter 15 (Foreign and Defense Policy)**—Naturally, the sections dealing with Iraq have been significantly revised and brought up to date. We now discuss the surge and recent developments. The section on China has been reworked to focus more on that country's explosive economic growth and the problem of Taiwan. We have rewritten the section on modern Russia. Other changes address terrorism, the Israeli-Palestinian conflict, and nuclear proliferation. One of the many new features asks *Which Side Are You On? Is a Nuclear-Free World Possible?* Another new feature is *Beyond Our Borders: The Impact of Population Growth on America's Future Role in the World.*

ACKNOWLEDGMENTS

Since we started this project a number of years ago, a sizable cadre of individuals has helped us in various phases of the undertaking. The following academic reviewers offered numerous constructive criticisms, comments, and suggestions during the preparation of all previous editions:

Danny M. Adkison
Oklahoma State University, Stillwater

Ahrar Ahmad
Black Hills State University, South Dakota

Sharon Z. Alter
William Rainey Harper College, Illinois

Hugh M. Arnold
Clayton College and State University, Georgia

William Arp III
Louisiana State University

Kevin Bailey
North Harris Community College, Texas

Evelyn Ballard
Houston Community College, Texas

Orlando N. Bama
McLennan Community College, Texas

Dr. Charles T. Barber
University of Southern Indiana, Evansville

Clyde W. Barrow
Texas A&M University

Shari Garber Bax
Central Missouri State University, Warrensburg

Dr. Joshua G. Behr
Old Dominion University, Norfolk, Virginia

David S. Bell
Eastern Washington University, Cheney

David C. Benford, Jr.
Tarrant County Junior College, Texas

Dr. Curtis Berry
Shippensburg University, Pennsylvania

John A. Braithwaite
Coastline College, California

Lynn R. Brink
North Lake College, Irving, Texas

Barbara L. Brown
Southern Illinois University at Carbondale

Richard G. Buckner
Santa Fe Community College

Kenyon D. Bunch
Fort Lewis College, Durango, Colorado

Ralph Bunch
Portland State University, Oregon

Carol Cassell
University of Alabama

Dewey Clayton
University of Louisville, Kentucky

Frank T. Colon
Lehigh University, Bethlehem, Pennsylvania

Frank J. Coppa
Union County College, Cranford, New Jersey

Irasema Coronado
University of Texas at El Paso

James B. Cottrill
Santa Clara University, California

Robert E. Craig
University of New Hampshire

Doris Daniels
Nassau Community College, New York

Carolyn Grafton Davis
North Harris County College, Texas

Paul B. Davis
Truckee Meadows Community College, Nevada

Richard D. Davis
Brigham Young University

Ron Deaton
Prince George's Community College, Maryland

Marshall L. DeRosa
Louisiana State University, Baton Rouge

Michael Dinneen
Tulsa Junior College, Oklahoma

Gavan Duffy
University of Texas at Austin

Don Thomas Dugi
Transylvania University, Louisville, Kentucky

George C. Edwards III
Texas A&M University

Gregory Edwards
Amarillo College, Texas

Mark C. Ellickson
Southwestern Missouri State University, Springfield

Larry Elowitz
Georgia College, Milledgeville

Jodi Empol
Montgomery County Community College, Blue Bell, Pennsylvania

John W. Epperson
Simpson College, Indianola, Indiana

Victoria A. Farrar-Myers
University of Texas at Arlington

Daniel W. Fleitas
University of North Carolina at Charlotte

Elizabeth N. Flores
Del Mar College, Texas

Joel L. Franke
Blinn College, Brenham, Texas

Barry D. Friedman
North Georgia College, Dahlonega

Robert S. Getz
SUNY–Brockport, New York

Kristina Gilbert
Riverside Community College, California

William A. Giles
Mississippi State University

Donald Gregory
Stephen F. Austin State University, Texas

Forest Grieves
University of Montana

Dale Grimnitz
Normandale Community College,
Bloomington, Minnesota

Stefan D. Haag
Austin Community College, Texas

Justin Halpern
Northeastern State University,
Oklahoma

Willie Hamilton
Mount San Jacinto College, California

Jean Wahl Harris
University of Scranton, Pennsylvania

David N. Hartman
Rancho Santiago College,
Santa Ana, California

Robert M. Herman
Moorpark College, California

Richard J. Herzog
Stephen F. Austin State University,
Nacogdoches, Texas

Paul Holder
McClennan Community College,
Waco, Texas

Michael Hoover
Seminole Community College,
Sanford, Florida

J. C. Horton
San Antonio College, Texas

Robert Jackson
Washington State University, Pullman

Willoughby Jarrell
Kennesaw State University, Georgia

Loch K. Johnson
University of Georgia

Donald L. Jordan
United States Air Force Academy,
Colorado

John D. Kay
Santa Barbara City College, California

Charles W. Kegley
University of South Carolina

Bruce L. Kessler
Shippensburg University, Pennsylvania

Robert King
Georgia Perimeter College

Jason F. Kirksey
Oklahoma State University, Stillwater

Nancy B. Kral
Tomball College, Texas

Dale Krane
Mississippi State University

Samuel Krislov
University of Minnesota

William W. Lamkin
Glendale Community College

Harry D. Lawrence
Southwest Texas Junior College,
Uvaide, Texas

Ray Leal
Southwest Texas State University,
San Marcos

Sue Lee
Center for Telecommunications, Dallas
County Community College District

Alan Lehmann
Blinn College, Texas

Carl Lieberman
University of Akron, Ohio

Orma Linford
Kansas State University, Manhattan

James J. Lopach
University of Montana

Eileen Lynch
Brookhaven College, Texas

William W. Maddox
University of Florida

S. J. Makielski, Jr.
Loyola University, New Orleans

Jarol B. Manheim
George Washington University,
District of Columbia

J. David Martin
Midwestern State University,
Wichita Falls, Texas

Bruce B. Mason
Arizona State University

Thomas Louis Masterson
Butte College, California

Steve J. Mazurana
University of Northern Colorado, Greeley

James D. McElyea
Tulsa Junior College, Oklahoma

Thomas J. McGaghie
Kellogg Community College, Michigan

William P. McLauchlan
Purdue University, Indiana

Stanley Melnick
Valencia Community College, Florida

Robert Mittrick
Luzurne County Community College,
Pennsylvania

Helen Molanphy
Richland College, Texas

James Morrow
Tulsa Community College

Keith Nicholls
University of Alabama

Sandra O'Brien
Florida Gulf Coast University, Fort Myers

Stephen Osofsky
Nassau Community College, New York

John P. Pelissero
Loyola University of Chicago

Neil A. Pinney
Western Michigan University, Kalamazoo

George E. Pippin
Jones County Community College,
Mississippi

Walter V. Powell
Slippery Rock University, Pennsylvania

Michael A. Preda
Midwestern State University,
Wichita Falls, Texas

Jeffrey L. Prewitt
Brewton-Parker College,
Mt. Vernon, Georgia

Mark E. Priewe
University of Texas at San Antonio

Charles Prysby
University of North Carolina

Donald R. Ranish
Antelope Valley College, California

John D. Rausch
Fairmont State University, West Virginia

Renford Reese
California State Polytechnic
University—Pomona

Curt Reichel
University of Wisconsin

Russell D. Renka
Southeast Missouri State University,
Cape Girardeau

Donna Rhea
Houston Community College–Northwest

Paul Rozycki
Charles Stewart Mott Community
College, Flint, Michigan

Bhim Sandhu
West Chester University, Pennsylvania

Gregory Schaller
Villanova University, Villanova,
Pennsylvania; and St. Joseph's University,
Philadelphia

Pauline Schloesser
Texas Southern University, Houston

Eleanor A. Schwab
South Dakota State University, Brookings

Charles R. Shedlak
Ivy Tech State College,
South Bend, Indiana

Len Shipman
Mount San Antonio College, California

Scott Shrewsbury
Mankato State University, Minnesota

Alton J. Slane
Muhlenberg College, Pennsylvania

Joseph L. Smith
Grand Valley State University, Michigan

Michael W. Sonnlietner
Portland Community College, Oregon

Gilbert K. St. Clair
University of New Mexico

Robert E. Sterken, Jr.
University of Texas, Tyler

Carol Stix
Pace University, Pleasantville, New York

Gerald S. Strom
University of Illinois at Chicago

Maxine Swaikowsky
Hubbard High School,
Chicago, Illinois

Regina Swopes
Northeastern Illinois University, Chicago

John R. Todd
North Texas State University

Ron Velton
Grayson County College, Texas

Albert C. Waite
Central Texas College

Benjamin Walter
Vanderbilt University, Tennessee

B. Oliver Walter
University of Wyoming, Laramie

Mark J. Wattier
Murray State University, Kentucky

Stella Webster
Wayne County Community College—
Downtown, Detroit, Michigan

Paul Weizer
Fitchburg State College, Massachusetts

Thomas L. Wells
Old Dominion University, Virginia

Jean B. White
Weber State College, Utah

Lance Widman
El Camino College, California

Allan Wiese
Mankato State University, Minnesota

J. David Woodard
Clemson University, South Carolina

Robert D. Wrinkle
Pan American University, Texas

In preparing this 2009–2010 Edition of *American Government and Politics Today: The Essentials,* we were the beneficiaries of the expert guidance of a skilled and dedicated team of publishers and editors. We have benefited greatly from the supervision and encouragement given by Carolyn Merrill, executive editor. Suzy Spivey, our developmental editor, also deserves our thanks for her efforts in coordinating reviews and in many other aspects of project development. We are also indebted to editorial assistant Nathan Gamache for his contributions to this project.

We are grateful to Bill Stryker, our production manager, for making it possible to get the text out on time. We also thank Anne Sheroff and Ann Hoffman for their work on photo issues and Ann Borman for her excellent efforts as senior content project manager. In addition, our gratitude goes to all of those who worked on the various supplements offered with this text, especially supplements coordinator Katie Hayes, and to Caitlin Holroyd, who coordinates the Web site. We would also like to thank Amy Whitaker, senior marketing manager, for her tremendous efforts in marketing the text. Additionally, we are indebted to the staff at Parkwood Composition Service. Their ability to generate the pages for this text quickly and accurately made it possible for us to meet our ambitious printing schedule.

Many other people helped during the research and editorial stages of this edition. Greg Scott provided excellent editorial and research assistance from the outset of the project to the end. Mary Berry's copyediting and Judy Kiviat's proofreading skills contributed greatly to the book. We also thank Roxie Lee for her assistance, which helped us to meet our printing schedule, and Sue Jasin of K&M Consulting for her contributions to the smooth running of the project.

Any errors remain our own. We welcome comments from instructors and students alike. Suggestions that we have received in the past have helped us to improve this text and to adapt it to the changing needs of instructors and students.

Barbara Bardes   **Mack Shelley**   **Steffen Schmidt**

ABOUT THE AUTHORS

BARBARA A. BARDES

Barbara A. Bardes is a professor of political science at the University of Cincinnati. She received her bachelor of arts degree and master of arts degree from Kent State University. After completing her Ph.D. at the University of Cincinnati, she held faculty positions at Mississippi State University and Loyola University in Chicago. She returned to the University of Cincinnati as dean of one of its colleges. She has also worked as a political consultant and directed polling for a research center.

Bardes has written articles on public opinion and foreign policy, and on women and politics. She has authored *Thinking about Public Policy; Declarations of Independence: Women and Political Power in Nineteenth-Century American Fiction;* and *Public Opinion: Measuring the American Mind* (with Robert W. Oldendick). Her current research interests include public opinion on terrorism and homeland security and media effects in elections.

Bardes's home is located in a very small hamlet in Kentucky called Rabbit Hash, famous for its 150-year-old general store. Her hobbies include traveling, gardening, needlework, and antique collecting.

MACK C. SHELLEY II

Mack C. Shelley II is professor of political science, professor of statistics, and director of the Research Institute for Studies in Education at Iowa State University. After receiving his bachelor's degree from American University in Washington, D.C., he completed graduate studies at the University of Wisconsin at Madison, where he received a master's degree in economics and a Ph.D. in political science. He taught for two years at Mississippi State University before arriving at Iowa State in 1979.

Shelley has published numerous articles, books, and monographs on public policy. From 1993 to 2002, he served as elected coeditor of the *Policy Studies Journal.* His published books include *The Permanent Majority: The Conservative Coalition in the United States Congress; Biotechnology and the Research Enterprise* (with William F. Woodman and Brian J. Reichel); *American Public Policy: The Contemporary Agenda* (with Steven G. Koven and Bert E. Swanson); and *Redefining Family Policy: Implications for the 21st Century* (with Joyce M. Mercier and Steven Garasky). Other recent work has focused on electronic government and the "digital divide," learning communities, how to improve student life (especially in residence halls), and public health.

His leisure time includes traveling, working with students, and playing with the family dog and three cats.

STEFFEN W. SCHMIDT

Steffen W. Schmidt is a professor of political science at Iowa State University. He grew up in Colombia, South America, and studied in Colombia, Switzerland, and France. He obtained his Ph.D. from Columbia University, New York, in public law and government.

Schmidt has published six books and more than 150 journal articles. He is also the recipient of numerous prestigious teaching prizes, including the Amoco Award for Lifetime Career Achievement in Teaching and the Teacher of the Year award. He is a pioneer in the use of Web-based and real-time video courses, as well as a member of the American Political Science Association's section on computers and multimedia. He is on the editorial board of the *Political Science Educator* and is the technology and teaching editor of the *Journal of Political Science Education.*

Schmidt has a political talk show on WOI radio, where he is known as Dr. Politics, streaming live once a week at www.woi.org. The show has been broadcast live from various U.S. and international venues. He is a frequent political commentator for *CNN en Español* and the British Broadcasting Corporation.

Schmidt likes to snow ski, ride hunter jumper horses, race sailboats, and scuba dive.

1 The Democratic Republic

Political candidates and parties often create proposed agendas that they promise to fulfill if elected. Here is a "checklist" showing some elements of the Democratic agenda during the 2008 presidential campaign. (Scott J. Ferrell/Congressional Quarterly/Getty Images)

whatif...we elected a dictator?

BACKGROUND

As you will read in this chapter, the framers of the Constitution created a *representative democracy*, a form of government in which the people govern. Citizens do not govern directly, of course, but indirectly—by electing others (such as members of Congress and the president) to govern the country on the people's behalf.

Through free elections, which underpin any democracy, the people can choose whomever they want to represent them. Citizens can even elect a dictator if they choose to do so—which voters in several countries have done. (A *dictator* is a ruler who governs absolutely, without being constrained by any institution or law—the dictator *is* the law.)

WHAT IF WE ELECTED A DICTATOR?

It is certainly possible that Americans could elect a dictator to the presidency. After all, there is never any guarantee that a president, once elected, will govern democratically.

Assume for the moment, however, that Americans elected a president with obvious dictatorial ambitions. What might happen? Would the elections be invalidated by the courts? Not likely, provided that the elections were fair and conducted in a legal manner. Free elections mean just that: the United States Supreme Court would be obligated to uphold the will of the people. As Justice Oliver Wendell Holmes, Jr., stated almost two centuries ago, "If my fellow citizens want to go to hell, I will help them. It's my job."

Once the new president began to exercise dictatorial powers, however, another question would come into play: Are our constitutional checks and balances strong enough to curb a president's dictatorial ambitions?

CONSTITUTIONAL CHECKS AND BALANCES

As you will learn in Chapter 2, to prevent the possibility of a dictatorship, the Constitution expressly limits the powers that a president can exercise. Indeed, the founders created a form of government specifically designed to prevent any one of the three branches of government (executive, legislative, and judicial) from gaining too much power.

If the new president ignored the wishes of the legislature (Congress), Congress could exercise its power to impeach and convict the president, thereby removing the president from office. Congress also has the so-called power of the purse. It could refuse to appropriate the funds necessary to implement the dictator's policies. The judiciary—the courts—can also exercise a check on the president by declaring presidential actions unconstitutional.

There is no guarantee that these congressional and judicial checks would be used, however. Suppose that the new president has succeeded in persuading the American people that the nation is facing a grave crisis. To protect the nation's security, the president asserts the need to be able to rule without facing constitutional restraints or interference from Congress or the courts.

Fear-mongering is one of the oldest, and most effective, dictatorial tools in the book. Dictators have learned that citizens are generally willing to sacrifice at least some of their civil rights and liberties to be safe and secure from external threats. If the dictator has overwhelming popular support, members of Congress might be reluctant to take action against the president for fear that they might not be reelected in the future.

Americans have had some experience with how a presidential administration can use fear to gain support for the expansion of executive powers. The administration of George W. Bush used fear of terrorist attacks to justify actions that some legal scholars contend were unconstitutional. These actions ranged from secret surveillance programs to the warrantless detention of terrorist suspects.

As legal scholar Stanley Fish noted, "The danger [of the terrorist threat] is not so much that terrorists will defeat democracies by force as it is that, in resisting terrorists, democracies will forgo the procedural safeguards . . . that make a democracy what it is."

CAN A DICTATOR BE "UNELECTED"?

If a dictator has strong public support, it may prove difficult to remove him or her from office. Once in a position of strength, a dictator can control the media and curb the influence of any significant opposition to the regime. Secret surveillance can be used to locate and then punish members of any political movement critical of the government.

Come election time, free elections could turn into "rigged" elections, in which the dictator would be ensured reelection. Ultimately, for a dictatorship to maintain itself, the nation's armed forces and police must obey the dictator, even when they are ordered to put down legitimate opposition. In many countries, the armed forces and police are willing to do just that.

FOR CRITICAL ANALYSIS

1. Is it possible to have a democracy and a dictatorship at the same time? Why or why not?
2. If a U.S. president is not held accountable for violations of the law, how might that affect future presidencies?

Politics, for many people, is the "great game"—better than soccer, better than chess. Scores may only be tallied every two years, at elections, but the play continues at all times. The game, furthermore, is played for high stakes. Politics can affect what you spend. It can determine what you can legally do in your spare time. In worst-case circumstances, it can even threaten your life. Few topics are so entertaining—and so important.

In our democratic republic, ordinary citizens have an important role to play by voting and participating in other ways. Many people have argued over the years that an active and informed citizenry is essential to maintaining our system of government. The nation's founders, in particular, were very much aware that the American political experiment might fail. Whether our democratic republic could be replaced by a dictatorship someday is a question that we examined in the *What If . . .* feature that opened this chapter.

Although voting is extremely important, it is only one of the ways that citizens can exercise their political influence. Americans can also join a political organization or interest group, stage a protest, or donate funds to a political campaign or cause. There are countless ways to become involved. Informed participation begins with knowledge, however, and this text aims to provide you with a strong foundation in American government and politics. We hope that this book helps introduce you to a lifetime of political awareness and activity.

didyouknow...

That the Greek philosopher Aristotle favored enlightened despotism over democracy, which to him meant mob rule?

POLITICS AND GOVERNMENT

What is politics? **Politics** can be understood as the process of resolving conflicts and deciding, as political scientist Harold Lasswell put it in his classic definition, "who gets what, when, and how."[1] More specifically, politics is the struggle over power or influence within organizations or informal groups that can grant or withhold benefits or privileges.

We can identify many such groups and organizations. In families, all members may meet together to decide on values, priorities, and actions. Wherever there is a community that makes decisions through formal or informal rules, politics exists. For example, when a church decides to construct a new building or hire a new minister, the decision may be made politically. Politics can be found in schools, social groups, and any other organized collection of people. Of all of the organizations that are controlled by political activity, however, the most important is the government.

What is the government? Certainly, it is an **institution**—that is, an ongoing organization that performs certain functions for society. An *organization* has a life separate from the lives of the individuals who are part of it at any given moment in time. The **government** can be defined as an institution in which decisions are made that resolve conflicts or allocate benefits and privileges. The government is also the *preeminent* institution within society. It is unique because it has the ultimate authority for making decisions and establishing political values.

WHY IS GOVERNMENT NECESSARY?

Perhaps the best way to assess the need for government is to examine circumstances in which government, as we normally understand it, does not exist. What happens when multiple groups compete with each other for power within a society? There are places around the world where such circumstances exist. A current example is the African nation of Somalia. Since 1991, Somalia has not had a central government capable of controlling the country. The regions of the country are divided among several warlords and factions, each controlling a block of territory. When Somali warlords compete for the control of

Politics
The process of resolving conflicts and deciding "who gets what, when, and how." More specifically, politics is the struggle over power or influence within organizations or informal groups that can grant or withhold benefits or privileges.

Institution
An ongoing organization that performs certain functions for society.

Government
The preeminent institution within society in which decisions are made that resolve conflicts or allocate benefits and privileges. It is unique because it has the ultimate authority for making decisions and establishing political values.

---

1. Harold Lasswell, *Politics: Who Gets What, When, and How* (New York: McGraw-Hill, 1936).

a particular locality, the result is war, widespread devastation, and famine. In general, multiple armed forces compete by fighting, and the absence of a unified government is equivalent to civil war.

THE NEED FOR SECURITY

As the example of Somalia shows, one of the original purposes of government is the maintenance of security, or **order.** By keeping the peace, the government protects the people from violence at the hands of private or foreign armies. It dispenses justice and protects the people against the violence of criminals. If order is not present, it is not possible for the government to provide any of the other benefits that people expect from it.

Consider the situation in Iraq. In March and April 2003, U.S. and British coalition forces invaded that nation, which was governed by the dictator Saddam Hussein. The relatively small number of coalition troops had little trouble in defeating their military opponents, but they experienced serious difficulties in establishing order within Iraq when the war was over.

Once it became clear that Saddam Hussein was no longer in control of the country, widespread looting broke out. Looters stole crucial supplies from hospitals, making it difficult to treat Iraqis injured during the war. Thieves stripped the copper from electrical power lines, which made it impossible to quickly restore electrical power. Iraqis continued to experience growing levels of violence from insurgent groups and even criminal gangs right up to the autumn of 2007, when the security situation finally began to improve. Iraq still has some distance to go before order is fully restored and reconstruction can truly begin. (Order is a political value to which we will return later in this chapter.)

LIMITING GOVERNMENT POWER

A complete collapse of order and security, as seen in Somalia, is actually an uncommon event. Much more common is the reverse—too much government control. In 2008, the human rights organization Freedom House judged that forty-three of the world's countries were "not free." These nations contain 36 percent of the world's population. Such countries may be controlled by individual dictators—Iraq's Saddam Hussein was one obvious example. Others include Libya's Muammar Qaddafi and Hosni Mubarak of Egypt. Alternatively, a political party, such as the Communist Party of China, may monopolize all the levers of power. The military may rule, as in Myanmar (formerly Burma). We look at how oil wealth props up dictators in this chapter's *Beyond Our Borders* feature.

In all of these examples, the individual or group running the country cannot be removed by legal means. Freedom of speech and the right to a fair trial are typically absent. Dictatorial governments often torture or execute their opponents. Such regimes may also suppress freedom of religion.

In short, protection from the violence of domestic criminals or foreign armies is not enough. Citizens also need protection from abuses of power by the government. To protect the liberties of the people, it is necessary to limit the powers of the government.

Liberty—the greatest freedom of the individual consistent with the freedom of other individuals—is a second major political value, along with order. We further discuss this value later in this chapter.

Roadside bombs
in Iraq have been a frequent event for the past few years. This one near Tayaran Square in central Baghdad occurred in the spring of 2008. The target was a local police patrol. Why are we witnessing these kinds of attacks in Iraq but not in, say, France, Germany, or the United States?
(AP Photo/Hadi Mizban)

Order
A state of peace and security. Maintaining order by protecting members of society from violence and criminal activity is the oldest purpose of government.

Liberty
The greatest freedom of the individual that is consistent with the freedom of other individuals in the society.

beyondourborders

GREASING THE WHEELS OF AUTOCRACY

Since the fall of the Soviet Union in 1991, democracy has been on the rise throughout the world. This democratic wave, however, has largely bypassed nations awash with oil wealth. At the beginning of 2008, the price per barrel of crude oil exceeded $100 for the first time. Oil has become more important than ever before to autocrats and dictators. Oil wealth allows these people to escape accountability. They can use it to buy off opponents. Oil income also makes it unnecessary for them to levy taxes directly on the people, thus eliminating a potential cause of unrest.

THE EXAMPLE OF LIBYA

Muammar Qaddafi is a typical oil-fueled dictator. Libya's oil revenues come directly to him, and he disposes of them by passing them on to his closest associates. Qaddafi has controlled Libya since 1969 and has cut it off from the outside world. Any would-be challengers to Qaddafi's rule are severely punished. His son is ready to take over in his place when he steps down or dies. Without high oil revenues, Qaddafi's rule might have been threatened years ago. As it is, he and his son are probably secure in their dictatorial rule for decades to come.

IRAN—LIKE MANY OTHERS, A MIDEAST POWER BECAUSE OF OIL

Iran is a theocracy—it has a clerical dictatorship run by religious leaders called mullahs. Oil forms the basis of the mullahs' dictatorship. The Iranian economy is more or less in shambles, but it would be in much worse shape without oil. Petroleum wealth fuels Iran's nuclear ambitions. Iran's government has been able to finance Palestinian terrorists and Syrian forays into Lebanon.

Throughout the rest of the Middle East, oil wealth has kept other autocrats in power. In the last five years alone, the Kingdom of Saudi Arabia has taken in more than $800 billion in oil revenues. The Saudi leaders can afford to put off economic and social modernization as long as oil yields so much in revenues. They do not have to worry whether their decisions make economic sense. For example, Saudi Arabia is able to remain the largest per capita consumer of energy in the world, even exceeding the United States—everything is air-conditioned.

RUSSIA AND VENEZUELA— ELECTED AUTOCRATS

When communism collapsed in the Soviet Union in the years leading up to 1991, everyone had high hopes for democracy in Russia. Vladimir Putin was democrati-cally elected as the president of Russia in 2000. This former head of the KGB (the Soviet Union's secret police) has used his elected position to become one of the most powerful autocrats in the world. In 2008, Putin's handpicked successor in the presidential post named him prime minister, so Putin was able to stay on as "the father of the nation." There are no free media left in Russia. There is no hope that anyone outside of Putin's circle of close associates could become politically powerful. Russia is a major oil exporter, and the windfall in oil prices gave Putin authority and confidence. He has become a modern-day czar because of high oil prices.

Iranian President
Mahmoud Ahmadinejad is shown here during a military parade in 2008. The autocratic Iranian government has had an easier time remaining in place because of high oil revenues. (AP Photo/Vahid Salemi)

The same is true of Venezuelan president Hugo Chávez. He, too, was democratically elected but used increasing oil revenues to eliminate any serious political opposition. This former lieutenant colonel in the army is slowly but surely wrecking Venezuela's economy. Chávez can get away with what he is doing because of the oil revenues that stream in every year—almost all of which he now controls.

FOR CRITICAL ANALYSIS

Norway is another country that has benefited greatly from huge increases in oil prices. Nonetheless, that country remains a true democracy, and no one individual has taken on any new powers because of increased oil wealth. Why not?

Authority
The right and power of a government or other entity to enforce its decisions and compel obedience.

Legitimacy
Popular acceptance of the right and power of a government or other entity to exercise authority.

Totalitarian Regime
A form of government that controls all aspects of the political and social life of a nation.

Authoritarianism
A type of regime in which only the government itself is fully controlled by the ruler. Social and economic institutions exist that are not under the government's control.

Aristocracy
Rule by the "best"; in reality, rule by an upper class.

Theocracy
Literally, rule by God or the gods; in practice, rule by religious leaders, typically self-appointed.

Oligarchy
Rule by a few.

Anarchy
The condition of no government.

Democracy
A system of government in which political authority is vested in the people. The term is derived from the Greek words *demos* ("the people") and *kratos* ("authority").

AUTHORITY AND LEGITIMACY

Every government must have **authority**—that is, the right and power to enforce its decisions. Ultimately, the government's authority rests on its control of the armed forces and the police. Virtually no one in the United States, however, bases his or her day-to-day activities on fear of the government's enforcement powers. Most people, most of the time, obey the law because this is what they have always done. Also, if they did not obey the law, they would face the disapproval of friends and family. Consider an example: Do you avoid injuring your friends or stealing their possessions because you are afraid of the police—or because if you did these things, you would no longer have friends?

Under normal circumstances, the government's authority has broad popular support. People accept the government's right to establish rules and laws. When authority is broadly accepted, we say that it has **legitimacy.** Authority without legitimacy is a recipe for trouble. Iraq can again serve as an example. Although many Iraqis were happy to see the end of Saddam Hussein's regime, they were not pleased that their nation was occupied by foreign troops. Many Iraqis, especially in districts inhabited by Sunni Arabs (the former politically dominant group in Iraq), did not accept the legitimacy of the U.S.-led Coalition Provisional Authority or the elected Iraqi government that followed it. The Shiite Arabs, longtime rivals of the Sunnis, dominated the elected government.

Terrorists and other groups hostile to the government and its American supporters could organize attacks on coalition troops or even on innocent civilians, knowing that their neighbors would not report their activities. The number of such attacks declined considerably by the end of 2007, but the crisis of legitimacy in Iraq remains unresolved.

DEMOCRACY AND OTHER FORMS OF GOVERNMENT

There are a variety of different types of government, which can be classified according to which person or group of people controls society through the government.

TYPES OF GOVERNMENT

At one extreme is a society governed by a **totalitarian regime.** In such a political system, a small group of leaders or a single individual—a dictator—makes all political decisions for the society. Every aspect of political, social, and economic life is controlled by the government. The power of the ruler is total (thus, the term *totalitarianism*).

A second type of system is authoritarian government. **Authoritarianism** differs from totalitarianism in that only the government itself is fully controlled by the ruler. Social and economic institutions exist that are not under the government's control.

Many of our terms for describing the distribution of political power are derived from the ancient Greeks, who were the first Western people to study politics systematically. One form of rule was known to the Greeks as **aristocracy,** literally meaning "rule by the best." In practice, this meant rule by leading members of wealthy families. Another term from the Greeks is **theocracy,** which literally means "rule by God" (or the gods). In practice, theocracy means rule by self-appointed religious leaders. Iran is a rare example of a country in which supreme power is in the hands of a religious leader, the grand ayatollah Ali Khamenei. One of the most straightforward Greek terms is **oligarchy,** which simply means "rule by a few."

Anarchy is a term derived from a Greek word meaning the absence of government. Advocates of anarchy envision a world in which each individual makes his or her own rules for behavior. In reality, the absence of government typically results in rule by competing armed factions, many of which are indistinguishable from gangsters. This is the state of affairs in Somalia, which we described earlier.

Finally, the Greek term for rule by the people was **democracy.** Within the limits of their culture, some of the Greek city-states operated as democracies. Today, in much (but not all) of the world, the people will not grant legitimacy to a government unless it is based on democracy.

DIRECT DEMOCRACY AS A MODEL

The system of government in the ancient Greek city-state of Athens is usually considered the purest model of **direct democracy** because the citizens of that community debated and voted directly on all laws, even those put forward by the ruling council of the city. The most important feature of Athenian democracy was that the **legislature** was composed of all of the citizens. Women, foreigners, and slaves, however, were excluded because they were not citizens. This form of government required a high level of participation from every citizen; that participation was seen as benefiting the individual and the city-state. The Athenians believed that although a high level of participation might lead to instability in government, citizens, if informed about the issues, could be trusted to make wise decisions.

Direct democracy has also been practiced in Switzerland and, in the United States, in New England town meetings. At these town meetings, which can include all of the voters who live in the town, important decisions—such as levying taxes, hiring city officials, and deciding local ordinances—are made by majority vote. Some states provide a modern adaptation of direct democracy for their citizens. Representative democracy is supplemented by the **initiative** or the **referendum**—processes by which the people may vote directly on laws or constitutional amendments. The **recall** process, which is available in many states, allows the people to vote to remove an official from state office.

THE DANGERS OF DIRECT DEMOCRACY

Although they were aware of the Athenian model, the framers of the U.S. Constitution were opposed to such a system. They regarded democracy as a dangerous idea that could lead to instability. Nevertheless, in the 1700s and 1800s, the idea of government based on the **consent of the people** gained increasing popularity. Such a government was the main aspiration of the American Revolution in 1775, the French Revolution in 1789, and many subsequent revolutions. At the time of the American Revolution, however, the masses were still considered to be too uneducated to govern themselves, too prone to the influence of demagogues (political leaders who manipulate popular prejudices), and too likely to subordinate minority rights to the tyranny of the majority.

James Madison, while defending the new scheme of government set forth in the U.S. Constitution, warned of the problems inherent in a "pure democracy":

A common passion or interest will, in almost every case, be felt by a majority of the whole . . . and there is nothing to check the inducements to sacrifice the weaker party or an obnoxious individual. Hence it is that such democracies have ever been spectacles of turbulence and contention, and have ever been found incompatible with personal security or the rights of property; and have in general been as short in their lives as they have been violent in their deaths.[2]

Like other politicians of his time, Madison feared that pure, or direct, democracy would deteriorate into mob rule. What would keep the majority of the people, if given direct decision-making power, from abusing the rights of minority groups?

The closest we have to direct democracy

in America is the New England town meeting. Here, residents have come to the Strafford Meeting Hall in Strafford, Vermont, for their town meeting. They will discuss the election of town clerks, as well as local issues. Why do you think relatively few town meetings take place in America? (AP Photo/Toby Talbot)

Direct Democracy
A system of government in which political decisions are made by the people directly, rather than by their elected representatives; probably attained most easily in small political communities.

Legislature
A governmental body primarily responsible for the making of laws.

Initiative
A procedure by which voters can propose a law or a constitutional amendment.

Referendum
An electoral device whereby legislative or constitutional measures are referred by the legislature to the voters for approval or disapproval.

Recall
A procedure allowing the people to vote to dismiss an elected official from state office before his or her term has expired.

Consent of the People
The idea that governments and laws derive their legitimacy from the consent of the governed.

2. James Madison, in Alexander Hamilton, James Madison, and John Jay, *The Federalist Papers*, No. 10 (New York: Mentor Books, 1964), p. 81. See Appendix C of this textbook.

Republic
A form of government in which sovereign power rests with the people, rather than with a king or a monarch.

Popular Sovereignty
The concept that ultimate political authority is based on the will of the people.

Democratic Republic
A republic in which representatives elected by the people make and enforce laws and policies.

Representative Democracy
A form of government in which representatives elected by the people make and enforce laws and policies; may retain the monarchy in a ceremonial role.

Universal Suffrage
The right of all adults to vote for their representatives.

Majority
More than 50 percent.

Majority Rule
A basic principle of democracy asserting that the greatest number of citizens in any political unit should select officials and determine policies.

A DEMOCRATIC REPUBLIC

The framers of the U.S. Constitution chose to craft a **republic,** meaning a government in which sovereign power rests with the people, rather than with a king or a monarch. A republic is based on **popular sovereignty.** To Americans of the 1700s, the idea of a republic also meant a government based on common beliefs and virtues that would be fostered within small communities. The rulers were to be amateurs—good citizens who would take turns representing their fellow citizens.

The U.S. Constitution created a form of republican government that we now call a **democratic republic.** The people hold the ultimate power over the government through the election process, but all policy decisions are made by elected officials. For the founders, even this distance between the people and the government was not sufficient. The Constitution made sure that the Senate and the president would be selected by political elites rather than by the people, although later changes to the Constitution allowed the voters to elect members of the Senate directly.

Despite these limits, the new American system was unique in the amount of power it granted to the ordinary citizen. Over the course of the following two centuries, democratic values became more and more popular, at first in the Western nations and then throughout the rest of the world. The spread of democratic principles gave rise to another name for our system of government—**representative democracy.** The term *representative democracy* has almost the same meaning as *democratic republic,* with one exception. In a republic, not only are the people sovereign, but there is no king. What if a nation develops into a democracy but preserves the monarchy as a largely ceremonial institution? This is exactly what happened in Britain. Not surprisingly, the British found the term *democratic republic* to be unacceptable, and they described their system as a representative democracy instead.

Principles of Democratic Government. All representative democracies rest on the rule of the people as expressed through the election of government officials. In the 1790s in the United States, only free white males were able to vote, and in some states they had to be property owners as well. Women did not receive the right to vote in national elections in the United States until 1920, and the right to vote was not secured in all states by African Americans until the 1960s. Today, **universal suffrage** is the rule.

Because everyone's vote counts equally, the only way to make fair decisions is by some form of **majority** will. But to ensure that **majority rule** does not become oppressive, modern democracies also provide guarantees of minority rights. If political minorities were not protected, the majority might violate the fundamental rights of members of certain groups—especially groups that are unpopular or that differ from the majority population, such as racial minorities.

To guarantee the continued existence of a representative democracy, there must be free, competitive elections. Thus, the opposition always has the opportunity to win elective office. For such elections to be totally open, freedom of the press and speech must be preserved so that opposition candidates may present their criticisms of the government.

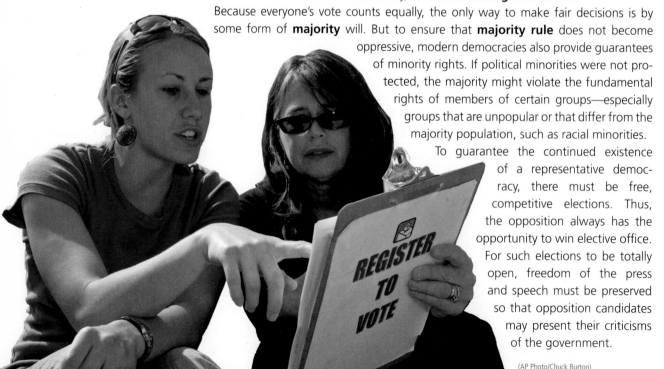

(AP Photo/Chuck Burton)

Constitutional Democracy. Yet another key feature of Western representative democracy is that it is based on the principle of **limited government.** Not only is the government dependent on popular sovereignty, but the powers of the government are also clearly limited, either through a written document or through widely shared beliefs. The U.S. Constitution sets down the fundamental structure of the government and the limits to its activities. Such limits are intended to prevent political decisions based on the whims or ambitions of individuals in government rather than on constitutional principles.

WHAT KIND OF DEMOCRACY DO WE HAVE?

Political scientists have developed a number of theories about American democracy, including *majoritarian* theory, *elite* theory, and theories of *pluralism*. Advocates of these theories use them to describe American democracy either as it actually is or as they believe it should be.

Some scholars argue that none of these three theories, which we discuss next, fully describes the workings of American democracy. These experts say that each theory captures a part of the true reality but that we need all three theories to gain a full understanding of American politics.

DEMOCRACY FOR EVERYONE

Many people believe that in a democracy, the government ought to do what the majority of the people want. This simple proposition is the heart of majoritarian theory. As a theory of what democracy should be like, **majoritarianism** is popular among both political scientists and ordinary citizens. Many scholars, however, consider majoritarianism to be a surprisingly poor description of how U.S. democracy actually works. In particular, they point to the low level of turnout for elections. Polling data have shown that many Americans are neither particularly interested in politics nor well informed. Few are able to name the persons running for Congress in their districts, and even fewer can discuss the candidates' positions.

DEMOCRACY FOR THE FEW

If ordinary citizens are not really making policy decisions with their votes, who is? One theory suggests that elites really govern the United States. This **elite theory** holds that society is ruled by a small number of people who exercise power to further their self-interest. American government, in other words, is a sham democracy. Elite theory is usually used simply to describe the American system. Few people today believe it is a good idea for the country to be run by a privileged minority. In the past, however, many people believed that it was appropriate for the country to be run by an elite. Consider the words of Alexander Hamilton, one of the framers of the Constitution:

> *All communities divide themselves into the few and the many. The first are the rich and the wellborn, the other the mass of the people. . . . The people are turbulent and changing; they seldom judge or determine right. Give therefore to the first class a distinct, permanent share in the government. They will check the unsteadiness of the second, and as they cannot receive any advantage by a change, they therefore will ever maintain good government.*[3]

Some versions of elite theory posit a small, cohesive elite class that makes almost all the important decisions for the nation,[4] whereas others suggest that voters choose among

Limited Government
A government with powers that are limited either through a written document or through widely shared beliefs.

Majoritarianism
A political theory holding that in a democracy, the government ought to do what the majority of the people want.

Elite Theory
A perspective holding that society is ruled by a small number of people who exercise power to further their self-interest.

didyouknow...

That there are over 500,000 elected officials in the United States, which is more than all the bank tellers in the country?

---

3. Alexander Hamilton, "Speech in the Constitutional Convention on a Plan of Government," in *Writings,* ed. Joanne B. Freeman (New York: Library of America, 2001).
4. Michael Parenti, *Democracy for the Few,* 8th ed. (Belmont, Calif.: Wadsworth Publishing, 2007).

competing elites. New members of the elite are recruited through the educational system so that the brightest children of the masses allegedly have the opportunity to join the elite stratum.

Does the existence of political dynasties constitute an argument in favor of elite theory? We look at such dynasties in this chapter's *Which Side Are You On?* feature.

DEMOCRACY FOR GROUPS

A different school of thought holds that our form of democracy is based on group interests. Even if the average citizen cannot keep up with political issues or cast a deciding vote in any election, the individual's interests will be protected by groups that represent her or him.

Theorists who subscribe to **pluralism** see politics as a struggle among groups to gain benefits for their members. Given the structures of the American political system, group conflicts tend to be settled by compromise and accommodation. Because there are a multitude of interests, no one group can dominate the political process. Furthermore, because most individuals have more than one interest, conflict among groups need not divide the nation into hostile camps.

Many political scientists believe that pluralism works very well as a descriptive theory. As a theory of how democracy *should* function, however, pluralism has problems. Poor citizens are rarely represented by interest groups. At the same time, rich citizens are often overrepresented. As political scientist E. E. Schattschneider once observed, "The flaw in the pluralist heaven is that the heavenly chorus sings with a strong upper-class accent."[5] There are also serious doubts as to whether group decision making always reflects the best interests of the nation.

Indeed, critics see a danger that groups may become so powerful that all policies become compromises crafted to satisfy the interests of the largest groups. The interests of the public as a whole, then, are not considered. Critics of pluralism have suggested that a democratic system can be virtually paralyzed by the struggle among interest groups. We discuss interest groups at greater length in Chapter 7.

FUNDAMENTAL VALUES

The writers of the American Constitution believed that the structures they had created would provide for both democracy and a stable political system. They also believed that the nation would be sustained by its **political culture**—a concept defined as a patterned set of ideas, values, and ways of thinking about government and politics.

Even today, there is considerable consensus among American citizens about certain concepts—including the rights to liberty, equality, and property—that are deemed to be basic to the U.S. political system. Given that the vast majority of Americans are descendants of immigrants having diverse cultural and political backgrounds, how can we account for this consensus? Primarily, it is the result of **political socialization**—the process by which political beliefs and values are transmitted to new immigrants and to our children. The two most important sources of political socialization are the family and the educational system. (See Chapter 6 for a more detailed discussion of the political socialization process.)

The most fundamental concepts of the American political culture are those of the *dominant culture*. The term **dominant culture** refers to the values, customs, and language established by the group or groups that traditionally have controlled politics and government in a society. The dominant culture in the United States has its roots in Western

---

Pluralism
A theory that views politics as a conflict among interest groups. Political decision making is characterized by compromise and accommodation.

Political Culture
A patterned set of ideas, values, and ways of thinking about government and politics.

Political Socialization
The process by which political beliefs and values are transmitted to new immigrants and to our children. The family and the educational system are two of the most important forces in the political socialization process.

Dominant Culture
The values, customs, and language established by the group or groups that traditionally have controlled politics and government in a society.

---

didyouknow...

That the phrase "In God We Trust" was made the national motto on July 30, 1956, but had appeared on U.S. coins as early as 1864?

---

5. E. E. Schattschneider, *The Semi-Sovereign People* (Hinsdale, Ill.: The Dryden Press, 1975; originally published in 1960).

whichsideare**you**on?

DO FAMILY DYNASTIES HAVE ANY PLACE IN AMERICAN POLITICS?

In his 1792 best seller, *Common Sense,* Thomas Paine argued that there was no role for a hereditary monarchy in this new country:

> All men being originally equals, no one by birth could have a right to set up his own family in perpetual preference to all others forever, and though himself might deserve some decent degree of honors of his contemporaries, yet his descendants might be far too unworthy to inherit them.

Indeed, the framers of our national constitution gave the federal government the task of guaranteeing a "republican form of government" to the states. Neither the federal government nor any state would be allowed to lapse into monarchy. The Constitution also states that "No Title of Nobility shall be granted by the United States."

We have seen family dynasties in republics and dictatorships elsewhere in the world—India, North Korea, and Syria, to name only a few. Do such family dynasties have a place in American politics?

JUST SAY NO TO IMPLICIT INHERITED TITLES

When New York senator Hillary Clinton announced that she was running for president, she seemed to be extending a modern family dynastic tradition. The country had just seen four years of George H. W. Bush, eight years of Bill Clinton, eight years of George W. Bush—and then was facing perhaps eight years of Hillary Clinton. Note that this country does have a history of family dynasties.

In 1824, John Quincy Adams followed his father into the presidency (although twenty-four years later). Benjamin Harrison was the grandson of President William Henry Harrison, elected forty-nine years earlier.

In Congress, politics has been a family matter to a much greater extent. As of 2008, four sitting incumbents had joined Congress to replace their deceased spouses. Congress is littered with the sons and daughters of former members. Michigan representative John Dingle served in the House for twenty-two years, and John Dingle, Jr., took over in 1955. He's still there.

It's time to stop political dynasties in the United States. To this end, legal scholar Bruce Fein has created a draft of an amendment to the Constitution that would prohibit spouses, siblings, and children of an elected or appointed official from immediately succeeding that official in the same office.

THE DYNASTIC DISEASE IS ON THE DECLINE, SO DON'T WORRY

To be sure, relatives of presidents have been elected as president. Relatives of members of Congress have also been elected to the same congressional seats. Recent research, though, has shown that dynastic legislative seats are on the decline.

In congressional elections from 1789 on, increased competition has diminished the power of political dynasties over time. The record holder, the Breckinridge family of Kentucky, sent seventeen of its members to Congress between 1789 and 1978. The current record holder—the Kennedy family—has seen six members serve in a total of thirty-seven Congresses (and counting, because Massachusetts senator Ted Kennedy is still active). Just because there have been two Bushes in the White House recently doesn't mean that we are facing a new American aristocracy. In any event, the voters decide whom they want in each office. That's called democracy.

It is not worth introducing an amendment to the Constitution to prevent "dynastic disease" in American politics. Remember, in the end Hillary Clinton lost the Democratic presidential nomination to Illinois senator Barack Obama. Family ties are often a negative. Just ask Florida governor Jeb Bush, who despite his considerable popularity decided he had no chance at the Republican presidential nomination in 2008.

(U.S. Air Force Photo by Tech. Sgt. Bob Oldham)

A visitor to the McCormick Tribune Freedom Museum in Chicago examines a copy of the Constitution. On the left is a copy of the Declaration of Independence, and on the right is a copy of the Bill of Rights. What are some of the fundamental American values that these documents support? (AP Photo/ Charles Rex Arbogast)

European civilization. From that civilization, American politics has inherited a bias toward individualism, private property, and Judeo-Christian ethics. Other cultural heritages honor community or family over individualism and sometimes place far less emphasis on materialism. Additionally, changes in our own society have led to the erosion of some values, such as the sanctity of the family structure, and the acceptance of other values, such as women's pursuit of careers in the workplace.

LIBERTY VERSUS ORDER

In the United States, our **civil liberties** include religious freedom—both the right to practice whatever religion we choose and freedom from any state-imposed religion. Our civil liberties also include freedom of speech—the right to express our opinions freely on all matters, including government actions. Freedom of speech is perhaps one of our most prized liberties, because a democracy could not endure without it. These and many other basic guarantees of liberty are found in the **Bill of Rights,** the first ten amendments to the Constitution.

Liberty, however, is not the only value widely held by Americans. A substantial portion of the American electorate believes that certain kinds of liberty threaten the traditional social order. The right to privacy is a particularly controversial liberty. The United States Supreme Court has held that the right to privacy can be derived from other rights that are explicitly stated in the Bill of Rights. The Supreme Court has also held that under the right to privacy, the government cannot ban either abortion[6] or private homosexual behavior by consenting adults.[7] Some Americans believe that such rights threaten the sanctity of the family and the general cultural commitment to moral behavior. Of course, others disagree with this point of view.

Security is another issue. When Americans have felt particularly fearful or vulnerable, the government has emphasized national security over civil liberties. Following the terrorist attacks on the World Trade Center and the Pentagon on September 11, 2001, Congress passed legislation designed to provide greater security at the expense of some civil liberties. In particular, the USA Patriot Act gave law enforcement and intelligence-gathering agencies greater latitude to search out and investigate suspected terrorists. Many Americans objected to the Patriot Act, pointing out that it compromised numerous civil liberties, such as protection from unreasonable searches and seizures. Do national security concerns justify the government surveillance programs created since 9/11? We examine that question in this chapter's *Politics and the Cyber Sphere* feature.

EQUALITY VERSUS LIBERTY

The Declaration of Independence states, "All men are created equal." The proper meaning of equality, however, has been disputed by Americans since the Revolution.[8] Much of American history—and indeed, world history—is the story of how the value of **equality**— the idea that all people are of equal worth—has been extended and elaborated.

Civil Liberties
Those personal freedoms, including freedom of religion and freedom of speech, that are protected for all individuals. The civil liberties set forth in the U.S. Constitution, as amended, restrain the government from taking certain actions against individuals.

Bill of Rights
The first ten amendments to the U.S. Constitution.

Equality
As a political value, the idea that all people are of equal worth.

---

6. *Roe v. Wade,* 410 U.S. 113 (1973).
7. *Lawrence v. Texas,* 539 U.S. 558 (2003).
8. Gary B. Nash, *The Unknown American Revolution: The Unruly Birth of Democracy and the Struggle to Create America* (New York: Viking, 2005); and Alfred F. Young, ed., *Beyond the American Revolution: Explorations in the History of American Radicalism* (DeKalb, Ill.: Northern Illinois University Press, 1993).

POLITICS AND...
the cyber sphere

DOES THE NATIONAL SECURITY AGENCY KNOW TOO MUCH ABOUT YOU?

In 1952, President Harry Truman, through a classified presidential order, created the National Security Agency (NSA). Since then, it has been this nation's most secretive intelligence agency. Truman's order limited the NSA to spying on foreign governments, and in 1978, Congress passed legislation that explicitly banned NSA eavesdropping in the United States without a warrant. After the terrorist attacks of 9/11, though, the NSA quietly expanded its role.

THE NSA AND DOMESTIC INTELLIGENCE

Many domestic agencies, including the Department of Justice, the Department of Homeland Security, and the Treasury Department, send huge quantities of data from their own surveillance programs to the NSA. The resulting data collection about individuals in the United States is used for *social-network analysis.* For example, the NSA's Terrorism Information Awareness Program analyzes as much and as many kinds of data as possible. The program sifts through the data looking for patterns that might point to a terrorist suspect or organization. Once these data are processed by the program's complicated software, the results may be shared with other domestic security agencies.

WHAT THE NSA CAN DO WITHOUT A WARRANT

The data that the NSA can access without a traditional warrant include, but are not limited to:

- The Internet—locating searches an individual may have conducted and sites the person may have visited.
- Airlines—which passengers flew on which flights, and when.
- E-mails—the senders' and recipients' addresses, the subject line, and the time and date sent.
- Cell and landline phones—incoming and outgoing numbers and the length of calls.
- Banking—large transfers of funds between banks.

A Supreme Court decision allows the government to collect records of phone calls—as opposed to actual conversations—without a warrant. The government's ability to obtain records of electronic communications was greatly expanded by the 2001 USA Patriot Act. When the government pulls together a widely based set of transactional data on an individual, it is able to paint a very detailed profile of that individual's behavior.

Although the government jus-tifies these data collection activities as important to the war on terror, the procedures are also used to pursue white-collar criminals. A striking example in 2008 was the government's use of banking records to determine that New York governor Eliot Spitzer had purchased the services of high-priced prostitutes. Spitzer was forced to resign.

FOR CRITICAL ANALYSIS

Some argue that domestic spying by the NSA should never be allowed. Others are not so sure. Those who support NSA domestic efforts argue that we should do everything possible to counter fanatical fundamentalists of all stripes. How do we, as a nation, determine what amount of domestic surveillance is necessary?

(© Studioxil/istockphotos.com)

First, the right to vote was granted to all adult white males regardless of whether they owned property. The Civil War resulted in the end of slavery and established that, in principle at least, all citizens were equal before the law. The civil rights movement of the 1950s and 1960s sought to make that promise of equality a reality for African Americans. Other movements have sought equality for other racial and ethnic groups, for women, for persons with disabilities, and for gay men and lesbians. We discuss these movements in Chapter 5.

To promote equality, it is often necessary to place limits on the desire by some to treat people unequally. In this sense, equality and liberty are conflicting values. Today, the denial of equal treatment to members of a particular race has very few defenders. As recently as sixty years ago, though, such denial was a cultural norm.

Economic Equality. Equal treatment regardless of race, religion, gender, and other characteristics is a popular value today. Equal opportunity for individuals to develop their talents and skills is another value with substantial support. Equality of economic status, however, is a controversial value.

For much of history, few people even contemplated the idea that the government could do something about the division of society between rich and poor. Most people assumed that such an effort was either impossible or undesirable. This assumption began to lose its force in the 1800s. As a result of the growing wealth of the Western world and a visible increase in the ability of government to take on large projects, some people began to advocate the value of universal equality. Some radicals dreamed of a revolutionary trans-

While in office, former President George W. Bush
often promoted increased eavesdropping on phone calls and e-mails of suspected terrorists. Why were so many Americans against this? (AP Photo/Ron Edmonds)

formation of society that would establish an *egalitarian system*—that is, a system in which wealth and power would be redistributed on a more equal basis.

Many others rejected this vision but still came to indorse the values of eliminating poverty and at least reducing the degree of economic inequality in society. Antipoverty advocates believed then and believe now that such a program could alleviate much suffering. In addition, they believed that reducing economic inequality would promote fairness and enhance the moral tone of society generally.

Property
Anything that is or may be subject to ownership. As conceived by the political philosopher John Locke, the right to property is a natural right superior to human law (laws made by government).

Capitalism
An economic system characterized by the private ownership of wealth-creating assets, free markets, and freedom of contract.

This protester believes that the government is abusing its eminent domain power. From what part of the Constitution does the government get this power? (AP Photo / Matt Rourke)

Property Rights and Capitalism. The value of reducing economic inequality is in conflict with the right to **property.** This is because reducing economic inequality typically involves the transfer of property (usually in the form of money) from some people to others. For many people, liberty and property are closely entwined. Our capitalist system is based on private property rights. Under **capitalism,** property consists not only of personal possessions but also of wealth-creating assets such as farms and factories. The investor-owned corporation is in many ways the preeminent capitalist institution. The funds invested by the owners of a corporation are known as *capital*—hence, the very name of the system. Capitalism is also typically characterized by considerable freedom to make binding contracts and by relatively unconstrained markets for goods, services, and investments.

Property—especially wealth-creating property—can be seen as giving its owner political power and the liberty to do whatever he or she wants. At the same time, the ownership of property immediately creates inequality in society. The desire to own property, however, is so widespread among all

(AP Photo/Matt Rourke)

classes of Americans that radical egalitarian movements have had a difficult time securing a wide following here.

THE PROPER SIZE OF GOVERNMENT

Opposition to "big government" has been a constant theme in American politics. Indeed, the belief that government is overreaching its power dates back to the years before the American Revolution. Tensions over the size and scope of government have plagued Americans ever since. American citizens often express contradictory opinions on the size of government and the role that it should play in their lives. Those who complain about the amount of taxes that they pay each year may also worry over the lack of funds for more teachers in the local schools. Individuals who fear future terrorist attacks may react with outrage at the thought of a government official snooping through their e-mail correspondence.

Big Government in Times of Crisis. Americans are most likely to call for the benefits of big government when they are reacting to a crisis. After the terrorist attacks of 9/11, the Bush administration substantially increased the scope of federal authority, and government spending went up as well. Likewise, other recent crises have resulted in demands for an active government. One example was the devastation caused by Hurricane Katrina in 2005. When the levees that protected New Orleans failed, floods covered most of the city. Thousands of poor people were stranded in horrific conditions, and many died. Americans blamed governments at all levels for the catastrophe. Many believed that repairing the devastation was a federal responsibility, and such activity inevitably requires tremendous government power and resources.

The Financial Crisis of 2008. In recent years, many mortgage holders took out loans that they could pay back only if the value of their homes continued to rise. When housing prices fell in 2007, these people faced foreclosure. Elaborate financial instruments based on these mortgages suddenly became nearly worthless. Institutions that held or guaranteed these securities faced bankruptcy. Naturally, the public demanded that the government do something. In 2008, the government rescued investment bank Bear Stearns, insurance giant AIG, and the government-sponsored mortgage firms Fannie Mae and Freddie Mac. Two banks—Lehman Brothers and Washington Mutual—failed, however. Banks began to refuse to lend to each other, fearing that the loans would not be repaid. Treasury secretary Hank Paulson was forced to demand that Congress pass a $700 billion bailout bill for financial institutions.

Big Government and Civil Liberties. Still, Americans value limited government when it comes to their private lives and civil liberties, often to a greater degree than people in other democratic countries. Americans prize freedom of speech and will not accept government restrictions on speech that are common elsewhere. For example, display of the Nazi swastika is banned so completely in democratic Germany that hobbyists may not affix historically accurate swastika decals to plastic models of World War II–era aircraft. Americans would find such a law to be absurd, not to mention unconstitutional. Many Americans worry about crime, but most would be even more

Americans often expect "big government" to handle major nationwide problems. These demonstrators wanted the federal government to "fix" the subprime mortgage crisis, which had caused many people to face foreclosure on their homes. Why do Americans often turn to the federal government to solve big problems? (AP Photo/Matt Rourke)

Ideology
A comprehensive set of beliefs about the nature of people and about the role of an institution or government.

Conservatism
A set of beliefs that includes a limited role for the national government in helping individuals, support for traditional values and lifestyles, and a cautious response to change.

Liberalism
A set of beliefs that includes the advocacy of positive government action to improve the welfare of individuals, support for civil rights, and tolerance for political and social change.

concerned about possible miscarriages of justice if they learned that 99.8 percent of all criminal prosecutions result in a conviction. Yet that is exactly what happens in democratic Japan. As a final example, the right to own firearms enjoys more protection in the United States than elsewhere—any government measure to limit gun ownership results in a storm of controversy.

POLITICAL IDEOLOGIES

A political **ideology** is a closely linked set of beliefs about politics. Political ideologies offer their adherents well-organized theories that propose goals for the society and the means by which those goals can be achieved. At the core of every political ideology is a set of guiding values. The two ideologies most commonly referred to in discussions of American politics are *conservatism* and *liberalism*.

CONSERVATISM VERSUS LIBERALISM

The set of beliefs called **conservatism** includes a limited role for the government in helping individuals. Conservatism also includes support for traditional values. These values usually include a strong sense of patriotism. Conservatives believe that the private sector probably can outperform the government in almost any activity. Believing that the individual is primarily responsible for his or her own well-being, conservatives typically oppose government programs to redistribute income or change the status of individuals.

Conservatives have enjoyed considerable political success in recent decades. Although the elections of 2006 and 2008 represented a swing away from conservatism, the long-time success of this philosophy will leave its mark for years to come. We look at the likely continuing influence of young, conservative Christian evangelicals who held positions in the Bush administration in this chapter's *Politics and Ideology* feature.

The set of beliefs called **liberalism** includes advocacy of government action to improve the welfare of individuals, support for civil rights, and tolerance for political and social change. American liberals believe that government should take positive action to reduce poverty, to redistribute income from wealthier classes to poorer ones, and to regulate the economy. Liberals are often seen as an influential force within the Democratic Party, and conservatives are often regarded as the most influential force in the Republican Party.[9]

THE TRADITIONAL POLITICAL SPECTRUM

A traditional method of comparing political ideologies is to array them on a continuum from left to right, based primarily on how much power the government should exercise to promote economic equality. Table 1–1 shows how ideologies can be arrayed in a traditional political spectrum. In addition to liberalism and conservatism, the table includes the ideologies of socialism and libertarianism.

---

9. For an insightful analysis of the differences between progressive and conservative beliefs, see George Lakoff, *Don't Think of an Elephant: Know Your Values and Frame the Debate* (White River Junction, Vt.: Chelsea Green Publishing Co., 2004).

TABLE 1–1: The Traditional Political Spectrum

	Socialism	Liberalism	Conservatism	Libertarianism
How much power should the government have over the economy?	Active government control over major economic sectors.	Positive government action in the economy.	Positive government action to support capitalism.	Almost no regulation over the economy.
What should the government promote?	Economic equality, community.	Economic security, equal opportunity, social liberty.	Economic liberty, morality, social order.	Total economic and social liberty.

politicsand...ideology

THE FAITHFUL CONSERVATIVES

According to some observers, George W. Bush created the first generation of conservative evangelical Christians who were enthusiastically and deeply involved in political administration. During the Bush presidency, numerous executive assistants, junior press secretaries, and interns throughout the White House had one thing in common: they were conservative evangelicals. Many were graduates of colleges with a strong Christian identity.

CHRISTIAN COLLEGES WITH A MISSION

These evangelical colleges often have a mission that they state explicitly in their campus handbooks and marketing materials. Regent University is one. Its mission is expressed in its motto: "Christian leadership to change the world." Another school, Patrick Henry College, wants its students to "lead our nation and shape our culture." These evangelical institutions of higher learning encourage their students to take part in political activities both during school and after graduation.

THE EVANGELICALS ARE HERE TO STAY

Some historians contend that it took the conservative political movement thirty years to become part of the Washington establishment. It may have taken about the same time for evangelicals to gain influence in that same establishment. (Note that not all conservatives are Christian evangelicals—and not all evangelicals are conservative.)

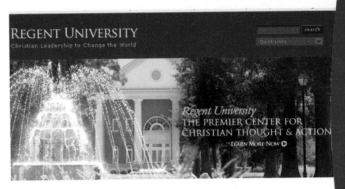

http://www.regent.edu

If evangelical political operatives can't work for Bush's successor, Barack Obama, they have alternatives. Dozens of members of Congress identify themselves as evangelicals, according to James L. Guth, a Furman University political science professor. Guth points out that evangelicals also sponsor an increasingly important network of think tanks and interest groups that will hire former White House junior officials—provided, of course, that they have the right credentials.

FOR CRITICAL ANALYSIS

In what ways can evangelical, conservative-minded junior government officials actually affect policy?

Socialism falls on the left side of the spectrum.[10] Socialists play a minor role in the American political arena, although socialist parties and movements have been important in other countries around the world. In the past, socialists typically advocated replacing investor ownership of major businesses with either government ownership or ownership by employee cooperatives. Socialists believed that such steps would break the power of the very rich and lead to an egalitarian society. In more recent times, socialists in Western Europe have advocated more limited programs that redistribute income.

On the right side of the spectrum is **libertarianism,** a philosophy of skepticism toward most government activities. Libertarians strongly support property rights and typically oppose regulation of the economy and redistribution of income. Libertarians support *laissez-faire* capitalism. (*Laissez faire* is French for "let it be.") Libertarians also tend to oppose government attempts to regulate personal behavior and promote moral values.

"CLASSICAL" LIBERALISM

The word *liberal* has an odd history. It comes from the same root as *liberty,* and originally it simply meant "free." In that broad sense, the United States as a whole is a *liberal* country, and all popular American ideologies are variants of liberalism. In a more restricted

Socialism
A political ideology based on strong support for economic and social equality. Socialists traditionally envisioned a society in which major businesses were taken over by the government or by employee cooperatives.

Libertarianism
A political ideology based on skepticism or opposition toward most government activities.

---

10. The terms *left* and *right* in the traditional political spectrum originated during the French Revolution, when liberal deputies to the Legislative Assembly sat to the left of the president and conservative deputies sat to the right of the president.

didyouknow...

That about 14 percent of all legal immigrants to the United States plan to live in the Los Angeles/Long Beach, California, area?

definition, a *liberal* was a person who believed in limited government and who opposed religion in politics. A hundred years ago, liberalism referred to a philosophy that in some ways resembled modern-day libertarianism. For that reason, many libertarians today refer to themselves as *classical liberals.*

How did the meaning of the word *liberal* change? In the 1800s, the Democratic Party was seen as the more liberal of the two parties. The Democrats of that time stood for limited government and opposition to moralism in politics. Democrats opposed Republican projects such as building roads, freeing the slaves, and prohibiting the sale of alcoholic beverages. Beginning with Democratic president Woodrow Wilson (1913–1921), however, the party's economic policies began to change. By the time of President Franklin Delano Roosevelt (1933–1945), the Democrats stood for positive government action to help the economy. Although Roosevelt called for new policies, he kept the old language—as Democrats had long done, he called himself a liberal. We will discuss the history of the two parties in greater detail in Chapter 8.

Outside the United States and Canada, the meaning of the word *liberal* never changed. For this reason, you might hear a left-of-center European denounce U.S. president Ronald Reagan (1981–1989) or British prime minister Margaret Thatcher (1979–1990) for their "liberalism." What is meant, of course, is that these two leaders were enthusiastic advocates of *laissez-faire* capitalism.

PROBLEMS WITH THE TRADITIONAL POLITICAL SPECTRUM

Many political scientists believe that the traditional left-to-right spectrum does not reflect the complexities of today's political ideologies. Take the example of libertarians. In Table 1–1 on page 18, libertarians are placed to the right of conservatives. If the only question is how much power the government should have over the economy, this is where they belong. Libertarians, however, advocate the most complete freedom possible in social matters. They oppose government action to promote traditional moral values, although such action is often favored by other groups on the political right. Libertarians' strong support for civil liberties seems to align them more closely with modern liberals than with conservatives.

Liberalism is often described as an ideology that supports "big government." If the objective is to promote equality, the description has some validity. In the moral sphere, however, conservatives tend to support more government regulation of social values and moral decisions than do liberals. Thus, conservatives tend to oppose gay rights legislation and propose stronger curbs on pornography. Liberals usually show greater tolerance for alternative lifestyle choices and oppose government attempts to regulate personal behavior and morals.

FIGURE 1–1:
A Four-Cornered Ideological Grid

In this grid, the colored squares represent four different political ideologies. The vertical choices range from cultural order to cultural liberty. The horizontal choices range from economic equality to economic liberty.

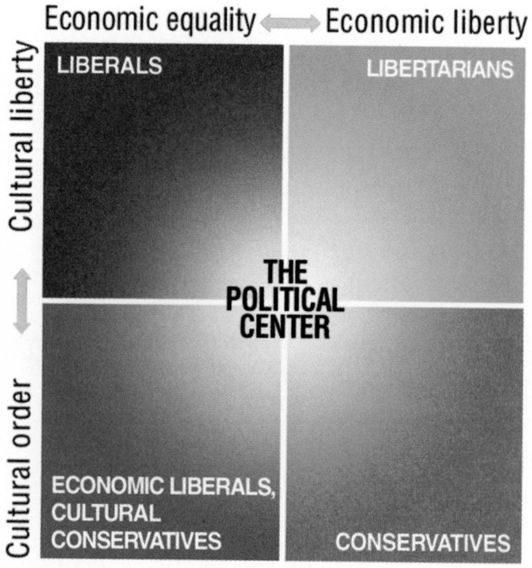

A FOUR-CORNERED IDEOLOGICAL GRID

For a more sophisticated breakdown of American popular ideologies, many scholars use a four-cornered grid, as shown in Figure 1–1. The grid provides four possible ideologies. Each quadrant contains a substantial portion of the American electorate. Individual voters may fall anywhere on the grid, depending on the strength of their beliefs about economic and cultural issues.

Note that there is no generally accepted term for persons in the lower-left position, which we have labeled "economic liberals, cultural conservatives." Some scholars have used terms such as *populist* to describe this point of view, but such terms can be misleading.

Individuals who are economic liberals and cultural conservatives tend to support government action both to promote the values of economic equality and fairness and to defend traditional values, such as the family and marriage. These individuals may describe themselves as conservative or moderate. They may be Democrats due to their support of economic liberalism, or they may vote for a Republican candidate due to their conservative values.

Libertarian, as a position on our four-way grid, does not refer to the small Libertarian Party, which has only a minor role in the American political arena. Rather, libertarians more typically support the Republican Party. They are more likely than conservatives to vote for a compatible Democrat, however.

Classifying the Voters. If the traditional political spectrum held, most voters would fall into the liberal or conservative quarter of our ideological grid. Actually, there are a substantial number of voters in each quadrant. Asking whether the government should guarantee everyone a job, for example, divides the electorate roughly in half on the economic dimension. A question about abortion also divides the electorate roughly in half on the social dimension. Knowing how a voter answered one of these questions, however, does not tell us how he or she answered the other one. Many people would give a "liberal" answer to the jobs question but a "conservative" answer to the abortion question; also, many people would give a "conservative" answer to the jobs question and a "liberal" answer on abortion.

Conservative Popularity. Even though all four ideologies are popular, it does not follow that the various labels we have used in the four-cornered grid are equally favored. Voters are much more likely to describe themselves as conservative than as liberal. There are a variety of reasons for this, but one is that *liberal* has come to imply "radical" to many people, whereas *conservative* often implies "moderate." Because most Americans value moderation, the conservative label has an advantage. Indeed, few politicians today willingly describe themselves as liberal, and many liberals prefer to describe themselves as *progressives* instead. The designation *libertarian* has an even more radical flavor than *liberal,* and the number of voters with obvious libertarian tendencies far exceeds the number who are willing to adopt the label. We will look further at popular ideologies in Chapter 6.

TOTALITARIAN IDEOLOGIES

Three other important ideologies fit poorly into the traditional political spectrum. These are *communism, fascism,* and *Islamism.* None of these ideologies has had a significant following in the United States. Their impact on Europe and Asia, however, has determined the course of world history over the last hundred years.

Communism. A variant of socialism is **communism.** Communists favor a partisan dictatorship, government control of all enterprises, and the replacement of free markets with central planning. The first communists were a radical faction that broke away from the socialist movement. Traditionally, socialists had always considered themselves to be democrats. The communists, however, believed that they could abolish capitalism and institute socialism through a severe partisan dictatorship. The Soviet Union, founded by Russian Communists after World War I (1914–1918), succeeded in establishing government control of farms, factories, and businesses of all kinds and in replacing the market system with central planning. Under Joseph Stalin (1924–1953), the Soviet Union also developed into a brutal totalitarian regime.

Fascism. The most famous example of **fascism** was Nazi Germany (1933–1945). As with communism, the success of fascism depended on a large body of disciplined followers and a populist appeal. Fascism, however, championed elitism rather than egalitarianism. It was strongly influenced by Charles Darwin's concept of "the survival of the fittest." It valued

didyouknow...

That a poll of New York University students revealed that one-fifth of them would give up their vote in the next election for an iPod and that half of them would renounce their vote permanently for $1 million?

Communism
A variant of socialism that favors a partisan (and often totalitarian) dictatorship, government control of all enterprises, and the replacement of free markets with central planning.

Fascism
A twentieth-century ideology—often totalitarian—that exalts the national collective united behind an absolute ruler. Fascism rejects liberal individualism, values action over rational deliberation, and glorifies war.

action over rational deliberation and explicitly rejected liberal individualism—it exalted the national collective, united behind an absolute ruler. Fascism appealed to patriotism or nationalism, but it shaped these common sentiments into virulent racism.

Islamism
A political ideology based on a radical and fundamentalist interpretation of Islam. Islamists reject all Western democratic values and often call for a worldwide Islamist political order. Radical Islamists have provided the membership of many recent terrorist groups.

Islamism. The terrorists who attacked the World Trade Center and the Pentagon on September 11, 2001, were ideologically motivated. These terrorists were members of the al Qaeda[11] network led by Osama bin Laden. Al Qaeda's ideology is based on a radical and fundamentalist interpretation of Islam, an interpretation sometimes called **Islamism.** Many recent terrorist groups other than al Qaeda have also had an Islamist orientation. Radical Islamists reject all Western democratic values. Many of them call for the establishment of a worldwide Islamic theocracy, the *caliphate.* (We described theocracy as a form of government on page 8.) The Taliban in Afghanistan were, in fact, able to impose an Islamist government on that country until they were brought down in late 2001 by a U.S.-led invasion and internal opponents supported by Western nations. Radical Islamism has become an increasingly widespread ideology, and the United States may be responding to Islamist movements for many years to come.

Shiite Cleric Muqtada al Sadr
is shown delivering a sermon at the Kufa Mosque near the holy city of Najaf in Iraq. Al Sadr represents a large faction of the Shiite Muslim sect in Iraq. The other sect is called the Sunnis (there are Kurds, too). Why does religion enter into politics much more in countries such as Iraq than it does in Europe or the United States? (AP Photo/Alaa al-Marjani)

"A REPUBLIC, IF YOU CAN KEEP IT"

In 1787, after the Constitutional Convention had ended, a woman stopped Benjamin Franklin on his way out of Independence Hall in Philadelphia and asked him, "Well, Doctor, what have we got—a republic or a monarchy?" Franklin replied: "A republic, if you can keep it." The quote reveals Franklin's concern over whether the new republic would last. It also reflects the founders' belief that a free government is not simply based on the consent of the people but depends on the people's active participation for its continued good health. In the words of a statement often attributed to Thomas Jefferson, "The price of liberty is eternal vigilance." It is reasonable to ask whether Americans have been sufficiently vigilant with respect to their government. How healthy is our democratic republic today?

DECLINING TRUST IN GOVERNMENT

While citizen trust in government peaked in the wake of the terrorist attacks of September 11, 2001, it then fell, apparently returning to a downward trajectory that dates back to the 1960s. In 2007, a *New York Times*/CBS News poll put it at 24 percent—the lowest percentage recorded in the poll during its seventeen-year history. In 2008, in a *Times* poll, 81 percent of the public agreed that "things have pretty seriously gotten off on the wrong track." In other polls, a majority of respondents agreed that "the government does not listen to people like me."

By the beginning of George W. Bush's second term as president, many Americans had come to believe that they were helpless in the face of a government that felt no need to be accountable to the public. The 2006 congressional elections showed that the public wanted to alter the nation's course. Democrats gained a majority in Congress, yet they did not have enough votes to change the administration's direction.

Negative attitudes toward the U.S. government also grew in many foreign countries. According to the Pew Global Attitudes Project, from 2002 to 2007 favorable views of America fell in twenty-six of the thirty-three countries for which it collected data. Muslim countries were particularly anti-American, but unfavorable attitudes also increased in Western Europe.

---

11. *Al Qaeda,* sometimes transliterated as al Qaida or al-Qa'idah, is Arabic for "the base."

STRENGTHENING GOVERNMENT

Even as popular disaffection with the U.S. government grew, the Bush administration continued its expansion of the powers of the executive. Although Vice President Dick Cheney was the administration's most prominent advocate of the expanded powers, he clearly had the backing of Bush himself. The essence of the new doctrine was that presidential power could not be limited by any law or treaty when the president acts to protect the national security. Furthermore, the president alone decides what constitutes a threat to the national security. Members of the administration strongly believed that these powers were essential to protect the nation from the threat of Islamist terrorism.

During the first six years of Bush's presidency, Congress and the courts for the most part did not question these unprecedented claims of authority. Actions based on the new doctrine included the following:

- Refusing to implement the Geneva Convention Relative to the Treatment of Prisoners of War, to which the United States is a signatory.
- Approving interrogation techniques generally considered to constitute torture.
- Surveilling U.S. citizens without obtaining a warrant from a court.
- Arresting a U.S. citizen on U.S. soil as an alleged "unlawful enemy combatant" and holding that person indefinitely without review by any court. (This action suspends a fundamental constitutional right known as *habeas corpus,* under which those arrested have the right to appear in court and challenge their detention.)

This last action was striking, because it suggested that the government could indefinitely imprison—and, indeed, mistreat—anyone at the president's sole discretion. In 2007, Attorney General Alberto Gonzales claimed before a Senate committee that the U.S. Constitution does not guarantee *habeas corpus* rights to U.S. citizens.

In addition to expanding presidential powers, the Bush administration also increased federal spending to a degree not seen in half a century. Even setting aside the costs of the Iraq War and the war on terror, spending increased at an unprecedented rate. Republican columnist David Brooks approvingly described the results as "big government conservatism," a reversal of previous conservative attitudes toward government spending.

elections2008
WERE THE 2008 ELECTIONS A TURNING POINT?

Leading Republicans in Congress attributed the party's reverses in the 2006 elections to its abandonment of traditional conservative principles on issues such as spending. Actually, popular disapproval of the war in Iraq was almost certainly the real problem, but the nostalgia for traditional Republican values did suggest that big government conservatism was on its way out.

Both of the two major-party candidates for president in 2008 seemed well placed to improve the government's standing in the eyes of the American people and the people of the world. Both also rejected the Bush administration's views on presidential authority. The Republican candidate, Arizona senator John McCain, declared that "to impinge on the rights of our own citizens or restrict the freedoms for which our nation stands would be to give terrorists the victory they seek." McCain, who suffered years of torture himself while a prisoner of war in North Vietnam, criticized the Bush administration's interrogation policies and argued that the detainees at the U.S.

naval base in Guantánamo Bay, Cuba, should be brought to trial rather than held indefinitely.

It was Illinois senator Barack Obama who won the election, however, and his rejection of the imperial presidency was even stronger than McCain's. Likewise, New York senator Hillary Clinton, who lost the Democratic nomination by the narrowest of margins, devoted an entire speech to defending *habeas corpus.* For his part, Obama ended one speech with the applause line: "We will close Guantánamo, we will restore *habeas corpus,* we will have a president who will respect and obey the Constitution." Law professor Jeffrey Rosen called Obama "our first president who is a civil libertarian." Of course, civil liberties were a minor issue in a campaign dominated by the economic crisis of 2008. Despite the nation's many troubles, Obama's supporters were buoyed by a wave of optimism that, as president, Obama would usher in a new American era.

Barack Obama
(AP Photo/ Charles Dharapak)

WHY SHOULD YOU CARE ABOUT
ourdemocracy?

Americans, for the most part, take our democracy for granted. We assume that our leaders, including the president, will uphold our democratic traditions when elected to office. Nonetheless, the history of other nations has shown that even leaders voted into office can become overbearing. Elected leaders can move a country away from its democratic underpinnings. In America, however, because most of us take democracy for granted, many of us do not even bother to vote. We never really worry very much that our elected leaders might corrupt our democratic system.

In any democracy, citizens must, nonetheless, remain vigilant. A lot is at stake—our way of life in particular. How does an individual stay vigilant? One important activity is staying informed about what's going on in government. You cannot hold your government leaders accountable if you do not know what they are doing. Staying informed is a lot easier today than it was, say, a hundred years ago. Newspapers and news magazines are everywhere. Perhaps more importantly, the Internet allows you to stay in constant touch with what your government is doing. There are blogs galore of all political stripes. There are Web pages created by Democrats, Republicans, independents, libertarians, and socialists. Even in the fantasy world of Second Life, political debates continue well after the elections are over.

OUR DEMOCRACY AND YOUR LIFE

Consider state and local legislative bodies. They can have a direct impact on your life. For example, local councils or commissions typically oversee the police, and the behavior of the police is a matter of interest even if you live on campus. If you live off campus, local authorities are responsible for an even greater number of issues that affect you directly. Are there items that your local sanitation department refuses to pick up? You might be able to change its policies by lobbying your councilperson.

Even if there are no local issues that concern you, there are still benefits to be gained from observing a local legislative session. You may discover that local government works rather differently from what you expected. You might learn, for example, that the representatives of your political party do not serve your interests as well as you thought—or that the other party is much more sensible than you had presumed.

HOW YOU CAN MAKE A DIFFERENCE

If you truly want to affect our democracy, you have to learn firsthand how a democratic government works. The easiest way is to attend a session of a local legislative body. To do so, look up the phone number of the city hall or county building on the Internet. Call the clerk of your local council or city commission. Find out when the next city council or county board meeting is. In many cities, you don't physically have to attend because you can watch these meetings on public access TV channels.

Before attending a business session of the local council or commission, try to find out how the members are elected. Are the members chosen by the "at-large" method of election, so that each member represents the whole community? Or are they chosen by specific geographic districts or wards? Is there a chairperson or official leader who controls the meetings? What are the responsibilities of this local legislature?

When you visit the local legislature, keep in mind the theory of representative democracy. The legislators or council members are elected to represent their constituents (those who live in the geographic area). Observe how often the members refer to their constituents or to the special needs of their community or electoral district. Listen for sources of conflict within a community. If, for example, there is a debate over a zoning proposal that involves the issue of land use, try to figure out why some members oppose the proposal.

If you want to follow up on your visit, try to get a brief interview with one of the members of the council or board. In general, legislators are very willing to talk to students, particularly students who also are voters. Ask the member how he or she sees the job of representative. How can the wishes of constituents be identified? How does the representative balance the needs of the particular ward or district that he or she represents with the good of the entire community? You can write to many legislators via e-mail. You might ask how much e-mail they receive and who actually answers it.

QUESTIONS FOR
discussionandanalysis

1. Review the *Which Side Are You On?* feature on page 13. Do you believe that family dynasties in American politics present enough of a problem that we should have a constitutional amendment to prevent them? Why or why not?

2. In Australia and Belgium, citizens are legally required to vote in elections. Would such a requirement be a good idea in the United States? What changes might take place if such a rule were in effect?

3. In your own life, what factors have contributed to your political socialization? To what extent were your political values shaped by your family, by school experiences, by friends, and by the media?

4. Following the terrorist attacks of September 11, 2001, the U.S. government imposed various restrictions, notably on airline passengers, in the belief that these measures would enhance our national security. How effective do you think these measures have been? In general, what limits on liberty should we accept as the price of security?

5. Should the government have a role in combating poverty or economic inequality? If so, what should that role be? What limits on property rights are acceptable as part of an effort to reduce poverty or economic inequality?

keyterms

anarchy 8
aristocracy 8
authoritarianism 8
authority 8
Bill of Rights 14
capitalism 16
civil liberties 14
communism 21
consent of the people 9
conservatism 18
democracy 8
democratic republic 10

direct democracy 9
dominant culture 12
elite theory 11
equality 14
fascism 21
government 5
ideology 18
initiative 9
institution 5
Islamism 22
legislature 9
legitimacy 8

liberalism 18
libertarianism 19
liberty 6
limited government 11
majoritarianism 11
majority 10
majority rule 10
oligarchy 8
order 6
pluralism 12
political culture 12
political socialization 12

politics 5
popular sovereignty 10
property 16
recall 9
referendum 9
representative
   democracy 10
republic 10
socialism 19
theocracy 8
totalitarian regime 8
universal suffrage 10

chaptersummary

1. Politics is the process by which people decide which members of society get certain benefits or privileges and which members do not. It is the struggle over power or influence within institutions and organizations that can grant benefits or privileges. Government is the institution within which decisions are made that resolve conflicts or allocate benefits and privileges. It is unique because it has the ultimate authority within society.

2. Two fundamental political values are order, which includes security against violence, and liberty, the greatest freedom of the individual consistent with the freedom of other individuals. Liberty can be both promoted by government and invoked against government. To be effective, government authority must be backed by legitimacy.

3. Many of our terms for describing forms of government came from the ancient Greeks. In a direct democracy, such as ancient Athens, the people themselves make the important political decisions. The United States is a representative democracy, in which the people elect representatives to make the decisions.

4. Theories of American democracy include majoritarianism, in which the government does what the majority wants; elite theory, in which the real power

lies with one or more elites; and pluralist theory, in which organized interest groups contest for power.

5. Fundamental American values include liberty, order, equality, and property. Not all of these values are fully compatible. The value of order often competes with civil liberties, and economic equality competes with property rights.

6. Popular political ideologies can be arrayed from left (liberal) to right (conservative). We can also analyze economic liberalism and conservatism separately from cultural liberalism and conservatism. Totalitarian ideologies, such as communism, fascism, and Islamism, do not fit easily into the American political spectrum.

selectedprint&mediaresources

SUGGESTED READINGS

Fineman, Howard. *The Thirteen American Arguments: Enduring Debates That Define and Inspire Our Country.* New York: Random House Trade Paperbacks, 2009. Fineman, the senior Washington correspondent for *Newsweek,* describes questions that have divided Americans since the Revolution. Examples include: "Who is an American," "The Role of Faith," and "America in the World." The book has won praise from Republicans and Democrats alike.

Hodgson, Godfrey. *The Myth of American Exceptionalism.* New Haven, Conn.: Yale University Press, 2009. A respected British commentator, Hodgson argues that America's history and political philosophy have always been more heavily influenced by the Old World than we have been willing to acknowledge.

Lasswell, Harold. *Politics: Who Gets What, When and How.* New York: McGraw-Hill, 1936. This classic work defines the nature of politics.

Lichtblau, Eric. *Bush's Law: The Remaking of American Justice.* New York: Pantheon, 2008. Lichtblau, a *New York Times* journalist, describes how the Bush administration, in the name of the war on terror, undertook the most radical remaking of American justice in generations.

McCain, John, and Mark Salter. *Faith of My Fathers: A Family Memoir.* New York: Harper, 2008 (paperback edition). Both 2008 presidential candidates have written exceptional autobiographies. McCain tells of his father and grandfather, both admirals in the U.S. Navy, and of his imprisonment in North Vietnam. The book, a fine depiction of American military culture, concludes before the beginning of McCain's political career.

Obama, Barack. *Dreams from My Father: A Story of Race and Inheritance.* New York: Three Rivers Press, 2004. Obama's best-selling autobiography also ends before his political career begins. He describes the sense of isolation resulting from his unusual background, and how he came to identify with the African American community. Like McCain's story, Obama's account provides fascinating insights into the many-sided American experience.

Tocqueville, Alexis de. *Democracy in America.* Edited by Phillips Bradley. New York: Vintage Books, 1945. Life in the United States is described by a French writer who traveled through the nation in the 1820s.

MEDIA RESOURCES

All Things Considered—A daily broadcast of National Public Radio that provides extensive coverage of political, economic, and social news stories.

The Conservatives—A program that shows the rise of the conservative movement in America from the 1940s, through the presidential candidacy of Barry Goldwater, to the presidency of Ronald Reagan. In addition to Goldwater and Reagan, leaders interviewed include William F. Buckley, Jr., Norman Podhoretz, and Milton Friedman.

Liberalism vs. Conservatism—A 2001 film from Teacher's Video that focuses on two contrasting views of the role of government in society.

Mr. Smith Goes to Washington—A classic movie, produced in 1939, starring Jimmy Stewart as the honest citizen who goes to Congress trying to represent his fellow citizens. The movie dramatizes the clash between representing principles and representing corrupt interests.

The Values Issue and American Politics: Values Matter Most—Ben Wattenberg travels around the country in this 1995 program speaking to a broad range of ordinary Americans. He examines what he calls the "values issue"—the issues of crime, welfare, race, discipline, drugs, and prayer in the schools. Wattenberg believes that candidates who can best address these issues will win elections.

e-mocracy

CONNECTING TO AMERICAN GOVERNMENT AND POLITICS

The Web has become a virtual library, a telephone directory, a contact source, and a vehicle to improve your understanding of American government and politics today.

Increasingly, governments at all levels are beginning to use the Web to do business and communicate with citizens. In some states, individuals filing for unemployment compensation do so entirely online. Other states are using the Web to post public notices that in the past were published in newspapers.

To help you become familiar with Web resources, we conclude each chapter in this book with an *E-mocracy* feature. The *Logging On* section in each of these features includes Internet addresses, or uniform resource locators (URLs), that will take you to Web sites focusing on topics or issues discussed in the chapter. Realize that Web sites come and go continually, so some of the Web sites that we include in the *Logging On* section may not exist by the time you read this book.

A word of caution about Internet use: Many students surf the Web for political resources. When doing so, you need to remember to approach these sources with care. For one thing, you should be very careful when giving out information about yourself. You also need to use good judgment, because the reliability or intent of any given Web site is often unknown. Some sites are more concerned with accuracy than others, and some sites are updated to include current information while others are not.

LOGGING ON

We have a powerful and interesting Web site for the textbook, which you can access through the Wadsworth American Government Resource Center. Go to **www.politicalscience.wadsworth.com/amgov**.

You may also want to visit the home page of Dr. Politics—offered by Steffen Schmidt, one of the authors of this book—for some interesting ideas and activities relating to American government and politics. Go to **www.public.iastate.edu/~sws/homepage.html**.

Information about the rules and requirements for immigration and citizenship can be found at the Web site of the U.S. Citizenship and Immigration Services: **www.uscis.gov/portal/site/uscis**.

For a basic "front door" to almost all U.S. government Web sites, click onto the very useful site maintained by the University of Michigan: **www.lib.umich.edu/govdocs/govweb.html**.

For access to federal government offices and agencies, go to the U.S. government's official Web site at **www.usa.gov**.

The Web is a good place to learn about political science as a profession. The URL for the American Political Science Association is **www.apsanet.org**.

You can find the Web site of the International Political Science Organization at **www.ipsa.org**.

We the People
he United States,
form a mo
ce, insure domestic Tranquility

2 The Constitution

CHAPTER CONTENTS

A large crowd attends one of the debates held by the Democratic presidential candidates in 2008. This debate was held at the National Constitution Center in Philadelphia. (John Anderson/UPI/Landov)

whatif...guns were allowed on campus?

BACKGROUND

In 2007, an unstable former student killed thirty-two students and professors at Virginia Tech University. A year later, a gunman (again a former student) opened fire during a lecture at Northern Illinois University, killing five, wounding fifteen, and then killing himself. There were four other school shootings in that same week. People have reacted to these events based on which side they take in a thorny controversy—what kinds of gun laws are appropriate. The Second Amendment to the Constitution makes this a constitutional issue.

On one side are those who argue that school shootings call out for more gun control—or even an outright ban on privately owned guns. These people do not believe that the Second Amendment's guarantee of the "right of the people to keep and bear Arms" applies to individuals.

On the other side are those who argue that school shootings cry out for new laws that allow persons with concealed-weapons permits to carry guns on campus. Students for Concealed Carry on Campus is a group with more than 12,000 members who believe that licensed gun owners should be able to bring guns to school. Utah already allows guns on campus. Colorado does not explicitly ban students and faculty from carrying hidden weapons if they are licensed to do so. At least fifteen other states are currently considering some form of "concealed carry" legislation directed at college campuses.

WHAT IF GUNS WERE ALLOWED ON CAMPUS?

All existing and proposed legislation would allow only those with concealed-weapons licenses to carry concealed weapons on campus. Most states do not issue such licenses to individuals under twenty-one years of age. (A few states license nineteen-year-olds.)

State proposals vary widely. In Arizona, Kentucky, Michigan, Ohio, and Washington, legislation would allow concealed-carry for everyone. In Alabama, Tennessee, and Virginia, only professors at public colleges and universities would be permitted to carry concealed weapons. Oklahoma's proposed legislation would apply only to students at public colleges and universities.

THE POTENTIAL FOR STOPPING MASS MURDERS ON CAMPUSES

Supporters of concealed guns on campus point out that several hours passed while the shooter at Virginia Tech completed his deadly mission. Had a student, professor, or employee of the university been armed, the gunman might have been taken down and prevented from killing more people.

Consider the incident at Northern Illinois University. Even though the police arrived within two minutes after the shooting began, the shooter had already fired off forty-eight bullets and six shotgun blasts. Only an armed person on the spot could have prevented the perpetrator from completing his deadly spree.

Many churches have physical settings that share the characteristics of a closed classroom. At the New Life Church in Colorado Springs, Jeanne Assam, a church member and security guard, was able to shoot a man walking through the door who was armed with several rifles and handguns. The man had already killed two parishioners in the parking lot and had earlier killed two people at a church school in another city. The church's leadership stated that Assam may have saved as many as one hundred lives by her actions.

Already, a dozen universities allow concealed-carry. To date, there have been no reported incidences of gun thefts, gun violence, or gun accidents.

THE OTHER SIDE OF THIS WHAT IF . . . SCENARIO

Not everyone, of course, agrees with the predictions outlined above. Many believe that the attempted use of weapons by persons who are not trained law enforcement officers is likely to increase the threat to bystanders, rather than reduce it. An untrained gun owner could end up injuring or killing additional students and faculty.

The Brady Campaign to Prevent Gun Violence has argued that allowing firearms on college campuses would heighten the danger of violence. Why? Because college campuses are locations where young people drink heavily and live communally.

FOR CRITICAL ANALYSIS

1. Does the Second Amendment's right to bear arms imply a right to defend oneself at all times with a gun? Why or why not?
2. Why does the proposed legislation single out campuses, as opposed to other public places?

We the People of the United States, in Order to form a more perfect Union, establish Justice, insure domestic Tranquility, provide for the common defence, promote the general Welfare, and secure the Blessings of Liberty to ourselves and our Posterity, do ordain and establish this Constitution for the United States of America.

Every schoolchild in America has at one time or another been exposed to these famous words from the Preamble to the U.S. Constitution. The document itself is remarkable. The U.S. Constitution, compared with others in the fifty states and in the world, is relatively short. Because amending it is difficult, it also has relatively few amendments. The Constitution has remained largely intact for over two hundred years. To a great extent, this is because the principles set forth in the Constitution are sufficiently broad that they can be adapted to meet the needs of a changing society. (Sometimes questions arise over whether and how the Constitution should be adapted, as you read in this chapter's *What If . . .* feature.)

> ## didyouknow...
>
> **That the first** English claim to territory in North America was made by John Cabot, on behalf of King Henry VII, on June 24, 1497?

How and why the U.S. Constitution was created is a story that has been told and retold. It is worth repeating, because knowing the historical and political context in which this country's governmental machinery was formed is essential to understanding American government and politics today. The Constitution did not result just from creative thinking. Many of its provisions were grounded in the political philosophy of the time. The delegates to the Constitutional Convention in 1787 brought with them two important sets of influences: their political culture and their political experience. In the years between the first settlements in the New World and the writing of the Constitution, Americans had developed a political philosophy about how people should be governed and had tried out several forms of government. These experiences gave the founders the tools with which they constructed the Constitution.

THE COLONIAL BACKGROUND

In 1607, the English government sent a group of farmers to establish a trading post, Jamestown, in what is now Virginia. The Virginia Company of London was the first to establish a permanent English colony in the Americas. The king of England gave the backers of this colony a charter granting them "full power and authority" to make laws "for the good and welfare" of the settlement. The colonists at Jamestown instituted a **representative assembly,** a legislature composed of individuals who represent the population, thus setting a precedent in government that was to be observed in later colonial adventures.

Jamestown was not an immediate success. Of the 105 men who landed, 67 died within the first year. But 800 new arrivals in 1609 added to their numbers. By the spring of the next year, frontier hazards had cut their numbers to 60. Of the 6,000 people who left England for Virginia between 1607 and 1623, 4,800 perished. This period is sometimes referred to as the "starving time for Virginia." Climatological researchers suggest that this "starving time" may have been brought about by a severe drought in the Jamestown area, which lasted from 1607 to 1612.

SEPARATISTS, THE *MAYFLOWER*, AND THE COMPACT

The first New England colony was established in 1620. A group made up mostly of extreme Separatists, who wished to break with the Church of England, came over on the ship *Mayflower* to the New World, landing at Plymouth (Massachusetts). Before going onshore, the adult males—women were not considered to have any political status—drew up the Mayflower Compact, which was signed by forty-one of the forty-four men aboard the ship on November 21, 1620. The reason for the compact was obvious. This group was outside the jurisdiction of the Virginia Company of London, which had chartered its settlement in Virginia, not Massachusetts. The Separatist leaders feared that

Representative Assembly
A legislature composed of individuals who represent the population.

The signing of the compact aboard the *Mayflower*.

In 1620, the Mayflower Compact was signed by almost all of the men aboard the *Mayflower* just before they disembarked at Plymouth, Massachusetts. It stated, "We . . . covenant and combine ourselves togeather into a civil body politick . . . ; and by vertue hearof to enacte, constitute, and frame such just and equal laws : . . as shall be thought [necessary] for the generall good of the Colonie." (Library of Congress)

some of the *Mayflower* passengers might conclude that they were no longer under any obligations of civil obedience. Therefore, some form of public authority was imperative. As William Bradford (one of the Separatist leaders) recalled in his accounts, there were "discontented and mutinous speeches that some of the strangers amongst them had let fall from them in the ship; That when they came a shore they would use their owne libertie; for none had power to command them."[1]

The compact was not a constitution. It was a political statement in which the signers agreed to create and submit to the authority of a government, pending the receipt of a royal charter. The Mayflower Compact's historical and political significance is twofold: it depended on the consent of the affected individuals, and it served as a prototype for similar compacts in American history. According to Samuel Eliot Morison, the compact proved the determination of the English immigrants to live under the rule of law, based on the *consent of the people*.[2]

MORE COLONIES, MORE GOVERNMENT

Another outpost in New England was set up by the Massachusetts Bay Colony in 1630. Then followed Rhode Island, Connecticut, New Hampshire, and others. By 1732, the last of the thirteen colonies, Georgia, was established. During the colonial period, Americans developed a concept of limited government, which followed from the establishment of the first colonies under Crown charters. Theoretically, London governed the colonies. In practice, owing partly to the colonies' distance from London, the colonists exercised a large measure of self-government. The colonists were able to make their own laws, as in the Fundamental Orders of Connecticut in 1639. The Massachusetts Body of Liberties in 1641 supported the protection of individual rights and was made a part of colonial law. In 1682, the Pennsylvania Frame of Government was passed. Along with the Pennsylvania Charter of Privileges of 1701, it foreshadowed our modern Constitution and Bill of Rights. All of this legislation enabled the colonists to acquire crucial political experience. After independence was declared in 1776, the states quickly set up their own new constitutions.

BRITISH RESTRICTIONS AND COLONIAL GRIEVANCES

The conflict between Britain and the American colonies, which ultimately led to the Revolutionary War, began in the 1760s when the British government decided to raise revenues by imposing taxes on the American colonies. Policy advisers to Britain's young King George III, who ascended the throne in 1760, decided that it was only logical to require the American colonists to help pay the costs of Britain's defending them during the French and Indian War (1756–1763). The colonists, who had grown accustomed to a large degree of self-government and independence from the British Crown, viewed the matter differently.

In 1764, the British Parliament passed the Sugar Act. Many colonists were unwilling to pay the tax imposed by the act. Further regulatory legislation was to come. In 1765, Parliament passed the Stamp Act, providing for internal taxation—or, as the colonists' Stamp Act Congress, assembled in 1765, called it, "taxation without representation." The colo-

---

1. John Camp, *Out of the Wilderness: The Emergence of an American Identity in Colonial New England* (Middleton, Conn.: Wesleyan University Press, 1990).
2. See Morison's "The Mayflower Compact" in Daniel J. Boorstin, ed., *An American Primer* (Chicago: University of Chicago Press, 1966), p. 18.

nists boycotted the purchase of English commodities in return. The success of the boycott (the Stamp Act was repealed a year later) generated a feeling of unity within the colonies. The British, however, continued to try to raise revenues in the colonies. When Parliament passed duties on glass, lead, paint, and other items in 1767, the colonists again boycotted British goods. The colonists' fury over taxation climaxed in the Boston Tea Party: colonists dressed as Mohawk Indians dumped close to 350 chests of British tea into Boston Harbor as a gesture of tax protest. In retaliation, Parliament passed the Coercive Acts (the "Intolerable Acts") in 1774, which closed Boston Harbor and placed the government of Massachusetts under direct British control. The colonists were outraged—and they responded.

THE COLONIAL RESPONSE: THE CONTINENTAL CONGRESSES

New York, Pennsylvania, and Rhode Island proposed the convening of a colonial congress. The Massachusetts House of Representatives requested that all colonies hold conventions to select delegates to be sent to Philadelphia for such a congress.

THE FIRST CONTINENTAL CONGRESS

The First Continental Congress was held at Carpenter's Hall on September 5, 1774. It was a gathering of delegates from twelve of the thirteen colonies (delegates from Georgia did not attend until 1775). At that meeting, there was little talk of independence. The Congress passed a resolution requesting that the colonies send a petition to King George III expressing their grievances. Resolutions were also passed requiring that the colonies raise their own troops and boycott British trade. The British government condemned the Congress's actions, treating them as open acts of rebellion.

The delegates to the First Continental Congress declared that in every county and city, a committee was to be formed whose mission was to spy on the conduct of friends and neighbors and to report to the press any violators of the trade ban. The formation of these committees was an act of cooperation among the colonies, which represented a step toward the creation of a national government.

THE SECOND CONTINENTAL CONGRESS

By the time the Second Continental Congress met in May 1775 (this time all of the colonies were represented), fighting already had broken out between the British and the colonists. One of the main actions of the Second Congress was to establish an army. It did this by declaring the militia that had gathered around Boston an army and naming George Washington as commander in chief. The participants in that Congress still attempted to reach a peaceful settlement with the British Parliament. One declaration of the Congress stated explicitly that "we have not raised armies with ambitious designs of separating from Great Britain, and establishing independent states." But by the beginning of 1776, military encounters had become increasingly frequent. Public debate was acrimonious. Then Thomas Paine's *Common Sense* appeared in Philadelphia

King George III

(1738–1820) was king of Great Britain and Ireland from 1760 until his death on January 29, 1820. Under George III, the British Parliament attempted to tax the American colonies. Ultimately, the colonies, exasperated at repeated attempts at taxation, proclaimed their independence on July 4, 1776. (National Portrait Gallery)

Milestones in Early U.S. Political History	
1607	Jamestown established; Virginia Company lands settlers.
1620	Mayflower Compact signed.
1630	Massachusetts Bay Colony set up.
1639	Fundamental Orders of Connecticut adopted.
1641	Massachusetts Body of Liberties adopted.
1682	Pennsylvania Frame of Government passed.
1701	Pennsylvania Charter of Privileges written.
1732	Last of the thirteen colonies (Georgia) established.
1756	French and Indian War declared.
1765	Stamp Act; Stamp Act Congress meets.
1774	First Continental Congress.
1775	Second Continental Congress; Revolutionary War begins.
1776	Declaration of Independence signed.
1777	Articles of Confederation drafted.
1781	Last state (Maryland) signs Articles of Confederation.
1783	"Critical period" in U.S. history begins; weak national government until 1789.
1786	Shays' Rebellion.
1787	Constitutional Convention.
1788	Ratification of Constitution.
1791	Ratification of Bill of Rights.

bookstores. The pamphlet was a colonial best seller. (To do relatively as well today, a book would have to sell between 9 million and 11 million copies in its first year of publication.) Many agreed that Paine did make common sense when he argued that

> *a government of our own is our natural right: and when a man seriously reflects on the precariousness [instability, unpredictability] of human affairs, he will become convinced, that it is infinitely wiser and safer, to form a constitution of our own in a cool and deliberate manner, while we have it in our power, than to trust such an interesting event to time and chance.*[3]

Paine further argued that "nothing can settle our affairs so expeditiously as an open and determined declaration for Independence."[4]

Students of Paine's pamphlet point out that his arguments were not new—they were common in tavern debates throughout the land. Rather, it was the near poetry of his words—which were at the same time as plain as the alphabet—that struck his readers.

DECLARING INDEPENDENCE

On April 6, 1776, the Second Continental Congress voted for free trade at all American ports with all countries except Britain. This act could be interpreted as an implicit declaration of independence. The next month, the Congress suggested that each of the colonies establish state governments unconnected to Britain. Finally, in July, the colonists declared their independence from Britain.

THE RESOLUTION OF INDEPENDENCE

On July 2, the Resolution of Independence was adopted by the Second Continental Congress:

> *RESOLVED, That these United Colonies are, and of right ought to be free and independent States, that they are absolved from allegiance to the British Crown, and that all political connection between them and the state of Great Britain is, and ought to be, totally dissolved.*

Already by June 1776, Thomas Jefferson was writing drafts of the Declaration of Independence in the second-floor parlor of a bricklayer's house in Philadelphia. On adoption of the Resolution of Independence, Jefferson argued that a declaration clearly putting forth the causes that compelled the colonies to separate from Britain was necessary. The Second Congress assigned the task to him.

JULY 4, 1776—THE DECLARATION OF INDEPENDENCE

Jefferson's version of the declaration was amended to gain unanimous acceptance (for example, his condemnation of the slave trade was eliminated to satisfy Georgia and North Carolina), but the bulk of it was passed intact on July 4, 1776. On July 19, the modified draft became "the unanimous declaration of the thirteen United States of America." On August 2, it was signed by the members of the Second Continental Congress.

Universal Truths. The Declaration of Independence has become one of the world's most famous and significant documents. The words opening the second paragraph of the Declaration are known most widely:

> *We hold these Truths to be self-evident, that all Men are created equal, that they are endowed by their Creator with certain unalienable Rights, that among these are Life, Liberty, and the Pursuit of Happiness—That to secure these Rights,*

didyouknow...

That the word *democracy* **does not appear once in the Constitution?**

---

3. *The Political Writings of Thomas Paine,* Vol. 1 (Boston: J. P. Mendum Investigator Office, 1870), p. 46.
4. Ibid., p. 54.

Governments are instituted among Men, deriving their just Powers from the Consent of the Governed, that whenever any Form of Government becomes destructive of these Ends, it is the Right of the People to alter or abolish it, and to institute new Government.

Natural Rights and a Social Contract. The assumption that people have **natural rights** ("unalienable Rights"), including the rights to "Life, Liberty, and the Pursuit of Happiness," was a revolutionary concept at that time. Its use by Jefferson reveals the influence of the English philosopher John Locke (1632–1704), whose writings were familiar to educated American colonists, including Jefferson.[5] In his *Two Treatises on Government,* published in 1690, Locke had argued that all people possess certain natural rights, including the rights to life, liberty, and property, and that the primary purpose of government was to protect these rights. Furthermore, government was established by the people through a **social contract**—an agreement among the people to form a government and abide by its rules. As you read earlier, such contracts, or compacts, were not new to Americans. The Mayflower Compact was the first of several documents that established governments or governing rules based on the consent of the governed. In citing the "pursuit of happiness" instead of "property" as a right, Jefferson clearly meant to go beyond Locke's thinking.

After setting forth these basic principles of government, the Declaration of Independence goes on to justify the colonists' revolt against Britain. Much of the remainder of the document is a list of what "He" (King George III) had done to deprive the colonists of their rights. (See Appendix A at the end of this book for the complete text of the Declaration of Independence.)

The Significance of the Declaration. The concepts of universal truths, natural rights, and government being established by a social contract expressed in the Declaration of Independence were to have a lasting impact on American life. The Declaration set forth ideals that have since become a fundamental part of our national identity. The Declaration of Independence also became a model for use by other nations around the world. The Declaration of Independence, the Constitution, and eventually the Bill of Rights made America an exceptional country from the outset. Have we lost that status in recent years? That is the topic of this chapter's *Beyond Our Borders* feature on the next page.

Certainly, most Americans are familiar with the words of the Declaration. Yet, as Harvard historian David Armitage noted in his study of the Declaration of Independence in the international context,[6] few Americans ponder the obvious question: What did these assertions in the Declaration have to do with independence? Clearly, independence could have been declared without these words. Even as late as 1857, Abraham Lincoln admitted, "The assertion that 'all men are created equal' was of no practical use in effecting our separation from Great Britain; and it was placed in the Declaration, not for that, but for future use."[7]

Essentially, the immediate significance of the Declaration of Independence, in 1776, was that it established the legitimacy of the new nation in the eyes of foreign governments, as well as in the eyes of the colonists themselves. What the new nation needed most were

Members of the Second Continental Congress adopted the Declaration of Independence on July 4, 1776. Minor changes were made in the document in the following two weeks. On July 19, the modified draft became the "unanimous declaration of the thirteen United States of America." On August 2, the members of the Second Continental Congress signed it. The first official printed version carried only the signatures of the Congress's president, John Hancock, and its secretary, Charles Thompson. (Painting by John Trumbull, 1819/Library of Congress)

Natural Rights
Rights held to be inherent in natural law, not dependent on governments. John Locke stated that natural law, being superior to human law, specifies certain rights of "life, liberty, and property." These rights, altered to become "life, liberty, and the pursuit of happiness," are asserted in the Declaration of Independence.

Social Contract
A voluntary agreement among individuals to secure their rights and welfare by creating a government and abiding by its rules.

---

5. Not all scholars believe that Jefferson was truly influenced by Locke. For example, Jay Fliegelman states that "Jefferson's fascination with Homer, Ossian, Patrick Henry, and the violin is of greater significance than his indebtedness to Locke." Jay Fliegelman, *Declaring Independence: Jefferson, Natural Language, and the Culture of Performance* (Palo Alto, Calif.: Stanford University Press, 1993).
6. David Armitage, *The Declaration of Independence: A Global History* (Cambridge, Mass.: Harvard University Press, 2007).
7. As cited in Armitage, *The Declaration of Independence,* p. 26.

beyondourborders

AMERICANS NO LONGER HAVE "EXCEPTIONAL" VIEWS

The United States has always thought of itself as exceptional. In the early years, Americans believed they had a unique commitment to liberty and to free institutions. Today, of course, many of the world's nations are representative democracies.

Americans also have long believed that their views were more modern, more accepting, and more tolerant than those in most of the rest of the world. The United States has been seen as the place where the boundaries of personal freedom were stretched, where the first modern feminist organizations and groups were founded, and where wacky new lifestyles and crazes were most enthusiastically adopted. For much of the world, America was the future.

AMERICAN TOLERANCE?

You would not get the impression that America is particularly tolerant from the latest Pew Global Attitudes Survey, however. For example, the United States has a rather chilly attitude on whether homosexuality should be accepted (which ought to elicit more positive responses than a question on whether there should be civil unions or gay marriages). On the acceptance issue, 49 percent of Americans say yes, and 41 percent say no. The United States has a smaller share of the public responding positively than does any Western European country, as well as many Eastern European and most Latin American countries. For example, in Mexico, 60 percent say yes, and 31 percent, no.

I'M IN, SO CLOSE THE DOOR

The Pew survey also suggests that Americans are much more pessimistic than other nations on "globalization" issues. Consider immigration. It's been repeated so many times that it's a terrible cliché—we are a nation of immigrants. Today, however, anti-immigration sentiment is stronger in the United States than almost anywhere else. The Pew study finds more anti-immigration sentiment in the United States than in France or Germany, which have also taken in large numbers of immigrants in recent years. Some of those running for election or reelection to Congress during the campaigns of 2004 and 2008 may have won, at least in part, because of harsh stands against immigration.

FREE TRADE NO LONGER SHOULD BE FREE

Because the Constitution prohibits restrictions on trade between and among the fifty states, the United States is a gigantic free trade zone. For decades, most Americans understood the importance of free trade and saw the benefits of trade among nations. Today, in contrast, a majority of Americans take the opposite view. In the Pew study just cited, of the forty-seven countries surveyed, the United States had the most negative view of world trade. Americans also express negative views of foreign companies, whereas most people in the rest of the world have positive views. And consider that the richest people in the world are no longer all Americans. Indeed, of the ten richest people in the world, eight are *not* Americans.

(Creative Commons)

FOR CRITICAL ANALYSIS

When surveyed, Americans have positive attitudes toward the free movement of people and goods throughout the United States. But when queried about the free movement of people and goods from foreign countries, those attitudes become negative. What is the difference?

supplies for its armies and a commitment of foreign military aid. Unless it appeared to the world as a political entity separate and independent from Britain, no foreign government would enter into an agreement with its leaders. Once the Declaration had fulfilled its purpose of legitimizing the American Revolution, the document was all but forgotten for many years. The lasting significance of the Declaration—as a founding document setting forth American ideals—came much later. According to scholar Pauline Maier, the Declaration did not become enshrined as what she calls "American Scripture" until the late 1800s.[8]

8. See Pauline Maier, *American Scripture: Making the Declaration of Independence* (New York: Knopf, 1997).

THE RISE OF REPUBLICANISM

Although the colonists had formally declared independence from Britain, the fight to gain actual independence continued for five more years—until the British general Cornwallis surrendered at Yorktown in 1781. In 1783, after Britain formally recognized the independent status of the United States in the Treaty of Paris, Washington disbanded the army. During these years of military struggles, the states faced the additional challenge of creating a system of self-government for an independent United States.

Some colonists had demanded that independence be preceded by the formation of a strong central government. But others, who called themselves Republicans, were against a strong central government. They opposed monarchy, executive authority, and virtually any form of restraint on the power of local groups.

From 1776 to 1780, all of the states adopted written constitutions. Eleven of the constitutions were completely new. Two of them—those of Connecticut and Rhode Island—were old royal charters with minor modifications. Republican sentiment led to increased power for the legislatures. In Georgia and Pennsylvania, **unicameral** (one-body) **legislatures** were unchecked by executive or judicial authority. Basically, the Republicans attempted to maintain the politics of 1776. In almost all states, the legislature was predominant.

THE ARTICLES OF CONFEDERATION: THE FIRST FORM OF GOVERNMENT

The fear of a powerful central government led to the passage of the Articles of Confederation, which created a weak central government. The term **confederation** is important; it means a voluntary association of *independent* **states,** in which the member states agree to only limited restraints on their freedom of action. As a result, confederations seldom have an effective executive authority.

In June 1776, the Second Continental Congress began the process of drafting what would become the Articles of Confederation. The final form of the Articles was achieved by November 15, 1777. It was not until March 1, 1781, however, that the last state, Maryland, agreed to ratify what was called the Articles of Confederation and Perpetual Union. Well before the final ratification of the Articles, however, many of them were implemented: the Continental Congress and the thirteen states conducted American military, economic, and political affairs according to the standards and the form specified by the Articles.[9]

Under the Articles, the thirteen original colonies, now states, established on March 1, 1781, a government of the states—the Congress of the Confederation. The Congress was a unicameral assembly of so-called ambassadors from each state, with each state possessing a single vote. Each year, the Congress would choose one of its members as its president (that is, presiding officer), but the Articles did not provide for a president of the United States.

The Congress was authorized in Article X to appoint an executive committee of the states "to execute in the recess of Congress, such of the powers of Congress as the United States, in Congress assembled, by the consent of nine [of the thirteen] states, shall from time to time think expedient to vest with them." The Congress was also allowed to appoint other committees and civil officers necessary for managing the general affairs of the United States. In addition, the Congress could regulate foreign affairs and establish coinage and weights and measures. But it lacked an independent source of revenue and the necessary executive machinery to enforce its decisions throughout the land. Article II

Unicameral Legislature
A legislature with only one legislative chamber, as opposed to a bicameral (two-chamber) legislature, such as the U.S. Congress. Today, Nebraska is the only state in the Union with a unicameral legislature.

Confederation
A political system in which states or regional governments retain ultimate authority except for those powers they expressly delegate to a central government; a voluntary association of independent states, in which the member states agree to limited restraints on their freedom of action.

State
A group of people occupying a specific area and organized under one government; may be either a nation or a subunit of a nation.

didyouknow...

That the Articles of Confederation specified that Canada could be admitted to the Confederation if it ever wished to join?

---

9. Robert W. Hoffert, *A Politics of Tensions: The Articles of Confederation and American Political Ideas* (Niwot, Colo.: University Press of Colorado, 1992).

FIGURE 2–1:
The Confederal
Government
Structure under
the Articles of
Confederation

Congress
Congress had one house. Each state had two to seven members, but only one vote. The exercise of most powers required approval of at least nine states. Amendments to the Articles required the consent of all the states.

⬇

Committee of the States
A committee of representatives from all the states was empowered to act in the name of Congress between sessions.

⬇

Officers
Congress appointed officers to do some of the executive work.

⬇

The States

of the Articles of Confederation guaranteed that each state would retain its sovereignty. Figure 2–1 illustrates the structure of the government under the Articles of Confederation; Table 2–1 summarizes the powers—and the lack of powers—of Congress under the Articles of Confederation.

ACCOMPLISHMENTS UNDER THE ARTICLES

The new government had some accomplishments during its eight years of existence under the Articles of Confederation. Certain states' claims to western lands were settled. Maryland had objected to the claims of the Carolinas, Connecticut, Georgia, Massachusetts, New York, and Virginia. It was only after these states consented to give up their land claims to the United States as a whole that Maryland signed the Articles of Confederation. Another accomplishment under the Articles was the passage of the Northwest Ordinance of 1787, which established a basic pattern of government for new territories north of the Ohio River. All in all, the Articles represented the first real pooling of resources by the American states.

WEAKNESSES OF THE ARTICLES

In spite of these accomplishments, the Articles of Confederation had many defects. Although Congress had the legal right to declare war and to conduct foreign policy, it did not have the right to demand revenues from the states. It could only ask for them. Additionally, the actions of Congress required the consent of nine states. Any amendments to the Articles required the unanimous consent of the Congress and confirmation by every state legislature. Furthermore, the Articles did not create a national system of courts.

Basically, the functioning of the government under the Articles depended on the goodwill of the states. Article III of the Articles simply established a "league of friendship" among the states—no national government was intended.

Probably, the most fundamental weakness of the Articles, and the most basic cause of their eventual replacement by the Constitution, was the lack of power to raise funds for the militia. The Articles contained no language giving Congress coercive power to raise revenues (by levying taxes) to provide adequate support for the military forces controlled by Congress. When states refused to send revenues to support the government (not one state met the financial requests made by Congress under the Articles), Congress resorted

TABLE 2–1: Powers of the Congress of the Confederation

Congress Had Power to	Congress Lacked Power to
• Declare war and make peace.	• Provide for effective treaty-making power and control foreign relations; it could not compel states to respect treaties.
• Enter into treaties and alliances.	
• Establish and control armed forces.	
• Requisition men and revenues from states.	• Compel states to meet military quotas; it could not draft soldiers.
• Regulate coinage.	
• Borrow funds and issue bills of credit.	• Regulate interstate and foreign commerce; it left each state free to set up its own tariff system.
• Fix uniform standards of weight and measurement.	
• Create admiralty courts.	• Collect taxes directly from the people; it had to rely on states to collect and forward taxes.
• Create a postal system.	
• Regulate Indian affairs.	• Compel states to pay their share of government costs.
• Guarantee citizens of each state the rights and privileges of citizens in the several states when in another state.	• Provide and maintain a sound monetary system or issue paper money; this was left up to the states, and monies in circulation differed tremendously in value.
• Adjudicate disputes between states on state petition.	

to selling off western lands to speculators or issuing bonds that sold for less than their face value. Due to a lack of resources, the Continental Congress was forced to disband the army, even in the face of serious Spanish and British military threats.

SHAYS' REBELLION AND THE NEED FOR REVISION OF THE ARTICLES

Because of the weaknesses of the Articles of Confederation, the central government could do little to maintain peace and order in the new nation. The states bickered among themselves and increasingly taxed each other's goods. At times they prevented trade altogether. By 1784, the country faced a serious economic depression. Banks were calling in old loans and refusing to give new ones. People who could not pay their debts were often thrown into prison.

By 1786, in Concord, Massachusetts, the scene of one of the first battles of the Revolution, there were three times as many people in prison for debt as there were for all other crimes combined. In Worcester County, Massachusetts, the ratio was even higher—twenty to one. Most of the prisoners were small farmers who could not pay their debts because of the disorganized state of the economy.

In August 1786, mobs of musket-bearing farmers led by former revolutionary captain Daniel Shays seized county courthouses and disrupted the trials of debtors in Springfield, Massachusetts. Shays and his men then launched an attack on the federal arsenal at Springfield, but they were repulsed. Shays' Rebellion demonstrated that the central government could not protect the citizenry from armed rebellion or provide adequately for the public welfare. The rebellion spurred the nation's political leaders to action. As John Jay wrote to Thomas Jefferson,

> *Changes are Necessary, but what they ought to be, what they will be, and how and when to be produced, are arduous Questions. I feel for the Cause of Liberty. . . . If it should not take Root in this Soil[,] Little Pains will be taken to cultivate it in any other.*[10]

This colorized engraving shows a mob of discontents seizing a Massachusetts courthouse during Shays' Rebellion in the summer of 1786. In what way did Shays' Rebellion show the weaknesses of the Articles of Confederation?
(Bettmann/Corbis)

DRAFTING THE CONSTITUTION

The Virginia legislature called for a meeting of all the states to be held at Annapolis, Maryland, on September 11, 1786—ostensibly to discuss commercial problems only. It was evident to those in attendance (including Alexander Hamilton and James Madison) that the national government had serious weaknesses that had to be addressed if it was to survive. Among the important problems to be solved were the relationship between the states and the central government, the powers of the national legislature, the need for executive leadership, and the establishment of policies for economic stability.

The result of this meeting was a petition to the Continental Congress for a general convention to meet in Philadelphia in May 1787 "to consider the exigencies of the union." Congress approved the convention in February 1787. When those who favored a weak central government realized that the Philadelphia meeting would in fact take place, they endorsed the convention. They made sure, however, that the convention would be summoned "for the sole and express purpose of revising the Articles of Confederation." Those in favor of a stronger national government had different ideas.

The designated date for the opening of the convention at Philadelphia, now known as the Constitutional Convention, was May 14, 1787. Because few of the delegates had actually arrived in Philadelphia by that time, however, the convention was not formally

didyouknow...

That the 1776 constitution of New Jersey granted the vote to "all free inhabitants," including women, but the large number of women who turned out to vote resulted in male protests and a new law limiting the right to vote to "free white male citizens"?

---

10. Excerpt from a letter from John Jay to Thomas Jefferson written in October 1786, as reproduced in Winthrop D. Jordan *et al., The United States,* combined ed., 6th ed. (Englewood Cliffs, N.J.: Prentice Hall, 1987), p. 135.

opened in the East Room of the Pennsylvania State House until May 25.[11] Fifty-five of the seventy-four delegates chosen for the convention actually attended. (Of those fifty-five, only about forty played active roles at the convention.) Rhode Island was the only state that refused to send delegates.

WHO WERE THE DELEGATES?

Who were the fifty-five delegates to the Constitutional Convention? They certainly did not represent a cross section of American society in the 1700s. Indeed, most were members of the upper class. Consider the following facts:

1. Thirty-three were members of the legal profession.
2. Three were physicians.
3. Almost 50 percent were college graduates.
4. Seven were former chief executives of their respective states.
5. Six were owners of large plantations.
6. Eight were important businesspersons.

They were also relatively young by today's standards: James Madison was thirty-six, Alexander Hamilton was only thirty-two, and Jonathan Dayton of New Jersey was twenty-six. The venerable Benjamin Franklin, however, was eighty-one and had to be carried in on a portable chair borne by four prisoners from a local jail. Not counting Franklin, the average age was just over forty-two.

THE WORKING ENVIRONMENT

The conditions under which the delegates worked for 115 days were far from ideal and were made even worse by the necessity of maintaining total secrecy. The framers of the Constitution believed that if public debate took place on particular positions, delegates would have a more difficult time compromising or backing down to reach agreement. Consequently, the windows were usually shut in the East Room of the State House. Summer quickly arrived, and the air became heavy, humid, and hot by noon of each day. Also, when the windows were open, flies swarmed into the room. The delegates did, however, have a nearby tavern and inn to which they retired each evening. The Indian Queen became the informal headquarters of the delegates.

didyouknow...

That James Madison was the only delegate to attend every meeting of the Constitutional Convention?

FACTIONS AMONG THE DELEGATES

We know much about the proceedings at the convention because James Madison kept a daily, detailed personal journal. A majority of the delegates were strong nationalists—they wanted a central government with real power, unlike the central government under the Articles of Confederation. George Washington and Benjamin Franklin preferred limited national authority based on a separation of powers. They were apparently willing to accept any type of national government, however, as long as the other delegates approved it. A few advocates of a strong central government, led by Gouverneur Morris of Pennsylvania and John Rutledge of South Carolina, distrusted the ability of the common people to engage in self-government.

Among the nationalists, several went so far as to support monarchy. This group included Alexander Hamilton, who was chiefly responsible for the Annapolis Convention's call for the Constitutional Convention. In a long speech on June 18, he presented his views: "I have no scruple in declaring . . . that the British government is the best in the world and that I doubt much whether anything short of it will do in America."

Another important group of nationalists were of a more democratic stripe. Led by James Madison of Virginia and James Wilson of Pennsylvania, these democratic nationalists wanted a central government founded on popular support.

---

11. The State House was later named Independence Hall. This was the same room in which the Declaration of Independence had been signed eleven years earlier.

Still another faction consisted of nationalists who were less democratic in nature and who would support a central government only if it was founded on very narrowly defined republican principles. This group was made up of a relatively small number of delegates, including Edmund Randolph and George Mason of Virginia, Elbridge Gerry of Massachusetts, and Luther Martin and John Francis Mercer of Maryland.

Many of the other delegates from Connecticut, Delaware, Maryland, New Hampshire, and New Jersey were concerned about only one thing—claims to western lands. As long as those lands became the common property of all of the states, these delegates were willing to support a central government.

Finally, there was a group of delegates who were totally against a national authority. Two of the three delegates from New York quit the convention when they saw the nationalist direction of its proceedings.

Elbridge Gerry
(1744–1814), from Massachusetts, was a patriot during the Revolution. He was a signatory of the Declaration of Independence and later became governor of Massachusetts (1810–1812). He became James Madison's vice president when Madison was reelected in December 1812.
(Library of Congress)

POLITICKING AND COMPROMISES

The debates at the convention started on the first day. James Madison had spent months reviewing European political theory. When his Virginia delegation arrived ahead of most of the others, it got to work immediately. By the time George Washington opened the convention, Governor Edmund Randolph of Virginia was prepared to present fifteen resolutions. In retrospect, this was a masterful stroke on the part of the Virginia delegation. It set the agenda for the remainder of the convention—even though, in principle, the delegates had been sent to Philadelphia for the sole purpose of amending the Articles of Confederation. They had not been sent to write a new constitution.

The Virginia Plan. Randolph's fifteen resolutions proposed an entirely new national government under a constitution. It was, however, a plan that favored the large states, including Virginia. Basically, it called for the following:

1. A **bicameral** (two-chamber) **legislature,** with the lower chamber chosen by the people and the smaller upper chamber chosen by the lower chamber from nominees selected by state legislatures. The number of representatives would be proportional to a state's population, thus favoring the large states. The legislature could void any state laws.
2. The creation of an unspecified national executive, elected by the legislature.
3. The creation of a national judiciary, appointed by the legislature.

It did not take long for the smaller states to realize they would fare poorly under the Virginia plan, which would enable Massachusetts, Pennsylvania, and Virginia to form a majority in the national legislature. The debate on the plan dragged on for a number of weeks. It was time for the small states to come up with their own plan.

The New Jersey Plan. On June 15, lawyer William Paterson of New Jersey offered an alternative plan. After all, argued Paterson, under the Articles of Confederation all states had equality; therefore, the convention had no power to change this arrangement. He proposed the following:

1. The fundamental principle of the Articles of Confederation—one state, one vote—would be retained.
2. Congress would be able to regulate trade and impose taxes.
3. All acts of Congress would be the supreme law of the land.
4. Several people would be elected by Congress to form an executive office.
5. The executive office would appoint a Supreme Court.

Basically, the New Jersey plan was simply an amendment of the Articles of Confederation. Its only notable feature was its reference to the **supremacy doctrine,** which was later included in the Constitution.

Bicameral Legislature
A legislature made up of two parts, called chambers. The U.S. Congress, composed of the House of Representatives and the Senate, is a bicameral legislature.

Supremacy Doctrine
A doctrine that asserts the priority of national law over state laws. This principle is rooted in Article VI of the Constitution, which provides that the Constitution, the laws passed by the national government under its constitutional powers, and all treaties constitute the supreme law of the land.

George Washington

presided over the Constitutional Convention of 1787. Although the convention was supposed to start on May 14, 1787, few of the delegates had actually arrived in Philadelphia by that date. The convention formally opened in the East Room of the Pennsylvania State House (later named Independence Hall) on May 25. Only Rhode Island did not send any delegates. (Corbis)

Great Compromise

The compromise between the New Jersey and Virginia plans that created one chamber of the Congress based on population and one chamber representing each state equally; also called the Connecticut Compromise.

The "Great Compromise." The delegates were at an impasse. Most wanted a strong national government and were unwilling even to consider the New Jersey plan. But when the Virginia plan was brought up again, the small states threatened to leave. It was not until July 16 that a compromise was achieved. Roger Sherman of Connecticut proposed the following:

1. A bicameral legislature in which the lower chamber, the House of Representatives, would be apportioned according to the number of free inhabitants in each state, plus three-fifths of the slaves.
2. An upper chamber, the Senate, which would have two members from each state elected by the state legislatures.

This plan, known as the **Great Compromise** (it is also called the Connecticut Compromise because of the role of the Connecticut delegates in the proposal), broke the deadlock. It did exact a political price, however, because it permitted each state to have equal representation in the Senate. Having two senators represent each state in effect diluted the voting power of citizens living in more heavily populated states and gave the smaller states disproportionate political powers. But the Connecticut Compromise resolved the large-state/small-state controversy. In addition, the Senate acted as part of a checks-and-balances system against the House, which many feared would be dominated by, and responsive to, the masses.

The Three-Fifths Compromise. The Great Compromise also settled another major issue—how to deal with slaves in the representational scheme. Slavery was still legal in many northern states, but it was concentrated in the South. Many delegates were opposed to slavery and wanted it banned entirely in the United States. Charles Pinckney of South Carolina led strong southern opposition to a ban on slavery. Furthermore, the South wanted slaves to be counted along with free persons in determining representation in Congress. Delegates from the northern states objected. Sherman's three-fifths proposal was a compromise between northerners who did not want the slaves counted at all and southerners who wanted them counted in the same way as free whites. Actually, Sherman's Connecticut plan spoke of three-fifths of "all other persons" (and that is the language of the Constitution itself). It is not hard to figure out, though, who those other persons were.

The three-fifths compromise illustrates the power of the southern states at the convention.[12] The three-fifths rule meant that the House of Representatives and the electoral college would be apportioned in part on the basis of *property*—specifically, property in slaves. Modern commentators have referred to the three-fifths rule as valuing African Americans only three-fifths as much as whites. Actually, the additional southern representatives elected because of the three-fifths rule did not represent the slaves at all. Rather, these extra representatives were a gift to the slave owners—the additional representatives enhanced the power of the South in Congress.

didyouknow...

That during the four centuries of slave trading, an estimated 10 million to 11 million Africans were transported to North and South America—and that only 6 percent of those slaves were imported into the United States?

The Slave Trade and the Future of Slavery. The three-fifths compromise did not completely settle the slavery issue. There was also the question of the slave trade. Eventually, the delegates agreed that Congress could not ban the importation of slaves until after 1808.

The compromise meant that the matter of slavery itself was never addressed directly. The South won twenty years of unrestricted slave trade and a requirement that escaped slaves in free states be returned to their owners in slave states.

Clearly, many delegates, including George Washington and James Madison, had serious doubts about slavery. Why, then, did they allow slavery to continue?

12. See Garry Wills, *"Negro President": Jefferson and the Slave Power* (New York: Houghton Mifflin, 2003).

Historians have long maintained that the framers had no choice—that without a slavery compromise, the delegates from the South would have abandoned the convention. Indeed, this was the fear of a number of the antislavery delegates to the convention. Madison, for example, said, "Great as the evil is, a dismemberment of the Union would be even worse."[13] Other scholars, however, contend that not only would it have been possible for the founders to ban slavery, but by doing so they would have achieved greater unity for the new nation.[14]

didyouknow...

That the U.S. Constitution, at 4,400 words, is the shortest written constitution of any major nation?

Other Issues. The South also worried that the northern majority in Congress would pass legislation unfavorable to its economic interests. Because the South depended on agricultural exports, it feared the imposition of export taxes. In return for acceding to the northern demand that Congress be able to regulate commerce among the states and with other nations, the South obtained a promise that export taxes would not be imposed. As a result, the United States is among the few countries that do not tax their exports.

There were other disagreements. The delegates could not decide whether to establish only a Supreme Court or to create lower courts as well. They deferred the issue by mandating a Supreme Court and allowing Congress to establish lower courts. They also disagreed over whether the president or the Senate would choose the Supreme Court justices. A compromise was reached with the agreement that the president would nominate the justices and the Senate would confirm the nominations.

These compromises, as well as others, resulted from the recognition that if one group of states refused to ratify the Constitution, it was doomed.

WORKING TOWARD FINAL AGREEMENT

The Connecticut Compromise was reached by mid-July. The makeup of the executive branch and the judiciary, however, was left unsettled. The remaining work of the convention was turned over to a five-man Committee of Detail, which presented a rough draft of the Constitution on August 6. It made the executive and judicial branches subordinate to the legislative branch.

The Madisonian Model—Separation of Powers. The major issue of **separation of powers** had not yet been resolved. The delegates were concerned with structuring the government to prevent the imposition of tyranny—either by the majority or by a minority. It was Madison who proposed a governmental scheme—sometimes called the **Madisonian model**—to achieve this: the executive, legislative, and judicial powers of government were to be separated so that no one branch had enough power to dominate the others. The separation of powers was by function, as well as by personnel, with Congress passing laws, the president enforcing and administering laws, and the courts interpreting laws in individual circumstances.

Each of the three branches of government would be independent of the others, but they would have to cooperate to govern. According to Madison, in *Federalist Paper* No. 51 (see Appendix C), "the great security against a gradual concentration of the several powers in the same department consists in giving to those who administer each department the necessary constitutional means and personal motives to resist encroachments of the others."

The Madisonian Model—Checks and Balances. The "constitutional means" Madison referred to is a system of **checks and balances** through which each branch of the government can check the actions of the others. For example, Congress can enact laws, but the president has veto power over congressional acts. The Supreme Court has the

Separation of Powers
The principle of dividing governmental powers among different branches of government.

Madisonian Model
A structure of government proposed by James Madison in which the powers of the government are separated into three branches: executive, legislative, and judicial.

Checks and Balances
A major principle of the American system of government whereby each branch of the government can check the actions of the others.

---

13. Speech before the Virginia ratifying convention on June 17, 1788, as cited in Bruno Leone, ed., *The Creation of the Constitution* (San Diego: Greenhaven Press, 1995), p. 159.
14. See, for example, Paul Finkelman, *Slavery and the Founders: Race and Liberty in the Age of Jefferson*, 2d ed. (Armonk, N.Y.: M. E. Sharpe, 2001); and Gary B. Nash, *The Forgotten Fifth: African Americans in the Age of Revolution* (Cambridge, Mass.: Harvard University Press, 2006).

James Madison

(1751–1836) earned the title "master builder of the Constitution" because of his persuasive logic during the Constitutional Convention. His contributions to the *Federalist Papers* showed him to be a brilliant political thinker and writer. (Library of Congress)

power to declare acts of Congress and of the executive unconstitutional, but the president appoints the justices of the Supreme Court, with the advice and consent of the Senate. (The Supreme Court's power to declare acts unconstitutional was not mentioned in the Constitution, although arguably the framers assumed that the Court would have this power—see the discussion of *judicial review* later in this chapter.) Figure 2–2 outlines these checks and balances.

Madison's ideas of separation of powers and checks and balances were not new. Indeed, the influential French political thinker Baron de Montesquieu (1689–1755) had explored these concepts in his book *The Spirit of the Laws,* published in 1748. Montesquieu not only discussed the "three sorts of powers" (executive, legislative, and judicial) that were necessarily exercised by any government but also gave examples of how, in some nations, certain checks on these powers had arisen and had been effective in preventing tyranny.

In the years since the Constitution was ratified, the checks and balances built into it have evolved into a sometimes complex give-and-take among the branches of government. Generally, for nearly every check that one branch has over another, the branch that has been checked has found a way of getting around it. For example, suppose that the president checks Congress by vetoing a bill. Congress can override the presidential veto by a two-thirds vote. Additionally, Congress holds the "power of the purse." If it disagrees with a program endorsed by the executive branch, it can simply refuse to appropriate the funds necessary to operate that program. Similarly, the president can impose a countercheck on Congress if the Senate refuses to confirm a presidential appointment, such as a judicial appointment. The president can simply wait until Congress is in recess and then make what is called a "recess appointment," which does not require the Senate's approval.

FIGURE 2–2: Checks and Balances

The major checks and balances among the three branches are illustrated here. The U.S. Constitution does not mention some of these checks, such as judicial review—the power of the courts to declare federal or state acts unconstitutional—and the president's ability to refuse to enforce judicial decisions or congressional legislation. Checks and balances can be thought of as a confrontation of powers or responsibilities. Each branch checks the action of another; two branches in conflict have powers that can result in balances or stalemates, requiring one branch to give in or both to reach a compromise.

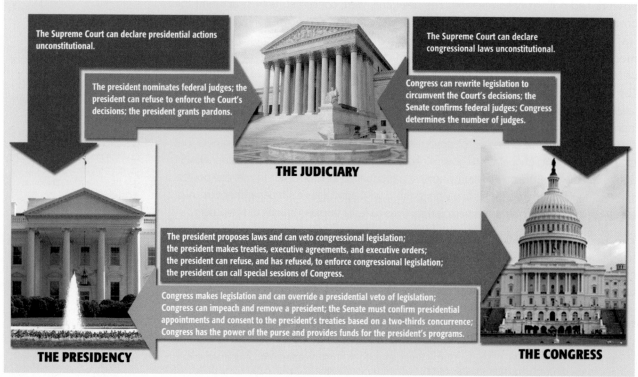

The Supreme Court can declare presidential actions unconstitutional.

The Supreme Court can declare congressional laws unconstitutional.

The president nominates federal judges; the president can refuse to enforce the Court's decisions; the president grants pardons.

Congress can rewrite legislation to circumvent the Court's decisions; the Senate confirms federal judges; Congress determines the number of judges.

THE JUDICIARY

The president proposes laws and can veto congressional legislation; the president makes treaties, executive agreements, and executive orders; the president can refuse, and has refused, to enforce congressional legislation; the president can call special sessions of Congress.

Congress makes legislation and can override a presidential veto of legislation; Congress can impeach and remove a president; the Senate must confirm presidential appointments and consent to the president's treaties based on a two-thirds concurrence; Congress has the power of the purse and provides funds for the president's programs.

THE PRESIDENCY

THE CONGRESS

Photos Creative Commons

The Executive. Some delegates favored a plural executive made up of representatives from the various regions. This was abandoned in favor of a single chief executive. Some argued that Congress should choose the executive. To make the presidency completely independent of the proposed Congress, however, an **Electoral College** was adopted. To be sure, the Electoral College created a cumbersome presidential election process (see Chapter 9). The process even made it possible for a candidate who comes in second in the popular vote to become president by being the top vote getter in the electoral college, which happened in 2000. The electoral college insulated the president, however, from direct popular control. The seven-year single term that some of the delegates had proposed was replaced by a four-year term and the possibility of reelection.

THE FINAL DOCUMENT

On September 17, 1787, the Constitution was approved by thirty-nine delegates. Of the fifty-five who had attended originally, only forty-two remained. Three delegates refused to sign the Constitution. Others disapproved of at least parts of it but signed anyway to begin the ratification debate.

The Constitution that was to be ratified established the following fundamental principles:

1. Popular sovereignty, or control by the people.
2. A republican government in which the people choose representatives to make decisions for them.
3. Limited government with written laws, in contrast to the powerful British government against which the colonists had rebelled.
4. Separation of powers, with checks and balances among branches to prevent any one branch from gaining too much power.
5. A federal system that allows for states' rights, because the states feared too much centralized control.

The U.S. Constitution.
(www.ourdocuments.gov.)

You will read about federalism in detail in Chapter 3. Suffice it to say here that in the **federal system** established by the founders, sovereign powers—ruling powers—are divided between the states and the national government. The Constitution expressly granted certain powers to the national government. For example, the national government was given the power to regulate commerce among the states. The Constitution also declared that the president is the nation's chief executive and the commander in chief of the armed forces. Additionally, the Constitution made it clear that laws made by the national government take priority over conflicting state laws. At the same time, the Constitution provided for extensive states' rights, including the right to control commerce within state borders and to exercise those governing powers that were not delegated to the national government.

The federal system created by the founders was a novel form of government at that time—no other country in the world had such a system. It was invented by the founders as a compromise solution to the controversy over whether the states or the central government should have ultimate sovereignty. As you will read in Chapter 3, the debate over where the line should be drawn between states' rights and the powers of the national government has characterized American politics ever since. The founders did not go into detail about where this line should be drawn, thus leaving it up to scholars and court judges to divine the founders' intentions.

Electoral College
A group of persons called *electors* selected by the voters in each state and the District of Columbia (D.C.); this group officially elects the president and vice president of the United States. The number of electors in each state is equal to the number of each state's representatives in both chambers of Congress. The Twenty-third Amendment to the Constitution grants D.C. as many electors as the state with the smallest population.

Federal System
A system of government in which power is divided between a central government and regional, or subdivisional, governments. Each level must have some domain in which its policies are dominant and some genuine political or constitutional guarantee of its authority.

THE DIFFICULT ROAD TO RATIFICATION

The founders knew that **ratification** of the Constitution was far from certain. Indeed, because it was almost guaranteed that many state legislatures would not ratify it, the delegates agreed that each state should hold a special convention. Elected delegates to these conventions would discuss and vote on the Constitution. Further departing from the Articles of Confederation, the delegates agreed that as soon as nine states (rather than all thirteen) approved the Constitution, it would take effect, and Congress could begin to organize the new government.

THE FEDERALISTS PUSH FOR RATIFICATION

The two opposing forces in the battle over ratification were the Federalists and the Anti-Federalists. The **Federalists**—those in favor of a strong central government and the new Constitution—had an advantage over their opponents, called the **Anti-Federalists,** who wanted to prevent the Constitution as drafted from being ratified. In the first place, the Federalists had assumed a positive name, leaving their opposition the negative label of *Anti*-Federalist.[15] More important, the Federalists had attended the Constitutional Convention and knew of all the deliberations that had taken place. Their opponents had no such knowledge, because those deliberations had not been open to the public. Thus, the Anti-Federalists were at a disadvantage in terms of information about the document. The Federalists also had time, power, and money on their side. Communications were slow. Those who had access to the best communications were Federalists—mostly wealthy bankers, lawyers, plantation owners, and merchants living in urban areas, where communications were better. The Federalist campaign was organized relatively quickly and effectively to elect Federalists as delegates to the state ratifying conventions.

The Anti-Federalists, however, had at least one strong point in their favor: they stood for the status quo. In general, the greater burden is always placed on those advocating change.

The *Federalist Papers*. In New York, opponents of the Constitution were quick to attack it. Alexander Hamilton answered their attacks in newspaper columns over the signature "Caesar." When the Caesar letters had little effect, Hamilton switched to the pseudonym Publius and secured two collaborators—John Jay and James Madison. In a very short time, those three political figures wrote a series of eighty-five essays in defense of the Constitution and of a republican form of government.

These widely read essays, called the *Federalist Papers,* appeared in New York newspapers from October 1787 to August 1788 and were reprinted in the newspapers of other states. Although we do not know for certain who wrote every one, it is apparent that Hamilton was responsible for about two-thirds of the essays. These included the most important ones interpreting the Constitution, explaining the various powers of the three branches, and presenting a theory of *judicial review*—to be discussed later in this chapter. Madison's *Federalist Paper* No. 10 (see Appendix C), however, is considered a classic in political theory; it deals with the nature of groups—or factions, as he called them. We discuss the ways in which groups influence our government in Chapter 7. In spite of the rapidity with which the *Federalist Papers* were written, they are considered by many to be perhaps the best example of political theorizing ever produced in the United States.[16]

Ratification
Formal approval.

Federalist
The name given to one who was in favor of the adoption of the U.S. Constitution and the creation of a federal union with a strong central government.

Anti-Federalist
An individual who opposed the ratification of the new Constitution in 1787. The Anti-Federalists were opposed to a strong central government.

---

15. There is some irony here. At the Constitutional Convention, those opposed to a strong central government pushed for a federal system because such a system would allow the states to retain some of their sovereign rights (see Chapter 3). The label Anti-Federalists thus contradicted their essential views.
16. Some scholars believe that the *Federalist Papers* played only a minor role in securing ratification of the Constitution. Even if this is true, they still have lasting value as an authoritative explanation of the Constitution.

The Anti-Federalist Response. The Anti-Federalists used such pseudonyms as Montezuma and Philadelphiensis in their replies. Many of their attacks on the Constitution were also brilliant. The Anti-Federalists claimed that the Constitution was written by aristocrats and would lead to aristocratic tyranny. More important, the Anti-Federalists believed that the Constitution would create an overbearing and overburdening central government hostile to personal liberty. (The Constitution said nothing about freedom of the press, freedom of religion, or any other individual liberty.) They wanted to include a list of guaranteed liberties, or a bill of rights. Finally, the Anti-Federalists decried the weakened power of the states.

The Anti-Federalists cannot be dismissed as unpatriotic extremists. They included such patriots as Patrick Henry and Samuel Adams. They were arguing what had been the most prevalent contemporary opinion. This view derived from the French political philosopher Montesquieu, who, as mentioned earlier, was an influential political theorist at that time. Montesquieu believed that liberty was safe only in relatively small societies governed by direct democracy or by a large legislature with small districts. The Madisonian view favoring a large republic, particularly expressed in *Federalist Papers* No. 10 and No. 51 (see Appendix C), was actually the more *un*popular view at the time. Madison was probably convincing because citizens were already persuaded that a strong national government was necessary to combat foreign enemies and to prevent domestic insurrections. Still, some researchers believe it was mainly the bitter experiences with the Articles of Confederation, rather than Madison's arguments, that persuaded the state conventions to ratify the Constitution.[17]

Patrick Henry was part of a group that called themselves the Anti-Federalists. They opposed the ratification of the Constitution. Henry is shown here giving his speech before the Virginia Assembly on March 23, 1775. He concluded that speech with his famous statement, "Give me liberty or give me death!" What were some of the arguments that the Anti-Federalists used to oppose the Constitution? (Library of Congress)

THE MARCH TO THE FINISH

The struggle for ratification continued. Strong majorities were procured in Delaware, Pennsylvania, New Jersey, Georgia, and Connecticut. After a bitter struggle in Massachusetts, that state ratified the Constitution by a narrow margin on February 6, 1788. By the spring, Maryland and South Carolina had ratified by sizable majorities. Then on June 21 of that year, New Hampshire became the ninth state to ratify the Constitution. Although the Constitution was formally in effect, this meant little without Virginia and New York—the latter did not ratify for another month (see Table 2–2 on the following page).

DID THE MAJORITY OF AMERICANS SUPPORT THE CONSTITUTION?

In 1913, historian Charles Beard published *An Economic Interpretation of the Constitution of the United States.*[18] This book launched a debate that has continued ever since—the debate over whether the Constitution was supported by a majority of Americans.

Beard's Thesis. Beard's central thesis was that the Constitution had been produced primarily by wealthy property owners who desired a stronger government able to protect their property rights. Beard also claimed that the Constitution had been imposed by undemocratic methods to prevent democratic majorities from exercising real power. He pointed out that there was never any popular vote on whether to hold a constitutional convention in the first place.

Furthermore, even if such a vote had been taken, state laws generally restricted voting rights to property-owning white males, meaning that most people in the country (white

---

17. Of particular interest is the view of the Anti-Federalist position contained in Herbert J. Storing, *What the Anti-Federalists Were For* (Chicago: University of Chicago Press, 1981). Storing also edited seven volumes of the Anti-Federalist writings, *The Complete Anti-Federalist* (Chicago: University of Chicago Press, 1981). See also Josephine F. Pacheco, *Antifederalism: The Legacy of George Mason* (Fairfax, Va.: George Mason University Press, 1992).
18. Charles A. Beard, *An Economic Interpretation of the Constitution of the United States* (New York: Macmillan, 1913; New York: Free Press, 1986).

TABLE 2-2: Ratification of the Constitution

State	Date	Vote For–Against
Delaware	Dec. 7, 1787	30–0
Pennsylvania	Dec. 12, 1787	43–23
New Jersey	Dec. 18, 1787	38–0
Georgia	Jan. 2, 1788	26–0
Connecticut	Jan. 9, 1788	128–40
Massachusetts	Feb. 6, 1788	187–168
Maryland	Apr. 28, 1788	63–11
South Carolina	May 23, 1788	149–73
New Hampshire	June 21, 1788	57–46
Virginia	June 25, 1788	89–79
New York	July 26, 1788	30–27
North Carolina	Nov. 21, 1789*	194–77
Rhode Island	May 29, 1790	34–32

*Ratification was initially defeated on August 4, 1788, by a vote of 84–184.

didyouknow...

That 64 percent of Americans believe that the Constitution declared English to be the national language of the United States?

males without property, women, Native Americans, and slaves) were not eligible to vote. Finally, Beard pointed out that even the word *democracy* was distasteful to the founders. The term was often used by conservatives to smear their opponents.

State Ratifying Conventions. As for the various state ratifying conventions, the delegates had been selected by only 150,000 of the approximately 4 million citizens. That does not seem very democratic—at least not by today's standards. Some historians have suggested that if a Gallup poll could have been taken at that time, the Anti-Federalists would probably have outnumbered the Federalists.[19]

Certainly, some of the delegates to state ratifying conventions from poor, agrarian areas feared that an elite group of Federalists would run the country just as oppressively as the British had governed the colonies. Amos Singletary, a delegate to the Massachusetts ratifying convention, contended that those who urged the adoption of the Constitution "expect to get all the power and all the money into their own hands, and then they will swallow up all us little folks . . . just as the whale swallowed Jonah."[20] Others who were similarly situated, though, felt differently. Jonathan Smith, who was also a delegate to the Massachusetts ratifying convention, regarded a strong national government as a "cure for disorder"—referring to the disorder caused by the rebellion of Daniel Shays and his followers.[21]

Support Was Probably Widespread. Much has also been made of the various machinations used by the Federalists to ensure the Constitution's ratification (and they did resort to a variety of devious tactics, including purchasing at least one printing press to prevent the publication of Anti-Federalist sentiments). Yet the perception that a strong central government was necessary to keep order and protect the public welfare appears to have been fairly pervasive among all classes—rich and poor alike.

---

19. Jim Powell, "James Madison—Checks and Balances to Limit Government Power," *The Freeman*, March 1996, p. 178.
20. As quoted in Leone, ed., *The Creation of the Constitution*, p. 215.
21. *Ibid.*, p. 217.

Further, although the need for strong government was a major argument in favor of adopting the Constitution, even the Federalists sought to craft a limited government. Compared with constitutions adopted by other nations in later years, the U.S. Constitution, through its checks and balances, favors limited government over "energetic" government to a marked degree.

THE BILL OF RIGHTS

The U.S. Constitution would not have been ratified in several important states if the Federalists had not assured the states that amendments to the Constitution would be passed to protect individual liberties against incursions by the national government. Many of the recommendations of the state ratifying conventions included specific rights that were considered later by James Madison as he labored to draft what became the Bill of Rights.

"Remember, gentlemen, we aren't here just to draft a constitution. We're here to draft the best damned constitution in the world."

A "BILL OF LIMITS"

Although called the Bill of Rights, essentially the first ten amendments to the Constitution were a "bill of limits," because the amendments limited the powers of the national government over the rights and liberties of individuals.

Ironically, a year earlier Madison had told Jefferson, "I have never thought the omission [of the Bill of Rights] a material defect" of the Constitution. Madison was not the only founder who believed a bill of rights to be unnecessary. We discuss the reasons for this in the *Politics and the Constitution* feature on the next page. Jefferson's enthusiasm for a bill of rights apparently influenced Madison, however, as did Madison's desire to gain popular support for his election to Congress. Madison promised in his campaign letter to voters that once elected, he would force Congress to "prepare and recommend to the states for ratification, the most satisfactory provisions for all essential rights."

Madison had to cull through more than two hundred state recommendations.[22] It was no small task, and in retrospect he chose remarkably well. One of the rights appropriate for constitutional protection that he left out was equal protection under the laws—but that was not commonly regarded as a basic right at that time. Not until 1868 did the states ratify an amendment guaranteeing that no state shall deny equal protection to any person. (The Supreme Court has since applied this guarantee to certain actions of the federal government as well.)

The final number of amendments that Madison and a specially appointed committee came up with was seventeen. Congress tightened the language somewhat and eliminated five of the amendments. Of the remaining twelve, two—dealing with the apportionment of representatives and the compensation of the members of Congress—were not ratified immediately by the states. Eventually, Supreme Court decisions led to reform of the apportionment process. The amendment on the compensation of members of Congress was ratified 203 years later—in 1992!

ADOPTION OF THE BILL OF RIGHTS

On December 15, 1791, the national Bill of Rights was adopted when Virginia agreed to ratify the ten amendments. On ratification, the Bill of Rights became part of the U.S. Constitution. The basic structure of American government had already been established. Now the fundamental rights and liberties of individuals were protected, at least in theory, at the national level. The proposed amendment that Madison characterized as "the most valuable amendment in the whole lot"—which would have prohibited the states from infringing on the freedoms of conscience, press, and jury trial—had been eliminated by

didyouknow...

That 52 percent of Americans do not know what the Bill of Rights is?

---

22. For details on these recommendations, including their sources, see Leonard W. Levy, *Origins of the Bill of Rights* (New Haven, Conn.: Yale University Press, 1999).

politicsand...the constitution

WHY DIDN'T THE FOUNDERS THINK THAT A BILL OF RIGHTS WAS NECESSARY?

All Americans know about our rights to freedom of speech, freedom of the press, freedom of religion, and other freedoms. Indeed, we take these freedoms for granted. In the original Constitution, however, the framers did not include any of these rights. How could they have left them out?

RIGHTS IN THE MAIN BODY OF THE CONSTITUTION

Many of the framers felt that specific guarantees of fundamental rights were unnecessary because the Constitution already included certain prohibitions. Article 1, Section 9, for example, prohibits so-called *bills of attainder*. These are acts of the legislature that allow capital punishment for accused criminals without normal judicial proceedings. In that same section of the Constitution, there is a prohibition against *ex post facto* laws, which are laws passed after the commission of an act that retroactively make that act illegal.

In Article 1, Section 9, the framers included a prohibition against government detention of individuals without due process of law. They did so by allowing a judge to inquire of an arresting officer or jailer about a person who was in custody (called a writ of *habeas corpus*). When

no proper explanation is given, the judge can order the person's release. Finally, Article 3, Section 2, imposes a requirement of a trial by jury in federal criminal cases.

In other words, the framers had already created a number of guarantees of civil liberties. The founders believed that these guarantees were sufficient.

SPECIFIC LIMITATIONS VIEWED AS DANGEROUS

Many framers also had something else in mind when they did not include a bill of rights in the original Constitution. They believed that there was a danger in enumerating specific civil liberties. The danger lay in the possibility that future governments might assume that rights that were *not* listed in a bill of rights did not exist. The framers wanted to avoid a view of the federal government under which it could do anything that wasn't explicitly prohibited.

FOR CRITICAL ANALYSIS

If there were no Bill of Rights, would that necessarily mean that residents of this country would not enjoy freedom of speech or freedom of the press? Why or why not?

the Senate. Thus, the Bill of Rights as adopted did not limit state power, and individual citizens had to rely on the guarantees contained in a particular state constitution or state bill of rights. The country had to wait until the violence of the Civil War before significant limitations on state power in the form of the Fourteenth Amendment became part of the national Constitution.

You can read through the Bill of Rights by going to the appendix following this chapter. In addition to the rights and liberties specified in these first ten amendments to the Constitution, the courts have concluded that several of these amendments imply that our civil liberties also include a right to privacy. For many, the right to privacy—the right to be free of the government's prying eyes—is one of our most important rights. Balancing this right against the government's need to protect society from criminal actions has become one of the significant challenges of our time. (See this chapter's *Politics and the Cyber Sphere* feature for an example of how a law might create a conflict between security and privacy rights.)

ALTERING THE CONSTITUTION: THE FORMAL AMENDMENT PROCESS

The U.S. Constitution consists of 7,000 words. It is shorter than any state constitution except that of Vermont, which has 6,880 words. One of the reasons the federal Constitution is short is that the founders intended it to be only a framework for the new government, to be interpreted by succeeding generations. One of the reasons it has

POLITICS AND...
the cyber sphere

HOW EXTENSIVE SHOULD DNA SAMPLING BE?

Everyone has heard of DNA sampling. It not only has helped police solve crimes that happened in the distant past but also has helped release innocent individuals held behind bars for years.

A DNA sample contains our genetic codes—our most private information. For years, states have collected DNA samples from individuals charged with, indicted for, or convicted of a crime. This information has been included in state DNA databases. States have been allowed to use DNA samples to search the federal DNA Index System database for a possible "hit."

Beginning in 2007, states began to collect samples from individuals who are arrested but not formally charged with a crime. The legal basis for the expansion was an amendment added to the federal Violence against Women Act when that legislation was renewed. The new amendment requires DNA sampling of anyone who is arrested by federal authorities and of unauthorized immigrants detained by federal agents. States may participate in the program. Within a year, twelve states had approved sampling of arrestees, and twenty-two state legislatures were considering legislation to introduce the practice. Federal courts have not ruled on the expanded collections. The Virginia Supreme Court upheld the practice in 2007, but a state appeals court in Minnesota struck it down in that state in 2006.

In a number of states, law enforcement officers have even introduced the practice of "surreptitious sampling." Officers can collect DNA samples from discarded cigarette butts or soda cans without ever having to arrest the suspect. In a dozen recent cases, judges have ruled that items discarded in public places are fair game for investigators.

BENEFITS OF EXPANDED DNA SAMPLING

Proponents of this expanded DNA sampling, who include crime victims' organizations and some women's groups, argue that the bigger the DNA database, the better.

Advocates believe that an expansion of the DNA database will help law enforcement agencies identify sexual predators and also dangerous criminals among unauthorized immigrants. In a typical year, the Border Patrol detains 1.2 million undocumented aliens. In recent years, about 13 percent of all unauthorized immigrants detained in Arizona had criminal records. To the claim that expanded DNA sampling intrudes on privacy rights, supporters respond that DNA sampling is no different in principle than collecting fingerprints.

PROBLEMS WITH EXPANDED SAMPLING

Those who oppose the expanded DNA sampling argue that such expansion may violate the constitutional right to privacy. People whose DNA is collected might be seen as criminals even if they had committed no felony. Most immigration violations, for example, are civil, not criminal, offenses.

Beyond that, there are practical problems involved with the expanded sampling. The Federal Bureau of Investigation (FBI) estimates that when the expanded sampling plan is fully implemented, the Bureau will have to process up to a million additional samples each year. Before the expansion, the FBI laboratory that handles the samples received fewer than 100,000 samples per year. As of 2008, the laboratory had received no additional funding, and the FBI admitted that severe backlogs were likely. Backlogs increase the possibility of errors that could lead to the imprisonment or even execution of innocent persons. Both the FBI lab and a lab used by the state of Texas have experienced such catastrophes.

It is also hard for innocent people to have their DNA samples removed from the database—this requires a court order. DNA profiles have the potential to reveal individuals' physical diseases and mental disorders. In 2008, however, Congress passed legislation that prohibits discrimination by health insurers and based on DNA profiles.

FOR CRITICAL ANALYSIS

The basic issue here is whether acquiring more information about actual or potential criminals is worth invading the privacy of innocent people. Which is more important, and why?

CODIS is the Federal Bureau of Investigation's Combined DNA Index System, which holds millions of offender profiles. (FBI Photo)

remained short is that the formal amending procedure does not allow for changes to be made easily. Article V of the Constitution outlines the ways in which amendments may be proposed and ratified (see Figure 2–3).

Two formal methods of proposing an amendment to the Constitution are available: (1) a two-thirds vote in each chamber of Congress or (2) a national convention that is called by Congress at the request of two-thirds of the state legislatures (the second method has never been used).

Ratification can occur by one of two methods: (1) by a positive vote in three-fourths of the legislatures of the various states or (2) by special conventions called in the states and a positive vote in three-fourths of them. The second method has been used only once, to repeal Prohibition (the ban on the production and sale of alcoholic beverages). That situation was exceptional because it involved an amendment (the Twenty-first) to repeal an amendment (the Eighteenth, which had created Prohibition). State conventions were necessary for repeal of the Eighteenth Amendment because the "pro-dry" legislatures in the most conservative states would never have passed the repeal. (Note that Congress determines the method of ratification to be used by all states for each proposed constitutional amendment.)

MANY AMENDMENTS PROPOSED, FEW ACCEPTED

Congress has considered more than eleven thousand amendments to the Constitution. Many proposed amendments have been advanced to address highly specific problems. An argument against such "narrow" amendments has been that amendments ought to embody broad principles, in the way that the existing Constitution does. For that reason, many people have opposed such narrow amendments as one to protect the American flag.

Only thirty-three amendments have been submitted to the states after having been approved by the required two-thirds vote in each chamber of Congress, and only twenty-seven have been ratified—see Table 2–3. (The full, annotated text of the U.S. Constitution, including its amendments, is presented in a special appendix at the end of this chapter.) It should be clear that the amendment process is much more difficult than a graphic depiction such as Figure 2–3 can indicate. Because of competing social and economic interests, the requirement that two-thirds of both the House and the Senate approve the

FIGURE 2–3: The Formal Constitutional Amending Procedure

There are two ways of proposing amendments to the U.S. Constitution and two ways of ratifying proposed amendments. Among the four possibilities, the usual route has been proposal by Congress and ratification by state legislatures.

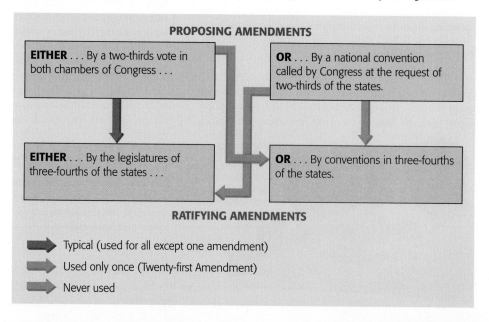

TABLE 2–3: Amendments to the Constitution

Amendment	Subject	Year Adopted	Time Required for Ratification
1st–10th	The Bill of Rights	1791	2 years, 2 months, 20 days
11th	Immunity of states from certain suits	1795	11 months, 3 days
12th	Changes in Electoral College procedure	1804	6 months, 3 days
13th	Prohibition of slavery	1865	10 months, 3 days
14th	Citizenship, due process, and equal protection	1868	2 years, 26 days
15th	No denial of vote because of race, color, or previous condition of servitude	1870	11 months, 8 days
16th	Power of Congress to tax income	1913	3 years, 6 months, 22 days
17th	Direct election of U.S. senators	1913	10 months, 26 days
18th	National (liquor) prohibition	1919	1 year, 29 days
19th	Women's right to vote	1920	1 year, 2 months, 14 days
20th	Change of dates for congressional and presidential terms	1933	10 months, 21 days
21st	Repeal of the Eighteenth Amendment	1933	9 months, 15 days
22d	Limit on presidential tenure	1951	3 years, 11 months, 3 days
23d	District of Columbia electoral vote	1961	9 months, 13 days
24th	Prohibition of tax payment as a qualification to vote in federal elections	1964	1 year, 4 months, 9 days
25th	Procedures for determining presidential disability and presidential succession and for filling a vice-presidential vacancy	1967	1 year, 7 months, 4 days
26th	Prohibition of setting the minimum voting age above eighteen in any election	1971	3 months, 7 days
27th	Prohibition of Congress's voting itself a raise that takes effect before the next election	1992	203 years

amendments is difficult to achieve. Thirty-four senators, representing only seventeen sparsely populated states, could block any amendment. For example, the Republican-controlled House approved the Balanced Budget Amendment within the first one hundred days of the 104th Congress in 1995, but it was defeated in the Senate by one vote.

After an amendment has been approved by Congress, the process becomes even more arduous. Three-fourths of the state legislatures must approve the amendment. Only those amendments that have wide popular support across parties and in all regions of the country are likely to be approved.

Why was the amendment process made so difficult? The framers feared that a simple amendment process could lead to a tyranny of the majority, which could pass amendments to oppress disfavored individuals and groups. The cumbersome amendment process does not seem to stem the number of amendments that are proposed each year in Congress, however, particularly in recent years. Whether the amendment procedure is too difficult is discussed in the *Which Side Are You On?* feature on the next page.

LIMITS ON RATIFICATION

A reading of Article V of the U.S. Constitution reveals that the framers of the Constitution specified no time limit on the ratification process. The Supreme Court has held that Congress can specify a time for ratification as long as it is "reasonable." Since 1919, most proposed amendments have included a requirement that ratification be obtained within seven years. This was the case with the proposed Equal Rights Amendment, which sought to guarantee equal rights for women. When three-fourths of the states had not ratified in the allotted seven years, however, Congress extended the limit by an additional three years and three months. That extension expired on June 30, 1982, and the amendment

whichsideareyouon?

IS THE AMENDMENT PROCESS TOO DIFFICULT?

Constitutions throughout the world are amended once they become law. The constitution in your state has, almost undoubtedly, been amended many times. The U.S. Constitution, however, has been amended only twenty-seven times in more than two hundred years. That could mean the framers created a document so perfect that it hasn't needed amending. In reality, the small number of amendments over such a long time is a result of the very difficult amending process built into the Constitution. Is the amendment process too difficult? If so, should the Constitution be amended to make this process easier?

MAKE THE AMENDMENT PROCESS SIMPLER

When the framers created the U.S. Constitution, the United States (and the world) was much different than it is today. Most residents were farmers. There were no railroads, much less automobiles, and no long-distance communications—not even the telegraph. Technology as we know it did not yet exist. The framers could not have imagined what issues the government would face in the twenty-first century. We need amendments to our Constitution that take account of all of the new situations facing us today, such as wiretapping, data mining for information about all individuals, and increased equality between men and women.

Consider the Equal Rights Amendment, which had significant public support. That amendment could not meet the stiff amendment requirements that the framers included in our Constitution.

Consider also the system we use to elect the president. We don't vote directly for presidential candidates but use something called the Electoral College (see Chapter 9). Many people want the president to be elected by popular vote, yet it is virtually impossible to amend the Constitution to allow this.

Also, because almost no proposed amendments are ever adopted, members of Congress propose thousands of largely frivolous amendments that appeal to popular prejudices, knowing that little danger exists that they will actually be approved. It's time to change the amending process to make it easier.

THE FEWER THE NUMBER OF AMENDMENTS, THE BETTER

Not everyone finds it a problem that the Constitution has been amended only twenty-seven times. Indeed, the very existence of a procedure for amending the Constitution was already a novel departure from the state constitutions under the Articles of Confederation. Most state constitutions at the time had no provision for amendments.

We also know what happens when it is easy to amend a constitution. In many states, the number of amendments submitted to the voters borders on the absurd. Alabama, for example, has adopted about eight hundred amendments to its state constitution. Many states use the amending process to create what are, in effect, new and very specific statutes (laws). Is it really necessary for South Dakota's constitution to authorize a cordage twine plant at the state prison, for example? The U.S. Constitution, fortunately, contains no such details. It leaves to the Congress the nuts-and-bolts activity of enacting specific statutory laws. The U.S. Constitution is admirably short. Let's keep it that way.

still had not been ratified. Another proposed amendment, which would have guaranteed congressional representation to the District of Columbia, fell far short of the thirty-eight state ratifications needed before its August 22, 1985, deadline.

On May 7, 1992, Michigan became the thirty-eighth state to ratify the Twenty-seventh Amendment (on congressional compensation)—one of the two "lost" amendments of the twelve that originally were sent to the states in 1789. Because most of the amendments proposed in recent years have been given a time limit of only seven years by Congress, it was questionable for a time whether the amendment would take effect even if the necessary number of states ratified it. Is 203 years too long a lapse of time between the proposal and the final ratification of an amendment? It apparently was not, because the amendment was certified as legitimate by archivist Don Wilson of the National Archives on May 18, 1992.

THE NATIONAL CONVENTION PROVISION

The Constitution provides that a national convention requested by the legislatures of two-thirds of the states can propose a constitutional amendment. Congress has received approximately 400 convention applications since the Constitution was ratified; every state has applied at least once. Fewer than 20 applications were submitted during the Constitution's first hundred years, but more than 150 have been filed in the last two decades. No national convention has been held since 1787, and many national political and judicial leaders are uneasy about the prospect of convening a body that conceivably could do as the Constitutional Convention did—create a new form of government. The state legislative bodies that originate national convention applications, however, do not appear to be uncomfortable with such a constitutional modification process; more than 230 state constitutional conventions have been held.

INFORMAL METHODS OF CONSTITUTIONAL CHANGE

Formal amendments are one way of changing our Constitution, and, as is obvious from their small number, they have been resorted to infrequently. If we discount the first ten amendments (the Bill of Rights), which were adopted soon after the ratification of the Constitution, there have been only seventeen formal alterations of the Constitution in the more than two hundred years of its existence.

The U.S. Constitution is silent on laws relating to marriage. Consequently, the states govern in this area. This recent demonstration outside the Massachusetts State House in Boston clearly involves the question of marriage. Present were those who were in favor of legalizing gay marriages as well as those who were against it. (Brian Snyder/Reuters/Landov)

But looking at the sparse number of formal constitutional amendments gives us an incomplete view of constitutional change. The brevity and ambiguity of the original document have permitted great alterations in the Constitution by way of varying interpretations over time. As the United States grew, both in population and in territory, new social and political realities emerged. Congress, presidents, and the courts found it necessary to interpret the Constitution's provisions in light of these new realities. The Constitution has proved to be a remarkably flexible document, adapting itself time and again to new events and concerns.

CONGRESSIONAL LEGISLATION

The Constitution gives Congress broad powers to carry out its duties as the nation's legislative body. For example, Article I, Section 8, of the Constitution gives Congress the power to regulate foreign and interstate commerce. Although there is no clear definition of foreign commerce or interstate commerce in the Constitution, Congress has cited the *commerce clause* as the basis for passing thousands of laws that have defined the meaning of foreign and interstate commerce.

Similarly, Article III, Section 1, states that the national judiciary shall consist of one supreme court and "such inferior courts, as Congress may from time to time ordain and establish." Through a series of acts, Congress has used this broad provision to establish the federal court system of today.

In addition, Congress has frequently delegated to federal agencies the legislative power to write regulations. These regulations become law unless challenged in the court system. Nowhere does the Constitution outline this delegation of legislative authority.

didyouknow...

That the states have still not ratified an amendment (introduced by Congress in 1810) barring U.S. citizens from accepting titles of nobility from foreign governments?

Executive Agreement
An international agreement between chiefs of state that does not require legislative approval.

Judicial Review
The power of the Supreme Court and other courts to declare unconstitutional federal or state laws and other acts of government.

PRESIDENTIAL ACTIONS

Even though the Constitution does not expressly authorize the president to propose bills or even budgets to Congress,[23] presidents since the time of Woodrow Wilson (who served as president from 1913 to 1921) have proposed hundreds of bills to Congress each year. Presidents have also relied on their Article II authority as commander in chief of the nation's armed forces to send American troops abroad into combat, although the Constitution provides that Congress has the power to declare war.

The president's powers in wartime have waxed and waned through the course of American history. President George W. Bush significantly expanded presidential power in the wake of the terrorist attacks of 2001. Until then, there had been a period of decline in the latitude given to presidents since the Vietnam War ended in 1975.

Presidents have also conducted foreign affairs by the use of **executive agreements,** which are legally binding documents made between the president and a foreign head of state. The Constitution does not mention such agreements.

JUDICIAL REVIEW

Another way of changing the Constitution—or of making it more flexible—is through the power of judicial review. **Judicial review** refers to the power of U.S. courts to examine the constitutionality of actions undertaken by the legislative and executive branches of government. A state court, for example, may rule that a statute enacted by the state legislature is unconstitutional. Federal courts (and ultimately, the United States Supreme Court) may rule unconstitutional not only acts of Congress and decisions of the national executive branch but also state statutes, state executive actions, and even provisions of state constitutions.

Not a Novel Concept. The Constitution does not specifically mention the power of judicial review. Those in attendance at the Constitutional Convention, however, probably expected that the courts would have some authority to review the legality of acts by the executive and legislative branches, because, under the common law tradition inherited from England, courts exercised this authority. Indeed, Alexander Hamilton, in *Federalist Paper* No. 78 (see Appendix C), explicitly outlined the concept of judicial review. Whether the power of judicial review can be justified constitutionally is a question that has been subject to some debate, particularly in recent years. For now, suffice it to say that in 1803, the Supreme Court claimed this power for itself in *Marbury v. Madison,*[24] in which the Court ruled that a particular provision of an act of Congress was unconstitutional.

Allows Court to Adapt the Constitution. Through the process of judicial review, the Supreme Court adapts the Constitution to modern situations. Electronic technology, for example, did not exist when the Constitution was ratified. Nonetheless, the Court has used the Fourth Amendment guarantees against unreasonable searches and seizures to place limits on the use of wiretapping and other electronic eavesdropping methods. The Court has needed to decide whether antiterrorism laws passed by Congress or state legislatures, or measures instituted by the president, violate the Fourth Amendment or other constitutional provisions. Additionally, the Court has changed its interpretation of the Constitution in accordance with changing values. It ruled in 1896 that "separate-but-equal" public facilities for African Americans were constitutional; but by 1954 the times had changed, and the Court reversed that decision.[25] Woodrow Wilson summarized the Court's work when he described it as "a constitutional convention in continuous session." Basically, the law is what the Supreme Court says it is at any given time.

23. Note, though, that the Constitution, in Article II, Section 3, does state that the president "shall from time to time . . . recommend to [Congress's] Consideration such Measures as he shall judge necessary and expedient." Some scholars interpret this phrase to mean that the president has the constitutional authority to propose bills and budgets to Congress for consideration.
24. 5 U.S. 137 (1803). See Chapter 13 for a further discussion of the *Marbury v. Madison* case.
25. *Brown v. Board of Education of Topeka,* 347 U.S. 483 (1954).

Stephen Breyer

Ruth Bader Ginsburg

Samuel Alito, Jr.

Anthony Kennedy

Chief Justice John Roberts, Jr.

Antonin Scalia

Clarence Thomas

David Souter

John Paul Stevens

The justices of the United States Supreme Court in 2008
are shown in these nine photographs. The newest members of the Court are Chief Justice John Roberts, Jr. (shown in the center), and Justice Samuel Alito, Jr. (shown on the upper left). The longest-sitting member of the Court is Justice John Paul Stevens (shown on the bottom right). There is only one female justice, Ruth Bader Ginsburg. What is the relationship between the U.S. Constitution and the work that the Supreme Court does? (U.S. Supreme Court)

INTERPRETATION, CUSTOM, AND USAGE

The Constitution has also been changed through interpretation by both Congress and the president. Originally, the president had a staff consisting of personal secretaries and a few others. Today, because Congress delegates specific tasks to the president and the chief executive assumes political leadership, the executive office staff alone has increased to several thousand persons. The executive branch provides legislative leadership far beyond the expectations of the founders.

One of the ways in which presidents have expanded their powers is through **executive orders.** (Executive orders will be discussed in Chapter 11, in the context of the presidency.) Executive orders have the force of legislation and allow presidents to significantly affect the political landscape. Consider, for example, that affirmative action programs have their origin in executive orders.

Changes in the ways of doing political business have also altered the Constitution. The Constitution does not mention political parties, yet these informal, "extraconstitutional" organizations make the nominations for offices, run the campaigns, organize the members of Congress, and in fact change the election system from time to time. The emergence and evolution of the party system, for example, have changed the way the president is elected. The Constitution calls for the Electoral College to choose the president. Today, the people vote for electors who are pledged to the candidate of their party, effectively choosing the president themselves. Perhaps most striking, the Constitution has been adapted from serving the needs of a small, rural republic to providing a framework of government for an industrial giant with vast geographic, natural, and human resources.

Executive Order
A rule or regulation issued by the president that has the effect of law. Executive orders can implement and give administrative effect to provisions in the U.S. Constitution, treaties, or statutes.

WHY SHOULD YOU CARE ABOUT
theconstitution?

(www.ourdocuments.gov.)

The U.S. Constitution is an enduring document that has survived more than two hundred years of turbulent history. It is also a changing document, however. Twenty-seven amendments have been added to the original Constitution. Why should you, as an individual, care about the Constitution?

THE CONSTITUTION AND YOUR LIFE

The laws of the nation have a direct impact on your life, and none more so than the Constitution—the supreme law of the land. The most important issues in society are often settled by the Constitution. For example, for the first seventy-five years of the republic, the Constitution implicitly protected the institution of slavery. If the Constitution had never been changed through the amendment process, slavery might still be legal today.

Since the passage of the Fourteenth Amendment in 1868, the Constitution has defined who is a citizen and who is entitled to the protections the Constitution provides. Constitutional provisions define our liberties. The First Amendment protects our freedom of speech more thoroughly than do the laws of many other nations. Few other countries have constitutional provisions governing the right to own firearms (the Second Amendment). All of these are among the most fundamental issues we face.

HOW YOU CAN MAKE A DIFFERENCE

Consider how one person decided to affect the Constitution. Shirley Breeze, head of the Missouri Women's Network, decided to bring the Equal Rights Amendment (ERA) back to life after its "death" in 1982. She spearheaded a movement that has gained significant support. Today, bills to ratify the ERA have been introduced not only in Missouri but also in other states that did not ratify it earlier, including Illinois, Oklahoma, and Virginia.

At the time of this writing, national coalitions of interest groups are supporting or opposing a number of proposed amendments. One hotly debated proposed amendment concerns abortion. If you are interested in this issue and would like to make a difference, you can contact one of several groups.

An organization whose primary goal is to secure the passage of the Human Life Amendment is

American Life League
P.O. Box 1350
Stafford, VA 22555
540-659-4171
www.all.org.

The Human Life Amendment would recognize in law the "personhood" of the unborn, secure human rights protections for an unborn child from the time of fertilization, and prohibit abortion under any circumstances.

A political action and information organization working on behalf of "pro-choice" issues—that is, the right of women to have control over reproduction—is

NARAL Pro-Choice America (formerly the National Abortion and Reproductive Rights Action League)
1156 15th St., Suite 700
Washington, DC 20005
202-973-3000
www.naral.org.

There is also another way that you can affect the Constitution—by protecting your existing rights and liberties under it. In the wake of the 9/11 attacks, a number of new laws have been enacted that many believe go too far in curbing our constitutional rights. If you agree and want to join with others who are concerned about this issue, a good starting point is the Web site of the American Civil Liberties Union (ACLU) at **www.aclu.org**.

QUESTIONS FOR
discussion**and**analysis

1. Review the *Which Side Are You On?* feature on page 54. Do you believe that the process of amending the Constitution should become easier? If so, what changes would you recommend? If not, why not?

2. Naturalized citizens—immigrants—have almost all of the rights of natural-born citizens, but under the Constitution they cannot be elected president. If the Constitution were changed to allow an immigrant to become president, do you think that today's voters would be reluctant to vote for such an individual? Why might a naturalized leader be more nationalistic than a natural-born one?

3. As you have learned, historian Charles Beard argued that the Constitution was produced primarily by wealthy property owners who wanted a stronger government that could protect their property rights. Do you see any provisions in the text of the Constitution that would support Beard's argument? Even if Beard is right, is this in any way a problem?

4. Consider what might have happened if Georgia and the Carolinas had stayed out of the Union because of a desire to protect slavery. What would subsequent American history have been like? Would the eventual freedom of the slaves have been delayed—or advanced?

5. A result of the Great Compromise is that representation in the Senate dramatically departs from the one-person one-vote rule. The almost 40 million people who live in California elect two senators, as do the half a million people living in Wyoming. What political results might occur when the citizens of small states are much better represented than the citizens of large ones? Do you see any signs that your predictions have actually come true?

key**terms**

Anti-Federalist 46
bicameral legislature 41
checks and balances 43
confederation 37
Electoral College 45
executive agreement 56

executive order 57
federal system 45
Federalist 46
Great Compromise 42
judicial review 56
Madisonian model 43

natural rights 34
ratification 46
representative
    assembly 31
separation of powers 43
social contract 35

state 37
supremacy doctrine 41
unicameral
    legislature 37

chapter**summary**

1. The first permanent English colonies were established at Jamestown in 1607 and Plymouth in 1620. The Mayflower Compact created the first formal government for the English colonists. By the mid-1700s, thirteen other British colonies had been established along the Atlantic seaboard.

2. In the 1760s, the British began to impose a series of taxes and legislative acts on their increasingly independent-minded colonies. The colonists responded with boycotts of British products and protests. Representatives of the colonies formed the First Continental Congress in 1774. The delegates sent a petition to the British king expressing their grievances. The Second Continental Congress established an army in 1775 to defend the colonists against attacks by British soldiers.

3. On July 4, 1776, the Second Continental Congress approved the Declaration of Independence. Perhaps the most revolutionary aspects of the Declaration were its assumptions that people have natural rights to life, liberty, and the pursuit of happiness; that governments derive their power from the consent of the governed; and that people have a right to overthrow oppressive governments. During the Revolutionary War, the colonies adopted written constitutions that severely curtailed the power of executives, thus giving their legislatures predominant powers. By the end of the Revolutionary War, the states had signed the Articles of Confederation, creating a weak central government with few powers. The Articles proved to be unworkable because the national government had no way to ensure compliance by the states with such measures as securing tax revenues.

4. General dissatisfaction with the Articles of Confederation prompted the call for a convention at Philadelphia in 1787. Although the delegates ostensibly convened to amend the Articles, the discussions soon focused on creating a constitution for a new form of government. The Virginia plan and the New Jersey plan did not garner widespread support. A compromise offered by Connecticut helped to break the large-state/small-state disputes dividing the delegates. The final version of the Constitution provided for the separation of powers, checks and balances, and a federal form of government.

5. Fears of a strong central government prompted the addition of the Bill of Rights to the Constitution. The Bill of Rights secured for Americans a wide variety of freedoms, including the freedoms of religion, speech, and assembly. It was initially applied only to the federal government, but amendments to the Constitution following the Civil War made it clear that the Bill of Rights would apply to the states as well.

6. An amendment to the Constitution may be proposed either by a two-thirds vote in each house of Congress or by a national convention called by Congress at the request of two-thirds of the state legislatures. Ratification can occur either by a positive vote in three-fourths of the legislatures of the various states or by special conventions called in the states for the specific purpose of ratifying the proposed amendment and a positive vote in three-fourths of these state conventions. Informal methods of constitutional change include congressional legislation, presidential actions, judicial review, and changing interpretations of the Constitution.

selected**print&media**resources

SUGGESTED READINGS

Breyer, Stephen G. *Active Liberty: Interpreting Our Democratic Constitution.* New York: Knopf, 2005. Supreme Court justice Stephen Breyer offers his thoughts on the Constitution as a living document. He argues that the genius of the Constitution rests in the adaptability of its great principles to cope with current problems.

Daniel, Marcus. *Scandal and Civility: Journalism and the Birth of American Democracy.* New York: Oxford University Press, 2009. The American Revolution led to a new breed of journalists who were partisan, irreverent, and satirical—and who ignited debates over the very nature of the country. Daniel gives us a fuller view of the times through the careers of these journalists, who were quite different from the often straight-laced founders.

McCullough, David. *1776.* New York: Simon and Schuster, 2006. McCullough, an esteemed historian, covers the military side of the nation's first year, when the fate of the independence movement hung in the balance. McCullough provides unusually sharp portraits both of George Washington and Britain's King George III.

Philbrick, Nathaniel. *Mayflower: A Story of Courage, Community, and War.* New York: Penguin, 2007. The author delves into many myths surrounding the *Mayflower* and the early years of the Plymouth Plantation, shedding much light on what some call a largely "forgotten chapter" in American history.

MEDIA RESOURCES

In the Beginning—A 1987 Bill Moyers program that features discussions with three prominent historians about the roots of the Constitution and its impact on our society.

John Adams—A widely admired 2008 HBO miniseries on founder John Adams and his wife, Abigail Adams, and other prominent Americans of the revolutionary period. The series is largely based on David McCullough's book *John Adams*.

John Locke—A 1994 video exploring the character and principal views of John Locke.

Thomas Jefferson—A 1996 documentary by acclaimed director Ken Burns. The film covers Jefferson's entire life, including his writing of the Declaration of Independence, his presidency, and his later years in Virginia. Historians and writers interviewed include Daniel Boorstin, Garry Wills, Gore Vidal, and John Hope Franklin.

e-mocracy

THE INTERNET AND OUR CONSTITUTION

Today, you can find online many important documents from the founding period, including descriptions of events leading up to the American Revolution, the Articles of Confederation, notes on the Constitutional Convention, the Federalists' writings, and the Anti-Federalists' responses.

You are able to access the Internet and explore a variety of opinions on every topic imaginable because you enjoy the freedoms—including freedom of speech—guaranteed by our Constitution. Even today, more than two hundred years after the U.S. Bill of Rights was ratified, citizens in some countries do not enjoy the right to free speech. Nor can they surf the Web freely, as U.S. citizens do.

For example, the Chinese government employs a number of methods to control Internet use. One method is to use filtering software to block electronic pathways to objectionable sites, including the sites of Western news organizations. Another technique is to prohibit Internet users from sending or discussing information that has not been publicly released by the government. Still another practice is to monitor the online activities of Internet users. None of these methods is foolproof, however. Indeed, some observers claim that the Internet, by exposing citizens in politically oppressive nations to a variety of views on politics and culture, will eventually transform those nations.

We should note that such restrictions also can exist in the United States. For example, there have been persistent efforts by Congress and many courts to limit access to Web sites deemed pornographic. Free speech advocates have attacked these restrictions as unconstitutional, as you will read in Chapter 4.

LOGGING ON

For U.S. founding documents, including the Declaration of Independence, scanned originals of the U.S. Constitution, and the *Federalist Papers,* go to Emory University School of Law's Web site at
www.law.emory.edu/erd/docs/federalist.

The University of Oklahoma Law Center has a number of U.S. historical documents online, including many of those discussed in this chapter. Go to
www.law.ou.edu/hist.

The National Constitution Center provides information on the Constitution—including its history, current debates over constitutional provisions, and news articles—at the following site:
www.constitutioncenter.org.

To look at state constitutions, go to
www.findlaw.com/casecode/state.html.

APPENDIX TO CHAPTER 2

THE CONSTITUTION OF THE UNITED STATES*

The Preamble

We the People of the United States, in Order to form a more perfect Union, establish Justice, insure domestic Tranquility, provide for the common defence, promote the general Welfare, and secure the Blessings of Liberty to ourselves and our Posterity, do ordain and establish this Constitution for the United States of America.

The Preamble declares that "We the People" are the authority for the Constitution (unlike the Articles of Confederation, which derived their authority from the states). The Preamble also sets out the purposes of the Constitution.

ARTICLE I. (Legislative Branch)

The first part of the Constitution, Article I, deals with the organization and powers of the lawmaking branch of the national government, the Congress.

Section 1. Legislative Powers

All legislative Powers herein granted shall be vested in a Congress of the United States, which shall consist of a Senate and House of Representatives.

Section 2. House of Representatives

Clause 1: Composition and Election of Members. The House of Representatives shall be composed of Members chosen every second Year by the People of the several States, and the Electors in each State shall have the Qualifications requisite for Electors of the most numerous Branch of the State Legislature.

Each state has the power to decide who may vote for members of Congress. Within each state, those who may vote for state legislators may also vote for members of the House of Representatives (and, under the Seventeenth Amendment, for U.S. senators). When the Constitution was written, nearly all states limited voting rights to white male property owners or taxpayers at least twenty-one years old. Subsequent amendments granted voting power to African American men, all women, and everyone at least eighteen years old.

Clause 2: Qualifications. No Person shall be a Representative who shall not have attained to the Age of twenty five Years, and been seven Years a Citizen of the United States, and who shall not, when elected, be an Inhabitant of that State in which he shall be chosen.

Each member of the House must be at least twenty-five years old, a citizen of the United States for at least seven years, and a resident of the state in which she or he is elected.

Clause 3: Apportionment of Representatives and Direct Taxes. Representatives [and direct Taxes][1] shall be apportioned among the several States which may be included within this Union, according to their respective Numbers [which shall be determined by adding to the whole Number of free Persons, including those bound to Service for a Term of Years, and excluding Indians not taxed, three fifths of all other Persons].[2] The actual Enumeration shall be made within three Years after the first Meeting of the Congress of the United States, and within every subsequent Term of ten Years, in such Manner as they shall by Law direct. The Number of Representatives shall not exceed one for every thirty Thousand, but each State shall have at Least one Representative; and until such enumeration shall be made, the State of New Hampshire shall be entitled to chuse three, Massachusetts eight, Rhode Island and Providence Plantations one, Connecticut five, New York six, New Jersey four, Pennsylvania eight, Delaware one, Maryland six, Virginia ten, North Carolina five, South Carolina five, and Georgia three.

A state's representation in the House is based on the size of its population. Population is counted in each decade's census, after which Congress reapportions House seats. Since early in the twentieth century, the number of seats has been limited to 435.

Clause 4: Vacancies. When vacancies happen in the Representation from any State, the Executive Authority thereof shall issue Writs of Election to fill such Vacancies.

The "Executive Authority" is the state's governor. When a vacancy occurs in the House, the governor calls a special election to fill it.

Clause 5: Officers and Impeachment. The House of Representatives shall chuse their Speaker and other Officers; and shall have the sole Power of Impeachment.

The power to impeach is the power to accuse. In this case, it is the power to accuse members of the executive or judicial branch of wrongdoing or abuse of power. Once a bill of impeachment is issued, the Senate holds the trial.

Section 3. The Senate

Clause 1: Term and Number of Members. The Senate of the United States shall be composed of two Senators from each State [chosen by the Legislature thereof],[3] for six Years; and each Senator shall have one Vote.

Every state has two senators, each of whom serves for six years and has one vote in the upper chamber. Since the Seventeenth Amendment was passed in 1913, all

---

* The spelling, capitalization, and punctuation of the original have been retained here. Brackets indicate passages that have been altered by amendments to the Constitution. We have added article titles (in parentheses), section titles, and clause designations. We have also inserted annotations in blue italic type.

---

1. Modified by the Sixteenth Amendment.
2. Modified by the Fourteenth Amendment.
3. Repealed by the Seventeenth Amendment.

senators have been elected directly by voters of the state during the regular election.

Clause 2: Classification of Senators. Immediately after they shall be assembled in Consequence of the first Election, they shall be divided as equally as may be into three Classes. The Seats of the Senators of the first Class shall be vacated at the Expiration of the second Year, of the second Class at the Expiration of the fourth Year, and of the third Class at the Expiration of the sixth Year, so that one third may be chosen every second Year; [and if Vacancies happen by Resignation, or otherwise, during the Recess of the Legislature of any State, the Executive thereof may make temporary Appointments until the next Meeting of the Legislature, which shall then fill such Vacancies].[4]

One-third of the Senate's seats are open to election every two years (in contrast, all members of the House are elected simultaneously).

Clause 3: Qualifications. No Person shall be a Senator who shall not have attained to the Age of thirty Years, and been nine Years a Citizen of the United States, and who shall not, when elected, be an Inhabitant of that State for which he shall be chosen.

Every senator must be at least thirty years old, a citizen of the United States for a minimum of nine years, and a resident of the state in which he or she is elected.

Clause 4: The Role of the Vice President. The Vice President of the United States shall be President of the Senate, but shall have no Vote, unless they be equally divided.

The vice president presides over meetings of the Senate but cannot vote unless there is a tie. The Constitution gives no other official duties to the vice president.

Clause 5: Other Officers. The Senate shall chuse their other Officers, and also a President pro tempore, in the Absence of the Vice President, or when he shall exercise the Office of President of the United States.

The Senate votes for one of its members to preside when the vice president is absent. This person is usually called the president pro tempore because of the temporary nature of the position.

Clause 6: Impeachment Trials. The Senate shall have the sole Power to try all Impeachments. When sitting for that Purpose, they shall be on Oath or Affirmation. When the President of the United States is tried, the Chief Justice shall preside: And no Person shall be convicted without the Concurrence of two thirds of the Members present.

The Senate conducts trials of officials that the House impeaches. The Senate sits as a jury, with the vice president presiding if the president is not on trial.

Clause 7: Penalties for Conviction. Judgment in Cases of Impeachment shall not extend further than to removal from Office, and disqualification to hold and enjoy any Office of honor, Trust, or Profit under the United States: but the Party convicted shall nevertheless be liable and subject to Indictment, Trial, Judgment, and Punishment, according to Law.

On conviction of impeachment charges, the Senate can only force an official to leave office and prevent him or her from holding another office in the federal government. The individual, however, can still be tried in a regular court.

Section 4. Congressional Elections: Times, Manner, and Places

Clause 1: Elections. The Times, Places and Manner of holding Elections for Senators and Representatives, shall be prescribed in each State by the Legislature thereof; but the Congress may at any time by Law make or alter such Regulations, except as to the Places of chusing Senators.

Congress set the Tuesday after the first Monday in November in even-numbered years as the date for congressional elections. In states with more than one seat in the House, Congress requires that representatives be elected from districts within each state. Under the Seventeenth Amendment, senators are elected at the same places as other officials.

Clause 2: Sessions of Congress. [The Congress shall assemble at least once in every Year, and such Meeting shall be on the first Monday in December, unless they shall by Law appoint a different Day.][5]

Congress has to meet every year at least once. The regular session now begins at noon on January 3 of each year, subsequent to the Twentieth Amendment, unless Congress passes a law to fix a different date. Congress stays in session until its members vote to adjourn. Additionally, the president may call a special session.

Section 5. Powers and Duties of the Houses

Clause 1: Admitting Members and Quorum. Each House shall be the Judge of the Elections, Returns, and Qualifications of its own Members, and a Majority of each shall constitute a Quorum to do Business; but a smaller Number may adjourn from day to day, and may be authorized to compel the Attendance of absent Members, in such Manner, and under such Penalties as each House may provide.

Each chamber may exclude or refuse to seat a member-elect.

The quorum rule requires that 218 members of the House and 51 members of the Senate be present to conduct business. This rule normally is not enforced in the handling of routine matters.

Clause 2: Rules and Discipline of Members. Each House may determine the Rules of its Proceedings, punish

---

4. Modified by the Seventeenth Amendment.

5. Changed by the Twentieth Amendment.

its Members for disorderly Behaviour, and, with the Concurrence of two thirds, expel a Member.

The House and the Senate may adopt their own rules to guide their proceedings. Each may also discipline its members for conduct that is deemed unacceptable. No member may be expelled without a two-thirds majority vote in favor of expulsion.

Clause 3: Keeping a Record. Each House shall keep a Journal of its Proceedings, and from time to time publish the same, excepting such Parts as may in their Judgment require Secrecy; and the Yeas and Nays of the Members of either House on any question shall, at the Desire of one fifth of those Present, be entered on the Journal.

The journals of the two chambers are published at the end of each session of Congress.

Clause 4: Adjournment. Neither House, during the Session of Congress, shall, without the Consent of the other, adjourn for more than three days, nor to any other Place than that in which the two Houses shall be sitting.

Congress has the power to determine when and where to meet, provided, however, that both chambers meet in the same city. Neither chamber may recess for more than three days without the consent of the other.

Section 6. Rights of Members

Clause 1: Compensation and Privileges. The Senators and Representatives shall receive a Compensation for their services, to be ascertained by Law, and paid out of the Treasury of the United States. They shall in all Cases, except Treason, Felony and Breach of the Peace, be privileged from Arrest during their Attendance at the Session of their respective Houses, and in going to and returning from the same; and for any Speech or Debate in either House, they shall not be questioned in any other Place.

Congressional salaries are to be paid by the U.S. Treasury rather than by the members' respective states. The original salaries were $6 per day; in 1857 they were $3,000 per year. Both representatives and senators were paid $165,200 in 2007.

Treason is defined in Article III, Section 3. A felony is any serious crime. A breach of the peace is any indictable offense less than treason or a felony. Members cannot be arrested for things they say during speeches and debates in Congress. This immunity applies to the Capitol Building itself and not to their private lives.

Clause 2: Restrictions. No Senator or Representative shall, during the Time for which he was elected, be appointed to any civil Office under the Authority of the United States, which shall have been created, or the Emoluments whereof shall have been encreased during such time; and no Person holding any Office under the United States, shall be a Member of either House during his Continuance in Office.

During the term for which a member was elected, he or she cannot concurrently accept another federal government position.

Section 7. Legislative Powers: Bills and Resolutions

Clause 1: Revenue Bills. All Bills for raising Revenue shall originate in the House of Representatives; but the Senate may propose or concur with Amendments as on other Bills.

All tax and appropriation bills for raising money have to originate in the House of Representatives. The Senate, though, often amends such bills and may even substitute an entirely different bill.

Clause 2: The Presidential Veto. Every Bill which shall have passed the House of Representatives and the Senate, shall, before it becomes a Law, be presented to the President of the United States; If he approve he shall sign it, but if not he shall return it, with his Objections to the House in which it shall have originated, who shall enter the Objections at large on their Journal, and proceed to reconsider it. If after such Reconsideration two thirds of that House shall agree to pass the Bill, it shall be sent together with the Objections, to the other House, by which it shall likewise be reconsidered, and if approved by two thirds of that House, it shall become a Law. But in all such Cases the Votes of both Houses shall be determined by Yeas and Nays, and the Names of the Persons voting for and against the Bill shall be entered on the Journal of each House respectively. If any Bill shall not be returned by the President within ten Days (Sundays excepted) after it shall have been presented to him, the Same shall be a Law, in like Manner as if he had signed it, unless the Congress by their Adjournment prevent its Return in which Case it shall not be a Law.

When Congress sends the president a bill, he or she can sign it (in which case it becomes law) or send it back to the chamber in which it originated. If it is sent back, a two-thirds majority of each chamber must pass it again for it to become law. If the president neither signs it nor sends it back within ten days, it becomes law anyway, unless Congress adjourns in the meantime.

Clause 3: Actions on Other Matters. Every Order, Resolution, or Vote to which the Concurrence of the Senate and House of Representatives may be necessary (except on a question of Adjournment) shall be presented to the President of the United States; and before the Same shall take Effect, shall be approved by him, or being disapproved by him, shall be repassed by two thirds of the Senate and House of Representatives, according to the Rules and Limitations prescribed in the Case of a Bill.

The president must have the opportunity to either sign or veto everything that Congress passes, except votes to adjourn and resolutions not having the force of law.

Section 8. The Powers of Congress

Clause 1: Taxing. The Congress shall have Power to lay and collect Taxes, Duties, Imposts and Excises, to pay the Debts and provide for the common Defence and general Welfare of the United States; but all Duties, Imposts and Excises shall be uniform throughout the United States;

Duties *are taxes on imports and exports. Impost is a generic term for tax. Excises are taxes on the manufacture, sale, or use of goods.*

Clause 2: Borrowing. To borrow Money on the credit of the United States;

Congress has the power to borrow money, which is normally carried out through the sale of U.S. Treasury bonds on which interest is paid. Note that the Constitution places no limit on the amount of government borrowing.

Clause 3: Regulation of Commerce. To regulate Commerce with foreign Nations, and among the several States, and with the Indian Tribes;

This is the commerce clause, which gives to Congress the power to regulate interstate and foreign trade. Much of the activity of Congress is based on this clause.

Clause 4: Naturalization and Bankruptcy. To establish an uniform Rule of Naturalization, and uniform Laws on the subject of Bankruptcies throughout the United States;

Only Congress may determine how aliens can become citizens of the United States. Congress may make laws with respect to bankruptcy.

Clause 5: Money and Standards. To coin Money, regulate the Value thereof, and of foreign Coin, and fix the Standard of Weights and Measures;

Congress mints coins and prints and circulates paper money. Congress can establish uniform measures of time, distance, weight, and so on. In 1838, Congress adopted the English system of weights and measurements as our national standard.

Clause 6: Punishing Counterfeiters. To provide for the Punishment of counterfeiting the Securities and current Coin of the United States;

Congress has the power to punish those who copy American money and pass it off as real. Currently, the fine is up to $5,000 and/or imprisonment for up to fifteen years.

Clause 7: Roads and Post Offices. To establish Post Offices and post Roads;

Post roads include all routes over which mail is carried—highways, railways, waterways, and airways.

Clause 8: Patents and Copyrights. To promote the Progress of Science and useful Arts, by securing for limited Times to Authors and Inventors the exclusive Right to their respective Writings and Discoveries;

Authors' and composers' works are protected by copyrights established by copyright law, which currently is the Copyright Act of 1976, as amended. Copyrights are valid for the life of the author or composer plus seventy years. Inventors' works are protected by patents, which vary in length of protection from fourteen to twenty years. A patent gives a person the exclusive right to control the manufacture or sale of her or his invention.

Clause 9: Lower Courts. To constitute Tribunals inferior to the supreme Court;

Congress has the authority to set up all federal courts, except the Supreme Court, and to decide what cases those courts will hear.

Clause 10: Punishment for Piracy. To define and punish Piracies and Felonies committed on the high Seas, and Offences against the Law of Nations;

Congress has the authority to prohibit the commission of certain acts outside U.S. territory and to punish certain violations of international law.

Clause 11: Declaration of War. To declare War, grant Letters of Marque and Reprisal, and make Rules concerning Captures on Land and Water;

Only Congress can declare war, although the president, as commander in chief, can make war without Congress's formal declaration. Letters of marque and reprisal authorized private parties to capture and destroy enemy ships in wartime. Since the middle of the nineteenth century, international law has prohibited letters of marque and reprisal, and the United States has honored the ban.

Clause 12: The Army. To raise and support Armies, but no Appropriation of Money to that Use shall be for a longer Term than two Years;

Congress has the power to create an army; the money used to pay for it must be appropriated for no more than two-year intervals. This latter restriction gives ultimate control of the army to civilians.

Clause 13: Creation of a Navy. To provide and maintain a Navy;

This clause allows for the maintenance of a navy. In 1947, Congress created the U.S. Air Force.

Clause 14: Regulation of the Armed Forces. To make Rules for the Government and Regulation of the land and naval Forces;

Congress sets the rules for the military mainly by way of the Uniform Code of Military Justice, which was enacted in 1950 by Congress.

Clause 15: The Militia. To provide for calling forth the Militia to execute the Laws of the Union, suppress Insurrections and repel Invasions;

The militia is known today as the National Guard. Both Congress and the president have the authority to call the National Guard into federal service.

Clause 16: How the Militia Is Organized. To provide for organizing, arming, and disciplining the Militia, and for governing such Part of them as may be employed in the Service of the United States, reserving to the States respectively, the Appointment of the Officers, and the Authority of training the Militia according to the discipline prescribed by Congress;

This clause gives Congress the power to "federalize" state militia (National Guard). When called into such service, the National Guard is subject to the same rules that Congress has set forth for the regular armed services.

Clause 17: Creation of the District of Columbia. To exercise exclusive Legislation in all Cases whatsoever, over such District (not exceeding ten Miles square) as may, by Cession of particular States, and the Acceptance of Congress, become the Seat of the Government of the United States, and to exercise like Authority over all Places purchased by the Consent of the Legislature of the State in which the Same shall be, for the Erection of Forts, Magazines, Arsenals, dock-Yards, and other needful Buildings;—And

Congress established the District of Columbia as the national capital in 1791. Virginia and Maryland had granted land for the District, but Virginia's grant was returned because it was believed it would not be needed. Today, the District covers sixty-nine square miles.

Clause 18: The Elastic Clause. To make all Laws which shall be necessary and proper for carrying into Execution the foregoing Powers, and all other Powers vested by this Constitution in the Government of the United States, or in any Department or Officer thereof.

This clause—the necessary and proper clause, or the elastic clause—grants no specific powers, and thus it can be stretched to fit different circumstances. It has allowed Congress to adapt the government to changing needs and times.

Section 9. The Powers Denied to Congress

Clause 1: Question of Slavery. The Migration or Importation of such Persons as any of the States now existing shall think proper to admit, shall not be prohibited by the Congress prior to the Year one thousand eight hundred and eight, but a Tax or duty may be imposed on such Importation, not exceeding ten dollars for each Person.

"Persons" referred to slaves. Congress outlawed the slave trade in 1808.

Clause 2: Habeas Corpus. The privilege of the Writ of Habeas Corpus shall not be suspended, unless when in Cases of Rebellion or Invasion the public Safety may require it.

A writ of habeas corpus is a court order directing a sheriff or other public officer who is detaining another person to "produce the body" of the detainee so the court can assess the legality of the detention.

Clause 3: Special Bills. No Bill of Attainder or ex post facto Law shall be passed.

A bill of attainder is a law that inflicts punishment without a trial. An ex post facto law is a law that inflicts

punishment for an act that was not illegal when it was committed.

Clause 4: Direct Taxes. [No Capitation, or other direct, Tax shall be laid, unless in Proportion to the Census or Enumeration herein before directed to be taken.][6]

A capitation is a tax on a person. A direct tax is a tax paid directly to the government, such as a property tax. This clause was intended to prevent Congress from levying a tax on slaves per person and thereby taxing slavery out of existence.

Clause 5: Export Taxes. No Tax or Duty shall be laid on Articles exported from any State.

Congress may not tax any goods sold from one state to another or from one state to a foreign country. (Congress does have the power to tax goods that are bought from other countries, however.)

Clause 6: Interstate Commerce. No Preference shall be given by any Regulation of Commerce or Revenue to the Ports of one State over those of another: nor shall Vessels bound to, or from, one State, be obliged to enter, clear, or pay Duties in another.

Congress may not treat different ports within the United States differently in terms of taxing and commerce powers. Congress may not give one state's port a legal advantage over the ports of another state.

Clause 7: Treasury Withdrawals. No Money shall be drawn from the Treasury, but in Consequence of Appropriations made by Law; and a regular Statement and Account of the Receipts and Expenditures of all public Money shall be published from time to time.

Federal funds can be spent only as Congress authorizes. This is a significant check on the president's power.

Clause 8: Titles of Nobility. No Title of Nobility shall be granted by the United States: And no Person holding any Office of Profit or Trust under them, shall, without the Consent of the Congress, accept of any present, Emolument, Office, or Title, of any kind whatever, from any King, Prince, or foreign State.

No person in the United States may hold a title of nobility, such as duke or duchess. This clause also discourages bribery of American officials by foreign governments.

Section 10. Those Powers Denied to the States

Clause 1: Treaties and Coinage. No State shall enter into any Treaty, Alliance, or Confederation; grant Letters of Marque and Reprisal; coin Money; emit Bills of Credit; make any Thing but gold and silver Coin a Tender in Payment of Debts; pass any Bill of Attainder, ex post facto Law, or Law impairing the Obligation of Contracts, or grant any Title of Nobility.

---

6. Modified by the Sixteenth Amendment.

Prohibiting state laws "impairing the Obligation of Contracts" was intended to protect creditors. (Shays' Rebellion—an attempt to prevent courts from giving effect to creditors' legal actions against debtors—occurred only one year before the Constitution was written.)

Clause 2: Duties and Imposts. No State shall, without the Consent of the Congress, lay any Imposts or Duties on Imports or Exports, except what may be absolutely necessary for executing its inspection Laws; and the net Produce of all Duties and Imposts, laid by any State on Imports or Exports, shall be for the Use of the Treasury of the United States; and all such Laws shall be subject to the Revision and Controul of the Congress.

Only Congress can tax imports. Further, the states cannot tax exports.

Clause 3: War. No State shall, without the Consent of Congress, lay any Duty of Tonnage, keep Troops, or Ships of War in time of Peace, enter into any Agreement or Compact with another State, or with a foreign Power or engage in War, unless actually invaded, or in such imminent Danger as will not admit of delay.

A duty of tonnage is a tax on ships according to their cargo capacity. No states may tax ships according to their cargo unless Congress agrees. Additionally, this clause forbids any state to keep troops or warships during peacetime or to make a compact with another state or foreign nation unless Congress so agrees. A state, in contrast, can maintain a militia, but its use has to be limited to disorders that occur within the state—unless, of course, the militia is called into federal service.

ARTICLE II. (Executive Branch)

Section 1. The Nature and Scope of Presidential Power

Clause 1: Four-Year Term. The executive Power shall be vested in a President of the United States of America. He shall hold his Office during the Term of four Years, and, together with the Vice President, chosen for the same Term, be elected, as follows.

The president has the power to carry out laws made by Congress, called the executive power. He or she serves in office for a four-year term after election. The Twenty-second Amendment limits the number of times a person may be elected president.

Clause 2: Choosing Electors from Each State. Each State shall appoint, in such Manner as the Legislature thereof may direct, a Number of Electors, equal to the whole Number of Senators and Representatives to which the State may be entitled in the Congress; but no Senator or Representative, or Person holding an Office of Trust or Profit under the United States, shall be appointed an Elector.

The "Electors" are known more commonly as the "electoral college." The president is elected by electors—that is, representatives chosen by the people—rather than by the people directly.

Clause 3: The Former System of Elections. [The Electors shall meet in their respective States, and vote by Ballot for two Persons, of whom one at least shall not be an Inhabitant of the same State with themselves. And they shall make a List of all the Persons voted for, and of the Number of Votes for each; which List they shall sign and certify, and transmit sealed to the Seat of the Government of the United States, directed to the President of the Senate. The President of the Senate shall, in the Presence of the Senate and House of Representatives, open all the Certificates, and the Votes shall then be counted. The Person having the greatest Number of Votes shall be the President, if such Number be a Majority of the whole Number of Electors appointed; and if there be more than one who have such Majority, and have an equal Number of Votes, then the House of Representatives shall immediately chuse by Ballot one of them for President; and if no Person have a Majority, then from the five highest on the List the said House shall in like Manner chuse the President. But in chusing the President, the Votes shall be taken by States, the Representation from each State having one Vote; A quorum for this Purpose shall consist of a Member or Members from two thirds of the States, and a Majority of all the States shall be necessary to a Choice. In every Case, after the Choice of the President, the Person having the greater Number of Votes of the Electors shall be the Vice President. But if there should remain two or more who have equal Votes, the Senate shall chuse from them by Ballot the Vice President.][7]

The original method of selecting the president and vice president was replaced by the Twelfth Amendment. Apparently, the framers did not anticipate the rise of political parties and the development of primaries and conventions.

Clause 4: The Time of Elections. The Congress may determine the Time of chusing the Electors, and the Day on which they shall give their Votes; which Day shall be the same throughout the United States.

Congress set the Tuesday after the first Monday in November every fourth year as the date for choosing electors. The electors cast their votes on the Monday after the second Wednesday in December of that year.

Clause 5: Qualifications for President. No person except a natural born Citizen, or a Citizen of the United States, at the time of the Adoption of this Constitution, shall be eligible to the Office of President; neither shall any Person be eligible to that Office who shall not have attained to the Age of thirty five Years, and been fourteen Years a Resident within the United States.

The president must be a natural-born citizen, be at least thirty-five years of age when taking office, and have been a resident within the United States for at least fourteen years.

Clause 6: Succession of the Vice President. [In Case of the Removal of the President from Office, or of his Death,

---

7. Changed by the Twelfth Amendment.

Resignation or Inability to discharge the Powers and Duties of the said Office, the same shall devolve on the Vice President, and the Congress may by Law provide for the Case of Removal, Death, Resignation or Inability, both of the President and Vice President, declaring what Officer shall then act as President, and such Officer shall act accordingly, until the Disability be removed, or a President shall be elected.][8]

This section provided for the method by which the vice president was to succeed to the presidency, but its wording is ambiguous. It was replaced by the Twenty-fifth Amendment.

Clause 7: The President's Salary. The President shall, at stated Times, receive for his Services, a Compensation, which shall neither be encreased nor diminished during the Period for which he shall have been elected, and he shall not receive within that Period any other Emolument from the United States, or any of them.

The president maintains the same salary during each four-year term. Moreover, she or he may not receive additional cash payments from the government. Originally set at $25,000 per year, the salary is currently $400,000 a year plus a $50,000 nontaxable expense account.

Clause 8: The Oath of Office. Before he enter on the Execution of his Office, he shall take the following Oath or Affirmation: "I do solemnly swear (or affirm) that I will faithfully execute the Office of President of the United States, and will to the best of my Ability, preserve, protect and defend the Constitution of the United States."

The president is "sworn in" prior to beginning the duties of the office. The taking of the oath of office occurs on January 20, following the November election. The ceremony is called the inauguration. The oath of office is administered by the chief justice of the United States Supreme Court.

Section 2. Powers of the President

Clause 1: Commander in Chief. The President shall be Commander in Chief of the Army and Navy of the United States, and of the Militia of the several States, when called into the actual Service of the United States; he may require the Opinion, in writing, of the principal Officer in each of the executive Departments, upon any Subject relating to the Duties of their respective Offices, and he shall have Power to grant Reprieves and Pardons for Offences against the United States, except in Cases of Impeachment.

The armed forces are placed under civilian control because the president is a civilian but still commander in chief of the military. The president may ask for the help of the head of each of the executive departments (thereby creating the cabinet). The cabinet members are chosen by the president with the consent of the Senate, but they can be removed without Senate approval.

The president's clemency powers extend only to federal cases. In those cases, he or she may grant a full or conditional pardon, or reduce a prison term or fine.

---

8. Modified by the Twenty-fifth Amendment.

Clause 2: Treaties and Appointment. He shall have Power, by and with the Advice and Consent of the Senate, to make Treaties, provided two thirds of the Senators present concur; and he shall nominate, and by and with the Advice and Consent of the Senate, shall appoint Ambassadors, other public Ministers and Consuls, Judges of the supreme Court, and all other Officers of the United States, whose Appointments are not herein otherwise provided for, and which shall be established by Law; but the Congress may by Law vest the Appointment of such inferior Officers, as they think proper, in the President alone, in the Courts of Law, or in the Heads of Departments.

Many of the major powers of the president are identified in this clause, including the power to make treaties with foreign governments (with the approval of the Senate by a two-thirds vote) and the power to appoint ambassadors, Supreme Court justices, and other government officials. Most such appointments require Senate approval.

Clause 3: Vacancies. The President shall have Power to fill up all Vacancies that may happen during the Recess of the Senate, by granting Commissions which shall expire at the end of their next Session.

The president has the power to appoint temporary officials to fill vacant federal offices without Senate approval if the Congress is not in session. Such appointments expire automatically at the end of Congress's next term.

Section 3. Duties of the President

He shall from time to time give to the Congress Information of the State of the Union, and recommend to their Consideration such Measures as he shall judge necessary and expedient; he may, on extraordinary Occasions, convene both Houses, or either of them, and in Case of Disagreement between them, with Respect to the Time of Adjournment, he may adjourn them to such Time as he shall think proper; he shall receive Ambassadors and other public Ministers; he shall take Care that the Laws be faithfully executed, and shall Commission all the Officers of the United States.

Annually, the president reports on the state of the union to Congress, recommends legislative measures, and proposes a federal budget. The State of the Union speech is a statement not only to Congress but also to the American people. After it is given, the president proposes a federal budget and presents an economic report. At any time, the president may send special messages to Congress while it is in session. The president has the power to call special sessions, to adjourn Congress when its two chambers do not agree on when to adjourn, to receive diplomatic representatives of other governments, and to ensure the proper execution of all federal laws. The president further has the ability to empower federal officers to hold their positions and to perform their duties.

Section 4. Impeachment

The President, Vice President and all civil Officers of the United States, shall be removed from Office on Impeachment for, and Conviction of, Treason, Bribery, or other high Crimes and Misdemeanors.

Treason *denotes giving aid to the nation's enemies. The phrase* high crimes and misdemeanors *is usually considered to mean serious abuses of political power. In either case, the president or vice president may be accused by the House (called an* impeachment*) and then removed from office if convicted by the Senate. (Note that impeachment does not mean removal but rather refers to an accusation of treason or high crimes and misdemeanors.)*

ARTICLE III. (Judicial Branch)

Section 1. Judicial Powers, Courts, and Judges

The judicial Power of the United States, shall be vested in one supreme Court, and in such inferior Courts as the Congress may from time to time ordain and establish. The Judges, both of the supreme and inferior Courts, shall hold their Offices during good Behaviour, and shall, at stated Times, receive for their Services a Compensation, which shall not be diminished during their Continuance in Office.

The Supreme Court is vested with judicial power, as are the lower federal courts that Congress creates. Federal judges serve in their offices for life unless they are impeached and convicted by Congress. The payment of federal judges may not be reduced during their time in office.

Section 2. Jurisdiction

Clause 1: Cases under Federal Jurisdiction. The judicial Power shall extend to all Cases, in Law and Equity, arising under this Constitution, the Laws of the United States, and Treaties made, or which shall be made, under their Authority;—to all Cases affecting Ambassadors, other public Ministers and Consuls;—to all Cases of admiralty and maritime Jurisdiction;—to Controversies to which the United States shall be a Party;—to Controversies between two or more States; [—between a State and Citizens of another State;—][9] between Citizens of different States;—between Citizens of the same State claiming Lands under Grants of different States, [and between a State, or the Citizens thereof, and foreign States, Citizens or Subjects.][10]

The federal courts take on cases that concern the meaning of the U.S. Constitution, all federal laws, and treaties. They also can take on cases involving citizens of different states and citizens of foreign nations.

Clause 2: Cases for the Supreme Court. In all Cases affecting Ambassadors, other public Ministers and Consuls, and those in which a State shall be a Party, the supreme Court shall have original Jurisdiction. In all the other Cases before mentioned, the supreme Court shall have appellate Jurisdiction, both as to Law and Fact, with such Exceptions, and under such Regulations as the Congress shall make.

In a limited number of situations, the Supreme Court acts as a trial court and has original jurisdiction. These cases involve a representative from another country or involve *a state. In all other situations, the cases must first be tried in the lower courts and then can be appealed to the Supreme Court. Congress may, however, make exceptions. Today, the Supreme Court acts as a trial court of first instance on rare occasions.*

Clause 3: The Conduct of Trials. The Trial of all Crimes, except in Cases of Impeachment, shall be by Jury; and such Trial shall be held in the State where the said Crimes shall have been committed; but when not committed within any State, the Trial shall be at such Place or Places as the Congress may by Law have directed.

Any person accused of a federal crime is granted the right to a trial by jury in a federal court in that state in which the crime was committed. Trials of impeachment are an exception.

Section 3. Treason

Clause 1: The Definition of Treason. Treason against the United States, shall consist only in levying War against them, or, in adhering to their Enemies, giving them Aid and Comfort. No Person shall be convicted of Treason unless on the Testimony of two Witnesses to the same overt Act, or on Confession in open Court.

Treason is the making of war against the United States or giving aid to its enemies.

Clause 2: Punishment. The Congress shall have Power to declare the Punishment of Treason, but no Attainder of Treason shall work Corruption of Blood, or Forfeiture except during the Life of the Person attainted.

Congress has provided that the punishment for treason ranges from a minimum of five years in prison and/or a $10,000 fine to a maximum of death. "No Attainder of Treason shall work Corruption of Blood" prohibits punishment of the traitor's heirs.

ARTICLE IV. (Relations among the States)

Section 1. Full Faith and Credit

Full Faith and Credit shall be given in each State to the public Acts, Records, and judicial Proceedings of every other State. And the Congress may by general Laws prescribe the Manner in which such Acts, Records and Proceedings shall be proved, and the Effect thereof.

All states are required to respect one another's laws, records, and lawful decisions. There are exceptions, however. A state does not have to enforce another state's criminal code. Nor does it have to recognize another state's grant of a divorce if the person obtaining the divorce did not establish legal residence in the state in which it was given.

Section 2. Treatment of Citizens

Clause 1: Privileges and Immunities. The Citizens of each State shall be entitled to all Privileges and Immunities of Citizens in the several States.

A citizen of a state has the same rights and privileges as the citizens of another state in which he or she happens to be.

---

9. Modified by the Eleventh Amendment.
10. Modified by the Eleventh Amendment.

Clause 2: Extradition. A Person charged in any State with Treason, Felony, or other Crime, who shall flee from Justice, and be found in another State, shall on Demand of the executive Authority of the State from which he fled, be delivered up, to be removed to the State having Jurisdiction of the Crime.

Any person accused of a crime who flees to another state must be returned to the state in which the crime occurred.

Clause 3: Fugitive Slaves. [No Person held to Service or Labour in one State, under the Laws thereof, escaping into another, shall, in Consequence of any Law or Regulation therein, be discharged from such Service or Labour, but shall be delivered up on Claim of the Party to whom such Service or Labour may be due.][11]

This clause was struck down by the Thirteenth Amendment, which abolished slavery in 1865.

Section 3. Admission of States

Clause 1: The Process. New States may be admitted by the Congress into this Union; but no new State shall be formed or erected within the Jurisdiction of any other State; nor any State be formed by the Junction of two or more States, or Parts of States, without the Consent of the Legislatures of the States concerned as well as of the Congress.

Only Congress has the power to admit new states to the union. No state may be created by taking territory from an existing state unless the state's legislature so consents.

Clause 2: Public Land. The Congress shall have Power to dispose of and make all needful Rules and Regulations respecting the Territory or other Property belonging to the United States; and nothing in this Constitution shall be so construed as to Prejudice any Claims of the United States, or of any particular State.

The federal government has the exclusive right to administer federal government public lands.

Section 4. Republican Form of Government

The United States shall guarantee to every State in this Union a Republican Form of Government, and shall protect each of them against Invasion; and on Application of the Legislature, or of the Executive (when the Legislature cannot be convened) against domestic Violence.

Each state is promised a republican form of government—that is, one in which the people elect their representatives. The federal government is bound to protect states against any attack by foreigners or during times of trouble within a state.

ARTICLE V. (Methods of Amendment)

The Congress, whenever two thirds of both Houses shall deem it necessary, shall propose Amendments to this Constitution, or on the Application of the Legislatures of two thirds of the several States, shall call a Convention for proposing Amendments, which, in either Case, shall be valid to all Intents and Purposes, as Part of this Constitution, when ratified by the Legislatures of three fourths of the several States, or by Conventions in three fourths thereof, as the one or the other Mode of Ratification may be proposed by the Congress; Provided that no Amendment which may be made prior to the Year One thousand eight hundred and eight shall in any Manner affect the first and fourth Clauses in the Ninth Section of the First Article; and that no State, without its Consent, shall be deprived of its equal Suffrage in the Senate.

Amendments may be proposed in either of two ways: by a two-thirds vote of each chamber (Congress) or at the request of two-thirds of the states. Ratification of amendments may be carried out in two ways: by the legislatures of three-fourths of the states or by the voters in three-fourths of the states. No state may be denied equal representation in the Senate.

ARTICLE VI. (National Supremacy)

Clause 1: Existing Obligations. All Debts contracted and Engagements entered into, before the Adoption of this Constitution shall be as valid against the United States under this Constitution, as under the Confederation.

During the Revolutionary War and the years of the Confederation, Congress borrowed large sums. This clause pledged that the new federal government would assume those financial obligations.

Clause 2: Supreme Law of the Land. This Constitution, and the Laws of the United States which shall be made in Pursuance thereof; and all Treaties made, or which shall be made, under the Authority of the United States, shall be the supreme Law of the Land; and the Judges in every State shall be bound thereby, any Thing in the Constitution or Laws of any State to the Contrary notwithstanding.

This is typically called the supremacy clause; it declares that federal law takes precedence over all forms of state law. No government at the local or state level may make or enforce any law that conflicts with any provision of the Constitution, acts of Congress, treaties, or other rules and regulations issued by the president and his or her subordinates in the executive branch of the federal government.

Clause 3: Oath of Office. The Senators and Representatives before mentioned, and the Members of the several State Legislatures, and all executive and judicial Officers, both of the United States and of the several States, shall be bound by Oath or Affirmation, to support this Constitution; but no religious Test shall ever be required as a Qualification to any Office or public Trust under the United States.

Every federal and state official must take an oath of office promising to support the U.S. Constitution. Religion may not be used as a qualification to serve in any federal office.

---

11. Repealed by the Thirteenth Amendment.

ARTICLE VII. (Ratification)

The Ratification of the Conventions of nine States shall be sufficient for the Establishment of this Constitution between the States so ratifying the Same.

Nine states were required to ratify the Constitution. Delaware was the first and New Hampshire the ninth.

Done in Convention by the Unanimous Consent of the States present the Seventeenth Day of September in the Year of our Lord one thousand seven hundred and Eighty seven and of the Independence of the United States of America the Twelfth. In witness whereof we have hereunto subscribed our Names,

Go. WASHINGTON
Presid't.
and deputy from Virginia

Attest William Jackson Secretary

DELAWARE
{ Geo. Read
Gunning Bedford jun
John Dickinson
Richard Bassett
Jaco. Broom

MARYLAND
{ James McHenry
Dan of St. Thos. Jenifer
Danl. Carroll

VIRGINIA
{ John Blair
James Madison Jr.

NORTH CAROLINA
{ Wm. Blount
Richd. Dobbs Spaight
Hu. Williamson

SOUTH CAROLINA
{ J. Rutledge
Charles Cotesworth Pinckney
Charles Pinckney
Pierce Butler

GEORGIA
{ William Few
Abr. Baldwin

NEW HAMPSHIRE
{ John Langdon
Nicholas Gilman

MASSACHUSETTS
{ Nathaniel Gorham
Rufus King

CONNECTICUT
{ Wm. Saml. Johnson
Roger Sherman

NEW YORK Alexander Hamilton

NEW JERSEY
{ Wh. Livingston
David Brearley
Wm. Paterson
Jona. Dayton

PENNSYLVANIA
{ B. Franklin
Thomas Mifflin
Robt. Morris
Geo. Clymer
Thos. FitzSimons
Jared Ingersoll
James Wilson
Gouv. Morris

AMENDMENTS TO THE CONSTITUTION OF THE UNITED STATES[12]

Articles in addition to, and amendment of, the Constitution of the United States of America, proposed by Congress and ratified by the Legislatures of the several states, pursuant to the Fifth Article of the original Constitution.

AMENDMENT I.
(Religion, Speech, Assembly, and Petition)
Congress shall make no law respecting an establishment of religion, or prohibiting the free exercise thereof; or abridging the freedom of speech, or of the press; or the right of the people peaceably to assemble, and to petition the Government for a redress of grievances.

Congress may not create an official church or enact laws limiting the freedom of religion, speech, the press, assembly, and petition. These guarantees, like the others in the Bill of Rights (the first ten amendments), are not absolute—each may be exercised only with regard to the rights of other persons.

AMENDMENT II.
(Militia and the Right to Bear Arms)
A well regulated Militia, being necessary to the security of a free State, the right of the people to keep and bear Arms, shall not be infringed.

To protect itself, each state has the right to maintain a volunteer armed force. States and the federal government regulate the possession and use of firearms by individuals.

AMENDMENT III.
(The Quartering of Soldiers)
No Soldier shall, in time of peace be quartered in any house, without the consent of the Owner, nor in time of war, but in a manner to be prescribed by law.

Before the Revolutionary War, it had been common British practice to quarter soldiers in colonists' homes. Military troops do not have the power to take over private houses during peacetime.

AMENDMENT IV.
(Searches and Seizures)
The right of the people to be secure in their persons, houses, papers, and effects, against unreasonable searches and seizures, shall not be violated, and no Warrants shall issue, but upon probable cause, supported by Oath or affirmation, and particularly describing the place to be searched, and the persons or things to be seized.

Here the word warrant means "justification" and refers to a document issued by a magistrate or judge indicat-

ing the name, address, and possible offense committed. Anyone asking for the warrant, such as a police officer, must be able to convince the magistrate or judge that an offense probably has been committed.

AMENDMENT V.
(Grand Juries, Self-Incrimination, Double Jeopardy, Due Process, and Eminent Domain)
No person shall be held to answer for a capital, or otherwise infamous crime, unless on a presentment or indictment of a Grand Jury, except in cases arising in the land or naval forces, or in the Militia, when in actual service in time of War or public danger; nor shall any person be subject for the same offence to be twice put in jeopardy of life or limb; nor shall be compelled in any criminal case to be a witness against himself, nor be deprived of life, liberty, or property, without due process of law; nor shall private property be taken for public use, without just compensation.

There are two types of juries. A grand jury considers physical evidence and the testimony of witnesses and decides whether there is sufficient reason to bring a case to trial. A petit jury hears the case at trial and decides it. "For the same offence to be twice put in jeopardy of life or limb" means to be tried twice for the same crime. A person may not be tried for the same crime twice or forced to give evidence against herself or himself. No person's right to life, liberty, or property may be taken away except by lawful means, called the due process of law. *Private property taken for public use must be paid for by the government.*

AMENDMENT VI.
(Criminal Court Procedures)
In all criminal prosecutions, the accused shall enjoy the right to a speedy and public trial, by an impartial jury of the State and district wherein the crime shall have been committed, which district shall have been previously ascertained by law, and to be informed of the nature and cause of the accusation; to be confronted with the witnesses against him; to have compulsory process for obtaining witnesses in his favor, and to have the Assistance of Counsel for his defence.

Any person accused of a crime has the right to a fair and public trial by a jury in the state in which the crime took place. The charges against that person must be indicated. Any accused person has the right to a lawyer to defend him or her and to question those who testify against him or her, as well as the right to call people to speak in his or her favor at trial.

AMENDMENT VII.
(Trial by Jury in Civil Cases)
In Suits at common law, where the value in controversy shall exceed twenty dollars, the right of trial by jury shall be preserved, and no fact tried by jury, shall be otherwise re-examined in any Court of the United States, than according to the rules of the common law.

---

12. On September 25, 1789, Congress transmitted to the state legislatures twelve proposed amendments, two of which, having to do with congressional representation and congressional pay, were not adopted. The remaining ten amendments became the Bill of Rights. In 1992, the amendment concerning congressional pay was adopted as the Twenty-seventh Amendment.

A jury trial may be requested by either party in a dispute in any case involving more than $20. If both parties agree to a trial by a judge without a jury, the right to a jury trial may be put aside.

AMENDMENT VIII.
(Bail, Cruel and Unusual Punishment)

Excessive bail shall not be required, nor excessive fines imposed, nor cruel and unusual punishments inflicted.

Bail is an amount of money that a person accused of a crime may be required to deposit with the court as a guaranty that she or he will appear in court when requested. The amount of bail required or the fine imposed as punishment for a crime must be reasonable compared with the seriousness of the crime involved. Any punishment judged to be too harsh or too severe for a crime is prohibited.

AMENDMENT IX.
(The Rights Retained by the People)

The enumeration in the Constitution, of certain rights, shall not be construed to deny or disparage others retained by the people.

Many civil rights that are not explicitly enumerated in the Constitution are still held by the people.

AMENDMENT X.
(Reserved Powers of the States)

The powers not delegated to the United States by the Constitution, nor prohibited by it to the States, are reserved to the States respectively, or to the people.

Those powers not delegated by the Constitution to the federal government or expressly denied to the states belong to the states and to the people. This amendment in essence allows the states to pass laws under their "police powers."

AMENDMENT XI.
(Ratified on February 7, 1795—
Suits against States)

The Judicial power of the United States shall not be construed to extend to any suit in law or equity, commenced or prosecuted against one of the United States by Citizens of another State, or by Citizens or Subjects of any Foreign State.

This amendment has been interpreted to mean that a state cannot be sued in federal court by one of its own citizens, by a citizen of another state, or by a foreign country.

AMENDMENT XII.
(Ratified on June 15, 1804—
Election of the President)

The Electors shall meet in their respective states, and vote by ballot for President and Vice-President, one of whom, at least, shall not be an inhabitant of the same State with themselves; they shall name in their ballots the person voted for as President, and in distinct ballots the person voted for as Vice-President, and they shall make distinct lists of all persons voted for as President, and of all persons voted for as Vice-President, and of the number of votes for each, which lists they shall sign and certify, and transmit sealed to the seat of the government of the United States, directed to the President of the Senate;—The President of the Senate shall, in the presence of the Senate and House of Representatives, open all the certificates and the votes shall then be counted;—The person having the greatest number of votes for President, shall be the President, if such number be a majority of the whole number of Electors appointed; and if no person have such majority, then from the persons having the highest numbers not exceeding three on the list of those voted for as President, the House of Representatives shall choose immediately, by ballot, the President. But in choosing the President, the votes shall be taken by States, the representation from each State having one vote; a quorum for this purpose shall consist of a member or members from two-thirds of the States, and a majority of all States shall be necessary to a choice. [And if the House of Representatives shall not choose a President whenever the right of choice shall devolve upon them, before the fourth day of March next following, then the Vice-President shall act as President, as in the case of the death or other constitutional disability of the President.][13]—The person having the greatest number of votes as Vice-President, shall be the Vice-President, if such number be a majority of the whole number of Electors appointed, and if no person have a majority, then from the two highest numbers on the list, the Senate shall choose the Vice-President; a quorum for the purpose shall consist of two-thirds of the whole number of Senators, and a majority of the whole number shall be necessary to a choice. But no person constitutionally ineligible to the office of President shall be eligible to that of Vice-President of the United States.

The original procedure set out for the election of president and vice president in Article II, Section 1, resulted in a tie in 1800 between Thomas Jefferson and Aaron Burr. It was not until the next year that the House of Representatives chose Jefferson to be president. This amendment changed the procedure by providing for separate ballots for president and vice president.

AMENDMENT XIII.
(Ratified on December 6, 1865—
Prohibition of Slavery)

Section 1.

Neither slavery nor involuntary servitude, except as a punishment for crime whereof the party shall have been duly convicted, shall exist within the United States, or any place subject to their jurisdiction.

Some slaves had been freed during the Civil War. This amendment freed the others and abolished slavery.

Section 2.

Congress shall have power to enforce this article by appropriate legislation.

---

13. Changed by the Twentieth Amendment.

AMENDMENT XIV.
(Ratified on July 9, 1868—
Citizenship, Due Process, and
Equal Protection of the Laws)

Section 1.

All persons born or naturalized in the United States, and subject to the jurisdiction thereof, are citizens of the United States and of the State wherein they reside. No State shall make or enforce any law which shall abridge the privileges or immunities of citizens of the United States; nor shall any State deprive any person of life, liberty, or property, without due process of law; nor deny to any person within its jurisdiction the equal protection of the laws.

Under this provision, states cannot make or enforce laws that take away rights given to all citizens by the federal government. States cannot act unfairly or arbitrarily toward, or discriminate against, any person.

Section 2.

Representatives shall be apportioned among the several States according to their respective numbers, counting the whole number of persons in each State, excluding Indians not taxed. But when the right to vote at any election for the choice of electors for President and Vice President of the United States, Representatives in Congress, the Executive and Judicial officers of a State, or the members of the Legislature thereof, is denied to any of the male inhabitants of such State, being [twenty-one][14] years of age, and citizens of the United States, or in any way abridged, except for participation in rebellion, or other crime, the basis of representation therein shall be reduced in the proportion which the number of such male citizens shall bear to the whole number of male citizens twenty-one years of age in such State.

Section 3.

No person shall be a Senator or Representative in Congress, or elector of President and Vice President, or hold any office, civil or military, under the United States, or under any State, who having previously taken an oath, as a member of Congress, or as an officer of the United States, or as a member of any State legislature, or as an executive or judicial officer of any State, to support the Constitution of the United States, shall have engaged in insurrection or rebellion against the same, or given aid or comfort to the enemies thereof. But Congress may by a vote of two-thirds of each House, remove such disability.

This provision forbade former state or federal government officials who had acted in support of the Confederacy during the Civil War to hold office again. It limited the president's power to pardon those persons. Congress removed this "disability" in 1898.

Section 4.

The validity of the public debt of the United States, authorized by law, including debts incurred for payment of pensions and bounties for services in suppressing insur-

rection or rebellion, shall not be questioned. But neither the United States nor any State shall assume or pay any debt or obligation incurred in aid of insurrection or rebellion against the United States, or any claim for the loss or emancipation of any slave, but all such debts, obligations and claims shall be held illegal and void.

Section 5.

The Congress shall have power to enforce, by appropriate legislation, the provisions of this article.

AMENDMENT XV.
(Ratified on February 3, 1870—
The Right to Vote)

Section 1.

The right of citizens of the United States to vote shall not be denied or abridged by the United States or by any State on account of race, color, or previous condition of servitude.

No citizen can be refused the right to vote simply because of race or color or because that person was once a slave.

Section 2.

The Congress shall have power to enforce this article by appropriate legislation.

AMENDMENT XVI.
(Ratified on February 3, 1913—
Income Taxes)

The Congress shall have power to lay and collect taxes on incomes, from whatever source derived, without apportionment among the several States, and without regard to any census or enumeration.

This amendment allows Congress to tax income without shar-ing the revenue so obtained with the states according to their population.

AMENDMENT XVII.
(Ratified on April 8, 1913—
The Popular Election of Senators)

Section 1.

The Senate of the United States shall be composed of two Senators from each State, elected by the people thereof, for six years; and each Senator shall have one vote. The electors in each State shall have the qualifications requisite for electors of the most numerous branch of the State legislatures.

Section 2.

When vacancies happen in the representation of any State in the Senate, the executive authority of such State shall issue writs of election to fill such vacancies: *Provided,* That the legislature of any State may empower the executive thereof to make temporary appointments until the people fill the vacancies by election as the legislature may direct.

Section 3.

This amendment shall not be so construed as to affect the election or term of any Senator chosen before it becomes valid as part of the Constitution.

---

14. Changed by the Twenty-sixth Amendment.

This amendment modified portions of Article I, Section 3, that related to election of senators. Senators are now elected by the voters in each state directly. When a vacancy occurs, either the state may fill the vacancy by a special election, or the governor of the state involved may appoint someone to fill the seat until the next election.

AMENDMENT XVIII.
(Ratified on January 16, 1919— Prohibition)

Section 1.

After one year from the ratification of this article the manufacture, sale, or transportation of intoxicating liquors within, the importation thereof into, or the exportation thereof from the United States and all territory subject to the jurisdiction thereof for beverage purposes is hereby prohibited.

Section 2.

The Congress and the several States shall have concurrent power to enforce this article by appropriate legislation.

Section 3.

This article shall be inoperative unless it shall have been ratified as an amendment to the Constitution by the legislatures of the several States, as provided in the Constitution, within seven years from the date of the submission hereof to the States by the Congress.[15]

This amendment made it illegal to manufacture, sell, and transport alcoholic beverages in the United States. It was repealed by the Twenty-first Amendment.

AMENDMENT XIX.
(Ratified on August 18, 1920— Women's Right to Vote)

Section 1.

The right of citizens of the United States to vote shall not be denied or abridged by the United States or by any State on account of sex.

Section 2.

Congress shall have power to enforce this article by appropriate legislation.

Women were given the right to vote by this amendment, and Congress was given the power to enforce this right.

AMENDMENT XX.
(Ratified on January 23, 1933— The Lame Duck Amendment)

Section 1.

The terms of the President and Vice President shall end at noon on the 20th day of January, and the terms of Senators and Representatives at noon on the 3d day of January, of the years in which such terms would have ended if this article had not been ratified; and the terms of their successors shall then begin.

This amendment modified Article I, Section 4, Clause 2, and other provisions relating to the president in the

Twelfth Amendment. The taking of the oath of office was moved from March 4 to January 20.

Section 2.

The Congress shall assemble at least once in every year, and such meeting shall begin at noon on the 3d day of January, unless they shall by law appoint a different day.

Congress changed the beginning of its term to January 3. The reason the Twentieth Amendment is called the Lame Duck Amendment is that it shortens the time between when a member of Congress is defeated for reelection and when he or she leaves office.

Section 3.

If, at the time fixed for the beginning of the term of the President, the President elect shall have died, the Vice President elect shall become President. If a President shall not have been chosen before the time fixed for the beginning of his term, or if the President elect shall have failed to qualify, then the Vice President elect shall act as President until a President shall have qualified; and the Congress may by law provide for the case wherein neither a President elect nor a Vice President elect shall have qualified, declaring who shall then act as President, or the manner in which one who is to act shall be selected, and such person shall act accordingly until a President or Vice President shall have qualified.

This part of the amendment deals with problem areas left ambiguous by Article II and the Twelfth Amendment. If the president dies before January 20 or fails to qualify for office, the presidency is to be filled as described in this section.

Section 4.

The Congress may by law provide for the case of the death of any of the persons from whom the House of Representatives may choose a President whenever the right of choice shall have devolved upon them, and for the case of the death of any of the persons from whom the Senate may choose a Vice President whenever the right of choice shall have devolved upon them.

Congress has never created legislation pursuant to this section.

Section 5.

Sections 1 and 2 shall take effect on the 15th day of October following the ratification of this article.

Section 6.

This article shall be inoperative unless it shall have been ratified as an amendment to the Constitution by the legislatures of three-fourths of the several States within seven years from the date of its submission.

AMENDMENT XXI.
(Ratified on December 5, 1933— The Repeal of Prohibition)

Section 1.

The eighteenth article of amendment to the Constitution of the United States is hereby repealed.

---

15. The Eighteenth Amendment was repealed by the Twenty-first Amendment.

Section 2.

The transportation or importation into any State, Territory, or possession of the United States for delivery or use therein of intoxicating liquors, in violation of the laws thereof, is hereby prohibited.

Section 3.

This article shall be inoperative unless it shall have been ratified as an amendment to the Constitution by conventions in the several States, as provided in the Constitution, within seven years from the date of the submission hereof to the States by the Congress.

The amendment repealed the Eighteenth Amendment but did not make alcoholic beverages legal everywhere. Rather, they remained illegal in any state that so designated them. Many such "dry" states existed for a number of years after 1933. Today, there are still "dry" counties within the United States, in which the sale of alcoholic beverages is illegal.

AMENDMENT XXII.
(Ratified on February 27, 1951— Limitation of Presidential Terms)

Section 1.

No person shall be elected to the office of the President more than twice, and no person who has held the office of President, or acted as President, for more than two years of a term to which some other person was elected President shall be elected to the office of President more than once. But this Article shall not apply to any person holding the office of President when this Article was proposed by the Congress, and shall not prevent any person who may be holding the office of President, or acting as President, during the term within which this Article becomes operative from holding the office of President or acting as President during the remainder of such term.

Section 2.

This article shall be inoperative unless it shall have been ratified as an amendment to the Constitution by the legislatures of three-fourths of the several States within seven years from the date of its submission to the States by the Congress.

No president may serve more than two elected terms. If, however, a president has succeeded to the office after the halfway point of a term in which another president was originally elected, then that president may serve for more than eight years, but not to exceed ten years.

AMENDMENT XXIII.
(Ratified on March 29, 1961— Presidential Electors for the District of Columbia)

Section 1.

The District constituting the seat of Government of the United States shall appoint in such manner as the Congress may direct:

A number of electors of President and Vice President equal to the whole number of Senators and Representatives in Congress to which the District would be entitled if it were a State, but in no event more than the least populous State; they shall be in addition to those appointed by the States, but they shall be considered, for the purposes of the election of President and Vice President, to be electors appointed by a State; and they shall meet in the District and perform such duties as provided by the twelfth article of amendment.

Section 2.

The Congress shall have power to enforce this article by appropriate legislation.

Citizens living in the District of Columbia have the right to vote in elections for president and vice president. The District of Columbia has three presidential electors, whereas before this amendment it had none.

AMENDMENT XXIV.
(Ratified on January 23, 1964— The Anti–Poll Tax Amendment)

Section 1.

The right of citizens of the United States to vote in any primary or other election for President or Vice President, for electors for President or Vice President, or for Senator or Representative in Congress, shall not be denied or abridged by the United States, or any State by reason of failure to pay any poll tax or other tax.

Section 2.

The Congress shall have power to enforce this article by appropriate legislation.

No government shall require a person to pay a poll tax to vote in any federal election.

AMENDMENT XXV.
(Ratified on February 10, 1967— Presidential Disability and Vice Presidential Vacancies)

Section 1.

In case of the removal of the President from office or of his death or resignation, the Vice President shall become President.

Whenever a president dies or resigns from office, the vice president becomes president.

Section 2.

Whenever there is a vacancy in the office of the Vice President, the President shall nominate a Vice President who shall take office upon confirmation by a majority vote of both Houses of Congress.

Whenever the office of the vice presidency becomes vacant, the president may appoint someone to fill this office, provided Congress consents.

Section 3.

Whenever the President transmits to the President pro tempore of the Senate and the Speaker of the House of Representatives his written declaration that he is unable to discharge the powers and duties of his office, and until he transmits to them a written declaration to the contrary, such powers and duties shall be discharged by the Vice President as Acting President.

Whenever the president believes she or he is unable to carry out the duties of the office, she or he shall so indicate to Congress in writing. The vice president then acts as president until the president declares that she or he is again able to carry out the duties of the office.

Section 4.

Whenever the Vice President and a majority of either the principal officers of the executive departments or of such other body as Congress may by law provide, transmit to the President pro tempore of the Senate and the Speaker of the House of Representatives their written declaration that the President is unable to discharge the powers and duties of his office, the Vice President shall immediately assume the powers and duties of the office as Acting President.

Thereafter, when the President transmits to the President pro tempore of the Senate and the Speaker of the House of Representatives his written declaration that no inability exists, he shall resume the powers and duties of his office unless the Vice President and a majority of either the principal officers of the executive department or of such other body as Congress may by law provide, transmit within four days to the President pro tempore of the Senate and the Speaker of the House of Representatives their written declaration that the President is unable to discharge the powers and duties of his office. Thereupon Congress shall decide the issue, assembling within forty-eight hours for that purpose if not in session. If the Congress, within twenty-one days after receipt of the latter written declaration, or, if Congress is not in session, within twenty-one days after Congress is required to assemble, determines by two-thirds vote of both Houses that the President is unable to discharge the powers and duties of his office, the Vice President shall continue to discharge the same as Acting President; otherwise, the President shall resume the powers and duties of his office.

Whenever the vice president and a majority of the members of the cabinet believe that the president cannot carry out her or his duties, they shall so indicate in writing to Congress. The vice president shall then act as president. When the president believes that she or he is able to carry out her or his duties again, she or he shall so indicate to the Congress. However, if the vice president and a majority of the cabinet do not agree, Congress must decide by a two-thirds vote within three weeks who shall act as president.

AMENDMENT XXVI.
(Ratified on July 1, 1971—
The Eighteen-Year-Old Vote)

Section 1.

The right of citizens of the United States, who are eighteen years of age or older, to vote shall not be denied or abridged by the United States or by any State on account of age.

No one over eighteen years of age can be denied the right to vote in federal or state elections by virtue of age.

Section 2.

The Congress shall have power to enforce this article by appropriate legislation.

AMENDMENT XXVII.
(Ratified on May 7, 1992—
Congressional Pay)

No law, varying the compensation for the services of the Senators and Representatives, shall take effect, until an election of representatives shall have intervened.

This amendment allows the voters to have some control over increases in salaries for congressional members. Originally submitted to the states for ratification in 1789, it was not ratified until 203 years later, in 1992.

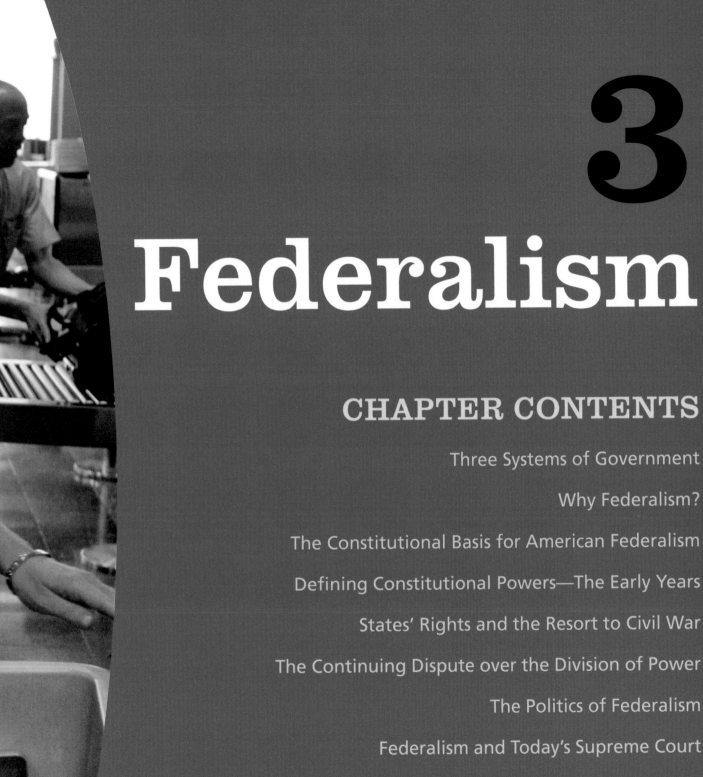

3

Federalism

CHAPTER CONTENTS

A Transportation Security Administration employee places luggage in a screening X-ray machine at Washington's Ronald Reagan National Airport. (AP Photo/Pablo Martinez Monsivais)

what if...state lotteries were privatized?

BACKGROUND

For many, gambling constitutes inappropriate behavior and should always be illegal. Most of the time, the states and the federal government agree—except when government profits from the games. In 1964, New Hampshire created the first modern state lottery. Today, forty-two states plus the District of Columbia and the Virgin Islands have lotteries. Certain states have even joined together to offer larger jackpots—the best known of these is the Powerball drawing. Many states have instant lottery tickets (scratch cards) that have become a major source of state lottery revenues. Often, the justification for state lotteries has been to raise funds for public education. In any event, states earn, after expenses, many billions of dollars a year from their lotteries. These revenue streams don't vary much from year to year. Some cash-strapped states are now contemplating whether they should privatize their state lotteries in order to raise large sums instantly.

WHAT IF STATE LOTTERIES WERE PRIVATIZED?

In general, the right to any stream of annual revenues can be sold in the open market. A corporation often sells the right to receive, say, 5 percent interest every year for ten years. This is called a bond. Some states have already sold the stream of revenues from toll roads to private companies. Chicago sold its 7.8-mile Skyway for $1.8 billion to a private company. The new operator must improve the highway's financial performance to make such a large investment pay off. Indiana and Virginia have undertaken similar actions.[a]

Privatization of a state lottery system would work in the same way. A state would sell the right to run the lottery to a private company or a group of private investors. In return for paying the state for this "asset," the purchaser would receive revenues from the lottery year after year.

CALIFORNIA WANTS TO BE THE FIRST

California wants to become the first state to privatize its lottery. It estimates that it can sell it for at least $37 billion. Governor Arnold Schwarzenegger wants to use part of these funds to pay for his proposed health-care reforms.

California hopes that the results will be similar to what happened in Britain after it transferred its national lottery to a private company. Under the Schwarzenegger plan, whoever bought California's lottery would have the right to run it for forty years, although the state would still regulate it. California's proposed lottery privatization would have to be ratified by a public ballot. A number of other states are likely to follow suit if the California plan succeeds.

PRIVATE LOTTERIES: NEW GAMES AND ADVERTISING GALORE

If state lotteries were owned and run by private companies, we could be sure of one thing—additional new, popular games would be introduced almost immediately. Variations on existing games would multiply. Games of chance that were not sufficiently profitable would eventually be dropped, and others would be introduced.

We also can be certain that there would be more retail sales outlets. Just imagine: you might be able to buy lottery tickets in shopping malls; in department stores; at large, members-only businesses, such as Costco or Sam's Club; and perhaps even in large restaurants.

You may think you see a lot of ads for the lottery now, but you would see many more if lotteries were privatized. The new private owners would surely advertise in every possible way—by sponsoring sporting events, employing billboards, purchasing ads on TV shows, and, of course, using the Internet.

Indeed, the Internet may become a key aspect of legalized gambling. Not only would private lottery owners use standard display and pop-up ads; they would probably also figure out a way to sell lottery tickets on the Internet. Remember, the goal of the private owners would be to maximize the return on their multibillion-dollar investment in a state lottery system.

FOR CRITICAL ANALYSIS

1. Although casino gambling is legal in many locations, only individuals over twenty-one years of age can enter casinos. If privatized lotteries started selling tickets on the Internet, how could they prevent those under twenty-one from purchasing them?
2. Why are some forms of gambling still illegal while other forms are completely legal?

---

a. Actually, these "sales" were ninety-nine-year leases.

In the United States, rights and powers are reserved to the states by the Tenth Amendment. It may appear that since the terrorist attacks of September 11, 2001, the federal government, sometimes called the national or central government, predominates. Nevertheless, that might be a temporary exaggeration, for there are 88,576 separate governmental units in this nation, as you can see in Table 3–1.

Visitors from France or Spain are often awestruck by the complexity of our system of government. Consider that a criminal action can be defined by state law, by national law, or by both. Thus, a criminal suspect can be prosecuted in the state court system or in the federal court system (or both). Often, economic regulation over exactly the same matter exists at the local level, the state level, and the national level—generating multiple forms to be completed, multiple procedures to be followed, and multiple laws to be obeyed. Many programs are funded by the national government but administered by state and local governments.

Relations between central governments and local units are structured in various ways. *Federalism* is one of these ways. Understanding federalism and how it differs from other forms of government is important in understanding the American political system. Indeed, many political issues today, including the lottery privatization issue discussed in this chapter's opening *What If . . .* feature, would be substantially different if we did not have a federal form of government in which governmental authority is divided between the central government and various subunits.

THREE SYSTEMS OF GOVERNMENT

There are nearly two hundred independent nations in the world today. Each of these nations has its own system of government. Generally, though, we can describe how nations structure relations between central governments and local units in terms of three models: (1) the unitary system, (2) the confederal system, and (3) the federal system. The most popular, both historically and today, is the unitary system.

A UNITARY SYSTEM

A **unitary system** of government is the easiest to define. Unitary systems allow ultimate governmental authority to rest in the hands of the national, or central, government. Consider a typical unitary system—France. There are regions, departments, and municipalities (communes) in France. The regions, departments, and communes have elected and appointed officials. So far, the French system appears to be very similar to the U.S. system, but the similarity is only superficial. Under the unitary French system, the decisions of the lower levels of government can be overruled by the national government. The

TABLE 3–1:
Governmental Units in the United States

With almost 89,000 separate governmental units in the United States today, it is no wonder that intergovernmental relations in the United States are so complicated. Actually, the number of school districts has decreased over time, but the number of special districts created for single purposes, such as flood control, has increased from only about 8,000 during World War II to over 36,000 today.

Federal government	1
State governments	50
Local governments	88,525
Counties	3,034
Municipalities	19,429
(mainly cities or towns)	
Townships	16,504
(less extensive powers)	
Special districts	36,052
(water, sewer, and so on)	
School districts	13,506
TOTAL	88,576

Source: U.S. Census Bureau.

Unitary System
A centralized governmental system in which ultimate governmental authority rests in the hands of the national, or central, government.

These lucky co-workers show off their 2008 Powerball winnings at the West Virginia Lottery Office in Charleston, the state capital. How do state lotteries indicate that we have a federal system of government? (AP Photo/Bob Bird)

national government also can cut off the funding of many local government activities. Moreover, in a unitary system such as that in France, all questions of education, police, the use of land, and welfare are handled by the national government. Britain, Egypt, Ghana, Israel, Japan, the Philippines, and Sweden—in fact, most countries today—have unitary systems of government.[1]

A CONFEDERAL SYSTEM

You were introduced to the elements of a **confederal system** of government in Chapter 2, when we examined the Articles of Confederation. A *confederation* is the opposite of a unitary governing system. It is a league of independent states, each having essentially sovereign powers. In a confederation, a central government or administration handles only those matters of common concern expressly delegated to it by the member states. The central government has no ability to make laws directly applicable to member states unless the members explicitly support such laws. The United States under the Articles of Confederation was a confederal system.

Few, if any, confederations of this kind exist. One possible exception is the European Union, a league of countries that is developing unifying institutions, such as a common currency. Nations have also formed organizations with one another for limited purposes, such as military or peacekeeping cooperation. Examples are the North Atlantic Treaty Organization (NATO) and the United Nations (UN). These organizations, however, are not true confederations.

A FEDERAL SYSTEM

The federal system lies between the unitary and confederal forms of government. As mentioned in Chapter 2, in a *federal system,* authority is divided, usually by a written constitution, between a central government and regional, or subdivisional, governments (often called *constituent governments*). The central government and the constituent governments both act directly on the people through laws and through the actions of elected and appointed governmental officials. Within each government's sphere of authority, each is supreme, in theory. Thus, a federal system differs sharply from a unitary one, in which the central government is supreme and the constituent governments derive their authority from it. Australia, Brazil, Canada, Germany, India, and Mexico are examples of other nations with federal systems. See Figure 3–1 for a comparison of the three systems.

WHY FEDERALISM?

Why did the United States develop in a federal direction? We look here at that question, as well as at some of the arguments for and against a federal form of government.

A PRACTICAL SOLUTION

As you saw in Chapter 2, the historical basis of our federal system was laid down in Philadelphia at the Constitutional Convention, where advocates of a strong national government opposed states' rights advocates. This dichotomy continued through to the ratifying conventions in the several states. The resulting federal system was a compromise. The supporters of the new Constitution were political pragmatists—they realized that without a federal arrangement, the new Constitution would not be ratified. The appeal of federalism was that it retained state traditions and local power while establishing a strong national government capable of handling common problems.

Even if the founders had agreed on the desirability of a unitary system, size and regional isolation would have made such a system difficult operationally. At the time

Confederal System
A system consisting of a league of independent states, each having essentially sovereign powers. The central government created by such a league has only limited powers over the states.

---

1. Recent legislation has altered somewhat the unitary character of the French political system. In Britain, the unitary nature of the government has been modified by the creation of the Scottish Parliament.

FIGURE 3–1: The Flow of Power in Three Systems of Government

In a unitary system, power flows from the central government to the local and state governments. In a confederal system, power flows in the opposite direction—from the state governments to the central government. In a federal system, the flow of power, in principle, goes both ways.

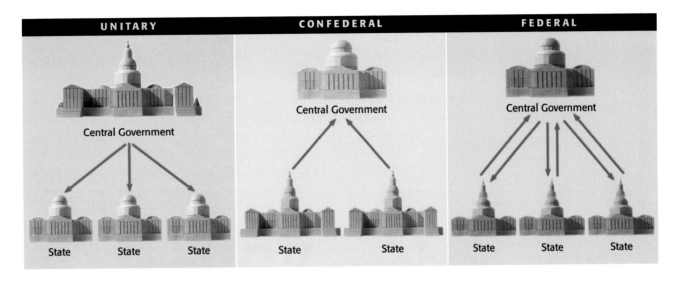

of the Constitutional Convention, the thirteen states taken together were much larger geographically than England or France. Slow travel and communication, combined with geographic spread, contributed to the isolation of many regions within the states. It could take several weeks for all of the states to be informed about a particular political decision.

OTHER ARGUMENTS FOR FEDERALISM

The arguments for federalism in the United States and elsewhere involve a complex set of factors, some of which we have already noted. First, for big countries, such as Canada, India, and the United States, federalism allows many functions to be "farmed out" by the central government to the states or provinces. The lower levels of government that accept these responsibilities thereby can become the focus of political dissatisfaction rather than the national authorities. Second, even with modern transportation and communications systems, the large area or population of some nations makes it impractical to locate all political authority in one place. Finally, federalism brings government closer to the people. It allows more direct access to, and influence on, government agencies and policies, rather than leaving the population restive and dissatisfied with a remote, faceless, all-powerful central authority.

didyouknow...

That **state governments** in the United States are unitary governments and, as a result, most local governments are mere creatures of the states.

Benefits for the United States. In the United States, federalism historically has yielded many benefits. State governments long have been a training ground for future national leaders. Many presidents made their political mark as state governors. The states themselves have been testing grounds for new government initiatives. As United States Supreme Court justice Louis Brandeis once observed:

> It is one of the happy incidents of the federal system that a single courageous state may, if its citizens choose, serve as a laboratory and try novel social and economic experiments without risk to the rest of the country.[2]

Examples of programs pioneered at the state level include unemployment compensation, which began in Wisconsin, and air-pollution control, which was initiated in California.

2. *New State Ice Co. v. Liebmann,* 285 U.S. 262 (1932).

Today, states are experimenting with policies ranging from education reforms, to health insurance for all residents, to homeland security defense strategies. Since the passage of the 1996 welfare reform legislation—which gave more control over welfare programs to state governments—states also have been experimenting with different methods of delivering welfare assistance. One example of how the federal government has recently deferred to the states is a 2007 law allowing state governors to decide when the flag should be lowered, even at federal facilities. We discuss controversies around this law in this chapter's *Which Side Are You On?* feature.

Allowance for Many Political Subcultures. The American way of life always has been characterized by a number of political subcultures, which divide along the lines of race and ethnic origin, region, wealth, education, and, more recently, degree of religious fundamentalism and sexual preference. The existence of diverse political subcultures would appear to be incompatible with a political authority concentrated solely in a central gov-

whichsideare**YOU**on?

SHOULD WE LOWER THE FLAG FOR EVERY FALLEN SOLDIER?

Lowering the flag to half-mast is a common act after the death of a well-known politician or government official, such as a former president. After the start of the Iraq War, more than half the states decided to lower their flags for twenty-four hours or more whenever a soldier from the state was killed in action. Some believe that so much flag lowering is overkill and cheapens the tribute. Others see it as a subtle antiwar gesture and point out that the practice is contrary to federal guidelines, which indicate that the flag should be lowered for "officials," not soldiers. For a time, the flag-lowering controversy also involved a federal issue: If a state governor ordered federal buildings to lower their flags, were the federal officials obligated to comply with the order? This part of the controversy is now moot because Congress passed a law that requires federal officials to comply with governors' requests to lower flags.

HONOR OUR FALLEN SOLDIERS

Many believe that it is quite appropriate that the states lower their state flags for twenty-four hours or more when a local soldier dies in combat, and that the U.S. flag should be lowered at the same time. After all, how can we say that an "official" is more important than one of our soldiers who has died in the line of duty? The head of the legislative unit of the Society for Military Widows believes that when a soldier gives his or her life, any sign, such as lowering a flag, shows respect that is greatly appreciated.

Thoughtful governors have realized the importance of lowering the flag for fallen soldiers for several years. California lowers both the U.S. flag and the state flag at all buildings at the capitol, as does Wisconsin. New Mexico and Virginia lower only their state flags. Michigan has lowered all flags at state buildings more than 130 times since

December 2003. Michigan governor Jennifer Granholm put it succinctly: "It is not a statement about the war, but it is a statement about service and about soldiers who have made the ultimate sacrifice."

DO WHAT IS RIGHT— DON'T LOWER THE U.S. FLAG

Critics of the flag lowering argue that the U.S. flag, at least, should not be lowered. The executive director of the National Flag Foundation, Joyce Doody, argues against lowering U.S. flags for fallen soldiers. She believes that in times of conflict, the flag should remain at full staff except when a significant number of lives are lost.

Many believe that lowering a flag to honor fallen soldiers today is simply "cheap patriotism." Others contend that lowering flags for a fallen soldier displays an antiwar sentiment that governors should not express. Although national law now requires federal officials to follow requests by governors to fly the U.S. flag at half-mast, critics complain that this gives the states power over the federal government that is contrary to the spirit of the Constitution.

(Jeff Banke, 2008/Used under license from Shutterstock.com)

ernment. Had the United States developed into a unitary system, various political subcultures certainly would be less able to influence government behavior than they have been, and continue to be, in our federal system.

In his classic work on American federalism, political scientist Daniel Elazar claimed that one of federalism's greatest virtues is that it encourages the development of distinct political subcultures. These political subcultures reflect differing needs and desires for government, which vary from region to region. Federalism, he argues, allows for "a unique combination of governmental strength, political flexibility, and individual liberty."[3] Indeed, the existence of political subcultures allows a wider variety of factions to influence government. As a result, political subcultures have proved instrumental in driving reform even at the national level.

ARGUMENTS AGAINST FEDERALISM

Not everyone thinks federalism is such a good idea. Some see it as a way for powerful state and local interests to block progress and impede national plans. Smaller political units are more likely to be dominated by a single political group. (This was essentially the argument that James Madison put forth in *Federalist Paper* No. 10, which you can read in Appendix C of this text.) The dominant groups in some cities and states have resisted implementing equal rights for minority groups. Some argue, however, that the dominant factions in other states have been more progressive than the national government in many areas, such as the environment.

Critics of federalism also argue that too many Americans suffer as a result of the inequalities across the states. Individual states differ markedly in educational spending and achievement, crime and crime prevention, and even the safety of their buildings. Not surprisingly, these critics argue for increased federal legislation and oversight. This might involve creating national standards for education and building codes, national expenditure minimums for crime control, and similar measures.

Others see dangers in the expansion of national powers at the expense of the states. President Ronald Reagan (1981–1989) said, "The Founding Fathers saw the federalist system as constructed something like a masonry wall. The States are the bricks, the national government is the mortar. . . . Unfortunately, over the years, many people have increasingly come to believe that Washington is the whole wall."[4]

The pollution restrictions on the cars traveling on the Golden Gate Bridge in San Francisco are stricter than those mandated by the Federal Clean Air Act and its amendments. How is it possible for California's pollution standards to be stricter than federal standards? (AP Photo/Eric Risberg)

THE CONSTITUTIONAL BASIS FOR AMERICAN FEDERALISM

The term *federal system* cannot be found in the U.S. Constitution. Nor is it possible to find a systematic division of governmental authority between the national and state governments in that document. Rather, the Constitution sets out different types of powers. These powers can be classified as (1) the powers of the national government, (2) the powers of the states, and (3) prohibited powers. The Constitution also makes it clear that if a state or local law conflicts with a national law, the national law will prevail.

POWERS OF THE NATIONAL GOVERNMENT

The powers delegated to the national government include both expressed and implied powers, as well as the special category of inherent powers. Most of the powers expressly delegated to the national government are found in the first seventeen clauses of Article I,

3. Daniel Elazar, *American Federalism: A View from the States,* 3d ed. (New York: Crowell, 1984).
4. Text of the address by the president to the National Conference of State Legislatures, Atlanta, Georgia (Washington, D.C.: The White House, Office of the Press Secretary, July 30, 1981), as quoted in Edward Millican, *One United People: The Federalist Papers and the National Idea* (Lexington, Ky.: The University Press of Kentucky, 1990).

Section 8, of the Constitution. These **enumerated powers** include coining money, setting standards for weights and measures, making uniform naturalization laws, admitting new states, establishing post offices, and declaring war. Another important enumerated power is the power to regulate commerce among the states—a topic we deal with later in this chapter.

The Necessary and Proper Clause. The implied powers of the national government are also based on Article I, Section 8, which states that Congress shall have the power

to make all Laws which shall be necessary and proper for carrying into Execution the foregoing Powers, and all other Powers vested by this Constitution in the Government of the United States, or in any Department or Officer thereof.

This clause is sometimes called the **elastic clause,** or the **necessary and proper clause,** because it provides flexibility to the U.S. constitutional system. It gives Congress the power to do whatever is necessary to execute its specifically designated powers. The clause was first used in the Supreme Court decision of *McCulloch v. Maryland*[5] (discussed later in this chapter) to develop the concept of implied powers. Through this concept, the national government has succeeded in strengthening the scope of its authority to meet the numerous problems that the framers of the Constitution did not, and could not, anticipate.

Inherent Powers. A special category of national powers that is not implied by the necessary and proper clause consists of what have been labeled the inherent powers of the national government. These powers derive from the fact that the United States is a sovereign power among nations, and so its national government must be the only government that deals with other nations. Under international law, it is assumed that all nation-states, regardless of their size or power, have an inherent right to ensure their own survival. To do this, each nation must have the ability to act in its own interest among and with the community of nations—by, for instance, making treaties, waging war, seeking trade, and acquiring territory.

Note that no specific clause in the Constitution says anything about the acquisition of additional land. Nonetheless, through the federal government's inherent powers, we made the Louisiana Purchase in 1803 and then went on to acquire Florida, Texas, Oregon, Alaska, Hawaii, and other lands. The United States grew from a mere thirteen states to fifty states, plus several territories.

The national government has these inherent powers whether or not they have been enumerated in the Constitution. Some constitutional scholars categorize inherent powers as a third type of power, completely distinct from the delegated powers (both expressed and implied) of the national government.

POWERS OF THE STATE GOVERNMENTS

The Tenth Amendment states that the powers not delegated to the United States by the Constitution, nor prohibited by it to the states, are reserved to the states, or to the people. These are the reserved powers that the national government cannot deny to the states. Because these powers are not expressly listed—and because they are not limited to powers that are expressly listed—there is sometimes a question as to whether a certain power is delegated to the national government or reserved to the states.

State powers have been held to include each state's right to regulate commerce within its borders and to provide for a state militia. States also have the reserved power to make laws on all matters not prohibited to the states by the U.S. Constitution or state constitutions and not expressly, or by implication, delegated to the national government.

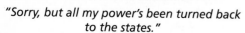

"Sorry, but all my power's been turned back to the states."

5. 17 U.S. 316 (1819).

Furthermore, the states have **police power**—the authority to legislate for the protection of the health, morals, safety, and welfare of the people. Their police power enables states to pass laws governing such activities as crimes, marriage, contracts, education, intrastate transportation, and land use.

The ambiguity of the Tenth Amendment has allowed the reserved powers of the states to be defined differently at different times in our history. When there is widespread support for increased regulation by the national government, the Tenth Amendment tends to recede into the background. When the tide turns the other way (in favor of states' rights), the Tenth Amendment is resurrected to justify arguments supporting increased states' rights.

CONCURRENT POWERS

In certain areas, the states share **concurrent powers** with the national government. Most concurrent powers are not specifically listed in the Constitution; they are only implied. An example of a concurrent power is the power to tax. The types of taxation are divided between the levels of government. For example, states may not levy a tariff (a set of taxes on imported goods); only the national government may do this. Neither government may tax the facilities of the other. If the state governments did not have the power to tax, they would not be able to function other than on a ceremonial basis. Other concurrent powers include the power to borrow funds, to establish courts, and to charter banks and corporations. To a limited extent, the national government exercises police power, and to the extent that it does, police power is also a concurrent power. Concurrent powers exercised by the states are normally limited to the geographic area of each state and to those functions not granted by the Constitution exclusively to the national government (such exclusive functions include the coinage of money and the negotiation of treaties).

We often think of tapping telephone lines as a federal activity, which it is in cases of national security. The states, however, actually undertake more wiretapping than does the federal government, you will read in this chapter's *Politics and the Cyber Sphere* feature on the following page.

PROHIBITED POWERS

The Constitution prohibits, or denies, a number of powers to the national government. For example, the national government expressly has been denied the power to impose taxes on goods sold to other countries (exports). Moreover, any power not granted expressly or implicitly to the federal government by the Constitution is prohibited to it. For example, many legal experts believe that the national government could not create a national divorce law system without a constitutional amendment. The states are also denied certain powers. For example, no state is allowed to enter into a treaty on its own with another country.

THE SUPREMACY CLAUSE

The supremacy of the national constitution over subnational laws and actions is established in the **supremacy clause** of the Constitution. The supremacy clause (Article VI, Clause 2) states the following:

> *This Constitution, and the Laws of the United States which shall be made in Pursuance thereof; and all Treaties made . . . under the Authority of the United States, shall be the supreme Law of the Land; and the Judges in every State shall be bound thereby, any Thing in the Constitution or Laws of any State to the Contrary notwithstanding.*

In other words, states cannot use their reserved or concurrent powers to thwart national policies. All national and state officers, including judges, must be bound by oath to support the Constitution. Hence, any legitimate exercise of national governmental

POLITICS AND...
the cyber sphere

THE STATES EXPAND THE ART OF WIRETAPPING

In the last few years, the press has paid much attention to allegedly illegal warrantless wiretapping by the federal government. Indeed, with or without warrants, the federal government has focused more of its resources on national security investigations and has devoted a lesser share of its effort to other types of investigations, such as those delving into suspected drug transactions and white-collar crimes. Federal wiretapping for criminal investigations is still a significant activity, but it is the number of federal wiretaps on possible terrorist suspects that has grown rapidly.

(Vladi, 2008/Used under license from Shutterstock.com)

WHAT THE NUMBERS SAY

Ten years ago, state and federal investigators requested about the same number of wiretaps. Remember that before tapping someone's phone, a prosecutor has to persuade a judge that there is probable cause that the person might be breaking the law. In the last ten years, however, judges have denied only 5 of the more than 15,000 wiretapping applications filed.

One consequence of the federal government's increased attention to the war on terrorism is that in recent years, state prosecutors have obtained more than three times as many wiretap authorizations as their federal counterparts. In 2006, the number of phones secretly wiretapped by Colorado police exceeded the number tapped in the previous nine years combined.

Technological advances in the 1980s initially made it more difficult for federal and local investigators to tap phones, especially the new cell phones. In 1994, however, Congress passed the Communications Assistance for Law Enforcement Act, or CALEA. Under CALEA, the telecommunications industry was required to design systems that would let law enforcement personnel place wiretaps, but the industry could set its own standards and design its own equipment to meet the requirement. Today, more than 90 percent of all wiretaps involve cell phones. The average cost of a wiretap has fallen dramatically in the last few years. Officers no longer need to visit a telephone switching station, but can monitor a wiretap from the computer in their office.

NEW YORK STATE SETS THE RECORD

Most authorized wiretaps last a relatively short time. Consider, in contrast, that in New York City, a wiretap used in a racketeering investigation was put in place for 519 days straight. The results? The interception of 105,000 cellular phone messages, of which more than 75,000 were incriminating. The states are clearly filling the wiretapping void left by the federal government.

FOR CRITICAL ANALYSIS

The majority of wiretaps today are used to catch drug dealers. Why might people who are not involved in illegal drug transactions be worried, nonetheless, about potential violations of their civil liberties?

---

power supersedes any conflicting state action.[6] Of course, deciding whether a conflict actually exists is a judicial matter, as you will see when we discuss the case of *McCulloch v. Maryland*.

National government legislation in a concurrent area is said to *preempt* (take precedence over) conflicting state or local laws or regulations in that area. One of the ways in which the national government has extended its powers, particularly during the twentieth century, is through the preemption of state and local laws by national legislation. In the first decade of the twentieth century, fewer than twenty national laws preempted laws and regulations issued by state and local governments. By the beginning of the twenty-first century, the number had grown into the hundreds.

---

6. An example of this is President Dwight Eisenhower's disciplining of Arkansas governor Orval Faubus in 1957 by federalizing the National Guard to enforce the court-ordered desegregation of Little Rock High School.

Some political scientists believe that national supremacy is critical for the longevity and smooth functioning of a federal system. Nonetheless, the application of this principle has been a continuous source of conflict. Indeed, as you will see, the most extreme example of this conflict was the Civil War.

VERTICAL CHECKS AND BALANCES

Recall from Chapter 2 that one of the concerns of the founders was to prevent the national government from becoming too powerful. For that reason, they divided the government into three branches—legislative, executive, and judicial. They also created a system of checks and balances that allowed each branch to check the actions of the others. The federal form of government created by the founders also involves checks and balances. These are sometimes called *vertical checks and balances* because they involve relationships between the states and the national government. They can be contrasted with *horizontal checks and balances,* in which the branches of government that are on the same level—either state or national—can check one other.

For example, the reserved powers of the states act as a check on the national government. Additionally, the states' interests are represented in the national legislature (Congress), and the citizens of the various states determine who will head the executive branch (the presidency). The founders also made it impossible for the central government to change the Constitution without the states' consent, as you read in Chapter 2. Finally, many national programs and policies are administered by the states, which gives the states considerable control over the ultimate shape of those programs and policies.

The national government, in turn, can check state policies by exercising its constitutional powers under the clauses just discussed, as well as under the commerce clause (to be examined later). Furthermore, the national government can influence state policies indirectly through federal grants, as you will learn later in this chapter.

INTERSTATE RELATIONS

So far we have examined only the relationship between central and state governmental units. The states, however, have constant commercial, social, and other dealings among themselves. The national Constitution imposes certain "rules of the road" on interstate relations. These rules have had the effect of preventing any one state from setting itself apart from the other states. The three most important clauses governing interstate relations in the Constitution, all taken from the Articles of Confederation, require each state to do the following:

1. Give full faith and credit to every other state's public acts, records, and judicial proceedings (Article IV, Section 1).
2. Extend to every other state's citizens the privileges and immunities of its own citizens (Article IV, Section 2).
3. Agree to return persons who are fleeing from justice in another state back to their home state when requested to do so (Article IV, Section 2).

Following these constitutional mandates is not always easy for the states. For example, one question that has arisen in recent years is whether states will be constitutionally obligated to recognize same-sex marriages performed in other states.

Additionally, states may enter into agreements called **interstate compacts**—if consented to by Congress. In reality, congressional consent is necessary only if such a compact increases the power of the contracting states relative to other states (or to the national government). Typical examples of interstate compacts are the establishment of the Port Authority of New York and New Jersey by a compact between those two states in 1921 and the regulation of the production of crude oil and natural gas by the Interstate Oil and Gas Compact of 1935.

Interstate Compact
An agreement between two or more states. Agreements on minor matters are made without congressional consent, but any compact that tends to increase the power of the contracting states relative to other states or relative to the national government generally requires the consent of Congress.

DEFINING CONSTITUTIONAL POWERS—THE EARLY YEARS

Recall from Chapter 2 that constitutional language, to be effective and to endure, must have some degree of ambiguity. Certainly, the powers delegated to the national government and the powers reserved to the states contain elements of ambiguity, thus leaving the door open for different interpretations of federalism. Disputes over the boundaries of national versus state powers have characterized this nation from the beginning. In the early 1800s, the most significant disputes arose over differing interpretations of the implied powers of the national government under the necessary and proper clause and over the respective powers of the national government and the states to regulate commerce.

This new train car replaces older cars on the Port Authority Trans-Hudson (PATH) rapid transit line, which is run by the Port Authority of New York and New Jersey. These new PATH cars are equipped with television screens showing news, weather, and sports. What political device did the governments of New York and New Jersey utilize in order to create the Port Authority? (AP Photo/ Mike Derer)

Although political bodies at all levels of government play important roles in the process of settling such disputes, ultimately it is the Supreme Court that casts the final vote. As might be expected, the character of the referee will have an impact on the ultimate outcome of any dispute. From 1801 to 1835, the Supreme Court was headed by Chief Justice John Marshall, a Federalist who advocated a strong central government. We look here at two cases decided by the Marshall Court: *McCulloch v. Maryland*[7] and *Gibbons v. Ogden.*[8] Both cases are considered milestones in the movement toward national government supremacy.

McCULLOCH V. MARYLAND (1819)

The U.S. Constitution says nothing about establishing a national bank. Nonetheless, at different times Congress chartered two banks—the First and Second Banks of the United States—and provided part of their initial capital; thus, they were national banks. The government of Maryland imposed a tax on the Second Bank's Baltimore branch in an attempt to put that branch out of business. The branch's cashier, James William McCulloch, refused to pay the Maryland tax. When Maryland took McCulloch to its state court, the state of Maryland won. The national government appealed the case to the Supreme Court.

One of the issues before the Court was whether the national government had the implied power, under the necessary and proper clause, to charter a bank and contribute capital to it. The other important question before the Court was the following: If the bank was constitutional, could a state tax it? In other words, was a state action that conflicted with a national government action invalid under the supremacy clause?

Chief Justice Marshall held that if establishing such a national bank aided the national government in the exercise of its designated powers, then the authority to set up such a bank could be implied. Having established this doctrine of implied powers, Marshall then answered the other important question before the Court and established the doctrine of national supremacy. Marshall ruled that no state could use its taxing power to tax an arm of the national government. If it could, "the declaration that the Constitution . . . shall be the supreme law of the land, is [an] empty and unmeaning [statement]."

Marshall's decision enabled the national government to grow and to meet problems that the Constitution's framers were unable to foresee. Today, practically every expressed

---

7. 17 U.S. 316 (1819).
8. 22 U.S. 1 (1824).

power of the national government has been expanded in one way or another by use of the necessary and proper clause.

GIBBONS V. OGDEN (1824)

One of the most important parts of the Constitution included in Article I, Section 8, is the so-called **commerce clause,** in which Congress is given the power "to regulate Commerce with foreign Nations, and among the several States, and with the Indian Tribes." The meaning of this clause was at issue in *Gibbons v. Ogden.*

The Background of the Case. Robert Fulton and Robert Livingston secured a monopoly on steam navigation on the waters in New York State from the New York legislature in 1803. They licensed Aaron Ogden to operate steam-powered ferryboats between New York and New Jersey. Thomas Gibbons, who had obtained a license from the U.S. government to operate boats in interstate waters, decided to compete with Ogden, but he did so without New York's permission. Ogden sued Gibbons. The New York state courts prohibited Gibbons from operating in New York waters. Gibbons appealed to the Supreme Court.

There were actually several issues before the Court in this case. The first issue was how the term *commerce* should be defined. New York's highest court had defined the term narrowly to mean only the shipment of goods or the interchange of commodities, *not* navigation or the transport of people. The second issue was whether the national government's power to regulate interstate commerce extended to commerce within a state (*intra*state commerce) or was limited strictly to commerce among the states (*inter*state commerce). The third issue was whether the power to regulate interstate commerce was a concurrent power (as the New York court had concluded) or an exclusive national power.

Marshall's Ruling. Marshall defined *commerce* as all commercial intercourse—all business dealings—including navigation and the transport of people. Marshall also held that the commerce power of the national government could be exercised in state jurisdictions, even though it cannot reach *solely* intrastate commerce. Finally, Marshall emphasized that the power to regulate interstate commerce was an *exclusive* national power. Marshall held that because Gibbons was duly authorized by the national government to navigate in interstate waters, he could not be prohibited from doing so by a state court.

Marshall's expansive interpretation of the commerce clause in *Gibbons v. Ogden* allowed the national government to exercise increasing authority over all areas of economic affairs throughout the land. Congress did not immediately exploit this broad grant of power. In the 1930s and subsequent decades, however, the commerce clause became the primary constitutional basis for national government regulation—as you will read later in this chapter.

STATES' RIGHTS AND THE RESORT TO CIVIL WAR

The controversy over slavery that led to the Civil War took the form of a dispute over national government supremacy versus the rights of the separate states. Essentially, the Civil War brought to an ultimate and violent climax the ideological debate that had been outlined by the Federalist and Anti-Federalist parties even before the Constitution was ratified.

THE SHIFT BACK TO STATES' RIGHTS

As we have seen, while John Marshall was chief justice of the Supreme Court, he did much to increase the power of the national government and to reduce that of the states. During the Jacksonian era (1829–1837), however, a shift

Commerce Clause
The section of the Constitution in which Congress is given the power to regulate trade among the states and with foreign countries.

didyouknow...

That the Liberty Bell cracked when it was rung at the funeral of John Marshall in 1835?

This statue of John Marshall
is located outside the Philadelphia Art Museum. John Marshall was the chief justice of the United States Supreme Court from 1801 to 1835. Was he in favor of a strong or a weak national government? (Richard Cummins/Corbis)

back to states' rights began. The question of the regulation of commerce became one of the major issues in federal-state relations. When Congress passed a tariff in 1828, the state of South Carolina unsuccessfully attempted to nullify the tariff (render it void), claiming that in cases of conflict between a state and the national government, the state should have the ultimate authority over its citizens.

Over the next three decades, the North and South became even more sharply divided—over tariffs that mostly benefited northern industries and over the slavery issue. On December 20, 1860, South Carolina formally repealed its ratification of the Constitution and withdrew from the Union. On February 4, 1861, representatives from six southern states met at Montgomery, Alabama, to form a new government called the Confederate States of America.

WAR AND THE GROWTH OF THE NATIONAL GOVERNMENT

The ultimate defeat of the South in 1865 permanently ended any idea that a state could successfully claim the right to secede, or withdraw, from the Union. Ironically, the Civil War—brought about in large part because of the South's desire for increased states' rights—resulted in the opposite: an increase in the political power of the national government.

didyouknow...

That only after the Civil War did people commonly refer to the United States as "it" instead of "they"?

The War Effort. Thousands of new employees were hired to run the Union war effort and to deal with the social and economic problems that had to be handled in the aftermath of war. A billion-dollar ($1.3 billion, which is more than $17 billion in today's dollars) national government budget was passed for the first time in 1865 to cover the increased government expenditures. The first (temporary) income tax was imposed on citizens to help pay for the war. This tax and the increased national government spending were precursors to the expanded future role of the national government in the American federal system. Civil liberties were curtailed in the Union and in the Confederacy in the name of the wartime emergency. The distribution of pensions and widows' benefits also boosted the national government's social role. Many scholars contend that the North's victory set the nation on the path to a modern industrial economy and society.

The Civil War Amendments. The expansion of the national government's authority during the Civil War was reflected in the passage of the Civil War amendments to the Constitution. Before the war, it was a bedrock constitutional principle that the national government should not interfere with slavery in the states. The Thirteenth Amendment, ratified in 1865, did more than interfere with slavery—it abolished the institution altogether. By abolishing slavery, the amendment also in effect abolished the rule by which three-fifths of the slaves were counted when apportioning seats in the House of Representatives (see Chapter 2). African Americans were now counted in full.

The Fourteenth Amendment, ratified in 1868, defined who was a citizen of each state. It sought to guarantee equal rights under state law, stating that

[no] State [shall] deprive any person of life, liberty, or property, without due process of law; nor deny to any person within its jurisdiction the equal protection of the laws.

President Lincoln

meets with some of his generals and other troops on October 3, 1862. While many believe that the Civil War was fought over the issue of slavery, others point out that it was also a battle over the supremacy of the national government. In any event, once the North won the war, what happened to the size and power of our national government? (Library of Congress)

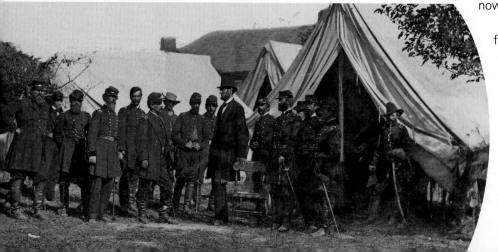

In time, the courts interpreted these words to mean that the national Bill of Rights applied to state governments, a development that we will examine in Chapter 4. The Fourteenth Amendment also confirmed the abolition of the three-fifths rule. Finally, the Fifteenth Amendment (1870) gave African Americans the right to vote in all elections, including state elections—although a century would pass before that right was enforced in all states.

THE CONTINUING DISPUTE OVER THE DIVISION OF POWER

Although the outcome of the Civil War firmly established the supremacy of the national government and put to rest the idea that a state could secede from the Union, the war by no means ended the debate over the division of powers between the national government and the states. The debate over the division of powers in our federal system can be viewed as progressing through at least two general stages since the Civil War: dual federalism and cooperative federalism.

Lincoln's Emancipation Proclamation freed slaves in each slave state as it came under the control of the North. The federal government created so-called Freedmen's Villages for these African Americans. What amendment to the Constitution guaranteed equal rights under state law to all Americans? (Corbis)

DUAL FEDERALISM AND THE RETREAT OF NATIONAL AUTHORITY

During the decades following the Civil War, the prevailing model was what political scientists have called **dual federalism**—a doctrine that emphasizes a distinction between federal and state spheres of government authority. The doctrine looks on nation and state as co-equal sovereign powers. Neither the state government nor the national government should interfere in the other's sphere.

Various images have been used to describe different configurations of federalism over time. Dual federalism is commonly depicted as a layer cake, because the state governments and the national government are viewed as separate entities, like separate layers in a cake. The national government is the top layer of the cake; the state government is the bottom layer. The two layers are physically separate. They do not mix. For the most part, advocates of dual federalism believed that the state and national governments should not exercise authority in the same areas.

A Return to Normal Conditions. The doctrine of dual federalism represented a revival of states' rights following the expansion of national authority during the Civil War. Dual federalism, after all, was a fairly accurate model of the prewar consensus on state-national relations. For many people, it therefore represented a return to normal. The national income tax, used to fund the war effort and the reconstruction of the South, was ended in 1872. The most significant step to reverse the wartime expansion of national power took place in 1877, when President Rutherford B. Hayes withdrew the last federal troops from the South. This meant that the national government was no longer in a position to regulate state actions that affected African Americans. Although the black population was no longer enslaved, it was again subject to the authority of southern whites.

The Role of the Supreme Court. The Civil War crisis drastically reduced the influence of the United States Supreme Court. In the prewar *Dred Scott* decision,[9] the Court had attempted to abolish the power of the national government to restrict slavery in the territories. In so doing, the Court placed itself on the losing side of the impending conflict.

Dual Federalism
A model of federalism in which the states and the national government each remain supreme within their own spheres. The doctrine looks on nation and state as co-equal sovereign powers. Neither the state government nor the national government should interfere in the other's sphere.

---

9. *Dred Scott v. Sandford,* 60 U.S. 393 (1856).

These children were working at a

Delaware canning factory in 1910. Their ages ranged from seven to fifteen years old. At that time, only the states, not the federal government, could regulate the working conditions of all citizens, including child laborers. In 1916, the United States Supreme Court struck down a federal law banning child labor. What was the basis of the Court's decision? (Lewis W. Hine/Library of Congress)

After the war, Congress took the unprecedented step of exempting the entire process of southern reconstruction from judicial review. The Court had little choice but to acquiesce.

In time, the Supreme Court reestablished itself as the legitimate constitutional umpire. Its decisions tended to support dual federalism, defend states' rights, and limit the powers of the national government. In 1895, for example, the Court ruled that a national income tax was unconstitutional.[10] In subsequent years, the Court gradually backed away from this decision and eventually might have overturned it. In 1913, however, the Sixteenth Amendment explicitly authorized a national income tax.

For the Court, dual federalism meant that the national government could intervene in state activities through grants and subsidies, but for the most part, it was barred from regulating matters that the Court considered to be purely local. The Court generally limited the exercise of police power to the states. For example, in 1918, the Court ruled that a 1916 national law banning child labor was unconstitutional because it attempted to regulate a local problem.[11] In effect, the Court placed severe limits on the ability of Congress to legislate under the commerce clause of the Constitution.

THE NEW DEAL AND COOPERATIVE FEDERALISM

The doctrine of dual federalism receded into the background in the 1930s as the nation attempted to deal with the Great Depression. Franklin D. Roosevelt was inaugurated on March 4, 1933, as the thirty-second president of the United States. In the previous year, nearly 1,500 banks had failed (and 4,000 more would fail in 1933). Thirty-two thousand businesses had closed down, and almost one-fourth of the labor force was unemployed. The public expected the national government to do something about the disastrous state of the economy. But for the first three years of the Great Depression (1930–1932), the national government had done very little.

The "New Deal." President Herbert Hoover (1929–1933) clung to the doctrine of dual federalism and insisted that unemployment and poverty were local issues. The states, not the national government, had the sole responsibility for combating the effects of unemployment and providing relief to the poor. Roosevelt, however, did not feel bound by this doctrine, and his new Democratic administration energetically intervened in the economy. Roosevelt's "New Deal" included large-scale emergency antipoverty programs. In addition, the New Deal introduced major new laws regulating economic activity, such as the National Industrial Recovery Act of 1933, which established the National Recovery Administration (NRA). The NRA, initially the centerpiece of the New Deal, provided codes for every industry to restrict competition and regulate labor relations.

The End of Dual Federalism. Roosevelt's expansion of national authority was challenged by the Supreme Court, which continued to adhere to the doctrine of dual federalism. In 1935, the Court ruled that the NRA program was unconstitutional.[12] The NRA had turned out to be largely unworkable and was unpopular. The Court, however, rejected the pro-

---

10. *Pollock v. Farmers' Loan & Trust Co.,* 157 U.S. 429 (1895); *Pollock v. Farmers' Loan & Trust Co.,* 158 U.S. 601 (1895).
11. *Hammer v. Dagenhart,* 247 U.S. 251 (1918). This decision was overruled in *United States v. Darby,* 312 U.S. 100 (1940).
12. *Schechter Poultry Corp. v. United States,* 295 U.S. 495 (1935).

gram on the ground that it regulated intrastate, not interstate, commerce. This position appeared to rule out any alternative recovery plans that might be better designed. Subsequently, the Court struck down the Agricultural Adjustment Act, the Bituminous Coal Act, a railroad retirement plan, legislation to protect farm mortgages, and a municipal bankruptcy act.

In 1937, Roosevelt proposed legislation that would allow him to add up to six new justices to the Supreme Court. Presumably, the new justices would be more friendly to the exercise of national power than the existing members were. Roosevelt's move was widely seen as an assault on the Constitution. Congressional Democrats refused to support the measure, and it failed. Nevertheless, the "court-packing scheme" had its intended effect. Although the membership of the Court did not change, after 1937 the Court ceased its attempts to limit the national government's powers under the commerce clause. For the next fifty years, the commerce clause would provide Congress with an essentially unlimited justification for regulating the economic life of the country.

Cooperative Federalism. Some political scientists have described the era since 1937 as characterized by **cooperative federalism,** in which the states and the national government cooperate in solving complex common problems. Roosevelt's New Deal programs, for example, often involved joint action between the national government and the states. The pattern of national-state relationships during these years gave rise to a new metaphor for federalism—that of a marble cake. Unlike a layer cake, in a marble cake the two types of cake are intermingled, and any bite contains cake of both flavors.

As an example of how national and state governments work together under the cooperative federalism model, consider Aid to Families with Dependent Children (AFDC), a welfare program that was established during the New Deal. (In 1996, AFDC was replaced by Temporary Assistance to Needy Families—TANF.) Under the AFDC program, the national government provided most of the funding, but state governments established benefit levels and eligibility requirements for recipients. Local welfare offices were staffed by state, not national, employees. In return for national funding, the states had to conform to a series of regulations on how the program was to be carried out. These regulations tended to become more elaborate over time.

The 1960s and 1970s were a time of even greater expansion of the national government's role in domestic policy. The evolving pattern of national-state-local government relationships during the 1960s and 1970s gave rise to yet another metaphor—**picket-fence federalism,** a concept devised by political scientist Terry Sanford. The horizontal boards in the fence represent the different levels of government (national, state, and local), while the vertical pickets represent the various programs and policies in which each level of government is involved. Officials at each level of government work together to promote and develop the policy represented by each picket.

METHODS OF IMPLEMENTING COOPERATIVE FEDERALISM

Even before the Constitution was adopted, the national government gave grants to the states in the form of land to finance education. The national government also provided land grants for canals, railroads, and roads. In the twentieth century, federal grants increased significantly, especially during Roosevelt's administration during the Great Depression and again in the 1960s, when the dollar amount of grants quadrupled. These funds were used for improvements in education, pollution control, recreation, and highways. With this increase in grants, however, came a bewildering number of restrictions and regulations.

These women are working at the Newport Canning Project, which was a small part of the Works Progress Administration (WPA) program implemented by President Franklin Roosevelt during the Great Depression. Why do you think that the federal government created the WPA? (AP Photo/Works Progress Administration)

Cooperative Federalism
A model of federalism in which the states and the national government cooperate in solving problems.

Picket-Fence Federalism
A model of federalism in which specific programs and policies (depicted as vertical pickets in a picket fence) involve all levels of government—national, state, and local (depicted by the horizontal boards in a picket fence).

Categorical Grants
Federal grants to states or local governments that are for specific programs or projects.

Categorical Grants. By 1985, **categorical grants** amounted to more than $100 billion a year. They were spread out across four hundred separate programs, but the five largest accounted for over 50 percent of the revenues spent. These five programs involved Medicaid (health care for the poor), highway construction, unemployment benefits, housing assistance, and welfare programs to assist mothers with dependent children and people with disabilities. For fiscal year 2008, the national government gave an estimated $230 billion to the states through federal grants. The shift toward a greater role for the central government in the United States can be seen in Figure 3–2, which shows the increase in central government spending as a percentage of total government spending.

Before the 1960s, most categorical grants by the national government were *formula grants*. These grants take their name from the method used to allocate funds. They fund state programs using a formula based on such variables as the state's needs, population, or willingness to come up with matching funds. Beginning in the 1960s, the national government began increasingly to offer *program grants*. This funding requires states to apply for grants for specific programs. The applications are evaluated by the national government, and the applications may compete with one another. Program grants give the national government a much greater degree of control over state activities than do formula grants.

Federal grants to the states have increased significantly, as shown in Figure 3–3. One reason for this increase is that Congress has decided to offload some programs to the states and provide a major part of the funding for them. Also, Congress continues to use grants to persuade states and cities to operate programs devised by the federal government. Finally, states often are happy to apply for grants because they are relatively "free," requiring only that the state match a small portion of each grant. States can still face criticism for accepting the grants, because their matching funds may be diverted from other state projects.

Feeling the Pressure—The Strings Attached to Federal Grants. No dollars sent to the states are completely free of "strings," however; all funds come with requirements that must be met by the states. Often, through the use of grants, the national government has been able to exercise substantial control over matters that traditionally have been under the

FIGURE 3–2: The Shift toward Central Government Spending

In the years before the Great Depression, local governments accounted for close to three-fifths of all government spending, and the federal government only accounted for about 30 percent. After Franklin D. Roosevelt's New Deal, federal spending began to rival state and local spending combined. The federal share is still about 46 percent today, not counting transfers to state and local governments. The size of the pies reflects total spending.

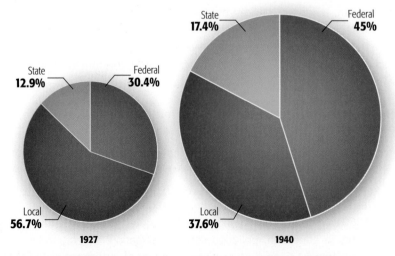

1927	1940
State 12.9%	State 17.4%
Federal 30.4%	Federal 45%
Local 56.7%	Local 37.6%

Source: *Historical Statistics of the United States,* Bureau of the Census, and authors' calculations.

FIGURE 3–3: The Rise in Federal Transfers to State and Local Governments

The chart shows the percentage of the nation's state and local revenues supplied by the federal government. The federal government has gained leverage over state and local governments by supplying an increasing share of their revenues. The drop in federal transfers from 1980 to 1990 took place during the presidency of Ronald Reagan, as we explain in "The 'New Federalism'" on page 99.

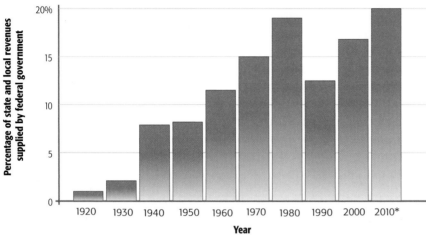

*The figure for 2010 is a projection.

Sources: *Historical Statistics of the United States; Statistical Abstract of the United States, 2008;* and *Budget of the United States Government, FY 2009.*

purview of state governments. When the federal government gives federal funds for highway improvements, for example, it may condition the funds on the state's cooperation with a federal policy. This is exactly what the federal government did in the 1980s and 1990s to force the states to raise their minimum drinking age to twenty-one.

Such carrot-and-stick tactics have been used as a form of coercion in recent years as well. In 2002, for example, President George W. Bush signed the No Child Left Behind (NCLB) Act into law. Under the NCLB, Bush promised billions of dollars to the states to bolster their education budgets. The funds would only be delivered, however, if states agreed to hold schools accountable on standardized tests. Education traditionally had been under state control, and the conditions for receiving NCLB funds effectively stripped the states of some autonomy in creating standards for public schools.

Block Grants. **Block grants** lessen the restrictions on federal grants given to state and local governments by grouping a number of categorical grants under one broad heading. Governors and mayors generally prefer block grants because such grants give the states more flexibility in how the funds are spent.

One major set of block grants provides aid to state welfare programs. The Personal Responsibility and Work Opportunity Reconciliation Act of 1996 ended the AFDC program. The TANF program that replaced AFDC provided a welfare block grant to each state. Each grant has an annual cap. According to some, this is one of the most successful block grant programs. Although state governments prefer block grants, Congress generally favors categorical grants because the expenditures can be targeted according to congressional priorities.

Federal Mandates. For years, the federal government has passed legislation requiring that states improve environmental conditions and the civil rights of certain groups. Since the 1970s, the national government has enacted literally hundreds of **federal mandates** requiring

Block Grants
Federal programs that provide funds to state and local governments for broad functional areas, such as criminal justice or mental-health programs.

Federal Mandate
A requirement in federal legislation that forces states and municipalities to comply with certain rules.

"The Feds have authorized me to leave your child behind."

the states to take some action in areas ranging from the way voters are registered, to ocean-dumping restrictions, to the education of persons with disabilities. The Unfunded Mandates Reform Act of 1995 requires the Congressional Budget Office to identify mandates that cost state and local governments more than $50 million to implement. Nonetheless, the federal government routinely continues to pass mandates for state and local governments that cost more than that to implement.

For example, the National Conference of State Legislatures has identified federal mandates to the states in transportation, health care, education, environment, homeland security, election laws, and other areas with a total cost of $29 billion per year. Water quality mandates appear to be particularly expensive.

One way in which the national government has moderated the burden of federal mandates is by granting *waivers,* which allow individual states to try out innovative approaches to carrying out the mandates. For example, Oregon received a waiver to experiment with a new method of rationing health-care services under the federally mandated Medicaid program.

THE POLITICS OF FEDERALISM

As we have observed, the allocation of powers between the national and state governments continues to be a major issue. We look here at some further aspects of the ongoing conflict between national authority and states' rights in our federal system.

WHAT HAS NATIONAL AUTHORITY ACCOMPLISHED?

Why is it that conservatives have favored the states and liberals have favored the national government? One answer is that throughout American history, the expansion of national authority typically has been an engine of social change. Far more than the states, the national government has been willing to alter the status quo. The expansion of national authority during the Civil War freed the slaves—a major social revolution. During the New Deal, the expansion of national authority meant unprecedented levels of government intervention in the economy. In both the Civil War and New Deal eras, support for states' rights was a method of opposing these changes and supporting the status quo.

Another example of the use of national power to change society was the presidency of Lyndon B. Johnson (1963–1969). Johnson oversaw the greatest expansion of national authority since the New Deal. Under Johnson, a series of civil rights acts forced the states to grant African Americans equal treatment under the law. Crucially, these acts included the abolition of all measures designed to prevent African Americans from voting. Johnson's Great Society and War on Poverty programs resulted in major increases in spending by the national government. As before, states' rights were invoked to support the status quo— states' rights meant no action on civil rights and no increase in antipoverty spending.

WHY SHOULD THE STATES WANT TO LIMIT NATIONAL AUTHORITY?

When state governments have authority in a particular field, there may be great variations from state to state in how the issues are handled. Inevitably, some states will be more conservative than others. Therefore, bringing national authority to bear on a particular issue may have the effect of imposing national standards on states that, for whatever reason, have not adopted such standards. One example is the voting rights legislation passed under President Johnson. By the 1960s, there was a national consensus that all citizens, regardless of race, should have the right to vote. A majority of the white electorate in certain states, however, did not share this view. National legislation was deemed necessary to impose the national consensus on the recalcitrant states.

Another factor that may make the states more receptive to limited government, especially on economic issues, is competition among the states. It is widely believed that major corporations are more likely to establish new operations in states with a "favorable business climate." National legislation regulating business activities within all states will make it more difficult for an individual state to create a more favorable business climate within its borders relative to other states. Yet another factor that may encourage the states to favor limited national authority is the relative power of local economic interests. A large corporation in a small state, for example, may have a substantial amount of political influence. Such a corporation, which has experienced success within the existing economic framework, may be opposed to any changes to that framework. These local economic interests may have less influence at the national level.

These voters are going to the polls in the primary elections in 2008 in Gary, Indiana. Each state, along with the two major political parties, determines the dates and manner in which primaries are held. Why doesn't the federal government have more control over primary elections? (AP Photo/Joe Raymond)

Finally, the states may simply feel that they can do a better job of regulating activities in the states than the federal government can. After all, state governments are closer to, and more knowledgeable about, problems affecting the population within their borders. Uniform standards imposed by the national government may not be as effective as state regulations in addressing these problems. Alternatively, the states may conclude that national regulations do not go far enough in curbing certain problems, such as air pollution.

At times, state and local governments take action on matters normally considered to be a federal responsibility. One example is immigration, as we see in the *Politics and Immigration* feature on the following page.

THE "NEW FEDERALISM"

In the years after 1968, the **devolution** of power from the national government to the states became a major ideological theme for the Republican Party. Republican president Richard Nixon (1969–1974) advocated what he called a "New Federalism" that would devolve authority from the national government to the states. In part, the New Federalism involved the conversion of categorical grants into block grants, thereby giving state governments greater flexibility in spending. A second part of Nixon's New Federalism was *revenue sharing.* Under the revenue-sharing plan, the national government provided direct, unconditional financial support to state and local governments.

Nixon was able to obtain only a limited number of block grants from Congress. The block grants he did obtain, plus revenue sharing, substantially increased financial support to state governments. Republican president Ronald Reagan (1981–1989) was also a strong advocate of federalism, but some of his policies withdrew certain financial support from the states. Reagan was more successful than Nixon in obtaining block grants, but Reagan's block grants, unlike Nixon's, were less generous to the states than the categorical grants they replaced. Under Reagan, revenue sharing was eliminated. You can see the results of these actions in Figure 3–3 on page 97.

FEDERALISM TODAY

Today, federalism (in the sense of limited national authority) no longer continues to be such an important element in conservative ideology. At this point, it is not clear whether competing theories of federalism divide the Republicans from the Democrats at all, at

Devolution
The transfer of powers from a national or central government to a state or local government.

politicsand...immigration

STATE AND LOCAL GOVERNMENTS TAKE ACTION

Immigration remains a "hot-button" issue throughout the United States. Perhaps as many as 12 to 13 million unauthorized immigrants now live in this country. (*Unauthorized immigrants* is the official term used by the Department of Homeland Security—depending on who is talking, these people may also be referred to as "illegal aliens" or "undocumented workers.") The federal government has failed to create a comprehensive immigration policy. Certain states and cities therefore are creating their own.

SANCTUARIES—NEW HAVEN AND SAN FRANCISCO

New Haven, Connecticut, is at the forefront of "regularizing" the status of unauthorized immigrants and has ordered its police not to inquire about immigrants' status. It offers all city residents, regardless of immigration status, an official city identification card. Any of the 125,000 New Haven residents can have one, including foreign citizens, both adults and children. Holders of the New Haven ID card can use city beaches and libraries. This official ID can even be used as a debit card at certain stores and restaurants and for parking meters. Several banks will accept this ID card for opening bank accounts.

(Courtesy of the Mayor, City of New Haven, CT)

San Francisco has gone one step further—it advertises throughout the state that it will not inquire into any immigrant's legal status. Not everyone agrees with such policies. When New York's governor suggested offering driver's licenses to unauthorized immigrants, the uproar was so loud he had to withdraw his idea.

CRACKING DOWN ON UNAUTHORIZED IMMIGRATION

A much greater number of states and cities are cracking down on unauthorized immigrants. A section in the 1996 Illegal Immigration Reform Act—Section 287(g)—allows state officers and employees to perform immigration officer functions. The Department of Homeland Security has entered into a large number of agreements with state and local enforcement agencies, allowing them to designate their officers to perform immigration law enforcement functions. Consider Phoenix, Arizona. Maricopa County sheriff Joe Arpaio has 160 officers trained to enforce federal immigration laws. Their efforts are supplemented by the city's 3,000-member "posse," of whom 500 carry guns. These 3,000 members have their own motorcycles, jeeps, and airplanes. State and county officials claim that "Sheriff Joe" has ignored tens of thousands of outstanding criminal warrants while chasing Mexican day laborers.

LAWS AGAINST HIRING UNDOCUMENTED WORKERS

A number of states (and cities), including Arizona, have passed laws that impose severe penalties on employers who knowingly hire undocumented workers. When challenged in court, these laws in Arizona, Missouri, and Oklahoma were judged legal.

In other jurisdictions, judicial decisions have gone the other way. The result is a nationwide checkerboard of conflicting laws. As long as Congress doesn't reform current federal immigration law, the number of these conflicting laws will continue to grow.

FOR CRITICAL ANALYSIS

Critics of state and local laws governing unauthorized immigrants argue that such laws generate discrimination against Hispanics who are *not* illegally in this country. Why might this be true?

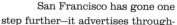

least in practice. Consider that the passage of welfare reform legislation in 1996, which involved transferring significant control over welfare programs to the states, took place under Democratic president Bill Clinton (1993–2001). In contrast, under Republican president George W. Bush, Congress enacted the No Child Left Behind Act of 2001, which was signed into law in 2002. This act increased federal control over education and educational funding, which had traditionally been under the purview of state governments. Indeed, the Bush administration often exercised federal control over areas—such as health, safety, and the environment—that traditionally had been the preserve of state governments.

FEDERALISM AND TODAY'S SUPREME COURT

The United States Supreme Court, which normally has the final say on constitutional issues, necessarily plays a significant role in determining the line between federal and state powers. Consider the decisions rendered by Chief Justice John Marshall in the cases discussed earlier in this chapter. Since the 1930s, Marshall's broad interpretation of the commerce clause has made it possible for the national government to justify its regulation of virtually any activity, even when an activity would appear to be purely local in character. In the 1990s and 2000s, however, the Court has evidenced a willingness to impose some limits on the national government's authority under the commerce clause and other constitutional provisions. As a result, it is difficult to predict how today's Court might rule on a particular case involving federalism.

THE TREND TOWARD STATES' RIGHTS

Since the 1990s, there has been a modest trend on the part of the Supreme Court to give greater weight to states' rights than was true for most of the twentieth century. In a widely publicized 1995 case, *United States v. Lopez*,[13] the Supreme Court held that Congress had exceeded its constitutional authority under the commerce clause when it passed the Gun-Free School Zones Act in 1990. The Court stated that the act, which banned the possession of guns within one thousand feet of any school, was unconstitutional because it attempted to regulate an area that had "nothing to do with commerce, or any sort of economic enterprise." This marked the first time in sixty years that the Supreme Court had placed a limit on the national government's authority under the commerce clause. The Court subsequently invalidated portions of another law on the ground that Congress had exceeded its authority under the commerce clause.[14]

In 1999 and the early 2000s, the Court also issued decisions that bolstered the authority of state governments under the Eleventh Amendment to the Constitution. The cases involved employees and others who sought redress for state-government violations of federal laws regulating employment. The Court held that the Eleventh Amendment, in most circumstances, precludes lawsuits against state governments for violations of rights established by federal laws unless the states consent to be sued.[15] Additionally, the Court supported states' rights under the Tenth Amendment when it invalidated, in 1997, provisions of a federal law that required state employees to check the backgrounds of prospective handgun purchasers.[16]

These first-grade students are performing a science experiment in a classroom in the Coachella Valley Unified School District in Thermal, California. Because the students in this school district have not fared very well on standardized tests, the district faces sanctions under the federal No Child Left Behind Act. Normally, we think of education as a local and state effort. Why did the No Child Left Behind Act seem to announce a new trend in public education? (AP Photo/Damian Dovarganes)

---

13. 514 U.S. 549 (1995).
14. *United States v. Morrison,* 529 U.S. 598 (2000).
15. See, for example, *Alden v. Maine,* 527 U.S. 706 (1999); and *Kimel v. Florida Board of Regents,* 528 U.S. 62 (2000).
16. *Printz v. United States,* 521 U.S. 898 (1997).

THE COURT SENDS MIXED MESSAGES

Although the Court has tended to favor states' rights in many decisions, in other decisions it has backed the federal government's position. For example, in two cases decided in 2003 and 2004, the Court, in contrast to its earlier rulings involving the Eleventh Amendment, ruled that the amendment could not shield states from suits by individuals complaining of discrimination based on gender and disability, respectively.[17] Also, in 2005 the Court held that the federal government's power to seize and destroy illegal drugs trumped California's law legalizing the use of marijuana for medical treatment.[18] Yet less than a year later, the Court favored states' rights when it upheld Oregon's controversial "death with dignity" law, which allows patients with terminal illnesses to choose to end their lives early and thus alleviate suffering.[19]

The Supreme Court also supported state claims in a 2007 case, *Massachusetts v. EPA*.[20] This case, which many have since hailed as the most significant decision on environmental law for decades, was brought against the Environmental Protection Agency (EPA) by Massachusetts and several other states, as well as various cities and environmental groups. The groups claimed that the EPA, which administers the Clean Air Act and other laws regulating the environment, had the authority to—and should—regulate carbon dioxide and other greenhouse gases. The EPA maintained that it lacked the authority to do so, arguing that members of Congress, when passing the Clean Air Act, had not envisioned a massive greenhouse-gas control program. The Court, however, held that the EPA *did* have such regulatory authority. The Court stated that the EPA could choose not to regulate auto emissions and other heat-trapping gases, but only if it could provide a scientific basis for its refusal. The close (five-to-four) decision was a strong rebuke to the Bush administration, which had refused to regulate carbon dioxide and other greenhouse gases under the Clean Air Act.

One year after this Supreme Court ruling, Massachusetts and the other states were back in federal court, suing the EPA for dragging its feet on issuing a carbon dioxide recommendation. Apparently, the EPA had prepared a recommendation by the end of 2007, but the White House blocked its release.

---

17. *Nevada v. Hibbs,* 538 U.S. 721 (2003); and *Tennessee v. Lane,* 541 U.S. 509 (2004).
18. *Gonzales v. Raich,* 545 U.S. 1 (2005).
19. *Gonzales v. Oregon,* 546 U.S. 243 (2006).
20. 127 S.Ct. 1438 (2007).

WHY SHOULD YOU CARE ABOUT
thefederalsystem?

Why should you, personally, care about the federal system? The system encourages debate over whether a particular issue should be a national, state, or local question. Because many questions are, in fact, state or local ones, it is easier for you to make a significant contribution to the discussion on these issues. Even in the largest states, there are many fewer people to persuade than in the nation as a whole. Attempts to influence your fellow citizens, by writing letters to the editor or other methods, can therefore be more effective.

THE FEDERAL SYSTEM AND YOUR LIFE

In this chapter, we have described a variety of issues arising from our federal system that may concern you directly. Although the national government provides aid to educational programs, education is still primarily a state and local responsibility. The total amount of money spent on education is determined by state and local governments. Therefore, you can address this issue at the state or local level. Welfare payments and sentences for crimes are also set at the state level. Gambling laws are another state responsibility. Do you enjoy gambling—or do you believe that the effects of gambling make it a social disaster? State law—or state negotiations with American Indian tribes—determines the availability of gambling.

The question of which level of government should handle an issue also may affect you directly. Are you concerned with current state laws regarding same-sex marriage and civil unions? Or do you believe that Congress needs to create a uniform national policy either in favor of or against such unions? Either way, in any state that seeks to permit same-sex marriage, the question of national versus state authority will determine the outcome of the debate.

HOW YOU CAN MAKE A DIFFERENCE

One of the best ways to make your point on these or other issues is by writing an effective letter to the editor of your local newspaper (or even to a national newspaper, such as the *New York Times*). First, you should familiarize yourself with the kinds of letters that are accepted by the newspapers to which you want to write. Then use the following rules for writing an effective letter:

1. Use a computer, and double-space the lines. If possible, use a spelling checker and grammar checker.
2. Include a lead topic sentence that is short, to the point, and powerful.
3. Keep your thoughts on target—choose only one topic to discuss in your letter. Make sure it is newsworthy and timely.
4. Make sure your letter is concise; never let your letter exceed a page and a half in length (double- spaced).
5. If you know that facts were misstated or left out in current news stories about your topic, supply the facts. The public wants to know.
6. Don't be afraid to express moral judgments. You can go a long way by appealing to the readers' sense of justice.
7. Personalize the letter by bringing in your own experiences, if possible.
8. Sign your letter, and give your address (including your e-mail address, if you have one) and your telephone number.
9. Send or e-mail your letter to the editorial office of the newspaper or magazine of your choice. Virtually all publications now have e-mail addresses and home pages on the Web. The Web sites usually give information on where you can send mail.

(©Liv Friis-Larsen, 2008. Used under license from Shutterstock.com.)

QUESTIONS FOR
discussion**and**analysis

1. Review the *Which Side Are You On?* feature on page 84. Should federal officials be required to lower the flags on federal buildings at the request of state authorities? Is it appropriate for the flag to be lowered for every fallen soldier? Why or why not?

2. The Constitution requires that each state give full faith and credit to every other state's public acts. Normally, those acts include marriages. According to the federal government's 1996 Defense of Marriage Act, however, states are not required to recognize other states' same-sex marriages. Do you think the Defense of Marriage Act is constitutional? If it were found unconstitutional, what results might follow?

3. While federal funding of primary and secondary education and federal influence on local schools have both grown considerably in recent years, K–12 education is still largely under the control of state and local governments. How might U.S. public schools be different if, like France, we had a unitary system of government?

4. The United States Supreme Court has interpreted the Fourteenth Amendment to the Constitution, adopted after the Civil War, to mean that most provisions of the Bill of Rights apply to state governments. If the First Amendment, with its guarantees of freedom of speech and religion, did not apply to the states, might some states seek to abridge these rights? If so, how might they do this?

5. Traditionally, conservatives have favored states' rights and liberals have favored national authority. Can you think of modern-day issues in which these long-standing preferences might be reversed, with conservatives favoring national authority and liberals favoring states' rights? Explain.

key**terms**

block grants 97
categorical grants 96
commerce clause 91
concurrent powers 87
confederal system 82
cooperative
    federalism 95

devolution 99
dual federalism 93
elastic clause, or
    necessary and
    proper clause 86
enumerated powers 86

federal mandate 97
interstate compact 89
picket-fence
    federalism 95
police power 87

supremacy clause 87
unitary system 81

chapter**summary**

1. There are three basic models for ordering relations between central governments and local units: (a) a unitary system (in which ultimate power is held by the national government), (b) a confederal system (in which ultimate power is retained by the states), and (c) a federal system (in which governmental powers are divided between the national government and the states). A major reason for the creation of a federal system in the United States is that it reflected a compromise between the views of the Federalists (who wanted a strong national government) and those of the Anti-Federalists (who wanted the states to retain their sovereignty).

2. The Constitution expressly delegated certain powers to the national government in Article I, Section 8. In addition to these expressed powers, the national government has implied and inherent powers.

Implied powers are those that are reasonably necessary to carry out the powers expressly delegated to the national government. Inherent powers are those held by the national government by virtue of its being a sovereign state with the right to preserve itself.

3. The Tenth Amendment to the Constitution states that powers not delegated to the United States by the Constitution, nor prohibited by it to the states, are reserved to the states, or to the people. In certain areas, the Constitution provides for concurrent powers (such as the power to tax), which are powers that are held jointly by the national and state governments. The Constitution also denies certain powers to both the national government and the states.

4. The supremacy clause of the Constitution states that the Constitution, congressional laws, and national treaties are the supreme law of the land. States cannot use their reserved or concurrent powers to override national policies. "Vertical" checks and balances allow the states to influence the national government and vice versa.

5. The three most important clauses in the Constitution on interstate relations require that (a) each state give full faith and credit to every other state's public acts, records, and judicial proceedings; (b) each state extend to every other state's citizens the privileges and immunities of its own citizens; and (c) each state agree to return persons who are fleeing from justice back to their home state when requested to do so.

6. Two landmark Supreme Court cases expanded the constitutional powers of the national government. Chief Justice John Marshall's expansive interpretation of the necessary and proper clause of the Constitution in *McCulloch v. Maryland* (1819) enhanced the implied power of the national government. Marshall's broad interpretation of the commerce clause in *Gibbons v. Ogden* (1824) further extended the constitutional regulatory powers of the national government.

7. The controversy over slavery that led to the Civil War took the form of a fight over national government supremacy versus the rights of the separate states. Ultimately, the effect of the South's desire for increased states' rights and the subsequent Civil War was an increase in the political power of the national government.

8. Since the Civil War, federalism has evolved through at least two general phases: dual federalism and cooperative federalism. In dual federalism, each of the states and the federal government remain supreme within their own spheres. The era since the Great Depression has sometimes been labeled one of cooperative federalism, in which states and the national government cooperate in solving complex common problems.

9. Categorical grants from the federal government to state governments help finance many projects, such as Medicaid, highway construction, unemployment benefits, and welfare programs. By attaching special conditions to the receipt of federal grants, the national government can effect policy changes in areas typically governed by the states. Block grants, which group a number of categorical grants together, usually have fewer strings attached, thus giving state and local governments more flexibility in using funds. Federal mandates—laws requiring states to implement certain policies, such as policies to protect the environment—have generated controversy because of their cost.

10. Traditionally, conservatives have favored states' rights, and liberals have favored national authority. In part, this is because the national government has historically been an engine of change, whereas state governments have favored limited national authority.

11. In response to the liberal movements and programs of the 1950s and 1960s (including the civil rights movement and Lyndon Johnson's Great Society and War on Poverty programs), Republicans indorsed what became known as the New Federalism. The New Federalism emphasized states' rights and devolution—returning power to the states. In the 1970s and 1980s, Republican presidents Richard Nixon and Ronald Reagan sought to return power to the states through block grants and other programs.

12. Today, at least in practice, the Republicans have backed away from a states' rights approach to federalism. During the Bush administration, the federal government exercised a significant degree of control over the states through national legislation and regulations.

13. The United States Supreme Court plays a significant role in determining the line between state and federal powers. Since the 1990s, there has been a trend on the part of the Court to support states' rights. Yet the Court has also issued several rulings in support of the federal government, making it difficult to predict how the Court will rule in a particular case involving issues of federalism.

selectedprint&mediaresources

SUGGESTED READINGS

Anderson, Lee W. *Congress and the Classroom: Ideology and the Expanding Federal Role in Schools from the Cold War to "No Child Left Behind."* University Park, Pa.: Penn State University Press, 2007. Anderson's volume gives a detailed account of the passage of the No Child Left Behind Act. He shows how the Republican Party, despite its conservative ideology, has moved from federal nonintervention to federal intervention in education.

Hamilton, Alexander, *et al. The Federalist: The Famous Papers on the Principles of American Government.* Benjamin F. Wright, ed. New York: Friedman/ Fairfax Publishing, 2002. These essays remain an authoritative exposition of the founders' views on federalism.

King, Preston. *Federalism and Federation.* London: Frank Cass & Co., 2008. This analysis of federalism and federation distinguishes these two forms of government and examines the different types of federalism now in existence.

Simon, Scott. *Windy City: A Novel of Politics.* New York: Random House Trade Paperbacks, 2009. The mayor of Chicago is dead, face down in a pizza, and Alderman Sundaran "Sunny" Roopini, the interim mayor, has more than one problem on his hands. Simon's comic novel portrays the gritty urban politics that Barack Obama emerged from as an Illinois state senator.

MEDIA RESOURCES

Can the States Do It Better?—A 1996 film in which various experts discuss how much power the national government should have. The film uses documentary footage and other resources to illustrate this debate.

The Civil War—The PBS documentary series that made director Ken Burns famous. *The Civil War,* first shown in 1990, marked a revolution in documentary technique. Photographs, letters, eyewitness memoirs, and music are used to bring the war to life. The DVD version was released in 2002.

Last Man Standing: Politics, Texas Style—A hilarious look at two Texas races, one for a legislative seat and one for governor. The winning Republican gubernatorial candidate is none other than George W. Bush. Paul Stekler's 2004 film includes enlightening interviews with Bush adviser Karl Rove and the late Molly Ivins, a much-beloved liberal commentator.

McCulloch v. Maryland and *Gibbons v. Ogden*—These programs are part of the series *Equal Justice under Law: Landmark Cases in Supreme Court History.* They provide more details on cases that defined our federal system.

Street Fight—A 2005 documentary by Marshall Curry, this film chronicles the unsuccessful attempt by young City Council member Cory Booker to unseat long-time Newark mayor Sharpe James in 2002. Curry captures on film James's abuse of police and code enforcement officers to sabotage Booker's campaign. In 2006, the voters elected Booker mayor of New York. In 2008, James was sentenced to twenty-seven months in prison on unrelated corruption charges.

e-mocracy

YOUR FEDERAL, STATE, AND LOCAL GOVERNMENTS ARE AVAILABLE WITH A CLICK OF YOUR MOUSE

Although online voting remains rare, your access to federal, state, and local government offices has improved dramatically since the Internet entered just about everybody's life. The number of government services available online is growing rapidly. Some researchers now talk about *e-government*. Instead of waiting in line to renew car registrations, residents of Scottsdale, Arizona, can renew online. In Colorado, heating and air-conditioning contractors can obtain permits from a Web site run by NetClerk, Inc. In many jurisdictions, all parking tickets can be handled with a credit card and a computer connected to the Internet.

It is now possible for students to apply online for financial aid. The federal government allows online applications for Social Security benefits and strongly encourages taxpayers to file their income tax returns electronically. Many citizens find that e-government programs such as these make interactions with the government much simpler. It is no longer necessary to wait in line or to put up with the "bureaucratic shuffle."

LOGGING ON

Federalism is an important aspect of our democracy. To learn more about the establishment of our federal form of government and about current issues relating to federalism, visit the Web sites listed in the remainder of this section.

To learn the founders' views on federalism, you can access the Federalist Papers online at
www.law.emory.edu/erd/docs/federalist.

The University of Richmond offers links to the constitutions of many nations around the globe through its Web site. Go to
confinder.richmond.edu.

The Council of State Governments is a good source for information on state responses to federalism issues. Go to
www.csg.org.

Another good source of information on issues facing state governments and federal-state relations is the National Governors Association's Web site at
www.nga.org.

The Brookings Institution's policy analyses and recommendations on a variety of issues, including federalism, can be accessed at
www.brookings.edu.

For a libertarian approach to issues relating to federalism, go to the Cato Institute's Web page at
www.cato.org.

4 Civil Liberties

CHAPTER CONTENTS

These demonstrators recite the Pledge of Allegiance
while displaying the Ten Commandments during a
rally at the Alabama capitol in Montgomery. They were
supporting the public display of the Ten Commandments
in the state judicial building. (AP Photo/Dave Martin)

what if...*Roe v. Wade* were overturned?

BACKGROUND

The Bill of Rights and other provisions of the U.S. Constitution are the ultimate protections of our civil rights and liberties. But how do these rights work out in practice? How do we determine what our rights are in any given situation? One way is through *judicial review,* the power of the United States Supreme Court or other courts to declare laws and other acts of government unconstitutional. Supreme Court cases are often hotly contested, and the decision in the 1973 case *Roe v. Wade* is one of the most contentious ever handed down. In the *Roe v. Wade* case, the Court declared that a woman's constitutionally protected right to privacy includes the right to have an abortion. The Court concluded that the states cannot restrict a woman's right to an abortion during the first three months of pregnancy. More than thirty years later, however, the debate over the legality of abortion still rages in the United States.

WHAT IF *ROE v. WADE* WERE OVERTURNED?

If the Supreme Court overturned *Roe v. Wade,* the authority to regulate abortion would fall again to the states. Before the *Roe v. Wade* case, each state decided whether abortion would be legal within its borders. State legislatures made the laws that covered abortion. Some critics of *Roe v. Wade*'s constitutional merits have argued that allowing the Supreme Court to decide the legality of abortion nationwide is undemocratic because the justices are not elected officials. In contrast, if state legislatures regained the power to create abortion policy, the resulting laws would reflect the majority opinion of each state's voters. Legislators would have to respect popular sentiment on the issue or risk losing their next reelection bids.

THE POSSIBILITY OF STATE BANS ON ABORTION

Simply overturning *Roe v. Wade* would not make abortion in the United States illegal overnight. In many states, abortion rights are very popular, and the legislatures in those states would not consider measures to ban abortion or to further restrict access to abortion. Some states have laws that would protect abortion rights even if *Roe v. Wade* were overturned. Access to abortions would likely continue in the West Coast states and in much of the Northeast. In much of the South and the Midwest, however, abortion could be seriously restricted or even banned. Some states have "trigger laws" that would immediately outlaw abortion if *Roe v. Wade* were overturned.

Women living in conservative states such as the Dakotas, Kentucky, and Mississippi already face serious difficulties in obtaining an abortion. In each of these states, 98 percent of the counties do not have an abortion clinic. Many women desiring the procedure already have to travel long distances. If abortion were banned, these women could still cross state lines to obtain an abortion. If twenty-one of the most conservative states banned abortion, only 170 providers would be affected—less than 10 percent of the national total.

STATE CHALLENGES TO *ROE v. WADE*

Undoubtedly feeling optimistic because of President George W. Bush's conservative Supreme Court appointments (John Roberts and Samuel Alito), South Dakota's legislature passed a law in February 2006 banning abortion. The new law was unconstitutional given the *Roe v. Wade* decision, but its supporters clearly hoped that the newly constituted Court would overturn *Roe v. Wade.* "Freedom of choice" groups were able to place the ban on the state ballot in 2006, however, and the voters repealed the act.

In 2008, "right-to-life" activists in a number of states placed antiabortion measures on the ballot. In Colorado, for example, citizens voted on whether the state constitution should declare a fertilized egg a "person" who enjoys "inalienable rights, equality of justice, and due process of law." Such a measure would not ban abortion directly, but it would undercut the legal reasoning used in deciding *Roe v. Wade.* The measure was voted down by a three-to-one margin. In South Dakota, voters faced a new antiabortion measure that was less restrictive than the 2006 law. It was also defeated.

FOR CRITICAL ANALYSIS

1. Why do you think that abortion remains a contentious topic more than thirty years after the *Roe v. Wade* decision? Should that decision be revisited? Why or why not?
2. How significant a role should the courts play in deciding constitutional questions about abortion? Do you feel that individual states should have a say in the legality of abortion within their own borders? Why or why not?

"The land of the free." When asked what makes the United States distinctive, Americans commonly say that it is a free country. Americans have long believed that limits on the power of government are an essential part of what makes this country free. Recall from Chapter 1 that restraints on the actions of government against individuals are generally referred to as *civil liberties*. The first ten amendments to the U.S. Constitution—the Bill of Rights—place such restraints on the national government. Of these amendments, none is more famous than the First Amendment, which guarantees freedom of religion, speech, and the press, as well as other rights.

Most other democratic nations have laws to protect these and other civil liberties, but none of the laws is quite like the First Amendment. Take the issue of "hate speech." What if someone makes statements that stir up hatred toward a particular race or other group of people? In Germany, where memories of Nazi anti-Semitism remain alive, such speech is unquestionably illegal. In the United States, the issue is not so clear. The courts have often extended constitutional protection to this kind of speech.

In this chapter, we describe the civil liberties provided by the Bill of Rights and some of the controversies that surround them. We look first at the First Amendment, including the establishment clause. We also discuss the right to privacy, which is at the heart of the abortion issue introduced in the *What If . . .* feature that opened this chapter. We also examine the rights of defendants in criminal cases.

THE BILL OF RIGHTS

As you read through this chapter, bear in mind that the Bill of Rights, like the rest of the Constitution, is relatively brief. The framers set forth broad guidelines, leaving it up to the courts to interpret these constitutional mandates and apply them to specific situations. Thus, judicial interpretations shape the true nature of the civil liberties and rights that we possess. Because judicial interpretations change over time, so do our liberties and rights. As you will read in the following pages, there have been many conflicts over the meaning of such simple phrases as *freedom of religion* and *freedom of the press*. Recently, the war on terrorism has had an impact on how we view our civil liberties, as you'll see in this chapter's *Politics and the War on Terrorism* feature on the following page.

To understand what freedoms we actually have, we need to examine how the courts—and particularly the United States Supreme Court—have resolved some of those conflicts. One important conflict was over the issue of whether the Bill of Rights in the federal Constitution limited the powers of state governments as well as those of the national government.

EXTENDING THE BILL OF RIGHTS TO STATE GOVERNMENTS

Many citizens do not realize that, as originally intended, the Bill of Rights limited only the powers of the national government. At the time the Bill of Rights was ratified, there was little concern over the potential of state governments to curb civil liberties. For one thing, state governments were closer to home and easier to control. For another, most state constitutions already had bills of rights. Rather, the fear was of the potential tyranny of the national government. The Bill of Rights begins with the

These school choice supporters hold a rally at the capitol in Madison, Wisconsin. They are showing their support for the Milwaukee Parental Choice Program. Freedom of speech is granted to U.S. residents in what part of the Bill of Rights? (AP Photo/Wisconsin State Journal, Steve Apps)

politicsand...the war on terrorism

CURTAILING CIVIL LIBERTIES WHEN WAGING THE WAR ON TERRORISM

During World War II, the United States interned tens of thousands of Japanese Americans, as well as a significant number of Italian Americans. Indeed, during the Second World War, many democracies spied on their own citizens, imposed censorship, and used torture to obtain information from enemy combatants. Civil liberties have again suffered during the war on terror that started in September 2001.

IS THE WAR ON TERROR REALLY LIKE THE SECOND WORLD WAR?

Even though World War II may have seemed extraordinarily long lasting for those fighting it and suffering from it, it came to an end in a few years. The so-called Cold War—the ideological battle between Western democracies and Communist countries, particularly the Soviet Union—lasted for more than four decades, but it, too, came to an end. During the Second World War, the curtailment of domestic civil liberties was short-lived. During the Cold War, there was relatively little curtailment of civil liberties, at least after the initial Communist scare of the early 1950s. But when will the war on terror end? No one knows, but it certainly could be never.

One of the casualties of the war on terror appears to be an erosion of our civil liberties. On occasion, the government has suspended *habeas corpus*, as you learned in Chapter 1. We have seen indefinite detention of enemy combatants without trial. We have seen the use of torture to obtain information about potential future terrorist acts.

Some say that if a suspected terrorist has information on a "ticking nuclear bomb," torture is justified to save hundreds of thousands, if not millions, of lives. Others argue that police personnel rarely, if ever, know if someone they have in custody might have such valuable knowledge. Torture may yield little valuable information, because those who are tortured will say whatever they think their captors want to hear.

Consider also locking up suspected terrorists. One could argue that we should lock up potential rapists and murderers as well. Why? Because in so doing, we would make society safer. In contrast, those who are against restricting civil liberties in the name of the war on terror claim that when we curtail U.S. residents' civil liberties, we are playing right into the terrorists' hands. Terrorists would love to see the "American way of life" disappear.

FOR CRITICAL ANALYSIS

Under what circumstances do you think our government has a duty to curtail civil liberties in the name of fighting the war on terror?

didyouknow...

words, "Congress shall make no law . . . ." It says nothing about *states* making laws that might abridge citizens' civil liberties. In 1833, in *Barron v. Baltimore*,[1] the United States Supreme Court held that the Bill of Rights did not apply to state laws.

We mentioned that most states had bills of rights. These bills of rights were similar to the national one, but there were some differences. Furthermore, each state's judicial system interpreted the rights differently. Citizens in different states, therefore, effectively had different sets of civil rights. It was not until after the Fourteenth Amendment was ratified in 1868 that civil liberties guaranteed by the national Constitution began to be applied to the states. Section 1 of that amendment provides, in part, as follows:

No State shall . . . deprive any person of life, liberty, or property, without due process of law.

---

1. 7 Peters 243 (1833).

INCORPORATION OF THE FOURTEENTH AMENDMENT

There was no question that the Fourteenth Amendment applied to state governments. For decades, however, the courts were reluctant to define the liberties spelled out in the national Bill of Rights as constituting "due process of law," which was protected under the Fourteenth Amendment. Not until 1925, in *Gitlow v. New York,*[2] did the United States Supreme Court hold that the Fourteenth Amendment protected the freedom of speech guaranteed by the First Amendment to the Constitution.

Only gradually, and never completely, did the Supreme Court accept the **incorporation theory**—the view that most of the protections of the Bill of Rights are incorporated into the Fourteenth Amendment's protection against state government actions. Table 4–1 shows the rights that the Court has incorporated into the Fourteenth Amendment and the case in which it first applied each protection. As you can see in that table, in the fifteen years following the *Gitlow* decision, the Supreme Court incorporated into the Fourteenth Amendment the other basic freedoms (of the press, assembly, the right to petition, and religion) guaranteed by the First Amendment. These and the later Supreme Court decisions listed in Table 4–1 have bound the fifty states to accept for their citizens most of the rights and freedoms that are set forth in the U.S. Bill of Rights. We now look at some of those rights and freedoms, beginning with the freedom of religion.

FREEDOM OF RELIGION

In the United States, freedom of religion consists of two main principles as they are presented in the First Amendment. The **establishment clause** prohibits the establishment of a church that is officially supported by the national government, thus guaranteeing a division between church and state. The **free exercise clause** constrains the national

Incorporation Theory
The view that most of the protections of the Bill of Rights apply to state governments through the Fourteenth Amendment's due process clause.

Establishment Clause
The part of the First Amendment prohibiting the establishment of a church officially supported by the national government. It is applied to questions of the legality of giving state and local government aid to religious organizations and schools, allowing or requiring school prayers, and teaching evolution versus intelligent design.

Free Exercise Clause
The provision of the First Amendment guaranteeing the free exercise of religion. The provision constrains the national government from prohibiting individuals from practicing the religion of their choice.

2. 268 U.S. 652 (1925).

TABLE 4–1: Incorporating the Bill of Rights into the Fourteenth Amendment

Year	Issue	Amendment Involved	Court Case
1925	Freedom of speech	I	*Gitlow v. New York*, 268 U.S. 652.
1931	Freedom of the press	I	*Near v. Minnesota*, 283 U.S. 697.
1932	Right to a lawyer in capital punishment cases	VI	*Powell v. Alabama*, 287 U.S. 45.
1937	Freedom of assembly and right to petition	I	*De Jonge v. Oregon*, 299 U.S. 353.
1940	Freedom of religion	I	*Cantwell v. Connecticut*, 310 U.S. 296.
1947	Separation of church and state	I	*Everson v. Board of Education*, 330 U.S. 1.
1948	Right to a public trial	VI	*In re Oliver*, 333 U.S. 257.
1949	No unreasonable searches and seizures	IV	*Wolf v. Colorado*, 338 U.S. 25.
1961	Exclusionary rule	IV	*Mapp v. Ohio*, 367 U.S. 643.
1962	No cruel and unusual punishment	VIII	*Robinson v. California*, 370 U.S. 660.
1963	Right to a lawyer in all criminal felony cases	VI	*Gideon v. Wainwright*, 372 U.S. 335.
1964	No compulsory self-incrimination	V	*Malloy v. Hogan*, 378 U.S. 1.
1965	Right to privacy	I, III, IV, V, IX	*Griswold v. Connecticut*, 381 U.S. 479.
1966	Right to an impartial jury	VI	*Parker v. Gladden*, 385 U.S. 363.
1967	Right to a speedy trial	VI	*Klopfer v. North Carolina*, 386 U.S. 213.
1969	No double jeopardy	V	*Benton v. Maryland*, 395 U.S. 784.

government from prohibiting individuals from practicing the religion of their choice. These two precepts can inherently be in tension with each other, however. For example, would prohibiting a group of students from holding prayer meetings in a public school classroom infringe on the students' right to free exercise of religion? Or would allowing the meetings amount to unconstitutional government support for religion? You will read about a number of difficult freedom of religion issues in the following discussion.

THE SEPARATION OF CHURCH AND STATE—THE ESTABLISHMENT CLAUSE

The First Amendment to the Constitution states, in part, that "Congress shall make no law respecting an establishment of religion." In the words of Thomas Jefferson, the *establishment clause* was designed to create a "wall of separation of Church and State." Perhaps Jefferson was thinking about the religious intolerance that characterized the first colonies. Many of the American colonies were founded by groups that were in pursuit of religious freedom. Nonetheless, the early colonists were quite intolerant of religious beliefs that did not conform to those held by the majority of citizens within their own communities. Jefferson undoubtedly was also aware that state churches (denominations) were the rule; among the original thirteen American colonies, nine had *official* churches.

As interpreted by the United States Supreme Court, the establishment clause in the First Amendment means at least the following:

> *Neither a state nor the federal government can set up a church. Neither can pass laws which aid one religion, aid all religions, or prefer one religion over another. Neither can force nor influence a person to go to or to remain away from church against his will or force him to profess a belief or disbelief in any religion. No person can be punished for entertaining or professing religious beliefs or disbeliefs, for church attendance or nonattendance. No tax in any amount, large or small, can be levied to support any religious activities or institutions, whatever they may be called, or whatever form they may adopt to teach or practice religion. Neither a state nor the federal government can, openly or secretly, participate in the affairs of any religious organizations or groups and vice versa.[3]*

The establishment clause covers all conflicts about such matters as the legality of giving state and local government aid to religious organizations and schools, allowing or requiring school prayers, teaching evolution versus intelligent design, posting the Ten Commandments in schools or public places, and discriminating against religious groups in publicly operated institutions. The establishment clause's mandate that government can neither promote nor discriminate against religious beliefs raises particularly knotty questions at times.

In contrast to the United States, many other nations have established churches or religions. We look at one of the most extreme examples in this chapter's *Beyond Our Borders* feature.

Aid to Church-Related Schools. Throughout the United States, all property owners except religious, educational, fraternal, and similar nonprofit institutions must pay property taxes. A large part of the proceeds of such taxes goes to support public schools. But fully 13 percent of school-aged children attend *private* schools, of which 80 percent have religious affiliations. In many cases, the United States Supreme Court has tried to draw a fine line between permissible public aid to students in these schools and impermissible public aid to religion. These issues have arisen most often at the elementary and secondary levels.

didyouknow...

That on the eve of the American Revolution, fewer than 20 percent of American adults adhered to a church in any significant way, compared with the 55 percent that do so today?

---

3. *Everson v. Board of Education,* 330 U.S. 1 (1947).

beyondourborders

THE RELIGIOUS POLICE IN SAUDI ARABIA

In the United States, the Bill of Rights prevents the government from establishing a state religion. In other countries, the opposite is true. Some nations have state-sponsored religions. One of those is Saudi Arabia. Indeed, in that country the government has established a bureaucracy to enforce Islamic religious beliefs. This body, the Committee for the Propagation of Virtue and the Prevention of Vice, employs a religious police known as the Mutaween. There are at least 3,500 officers in the Mutaween, helped by tens of thousands of volunteers.

THE RELIGIOUS POLICE TAKE THEIR JOB SERIOUSLY

Those in the Mutaween take their job so seriously that sometimes tragedy results. In 2002, the world was shocked to learn that Saudi Arabia's religious police had prevented schoolgirls from leaving a blazing building because they were not wearing correct Islamic dress. Fifteen girls died in the fire. The religious police even stopped others who attempted to help save the girls.

As many Westerners know, Saudi Arabia has the world's strictest religious code of separation of the sexes. As a consequence, couples seen in public are routinely questioned. They must show proof that they are related by blood or marriage to justify their being together in public. Stories of severe beatings and imprisonment for those couples without a family link are numerous. The religious police go even further. In 2008, the Mutaween arrested fifty-seven young men in front of a shopping mall in Mecca. Their crimes? Improper clothing, dancing to pop music, and flirting with women. Suppressing any celebration of Valentine's Day is also a Mutaween preoccupation.

Saudi Arabia strictly forbids the sale, possession, and consumption of alcoholic beverages. Although rich and well-connected Saudis have little difficulty violating this law inside their own homes, the less well connected are at greater risk. In 2007, the Mutaween beat a man to death who was alleged to have alcohol in his home.

Most recently, one of the jobs of the Mutaween has been to enforce the ban on the sale of dogs and cats. Although the reasoning behind this ban is not completely clear, it appears that some young Saudis have been seen parading their pets in public. These actions "smell" of imitating the West.

TIMES COULD BE CHANGING (BUT DON'T BET ON IT)

A new government-sponsored organization has been created recently to counter the fervor of the religious police. The National Society for Human Rights has criticized the behavior of the Mutaween. The new group publicly argues that there appears to be a pattern of abuses by the religious police. They have "exceeded their limits." Further, they have not obtained proper orders from the government before engaging in their policing activities.

Outsiders do not believe that the new human rights organization will change much in Saudi Arabia. It is, after all, a country where women are still not allowed to drive.

FOR CRITICAL ANALYSIS

The United States has never had anything like a religious police. Yet during Puritan times, public and private morals were often policed by what today we would call busybodies. Why do you think that in modern America, there is little public or private monitoring of morals?

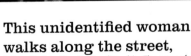

This unidentified woman walks along the street, fully veiled, in Riyadh, Saudi Arabia. The powerful Mutaween—the religious police—have virtually unlimited authority to ensure that women cover themselves in this manner. The Mutaween also enforce a strict moral code on both men and women. Are there any "moral codes" that are enforced in the United States? (AP Photo/Hasan Jamali)

In 1971, in *Lemon v. Kurtzman,*[4] the Court ruled that direct state aid could not be used to subsidize religious instruction. The Court in the *Lemon* case gave its most general statement on the constitutionality of government aid to religious schools, stating that the aid had to be secular (nonreligious) in aim, that it could not have the primary effect

4. 403 U.S. 602 (1971).

"We seem to be getting away from the separation of church and state."
(©The New Yorker Collection, 1991. James Stevenson, from cartoonbank.com. All Rights Reserved.)

of advancing or inhibiting religion, and that the government must avoid "an excessive government entanglement with religion." All laws under the establishment clause are now subject to the three-part *Lemon* test. How the test is applied, however, has varied over the years.

In a number of cases, the Supreme Court has held that state programs helping church-related schools are unconstitutional. The Court also has denied state reimbursements to religious schools for field trips and for developing achievement tests. In a series of other cases, however, the Supreme Court has allowed states to use tax funds for lunches, textbooks, diagnostic services for speech and hearing problems, standardized tests, computers, and transportation for students attending church-operated elementary and secondary schools, as well as for special educational services for disadvantaged students attending religious schools.

School Vouchers. An ongoing controversial issue concerning the establishment clause has to do with school vouchers. One solution to the problem of poor educational performance has been for state and local governments to issue school vouchers (representing state-issued funds) that can be used to "purchase" education at any school, public or private. At issue is whether voucher programs violate the establishment clause.

In 2002, the United States Supreme Court held that a voucher program in Cleveland, Ohio, did not violate the establishment clause. The Court concluded that because the vouchers could be used for public as well as private schools, the program did not unconstitutionally entangle church and state.[5] The Court's 2002 decision was encouraging to those who support school choice, whether it takes the form of school vouchers or tuition tax credits to offset educational expenses in private schools.

Today, thirteen states and the District of Columbia allow public funds to be used for private education. Six states and the District of Columbia have small-scale voucher programs for a limited number of students. Seven states offer tuition tax-subsidy programs. At the national level, President George W. Bush urged Congress to pass legislation that would allow public funds to be used for education in either a private religious school or a public secular institution. Nonetheless, some state courts, such as those in Florida and Colorado, have held that school vouchers violate state constitutions, and the nation's lawmakers remain divided on the issue.

The Issue of School Prayer—*Engel v. Vitale*. Do the states have the right to promote religion in general, without making any attempt to establish a particular religion? That is the question raised by school prayer and was the precise issue presented in 1962 in *Engel v. Vitale*,[6] the so-called Regents' Prayer case in New York. The State Board of Regents of New York had suggested that a prayer be spoken aloud in the public schools at the beginning of each day. The recommended prayer was as follows:

*Almighty God, we acknowledge our dependence upon Thee,
And we beg Thy blessings upon us, our parents, our teachers,
and our Country.*

Such a prayer was implemented in many New York public schools.

The parents of a number of students challenged the action of the regents, maintaining that it violated the establishment clause of the First Amendment. At trial, the parents lost. The Supreme Court, however, ruled that the regents' action was unconstitutional because "the constitutional prohibition against laws respecting an establishment of a religion must mean at least that in this country it

didyouknow...

That in 1657, more than a century before the First Amendment, thirty citizens of the Netherlands on Manhattan Island signed the Flushing Remonstrance, a document that called for religious tolerance?

---

5. *Zelman v. Simmons-Harris,* 536 U.S. 639 (2002).
6. 370 U.S. 421 (1962).

is no part of the business of government to compose official prayers for any group of the American people to recite as part of a religious program carried on by any government." The Court's conclusion was based in part on the "historical fact that governmentally established religions and religious persecutions go hand in hand." In *Abington School District v. Schempp,*[7] the Supreme Court outlawed officially sponsored daily readings of the Bible and recitation of the Lord's Prayer in public schools.

The Debate over School Prayer Continues. Although the Supreme Court has ruled repeatedly against officially sponsored prayer and Bible-reading sessions in public schools, other means for bringing some form of religious expression into public education have been attempted. In 1983, the Tennessee legislature passed a bill requiring public school classes to begin each day with a minute of silence. Alabama had a similar law. In 1985, in *Wallace v. Jaffree,*[8] the Supreme Court struck down as unconstitutional the Alabama law authorizing one minute of silence for prayer or meditation in all public schools. Applying the three-part *Lemon* test, the Court concluded that the law violated the establishment clause because it was "an endorsement of religion lacking any clearly secular purpose."

Since then, the lower courts have interpreted the Supreme Court's decision to mean that states can require a moment of silence in the schools as long as they make it clear that the purpose of the law is secular, not religious.

Prayer outside the Classroom. The courts have also dealt with cases involving prayer in public schools outside the classroom, particularly prayer during graduation ceremonies. In 1992, in *Lee v. Weisman,*[9] the United States Supreme Court held that it was unconstitutional for a school to invite a rabbi to deliver a nonsectarian prayer at graduation. The Court said nothing about *students* organizing and leading prayers at graduation ceremonies and other school events, however, and these issues continue to come before the courts. A contentious question has been the constitutionality of student-initiated prayers before sporting events, such as football games. In 2000, the Supreme Court held that while school prayer at graduation did not violate the establishment clause, students could not use a school's public-address system to lead prayers at sporting events.[10]

---

7. 374 U.S. 203 (1963).
8. 472 U.S. 38 (1985).
9. 505 U.S. 577 (1992).
10. *Santa Fe Independent School District v. Doe,* 530 U.S. 290 (2000).

At certain schools, such as the Chambersburg Area Senior High School in Pennsylvania, shown in this photo, students celebrate their faith by praying around a flagpole outside school before classes. Is there anything in the Constitution that prohibits such group religious activity? (AP Photo/Chambersburg Public Opinion, Christopher Shatzer)

A Ten Commandments monument is removed from a high school in West Union, Ohio. Why have federal judges ordered the removal of such monuments from public schools and county courthouses? (AP Photo/Al Behrman)

In spite of the Court's ruling, students in a number of schools in Texas continue to pray over public-address systems at sporting events. In other areas, the Court's ruling is skirted by avoiding the use of the public-address system. For example, in a school in North Carolina, a pregame prayer was broadcast over a local radio station and heard by fans who took radios to the game for that purpose.

The Ten Commandments. A related church-state issue is whether the Ten Commandments may be displayed in public schools—or on any public property. In recent years, a number of states have considered legislation that would allow or even require schools to post the Ten Commandments in school buildings. Supporters of the "Hang Ten" movement claim that schoolchildren are not being taught the fundamental religious and family values that frame the American way of life. They argue further that the Ten Commandments are more than just religious documents. The commandments are also secular in nature because they constitute a part of the official and permanent history of American government.

Opponents of such laws claim that they are an unconstitutional government entanglement with the religious life of citizens. Still, various Ten Commandments installations have been found to be constitutional. For example, the Supreme Court ruled in 2005 that a granite monument on the grounds of the Texas state capitol that contained the commandments was constitutional because the monument as a whole was secular in nature.[11] In another 2005 ruling, however, the Court ordered that displays of the Ten Commandments in front of two Kentucky county courthouses be removed because they were overtly religious.[12]

The Ten Commandments controversy took an odd twist in 2003 when, in the middle of the night, then Alabama chief justice Roy Moore installed a two-and-a-half-ton granite monument featuring the commandments in the rotunda of the state courthouse. When Moore refused to obey a federal judge's order to remove the monument, the Alabama Court of the Judiciary was forced to expel him from the judicial bench. The monument was wheeled away to a storage room.

Forbidding the Teaching of Evolution. For many decades, certain religious groups, particularly in southern states, have opposed the teaching of evolution in the schools. To these groups, evolutionary theory directly counters their religious belief that human beings did not evolve but were created fully formed, as described in the biblical story of the creation. State and local attempts to forbid the teaching of evolution, however, have not passed constitutional muster in the eyes of the United States Supreme Court. For example, in 1968 the Supreme Court held, in *Epperson v. Arkansas,*[13] that an Arkansas law prohibiting the teaching of evolution violated the establishment clause, because it imposed religious beliefs on students. The Louisiana legislature passed a law requiring the teaching of the biblical story of the creation alongside the teaching of evolution. In 1987, in *Edwards v. Aguillard,*[14] the Supreme Court declared that this law was unconstitutional, in part because it had as its primary purpose the promotion of a particular religious belief.

Nonetheless, state and local groups around the country, particularly in the so-called Bible Belt, continue their efforts against the teaching of evolution. The Cobb County school system in Georgia attempted to include a disclaimer in its biology textbooks that proclaims, "Evolution is a theory, not a fact, regarding the origin of living things." A federal judge later ruled that the disclaimer stickers must be removed. Other

didyouknow...

That according to Gallup polls, only 10 percent of Americans say they hold a secular evolutionist view of the world, while 44 percent believe in strict biblical creationism?

---

11. *Van Orden v. Perry,* 545 U.S. 677 (2005).
12. *McCreary County v. American Civil Liberties Union,* 545 U.S. 844 (2005).
13. 393 U.S. 97 (1968).
14. 482 U.S. 578 (1987).

school districts have considered teaching "intelligent design" as an alternative explanation of the origin of life. Indeed, in 2005 the Kansas state board of education rewrote its science standards to implement the teaching of intelligent design in Kansas schools. (New board members elected in 2006, however, reversed this decision in early 2007.) Proponents of intelligent design contend that evolutionary theory has "gaps" that can be explained only by the existence of an intelligent creative force (God).

The federal courts took up the issue of intelligent design in 2005. The previous year, the Dover Area Board of Education in Pennsylvania had voted to require the presentation of intelligent design as an explanation of the origin of life. In December 2005, a U.S. district court ruled that the Dover mandate was unconstitutional. Judge John E. Jones III, appointed in 2002 by President George W. Bush, issued a 139-page decision that criticized the intelligent design theory in depth.[15] All of the school board members who indorsed intelligent design were voted out of office, and the new school board declined to appeal the decision.

Religious Speech. Another controversy in the area of church-state relations concerns religious speech in public schools or universities. For example, in *Rosenberger v. University of Virginia,*[16] the issue was whether the University of Virginia violated the establishment clause when it refused to fund a Christian group's newsletter but granted funds to more than one hundred other student organizations. The Supreme Court ruled that the university's policy unconstitutionally discriminated against religious speech. The Court pointed out that the funds came from student fees, not general taxes, and were used for the "neutral" payment of bills for student groups.

Later, the Supreme Court reviewed a case involving a similar claim of discrimination against a religious group, the Good News Club. The club offers religious instruction to young schoolchildren. The club sued the school board of a public school in Milford, New York, when the board refused to allow the club to meet on school property after the school day ended. The club argued that the school board's refusal to allow the club to meet on school property, when other groups—such as the Girl Scouts and the 4-H Club—were permitted to do so, amounted to discrimination on the basis of religion. Ultimately, the Supreme Court agreed, ruling in *Good News Club v. Milford Central School*[17] that the Milford school board's decision violated the establishment clause.

THE FREE EXERCISE CLAUSE

The First Amendment constrains Congress from prohibiting the free exercise of religion. Does this *free exercise clause* mean that no type of religious practice can be prohibited or restricted by government? Certainly, a person can hold any religious belief that he or she wants, or a person can have no religious belief. When, however, religious *practices* work against public policy and the public welfare, the government can act. For example, regardless of a child's or parent's religious beliefs, the government can require certain types of vaccinations. Additionally, public school students can be required to study from textbooks chosen by school authorities.

The extent to which government can regulate religious practices has always been a subject of controversy. For example, in 1990, in *Oregon v. Smith,*[18] the United States Supreme Court ruled that the state of Oregon could deny unemployment benefits to two

This demonstrator is showing her disapproval of the teaching of "intelligent design" as an alternative to the theory of evolution. This religious-based alternative claims that life is so complex that it must have been created by an all-knowing being. Why have some courts ruled that schools cannot teach intelligent design in the classroom? (AP Photo/Niklas Larsson)

---

15. *Kitzmiller v. Dover Area School District,* 400 F.Supp.2d 707 (M.D. Pa. 2005).
16. 515 U.S. 819 (1995).
17. 533 U.S. 98 (2001).
18. 494 U.S. 872 (1990).

drug counselors who had been fired for using peyote, an illegal drug, in their religious services. The counselors had argued that using peyote was part of the practice of a Native American religion. Many criticized the decision as going too far in the direction of regulating religious practices.

The Religious Freedom Restoration Act. In 1993, Congress responded to the public's criticism by passing the Religious Freedom Restoration Act (RFRA). One of the specific purposes of the act was to overturn the Supreme Court's decision in *Oregon v. Smith*. The act required national, state, and local governments to "accommodate religious conduct" unless the government could show that there was a *compelling* reason not to do so. Moreover, if the government did regulate a religious practice, it had to use the least restrictive means possible.

Some people believed that the RFRA went too far in the other direction—it accommodated practices that were contrary to the public policies of state governments. Proponents of states' rights complained that the act intruded into an area traditionally governed by state laws, not by the national government. In 1997, in *City of Boerne v. Flores,*[19] the Supreme Court agreed and held that Congress had exceeded its constitutional authority when it passed the RFRA. According to the Court, the act's "sweeping coverage ensures its intrusion at every level of government, displacing laws and prohibiting official actions of almost every description and regardless of subject matter."

A fascinating recent issue involving the accommodation of religion is to what extent public colleges and universities ought to accommodate the religious practices of Muslim students. We look at this controversial topic in the *Which Side Are You On?* feature on the facing page.

Free Exercise in the Public Schools. The courts have repeatedly held that U.S. governments at all levels must remain neutral on issues of religion. In the *Good News Club* decision discussed earlier, the Supreme Court ruled that "state power is no more to be used to handicap religions than it is to favor them." Nevertheless, by overturning the RFRA, the Court cleared the way for public schools to set regulations that, while ostensibly neutral, effectively limited religious expression by students. An example is a rule banning hats, which has been instituted by many schools as a way of discouraging the display of gang insignia. This rule has also been interpreted as barring yarmulkes, the small caps worn by strictly observant Jewish boys and men.

The national government has found a new way to ensure that public schools do not excessively restrict religion. To receive funds under the No Child Left Behind Act of 2001, schools must certify in writing that they do not ban prayer or other expressions of religion as long as they are made in a constitutionally appropriate manner.

FREEDOM OF EXPRESSION

Perhaps the most frequently invoked freedom that Americans have is the right to free speech and a free press without government interference. Each of us has the right to have our say, and all of us have the right to hear what others say. For the most part, Americans can criticize public officials and their actions without fear of reprisal by any branch of government.

NO PRIOR RESTRAINT

Prior Restraint
Restraining an activity before it has actually occurred. When expression is involved, this means censorship.

Restraining an activity before that activity has actually occurred is called **prior restraint.** When expression is involved, prior restraint means censorship, as opposed to subsequent punishment. Prior restraint of expression would require, for example, that a permit be obtained before a speech could be made, a newspaper published, or a movie or TV show

---

19. 521 U.S. 507 (1997).

whichsideare**you**on?

SHOULD MUSLIMS' RELIGIOUS NEEDS BE ACCOMMODATED ON CAMPUS?

The United States is known as a land of religious tolerance. Americans practice many minority religions in addition to the major faiths. So long as religious practices do not interfere with the rights of others, they are legally acceptable. The courts have drawn the line, though, when religious practices involve illegal activities, such as leaving beheaded animals on the side of the road or using prohibited drugs.

Recently, college campuses have been asked to accommodate the religious needs of Muslim students. Observant Muslims seek to wash their feet before they pray. Should universities build footbaths that Muslim students can then use? The Dearborn campus of the University of Michigan, where 16 percent of the students are Muslim, decided to do just that, in part to keep students from washing their feet in the restroom sinks. The university spent more than $25,000 to install foot-washing stations in a number of restrooms.

And what about separate prayer rooms for Muslim students in public schools? There is also the issue of whether food in cafeterias conforms to Muslims' religious requirements. Finally, what about religious holidays? School calendars already accommodate Christians with vacations around Easter and Christmas. Why not also Muslim holidays?

CAMPUS OFFICIALS SHOULD BE TOLERANT

While providing footbaths for Muslims on college campuses may seem strange, that is only because most students are not used to having Muslims around them. Just because America is basically a nation whose major religions are based on Judeo-Christian doctrines does not mean that we can't accommodate a growing alternative religion. One of the fastest-growing religions in the United States is indeed Islam. We should consider most Muslim student requests for accommodation on campuses as simply part of those students' right to practice their religion.

Campus authorities are going to have to face the issue of accommodating Muslim religious practices sooner or later anyway. In addition to the University of Michigan, at least fifteen other universities have installed footbaths in new buildings. The footbaths can be used by anyone, including sweaty athletes and janitors who fill buckets. They are not for the exclusive use of Muslim students. Such footbaths have no symbolic value; they are not stylized in a religious manner.

(Creative Commons)

WHAT ABOUT SEPARATION OF CHURCH AND STATE?

Those who oppose religious accommodation for Muslims argue that, at least on public college campuses, the funding of such actions necessarily violates the constitutionally mandated separation of church and state. Footbaths are essentially structures for a particular religious tradition. The Constitution prohibits the government from endorsing any particular religion. On college campuses, the footbaths are being financed out of building-maintenance fees paid by students. Students aren't given any voice in the decision, and that is wrong. Many colleges no longer sponsor Christmas music on campus, so why would those universities behave any differently when it comes to accommodating Muslims? The Constitution should be our guide.

---

exhibited. Most, if not all, Supreme Court justices have been very critical of any governmental action that imposes prior restraint on expression. The Court clearly displayed this attitude in *Nebraska Press Association v. Stuart,*[20] a case decided in 1976:

> A prior restraint on expression comes to this Court with a "heavy presumption" against its constitutionality. . . . The government thus carries a heavy burden of showing justification for the enforcement of such a restraint.

---

20. 427 U.S. 539 (1976). See also *Near v. Minnesota,* 283 U.S. 697 (1931).

Symbolic Speech
Expression made through articles of clothing, gestures, movements, and other forms of nonverbal conduct. Symbolic speech is given substantial protection by the courts.

One of the most famous cases concerning prior restraint was *New York Times v. United States*,[21] the so-called Pentagon Papers case. In 1971, the *Times* and the *Washington Post* were about to publish the Pentagon Papers, an elaborate secret history of the U.S. government's involvement in the Vietnam War (1964–1975). The secret documents had been obtained illegally by a disillusioned former Pentagon official. The government wanted a court order to bar publication of the documents, arguing that national security was threatened and that the documents had been stolen. The newspapers argued that the public had a right to know the information contained in the papers and that the press had the right to inform the public. The Supreme Court ruled six to three in favor of the newspapers' right to publish the information. This case affirmed the no-prior-restraint doctrine.

THE PROTECTION OF SYMBOLIC SPEECH

Not all expression is in words or in writing. Articles of clothing, gestures, movements, and other forms of nonverbal expressive conduct are considered **symbolic speech.** Such speech is given substantial protection today by our courts. For example, in a landmark decision issued in 1969, *Tinker v. Des Moines School District,*[22] the United States Supreme Court held that the wearing of black armbands by students in protest against the Vietnam War was a form of speech protected by the First Amendment. The case arose after a school administrator in Des Moines, Iowa, issued a regulation prohibiting students in the Des Moines School District from wearing the armbands. The Supreme Court reasoned that the school district was unable to show that the wearing of the armbands had disrupted normal school activities. Furthermore, the school district's policy was discriminatory, as it banned only certain forms of symbolic speech (the black armbands) and not others (such as lapel crosses and fraternity rings).

In 1989, in *Texas v. Johnson,*[23] the Supreme Court ruled that state laws that prohibited the burning of the American flag as part of a peaceful protest also violated the freedom of expression protected by the First Amendment. Congress responded by passing the Flag Protection Act of 1989, which was ruled unconstitutional by the Supreme Court in June 1990.[24] Congress and President George H. W. Bush immediately pledged to work for a constitutional amendment to "protect our flag"—an effort that has yet to be successful.

In 2003, however, the Supreme Court held that a Virginia statute prohibiting the burning of a cross with "an intent to intimidate" did not violate the First Amendment. The Court concluded that a burning cross is an instrument of racial terror so threatening that it overshadows free speech concerns.[25]

These rock fans at the Coachella Valley Music and Arts Festival in Indio, California, burn the American flag. Is such an action illegal? Why or why not? (AP Photo/Branimir Kvartuc)

21. 403 U.S. 713 (1971).
22. 393 U.S. 503 (1969).
23. 488 U.S. 884 (1989).
24. *United States v. Eichman,* 496 U.S. 310 (1990).
25. *Virginia v. Black,* 538 U.S. 343 (2003).

THE PROTECTION OF COMMERCIAL SPEECH

Commercial speech usually is defined as advertising statements. Can advertisers use their First Amendment rights to prevent restrictions on the content of commercial advertising? Until the 1970s, the Supreme Court held that such speech was not protected at all by the First Amendment. By the mid-1970s, however, more and more commercial speech had been brought under First Amendment protection. According to Justice Harry A. Blackmun, "Advertising, however tasteless and excessive it sometimes may seem, is nonetheless dissemination of information as to who is producing and selling what product for what reason and at what price."[26] Nevertheless, the Supreme Court will consider a restriction on commercial speech valid as long as it (1) seeks to implement a substantial government interest, (2) directly advances that interest, and (3) goes no further than necessary to accomplish its objective. In particular, a business engaging in commercial speech can be subject to liability for factual inaccuracies in ways that do not apply to noncommercial speech.

PERMITTED RESTRICTIONS ON EXPRESSION

At various times, restrictions on expression have been permitted. A description of several such restrictions follows.

Clear and Present Danger. When a person's remarks create a clear and present danger to the peace or public order, they can be curtailed constitutionally. Justice Oliver Wendell Holmes used this reasoning in 1919 when examining the case of a socialist who had been convicted for violating the Espionage Act by distributing a leaflet that opposed the military draft. Holmes stated:

> *The question in every case is whether the words are used in such circumstances and are of such a nature as to create a* clear and present danger *that they will bring about the substantive evils that Congress has a right to prevent. It is a question of proximity and degree.*[27] [Emphasis added.]

According to the **clear and present danger test,** then, expression may be restricted if evidence exists that such expression would cause a dangerous condition, actual or imminent, that Congress has the power to prevent. Commenting on this test, Justice Louis D. Brandeis in 1920 said, "Correctly applied, it will reserve the right of free speech . . . from suppression by tyrannists, well-meaning majorities, and from abuse by irresponsible, fanatical minorities."[28]

Modifications to the Clear and Present Danger Rule. Over the course of the twentieth century, the United States Supreme Court modified the clear and present danger rule, limiting the constitutional protection of free speech in 1925 and 1951, and then broadening it substantially in 1969. In *Gitlow v. New York,*[29] the Court introduced the *bad-tendency rule.* According to this rule, speech or other First Amendment freedoms may be curtailed if there is a possibility that such expression might lead to some "evil." In the *Gitlow* case, a member of a left-wing group was convicted of violating New York State's criminal anarchy statute when he published and distributed a pamphlet urging the violent overthrow of the U.S. government. In its majority opinion, the Supreme Court held that although the First Amendment afforded protection against state incursions on freedom of expression, Gitlow could be punished legally in this particular instance because his expression would tend to bring about evils that the state had a right to prevent.

Commercial Speech
Advertising statements, which increasingly have been given First Amendment protection.

Clear and Present Danger Test
The test proposed by Justice Oliver Wendell Holmes for determining when government may restrict free speech. Restrictions are permissible, he argued, only when speech creates a *clear and present danger* to the public order.

---

26. *Virginia State Board of Pharmacy v. Virginia Citizens Consumer Council, Inc.,* 425 U.S. 748 (1976).
27. *Schenck v. United States,* 249 U.S. 47 (1919).
28. *Schaefer v. United States,* 251 U.S. 466 (1920).
29. 268 U.S. 652 (1925).

The Supreme Court again modified the clear and present danger test in a 1951 case, *Dennis v. United States*.[30] At the time, there was considerable tension between the United States and the Soviet Union, a Communist-ruled country that included Russia and several other modern-day nations. Twelve members of the American Communist Party were convicted of violating a statute that made it a crime to conspire to teach, advocate, or organize the violent overthrow of any government in the United States. The Supreme Court affirmed the convictions, significantly modifying the clear and present danger test in the process. The Court applied a *grave and probable danger rule*. Under this rule, "the gravity of the 'evil' discounted by its improbability justifies such invasion of free speech as is necessary to avoid the danger." This rule gave much less protection to free speech than did the clear and present danger test.

Some claim that the United States did not achieve true freedom of political speech until 1969. In that year, in *Brandenburg v. Ohio*,[31] the Supreme Court overturned the conviction of a Ku Klux Klan leader for violating a state statute. The statute prohibited anyone from advocating "the duty, necessity, or propriety of sabotage, violence, or unlawful methods of terrorism as a means of accomplishing industrial or political reform." The Court held that the guarantee of free speech does not permit a state "to forbid or proscribe advocacy of the use of force or of law violation except where such advocacy is directed to inciting or producing imminent lawless actions and is likely to incite or produce such action." The incitement test enunciated by the Court in this case is a difficult one for prosecutors to meet. As a result, the Court's decision significantly broadened the protection given to advocacy speech.

UNPROTECTED SPEECH: OBSCENITY

A large number of state and federal statutes make it a crime to disseminate obscene materials. Generally, the courts have not been willing to extend constitutional protections of free speech to what they consider obscene materials. But what is obscenity? Justice Potter Stewart once stated, in *Jacobellis v. Ohio*,[32] a 1964 case, that even though he could not define *obscenity,* "I know it when I see it." The problem, of course, is that even if it were agreed on, the definition of *obscenity* changes with the times. Victorians deeply disapproved of the "loose" morals of the Elizabethan Age. The works of Mark Twain and Edgar Rice Burroughs at times have been considered obscene (after all, Tarzan and Jane were not legally wedded).

Definitional Problems. The Supreme Court has grappled from time to time with the difficulty of specifying an operationally effective definition of *obscenity.* In 1973, in *Miller v. California*,[33] Chief Justice Warren Burger created a formal list of requirements that must be met for material to be legally obscene. Material is obscene if (1) the average person finds that it violates contemporary community standards; (2) the work taken as a whole appeals to a prurient interest in sex; (3) the work shows patently offensive sexual conduct; and (4) the work lacks serious redeeming literary, artistic, political, or scientific merit. The problem, of course, is that one person's prurient interest is another person's medical interest or artistic pleasure. The Court went on to state that the definition of *prurient interest* would be determined by the community's standards. The Court avoided presenting a definition of *obscenity,* leaving this determination to local and state authorities. Consequently, the *Miller* case has been applied in a widely inconsistent manner.

Protecting Children. The Supreme Court has upheld state laws making it illegal to sell materials showing sexual performances by minors. In 1990, in *Osborne v. Ohio*,[34] the

---

30. 341 U.S. 494 (1951).
31. 395 U.S. 444 (1969).
32. 378 U.S. 184 (1964).
33. 413 U.S. 5 (1973).
34. 495 U.S. 103 (1990).

Court ruled that states can outlaw the possession of child pornography in the home. The Court reasoned that the ban on private possession is justified because owning the material perpetuates commercial demand for it and for the exploitation of the children involved. At the federal level, the Child Protection Act of 1984 made it a crime to receive knowingly through the mails sexually explicit depictions of children.

Pornography on the Internet. A significant problem facing Americans and their lawmakers today is how to control obscenity and child pornography that are disseminated by way of the Internet. In 1996, Congress first attempted to protect minors from pornographic materials on the Internet by passing the Communications Decency Act (CDA). The act made it a crime to make available to minors online any "obscene or indecent" message

that "depicts or describes, in terms patently offensive as measured by contemporary community standards, sexual or excretory activities or organs." The act was immediately challenged in court as an unconstitutional infringement on free speech. The Supreme Court held that the act imposed unconstitutional restraints on free speech and was therefore invalid.[35] In the eyes of the Court, the terms *indecent* and *patently offensive* covered large amounts of nonpornographic material with serious educational or other value.

A second attempt to protect children from online obscenity, the Child Online Protection Act (COPA) of 1998, met with a similar fate. Although the COPA was more narrowly tailored than its predecessor, the CDA, it still used "contemporary community standards" to define which material was obscene and harmful to minors. Ultimately, in 2004 the Supreme Court concluded that it was likely that the COPA did violate the right to free speech, and the Court prevented enforcement of the act.[36] In 2002, the Supreme Court invalidated a 1996 law banning virtual pornography, which involves only digitally rendered images and no actual children.[37] In 2008, however, the Court upheld the legality of a 2003 federal law that made it a crime to offer child pornography, even if the pornography in question does not actually exist.[38]

In 2000, Congress enacted the Children's Internet Protection Act (CIPA), which requires public schools and libraries to install filtering software to prevent children from viewing Web sites with "adult" content. The CIPA was also challenged on constitutional grounds, but in 2003 the Supreme Court held that the act did not violate the First Amendment. The Court concluded that because libraries can disable the filters for any patrons who ask, the system does not burden free speech to an unconstitutional extent.[39]

UNPROTECTED SPEECH: SLANDER

Can you say anything you want about someone else? Not really. Individuals are protected from **defamation of character,** which is defined as wrongfully hurting a person's good reputation. The law imposes a general duty on all persons to refrain from making false,

First Assistant U.S. Attorney
Marc Haws discusses the formation of a statewide Idaho Internet Crimes Against Children Task Force during a press conference in January 2008. What has the federal government done in an attempt to prevent online crimes against children, such as child pornography? (AP Photo/*Idaho Press-Tribune*/Mike Vogt)

Defamation of Character
Wrongfully hurting a person's good reputation. The law imposes a general duty on all persons to refrain from making false, defamatory statements about others.

---

35. *Reno v. American Civil Liberties Union,* 521 U.S. 844 (1997).
36. *American Civil Liberties Union v. Ashcroft,* 542 U.S. 646 (2004).
37. *Ashcroft v. Free Speech Coalition,* 535 U.S. 234 (2002).
38. *United States v. Williams,* 128 S.Ct. 1830 (2008).
39. *United States v. American Library Association,* 539 U.S. 194 (2003).

Slander
The public uttering of a false statement that harms the good reputation of another. The statement must be made to, or within the hearing of, persons other than the defamed party.

defamatory statements about others. Breaching this duty orally is the wrongdoing called *slander.* Breaching it in writing is the wrongdoing called *libel,* which we discuss later. The government itself does not bring charges of slander or libel. Rather, the defamed person may bring a civil suit for damages.

Legally, **slander** is the public uttering of a false statement that harms the good reputation of another. Slanderous public uttering means that the defamatory statements are made to, or within the hearing of, persons other than the defamed party. If one person calls another dishonest, manipulative, and incompetent to his or her face when no one else is around, that does not constitute slander. The message is not communicated to a third party. If, however, a third party accidentally overhears defamatory statements, the courts have generally held that this constitutes a public uttering and therefore slander, which is prohibited.

STUDENT SPEECH

In recent years, high school and university students at public institutions have faced a variety of free speech challenges. Court rulings on these issues have varied by the level of school involved. Elementary schools, in particular, have great latitude in determining what kinds of speech are appropriate for their students. High school students have greater free speech rights, and college students have the most rights of all.

Rights of Public School Students. High schools can impose restrictions on speech that would not be allowed in a college setting or in the general society. For example, high school officials may censor publications such as newspapers and yearbooks produced by the school's students. Courts have argued that a school newspaper is an extension of the school's educational mission, and thus subject to control by the school administration. One of the most striking rulings to illustrate the power of school officials was handed down by the United States Supreme Court in 2007. An Alaska high school student had displayed a banner reading "Bong Hits 4 Jesus" on private property across from the school as students on the school grounds watched the Winter Olympics torch relay. The school principal crossed the street, seized the banner, and suspended the student from school. The Supreme Court later held that the school had an "important—indeed, perhaps compelling—interest" in combating drug use that allowed it to suppress the banner.[40] The Court's decision was widely criticized.

Former Juneau, Alaska, high school principal Deborah Morse is shown in front of the Supreme Court building after she successfully defended her actions in suspending a student. That student had displayed a banner reading "Bong Hits 4 Jesus" after a winter Olympics torch relay on a downtown street. Why did the Supreme Court uphold her actions? (AP Photo/Evan Vucci)

College Student Activity Fees. At the college level, one speech issue is whether a student should have to subsidize, through student activity fees, organizations that promote causes that the student finds objectionable. In 2000, this question came before the Supreme Court in a case brought by several University of Wisconsin students. The students argued that their mandatory student activity fees—which helped to fund liberal causes with which they disagreed, including gay rights—violated their First Amendment rights of free speech, free association, and free exercise of religion. They contended that they should have the right to choose whether to fund organizations that promoted political and ideological views that were offensive to their personal beliefs.

To the surprise of many, the Supreme Court rejected the students' claim and ruled in favor of the university. The Court stated that "the university may determine that its mission is well served if students have the means to engage in dynamic discussions of philosophical, religious, scientific, social and political subjects in their extracurricular life. If the

---

40. *Morse v. Frederick,* 127 S. Ct. 2618 (2007).

university reaches this conclusion, it is entitled to impose a mandatory fee to sustain an open dialogue to these ends."[41]

Campus Speech and Behavior Codes. Another free speech issue is the legitimacy of campus speech and behavior codes. Some state universities have established codes that challenge the boundaries of the protection of free speech provided by the First Amendment. These codes are designed to prohibit so-called hate speech—abusive speech attacking persons on the basis of their ethnicity, race, or other criteria. For example, a University of Michigan code banned "any behavior, verbal or physical, that stigmatizes or victimizes an individual on the basis of race, ethnicity, religion, sex, sexual orientation, creed, national origin, ancestry, age, marital status, handicap," or Vietnam-veteran status. A federal court found that the code violated students' First Amendment rights.[42]

Although the courts generally have held, as in the University of Michigan case, that campus speech codes are unconstitutional restrictions on the right to free speech, such codes continue to exist. Whether hostile speech should be banned on high school campuses has also become an issue. In view of school shootings and other violent behavior in the schools, school officials have become concerned about speech that consists of veiled threats or that could lead to violence. Some schools have even prohibited students from wearing T-shirts bearing verbal messages (such as sexist or racist comments) or symbolic messages (such as the Confederate flag) that might generate "ill will or hatred."

Defenders of campus speech codes argue that they are necessary not only to prevent violence but also to promote equality among different cultural, ethnic, and racial groups on campus and greater sensitivity to the needs and feelings of others. Most educators acknowledge that a certain degree of civility is required for productive campus discourse. Moreover, some hostile speech can rise to the level of illegal threats or illegal forms of harassment. A number of students also support restraints on campus hate speech. In 2002, for example, the student assembly at Wesleyan University passed a resolution declaring that the "right to speech comes with implicit responsibilities to respect community standards."

This University of Arizona student demonstrates in favor of what he calls intellectual diversity in the classroom. Some college students believe that their grades will suffer if they are vocal in challenging their professors' political views. Do you believe that this is a serious problem on campus? (AP Photo/The Arizona Daily Wildcat, Roxana Vasquez)

HATE SPEECH ON THE INTERNET

Extreme hate speech appears on the Internet, including racist materials and denials of the Holocaust (the murder of millions of Jews by the Nazis during World War II). Can the federal government restrict this type of speech? Should it? Consider that even if Congress succeeded in passing a law prohibiting particular speech on the Internet, an army of "Internet watchers" would be needed to enforce it. Also, what if other countries attempt to impose on U.S. Web sites their laws that restrict speech? This is not a theoretical issue. In 2000, a French court found Yahoo in violation of French laws banning the display of Nazi memorabilia. In 2001, however, a U.S. district court held that this ruling could not be enforced against Yahoo in the United States.[43]

These students at the University of Michigan at Ann Arbor show their support for, or anger against, a proposal involving a ban on certain types of affirmative action programs on campus. (AP Photo/Carlos Osorio)

41. *Board of Regents of the University of Wisconsin System v. Southworth,* 529 U.S. 217 (2000).
42. *Doe v. University of Michigan,* 721 F. Supp. 852 (1989).
43. *Yahoo!, Inc. v. La Ligue Contre le Racisme et l'Antisémitisme,* 169 F.Supp.2d 1181 (N.D.Cal. 2001).

Libel

A written defamation of a person's character, reputation, business, or property rights.

Actual Malice

Either knowledge of a defamatory statement's falsity or a reckless disregard for the truth.

Public Figure

A public official, a public employee who exercises substantial governmental power, or any other person, such as a movie star, known to the public because of his or her position or activities.

Gag Order

An order issued by a judge restricting the publication of news about a trial or a pretrial hearing to protect the accused's right to a fair trial.

FREEDOM OF THE PRESS

Freedom of the press can be regarded as a special instance of freedom of speech. Of course, at the time of the framing of the Constitution, the press meant only newspapers, magazines, and books. As technology has modified the ways in which we disseminate information, the laws touching on freedom of the press have been modified. What can and cannot be printed still occupies an important place in constitutional law, however.

DEFAMATION IN WRITING

Libel is defamation in writing (or in pictures, signs, films, or any other communication that has the potentially harmful qualities of written or printed words). As with slander, libel occurs only if the defamatory statements are observed by a third party. If one person writes a private letter to another wrongfully accusing him or her of embezzling funds, that does not constitute libel. It is interesting that the courts have generally held that dictating a letter to a secretary constitutes communication of the letter's contents to a third party, and therefore, if defamation has occurred, the wrongdoer can be sued.

A 1964 case, *New York Times Co. v. Sullivan,*[44] explored an important question regarding libelous statements made about public officials. The Supreme Court held that only when a statement against a public official was made with **actual malice**—that is, with either knowledge of its falsity or a reckless disregard for the truth—could damages be obtained.

The standard set by the Court in the *New York Times* case has since been applied to **public figures** generally. Public figures include not only public officials but also public employees who exercise substantial governmental power and any persons, such as movie stars, who are generally in the public limelight. Statements made about public figures, especially when they are made through a public medium, usually are related to matters of general public interest; they are made about people who substantially affect all of us. Furthermore, public figures generally have some access to a public medium for answering disparaging falsehoods about themselves, whereas private individuals do not. For these reasons, public figures have a greater burden of proof in defamation cases than do private individuals; they must prove that the statements were made with actual malice.

A FREE PRESS VERSUS A FAIR TRIAL: GAG ORDERS

Another major issue relating to freedom of the press concerns media coverage of criminal trials. The Sixth Amendment to the Constitution guarantees the right of criminal suspects to a fair trial. In other words, the accused have rights. The First Amendment guarantees freedom of the press. What if the two rights appear to be in conflict? Which one prevails?

Jurors certainly may be influenced by reading news stories about the trial in which they are participating. In the 1970s, judges increasingly issued **gag orders,** orders that restricted the publication of news about a trial in progress or even a pretrial hearing to protect the accused's right to a fair trial. In a landmark 1976 case, *Nebraska Press Association v. Stuart,*[45] the Supreme Court unanimously ruled that a Nebraska judge's gag order had violated the First Amendment's guarantee of freedom of the press. Chief Justice Warren Burger indicated that even pervasive adverse pretrial publicity did not necessarily lead to an unfair trial and that prior restraints on publication were not justified. Some justices even went so far as to suggest that gag orders are never justified.

Students at Oakridge High School in Tennessee show their displeasure at the seizure of the student-produced newspaper. Do you think that the same rights of freedom of the press that are applied off campus should also be applied on campus? Why or why not? (AP Photo/Knoxville News Sentinel, Bob Fowler)

44. 376 U.S. 254 (1964).
45. 427 U.S. 539 (1976).

In spite of the *Nebraska Press Association* ruling, the Court has upheld certain types of gag orders. In *Gannett Co. v. De Pasquale*[46] in 1979, for example, the highest court held that if a judge found a reasonable probability that news publicity would harm a defendant's right to a fair trial, the court could impose a gag rule: "Members of the public have no constitutional right under the Sixth and Fourteenth Amendments to attend criminal trials."

The *Nebraska* and *Gannett* cases, however, involved pretrial hearings. Could a judge impose a gag order on an entire trial, including pretrial hearings? In 1980, in *Richmond Newspapers, Inc. v. Virginia*,[47] the Court ruled that actual trials must be open to the public except under unusual circumstances.

FILMS, RADIO, AND TV

As we have noted, in only a few cases has the Supreme Court upheld prior restraint of published materials. The Court's reluctance to accept prior restraint is less evident with respect to motion pictures. In the first half of the twentieth century, films were routinely submitted to local censorship boards. In 1968, the Supreme Court ruled that a film can be banned only under a law that provides for a prompt hearing at which the film is shown to be obscene. Today, few local censorship boards exist. Instead, the film industry regulates itself primarily through the industry's rating system.

Radio and television broadcasting has the least First Amendment protection. Broadcasting initially received less protection than the printed media because, at that time, the number of airwave frequencies was limited. In 1934, the national government established the Federal Communications Commission (FCC) to regulate electromagnetic wave frequencies. No one has a right to use the airwaves without a license granted by the FCC. The FCC grants licenses for limited periods and imposes a variety of regulations on broadcasting. For example, the FCC can impose sanctions on radio or TV stations that broadcast "filthy words," even if the words are not legally obscene.

THE RIGHT TO ASSEMBLE AND TO PETITION THE GOVERNMENT

The First Amendment prohibits Congress from making any law that abridges "the right of the people peaceably to assemble, and to petition the Government for a redress of grievances." Inherent in such a right is the ability of private citizens to communicate their ideas on public issues to government officials, as well as to other individuals. The Supreme Court has often put this freedom on a par with freedom of speech and freedom of the press. Nonetheless, it has allowed municipalities to require permits for parades, sound trucks, and demonstrations so that public officials can control traffic or prevent demonstrations from turning into riots.

The freedom to demonstrate became a major issue in 1977 when the American Nazi Party sought to march through Skokie, Illinois, a largely Jewish suburb where many Holocaust survivors resided. The American Civil Liberties Union defended the Nazis' right to march (in spite of its opposition to the Nazi philosophy). The Supreme Court let stand a lower court's ruling that the city of Skokie had violated the Nazis' First Amendment guarantees by denying them a permit to march.[48]

This student in West Virginia shows two popular books written by Pat Conroy that were banned from use in English classes in Nitro High School in Charleston, West Virginia. The ban occurred after several parents of students complained about the author's depiction of violence, suicide, and sexual assault. Should high school English teachers be able to use any works of fiction they wish to in their classes? (AP Photo/Jeff Gentner)

---

46. 443 U.S. 368 (1979).
47. 448 U.S. 555 (1980).
48. *Smith v. Collin,* 439 U.S. 916 (1978).

A member of the National Socialist (Nazi) Movement is seen holding the hand of a young child in front of the U.S. Capitol in Washington, D.C. According to the Supreme Court's interpretation of the Bill of Rights, do Nazis have the right to assemble openly?
(AP Photo/Haraz N. Ghanbari)

STREET GANGS

An issue that has surfaced in recent years is whether communities can prevent gang members from gathering together on the streets without violating their right of assembly or associated rights. Although some actions taken by cities to prevent gang members from gathering together or "loitering" in public places have passed constitutional muster, others have not. For example, in a 1997 case, the California Supreme Court upheld a lower court's order preventing gang members from appearing in public together.[49] In 1999, however, the United States Supreme Court held that Chicago's "antiloitering" ordinance violated the constitutional right to due process of law because, among other things, it left too much power to the police to determine what constituted "loitering."[50]

ONLINE ASSEMBLY

A question for Americans today is whether individuals should have the right to "assemble" online for the purpose of advocating violence against certain groups (such as physicians who perform abortions) or advocating values that are opposed to our democracy (such as terrorism). While some online advocacy groups promote interests consistent with American political values, other groups have as their goal the destruction of those values. Whether First Amendment freedoms should be sacrificed (by the government's monitoring of Internet communications, for example) in the interests of national security is a question that will no doubt be debated for some time to come.

MORE LIBERTIES UNDER SCRUTINY: MATTERS OF PRIVACY

No explicit reference is made anywhere in the Constitution to a person's right to privacy. Until the second half of the 1900s, the courts did not take a very positive approach toward the right to privacy. For example, during Prohibition, suspected bootleggers' telephones were tapped routinely, and the information obtained was used as a legal basis for prosecution. In *Olmstead v. United States*[51] in 1928, the Supreme Court upheld such an invasion of privacy. Justice Louis Brandeis, a champion of personal freedoms, strongly dissented from the majority decision in this case, though. He argued that the framers of the Constitution gave every citizen the right to be left alone. He called such a right "the most comprehensive of rights and the right most valued by civilized men."

In the 1960s, the highest court began to modify the majority view. In 1965, in *Griswold v. Connecticut*,[52] the Supreme Court overturned a Connecticut law that effectively prohibited the use of contraceptives, holding that the law violated the right to privacy. Justice William O. Douglas formulated a unique way of reading this right into the Bill of Rights. He claimed that the First, Third, Fourth, Fifth, and Ninth Amendments created "penumbras [shadows], formed by emanations [things sent out] from those guarantees that help give them life and substance," and he went on to describe zones of privacy that are guaranteed by these rights. When we read the Ninth Amendment, we can see the

---

49. *Gallo v. Acuna,* 14 Cal.4th 1090 (1997).
50. *City of Chicago v. Morales,* 527 U.S. 41 (1999).
51. 277 U.S. 438 (1928). This decision was overruled later in *Katz v. United States,* 389 U.S. 347 (1967).
52. 381 U.S. 479 (1965).

foundation for his reasoning: "The enumeration in the Constitution, of certain rights, shall not be construed to deny or disparage [belittle] others retained by the people." In other words, just because the Constitution, including its amendments, does not specifically talk about the right to privacy does not mean that this right is denied to the people.

Some of today's most controversial issues relate to privacy rights. One issue involves the erosion of privacy rights in an information age, as computers make it easier to compile and distribute personal information. Other issues concern abortion and the "right to die." Since the terrorist attacks of September 11, 2001, Americans have faced another crucial question regarding privacy rights: To what extent should Americans sacrifice privacy rights in the interests of national security?

PRIVACY RIGHTS IN AN INFORMATION AGE

An important privacy issue, created in part by new technology, is the amassing of information on individuals by government agencies and private businesses such as marketing firms. Personal information on the average American citizen is filed away in dozens of agencies—such as the Social Security Administration and the Internal Revenue Service. Because of the threat of indiscriminate use of private information by unauthorized individuals, Congress passed the Privacy Act in 1974. This was the first law regulating the use of federal government information about private individuals. Under the Privacy Act, every citizen has the right to obtain copies of personal records collected by federal agencies and to correct inaccuracies in such records.

The ease with which personal information can be obtained by using the Internet for marketing and other purposes has led to unique privacy issues. Some fear that privacy rights in personal information may soon be a thing of the past. Whether privacy rights can survive in an information age is a question that Americans continue to confront.

PRIVACY RIGHTS AND ABORTION

Historically, abortion was not a criminal offense before the "quickening" of the fetus (the first movement of the fetus in the uterus, usually between the sixteenth and eighteenth weeks of pregnancy). During the last half of the nineteenth century, however, state laws became more severe. By 1973, performing an abortion at any time during pregnancy was a criminal offense in a majority of the states.

Roe v. Wade. In 1973, in *Roe v. Wade,*[53] the United States Supreme Court accepted the argument that the laws against abortion violated "Jane Roe's" right to privacy under the Constitution. The Court held that during the first trimester (three months) of pregnancy, abortion was an issue solely between a woman and her physician. The state could not limit abortions except to require that they be performed by licensed physicians. During the second trimester, to protect the health of the mother, the state was allowed to specify the conditions under which an abortion could be performed. During the final trimester, the state could regulate or even outlaw abortions except when necessary to preserve the life or health of the mother.

After the *Roe* case, the Supreme Court issued decisions in a number of cases defining and redefining the boundaries of state regulation of abortion. During the 1980s, the Court twice struck down laws that required a woman who wished to have an abortion to undergo counseling designed to discourage abortions. In the late 1980s and early 1990s, however, the Court took a more conservative approach. For example, in *Webster v. Reproductive Health Services*[54] in 1989, the Court upheld a Missouri statute that, among other things, banned the use of public hospitals or other taxpayer-supported facilities for

---

53. 410 U.S. 113 (1973). Jane Roe was not the real name of the woman in this case. It is a common legal pseudonym used to protect a person's privacy.
54. 492 U.S. 490 (1989).

performing abortions. And, in *Planned Parenthood v. Casey*[55] in 1992, the Court upheld a Pennsylvania law that required preabortion counseling, a waiting period of twenty-four hours, and, for girls under the age of eighteen, parental or judicial permission. As a result, abortions are now more difficult to obtain in some states than others.

Protests at Abortion Clinics. Abortion continues to be a divisive issue. Right-to-life forces continue to push for laws banning abortion, to endorse political candidates who support their views, and to organize protests. Because of several episodes of violence attending protests at abortion clinics, in 1994 Congress passed the Freedom of Access to Clinic Entrances Act. The act prohibits protesters from blocking entrances to such clinics. The Supreme Court ruled in 1993 that such protesters can be prosecuted under laws governing racketeering, and in 1998 a federal court in Illinois convicted right-to-life protesters under these laws. In 2006, however, the Supreme Court unanimously reversed its earlier decision that right-to-life protesters could be prosecuted under laws governing racketeering.[56]

In 1997, the Supreme Court upheld the constitutionality of prohibiting protesters from entering a fifteen-foot "buffer zone" around abortion clinics and from giving unwanted counseling to those entering the clinics.[57] In a 2000 decision, the Court upheld a Colorado law requiring demonstrators to stay at least eight feet away from people entering and leaving clinics unless people consented to be approached. The Court concluded that the law's restrictions on speech-related conduct did not violate the free speech rights of abortion protesters.[58]

The North Lee County Right to Life Organization sponsored an anti-abortion rally in Fort Madison, Iowa, in 2008. What Supreme Court case do pro-life supporters want to have overturned? (AP Photo/The Hawk Eye, John Lovretta)

Partial-Birth Abortion. Another issue in the abortion controversy concerns partial-birth abortion. A partial-birth abortion, which physicians call intact dilation and extraction, is a procedure that can be used during the second trimester of pregnancy. Abortion rights advocates claim that in limited circumstances the procedure is the safest way to perform an abortion and that the government should never outlaw specific medical procedures. Opponents argue that the procedure has no medical merit and that it ends the life of a fetus that might be able to live outside the womb.

In 2000, the Supreme Court addressed this issue when it reviewed a Nebraska law banning partial-birth abortions. Similar laws had been passed by at least twenty-seven states. The Court invalidated the Nebraska law on the ground that, as written, the law could be used to ban other abortion procedures and contained no provisions for protecting the health of the pregnant woman.[59] In 2007, the Supreme Court revisited the issue of partial-birth abortion when it reviewed two cases involving a 2003 federal law similar to the Nebraska statute. In 2007, however, in a close (five-to-four) vote, the Supreme Court upheld the federal law. The Court stated that the opponents of the act "have not demonstrated that the act would be unconstitutional in a large fraction of relevant cases." Furthermore, said the Court, "government has a legitimate and substantial interest in

---

55. 505 U.S. 833 (1992).
56. *Scheidler v. National Organization for Women,* 547 U.S. 9 (2006).
57. *Schenck v. ProChoice Network,* 519 U.S. 357 (1997).
58. *Hill v. Colorado,* 530 U.S. 703 (2000).
59. *Stenberg v. Carhart,* 530 U.S. 914 (2000).

preserving and promoting fetal life." The Court also noted that there was an alternative (though less safe, according to the act's opponents) abortion procedure that could be used in the second trimester. Also, the Court emphasized that the law allowed partial-birth abortion to be performed when a woman's life was in jeopardy.

Note that the Court's 2007 ruling concerned how abortions could be effected, not whether abortions were legal—the central issue in *Roe v. Wade*. The Court emphasized this by stating that although the government may not forbid abortion outright, it "may use its voice and its regulatory authority" to dissuade women from ending pregnancies. In her dissent to the majority opinion, Justice Ruth Bader Ginsburg said that the ruling "cannot be understood as anything other than an effort to chip away at a right declared again and again by this Court"—that right being a woman's right to choose.[60]

PRIVACY RIGHTS AND THE "RIGHT TO DIE"

A 1976 case involving Karen Ann Quinlan was one of the first publicized right-to-die cases.[61] The parents of Quinlan, a young woman who had been in a coma for nearly a year and who had been kept alive during that time by a respirator, wanted her respirator removed. In 1976, the New Jersey Supreme Court ruled that the right to privacy includes the right of a patient to refuse treatment and that patients unable to speak can exercise that right through a family member or guardian. In 1990, the Supreme Court took up the issue. In *Cruzan v. Director, Missouri Department of Health,*[62] the Court stated that a patient's life-sustaining treatment can be withdrawn at the request of a family member only if there is "clear and convincing evidence" that the patient did not want such treatment.

What If There Is No Living Will? Since the 1976 *Quinlan* decision, most states have enacted laws permitting people to designate their wishes concerning life-sustaining procedures in "living wills" or durable health-care powers of attorney. These laws and the Supreme Court's *Cruzan* decision have resolved the right-to-die controversy for situations in which the patient has drafted a living will. Disputes are still possible if there is no living will. An example is the case of Terri Schiavo. The husband of the Florida woman who had been in a persistent vegetative state for over a decade sought to have her feeding tube removed on the basis of oral statements that she would not want her life prolonged in such circumstances. Schiavo's parents fought this move in court but lost on the ground that a spouse, not a parent, is the appropriate legal guardian for a married person. Although the Florida legislature passed a law allowing Governor Jeb Bush to overrule the courts, the state supreme court held that the law violated the state constitution.[63]

In March 2005, the U.S. Congress intervened and passed a law allowing Schiavo's case to be heard in the federal court system. The federal courts, however, essentially agreed with the Florida state courts and refused to order the reconnection of the feeding tube, which had been disconnected a few days earlier. After twice appealing to the United States Supreme Court without success, the parents gave up hope, and Schiavo died shortly thereafter.

Physician-Assisted Suicide. In the 1990s, another issue surfaced: Do privacy rights include the right of terminally ill people to end their lives through physician-assisted suicide? Until 1996, the courts consistently upheld state laws that prohibited this practice, either through specific statutes or under their general homicide statutes. In 1996, after two federal appellate courts ruled that state laws banning assisted suicide (in Washington and New York) were unconstitutional, the issue reached the United States Supreme Court.

60. *Gonzales v. Carhart,* 127 S.Ct. 1610 (2007); and *Gonzales v. Planned Parenthood,* 127 S.Ct. 1610 (2007).
61. *In re Quinlan,* 70 N.J. 10 (1976).
62. 497 U.S. 261 (1990).
63. *Bush v. Schiavo,* 885 So.2d 321 (Fla. 2004).

In 1997, in *Washington v. Glucksberg*,[64] the Court stated that the liberty interest protected by the Constitution does not include a right to commit suicide, with or without assistance. In effect, the Supreme Court left the decision to the states. Since then, assisted suicide has been allowed in only two states—Oregon and Washington. In 2006, the Supreme Court upheld Oregon's physician-assisted suicide law against a challenge from the Bush administration.[65]

PRIVACY RIGHTS VERSUS SECURITY ISSUES

As former Supreme Court justice Thurgood Marshall once said, "Grave threats to liberty often come in times of urgency, when constitutional rights seem too extravagant to endure." Not surprisingly, antiterrorist legislation since the attacks on September 11, 2001, has eroded certain basic rights, in particular the Fourth Amendment protections against unreasonable searches and seizures.

Physician-assisted suicide continues to be an emotional issue for many Americans. Only the state of Oregon has legislation supporting such action by physicians. Does the Constitution give any guidelines about the "right to die" controversy? (AP Photo/ Charles Dharapak)

Current legislation allows the government to conduct "roving" wiretaps. Previously, roving wiretaps could be requested only for persons suspected of one of a small number of serious crimes. Now if persons are suspected of planning a terrorist attack, they can be monitored no matter what form of electronic communication they use. Such roving wiretaps contravene the Supreme Court's interpretation of the Fourth Amendment, which requires a judicial warrant to describe the *place* to be searched, not just the person. One of the goals of the framers was to avoid *general* searches. Further, once a judge approves an application for a roving wiretap, when, how, and where the monitoring occurs will be left to the discretion of law enforcement agents. Supporters of these new procedures say that they allow agents to monitor individuals as they move about the nation. Previously, a warrant issued in one federal district might not be valid in another.

The USA Patriot Act. Much of the government's failure to anticipate the attacks of September 11, 2001, has been attributed to a lack of cooperation among government agencies. At that time, barriers prevented information sharing between the law enforcement and intelligence arms of the government. Lawmakers claimed that the USA Patriot Act of 2001 would improve lines of communication between agencies such as the Federal Bureau of Investigation (FBI) and the Central Intelligence Agency (CIA), allowing the government to better anticipate terrorist plots.

In addition, the Patriot Act eased restrictions on the government's ability to investigate and arrest suspected terrorists. Because of the secretive nature of terrorist groups, supporters of the Patriot Act argue that the government must have greater latitude in pursuing leads on potential terrorist activity. The act authorizes law enforcement officials to secretly search a suspected terrorist's home. It also allows the government to monitor a suspect's Internet activities, phone conversations, financial records, and book purchases. For the first time in American history, the government can even open a suspect's mail. Although a number of these search and surveillance tactics have long been a part of criminal investigations, the Patriot Act expanded their scope and streamlined the process of obtaining warrants to use them.

64. 521 U.S. 702 (1997).
65. *Gonzales v. Oregon,* 546 U.S. 243 (2006).

Civil Liberties and the Patriot Act. Proponents of the Patriot Act insist that ordinary, law-abiding citizens have nothing to fear from the government's increased search and surveillance powers. Groups such as the American Civil Liberties Union have objected to the Patriot Act, however, arguing that it poses a grave threat to constitutionally guaranteed rights and liberties. Under the Patriot Act, FBI agents are required to certify the need for search warrants to the court, but the court cannot, in fact, reject the request for a warrant.

The Patriot Act also authorized National Security Letters (NSLs), which are subpoenas issued by the FBI itself and which do not require probable cause or judicial oversight. In addition, an individual or financial institution that is served with such a warrant cannot speak about the government's investigation to anyone. Thus, many argue that this provision of the Patriot Act contradicts the First Amendment by making free speech a crime. In addition to First Amendment issues, this provision raises the concern that no one would be allowed to blow the whistle on abuses of the government's powers. As a result of these concerns, a U.S. district court found the NSL provisions of the Patriot Act to be unconstitutional in 2004 and again in 2007.[66]

Finally, if the government decides to take a suspected terrorist into custody, the suspect can be summarily denied bail—a breach of the Eighth Amendment. Opponents of the Patriot Act fear that these expanded powers of investigation might be used to silence government critics or to threaten members of interest groups who oppose government policies today or in the future. Congress debated all of these issues in 2005 and then renewed most of the provisions of the act in 2006. It is certainly true that the government has used the Patriot Act to develop cases that have nothing at all to do with terrorism, as we show in this chapter's *Politics and the Cyber Sphere* feature on the next page.

Secret Surveillance. Shortly after 9/11, President George W. Bush issued an executive order authorizing the National Security Agency (NSA) to conduct secret surveillance. The NSA was ordered to monitor, without obtaining warrants, phone calls and other communications between foreign parties and persons within the United States when one of the parties had suspected links to a terrorist organization. When the American public learned of this secret program in December 2005, the news led to intense criticism by civil rights groups. These groups and other Americans called for the immediate termination of the allegedly illegal surveillance.

In 2007, Congress passed a law to authorize the warrantless NSA wiretaps. The law expired in 2008, however, and its reauthorization was held up by a dispute between Congress and the Bush administration as to whether telephone companies should receive blanket immunity from lawsuits stemming from their past cooperation with the wiretaps. President Bush threatened to veto any reauthorization that did not grant the immunity. As of mid-2008, the courts had not yet ruled on the constitutionality of the warrantless wiretaps.

This is a photo of the Threat Operation Center of the National Security Agency (NSA), which is located at Fort Meade, Maryland. Not much is known about how the ultra-secret NSA operates, although investigative reporters learned in December 2005 that the NSA was secretly monitoring domestic phone calls without obtaining warrants. What part of the Constitution might have been violated by such actions? (Jason Reed/Reuters/Corbis)

---

66. *Doe v. Ashcroft,* 334 F.Supp.2d 471 (S.D.N.Y. 2004); and *Doe v. Gonzales,* 500 F.Supp.2d 379 (S.D.N.Y. 2007).

POLITICS AND...
the cyber sphere

SOME UNINTENDED CONSEQUENCES OF THE PATRIOT ACT

"Client 9" had arranged to meet a prostitute named "Kristen" in room 871 of the Mayflower Hotel in Washington, D.C. Kristen reported back to her employer that Client 9 had paid her $4,300 (part of this amount was offered as a "down payment" for the next encounter). Not too long afterward, federal investigators informed the governor of New York, Eliot Spitzer, that they knew he was Client 9. Spitzer eventually resigned in one of the most high-profile sex scandals in his state's history. Less widely known is the fact that it was the USA Patriot Act that caused him to be snagged by the federal government.

AFTER THE 9/11 ATTACKS, CONGRESS PASSED THE PATRIOT ACT

Most law enforcement agencies hailed the Patriot Act as a powerful tool that would allow them to track down the accomplices of Osama bin Laden, the mastermind behind the suicide attacks against the World Trade Center Towers in New York City and the Pentagon in Washington, D.C. The Patriot Act gave the Federal Bureau of Investigation (FBI) increased authority to snoop on unsuspecting terrorists.

In the fine print of that act, the Treasury Department was authorized to demand more information from banks about financial transactions. The goal was to seek out terrorists who were laundering money through the U.S. banking system. Banks are now required to report any unusual transactions by submitting Suspicious Activity Reports (SARs). Banks spent tens of millions of dollars to develop sophisticated software to do just that. In 2001, they submitted 200,000 SARs, and that number has jumped to about 1.5 million today. These data are stored in an Internal Revenue Service (IRS) building in Detroit and are accessible by law enforcement agencies throughout the country.

THE NET CLOSES AROUND ELIOT SPITZER

In the summer of 2007, New York's North Force Bank filed a SAR about money transfers that Governor Spitzer had made. Spitzer had asked the bank to transfer funds in someone else's name. Federal authorities became curious enough to follow the money trail. They ultimately discovered that New York's governor had wired $80,000 to various accounts that looked suspicious. The authorities then learned that the accounts were owned by an Internet prostitution service. The rest is now part of New York's colorful history.

FOR CRITICAL ANALYSIS

Why do you think banks in this country cooperate so completely with the federal government?

THE GREAT BALANCING ACT: THE RIGHTS OF THE ACCUSED VERSUS THE RIGHTS OF SOCIETY

The United States has one of the highest murder rates in the industrialized world. It is not surprising, therefore, that many citizens have extremely strong opinions about the rights of those accused of violent crimes. When an accused person, especially one who has confessed to some criminal act, is set free because of an apparent legal "technicality," many people believe that the rights of the accused are being given more weight than the rights of society and of potential or actual victims. Why, then, give criminal suspects rights? The answer is partly to avoid convicting innocent people, but mostly because due process of law and fair treatment benefit everyone who comes in contact with law enforcement or the courts.

The courts and the police must constantly engage in a balancing act of competing rights. At the basis of all discussions about the appropriate balance is, of course, the U.S. Bill of Rights. The Fourth, Fifth, Sixth, and Eighth Amendments deal specifically with the rights of criminal defendants. (You will learn about some of your rights under the Fourth Amendment in the *Why Should You Care about Civil Liberties?* feature at the end of this chapter.)

RIGHTS OF THE ACCUSED

The basic rights of criminal defendants are outlined next. When appropriate, the specific constitutional provision or amendment on which a right is based is also given.

Limits on the Conduct of Police Officers and Prosecutors

- No unreasonable or unwarranted searches and seizures (Amend. IV).
- No arrest except on probable cause (Amend. IV).
- No coerced confessions or illegal interrogation (Amend. V).
- No entrapment.
- On questioning, a suspect must be informed of her or his rights.

Defendant's Pretrial Rights

- **Writ of *habeas corpus*** (Article I, Section 9).
- Prompt **arraignment** (Amend. VI).
- Legal counsel (Amend. VI).
- Reasonable bail (Amend. VIII).
- To be informed of charges (Amend. VI).
- To remain silent (Amend. V).

Trial Rights

- Speedy and public trial before a jury (Amend. VI).
- Impartial jury selected from a cross section of the community (Amend. VI).
- Trial atmosphere free of prejudice, fear, and outside interference.
- No compulsory self-incrimination (Amend. V).
- Adequate counsel (Amend. VI).
- No cruel and unusual punishment (Amend. VIII).
- Appeal of convictions.
- No double jeopardy (Amend. V).

EXTENDING THE RIGHTS OF THE ACCUSED

During the 1960s, the Supreme Court, under Chief Justice Earl Warren, significantly expanded the rights of accused persons. In *Gideon v. Wainwright*,[67] a case decided in 1963, the Court held that if a person is accused of a felony and cannot afford an attorney, an attorney must be made available to the accused person at the government's expense. Although the Sixth Amendment to the Constitution provides for the right to counsel, the Supreme Court had established a precedent twenty-one years earlier in *Betts v. Brady*,[68] when it held that only criminal defendants in capital (death penalty) cases automatically had a right to legal counsel.

Miranda v. Arizona. In 1966, the Court issued its decision in *Miranda v. Arizona*.[69] The case involved Ernesto Miranda, who was arrested and charged with the kidnapping and rape of a young woman. After two hours of questioning, Miranda confessed and was later convicted. Miranda's lawyer appealed his conviction, arguing that the police had never informed Miranda that he had a right to remain silent and a right to be represented by counsel. The Court, in ruling in Miranda's favor, enunciated the *Miranda* rights that are now familiar to virtually all Americans:

> *Prior to any questioning, the person must be warned that he has a right to remain silent, that any statement he does make may be used against him, and that he has a right to the presence of an attorney, either retained or appointed.*

Writ of *Habeas Corpus*
Habeas corpus means, literally, "you have the body." A writ of *habeas corpus* is an order that requires jailers to bring a prisoner before a court or a judge and explain why the person is being held.

Arraignment
The first act in a criminal proceeding, in which the defendant is brought before a court to hear the charges against him or her and enter a plea of guilty or not guilty.

---

67. 372 U.S. 335 (1963).
68. 316 U.S. 455 (1942).
69. 384 U.S. 436 (1966).

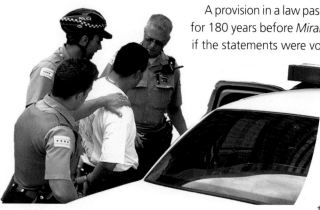

These three police officers are taking a man into custody outside the Chicago Art Institute. While he is in the patrol car, can the police officers legally interrogate him? Why or why not? (grendelkhan/Creative Commons)

A provision in a law passed by Congress in 1968 reinstated a rule that had been in effect for 180 years before *Miranda*—that statements by defendants can be used against them if the statements were voluntarily made. The Justice Department refused to enforce the provision, however, and in 2000 the Supreme Court held that the Miranda warnings were constitutionally based and could not be overruled by a legislative act.[70]

Exceptions to the Miranda Rule. As part of a continuing attempt to balance the rights of accused persons against the rights of society, the Supreme Court has made a number of exceptions to the *Miranda* rule. In 1984, for example, the Court recognized a "public-safety" exception to the rule. The need to protect the public warranted the admissibility of statements made by the defendant (in this case, indicating where he had placed a gun) as evidence in a trial, even though the defendant had not been informed of his *Miranda* rights.

In 1985, the Court further held that a confession need not be excluded even though the police failed to inform a suspect in custody that his attorney had tried to reach him by telephone. In an important 1991 decision, the Court stated that a suspect's conviction will not be automatically overturned if the suspect was coerced into making a confession. If the other evidence admitted at trial is strong enough to justify the conviction without the confession, then the fact that the confession was obtained illegally in effect can be ignored. In yet another case, in 1994, the Supreme Court ruled that suspects must unequivocally and assertively state their right to counsel in order to stop police questioning. Saying, "Maybe I should talk to a lawyer" during an interrogation after being taken into custody is not enough. The Court held that police officers are not required to decipher the suspect's intentions in such situations.

Video Recording of Interrogations. In view of the numerous exceptions, there are no guarantees that the *Miranda* rule will survive indefinitely. Increasingly, though, law enforcement personnel are using digital movie cameras to record interrogations. According to some scholars, the recording of *all* custodial interrogations would satisfy the Fifth Amendment's prohibition against coercion and in the process render the *Miranda* warnings unnecessary. Others argue, however, that recorded interrogations can be misleading.

THE EXCLUSIONARY RULE

At least since 1914, judicial policy has prohibited the admission of illegally seized evidence at trials in federal courts. This is the so-called **exclusionary rule.** Improperly obtained evidence, no matter how telling, cannot be used by prosecutors. This includes evidence obtained by police in violation of a suspect's *Miranda* rights or of the Fourth Amendment. The Fourth Amendment protects against unreasonable searches and seizures and provides that a judge may issue a search warrant to a police officer only on *probable cause* (a demonstration of facts that permit a reasonable belief that a crime has been committed). The courts must determine what constitutes an "unreasonable" search and seizure.

The reasoning behind the exclusionary rule is that it forces police officers to gather evidence properly, in which case their due diligence will be rewarded by a conviction. Nevertheless, the exclusionary rule has always had critics who argue that it permits guilty persons to be freed because of innocent errors.

Exclusionary Rule
A judicial policy prohibiting the admission at trial of illegally seized evidence.

This rule was first extended to state court proceedings in a 1961 United States Supreme Court decision, *Mapp v. Ohio.*[71] In this case, the Court overturned the conviction of Dollree Mapp for the possession of obscene materials. Police found pornographic books

---

70. *Dickerson v. United States,* 530 U.S. 428 (2000).
71. 367 U.S. 643 (1961).

in her apartment after searching it without a search warrant and despite her refusal to let them in.

Over the last several decades, the Supreme Court has diminished the scope of the exclusionary rule by creating some exceptions to its applicability. For example, in 1984 the Court held that illegally obtained evidence could be admitted at trial if law enforcement personnel could prove that they would have obtained the evidence legally anyway. In another case decided in the same year, the Court held that a police officer who used a technically incorrect search warrant form to obtain evidence had acted in good faith and therefore the evidence was admissible at trial. The Court thus created the "good faith" exception to the exclusionary rule.

Under the Fourth Amendment, search warrants must describe the persons or things to be seized. In addition, however, officers are entitled to seize items not mentioned in the search warrant if the materials are in "plain view" and reasonably appear to be contraband or evidence of a crime.[72]

THE DEATH PENALTY

Capital punishment remains one of the most debated aspects of our criminal justice system. Those in favor of the death penalty maintain that it serves as a deterrent to serious crime and satisfies society's need for justice and fair play. Those opposed to the death penalty do not believe it has any deterrent value and hold that it constitutes a barbaric act in an otherwise civilized society.

CRUEL AND UNUSUAL PUNISHMENT?

The Eighth Amendment prohibits cruel and unusual punishment. Throughout history, "cruel and unusual" referred to punishments that were more serious than the crimes—the phrase referred to torture and to executions that prolonged the agony of dying. The Supreme Court never interpreted "cruel and unusual" to prohibit all forms of capital punishment in all circumstances. Indeed, a number of states had imposed the death penalty for a variety of crimes and allowed juries to decide when the condemned could be sentenced to death. Many believed, however, that the imposition of the death penalty was random and arbitrary, and in 1972 the Supreme Court agreed, in *Furman v. Georgia*.[73]

The Supreme Court's 1972 decision stated that the death penalty, as then applied, violated the Eighth and Fourteenth Amendments. The Court ruled that capital punishment is not necessarily cruel and unusual if the criminal has killed or attempted to kill someone. In its opinion, the Court invited the states to enact more precise laws so that the death penalty would be applied more consistently. By 1976, twenty-five states had adopted a two-stage, or *bifurcated*, procedure for capital cases. In the first stage, a jury determines the guilt or innocence of the defendant for a crime that has been determined by statute to be punishable by death. If the defendant is found guilty, the jury reconvenes in the second stage and considers all relevant evidence to decide whether the death sentence is, in fact, warranted.

In 1976, in *Gregg v. Georgia*,[74] the Supreme Court ruled in favor of Georgia's bifurcated process, holding that the state's legislative guidelines had removed the ability of a jury to "wantonly and freakishly impose the death penalty." The Court upheld similar procedures in Texas and Florida, establishing a "road map" for all states to follow that would assure them protection from lawsuits based on Eighth Amendment grounds.

didyouknow...

That in eighteenth-century England, pocket picking and similar crimes were punishable by the death penalty?

Capital punishment elicits strong sentiment by those who are for or against this criminal penalty. Is the death penalty a "cruel and unusual" punishment and therefore prohibited by the Eighth Amendment? (AP Photo/Charles Smith)

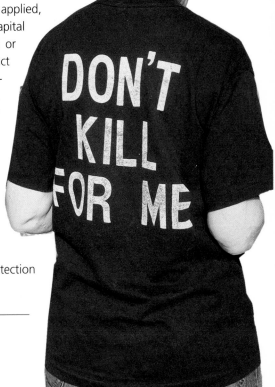

---

72. *Texas v. Brown,* 460 U.S. 730 (1983); and *Horton v. California,* 496 U.S. 128 (1990).
73. 408 U.S. 238 (1972).
74. 428 U.S. 153 (1976).

THE DEATH PENALTY TODAY

Today, thirty-seven states (see Figure 4–1) and the federal government have capital punishment laws based on the guidelines established by the *Gregg* case. State governments are responsible for almost all executions in this country. The executions of Timothy McVeigh and Juan Raul Garza in 2001 marked the first death sentences carried out by the federal government since 1963. At this time, there are about 3,350 prisoners on death row across the nation.

The number of executions per year reached a high in 1998 at ninety-eight and then began to fall. Some believe that the declining number of executions reflects the waning support among Americans for the imposition of the death penalty. In 1994, polls indicated that 80 percent of Americans supported the death penalty in cases involving murder. Recent polls, however, suggest that this number has dropped to about 65 percent.

The decline in the number of executions may be due in part to the Supreme Court's 2002 ruling in *Ring v. Arizona*.[75] The Court held that only juries, not judges, could impose the death penalty, thus invalidating the laws of five states that allowed judges to make this decision. The ruling meant that the death sentences of 168 death row inmates would have to be reconsidered by the relevant courts. The sentences of many of these inmates have been commuted to life in prison. (For a further discussion of why the death penalty is in retreat, see this chapter's *Politics and the Death Penalty* feature.)

---

75. 536 U.S. 548 (2002).

FIGURE 4–1: The States and the Death Penalty: Executions since 1976 and the Death Row Population

Today, as shown in this figure, thirteen states have abolished the death penalty. The most recent state to act was New Jersey, which abolished the penalty in 2007. The District of Columbia, Puerto Rico, Guam, and the U.S. Virgin Islands also have no death penalty. In two states—New York in 2004 and Nebraska in 2008—the state supreme court has ruled the existing death penalty law unconstitutional. In neither state has the legislature attempted to pass a new law. New Hampshire has the death penalty but has not sentenced anyone to death since 1972. Kansas and the U.S. military both have inmates on death row but have not actually executed anyone since 1972.

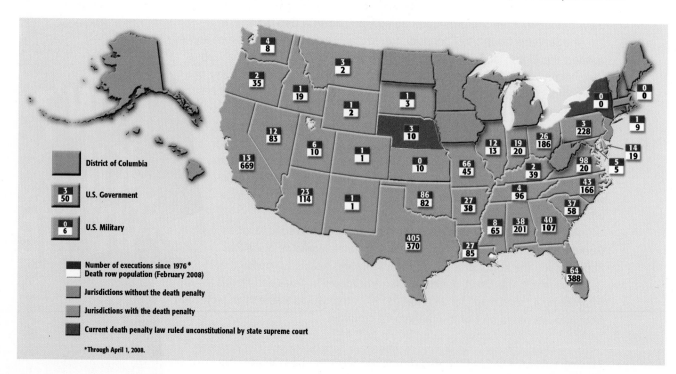

Source: Death Penalty Information Center.

politicsand...the death penalty

THE HIGH COST OF DEFENSE COUNSEL OFTEN MAKES CAPITAL PUNISHMENT IMPRACTICAL

In 2005, before multiple witnesses, Brian Nichols shot and killed a judge, a court reporter, a sheriff's deputy, and a federal agent in an Atlanta, Georgia, courthouse. State prosecutors asked for the death penalty. In July 2007, however, the Georgia agency that pays the lawyers of indigent defendants ran out of funds for Nichols's defense, and in October the presiding judge suspended the trial indefinitely. Between the costs of the prosecution and the defense, Nichols's case is expected to cost more than $5 million.

Enter into the world of the death penalty cases. They are expensive and getting more so. The New Jersey Policy Perspective, a research group, estimated that capital punishment cost the state $256 million since 1983, including $60 million for defense. By 2007, when the death penalty was abolished in New Jersey, the state had yet to execute a single inmate.

WHY THE HIGH COST OF DEFENDING MURDERERS?

In 2003, the American Bar Association outlined guidelines for defense attorneys taking on death penalty cases. Those attorneys must have special skills and undertake "extraordinary efforts" because of the irreversible nature of the punishment. There must be at least two lawyers on the case at all times. The defense must undertake independent investigations at every phase of the appeals process.

The Supreme Court has cited these guidelines when reversing a trial court's imposition of the death penalty. In one case, the Court found that a "more thorough review by the defense" might have unearthed information that the jury should have heard before imposing the death penalty.

WHAT EACH DEFENSE TEAM MUST DO

The long and the short of the problem is that every defense team helping a convicted criminal who faces the death penalty has to review all of the information and investigate every witness. In the case against Brian Nichols, there were 400 potential witnesses for the prosecution. The defense team also had to read 32,000 pages of documents and review 400 hours of taped telephone calls.

One New Mexico Supreme Court case was suspended recently because the court believed that the defense team's lawyers were being paid so little by the state that it was unlikely that they would be effective. One judge in Utah wondered how well a death penalty appeal would be carried out when the effective wage rate for a defense attorney from the public defender's office was only $10 an hour. In Arizona, California, Louisiana, and Texas, death row inmates wait more than three years to have lawyers assigned to their cases because those states won't raise their hourly rates.

FOR CRITICAL ANALYSIS

Some argue that even though the Supreme Court recently ruled that legal injection is allowed—and therefore, death penalty cases that had been on hold for many months can now go forward—there will be almost no executions, because few convicted killers will be able to obtain "effective" defense counsel. Why do you think the right to counsel is so fundamental?

TIME LIMITS FOR DEATH ROW APPEALS

In 1996, Congress passed the Anti-Terrorism and Effective Death Penalty Act. The law limits access to the federal courts for all defendants convicted in state courts. It also imposes a severe time limit on death row appeals. The law requires federal judges to hear these appeals and issue their opinions within a specified time period. Many are concerned that the shortened appeals process increases the possibility that innocent persons may be put to death. Recently, DNA testing has shown that some innocent people may have been convicted unjustly of murder. Since 1973, more than one hundred prisoners have been freed from death row after new evidence suggested that they were convicted wrongfully. On average, it takes about seven years to exonerate someone on death row. Currently, however, the time between conviction and execution has been shortened from an average of ten to twelve years to an average of six to eight years.

WHY SHOULD YOU CARE ABOUT
civil liberties?

(AP Photo/Carlos Osorio)

Our civil liberties include numerous provisions, many of them listed in the Bill of Rights, that protect persons who are suspected of criminal activity. Among these are limits on how the police—as agents of the government—can conduct searches and seizures.

CIVIL LIBERTIES AND YOUR LIFE

You may be the most law-abiding person in the world, but that will not guarantee that you will never be stopped, arrested, or searched by the police. Sooner or later, the great majority of all citizens will have some kind of interaction with the police. People who do not understand their rights or how to behave toward law enforcement officers can find themselves in serious trouble. The words of advice in this feature actually provide you with key survival skills for life in the modern world.

HOW YOU CAN MAKE A DIFFERENCE

How should you behave if you are stopped by police officers? Your civil liberties protect you from having to provide information other than your name and address. Normally, even if you have not been placed under arrest, the officers have the right to frisk you for weapons, and you must let them proceed. The officers cannot, however, check your person or your clothing further if, in their judgment, no weaponlike object is produced.

The officers may search you only if they have a search warrant or probable cause to believe that a search will likely produce incriminating evidence. What if the officers do not have probable cause or a warrant? Physically resisting their attempt to search you can lead to disastrous results. It is best simply to refuse orally to give permission for the search, preferably in the presence of a witness. Being polite is better than acting out of anger and making the officers irritable. It is usually advisable to limit what you say to the officers. If you are arrested, it is best to keep quiet until you can speak with a lawyer.

If you are in your car and are stopped by the police, the same fundamental rules apply. Always be ready to show your driver's license and car registration. You may be asked to get out of the car. The officers may use a flashlight to peer inside if it is too dark to see otherwise. None of this constitutes a search. A true search requires either a warrant or probable cause. No officer has the legal right to search your car simply to find out if you may have committed a crime. Police officers can conduct searches that are incident to lawful arrests, however.

If you are in your home and a police officer with a search warrant appears, you can ask to examine the warrant before granting entry. A warrant that is correctly made out will state the place or persons to be searched, the object sought, and the date of the warrant (which should be no more than ten days old); and it will bear the signature of a judge or magistrate. If the warrant is in order, you need not make any statement. If you believe the warrant to be invalid, or if no warrant is produced, you should make it clear orally that you have not consented to the search, preferably in the presence of a witness. If the search later is proved to be unlawful, normally any evidence obtained cannot be used in court.

Officers who attempt to enter your home without a search warrant can do so only if they are pursuing a suspected felon into the house. Rarely is it advisable to give permission for a warrantless search. You, as the resident, must be the one to give permission if any evidence obtained is to be considered legal. The landlord, manager, or head of a college dormitory cannot give legal permission. A roommate, however, can give permission for a search of his or her room, which may allow the police to search areas where you have belongings.

If you are a guest in a place that is being legally searched, you may be legally searched as well. But unless you have been placed under arrest, you cannot be compelled to go to the police station or get into a squad car.

If you would like to find out more about your rights and obligations under the laws of searches and seizures, you might want to contact the following organization:

American Civil Liberties Union
125 Broad St., 18th Floor
New York, NY 10004
212-549-2500
www.aclu.org

QUESTIONS FOR
discussionandanalysis

1. Review the *Which Side Are You On?* feature on page 121. To what extent should college campuses accommodate the religious needs of students? Does installing footbaths that especially benefit Muslims (although the footbaths can be used by anyone) go too far? Why or why not?

2. If freedom of speech were not a constitutional right, but merely a matter of tradition and custom, in what ways might the government be tempted to limit it?

3. The courts have never held that the provision of military chaplains by the armed forces is unconstitutional, despite the fact that chaplains are religious leaders who are employed by and under the authority of the U.S. government. What arguments might the courts use to defend the military chaplain system?

4. The courts have banned the teaching of the theory of creation by intelligent design in public school biology classes, arguing that the theory is based on religion, not science. Indeed, it is not hard to detect a religious basis in the classroom materials recently disseminated by the intelligent design movement. Is it possible to make an argument in favor of intelligent design that would not promote a religious belief?

5. In a surprisingly large number of cases, arrested individuals do not choose to exercise their right to remain silent. Why might a person not exercise his or her *Miranda* rights?

keyterms

actual malice 128
arraignment 137
clear and present
    danger test 123
commercial speech 123
defamation of
    character 125

establishment
    clause 113
exclusionary rule 138
free exercise clause 113
gag order 128

incorporation
    theory 113
libel 128
prior restraint 120
public figure 128

slander 126
symbolic speech 122
writ of *habeas
    corpus* 137

chaptersummary

1. Originally, the Bill of Rights limited only the power of the national government, not that of the states. Gradually and selectively, however, the Supreme Court accepted the incorporation theory, under which no state can violate most provisions of the Bill of Rights.

2. The First Amendment protects against government interference with freedom of religion by requiring a separation of church and state (under the establishment clause) and by guaranteeing the free exercise of religion. Controversial issues that arise under the establishment clause include the following: aid to church-related schools, school prayer, the teaching of evolution versus intelligent design, school vouchers, the posting of the Ten Commandments in public places, and discrimination against religious speech. The government can interfere with the free exercise of religion only when religious practices work against public policy or the public welfare.

3. The First Amendment protects against government interference with freedom of speech, which includes symbolic speech (expressive conduct). The Supreme Court has been especially critical of government actions that impose prior restraint on expression. Commercial speech (advertising) by businesses has received limited First Amendment protection. Restrictions on expression are permitted when the expression creates a clear and present danger to the peace or public order. Speech that has not received First Amendment protection includes expression judged to be obscene or slanderous.

4. The First Amendment protects against government interference with the freedom of the press, which can be regarded as a special instance of freedom of speech. Speech by the press that does not receive protection includes libelous statements. Publication of news about a criminal trial may be restricted by a gag order in some circumstances.

5. The First Amendment protects the right to assemble peaceably and to petition the government. Permits may be required for parades, sound trucks, and demonstrations to maintain the public order, and a permit may be denied to protect the public safety.

6. Under the Ninth Amendment, rights not specifically mentioned in the Constitution are not necessarily denied to the people. Among these unspecified rights protected by the courts is a right to privacy, which has been inferred from the First, Third, Fourth, Fifth, and Ninth Amendments. A major privacy issue today is how best to protect privacy rights in cyberspace. Whether an individual's privacy rights include a right to an abortion or a "right to die" continues to provoke controversy. Another major challenge concerns the extent to which Americans must forfeit privacy rights to control terrorism.

7. The Constitution includes protections for the rights of persons accused of crimes. Under the Fourth Amendment, no one may be subject to an unreasonable search or seizure or be arrested except on probable cause. Under the Fifth Amendment, an accused person has the right to remain silent.

Under the Sixth Amendment, an accused person must be informed of the reason for his or her arrest. The accused also has the right to adequate counsel, even if he or she cannot afford an attorney, and the right to a prompt arraignment and a speedy and public trial before an impartial jury selected from a cross section of the community.

8. In *Miranda v. Arizona* (1966), the Supreme Court held that criminal suspects, before interrogation by law enforcement personnel, must be informed of certain constitutional rights, including the right to remain silent and the right to be represented by counsel.

9. The exclusionary rule forbids the admission in court of illegally seized evidence. There is a "good faith exception" to the exclusionary rule: illegally seized evidence need not be thrown out owing to, for example, a technical defect in a search warrant. Under the Eighth Amendment, cruel and unusual punishment is prohibited. Whether the death penalty is cruel and unusual punishment continues to be debated.

selectedprint&mediaresources

SUGGESTED READINGS

Dowbiggin, Ian. *A Concise History of Euthanasia: Life, Death, God, and Medicine.* Lanham, Md.: Rowman & Littlefield, 2007. This brief book offers a clearly written and useful history of the practice of euthanasia and the reasons underlying its advocacy.

Hamadi, Rob. *Privacy Wars: Who Holds Information on You and What They Do with It.* London: Vision Paperbacks, 2009. Hamadi sounds an alarm about the current extent of surveillance in the United States. He also provides recommendations that citizens can use to protect their own privacy.

Kitcher, Philip. *Living with Darwin: Evolution, Design, and the Future of Faith.* New York: Oxford University Press, 2007. This brief book looks at the history of the controversy over evolution as part of a larger conflict between religious faith and the discoveries of modern science.

Lewis, Anthony. *Freedom for the Thought We Hate: Tales of the First Amendment.* New York: Basic Books, 2008. Pulitzer Prize–winning journalist Anthony Lewis writes eloquently on the value of free expression and the resulting need for "activist judges." He provides a series of engaging stories of how the courts came to give real life to the First Amendment.

Mayer, Jane. *The Dark Side: The Inside Story of How the War on Terror Turned into a War on American Ideals.* New York: Doubleday, 2008. Mayer, a staff writer for the *New Yorker,* provides a dramatic account in which she alleges that torture became an unofficial policy of the George W. Bush administration. Mayer contends that up to half of the mistreated individuals were in fact imprisoned by mistake.

MEDIA RESOURCES

The Abortion War: Thirty Years after Roe v. Wade—An ABC News program released in 2003 that examines the abortion issue.

Gideon's Trumpet—An excellent 1980 movie about the *Gideon v. Wainwright* case. Henry Fonda plays the role of the convicted petty thief Clarence Earl Gideon.

God's Christian Warriors—A controversial 2007 CNN special on how evangelical Christians seek to influence American politics and society. Reported by CNN chief international correspondent Christine Amanpour, the two-hour show is part of a broader series that includes *God's Jewish Warriors* and *God's Muslim Warriors.*

May It Please the Court: The First Amendment—A set of audiocassette recordings and written transcripts of the oral arguments made before the Supreme Court in sixteen key First Amendment cases. Participants in the recording include nationally known attorneys and several Supreme Court justices.

The People versus Larry Flynt—An R-rated 1996 film that clearly articulates the conflict between freedom of the press and how a community defines pornography.

Skokie: Rights or Wrong?—A documentary by Sheila Chamovitz. The film documents the legal and moral crisis created when American Nazis attempted to demonstrate in Skokie, Illinois, a predominantly Jewish suburb that was home to many concentration camp survivors.

Taxi to the Dark Side—Winner of the 2008 Academy Award for best documentary. Director Alex Gibney focuses on an Afghan taxi driver named Dilawar who was apparently beaten to death by U.S. soldiers at Bagram Air Base. The film goes on to examine America's policy on torture and interrogation in general.

e-mocracy

UNDERSTANDING YOUR CIVIL LIBERTIES

Today, the online world offers opportunities for Americans to easily access information concerning the nature of their civil liberties, how they originated, and how they may be threatened by various government actions. Several of the Web sites in the *Logging On* section of Chapter 2 present documents that set forth and explain the civil liberties guaranteed by the Constitution. In the *Logging On* section that follows, we list other Web sites you can visit to gain insights into the nature of these liberties.

LOGGING ON

The American Civil Liberties Union (ACLU), the nation's leading civil liberties organization, provides an extensive array of information and links concerning civil rights issues at
www.aclu.org.

The Liberty Counsel describes itself as "a nonprofit religious civil liberties education and legal defense organization established to preserve religious freedom." The URL for its Web site is
www.lc.org.

Summaries and the full text of Supreme Court decisions concerning constitutional law, plus a virtual tour of the Supreme Court, are available at
www.oyez.org.

If you want to read historic Supreme Court decisions, you can search for them at
supct.law.cornell.edu/supct/search/index.html.

The Center for Democracy and Technology (CDT) focuses on how developments in communications technology are affecting the constitutional liberties of Americans. You can access the CDT's site at
www.cdt.org.

The American Library Association's Web site provides information on free speech issues, especially issues of free speech on the Internet. Go to
www.ala.org/ala/issues/fedissues.cfm.

You can find current information on Internet privacy issues at the Electronic Privacy Information Center's Web site. Go to
www.epic.org/privacy.

For information on the history of flag protection and the First Amendment, as well as the status of the proposed flag amendment in Congress, go to
**www.freedomforum.org/
packages/first/Flag/timeline.htm**.

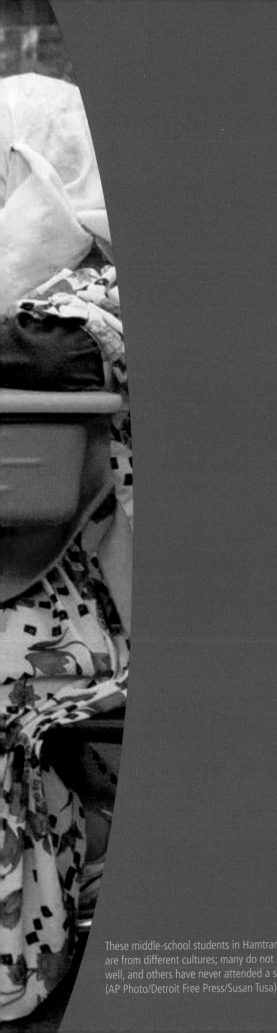

These middle-school students in Hamtramck, Michigan, are from different cultures; many do not speak English well, and others have never attended a school before. (AP Photo/Detroit Free Press/Susan Tusa)

5 Civil Rights

CHAPTER CONTENTS

whatif...unauthorized immigrants were granted citizenship?

BACKGROUND

By common estimates, there may be as many as 12 million unauthorized immigrants living in the United States. The majority of these people, who are also called illegal immigrants, illegal aliens, or undocumented workers, came to the United States from Latin American countries, with more than half coming from Mexico. In 2006, many unauthorized immigrants and their advocates took to the streets to protest legislation that would have raised penalties for illegal immigration and classified as felons all unauthorized immigrants and anyone who helped them. (The legislation did not pass.) The protesters also voiced an overriding request: the desire to obtain U.S. citizenship for illegal immigrants.

WHAT IF UNAUTHORIZED IMMIGRANTS WERE GRANTED CITIZENSHIP?

Granting citizenship to every unauthorized immigrant now living in the United States would have significant repercussions. The immigrants' sheer numbers would command attention from both political parties. The already important "Hispanic vote" would take on even greater significance.

A massive grant of citizenship would make employment and income tax practices (or lack thereof) associated with undocumented workers more transparent. Finally, by granting citizenship to those who had entered the country illegally, the United States would likely face an additional tide of new immigrants.

INCREASED POLITICAL CLOUT FOR THE HISPANIC COMMUNITY

In recent years, voter participation within the Hispanic, or Latino, community has increased. Latinos have become more politically active and outspoken. A growing number of individuals of Hispanic descent hold public office as mayors of major cities, governors, and members of Congress.

That granting citizenship to unauthorized immigrants is even a topic of discussion represents a significant turn of events for Hispanic Americans. Factions within both major parties have proposed different measures that would lead to citizenship for these people. Political interest groups have formed to champion immigrant rights. Some broader-based groups have advocated on behalf of both legal and unauthorized immigrants of Hispanic origin.

EMPLOYMENT AND TAXES

Most illegal immigrants come to the United States to work. Many of them send part of their earnings in America back to relatives in their home countries. The wages sent home to family members by individuals working in the United States (both legally and illegally) are the second-largest source of foreign income in Mexico.

The Internal Revenue Service has had difficulty collecting taxes on the wages that unauthorized immigrants earn, however. Some employers who knowingly hire undocumented workers simply pay those workers "under the table" to avoid a paper trail. Often, the arrangement is a cash transaction, which is difficult to track. If all unauthorized immigrants were granted citizenship, most employers would no longer be able to engage in such tax-evasion schemes.

Employers sometimes take advantage of undocumented workers by refusing to pay them for work or changing the terms of work agreements. Other employers use illegal immigrants as employees because they often accept lower wages than American citizens would. Some employers break the law by hiring unauthorized immigrants to get around paying state or federal minimum wages. If citizenship were granted to unauthorized immigrants, employers would have to reconsider their practices. Moreover, as wages were properly reported, tax revenues would increase.

U.S. IMMIGRATION POLICY

Obviously, unauthorized immigrants violate U.S. immigration laws. Anyone seeking to enter the United States legally faces a lengthy application process and annual quota limitations that depend on national origin. Enforcement of immigration law has always been difficult. Record numbers of illegal aliens continue to enter the United States despite efforts to control the borders.

Granting citizenship to all unauthorized immigrants now living in the United States could be considered unfair to all those who are waiting for legal entry. It would be difficult for the United States to justify keeping its borders closed if citizenship were granted to those already within its borders illegally.

FOR CRITICAL ANALYSIS

1. Some politicians have advocated a "gradual" process for granting citizenship to unauthorized immigrants. Would a gradual process be more appropriate than an automatic grant of citizenship? Or do you oppose offering citizenship to such immigrants? Explain your position.

2. Do you think immigration would significantly increase if the United States unveiled some type of policy to grant citizenship to unauthorized immigrants? Why or why not?

In spite of the words set forth in the Declaration of Independence that "all Men are created equal," the concept of equal treatment under the law was a distant dream in our nation's early years. In fact, the majority of the population had few rights at that time. As you learned in Chapter 2, the framers of the Constitution permitted slavery to continue. Slaves thus were excluded from the political process. Women also were excluded for the most part, as were Native Americans, African Americans who were not slaves, and even white men who did not own property.

Today, in contrast, we have numerous civil rights. Equality is at the heart of the concept of civil rights. Generally, the term **civil rights** refers to the rights of all Americans to equal protection under the law, as provided for by the Fourteenth Amendment to the Constitution. Although the terms *civil rights* and *civil liberties* are sometimes used interchangeably, scholars make a distinction between the two. As you learned in Chapter 4, civil liberties are basically limitations on government; they specify what the government *cannot* do. Civil rights, in contrast, specify what the government *must* do—to ensure equal protection and freedom from discrimination.

Essentially, the history of civil rights in America is the story of the struggle of various groups to be free from discriminatory treatment. In this chapter, we first look at two movements that had significant consequences for the history of civil rights in America: the civil rights movement of the 1950s and 1960s and the women's movement, which began in the mid-1800s and continues today. Each of these movements resulted in legislation that secured important basic rights for all Americans—the right to vote and the right to equal protection under the laws.

As you read in the chapter-opening *What If . . .* feature, the Hispanic American population has grown rapidly over the past two decades. In this chapter, we look at some of the issues related to Hispanic Americans and immigration. Note that most minorities in this nation have suffered—and some continue to suffer—from discrimination. Native Americans, Asian Americans, Arab Americans, and persons from India all have had to struggle for equal treatment, as have people from various island nations and other countries. The fact that these groups are not singled out for special attention in the following pages should not be construed to mean that their struggle for equality is any less significant than the struggles of those groups that we do discuss.

AFRICAN AMERICANS AND THE CONSEQUENCES OF SLAVERY IN THE UNITED STATES

Before 1863, the Constitution protected slavery and made equality impossible in the sense in which we use the word today. African American leader Frederick Douglass pointed out that "Liberty and Slavery—opposite as Heaven and Hell—are both in the Constitution." As Abraham Lincoln stated sarcastically, "All men are created equal, except Negroes."

The constitutionality of slavery was confirmed just a few years before the outbreak of the Civil War in the famous *Dred Scott v. Sandford*[1] case of 1857. The Supreme Court held that slaves were not citizens of the United States, nor were they entitled to the rights and privileges of citizenship. The Court also ruled that the Missouri Compromise, which banned slavery in the territories north of 36°30' latitude (the southern border of Missouri), was unconstitutional. The *Dred Scott* decision had grave consequences. Most observers contend that the ruling contributed to making the Civil War inevitable.

---

didyouknow...

That at the time of the American Revolution, African Americans made up nearly 25 percent of the American population of about 3 million?

Civil Rights
Generally, all rights rooted in the Fourteenth Amendment's guarantee of equal protection under the law.

This is a portrait of Dred Scott (1795–1858), an American slave who was born in Virginia and who later moved with his owner to Illinois, where slavery was illegal. He was the nominal plaintiff in a test case that sought to obtain his freedom on the ground that he lived in the free state of Illinois. Although the United States Supreme Court ruled against him, he was soon emancipated and became a hotel porter in St. Louis. (Missouri Historical Society)

---

1. 60 U.S. 393 (1857).

didyouknow...

That slaves in several states, including Arkansas, Louisiana, Oklahoma, and Texas, did not learn about the Emancipation Proclamation until more than two years after it had taken effect in 1863?

ENDING SERVITUDE

With the emancipation of the slaves by President Lincoln's Emancipation Proclamation in 1863 and the passage of the Thirteenth, Fourteenth, and Fifteenth Amendments during the Reconstruction period following the Civil War, constitutional inequality was ended.

The Thirteenth Amendment (1865) states that neither slavery nor involuntary servitude shall exist within the United States. The Fourteenth Amendment (1868) tells us that *all* persons born or naturalized in the United States are citizens of the United States. It states, furthermore, that "no State shall make or enforce any law which shall abridge the privileges or immunities of citizens of the United States; nor shall any State deprive any person of life, liberty, or property, without due process of law; nor deny to any person within its jurisdiction the equal protection of the laws." Note the use of the terms *citizen* and *person* in this amendment. *Citizens* have political rights, such as the right to vote and run for political office. Citizens also have certain privileges or immunities (see Chapter 3). All *persons,* however, including noncitizen immigrants, have a right to due process of law and equal protection under the law.

The Fifteenth Amendment (1870) reads as follows: "The right of citizens of the United States to vote shall not be denied or abridged by the United States or by any State on account of race, color, or previous condition of servitude."

THE CIVIL RIGHTS ACTS OF 1865 TO 1875

In 1865, southern state legislatures responded to the freeing of the slaves by enacting "Black Codes" to regulate the African American freedmen. The codes were so severe that they almost amounted to a new form of slavery. Typically, African Americans were required to enter into annual labor contracts and were subject to close regulation by their employers. Corporal punishment was permitted. In 1866, however, the U.S. Congress placed all the rebellious states except Tennessee under military rule, and the Black Codes were revoked.

From 1865 to 1875, Congress passed a series of civil rights acts to negate the Black Codes and enforce the Thirteenth, Fourteenth, and Fifteenth Amendments. The Civil Rights Act of 1866 extended citizenship to anyone born in the United States and gave African Americans full equality before the law. The act further authorized the president to enforce the law with national armed forces. The Enforcement Act of 1870 set out specific criminal sanctions for interfering with the right to vote as protected by the Fifteenth Amendment and by the Civil Rights Act of 1866. Equally important was the Civil Rights Act of 1872, known as the Anti–Ku Klux Klan Act. This act made it a federal crime for anyone to use law or custom to deprive an individual of rights, privileges, and immunities secured by the Constitution or by any federal law. The Second Civil Rights Act, passed in 1875, declared that everyone is entitled to full and equal enjoyment of public accommodations, theaters, and other places of public amusement, and it imposed penalties for violators.

Abraham Lincoln reads the Emancipation Proclamation on July 22, 1862. The Emancipation Proclamation did not abolish slavery (that was done by the Thirteenth Amendment, in 1865), but it ensured that slavery would be abolished if and when the North won the Civil War. After the Battle of Antietam on September 17, 1862, Lincoln publicly announced the Emancipation Proclamation and declared that all slaves residing in states that were still in rebellion against the United States on January 1, 1863, would be freed once those states came under the military control of the Union Army. (Library of Congress)

THE INEFFECTIVENESS OF THE CIVIL RIGHTS LAWS

The Reconstruction statutes, or civil rights acts, ultimately did little to secure equality for African Americans. Both the *Civil Rights Cases* and the case of *Plessy v. Ferguson* (discussed next) effectively nullified these acts. Additionally, various barriers were erected that prevented African Americans from exercising their right to vote.

The *Civil Rights Cases*. The United States Supreme Court invalidated the 1875 Civil Rights Act when it held, in the *Civil Rights Cases*[2] of 1883, that the enforcement clause of the Fourteenth Amendment (which states that "no State shall make or enforce any law which shall abridge the privileges or immunities of citizens") was limited to correcting actions by states in their *official* acts; thus, the discriminatory acts of *private* citizens were not illegal. ("Individual invasion of individual rights is not the subject matter of the Amendment.") The 1883 Supreme Court decision met with widespread approval throughout most of the United States.

Twenty years after the Civil War, the white majority was all too willing to forget about the three Civil War amendments and the civil rights legislation of the 1860s and 1870s. The other civil rights laws that the Court did not specifically invalidate became dead letters in the statute books, although they were never repealed by Congress. At the same time, many former pro-slavery secessionists had regained political power in the southern states.

Plessy v. Ferguson: Separate but Equal. A key decision during this period concerned Homer Plessy, a Louisiana resident who was one-eighth African American. In 1892, he boarded a train in New Orleans. The conductor made him leave the car, which was restricted to whites, and directed him to a car for nonwhites. At that time, Louisiana had a statute providing for separate railway cars for whites and African Americans.

Plessy went to court, claiming that such a statute was contrary to the Fourteenth Amendment's equal protection clause. In 1896, the United States Supreme Court rejected Plessy's contention. The Court concluded that the Fourteenth Amendment "could not have been intended to abolish distinctions based upon color, or to enforce social . . . equality." The Court stated that segregation alone did not violate the Constitution: "Laws permitting, and even requiring, their separation in places where they are liable to be brought into contact do not necessarily imply the inferiority of either race to the other."[3] So was born the **separate-but-equal doctrine.**

Plessy v. Ferguson became the judicial cornerstone of racial discrimination throughout the United States. Even though *Plessy* upheld segregated facilities in railway cars only, it was assumed that the Supreme Court was upholding segregation everywhere as long as the separate facilities were equal. The result was a system of racial segregation, particularly in the South—supported by laws collectively known as Jim Crow laws—that required separate drinking fountains; separate seats in theaters, restaurants, and hotels; separate public toilets; and separate waiting rooms for the two races. "Separate" was indeed the rule, but "equal" was never enforced, nor was it a reality.

Voting Barriers. The brief voting enfranchisement of African Americans ended after 1877, when the federal troops that occupied the South during the Reconstruction era were withdrawn. Southern politicians regained control of state governments and, using

Separate-but-Equal Doctrine
The doctrine holding that separate-but-equal facilities do not violate the equal protection clause of the Fourteenth Amendment to the U.S. Constitution.

Segregated drinking fountains were common in southern states in the late 1800s and during the first half of the twentieth century. What landmark Supreme Court case made such segregated facilities legal? (Bettmann/Corbis)

---

2. 109 U.S. 3 (1883).
3. *Plessy v. Ferguson*, 163 U.S. 537 (1896).

White Primary
A state primary election that restricts voting to whites only; outlawed by the Supreme Court in 1944.

Grandfather Clause
A device used by southern states to disenfranchise African Americans. It restricted voting to those whose grandfathers had voted before 1867.

Poll Tax
A special tax that must be paid as a qualification for voting. In 1964, the Twenty-fourth Amendment to the Constitution outlawed the poll tax in national elections, and in 1966 the Supreme Court declared it unconstitutional in all elections.

Literacy Test
A test administered as a pre-condition for voting, often used to prevent African Americans from exercising their right to vote.

didyouknow...

That the original Constitution failed to describe the status of *citizen* or how this status could be acquired?

Linda Brown Smith
was only eight years old when her father started a lawsuit to allow her to attend a nearby white grammar school. The result was the landmark decision *Brown v. Board of Education of Topeka,* rendered in 1954. What was the impact of this Supreme Court decision?
(AP Photo)

everything except race as a formal criterion, passed laws that effectively deprived African Americans of the right to vote. By using the ruse that political parties were private bodies, the Democratic Party was allowed to keep black voters from its primaries. The **white primary** was upheld by the United States Supreme Court until 1944 when, in *Smith v. Allwright,*[4] the Court ruled that it violated the Fifteenth Amendment.

Another barrier to African American voting was the **grandfather clause,** which restricted voting to those who could prove that their grandfathers had voted before 1867. **Poll taxes** required the payment of a fee to vote; thus, poor African Americans—as well as poor whites—who could not afford to pay the tax were excluded from voting. Not until the Twenty-fourth Amendment to the Constitution was ratified in 1964 was the poll tax eliminated as a precondition to voting. **Literacy tests** were also used to deny the vote to African Americans. Such tests asked potential voters to read, recite, or interpret complicated texts, such as a section of the state constitution, to the satisfaction of local registrars—who were, of course, never satisfied with the responses of African Americans.

Extralegal Methods of Enforcing White Supremacy. The second-class status of African Americans was also a matter of social custom, especially in the South. In their interactions with southern whites, African Americans were expected to observe an informal but detailed code of behavior that confirmed their inferiority. The most serious violation of the informal code was "familiarity" toward a white woman by an African American man or boy. The code was backed up by the common practice of *lynching*—mob action to murder an accused individual, usually by hanging and sometimes accompanied by torture. Lynching was a common response to an accusation of "familiarity." Of course, lynching was illegal, but southern authorities rarely prosecuted these cases, and white juries would not convict.[5]

African Americans outside the South were subject to a second kind of violence—race riots. In the early twentieth century, race riots were typically initiated by whites. Frequently, the riots were caused by competition for employment. For example, there were a number of serious riots during World War II (1939–1945), when labor shortages forced northern employers to hire more black workers.

THE END OF THE SEPARATE-BUT-EQUAL DOCTRINE

A successful attack on the separate-but-equal doctrine began with a series of lawsuits in the 1930s that sought to admit African Americans to state professional schools. By 1950, the United States Supreme Court had ruled that African Americans who were admitted to a state university could not be assigned to separate sections of classrooms, libraries, and cafeterias.

In 1951, Oliver Brown decided that his eight-year-old daughter, Linda Carol Brown, should not have to go to an all-nonwhite elementary school twenty-one blocks from her home, when there was a white school only seven blocks away. The National Association for the Advancement of Colored People (NAACP), formed in 1909, decided to support Oliver Brown. The outcome would have a monumental impact on American society.

Brown v. Board of Education of Topeka. The 1954 unanimous decision of the United States Supreme Court in *Brown v. Board of Education of Topeka*[6] established that segregation of races in the public schools violates the equal protection clause of the Fourteenth Amendment. Chief Justice Earl Warren said that separation implied inferiority, whereas the majority opinion in *Plessy v. Ferguson* had said the opposite.

4. 321 U.S. 649 (1944).
5. One of the most notorious organizations enforcing white supremacy was the Ku Klux Klan, which made its first appearance in 1866.
6. 347 U.S. 483 (1954).

"With All Deliberate Speed." The following year, in *Brown v. Board of Education*[7] (sometimes called the second *Brown* decision), the Court declared that the lower courts needed to ensure that African Americans would be admitted to schools on a nondiscriminatory basis "with all deliberate speed." The district courts were to consider devices in their desegregation orders that might include "the school transportation system, personnel, [and] revision of school districts and attendance areas into compact units to achieve a system of determining admission to the public schools on a nonracial basis."

REACTIONS TO SCHOOL INTEGRATION

The white South did not let the Supreme Court ruling go unchallenged. Governor Orval Faubus of Arkansas used the state's National Guard to block the integration of Central High School in Little Rock in September 1957. The federal court demanded that the troops be withdrawn. Finally, President Dwight Eisenhower had to federalize the Arkansas National Guard and send in the Army's 101st Airborne Division to quell the violence. Central High became integrated.

The universities in the South, however, remained segregated. When James Meredith, an African American student, attempted to enroll at the University of Mississippi in Oxford in 1962, violence flared there, as it had in Little Rock. The white riot at Oxford was so intense that President John Kennedy was forced to send in 30,000 U.S. combat troops, a larger force than the one then stationed in Korea. There were 375 military and civilian injuries, many from gunfire, and two bystanders were killed. Ultimately, peace was restored, and Meredith began attending classes.[8]

These two African American students were attempting to enter an all-white high school in Little Rock, Arkansas, in 1957. Did such actions ultimately lead to the integration of high schools in that state? (AP Photo)

AN INTEGRATIONIST ATTEMPT AT A CURE: BUSING

In most parts of the United States, residential concentrations by race have made it difficult to achieve racial balance in schools. Although it is true that a number of school boards in northern districts created segregated schools by drawing school district lines arbitrarily, the residential concentration of African Americans and other minorities in well-defined geographic locations has contributed to the difficulty of achieving racial balance. This concentration results in ***de facto* segregation,** as distinct from ***de jure* segregation,** which results from laws or administrative decisions.

Court-Ordered Busing. The obvious solution to both *de facto* and *de jure* segregation seemed to be transporting some African American schoolchildren to white schools and some white schoolchildren to African American schools. Increasingly, the courts ordered school districts to engage in such **busing** across neighborhoods. Busing led to violence in some northern cities, such as in south Boston, where African American students were bused into blue-collar Irish Catholic neighborhoods. Indeed, busing was unpopular with many groups. In the mid-1970s, almost 50 percent of African Americans interviewed were opposed to busing, and approximately three-fourths of the whites interviewed held the same opinion. Nonetheless, through the next decade, the United States Supreme Court fairly consistently upheld busing plans in the cases it decided.

The End of Integration? During the 1980s and the early 1990s, the Supreme Court tended to back away from its earlier commitment to busing and other methods of desegregation. By the late 1990s and early 2000s, the federal courts were increasingly unwilling to uphold race-conscious policies designed to further school integration and diversity—outcomes that are not mandated by the Constitution. For example, in 2001, a federal

De Facto **Segregation**
Racial segregation that occurs because of past social and economic conditions and residential racial patterns.

De Jure **Segregation**
Racial segregation that occurs because of laws or administrative decisions by public agencies.

Busing
In the context of civil rights, the transportation of public school students from areas where they live to schools in other areas to eliminate school segregation based on residential patterns.

---

7. 349 U.S. 294 (1955).
8. William Doyle, *An American Insurrection: James Meredith and the Battle of Oxford, Mississippi, 1962* (New York: Anchor, 2003).

Civil Disobedience
A nonviolent, public refusal to obey allegedly unjust laws.

appellate court held that the Charlotte-Mecklenburg school district in North Carolina had achieved the goal of integration,[9] meaning that race-based admission quotas could no longer be imposed constitutionally. Indeed, today, school admissions policies that favor minority applicants in any way may end up being challenged on equal protection grounds. (For a further discussion of this issue, see the section on affirmative action later in this chapter.)

didyouknow...

That during the Mississippi Summer Project in 1964, organized by students to register African American voters, 1,000 students and voters were arrested, 80 were beaten, 35 were shot, and 6 were murdered; 30 buildings were bombed; and 25 churches were burned?

The Resurgence of Minority Schools. Today, schools around the country are becoming segregated again, in large part because of *de facto* segregation. The rapid decline in the relative proportion of whites who live in large cities and high minority birthrates have increased the minority presence in those urban areas. Today, one out of every three African American and Latino students goes to a school with more than 90 percent minority enrollment. In the largest U.S. cities, fifteen out of sixteen African American and Hispanic students go to schools with almost no non-Hispanic whites.

Generally, Americans are now taking another look at what desegregation means. The attempt to integrate the schools, particularly through busing, has largely failed to improve educational resources and achievement for African American children. The goal of racially balanced schools envisioned in the 1954 *Brown v. Board of Education of Topeka* decision is giving way to the goal of better education for children, even if that means educating them in schools in which students are of the same race or in which race is not considered.

THE CIVIL RIGHTS MOVEMENT

The *Brown* decision applied only to public schools. Not much else in the structure of existing segregation was affected. In December 1955, a forty-three-year-old African American woman, Rosa Parks, boarded a public bus in Montgomery, Alabama. When the bus became crowded and several white people stepped aboard, Parks was asked to move to the rear of the bus (the "colored" section). She refused, was arrested, and was fined $10; but that was not the end of the matter. For an entire year, African Americans boycotted the Montgomery bus line. The protest was headed by a twenty-seven-year-old Baptist minister, Dr. Martin Luther King, Jr. During the protest period, he went to jail, and his house was bombed. In the face of overwhelming odds, King won. In 1956, a federal district court issued an injunction prohibiting the segregation of buses in Montgomery. The era of civil rights protests had begun.

This Montgomery, Alabama, sheriff's department booking photo of Rosa Parks shows her after she was arrested for refusing to give up her seat on a bus and move to the "colored" section in 1955. What happened after her arrest? (AP Photo/Montgomery County Sheriff's office)

KING'S PHILOSOPHY OF NONVIOLENCE

The following year, in 1957, King formed the Southern Christian Leadership Conference (SCLC). King advocated nonviolent **civil disobedience** as a means to achieve racial justice. King's philosophy of civil disobedience was influenced, in part, by the life and teachings of Mahatma Gandhi (1869–1948). Gandhi had led resistance to the British colonial system in India from 1919 to 1947. He used tactics such as demonstrations and marches, as well as nonviolent, public disobedience to unjust laws. King's followers successfully used these methods to gain wider public acceptance of their cause.

Nonviolent Demonstrations. For the next decade, African Americans and sympathetic whites engaged in sit-ins, freedom rides, and freedom marches. In the beginning, such demonstrations were often met with vio-

---

9. *Belk v. Charlotte-Mecklenburg Board of Education,* 269 F.3d 305 (4th Cir. 2001).

lence, and the contrasting image of nonviolent African Americans and violent, hostile whites created strong public support for the civil rights movement. When African Americans in Greensboro, North Carolina, were refused service at a Woolworth's lunch counter, they organized a sit-in that was aided day after day by sympathetic whites and other African Americans. Enraged customers threw ketchup on the protesters. Some spat in their faces. The sit-in movement continued to grow, however. Within six months of the first sit-in at the Greensboro Woolworth's, hundreds of lunch counters throughout the South were serving African Americans.

The sit-in technique also was successfully used to integrate interstate buses and their terminals, as well as railroads engaged in interstate transportation. Although buses and railroads engaged in interstate transportation were prohibited by law from segregating African Americans from whites, they stopped doing so only after the sit-in protests.

Marches and Demonstrations. One of the most famous of the violence-plagued protests occurred in Birmingham, Alabama, in 1963, when Police Commissioner Eugene "Bull" Connor unleashed police dogs and used electric cattle prods against the protesters. People throughout the country viewed the event on television with indignation and horror. King himself was thrown in jail. The media coverage of the Birmingham protest and the violent response by the city government played a key role in the process of ending Jim Crow laws in the United States. The ultimate result was the most important civil rights act in the nation's history, the Civil Rights Act of 1964 (to be discussed shortly).

In August 1963, African American leaders A. Philip Randolph and Bayard Rustin organized the massive March on Washington for Jobs and Freedom. Before nearly a quarter-million white and African American spectators and millions watching on television, King told the world his dream: "I have a dream that my four little children will one day live in a nation where they will not be judged by the color of their skin but by the content of their character."

ANOTHER APPROACH—BLACK POWER

Not all African Americans agreed with King's philosophy of nonviolence or with the idea that King's strong Christian background should represent the core spirituality of African Americans. Black Muslims and other African American separatists advocated a more militant stance and argued that desegregation should not result in cultural assimilation. During the 1950s and 1960s, when King was spearheading nonviolent protests and demonstrations to achieve civil rights for African Americans, black power leaders insisted that African Americans should "fight back" instead of turning the other cheek. Indeed, some would argue that without the fear generated by black militants, a "moderate" such as King would not have garnered such widespread support from white America.

Malcolm Little (who became Malcolm X when he joined the Black Muslims in 1952) and other leaders in the black power movement believed that African Americans fell into two groups: the "Uncle Toms," who peaceably accommodated the white establishment, and the "New Negroes," who took pride in their color and culture and who preferred and demanded racial separation as well as power. Malcolm X was assassinated in 1965, but he became an important reference point for a new generation of African Americans and a symbol of African American identity.

In August 1963, a quarter of a million whites and blacks descended on Washington, D.C., for a massive March for Jobs and Freedom. Who was the most important speaker at that event? (AP Photo)

THE CLIMAX OF THE CIVIL RIGHTS MOVEMENT

Police-dog attacks, the use of cattle prods and high-pressure water hoses against non-violent protesters, beatings, bombings, the March on Washington, and black militancy—all of these events and developments led to an environment in which Congress felt compelled to act on behalf of African Americans. The second era of civil rights acts, sometimes referred to as the second Reconstruction period, was under way.

CIVIL RIGHTS LEGISLATION

As the civil rights movement mounted in intensity, equality before the law came to be "an idea whose time has come," in the words of then Republican Senate minority leader Everett Dirksen.

The Civil Rights Act of 1964. The Civil Rights Act of 1964, the most far-reaching bill on civil rights in modern times, forbids discrimination on the basis of race, color, religion, gender, or national origin. The major provisions of the act are as follows:

1. It outlawed arbitrary discrimination in voter registration.
2. It barred discrimination in public accommodations, such as hotels and restaurants, whose operations affect interstate commerce.
3. It authorized the federal government to bring suits to desegregate public schools and facilities.
4. It expanded the power of the Civil Rights Commission and extended its life.
5. It provided for the withholding of federal funds from programs administered in a discriminatory manner.
6. It established the right to equality of opportunity in employment.

Title VII of the Civil Rights Act of 1964 is the cornerstone of our employment-discrimination laws. It prohibits discrimination in employment based on race, color, religion, gender, or national origin. Under Title VII, executive orders were issued that banned employment discrimination by firms that received any federal funding. The 1964 Civil Rights Act created a five-member commission, the Equal Employment Opportunity Commission (EEOC), to administer Title VII.

At its inception, the EEOC relied on conciliation, education, outreach, and technical assistance, because that was all that the law permitted. In 1972, however, Congress gave the EEOC the right to sue employers, unions, and employment agencies, and litigation became a focal point for the agency. Congress also expanded Title VII to cover federal, state, and local governments, as well as schools and colleges. The EEOC has broad authority to require the production of documentary evidence, to hold hearings, and to serve a **subpoena** and examine witnesses under oath.

Here, we see the only face-to-face meeting between Martin Luther King, Jr., and Malcolm X. What differences in tactics did these two men represent? (Bettmann/Corbis)

The Voting Rights Act of 1965. As late as 1960, only 29.1 percent of African Americans of voting age were registered in the southern states, in stark contrast to 61.1 percent of whites. The Voting Rights Act of 1965 addressed this issue. The act had two major provisions. The first one outlawed discriminatory voter-registration tests. The second authorized federal registration of voters and federally administered voting procedures in any political subdivision or state that discriminated electorally against a particular group. In part, the act provided that certain political subdivisions could not change their voting procedures and election laws without federal approval. The act targeted counties, mostly in the South, in which less than 50 percent of the eligible population was registered to vote. Federal voter registrars were sent to these areas to register African Americans who had been kept from voting by local registrars. Within one week after the act was passed, forty-five federal examiners were sent to the South. A massive voter-registration drive covered the country.

Urban Riots. Even as the civil rights movement was experiencing its greatest victories, a series of riots swept through African American inner-city neighborhoods. These urban riots were different in character from the race riots described earlier in this chapter. The riots in the first half of the twentieth century were street battles between whites and blacks. The urban riots of the late 1960s and early 1970s, however, were not directed against individual whites—in some instances, whites actually participated in small numbers. The riots were primarily civil insurrections, although these disorders were accompanied by large-scale looting of stores. Inhabitants of the affected neighborhoods attributed the riots to racial discrimination.[10] The riots dissipated much of the goodwill toward the civil rights movement that had been built up earlier in the decade among northern whites. Together with widespread student demonstrations against the Vietnam War (1964–1975), the riots pushed many Americans toward conservatism.

The Civil Rights Act of 1968 and Other Housing Reform Legislation. Martin Luther King, Jr., was assassinated on April 4, 1968. Despite King's message of peace, his death was followed by the most widespread rioting to date. Nine days after King's death, President Johnson signed the Civil Rights Act of 1968, which forbade discrimination in most housing and provided penalties for those attempting to interfere with individual civil rights (giving protection to civil rights workers, among others). Subsequent legislation added enforcement provisions to the federal government's rules against discriminatory mortgage-lending practices. Today, all lenders must report to the federal government the race, gender, and income of all mortgage-loan seekers, along with the final decision on their loan applications.

CONSEQUENCES OF CIVIL RIGHTS LEGISLATION

As a result of the Voting Rights Act of 1965 and its amendments, and the large-scale voter-registration drives in the South, the number of African Americans registered to vote climbed dramatically. By 1980, 55.8 percent of African Americans of voting age in the

During the spring of 1968, there were riots in many inner-city neighborhoods throughout America like this one in Baltimore, Maryland. Were such riots directed at individual whites? (AP Photo)

President Lyndon Johnson is shown signing the Civil Rights Act of 1968. What are some of the provisions of that far-reaching law? (Bettmann/Corbis)

---

10. Angus Campbell and Howard Schuman, *ICPSR 3500: Racial Attitudes in Fifteen American Cities, 1968* (Ann Arbor, Mich.: Inter-University Consortium for Political and Social Research, 1997). Campbell and Schuman's survey documented both white participation and the attitudes of the inhabitants of affected neighborhoods.

Hispanic
Someone who can claim a heritage from a Spanish-speaking country (other than Spain). The term is used only in the United States or other countries that receive immigrants—Spanish-speaking persons living in Spanish-speaking countries do not normally apply the term to themselves.

Latino
An alternative to the term *Hispanic* that is preferred by many.

South were registered. In recent elections, the percentage of voting-age African Americans who have registered to vote has been just slightly less than the percentage of voting-age whites who have done so. Some of the provisions in the Voting Rights Act of 1965 were due to "sunset" (expire) in 2007. In July 2006, President George W. Bush signed a twenty-five-year extension of these provisions following heated congressional debate.

Political Participation by African Americans. Today, there are more than 9,100 African American elected officials in the United States. The movement of African American citizens into high elected office has been sure, if exceedingly slow. Notably, recent polling data show that most Americans do not consider race a significant factor in choosing a president. In 1958, when a Gallup poll first asked whether respondents would be willing to vote for an African American as president, only 38 percent of the public said yes. By 2008, this number had reached 94 percent. This high figure may have been attained, at least in part, because of the emergence of several African Americans of presidential caliber. Indeed, Illinois senator Barack Obama was elected president in 2008 on the Democratic ticket. Republicans of note include Colin Powell, formerly chair of the Joint Chiefs of Staff and later secretary of state under President George W. Bush; and Condoleezza Rice, who succeeded Powell at the State Department.

Political Participation by Other Minorities. As mentioned earlier, the civil rights movement focused primarily on the rights of African Americans. Yet the legislation resulting from the movement has ultimately benefited virtually all minority groups. The Civil Rights Act of 1964, for example, prohibits discrimination against any person because of race, color, or national origin. Subsequent amendments to the Voting Rights Act of 1965 extended its protections to other minorities, including **Hispanics** (or **Latinos**), Asian Americans, Native Americans, and Native Alaskans. To further protect the voting rights of minorities, the law now provides that states must make bilingual ballots available in counties where 5 percent or more of the population speaks a language other than English.

The political participation of other minority groups in the United States has also been increasing. Hispanics are gaining political power in several states. The growth in Latino political power, however, has not come without frictions of various kinds, as will be discussed in this chapter's *Politics and Diversity* feature.

Even though political participation by minorities has increased dramatically since the 1960s, the number of political offices held by members of minority groups remains disproportionately low compared with their numbers in the overall population. This will likely change in the future due to the continued influx of immigrants, particularly from Mexico.

A decade ago, not
even 40 percent of Americans said they would vote for an African American for president. Since then, numerous African Americans emerged as high government officials, including Colin Powell, secretary of state, and Condoleezza Rice, who succeeded him in that office during the Bush administration. Of course, today America has its first African American president. What does Barack Obama's victory in the 2008 presidential elections tell you about changing racial attitudes in this country? (From left to right, Charles Haynes/Creative Commons, AP Photo/ J.J. Guillen and AP Photo/Jae C. Hong)

politicsand...diversity

THE ZERO-SUM POLITICAL STRUGGLE BETWEEN LATINOS AND AFRICAN AMERICANS

For a long time, the term *biracial* signified a community or an organization that contained both whites and blacks. Increasingly, according to researcher Earl Ofari Hutchinson, in certain cities this term refers to African Americans and Latinos (or Hispanics). But how often do these two minority groups actually ally?

FEW POLITICAL ALLIANCES BETWEEN BLACKS AND LATINOS

For decades, African Americans have been building their political power base. Starting with the civil rights struggle in the South, they have gradually asserted their legal rights and reduced the barriers to voting. The struggles within Latino communities are quite different. Because so many Latinos are unauthorized (undocumented) immigrants, they often push for the nonenforcement of immigration laws. They want, as an example, local police in certain cities *not* to cooperate with federal immigration agents.

The number of Latinos in particular cities does not give much indication of their political power. A good example is Compton, California (south of Los Angeles). Latinos constitute almost 60 percent of the population. Nonetheless, the mayor and the members of the city council are all African American. In nearby Lynnwood, Latinos were kept out of power until they became a large majority. The African American political machine in that city has since been practically pulverized.

The fact is that many African Americans and Latinos view urban politics as a zero-sum game. Rarely do the two groups work toward electing a common candidate. During the Democratic presidential primaries in 2008, for example, African American Democrats strongly favored Barack Obama, whereas Hispanic Democrats favored Hillary Clinton.

TENSIONS AMONG BLACKS AND LATINOS IN CERTAIN CITIES

While civil rights activist Martin Luther King, Jr., called blacks and Latinos "brothers in the fight for equality," such an attitude cannot be found on the streets of some cities today. Consider Choose Black America, an activist group in south-central Los Angeles. This group has been at the forefront of anti-immigration demonstrations. A Pew report found that one-third of African Americans believe that immigrants take jobs from other Americans. A survey taken in Durham, North Carolina, found that almost 60 percent of Latinos believe that African Americans are not as hardworking as they are. Similar surveys taken twenty years ago did not show these negative views.

Biracial crime in Los Angeles is now quite rampant. Of the 400 racial hate crimes registered in a recent year, almost 60 percent of the victims were African Americans—even though African Americans constituted only 9 percent of the population. Seventy percent of the time the perpetrators were Latino. In turn, Latinos were targeted by African Americans in 80 percent of the hate crimes in which Latinos were the victims.

FOR CRITICAL ANALYSIS

In the past, the term *race relations* had only one meaning. What was that meaning, and how does it differ from the use of this term today?

Collectively, Hispanics, African Americans, Native Americans, and Asian Americans are now a majority of the populations in California, Hawaii, and New Mexico. It is estimated that by 2015, minority populations will collectively outnumber whites in Texas as well. The impact of immigration will be discussed in more detail later in the chapter.

Lingering Social and Economic Disparities. According to recent census data, social and economic disparities between whites and blacks (and other minorities) persist. Data released by the U.S. Census Bureau in August 2007 (the latest data available) showed that incomes in non-Hispanic white households were 62 percent higher than in black households and 39 percent higher than in Hispanic households. White adults were also more likely than black and Hispanic adults to have college degrees and to own their own homes. Whites are also less likely to live in poverty. Consider that the poverty rate for non-Hispanic white residents was 8.2 percent, compared with a poverty rate of 24.5 percent for blacks and 21.5 percent for Hispanics.

Finally, even today, race consciousness continues to divide African Americans and white Americans. Whether we are talking about college attendance, media stereotyping, racial profiling, or academic achievement, the black experience is different from the white one. As a result, African Americans view the nation and many specific issues differently than their white counterparts do. In survey after survey, when blacks are asked whether they have achieved racial equality, few believe that they have. In contrast, whites are much more likely than blacks to believe that racial equality has been achieved. In spite of the civil rights movement and civil rights legislation, African Americans continue to feel a sense of injustice in matters of race, and this feeling is often not apparent to, or appreciated by, the majority of white Americans.

One response to lingering social and economic disparities that has garnered considerable attention among liberals is to focus on differences of socioeconomic class, regardless of race. The resulting programs would attempt to lift up poor and lower-class families regardless of whether they were white, black, Hispanic, Native American, or Asian. For example, some cities have attempted to integrate their school systems based on economic class, rather than race. Indeed, the 2005 National Assessment of Educational Progress appeared to show that low-income students attending more affluent schools scored almost two grade levels higher than low-income students attending high-poverty schools.

A number of conservatives have proposed class-based programs in education, such as admitting the best students from every high school to the state university. (Such a move benefits both students from minority high schools *and* low-income rural whites.) Support for further measures has been limited by the widespread belief among conservatives that economic inequality is the legitimate result of differences in ability and effort. We examine these ideas in this chapter's *Which Side Are You On?* feature.

WOMEN'S STRUGGLE FOR EQUAL RIGHTS

Like African Americans and other minorities, women also have had to struggle for equality. During the first phase of this struggle, the primary goal of women was to obtain the right to vote. Some women had hoped that the founders would provide such a right in the Constitution. The Constitution did not include a provision guaranteeing women the right to vote, but neither did it deny to women—or to any others—this right. Rather, the founders left it up to the states to decide such issues, and, as mentioned earlier, by and large, the states limited the franchise to adult white males who owned property.

EARLY WOMEN'S POLITICAL MOVEMENTS

The first political cause in which women became actively engaged was the movement to abolish slavery. Yet male abolitionists felt that women should not take an active role in public. When the World Antislavery Convention was held in London in 1840, women delegates were barred from active participation. Partly in response to this rebuff, two American delegates, Lucretia Mott and Elizabeth Cady Stanton, returned from that meeting with plans to work for women's rights in the United States.

In 1848, Mott and Stanton organized the first women's rights convention in Seneca Falls, New York. The three hundred people who attended approved a Declaration of Sentiments: "We hold these truths to be self-evident: that all men and women are created equal." In the following twelve years, groups that supported women's rights held seven conventions in different cities in the Midwest and

Women did not get the right to vote in the United States until 1920. Prior to that, though, there was a strong women's suffrage movement. This cardboard poster is asking voters to support candidates who favor women's right to vote. (David J. & Janice L. Frent Collection/Corbis)

whichsideare**you**on?

IS INEQUALITY NECESSARILY A BAD THING?

This nation was founded on a belief that everyone is created equal. Clearly, this does not mean that everybody should have exactly the same income or wealth. Income inequality exists today, as it always has. The courageous immigrants coming to our shores from England in the 1600s certainly knew about income inequality. England was a class-based society then. Not only did a limited number of families control most of the nation's wealth, but members of the aristocracy had specified privileges written into the law. To be sure, modern-day America isn't seventeenth-century England. Nonetheless, many studies show that in recent years, the incomes of the richest few percent of families have grown much faster than the incomes of everyone else.

THE AMERICAN DREAM IS DEAD

The gap between the rich and the poor has increased dramatically in the last twenty years in the United States. The American dream was once that "a rising tide lifts all boats." That may have occurred during the first several hundred years in American history, but it is not happening today. Many of the boats are simply being swamped. We are increasingly becoming a class society. A small minority live in opulence while the majority struggle with little hope of getting rich. Just take the last ten years. The salaries of average workers, corrected for inflation, have barely risen. At the other extreme, the number of millionaires and billionaires has skyrocketed. Inequality is bad for the economy, the society, and the body politic.

GREATER INEQUALITY MAY BE FAIR AND BENEFICIAL

Three economists recently looked at rising inequality and found one very good reason that the rich have become richer: over the last twenty years, an increasing number of companies have started to use performance-pay systems. These economists contend that the growing incidence of performance pay explains about a quarter of the growth in the inequality of male wages in recent decades, and nearly all of the growth in wage differences among the best paid.[a]

In other words, the harder employees work, the more they are being paid. Ours has become an economy that increasingly rewards hard work. That can't be bad, even if it leads to more income inequality. There is nothing wrong with more employers using productivity-

"I'VE NEVER SEEN A TIDE RISE LIKE *THAT* BEFORE!"

(© R. J. Matson, *St Louis Post-Dispatch*)

oriented pay plans such as piece-rate bonuses, commissions based on sales, and stock options. More than 50 percent of salaried employees today receive at least part of their pay based on performance. Finally, it is not true that rising inequality means the poor cannot get ahead. Rather, because of performance pay systems, increased inequality also means increased opportunities to "hit it big."

---

a. Thomas Lemieux, W. Bentley MacLeod, and Daniel Parent, "Performance Pay and Wage Inequality" (working paper no. 13128, National Bureau of Economic Research, April 2007).

East. With the outbreak of the Civil War, however, advocates of women's rights were urged to put their support behind the war effort, and most agreed.

WOMEN'S SUFFRAGE ASSOCIATIONS

Susan B. Anthony and Elizabeth Cady Stanton formed the National Woman Suffrage Association in 1869. In their view, women's **suffrage**—the right to vote—was a means to achieve major improvements in the economic and social situation of women in the United States. In other words, the vote was to be used to seek broader goals. Nowadays, we

Suffrage
The right to vote; the franchise.

Feminism
The movement that supports political, economic, and social equality for women.

commonly see the women's rights movement as a liberal cause, but many of the broader goals of the suffrage advocates would not be regarded as liberal today. An example was the prohibition of alcoholic beverages, which received widespread support among women in general and women's rights activists in particular. It should be noted that many women considered prohibition to be a method of combating domestic violence.

Unlike Anthony and Stanton, Lucy Stone, a key founder of the rival American Woman Suffrage Association, believed that the vote was the only major issue. Members of the American Woman Suffrage Association traveled to each state; addressed state legislatures; and wrote, published, and argued their convictions. They achieved only limited success. In 1880, the two organizations joined force. The resulting National American Woman Suffrage Association had only one goal—the enfranchisement of women—but it made little progress.

The Congressional Union, founded in the early 1900s by Alice Paul, rejected the state-by-state approach. Instead, the Union adopted a national strategy of obtaining an amendment to the U.S. Constitution. The Union also employed militant tactics. It sponsored large-scale marches and civil disobedience—which resulted in hunger strikes, arrests, and jailings. Finally, in 1920, the Nineteenth Amendment was passed: "The right of citizens of the United States to vote shall not be denied or abridged by the United States or by any State on account of sex." (Today, the word *gender* is typically used instead of *sex*.) Although it may seem that the United States was slow to give women the vote, it was really not too far behind the rest of the world (see Table 5–1).

THE MODERN WOMEN'S MOVEMENT

Historian Nancy Cott contends that the word *feminism* first began to be used around 1910. At that time, **feminism** meant, as it does today, political, social, and economic equality for women—a radical notion that gained little support among members of the suffrage movement.

didyouknow...

That in 1916, four years before the Nineteenth Amendment gave women the right to vote, Jeannette Rankin became the first woman to be elected to the U.S. House of Representatives?

After gaining the right to vote in 1920, women engaged in little independent political activity until the 1960s. The civil rights movement of that decade resulted in a growing awareness of rights for all groups, including women. Increased participation in the workforce gave many women greater self-confidence. Additionally, the publication of Betty Friedan's *The Feminine Mystique* in 1963 focused national attention on the unequal status of women in American life.

In 1966, Friedan and others who were dissatisfied with existing women's organizations, and especially with the failure of the Equal Employment Opportunity Commission to address discrimination against women, formed the National Organization for Women (NOW). Many observers consider the founding of NOW to be the beginning of the modern women's movement—the feminist movement. NOW's goal

TABLE 5–1: Years, by Country, in Which Women Gained the Right to Vote

1893: New Zealand	**1919:** Germany	**1945:** Italy	**1953:** Mexico
1902: Australia	**1920:** United States	**1945:** Japan	**1956:** Egypt
1913: Norway	**1930:** South Africa	**1947:** Argentina	**1963:** Kenya
1918: Britain	**1932:** Brazil	**1950:** India	**1971:** Switzerland
1918: Canada	**1944:** France	**1952:** Greece	**1984:** Yemen

Source: Center for the American Woman and Politics.

was "to bring women into full participation in the mainstream of American society *now,* exercising all the privileges and responsibilities thereof in truly equal partnership with men."

Feminism gained additional impetus from young women who entered politics to support the civil rights movement or to oppose the Vietnam War. Many of them found that despite the egalitarian principles of these movements, women remained in second-class positions. These young women sought their own movement. In the late 1960s, "women's liberation" organizations began to spring up on college campuses. Women also began organizing independent "consciousness-raising groups" in which they discussed how gender issues affected their lives. The new women's movement experienced explosive growth, and by 1970 it had emerged as a major social force.

A rally was held in Washington, D.C., on July 9, 1978, in favor of extending the time for ratification of the Equal Rights Amendment (ERA). How many years had Congress given the states to ratify the ERA? (AP Photo/Greg Smith)

The Equal Rights Amendment. The initial focus of the modern women's movement was not on expanding the political rights of women. Rather, leaders of NOW and other liberal women's rights advocates sought to eradicate gender inequality through a constitutional amendment. The proposed Equal Rights Amendment (ERA), which was first introduced in Congress in 1923 by leaders of the National Women's Party (a successor to the Congressional Union), states as follows: "Equality of rights under the law shall not be denied or abridged by the United States or by any state on account of sex." For years the amendment was not even given a hearing in Congress, but finally it was approved by both chambers and sent to the state legislatures for ratification in 1972.

As was noted in Chapter 2, any constitutional amendment must be ratified by the legislatures (or conventions) in three-fourths of the states before it can become law. Since the early 1900s, most proposed amendments have required that ratification occur within seven years of Congress's adoption of the amendment. The necessary thirty-eight states failed to ratify the ERA within the seven-year period specified by Congress, even though it was supported by numerous national party platforms, six presidents, and both chambers of Congress. To date, efforts to reintroduce the amendment have not succeeded.

During the national debate over the ratification of the ERA, a women's counter-movement emerged. Some women perceived the goals pursued by NOW and other liberal women's organizations as a threat to their way of life. One leader of the countermovement was Republican Phyllis Schlafly and her conservative organization, Eagle Forum. Eagle Forum's "Stop ERA" campaign found significant support among fundamentalist religious groups and various other conservative organizations.

Additional Women's Issues. While NOW concentrated on the ERA, a large number of other women's groups, many of them entirely local, addressed a spectrum of added issues. One of these was the issue of *domestic violence*—that is, assaults within the family. Typically, this meant husbands or

didyouknow...

That in 1922, at age eighty-seven, Rebecca Latimer Felton was the first and oldest woman to serve in the U.S. Senate—although she was appointed as a token gesture and was allowed to serve only one day?

Conservative activist Phyllis Schlafly led a nationwide campaign against the passage of the Equal Rights Amendment. (AP Photo/Barry Thumma)

Gender Discrimination
Any practice, policy, or procedure that denies equality of treatment to an individual or to a group because of gender.

didyouknow...

That a Gallup poll taken in early 2000 found that 15 percent of the women polled described themselves as homemakers, but not one man described himself as such?

boyfriends assaulting their wives or girlfriends. During the 1970s, feminists across the country began opening *battered women's shelters* to house victims of abuse.

Abortion soon emerged as a key concern. Virtually the entire organized women's movement united behind the "freedom-of-choice" position, at the cost of alienating potential women's rights supporters who favored the "right-to-life" position instead. Because abortion was a national issue, the campaign was led by national organizations such as NARAL Pro-Choice America, formerly the National Abortion and Reproductive Rights Action League. (For information about organizations on both sides of this debate, see the *Why Should You Care about the Constitution?* feature on page 58 in Chapter 2.)

Another issue—pornography—tended to divide the women's movement rather than unite it. While a majority of feminists found pornography demeaning to women, many were also strong supporters of free speech. Others, notably activists Andrea Dworkin and Catharine Mackinnon, believed that pornography was so central to the subjugation of women that First Amendment protections should not apply. In some ways, the campaign against pornography was reminiscent of the "social control" tendencies of the suffrage movement that had been expressed in such issues as prohibition.

Challenging Gender Discrimination in the Courts. When the ERA failed to be ratified, women's rights organizations began a campaign to win more limited national and state laws that would guarantee the equality of women. This more limited campaign met with much success. Women's rights organizations also challenged discriminatory statutes and policies in the federal courts, contending that **gender discrimination** violated the Fourteenth Amendment's equal protection clause. Since the 1970s, the United States Supreme Court has tended to scrutinize gender classifications closely and has invalidated a number of such statutes and policies. For example, in 1977 the Court held that police and firefighting units cannot establish arbitrary rules, such as height and weight requirements, that tend to keep women from joining those occupations.[11] In 1983, the Court ruled that life insurance companies cannot charge different rates for women and men.[12]

This woman is a trained medical technician in the Marines. Could she join an infantry direct-combat unit? (AP Photo, John Althouse/The Daily News)

Congress sought to guarantee equality of treatment in education by passing Title IX of the Education Amendments of 1972, which states: "No person in the United States shall, on the basis of sex, be excluded from participation in, be denied the benefits of, or be subjected to discrimination under any education program or activity receiving Federal financial assistance." Title IX's best known and most controversial impact has been on high school and collegiate athletics, although the original statute made no reference to athletics.

A question that the Supreme Court has not ruled on is whether women should be allowed to participate in military combat. Generally, the Court has left this decision up to Congress and the Department of Defense. Recently, women have been allowed to serve as combat pilots and on naval warships. To date, however, they have not been allowed to join infantry direct-combat units, although they are now permitted to serve in combat-support units. In 1996, the Supreme Court held that the state-financed Virginia Military Institute's policy of accepting only males violated the equal protection clause.[13]

---

11. *Dothard v. Rawlinson,* 433 U.S. 321 (1977).
12. *Arizona v. Norris,* 463 U.S. 1073 (1983).
13. *United States v. Virginia,* 518 U.S. 515 (1996).

WOMEN IN POLITICS TODAY

The efforts of women's rights advocates have helped to increase the number of women holding political offices at all levels of government. In 2008, eight women served as state governors, and women made up almost a quarter of the nation's state legislators.

Women in Congress. Although a men's club atmosphere still prevails in Congress, the number of women holding congressional seats has increased significantly in recent years. Elections during the 1990s brought more women to Congress than either the Senate or the House had seen before. In 2001, for the first time, a woman was elected to a leadership post in Congress. Nancy Pelosi of California was elected as the Democrats' minority whip in the House of Representatives. In 2002, she became minority leader, and in 2006, she was chosen to be the first woman Speaker of the House in the history of the United States. In all, 133 women ran for Congress in 2008 on major-party tickets. In 2009, the House contained 74 women. Following the 2008 elections, the Senate included 17 women, up from 16 in the previous Congress—and an all-time record.

This is a photo of the sixteen female senators who served in the 110th Congress. What are some of the hurdles still facing women who seek high government offices? (Courtesy of Senator Mikulski's office)

Women in the Executive and Judicial Branches. In 1984, for the first time, a woman, Geraldine Ferraro, became the Democratic nominee for vice president. Another woman, Elizabeth Dole, made a serious run for the Republican presidential nomination in the 2000 campaigns. In 2008, Hillary Clinton mounted a major campaign for the presidency, and Sarah Palin became the Republican nominee for vice president. Recent Gallup polls show that close to 90 percent of Americans say they would vote for a qualified woman for president if she was nominated by their party.

Increasing numbers of women are also being appointed to cabinet posts. President Bill Clinton (1993–2001) appointed four women to his cabinet, more than any previous president. Madeleine Albright was appointed to the important post of secretary of state. President George W. Bush also appointed several women to cabinet positions, including

elections2008
POLITICAL LEADERSHIP BY WOMEN

In 2008, the two biggest stories that involved women featured New York senator Hillary Clinton and Alaska governor Sarah Palin. Clinton was the early favorite to win the 2008 Democratic nomination for president. Had she won, she would have been the first women nominated for president by a major party, and she may well have become the first woman president. Clinton's campaign organization and fund-raising were strong, but in the end, Illinois senator Barack Obama's campaign proved to be stronger. Still, the Obama-Clinton race was the closest primary contest in memory. In late August, Republican presidential candidate John McCain selected Palin as the first woman ever to run for vice president

on the Republican ticket. A staunch social conservative, Palin was greeted with enormous enthusiasm by the many voters who shared her views. Palin soon ran into trouble, however. In interviews with Charles Gibson on "Good Morning, America" and later with CBS anchor Katie Couric, Palin had trouble with questions about domestic and foreign policy. Although intelligent and politically sharp, Palin seemed to have paid insufficient attention to national issues before she was nominated. By the time of the general election, polls suggested that Palin was losing votes for the Republican ticket.

Hillary Clinton
(Paul J. Richards/AFP/ Getty Images)

Sexual Harassment
Unwanted physical or verbal conduct or abuse of a sexual nature that interferes with a recipient's job performance, creates a hostile work environment, or carries with it an implicit or explicit threat of adverse employment consequences.

Condoleezza Rice as his secretary of state in 2005, and a number of other women to various federal offices.

Increasing numbers of women are sitting on federal judicial benches as well. President Ronald Reagan (1981–1989) was credited with a historic first when he appointed Sandra Day O'Connor to the United States Supreme Court in 1981. President Clinton appointed a second woman, Ruth Bader Ginsburg, to the Court. O'Connor retired from the Court in 2006. President Bush initially nominated another woman, Harriet Miers, to take her place on the bench. Miers, however, later withdrew her nomination.

Continuing Disproportionate Leadership. For all the achievements of women in the political arena, the number of them holding political offices remains disproportionately low compared with their participation as voters, and the number of women holding elective office may have leveled off in the last few years. In recent elections, the turnout of female voters nationally has been slightly higher than that of male voters.

GENDER-BASED DISCRIMINATION IN THE WORKPLACE

Traditional cultural beliefs concerning the proper role of women in society continue to be evident not only in the political arena but also in the workplace. Since the 1960s, however, women have gained substantial protection against discrimination through laws mandating equal employment opportunities and equal pay.

TITLE VII OF THE CIVIL RIGHTS ACT OF 1964

Title VII of the Civil Rights Act of 1964 prohibits gender discrimination in employment and has been used to strike down employment policies that discriminate against employees on the basis of gender. Even so-called protective policies have been held to violate Title VII if they have a discriminatory effect. In 1991, for example, the United States Supreme Court held that a fetal protection policy established by Johnson Controls, Inc., the country's largest producer of automobile batteries, violated Title VII. The policy required all women of childbearing age working in jobs that entailed periodic exposure to lead or other hazardous materials to prove that they were infertile or to transfer to other positions. Women who agreed to transfer often had to accept cuts in pay and reduced job responsibilities. The Court concluded that women who are "as capable of doing their jobs as their male counterparts may not be forced to choose between having a child and having a job."[14]

In 1978, Congress amended Title VII to expand the definition of gender discrimination to include discrimination based on pregnancy. Pregnancy and related conditions must be treated—for all employment-related purposes, including the receipt of benefits under employee benefit programs—the same as any other health issue.

SEXUAL HARASSMENT

The United States Supreme Court has also held that Title VII's prohibition of gender-based discrimination extends to **sexual harassment** in the workplace. Sexual harassment occurs when job opportunities, promotions, salary increases, and the like are given in return for sexual favors. A special form of sexual harassment, called hostile-environment harassment, occurs when an employee is subjected to sexual conduct or comments that interfere with the employee's job performance or are so pervasive or severe as to create an intimidating, hostile, or offensive environment.

In two 1998 cases, the Supreme Court clarified the responsibilities of employers in preventing sexual harassment. In *Faragher v. City of Boca Raton,* the question was the following: Should an employer be held liable for a supervisor's sexual harassment of an employee even though the employer was unaware of the harassment? The Court ruled

---

14. *United Automobile Workers v. Johnson Controls, Inc.,* 499 U.S. 187 (1991).

that the employer in this case was liable but stated that the employer might have avoided such liability if it had taken reasonable care to prevent harassing behavior—which the employer had not done. In the second case, *Burlington Industries v. Ellerth,* the Court made a similar finding.[15]

In another 1998 case, *Oncale v. Sundowner Offshore Services, Inc.,*[16] the Supreme Court addressed a further issue: Should Title VII protection be extended to cover situations in which individuals are harassed by members of the same gender? The Court answered this question in the affirmative.

WAGE DISCRIMINATION

By 2010, women will constitute a majority of U.S. workers. Although Title VII and other legislation since the 1960s have mandated equal employment opportunities for men and women, women continue to earn less, on average, than men do.

The Equal Pay Act of 1963. The issue of wage discrimination was first addressed during World War II (1939–1945), when the War Labor Board issued an "equal pay for women" policy. In implementing the policy, the board often evaluated jobs for their comparability and required equal pay for comparable jobs. The board's authority ended with the war. Although it was supported by the next three presidential administrations, the Equal Pay Act was not enacted until 1963 as an amendment to the Fair Labor Standards Act of 1938.

Basically, the Equal Pay Act requires employers to provide equal pay for substantially equal work. In other words, males cannot legally be paid more than females who perform essentially the same job. The Equal Pay Act did not address the fact that certain types of jobs traditionally held by women pay lower wages than the jobs usually held by men. For example, more women than men are salesclerks and nurses, whereas more men than women are construction workers and truck drivers. Even if all clerks performing substantially similar jobs for a company earned the same salaries, they typically would still be earning less than the company's truck drivers.

When Congress passed the Equal Pay Act in 1963, a woman, on average, made 59 cents for every dollar earned by a man. By the mid-1990s, this amount had risen to 75 cents. Figures recently released by the U.S. Department of Labor indicate, though, that since then there has been little change. By 2009, women were still earning, on average, 77 cents for every dollar earned by men.

The Glass Ceiling. Although greater numbers of women are holding jobs in professions or business enterprises that were once dominated by men, few women hold top positions in their firms. Women now hold only 15 percent of the top corporate officer positions in Fortune 500 companies—the nation's leading corporations. Although this percentage has grown from 8.7 percent in 1995, women continue to face barriers to advancement in the corporate world. Because these barriers are subtle and not easily pinpointed, they have been referred to as the "glass ceiling."

Over the last decade, women have been breaking through the glass ceiling in far greater numbers than before. Alternatively, some corporations have offered a "mommy track" to high-achieving women. The mommy track allows a woman more time to pursue a family life but usually rules out promotion to top jobs. The mommy track therefore tends to reinforce the glass ceiling.

These Vermont citizens attend a rally on National Equal Pay Day in front of the statehouse in Montpellier. What are some of the reasons that women typically earn less than men do? (AP Photo/Toby Talbot)

---

15. 524 U.S. 775 (1998); and 524 U.S. 742 (1998).
16. 523 U.S. 75 (1998).

TABLE 5–2:

Top Ten Countries of Origin for the Foreign-Born Population

Hispanic countries are marked in red.

Mexico	11,534,972
Philippines	1,634,117
India	1,505,351
China	1,357,482
Vietnam	1,116,156
El Salvador	1,042,218
Korea	1,021,212
Cuba	932,563
Canada	847,228
Dominican Republic	764,930
ALL COUNTRIES	37,469,387

Source: Pew Hispanic Center tabulations of the 2006 American Community Survey.

TABLE 5–3:

Top Ten Countries of Birth for Unauthorized Immigrants

Also referred to as "illegal" or "undocumented" immigrants. Of necessity, these figures are rough estimates. Hispanic countries are marked in red.

Mexico	5,970,000
El Salvador	470,000
Guatemala	370,000
India	280,000
China	230,000
Korea	210,000
Philippines	210,000
Honduras	180,000
Brazil*	170,000
Vietnam	160,000
ALL COUNTRIES	10,500,000

*Although Brazil is located in South America, its language is Portuguese, and the Bureau of the Census does not consider it a Hispanic country.

Source: U.S. Department of Homeland Security.

IMMIGRATION, LATINOS, AND CIVIL RIGHTS

Time and again, this nation has been challenged and changed—and culturally enriched—by immigrant groups. All of these immigrants have faced the challenges involved in living in a new and different political and cultural environment. Most of them have had to overcome language barriers, and many have had to deal with discrimination in one form or another because of their color, their inability to speak English fluently, or their customs.

Immigration, and in particular unauthorized immigration, has become one of the hottest political issues under debate. Issues include whether we should create a path toward citizenship for unauthorized immigrants, as discussed in the *What If . . .* feature at the beginning of this chapter, or whether such a move amounts to an unacceptable amnesty for lawbreakers. A second major issue is how to limit unauthorized immigration in the first place. Closely allied to these issues are those affecting legal immigrants. Are we admitting too many legal immigrants—or not enough? Are laws restricting the rights of immigrants appropriate—or too tough? We examine immigration issues in detail in Chapter 14.

A century ago, most immigrants to the United States came from Europe. Today, however, most come from Latin America and Asia. Tables 5–2, 5–3, and 5–4 show the top countries of origin for immigrants, both legal and unauthorized, entering the United States. Note the large number of immigrants from Spanish-speaking countries, or "Hispanic" countries, which are marked in red on the tables.

The large number of new immigrants from Spanish-speaking countries increases the Hispanic proportion of the U.S. population. The number of persons who identify themselves as *multiracial* is also growing due to interracial marriages. Those who consider themselves as multiracial may have one parent of Chinese descent and another of Mexican descent, for example.

HISPANIC v. LATINO

To the U.S. Census Bureau, Hispanics are those who identify themselves by that term. Hispanics can be of any race. Hispanics can be new immigrants or the descendants of families that have lived in the United States for centuries. Hispanics may come from any of about twenty primarily Spanish-speaking countries,[17] and they differ among themselves in many ways. Hispanic Americans, as a result, are a highly diverse population. The three largest Hispanic groups are Mexican Americans, at 63.9 percent of all Hispanics; Puerto Ricans (all of whom are U.S. citizens), at 9.1 percent of the total; and Cuban Americans, at 3.5 percent.

The term *Hispanic* itself, although used by the government, is not particularly popular among Hispanic Americans. Many prefer the term *Latino,* and for that reason we frequently use that term throughout this text. When possible, Latinos prefer a name that identifies their heritage more specifically—for example, many Mexican Americans would rather be called that than *Latino* or *Hispanic.* Some Mexican Americans prefer the term *Chicano.*

THE CHANGING FACE OF AMERICA

As a result of immigration, the ethnic makeup of the United States is changing. The percentage of Latinos and Asian Americans in the population is growing rapidly. At the same time, the percentage of African Americans is staying relatively constant and the percentage of European Americans is dropping, though both groups continue to grow in absolute numbers.

---

17. According to the census definition, *Hispanic* includes the relatively small number of Americans whose ancestors came directly from Spain itself. Few of these people are likely to check the "Hispanic" box on a census form, however.

Immigration is not the only factor contributing to changes in the American ethnic mosaic. Another factor is ethnic differences in the *fertility rate*. The **fertility rate** measures the average number of children that women in a given group are expected to have over the course of a lifetime. A fertility rate of 2.1 is the "long-term replacement rate." In other words, if a nation or group maintains a fertility rate of 2.1, its population will eventually stabilize. This can take a long time. Because of past growth, the median age of the population may be younger than it would otherwise be. This means that there are more potential mothers and fathers. Only after its residents age will the population of a group or country stabilize.

Today, the United States actually has a fertility rate of 2.1 children per woman. Hispanic Americans, however, have a current fertility rate of 2.9. (The fertility rate in Mexico itself is only 2.4.) African Americans have a fertility rate of 2.1. Non-Hispanic white Americans have a fertility rate of 1.86. Figure 5–1 on the following page shows the projected changes in the U.S. ethnic distribution in future years.

THE CIVIL RIGHTS OF IMMIGRANTS

Citizens who are Hispanic Americans have the same rights as all other Americans. Further, the law recognizes that in years past, Latinos have been subjected to many of the same forms of ill treatment as African Americans, so Latinos are usually grouped with African Americans and American Indians (Native Americans) in laws and programs that seek to protect minorities from discrimination or to address the results of past discrimination. Such programs often cover Asian Americans as well.

Immigrants who are not yet citizens, however, possess fewer civil rights than any other identifiable group in the United States. The rights of unauthorized immigrants are fewer still. As one example, even most legal immigrants are not eligible for various federal antipoverty programs such as food stamps. The terrorist attacks on September 11, 2001, reinforced the belief that the rights of noncitizens should be limited. Among the most obvious characteristics of the terrorists who perpetrated the 9/11 attacks is that they were all foreign citizens.

The Constitutional Rights of Noncitizens. Legal immigrants are not entirely without rights. The Bill of Rights contains no language that limits its protections to citizens. The Fourteenth Amendment specifies that all *persons* (as opposed to *citizens*) shall enjoy "due process of law." In decisions spanning more than a century, the United States Supreme Court has ruled that there are constitutional guarantees that apply to every person within our borders, including "aliens whose presence in this country is unlawful." The Court has also said, however, that in supervising immigration, the federal government can discriminate on the basis of citizenship.

Immigrants who are not here legally are subject to deportation. In 1903, however, the Supreme Court ruled that the government could not deport someone without a hearing that meets constitutional due process standards.[18] Today, most people facing deportation are entitled to a hearing before an immigration judge, to representation by a lawyer, and to the right to see the evidence presented against them. The government must prove that its grounds for deportation are valid.

---

18. *Yamataya v. Fisher*, 189 U.S. 86 (1903).

Fertility Rate
A statistic that measures the average number of children that women in a given group are expected to have over the course of a lifetime.

TABLE 5-4:
Top Ten Countries of Origin for Legal Immigrants

The following figures are for a single year only. Legal immigrants in 2006 are persons obtaining official permanent resident status in that year. Hispanic countries are marked in red.

Mexico	173,753
China	87,345
Philippines	74,607
India	61,369
Cuba	45,614
Colombia	43,151
Dominican Republic	38,069
El Salvador	31,783
Vietnam	30,695
Jamaica	24,976
ALL COUNTRIES	1,266,264

Source: U.S. Department of Homeland Security.

These immigrants and activists carry flags in downtown Chicago during a rally for comprehensive immigration reform. What might some of their reform demands be? (AP Photo/M. Spencer Green)

FIGURE 5-1: Projected Changes in U.S. Ethnic Distribution

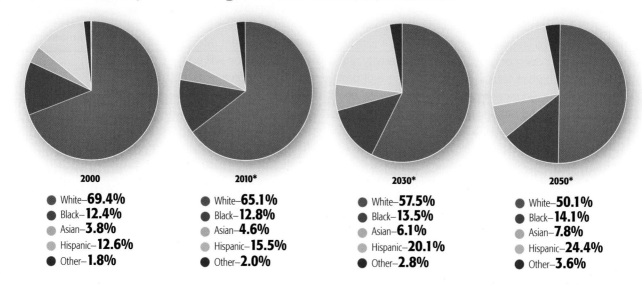

2000
- White–**69.4%**
- Black–**12.4%**
- Asian–**3.8%**
- Hispanic–**12.6%**
- Other–**1.8%**

2010*
- White–**65.1%**
- Black–**12.8%**
- Asian–**4.6%**
- Hispanic–**15.5%**
- Other–**2.0%**

2030*
- White–**57.5%**
- Black–**13.5%**
- Asian–**6.1%**
- Hispanic–**20.1%**
- Other–**2.8%**

2050*
- White–**50.1%**
- Black–**14.1%**
- Asian–**7.8%**
- Hispanic–**24.4%**
- Other–**3.6%**

*Data for 2010, 2030, and 2050 are projections.
Hispanics may be of any race. The chart categories *White, Black, Asian,* and *Other* are limited to non-Hispanics.
Other consists of the following non-Hispanic groups: *American Indian, Native Alaskan, Native Hawaiian, Other Pacific Islander,* and *Two or more races.*

Source: U.S. Bureau of the Census and authors' calculations.

Limits to the Rights of Deportees: Due Process. Despite the language of the Fourteenth Amendment, the courts have often deferred to government assertions that noncitizens cannot make constitutional claims. The Supreme Court has stated, "In exercise of its broad power over naturalization and immigration, Congress may make rules as to aliens that would be unacceptable if applied to citizens."[19] Immigration and antiterrorism laws passed by Congress in 1996 were especially restrictive. The government was given the right to deport noncitizens in cases of alleged terrorism without any federal court review of the deportation order. Further, the government is now allowed to deport noncitizens based on secret evidence that the deportee is not permitted to see.

Immediately after 9/11, the government arrested more than 1,200 foreign citizens on suspicion of terrorism. These persons were cleared of terrorism, but most were deported for violating immigration rules. The deportation hearings were secret—a reversal of past procedure. Even the names of the persons held were not released. In June 2003, a federal appellate court ruled that the government was within its rights to maintain such secrecy.[20] The Supreme Court refused to review the issue. As a result, the public will never know how these cases were handled.

Limits to the Rights of Deportees: Freedom of Speech. A case in 1999 involved a group of noncitizens associated with the Popular Front for the Liberation of Palestine (PFLP). The PFLP has carried out terrorist acts in Israel, but there was no evidence of criminal conduct by the group arrested in the United States. In *Reno v. American-Arab Anti-Discrimination Committee,*[21] the Supreme Court ruled that aliens have no First Amendment rights to object to deportation, even if the deportation is based on their political associations. This ruling also covers permanent residents—noncitizens with "green cards" that allow them to live and work in the United States on a long-term basis.

Limits to the Rights of Deportees: *Ex Post Facto* Laws. Article I, Section 9, of the Constitution prohibits *ex post facto* laws—laws that inflict punishments for acts that were

---

19. See, for example, *Demore v. Hyung Joon Kim,* 538 U.S. 510 (2003).
20. *Center for National Security Studies v. U.S. Dept. of Justice,* 331 F.3d 918 (D.C.Cir. 2003).
21. 525 U.S. 471 (1999).

not illegal when they were committed. This provision may not apply to deportation cases, however. The 1996 immigration and antiterrorism laws mentioned earlier provide mandatory deportation for noncitizens convicted of an aggravated felony, even if the crime took place before 1996. The term *aggravated felony* sounds serious, but under immigration law it can include misdemeanors. Until recently, mere possession of marijuana was usually an aggravated felony. Under the 1996 laws, permanent residents have been deported to nations that they left when they were small children. In some cases, deported persons did not even speak the language of the country to which they were deported.

BILINGUAL EDUCATION

The continuous influx of immigrants into this country presents another ongoing challenge—how to overcome language barriers. About half of the states have responded to this challenge by passing "English-only" laws, making English the official language of those states. Language issues have been particularly difficult for the schools. Throughout our history, educators have been faced with the question of how best to educate children who do not speak English or do not speak it very well.

During the 1950s, increased immigration from Mexico and Latin American countries caused many educators to be concerned about the language problems facing these immigrants. Spanish had effectively become America's second language, yet local school districts in some parts of the Southwest prohibited children from speaking Spanish, even on school playgrounds. In the 1960s, bilingual education programs began to be implemented as a solution to the language problems facing immigrants.

In Palo Alto, California, these grade school students participate in a Spanish immersion class. What are the pros and cons of bilingual education? (AP Photo/ Marcio Jose Sanchez)

Accommodating Diversity with Bilingual Education. Bilingual education programs teach children in their native language while also teaching them English. To some extent, today's bilingual education programs are the result of the government policies favoring multiculturalism that grew out of the civil rights movement. Multiculturalism involves the belief that the government should accommodate the needs of different cultural groups and should protect and encourage ethnic and cultural differences.

Congress authorized bilingual education programs in 1968 when it passed the Bilingual Education Act, which was intended primarily to help Hispanic children learn English. In a 1974 case, *Lau v. Nichols,*[22] the Supreme Court bolstered the claim that children have a right to bilingual education. In that case, the Court ordered a California school district to provide special programs for Chinese students with language difficulties if a substantial number of these children attended school in the district. Today, most bilingual education programs are for Hispanic American children, particularly in areas of the country, such as California and Texas, where there are large numbers of Latino residents.

Controversy over Bilingual Education. The bilingual programs established in the 1960s and subsequently have increasingly come under attack. Indeed, in 1998 California residents passed a ballot initiative that called for the end of bilingual education programs in that state. The law allowed schools to implement "English-immersion" programs instead.

---

22. 414 U.S. 563 (1974).

Affirmative Action
A policy in educational admissions or job hiring that gives special attention or compensatory treatment to traditionally disadvantaged groups in an effort to overcome present effects of past discrimination.

Reverse Discrimination
The situation in which an affirmative action program discriminates against those who do not have minority status.

In these programs, students are given intensive instruction in English for a limited period of time and then placed in regular classrooms.

The law was immediately challenged in court on the ground that it unconstitutionally discriminated against non-English-speaking groups. A federal district court, however, concluded that the law did not violate the equal protection clause and allowed the law to stand, thus ending bilingual education efforts in California.

AFFIRMATIVE ACTION

As noted earlier in this chapter, the Civil Rights Act of 1964 prohibited discrimination against any person on the basis of race, color, national origin, religion, or gender. The act also established the right to equal opportunity in employment. A basic problem remained, however: minority groups and women, because of past discrimination, often lacked the education and skills to compete effectively in the marketplace. In 1965, the federal government attempted to remedy this problem by implementing the concept of affirmative action. **Affirmative action** policies attempt to "level the playing field" by giving special preferences in educational admissions and employment decisions to groups that have been discriminated against in the past.

In 1965, President Lyndon Johnson issued Executive Order 11246, which mandated affirmative action policies to remedy the effects of past discrimination. All government agencies, including those of state and local governments, were required to implement such policies. Additionally, affirmative action requirements were imposed on companies that sell goods or services to the federal government and on institutions that receive federal funds. Affirmative action policies were also required whenever an employer had been ordered to develop such a plan by a court or by the Equal Employment Opportunity Commission because of evidence of past discrimination. Finally, labor unions that had been found to discriminate against women or minorities in the past were required to establish and follow affirmative action plans.

(Walt Handelsman/Newsday)

Affirmative action programs have been controversial because they allegedly result in discrimination against majority groups, such as white males (or discrimination against other minority groups that may not be given preferential treatment under a particular affirmative action program). At issue in the current debate over affirmative action programs is whether such programs, because of their discriminatory nature, violate the equal protection clause of the Fourteenth Amendment to the Constitution.

While the term *affirmative action* was coined in the United States, other countries, such as India, Malaysia, and South Africa, have attempted to implement similar policies. We look at India's program of affirmative action for the lower castes in its society in this chapter's *Beyond Our Borders* feature.

THE *BAKKE* CASE

The first United States Supreme Court case addressing the constitutionality of affirmative action plans examined a program implemented by the University of California at Davis. Allan Bakke, a white student who had been turned down for medical school at the Davis campus, discovered that his academic record was better than those of some of the minority applicants who had been admitted to the program. He sued the University of California regents, alleging **reverse discrimination.** The UC-Davis Medical School had held sixteen places out of one hundred for educationally "disadvantaged students" each year, and the administrators at that campus admitted to using race as a criterion for admission for these

beyondourborders

HIRING QUOTAS IN INDIA

Americans have become used to affirmative action systems designed to eradicate discrimination in the workplace. In the past, such systems sometimes involved actual quotas for hiring members of racial minorities or admitting them into college. Over the years, the courts have struck down systems that established outright quotas, while permitting plans that consider race as one factor among many. Some states have passed laws prohibiting any consideration of race in admissions to public universities.

In India, the world's most populous democracy with more than a billion inhabitants, however, quotas for hiring and college admissions are widespread. Preferences are based not on minority status, as in the United States, but rather on Hinduism's caste system.

These technology workers attend a training center at the Infosys corporate campus in Mysore, India. Some Indian government officials would like to extend a quota system to the private sector so that more of those in the lower classes have access to better jobs. (AP Photo/Gurinder Osan, File)

THE CASTE SYSTEM

India's traditional caste system is bound up with its dominant religion. For millennia, Hindu teachings have endorsed a rigid social hierarchy. One ancient Hindu text, the Laws of Manu, states that individuals from the "lower orders" are not even allowed to mention the name of higher castes, such as the highest—the Brahman. Today, the caste system is strongest in India's rural villages, but its effects are felt throughout the country. Members of the upper castes get the larger share of good jobs. The untouchables—the *Dalits*—get few.

QUOTAS IN THE PUBLIC SECTOR

Currently, almost 25 percent of public sector jobs and university admissions are reserved for *Dalits* and for members of tribes that fall outside the caste system. In 1993, another 25 percent of university admissions and public sector jobs were reserved for "other backward classes," low-ranking subcastes that nonetheless have higher status than the *Dalits*. Not everyone is happy about such quotas. There have been riots by those in India who have lost out because they are not designated as either untouchables or part of "other backward classes."

EXTENDING QUOTAS TO THE PRIVATE SECTOR

Recently, some members of India's government have argued that quotas should be applied to private companies. One *Dalit* leader has said that he believes that 30 percent of company jobs should be reserved for *Dalits*, members of "other backward classes," and the Muslim poor. Indian businesses argue against such preferences. They contend that those employees who are given a right to a job tend not to work very hard. Some enterprises, however, have responded to these arguments by setting up affirmative action programs for *Dalits* that are not based on quotas.

India has not seen the kind of reverse discrimination cases that have come before U.S. courts over the last twenty years. Nonetheless, some Indian attorneys are starting to prepare their arguments.

FOR CRITICAL ANALYSIS

Given that any quota system means that someone loses out on university admission or employment because of that system, is there any procedure that can be used to reduce the frictions among affected groups?

particular minority slots. At trial in 1974, Bakke said that his exclusion from medical school violated his rights under the Fourteenth Amendment's provision for equal protection of the laws. The trial court agreed. On appeal, the California Supreme Court agreed also. Finally, the regents of the university appealed to the United States Supreme Court.

In 1978, the Supreme Court handed down its decision in *Regents of the University of California v. Bakke.*[23] The Court did not rule against affirmative action programs. Rather, it held that Bakke must be admitted to the medical school because its admissions policy had used race as the sole criterion for the sixteen "minority" positions. Justice Lewis Powell, speaking for the Court, indicated that while race can be considered "as a factor" among others in admissions (and presumably hiring) decisions, race cannot be the sole factor. So affirmative action programs, but not quota systems, were upheld as constitutional.

FURTHER LIMITS ON AFFIRMATIVE ACTION

A number of cases decided during the 1980s and 1990s placed further limits on affirmative action programs. In a landmark decision in 1995, *Adarand Constructors, Inc. v. Peña,*[24] the Supreme Court held that any federal, state, or local affirmative action program that uses racial or ethnic classifications as the basis for making decisions is subject to "strict scrutiny" by the courts. Under a strict-scrutiny analysis, to be constitutional, a discriminatory law or action must be narrowly tailored to meet a *compelling* government interest. In effect, the Court's opinion in *Adarand* means that an affirmative action program cannot make use of quotas or preferences for unqualified persons. Furthermore, once the program has succeeded in achieving its purpose, it must be changed or dropped.

In 1996, a federal appellate court went even further. In *Hopwood v. State of Texas,*[25] two white law school applicants sued the University of Texas School of Law in Austin, alleging that they had been denied admission because of the school's affirmative action program. The program allowed admissions officials to take race and other factors into consideration. The federal appellate court held that the program violated the equal protection clause because it discriminated in favor of minority applicants. Significantly, the court directly challenged the *Bakke* decision by stating that the use of race even as a means of achieving diversity on college campuses "undercuts the Fourteenth Amendment."

In 2003, however, in two cases involving the University of Michigan, the Supreme Court indicated that limited affirmative action programs continue to be acceptable and that diversity is a legitimate goal. The Court struck down the affirmative action plan used for undergraduate admissions at the university, which automatically awarded a substantial number of points to applicants based on minority status.[26] At the same time, it approved the admissions plan used by the law school, which took race into consideration as part of a complete examination of each applicant's background.[27]

THE END OF AFFIRMATIVE ACTION?

Although in 2003 the United States Supreme Court upheld the admissions plan used by the University of Michigan Law School, a Michigan ballot initiative passed in 2006 prohibited affirmative action programs in all public universities and state government positions.

In addition to Michigan, other states, including California, Florida, Nebraska, and Washington, have banned all state-sponsored affirmative action programs. In 2008, however, Colorado voters rejected such a ban.

In 2007, the United States Supreme Court heard a case involving voluntary integration plans in school districts in Seattle, Washington, and in

These concerned Seattle residents
listen to a news conference that discussed the Supreme Court's 2000 decision concerning the voluntary integration plans for school districts in Seattle. The Court ruled that race could not be the deciding factor in denying admission to a particular school. How does the Fourteenth Amendment to the Constitution enter into this discussion?
(AP Photo/Joe Nicholson)

---

23. 438 U.S. 265 (1978).
24. 515 U.S. 200 (1995).
25. 84 F.3d 720 (5th Cir. 1996).
26. *Gratz v. Bollinger,* 539 U.S. 244 (2003).
27. *Grutter v. Bollinger,* 539 U.S. 306 (2003).

Louisville, Kentucky. The schools' racial-integration guidelines permitted race to be a deciding factor if, say, two persons sought to be admitted to the school and there was space for only one. The schools' policies were challenged by parents of students, most of them white, who were denied admission because of their race. In a close (five-to-four) decision, the Court ruled that the schools' policies violated the Constitution's equal protection clause. (The Court did not, however, go so far as to invalidate the use of race as a factor in university admissions policies.)[28]

SPECIAL PROTECTION FOR OLDER AMERICANS

Americans are getting older. About half the population living in colonial times were under the age of sixteen. By 2000, fewer than one in four Americans were under the age of sixteen. The "aging of America" is a weaker phenomenon than in many other wealthy countries, however. Today, the median age of the population is thirty-seven in the United States and thirty-nine in Europe. By 2050, the median age in the United States is expected to rise slightly, to thirty-nine. In Europe, it is expected to surpass forty-seven. Figure 5–2 shows the predicted change in the proportion of the retirement-age population in the United States over the next half century. By 2025, that proportion is expected to be almost one and a half times what it is today.

As a result, the government will be under pressure to revise the Social Security system. A larger portion of each worker's wages will have to go toward taxes to support benefits for the retired population—or else the benefits may be reduced. The larger number of older persons will also strain health-care budgets. Not only do older persons require more medical care, but we can expect that advances in medical science will cause the demand for medical services to rise in future years. We discuss these issues in Chapter 14.

Older citizens face a variety of other difficulties unique to their group. One problem that seems to endure, despite government legislation designed to prevent it, is age discrimination in employment.

AGE DISCRIMINATION IN EMPLOYMENT

Age discrimination is potentially the most widespread form of discrimination, because almost anyone—regardless of race, color, national origin, or gender—could be a victim at some point in life. The unstated policies of some companies not to hire or to demote or dismiss people they feel are "too old" have made it difficult for some older workers to succeed in their jobs or continue with their careers. Additionally, older workers have fallen victim at times to cost-cutting efforts by employers. To reduce operational costs, companies may replace older, higher-salaried workers with younger, lower-salaried workers.

THE AGE DISCRIMINATION IN EMPLOYMENT ACT OF 1967

In an attempt to protect older employees from such discriminatory practices, Congress passed the Age Discrimination in Employment Act (ADEA) in 1967. The act, which applies to employers, employment agencies, and labor organizations and covers individuals over the age of forty, prohibits discrimination against individuals on the basis of age unless age is shown to be a bona fide occupational qualification reasonably necessary to the normal operation of the particular business.

To succeed in a suit for age discrimination, an employee must prove that the employer's action, such as a decision to fire the employee, was motivated, at least in part, by age

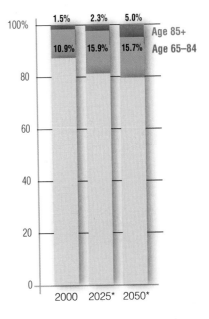

FIGURE 5–2:

The Aging of America

This figure shows that the portion of the population over age sixty-five will increase during the next half century. Growth in the proportion of the elderly may slow by 2050 due to the effects of immigration.

*Data for 2025 and 2050 are projections.
Source: U.S. Bureau of the Census.

---

28. *Parents Involved in Community Schools v. Seattle School District No. 1,* 127 S.Ct. 2738 (2007).

bias. Even if an older worker is replaced by a younger worker who is also over the age of forty, the older worker is entitled to bring a suit under the ADEA. In 2000, the United States Supreme Court limited the applicability of the ADEA by holding that the sovereign immunity granted to the states by the Eleventh Amendment to the Constitution precluded suits against a state by private parties alleging violations of the ADEA. Victims of age discrimination can bring actions under state statutes, however.[29] In 2008, the Supreme Court made it clear that the sovereign immunity defense does not apply to federal employers. Federal employees can sue their employers (federal agencies) not only for age discrimination but also for retaliation (which occurs when an employer fires or demotes an employee who complains of age discrimination).[30]

To address another problem facing older workers, in 1978, in an amendment to the ADEA, Congress prohibited **mandatory retirement** rules for most employees under the age of seventy. In 1986, Congress outlawed mandatory retirement rules entirely for all but a few selected occupations, such as firefighting.

SECURING RIGHTS FOR PERSONS WITH DISABILITIES

Like older Americans, persons with disabilities did not fall under the protective umbrella of the Civil Rights Act of 1964. In 1973, however, Congress passed the Rehabilitation Act, which prohibited discrimination against persons with disabilities in programs receiving federal aid. A 1978 amendment to the act established the Architectural and Transportation Barriers Compliance Board. Regulations for ramps, elevators, and the like in all federal buildings were implemented. Congress passed the Education for All Handicapped Children Act in 1975. It guarantees that all children with disabilities will receive an "appropriate" education. The most significant federal legislation to protect the rights of persons with disabilities, however, is the Americans with Disabilities Act (ADA), which Congress passed in 1990.

THE AMERICANS WITH DISABILITIES ACT OF 1990

The ADA requires that all public buildings and public services be accessible to persons with disabilities. The act also mandates that employers must reasonably accommodate the needs of workers or potential workers with disabilities. Physical access means ramps; handrails; wheelchair-accessible restrooms, counters, drinking fountains, telephones, and doorways; and easily accessible mass transit. In addition, other steps must be taken to comply with the act. Car rental companies must provide cars with hand controls for disabled drivers. Telephone companies are required to have operators to pass on messages from speech-impaired persons who use telephones with keyboards.

The ADA requires employers to "reasonably accommodate" the needs of persons with disabilities unless to do so would cause the employer to suffer an "undue hardship." The ADA defines persons with disabilities as persons who have physical or mental impairments that "substantially limit" their everyday activities. Health conditions that have been considered disabilities under federal law include blindness, alcoholism, heart disease, cancer, muscular dystrophy, cerebral palsy, paraplegia, diabetes, acquired immune deficiency syndrome (AIDS), and infection with the human immunodeficiency virus (HIV) that causes AIDS.

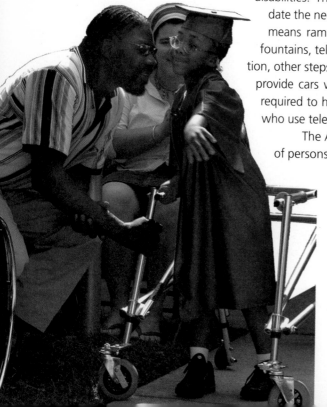

This child, who uses a walker for mobility assistance, is a beneficiary of the Education for All Handicapped Children Act of 1975. What other federal legislation was passed to help persons with disabilities in the United States? (Realistic Reflections)

29. *Kimel v. Florida Board of Regents,* 528 U.S. 62 (2000).
30. *Gomez-Perez v. Potter,* 128 S.Ct. 1931 (2008).

The ADA does not require that *unqualified* applicants with disabilities be hired or retained. If a job applicant or an employee with a disability, with reasonable accommodation, can perform essential job functions, however, then the employer must make the accommodation. Required accommodations may include installing ramps for a wheelchair, establishing more flexible working hours, creating or modifying job assignments, and creating or improving training materials and procedures.

LIMITING THE SCOPE AND APPLICABILITY OF THE ADA

Beginning in 1999, the United States Supreme Court has issued a series of decisions that effectively limit the scope of the ADA. In 1999, for example, the Court held in *Sutton v. United Airlines, Inc.*[31] that a condition (in this case, severe nearsightedness) that can be corrected with medication or a corrective device (in this case, eyeglasses) is not considered a disability under the ADA. In other words, the determination of whether a person is substantially limited in a major life activity is based on how the person functions when taking medication or using corrective devices, not on how the person functions without these measures. Since then, the courts have held that plaintiffs with bipolar disorder, epilepsy, diabetes, and other conditions do not fall under the ADA's protections if the conditions can be corrected with medication or corrective devices—even though the plaintiffs contended that they were discriminated against because of their conditions.

In a 2002 decision, the Court held that carpal tunnel syndrome did not constitute a disability under the ADA. The Court stated that although an employee with carpal tunnel syndrome could not perform the manual tasks associated with her job, the injury did not constitute a disability under the ADA because it did not "substantially limit" the major life activity of performing manual tasks.[32]

The Supreme Court has also limited the applicability of the ADA by holding that lawsuits under the ADA cannot be brought against state government employers.[33] In a 2001 case, the Court concluded—as it did with the ADEA, as mentioned earlier—that states, as sovereigns, are immune from lawsuits brought against them by private parties under the federal ADA.

THE RIGHTS AND STATUS OF GAY MALES AND LESBIANS

On June 27, 1969, patrons of the Stonewall Inn, a New York City bar popular with gay men and lesbians, responded to a police raid by throwing beer cans and bottles because they were angry at what they felt was unrelenting police harassment. In the ensuing riot, which lasted two nights, hundreds of gay men and lesbians fought with police. Before Stonewall, the stigma attached to homosexuality and the resulting fear of exposure had tended to keep most gay men and lesbians quiescent. In the months immediately after Stonewall, however, "gay power" graffiti began to appear in New York City. The Gay Liberation Front and the Gay Activist Alliance were formed, and similar groups

In the summer of 1969, gay men and lesbians who frequented a New York City bar called the Stonewall Inn had had enough. They were tired of unrelenting police harassment. For two nights, they fought with police. Out of these riots came a "gay power" movement. ("DoctorWho," Creative Commons)

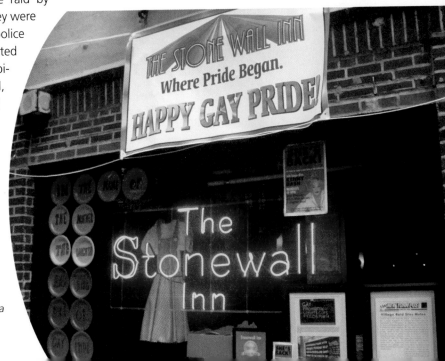

31. 527 U.S. 471 (1999).
32. *Toyota Manufacturing, Kentucky, Inc. v. Williams,* 534 U.S. 184 (2002).
33. *Board of Trustees of the University of Alabama v. Garrett,* 531 U.S. 356 (2001).

sprang up in other parts of the country. Thus, Stonewall has been called "the shot heard round the homosexual world."

GROWTH IN THE GAY MALE AND LESBIAN RIGHTS MOVEMENT

The Stonewall incident marked the beginning of the movement for gay and lesbian rights. Since then, gay men and lesbians have formed thousands of organizations to exert pressure on legislatures, the media, schools, churches, and other organizations to recognize their right to equal treatment.

To a great extent, lesbian and gay groups have succeeded in changing public opinion—and state and local laws—that pertain to their status and rights. Nevertheless, they continue to struggle against age-old biases against homosexuality, often rooted in deeply held religious beliefs, and the rights of gay men and lesbians remain an extremely divisive issue in American society. These attitudes were clearly illustrated in a widely publicized case involving the Boy Scouts of America. The case arose after a Boy Scout troop in New Jersey refused to allow gay activist James Dale to be a Scout leader. In 2000, the case came before the United States Supreme Court, which held that, as a private organization, the Boy Scouts had the right to determine the requirements for becoming a Scout leader.[34]

STATE AND LOCAL LAWS TARGETING GAY MEN AND LESBIANS

Before the Stonewall incident, forty-nine states had sodomy laws that made various kinds of sexual acts, including homosexual acts, illegal (Illinois, which had repealed its sodomy law in 1962, was the only exception). During the 1970s and 1980s, more than half of these laws were either repealed or struck down by the courts.

The trend toward repealing state antigay laws was suspended in 1986 with the Supreme Court's decision in *Bowers v. Hardwick*.[35] In that case, the Court upheld, by a five-to-four vote, a Georgia law that made homosexual conduct between two adults a crime. In 2003, the Court reversed its earlier position on sodomy with its decision in *Lawrence v. Texas*.[36] In this case, the Court held that laws against sodomy violate the due process clause of the Fourteenth Amendment. The Court stated: "The liberty protected by the Constitution allows homosexual persons the right to choose to enter upon relationships in the confines of their homes and their own private lives and still retain their dignity as free persons." The result of *Lawrence v. Texas* was to invalidate all remaining sodomy laws throughout the country.

Today, twenty states, the District of Columbia, and more than 140 cities and counties have enacted laws protecting lesbians and gay men from discrimination in employment. Many of these laws also ban discrimination in housing, public accommodation, and other contexts. At one point, Colorado adopted a constitutional amendment to invalidate all state and local laws protecting homosexuals from discrimination. Ultimately, however, the Supreme Court, in

didyouknow...

That in October 1999, Scouts Canada, the Canadian equivalent of the Boy Scouts of America, officially approved North America's first gay Scout troop?

For three days in June every year, Atlanta, Georgia, holds a gay pride festival parade. At the same time, there are rock bands, fashion shows, and shopping at hundreds of vendors' booths. (AP Photo/Gregory Smith)

---

34. *Boy Scouts of America v. Dale,* 530 U.S. 640 (2000).
35. 478 U.S. 186 (1986).
36. 539 U.S. 558 (2003).

Romer v. Evans,[37] invalidated the amendment, ruling that it violated the equal protection clause of the U.S. Constitution because it denied to homosexuals in Colorado—but to no other Colorado residents—"the right to seek specific protection of the law." Several laws at the national level have also been changed over the past two decades. Among other things, the government has lifted a ban on hiring gay men and lesbians and voided a 1952 law prohibiting gay men and lesbians from immigrating to the United States.

THE GAY COMMUNITY AND POLITICS

Politicians at the national level have not overlooked the potential significance of homosexual issues in American politics. While conservative politicians generally have been critical of efforts to secure gay and lesbian rights, liberals, by and large, have been speaking out for gay rights in the last twenty-five years. In 1980, the Democratic platform included a gay plank for the first time.

President Bill Clinton was the first sitting president to address a gay rights organization. In 1997, in a speech intentionally reminiscent of Harry Truman's 1947 speech to an African American civil rights group, Clinton pledged his support for equal rights for gay and lesbian Americans at a fund-raiser sponsored by the Human Rights Campaign Fund. In 2000, George W. Bush became the first Republican presidential candidate to meet with a large group of openly gay leaders to discuss their issues. Although Bush asserted that he would continue to oppose gay marriage and adoption, he also said that being openly gay would not disqualify a person from serving in a prominent position in his administration.

To date, twelve openly gay men and lesbians have been elected to the House of Representatives, although only three were seated in 2009.[38] None has succeeded yet in gaining a seat in the Senate. Gay rights groups continue to work for increased political representation in Congress.

GAY MEN AND LESBIANS IN THE MILITARY

The U.S. Department of Defense traditionally has viewed homosexuality as incompatible with military service. Supporters of gay and lesbian rights have attacked this policy in recent years, and in 1993 the policy was modified. In that year, President Clinton announced that a new policy, generally characterized as "don't ask, don't tell," would be in effect. Enlistees would not be asked about their sexual orientation, and gay men and lesbians would be allowed to serve in the military so long as they did not declare that they were gay or lesbian or commit homosexual acts. Military officials endorsed the new policy, after opposing it initially, but supporters of gay rights were not enthusiastic. Clinton had promised during his presidential campaign to repeal outright the long-standing ban.

Several gay men and lesbians who have been discharged from military service have protested their discharges by bringing suit against the Defense Department. Often at issue in these cases are the constitutional rights to free speech, privacy, and the equal protection of the laws. A widely publicized 1998 case involved the Navy's dismissal of a naval officer, Timothy McVeigh,[39] on the ground that he had entered "gay" on a profile page for his account with America Online (AOL). Naval officers claimed that this amounted to a public declaration of McVeigh's gay status and thus justified his

> **didyouknow...**
>
> **That Albert Einstein** was among six thousand persons in Germany in 1903 who signed a petition to repeal a portion of the German penal code that made homosexuality illegal?

A group of retired gay and lesbian veterans and activists held a parade on Veterans Day in 2005 to honor the contributions of gay men and lesbians in the military. They also protested the Pentagon's "Don't ask, don't tell" policy. What does this policy involve? (AP Photo/Paul Sakuma)

37. 517 U.S. 620 (1996).
38. Tammy Baldwin (D., Wisc.), Barney Frank (D., Mass.), and Jared Polis (D., Colo.).
39. This is not the Timothy McVeigh who was convicted for the 1995 bombing of the Alfred P. Murrah Federal Building in Oklahoma City.

discharge. McVeigh argued that it was not a public declaration. Furthermore, contended McVeigh, the Navy had violated a 1986 federal privacy law governing electronic communications by obtaining information from AOL without a warrant or a court order. In 1998, a federal court judge agreed and ordered the Navy to reinstate McVeigh.[40]

Recent polling data show that military personnel may be more accepting of gay men and lesbians today than they were in years past. For example, in one poll of more than five hundred service members returning from Afghanistan and Iraq, 75 percent of those responding indicated that they would be comfortable interacting with gay people.[41]

SAME-SEX MARRIAGE

Perhaps one of the hottest political issues concerning the rights of gay and lesbian couples is whether they should be allowed to marry, just as heterosexual couples are.

Defense of Marriage Act. The controversy over this issue in the United States began in 1993 when the Hawaii Supreme Court ruled that denying marriage licenses to gay couples might violate the equal protection clause of the Hawaii constitution.[42] In the wake of this event, other states began to worry about whether they might have to treat gay men or lesbians who were legally married in another state as married couples in their state as well. Opponents of gay rights pushed for state laws banning same-sex marriages, and a number of states enacted such laws. At the federal level, Congress passed the Defense of Marriage Act of 1996, which bans federal recognition of lesbian and gay couples and allows state governments to ignore same-sex marriages performed in other states.

The controversy over gay marriages was fueled again by developments in the state of Vermont. In 1999, the Vermont Supreme Court ruled that gay couples are entitled to the same benefits of marriage as opposite-sex couples.[43] Subsequently, in April 2000, the Vermont legislature passed a law permitting gay and lesbian couples to form "civil unions." The law entitled partners forming civil unions to receive some three hundred state benefits available to married couples, including the rights to inherit a partner's property and to decide on medical treatment for an incapacitated partner. It did not, however, entitle those partners to receive any benefits allowed to married couples under federal law, such as spousal Social Security benefits. As of 2008, seven states have approved some form of spousal rights for same-sex couples.[44]

---

40. *McVeigh v. Cohen,* 983 F.Supp. 215 (D.C. 1998).
41. As cited in John M. Shalikashvili, "Second Thoughts on Gays in the Military," *The New York Times,* January 2, 2007.
42. *Baehr v. Lewin,* 852 P.2d 44 (Hawaii 1993).
43. *Baker v. Vermont,* 744 A.2d 864 (Vt. 1999).
44. Hawaii, Maine, New Hampshire, New Jersey, Oregon, Vermont, and Washington. The list does not include California, Connecticut, and Massachusetts, which allow full same-sex marriage.

Same-sex marriages have traditionally not been legal throughout the United States. In the last few years, some states have passed laws outlawing them. On May 15, 2008, the California Supreme Court overturned a voter-approved ban on gay marriages. Do same-sex civil-union laws provide the same benefits to gay and lesbian couples as same-sex marriages?
(AP Photo/Nick Ut)

State Recognition of Gay Marriages. In November 2003, the Massachusetts Supreme Judicial Court ruled that same-sex couples have a right to civil marriage under the Massachusetts state constitution.[45] The court also ruled that civil unions would not suffice. In 2005, the Massachusetts legislature voted down a proposed ballot initiative that would have amended the state constitution to explicitly state that marriage could only be between one man and one woman (but would have extended civil union status to same-sex couples). In May 2008, the California Supreme Court invalidated a voter-approved ban on same-sex marriage, effectively legalizing such marriages in California. In October, the Connecticut Supreme Court issued a similar ruling. In the November general elections, however, California voters overruled the Court by passing an amendment to the state constitution that banned gay marriage. Twenty-six states now have constitutional amendments explicitly barring the recognition of same-sex marriage. Same-sex marriage is currently accepted nationwide in Canada and several other countries.

CHILD CUSTODY AND ADOPTION

Gay men and lesbians have also faced difficulties in obtaining child-custody and adoption rights. Courts around the country, when deciding which of two parents should have custody, have wrestled with how much weight, if any, should be given to a parent's sexual orientation. For some time, the courts were split fairly evenly on this issue. In about half the states, courts held that a parent's sexual orientation should not be a significant factor in determining child custody. Courts in other states, however, tended to give more weight to sexual orientation. In one case, a court even went so far as to award custody to a father because the child's mother was a lesbian, even though the father had served eight years in prison for killing his first wife. Today, however, courts in the majority of states no longer deny custody or visitation rights to persons solely on the basis of their sexual orientation.

The last decade has also seen a sharp climb in the number of gay men and lesbians who are adopting children. Today, nearly half the states allow lesbians and gay men to adopt children through state-operated or private adoption agencies. Single-parent adoptions by gay men or lesbians are now legal in every state but Florida.

This lesbian couple in New York State succeeded in adopting a child, whom they brought to New York's Gay Pride Parade in June 2008. (AP Photo/Tina Fineberg)

THE RIGHTS AND STATUS OF JUVENILES

Approximately 88 million Americans—about 28 percent of the total population—are under twenty-one years of age. The definition of *children* ranges from persons under age sixteen to persons under age twenty-one. However defined, children in the United States have fewer rights and protections than adults.

The reason for this lack of rights is the presumption of society that children basically are protected by their parents. This is not to say that children are the exclusive property of the parents. Rather, an overwhelming case in favor of *not* allowing parents to control the actions of their children must be presented before children can be given authorization to act without parental consent (or before the state can be authorized to act on children's behalf without regard to their parents' wishes).

Supreme Court decisions affecting children's rights began a process of slow evolution with *Brown v. Board of Education of Topeka,* the landmark civil rights case of 1954 discussed earlier in this chapter. In the *Brown* case, the Court granted children the status of rights-bearing persons. In 1967, in *In re Gault,*[46] the Court expressly held that children have a constitutional right to be represented by counsel at the government's expense

didyouknow...

That the United Nations Convention on the Rights of the Child calls for the provision of effective legal assistance for children so that their interests can be "heard directly"?

---

45. *Goodridge v. Department of Public Health,* 798 N.E.2d 941 (Mass. 2003).
46. 387 U.S. 1 (1967).

Since 1971, those over the age of eighteen have been allowed to vote. Students on many college campuses, such as those pictured here at the University of Pennsylvania, volunteer to "get out the vote." They are helping a university employee fill out his voter registration form. Which amendment to the Constitution gave eighteen-year-olds the right to vote?

(AP Photo/Manuel Balce Ceneta, File)

in a criminal action. Five years later, the Court acknowledged that "children are 'persons' within the meaning of the Bill of Rights. We have held so over and over again."[47]

VOTING RIGHTS AND THE YOUNG

The Twenty-sixth Amendment to the Constitution, ratified on July 1, 1971, reads as follows:

> *The right of citizens of the United States, who are eighteen years of age or older, to vote shall not be denied or abridged by the United States or by any State on account of age.*

Before this amendment was ratified, the age at which citizens could vote was twenty-one in most states. Why did the Twenty-sixth Amendment specify age eighteen? Why not seventeen or sixteen? And why did it take until 1971 to allow those between the ages of eighteen and twenty-one to vote? One of the arguments used for granting suffrage to eighteen-year-olds was that, because they could be drafted to fight in the country's wars, they had a stake in public policy. At the time, the example of the Vietnam War (1964–1975) was paramount.

Have eighteen- to twenty-year-olds used their right to vote? Yes and no. In 1972, immediately after the passage of the Twenty-sixth Amendment, 58 percent of eighteen- to twenty-year-olds were registered to vote, and 48.4 percent reported that they had voted. But by the 2004 presidential elections, of the 11.5 million U.S. residents in the eighteen-to-twenty age bracket, just 50.7 percent were registered, and only 41 percent reported that they had voted. Subsequent elections have shown similar results. In contrast, voter turnout among Americans aged sixty-five or older is very high, usually between 60 and 70 percent.

THE RIGHTS OF CHILDREN IN CIVIL AND CRIMINAL PROCEEDINGS

Civil Law
The law regulating conduct between private persons over noncriminal matters, including contracts, domestic relations, and business interactions.

Criminal Law
The law that defines crimes and provides punishment for violations. In criminal cases, the government is the prosecutor.

Children today have limited rights in civil and criminal proceedings in our judicial system. Different procedural rules and judicial safeguards apply under civil and criminal laws. **Civil law** relates to such matters as contracts among private individuals, domestic relations, and business transactions between private parties. **Criminal law** relates to crimes against society that are defined by society acting through its legislatures and prosecuted by a public official, such as a district attorney.

---

47. *Wisconsin v. Yoder,* 406 U.S. 205 (1972).

Civil Rights of Juveniles. The civil rights of children are defined exclusively by state laws that govern private contract negotiations, rights, and remedies. The legal definition of **majority**—the age at which a person is entitled by law to the right to manage his or her own affairs and to the full enjoyment of civil rights—varies from eighteen to twenty-one years of age, depending on the state. As a rule, an individual who is legally a minor cannot be held responsible for contracts that he or she forms with others. In most states, only contracts entered into for so-called **necessaries** (things necessary for subsistence, as determined by the courts) can be enforced against minors. Also, when minors engage in negligent behavior, typically their parents are liable. If, for example, a minor destroys a neighbor's fence, the neighbor may bring suit against the child's parent but not against the child.

Civil law also encompasses the area of child custody. Child-custody rulings traditionally have given little weight to the wishes of the child. Courts have maintained the right to act on behalf of the child's "best interests" but have sometimes been constrained from doing so by the "greater" rights possessed by adults. For instance, a widely publicized Michigan Supreme Court ruling awarded legal custody of a two-and-a-half-year-old Michigan resident to an Iowa couple, the child's biological parents. A Michigan couple, who had cared for the child since shortly after her birth and who had petitioned to adopt the child, lost out in the custody battle. The court said that the law had allowed it to consider only the parents' rights and not the child's best interests.

Children's rights and their ability to articulate their rights for themselves in custody matters were strengthened, however, by several well-publicized rulings involving older children. In one case, for example, an eleven-year-old Florida boy filed suit in his own name, assisted by his own privately retained legal counsel, to terminate his relationship with his biological parents and to have the court affirm his right to be adopted by foster parents. The court granted his request, although it did not agree procedurally with the method by which the boy initiated the suit.[48] The news media characterized the case as the first instance in which a minor child had "divorced" himself from his parents.

Criminal Rights of Juveniles. One of the main requirements for an act to be criminal is intent. The law has given children certain defenses against criminal prosecution because of their presumed inability to have criminal intent. Under the **common law,** children up to seven years of age were considered incapable of committing a crime because they did not have the moral sense to understand that they were doing wrong. Children between the ages of seven and fourteen were also presumed to be incapable of committing a crime, but this presumption could be challenged by showing that the child understood the wrongful nature of the act. Today, states vary in their approaches. Most states retain the common law approach, although age limits vary from state to state. Other states have simply set a minimum age for criminal responsibility.

All states have juvenile court systems that handle children below the age of criminal responsibility who commit delinquent acts. The aim of juvenile courts is allegedly to reform rather than to punish. In states that retain the common law approach, children who are above the minimum age but are still juveniles can be turned over to the criminal courts if the juvenile court determines that they should be treated as adults. Children sent to juvenile court still do not have the right to trial by jury or to post bail. Also, in most states parents can commit their minor children to state mental institutions without allowing the child a hearing.

Although minors usually do not have the full rights of adults in criminal proceedings, they have certain advantages. In felony, manslaughter, murder, armed robbery, and assault cases, traditionally juveniles were not tried as adults. They were

Majority
The age at which a person is entitled by law to the right to manage her or his own affairs and to the full enjoyment of civil rights.

Necessaries
Things necessary for existence. In contract law, necessaries include whatever is reasonably necessary for suitable subsistence as measured by age, state, condition in life, and the like.

Common Law
Judge-made law that originated in England from decisions shaped according to prevailing customs. Decisions were applied to similar situations and thus gradually became common to the nation.

didyouknow...

That the first juvenile court in the United States opened in Chicago on July 3, 1899?

Juvenile criminal defendants typically appear in juvenile court, which is separate from our adult court system. If the alleged crime is serious enough, such as murder, the juvenile may be waived into the adult court system, however. This sixteen-year-old youth was accused of shooting his parents, killing his mother and critically wounding his father as a result. Nonetheless, his case was handled through the juvenile court system. Is it fair that some juveniles are prosecuted as adults but others are not? Explain. (AP Photo/Chronicle-Telegram, Bruce Bishop)

48. *Kingsley v. Kingsley,* 623 So.2d 780 (Fla.App. 1993).

A sheriff's officer

leads sixteen-year-old Shahid Baskerville out of the county courthouse in Newark, New Jersey, in April 2008. Baskerville and another youth were charged with the murder of three college students in a Newark schoolyard the previous summer. Are there any advantages to being prosecuted as an adult, rather than as a juvenile, in criminal proceedings?

(AP Photo/Mike Derer)

didyouknow...

That the number of juveniles sent to adult prisons for violent offenses in the United States has tripled since 1985?

often sentenced to probation or "reform" school for a relatively short term regardless of the seriousness of their crimes. Today, however, most states allow juveniles to be tried as adults (often at the discretion of the judge) for certain crimes, such as murder. When they are tried as adults, they are given due process of law and tried for the crime, rather than being given the paternalistic treatment reserved for the juvenile delinquent. Juveniles who are tried as adults may also face adult penalties. These used to include the death penalty. In 2005, however, the United States Supreme Court ruled that executing persons who were under the age of eighteen when they committed their crimes would constitute cruel and unusual punishment. The Court opined that sixteen- and seventeen-year-olds do not have a fully developed sense of right and wrong, nor do they necessarily understand the full gravity of their misdeeds.[49]

Approaches to Dealing with Crime by Juveniles. What to do about crime committed by juveniles is a pressing problem for today's political leaders. One approach to the problem is to treat juveniles as adults, which more and more judges seem to be doing. There appears to be widespread public support for this approach, as well as for lowering the age at which juveniles should receive adult treatment in criminal proceedings. Polling data show that two-thirds of U.S. adults think that juveniles under the age of thirteen who commit murder should be tried as adults. Another method is to hold parents responsible for the crimes of their minor children (a minority of the states do so under so-called parental-responsibility laws). These are contradictory approaches, to be sure. Yet they perhaps reflect the divided opinion in our society concerning the rights of children versus the rights of parents.

---

49. *Roper v. Simmons,* 543 U.S. 551 (2005).

WHY SHOULD YOU CARE ABOUT
civilrights?

Why should you, as an individual, care about civil rights? Anyone applying for a job may be subjected to a variety of possibly discriminatory practices based on race, color, gender, religion, age, sexual preference, or disability. There may be tests, some of which could have a discriminatory effect. At both the state and federal levels, the government continues to examine the fairness and validity of criteria used in screening job applicants. As a result, there are ways of addressing the problem of discrimination.

CIVIL RIGHTS AND YOUR LIFE

Some people may think that discrimination is only a problem for members of racial or ethnic minorities. Actually, almost everyone can be affected. Consider that in some instances, white men have actually experienced "reverse discrimination"—and have obtained redress for it. Also, discrimination against women is common, and women constitute half the population. Even if you are male, you probably have female friends whose well-being is of interest to you. Therefore, the knowledge of how to proceed when you suspect discrimination is another useful tool to have when living in the modern world.

HOW YOU CAN MAKE A DIFFERENCE

If you believe that you have been discriminated against by a potential employer, consider the following steps:

1. Evaluate your own capabilities, and determine if you are truly qualified for the position.
2. Analyze the reasons why you were turned down. Would others agree with you that you have been the object of discrimination, or would they uphold the employer's claim?
3. If you still believe that you have been treated unfairly, you have recourse to several agencies and services.

You should first speak to the personnel director of the company and explain politely that you believe you have not been evaluated adequately. If asked, explain your concerns clearly. If necessary, go into explicit detail, and indicate that you may have been discriminated against.

If a second evaluation is not forthcoming, contact your local state employment agency. If you still do not obtain adequate help, contact one or more of the following state agencies, usually listed in your telephone directory under "State Government":

(AP Photo/Javier Galeano)

1. If a government entity is involved, a state ombudsperson or citizen aide may be available to mediate.
2. You can contact the state civil rights commission, which at least will give you advice even if it does not wish to take up your case.
3. The state attorney general's office normally has a division dealing with discrimination and civil rights.
4. There may be a special commission or department specifically set up to help you, such as a women's status commission or a commission on Hispanics or Asian Americans. If you are a woman or a member of such a minority group, contact these commissions.

Finally, at the national level, you can contact:

American Civil Liberties Union
125 Broad St., 18th Floor
New York, NY 10004-2400
212-549-2500
www.aclu.org

You can also contact the most appropriate federal agency:

Equal Employment Opportunity Commission
1801 L St. NW
Washington, DC 20507
202-663-4900
www.eeoc.gov

QUESTIONS FOR
discussion**and**analysis

1. Review the *Which Side Are You On?* feature on page 161. Does inequality of wealth and income necessarily lead to negative consequences? If so, what are they? Are arguments about the benefits of inequality credible? Why or why not?

2. Not all African Americans agreed with the philosophy of nonviolence espoused by Dr. Martin Luther King, Jr. Advocates of black power called for a more militant approach. Can militancy make a movement more effective (possibly by making a more moderate approach seem like a reasonable compromise), or is it typically counterproductive? Either way, why?

3. Women in the military are currently barred from assignments that are likely to place them in active combat. (Of course, the nature of war is such that support units sometimes find themselves in combat, regardless of assignment.) Such barriers can keep female officers from advancing to the highest levels within the armed services. Are these barriers appropriate? Why or why not?

4. While polls of military personnel suggest that rank-and-file soldiers are more accepting of gay men and lesbians than in years past, the current policy, known as "don't ask, don't tell," continues to result in the discharge of large numbers of military personnel on the basis of their sexual orientation. Is the current policy appropriate, or should it be liberalized? Either way, why? If a different policy were adopted, what should it be?

5. The prevention of terrorist acts committed by adherents of radical Islamism is a major policy objective today. Can we defend ourselves against such acts without abridging the civil rights and liberties of American Muslims and immigrants from predominantly Muslim countries? What measures that might be undertaken by the authorities are legitimate? Which are not?

key**terms**

affirmative action 172
busing 153
civil disobedience 154
civil law 182
civil rights 149
common law 183
criminal law 182
de facto segregation 153

de jure segregation 153
feminism 162
fertility rate 169
gender discrimination 164
grandfather clause 152
Hispanic 158
Latino 158

literacy test 152
majority 183
mandatory retirement 176
necessaries 183
poll tax 152
reverse discrimination 172

separate-but-equal doctrine 151
sexual harassment 166
subpoena 156
suffrage 161
white primary 152

chapter**summary**

1. The civil rights movement started with the struggle by African Americans for equality. Before the Civil War, most African Americans were slaves, and slavery was protected by the Constitution and the Supreme Court. Constitutional amendments after the Civil War legally ended slavery, and African Americans gained citizenship, the right to vote, and other rights. This legal protection was largely a dead letter by the 1880s, however, and politically and socially, African American inequality continued.

2. Legal segregation was declared unconstitutional by the Supreme Court in *Brown v. Board of Education of Topeka* (1954), in which the Court stated that separation implied inferiority. In *Brown v. Board of Education* (1955), the Supreme Court ordered federal courts to ensure that public schools were desegregated "with all deliberate speed." Also in 1955, the modern civil rights movement began with a boycott of segregated public transportation in Montgomery, Alabama. Of particular impact was

the Civil Rights Act of 1964. The act bans discrimination on the basis of race, color, religion, gender, or national origin in employment and public accommodations.

3. The Voting Rights Act of 1965 outlawed discriminatory voter-registration tests and authorized federal registration of persons and federally administered procedures in any state or political subdivision evidencing electoral discrimination or low registration rates. The Voting Rights Act and other protective legislation passed during and since the 1960s apply not only to African Americans but to other ethnic groups as well. Minorities have been increasingly represented in national and state politics, although they have yet to gain representation proportionate to their numbers in the U.S. population. Lingering social and economic disparities continue to exist.

4. In the early history of the United States, women were considered citizens, but by and large they had no political rights. After the first women's rights convention in 1848, the women's movement gained momentum. Not until 1920, however, when the Nineteenth Amendment was ratified, did women finally obtain the right to vote. The modern women's movement began in the 1960s in the wake of the civil rights and anti–Vietnam War movements. The National Organization for Women (NOW) was formed in 1966 to bring about complete equality for women in all walks of life. Efforts to secure the ratification of the Equal Rights Amendment failed, but the women's movement has been successful in obtaining new laws, changes in social customs, and increased political representation for women.

5. Although women have found it difficult to gain positions of political leadership, their numbers in Congress and in other government bodies increased significantly in the 1990s and 2000s. Women continue to struggle against gender discrimination in employment. Federal government efforts to eliminate gender discrimination in the workplace include Title VII of the Civil Rights Act of 1964, which prohibits, among other things, gender-based discrimination, including sexual harassment on the job. Wage discrimination also continues to be a problem for women, as does the "glass ceiling" that prevents them from rising to the top of business or professional firms.

6. Today, most immigrants come from Asia and Latin America, especially Mexico. Many are unauthorized immigrants (also called illegal aliens or undocumented workers). The large number of Spanish-speaking immigrants means that the percentage of Latinos, or Hispanic Americans, in the population is growing rapidly. This population is also growing because of a high fertility rate—on average, Hispanic families have more children than other Americans. By 2050, non-Hispanic whites will make up only half of the nation's residents. While Latinos who are citizens benefit from the same antidiscrimination measures as African Americans, immigrants who are not citizens have few civil rights. The Fourteenth Amendment to the Constitution says that all *persons,* as opposed to *citizens,* deserve due process of law, but the government possesses sweeping powers to deport noncitizens.

7. Affirmative action programs have been controversial because they can lead to reverse discrimination against majority groups or even other minority groups. United States Supreme Court decisions have limited affirmative action programs, and several states now ban state-sponsored affirmative action. Two 2003 Supreme Court decisions in cases brought against the University of Michigan have confirmed the principle that limited affirmative action programs are constitutional.

8. Problems associated with aging and retirement are becoming increasingly important as the number of older persons in the United States increases. The Age Discrimination in Employment Act of 1967 prohibited job-related discrimination against individuals who are over forty years old on the basis of age, unless age is shown to be a bona fide occupational qualification reasonably necessary to the normal operation of the business. Amendments to the act prohibit mandatory retirement except in a few selected professions.

9. The Rehabilitation Act of 1973 prohibited discrimination against persons with disabilities in programs receiving federal aid. Regulations implementing the act provide for ramps, elevators, and the like in federal buildings. The Education for All Handicapped Children Act (1975) provides that children with disabilities should receive an "appropriate" education. The Americans with Disabilities Act of 1990 prohibits job discrimination against persons with physical and mental disabilities, requiring that positive steps be taken to comply with the act. The act also requires expanded access to public facilities, including transportation, and to services offered by such private concerns as car rental and telephone companies. The courts have limited the impact of this law, however.

10. Gay and lesbian rights groups, which first began to form in 1969, now number in the thousands. During the 1970s and 1980s, sodomy laws that criminalized specific sexual practices were repealed or struck down by the courts in nearly half of the states. In 2003, a United States Supreme Court decision effectively invalidated all remaining sodomy laws nationwide. Twenty states and more than 140 cities and counties now have laws prohibiting discrimination based on sexual orientation. Gay men and lesbians are no

longer barred from federal employment or from immigrating to this country. Since 1980, liberal Democrats at the national level have supported gay and lesbian rights and sought electoral support from these groups. The military's "don't ask, don't tell" policy has fueled extensive controversy, as have same-sex marriages and child-custody issues.

11. Children have few rights and protections, in part because it is commonly presumed that their parents protect them. The Twenty-sixth Amendment grants the right to vote to those aged eighteen or older. In most states, only contracts entered into for necessaries can be enforced against minors. When minors engage in negligent acts, their parents may be held liable. Minors have some defense against criminal prosecution because of their presumed inability to have criminal intent below certain ages. For those under the age of criminal responsibility, there are state juvenile courts. When minors are tried as adults, they are entitled to the procedural protections afforded to adults and are sometimes subject to adult penalties.

selectedprint&mediaresources

SUGGESTED READINGS

Friedan, Betty. *The Feminine Mystique.* New York: W. W. Norton, 2001. Betty Friedan's work is the feminist classic that helped launch the modern women's movement in the United States. This edition contains an up-to-date introduction by columnist Anna Quindlen.

Gilmore, Glenda Elizabeth. *Defying Dixie: The Radical Roots of Civil Rights, 1919–1950.* New York: Norton, 2008. Gilmore, an award-winning history professor at Yale, looks at the radicalism of those who sought to overthrow Jim Crow laws before the time of the civil rights movement. In 2002, Gilmore gained national attention for strongly opposing the war in Iraq before it had even begun.

Litwack, Leon F. *How Free Is Free? The Southern Black Experience.* Cambridge, Mass.: Harvard University Press, 2009. The African American struggle for freedom and dignity has lasted for generations and continues today. Litwack, a prize-winning University of California history professor, confronts a painful history in a series of inspiring lectures.

Moats, David. *Civil Wars: A Battle for Gay Marriage.* New York: Harcourt, 2004. Moats, a Pulitzer Prize–winning Vermont journalist, chronicles the battle over same-sex marriage in Vermont. The result was a law legalizing civil unions.

Riley, Glenda. *Inventing the American Woman: An Inclusive History,* 4th ed. Wheeling, Ill.: Harlan Davidson, 2007. This updated edition covers a wide range of women's experiences in the United States from colonial times to the present.

Risen, Clay. *A Nation on Fire: America in the Wake of the King Assassination.* Hoboken, N.J.: Wiley, 2009. The riots that blazed through city after city following the murder of the Reverend Dr. Martin Luther King, Jr., may have marked the end of the liberal dreams of the 1960s. Risen explains why these riots took place, how they played out, and what results followed.

MEDIA RESOURCES

Beyond the Glass Ceiling—A CNN-produced program showing the difficulties women face in trying to rise to the top in corporate America.

G.I. Jane—A 1997 film about a woman who is out to prove that she can survive Navy SEAL training that is so rigorous that many (60 percent) of the men do not make it.

King: Man of Peace in a Time of War—This 2006 release contains much rare footage. The "I Have a Dream" speech is here, of course, but so is a 1967 interview from the Mike Douglas show in which King answers pointed questions about race riots, patriotism, communism, and the Vietnam War.

Malcolm X—A 1992 film, directed by Spike Lee and starring Denzel Washington, that depicts the life of the controversial "black power" leader Malcolm X. Malcolm X, who was assassinated on February 21, 1965, clearly had a different vision from that of Martin Luther King, Jr., regarding how to achieve civil rights, respect, and equality for black Americans.

Separate but Equal—A video focusing on Thurgood Marshall, the African American lawyer (and later Supreme Court justice) who took the struggle for equal rights to the Supreme Court, and on the rise and demise of segregation in America.

Shot by a Kid—A film documenting the relationship among children, guns, and violence in four major U.S. cities.

e-mocracy

CIVIL RIGHTS INFORMATION ONLINE

Today, thanks to the Internet, information on civil rights issues is literally at your fingertips. By simply accessing the American Civil Liberties Union's Web site (the URL for this organization is given below, in the *Logging On* section), you can learn about the major civil rights issues facing Americans today. A host of other Web sites offer data on the extent to which groups discussed in this chapter are protected under state and federal laws. You can also find numerous advocacy sites that indicate what you can do to help promote the rights of a certain group.

LOGGING ON

For information on, and arguments in support of, affirmative action and the rights of the groups discussed in this chapter, a good source is the American Civil Liberties Union's Web site. Go to
www.aclu.org.

The National Organization for Women (NOW) offers online information and updates on the status of women's rights, including affirmative action cases involving women. Go to
www.now.org.

An excellent source of information on issues facing African Americans is the Web site of the National Association for the Advancement of Colored People at
www.naacp.org.

You can find information on the Americans with Disabilities Act (ADA) of 1990, including the act's text, at
www.jan.wvu.edu/links/adalinks.htm.

You can access the Web site of the Human Rights Campaign Fund, the nation's largest gay and lesbian political organization, at
www.hrc.org.

If you are interested in children's rights and wefare, a good starting place is the Web site of the Child Welfare Institute. Go to
www.gocwi.org.

6 Public Opinion and Political Socialization

The head of Marist College's Institute for Public Opinion sits among his students as they call people in New York State with poll questions. (AP Photo/Jim McKnight)

what if ...voters could accept or reject national policies via the Internet?

BACKGROUND

In recent years, public opinion has not had as much influence on government decision making as many people would like. Voters appear to have rejected the Iraq War policy of President George W. Bush when they handed control of Congress to the Democrats in 2006. No change in policy followed, however, because the Democrats in Congress still did not have enough votes to force a change on the administration. Indeed, in March 2008, when ABC News reporter Martha Raddatz informed Vice President Dick Cheney that a two-thirds majority of Americans disapproved of the Iraq War policy, Cheney responded, "So?" He went on to say that "we cannot be blown off course by the fluctuations of public opinion polls."

What if the public had a chance to vote on important national issues in referenda? Such national votes could be arranged using the Internet. Today, most people can access the Internet at home, at school, or at work. If not, they can do so at an Internet café or the local public library. Use of the Internet could provide extremely rapid voter feedback. Of course, steps would have to be taken to protect the integrity of the process and prevent voter fraud. An alternative would be to allow voting through the mail, as is done in Oregon. This, too, would require security measures.

WHAT IF VOTERS COULD ACCEPT OR REJECT NATIONAL POLICIES VIA THE INTERNET?

Many states allow their citizens to vote on policy issues by means of the referendum and citizens' initiative procedures that we described in Chapter 1. In 2006, for example, Arizona voters approved an initiative that guaranteed a minimum living space for pregnant pigs and calves. In all states, constitutions can be amended by referenda. By these means, public opinion can directly affect government policy on many issues. In a true direct democracy, however, like that of ancient Athens, citizens would be able to vote on all policy issues as they arise.

Assume for a moment that the U.S. Congress had to submit all important policy issues to the voters on a regular basis, such as every three or six months, or every year. Obviously, each single piece of legislation could not be presented to the electorate. More than twenty thousand bills are submitted in Congress annually. Thus, the country would need to somehow determine which policy issues were important enough to be settled by a popular vote. Herein lies a major policy issue in and of itself: What constitutes an "important" policy issue?

Additionally, congressional bills are very detailed and are often written in a way that is difficult for the average person to understand. Voters would need summaries of the bills and their likely consequences, which they could receive through the Internet or by mail. It might also be desirable to control the length of the referenda text and the complexity of the language.

A CHANGE IN HOW CONGRESS OPERATES

If important issues were presented for nationwide voting, those who favor a given policy would have to engage in a nationwide campaign. Rather than merely pressuring legislators and other government officials in Washington, D. C., interest groups would try to shape public opinion directly through advertising, opinion polling, and all the techniques used by marketing firms in creating demand for various products and services.

This is exactly what has happened in states with frequent referenda and initiatives. In California, for example, interest groups spend ever-increasing amounts on advertising and other strategies to garner support for their position on particular ballot items.

IN THE END, WOULD WE HAVE BETTER POLICIES?

In the final analysis, whether we would have better policies would depend on the extent to which citizens actually attempt to understand the policy issues on which they would be voting. If only a small percentage of Americans actually bothered to vote on national policy issues, then the resulting policies would not truly reflect public opinion. Instead, the results would tend to favor those citizens who are most likely to vote. That includes voters who are older, better educated, and wealthier than the average American—although voting via the Internet may increase participation by other groups, especially younger Americans.

FOR CRITICAL ANALYSIS

1. What do you think the criteria should be for deciding which policy issues are "important"?
2. If all citizens could vote on policy issues, including taxes, would it ever be possible to enact laws imposing higher federal taxes?

In a democracy, the ability of the people to freely express their opinions is fundamental. Americans can express their opinions in many ways. They can write letters to newspapers. They can share their ideas in online forums. They can organize politically. They can vote. They can respond to opinion polls. Public opinion clearly plays an important role in our political system, just as it does in any democracy.

In 2008, President George W. Bush and members of Congress from both parties showed that they knew how important public opinion can be. Not only was 2008 an election year, it was also a year in which the nation's economy experienced a serious slowdown. A crisis in the housing market led to an almost unprecedented increase in foreclosures. Financial institutions that had invested in mortgages lost hundreds of billions of dollars. Voters naturally wanted the government to "do something about the economy." Fixing the housing market would be difficult, however. Just what should the government do? Giving away money was much easier, so at the beginning of 2008, Congress and the Bush administration quickly forged a deal to rush income tax rebates of $600 to $1,200 to most tax filers by spring.

There is no doubt that public opinion can be powerful. Political scientists often point to two presidential decisions to illustrate this power. In 1968, President Lyndon Johnson decided not to run for reelection because of the intense and negative public reaction to the war in Vietnam. In 1974, President Richard Nixon resigned in the wake of a scandal when it was obvious that public opinion no longer supported him. The extent to which public opinion affects policymaking is not always so clear, however. For example, suppose that public opinion strongly supports a certain policy. If political leaders adopt that position, is it because they are responding to public opinion or to their own views on the issue? In addition, to some extent, political leaders themselves can shape public opinion. For these and other reasons, scholars must deal with many uncertainties when analyzing the impact of public opinion on policymaking.

DEFINING PUBLIC OPINION

There is no single public opinion, because there are many different "publics." In a nation of more than 300 million people, there may be innumerable gradations of opinion on an issue. What we do is describe the distribution of opinions among the members of the public about a particular question. Thus, we define **public opinion** as the aggregate of individual attitudes or beliefs shared by some portion of the adult population.

Public Opinion
The aggregate of individual attitudes or beliefs shared by some portion of the adult population.

One way for Americans to express their opinions is through demonstrations. Here, some Americans are expressing their strong opinion against the war in Iraq outside the White House. (AP Photo/Jose Luis Magana)

Consensus
General agreement among the citizenry on an issue.

Divided Opinion
Public opinion that is polarized between two quite different positions.

Political Socialization
The process by which people acquire political beliefs and values.

Typically, public opinion is distributed among several different positions, and the distribution of opinion can tell us how divided the public is on an issue and whether compromise is possible. When a poll shows that a large proportion of the American public appears to express the same view on an issue, we say that a **consensus** exists, at least at the moment the poll was taken. Figure 6–1 shows a pattern of opinion that might be called consensual. Issues on which the public holds widely differing attitudes result in **divided opinion** (see Figure 6–2). Sometimes, a poll shows a distribution of opinion indicating that most Americans either have no information about the issue or are not interested enough in the issue to formulate a position. Politicians may believe that the public's lack of knowledge about an issue gives them more room to maneuver, or they may be wary of taking any action for fear that opinion will crystallize after a crisis.

An interesting question arises as to when private opinion becomes public opinion. Everyone probably has a private opinion about the competence of the president, as well as private opinions about more personal concerns, such as the state of a neighbor's lawn. We say that private opinion becomes public opinion when the opinion is publicly expressed and concerns public issues. When someone's private opinion becomes so strong that the individual is willing to go to the polls to vote for or against a candidate or an issue—or is willing to participate in a demonstration, discuss the issue at work, speak out on television or radio, or participate in the political process in any one of a dozen other ways—then the opinion becomes public opinion.

HOW PUBLIC OPINION IS FORMED: POLITICAL SOCIALIZATION

Most Americans are willing to express opinions on political issues when asked. How do people acquire these opinions and attitudes? Typically, views that are expressed as political opinions are acquired through the process of **political socialization.** By this we mean

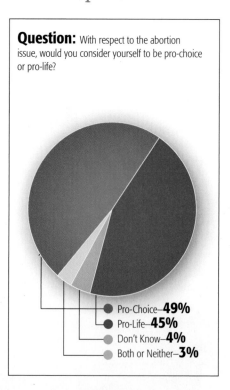

FIGURE 6–1:
Consensus Opinion

Question: Do you approve or disapprove of the way George W. Bush handled his job as president in the first few weeks after the September 11 terrorist attacks?

● Approve–**88%**
● Disapprove–**10%**
● No Opinion–**2%**

Source: Gallup poll, January 23–25, 2003.

FIGURE 6–2:
Divided Opinion

Question: With respect to the abortion issue, would you consider yourself to be pro-choice or pro-life?

● Pro-Choice–**49%**
● Pro-Life–**45%**
● Don't Know–**4%**
● Both or Neither–**3%**

Source: Gallup poll, May 10–13, 2007.

that people acquire their political beliefs and values, often including their party identification, through relationships with their families, friends, and co-workers.

MODELS OF POLITICAL SOCIALIZATION

The most important early sources of political socialization are found in the family and the schools. Individuals' basic political orientations are formed in the family if the family members hold strong views. When the adults in a family view politics as relatively unimportant and describe themselves as independent voters or disaffected from the political system, children receive very little political socialization.

In the last few decades, more and more sources of information about politics have become available to all Americans, and especially to young people. Although their basic outlook on the political system may be formed by early family influences, young people are now exposed to many other sources of information about issues and values. Scholars believe that this greater access to information may explain why young Americans are more liberal than their parents on many social issues. We look at one major source of online information that is popular among younger people in this chapter's *Politics and the Cyber Sphere* feature on the following page.

THE FAMILY AND THE SOCIAL ENVIRONMENT

Not only do our parents' political beliefs, values, and actions affect our opinions, but the family also links us to other factors that affect opinion, such as race, social class, educational environment, and religious beliefs. How do parents transmit their political values to their offspring?

Studies suggest that the influence of parents is due to two factors: communication and receptivity. Parents communicate their feelings and preferences to children constantly. Because children have such a strong need for parental approval, they are very receptive to their parents' views. Children are less likely to influence their parents, because parents expect deference from their children.[1]

Nevertheless, other studies show that if children are exposed to political ideas at school and in the media, they will share these ideas with their parents, giving the parents what some scholars call a "second chance" at political socialization. Children can also expose their parents to new media, such as the Internet.[2]

Education as a Source of Political Socialization. From the early days of the republic, schools were perceived to be important transmitters of political information and attitudes. Children in the primary grades learn about their country mostly in patriotic ways. They learn about the Pilgrims, the flag, and some of the nation's presidents. They also learn to celebrate national holidays. Later, in the middle grades, children learn more historical facts and come to understand the structure of government and the functions of the president, judges, and Congress. By high school, students have a more complex understanding of the political system, may identify with a political party, and may take positions on issues.

Generally, education is closely linked to political participation. The more education a person receives, the more likely that person will be interested in politics, be confident in his or her ability to understand political issues, and be an active participant in the political process. Public opinion polls, however, suggest that even well-educated younger Americans are not strongly interested in politics.[3]

These children show their support for Barack Obama at a campaign rally at Memorial Hall in Racine, Wisconsin, in 2008. How do children acquire their political attitudes?
(AP Photo/Journal Times, Mark Hertzberg)

1. Barbara A. Bardes and Robert W. Oldendick, *Public Opinion: Measuring the American Mind,* 3d ed. (Belmont, Calif.: Wadsworth Publishing Co., 2006), p. 73.
2. For a pioneering study in this area, see Michael McDevitt and Steven H. Chaffee, "Second Chance Political Socialization: 'Trickle-up' Effects of Children on Parents," in Thomas J. Johnson *et al.,* eds., *Engaging the Public: How Government and the Media Can Reinvigorate American Democracy* (Lanham, Md.: Rowman & Littlefield Publishers, 1998), pp. 57–66.
3. Jane Eisner, *Taking Back the Vote: Getting American Youth Involved in Our Democracy* (Boston: Beacon Press, 2004).

POLITICS AND...
the cyber sphere

THE YOUTUBE AND MYSPACE GENERATION ROCKS THE VOTE

(www.YouTube.com)

What group watches collectively as many as 2.5 billion online videos a month? The answer is, of course, the more than 75 million users of YouTube. A significant amount of political content appears on YouTube. Much of it, as you might imagine, is not very serious—a video that stars the "Obama girl" or that mocks New York senator Hillary Clinton's laugh doesn't have much real content. But YouTube is coming of political age.

YOUTUBE SPONSORS SERIOUS DEBATES

During the 2007–2008 presidential primary season, YouTube helped sponsor many of the debates among those candidates hoping to become the next Republican or Democratic nominee. Some of the questions were relayed to the candidates through YouTube videos on big screens. While some of the questions were off the wall, others were serious and addressed issues such as gun control and global warming. For the YouTube generation, this all seemed quite normal. But consider that YouTube had only been in existence for four years.

Currently, YouTube offers each candidate a "You-Choose" channel. Candidates can then interact with YouTube members using video clips. YouTube users can respond to candidates by posting their own video responses. Candidates themselves have discovered the power of YouTube. In January 2008, Illinois senator Barack Obama, at that time one of the less well-known Democratic candidates, videotaped his response to President George W. Bush's last State of the Union address. It was five minutes long and poorly lit. Television

and newspaper reporters essentially ignored it. Then it was posted on YouTube. Within two months, it was viewed almost 1.5 million times. More than 500 blogs posted links to the speech on YouTube. It was also distributed on social networking sites such as MySpace and Facebook.

CANDIDATES BEWARE—THE NEW GENERATION IS NOT PASSIVE

Many young people today (and some older ones, too) use YouTube, blogs, MySpace, Facebook, and other social networking sites to promote their favorite candidates or to identify weaknesses in opposing candidates' characters and policies. Obama found that out, too, much to his chagrin. Clips of sermons by his former pastor, the Reverend Jeremiah Wright, were widely disseminated through YouTube. Wright's sermons included harsh statements, such as "Not God bless America, God damn America," that seemed to say that the United States deserved 9/11. Obama was forced to disassociate himself completely from Wright and to repeatedly defend himself for remaining a member of that particular church for more than twenty years.

MILLIONS OF FRIENDS

MySpace and Facebook work because they create a sense of connection between people who use these social networking sites to link to their numerous online "friends." By the summer of 2008, Obama had 1 million "friends." Hillary Clinton had fewer, but they still numbered in the hundreds of thousands. Arizona senator John McCain, the Republican candidate, also had several hundred thousand. What started as a college networking system for students has ended up as a networking system for politicians as well.

FOR CRITICAL ANALYSIS

When promoting a candidate, what is the difference between social networking on the Internet and the traditional word-of-mouth approach?

Peer Group
A group consisting of members sharing common social characteristics. These groups play an important part in the socialization process, helping to shape attitudes and beliefs.

Peers and Peer Group Influence. Once a child enters school, the child's friends become an important influence on behavior and attitudes. For children and for adults, friendships and associations in **peer groups** affect political attitudes. We must, however, separate the effects of peer group pressure on opinions and attitudes in general from the effects of peer group pressure on political opinions. For the most part, associations among peers are nonpolitical. Political attitudes are more likely to be shaped by peer groups when the peer groups are involved directly in political activities.

Individuals who join interest groups based on ethnic identity may find, for example, a common political bond through working for the group's civil liberties and rights. African American activist groups may consist of individuals who join together to support government programs that will aid the African American population. Members of a labor union may be strongly influenced to support certain pro-labor candidates.

Opinion Leaders' Influence. We are all influenced by those with whom we are closely associated or whom we hold in high regard—friends at school, family members and other relatives, and teachers. In a sense, these people are **opinion leaders,** but on an *informal* level; that is, their influence on our political views is not necessarily intentional or deliberate. We are also influenced by *formal* opinion leaders, such as presidents, lobbyists, congresspersons, news commentators, and religious leaders, who have as part of their jobs the task of swaying people's views. Their interest lies in defining the political agenda in such a way that discussions about policy options will take place on their terms.

THE IMPACT OF THE MEDIA

Clearly, the **media**—newspapers, television, radio, and Internet sources—strongly influence public opinion. This is because the media inform the public about the issues and events of our times and thus have an **agenda-setting** effect. In other words, to borrow from Bernard Cohen's classic statement about the media and public opinion, the media may not be successful in telling people what to think, but they are "stunningly successful in telling their audience what to think about."[4] For competing views on the media's role in agenda setting, see the *Which Side Are You On?* feature on the next page.

Today, many contend that the media's influence on public opinion has grown to equal that of the family. For example, in her analysis of the role played by the media in American politics,[5] media scholar Doris A. Graber points out that high school students, when asked where they obtain the information on which they base their attitudes, mention the mass media far more than they mention their families, friends, and teachers. This trend, combined with the increasing popularity of such information sources as talk shows and the Internet, may significantly alter the nature of the media's influence on public debate in the future. The media's influence will be discussed in more detail in Chapter 9.

THE INFLUENCE OF POLITICAL EVENTS

Generally, older Americans tend to be somewhat more conservative than younger Americans, particularly on social issues but also, to some extent, on economic issues. This effect is known as the **lifestyle effect.** It probably occurs because older adults are concerned about their own economic situations and are likely to retain the social values that they learned at a younger age. Young people, especially today, are more liberal than their grandparents on social issues, such as the rights of gay men and lesbians and racial and gender equality. Nevertheless, a more important factor than a person's age is the impact of significant political events that shape the political attitudes of an entire generation. When events produce such a long-lasting result, we refer to it as a **generational effect** (also called a *cohort effect*).

Opinion Leader
One who is able to influence the opinions of others because of position, expertise, or personality.

Media
The channels of mass communication.

Agenda Setting
Determining which public-policy questions will be debated or considered.

Lifestyle Effect
A phenomenon in which certain attitudes occur at certain chronological ages.

Generational Effect
A long-lasting effect of the events of a particular time on the political opinions of those who came of political age at that time.

didyouknow...

That CNN reaches more than 1.5 billion people in more than 200 countries?

Oprah Winfrey
gave her support to presidential candidate Barack Obama (shown with his wife, Michelle) in 2007. To what extent do media stars such as Winfrey influence public opinion? (AP Photo/ Kristie Bull/Graylock.com)

4. *The Press and Foreign Policy* (Princeton, N.J.: Princeton University Press, 1963), p. 81.
5. Doris A. Graber, *Mass Media and American Politics,* 7th ed. (Chicago: University of Chicago Press, 2005).

whichsideare**YOU**on?

THE MEDIA AND AGENDA SETTING

The media clearly have a significant impact on the way that Americans think about politics. As you have read in this chapter, the media play a considerable role in *agenda setting*—determining which public-policy issues will be debated or considered. Traditional outlets such as television, radio, and the daily newspaper have long influenced what information reaches the public and how that information is packaged. Some Americans claim that in setting agendas, the media try to impose their own political views on the public. Others disagree, arguing that the rise of the "new" media of the Internet, such as blogs, has provided a wider selection of viewpoints in the information marketplace.

THE MEDIA IMPOSE AN AGENDA

Some Americans believe that the media have improper motives when they determine what information the public receives. Some argue that the public does not have access to a full spectrum of information about issues and events important to American politics and government.

Some even argue that the growth of media monopolies in recent years has created a collusive environment in which corporate interests dictate which information will be disseminated. Indeed, sometimes financial motives do influence the information that is presented to the public. For example, a media outlet might ignore a potential news story that reflects poorly on one of its major advertisers.

More often, news outlets determine which topics to cover based on entertainment or ratings value. In other words, the media devote the most attention to stories that will draw the widest audience. Some say this leads to a "dumbing down" of the news. For example, supporters of Democratic presidential candidate Barack Obama contended in 2008 that the media's obsessive interest in the controversial opinions of the Reverend Jeremiah Wright, Obama's former pastor, interfered with Obama's ability to present his own positions, which were quite different from Wright's.

At other times, content decisions may be driven by the political biases of the media outlet itself. Critics argue that some media outlets, such as Fox News, cater specifically to one political ideology or party.

THE MEDIA ARE TOO BROAD FOR A SPECIFIC AGENDA

Others disagree with the notion that the media can impose a point of view. Spotlighting the information revolution brought about by the Internet, these people argue that anyone can pursue his or her information-gathering agenda. Rather than being forced to sit through a predetermined set of stories on the evening news, Americans can surf countless Web sites, blogs, and chat rooms dedicated to political events and issues. If anyone believes that a source is biased, many other sources are at that Internet user's fingertips.

Obviously, most Americans still utilize traditional news sources. More and more homes have Internet access, however, so an ever-increasing portion of the public has a wide variety of outlets available. The sheer number of potential sources of information makes it nearly impossible for a concerted agenda to be foisted on the public as a whole.

Voters who grew up in the 1930s during the Great Depression were likely to form lifelong attachments to the Democratic Party, the party of Franklin D. Roosevelt. In the 1960s and 1970s, the war in Vietnam and the **Watergate break-in** and the subsequent presidential cover-up fostered widespread cynicism toward government. There is evidence that the years of economic prosperity under President Ronald Reagan during the 1980s led many young people to identify with the Republican Party. It is less clear whether more recent presidents—including Democrat Bill Clinton (1993–2001) and Republican George W. Bush—were able to affect the party identification of young voters.

POLITICAL PREFERENCES AND VOTING BEHAVIOR

A major indicator of voting behavior is, of course, party identification. In addition, however, there are a variety of socioeconomic and demographic factors that also appear to influence political preferences. These factors include education, income and **socioeconomic status,** religion, race, gender, geographic region, and similar traits. People who share the same

Watergate Break-In
The 1972 illegal entry into the Democratic National Committee offices by participants in President Richard Nixon's reelection campaign.

Socioeconomic Status
The value assigned to a person due to occupation or income. An upper-class person, for example, has high socioeconomic status.

TABLE 6–1: Votes by Groups in Presidential Elections, 1992–2008 (in Percentages)

	1992			1996		2000		2004		2008	
	Clinton (Dem.)	Bush (Rep.)	Perot (Ref.)	Clinton (Dem.)	Dole (Rep.)	Gore (Dem.)	Bush (Rep.)	Kerry (Dem.)	Bush (Rep.)	Obama (Dem.)	McCain (Rep.)
Total Vote	43	38	19	49	41	48	48	48	51	53	46
Gender											
Men	41	38	21	43	44	42	53	44	55	49	48
Women	46	37	17	54	38	54	43	51	48	56	43
Race											
White	39	41	20	43	46	42	54	41	58	43	55
Black	82	11	7	84	12	90	8	88	11	95	4
Hispanic	62	25	14	72	21	67	31	58	40	67	31
Educational Attainment											
Not a high school graduate	55	28	17	59	28	59	39	50	50	63	35
High school graduate	43	36	20	51	35	48	49	47	52	52	46
College graduate	40	41	19	44	46	45	51	46	52	50	48
Postgraduate education	49	36	15	52	40	52	44	54	45	58	40
Religion											
White Protestant	33	46	21	36	53	34	63	32	68	34	65
Catholic	44	36	20	53	37	49	47	47	52	54	45
Jewish	78	12	10	78	16	79	19	75	24	78	21
White evangelical	23	61	15	NA	NA	NA	NA	21	79	24	74
Union Status											
Union household	55	24	21	59	30	59	37	59	40	59	39
Family Income											
Under $15,000	59	23	18	59	28	57	37	63	37	73	25
$15,000–29,000	45	35	20	53	36	54	41	57	41	60	37
$30,000–49,000	41	38	21	48	40	49	48	50	49	55	43
Over $50,000	40	42	18	44	48	45	52	43	56	49	49
Size of Place of Residence											
Population over 500,000	58	28	13	68	25	71	26	60	40	70	28
Population 50,000 to 500,000	50	33	16	50	39	57	40	50	50	59	39
Population 10,000 to 50,000	39	42	20	48	41	38	59	48	51	45	53
Rural	39	40	20	44	46	37	59	39	60	45	53

NA = Not asked.

Sources: *The New York Times;* Voter News Service; CBS News, and the National Election Pool.

religion, occupation, or any other demographic trait are likely to influence one another and may also have common political concerns that follow from the common characteristic. Other factors, such as perception of the candidates and issue preferences, are closely connected to the electoral process itself. Table 6–1 illustrates the impact of some of these variables on voting behavior.

Because of the relationship between various groups and voting behavior, campaign managers often target particular groups when creating campaign advertising. Today, campaign managers and consultants are going even further in this attempt to "sell" their candidate to very specific groups by using "microtargeting" (see Chapter 9).

PARTY IDENTIFICATION AND
DEMOGRAPHIC INFLUENCES

With the possible exception of race, party identification has been the most important determinant of voting behavior in national elections. Party affiliation is influenced by family and peer groups, by generational effects, by the media, and by the voter's assessment of candidates and issues.

In the middle to late 1960s, party attachment began to weaken. Whereas independent voters were only a little more than 20 percent of the eligible electorate during the 1950s, they constituted more than 30 percent of all voters by the mid-1990s, and their numbers have remained constant since that time. New voters are likely to identify themselves as independent voters, although they may be more ready to identify with one of the major parties by their mid-thirties. There is considerable debate among political scientists over whether those who call themselves independents are truly so: when asked, a majority say that they are "leaning" toward one party or the other. (For further discussion of party affiliation, see Chapter 8.)

Demographic influences reflect the individual's personal background and place in society. Some factors have to do with the family into which a person was born: race and (for most people) religion. Others may be the result of choices made throughout an individual's life: place of residence, educational achievement, and profession. It is also clear that many of these factors are interrelated. People who have more education are likely to have higher incomes and to hold professional jobs. Similarly, children born into wealthier families are far more likely to complete college than children from poor families.

Education. In the past, having a college education tended to be associated with voting for Republicans. In recent years, however, this correlation has become weaker. In particular, individuals with a postgraduate education—more than a bachelor's degree—have voted predominantly Democratic. Also, in recent years (with the exception of the 2008 presidential elections), voters with only a high school education have cast their ballots for Republican presidential candidates more frequently than they did in the 1960s and 1970s, when such voters tended to favor Democrats.

Many people with postgraduate degrees are professionals, such as physicians, attorneys, and college instructors. Typically, a postgraduate degree is an occupational requirement for professionals. Despite the recent popularity of the master of business administration (MBA) degree, businesspersons are more likely to have only a bachelor's degree or no degree at all. They are also much more likely to vote Republican.

The Influence of Economic Status. Family income is a strong predictor of economic liberalism or conservatism. Those with low incomes tend to favor government action to benefit the poor or to promote economic equality. Those with high incomes tend to oppose government intervention in the economy or to support it only when it benefits business. On political issues, therefore, the traditional political spectrum described in Chapter 1 on page 18 is a useful tool. The rich tend toward the right; the poor tend toward the left.

If we examine cultural as well as economic issues, however, the four-cornered ideological grid discussed in Chapter 1 on page 20 becomes important. It happens that upper-class voters are more likely to endorse cultural liberalism and lower-class individuals are more likely to favor cultural conservatism. Support for the right to have an abortion, for example, rises with income. It follows that libertarians—those who oppose government action on both economic and social issues—are concentrated among the wealthier members of the population. (Libertarians constitute the upper-right-hand corner of the grid in Figure 1–1 in Chapter 1.) Those who favor government action both to promote traditional moral values and to promote economic equality—economic liberals, cultural conservatives—are concentrated among groups that are less well off. (This group fills up the lower-left-hand corner of the grid.)

Economic Status and Voting Behavior. Normally, the higher a person's income, the more likely the person will be to vote Republican. Manual laborers, factory workers, and especially union members are more likely to vote Democratic. There are no hard-and-fast rules, however. Some very poor individuals are devoted Republicans, just as some extremely wealthy people support the Democratic Party.

Religious Influence: Denomination. Traditionally, scholars have examined the impact of religion on political attitudes by dividing the population into such categories as Protestant, Catholic, and Jewish. In recent decades, however, such a breakdown has become less valuable as a means of predicting someone's political preferences. It is true that in the past, Jewish voters were notably more liberal than members of other groups, on both economic and cultural issues, and they continue to be more liberal today. Persons reporting no religion are very liberal on social issues but have mixed economic views. Northern Protestants and Catholics, however, have grown closer to each other politically in recent years, and so have southern Protestants and Catholics. This represents something of a change—in the late 1800s and early 1900s, northern Protestants were distinctly more likely to vote Republican, and northern Catholics were more likely to vote Democratic. Yet even today, in a few parts of the country, Protestants and Catholics tend to line up against each other when choosing a political party.

Religious Influence: Religiosity and Evangelicals. Today, two factors turn out to be major predictors of political attitudes among members of the various Christian denominations. One is the degree of *religiosity,* or practice of beliefs, and the other is whether the person holds fundamentalist or evangelical views. A high degree of *religiosity* is usually manifested by very frequent attendance at church services—that is, attending church at least once or twice a week.

Voters who are more devout, regardless of their church affiliation, tend to vote Republican, while voters who are less devout are more often Democrats. In the 2008 presidential elections, for example, Protestants who regularly attended church gave 67 percent of their votes to Republican candidate John McCain, compared with 54 percent of those who attended church less often. Among Catholics, there was a similar pattern: a majority of Catholics who attended church regularly voted Republican, while a slim majority of Catholics who were not regular churchgoers voted for Democratic candidate Barack Obama. Exit polls following the 2006 congressional elections showed the same pattern. A majority (55 percent) of those who attended church at least once a week voted for Republicans, while a majority (60 percent) of those who attended church less than once a week voted Democratic. There is an exception to this trend: African Americans of all religions have been strongly supportive of Democrats.

Another distinctive group of voters are those Protestant Americans who can be identified as holding evangelical or

A Jewish Family Celebrates Their Daughter Becoming a Bat Mitzvah by reading from the Torah. Despite their modern-day prosperity, a majority of American Jews continue to support liberal politics. Why might Jewish voters continue to be more interested in traditionally liberal values than in "voting their pocketbooks"? (Alan Shavit-Lonstein)

This New Life Congregation of Pentecostals in Tucson, Arizona, has numerous weekly services in Spanish. To what extent can we predict voting behavior based on religious affiliation? (AP Photo/Arizona Daily Star, Chris Richards)

fundamentalist beliefs. Actually, a majority of American Protestants can be characterized as evangelical. Not all are politically conservative. Some are politically liberal, such as former Democratic presidents Jimmy Carter and Bill Clinton. Fundamentalists are a subset of evangelicals who believe in a number of doctrines not held by all evangelicals. In particular, fundamentalists believe in biblical inerrancy—that is, that every word of the Bible is literally true. In politics, fundamentalists are notably more conservative than other evangelicals—liberal fundamentalists are rare indeed.[6]

The Influence of Race and Ethnicity. Although African Americans are, on average, somewhat conservative on certain cultural issues, such as same-sex marriage and abortion, they tend to be more liberal than whites on social-welfare matters, civil liberties, and even foreign policy. African Americans voted principally for Republicans until Democrat Franklin Roosevelt's New Deal in the 1930s. Since then, they have largely identified with the Democratic Party. Indeed, Democratic presidential candidates have received, on average, more than 80 percent of the African American vote since 1956. Of course, Barack Obama's support among African Americans was overwhelming.

Most Asian American groups lean toward the Democrats, although often by narrow margins. Muslim American immigrants and their descendants are an interesting category.[7] In 2000, a majority of Muslim Americans of Middle Eastern ancestry voted for Republican George W. Bush because they shared his cultural conservatism. Beginning with the 2004 election campaign, however, the civil liberties issue drove many of these voters toward the Democrats.

The Hispanic Vote. The diversity among Hispanic Americans has resulted in differing political behavior. The majority of Hispanic Americans vote Democratic. Cuban Americans, however, are usually Republican. Most Cuban Americans left Cuba because of Fidel Castro's Communist regime, and their strong anticommunism translates into conservative politics.

These Hispanic protesters at the capitol in Jackson, Mississippi, are shown supporting immigration reform. (AP Photo/Rogelio Solis)

In 2000, Republican presidential candidate George W. Bush received 34 percent of the Hispanic vote. In 2004, Bush's Hispanic support may have approached 40 percent. (A widely quoted survey put Bush's support at 44 percent, but that figure was almost certainly erroneous.) Since his days as Texas governor, Bush had envisioned creating a stronger long-term Republican coalition by adding Hispanics. Indeed, Hispanic voters appeared to show considerable sympathy for Bush's campaign appeals based on religious and family values and patriotism.

In 2006, however, Hispanics favored Democratic candidates over Republicans by 73 percent to 26 percent. Why did Hispanic support for the Republicans fall so greatly? In a word: immigration. In 2008, Barack Obama won more than two-thirds of the Hispanic vote. Bush favored a comprehensive immigration reform that would have granted unauthorized immigrants (also known as illegal or undocumented immigrants) a path to citizenship. Most Republicans in Congress refused to support Bush on this issue, and instead called for a hard line against unauthorized immigration. Although many Hispanics are also concerned about unauthorized immigration, the harsh rhetoric of some Republicans on this issue convinced many Hispanics that the Republicans were hostile to Hispanic interests.

---

6. George M. Marsden, *Understanding Fundamentalism and Evangelicalism* (Grand Rapids, Mich.: Eerdmans Publishing Co., 1991); and Karen Armstrong, *The Battle for God* (New York: Ballantine Books, 2001).

7. At least one-third of U.S. Muslims actually are African Americans whose ancestors have been in this country for a long time. In terms of political preferences, African American Muslims are more likely to resemble other African American Muslims than Muslim immigrants from the Middle East.

The Gender Gap. Until the 1980s, there was little evidence that men's and women's political attitudes were different. Following the election of Ronald Reagan in 1980, however, scholars began to detect a **gender gap.** A May 1983 Gallup poll revealed that men were more likely than women to approve of Reagan's job performance. The gender gap has reappeared in subsequent elections, with women being more likely than men to support the Democratic candidate (see Figure 6–3). A gender gap has also been evident in recent midterm elections. In 2002, 55 percent of women favored Democratic candidates, compared with 43 percent of men. In the 2006 midterm elections, the gender gap appeared to have narrowed somewhat. Just as in 2002, 55 percent of women favored Democratic candidates. In 2006, however, 50 percent of the men favored Democrats as well.

Women also appear to hold different attitudes from their male counterparts on a range of issues other than presidential preferences. They are much more likely than men to oppose capital punishment and the use of force abroad. Studies also have shown that women are more concerned about risks to the environment, more supportive of social welfare, and more in agreement with extending civil rights to gay men and lesbians than are men. Notably, women are also more concerned than men about the security issues raised by the terrorist attacks of September 11, 2001. This last fact may have pushed women in a more conservative direction, at least for a time. As you can see in Figure 6–3, in both the 2004 presidential elections and the 2008 presidential elections, the gender gap was slightly narrower.

Geographic Region. Finally, where you live can influence your political attitudes. For example, the former solid Democratic South has now become the solid Republican South. Only 42 percent of the votes from the southern states went to Democrat John Kerry in 2004, while 58 percent went to Republican George W. Bush. Barack Obama did better than Kerry, but Obama still won only 45 percent of the southern vote.

Muslim American
immigrants of Middle Eastern ancestry tend to favor Democratic candidates. **Why?** (AP Photo/M. Spencer Green)

Gender Gap
The difference between the percentage of women who vote for a particular candidate and the percentage of men who vote for the candidate.

FIGURE 6–3: Gender Gap in Presidential Elections, 1984–2008

A gender gap in voting is apparent in the percentage of women and the percentage of men voting in the last seven presidential elections. Even when women and men favor the same candidate, they do so by different margins, resulting in a gender gap.

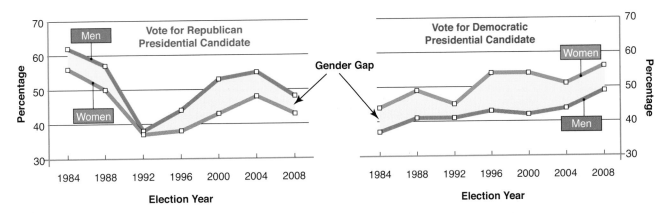

Note: Data in the chart include votes for Republican and Democratic candidates only. The effect of third party candidates on the gender gap was nominal except in 1992, when H. Ross Perot received 17 percent of the vote among women and 21 percent among men. Perot's impact, if factored into the data, would widen the gap pictured in the chart for 1992. To a lesser extent, it would also widen the gap shown for 1996, when his candidacy drew fewer votes.

Sources: Center for American Women and Politics (CAWP); Eagleton Institute of Politics; and Rutgers University.

There is a tendency today, at least in national elections, for the South, the Great Plains, and the Rocky Mountain states to favor the Republicans and for the West Coast and the Northeast to favor the Democrats. Perhaps more important than region is residence—urban, suburban, or rural. People in large cities tend to be liberal and Democratic. Those who live in smaller communities tend to be conservative and Republican.

ELECTION-SPECIFIC FACTORS

Factors such as perception of the candidates and issue preferences may have an effect on how people vote in particular elections. Candidates and issues can change greatly, and voting behavior can therefore change as well.

Perception of the Candidates. The image of the candidate seems to be important in a voter's choice, especially of a president. To some extent, voter attitudes toward candidates are based on emotions (such as trust) rather than on any judgment about experience or policy. In some years, voters have been attracted to a candidate who appeared to share their concerns and worries. In other years, voters have sought a candidate who appeared to have high integrity and honesty. Voters have been especially attracted to these candidates in elections that follow a major scandal, such as Richard Nixon's Watergate scandal (1972–1974) or Bill Clinton's sex scandal (1998–1999).

Issue Preferences. Issues make a difference in presidential and congressional elections. Although personality or image factors may be very persuasive, most voters have some notion of how the candidates differ on basic issues or at least know which candidates want a change in the direction of government policy.

Historically, economic concerns have been among the most powerful influences on public opinion. When the economy is doing well, it is very difficult for a challenger, especially at the presidential level, to defeat the incumbent. In contrast, inflation, unemployment, or high interest rates are likely to work to the disadvantage of the incumbent.

In the past several years, the Iraq War emerged as a dominant issue for voters. Certainly, the Bush administration's war policy had much to do with the outcome of the 2006 congressional elections, which gave control of Congress to the Democrats. By late 2008, however, relatively good news from Iraq tended to take the war off the table as an election issue. The worldwide financial crisis, which exploded into the headlines in mid-September, made the economy once again the issue of overwhelming importance to the voters.

MEASURING PUBLIC OPINION

In a democracy, people express their opinions in a variety of ways, as mentioned in this chapter's introduction. One of the most common means of gathering and measuring public opinion on specific issues is, of course, through the use of **opinion polls.**

THE HISTORY OF OPINION POLLS

During the 1800s, certain American newspapers and magazines spiced up their political coverage by doing face-to-face straw polls (unofficial polls indicating the trend of political opinion) or mail surveys of their readers' opinions. In the early twentieth century, the magazine *Literary Digest* further developed the technique of opinion polling by mailing large numbers of questionnaires to individuals, many of whom were its own subscribers, to determine their political opinions. From 1916 to 1936, more than 70 percent of the magazine's election predictions were accurate.

Literary Digest's polling activities suffered a setback in 1936, however, when the magazine predicted, based on more than 2 million returned questionnaires, that Republican candidate Alfred Landon would win over Democratic candidate Franklin D. Roosevelt. Landon won in only two states. A major problem with the *Digest's* polling technique was

Opinion Poll
A method of systematically questioning a small, selected sample of respondents who are deemed representative of the total population.

its use of nonrepresentative respondents. In 1936, at possibly the worst point of the Great Depression, the magazine's subscribers were, for one thing, considerably more affluent than the average American. In other words, they did not accurately represent all of the voters in the U.S. population.

Several newcomers to the public opinion poll industry accurately predicted Roosevelt's landslide victory. These newcomers are still active in the poll-taking industry today: the Gallup poll of George Gallup and the Roper poll founded by Elmo Roper. Gallup and Roper, along with Archibald Crossley, developed the modern polling techniques of market research. Using personal interviews with small samples of selected voters (less than two thousand), they showed that they could predict with accuracy the behavior of the total voting population.

By the 1950s, improved methods of sampling and a whole new science of survey research had been developed. Survey research centers sprang up throughout the United States, particularly at universities. Some of these survey groups are the American Institute of Public Opinion at Princeton, in New Jersey; the National Opinion Research Center at the University of Chicago; and the Survey Research Center at the University of Michigan.

didyouknow...

That 30 percent of people asked to participate in an opinion poll refuse?

SAMPLING TECHNIQUES

How can interviewing fewer than two thousand voters tell us what tens of millions of voters will do? Clearly, it is necessary that the sample of individuals be representative of all voters in the population. Consider an analogy. Let's say we have a large jar containing ten thousand pennies of various dates, and we want to know how many pennies were minted within certain decades (1960–1969, 1970–1979, and so on).

Representative Sampling. One way to estimate the distribution of the dates on the pennies—without examining all ten thousand—is to take a representative sample. This sample would be obtained by mixing the pennies up well and then removing a handful of them—perhaps one hundred pennies. The distribution of dates might be as follows:

- *1960–1969: 5 percent*
- *1970–1979: 5 percent*
- *1980–1989: 20 percent*
- *1990–1999: 30 percent*
- *2000–present: 40 percent*

If the pennies are very well mixed within the jar, and if you take a large enough sample, the resulting distribution will probably approach the actual distribution of the dates of all ten thousand coins.

The Principle of Randomness. The most important principle in sampling, or poll taking, is randomness. Every penny or every person should have a known chance, and especially an *equal chance,* of being sampled. If this happens, then a small sample should be representative of the whole group, both in demographic characteristics (age, religion, race, region, and the like) and in opinions. The ideal way to sample the voting population of the United States would be to put all voter names into a jar—or a computer—and randomly sample, say, two thousand of them. Because this is too costly and inefficient, pollsters have developed other ways to obtain good samples. One technique is simply to choose a random selection of telephone numbers and interview the respective households. This technique produces a relatively accurate sample at a low cost.

When public
opinion research centers gather information, they typically do so over the phone. How do such research centers decide whom to call?
(AP Photo/Jim McKnight)

didyouknow...

That public opinion pollsters typically measure national sentiment among the roughly 200 million adult Americans by interviewing only about 1,500 people?

To ensure that the random samples include respondents from relevant segments of the population—rural, urban, northeastern, southern, and so on—most survey organizations randomly choose, say, urban areas that they will consider as representative of all urban areas. Then they randomly select their respondents within those areas. A generally less accurate technique is known as *quota sampling*. Here, survey researchers decide how many persons of certain types they need in the survey—such as minorities, women, or farmers—and then send out interviewers to find the necessary number of these types. Not only is this method often less accurate, but it also may be biased if, say, the interviewer refuses to go into certain neighborhoods or will not interview after dark.

THE IMPORTANCE OF ACCURACY

Generally, the national survey organizations take great care to select their samples randomly, because their reputations rest on the accuracy of their results. The Gallup and Roper polls usually interview about 1,500 individuals, and their results have a very high probability of being correct—within a margin of 3 percentage points. The accuracy with which the Gallup poll has predicted presidential election results is shown in Figure 6–4.

Polling organizations have also had some notable successes in accurately predicting the results of midterm elections. Certainly, the 2006 election forecasts were mostly on the mark. Indeed, pollsters were publicly ecstatic about how closely their preelection forecasts matched the results. Two pollsters, Mark Blumenthal and John McIntyre, took the average of five polls conducted by major organizations (including Harris, Roper, and Gallup) on each of the last five days before the elections. The averaged forecasts were correct for every candidate. In addition, the average of polls had Democrats picking up six Senate seats, which they did. According to Blumenthal, "The reason polls continue to do reasonably well is that people who actually vote are people who take the trouble to be interviewed."

PROBLEMS WITH POLLS

Public opinion polls are snapshots of the opinions and preferences of the people at a specific moment in time and as expressed in response to a specific question. Given that definition, it is fairly easy to understand situations in which the polls are wrong. For example, opinion polls leading up to the 1980 presidential elections showed President Jimmy Carter defeating challenger Ronald Reagan. Only a few analysts noted the large number of "undecided" respondents a week before the elections. Those voters shifted massively to Reagan at the last minute, and Reagan won the elections.

FIGURE 6–4: Gallup Poll Accuracy Record

This chart compares the percentage of the vote received by the winning presidential candidate with Gallup's final prediction.

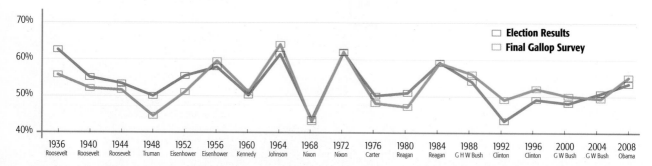

Sources: *The Gallup Poll Monthly*, November 1992; *Time*, November 21, 1994; *The Wall Street Journal*, November 6, 1996; and authors' updates.

elections2008
THE ACCURACY OF THE 2008 POLLS

By Election Day 2008, poll takers were nervous about the accuracy of their results, with good reason. Estimates of Barack Obama's margin of victory over John McCain ranged all the way from 2 percentage points to more than 12. In the end, Obama's margin was about 6.5 percentage points, which tended to vindicate the many pollsters whose results fell between the extremes. The polls were so divergent because polling firms faced a series of questions to which they had no good answers. Turnout was expected to be up, but no one knew by how much. Would young people vote in greater numbers? How efficient was Obama's get-out-the-vote operation? Many poll takers weight their samples to reflect the number of Republicans and Democrats in the population. If a sample contains too few Republicans, for example, pollsters will give Republican responses extra weight.

But how accurate are the estimates of support for the two parties? Weighting can introduce an extra source of error. Finally, some polling firms did not bother to call cell phone users. Under law, cell phones must be called by live people, not automated systems, and cell phones are therefore more expensive to reach. Given the problems that poll takers faced in 2008, it is remarkable that a majority of them were fairly accurate.

Gallup Website
(www.gallup.com/Home.aspx)

The famous photo of Harry Truman showing the front page of the newspaper that declared his defeat in the 1948 presidential elections is another tribute to the weakness of polling. Again, the poll that predicted his defeat was taken more than a week before Election Day. Truman won the election with 49.9 percent of the vote.

Sampling Errors. Polls may also report erroneous results because the pool of respondents was not chosen in a scientific manner; that is, the form of sampling and the number of people sampled may be too small to overcome **sampling error,** which is the difference between the sample result and the true result if the entire population had been interviewed. The sample would be biased, for example, if the poll interviewed people by telephone and did not correct for the fact that more women than men answer the telephone and that some populations (college students and very poor individuals, for example) cannot be found so easily by telephone.

As poll takers get close to Election Day, they become even more concerned about their sample of respondents. Some pollsters continue to interview eligible voters, meaning those over age eighteen and registered to vote. Many others use a series of questions in the poll and other methods to try to identify "likely voters" so that they can be more accurate in their election-eve predictions. When a poll changes its method from reporting the views of eligible voters to reporting those of likely voters, the results tend to change dramatically.

Sampling Error
The difference between a sample's results and the true result if the entire population had been interviewed.

President Harry Truman holds up the front page

of the *Chicago Daily Tribune* issue that predicted his defeat on the basis of a Gallup poll. The poll had indicated that Truman would lose the 1948 contest for his reelection by a margin of 55.5 to 44.5 percent. The Gallup poll was completed more than a week before the election, so it missed a shift by undecided voters to Truman.
(AP Photo/Byron Rollins)

"Is 'oblivious' the same as 'undecided'?"

False Precision. Often, surveys report very detailed results with percentages carried out to one or even two decimal places. For example, you may read about two candidates being within, say, 3.2 percentage points of each other. But if the survey has a margin of error of plus or minus 4 percentage points, then the difference between the candidates could be as much as 7 points or as little as zero. This is not a very comforting result if you are trying to make predictions about who will win.

Most national polling organizations will take an election sample of one thousand or so potential voters and state that the sampling error is plus or minus 3 percentage points for each candidate. So what does that tell you? If two candidates are evenly matched in the polls, it means that the final result could be 47 percent for one and 53 for the other.

Poll Questions. It makes sense to expect that the results of a poll will depend on the questions that are asked. Depending on what question is asked, voters could be said either to support a particular proposal or to oppose it. One of the problems with many polls is the yes/no answer format. For example, suppose the poll question asks, "Do you favor or oppose the war in Iraq?" Respondents might wish to answer that they favored the war at the beginning but not as it is currently being waged, or that they favor fighting terrorism but not a military occupation. They have no way of indicating their true position with a yes or no answer. Respondents also are sometimes swayed by the inclusion of certain words in a question: more of the respondents will answer in the affirmative if the question asks, "Do you favor or oppose the war in Iraq as a means of fighting terrorism?"

How a question is phrased can change the polling outcome dramatically. The Roper polling organization once asked a double-negative question that was very hard to understand: "Does it seem possible or does it seem impossible to you that the Nazi extermination of the Jews never happened?" The survey results showed that 20 percent of Americans seemed to doubt that the Holocaust ever occurred. When the Roper organization rephrased the question more clearly, the percentage of doubters dropped to less than 1 percent.

Furthermore, respondents' answers are also influenced by the order in which questions are asked, by the possible answers from which they are allowed to choose, and, in some cases, by their interaction with the interviewer. To a certain extent, people try to please the interviewer. They answer questions about which they have no information and avoid some answers to try to measure up to the interviewer's expectations.

Unscientific and Fraudulent Polls. Unscientific mail-in polls, telephone call-in polls, Internet polls, and polls conducted by the workers in a campaign office are usually biased and do not give an accurate picture of the public's views. The truthfulness of many polls has to be taken with a grain of salt. For example, when local retailers of alcoholic beverages who were opposed to Internet sales did a "landmark survey," they "proved" that "millions of teenagers" buy alcohol online. What they failed to point out was that the polling organization paid teenagers to be part of the sample and that the sample included only Internet users—this was hardly a random survey.

Interestingly, there is one unscientific method of forecasting election results that compares well with opinion polls in making accurate predictions. Markets that accept bets on who will win various election contests have a good history of identifying winners, as we explain in this chapter's *Politics and Campaigns* feature.

politicsand...campaigns

OPINION POLLING FACES COMPETITION

Not a day goes by, especially during an election year, without the results of another opinion poll being proudly announced in the media. One presidential candidate is pulling away from the other. Or perhaps the candidates are now neck and neck. Or maybe the Democrats might take six more seats in the house. As you have learned in this chapter, opinion polls use random sampling in an effort to make accurate predictions. There is a problem with opinion polls, though. People can say anything they want—there's no law that says they have to tell the truth. For example, a poll in Louisiana in 1991 reported that a measurable percentage of the state's African Americans planned to vote for Ku Klux Klan leader David Duke for governor. Analysts suspect the poll takers did not realize that their black respondents were being sarcastic.

BEFORE THERE WERE POLLS, WE HAD . . . GAMBLING!

Modern polling didn't really come into being until the 1940s. Nonetheless, newspapers frequently carried predictions about who would be elected president. Those predictions were often based on the latest betting odds. In the 1916 presidential election, for example, more than $150,000 (measured in 2009 dollars) was wagered on the election outcome. That sum constituted twice the amount spent on the election campaign itself. Newspapers routinely showed the odds on the two presidential candidates, Woodrow Wilson and Charles Evans Hughes. At that time, a variety of firms were in the business of receiving and placing bets on election outcomes. The betting favored Wilson by a slight margin. And, indeed, he did win. When various state and federal gambling laws were instituted later in the twentieth century, betting on political events became illegal.

ENTER THE IOWA ELECTRONIC MARKETS

In 1993, a group of researchers at the University of Iowa obtained permission from the federal government to establish an experimental academic program that allows betting on elections. The bets are limited to a maximum of $500. Iowa Electronic Markets (**www.biz.uiowa.edu/iem**) claims that since 1993, its results have been more accurate than the opinion polls 75 percent of the time. A competing organization, Intrade (**www.intrade.com**), based in Dublin, Ireland, claims that its betting operation predicted the results correctly in forty-nine states in the 2004 presidential elections.

THE DIFFERENCE BETWEEN OPINION POLLS AND BETTING

Well-crafted opinion polling requires, as stated above, not only a representative sample but truthful responses as well. Election prediction markets, in contrast, require neither. When a person can win or lose a $500 bet by predicting who will be the next president and what the margin will be, a lot more care goes into that prediction than might go into the answer to a polling question. The old saying "Put your money where your mouth is" turns out to result in good political predictions. Unfortunately, the Iowa Electronic Markets is the only legal market in the country for betting on elections.

FOR CRITICAL ANALYSIS

Is there any difference between "placing a bet" on the future value of a stock by buying it in the stock market and placing a bet on who will become president? Explain.

Push Polls. Some campaigns have been using "push polls," in which the respondents are given misleading information in the questions asked to persuade them to vote against a candidate. Indeed, the practice has spread throughout all levels of U.S. politics—local, state, and federal. In 1996, in a random survey of forty-five candidates, researchers found that thirty-five of them claimed to have been victimized by negative push-polling techniques used by their opponents.[8] Now even advocacy groups, as well as candidates for political offices, are using push polls.

During the 2000 presidential primaries, Republican presidential hopeful John McCain accused the Bush camp of making more than 200,000 "advocacy" calls, asking voters

---

8. Karl T. Feld, "When Push Comes to Shove: A Polling Industry Call to Arms," *Public Perspective,* September/October 2001, p. 38.

about their likely choices in the elections. The calls used long questions containing information about McCain's record. The Bush camp said that the information was accurate. In contrast, McCain saw this as negative "push polling."

Push polling continued during the campaigns in 2004, the congressional campaigns in 2006, and the 2008 presidential and congressional campaigns. Its use was widespread in campaigns for governorships and other state offices. Obviously, the answers given are likely to be influenced by such techniques.

Because of these problems with polls, you need to be especially careful when evaluating poll results. For some suggestions on how to be a critical consumer of public opinion polls, see the *Why Should You Care?* feature at the end of this chapter.

TECHNOLOGY AND OPINION POLLS

Public opinion polling is based on scientific principles, particularly the principle of randomness. Today, technological advances allow polls to be taken over the Internet, but serious questions have been raised about the ability of pollsters to obtain truly random samples using this medium. The same was said not long ago when another technological breakthrough changed public opinion polling—the telephone.

THE ADVENT OF TELEPHONE POLLING

During the 1970s, telephone polling began to predominate over in-person polling. Obviously, telephone polling is less expensive than sending interviewers to poll respondents in their homes. Additionally, telephone interviewers do not have to worry about safety problems, which is particularly important for interviewers working in high-crime areas. Finally, telephone interviews can be conducted relatively quickly. They allow politicians or the media to poll one evening and report the results the next day.

Telephone Polling Problems. Somewhat ironically, the success of telephone polling has created major problems for the technique. The telemarketing industry in general has become so pervasive that people increasingly refuse to respond to telephone polls. More than 40 percent of households now use either caller ID or some other form of call screening. This has greatly reduced the number of households that polling organizations can reach. Calls may be automatically rejected, or the respondent may not pick up the call.

Nonresponses in telephone polling include unreachable numbers, refusals, answering machines, and call-screening devices. The nonresponse rate has increased to as high as 80 percent for most telephone polls. Such a high nonresponse rate undercuts confidence in the survey results. In most cases, polling only 20 percent of those on the list cannot lead to a random sample. Even more important for politicians is the fact that polling organizations are not required to report their response rates.

The Cell Phone Problem. A potentially greater problem for telephone polling is the popularity of cell phones. Cellular telephone numbers are not yet included in random-digit dialing programs or listed in telephone directories. Furthermore, individuals with cell phones may be located anywhere in the United States or the world, thus confounding attempts to reach people in a particular area. As more people, and especially younger Americans, choose to use only a cell phone and do not have a landline at all, polling accuracy is further reduced because these individuals cannot be included in any sample for a poll.

ENTER INTERNET POLLING

Obviously, Internet polling is not done on a one-on-one basis, because there is no voice communication. In spite of the potential problems, the Harris poll, a widely respected national polling organization, conducted online polls during the 1998 elections. Its election predictions were accurate in many states. Nonetheless, it made a serious error in one southern gubernatorial election. The Harris group subsequently refined its techniques and continues to conduct online polls. This organization believes that proper weighting of the results will achieve the equivalent of a random-sampled poll.

Public opinion experts argue that the Harris poll procedure violates the mathematical basis of random sampling. Even so, the Internet population is looking more like the rest of America: almost as many women (71 percent) go online as men (74 percent), 61 percent of African American adults are online, and so are 72 percent of Hispanics (compared with 73 percent of non-Hispanic whites).[9]

"Nonpolls" on the Internet. Even if organizations such as the Harris poll succeed in obtaining the equivalent of a random sample when polling on the Internet, another problem will remain: the proliferation of "nonpolls" on the Internet. Every media outlet that maintains a Web site allows users to submit their opinions. Numerous organizations and for-profit companies send polls to individuals via e-mail. Mister Poll (**www.mrpoll.com**) bills itself as the Internet's largest online polling database. Mister Poll allows you to create your own polls just for fun and to include them on your home page. In general, Mister Poll, like many other polling sites, asks a number of questions on various issues and seeks answers from those who log on to its site. Although the Mister Poll Web site states, "None of these polls is scientific," sites such as this one undercut the efforts of legitimate pollsters to use the Internet scientifically.

Does Internet Polling Devalue Polling Results? Although nonpolls certainly existed before the Internet, the ease with which they can be conducted and disseminated is accelerating another trend: the indiscriminate use of polling by all concerned. Though Americans may not want to be bothered by telemarketers or unwanted telephone polls, they seem to continue to want reports of polling results during presidential elections and news stories about the president's approval ratings and similar topics. When asked, a majority of Americans say that polling results are interesting to them. Yet the proliferation of polls, often on the Internet, with little effort to ensure the accuracy of the results presents perhaps the greatest threat to the science of polling.

PUBLIC OPINION AND THE POLITICAL PROCESS

Public opinion affects the political process in many ways. Politicians, whether in office or in the midst of a campaign, see public opinion as important to their careers. The president, members of Congress, governors, and other elected officials realize that strong support by the public as expressed in opinion polls is a source of power in dealing with other politicians. It is far more difficult for a senator to say no to the president if the president is immensely popular and if polls show approval of the president's policies. Public opinion also helps political candidates identify the most important concerns among the people and may help them shape their campaigns successfully.

Nevertheless, surveys of public opinion are not equivalent to elections in the United States. Although opinion polls may influence political candidates or government officials, elections are the major vehicle through which Americans can bring about changes in their government.

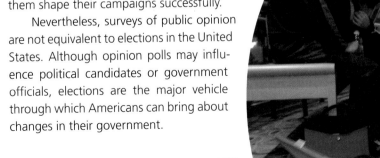

This freshman at Franklin & Marshall College in Lancaster, Pennsylvania, attempts to access the Internet in preparation for an online post-presidential-election debate. How representative would this student's opinion be if she had been polled on the Internet prior to the election? (AP Photo/Daniel Shanken)

9. Pew Internet and American Life Project, *May–June 2006 Tracking Survey.*

POLITICAL CULTURE AND PUBLIC OPINION

Americans are divided into a multitude of ethnic, religious, regional, and political subgroups. Given the diversity of American society and the wide range of opinions contained within it, how is it that the political process continues to function without being stalemated by conflict and dissension? One explanation is rooted in the concept of the American political culture, which can be described as a set of attitudes and ideas about the nation and the government. As discussed in Chapter 1, our political culture is widely shared by Americans of many different backgrounds. To some extent, it consists of symbols, such as the American flag, the Liberty Bell, and the Statue of Liberty. The elements of our political culture also include certain shared beliefs about the most important values in the American political system, including (1) liberty, equality, and property; (2) support for religion; and (3) community service and personal achievement. The structure of the government—particularly federalism, the political parties, the powers of Congress, and popular rule—is also an important value.

A person wearing a caricature mask

of George W. Bush expresses his desire to have Congress impeach Bush and Vice President Cheney. Does such strong expression of this individual's opinion have much effect on the actual political process? Why or why not?
(AP Photo/Mel Evans)

Political Culture and Support for Our Political System. The political culture provides a general environment of support for the political system. If the people share certain beliefs about the system and a reservoir of good feeling exists toward the institutions of government, the nation will be better able to weather periods of crisis. Such was the case after the 2000 presidential elections when, for several weeks, it was not certain who the next president would be and how that determination would be made. At the time, some contended that the nation was facing a true constitutional crisis. Certainly, in many nations of today's world this would be the case. In fact, however, the broad majority of Americans did not believe that the uncertain outcome of the elections had created a constitutional crisis. Polls taken during this time found that, on the contrary, most Americans were confident in our political system's ability to decide the issue peaceably and in a lawful manner.[10]

Political Trust
The degree to which individuals express trust in the government and political institutions, usually measured through a specific series of survey questions.

Political Trust. The political culture also helps Americans evaluate their government's performance. **Political trust,** the degree to which individuals express trust in political institutions, has been measured by a variety of polling questions. One of these is whether the respondent is satisfied with "the way things are going in the United States." Figure 6–5 shows the responses to this question over time, which correspond to political developments. During the presidency of Republican Ronald Reagan (1981–1989), satisfaction levels rose. Republican George H. W. Bush (1989–1993) enjoyed relatively high levels of satisfaction until 1992, when economic problems and other difficulties handed the presidency to Democrat Bill Clinton (1993–2001). Polling suggests that Clinton's two terms were largely successful. Under Republican George W. Bush

"Tell Washington we've lost Osama bin What's-His-Name's trail."

10. As reported in *Public Perspective,* March/April 2002, p. 11, summarizing the results of Gallup/CNN/*USA Today* polls conducted between November 11 and December 10, 2000.

FIGURE 6–5: Trends in Political Satisfaction

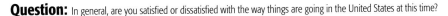

Question: In general, are you satisfied or dissatisfied with the way things are going in the United States at this time?

Sources: Gallup polls, February 2–5, 1979, through August 21–23, 2008.

(2001–2009), however, satisfaction levels have fallen, although the decline was inter-rupted by the terrorist attacks of September 11, 2001.

PUBLIC OPINION ABOUT GOVERNMENT

A vital component of public opinion in the United States is the considerable ambivalence with which the public regards many major national institutions. Table 6–2 shows trends from 1987 to 2008 in opinion polls asking respondents, over a number of years, how much confidence they had in the institutions listed. Over the years, military and religious organizations have ranked highest. Note, however, the decline in confidence in churches

TABLE 6–2: Confidence in Institutions Trend

Question: I am going to read a list of institutions in American society. Would you please tell me how much confidence you, yourself, have in each one—a great deal, quite a lot, some, or very little?

	Percentage Saying "A Great Deal" or "Quite a Lot"														
	1987	1989	1991	1993	1995	1997	1999	2001	2002	2003	2004	2005	2006	2007	2008
Military	61	63	69	67	64	60	68	66	79	82	75	74	73	69	71
Church or organized religion	61	52	56	53	57	56	58	60	45	50	53	53	52	46	48
Banks and banking	51	42	30	38	43	41	43	44	47	50	53	49	49	41	32
U.S. Supreme Court	52	46	39	43	44	50	49	50	50	47	46	41	40	34	32
Public schools	50	43	35	39	40	40	36	38	38	40	41	37	37	33	33
Television news	28	NA	24	21	33	34	34	34	35	35	30	28	31	23	24
Newspapers	31	NA	32	31	30	35	33	36	35	33	30	28	30	22	24
Congress	NA	32	18	19	21	22	26	26	29	29	30	22	19	14	12
Organized labor	26	NA	22	26	26	23	28	26	26	28	31	24	24	19	20
Big business	NA	NA	22	23	21	28	30	28	20	22	24	22	18	18	20

NA = Not asked.

Sources: Gallup polls over time.

didyouknow...

That in its "Cess Poll," an Iowa radio station assesses voters' preferences for presidential primary candidates by reading a candidate's name over the air, asking supporters of that candidate to flush their toilets, and measuring the resulting drop in water pressure?

in 2002 following a substantial number of sex-abuse allegations against Catholic priests. Note also the somewhat heightened regard for the military after the first Gulf War in 1991. Since that time, the public has consistently had more confidence in the military than in any of the other institutions shown in Table 6–2 on the previous page. In 2002 and 2003, confidence in the military soared even higher, most likely because Americans recognized the central role being played by the military in the war on terrorism. From 2004 to 2007, however, this confidence was waning.

The United States Supreme Court and the banking industry have scored well over time, although banking took a big hit in 2008 due to the mortgage industry crisis. Less confidence is expressed in newspapers, television, big business, and organized labor. In 1991, following a scandal involving congressional banking practices, confidence in Congress fell to 18 percent. Confidence in Congress dropped to a record low of 12 percent in 2008. Some 2008 polls showed an approval rating for Congress of only 9 percent.

At times, popular confidence in all institutions may rise or fall, reflecting optimism or pessimism about the general state of the nation. For example, a 2008 Gallup poll showed that the level of national satisfaction with the state of the nation had dropped to 14 percent—the lowest rating since 1992. This general dissatisfaction is clearly reflected in Table 6–2.

Although people may not have much confidence in government institutions, they nonetheless turn to government to solve what they perceive to be the major problems facing the country. Table 6–3, which is based on Gallup polls conducted from the years 1979 to 2008, shows that the leading problems have changed over time. The public tends to emphasize problems that are immediate and that have been the subject of many stories in the media. When coverage of a particular problem increases suddenly, the public is more likely to see that as the most important problem. Thus, the fluctuations in the "most important problem" cited in Table 6–3 may, in part, be attributed to media agenda setting. In 2008, the economy and, to a lesser extent, the war in Iraq were at the top of the list.

TABLE 6–3: Most Important Problem Trend, 1979 to Present

Year	Problem	Year	Problem
1979	High cost of living, energy problems	1994	Crime, violence, health care
1980	High cost of living, unemployment	1995	Crime, violence
1981	High cost of living, unemployment	1996	Budget deficit
1982	Unemployment, high cost of living	1997	Crime, violence
1983	Unemployment, high cost of living	1998	Crime, violence
1984	Unemployment, fear of war	1999	Crime, violence
1985	Fear of war, unemployment	2000	Morals, family decline
1986	Unemployment, budget deficit	2001	Economy, education
1987	Unemployment, economy	2002	Terrorism, economy
1988	Economy, budget deficit	2003	Terrorism, economy
1989	War on drugs	2004	War in Iraq, economy
1990	War in Middle East	2005	War in Iraq
1991	Economy	2006	War in Iraq, terrorism
1992	Unemployment, budget deficit	2007	War in Iraq, health care
1993	Health care, budget deficit	2008	Economy, war in Iraq

Sources: *New York Times*/CBS News poll, January 1996; and Gallup polls, 2000 through 2008.

PUBLIC OPINION AND POLICYMAKING

If public opinion is important for democracy, are policymakers really responsive to public opinion? A groundbreaking study by political scientists Benjamin I. Page and Robert Y. Shapiro in the early 1990s suggested that in fact the national government is very responsive to the public's demands for action.[11] In looking at changes in public opinion poll results over time, Page and Shapiro showed that when the public supports a policy change, the following occurs: policy changes in a direction consistent with the change in public opinion 43 percent of the time, policy changes in a direction opposite to the change in opinion 22 percent of the time, and policy does not change at all 33 percent of the time. Page and Shapiro also showed, as should be no surprise, that when public opinion changes dramatically—say, by 20 percentage points rather than by just 6 or 7 percentage points—government policy is much more likely to follow changing public attitudes.

Setting Limits on Government Action. Although opinion polls cannot give exact guidance on what the government should do in a specific instance, the opinions measured in polls do set an informal limit on government action. For example, consider the highly controversial issue of abortion. Most Americans are moderates on this issue; they do not approve of abortion as a means of birth control, but they do feel that it should be available under certain circumstances. Yet sizable groups of people express very intense feelings both for and against legalized abortion. Given this distribution of opinion, most elected officials would rather not try to change policy to favor either of the extreme positions. To do so would clearly violate the opinion of the majority of Americans. In this case, as in many others, *public opinion does not make public policy; rather, it restrains officials from taking truly unpopular actions.* If officials do act in the face of public opposition, the consequences will be determined at the ballot box.

To what degree should public opinion influence policymaking? It would appear that members of the public view this issue differently than policy leaders do. Polls indicate that whereas a majority of the public feel that public opinion should have a great deal of

---

11. Benjamin I. Page and Robert Y. Shapiro, *The Rational Public: Fifty Years of Trends in Americans' Policy Preferences* (Chicago: University of Chicago Press, 1992).

Speaker of the House Nancy Pelosi
(D., Calif.) speaks at a news conference concerning proposed additional health insurance for American children. To what extent do you think that public opinion about this important topic influences what Congress does?
(AP Photo/Caleb Jones)

influence on policy, a majority of policy leaders hold the opposite position. Why would a majority of policy leaders not want to be strongly influenced by public opinion? One answer to this question is that public opinion polls can provide only a limited amount of guidance to policymakers.

The Limits of Polling. Policymakers cannot always be guided by opinion polls. In the end, politicians must make their own choices. When they do so, their choices necessarily involve trade-offs. If politicians vote for increased spending to improve education, for example, by necessity fewer resources are available for other worthy projects.

Individuals who are polled do not have to make such trade-offs when they respond to questions. Indeed, survey respondents usually are not even given a choice of trade-offs in their policy opinions. Pollsters typically ask respondents whether they want more or less spending in a particular area, such as education. Rarely, though, is a dollar amount assigned. Additionally, broad poll questions often provide little guidance for policymakers. What does it mean if a majority of those polled want "free" medical treatment for everyone in need? Obviously, medical care is never free. Certain individuals may receive medical care free of charge, but society as a whole has to pay for it. In short, polling questions usually do not reflect the cost of any particular policy choice.

Moreover, to make an informed policy choice requires an understanding not only of the policy area but also of the consequences of any given choice. Virtually no public opinion polls make sure that those polled have such information.

Finally, government decisions cannot be made simply by adding up individual desires. Politicians engage in a type of "horse trading." All politicians know that they cannot satisfy every desire of every constituent. Therefore, each politician attempts to maximize the net benefits to his or her constituents, while keeping within whatever the politician believes the government can afford.

Every politician has different sets of constituents. For example, Representative Keith Ellison (D., Minn.) is shown here with three distinct groups of constituents from his home district in Minneapolis. The group shown in the top photo is the Alzheimer's Association of Minnesota; the group in the center photo shows representatives from the American Federation of State, County, and Municipal Employees; and the group in the bottom photo is the Amyotrophic Lateral Sclerosis Association. How does a member of Congress react to the varying demands of different groups of constituents? (All photographs courtesy of Representative Keith Ellison, Creative Commons)

WHY SHOULD YOU CARE ABOUT
pollsand
publicopinion?

Why should you, as an individual, care about public opinion and opinion polls? Americans are inundated with the results of public opinion polls. The polls purport to tell us a variety of things: whether the president's popularity is up or down, whether gun control is more in favor now than previously, or who is leading the pack for the next presidential nomination. What must be kept in mind with this blizzard of information is that poll results are not equally good or equally believable.

OPINION POLLS AND YOUR LIFE

As a critical consumer, you need to be aware of what makes one set of public opinion poll results valid and other results useless or even dangerously misleading. Knowing what makes a poll accurate is especially important if you plan to participate actively in politics. Successful participation depends on accurate information, and that includes knowing what your fellow citizens are thinking. If large numbers of other people really agree with you that a particular policy needs to be changed, there may be a good chance that the policy can actually be altered. If almost no one agrees with you on a particular issue, there may be no point in trying to change policy immediately; the best you can do is to try to sway the opinions of others, in the hope that someday enough people will agree with you to make policy changes possible.

HOW YOU CAN MAKE A DIFFERENCE

Pay attention only to opinion polls that are based on scientific, or random, samples. In these so-called *probability samples*, a known probability is used to select each person interviewed. Do not give credence to the results of opinion polls that consist of shopping-mall interviews or the like. The main problem with this kind of opinion taking is that not everyone has an equal chance of being in the mall when the interview takes place. Also, it is almost certain that the people in the mall are not a reasonable cross section of a community's entire population.

Probability samples are useful because you can calculate the range within which the results would have fallen if everybody had been interviewed. Well-designed probability samples will allow the pollster to say, for example, that he or she is 95 percent sure that 61 percent of the public, plus or minus 4 percentage points, supports the idea of universal health insurance. It turns out that if you want to be twice as precise about a poll result, you need to collect a sample four times as large. This tends to make accurate polls ex-pensive and difficult to conduct.

Pay attention as well to how people were contacted for the poll—by mail, by telephone, in person in their homes, or in some other way (such as via the Internet). Because of its lower cost, polling firms have turned more and more to telephone interviewing. This method

(Courtesy www.pollster.com)

can produce highly accurate results. Its disadvantage is that telephone interviews typically need to be short and to deal with questions that are fairly easy to answer. Interviews in person are better for getting useful information about why a particular response was given. They take much longer to complete, however. Results from mailed questionnaires should be taken with a grain of salt. Usually, only a small percentage of people send them back.

When viewers or listeners of television or radio shows are encouraged to call in their opinions to an 800 telephone number, the polling results are meaningless. Users of the Internet also have an easy way to make their views known. Only people who own computers and are interested in the topic will take the trouble to respond, however, and that group is not representative of the general public.

QUESTIONS FOR
discussionandanalysis

1. Review the *Which Side Are You On?* feature on page 198. In what ways, if at all, do you think the media have a set of biases that determine the issues and events that are discussed? Why would the media have such viewpoints in the first place?

2. In the 2000 presidential elections, Arab American votes were split almost evenly between the two major parties. By 2004 and 2006, the Arab American vote was heavily Democratic. Why, in the past, might Arab Americans have been more favorable than members of many other minority groups to the Republicans? Why might Republican Arab Americans have switched their allegiances?

3. In recent years, more and more Americans have begun refusing to talk to poll takers. Also, many people now rely on cell phones, which have numbers that are not available to telephone pollsters. What problems could these two developments pose for polling organizations? How might these developments bias polling results?

4. Some political scientists claim that individual polls are relatively meaningless but that a number of polls averaged together can be fairly accurate. Why would a number of polls averaged together have more predictive power?

5. Why do you think the American people express a relatively high degree of confidence in the military as an institution? Why do people express less confidence in Congress than in other major institutions? Could people be holding various institutions to different standards, and if so, what might these standards be?

keyterms

agenda setting 197
consensus 194
divided opinion 194
gender gap 203
generational effect 197

lifestyle effect 197
media 197
opinion leader 197
opinion poll 204
peer group 196

political
    socialization 194
political trust 212
public opinion 193
sampling error 207

socioeconomic
    status 198
Watergate break-in 198

chaptersummary

1. Public opinion is the aggregate of individual attitudes or beliefs shared by some portion of the adult population. A consensus exists when a large proportion of the public appears to express the same view on an issue. Divided opinion exists when the public holds widely different attitudes on an issue. Sometimes, a poll shows a distribution of opinion indicating that most people either have no information about an issue or are not interested enough in the issue to form a position on it.

2. People's opinions are formed through the political socialization process. Important factors in this process are the family, educational experiences, peer groups, opinion leaders, the media, and political events. The influence of the media as a socialization factor may be growing relative to the influence of the family. Party identification is one of the most important indicators of voting behavior. Voting behavior is also influenced by demographic factors, such as education, economic status, religion, race and ethnicity, gender, and region. Finally, voting behavior is influenced by election-specific factors, such as perception of the candidates and issue preferences.

3. Most descriptions of public opinion are based on the results of opinion polls. The accuracy of polls depends on sampling techniques. An accurate poll includes a representative sample of the population being polled and ensures randomness in the selection of respondents.

4. Problems with polls include sampling errors (which may occur when the pool of respondents is not chosen in a scientific manner), the difficulty of knowing the degree to which responses are influenced by the type and order of questions asked, the use of a yes/no format for answers to the questions, and the interviewer's techniques. Many are concerned about the use of "push polls" (in which the ques-

tions "push" the respondent toward a particular candidate).

5. Advances in technology have changed polling techniques over the years. During the 1970s, telephone polling came to be widely used. Today, largely because of extensive telemarketing, people often refuse to answer calls, and nonresponse rates in telephone polling have skyrocketed. Due to the difficulty of obtaining a random sample in the online environment, Internet polls are often "nonpolls." Whether Internet polls can overcome this problem remains to be seen.

6. Public opinion affects the political process in many ways. The political culture provides a general environment of support for the political system, allowing the nation to weather periods of crisis. The political culture also helps Americans to evaluate their government's performance. At times, the level of trust in government has been relatively high; at other times, the level of trust has declined steeply.

Similarly, Americans' confidence in government institutions varies over time, depending on a number of circumstances. Generally, though, Americans turn to government to solve what they perceive to be the major problems facing the country. In 2008, Americans ranked the economy and the war in Iraq as the two most significant problems facing the nation.

7. Public opinion also plays an important role in policymaking. Although polling data show that a majority of Americans would like policy leaders to be influenced to a great extent by public opinion, politicians cannot always be guided by opinion polls. This is because the respondents often do not understand the costs and consequences of policy decisions or the trade-offs involved in making such decisions. An important function of public opinion is to set limits on government action through public pressure.

selected print&media resources

SUGGESTED READINGS

Asher, Herbert. *Polling and the Public: What Every Citizen Should Know.* Washington, D.C.: CQ Press, 2004. This clearly written and often entertaining book explains what polls are, how they are conducted and interpreted, and how the wording and ordering of survey questions, as well as the interviewer's techniques, can significantly affect the respondents' answers.

Bishop, Bill. *The Big Sort: Why the Clustering of Like-Minded America Is Tearing Us Apart.* New York: Houghton Mifflin, 2008. Jam-packed with polling data, Bishop's book argues that we have clustered into like-minded communities as never before. Results include political polarization and an inability to understand Americans of different backgrounds or beliefs.

Grabe, Maria Elizabeth, and Erik Page Bucy. *Image Bite Politics: News and the Visual Framing of Elections.* New York: Oxford University Press, 2009. Grabe and Bucy examine the visual presentation of presidential candidates in news reports and connect these images to shifts in public opinion. They argue that "image bites" can be more influential than "sound bites."

Lewis-Beck, Michael S., Helmut Norpoth, William G. Jacoby, and Herbert F. Weisberg. *The American Voter Revisited.* Ann Arbor: University of Michigan Press, 2008. Four political scientists have recreated the 1960 classic *The American Voter* with up-to-date data and analysis. They find that voter behavior has been remarkably consistent, even over half a century.

Lynch, Marc. *Voices of the New Arab Public: Iraq, al-Jazeera, and Middle East Politics Today.* New York: Columbia University Press, 2006. The author takes an in-depth look at how al-Jazeera and other Arab satellite television stations have transformed Middle Eastern politics over the past decade. Lynch also discusses how this new era of political socialization has affected relations with the United States.

MEDIA RESOURCES

Faith and Politics: The Christian Right—A 1995 documentary hosted by Dan Rather and produced by CBS News. It focuses on the efforts of the Christian conservative movement to affect educational curricula and public policy. Members of the Christian right who are interviewed include Ralph Reed and Gary Bauer. Critics of the Christian right who are interviewed include Senator Arlen Specter.

Vox Populi: Democracy in Crisis—A PBS special focusing on why public confidence in government, which has plummeted during recent decades, still has not recovered.

Wag the Dog—A 1997 film that provides a very cynical look at the importance of public opinion. The film, which features Dustin Hoffman and Robert De Niro, follows the efforts of a presidential political consultant who stages a foreign policy crisis to divert public opinion from a sex scandal in the White House.

e-mocracy

ONLINE POLLING AND POLL DATA

News organizations, interest groups, not-for-profit groups, and online e-zines are now using online polling to gather the opinions of their readers and viewers. All the user has to do is log on to the Web site and click on the box indicating the preferred response. People can respond to online polls more easily than to call-in polls, and in most cases, online polls are free to the user. Realize, though, that online polls are totally nonscientific because the respondents are all self-selected. Essentially, Internet polls are nonpolls because only those who choose to do so respond, making the polls much more likely to be biased and based on an unrepresentative sample.

At the same time, the Internet is an excellent source for finding reliable polling reports and data. All of the major polling organizations have Web sites that include news releases about polls they have conducted. Some sites make the polling data available for free to users; others require that a user pay a subscription fee before accessing the polling archives on the site.

LOGGING ON

Yale University Library, one of the world's great research institutions, offers access to social science libraries and information services. If you want to browse through library sources of public opinion data, this is an interesting site to visit. Go to
www.library.yale.edu/socsci/opinion.

According to its home page, the mission of American National Election Studies (ANES) "is to produce high-quality data on voting, public opinion, and political participation that serves the research needs of social scientists, teachers, students, and policymakers concerned with understanding the theoretical and empirical foundations of mass politics in a democratic society." This is a good place to obtain information on public opinion. Find it at
www.electionstudies.org.

The Polling Report Web site offers polls and their results organized by topic. It is up to date and easy to use. Go to
www.pollingreport.com.

The Gallup organization's Web site offers not only polling data (although a user must pay a subscription fee to obtain access to many polling reports) but also information on how polls are constructed, conducted, and interpreted. Go to
www.gallup.com.

Another site that features articles and polling data on public opinion is the Web site of the Zogby poll at
www.zogby.com.

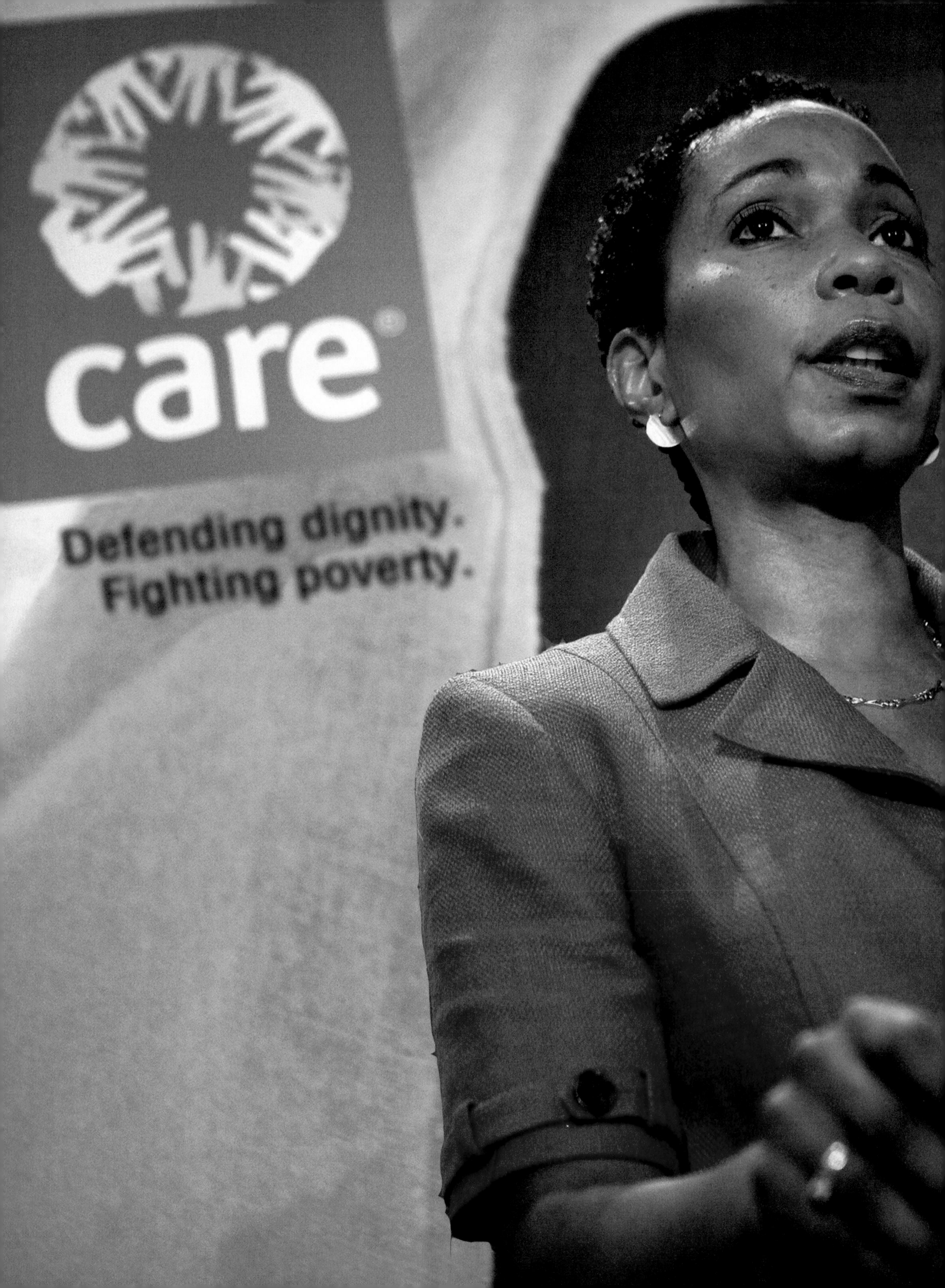
care
Defending dignity.
Fighting poverty.

7 Interest Groups

CHAPTER CONTENTS

The president of CARE, an international humanitarian organization, holds a news conference to speak about child labor and women's rights in Washington, D.C. (Brendan Smialowski/Getty Images)

what**if**...retired government employees could not work for interest groups?

BACKGROUND

Many interest groups employ lobbyists to influence legislation and the administrative decisions of government. About half of the paid lobbyists in Washington are former government employees or former members of Congress. Interest groups place a high value on lobbyists who "know their way around Washington." Former government employees and elected officials qualify in this regard. Often, retired government employees or congresspersons retain personal friendships with their former colleagues. There are rules in place to prevent former government employees from lobbying their former colleagues for a limited period of time after retirement. Congresspersons and their staff members also face such limits. Still, retirees can immediately engage in activities that do not technically qualify as lobbying, and they can begin full-scale lobbying as soon as the time limits expire.

WHAT IF RETIRED GOVERNMENT EMPLOYEES COULD NOT WORK FOR INTEREST GROUPS?

Some people have argued that interest groups gain improper influence by hiring former government employees. Therefore, these critics say, such hiring should not merely be restricted but should be banned altogether. If this were to happen, interest groups that frequently hire former government employees would be less effective. Which groups are these, and what do they seek to accomplish?

A large number of interest groups represent particular industries. Typically, such groups are concerned with legislation and administrative rules that are specific to their industry and are of little interest to the general public. Therefore, the press pays little attention to these laws and regulations. Industry lobbying can "fly under the radar." A retired government employee with expert knowledge of the specific subject matter and of the processes and people involved in making administrative rules can be a formidable lobbyist.

Likewise, a former member of Congress can offer invaluable assistance when an interest group seeks to affect lawmaking. If these knowledgeable retirees were not available to interest groups, those groups would have less influence on administrative rulemaking and on legislation. Of course, campaign contributions by interest groups are also part of the process of influencing Congress. (You will learn more about campaign finance later in this chapter and in Chapter 9.)

CORPORATE WELFARE

As an example of an interest group, the pharmaceutical industry spends nearly $100 million per year on lobbying, and more than half of its 600-plus registered lobbyists are former members of Congress or former government employees. The pharmaceutical industry has a history of slipping favorable elements into pending legislation. In 2004, for example, the Medicare Reform Bill was passed with a prescription drug benefits program that does not allow Medicare bureaucrats to negotiate the prices of approved drugs (as private health insurance companies normally do) to control costs.

Industry-specific legislation can include tariffs on imports, tax breaks, and direct subsidies. The cost of this legislation adds up. The Cato Institute, a libertarian research group, estimates that what it calls "corporate welfare" costs nearly $100 billion a year. Barring former government employees from working for interest groups might reduce these kinds of corporate subsidies.

Interest groups that address issues of broader concern generally do not need to hire experts with government experience to be effective. There can be little doubt, for example, that the influence of the National Rifle Association does not depend on its ability to hire retired government employees.

THE IMPACT ON FORMER EMPLOYEES

Some government employees—as well as many congresspersons—look forward to lobbying as a final stage of their careers. A government career may be more attractive if it ends with a few years of highly paid, comfortable employment. Banning such employment might make government service less appealing to some. The long-term result might be that fewer well-qualified individuals would choose to enter government and politics as a lifelong career.

FOR CRITICAL ANALYSIS

1. Why would interest groups argue that a ban on hiring retired government employees would be an unfair (or even an unconstitutional) restriction on their activities?

2. In what ways might a ban on hiring retired government employees be unfair to the former employees themselves?

The structure of American government invites the participation of **interest groups** at various stages of the policymaking process. For example, Americans can form groups in their neighborhoods or cities and lobby the city council and their state government. They can join statewide groups or national groups and try to influence government policy through Congress or through one of the executive agencies or cabinet departments. Representatives of large corporations may seek to influence the president personally at social events or fund-raisers. When attempts to influence government through the executive and legislative branches fail, interest groups can turn to the courts, filing suit in state or federal court to achieve their political objectives.

The many "pressure points" for interest group activity in American government help to explain why there are so many—more than one hundred thousand—interest groups at work in our society. Another reason is that the right to join a group is protected by the First Amendment to the U.S. Constitution (see Chapter 4). Not only are all people guaranteed the right "peaceably to assemble," but they are also guaranteed the right "to petition the Government for a redress of grievances." This constitutional provision encourages Americans to form groups and to express their opinions to the government or to their elected representatives as members of a group. Group membership makes the individual's opinions appear more powerful and strongly conveys the group's ability to vote for or against a representative.

Interest groups play a significant role in American government at all levels. As you will read later in this chapter and in Chapter 9, one of the ways in which interest groups attempt to influence government policies is through campaign contributions to members of Congress who intend to run for reelection. It is the interplay between campaign financial assistance and legislation favorable to specific interests that has caused some observers to claim that Congress has been sold to the highest bidder. Certainly, devising a system in which campaigns can be financed *without* jeopardizing objectivity on the part of members of Congress is a major challenge for our nation today. Recall from Chapter 1, however, that in our pluralist society, the competition by interest groups for access to lawmakers automatically checks the extent to which any one particular group can influence Congress.

These two former Senate leaders, Trent Lott (right) and Tom Daschle, work as lobbyists. Why do interest groups prefer to hire former members of Congress to influence legislation on their behalf? (AP Photo/Susan Walsh, File)

> **Interest Group**
> An organized group of individuals sharing common objectives who actively attempt to influence policymakers.

Alexis de Tocqueville was a French historian who wrote about the character of Americans, including American's propensity to join groups. (Réunion des Musées Nationaux/Art Resource)

INTEREST GROUPS: A NATURAL PHENOMENON

Alexis de Tocqueville observed in the early 1830s that "in no country of the world has the principle of association been more successfully used or applied to a greater multitude of objectives than in America."[1] The French traveler was amazed at the degree to which Americans formed groups to solve civic problems, establish social relationships, and speak for their economic or political interests. Perhaps James Madison, when he wrote *Federalist Paper* No. 10 (see Appendix C), had already judged the character of his country's citizens similarly. He supported the creation of a large republic with many states to encourage the formation of multiple interests. The multitude of interests, in Madison's view, would work to discourage the formation of an oppressive majority interest.

Surely, neither Madison nor de Tocqueville foresaw the formation of so many thousands of associations in the United States. Poll data show that more than two-thirds of all Americans belong to at least one group or association. Although the majority of these affiliations could not be classified as "interest groups" in the political sense, Americans do understand the principles of working in groups.

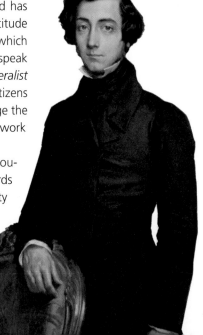

---

1. Alexis de Tocqueville, *Democracy in America,* Vol. 1 [1835], ed. Phillips Bradley (New York: Knopf, 1980), p. 191.

Today, interest groups range from the elementary school parent-teacher association and the local "Stop the Sewer Plant Association" to the state-wide association of insurance agents. They include small groups such as local environmental organizations and national groups such as the Boy Scouts of America, the American Civil Liberties Union, the National Education Association, and the American League of Lobbyists.

INTEREST GROUPS AND SOCIAL MOVEMENTS

Interest groups are often spawned by mass **social movements.** Such movements represent demands by a large segment of the population for change in the political, economic, or social system. Social movements are often the first expression of latent discontent with the existing system. They may be the authentic voice of weaker or oppressed groups in society that do not have the means or standing to organize as interest groups. For example, most mainstream political and social leaders disapproved of the women's movement of the 1800s. Because women were unable to vote or take an active part in the political system, it was difficult for women who desired greater freedom to organize formal groups. After the Civil War, when more women became active in professional life, the first real women's rights group, the National Woman Suffrage Association, came into being.

These women were part of a social movement to obtain the right to vote in the early 1900s. How do social movements sometimes lead to interest groups? (AP Photo)

African Americans found themselves in an even more disadvantaged situation after the end of the Reconstruction period (1865–1877). They were unable to exercise political rights in many southern and border states, and their participation in any form of organization could lead to economic ruin, physical harassment, or even death. The civil rights movement of the 1950s and 1960s was clearly a social movement. To be sure, the movement received support from several formal organizations—including the Southern Christian Leadership Conference, the National Association for the Advancement of Colored People, and the Urban League. Yet only a social movement could generate the kinds of civil disobedience that took place in hundreds of towns and cities across the country.

Social movements are often precursors of interest groups. They may generate interest groups with specific goals that successfully recruit members by offering certain incentives. In the example of the women's movement of the 1960s, the National Organization for Women was formed in part out of a demand to end gender-segregated job advertising in newspapers.

WHY DO AMERICANS JOIN INTEREST GROUPS?

One puzzle that has fascinated political scientists is why some people join interest groups, while many others do not. Everyone has some interest that could benefit from government action. For many individuals, however, those concerns remain unorganized interests, or **latent interests.**

According to political theorist Mancur Olson,[2] it simply may not be rational for individuals to join most groups. In his classic work on this topic, Olson introduced the idea of

Social Movement
A movement that represents the demands of a large segment of the public for political, economic, or social change.

Latent Interests
Public-policy interests that are not recognized or addressed by a group at a particular time.

---

2. Mancur Olson, *The Logic of Collective Action* (Cambridge, Mass.: Harvard University Press, 1965).

the "collective good." This concept refers to any public benefit that, if available to any member of the community, cannot be denied to any other member, whether or not he or she participated in the effort to gain the good.

Although collective benefits are usually thought of as coming from such public goods as clean air and national defense, benefits are also bestowed by the government on subsets of the public. Price subsidies to dairy farmers and loans to college students are examples. Olson used economic theory to propose that it is not rational for interested individuals to join groups that work for group benefits. In fact, it is often more rational for the individual to wait for others to procure the benefits and then share them. How many college students, for example, join the American Association of Community Colleges, an organization that lobbies the government for increased financial aid to students? The difficulty interest groups face in recruiting members when the benefits can be obtained without joining the groups is referred to as the **free rider problem.**

If so little incentive exists for individuals to join together, why are there thousands of interest groups lobbying in Washington? According to the logic of collective action, if the contribution of an individual *will* make a difference to the effort, then it is worth it to the individual to join. Thus, smaller groups, which seek benefits for only a small proportion of the population, are more likely to enroll members who will give time and funds to the cause. Larger groups, which represent general public interests (the women's movement or the American Civil Liberties Union, for example), will find it relatively more difficult to get individuals to join. People need an incentive—material or otherwise—to participate.

SOLIDARY INCENTIVES

Interest groups offer **solidary incentives** for their members. Solidary benefits include companionship, a sense of belonging, and the pleasure of associating with others. Although the National Audubon Society was originally founded to save the snowy egret from extinction, today most members join to learn more about birds and to meet and share their pleasure with other individuals who enjoy bird-watching as a hobby. Even though the incentive might be solidary for many members, this organization nonetheless also pursues an active political agenda, working to preserve the environment and to protect endangered species. Most members may not play any part in working toward larger, more national goals unless the organization can convince them to take political action or unless some local environmental issue arises.

MATERIAL INCENTIVES

For other individuals, interest groups offer direct **material incentives.** A case in point is AARP (formerly the American Association of Retired Persons), which provides discounts, insurance plans, and organized travel opportunities for its members. Because of its exceptionally low dues ($12.50 annually) and the benefits gained through membership, AARP has become the largest—and a very powerful—interest group in the United States. AARP can claim to represent the interests of millions of senior citizens and can show that they actually have joined the group. For most seniors, the material incentives outweigh the membership costs. Another example of an interest group is the American Automobile Association (AAA). Most people who join this organization do so

Do those who join the American Automobile Association (AAA) do so because of solidary incentives or material incentives? (Screen capture from AAA)

for its emergency roadside assistance and trip planning. Many members may not realize that the AAA is also a significant interest group seeking to shape laws that affect drivers.

Many other interest groups offer indirect material incentives for their members. Such groups as the American Dairy Association and the National Association of Automobile Dealers do not give discounts or freebies to their members, but they do offer indirect benefits and rewards by, for example, protecting the material interests of their members from government policymaking that is injurious to their industry or business.

PURPOSIVE INCENTIVES

Interest groups also offer the opportunity for individuals to pursue political, economic, or social goals through joint action. **Purposive incentives** offer individuals the satisfaction of taking action when the goals of a group correspond to their beliefs or principles. The individuals who belong to a group focusing on the abortion issue or gun control, for example, do so because they feel strongly enough about the issues to support the group's work with money and time.

Some scholars have argued that many people join interest groups simply for the discounts, magazine subscriptions, and other tangible benefits and are not really interested in the political positions taken by the groups. According to William P. Browne, however, research shows that people really do care about the policy stance of an interest group. Members of a group seek people who share the group's views and then ask them to join. As one group leader put it, "Getting members is about scaring the hell out of people."[3] People join the group and then feel that they are doing something about a cause that is important to them.

didyouknow...

That the activities of interest groups at the state level have been growing much faster than in the nation's capital, with more than 45,000 registered state lobbyists in 2009 and with a growth rate of 50 percent in California, Florida, and Texas in the last ten years?

TYPES OF INTEREST GROUPS

Thousands of groups exist to influence government. Among the major types of interest groups are those that represent the main sectors of the economy. In addition, a number of "public-interest" organizations have been formed to represent the needs of the general citizenry, including many "single-issue" groups. The interests of foreign governments and foreign businesses are also represented in the American political arena. The names and Web addresses of some major interest groups are shown in Tables 7–1 and 7–2 on the facing page.

ECONOMIC INTEREST GROUPS

More interest groups are formed to represent economic interests than any other set of interests. The variety of economic interest groups mirrors the complexity of the American economy. The major sectors that seek influence in Washington, D.C., include business, agriculture, labor unions, government workers, and professionals.

Business Interest Groups. Thousands of business groups and trade associations work to influence government policies that affect their respective industries. "Umbrella groups" represent certain types of businesses or companies that deal in a particular type of product. The U.S. Chamber of Commerce, for example, is an umbrella group that represents a wide variety of businesses, and the National Association of Manufacturers

Members of the Senate Health and Human Services Committee listen to a lobbyist for Planned Parenthood. Why is Planned Parenthood considered a single-issue group? (AP Photo/Doug Dreyer)

---

3. William P. Browne, *Groups, Interests, and U.S. Public Policy* (Washington, D.C.: Georgetown University Press, 1998), p. 23.

TABLE 7–1: *Fortune*'s "Power 25"—The Twenty-Five Most Effective Interest Groups

1. National Rifle Association of America (the NRA—opposed to gun control): **www.nra.org**
2. AARP (formerly the American Association of Retired Persons): **www.aarp.org**
3. National Federation of Independent Business: **www.nfib.com**
4. American Israel Public Affairs Committee (AIPAC—a pro-Israel group): **www.aipac.org**
5. American Association for Justice (formerly the Association of Trial Lawyers of America): **www.justice.org**
6. American Federation of Labor–Congress of Industrial Organizations (the AFL-CIO—the largest federation of U.S. labor unions): **www.aflcio.org**
7. Chamber of Commerce of the United States of America (an association of businesses): **www.uschamber.org**
8. National Beer Wholesalers Association: **www.nbwa.org**
9. National Association of Realtors: **www.realtor.org**
10. National Association of Manufacturers (NAM): **www.nam.org**
11. National Association of Home Builders of the United States: **www.nahb.org**
12. American Medical Association (the AMA—representing physicians): **www.ama-assn.org**
13. American Hospital Association: **www.aha.org**
14. National Education Association of the United States (the NEA—representing teachers): **www.nea.org**
15. American Farm Bureau Federation (representing farmers): **www.fb.org**
16. Motion Picture Association of America (representing movie studios): **www.mpaa.org**
17. National Association of Broadcasters: **www.nab.org**
18. National Right to Life Committee (opposed to legalized abortion): **www.nrlc.org**
19. America's Health Insurance Plans: **www.ahip.org**
20. National Restaurant Association: **www.restaurant.org**
21. National Governors Association: **www.nga.org**
22. Recording Industry Association of America: **www.riaa.com**
23. American Bankers Association: **www.aba.com**
24. Pharmaceutical Research and Manufacturers of America: **www.phrma.org**
25. International Brotherhood of Teamsters (a labor union): **www.teamster.org**

Source: *Fortune* Magazine.

is an umbrella group that represents only manufacturing concerns. The American Pet Products Manufacturers Association works for the good of manufacturers of pet food, pet toys, and other pet products, as well as for pet shops. This group strongly opposes increased regulation of stores that sell animals and restrictions on importing pets. Other major organizations that represent business interests, such as the Better Business Bureaus, take positions on policies but do not actually lobby in Washington, D.C.

Some business groups are decidedly more powerful than others. The U.S. Chamber of Commerce, which represents more than 3 million businesses and organizations, can bring constituent influence to bear on every member of Congress. Another powerful lobbying organization is the National Association of Manufacturers. With a staff of about 150 people in Washington, D.C., the organization can mobilize dozens of well-educated, articulate **lobbyists** to work the corridors of Congress on issues of concern to its members.

Lobbyist
An organization or individual who attempts to influence legislation and the administrative decisions of government.

TABLE 7–2: Some Other Important Interest Groups (Not on *Fortune*'s "Power 25" List)

American Cancer Society: **www.cancer.org**

American Civil Liberties Union (the ACLU): **www.aclu.org**

American Legion (a veterans group): **www.legion.org**

American Library Association: **www.ala.org**

American Society for the Prevention of Cruelty to Animals (the ASPCA): **www.aspca.org**

Amnesty International USA (promotes human rights): **www.amnesty.org**

Change to Win (a federation of labor unions): **www.changetowin.org**

Handgun Control, Inc. (favors gun control): **www.bradycampaign.org**

League of United Latin American Citizens (LULAC): **www.lulac.org**

Mothers Against Drunk Driving (MADD): **www.madd.org**

NARAL Pro-Choice America (formerly the National Abortion and Reproductive Rights Action League—favors legalized abortion): **www.naral.org**

National Association for the Advancement of Colored People (the NAACP—represents African Americans): **www.naacp.org**

National Audubon Society (an environmentalist group): **www.audubon.org**

National Gay and Lesbian Task Force: **www.thetaskforce.org**

National Organization for Women (NOW—a feminist group): **www.now.org**

National Urban League (a civil rights organization): **www.nul.org**

National Wildlife Federation: **www.nwf.org**

Nature Conservancy: **www.nature.org**

Sierra Club (an environmentalist group): **www.sierraclub.org**

Veterans of Foreign Wars of the United States: **www.vfw.org**

World Wildlife Fund: **www.wwf.org**

Agricultural Interest Groups. American farmers and their employees represent less than 1 percent of the U.S. population. Nevertheless, farmers' influence on legislation beneficial to their interests has been significant. Farmers have succeeded in their aims because they have very strong interest groups. They are geographically dispersed and therefore have many representatives and senators to speak for them.

The American Farm Bureau Federation, established in 1919, represents more than 5.5 million families (a majority of whom are not actually farm families) and is usually seen as conservative. It was instrumental in getting government guarantees of "fair" prices during the Great Depression in the 1930s.[4] Another important agricultural interest organization is the National Farmers' Union (NFU), which is considered more liberal. As farms have become larger and "agribusiness" has become a way of life, single-issue farm groups have emerged. The American Dairy Association, the Peanut Growers Group, and the National Soybean Association, for example, work to support their respective farmers and associated businesses. In recent years, agricultural interest groups have become active on many new issues. Among other things, they have opposed immigration restrictions and are very involved in international trade matters as they seek new markets. One of the newest agricultural groups is the American Farmland Trust, which supports policies to conserve farmland and protect natural resources.

Agricultural interest groups have probably been more successful than any other groups in obtaining subsidies from American taxpayers. U.S. farm subsidies cost taxpayers at least $20 billion a year directly, and another $12 billion a year in higher food prices. Republicans and Democrats alike supported the latest agricultural subsidy legislation, showing the success of agricultural lobbying groups. The latest legislation, passed in 2008, created the most expensive agricultural subsidy bill ever.

The farm bill, which was passed over the president's veto, had a price tag of about $300 billion over a five-year period. The bill included tax breaks for racehorse owners, marketing subsidies for fruit and vegetable growers, research funding for organic farmers, and increased price supports for domestic sugar producers. At the last minute, the salmon industry obtained $170 million. In spite of the highest prices for agricultural products ever recorded, the 2008 act provides for permanent disaster assistance for corn, wheat, cotton, rice, and soybean growers.

Labor Interest Groups. Interest groups representing the **labor movement** date back to at least 1886, when the American Federation of Labor (AFL) was formed. In 1955, the AFL joined forces with the Congress of Industrial Organizations (CIO). Today, the combined AFL-CIO is a large federation with a membership of nearly 10 million workers and an active political arm called the Committee on Political Education. In a sense, the AFL-CIO is a union of unions.

The AFL-CIO remained the predominant labor-union organization for fifty years. In 2005, however, seven unions with more than 45 percent of total AFL-CIO membership broke off to form a separate union organization called Change to Win. More recently, two construction industry unions also left the AFL-CIO and joined with

---

didyouknow...

That the names of many interest groups suggest goals opposite from the organization's true objectives—for example, the Palm Oil Truth Foundation does not seek to expose the dangers of palm oil use, but to expand the use of palm oil in food and oppose action against global warming?

Labor Movement
Generally, the economic and political expression of working-class interests; politically, the organization of working-class interests.

These farm workers demonstrate after the death of Maria Isabel Vasquez Jimenez, who died while working, apparently from dehydration. These workers argue that the working conditions on dozens of California's farms are "inhuman." How can the interests of these workers translate into action to help them? (AP Photo/Rich Pedroncelli)

---

4. The Agricultural Adjustment Act of 1933 (declared unconstitutional) was replaced by the 1938 Agricultural Adjustment Act and later changed and amended several times.

ironworkers and bricklayers unions to form the National Construction Alliance. Many labor advocates fear that these splits will further weaken organized labor's waning political influence. Indeed, the role of unions in American society has declined in recent years, as witnessed by the decrease in union membership (see Figure 7–1). In the age of automation and with the rise of the **service sector,** blue-collar workers in basic industries (autos, steel, and the like) represent a smaller and smaller percentage of the total working population.

Because of this decline in the industrial sector of the economy, national unions are looking to nontraditional areas for their membership, including migrant farmworkers, service workers, and especially public employees—such as police officers, firefighting personnel, and teachers, including college professors and graduate assistants. Indeed, public-sector unions are the fastest-growing labor organizations.

Although the proportion of the workforce that belongs to a union has declined over the years, American labor unions have not given up their efforts to support sympathetic candidates for Congress or for state office. Currently, the AFL-CIO, under the leadership of John J. Sweeney, has a large political budget, which it uses to help Democratic candidates nationwide. Although interest groups that favor Republicans continue to assist their candidates, the efforts of labor are more sustained and more targeted. Labor offers a candidate (such as Democratic presidential candidate Barack Obama in 2008) a corps of volunteers in addition to campaign contributions. A massive turnout by labor union members in critical elections can significantly increase the final vote totals for Democratic candidates. Currently, labor unions are pushing members of Congress to pass legislation that would make it easier for employees to join unions—and thus boost union membership.

Public Employee Unions. The degree of unionization in the private sector has declined over the past fifty years, but this has been partially offset by growth in the unionization of public employees. Figure 7–1 displays the growth in public-sector unionization. With

U.S. Senator Dick Durbin (D., Ill.) is shown addressing the annual convention of the AFL-CIO in Chicago. Why do you think that Democratic members of Congress support unions more than do Republican members? (AP Photo/Charles Rex Arbogast)

Service Sector
The sector of the economy that provides services—such as health care, banking, and education—in contrast to the sector that produces goods.

FIGURE 7–1:
Decline in Union Membership, 1948 to Present

As shown in this figure, the percentage of the total workforce that consists of labor union members has declined precipitously over the last forty years. Note, however, that in contrast to the decline in union membership in the private sector, the percentage of government workers who are union members increased significantly in the 1960s and 1970s and has remained stable since.

Source: Bureau of Labor Statistics.

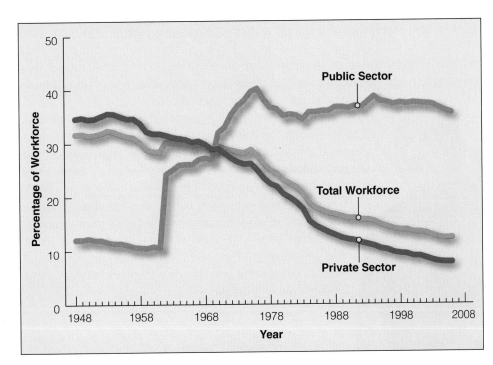

Hollywood writers
went on strike against television networks and movie studios in late 2007. This strike occurred after negotiations between the Writers Guild of America and the Alliance of Motion Picture and Television Producers failed to produce a new contract. (AP Photo/ Reed Saxon)

a total membership of more than 7.5 million, public-sector unions are likely to continue expanding.

Both the American Federation of State, County, and Municipal Employees and the American Federation of Teachers are members of the AFL-CIO's Public Employee Department. Over the years, public employee unions have become quite militant and are often involved in strikes. Most of these strikes are illegal, because almost no public employees have the right to strike.

A powerful interest group lobbying on behalf of public employees is the National Education Association (NEA), a nationwide organization of about 3.2 million teachers and others connected with education. Many NEA locals function as labor unions. The NEA lobbies intensively for increased public funding of education.

Interest Groups of Professionals. Numerous professional organizations exist, including the American Bar Association, the Association of General Contractors of America, the Institute of Electrical and Electronics Engineers, and others. Some professional groups, such as lawyers and physicians, are more influential than others because of their social status. Lawyers have a unique advantage—a large number of members of Congress share their profession. In terms of funds spent on lobbying, however, one professional organization stands head and shoulders above the rest—the American Medical Association (AMA). Founded in 1847, it is now affiliated with more than 1,000 local and state medical societies and has a total membership of about 250,000.

The Unorganized Poor. Some have argued that the system of interest group politics leaves out poor Americans and U.S. residents who are not citizens and cannot vote. Americans who are disadvantaged economically cannot afford to join interest groups; if they are members of the working poor, they may hold two or more jobs just to survive, leaving them no time to participate in interest groups. Other groups in the population—including non-English-speaking groups, resident aliens, single parents, Americans with disabilities, and younger voters—may not have the time or expertise even to find out what group might represent them. Consequently, some scholars suggest that interest groups and lobbyists are the privilege of upper-middle-class Americans and those who belong to unions or other special groups.

R. Allen Hays examines the plight of poor Americans in his book *Who Speaks for the Poor?*[5] Hays studied groups and individuals who have lobbied for public housing and other issues related to the poor and concluded that the poor depend largely on indirect representation. Most efforts on behalf of the poor come from a policy network of groups—including public housing officials, welfare workers and officials, religious groups, public-interest groups, and some liberal general interest groups—that speak loudly and persistently for the poor. Poor Americans themselves remain outside the interest group network and have little direct voice of their own.

Harold Lasso is the Director of
the Humanitarian Center for Workers. What group of workers do you think his organization represents? (AP Photo/ Will Powers)

---

5. R. Allen Hays, *Who Speaks for the Poor? National Interest Groups and Social Policy* (New York: Routledge, 2001).

ENVIRONMENTAL GROUPS

Environmental interest groups are not new. We have already mentioned the National Audubon Society, which was founded in 1905 to protect the snowy egret from the commercial demand for hat decorations. The patron of the Sierra Club, John Muir, worked for the creation of national parks more than a century ago. But the blossoming of national environmental groups with mass member-ships did not occur until the 1970s. Since the first Earth Day, organized in 1970, many interest groups have sprung up to protect the environment in general or unique eco-logical niches. The groups range from the National Wildlife Federation, with a member-ship of nearly 5 million and an emphasis on edu-cation, to the more elite Environmental Defense Fund, with a membership of 500,000 and a focus on influencing federal policy. Other groups include the Nature Conservancy, which uses members' contributions to buy up threatened natural areas and either give them to state or local govern-ments or manage them itself, and the more radical Greenpeace Society and Earth First.

These Sierra Club activists demonstrate in favor of reducing pollution in the Willamette River in Oregon. Whom are these activists trying to influence?
(AP Photo/Rick Bowmer)

In early 2007, twenty labor unions joined with the Theodore Roosevelt Conservation Partnership, a Republican-leaning group of conservationists, to form the Union Sportsmen's Alliance. This unlikely combination of union and conservation interests was a response to the limitations placed in recent years on prime hunting and fishing areas on federal lands in the West. Many hunters and fishers belong to the labor unions, and union leaders also looked at the alliance with the conservation group as a way to expand union membership. The conservation group, in turn, thought that it would benefit from the funds and lob-bying power of the unions. According to environmental expert Thomas Dunlap of Texas A&M University, the new alliance "may have a major effect in reshaping the environmen-tal movement for this decade."[6]

PUBLIC-INTEREST GROUPS

Public interest is a difficult term to define because, as we noted in Chapter 6, there are many publics in our nation of more than 300 million. It is almost impossible for one par-ticular public policy to benefit everybody, which makes it practically impossible to define the public interest. Nonetheless, over the past few decades, a variety of lobbying organiza-tions have been formed "in the public interest."

Nader Organizations. The best-known and perhaps the most effective public-interest groups are those founded under the leadership of consumer activist Ralph Nader. Nader's rise to the top began in 1965 with the publication of his book *Unsafe at Any Speed,* a lambasting critique of the purported attempt by General Motors (GM) to keep from the public detrimental information about its rear-engine Corvair. Partly as a result of Nader's book, Congress began to consider an automobile safety bill. GM made a clumsy attempt to discredit Nader's background. Nader sued, the media exploited the story, and when GM settled out of court for $425,000, Nader became a recognized champion of consumer interests. Since then, Nader has turned over much of his income to the more than sixty public-interest groups that he has formed or

Public Interest
The best interests of the overall community; the national good, rather than the narrow interests of a particular group.

---

6. As cited in Blaine Harden, "Unions, Conservationists Join Hands," *The Washington Post*, January 16, 2007.

sponsored. Nader ran for president in 2000 on the Green Party ticket and in 2004 and 2008 as an independent.

Other Public-Interest Groups. Partly in response to the Nader organizations, a variety of conservative public-interest law firms have sprung up that are often pitted against the consumer groups in court. Some of these are the Mountain States Legal Defense Foundation, the Pacific Legal Foundation, the National Right-to-Work Legal Defense Foundation, the Washington Legal Foundation, the Institute for Justice, and the Mid-Atlantic Legal Foundation.

One of the largest public-interest groups is Common Cause, founded in 1970. Its goal is to reorder national priorities toward "the public" and to make governmental institutions more responsive to the needs of the public. Anyone willing to pay dues of $20 a year can become a member. Members are polled regularly to obtain information about local and national issues requiring reassessment. Some of the activities of Common Cause have been (1) helping to ensure the passage of the Twenty-sixth Amendment (giving eighteen-year-olds the right to vote), (2) achieving greater voter registration in all states, (3) supporting the complete withdrawal of all U.S. forces from South Vietnam in the 1970s, and (4) promoting legislation that would limit campaign spending.

Ralph Nader, testifying on automobile safety before a Senate subcommittee

in 1966. Nader, author of the book *Unsafe at Any Speed,* campaigned for president in 2000, 2004, and 2008 but received only a small share of the votes. How might his political ambitions have affected the public-interest organizations that he helped found? (AP Photo)

Other public-interest groups include the League of Women Voters, founded in 1920. Although nominally nonpartisan, it has lobbied for the Equal Rights Amendment and for government reform. The Consumer Federation of America is an alliance of about three hundred nonprofit organizations interested in consumer protection. The American Civil Liberties Union dates back to World War I (1914–1918), when, under a different name, it defended draft resisters. It generally enters into legal disputes related to Bill of Rights issues.

OTHER INTEREST GROUPS

Single-interest groups, being narrowly focused, may be able to call attention to their causes because they have simple, straightforward goals and because their members tend to care intensely about the issues. Thus, such groups can easily motivate their

This member of

the Consumer Federation of America argues that all-terrain vehicles (ATVs) are unsafe for minors. This group wants the federal Consumer Product Safety Commission to prohibit the use of adult-sized ATVs by children under the age of sixteen. Why is the Consumer Federation of America called a public-interest lobbying group? (AP Photo/Ron Edmonds)

members to contact legislators or to organize demonstrations in support of their policy goals.

A number of interest groups focus on just one issue. The abortion debate has created various groups opposed to abortion (such as the National Right to Life Committee organization) and groups in favor of abortion rights (such as NARAL Pro-Choice America). Other single-issue groups are the National Rifle Association of America, the Right to Work Committee (an anti-union group), and the American Israel Public Affairs Committee (a pro-Israel group).

Still other groups represent Americans who share a common characteristic, such as age or ethnicity. Such interest groups may lobby for legislation that enhances the rights of their members or may just represent a viewpoint.

AARP, as mentioned earlier, is one of the most powerful interest groups in Washington, D.C., and, according to some, the strongest lobbying group in the United States. It is certainly the nation's largest interest group, with a membership of more than 38 million. AARP has accomplished much for its members over the years. It played a significant role in the creation of Medicare and Medicaid, as well as in obtaining cost-of-living increases in Social Security payments. In 2003, AARP supported the Republican bill to add prescription drug coverage to Medicare. (The plan also made other changes to the system.) Some observers believe that AARP's support tipped the balance and allowed Congress to pass the measure on a closely divided vote.

FOREIGN GOVERNMENTS

Homegrown interests are not the only players in the game. Washington, D.C., is also the center for lobbying by foreign governments as well as private foreign interests. The governments of the largest U.S. trading partners, such as Canada, the European Union (EU) countries, Japan, and South Korea, maintain substantial research and lobbying staffs. Even smaller nations, such as those in the Caribbean, engage lobbyists when vital legislation affecting their trade interests is considered. Frequently, these foreign interests hire former representatives or former senators to promote their positions on Capitol Hill. Should foreign interests be allowed to lobby Congress? We address this question in the *Which Side Are You On?* feature on the next page.

WHAT MAKES AN INTEREST GROUP POWERFUL?

At any time, thousands of interest groups are attempting to influence state legislatures, governors, Congress, and members of the executive branch of the U.S. government. What characteristics make some of those groups more powerful than others and more likely to have influence over government policy? Generally, interest groups attain a reputation for being powerful through their membership size, financial resources, leadership, and cohesiveness.

SIZE AND RESOURCES

No legislator can deny the power of an interest group that includes thousands of his or her own constituents among its members. Labor unions and organizations such as AARP and the American Automobile Association are able to claim voters in every congressional district. Having a large membership—nearly 10 million in the case of the AFL-CIO—carries a great deal of weight with government officials. AARP now has more than 38 million members and a budget of more than a billion dollars for its operations. In addition, AARP claims to represent all older Americans, who constitute close to 20 percent of the population, whether they join the organization or not.

Having a large number of members, even if the individual membership dues are relatively small, provides an organization with a strong financial base. Those funds pay for lobbyists, television advertisements, mailings to members, a Web site, and many

whichsideareYOUon?

SHOULD FOREIGN INTERESTS BE ALLOWED TO LOBBY CONGRESS?

No one doubts that lobbying is significant in our political system. Thousands of lobbyists ply the halls of Congress on a daily basis. That's part of American democracy. It's less well known, though, that a significant number of these lobbyists are working for foreign companies and, more important, for foreign governments. American lobbying firms are often used by foreign groups seeking to advance foreign agendas. The use of American lobbyists ensures greater access and increases the possibility of legislative success.

Because of the prominence of the United States in the global economy, international corporations—often owned by foreign governments—have taken a keen interest in influencing the U.S. government. Foreign corporations frequently hire former members of Congress to lobby on their behalf. Foreign governments like to present a better image of their countries, so they often hire "government affairs" consulting firms in Washington, D.C. That's exactly what Saudi Arabia did after 9/11. That government hired Qorvis Communications to spread the message that Saudi Arabia backed the U.S.-led war on terrorism. Qorvis garnered at least $15 million in fees from Saudi Arabia.

WE ARE AN OPEN COUNTRY— LET'S KEEP IT THAT WAY

Those who see no problem with foreign corporations or foreign governments hiring lobbyists to try to influence U.S. policy argue that we are an open democracy. We do business with the rest of the world, and the rest of the world does business with us. U.S. companies invest everywhere. Why shouldn't foreign companies be able to invest in the United States? And, if they must hire American lobbying firms to safeguard their investments, so be it. When Borse Dubai wanted to buy a 20 percent stake in NASDAQ (an important U.S. stock exchange), it spent millions on a lobbying push to boost the image of Dubai and the United Arab Emirates. Given that foreign ownership of a U.S. stock exchange could not conceivably constitute a security threat, why shouldn't Borse Dubai be able to attempt to influence U.S. legislators the same way that U.S. corporations do? We need foreign capital to keep America running smoothly. We should welcome foreign investors with open arms, so why not accept the lobbyists they hire just as we accept lobbyists for domestic corporations and interest groups?

U.S. LOBBYISTS SHOULD WORK FOR U.S. FIRMS

It all sounds so benign on paper—foreign governments and corporations simply wanting to get their "fair share" of U.S. business. Consider the Chinese government. It contacted U.S. lobbying firms in its attempt to purchase California-based Unocal Oil Company a few years ago. Not surprisingly, members of Congress claimed that foreign ownership of an American oil company would represent a national security risk. Consider also that overseas companies hired lobbyist Jack Abramoff. That well-known lobbyist is now in prison after having pleaded guilty to three felony charges involving fraud in his lobbying activities. Not too many years ago, Dubai Ports World attempted to buy the operations at six U.S. ports. Dubai Ports is under the control of the government of the United Arab Emirates. Opponents of this action pointed out that the United Arab Emirates had links in the past to the Taliban regime in Afghanistan and to Middle Eastern terrorist groups, such as al Qaeda. In a world of security concerns, we cannot allow foreign corporations and foreign governments to influence decisions on what is right for America.

other resources that help an interest group make its point to politicians. The business organization with the largest membership is probably the U.S. Chamber of Commerce, which represents more than 3 million businesses and organizations. The Chamber uses its members' dues to pay for staff and lobbyists, as well as a sophisticated communications network so that it can contact members in a timely way. All of the members can receive e-mail and check the Web site to get updates on the latest legislative proposals.

Other organizations may have fewer members but nonetheless can muster significant financial resources. The pharmaceutical lobby, which represents many of the major drug manufacturers, is one of the most powerful interest groups in Washington due to its financial resources. This lobby has more than 1,250 registered lobbyists and spent close to $200 million in the last presidential election cycle for lobbying and campaign expenditures.

LEADERSHIP

Money is not the only resource that interest groups need to have. Strong leaders who can develop effective strategies are also important. For example, the American Israel Public Affairs Committee (AIPAC) has long benefited from strong leadership. AIPAC lobbies Congress and the executive branch on issues related to U.S.-Israeli relations, as well as general foreign policy in the Middle East. AIPAC has been successful in promoting the close relationship that the two nations have enjoyed, which includes foreign aid that the United States annually bestows on Israel, now down to about $2.5 billion a year, but more than $4 billion as recently as 2000. Despite its modest membership size, AIPAC has won bipartisan support for its agenda and is consistently ranked among the most influential interest groups in America.

Other interest groups, including some with few financial resources, succeed in part because they are led by individuals with charisma and access to power, such as Jesse Jackson of the Rainbow Coalition. Sometimes, choosing a leader with a particular image can be an effective strategy for an organization. The National Rifle Association (NRA) had more than organizational skills in mind when it elected actor Charlton Heston as its president. The strategy of using an actor identified with powerful roles as the spokesperson for the organization worked to improve its national image.

Speaker of the House Nancy Pelosi (D., Calif.) addresses the American Israel Public Affairs Committee (AIPAC) policy conference. What issues might she be discussing? (AP Photo/Evan Vucci)

COHESIVENESS

Regardless of an interest group's size or the amount of funds in its coffers, the motivation of an interest group's members is a key factor in determining how powerful it is. If the members of a group hold their beliefs strongly enough to send letters to their representatives, join a march on Washington, or work together to defeat a candidate, that group is considered powerful. As described earlier, the American labor movement's success in electing Democratic candidates made the labor movement a more powerful lobby.

In contrast, although groups that oppose abortion rights have had modest success in influencing policy, they are considered powerful because their members are vocal and highly motivated. Other measures of cohesion include the ability of a group to get its members to contact Washington quickly or to give extra funds when needed. The U.S. Chamber of Commerce excels at both of these strategies. In comparison, AARP cannot claim that it can get its more than 38 million members to contact their congressional representatives, but it does seem to influence the opinions of older Americans and their views of political candidates.

The Reverend Jessie Jackson presides over the Rainbow Coalition. What do you think some of the goals of this group might be? (AP Photo/Damian Dovarganes)

Direct Technique
An interest group activity that involves interaction with government officials to further the group's goals.

Indirect Technique
A strategy employed by interest groups that uses third parties to influence government officials.

INTEREST GROUP STRATEGIES

Interest groups employ a wide range of techniques and strategies to promote their policy goals. Although few groups are successful at persuading Congress and the president to completely endorse their programs, many are able to block—or at least weaken—legislation injurious to their members. The key to success for interest groups is access to government officials. To gain such access, interest groups and their representatives try to cultivate long-term relationships with legislators and government officials. The best of these relationships are based on mutual respect and cooperation. The interest group provides the official with excellent sources of information and assistance, and the official in turn gives the group opportunities to express its views.

The techniques used by interest groups can be divided into direct and indirect techniques. With **direct techniques,** the interest group and its lobbyists approach the officials personally to present their case. With **indirect techniques,** in contrast, the interest group uses the general public or individual constituents to influence the government on behalf of the interest group.

DIRECT TECHNIQUES

Lobbying, publicizing ratings of legislative behavior, building coalitions, and providing campaign assistance are the four main direct techniques used by interest groups.

Lobbying Techniques. As might be guessed, the term *lobbying* comes from the activities of private citizens regularly congregating in the lobbies of legislative chambers before a session to petition legislators. In the latter part of the 1800s, railroad and industrial groups openly bribed state legislators to pass legislation beneficial to their interests, giving lobbying a well-deserved bad name. Most lobbyists today are professionals. They are either consultants to a company or interest group or members of one of the Washington, D.C., law firms that specialize in providing such services. As described in this chapter's opening *What If . . .* feature, such firms employ hundreds of former members of Congress and former government officials—for example, former presidential candidates Bob Dole and Walter Mondale. Lobbyists are valued for their network of contacts in Washington. As Ed Rollins, a former White House aide, put it, "I've got many friends who are all through the agencies and equally important, I don't have many enemies. . . . I tell my clients I can get your case moved to the top of the pile."[7] Lobbyists of all types are becoming more numerous. The number of lobbyists in Washington, D.C., has more than doubled since 2000.

Lobbyists engage in an array of activities to influence legislation and government policy. These include the following:

1. Engaging in private meetings with public officials, including the president's advisers, to make known the interests of the lobbyists' clients. Although acting on behalf of their clients, lobbyists often furnish needed information to senators and representatives (and government agency appointees) that these officials could not easily obtain on their own. It is to the lobbyists' advantage to provide accurate information so that policymakers will rely on this source in the future.
2. Testifying before congressional committees for or against proposed legislation.
3. Testifying before executive rulemaking agencies—such as the Federal Trade Commission or the Consumer Product Safety Commission—for or against proposed rules.
4. Assisting legislators or bureaucrats in drafting legislation or prospective regulations. Often, lobbyists furnish advice on the specific details of legislation.
5. Inviting legislators to social occasions, such as cocktail parties, boating expeditions, and other events, including conferences at exotic locations. Most lobbyists believe that meeting legislators in a relaxed social setting is effective.

---

7. As quoted in H. R. Mahood, *Interest Groups in American National Politics: An Overview* (New York: Prentice Hall, 2000), p. 51.

6. Providing political information to legislators and other government officials. Often, the lobbyists have better information than the party leadership about how other legislators are going to vote. In this case, the political information they furnish may be a key to legislative success.

7. Supplying nominations for federal appointments to the executive branch.

The Ratings Game. Many interest groups attempt to influence the overall behavior of legislators through their rating systems. Each year, the interest group selects legislation that it believes is most important to the organization's goals and then monitors how legislators vote on it. Each legislator is given a score based on the percentage of times that he or she voted in favor of the group's position. The usual rating scheme ranges from 0 to 100 percent. In the scheme of the liberal Americans for Democratic Action, for example, a rating of 100 means that a member of Congress voted with the group on every issue and is, by that measure, very liberal.

Ratings are a shorthand way of describing members' voting records for interested citizens. Voting records can also be used to embarrass members. For example, an environmental group identifies the twelve representatives who the group believes have the worst voting records on environmental issues and labels them "the Dirty Dozen," and a watchdog group describes those representatives who took home the most "pork" for their districts or states as the biggest "pigs."

Building Alliances. Another direct technique used by interest groups is to form a coalition with other groups concerned about the same legislation. Often, these groups will set up a paper organization with an innocuous name to represent their joint concerns. In the early 1990s, for example, environmental, labor, and consumer groups formed an alliance called the Citizens Trade Campaign to oppose the passage of the North American Free Trade Agreement.

Members of such a coalition share expenses and multiply the influence of their individual groups by combining their efforts. Other advantages of forming a coalition are that it blurs the specific interests of the individual groups involved and makes it appear that larger public interests are at stake. These alliances also are efficient devices for keeping like-minded groups from duplicating one another's lobbying efforts.

Another example of an alliance developed when the Republicans launched the K Street Project. The project, named for the street in Washington, D.C., where the largest lobbying firms have their headquarters, was designed to freeze Democrats out of the lobbying community. Republicans sought to pressure lobbying firms to hire Republicans in top positions, offering loyal lobbyists greater access to lawmakers in return. An indication of the success of the project was the increase in the donations given to Republican lawmakers by lobbyists, which rose from $1.2 million in 1994 to nearly $12 million in 2006. But the K Street Project also had a troubling aspect, as revelations of legislative favors being granted to special interests in return for campaign donations have made clear. This trend, and the many examples of corruption attendant on it, will be discussed further in Chapter 10.

The K Street Project essentially fell apart when the Democrats took control of Congress after the 2006 elections. With the likelihood that the Democrats would do even better in 2008, K Street lobbyists tilted to the Democrats in 2007 and 2008. Congress also passed new lobbying rules in 2007, described in detail later in this chapter. Among other things, the new rules criminalized efforts to influence private hiring at lobbying firms "solely on the basis of partisan political affiliation." This provision seeks to ensure that the K Street Project cannot be resurrected in the future by either party.

"Please understand. I don't sell access to the government. I merely sell access to the guys who <u>do</u> sell access to the government."

Interest groups from every imaginable ideological point of view

issue scorecards of individual legislators' voting records as they relate to their organization's agenda. Shown here are a few such scorecards. How much value can voters place on these kinds of ratings? (Photo illustration assembled from various Web sites.)

Assistance with Campaigns. Interest groups have additional strategies to use in their attempts to influence government policies. Groups recognize that the greatest concern of legislators is to be reelected, so they focus on the legislators' campaign needs. Associations with large memberships, such as labor unions, are able to provide workers for political campaigns, including precinct workers to get out the vote, volunteers to put up posters and pass out literature, and people to staff telephone banks for campaign headquarters.

In many states where certain interest groups have large memberships, candidates vie for the groups' endorsements in a campaign. Gaining those endorsements may be automatic, or it may require that the candidates participate in debates or interviews with the interest groups. Endorsements are important because an interest group usually publicizes its choices in its membership publication and because the candidate can use the endorsement in her or his campaign literature. Traditionally, labor unions have endorsed Democratic Party candidates. Republican candidates, however, often try to persuade union locals at least to refrain from any endorsement. Making no endorsement can then be perceived as disapproval of the Democratic Party candidate.

Despite attempts at campaign-finance reform, the 2008 elections boasted record campaign spending. The usual array of interest groups—labor unions, professional groups, and business associations—gathered contributions to their political action committees and distributed them to the candidates. Most labor contributions went to Democratic candidates, of course. For the first time in living memory, however, businesses, including the finance, health-care, and pharmaceutical industries, contributed larger sums to the Democrats than to their rivals. Clearly, 2008 was not a good year for the Republicans. At the same time, new campaign groups—the so-called 527 organizations, tax-exempt associations focused on influencing political elections—raised hundreds of millions of dollars in unregulated contributions and used them for campaign activities and advertising. Some national interest groups, such as the Laborers' Union, the National Association of Realtors, and the Sierra Club, created their own 527 organizations to spend funds for advertising and other political activities. The flood of unregulated funds supported massive advertising campaigns throughout the election season.

INDIRECT TECHNIQUES

Interest groups can also try to influence government policy by working through others, who may be constituents or the general public. Indirect techniques mask an interest group's own activities and make the effort appear to be spontaneous. Furthermore, legislators and government officials are often more impressed by contacts from constituents than from an interest group's lobbyist.

Generating Public Pressure. In some instances, interest groups try to produce a "groundswell" of public pressure to influence the government. Such efforts may include advertisements in national magazines and newspapers, mass mailings, television publicity, and demonstrations. The Internet and satellite links make communication efforts even more effective. Interest groups may commission polls to find out what the public's sentiments are and then publicize the results. The intent of this activity is to convince policy-makers that public opinion supports the group's position.

Some corporations and interest groups also engage in a practice that might be called **climate control.** With this strategy, public relations efforts are aimed at improving the public image of the industry or group and are not necessarily related to any specific political issue. Contributions by corporations and groups in support of public television programs, sponsorship of special events, and commercials extolling the virtues of corporate research are some ways of achieving climate control. For example, to improve its image in the wake of litigation against tobacco companies, Philip Morris began advertising its assistance to community agencies, including halfway houses for teen offenders and shelters for battered women. By building a reservoir of favorable public opinion, groups believe that their legislative goals will be less likely to encounter opposition from the public.

Using Constituents as Lobbyists. Interest groups also use constituents to lobby for their groups' goals. In the "shotgun" approach, the interest group tries to mobilize large numbers of constituents to write, phone, or send e-mails to their legislators or the president. Often, the group provides postcards or form letters for constituents to fill out and mail. These efforts are effective on Capitol Hill only when there are a great many responses, however, because legislators know that the voters did not initiate the communications on their own. Artificially manufactured grassroots activity has been aptly labeled *Astroturf lobbying.*

A more powerful variation of this technique uses only important constituents. With this approach, known as the "rifle" technique or the "Utah plant manager theory," the interest group might, for example, ask the manager of a local plant in Utah to contact the senator from Utah.[8] Because the constituent is seen as responsible for many jobs or other resources, the legislator is more likely to listen carefully to the constituent's concerns about legislation than to a paid lobbyist.

Unconventional Forms of Pressure. Sometimes, interest groups may employ forms of pressure that are outside the ordinary political process. These can include marches, rallies, civil disobedience, or demonstrations. Such assemblies, as long as they are peaceful, are protected by the First Amendment. In Chapter 5, we described the civil disobedience techniques of the African American civil rights movement in the 1950s and 1960s. The 1963 March on Washington in support of civil rights was one of the most effective demonstrations ever organized. The women's suffrage movement of the early 1900s also employed marches and demonstrations to great effect.

Demonstrations, however, are not always peaceable. Violent demonstrations have a long history in America, dating back to the antitax Boston Tea Party described in Chapter 2. The Vietnam War (1964–1975) provoked a large number of demonstrations, some of which were violent. In 1999, at a meeting of the World Trade Organization in Seattle, demonstrations against "globalization" turned violent. These demonstrations were

Climate Control
The use of public relations techniques to create favorable public opinion toward an interest group, industry, or corporation.

didyouknow...

That lobbyists have their own lobbying organization, the American League of Lobbyists?

During the war in Vietnam

(1964–1975), peace demonstrators engaged in marches and rallies such as this one in San Francisco on April 15, 1967. Why are such demonstrations considered "outside" the ordinary political process? (AP Photo/Robert W. Klein)

---

8. Kay Lehman Schlozman and John T. Tierney, *Organized Interests and American Democracy* (New York: Harper & Row, 1986), p. 293.

Boycott
A form of pressure or protest—an organized refusal to purchase a particular product or deal with a particular business.

repeated throughout the 2000s at various sites around the world. Violent demonstrations can be counterproductive—instead of putting pressure on the authorities, they may simply alienate the public. For example, historians continue to debate whether the demonstrations against the Vietnam War were effective or counterproductive.

Another unconventional form of pressure is the **boycott**—a refusal to buy a particular product or deal with a particular business. To be effective, boycotts must command widespread support. One example was the African American boycott of buses in Montgomery, Alabama, in 1955, described in Chapter 5. Another was the boycott of California grapes that were picked by nonunion workers, as part of a campaign to organize Mexican American farmworkers. The first grape boycott lasted from 1965 to 1970; a series of later boycotts was less effective.

REGULATING LOBBYISTS

Congress made its first attempt to control lobbyists and lobbying activities through Title III of the Legislative Reorganization Act of 1946, otherwise known as the Federal Regulation of Lobbying Act. The act actually provided for public disclosure more than for regulation, and it neglected to specify which agency would enforce its provisions. The 1946 legislation defined a *lobbyist* as any person or organization that received funds to be used principally to influence legislation before Congress. Such persons and individuals were supposed to "register" their clients and the purposes of their efforts and to report quarterly on their activities.

The legislation was tested in a 1954 Supreme Court case, *United States v. Harriss,*[9] and was found to be constitutional. The Court agreed that the lobbying law did not violate due process, freedom of speech or of the press, or the freedom to petition. The Court narrowly construed the act, however, holding that it applied only to lobbyists who were influencing federal legislation *directly.*

THE RESULTS OF THE 1946 ACT

The immediate result of the act was that a minimal number of individuals registered as lobbyists. National interest groups, such as the National Rifle Association and the American Petroleum Institute, could employ hundreds of staff members who were, of course, working on legislation but only register one or two lobbyists who were engaged *principally* in influencing Congress. There were no reporting requirements for lobbying the executive branch, federal agencies, the courts, or congressional staff. Approximately seven thousand individuals and organizations registered annually as lobbyists, although most experts estimated that ten times that number were actually employed in Washington to exert influence on the government.

THE REFORMS OF 1995

The reform-minded Congress of 1995–1996 overhauled the lobbying legislation, fundamentally changing the ground rules for those who seek to influence the federal government. The Lobbying Disclosure Act (LDA), passed in 1995, included the following provisions:

1. A *lobbyist* is defined as anyone who spends at least 20 percent of his or her time lobbying members of Congress, their staffs, or executive-branch officials.
2. Lobbyists must register with the clerk of the House and the secretary of the Senate within forty-five days of being hired or of making their first contacts. The registration requirement applies to organizations that spend more than $20,000 or to individuals who are paid more than $5,000 semiannually for lobbying work. These figures have since been raised to $24,500 and $6,000, respectively.

---

9. 347 U.S. 612 (1954).

3. Semiannual reports must disclose the general nature of the lobbying effort, the name of the client, specific issues and bill numbers, the estimated cost of the campaign, and a list of the branches of government contacted. The names of the individuals contacted need not be reported.

4. Representatives of U.S.-owned subsidiaries of foreign-owned firms and lawyers who represent foreign entities also are required to register.

5. The requirements exempt "grassroots" lobbying efforts and those of tax-exempt organizations, such as religious groups.

As they debated the 1995 law, both the House and the Senate adopted new rules on gifts and travel expenses provided by lobbyists: the House adopted a flat ban on gifts, and the Senate limited gifts to $50 in value and to no more than $100 in gifts from a single source in a year. There are exceptions for gifts from family members and for home-state products and souvenirs, such as T-shirts and coffee mugs. Both chambers banned all-expenses-paid trips, golf outings, and other such junkets. An exception applies for "widely attended" events, however, or if the member is a primary speaker at an event. These gift rules stopped the broad practice of taking members of Congress to lunch or dinner, but the various exemptions and exceptions have caused much controversy.

LOBBYING SCANDALS

The regulation of lobbying activity again surfaced as an issue in 2005 when a number of scandals came to light. At the center of many of the publicized incidents was a highly influential and corrupt lobbyist, Jack Abramoff. Using his ties with numerous Republican, and a handful of Democratic, lawmakers, Abramoff brokered many deals for the special interest clients that he represented in return for campaign donations, gifts, and various perks.

In January 2006, Abramoff pleaded guilty to three criminal felony counts alleging that he had defrauded American Indian tribes and engaged in the corruption of public officials. A number of politicians attempted to distance themselves from the embattled lobbyist by giving Abramoff's campaign donations to charity. To date, the only lawmaker to be convicted in connection with the Abramoff lobbying scandal is congressional representative Robert Ney (R., Ohio). On March 1, 2007, Ney began serving a thirty-month sentence in a federal prison for conspiracy and making false statements to investigators.

THE REFORMS OF 2007

The corruption and scandals that occurred while the Republicans controlled Congress certainly had some effect on the 2006 elections. When the Democrats took control of Congress in January 2007, one of their first undertakings was ethics and lobbying reform. In the first one hundred hours of the session, the House tightened its ethics rules on gifts and on travel funded by lobbyists. The Senate followed shortly thereafter.

In September 2007, President George W. Bush signed the Honest Leadership and Open Government Act. Under the new law, lobbyists must report quarterly, and the registration threshold becomes $10,000 per quarter. Organizations must report coalition activities if they contribute more than $5,000 to a coalition. The House and Senate must now post lobbying information in a searchable file on the Internet. In a significant alteration to legislative practices, "earmarked" expenditures, commonly called "pork," must now be identified and made public. This last change may not have its intended effect of reducing earmarks, however, because it turns out that many legislators are actually proud of their pork and happy to tell the folks back home all about it. Many observers doubt whether the new rules will really change the congressional culture in which favors flow in one direction and legislation flows in the other—as we explain in this chapter's *Politics and Ethics* feature on the next page.

Republican John Doolittle (R., Calif.) announces his retirement from Congress. Simultaneously, his wife was being investigated for her alleged participation in a congressional lobbying scandal that involved former lobbyist Jack Abramoff. Can regulation of lobbying activities prevent lobbying scandals? (AP Photo/Rich Pedroncelli)

politicsand...ethics

LOBBYING RULES—THE MORE THEY CHANGE, THE MORE THEY STAY THE SAME

Members of Congress have often vowed that they would "clean up the ethics mess." When the Democrats took control of Congress in 2006, after six years of Republican dominance, they were especially vehement in making this pledge. Ethics reform was at the top of the agenda. The 110th Congress proceeded to ban an assortment of apparently unethical practices. New lobbying rules were designed to prevent lobbyists from showering members of Congress with gifts. Lobbyists must now report more fully on contacts and contributions. The new rules also prohibited discounted trips on private jets for members of Congress. It didn't take long, though, for members of Congress to figure out ways to get around the new lobbying rules.

INNOVATION IS NOW THE WATCHWORD

Innovation was key in finding ways to skirt the new rules. Lobbyists can still contribute to political action committees (PACs). These committees then pay the lawmakers' expenses for such important events as wine-tasting tours, weekends at Disney World, and parties on South Beach in Miami Beach. Lobbyists then appear at these events.

What all this means is that under the new rules, members of Congress are not allowed to mingle with lobbyists who offer them a free meal in an expensive French restaurant near the U.S. Capitol building. Rather, they are allowed to mingle with lobbyists at social fund-raising events. Not surprisingly, firms that specialize in PACs have more business than they can handle—all due to the latest "ethical" lobbying rules. Fund-raising events have become more prevalent and more extravagant. They provide a safe haven for lobbyists to make contacts with members of Congress without violating ethics rules.

LOBBYISTS AND INTEREST GROUPS INVEST IN REAL ESTATE

To satisfy the increased demand for social fund-raising events, lobbying firms and special interest groups have purchased or leased scores of townhouses within blocks of the Capitol. United Parcel Service (UPS) has a beautiful townhouse near the Capitol, where in just one year it held fifty-seven events, none of which are reflected in federal campaign records. The American Council of Life Insurers held twenty-nine similar events. The lobbying group Van Scoyoc Associates held forty-seven. In a recent year, there were more than four hundred congressional fund-raisers at Capitol Hill facilities owned by labor organizations, corporate groups, or lobbyists. Almost half the members of Congress benefited from these events. Often, lobbying groups rent their townhouses to members of Congress at unusually low rates. Those members' campaign committees then pay for the catering costs.

While the Democrats who took control of the 110th Congress advocated "freeing Washington from the grip of lobbyists," they continue to rack up serious financial war chests from business interests. Indeed, Democratic members of Congress outraised Republicans among business interests by more than $100 million in 2007 alone—the year the new ethics rules were put into place.

FOR CRITICAL ANALYIS

Actual and potential members of Congress require large sums to finance their campaigns. Is there any neutral way that campaigns could be financed?

INTEREST GROUPS AND REPRESENTATIVE DEMOCRACY

The role played by interest groups in shaping national policy has caused many to question whether we really have a democracy at all. Most interest groups have a middle-class or upper-class bias. Members of interest groups can afford to pay the membership fees, are generally fairly well educated, and normally participate in the political process to a greater extent than the "average" American.

Furthermore, leaders of interest groups tend to constitute an "elite within an elite" in the sense that they usually are from a higher social class than other group members. The most powerful interest groups—those with the most resources and political influence—are primarily business, trade, and professional groups. In contrast, public-interest groups and civil rights groups make up only a small percentage of the interest groups lobbying Congress.

INTEREST GROUPS: ELITIST OR PLURALIST?

Remember from Chapter 1 that the elite theory of politics presumes that most Americans are uninterested in politics and are willing to let a small, elite group of citizens make decisions for them. Pluralist theory, in contrast, views politics as a struggle among various interest groups to gain benefits for their members. The pluralist approach views compromise among various competing interests as the essence of political decision making. In reality, neither theory fully describes American politics. If interest groups led by elite, upper-class individuals are the dominant voices in Congress, then what we see is a conflict among elite groups—which would lend as much support to the elitist theory as to the pluralist approach.

INTEREST GROUP INFLUENCE

The results of lobbying efforts—congressional legislation—do not always favor the interests of the most powerful groups, however. In part, this is because not all interest groups have an equal influence on government. Each group has a different combination of resources to use in the policymaking process. While some groups are composed of members who have high social status and significant economic resources, such as the National Association of Manufacturers, other groups derive influence from their large memberships. AARP, for example, has more members than any other interest group. Its large membership allows it to wield significant power over legislators. Still other groups, such as environmentalists, have causes that can claim strong public support even from people who have no direct stake in the issue. Groups such as the National Rifle Association are well organized and have highly motivated members. This enables them to channel a stream of letters or e-mails toward Congress with a few days' effort.

didyouknow...

That, on average, there are now sixty lobbyists for each member of Congress?

Even the most powerful interest groups do not always succeed in their demands. Whereas the U.S. Chamber of Commerce may be accepted as having a justified interest in the question of business taxes, many legislators might feel that the group should not engage in the debate over the future of Social Security. In other words, groups are seen as having a legitimate concern in the issues closest to their interests but not necessarily in broader issues. This may explain why some of the most successful groups are those that focus on very specific issues—such as tobacco farming, funding of abortions, and handgun control—and do not get involved in larger conflicts.

Complicating the question of interest group influence is the fact that many groups' lobbyists are former colleagues, friends, or family members of current members of Congress.

WHY SHOULD YOU CARE ABOUT
interestgroups?

Why should you, as an individual, care about interest groups? True, some interest groups focus on issues that concern only a limited number of people. Others, however, are involved in causes in which almost everyone has a stake. Gun control is one of the issues that concerns a large number of people. The question of whether the possession of handguns should be regulated or even banned is at the heart of a long-running heated battle among organized interest groups. The fight is fueled by the one million gun incidents occurring in the United States each year—murders, suicides, assaults, accidents, and robberies in which guns are involved.

Brady Gun Activist
(Mark Wilson/Getty Images)

INTEREST GROUPS AND YOUR LIFE

The passionate feelings that are brought to bear on both sides of the gun control issue are evidence of its importance. The problem of crime is central to the gun control issue. Public opinion poll respondents cited crime as one of the nation's most important problems throughout the 1990s, and it continues to be a major concern today.

Does the easy availability of handguns promote crime? Do people have a right to possess firearms to defend home and hearth? In other words, are guns part of the problem of crime—or part of the solution? Either way, the question is important to you personally. Even if you are fortunate enough not to be victimized by crime, you will probably find yourself limiting your activities from time to time out of a fear of crime.

HOW YOU CAN MAKE A DIFFERENCE

Almost every year, Congress and the various state legislatures debate measures that would alter gun laws for the nation or for the individual states. As a result, there are plenty of opportunities to get involved.

Issues in the debate include child-safety features on guns and the regulation of gun dealers who sell firearms at gun shows. Proponents of gun control seek safety locks and more restrictions on gun purchases—if not to ban handguns entirely. Proponents of firearms claim that possessing firearms is a constitutional right and meets a vital defense need for individuals. They contend that the problem lies not in the sale and ownership of weapons but in their use by criminals.

The National Coalition to Ban Handguns favors a total ban, taking the position that handguns "serve no valid purpose, except to kill people." Such a ban is opposed by the National Rifle Association (NRA) of America. The NRA, founded in 1871, is currently one of the most powerful single-issue groups in the United States. The NRA believes that gun laws will not reduce the number of crimes. It is illogical to assume, according to the NRA, that persons who refuse to obey laws prohibiting rape, murder, and other crimes will obey a gun law.

Many proponents of gun control insist that controlling the purchase of weapons would reduce the availability of guns to children. In response, some states have passed laws that hold adults liable for not locking away their firearms. In addition, a number of cities have sued gun manufacturers for not controlling the flow of their products to dealers who sell guns to criminals and gang members.

To find out more about the NRA's position, contact that organization at the following address:

The National Rifle Association
11250 Waples Mill Rd.
Fairfax, VA 22030
703-267-1000
www.nra.org

To learn about the positions of gun control advocates, contact:

The Coalition to Stop Gun Violence
1023 15th St. N.W., Suite 301
Washington, DC 20005
202-408-0061
www.csgv.org

Brady Center to Prevent Gun Violence
1225 Eye St. N.W., Suite 1100
Washington, DC 20005
202-289-7319
www.bradycampaign.org

QUESTIONS FOR
discussionandanalysis

1. Review the *Which Side Are You On?* feature on page 236. Should foreign corporations be allowed to lobby the U.S. Congress and executive-branch officials? Why or why not? Should foreign governments be barred from lobbying? Explain.

2. Some interest groups are much more influential than others. Some interest groups famous for their clout are the National Rifle Association, AARP, business groups such as the National Federation of Independent Business, the American Israel Public Affairs Committee, and the American Association for Justice (formerly the Association of Trial Lawyers of America). What factors might make each of these groups powerful?

3. After 9/11, Congress passed new laws to increase airport security. The legislation was the subject of intense lobbying by airlines that wanted the government to pick up the expense of hiring new staff, labor groups that wanted the new federal employees to have civil service protections, and other interest groups as well. Is it appropriate for interest groups to lobby for their positions in times of national emergency? Why or why not?

4. "If guns are outlawed, only outlaws will have guns." This is a key slogan used by opponents of gun control. How much truth do you think there is to this slogan? Explain your reasoning.

5. Often, special interests are much more interested in receiving tax breaks than in any kind of direct federal spending. Tax breaks to encourage various kinds of economic behavior are popular with the public, but they complicate the tax code and shift the tax burden to other taxpayers. Under what circumstances are tax breaks good public policy? Consider the deduction of mortgage interest from taxable income, popular with homeowners and the real estate industry. Should this be allowed for second homes? Why or why not?

keyterms

boycott 242
climate control 241
direct technique 238
free rider problem 227

indirect technique 238
interest group 225
labor movement 230
latent interests 226

lobbyist 229
material incentive 227
public interest 233
purposive incentive 228

service sector 231
social movement 226
solidary incentive 227

chaptersummary

1. An interest group is an organization whose members share common objectives and actively attempt to influence government policy. Interest groups proliferate in the United States because they can influence government at many points in the political structure and because they offer solidary, material, and purposive incentives to their members. Interest groups are often created out of social movements.

2. Major types of interest groups include business, agricultural, labor, public employee, professional, and environmental groups. Other important groups may be considered public-interest groups. In addition, foreign governments and corporations lobby our government.

3. Interest groups use direct and indirect techniques to influence government. Direct techniques include testifying before committees and rulemaking agencies, providing information to legislators, rating legislators' voting records, aiding political campaigns, and building alliances. Indirect techniques to influence government include campaigns to rally public sentiment, letter-writing campaigns, efforts to influence the climate of opinion, and the use of constituents to lobby for the group's interest. Unconventional methods of applying pressure include demonstrations and boycotts.

4. The 1946 Legislative Reorganization Act was the first attempt to control lobbyists and their activities through registration requirements. The United States Supreme Court narrowly construed the act as applying only to lobbyists who directly seek to influence federal legislation.

5. In 1995, Congress approved new legislation requiring anyone who spends 20 percent of his or her

time influencing legislation to register as a lobbyist. Also, any organization spending more than $24,500 (originally $20,000) semiannually and any individual who is paid more than $6,000 (originally $5,000) semiannually for his or her work must register. Semiannual reports must include the names of clients, the bills in which they are interested, and the branches of government contacted. Grassroots lobbying and the lobbying efforts of tax-exempt organizations are exempt from the rules.

6. In 2007, in response to lobbying scandals, Congress tightened rules on giving gifts to legislators and increased reporting requirements for lobbyists to four times a year. Under the 2007 reform legislation, lobbyists now have to report contributions to coalition efforts. Congress has created a searchable online database of lobbying information.

selected**print&media**resources

SUGGESTED READINGS

Battista, Andrew. *The Revival of Labor Liberalism.* Champaign, Ill.: University of Illinois Press, 2008. While labor unions have lost members in recent decades, it is still true that few interest groups are as large as organized labor. Until the late 1960s, the labor movement and political liberalism were close allies. Battista, a political science professor, analyzes the political decline of labor and liberalism, especially after the breakup of the labor-liberal coalition. He also looks at recent attempts to put the coalition back together.

Fleshler, Dan. *Transforming America's Israel Lobby: The Limits of Its Power and the Potential for Change.* Dulles, Va.: Potomac Books, 2009. Fleshler contends that America's Israel lobby, like many other lobbies, is more resistant to compromise than the people it represents. Fleshler proposes strategies to encourage moderation and promote the peace process.

Kaiser, Robert G. *So Damn Much Money: The Triumph of Lobbying and the Corrosion of American Government.* New York: Knopf, 2009. A *Washington Post* journalist, Kaiser shows how lobbyists satisfy politicians' ever-growing need for campaign funds. He argues that behavior once considered corrupt has become commonplace.

Nownes, Anthony J. *Total Lobbying: What Lobbyists Want (and How They Try to Get It).* New York: Cambridge University Press, 2006. This well-written survey of lobbying covers state and local governments, in addition to lobbying at the federal level. It concentrates on public policy, land use, and procurement.

Tushnet, Mark V. *Out of Range: Why the Constitution Can't End the Battle over Guns.* New York: Oxford University Press, 2007. The author, a Harvard law professor, looks at the ongoing debate between the National Rifle Association and gun control groups and offers a thoughtful analysis of both sides of the debate.

MEDIA RESOURCES

Bowling for Columbine—A documentary by Michael Moore won an Academy Award in 2003. Moore seeks to understand why the United States leads the industrialized world in firearms deaths. While the film is hilarious, it takes a strong position in favor of gun control and is critical of the National Rifle Association.

Norma Rae—A 1979 Hollywood movie about an attempt by a northern union organizer to unionize workers in the southern textile industry; stars Sally Field, who won an Academy Award for her performance.

Organizing America: The History of Trade Unions—A 1994 documentary that incorporates interviews, personal accounts, and archival footage to tell the story of the American labor movement. The film is a Cambridge Educational Production.

e-mocracy

INTEREST GROUPS AND THE INTERNET

The Internet may have a strong equalizing effect in the world of lobbying and government influence. The first organizations to use electronic means to reach their constituents and drum up support for action were the large economic coalitions, including the Chamber of Commerce and the National Association of Manufacturers. Groups such as these, as well as groups representing a single product such as tobacco, quickly realized that they could set up Web sites and mailing lists to provide information more rapidly to their members. Members could check the Web every day to see how legislation was developing in Congress or anywhere in the world. National associations could send e-mail to all of their members with one keystroke, mobilizing them to contact their representatives in Congress.

LOGGING ON

Almost every interest group or association has its own Web site. To find one, use your favorite search engine (Lycos, Google, or another search engine), and search for the association by name. For a sense of the breadth of the kinds of interest groups that have Web sites, take a look at one or two of those listed here.

Those interested in the gun control issue may want to visit the National Rifle Association's site at **www.nra.org**.

You can learn more about the labor movement by visiting the AFL-CIO's site at **www.aflcio.org**.

AARP (formerly the American Association of Retired Persons) has a site at **www.aarp.org**.

Information on environmental issues is available at a number of sites. The Environmental Defense Fund's site is **www.environmentaldefense.org/home.cfm**.

You can also go to the National Resources Defense Council's site for information on environmental issues. Its URL is **www.nrdc.org**.

MCCAIN

Courageous Service.
Experienced Leadership.
Bold Solutions.

www.JOHNMCCAIN.COM

Paid for by John McCain 2008

Obar

FOR PRES

Vote Janu

NH.BarackOb

8 Political Parties

CHAPTER CONTENTS

These campaign signs for the two presidential candidates are posted in the snow in Manchester, New Hampshire, during that state's primaries in 2008. (AP Photo/Alex Brandon)

whatif...parties were supported solely by public funding?

BACKGROUND

Today's major political parties are supported by hundreds of millions of dollars offered by unions, corporations, other groups, and individuals. Not surprisingly, some Americans lament that the winning candidates are merely the "best that money can buy." For years, members of both political parties have been linked to lobbying and campaign-contribution scandals, leading some critics to call for dramatic reforms. One of those reforms would be the public financing of political parties. Such public financing would, of course, come from taxpayers.

WHAT IF PARTIES WERE SUPPORTED SOLELY BY PUBLIC FUNDING?

If parties were supported solely by public funding, one question would immediately arise: What level of funding would be required? Both major political parties now spend many millions of dollars each year to educate the public, register voters, recruit candidates, and support election campaigns. If that amount were significantly reduced, the effectiveness of the political parties would also be reduced.

Also, if the public were funding the national parties, there would almost certainly be prohibitions on contributions from corporations, individuals, and interest groups. This situation would be much different from the one that exists now, because corporations and interest groups currently give to candidates who they believe will support their interests. For example, labor unions give to Democratic political action committees (PACs), and chambers of commerce normally give to Republican PACs. The number of paid employees of the major political parties would also fall if these parties were publicly funded, although more people might volunteer.

THE EFFECT ON LOBBYISTS

Fourteen states now provide direct public financing to candidates. An additional ten states provide minimal public financing to candidates or political parties, usually by collecting contributions to political parties from taxpayers through their state income tax returns. California, Indiana, and Ohio give some funds to the parties. The federal government currently provides a limited amount of public funding for presidential candidates.

All such public financing of candidates' campaigns carries with it restrictions on acceptable sources of other funds. If both the major parties and candidates for election were publicly financed, the role of lobbies and lobbyists would be changed. No longer would they be holding fund-raising social events for candidates and parties. Instead, they would have to rely on their ability to inform or persuade legislators.

THE FLOW OF FUNDS AND POWER

The public financing of the major national parties would most likely weaken their influence over candidates, voters, and campaigns. Contributors might channel their contributions to candidates and parties in those states that do not offer public financing.

In recent years, the United States has seen a rapid growth in nonparty political organizations that avoid regulation by not coordinating their activities with a party or campaign. If the political parties were limited to public funding, such nonparty groups would become vastly more important.

Candidates for the U.S. House and Senate would also increase their own fund-raising if they could not depend on the national parties to do it for them. Already, most politicians have their own PACs, and those would multiply. Forcing candidates to be responsible for their own funding might make them more independent of their parties, weakening party cohesion. In the long run, this might also weaken the attachment of voters to their party identification, making it possible for them to consider a third party.

MORE POLITICAL PARTIES MIGHT BE POSSIBLE

Who is to say that public funding of political parties would be limited to only the two major parties? If we adopted the French system, for example, public funds would be available for numerous political parties. The only requirement would be a minimum number of party members. As you might imagine, the result in France has been the emergence of dozens of small political parties. After all, if public funds are available, someone will figure out a way to obtain them.

Even if minor parties became more important, however, the major political parties would still be the only serious players in this country. In our winner-take-all electoral system, few independent party candidates can win public office.

FOR CRITICAL ANALYSIS

1. If political parties were publicly funded, what would be the appropriate level of funding—more than the parties are spending today, the same, or less?
2. Currently, both major political parties have paid employees who function as "upper management." Would the type of person seeking such a job change if the parties were supported solely by public funds? Why or why not?

Every two years, usually starting in early fall, the media concentrate on the state of the political parties. For example, during most of 2008 the media offered continuous commentaries on the relative fortunes of the Democrats and Republicans. Until the Democratic nominee was known, the media focused intensively on what impact the heated race between Illinois senator Barack Obama and New York senator Hillary Clinton might have on Democrats and the Democratic Party. As the elections drew near, the polls also concentrated on discovering to which political party each potential voter believed he or she "belonged." Prior to an election, a typical poll usually asks the following question: "Do you consider yourself to be a Republican, a Democrat, or an independent?" In recent years, the responses have shown that Americans divide fairly evenly among the three choices, with about a third describing themselves as **independents.** Of course, independents are not represented as such in Congress—for congressional purposes, they align themselves with either the Democratic Party or the Republican Party. In fact, almost half of all independents in 2008 leaned toward the Democrats, and almost a third leaned toward the Republicans. This situation could change if public funding allowed for the creation of more parties, as discussed in the chapter-opening *What If . . .* feature.

After the elections are over, the media publish the election results. Among other things, Americans learn which party controls the presidency and how many Democrats and Republicans will be sitting in the House of Representatives and the Senate when the new Congress convenes.

Notice that in the first paragraph, when discussing party membership, we put the word *belonged* in quotation marks. We did this because hardly anyone actually "belongs" to a political party in the sense of being a card-carrying member. To become a member of a political party, you do not have to pay dues, pass an examination, or swear an oath of allegiance. Therefore, at this point we can ask an obvious question: If it takes nothing to be a member of a political party, what, then, is a political party?

WHAT IS A POLITICAL PARTY?

A **political party** might be formally defined as a group of political activists who organize to win elections, operate the government, and determine public policy. This definition explains the difference between an interest group and a political party. Interest groups do not want to operate the government, and they do not put forth political candidates—even though they support candidates who will promote their interests if elected or reelected. Another important distinction is that interest groups tend to sharpen issues, whereas American political parties sometimes blur their issue positions to attract a broader range of voters.

Political parties differ from **factions,** which are smaller groups that are trying to obtain power or benefits.[1] Factions generally preceded the formation of political parties in American history, and the term is still used to refer to groups within parties that follow a particular leader or share a regional identification or an ideological viewpoint. For example, until fairly recently the Democratic Party was seen as containing a southern faction that was much more conservative than the rest of the party. Factions are subgroups within parties that may try to

---

1. See James Madison's comments on factions in *Federalist Paper* No. 10 in Appendix C at the end of this book.

Independent
A voter or candidate who does not identify with a political party.

Political Party
A group of political activists who organize to win elections, operate the government, and determine public policy.

Faction
A group or bloc in a legislature or political party that is trying to obtain power or benefits.

Candidates rely
on volunteers to operate the phones to get out the vote. These volunteers supported former Senator John Edwards (D., N.C.) during his attempt to become the Democratic Party's candidate in 2008. What motivates volunteers to do such work?
(AP Photo/Steven Senne)

capture a nomination or get a position adopted by the party. A key difference between factions and parties is that factions do not have a permanent organization, whereas political parties do.

Political parties in the United States engage in a wide variety of activities, many of which are discussed in this chapter. Through these activities, parties perform a number of functions for the political system. These functions include the following:

1. *Recruiting candidates for public office.* Because it is the goal of parties to gain control of government, they must work to recruit candidates for all elective offices. Often, this means recruiting candidates to run against powerful incumbents. If parties did not search out and encourage political hopefuls, far more offices would be uncontested, and voters would have limited choices.

2. *Organizing and running elections.* Although elections are a government activity, political parties actually organize the voter-registration drives, recruit the volunteers to work at the polls, provide much of the campaign activity to stimulate interest in the election, and work to increase voter participation.

3. *Presenting alternative policies to the electorate.* In contrast to factions, which are often centered on individual politicians or regions, parties are focused on a set of political positions. The Democrats or Republicans in Congress who vote together do so because they represent constituencies that have similar expectations and demands.

4. *Accepting responsibility for operating the government.* When a party elects the president or governor and members of the legislature, it accepts the responsibility for running the government. This includes staffing the executive branch with loyal party supporters and developing linkages among the elected officials to gain support for policies and their implementation.

5. *Acting as the organized opposition to the party in power.* The "out" party, or the one that does not control the government, is expected to articulate its own policies and oppose the winning party when appropriate. By organizing the opposition to the "in" party, the opposition party forces debate on the policy alternatives.

The major functions of American political parties are carried out by a small, relatively loose-knit nucleus of party activists. This arrangement is quite different from the more highly structured, mass-membership party organization typical of many European parties. American parties concentrate on winning elections rather than on signing up large numbers of deeply committed, dues-paying members who believe passionately in the party's program.

A HISTORY OF POLITICAL PARTIES IN THE UNITED STATES

Although it is difficult to imagine a political system in the United States with four, five, six, or seven major political parties, other democratic systems have three-party, four-party, or even ten-party systems. In some European nations, parties are clearly tied to ideological positions; parties that represent Marxist, socialist, liberal, conservative, and ultraconservative positions appear on the political continuum. Some nations have political parties representing regions of the nation that have separate cultural identities, such as the French-speaking and Flemish-speaking regions of Belgium. Some parties are rooted in religious differences. Parties also exist that represent specific economic interests, such as agricultural, maritime, or industrial interests. Still other parties, such as monarchist parties, speak for alternative political systems.

The United States has a **two-party system,** and that system has been around since about 1800. The function and character of the political parties, as well as the emergence of the two-party system itself, have much to do with the unique historical forces operating from this country's beginning as an independent nation. Indeed, James Madison (1751–

Two-Party System
A political system in which only two parties have a reasonable chance of winning.

1836) linked the emergence of political parties to the form of government created by the Constitution.

Generally, we can divide the evolution of the nation's political parties into seven periods:

1. The creation of parties, from 1789 to 1816.
2. The era of one-party rule, or personal politics, from 1816 to 1828.
3. The period from Andrew Jackson's presidency to just before the Civil War, from 1828 to 1856.
4. The Civil War and post–Civil War period, from 1856 to 1896.
5. The Republican ascendancy and the progressive period, from 1896 to 1932.
6. The New Deal period, from 1932 to about 1968.
7. The modern period, from approximately 1968 to the present.

THE FORMATIVE YEARS: FEDERALISTS AND ANTI-FEDERALISTS

The first partisan political division in the United States occurred before the adoption of the Constitution. As you will recall from Chapter 2, the Federalists were those who pushed for adoption of the Constitution, whereas the Anti-Federalists were against ratification.

In September 1796, George Washington, who had served as president for almost two full terms, decided not to run again. In his farewell address, he made a somber assessment of the nation's future. Washington felt that the country might be destroyed by the "baneful [harmful] effects of the spirit of party." He viewed parties as a threat to both national unity and the concept of popular government. Early in his career, Thomas Jefferson did not like political parties either. In 1789, he stated, "If I could not go to heaven but with a party, I would not go there at all."[2]

Nevertheless, in the years after the ratification of the Constitution, Americans came to realize that something more permanent than a faction would be necessary to identify candidates for office and represent political differences among the people. The result was two political parties.

One party was the Federalists, which included John Adams, the second president (1797–1801). The Federalists represented commercial interests such as merchants and large planters. They supported a strong national government.

Thomas Jefferson led the other party, which came to be called the Republicans, or Jeffersonian Republicans. These Republicans should not be confused with the later Republican Party of Abraham Lincoln.[3] Jefferson's Republicans represented artisans and farmers. They strongly supported states' rights. In 1800, when Jefferson defeated Adams in the presidential contest, one of the world's first peaceful transfers of power from one party to another was achieved.

Thomas Jefferson
was particularly adamant about his dislike of political parties. Nonetheless, he helped create a new party called the Jeffersonian Republicans. Why did he find it necessary to engage in party politics? (AP Photo)

THE ERA OF GOOD FEELINGS

From 1800 to 1820, a majority of U.S. voters regularly elected Republicans to the presidency and to Congress. By 1816, the Federalist Party had virtually collapsed, and two-party competition did not really exist. Although during elections the Republicans opposed the Federalists' call for a stronger, more active central government, they undertook such

2. Letter to Francis Hopkinson written from Paris while Jefferson was minister to France. In John P. Foley, ed., *The Jeffersonian Cyclopedia* (New York: Russell & Russell, 1967), p. 677.
3. To avoid confusion, some scholars refer to Jefferson's party as the Democratic-Republicans, but this name was never used during the time that the party existed.

Andrew Jackson
earned the name "Old Hickory" for exploits during the War of 1812. In 1828, Jackson was elected president as the candidate of the new Democratic Party. (Corbis/Bettmann)

active government policies as acquiring the Louisiana Territory and Florida and establishing a national bank. Because there was no real political opposition to the Republicans and thus little political debate, the administration of James Monroe (1817–1825) came to be known as the **era of good feelings.** Since political competition now took place among individual Republican aspirants, this period can also be called the *era of personal politics.*

NATIONAL TWO-PARTY RULE: DEMOCRATS AND WHIGS

Organized two-party politics returned in 1824. With the election of John Quincy Adams as president, the Republican Party split in two. The followers of Adams called themselves National Republicans. The followers of Andrew Jackson, who defeated Adams in 1828, formed the **Democratic Party.** Later, the National Republicans took the name **Whig Party,** which had been a traditional name for British liberals. The Whigs stood, among other things, for federal spending on "internal improvements," such as roads. The Democrats opposed this policy. The Democrats, who were the stronger of the two parties, favored personal liberty and opportunity for the "common man." It was understood implicitly that the "common man" was a white man—hostility toward African Americans was an important force holding the disparate Democratic groups together.[4]

The Democrats' success was linked to their superior efforts to involve common citizens in the political process. Mass participation in politics and elections was a new phenomenon in the 1820s, as the political parties began to appeal to popular enthusiasm and themes. The parties adopted the techniques of mass campaigns, including rallies and parades. Lavishing food and drink on voters at polling places also became a common practice. Perhaps of greatest importance, however, was the push to cultivate party identity and loyalty. In large part, the spirit that motivated the new mass politics was democratic pride in participation. By making citizens feel that they were part of the political process, the parties hoped to win lasting party loyalty at the ballot box.

THE CIVIL WAR CRISIS

In the 1850s, hostility between the North and South over the issue of slavery divided both parties. The Whigs were the first to split in two. The Whigs had been the party of an active federal government, but southerners had come to believe that "a government strong enough to build roads is a government strong enough to free your slaves." The southern Whigs therefore ceased to exist as an organized party. In 1854, the northern Whigs united with antislavery Democrats and members of the radical antislavery Free Soil Party to found the modern **Republican Party.**

THE POST–CIVIL WAR PERIOD

After the Civil War, the Democratic Party was able to heal its divisions. Southern resentment of the Republicans' role in defeating the South and fears that the federal government would intervene on behalf of African Americans ensured that the Democrats would dominate the white South for the next century.

"Rum, Romanism, and Rebellion." Northern Democrats feared a strong government for other reasons. The Republicans thought that the government should promote business and economic growth, but many Republicans also wanted to use the power of government to impose evangelical Protestant moral values on society. Democrats opposed what they saw as culturally coercive measures. Many Republicans wanted to limit or even prohibit the sale of alcohol. They favored the establishment of public schools—with a Protestant curriculum. As a result, Catholics were strongly Democratic. In 1884, Protestant minister Samuel Burchard described the Democrats as the party of "rum, Romanism, and rebellion." This remark was

Era of Good Feelings
The years from 1817 to 1825, when James Monroe was president and there was, in effect, no political opposition.

Democratic Party
One of the two major American political parties evolving out of the Republican Party of Thomas Jefferson.

Whig Party
A major party in the United States during the first half of the nineteenth century, formally established in 1836. The Whig Party was anti-Jackson and represented a variety of regional interests.

Republican Party
One of the two major American political parties. It emerged in the 1850s as an antislavery party and consisted of former northern Whigs and antislavery Democrats.

---

4. Edward Pessen, *Jacksonian America: Society, Personality, and Politics* (Homewood, Ill.: Dorsey Press, 1969). See especially pages 246–247. The small number of free blacks who could vote were overwhelmingly Whig.

offensive to Catholics, and Republican presidential candidate James Blaine later claimed that it cost him the White House.

The Triumph of the Republicans. In this period, the parties were very evenly matched in strength. The abolition of the three-fifths rule, described in Chapter 2, meant that African Americans would be counted fully when House seats and electoral votes were allocated to the South. The Republicans therefore had to carry almost every northern state to win, and this was not always possible. In the 1890s, however, the Republicans gained a decisive edge. In that decade, the populist movement emerged in the West and South to champion the interests of small farmers, who were often heavily in debt. Populists supported inflation, which benefited debtors by reducing the real value of outstanding debts. In 1896, when William Jennings Bryan became the Democratic candidate for president, the Democrats embraced populism.

As it turned out, the few western farmers who were drawn to the Democrats by this step were greatly outnumbered by urban working-class voters who believed that inflation would reduce the purchasing power of their paychecks and who therefore became Republicans. William McKinley, the Republican candidate, was elected with a solid majority of the votes. Figure 8–1 on the following page shows the states taken by Bryan and McKinley. The pattern of regional support shown in Figure 8–1 persisted for many years. From 1896 until 1932, the Republicans were successful at presenting themselves as the party that knew how to manage the economy.

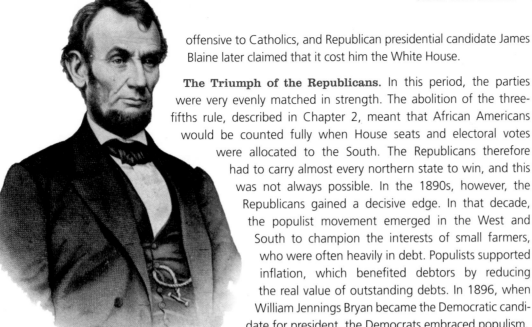

President Abraham Lincoln ran on the Republican ticket for president in 1860. What political groups banded together to form the modern Republican Party? (Ohio Historical Society/ www.ohiohistorycentral.org)

THE PROGRESSIVE INTERLUDE

In the early 1900s, a spirit of political reform arose in both major parties. Called *progressivism,* this spirit was compounded of a fear of the growing power of large corporations and a belief that honest, impartial government could regulate the economy effectively. In 1912, the Republican Party temporarily split as former Republican president Theodore Roosevelt campaigned for the presidency on a third-party Progressive, or Bull Moose, ticket. The Republican split permitted the election of Woodrow Wilson, the Democratic candidate, along with a Democratic Congress.

Like Roosevelt, Wilson considered himself a progressive, although he and Roosevelt did not agree on how progressivism ought to be implemented. Wilson's progressivism

In 1912, Theodore Roosevelt campaigned for the presidency on a third-party Progressive, or Bull Moose, ticket. Here, you see a charter membership certificate showing Roosevelt and his vice-presidential candidate, Hiram W. Johnson. What was the main result of Roosevelt's formation of this third party? (Bettmann/Corbis)

FIGURE 8–1: The 1896 Presidential Elections

In 1896, the agrarian, populist appeal of Democrat William Jennings Bryan (blue states) won western states for the Democrats at the cost of losing more populous eastern states to Republican William McKinley (red states). This pattern held in subsequent presidential elections.

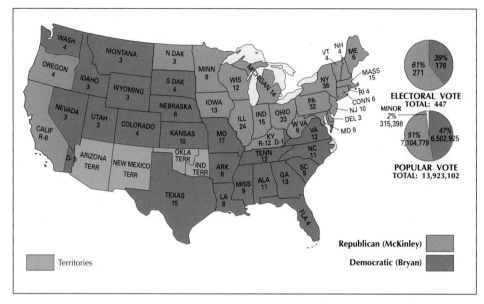

marked the beginning of a radical change in Democratic policies. Dating back to its very foundation, the Democratic Party had been the party of limited government. Under Wilson, the Democrats became for the first time at least as receptive as the Republicans to government action in the economy. (Wilson's progressivism did not extend to race relations—for African Americans, the Wilson administration was something of a disaster.)

In recent years, many Democrats have revived the term *progressive* to describe their politics and no longer call themselves *liberals*. We examine that phenomenon in the *Politics and Terminology* feature on the next page.

These Works Progress
Administration workers were paid by the federal government. (AP Photo/Works Progress Administration)

THE NEW DEAL ERA

The Republican ascendancy resumed after Wilson left office. It ended with the election of 1932, in the depths of the Great Depression. Republican Herbert Hoover was president when the depression began in 1929. Although Hoover took some measures to fight the depression, they fell far short of what the public demanded. Significantly, Hoover opposed federal relief for the unemployed and the destitute. In 1932, Democrat Franklin D. Roosevelt was elected president by an overwhelming margin.

The Great Depression shattered the working-class belief in Republican economic competence. Under Roosevelt, the Democrats began to make major interventions in the economy in an attempt to combat the depression and to relieve the suffering of the unemployed. Roosevelt's New Deal relief programs were open to all citizens, both black and white. As a result, African Americans began to support the Democratic Party in large numbers—a development that would have stunned any American politician of the 1800s.

politicsand...terminology

WHAT IS THE DIFFERENCE BETWEEN A *LIBERAL* AND A *PROGRESSIVE*?

During a CNN/YouTube debate, Senator Hillary Clinton observed that she did not like to use the word *liberal* because its meaning has been debased. Rather, she said that she preferred the word *progressive*. This word, she continued, "has a real American meaning, going back to the Progressive Era at the beginning of the twentieth century. I consider myself a modern progressive." Indeed, for some years now, Democrats have frequently described themselves as progressives or even populists rather than liberals.

LIBERALS VERSUS PROGRESSIVES IN EUROPE AND IN AMERICA

Those on the political left have long complained about conservatives' ability to make the word *liberal* an embarrassment. Indeed, most Americans today associate liberalism with big government, which is not a popular concept. In Europe, in contrast, politicians who call themselves liberals tend to support free-market, small-government policies. In Chapter 1, we described how American liberalism was transformed from a belief in limited government into a philosophy that supports strong government.

A hundred years ago, the word *liberal* still referred to limited government in the United States. In contrast, early-twentieth-century progressives were indeed in favor of a larger role for government. Progressive activist Jane Addams went so far as to say, "We must demand that the individual shall be willing to lose the sense of personal achievement, and shall be content to realize his activity

Jane Addams
(Library of Congress)

only in the connection with the activity of the many." Of course, no politician of any stripe would dare make such a statement today.

By the late 1940s, the term *progressive* had dropped out of fashion in the U.S. political arena, and *liberal* had become the term of choice. What Hillary Clinton was admitting, perhaps, is that in subsequent years Democrats overused the term *liberal*. Perhaps *progressive* or *populist* would sound fresher.

Hillary Clinton
(William Thomas Cain/Getty Images)

THE PROGRESSIVE LABEL SWEEPS THE BLOGS

In the blogosphere, liberals typically call themselves progressives. A highly respected liberal political research center calls itself the Progressive Policy Institute. Left-of-center journalists more frequently refer to themselves as progressives than liberals.

Time will tell how well modern progressivism will succeed at the ballot box. It's also too early to know whether the word *progressive*, like the word *liberal*, will eventually sink beneath the weight of accumulated historical baggage.

FOR CRITICAL ANALYSIS

Are the labels with which politicians identify their philosophies and their desired political programs important? Why or why not?

Roosevelt's political coalition was broad enough to establish the Democrats as the new majority party, in place of the Republicans. In the 1950s, Republican Dwight D. Eisenhower, the leading U.S. general during World War II, won two terms as president. Otherwise, with minor interruptions, the Democratic ascendancy lasted until 1968.

AN ERA OF DIVIDED GOVERNMENT

The New Deal coalition managed the unlikely feat of including both African Americans and whites who were hostile to African American advancement. This balancing act came to an end in the 1960s, a decade that was marked by the civil rights movement, by several years of "race riots" in major cities, and by increasingly heated protests against the Vietnam War (1964–1975). For many

didyouknow...

That the Democrats and Republicans each had exactly one woman delegate at their conventions in 1900?

" **The Democratic Party today changed its name to 'The Republican Party.'**"

economically liberal, socially conservative voters, especially in the South, social issues had become more important than economic ones, and these individuals left the Democrats. These voters outnumbered the new voters who joined the Democrats—newly enfranchised African Americans and former liberal Republicans in New England and the upper Midwest.

The Parties in Balance. The result, after 1968, was a nation almost evenly divided in politics. In presidential elections, the Republicans had more success than the Democrats. Until 1994, Congress remained Democratic, but official party labels can be misleading. Some of the Democrats were southern conservatives who normally voted with the Republicans on issues. As these conservative Democrats retired, they were largely replaced by Republicans.

In the forty years between the elections of 1968 and 2008, there were only ten years when one of the two major parties controlled the presidency, the House of Representatives, and the Senate. The Democrats controlled all three institutions during the presidency of Jimmy Carter (1977–1981) and during the first two years of the presidency of Bill Clinton (1993–2001). The Republicans controlled all three institutions during the third through sixth years of George W. Bush's presidency.[5] Before the 1992 elections, the electorate seemed to prefer, in most circumstances, to match a Republican president with a Democratic Congress. Under Bill Clinton, that state of affairs was reversed, with a Democratic president facing a Republican Congress.

Red State, Blue State. The pattern of a Republican Congress and a Democratic president would have continued after the elections of 2000 if Democratic presidential candidate Al Gore had prevailed. Gore won the popular vote, but lost the electoral college by a narrow margin. The extreme closeness of the vote in the Electoral College led the press to repeatedly publish the state map of the results. Commentators discussed at length the supposed differences between the Republican "red states" and the Democratic "blue states."

In the presidential elections of 2004, George W. Bush won the popular vote by a margin of more than 3 million votes over Democrat John F. Kerry. Yet only three states changed hands. Bush picked up Iowa and New Mexico, which had voted Democratic in 2000, and lost New Hampshire. Figure 8–2 shows the resulting map. Clearly, the parties continued to be closely matched.

An interesting characteristic of the 2000 and 2004 red state–blue state maps is that they are almost exact reversals of the map showing the presidential elections of 1896 (see Figure 8–1 on page 258), which established the Republican ascendancy that lasted until the Great Depression. Except for the state of Washington, every state that supported Democrat William Jennings Bryan in 1896 supported Republican George W. Bush in 2000 and 2004. This reversal parallels the transformation of the Democrats from an anti–civil rights to a pro–civil rights party and from a party that supported limited government to a party that favors positive government action.

TILTING TOWARD THE DEMOCRATS

By 2006, the Republicans were in trouble. The violence in Iraq, including attacks on American soldiers and the low-level civil war between the Sunni and Shiite communities, continued. Ever-larger numbers of voters came to believe that the U.S. occupation of Iraq had been a mistake and that American forces should be withdrawn quickly. Apparently, many voters were coming to view the Iraq conflict as an example of deeper problems with

---

5. The Republicans also were in control of all three institutions for the first four months after Bush's inauguration. This initial period of control came to an end when Senator James Jeffords of Vermont left the Republican Party, giving the Democrats control of the Senate.

FIGURE 8–2: The Presidential Elections of 2004

The 2004 presidential elections proved very close in the electoral college. Although Republican incumbent George W. Bush won the popular vote by more than 3 million votes, Democratic challenger John F. Kerry could have carried the election if the state of Ohio, and its twenty electoral votes, had fallen in his column.

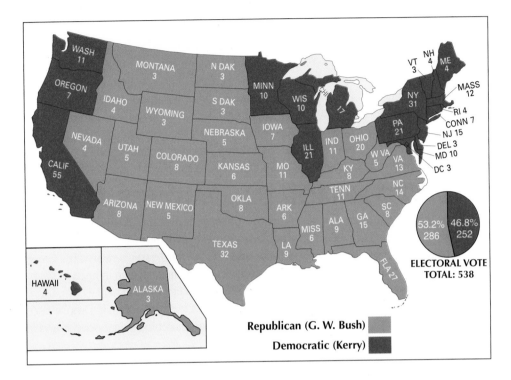

Republican (G. W. Bush)
Democratic (Kerry)

elections2008
PARTISAN TRENDS IN THE 2008 ELECTIONS

(Joe Raedle/Getty Images)

It was clear from the beginning that 2008 was not going to be a good year for the Republicans. Still, many experts believed that the party had a chance to hold on to the presidency. John McCain, the Republican candidate, had a history of opposing his party on important issues, such as campaign-financing reform and immigration. McCain had a proven track record in attracting independent voters. Indeed, in early September, McCain had a slight advantage over Democrat Barack Obama in many public opinion polls.

McCain's lead lasted only a week. After September 15, the financial crisis dominated the headlines, to the benefit of the Democrats. Another issue was the growing concern that Sarah Palin, McCain's running mate, was not adequately prepared to serve as president. A final factor concerned the two candidate's temperaments: McCain came across to many voters as heated and erratic, while Obama was strikingly calm.

Normally, a presidential candidate moves to the political center after the primary elections to appeal to independents. Obama did this to a degree, but surprisingly, McCain did not. He ran as a strong conservative— by favoring President Bush's tax cuts, for example—all the way to November. McCain never successfully separated himself from Bush and thereby lost much of his ability to appeal to independents. McCain's fellow Republicans cheered him on in this strategy. Campaign crowds pleaded with him to hit Obama harder— even as polling data showed that personal attacks on his opponent were hurting McCain among independents. In other polls, independents agreed that the Republicans were losing because they were too conservative. Republicans, in contrast, believed they were losing because their party was not conservative enough.

If these views prevail, the Republican Party will be poorly positioned to counteract the Democratic trend that manifested itself so strongly in 2008. No only did Obama, with almost 53 percent of the popular vote, win the strongest personal mandate of any Democrat in a generation, but the Democrats picked up seven seats in the U.S. Senate and twenty-one seats in the House. Back-to-back victories in Congress, such as the ones that the Democrats enjoyed in 2006 and 2008 are rare and are a strong indicator of public sentiment.

the Republican Party. In the 2006 midterm elections, the Democrats picked up thirty seats in the House, which gave them a majority in that chamber. The total popular vote for Democratic representatives exceeded the Republican vote by 6.4 percent. The Democrats also picked up six seats in the Senate, giving them a one-vote majority.[6]

By 2007 and 2008, half or more of those polled claimed either to be Democrats or independents leaning Democratic, compared with about 40 percent on the Republican side. Bush's approval ratings were among the lowest ever recorded for a president. Polls even suggested that voters were becoming more liberal on issues that had nothing to do with Iraq, such as support for antipoverty measures. This Democratic trend was reinforced by bad economic news. In late 2007, the housing market collapsed. Many homeowners could not pay their mortgages, which set off a financial contagion that brought down several major institutions in 2008. When Lehman Brothers failed on September 15, followed by Washington Mutual, it was clear that the country was in an economic crisis that would guarantee a Democratic victory in the 2008 elections, as shown in Figure 8–3.

THE TWO MAJOR U.S. PARTIES TODAY

It is sometimes said that the major American political parties are like Tweedledee and Tweedledum, the twins in Lewis Carroll's *Through the Looking Glass*. Labels such as "Repubocrats" are especially popular among supporters of third parties, such as the Green Party and the Libertarian Party. Third-party advocates, of course, have an interest in claiming that there is no difference between the two major parties—their chances of gaining support are much greater if the major parties are seen as indistinguishable. Despite such allegations, the major parties do have substantial differences, both in their policies and in their constituents.

---

6. The one-vote margin includes two independents who caucus with the Democrats, Joe Lieberman of Connecticut and Bernie Sanders of Vermont.

FIGURE 8–3: The Presidential Elections of 2008

In the 2008 presidential elections, Democrat Barack Obama received a majority of the electoral college votes, outdoing Republican John McCain by a large margin. Although Obama won nine more states than Democrat John Kerry had won in the 2004 presidential elections, the regional political preferences remained similar to those of previous elections.

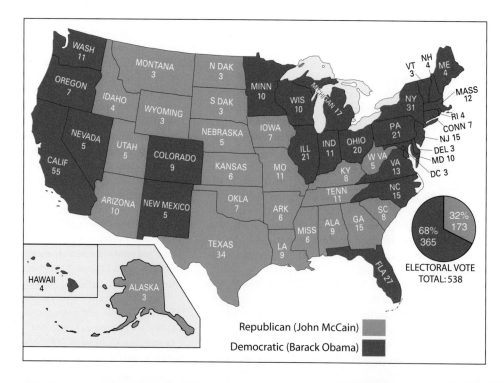

THE PARTIES' CORE CONSTITUENTS

You learned in Chapter 6 how demographic factors affect support for the two parties. Democrats receive disproportionate support not only from the least well-educated voters but also from individuals with advanced degrees. Upper-income voters are generally more Republican than lower-income voters; businesspersons are much more likely to vote Republican than labor union members. The Jewish electorate is heavily Democratic; white evangelical Christians who are regular churchgoers tend to be Republicans. Hispanics are strongly Democratic; African Americans are overwhelmingly so. Women are somewhat more Democratic than men. City dwellers tend to be Democrats; rural people tend to be Republicans. In presidential elections, the South, several of the Rocky Mountain states, and the Great Plains states typically vote Republican; the West Coast and the Northeast are more likely to favor the Democrats. These tendencies represent the influences of economic interests and cultural values, which are often in conflict with each other.

A coalition of the labor movement and various racial and ethnic minorities has been the core of Democratic Party support since the presidency of Franklin D. Roosevelt. The social programs and increased government intervention in the economy that made up Roosevelt's New Deal were intended to ease the pressure of economic hard times on these groups. This goal remains important for many Democrats today. In general, Democratic identifiers are more likely to approve of social-welfare spending, to support government regulation of business, to endorse measures to improve the situation of minorities, and to support assisting the elderly with their medical expenses. Republicans are more supportive of the private marketplace and believe more strongly in an ethic of self-reliance and limited government.

These traditional party beliefs are often reflected in public opinion poll results. For example, in a recent *New York Times*/CBS poll, respondents considered the Democrats more trustworthy than Republicans on economic and health-care issues. In past years, polls have ranked Republicans as the stronger party on national security issues. Since the terrorist attacks of 2001, when national security interests became paramount, the Republicans have been able to take advantage of this preference in their campaigns—until recently. Today, voters are more evenly divided in their opinions of which party can better handle security and defense. Indeed, some recent polls indicate that the Democrats are currently stronger than the Republicans in these areas.

ECONOMIC CONVERGENCE?

In his 1996 State of the Union address, Democratic president Bill Clinton announced that "the era of big government is over." One might conclude from this that both parties now favor limited government. Some political observers, however, argue that despite the tax cuts that Republicans have implemented, both parties in practice now favor "big government." Harvard University professor Jeffrey Frankel goes even further. "When it comes to White House economic policy," Frankel writes, "the Republican and Democratic parties have switched places since the 1960s." Frankel points out that budget deficits rose during the administrations of Republicans Ronald Reagan (1981–1989) and George W. Bush but fell under Bill Clinton. Federal employment grew under Reagan and George W. Bush but fell under Clinton. Reagan and Bush both introduced "protectionist" measures to restrict imports, such as Bush's tariffs on imported steel and timber. Clinton, despite the protectionist beliefs of many Democrats in Congress, was in practice more supportive of free trade.[7]

When President Bill Clinton announced in his 1996 State of the Union message that "the era of big government is over," what do you think he meant? Was he right? (AP Photo/Denis Paquin)

---

7. Jeffrey Frankel, "Republican and Democratic Presidents Have Switched Economic Policies," *Milken Institute Review,* Vol. 5, No. 1 (First Quarter 2003), pp. 18–25.

The 2008 Democratic

presidential primaries were long and drawn out. Senator Hillary Clinton (D., N.Y.) finally lost out to Senator Barack Obama (D., Ill.). Here the two candidates are shown at their first joint public appearance on June 27, 2008, in Unity, New Hampshire. Why was the 2008 primary season considered to be "historical"? (AP Photo/Elise Amendola)

Other observers have noted a similar reversal in traditional party roles with respect to spending. Consider that Reagan, who faced a Congress controlled by the Democrats, regularly submitted budgets larger than the ones that the Democratic Congress eventually passed. Clinton, however, who faced a Republican Congress for most of his administration, submitted budgets that were typically smaller than those approved by the Republican Congress.

During the presidency of George W. Bush, spending skyrocketed, in part due to the Iraq War. Bush signed into law more domestic government spending increases than any other president since World War II (even correcting for inflation). By the time he left office in January 2009, the federal budget deficit had hit a record.

CULTURAL POLITICS

In recent years, cultural values may have become more important than they previously were in defining the beliefs of the two major parties. For example, in 1987, Democrats were almost as likely to favor stricter abortion laws (40 percent) as Republicans were (48 percent). Today, Republicans are twice as likely to favor stricter abortion laws (50 percent to 25 percent).

Cultural Politics and Socioeconomic Status. Thomas Frank, writing in *Harper's Magazine,* reported seeing the following bumper sticker at a gun show in Kansas City: "A working person voting for the Democrats is like a chicken voting for Colonel Sanders." (Colonel Sanders is the iconic founder of KFC, the chain of fried chicken restaurants.) In light of the economic traditions of the two parties, this seems to be an odd statement. In fact, the sticker is an exact reversal of an earlier one directed against the Republicans.

You can make sense of such a sentiment by remembering what you learned in Chapter 6—although economic conservatism is associated with higher incomes, social conservatism is relatively more common among lower-income groups. The individual who displayed the bumper sticker, therefore, was in effect claiming that cultural concerns—in this example, presumably the right to own handguns—are far more important than economic ones. Frank argues that despite Republican control of both the White House and Congress during much of the George W. Bush administration, cultural conservatives continued to view themselves as embattled "ordinary Americans" under threat from a liberal, cosmopolitan elite.[8]

Also, according to Republican commentator Karl Zinsmeister, many police officers, construction workers, military veterans, and rural residents began moving toward the Republican Party in the 1960s and 1970s. In contrast, many of America's rich and superrich elite, including financiers, media barons, software millionaires, and entertainers, started slowly, but surely, drifting toward the Democratic Party. As a result, today it is difficult to stereotype what socioeconomic groups support which party.

The Regional Factor in Cultural Politics. Conventionally, some parts of the country are viewed as culturally liberal, and others as culturally conservative. On a regional basis, cultural liberalism (as opposed to economic liberalism) may be associated with economic dynamism. The San Francisco Bay Area can serve as an example. The greater Bay Area contains Silicon Valley, the heart of the microcomputer industry; it has the highest per capita personal income of any metropolitan area in America. It also is one of the most liberal regions of the country. San Francisco liberalism is largely cultural—one sign of this liberalism is that the city has a claim to be the "capital" of gay America.

---

8. Thomas Frank, "Lie Down for America," *Harper's Magazine,* April 2004, p. 33.

To further illustrate this point, we can compare the political preferences of relatively wealthy states with those of relatively poor ones. Of the fifteen states with the highest per capita personal incomes in 2008, fourteen voted for Democrat Barack Obama in the presidential elections of that year. Of the fifteen with the lowest per capita incomes in 2008, thirteen voted for Republican John McCain.

Given these data, it seems hard to believe that upper-income voters really are more Republican than lower-income ones. Still, within any given state or region, upscale voters are more likely to be Republican regardless of whether the area as a whole leans Democratic or Republican. States that vote Democratic are often northern states that contain large cities. At least part of this **reverse-income effect** may simply be that urban areas are more prosperous, culturally liberal, and Democratic than the countryside, and that the North is more prosperous, culturally liberal, and Democratic than the South.

Cultural Divisions within the Democratic Party. The extremely close and hard-fought Democratic presidential primary contest between Senator Barack Obama and Senator Hillary Clinton exposed a series of cultural divisions within the Democratic Party that political scientists have been aware of for some time. Of course, African Americans supported Obama strongly, and women tended to favor Clinton. Beyond these obvious patterns, Clinton appeared to do well among older people, white working-class voters, and Latinos, while Obama received more support from the young and from better-educated, upscale Democrats.

This division appears to be similar to the cultural divisions in the general population that we have just discussed. Yet the differences between the two candidates on policy issues were actually very small. Likewise, there was no evidence that Obama fans and the Clinton backers held significantly different positions on the issues—the two groups may have been somewhat different kinds of people, but they appeared to have similar politics. One difference was the relative importance the two groups placed on the issues: older, working-class Clinton supporters were more concerned with economic issues, while the younger, more prosperous Obama supporters gave somewhat greater weight to issues such as the war in Iraq. By far the greatest difference was that Clinton voters thought she had the right experience, whereas Obama supporters believed that he could best bring about change.

To a degree, Obama's narrow victory reflects changes in the Democrats' core constituencies. Traditionally, the candidate with a stronger working-class appeal could expect to win over the largest number of Democrats. As we have noted, however, in recent years well-educated, professional individuals have shifted to the Democrats even as voters without college degrees have grown more Republican. By 2008, Obama's upscale supporters made up a larger share of the Democratic Party than in years past. Still, Obama could not have won without strong support from African Americans of all classes. Indeed, Obama's black support grew as the campaign progressed. Apparently, many African Americans saw the harsh criticisms he received during the campaign as attacks on the black community as a whole.

Cultural Divisions among the Republicans. One wing of the Republican Party, often called the Religious Right, is energized by conservative religious beliefs. These conservatives are often evangelical Protestants but may also be Catholics,

Reverse-Income Effect
A tendency for wealthier states or regions to favor the Democrats and for less wealthy states or regions to favor the Republicans. The effect appears paradoxical because it reverses traditional patterns of support.

didyouknow...

That it took 103 ballots for John W. Davis to be nominated at the Democratic National Convention in 1924?

Party-in-the-Electorate
Those members of the general public who identify with a political party or who express a preference for one party over another.

Party Organization
The formal structure and leadership of a political party, including election committees; local, state, and national executives; and paid professional staff.

Party-in-Government
All of the elected and appointed officials who identify with a political party.

Mormons, or adherents of other faiths. For these voters, moral issues such as abortion and gay marriage are key. The other wing of the Republican Party is more oriented toward economic issues and business concerns. These voters often are small-business owners or have some other connection to commercial enterprise. Such voters oppose high taxes and are concerned about government regulations that interfere with the conduct of business.

In the current political environment, the differences among Republicans may have greater policy implications than the divisions among the Democrats. Of course, many Republicans are pro-business and also support the Religious Right. Some economically oriented Republicans, however, are strongly libertarian and dislike government regulation of social issues as well as economic ones. Likewise, some on the Religious Right are not particularly committed to the free-market ethos of the party's business wing and are willing to support a variety of government interventions into the economy.

Successful Republican presidential candidates, such as George W. Bush, have tried to appeal to both wings of the party. Senator John McCain of Arizona, the Republican candidate for president in 2008, initially found it hard to appeal to the Religious Right until he chose Sarah Palin as his running mate. McCain's maverick positions on a number of issues in the past had led many to doubt his conservatism (which was actually quite strong). In the end, however, McCain was able to unite his party behind him.

THE THREE FACES OF A PARTY

Although American parties are known by a single name and, in the public mind, have a common historical identity, each party really has three major components. The first component is the **party-in-the-electorate.** This phrase refers to all those individuals who claim an attachment to the political party. They need not participate in election campaigns. Rather, the party-in-the-electorate is the large number of Americans who feel some loyalty to the party or who use partisanship as a cue to decide who will earn their vote. Party membership is not really a rational choice; rather, it is an emotional tie somewhat analogous to identifying with a region or a baseball team. Although individuals may hold a deep loyalty to or identification with a political party, there is no need for members of the party-in-the-electorate to speak out publicly, to contribute to campaigns, or to vote all Republican or all Democratic. Needless to say, the party leaders pay close attention to their members in the electorate.

The second component, the **party organization,** provides the structural framework for the political party by recruiting volunteers to become party leaders; identifying potential candidates; and organizing caucuses, conventions, and election campaigns for its candidates, as will be discussed in more detail shortly. It is the party organization and its active workers that keep the party functioning between elections, as well as ensure that the party puts forth electable candidates and clear positions in the elections. If the party-in-the-electorate declines in numbers and loyalty, the party organization must try to find a strategy to rebuild the grassroots following.

The **party-in-government** is the third component of American political parties. The party-in-government consists of those elected and appointed officials who identify with a political party. Generally, elected officials do not also hold official party positions within the formal organization, although they often have the informal power to appoint party executives.

The Democratic National Convention in 2008 was held in Denver, Colorado. Do such political extravaganzas have much impact on how voters decide who is the best candidate for president? (AP Photo/Jeff Chiu)

PARTY ORGANIZATION

Each of the American political parties is often seen as having a pyramid-shaped organization, with the national chairperson and committee at the top and the local precinct chairperson on the bottom. This structure, however, does not accurately reflect the relative power of the individual components of the party organization. If it did, the national chairperson of the Democratic Party or the Republican Party, along with the national committee, could simply dictate how the organization was to be run, just as if it were the ExxonMobil Corporation or Ford Motor Company. In reality, the political parties have a confederal structure, in which each unit has significant autonomy and is linked only loosely to the other units.

The Republican National Convention was held in Minneapolis–St. Paul, Minnesota, in early September 2008. Does the choice of where a national party's convention is held have any significance? Why or why not? (AP Photo/ Ron Edmonds)

THE NATIONAL PARTY ORGANIZATION

Each party has a national organization, the most clearly institutional part of which is the **national convention,** held every four years. The convention is used to nominate the presidential and vice-presidential candidates. In addition, the **party platform** is developed at the national convention. The platform sets forth the party's position on the issues and makes promises to initiate certain policies if the party wins the presidency.

After the convention, the platform frequently is neglected or ignored by party candidates who disagree with it. Because candidates are trying to win votes from a wide spectrum of voters, it is counterproductive to emphasize the fairly narrow and sometimes controversial goals set forth in the platform. Political scientist Gerald M. Pomper discovered decades ago, however, that once elected, the parties do try to carry out platform promises and that roughly three-fourths of the promises eventually become law.[9] Of course, some general goals, such as economic prosperity, are included in the platforms of both parties.

Convention Delegates. The party convention provides the most striking illustration of the difference between the ordinary members of a party, or party identifiers, and party activists. As a series of studies by the *New York Times* shows, delegates to the national party conventions are different from ordinary party identifiers. Delegates to the Democratic National Convention, as shown in Table 8–1, take stands on many issues that are far more liberal than the positions of ordinary Democratic voters. Typically, delegates to the Republican National Convention are far more conservative than ordinary Republicans. Why does this happen? In part, it is because a person, to become a delegate, must gather votes in a primary election from party members who care enough to vote in a primary or be appointed by party leaders. Also, the primaries generally pit presidential candidates against each other on intraparty issues. Competition within each party tends to pull candidates away from the center, and delegates even more so. Often, the most important activity for the convention is making peace among the delegates who support different candidates and persuading them to accept a party platform that will appeal to the general electorate.

The National Committee. At the national convention, each of the parties formally chooses a national standing committee, elected by the individual state parties. This **national committee** directs and coordinates party activities during the following four

National Convention
The meeting held every four years by each major party to select presidential and vice-presidential candidates, write a platform, choose a national committee, and conduct party business.

Party Platform
A document drawn up at each national convention, outlining the policies, positions, and principles of the party.

National Committee
A standing committee of a national political party established to direct and coordinate party activities between national party conventions.

---

9. Gerald M. Pomper and Susan S. Lederman, *Elections in America: Control and Influence in Democratic Politics,* 2d ed. (New York: Longman, 1980).

TABLE 8–1: Convention Delegates and Voters: How Did They Compare on the Issues in 2008?

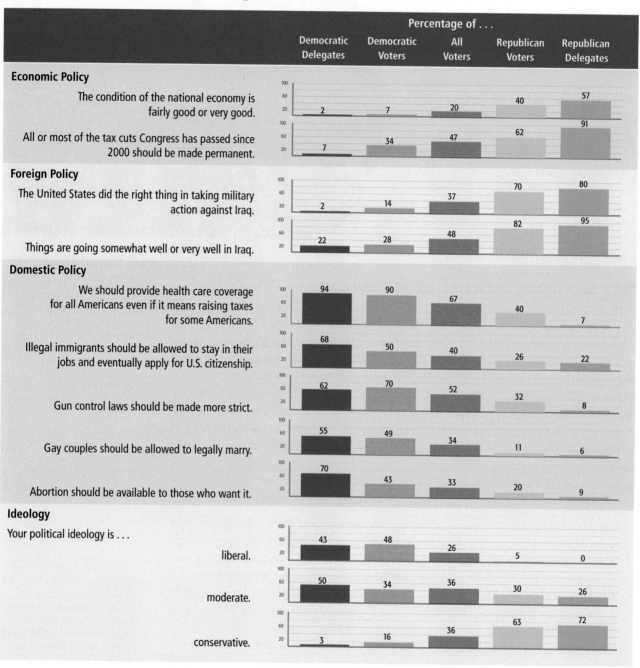

	Percentage of . . .				
	Democratic Delegates	Democratic Voters	All Voters	Republican Voters	Republican Delegates
Economic Policy					
The condition of the national economy is fairly good or very good.	2	7	20	40	57
All or most of the tax cuts Congress has passed since 2000 should be made permanent.	7	34	47	62	91
Foreign Policy					
The United States did the right thing in taking military action against Iraq.	2	14	37	70	80
Things are going somewhat well or very well in Iraq.	22	28	48	82	95
Domestic Policy					
We should provide health care coverage for all Americans even if it means raising taxes for some Americans.	94	90	67	40	7
Illegal immigrants should be allowed to stay in their jobs and eventually apply for U.S. citizenship.	68	50	40	26	22
Gun control laws should be made more strict.	62	70	52	32	8
Gay couples should be allowed to legally marry.	55	49	34	11	6
Abortion should be available to those who want it.	70	43	33	20	9
Ideology					
Your political ideology is . . .					
liberal.	43	48	26	5	0
moderate.	50	34	36	30	26
conservative.	3	16	36	63	72

Source: *The New York Times.*

years. The Democrats include at least two members (a man and a woman) from each state, from the District of Columbia, and from the several territories. Governors, members of Congress, mayors, and other officials may be included as at-large members of the national committee. The Republicans, in addition, include state chairpersons from every state carried by the Republican Party in the preceding presidential, gubernatorial, or congressional elections. The selections of national committee members are ratified by the delegations to the national convention.

One of the jobs of the national committee is to ratify the presidential nominee's choice of a national chairperson, who in principle acts as the spokesperson for the party.

Prior to the presidential elections of 2008, the chair of the Democratic National Committee was Howard Dean (left), and the chair of the Republican National Committee was Mike Duncan (right). Both chairs are likely to be replaced by early 2009. What are some of the jobs that national party chairs perform?

The national chairperson and the national committee plan the next campaign and the next convention, obtain financial contributions, and publicize the national party.

Picking a National Chairperson. In general, the party's presidential candidate chooses the national chairperson. (If that candidate loses, however, the chairperson is often changed.) The national chairperson performs such jobs as establishing a national party headquarters, raising campaign funds and distributing them to state parties and to candidates, and appearing in the media as a party spokesperson. The national chairperson, along with the national committee, attempts to maintain some sort of liaison among the different levels of the party organization. The fact, though, is that the real strength and power of the party is at the state level.

THE STATE PARTY ORGANIZATION

There are fifty states in the Union, plus the District of Columbia and the territories, and an equal number of party organizations for each major party. Therefore, there are more than a hundred state parties (and even more, if we include local parties and minor parties). Because every state party is unique, it is impossible to describe what an "average" state political party is like. Nonetheless, state parties have several organizational features in common.

Each state party has a chairperson, a committee, and a number of local organizations. In theory, the role of the **state central committee**—the principal organized structure of each political party within each state—is similar in the various states. The committee, usually composed of members who represent congressional districts, state legislative districts, or counties, has responsibility for carrying out the policy decisions of the party's state convention. In some states, the state committee can issue directives to the state chairperson.

Also, like the national committee, the state central committee has control over the use of party campaign funds during political campaigns. Usually, the state central committee has little, if any, influence on party candidates once they are elected. In fact, state parties are fundamentally loose alliances of local interests and coalitions of often bitterly opposed factions.

State parties are also important in presidential politics because of the **unit rule,** which awards a state's electoral votes in presidential elections as an indivisible bloc (except in Maine and Nebraska). Presidential candidates concentrate their efforts in states in which voter preferences seem to be evenly divided or in which large numbers of electoral votes are at stake.

State Central Committee
The principal organized structure of each political party within each state. This committee is responsible for carrying out policy decisions of the party's state convention.

Unit Rule
A rule by which all of a state's electoral votes are cast for the presidential candidate receiving a plurality of the popular vote in that state.

Patronage
Rewarding faithful party workers and followers with government employment or contracts.

LOCAL PARTY MACHINERY: THE GRASSROOTS

The lowest layer of party machinery is the local organization, supported by district leaders, precinct or ward captains, and party workers. Much of the work is coordinated by county committees and their chairpersons.

Patronage and City Machines. In the 1800s, the institution of **patronage**—rewarding the party faithful with government jobs or contracts—held the local organization together. For immigrants and the poor, the political machine often furnished important services and protections. The big-city machine was the archetypal example. Tammany Hall, or the Tammany Society, which dominated New York City government well into the twentieth century, was perhaps the most notorious example of this political form.

The last big-city local political machine to exercise substantial power was run by Chicago mayor Richard J. Daley, who was also an important figure in national Democratic politics. Daley, as mayor, ran the Chicago Democratic machine from 1955 until his death in 1976. The current mayor of Chicago, Richard M. Daley, son of the former mayor, does not have the kind of political machine that his father had.

City machines are now dead, mostly because their function of providing social services (and reaping the reward of votes) has been taken over by state and national agencies. This trend began in the 1930s, when the social legislation of the New Deal established Social Security and unemployment insurance. Today, local party organizations have little, if anything, to do with deciding who is eligible to receive these benefits.

Local Party Organizations Today. Local political organizations—whether located in cities, in townships, or at the county level—still can contribute a great deal to local election campaigns. These organizations are able to provide the foot soldiers of politics—individuals who pass out literature and get out the vote on election day, which can be crucial in local elections. In many regions, local Democratic and Republican organizations still exercise some patronage, such as awarding courthouse jobs, contracts for street repair, and other lucrative construction contracts. The constitutionality of awarding—or not awarding—contracts on the basis of political affiliation has been subject to challenge, however. The United States Supreme Court has ruled that firing or failing to hire individuals because of their political affiliation is an infringement of the employees' First Amendment rights to free expression.[10] Local party organizations are also the most important vehicles for recruiting young adults into political work, because political involvement at the local level offers activists many opportunities to gain experience.

didyouknow...

That it takes about 700,000 signatures to qualify to be on the ballot as a presidential candidate in all fifty states?

Geraldine Ferraro, on the left, was the Democratic vice-presidential nominee in 1984. Alongside her is actress Kerry Washington. They launched WE Vote '08 in late 2007. The goal of this organization was to register more than one million female voters prior to the 2008 elections. Why does this organization target potential female voters? (AP Photo/Stuart Ramson)

THE PARTY-IN-GOVERNMENT

After the election is over and the winners are announced, the focus of party activity shifts from getting out the vote to organizing and controlling the government. As you will learn in Chapter 10, party membership plays an important role in the day-to-day operations of Congress, with partisanship determining everything from office space to committee assignments and power on Capitol Hill. For the president, the political party furnishes the pool of qualified applicants for political appointments to run the govern-

10. *Rutan v. Republican Party of Illinois,* 497 U.S. 62 (1990).

President Bush, surrounded by members of Congress and of his Cabinet, signed the Economic Stimulus Act of 2008, which provided for, among other things, "rebate" checks to most tax-paying households. Why are such actions considered bipartisan? (AP Photo/Manuel Balce Ceneta)

ment. (Although it is uncommon to do so, presidents can and occasionally do appoint executive personnel, such as cabinet members, from the opposition party.) As we note in Chapter 11, there are not as many of these appointed positions as presidents might like, and presidential power is limited by the permanent bureaucracy.[11] Judicial appointments also offer a great opportunity to the winning party. For the most part, presidents are likely to appoint federal judges from their own party.

Divided Government. All of these party appointments suggest that the winning political party, whether at the national, state, or local level, has a great deal of control in the American system. The degree of control that a winning party can actually exercise, however, depends on several factors. At the national level, an important factor is whether the party also controls the executive branch of government. If it does, the party leadership may be reluctant to exercise congressional checks on presidential powers. If Congress is cooperating in implementing legislation approved by the president, the president, in turn, will not feel it necessary to exercise the veto power. Certainly, this situation existed while the Republicans controlled both the legislative and executive branches of government from 2001 through 2006.

The winning party has less control over the government when the government is divided. A **divided government** is one in which the executive and legislative branches are controlled by different parties. After the 2006 elections, this was the situation facing the Democrats in Congress. The Democrats were largely unable to pass any legislation that did not meet with President Bush's approval because they did not have sufficient votes (a two-thirds majority) to override a presidential veto. Although Bush exercised only one veto from 2001 through 2006, after the Democrats took control of Congress in January 2007 he vetoed eleven bills.

The Limits of Party Unity. There are other ways in which the power of the parties is limited. Consider how major laws are passed in Congress. Traditionally, legislation has rarely

Divided Government
A situation in which one major political party controls the presidency and the other controls the chambers of Congress, or in which one party controls a state governorship and the other controls the state legislature.

---

11. As noted in Chapter 2 and as you will read in Chapter 12, in 2007 President George W. Bush attempted to gain more influence over bureaucratic decision making by establishing a Regulatory Policy Office in each agency of the federal government. Each of these offices is headed by a political appointee.

"I think it was an election year."

This photo was taken when both John McCain and Barack Obama were active in the U.S. Senate. At that time, McCain unequivocally supported the war effort in Iraq whereas Obama did not. When they both became presidential candidates, national security and experience in foreign affairs became key points in their campaigns. Have American voters always been concerned about national security issues? (AP Photo/Dennis Cook, File)

been passed by a vote strictly along party lines. Although most Democrats may oppose a bill, for example, some Democrats may vote for it. Their votes, combined with the votes of Republicans, may be enough to pass the bill. Similarly, support from some Republicans may enable a bill sponsored by the Democrats to pass.

One reason that the political parties have traditionally found it so hard to rally all of their members in Congress to vote along party lines is that candidates who win most elections largely do so on their own, without significant help from a political party. A candidate generally gains a nomination through her or his own hard work and personal political organization. In many other countries, most candidates are selected by the party organization, not by primary elections. This means, though, that in the United States the parties have very little control over the candidates who run under the party labels. In fact, a candidate could run as a Republican, for example, and advocate beliefs repugnant to the national party, such as racism. No one in the Republican Party organization could stop this person from being nominated or even elected.

Party Polarization. Despite the forces that act against party-line voting, there have been times when the two parties in Congress have been polarized, and defections from the party line have been rare. Indeed, while the Republicans controlled Congress from 1994 through 2006, the party was able to achieve a great deal of unity, and voting along party lines was common. A notable example of such partisan voting occurred in the House of Representatives in 1998. The issue at hand was whether to impeach President Bill Clinton. Almost all votes during the course of the proceedings were strictly along party lines—Democrats against, and Republicans for.

This polarization in Congress has continued up to the present day. To be sure, after the Democrats took control of Congress in January 2007, Republicans cast fewer party-line votes as some members sought to distance themselves from the unpopularity of the Bush administration. The Democrats, however, responded to their new, dominant position with a greater degree of unity than they had shown previously. Are high degrees of partisanship good or bad for America? We examine this question in the *Which Side Are You On?* feature on the facing page.

WHY HAS THE TWO-PARTY SYSTEM ENDURED?

There are several reasons why two major parties have dominated the political landscape in the United States for almost two centuries. These reasons have to do with (1) the historical foundations of the system, (2) political socialization and practical considerations, (3) the winner-take-all electoral system, and (4) state and federal laws favoring the two-party system.

whichsideareyouon?

IS PARTISANSHIP GOOD FOR AMERICA?

Partisan politics have been a prominent part of the American political landscape for more than two centuries. Just consider that in the 1828 election, supporters of Andrew Jackson accused the opposing presidential candidate, John Quincy Adams, of being "a drunken fornicator who sold virgins into white slavery." On the other side, supporters of Adams accused Jackson of having committed eighteen murders. By comparison with this rhetoric, partisan "cat calls" in modern America seem tame.

Still, from the beginning of Barack Obama's campaign for the presidency, he seized on the public's distaste for Bush's divisive partisanship. Obama referred to such divisiveness as the "old politics" and pledged to change "politics as usual" in Washington, D.C. Is partisanship really that bad? Would America be better off if there weren't so much of it?

PARTISANSHIP IS GOOD FOR AMERICA

Partisanship offers voters "a choice, not an echo." Partisanship leads to more political participation. Divisive partisanship creates strong feelings for and against candidates, and that's good for America because such interest brings out the vote—witness the 2004 elections, in which participation increased by more than 6 percentage points compared with the 2000 presidential elections.

Further, when candidates compromise their positions to garner a majority of votes in an election, these compromises can lead to policies that "fall between the stools" and yield perverse results. Partisan solidarity can ensure that policies, whether conservative or liberal, are coherent and workable. We do not have a multiparty system. Therefore, we can only elect one president from one party. Each chamber in Congress is dominated by one party. Hence, we need partisanship to enable our political system to function well. We don't have a choice.

PARTISANSHIP IS ENDANGERING OUR POLITICAL SYSTEM

Many Americans find excessive partisanship offensive. As far back as George Washington's farewell speech in 1796, the dangers of "faction" have been well known. Washington observed that partisanship draws attention away from important questions, weakens the government, and "agitates the community with ill-founded jealousies and false alarms."

Partisanship alienates the 45 percent of voters who identify themselves as moderates. It weakens congressional checks and balances. For example, when Republicans controlled both chambers of Congress through 2006, they had no interest in scrutinizing the actions of Republican president George W. Bush. Partisanship has left Congress (and the president) unable to deal with such long-term problems as Social Security reform, because such reforms cannot pass without complex deal making and compromises. Even the nation's foreign policy can be affected—foreign governments have been known to stall negotiations in the hope that they can get a better deal from the other party after the next elections.

THE HISTORICAL FOUNDATIONS OF THE TWO-PARTY SYSTEM

As we have seen, at many times in American history there has been one preeminent issue or dispute that divided the nation politically. In the beginning, Americans were at odds over ratifying the Constitution. After the Constitution went into effect, the power of the federal government became the major national issue. Thereafter, the dispute over slavery divided the nation by section, North versus South. At times—for example, in the North after the Civil War—cultural differences have been important, with advocates of government-sponsored morality (such as banning alcoholic beverages) pitted against advocates of personal liberty.

During much of the twentieth century, economic differences were preeminent. In the New Deal period, the Democrats became known as the party of the working class, while the Republicans became known as the party of the middle and upper classes and commercial interests. When politics is based on an argument between two opposing points of view, advocates of each viewpoint can mobilize most effectively by forming a single, unified party, resulting in a two-party system. When such a system has been in existence for almost two centuries, it becomes difficult to imagine an alternative.

POLITICAL SOCIALIZATION AND PRACTICAL CONSIDERATIONS

Given that the majority of Americans identify with one of the two major political parties, it is not surprising that most children learn at a fairly young age to think of themselves as either Democrats or Republicans. This generates a built-in mechanism to perpetuate a two-party system. Also, many politically oriented people who aspire to work for social change consider that the only realistic way to capture political power in this country is to be either a Republican or a Democrat.

THE WINNER-TAKE-ALL ELECTORAL SYSTEM

At virtually every level of government in the United States, the outcome of elections is based on the **plurality,** winner-take-all principle. In a plurality system, the winner is the person who obtains the most votes, even if that person does not receive a majority (over 50 percent) of the votes. Whoever gets the most votes gets everything. Most legislators in the United States are elected from single-member districts in which only one person represents the constituency, and the candidate who finishes second in such an election receives nothing for the effort.

Presidential Voting. The winner-take-all system also operates in the election of the U.S president. Recall that the voters in each state do not vote for a president directly but vote for **Electoral College** delegates who are committed to the various presidential candidates. These delegates are called *electors*.

In all but two states (Maine and Nebraska), if a presidential candidate wins a plurality in the state, then *all* of the state's electoral votes go to that candidate. For example, let us say that the electors pledged to a particular presidential candidate receive a plurality of 40 percent of the votes in a state. That presidential candidate will receive all of the state's votes in the Electoral College. Minor parties have a difficult time competing under such a system. Because voters know that minor parties cannot win any electoral votes, they often will not vote for minor-party candidates, even if the candidates are in tune with them ideologically.

Popular Election of the Governors and the President. In most European countries, the chief executive (usually called the prime minister) is elected by the legislature, or parliament. If the parliament contains three or more parties, as is usually the situation, two or more of the parties can join together in a coalition to choose the prime minister and the other leaders of the government. In the United States, however, the people elect the president and the governors of all fifty states. There is no opportunity for two or more parties to negotiate a coalition. Here, too, the winner-take-all principle discriminates powerfully against any third party.

Proportional Representation. Many other nations use a system of proportional representation with multi-member districts. If, during the national election, party X obtains 12 percent of the vote, party Y gets 43 percent of the vote, and party Z gets the remaining 45

Plurality
A number of votes cast for a candidate that is greater than the number of votes for any other candidate but not necessarily a majority.

Electoral College
A group of persons, called electors, who are selected by the voters in each state. This group officially elects the president and the vice president of the United States.

Rutherford B. Hayes won the highly contested 1876 election in which he lost the popular vote but won the Electoral College vote. His opponent, Democrat Samuel J. Tilden, received 250,000 more popular votes out of the 8.5 million that were tallied. Have we seen a similar situation in modern times? (Library of Congress, Matthew Brady Photo)

percent of the vote, then party X gets 12 percent of the seats in the legislature, party Y gets 43 percent of the seats, and party Z gets 45 percent of the seats. Because even a minor party may still obtain at least a few seats in the legislature, the smaller parties have a greater incentive to organize under such electoral systems than they do in the United States.

The relative effects of proportional representation versus our system of single-member districts are so strong that many scholars have made them one of the few "laws" of political science. "Duverger's Law," named after French political scientist Maurice Duverger, states that electoral systems based on single-member districts tend to produce two parties, while systems of proportional representation produce multiple parties.[12] Still, many countries with single-member districts have more than two political parties—Britain and Canada are examples.

STATE AND FEDERAL LAWS FAVORING THE TWO PARTIES

Many state and federal election laws offer a clear advantage to the two major parties. In some states, the established major parties need to gather fewer signatures to place their candidates on the ballot than minor parties or independent candidates do. The criterion for determining how many signatures will be required is often based on the total party vote in the last general election, thus penalizing a new political party that did not compete in that election.

At the national level, minor parties face different obstacles. All of the rules and procedures of both houses of Congress divide committee seats, staff members, and other privileges on the basis of party membership. A legislator who is elected on a minor-party ticket, such as the Conservative Party of New York, must choose to be counted with one of the major parties to obtain a committee assignment. The Federal Election Commission (FEC) rules for campaign financing also place restrictions on minor-party candidates. Such candidates are not eligible for federal matching funds in either the primary or the general election. In the 1980 elections, John Anderson, running for president as an independent, sued the FEC for campaign funds. The commission finally agreed to repay part of his campaign costs after the election in proportion to the votes he received. Giving funds to a candidate when the campaign is over is, of course, much less helpful than providing funds while the campaign is still under way.

THE ROLE OF MINOR PARTIES IN U.S. POLITICS

For the reasons just discussed, minor parties have a difficult, if not impossible, time competing within the American two-party political system. Nonetheless, minor parties have played an important role in our political life. Parties other than the Republicans or Democrats are usually called **third parties.** (Technically, of course, there could be fourth, fifth, or sixth parties as well, but we use the term *third party* because it has endured.) Third parties can come into existence in a number of ways. They may be founded from scratch by individuals or groups who are committed to a particular interest, issue, or ideology. They can split off from one of the major parties when a group becomes dissatisfied with the major party's policies. Finally, they can be organized around a particular charismatic leader and serve as that person's vehicle for contesting elections.

Third parties have acted as barometers of changes in the political mood. Such barometric indicators have forced the major parties to recognize new issues or trends in the thinking of Americans. Political scientists believe that third parties have acted as safety

Third Party
A political party other than the two major political parties (Republican and Democratic).

didyouknow...

That the Reform Party, established in 1996, used a vote-by-mail process for the first step of its nominating convention and also accepted votes cast by e-mail?

12. As cited in Todd Landman, *Issues and Methods in Comparative Politics* (New York: Routledge, 2003), p. 14.

TABLE 8–2: The Most Successful Third-Party Presidential Campaigns Since 1864

The following list includes all third-party candidates winning more than 5 percent of the popular vote or any electoral votes since 1864. (We ignore isolated "unfaithful electors" in the Electoral College who failed to vote for the candidate to which they were pledged.)

Year	Major Third Party	Third-Party Presidential Candidate	Percent of the Popular Vote	Electoral Votes	Winning Presidential Candidate and Party
1892	Populist	James Weaver	8.5	22	Grover Cleveland (D)
1912	Progressive	Theodore Roosevelt	27.4	88	Woodrow Wilson (D)
	Socialist	Eugene Debs	6.0	—	
1924	Progressive	Robert LaFollette	16.6	13	Calvin Coolidge (R)
1948	States' Rights	Strom Thurmond	2.4	39	Harry Truman (D)
1960	Independent Democrat	Harry Byrd	0.4	15*	John Kennedy (D)
1968	American Independent	George Wallace	13.5	46	Richard Nixon (R)
1980	National Union	John Anderson	6.6	—	Ronald Reagan (R)
1992	Independent	Ross Perot	18.9	—	Bill Clinton (D)
1996	Reform	Ross Perot	8.4	—	Bill Clinton (D)

*Byrd received fifteen electoral votes from unpledged electors in Alabama and Mississippi.

Source: *Dave Leip's Atlas of U.S. Presidential Elections* at **www.uselectionatlas.org**.

valves for dissident groups, preventing major confrontations and political unrest. In some instances, third parties have functioned as way stations for voters en route from one of the major parties to the other. Table 8–2 lists significant third-party presidential campaigns in American history; Table 8–3 provides a brief description of third-party beliefs.

IDEOLOGICAL THIRD PARTIES

The longest-lived third parties have been those with strong ideological foundations that are typically at odds with the majority mind-set. The Socialist Party is an example. The party was founded in 1901 and lasted until 1972, when it was finally dissolved. (A smaller party later took up the name.)

TABLE 8–3: Policies of Selected American Third Parties since 1864

Populist: This pro-farmer party of the 1890s advocated progressive reforms. It also advocated replacing gold with silver as the basis of the currency in hopes of creating a mild inflation in prices. (It was believed by many that inflation would help debtors and stimulate the economy.)

Socialist: This party advocated a "cooperative commonwealth" based on government ownership of industry. It was pro-labor, often antiwar, and in later years, anti-Communist. It was dissolved in 1972 and replaced by nonparty advocacy groups (Democratic Socialists of America and Social Democrats USA).

Communist: This left-wing breakaway from the Socialists was the U.S. branch of the worldwide Communist movement. The party was pro-labor and advocated full equality for African Americans. It was also closely aligned with the Communist-led Soviet Union, which provoked great hostility among most Americans.

Progressive: This name was given to several successive splinter parties built around individual political leaders. Theodore Roosevelt, who ran in 1912, advocated federal regulation of industry to protect consumers, workers, and small businesses. Robert LaFollette, who ran in 1924, held similar viewpoints.

American Independent: Built around George Wallace, this party opposed any further promotion of civil rights and advocated a militant foreign policy. Wallace's supporters were mostly former Democrats who were soon to be Republicans.

Libertarian: This party opposes most government activity.

Reform: The Reform Party was initially built around businessman Ross Perot but later was taken over by others. Under Perot, the party was a middle-of-the-road group opposed to federal budget deficits. Under Patrick Buchanan, it came to represent right-wing nationalism and opposition to free trade.

Green: The Greens are a left-of-center pro-environmental party; they are also generally hostile to globalization.

Ideology has at least two functions. First, the members of the minor party regard themselves as outsiders and look to one another for support; ideology provides great psychological cohesiveness. Second, because the rewards of ideological commitment are partly psychological, these minor parties do not think in terms of immediate electoral success. A poor showing at the polls does not dissuade either the leadership or the grassroots participants from continuing their quest for change in American government (and, ultimately, American society).

Currently active ideological parties include the Libertarian Party and the Green Party. As you learned in Chapter 1, the Libertarian Party supports a *laissez-faire* ("let it be") capitalist economic program, together with a hands-off policy on regulating matters of moral conduct. The Green Party began as a grassroots environmentalist organization with affiliated political parties across North America and Western Europe. It was established in the United States as a national party in 1996 and nominated Ralph Nader to run for president in 2000. Nader campaigned against what he called "corporate greed," advocated universal health insurance, and promoted environmental concerns.[13] He ran again for president as an independent in 2004 and 2008.

SPLINTER PARTIES

Some of the most successful minor parties have been those that split from major parties. The impetus for these **splinter parties,** or factions, has usually been a situation in which a particular personality was at odds with the major party. The most successful of these splinter parties was the Bull Moose Progressive Party, formed in 1912 to support Theodore Roosevelt for president. The Republican national convention of that year denied Roosevelt the nomination, despite the fact that he had won most of the primaries. He therefore left the Republicans and ran against Republican "regular" William Howard Taft in the general election. Although Roosevelt did not win the election, he did split the Republican vote, enabling Democrat Woodrow Wilson to become president.

Third parties have also been formed to back individual candidates who were not rebelling against a particular party. Ross Perot, for example, who challenged Republican George H. W. Bush and Democrat Bill Clinton in 1992, had not previously been active in a major party. Perot's supporters probably would have split their votes between Bush and Clinton had Perot not been in the race. In theory, Perot ran in 1992 as a nonparty independent; in practice, he had to create a campaign organization. By 1996, Perot's organization was formalized as the Reform Party.

THE IMPACT OF MINOR PARTIES

Third parties have rarely been able to affect American politics by actually winning elections. (One exception is that third-party and independent candidates have occasionally won races for state governorships—for example, Jesse Ventura was elected governor of Minnesota on the Reform Party ticket in 1998.) Instead, the impact of third parties has taken two forms. First, third parties can influence one of the major parties to take up one or more issues. Second, third parties can determine the outcome of a particular election by pulling votes from one of the major-party candidates in what is called the "spoiler effect."

Influencing the Major Parties. One of the most clear-cut examples of a major party adopting the issues of a minor party took place in 1896, when the Democratic Party took over the Populist demand for "free silver"—that is, a policy of coining enough new money to create an inflation. As you

> **Splinter Party**
> A new party formed by a dissident faction within a major political party. Often, splinter parties have emerged when a particular personality was at odds with the major party.

Theodore Roosevelt served as president of the United States from 1901 to 1909 as a Republican. Later, after he was unable to secure the Republican nomination for president in 1912, Roosevelt formed a splinter group known as the Progressive Party. Roosevelt was ultimately unsuccessful in his bid to regain the presidency as a minor-party candidate. Does a minor-party candidate have a realistic chance of winning a presidential election today? (Library of Congress)

---

13. Ralph Nader offers his own entertaining account of his run for the presidency in 2000 in *Crashing the Party: How to Tell the Truth and Still Run for President* (New York: St. Martin's Press, 2002).

Ralph Nader
ran as the candidate for the Green Party and as an independent in several presidential elections. How important are third-party and independent candidates in our political system?
(AP Photo/George Ruhe)

learned on page 257, however, absorbing the Populists cost the Democrats votes overall.

Affecting the Outcome of an Election. The presidential elections of 2000 were one instance in which a minor party may have altered the outcome. Green candidate Ralph Nader received almost 100,000 votes in Florida, a majority of which would probably have gone to Democrat Al Gore if Nader had not been in the race.

The real question, however, is not whether the Nader vote had an effect—clearly, it did—but whether the effect was important. The problem is that in elections as close as the presidential elections of 2000, *any* factor with an impact on the outcome can be said to have determined the results of the elections. Discussing his landslide loss to Democrat Lyndon Johnson in 1964, Republican Barry Goldwater wrote, "When you've lost an election by that much, it isn't the case of whether you made the wrong speech or wore the wrong necktie. It was just the wrong time."[14] With the opposite situation, a humorist might speculate that Gore would have won the election had he worn a better tie! Nevertheless, given that Nader garnered almost 3 million votes, many believe that the Nader campaign was an important reason for Gore's loss.

MECHANISMS OF POLITICAL CHANGE

In the future, could one of the two parties decisively overtake the other and become the "natural party of government"? The Republicans held this status from 1896 until 1932, and the Democrats enjoyed it for many years after the election of Franklin D. Roosevelt in 1932.

REALIGNMENT

One mechanism by which a party might gain dominance is called **realignment.** In this process, major constituencies shift their allegiance from one party to another, creating a long-term alteration in the political environment. Realignment has often been associated with particular elections, called *realigning elections*. The election of 1896, which established a Republican ascendancy, was clearly a realigning election. So was the election of 1932, which made the Democrats the leading party.

Realignments in American Politics. A number of myths exist about the concept of realignment. One is that in realignment, a newly dominant party must replace the previously dominant party. Actually, realignment could easily strengthen an already dominant party. Alternatively, realignment could result in a tie. This has happened—twice. One example was the realignment of the 1850s, which resulted in Abraham Lincoln's election as president in 1860. After the Civil War, the Republicans and the Democrats were almost evenly matched nationally.

The most recent realignment—which also resulted in two closely matched parties—was a gradual process that took place over many years. In 1968, Republican president Nixon adopted a "southern strategy" aimed at drawing dissatisfied southern Democrats into the Republican Party.[15] At the presidential level, the strategy was an immediate success, although years would pass before the Republicans could gain dominance in the South's delegation to Congress or in state legislatures. Another milestone in the progress

Realignment
A process in which a substantial group of voters switches party allegiance, producing a long-term change in the political landscape.

---

14. Barry Goldwater, *With No Apologies* (New York: William Morrow, 1979).
15. The classic work on Nixon's southern strategy is Kirkpatrick Sales, *The Emerging Republican Majority* (New Rochelle, N.Y.: Arlington House, 1969).

FIGURE 8–4: Party Identification from 1944 to the Present

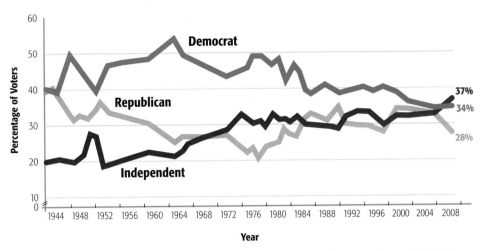

Sources: *Gallup Report,* August 1995; *New York Times/*CBS poll, June 1996; *Gallup Report,* February 1998; The Pew Research Center for the People and the Press, November 2003; Gallup polls, 2004 through 2008.

of the Republican realignment was Ronald Reagan's sweeping victory in the presidential elections of 1980.

Is Realignment Still Possible? The sheer size of our nation, combined with the inexorable pressure toward a two-party system, has resulted in parties made up of voters with conflicting interests or values. The pre–Civil War party system involved two parties—Whigs and Democrats—with support in both the North and the South. This system could survive only by burying, as deeply as possible, the issue of slavery. We should not be surprised that the structure eventually collapsed. The Republican ascendancy of 1896–1932 united capitalists and industrial workers under the Republican banner, despite serious economic conflicts between the two. The New Deal Democratic coalition after 1932 brought African Americans and ardent segregationists into the same party.

For realignment to occur, a substantial body of citizens must come to believe that their party can no longer represent their interests or values. The problem must be fundamental and not attributable to the behavior of an individual politician. Despite the divisions within the parties discussed earlier, it is not easy to identify groups of Republicans or Democrats today who might reach such a conclusion.

DEALIGNMENT

Among political scientists, one common argument has been that realignment is no longer likely because voters are not as committed to the two major parties as they were in the 1800s and early 1900s. In this view, called **dealignment** theory, large numbers of independent voters may result in political volatility, but the absence of strong partisan attachments means that it is no longer easy to "lock in" political preferences for decades.

Independent Voters. Figure 8–4 shows trends in **party identification,** as measured by standard polling techniques from 1944 to the present. The chart displays a rise in the number of independent voters throughout the period combined with a fall in support for the Democrats from the mid-1960s on. The decline in Democratic identification may be due to the consolidation of Republican support in the South since 1968, a process that by now is substantially complete. In any event, the traditional Democratic advantage in party identification has largely vanished. How has the growing number of independents affected recent election outcomes? We look at that issue in this chapter's *Politics and Ideology* feature on the next page.

Dealignment
A decline in party loyalties that reduces long-term party commitment.

Party Identification
Linking oneself to a particular political party.

politicsand...ideology

THE INCREASING SIGNIFICANCE OF INDEPENDENT VOTERS

This country has been dominated by two political parties for as long as anyone living today can remember. By March 2008, though, more potential voters identified themselves as independents (37 percent) than either as Democrats (34 percent) or as Republicans (28 percent). Does this mean that "the party is over"? First, who are these independents?

WHO ARE THE INDEPENDENTS?

There are differences between those who identify themselves as Democrats or Republicans and those who identify themselves as independents. The latter are better educated and younger than the average American. They appear to be anti-ideological. They are hostile toward "big government," but they still want to see the federal government take an active role in major problem areas such as climate change. Self-identified independents are typically results-oriented individuals.

THE CHANGING FACE OF PARTISAN POLITICS

In the first years of the twenty-first century, independents were often marginalized during elections. Candidates attempted to win by mobilizing their most partisan supporters. (A *partisan* is someone who believes strongly in a particular party's philosophy and the candidates put forward by that party.) In the presidential elections of 2004, for example, Republican George W. Bush enjoyed considerable success with a strategy of energizing "the faithful."

A recent *Washington Post* poll, however, showed that about 77 percent of voters would consider voting for an independent. Some say that in the 2006 midterm elections, the Republicans took a "thumping" (President Bush's description) because they no longer appealed to

" THEY'RE GOING AFTER THE INDEPENDENT VOTE."

(© Harley Schwadron/Cartoon Stock)

independent voters. As a result, the 2008 Republican presidential candidate, Arizona senator John McCain, capitalized on his image as a maverick, in part to appeal to independents. In 2008, McCain carried independents who voted in the Republican primaries by margins ranging from 10 to 31 percentage points. During the Democratic primaries, New York senator Hillary Clinton scored relatively poorly among independents, whereas Illinois senator Barack Obama, the eventual victor, scored well.

What does this all mean? Simply that political candidates can no longer win elections unless they impress independent voters.

FOR CRITICAL ANALYSIS

What problems do political candidates face when they attempt to appeal to independents? (Hint: How might their "loyal base" react?)

Straight-Ticket Voting
Voting exclusively for the candidates of one party.

Split-Ticket Voting
Voting for candidates of two or more parties for different offices, such as voting for a Republican presidential candidate and a Democratic congressional candidate.

Not only has the number of independents grown over the last half century, but voters are also less willing to vote a straight ticket—that is, to vote for all the candidates of one party. In the early 1900s, **straight-ticket voting** was nearly universal. By midcentury, 12 percent of voters engaged in **split-ticket voting**—voting for candidates of two or more parties for different offices, such as voting for a Republican presidential candidate and a Democratic congressional candidate. In recent presidential elections, between 20 and 40 percent of the voters engaged in split-ticket voting. This trend, along with the increase in voters who call themselves independents, suggests that parties have lost much of their hold on the voters' loyalty.

Not-So-Independent Voters. A problem with dealignment theory is that many of the "independent" voters are not all that independent. For some time, about one-third of the voters who classified themselves as independents typically voted Democratic, and another one-third typically voted Republican. The remaining third consisted of true independents and became known as **swing voters**—they could swing back and forth between the parties. Because of this, swing voters normally have been targeted with advertising campaigns by candidates of both parties.

The preferences of independent voters have changed significantly in the last few years, however. Democratic gains have come largely from independents, about two-thirds of whom now "lean" Democratic. Polls reveal that if the partisans and leaners among the independents are combined, the Democrats enjoy a significant advantage over the Republicans—at least 50 percent of the voters identify with the Democratic Party and about 40 percent with the Republican Party. These figures fluctuate somewhat from month to month and even from week to week, responding to the shifting winds of public opinion. (Fluctuations also occur because of the margin of error in all public opinion polls.)

TIPPING

Political transformation can also result from changes in the composition of the electorate. Even when groups of voters never change their party preferences, if one group becomes more numerous over time, it can become dominant for that reason alone. We call this kind of demographically based change **tipping.**

Tipping in Massachusetts and California. Consider Massachusetts, where for generations Irish Catholics confronted Protestant Yankees in the political arena. Most of the Yankees were Republicans; most of the Irish were Democrats. The Yankees were numerically dominant from the founding of the state until 1928. In that year, for the first time, Democratic Irish voters came to outnumber the Republican Yankees. Massachusetts, which previously had been one of the most solidly Republican states, became one of the most reliably Democratic states in the nation.

California may have experienced a tipping effect during the 1990s. From 1952 through 1988, California normally supported Republican presidential candidates. Since 1992, however, no Republican presidential candidate has managed to carry California. The improved performance of the Democrats in California is almost certainly a function of demography. In 1999, California became the third state, after Hawaii and New Mexico, in which non-Hispanic whites do not make up a majority of the population.

Tipping in the Twenty-First Century? It is possible that states other than California may tip to a different party in future years. In 2002, John B. Judis and Ruy Teixeira argued that the Democrats were poised to become the new majority party due to a growth in the number of liberal professionals and Hispanic immigrants.[16] This thesis attracted much ridicule in subsequent years, as the Republicans continued to triumph in midterm and presidential elections. By 2008, however, the thesis had become more credible. A growing Hispanic vote was clearly pushing several southwestern states, such as Nevada and Colorado, into the Democratic column, while larger numbers of upscale urban voters in the suburbs of Washington, D.C., brought an end to the traditional Republican dominance in Virginia.

Swing Voters
Voters who frequently swing their support from one party to another.

Tipping
A phenomenon that occurs when a group that is becoming more numerous over time grows large enough to change the political balance in a district, state, or country.

---

16. John B. Judis and Ruy Teixeira, *The Emerging Democratic Majority* (New York: Scribner, 2002).

WHY SHOULD YOU CARE ABOUT
political parties?

Why should you, as an individual, care about political parties? The most exciting political party event, staged every four years, is the national convention. State conventions also take place on a regular basis. These may seem like remote activities. Surprising as it might seem, though, there are opportunities for the individual voter to become involved in nominating delegates to a state or national convention or to become a delegate.

POLITICAL PARTIES AND YOUR LIFE

How would you like to exercise a small amount of real political power yourself—power that goes beyond simply voting in an election? You might be able to become a delegate to a county, district, or even state party convention. Many of these conventions nominate candidates for various offices. For example, in Michigan, the state party conventions nominate the candidates for the Board of Regents of the state's three top public universities. The regents set university policies, so these are nominations in which students have an obvious interest. In Michigan, if you are elected as a party precinct delegate, you can attend your party's state convention.

In much of the country, there are more openings for district-level delegates than there are people willing to serve. In such circumstances, almost anyone can become a delegate by collecting a handful of signatures on a nominating petition or by mounting a small-scale write-in campaign. You are then eligible to take part in one of the most educational political experiences available to an ordinary citizen. You will get a first-hand look at how political persuasion takes place, how resolutions are written and passed, and how candidates seek out support among their fellow party members. In some states, party caucuses bring debate even closer to the grassroots level.

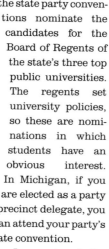

North Carolina delegate
Hiawatha Foster holds up a sign after Democratic presidential nominee Barack Obama (D., Ill.) gave his speech during the 2008 Democratic National Convention in Denver. (AP Photo/Matt Sayles)

HOW YOU CAN MAKE A DIFFERENCE

When the parties choose delegates for the national convention, the process begins at the local level—either the congressional district or the state legislative district. Delegates may be elected in party primary elections or chosen in neighborhood or precinct caucuses.

If the delegates are elected in a primary, persons who want to run for these positions must first file petitions with the board of elections. If you are interested in committing yourself to a particular presidential candidate and running for the delegate position, check with the local county committee or with the party's national committee about the rules you must follow.

It is even easier to get involved in the grassroots politics of presidential caucuses. In some states—Iowa being the earliest and most famous example—delegates are first nominated at the local precinct caucus. According to the rules of the Iowa caucuses, anyone can participate in a caucus if he or she is eighteen years old, a resident of the precinct, and registered as a party member. These caucuses, in addition to being the focus of national media attention in January or February, select delegates to the county conventions who are pledged to specific presidential candidates. This is the first step toward the national convention.

At both the county caucus and the convention levels, both parties try to find younger members to fill some of the seats. Contact the state or county political party to find out when the caucuses or primaries will be held. Then gather local supporters and friends, and prepare to join in an occasion during which political debate is at its best.

For further information about these opportunities (some states hold caucuses and state conventions in every election year), contact the state party office or your local state legislator for specific dates and regulations. You can also write to the national committee for information on how to become a delegate.

Republican National Committee
Republican National Headquarters
310 First St. S.E.
Washington, DC 20003
202-863-8500
www.rnc.org.

Democratic National Committee
Democratic National Headquarters
430 Capital St. S.E.
Washington, DC 20003
202-863-8000
www.democrats.org.

QUESTIONS FOR
discussion**and**analysis

1. Review the *Which Side Are You On?* feature on page 273. Has partisanship been good for America in recent years, perhaps by sharpening the issues under discussion? Or has partisanship been primarily negative, because it turns Americans against one another or for other reasons? Evaluate the pros and cons of partisanship.

2. In America, party candidates for national office are typically chosen through primary elections. In some other countries, a party's central committee picks the party's candidates. How might primary elections limit the ability of political parties to present a united front on the issues?

3. Do you support (or lean toward) one of the major political parties today? If so, would you have supported the same party in the late 1800s—or would you have supported a different party? Explain your reasoning.

4. During 2008, what political developments had an impact on the support that voters gave to the Republican and Democratic parties? To what extent were the Democrats able to take advantage of the unpopularity of the Bush administration?

5. Suppose that the United States Supreme Court were to reverse itself on *Roe v. Wade,* with the result that abortions became illegal in many states. What impact do you think such a ruling might have on Republicans with strongly libertarian beliefs? How likely is it that some of these Republicans might leave the party?

key**terms**

dealignment 279
Democratic Party 256
divided
   government 271
Electoral College 274
era of good feelings 256
faction 253
independent 253
national committee 267
national
   convention 267

party identification 279
party-in-
   government 266
party-in-the-
   electorate 266
party organization 266
party platform 267
patronage 270
plurality 274

political party 253
realignment 278
Republican Party 256
reverse-income
   effect 265
splinter party 277
split-ticket voting 280
state central
   committee 269

straight-ticket
   voting 280
swing voters 281
third party 275
tipping 281
two-party system 254
unit rule 269
Whig Party 256

chapter**summary**

1. A political party is a group of political activists who organize to win elections, operate the government, and determine public policy. Political parties recruit candidates for public office, organize and run elections, present alternative policies to the voters, assume responsibility for operating the government, and act as the opposition to the party in power.

2. The evolution of our nation's political parties can be divided into seven periods: (a) the creation and formation of political parties from 1789 to 1816; (b) the era of one-party rule, or personal politics, from 1816 to 1828; (c) the period from Andrew Jackson's presidency to the Civil War era, from 1828 to 1856; (d) the Civil War and post–Civil War period, from 1856 to 1896; (e) the Republican ascendancy and progressive period, from 1896 to 1932; (f) the New Deal period, from 1932 to about 1968; and (g) the modern period, from approximately 1968 to the present.

3. Many of the differences between the two parties date from the time of Franklin D. Roosevelt's New Deal. The Democrats have advocated government action to help labor and minorities, and the Republicans

have championed self-reliance and limited government. The constituents of the two parties continue to differ. A close look at policies actually enacted in recent years, however, suggests that despite rhetoric to the contrary, both parties are committed to a large and active government. Today, cultural differences are at least as important as economic issues in determining party allegiance.

4. A political party consists of three components: the party-in-the-electorate, the party organization, and the party-in-government. Each party component maintains linkages to the others to keep the party strong. Each level of the party—local, state, and national—has considerable autonomy. The national party organization is responsible for holding the national convention in presidential election years, writing the party platform, choosing the national committee, and conducting party business.

5. The party-in-government comprises all of the elected and appointed officeholders of a party. The linkage of party members is crucial to building support for programs among the branches and levels of government.

6. Two major parties have dominated the political landscape in the United States for almost two centuries. The reasons for this include (a) the historical foundations of the system, (b) political socialization and practical considerations, (c) the winner-take-all electoral system, and (d) state and federal laws favoring the two-party system. For these reasons, minor parties have found it extremely difficult to win elections.

7. Minor, or third, parties have emerged from time to time, sometimes as dissatisfied splinter groups from within major parties, and have acted as barometers of changes in the political mood. Splinter parties have emerged when a particular personality was at odds with the major party, as when Theodore Roosevelt's differences with the Republican Party resulted in the formation of the Bull Moose Progressive Party. Other minor parties, such as the Socialist Party, have formed around specific issues or ideologies. Third parties can affect the political process (even if they do not win) if major parties adopt their issues or if they determine which major party wins an election.

8. One mechanism of political change is realignment, in which major blocs of voters switch allegiance from one party to another. Realignments were manifested in the elections of 1896 and 1932. Some scholars speak of dealignment—that is, the loss of strong party attachments. In fact, during the past fifty years, the share of the voters who describe themselves as independents has grown, and the share of self-identified Democrats has shrunk. Many independents actually vote as if they were Democrats or Republicans, however. Demographic change can also "tip" a district or state from one party to another.

selected print & media resources

SUGGESTED READINGS

Amato, Theresa. *Grand Illusion: The Fantasy of Voter Choice in a Two-Party Tyranny.* New York: The New Press, 2009. As Ralph Nader's campaign manager during his 2000 and 2004 presidential runs, Amato was in an excellent position to see how the political system makes it almost impossible for third-party candidates to succeed. She also examines the experiences of other challengers, including John Anderson, Ross Perot, and Pat Buchanan.

Lublin, David. *The Republican South: Democratization and Partisan Change.* Ewing, N.J.: Princeton University Press, 2007. Lublin looks at the rise of Republicanism in the southern states, emphasizing the economic issues involved in the political realignment of the South.

Paul, Ron. *The Revolution: A Manifesto.* New York: Grand Central Publishing, 2008. Representative Paul (R., Tex.) ran for president on the Libertarian ticket in 2004 and as a Republican in 2008. His concise political statement is an eloquent defense of the libertarian cause. Among Paul's more striking proposals is the abolition of the Federal Reserve System, which, in his opinion, benefits only the rich.

Sager, Ryan. *The Elephant in the Room: Evangelicals, Libertarians, and the Battle to Control the Republican Party.* New York: Wiley, 2006. The author describes the current coalition of subgroups within the Republican Party and predicts an eventual splintering as the individual groups struggle for greater power within the party.

Schaller, Thomas F. *Whistling Past Dixie: How Democrats Can Win without the South.* New York: Simon & Schuster, 2008. Schaller, a professor of political science at the University of Maryland, argues that the Democrats are more likely to succeed by solidifying their support in northern states than by trying to rebuild their once-predominant position in the South.

MEDIA RESOURCES

The American President—A 1995 film starring Michael Douglas as a president who must balance partisanship and friendship (Republicans in Congress promise to approve the president's crime bill only if he modifies an environmental plan sponsored by his liberal girlfriend).

The Best Man—A 1964 drama based on Gore Vidal's play of the same name. The film, which deals with political smear campaigns by presidential party nominees, focuses on political party power and ethics.

Mr. Conservative: Goldwater on Goldwater—As the 1964 Republican presidential candidate, Arizona senator Barry Goldwater lost by a landslide. His conservative philosophy, however, transformed the Republican Party and triumphed in 1980 with the victory of Republican candidate Ronald Reagan. This 2006 production includes interviews with columnist George Will, United States Supreme Court Justice Sandra Day O'Connor, and others.

So Goes the Nation—As one observer correctly put it during the 2004 presidential election, "As goes Ohio, so goes the nation." This 2006 film provides a close-up of the Republican and Democratic presidential campaigns in that state. Viewers come away with a better understanding of the two major parties.

A Third Choice—A film that examines America's experience with third parties and independent candidates throughout the nation's political history.

e-mocracy

POLITICAL PARTIES AND THE INTERNET

Today's political parties use the Internet to attract voters, organize campaigns, obtain campaign contributions, and the like. Voters, in turn, can go online to learn more about specific parties and their programs. Those who use the Internet for information on the parties, though, need to exercise some caution. Even the official party sites are filled with misinformation or even outright lies about the policies and leaders of the other party. Besides the parties' official sites, there are satirical sites mimicking the parties, sites distributing misleading information about the parties, and sites that are raising money for their own causes rather than for political parties.

LOGGING ON

The political parties all have Web sites. The Democratic Party is online at
www.democrats.org.

The Republican National Committee is at
www.rnc.org.

The Libertarian Party has a Web site located at
www.lp.org.

The Green Party of the United States can be found at
www.gp.org.

Politics1.com offers extensive information on U.S. political parties, including the major parties and fifty minor parties. Go to
www.politics1.com/parties.htm.

The Pew Research Center for the People and the Press offers survey data online on how the parties fared during the most recent elections, voter typology, and numerous other issues. To access this site, go to
people-press.org.

9

Campaigns, Elections, and the Media

Campaign workers and the media attempt to capture a "newsworthy" moment at the Bonnet Lane Family Restaurant in Abington, Pennsylvania, during the presidential campaign. (Photo by Joe Raedle/Getty Images)

whatif...no limits were placed on campaign contributions?

BACKGROUND

In the early 1990s, a typical presidential primary campaign required about $20 million in funding. Fast-forward to 2008. By the end of March, Barack Obama had already raised $235 million. Obama collected a record number of "small" donations ($200 and under) especially through the Internet, but his take from $1,000-plus contributors was almost as great. All the presidential candidates together had raised a record $838 million, and the general election was still months away.

To date, one set of campaign reforms after another has aimed at "taking money out of politics." Clearly, money *is* politics. The latest campaign reform act, passed in 2002, is filled with loopholes. One allows independent groups, known as *527 committees* after the governing section of the tax code, to collect unlimited donations and support positions on issues, but not to support specific, named candidates. In the 2004 election, 527 committees spent $653 million.

In 2007–2008, wealthy donors began using a new type of group, the "exempt" 501(c)4 organization, which does support candidates by name and which does not have to disclose the identity of its contributors.

Political spending by independent groups during the 2007–2008 election cycle is estimated to have exceeded $1 billion. This sum represents increased influence by America's richest individuals, contrary to the intention of campaign reform laws. Some critics of current campaign restrictions argue for their total elimination, save for one requirement—a prompt posting on the Internet of the amount and the source of each contribution.

WHAT IF NO LIMITS WERE PLACED ON CAMPAIGN CONTRIBUTIONS?

Some contend that if there were no limits on campaign contributions, money would become even more important in politics. That is hard to believe, given how important it already is. The most likely result is that political action committees (PACs), 527 committees, 501(c)4 groups, and other independent bodies would become less important and might disappear.

The most certain change would be in the 501(c)4s. No longer would major political donors be able to conceal their participation in campaign finance. America's wealthiest citizens could continue to spend millions on elections. The difference would be that their donations to campaigns would become public information almost immediately.

Each candidate's campaign machine would change if there were no restrictions on campaign contributions.

Rather than spending much time wooing PACs, those responsible for campaign financing would focus directly on individuals.

The role of the campaign contribution packager would likely disappear, too. Currently, these "bundlers" agree to raise for a candidate a specified amount, say, $100,000. These packagers currently cannot go to one rich person and ask for that large amount because that is illegal. Rather, the packager puts together a group of hundreds of individuals who give the maximum amount of $2,300 per candidate. If we eliminated campaign limitations, campaign finance specialists would be free to raise those sums via the Internet and to go after individuals who are currently giving large amounts to independent political groups, such as 527s.

CONTRIBUTIONS AS A FORM OF SPEECH

Opponents of contribution limits argue that such limits violate the First Amendment, because campaign contributions are in essence a form of political speech. In America, free speech is hard to suppress. If campaign reform laws eliminated 527s, issue ads, and independent efforts to register voters, various groups would still find ways to raise their voices. The National Rifle Association would still operate a satellite radio station. Rich individuals could still buy television stations or newspapers to make sure that their voices were heard. Candidates would still write "life stories," get them published for big advances, and then be paid to go on book tours. Without any regulation of campaign contributions, in contrast, we would probably see a distinct decline over time in these indirect ways of influencing elections.

KNOWLEDGE IS POWER

If voters could go directly to the Internet and see how each candidate obtained every dollar in campaign funds, that information would allow them to make reasoned choices about each candidate. A candidate would have a difficult time arguing that he or she did not take "special interest money" if such donations were obvious and accessible, rather than concealed by the use of independent organizations.

FOR CRITICAL ANALYSIS

1. Would unlimited campaign contributions change the way elected politicians run the American government?
2. Would rich individuals have more or less influence in government if there were unlimited campaign contributions?

Free elections are the cornerstone of the American political system. Voters choose one candidate over another to hold political office by casting ballots in local, state, and federal elections. In 2008, the voters chose Barack Obama and Joe Biden to be president and vice president of the United States for the following four years. In addition, voters elected all of the members of the House of Representatives and one-third of the members of the Senate. The campaigns were bitter, long, and the most expensive in U.S. history. Five months of hard primary campaigning passed before the Democrats were able to settle on Obama as their presidential candidate. The contest between Obama and Republican John McCain was extremely close until the middle of September.

Voters and candidates frequently criticize the American electoral process. It is said to favor wealthier candidates, to further the aims of special interest groups, and to be dominated by older voters and those with better education and higher incomes. The most recent reforms of the campaign-finance laws were tested for the first time in 2004. Although the reforms had some effect on campaign strategy, fund-raising outside the system and extensive use of television advertising dominated the election season. During the congressional campaigns in 2006 and the presidential elections of 2008, television advertising continued to dominate. Some commentators have argued that our campaign-finance laws are counterproductive and should simply be repealed. We discussed that issue in this chapter's opening *What If . . .* feature.

> **Presidential Primary**
> A statewide primary election of delegates to a political party's national convention, held to determine a party's presidential nominee.

WHO WANTS TO BE A CANDIDATE?

There are thousands of elective offices in the United States. The major political parties strive to provide a slate of candidates for every election. Recruiting candidates is easier for some offices than for others. Political parties may have difficulty finding candidates for the board of the local water control district, for example, but they generally have a sufficient number of candidates for county commissioner or sheriff. The "higher" the office and the more prestige attached to it, the more candidates are likely to want to run. In many areas of the country, however, one political party may be considerably stronger than the other. In those situations, the minority party may have more difficulty finding nominees for elections in which victory is unlikely.

The presidential campaign provides the most colorful and exciting look at candidates and how they prepare to compete for office—in this instance, the highest office in the land. The men and women who wanted to be candidates in the 2008 presidential campaign faced a long and obstacle-filled path. First, they needed to raise sufficient funds to tour the nation, particularly the states with early **presidential primaries,** to see if they had enough local supporters. They needed funds to create an organization, to devise a plan to win primary votes, and to win the party's nomination at the national convention. Finally, when they were nominated as their parties' candidates, they required funds to finance a successful campaign for president. Always, at every turn, there was the question of whether they had enough funds to wage a campaign.

John Edwards
announced his withdrawal from the Democratic presidential race early in 2008. What drives individuals to attempt to become president?
(AP Photo/Alex Brandon)

WHY THEY RUN

People who choose to run for office can be divided into two groups—the "self-starters" and those who are recruited. The volunteers, or self-starters, get involved in political activities to further their careers, to carry out specific political programs, or in response to certain issues or events. For example, John Edwards, who had been the Democratic candidate for vice president in 2004, was inspired to run for president in the 2008

The Democratic primary season

lasted for well over a year. The ultimate winner, Barack Obama (left), fought off a hard-hitting group of contenders, including Senator Hillary Clinton (D., N.Y.). John McCain (right) almost ran out of campaign funds during his months-long attempt to be named the Republican nominee. He ultimately prevailed. Why do you think the nominating process today takes so long?

(AP Photo/Rick Bowmer, File)

(AP Photo/Jeff Chiu)

elections because he was strongly concerned about poverty in America. When Edwards dropped out of the race on January 30, 2008, he secured pledges from the remaining candidates, Barack Obama and Hillary Clinton, that they would address this issue.

Issues are important, but self-interest and personal goals—status, career objectives, prestige, and income—are central in motivating some candidates to enter political life. A lawyer or an insurance agent may run for office only once or twice and then return to private life with enhanced status. Other politicians may aspire to long-term political office—for example, an office such as county sheriff is in itself a career goal. Finally, ambition is a major motivator for those seeking higher office.

THE NOMINATION PROCESS

Individuals become official candidates through the process of nomination. Generally, nominating processes for all offices are controlled by state laws and usually favor the two major political parties. For most minor offices, individuals become candidates by submitting petitions to the local election board. In most states, a candidate from one of the two major parties faces far fewer requirements to get on the ballot than a candidate who is an independent or who represents a minor or new party.

The American system of nominations and primary elections is one of the most complex in the world. In a majority of European nations, the political party's choice of candidates is final, and no primary elections are ever held.

WHO IS ELIGIBLE?

There are few constitutional restrictions on who can become a candidate in the United States. As set out in the Constitution, the formal requirements for national office are as follows:

1. *President.* Must be a natural-born citizen, have attained the age of thirty-five years, and be a resident of the country for fourteen years by the time of inauguration.
2. *Vice president.* Must be a natural-born citizen, have attained the age of thirty-five years, and not be a resident of the same state as the candidate for president.[1]
3. *Senator.* Must be a citizen for at least nine years, have attained the age of thirty by the time of taking office, and be a resident of the state from which elected.

---

1. Technically, a presidential and vice-presidential candidate can be from the same state, but if they are, one of the two must forfeit the electoral votes of their home state.

4. *Representative.* Must be a citizen for at least seven years, have attained the age of twenty-five by the time of taking office, and be a resident of the state from which elected.

The qualifications for state legislators are set by the state constitutions and likewise include age, place of residence, and citizenship. (Usually, the requirements for the upper chamber of a legislature are somewhat more stringent than those for the lower chamber.) The legal qualifications for running for governor or other state office are similar.

WHO RUNS?

In spite of these minimal legal qualifications for office at both the national and state levels, a quick look at the slate of candidates in any election—or at the current members of the U.S. House of Representatives—will reveal that not all segments of the population take advantage of these opportunities. Holders of political office in the United States are overwhelmingly white and male. Until the twentieth century, presidential candidates were exclusively of northern European origin and of Protestant heritage.[2] Laws that effectively denied voting rights made it impossible to elect African American public officials in many areas in which African Americans constituted a significant portion of the population. As a result of the passage of major civil rights legislation in the 1960s, however, the number of African American public officials has increased throughout the United States.

Women as Candidates. Until recently, women generally were considered to be appropriate candidates only for lower-level offices, such as state legislator or school board member. The last twenty years have seen a tremendous increase in the number of women who run for office, not only at the state level but for the U.S. Congress as well. Figure 9–1 shows

> **did**you**know...**
>
> **That five women** received votes for vice president at the Democratic convention in 1924, the first held after women received the right to vote in 1920?

---

2. A number of early presidents were Unitarian. The Unitarian Church is not Protestant, but it is historically rooted in the Protestant tradition.

FIGURE 9–1: Women Running for Congress (and Winning)

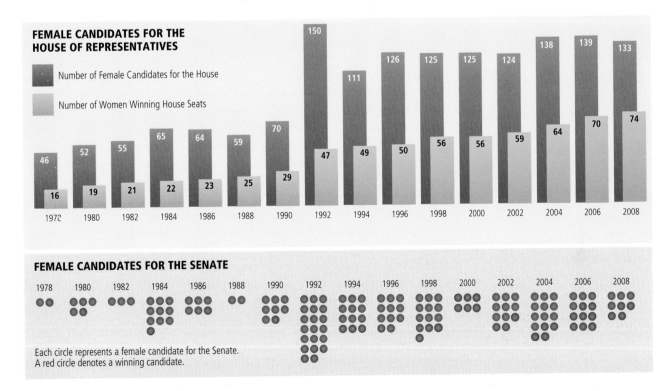

FEMALE CANDIDATES FOR THE HOUSE OF REPRESENTATIVES

- Number of Female Candidates for the House
- Number of Women Winning House Seats

	1978	1980	1982	1984	1986	1988	1990	1992	1994	1996	1998	2000	2002	2004	2006	2008
Candidates	46	52	55	65	64	59	70	150	111	126	125	125	124	138	139	133
Winning	16	19	21	22	23	25	29	47	49	50	56	56	59	64	70	74

FEMALE CANDIDATES FOR THE SENATE

1978 1980 1982 1984 1986 1988 1990 1992 1994 1996 1998 2000 2002 2004 2006 2008

Each circle represents a female candidate for the Senate.
A red circle denotes a winning candidate.

the increase in female candidates. In 2008, 141 women ran for Congress, and 78 were elected. Today, a majority of Americans say they would vote for a qualified woman for president of the United States.[3] Indeed, Hillary Clinton came close to winning the Democratic presidential nomination in 2008, a year in which the eventual Democratic nominee was heavily favored to win the general election.

Lawyers as Candidates. Candidates are likely to be professionals, particularly lawyers. Political campaigning and officeholding are simply easier for some occupational groups than for others, and political involvement can make a valuable contribution to certain careers. Lawyers, for example, have more flexible schedules than do many other professionals, can take time off for campaigning, and can leave their jobs to hold public office full-time. Furthermore, holding political office is good publicity for their professional practice, and they usually have partners or associates to keep the firm going while they are in office. Perhaps most important, many jobs that lawyers aspire to—federal or state judgeships, state's attorney offices, or work in a federal agency—can be attained by political appointment.

THE TWENTY-FIRST-CENTURY CAMPAIGN

After the candidates have been nominated, the most exhausting and expensive part of the election process begins—the general election campaign. The contemporary political campaign is becoming more complex and more sophisticated. Even with the most appealing of candidates, today's campaigns require a strong organization; expertise in political polling and marketing; professional assistance in fund-raising, accounting, and financial management; and technological capabilities in every aspect of the campaign.

THE CHANGING CAMPAIGN

The goal is the same for all campaigns—to convince voters to choose a candidate or a slate of candidates for office. Part of the reason for the increased intensity of campaigns in the last decade is that they are now centered on the candidate, not on the party. The candidate-centered campaign emerged in response to changes in the electoral system, the increased importance of television in campaigns, technological innovations such as computers, and the increased cost of campaigning.

To run a successful and persuasive campaign, the candidate's organization must be able to raise funds for the effort, obtain coverage from the media, produce and pay for political commercials and advertising, schedule the candidate's time effectively, convey the candidate's position on the issues to the voters, conduct research on the opposing candidate, and get the voters to go to the polls. When party identification was stronger among voters and before the advent of television campaigning, a strong party organization at the local, state, or national level could furnish most of the services and expertise that the candidate needed. Political parties provided the funds for campaigning until the 1970s. Parties used their precinct organizations to distribute literature, register voters, and get out the vote on election day. Less effort was spent on advertising each candidate's positions and character, because the party label presumably communicated that information to many voters.

One of the reasons that campaigns no longer depend on parties is that fewer people identify with them (see Chapter 8), as is evident from the increased number of political independents. In 1954, less than 20 percent of adults identified themselves as independents, whereas today that number exceeds 35 percent.

---

3. According to a Gallup poll conducted prior to the 2008 elections, this majority varied according to party affiliation and ideology, ranging from 76 percent (for conservative Republicans) to 98 percent (for liberal Democrats).

THE PROFESSIONAL CAMPAIGN

Whether the candidate is running for the state legislature, for the governor's office, for the U.S. Congress, or for the presidency, every campaign has some fundamental tasks to accomplish. Today, in national elections, the lion's share of these tasks is handled by paid professionals rather than volunteers or amateur politicians.

The most sought-after and possibly the most criticized campaign expert is the **political consultant,** who, for a large fee, devises a campaign strategy, thinks up a campaign theme, oversees the advertising, and possibly chooses the campaign colors and the candidate's official portrait. Political consultants began to displace volunteer campaign managers in the 1960s, about the same time that television became a force in campaigns. The paid consultant monitors the campaign's progress, plans all media appearances, and coaches the candidate for debates. The consultants and the firms they represent are not politically neutral; most will work only for candidates from one party.

THE STRATEGY OF WINNING

In the United States, unlike some European countries, there are no rewards for a candidate who comes in second; the winner takes all. A winner-take-all system is also known as a *plurality voting system.* In most situations, the winning candidate does not have to have a majority of the votes. If there are three candidates, the one who gets the most votes wins—that is, "takes it all"—and the other two candidates get nothing. Given this system, the campaign organization must plan a strategy that maximizes the candidate's chances of winning. Candidates seek to capture all the votes of their party's supporters, to convince a majority of the independent voters to vote for them, and to gain a few votes from supporters of the other party. To accomplish these goals, candidates must consider their visibility, their message, and their campaign strategy.

Candidate Visibility and Appeal. One of the most important concerns is how well known the candidate is. If she or he is a highly visible incumbent, there may be little need for campaigning except to remind the voters of the officeholder's good deeds. If, however, the candidate is an unknown challenger or a largely unfamiliar character attacking a well-known public figure, the campaign requires a strategy to get the candidate before the public.

In the case of the independent candidate or the candidate representing a minor party, the problem of name recognition is serious. Such candidates must present an overwhelming case for the voter to reject the major-party candidates. Both Democratic and Republican candidates will label third-party candidates as "not serious" and therefore not worth the voter's time.

The Use of Opinion Polls. Opinion polls are a major source of information for both the media and the candidates. Poll taking is widespread during the primaries. Presidential hopefuls have private polls taken to make sure that there is at least some chance they could be nominated and, if nominated, elected. During the presidential campaign itself, polling is even more frequent. Polls are taken not only by the regular pollsters—Roper, Harris, Gallup, and others—but also privately by each candidate's campaign organization. These private polls are for the exclusive and secret use of the candidate and his or her campaign organization. As the election approaches, many candidates use **tracking polls,** which are polls taken almost every day, to find out how well they are competing for votes. Tracking polls enable consultants to fine-tune the advertising and the candidate's speeches in the last days of the campaign.

In his recent book, *Politics Lost: How American Democracy Was Trivialized by People Who Think You're Stupid,* political

Political Consultant
A paid professional hired to devise a campaign strategy and manage a campaign.

Tracking Poll
A poll taken for the candidate on a nearly daily basis as election day approaches.

This researcher at the University of California
at Los Angeles believes that magnetic resonance imaging (MRI) can be used to judge the effectiveness of political ads on television. The graph he shows in this photo is the average of responses of Republicans (red line) and Democrats (blue line) as they watched a video supporting a Republican candidate. Clearly, the Republican viewers demonstrated a more positive response than did the Democrats. Why might political consultants be interested in such research? (AP Photo/ Reed Saxon)

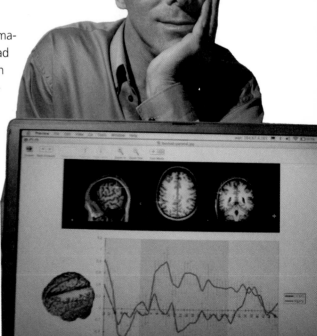

Focus Group
A small group of individuals who are led in discussion by a professional consultant in order to gather opinions on and responses to candidates and issues.

analyst and journalist Joe Klein laments the lack of spontaneous expression by today's political candidates. Instead of saying what they want to say, candidates are advised to change their image and positions in response to polling data. As an example of the negative effects of this process, Klein discusses how campaign advisers "sabotaged" Al Gore's 2000 presidential campaigns. Gore was told not to focus on global warming, an issue that he was passionate about, but on poll-tested issues such as Social Security and prescription drugs. As a result, states Klein, Gore was turned into a mere robot and lost the passion and conviction that might have had more appeal to voters.[4]

Focus Groups. Another tactic is to use a **focus group** to gain insights into public perceptions of the candidate. Professional consultants organize a discussion of the candidate or of certain political issues among ten to fifteen ordinary citizens. The citizens are selected from specific target groups in the population—for example, working women, blue-collar men, senior citizens, or young voters. Recent campaigns have tried to reach groups such as "soccer moms," "Wal-Mart shoppers," or "NASCAR dads."[5] The group discusses personality traits of the candidate, political advertising, and other candidate-related issues. Focus groups are expected to reveal more emotional responses to candidates or the deeper anxieties of voters—feelings that consultants believe often are not tapped by more impersonal telephone surveys. The campaign then can shape its messages to respond to those feelings and perceptions.

didyouknow...

That a candidate can buy lists of all the voters in a precinct, county, or state for a few cents per name from a commercial firm?

FINANCING THE CAMPAIGN

In a book published in 1932 entitled *Money in Elections,* Louise Overacker had the following to say about campaign financing:

> *The financing of elections in a democracy is a problem which is arousing increasing concern. Many are beginning to wonder if present-day methods of raising and spending campaign funds do not clog the wheels of our elaborately constructed mechanism of popular control, and if democracies do not inevitably become [governments ruled by small groups].[6]*

This congressional candidate hopes to attract votes based on his record. Do potential voters see many such print ads, or is there an alternative medium that dominates campaign advertising? *(AP Photo/Houston Chronicle)*

Although writing more than seventy-five years ago, Overacker touched on a sensitive issue in American political campaigns—the connection between money and elections. More than $3.5 billion was spent at all levels of campaigning during the 2003–2004 election cycle, and total spending reached unprecedented heights during the 2007–2008 election cycle. Total spending by the presidential candidates alone in 2008 reached $2.4 billion.

For the midterm senatorial elections in 2006 in New York State, the two candidates together amassed $50 million for their campaigns. Arizona, Michigan, Minnesota, Missouri, Nebraska, Pennsylvania, and Washington all saw senatorial campaigns costing between $15 million and $30 million. Candidates spend much less to retain or obtain a seat in the House of Representatives because representatives must run for election every two years, as opposed to six years for senators. (The seats are also less valuable because the House has many more members than the Senate.)

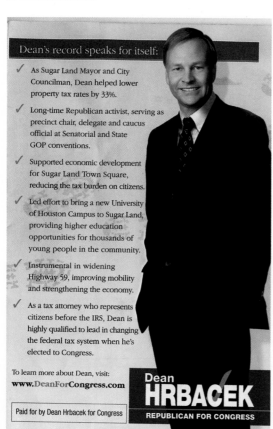

Dean's record speaks for itself:

✓ As Sugar Land Mayor and City Councilman, Dean helped lower property tax rates by 33%.

✓ Long-time Republican activist, serving as precinct chair, delegate and caucus official at Senatorial and State GOP conventions.

✓ Supported economic development for Sugar Land Town Square, reducing the tax burden on citizens.

✓ Led effort to bring a new University of Houston Campus to Sugar Land, providing higher education opportunities for thousands of young people in the community.

✓ Instrumental in widening Highway 59, improving mobility and strengthening the economy.

✓ As a tax attorney who represents citizens before the IRS, Dean is highly qualified to lead in changing the federal tax system when he's elected to Congress.

To learn more about Dean, visit: **www.DeanForCongress.com**

Paid for by Dean Hrbacek for Congress

Dean HRBACEK
REPUBLICAN FOR CONGRESS

---

4. Joe Klein, *Politics Lost: How American Democracy Was Trivialized by People Who Think You're Stupid* (New York: Doubleday, 2006).
5. NASCAR stands for the National Association of Stock Car Auto Racing.
6. Louise Overacker, *Money in Elections* (New York: Macmillan, 1932), p. vii.

Except for the presidential campaigns, all of these funds had to be provided by the candidates and their families, borrowed, or raised by contributions from individuals or *political action committees,* described later in this chapter. For the presidential campaigns, some of the funds may come from the federal government.

REGULATING CAMPAIGN FINANCING

The way campaigns are financed has changed dramatically in the last two and a half decades. Today, candidates and political parties must operate within the constraints imposed by complicated laws regulating campaign financing.

A variety of federal **corrupt practices acts** have been designed to regulate campaign financing. The first, passed in 1925, contained many loopholes and proved to be ineffective. The **Hatch Act** (Political Activities Act) of 1939 is best known for restricting the political activities of civil servants. The act also, however, made it unlawful for a political group to spend more than $3 million in any campaign and limited individual contributions to a political group to $5,000. Of course, such restrictions were easily circumvented by creating additional political groups.

THE FEDERAL ELECTION CAMPAIGN ACT

The Federal Election Campaign Act (FECA) of 1971, which became effective in 1972, essentially replaced all past laws. The act placed no limit on overall spending but restricted the amount that could be spent on mass media advertising, including television. It limited the amount that candidates could contribute to their own campaigns (a limit later ruled unconstitutional) and required disclosure of all contributions and expenditures over $100. In principle, the FECA limited the role of labor unions and corporations in political campaigns. It also provided for a voluntary $1 (now $3) check-off on federal income tax returns for general campaign funds to be used by major-party presidential candidates.

Further Reforms in 1974. For many, the 1971 act did not go far enough. Amendments to the FECA passed in 1974 did the following:

1. *Created the Federal Election Commission.* This commission consists of six nonpartisan administrators whose duties are to enforce compliance with the requirements of the act.
2. *Provided public financing for presidential primaries and general elections.* Any candidate running for president who is able to obtain sufficient contributions in at least twenty states can obtain a subsidy from the U.S. Treasury to help pay for primary campaigns. The government also subsidizes the national conventions of the two major parties. Candidates who accept federal funding for the general elections are limited to spending what the government provides and cannot raise funds privately. The system began to break down after 2000, when many candidates rejected public funding in the belief that they could raise larger sums privately. George W. Bush opted out of primary financing in 2000, as did John Kerry in 2004. In the 2008 primaries, most of the major candidates refused public financing, and Barack Obama became the first candidate since the program was founded to opt out of federal funding for the general elections as well. As a result, he was able to raise unprecedented sums.
3. *Limited presidential campaign spending.* Any candidate accepting federal support must agree to limit campaign expenditures to the amount prescribed by federal law.
4. *Limited contributions.* Under the 1974 amendments, citizens could contribute up to $1,000 to each candidate in each federal election or primary; the total limit on all contributions from an individual to all candidates was $25,000 per year. Groups could contribute up to a maximum of $5,000 to a candidate in any election. (As you will read shortly, some of these limits were changed by the 2002 campaign-reform legislation.)

Corrupt Practices Acts
A series of acts passed by Congress in an attempt to limit and regulate the size and sources of contributions and expenditures in political campaigns.

Hatch Act
An act passed in 1939 that restricted the political activities of government employees. It also prohibited a political group from spending more than $3 million in any campaign and limited individual contributions to a campaign committee to $5,000.

didyouknow...

That Abraham Lincoln sold pieces of fence rail that he had split as political souvenirs to finance his campaign?

Political Action Committee (PAC)
A committee set up by and representing a corporation, labor union, or special interest group. PACs raise and give campaign donations.

5. *Required disclosure.* Each candidate must file periodic reports with the Federal Election Commission, listing who contributed, how much was spent, and for what the funds were spent.

Buckley v. Valeo. The 1971 act had limited the amount that each individual could spend on his or her own behalf. The Supreme Court declared the provision unconstitutional in 1976, in *Buckley v. Valeo,*[7] stating that it was unconstitutional to restrict in any way the amount congressional candidates could spend on their own behalf: "The candidate, no less than any other person, has a First Amendment right to engage in the discussion of public issues and vigorously and tirelessly to advocate his own election." In 2006, in holding unconstitutional a 1997 Vermont law that limited the amount that candidates for Vermont state offices could spend on their own campaigns, the Court reaffirmed *Buckley v. Valeo* and extended its reach to candidates for state offices.[8]

PACs AND POLITICAL CAMPAIGNS

In the last two decades, interest groups and individual companies have found new, very direct ways to support elected officials through campaign donations. Elected officials, in turn, have become dependent on these donations to run increasingly expensive campaigns. Interest groups and corporations funnel money to political candidates through several devices, including **political action committees (PACs).**

Laws Governing PACs. The 1974 and 1976 amendments to the Federal Election Campaign Act of 1971 allow corporations, labor unions, and other interest groups to set up PACs to raise funds for candidates. For a federal PAC to be legitimate, the funds must be raised from at least fifty volunteer donors and must be given to at least five candidates in the federal election. PACs can contribute up to $5,000 to each candidate in each election. Each corporation or each union is limited to one PAC. Campaign-financing regulations limit the amount that a PAC can give to any one candidate, but there is no limit on the amount that a PAC can spend on issue advocacy, either on behalf of a candidate or party or in opposition to one.

PACs and Campaign Financing. The number of PACs grew significantly after 1976, as did the amounts that they spent on elections. There were about 1,000 PACs in 1976; today, there are more than 4,500. Since the 1990s, however, the number of PACs has leveled off. As you learned in the *What If . . .* feature at the beginning of this chapter, interest groups and activists have found alternate mechanisms for funneling resources into campaigns. Total spending by PACs exceeded $900 million in the 2003–2004 election cycle, when about 44 percent of all campaign funds raised by House candidates came from PACs. In subsequent years, the share of election financing provided by PACs fell even as the dollar amount of PAC contributions continued to climb.

Interest groups funnel PAC funds to the candidates they think can do the most good for them. Frequently, they make the maximum contribution of $5,000 per election to candidates who face little or no opposition. The great bulk of campaign contributions goes to incumbent candidates rather than to challengers. Table 9–1 shows the amounts contributed by the top twenty PACs during the 2007–2008 election cycle.

As Table 9–1 also shows, many PACs give most of their contributions to candidates of one party. Other PACs, particularly corporate PACs, tend to give funds to Democrats in Congress as well as to Republicans. Why, you might ask, would business leaders give to Democrats who may be more liberal than themselves? Interest groups see PAC contributions as a way to ensure *access* to powerful legislators, even though the groups may disagree with the legislators some of the time.

7. 424 U.S. 1 (1976).
8. *Randall v. Sorrell,* 548 U.S. 230 (2006).

TABLE 9–1: The Top Twenty Political Action Committees Contributing to Federal Candidates, 2007–2008 Election Cycle*

Political Action Committee Name	Total Amount	Dem. %	Rep. %
National Association of Realtors	$3,122,000	57	43
International Brotherhood of Electrical Workers	2,666,300	98	2
American Bankers Association	2,631,850	40	60
Operating Engineers Union	2,612,957	86	14
National Beer Wholesalers Association	2,426,500	53	47
AT&T, Inc.	2,415,200	41	59
Air Line Pilots Association	2,309,500	85	15
National Auto Dealers Association	2,280,000	34	66
American Association for Justice (trial lawyers)	2,277,500	95	5
International Association of Fire Fighters	2,149,900	76	24
Machinists/Aerospace Workers Union	1,964,300	96	4
Laborers Union	1,943,500	92	8
National Air Traffic Controllers Association	1,934,975	79	21
Credit Union National Association	1,914,049	52	48
Sheet Metal Workers Union	1,911,360	96	4
Plumbers/Pipefitters Union	1,855,925	94	6
Service Employees International Union	1,839,700	94	6
Honeywell International	1,815,616	53	47
American Dental Association	1,805,612	53	47
United Auto Workers	1,802,450	99	1

*Includes subsidiaries and affiliated PACs, if any.

Source: Center for Responsive Politics, 2008.

CAMPAIGN FINANCING BEYOND THE LIMITS

Within a few years after the establishment of the tight limits on contributions, new ways to finance campaigns were developed that skirted the reforms and made it possible for huge sums to be raised, especially by the major political parties.

Contributions to Political Parties. Candidates, PACs, and political parties found ways to generate **soft money**—that is, campaign contributions to political parties that escaped the limits of federal election law. Although the FECA limited contributions that would be spent on elections, there were no limits on contributions to political parties for activities such as voter education and voter-registration drives. This loophole enabled the parties to raise millions of dollars from corporations and individuals. It was not unusual for some corporations to give more than $1 million to the Democratic National Committee or to the Republican Party.

Each of the major parties raised about $200 million in soft money during the 1999–2000 presidential election cycle. The parties spent these funds for their conventions, for

Soft Money
Campaign contributions unregulated by federal or state law, usually given to parties and party committees to help fund general party activities.

Independent Expenditures
Nonregulated contributions from PACs, organizations, and individuals. The funds may be spent on advertising or other campaign activities so long as those expenditures are not coordinated with those of a candidate.

Issue Advocacy
Advertising paid for by interest groups that support or oppose a candidate or a candidate's position on an issue without mentioning voting or elections.

registering voters, and for advertising to promote the general party position. The parties also sent a great deal to state and local party organizations, which used the soft money to support their own tickets. Although soft money contributions to the national parties were outlawed after Election Day 2002 (as you will read shortly), political parties saw no contradiction in raising and spending as much soft money as possible during the 2001–2002 election cycle.

Independent Expenditures. Business corporations, labor unions, and other interest groups discovered that it was legal to make **independent expenditures** in an election campaign so long as the expenditures were not coordinated with those of the candidate or political party. Hundreds of unique committees and organizations blossomed to take advantage of this campaign tactic. Although a 1990 United States Supreme Court decision, *Austin v. Michigan State Chamber of Commerce,*[9] upheld the right of the states and the federal government to limit independent, direct corporate expenditures (such as for advertisements) on behalf of *candidates,* the decision did not stop business and other types of groups from making independent expenditures on *issues.*

Issue Advocacy. Indeed, **issue advocacy**—spending unregulated funds on advertising that promotes positions on issues rather than candidates—has become a common tactic in recent years. Interest groups routinely wage their own issue campaigns. For example, the Christian Coalition, which is incorporated, annually raises millions of dollars to produce and distribute voter guidelines and other direct-mail literature to describe candidates' positions on various issues and to promote its agenda. Before the 2008 elections, AARP, which represents older Americans, aired a series of ads showcasing people who had been ruined by health-care costs. Ostensibly bipartisan, the campaign in fact benefited the Democrats.

Although promoting issue positions is very close to promoting candidates who support those positions, the courts repeatedly have held, in accordance with the *Buckley v. Valeo* decision mentioned earlier, that interest groups have a First Amendment right to advocate their positions. The courts have also clarified that political parties may make independent expenditures on behalf of candidates—as long as the parties do so *independently* of the candidates. In other words, the parties must not coordinate such expenditures with the candidates' campaigns.

(Carlson © 2001 *The Philadelphia Inquirer.* Reprinted with permission of Universal Press Syndicate. All Rights Reserved.)

THE BIPARTISAN CAMPAIGN REFORM ACT OF 2002

Campaign reform had been in the air for so long that it was almost anticlimactic when President George W. Bush signed the Bipartisan Campaign Reform Act on March 27, 2002. This act, also known as the McCain-Feingold Act after its chief sponsors in the Senate, amended the 1971 FECA. The act took effect on the day after the congressional elections were held on November 5, 2002.

Key Elements of the New Law. The 2002 law banned the large, unlimited contributions to national political parties that are known as soft money. It placed curbs on, but did not entirely eliminate, the use of campaign ads by outside special interest groups advocating

---

9. 494 U.S. 652 (1990).

the election or defeat of specific candidates. Such ads were allowed up to sixty days before a general election and up to thirty days before a primary election. (As you will read shortly, this rule was eased by the Supreme Court in 2007.)

In 1974, contributions by individuals to federal candidates were limited to $1,000 per individual. The McCain-Feingold Act increased this to $2,000. Also, the maximum amount that an individual can give to all federal candidates was raised from $25,000 per year to $95,000 over a two-year election cycle. The act did not ban soft money contributions to state and local parties, which can accept such contributions as long as they are limited to $10,000 per year per individual.

Challenges to the 2002 Act. Almost immediately, the 2002 act faced a set of constitutional challenges brought by groups negatively affected. In December 2003, however, the Supreme Court upheld almost all of the clauses of the act.[10]

Soon thereafter, the antiabortion group Wisconsin Right to Life sued the Federal Election Commission (FEC), claiming that the 2002 act infringed on legitimate grassroots lobbying and free political speech. The group argued that the part of the act that restricts the broadcasting of issue ads just before an election was unconstitutional. A special federal court panel decided in favor of the antiabortion group, ruling that the ads' text and images did not show that they were "intended to influence the voters' decisions" but rather that they were "genuine issue ads" that the government could not keep off the air. The case ultimately reached the Supreme Court, and in 2007 the Court agreed with the federal court panel. According to the Court, only those ads "susceptible of no reasonable interpretation other than as an appeal to vote for or against a specific candidate" could be restricted prior to an election. To prohibit all ads paid for by corporations or unions amounted to censorship. The Court added, "Where the First Amendment is implicated, the tie goes to the speaker, not the censor."[11]

The Roberts Court and Campaign Financing. Many hailed the controversial decision as a clear victory for those who oppose campaign-finance regulation. Certainly, the ruling will make it more difficult to challenge issue ads, even when the intent behind them—and their effect—is to support a particular candidate in an election. Supreme Court observers also noted that the ruling, which contrasts so starkly with the Court's 2003 decision on this issue, underscores the influence of the two new conservative justices appointed to the Court by President George W. Bush—Chief Justice John Roberts, Jr., and Associate Justice Samuel Alito.

The Roberts Court again showed its skepticism concerning the constitutionality of campaign-finance regulation in a case decided in June 2008. The case involved a provision of the McCain-Feingold Act that was known as the "millionaire's amendment." Under this provision, opponents of certain wealthy candidates who fund their own campaigns could raise more funds from individual donors than federal law normally allows. The law also permitted opponents of wealthy candidates to coordinate finances with party officials in ways that normally would be prohibited. The law did not prevent rich individuals from spending as much as they wanted on their own campaigns—it simply allowed rival candidates to raise additional contributions. Essentially, the provision was meant to level the financial playing field when wealthy candidates pay for their own campaigns. The Court, however, concluded that the millionaire's amendment was unconstitutional. Said the Court: "Different candidates have different strengths. . . . Leveling electoral opportunities means making and implementing judgments about which strengths should be

A MoveOn.org television commercial that has an image of former President Richard M. Nixon morphing into the image of President George W. Bush. This ad was targeted generally against the Republican Party in the run-up to the 2006 elections. How can independent expenditures on political advertisements create problems for a party that is the apparent beneficiary of the ads? (Photos Courtesy of MoveOn.org)

10. *McConnell v. Federal Election Commission,* 540 U.S. 93 (2003).
11. *Federal Election Commission v. Wisconsin Right to Life, Inc.,* 127 S.Ct. 2652 (2007).

These four Republican presidential candidates started debating each other almost a year and a half before the general election in November 2008. From left to right are former Massachusetts governor Mitt Romney, former New York City mayor Rudolph W. Giuliani, Senator John McCain, and former Arkansas governor Mike Huckabee. (Photo by Darren McCollester/Getty Images)

permitted to contribute to the outcome of an election." The Court emphasized that the Constitution permits voters, not Congress, to make such decisions.[12]

The Rise of the 527s. Interest groups that previously gave soft money to the parties responded to the 2002 Bipartisan Campaign Reform Act by setting up new organizations outside the parties, called "527" organizations after the section of the tax code that provides for them. These tax-exempt organizations, which rely on soft money contributions for their funding and generally must report their contributions and expenditures to the Internal Revenue Service, first made a major impact in the 2003–2004 election cycle. The groups focus on encouraging voter registration and running issue ads aimed at energizing supporters. Often, 527 groups run ads that take a strong position for or against a candidate. These groups continued to be active during the 2007–2008 election cycle, as you can see in Table 9–2.

In the 2007–2008 election cycle, campaign-finance lawyers began recommending a new type of independent group—the 501(c)4 organization, which, like the 527 committee, is named after the relevant provision of the tax code. A 501(c)4 is ostensibly a "social welfare" group and, unlike a 527, is not required to disclose the identity of its donors or report spending to the FEC. Lawyers then began suggesting that 501(c)4 organizations claim an exemption under the 1996 Supreme Court ruling described earlier. This would allow the organization to ask people to vote for or against specific candidates as long as a majority of the group's effort was devoted to issues. Only those funds spent on direct campaigning had to be reported to the FEC, and the 501(c)4 could continue to conceal its donors.

One result of the 501(c)4 was to make it all but impossible to determine exactly how much was really spent on the 2007–2008 elections. Critics claimed that 501(c)4s were being used illegally. The FEC was unable to rule on their validity in 2008, however, because a partisan deadlock in the Senate had left the commission with only two members, two short of the number it needed to make a ruling.

---

12. *Davis v. Federal Election Commission*, 128 S.Ct. 2759 (2008).

TABLE 9–2: 527 Committee Activity in 2007–2008 by Type of Group or Interest

Type of Group or Interest	Total Receipts	Total Expenditures
Democratic/liberal	$53,294,910	$51,777,965
Republican/conservative	50,880,924	56,331,174
Miscellaneous unions	28,313,753	29,355,217
Women's issues	11,861,099	10,494,811
Building trade unions	10,624,855	8,196,634
Candidate committees	4,644,608	1,487,266
Human rights	4,552,478	5,827,950
Miscellaneous issues	3,790,252	3,626,483
Industrial unions	3,598,007	4,160,084
Public-sector unions	3,336,090	3,741,506

Source: Internal Revenue Service.

elections2008
CAMPAIGN FINANCING AND THE 2008 ELECTIONS

In 2008, Barack Obama's fund-raising operation obliterated every political fund-raising and spending record in history. By mid-October, Obama had raised more than $650 million from about three million donors, in large part over the Internet. While about half of the funds came from people giving less than $200, larger donors were also generous. Obama collected more contributions of $1,000 or more than George W. Bush did in 2004. Obama was able to raise so much because he opted out of the public funding system. John McCain, who relied on the public system, was limited to $84 million for the general election. McCain did have a way of raising additional sums, however—by coordinating with the Republican Party. The party faced no limits on how much it could raise and spend on advertisements favorable to McCain. Many journalists speculated that Obama's performance marked the death of the public financing system for presidential elections. Others were not so sure. Not all candidates can expect to match Obama's fund-raising prowess. Those who cannot may find a combination of public and party funds to be the best way to support a campaign. It is not clear, for example, whether McCain could have raised substantially more if he had relied entirely on private contributions.

(Screen capture from Obama Web site: www.barackobama.com)

RUNNING FOR PRESIDENT: THE LONGEST CAMPAIGN

The American presidential election is the culmination of two different campaigns: the presidential primary campaign and the final campaign following the party's national convention. Traditionally, both the primary campaigns and the final campaigns take place during the first ten months of an election year. Increasingly, though, the states are holding their primaries earlier in the year, which has motivated the candidates to begin their campaigns earlier as well. Indeed, candidates in the 2008 presidential races began campaigning in early 2007, thus launching the longest presidential campaign to date in U.S. history.

Primary elections were first mandated in 1903 in Wisconsin. The purpose of the primary was to open the nomination process to ordinary party members and to weaken the influence of party bosses. Until 1968, however, there were fewer than twenty primary elections for the presidency. They were often **"beauty contests"** in which the candidates competed for popular votes, but the results had little or no impact on the selection of delegates to the national convention. National conventions were meetings of the party elite—legislators, mayors, county chairpersons, and loyal party workers—who were mostly appointed to their delegations. National conventions saw numerous trades and bargains among competing candidates, and the leaders of large blocs of delegates could direct their delegates to support a favorite candidate.

didyouknow...

That in 1904, Florida became the first state to use primary elections to select delegates to the major party national conventions, and although New Hampshire began using primary elections in 1916, it did not have a contested election until 1952?

REFORMING THE PRIMARIES

In recent decades, the character of the primary process and the makeup of the national convention have changed dramatically. The public, rather than party elites, now generally controls the nomination process. After the disruptive riots outside the doors of the 1968 Democratic convention in Chicago, many party leaders pushed for serious reforms of the convention process. They saw the general dissatisfaction with the convention, and the riots in particular, as being caused by the inability of the average party member to influence the nomination system.

The Democratic National Committee appointed a special commission to study the problems of the primary system. Called the McGovern-Fraser Commission, during the

"Beauty Contest"
A presidential primary in which contending candidates compete for popular votes but the results do not control the selection of delegates to the national convention.

next several years the group formulated new rules for delegate selection that had to be followed by state Democratic parties.

The reforms instituted by the Democratic Party, which were imitated in most states by the Republicans, revolutionized the nomination process for the presidency. The most important changes require that a majority of the convention delegates not be nominated by party elites; they must be elected by the voters in primary elections, in caucuses held by local parties (to be discussed shortly), or at state conventions. Delegates are normally pledged to a particular candidate, although the pledge is not always formally binding at the convention. The delegation from each state must also include a proportion of women, younger party members, and representatives of the minority groups within the party. At first, virtually no special privileges were given to elected party officials, such as senators and governors. In 1984, however, many of these officials returned to the Democratic convention as superdelegates.

Many voters go to the polls twice

during an election year: once to vote in their state's primary election and once to vote in the general election in November. This Maryland voter is shown pausing before a voting booth during that state's primary elections. What motivates individuals to vote in the primaries? (AP Photo/Matthew S. Gunby/ *Salisbury Daily Times*)

PRIMARIES AND CAUCUSES

A variety of types of primaries are used by the states. One notable difference is between proportional and winner-take-all primaries. Another important consideration is whether independent voters can take part in a primary, as we will explain shortly. Some states also use **caucuses** and conventions to choose candidates for various offices.

Proportional and Winner-Take-All Primaries. Most primaries are *winner-take-all*. *Proportional* primaries are used mostly to elect delegates to the national conventions of the two major parties—delegates who are pledged to one or another candidate for president. In 2008, all Democratic Party presidential primaries and caucuses allocated delegates on a proportional basis. This meant that if one candidate for president won 40 percent of the vote in a primary, that candidate would receive about 40 percent of the pledged delegates. If a candidate won 60 percent of the vote, he or she would obtain about 60 percent of the delegates. In many states, the proportional share going to each candidate was decided partly at the district level, so the statewide vote percentages did not precisely match the percentages of pledged delegates. In contrast, the Republicans used the winner-take-all primary system in most, but not all, states. Under this system, the candidate who received the most votes won all of the states' delegates, no matter how narrow the margin of victory.

The use of different systems by the two major parties had a striking impact on the conduct and outcome of the 2008 presidential primaries. Because the Democratic contest between Barack Obama and Hillary Clinton was so close, the proportional distribution of delegates ensured that the winner was not established until June. Neither candidate actually accumulated enough delegates to win during the primary season—the nomination had to be settled by the unelected, unpledged **superdelegates** (party leaders, members of Congress, and others). Of course, a majority of the superdelegates eventually endorsed Obama, the candidate with the most pledged delegates.

On the Republican side, the winner-take-all system let John McCain sew up his party's nomination by March 4, allowing him several additional months in which he could campaign as his party's undisputed nominee. As an interesting note, if the Democrats had used the winner-take-all system, Clinton, not Obama, would have been their candidate. She would have won the nomination early on by collecting all of the delegates from large states, such as California and New York.

Closed Primary. A closed primary is one of several types of primaries distinguished by how independent voters are handled. In a **closed primary,** only avowed or declared mem-

Caucus

A meeting of party members designed to select candidates and propose policies.

Superdelegate

A party leader or elected official who is given the right to vote at the party's national convention. Superdelegates are not elected at the state level.

Closed Primary

A type of primary in which the voter is limited to choosing candidates of the party of which he or she is a member.

bers of a party can vote in that party's primary. In other words, voters must declare their party affiliation, either when they register to vote or at the primary election. A closed-primary system tries to make sure that registered voters cannot cross over into the other party's primary in order to nominate the weakest candidate of the opposing party or to affect the ideological direction of that party.

Open Primary. An **open primary** is a primary in which voters can vote in either party primary without disclosing their party affiliation. Basically, the voter makes the choice in the privacy of the voting booth. The voter must, however, choose one party's list from which to select candidates. Open primaries place no restrictions on independent voters.

Blanket Primary. A *blanket primary* is one in which the voter can vote for candidates of more than one party. Alaska and Louisiana have blanket primaries. Blanket-primary campaigns may be much more costly than other types because each candidate for every office is trying to influence all the voters, not just those in his or her party.

In 2000, the United States Supreme Court issued a decision that altered significantly the use of the blanket primary. The case arose when political parties in California challenged the constitutionality of a 1996 ballot initiative authorizing the use of the blanket primary in that state. The parties contended that the blanket primary violated their First Amendment right of association. Because the nominees represent the party, they argued, party members—not the general electorate—should have the right to choose the party's nominee. The Supreme Court ruled in favor of the parties, holding that the blanket primary violated parties' First Amendment associational rights.[13]

The Court's ruling called into question the constitutional validity of blanket primaries in other states as well. These states have since been devising primary election systems that comply with the Supreme Court's ruling yet offer independent voters a chance to participate in the primary elections.

Run-Off Primary. Some states have a two-primary system. If no candidate receives a majority of the votes in the first primary, the top two candidates must compete in another primary, called a *run-off primary*.

Conventions. While primary elections are the most common way in which a party's candidates are selected, there are other procedures in use. The Virginia Republican Party, for example, chose its 2008 candidate for the U.S. Senate at its state convention, whereas the Democrats in that state used a primary. In Connecticut, the major parties also choose candidates for the U.S. Senate and the governorship at their state conventions, but if two or more candidates receive more than 15 percent of the vote at a convention, the nomination is settled by a primary.

Meetings below the statewide level may help nominate candidates for local, state, or national office. The most famous of such meetings are the caucuses that help nominate a party's candidate for president of the United States.

Caucuses. In 2008, twelve states[14] relied entirely on the caucus system for choosing delegates to the Republican and Democratic national conventions—delegates committed to one presidential candidate or the other. Several other states used a combined system.[15] Strictly speaking, the caucus system is actually a caucus/convention system. In North

didyouknow...

That when David Leroy Gatchell changed his middle name to None of the Above and ran for the U.S. Senate representing Tennessee, a court ruled that he could not use his middle name on the ballot?

Open Primary
A primary in which any registered voter can vote (but must vote for candidates of only one party).

13. *California Democratic Party v. Jones,* 530 U.S. 567 (2000).
14. Alaska, Colorado, Hawaii, Iowa, Kansas, Maine, Minnesota, Nebraska, Nevada, North Dakota, Washington, and Wyoming.
15. Montana Republicans and Idaho Democrats employed the caucus system, whereas the other party in those states relied on a primary. Democrats in Texas and Republicans in Idaho and Louisiana used both primaries *and* caucuses to allocate delegates.

Dakota, for example, local citizens, who need not be registered as party members, gather in party meetings, called caucuses, at the precinct level. They choose delegates to district conventions, and the delegates are committed to one or the other of the candidates. The district conventions elect committed delegates to the state convention, and the state convention actually chooses the delegates to the national convention. The national delegates, however, are pledged to reflect the presidential preferences that voters expressed at the caucus level.

FRONT-LOADING THE PRIMARIES

When politicians and potential presidential candidates realized that winning as many primary elections as possible guaranteed them the party's nomination for president, their tactics changed dramatically. Candidates began to concentrate on building organizations in states that held early, important primary elections. By the 1970s, candidates recognized that winning early contests, such as the Iowa caucuses or the New Hampshire primary election (both now held in January), meant that the media instantly would label the winner as the **front-runner,** thus increasing the candidate's media exposure and escalating the pace of contributions to his or her campaign fund.

The Rush to Be First. The states and state political parties began to see that early primaries had a much greater effect on the outcome of the presidential election. As a result, for the last several decades, in every presidential election year more and more states have moved their presidential primaries or caucuses up toward the beginning of the calendar. In 1988, for example, nine southern states agreed to hold a regional primary on March 8 in the hopes that this early contest would maximize southern influence on the nominating process. This joint primary was dubbed "Super Tuesday." In subsequent elections, some groups of states organized a variety of Super Tuesdays in March and eventually even in February. In 1996, California, which formerly conducted one of the last major primaries, in June, moved its election up to March, **front-loading** the primary season drastically. In 2000, the presidential nominating process was over in March, with both George W. Bush and Al Gore having enough convention delegate votes to win their nominations. This meant that voters in the remaining primaries that year became largely irrelevant to the primary process.

By 2007, four states (Florida, Michigan, Nevada, and South Carolina) had decided to hold their primaries in January 2008, within the time frame of the Iowa caucuses and New Hampshire primary. Twenty-two states, including the most populous states, scheduled their primaries for February 5. This date was the new Super Tuesday. The remaining primaries continued until June 3, the date of the final primaries (in Montana and South Dakota).

The National Parties Try to Regain Control of the Process. Throughout 2007, the severe front-loading scheduled for 2008 was widely criticized. The general assumption was that the primary season would be drastically curtailed and that "establishment" candidates who could raise large amounts of funds would coast to an easy—and early—victory. Voters would not have the time to become acquainted with other, perhaps superior, candidates. One or both of the parties might even find themselves saddled with a candidate who, by the time of the general election, would be considered "damaged goods."

In 2007, the Democratic and Republican national committees sought to place some controls on the front-loading process. The parties adopted rules to prohibit states from holding primaries or caucuses before February 5, 2008, unless they received a special exemption from the national parties. (One result of these rules was that twenty-two states moved their contests to February 5, as was observed above.) The traditional early contests—the Iowa caucuses and the New Hampshire primary—were permitted to lead off the primary season, as usual. In addition, the parties allowed two other states with rela-

Front-Runner
The presidential candidate who appears to be ahead at a given time in the primary season.

Front-Loading
The practice of moving presidential primary elections to the early part of the campaign to maximize the impact of these primaries on the nomination.

tively small populations, Nevada and South Carolina, to go early. The plan was to conduct one early contest in each of the nation's four major regions—the Northeast, the Midwest, the South, and the West.

Unfortunately, state officials in Florida and Michigan refused to obey the rules set by the national parties, and the two states scheduled primaries in January. The Republicans penalized the two state delegations by cutting in half the number of votes they could cast at the national convention. Eventually, the Democrats did likewise. (At the convention, however, the Democrats counted the votes of these two states fully.)

The Unintended Consequences of Early Primaries. Because of the Republicans' winner-take-all rule, the Republican nomination was indeed decided with relative speed. In 2007, Senator John McCain's campaign had experienced serious financial trouble, and in that year McCain was well behind in the polls. By 2008, however, he prevailed easily in a widely divided field. Former Massachusetts governor Mitt Romney made a major pitch to the Religious Right, a constituency that viewed McCain with suspicion. Romney, however, wound up splitting the religious vote with Mike Huckabee, a former governor of Arkansas. Huckabee began the race as a relative unknown but rapidly gained popularity among evangelical voters due to his attractive personality and debating skills.

On the Democratic side, the front-loaded primary system yielded results that were the opposite of what most people had expected. Senator Hillary Clinton, the Democratic front-runner throughout 2007, was unable to land an early knockout blow on her chief opponent, Senator Barack Obama. Because of the proportional allocation of delegates, Obama actually came out of Super Tuesday slightly ahead of Clinton in pledged delegates. He then rode through the rest of the February contests on a wave of popular enthusiasm and established a lead that Clinton was never able to shake. Still, more than three months followed before Obama was able to "close the deal" and become the presumptive Democratic nominee.

As a result, every single Democratic contest was a true battle, and participation in the Democratic primaries and caucuses set new records. Late-voting states, such as Ohio, Texas, Pennsylvania, Indiana, and North Carolina, received major attention by the press and the candidates—attention they had not received in past elections. Officials in the Super Tuesday states began to realize that late-voting states were receiving much more attention than the Super Tuesday states—with twenty-two states all voting at once, the smaller Super Tuesday states were necessarily ignored by the campaigns and the media. Front-loading the nominating process had become counterproductive for the front-loaders.

Are Regional Primaries the Solution? In 2005, a private commission headed by former president Jimmy Carter and former secretary of state James A. Baker III proposed a number of steps to avoid the problems caused by early primaries. The commission argued in favor of keeping the Iowa caucuses and New Hampshire's early primary because "they test the candidates by genuine retail, door-to-door campaigning." After that, though, the commission had a radical suggestion—eliminate the state primaries and hold four regional presidential primaries. These regional primaries would be held at monthly intervals in March, April, May, and June, with the order rotated every four years. Other organizations have made similar proposals.

About every four years, there are new concerns relating to America's federal election system. Former president Jimmy Carter on the left and former secretary of state James A. Baker III are shown listening to testimony during a hearing at American University in Washington, D.C. Carter and Baker co-chaired the Commission on Federal Election Reform. What are some of the problems with the current federal election system? (Mark Wilson/Getty Images)

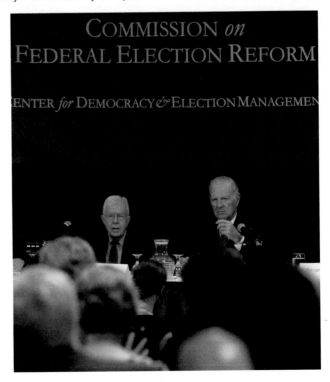

The Democrats

held their convention in Denver, Colorado, in 2008. Barack Obama gave his acceptance speech in a football stadium filled with 85,000 people.
(AP Photo/Jae C. Hong)

didyouknow...

That the **1976** Republican National Convention, where incumbent president Gerald Ford narrowly defeated former California governor Ronald Reagan, was the last major party convention at which the party's nominee was *not* decided before the convention began?

Credentials Committee

A committee used by political parties at their national conventions to determine which delegates may participate. The committee inspects the claim of each prospective delegate to be seated as a legitimate representative of his or her state.

Elector

A member of the Electoral College, which selects the president and vice president. Each state's electors are chosen in each presidential election year according to state laws.

ON TO THE NATIONAL CONVENTION

Presidential candidates have been nominated by the convention method in every election since 1832. Extra delegates are allowed from states that had voting majorities for the party in the preceding elections. Parties also accept delegates from the District of Columbia, the territories, and certain overseas groups.

Seating the Delegates. At the convention, each political party uses a **credentials committee** to determine which delegates may participate. Controversy may arise when rival groups claim to be the official party organization. For example, the Mississippi Democratic Party split in 1964 at the height of the civil rights movement, and two sets of delegates were selected. After much debate, the credentials committee seated the mixed-race, pro–civil rights delegation and excluded those who represented the traditional "white" party.

Convention Activities. Most delegates arrive at the convention committed to a presidential candidate. No convention since 1952 has required more than one ballot to choose a nominee. Conventions normally last four days. On each night, featured speakers seek to rally the party faithful and to draw in uncommitted voters who are watching on television. On day three, the vice-presidential nominee is featured; on day four the presidential candidate gives an acceptance speech. The national networks limit their coverage to the major speeches, but several cable networks and Internet sites provide gavel-to-gavel coverage. In 2008, more than 42 million people watched Democrat Barack Obama address an audience of 85,000 in Denver's Mile High Stadium. A week later, at least 37 million people tuned into the Republican vice-presidential candidate, Alaska governor Sarah Palin. For most viewers (and for most Republican delegates), this was their first introduction to Palin, who was previously little known outside Alaska. The next night, John McCain's ratings matched or beat Obama's. At both conventions, the speakers were effective. Polls taken immediately after each convention showed substantial gains for each party.

THE ELECTORAL COLLEGE

Some people who vote for the president and vice president think that they are voting directly for a candidate. In actuality, they are voting for **electors** who will cast their ballots in the Electoral College. Article II, Section 1, of the Constitution outlines in detail the method of choosing electors for president and vice president. The framers of the Constitution wanted to avoid the selection of president and vice president by the "excitable masses." Rather, they wished the choice to be made by a few supposedly dispassionate, reasonable men (but not women).

The Choice of Electors. Each state's electors are selected during each presidential election year. The selection is governed by state laws. After the national party convention, the electors normally are pledged to the candidates chosen. Each state's number of electors equals that state's number of senators (two) plus its number of representatives. The total number of electors today is 538, equal to 100 senators, 435 members of the House, and 3 electors for the District of Columbia (the Twenty-third Amendment, ratified in 1961, added electors for the District of Columbia).

The Electors' Commitment. When a plurality of voters in a state chooses a slate of electors (except in Maine and Nebraska, where electoral votes are based on congressional districts), those electors are pledged to cast their ballots on the first Monday after the second Wednesday in December in the state capital for the presidential and vice-presidential candidates of their party. The Constitution does not, however, *require* the electors to cast their ballots for the candidates of their party.

The ballots are counted and certified before a joint session of Congress early in January. The candidates who receive a majority of the electoral votes (270) are certified as president-elect and vice president–elect. According to the Constitution, if no candidate receives a majority of the electoral votes, the election of the president is decided in the House from among the candidates with the three highest numbers of votes, with each state having one vote (decided by a plurality of each state delegation). The selection of the vice president is determined by the Senate in a choice between the two candidates with the most votes, each senator having one vote. The House was required to choose the president in 1801 (Thomas Jefferson) and again in 1825 (John Quincy Adams).[16]

It is possible for a candidate to become president without obtaining a majority of the popular vote. There have been many presidents in our history who did not win a majority of the popular vote, including Abraham Lincoln, Woodrow Wilson, Harry Truman, John F. Kennedy, Richard Nixon (in 1968), Bill Clinton, and George W. Bush (in 2000). Such an event becomes more likely when there are important third-party candidates.

Perhaps more distressing is the possibility of a candidate's being elected when an opposing candidate receives a plurality of the popular vote. This has occurred on four occasions—in the elections of John Quincy Adams in 1824, Rutherford B. Hayes in 1876, Benjamin Harrison in 1888, and George W. Bush in 2000, all of whom won elections in which an opponent received a plurality of the popular vote.

Criticisms of the Electoral College. Besides the possibility of a candidate's becoming president even though an opponent obtains more popular votes, there are other complaints about the Electoral College. The idea of the Constitution's framers was to have electors use their own discretion to decide who would make the best president. But electors no longer perform the selecting function envisioned by the founders, because they are committed to the candidate who has a plurality of popular votes in their state in the general election.[17]

One can also argue that the current system, which in most states gives all of the electoral votes to the candidate who has a statewide plurality, is unfair to other candidates and their supporters. The current system of voting also means that presidential campaigning will be concentrated in those states that have the largest number of electoral votes and in those states in which the outcome is likely to be close. The other states may receive second-class treatment during the presidential campaign. It can also be argued that there is something of a bias favoring states with smaller populations, because including Senate

The Republicans

held their convention in Minneapolis–St. Paul, Minnesota. Most delegates indicated that the speech by vice-presidential candidate Sarah Palin was the highlight of the four days.
(AP Photo/Jae C. Hong)

didyouknow...

That forty-two states do not indicate on the ballot that the voter is casting a ballot for members of the Electoral College rather than for the president and vice president directly?

---

16. For a detailed account of the process, see Michael J. Glennon, *When No Majority Rules: The Electoral College and Presidential Succession* (Washington, D.C.: Congressional Quarterly Press, 1993), p. 20.
17. Note, however, that there have been revolts by so-called *faithless electors*—in 1796, 1820, 1948, 1956, 1960, 1968, 1972, 1976, 1988, 2000, and 2004.

didyouknow...

That when President Grover Cleveland lost the election of 1888, his wife told the White House staff to change nothing because the couple would be back in four years—and she was right?

seats in the electoral vote total partly offsets the edge of the more populous states in the House. Wyoming (with two senators and one representative) gets an electoral vote for roughly every 164,594 inhabitants (based on the 2000 census), for example, whereas Iowa gets one vote for every 418,046 inhabitants, and California has one vote for every 615,848 inhabitants. Note that many of the smallest states have Republican majorities.

Proposals to Reform the Electoral College. Many proposals to reform the Electoral College system have been advanced, particularly after the turmoil following the 2000 elections, when Al Gore lost to George W. Bush in the Electoral College despite having won the national popular vote. The most obvious is to get rid of it completely and allow candidates to be elected on a popular-vote basis—in other words, have a direct election, by the people, of the president and vice president. Abolishing the Electoral College would require a constitutional amendment, however, and the likelihood of such an amendment being adopted is remote. Additionally, the major parties are not in favor of eliminating the Electoral College, fearing that it would give minor parties a more influential role. Also, less populous states are not in favor of direct election of the president because they believe they would be overwhelmed by the large-state vote.

As an alternative, the National Popular Vote movement advocates an end-run around the Electoral College by the states. This proposal, which has been endorsed by four states and is pending in others, would require each participating state to cast all of its electoral votes for the candidate who receives the most popular votes nationwide. The plan, essentially an interstate compact, will go into effect if the number of participating states grows to the point at which these states can elect a majority of the Electoral College.

Another proposal is to choose 435 of the members of the Electoral College by U.S. congressional district and 100 of the members state by state, as is done for U.S. senators. As noted earlier, Maine and Nebraska use a congressional district system today. A group of Republicans attempted to put the district system on the June 2008 California ballot, but they failed to collect enough signatures. As it happens, allocating electors proportionally by congressional district in the nation's largest Democratic-leaning state, when the largest Republican-leaning states use the winner-take-all system, would guarantee that no Democrat could be elected U.S. president without a landslide. Indeed, some political scientists have observed that if such a system were used everywhere, it would still introduce a Republican bias into the Electoral College. One of the merits of the Electoral College is that it has no particular partisan bias—although it is certainly capable of delivering a result that does not match the national popular vote.

HOW ARE ELECTIONS CONDUCTED?

The United States uses the **Australian ballot**—a secret ballot that is prepared, distributed, and counted by government officials at public expense. Since 1888, all states have used the Australian ballot. Before that, many states used the alternatives of oral voting and differently colored ballots prepared by the parties. Obviously, knowing which way a person was voting made it easy to apply pressure on the person to change his or her vote, and vote buying was common.

OFFICE-BLOCK AND PARTY-COLUMN BALLOTS

Two types of Australian ballots are used in the United States in general elections. The first, called an **office-block ballot,** or sometimes a **Massachusetts ballot,** groups all the candidates for a particular elective office under the title of that office. Parties dislike the office-block ballot because it places more emphasis on the office than on the party; it discourages straight-ticket voting and encourages split-ticket voting.

A **party-column ballot** is a form of general election ballot in which all of a party's candidates are arranged in one column under the party's label and symbol. It is also called

Australian Ballot
A secret ballot prepared, distributed, and tabulated by government officials at public expense. Since 1888, all states have used the Australian ballot rather than an open, public ballot.

Office-Block, or Massachusetts, Ballot
A form of general election ballot in which candidates for elective office are grouped together under the title of each office. It emphasizes voting for the office and the individual candidate, rather than for the party.

Party-Column, or Indiana, Ballot
A form of general election ballot in which all of a party's candidates for elective office are arranged in one column under the party's label and symbol. It emphasizes voting for the party, rather than for the office or individual.

the **Indiana ballot.** In some states, it allows voters to vote for all of a party's candidates for local, state, and national offices by simply marking a single "X" or by pulling a single lever. Most states use this type of ballot. Because it encourages straight-ticket voting, the two major parties favor this form. When a party has an exceptionally strong presidential or gubernatorial candidate to head the ticket, the use of the party-column ballot increases the **coattail effect** (the influence of a popular candidate on the success of other candidates on the same party ticket).

VOTING BY MAIL

Although voting by mail has been accepted for absentee ballots for many decades (for example, for individuals who are doing business away from home or for members of the armed forces), recently several states have offered mail ballots to all of their voters. The rationale for using the mail ballot is to make voting easier for the voters. Oregon has gone one step further: since 1998, that state has employed postal ballots exclusively, and there are no polling places. (Voters who do not prepare their ballot in time for the U.S. Postal Service to deliver it can drop off their ballots at drop boxes on Election Day.) In addition, most counties in Washington State now use mail ballots exclusively. Supporters of the system contend that it has enhanced voter participation, but Oregon's turnout figure in the 2008 elections was only 66 percent, not much above the national average.

didyouknow...

That in August 2000, six people offered to sell their votes for president on eBay, the online auction site (eBay quickly canceled the bidding)?

VOTING FRAUD AND MISTAKES

Voting fraud is something regularly suspected but seldom proved. Voting in the 1800s, when secret ballots were rare and people had a cavalier attitude toward the open buying of votes, was probably much more conducive to fraud than modern elections are.

The Danger of Fraud. Some observers claim that the potential for voting fraud is high in many states, particularly through the use of phony voter registrations and absentee ballots. In California, for example, it is very difficult to remove a name from the polling list even if the person has not cast a ballot in the last two years. Thus, many persons are still on the rolls even though they no longer live in California. Enterprising political activists could use these names for absentee ballots. Other states have registration laws that are meant to encourage easy registration and voting. Such laws can be taken advantage of by those who seek to vote more than once.

After the 2000 elections, political scientist Larry Sabato emphasized the problem of voting fraud. "It's a silent scandal," said Sabato, "and the problem is getting worse with increases in absentee voting, which is the easiest way to commit fraud." Investigators in Milwaukee, Wisconsin, found that in the state's ultra-close 2004 presidential elections, more than two hundred felons voted illegally and more than one hundred people voted twice.[18]

Because voting fraud is always suspected, but difficult to prove, the Connecticut secretary of state developed a chart in an attempt to prove that no dead people were "voting" in elections in that state. How might dead people "vote"? (AP Photo/Bob Child)

Mistakes by Voting Officials. Some observers claim, however, that errors leading to fraud are trivial in number and that a few mistakes are inevitable in a system involving millions of voters. These people argue that an excessive concern with voting fraud makes it harder for minorities and poor people to vote.

For example, in 2000, Katherine Harris, Florida's top election official, oversaw a purge of the voter rolls while simultaneously serving as co-chair of the Florida Bush campaign. According to the *New York Times,* when attempting to remove the names of convicted felons from the list of voters:

VOTERS VERIFIED AS DECEASED

□ "Other" Means
■ Death Certificates

63% Verified through town documents, i.e. death certificates.
37% Verified through "other" resources, i.e. newspaper obits, probate records, internet resources, etc.

Current as of 3:00 p.m. Tuesday May 13, 2008

---

18. John Fund, "Voter-Fraud Showdown," *The Wall Street Journal,* January 9, 2008, p. A15.

> *Ms. Harris's office overruled the advice of the private firm that compiled the felon list and called for removing not just names that were an exact match, but ones that were highly inexact. Thousands of Florida voters wound up being wrongly purged . . . . In Missouri, elected officials charged for years that large numbers of St. Louis residents were casting votes from vacant lots. A study conducted by The [St. Louis] Post Dispatch in 2001 found that in the vast majority of cases, the voters lived in homes that had been wrongly classified by the city.*[19]

In both the Florida and Missouri examples, a majority of the affected voters were African American.

Voter ID Requirements. In recent years, many states have adopted laws requiring enhanced proof of identity before voters can cast their ballots. Indiana imposed the nation's toughest voter identification (ID) law in 2005, which was challenged in a case that reached the United States Supreme Court. In 2008, the Court upheld the Indiana voter ID law.[20] When legislators propose voter identification laws, are they truly motivated by a desire to prevent voting fraud—or are they really trying to suppress voter turnout among the groups least likely to possess adequate identification? We address that question in the *Which Side Are You On?* feature on the facing page.

These poll workers in Columbus, Ohio, gathered and recorded identification information presented by voters. What are the benefits of such a time-consuming process? Should all states require the presentation of a photo ID as a requirement for voting? (Jim Wilson/*The New York Times*/Redux Pictures)

Reforming the Voting Process. Getting an accurate vote count was crucial in the close 2000 presidential elections. Yet problems with outdated or malfunctioning voting equipment, along with questionable practices at some polling places, meant that not everyone's vote counted—and that some voters were barred from the polls. In response to these problems, Congress enacted the Help America Vote Act (HAVA) of 2002. The act provided funds to the states to help them implement a number of reforms. Among other things, the states were asked to replace outdated voting equipment with newer electronic voting systems, to create statewide computerized voter lists, to issue provisional ballots to voters in certain circumstances, and to increase access to the polling places for voters with disabilities.

Critics of HAVA point out that by urging the adoption of electronic voting equipment, the act may have traded old problems for newer, more complicated ones. This became particularly apparent during the 2006 midterm elections. Although, by and large, the elections went smoothly, more than twenty-five states reported problems at the polls on Election Day. Many of these problems involved failures in the new voting machines. According to election officials, some 20,000 people in Colorado gave up trying to vote after new online systems for verifying voter registrations crashed repeatedly. In Pennsylvania, electronic voting machinery refused to start or crashed, and vote-flipping (pressing one candidate's name but having another candidate's name appear on the computer screen) was a recurrent problem. In one Florida county, it was estimated that nearly 18,000 votes may have gone unrecorded by electronic voting machines, thus changing the outcome of a congressional election.[21]

---

19. "How America Doesn't Vote," *The New York Times: The News of the Week in Review,* February 15, 2004, p. 10.
20. *Crawford v. Marion County Election Board,* 128 S.Ct. 1610 (2008).
21. For a more detailed account of these and other problems encountered by voters during the 2006 elections, see Ian Urbina and Christopher Drew, "Experts Concerned as Ballot Problems Persist," *The New York Times,* November 26, 2006.

whichsideareYOUon?

ARE STIFF VOTER ID LAWS A GOOD THING?

In May 2008, immediately before the Indiana presidential primary, the United States Supreme Court ruled that Indiana's law requiring voters to show a photo identification (ID) card at the polls was constitutional. The Supreme Court ruling will surely encourage many of the twenty other states that are considering such a law. Note that almost all states require every voter to show some type of identification, such as proof of name, residence, and age, when they register to vote. The Indiana law, however, requires proof in the form of a government-issued photographic ID card at every election. Proponents of more stringent voter ID requirements argue that stricter laws would prevent voter fraud. Opponents claim that such stricter requirements reduce the turnout of eligible voters.

PHOTO IDS FOR VOTING ARE UNNECESSARY

Opponents of photo ID requirements for voters contend that claims of voter fraud, particularly voter fraud by noncitizens, are a myth. After all, illegal immigrants attempt to "remain in the shadows." They are not going to walk into a polling place to try to cast a ballot.

Indiana's photo ID law does not allow the use of private college photo IDs, utility bills, or other commonly used forms of identification. Only an Indiana driver's license, state-issued ID, U.S. passport, military ID, or photo ID from an Indiana state university is acceptable. U.S. passports currently cost $100, and an Indiana driver's license or state-issued ID requires a birth certificate plus an actual Social Security card (not just a number). If you do not already have such documentation, obtaining it is time-consuming and can also be expensive.

People without photo IDs are disproportionately poor and from minority groups, and they may lack the funds and time needed to secure acceptable documentation. Opponents of stiff voter photo ID laws therefore believe that these laws are simply a partisan scam perpetrated by Republicans to drive down voter turnout among groups that are likely to vote Democratic.

WHAT'S THE PROBLEM WITH VOTER PHOTO IDS, ANYWAY?

Today, if you don't have a government-issued photo ID, you cannot get on a commercial airplane, enter a federal court building, or at most institutions, cash a check. So what is the big deal about requiring the same type of ID to vote? A state study in Indiana found that 99 percent of the voting-age population already had the necessary photo IDs.

That state provides a photo ID for free to anyone who can prove his or her identity. In a recent mayoral election in Indianapolis, only 34 voters out of 165,000 did not have the proper ID. They were allowed to cast a provisional ballot. All they had to do was come back to the clerk's office within ten days to show a photo ID or to sign an affidavit. Since Indiana's voter photo ID law was passed, there has been no evidence that voter participation rates have declined in counties with poor or minority voters.

Not too many years ago, a grand jury in Brooklyn, New York, detailed a massive fourteen-year voter conspiracy in which groups of individuals were recruited to vote in the names of fraudulently registered and dead voters. Without a photo ID requirement, in-person voter fraud is extremely difficult to detect or investigate.

Because of problems with electronic voting machinery, Florida has decided to go back to the paper ballot, and some other states are considering doing likewise. Additionally, new legislation introduced into Congress is also calling for a "paper trail" that can be used to accurately verify the vote count.

TURNING OUT TO VOTE

In 2008, the number of Americans eligible to vote was about 213 million people. Of that number, about 130.8 million, or 61.4 percent of the eligible population, actually cast a ballot. When voter turnout is this low, it means, among other things, that the winner of a close presidential election may be voted in by less than a third of those eligible to vote (see Table 9–3 on the following page).

TABLE 9–3: Elected by a Majority?

Most presidents have won a majority of the votes cast in their election. We generally judge the extent of their victory by whether they have won more than 51 percent of the votes. Some presidential elections have been proclaimed *landslides*, meaning that the candidates won by an extraordinary majority of votes cast. As indicated below, however, no modern president has been elected by more than 38 percent of the population eligible to vote. The best showing was by Johnson in 1964.

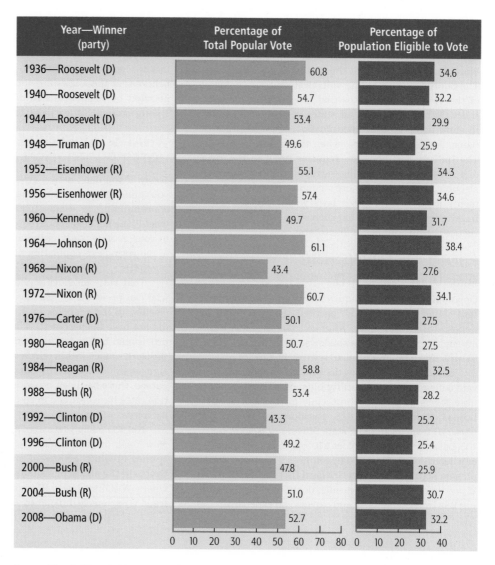

Year—Winner (party)	Percentage of Total Popular Vote	Percentage of Population Eligible to Vote
1936—Roosevelt (D)	60.8	34.6
1940—Roosevelt (D)	54.7	32.2
1944—Roosevelt (D)	53.4	29.9
1948—Truman (D)	49.6	25.9
1952—Eisenhower (R)	55.1	34.3
1956—Eisenhower (R)	57.4	34.6
1960—Kennedy (D)	49.7	31.7
1964—Johnson (D)	61.1	38.4
1968—Nixon (R)	43.4	27.6
1972—Nixon (R)	60.7	34.1
1976—Carter (D)	50.1	27.5
1980—Reagan (R)	50.7	27.5
1984—Reagan (R)	58.8	32.5
1988—Bush (R)	53.4	28.2
1992—Clinton (D)	43.3	25.2
1996—Clinton (D)	49.2	25.4
2000—Bush (R)	47.8	25.9
2004—Bush (R)	51.0	30.7
2008—Obama (D)	52.7	32.2

Sources: Historical Data Archive, Inter-university Consortium for Political and Social Research; Michael P. McDonald and Samuel L. Popkin, "The Myth of the Vanishing Voter," *American Political Science Review*, Vol. 95, No. 4 (December 2001), p. 966; and the United States Elections Project.

Figure 9–2 shows **voter turnout** for presidential and congressional elections from 1908 to 2008. Each of the peaks in the figure represents voter turnout in a presidential election. Thus, we can also see that turnout for congressional elections is influenced greatly by whether there is a presidential election in the same year. Whereas voter turnout during the presidential elections of 2008 was 61.4 percent, it was only 40.3 percent in the midterm elections of 2006.

The same is true at the state level. When there is a race for governor, more voters participate both in the general election for governor and in the election for state representatives. Voter participation rates in gubernatorial elections are also greater in presidential election years. The average turnout in state elections is about 14 percentage points higher when a presidential election is held.

Voter Turnout
The percentage of citizens taking part in the election process; the number of eligible voters that actually "turn out" on election day to cast their ballots.

FIGURE 9–2: Voter Turnout for Presidential and Congressional Elections, 1908–2008

The peaks represent voter turnout in presidential-election years; the troughs represent voter turnout in off-presidential-election years.

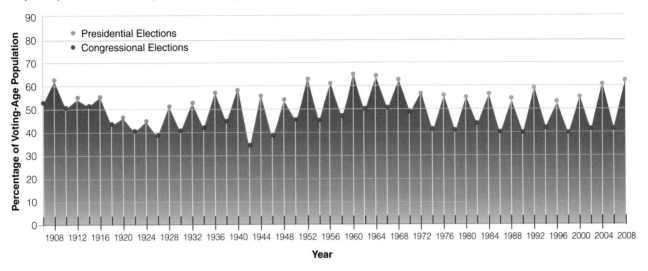

Note: Prior to 1948, the voting-age population is used as a proxy for the population eligible to vote.

Sources: Historical Data Archive, Inter-university Consortium for Political and Social Research; Michael P. McDonald and Samuel L. Popkin, "The Myth of the Vanishing Voter," *American Political Science Review,* Vol. 95, No. 4 (December 2001), p. 966; and the United States Elections Project.

Now consider local elections. In races for mayor, city council, county auditor, and the like, it is fairly common for only 25 percent or less of the electorate to vote. Is something amiss here? It would seem that people should be more likely to vote in elections that directly affect them. At the local level, each person's vote counts more (because there are fewer voters). Furthermore, the issues—crime control, school bonds, sewer bonds, and the like—touch the immediate interests of the voters. In reality, however, potential voters are most interested in national elections when a presidential choice is involved. Otherwise, voter participation in our representative government is very low (and, as we have seen, it is not overwhelmingly great even in presidential elections).

THE EFFECT OF LOW VOTER TURNOUT

There are two schools of thought concerning low voter turnout. Some view low voter participation as a threat to representative democratic government. Too few individuals are deciding who wields political power in society. In addition, low voter participation presumably signals apathy about the political system in general. It also may signal that potential voters simply do not want to take the time to learn about the issues.

Others are less concerned about low voter participation. They contend that low voter participation simply indicates more satisfaction with the status quo. Also, they believe that representative democracy is a reality even if a very small percentage of eligible voters vote. If everyone who does not vote thinks that the outcome of the election will accord with his or her own desires, then representative democracy is working. The nonvoters are obtaining the type of government—with the type of people running it—that they want to have anyway.

IS VOTER TURNOUT DECLINING?

During many recent elections, the media have voiced concern that voter turnout is declining. Indeed, Figure 9–2 shows relatively low voter turnout from 1972 through 2002—though turnout has gone back up in the last few elections. Pundits have blamed the low turnout on negative campaigning and broad public cynicism about the political process. But is voter turnout actually as low as it seems?

didyouknow...

That computer software now exists that can identify likely voters and likely campaign donors by town, neighborhood, and street?

One problem with widely used measurements of voter turnout is that they compare the number of people who actually vote with the voting-age population, not the population of *eligible voters*. These figures are not the same. The figure for the voting-age population includes felons and former felons who have lost the right to vote. Above all, it includes new immigrants who are not yet citizens. Finally, it does not include Americans living abroad, who can cast absentee ballots.

In 2008, the measured voting-age population included 3.4 million ineligible felons and former felons, and an estimated 19.9 million noncitizens. It did not include 5.0 million Americans abroad. The voting-age population in 2008 was 231.2 million people. The number of eligible voters, however, was only 213.0 million. Using the voting-age population to calculate national turnout would reduce the turnout percentage from 61.4 to 56.4.

As you learned in Chapter 5, the United States has experienced high rates of immigration in recent decades. Political scientists Michael McDonald and Samuel Popkin concluded that the very low voter turnout reported in many sources after 1972 was a function of the increasing size of the ineligible population, chiefly due to immigration.[22]

FACTORS INFLUENCING WHO VOTES

A clear association exists between voter participation and the following characteristics: age, educational attainment, minority status, income level, and the existence of two-party competition.

1. *Age.* Look at Table 9–4, which shows the breakdown of voter participation by age group for the 2006 congressional elections. It would appear from these figures that age is a strong factor in determining voter turnout on Election Day. The reported turnout increases with older age groups. Older voters are more settled in their lives, are already registered, and have had more time to experience voting as an expected activity.

2. *Educational attainment.* Education also influences voter turnout. In general, the more education you have, the more likely you are to vote. This pattern is clearly evident in the 2006 election results, as you can see in Table 9–5.

3. *Minority status.* Race and ethnicity are important, too, in determining the level of voter turnout. Non-Hispanic whites in 2006 voted at a 51.6 percent rate, whereas the non-Hispanic African American turnout rate was 41.0 percent. For Hispanics, the turnout rate was 32.3 percent, and for Asian Americans the rate was 32.4 percent. Of course, all reports suggest that in 2008 the black turnout rate took an enormous leap because an African American was running for president.

4. *Income level.* Differences in income also correlate with differences in voter turnout. Wealthier people tend to be overrepresented among voters who turn out on Election Day. In recent presidential elections, voter turnout for those with the highest annual family incomes has approached three times the turnout of those with the lowest annual family incomes.

5. *Two-party competition.* Another factor in voter turnout is the extent to which elections are competitive within a state. More competitive states generally have higher turnout rates, and turnout increases considerably in states where there is an extremely competitive race in a particular year.

TABLE 9–4: Voting in the 2006 Congressional Elections by Age Group

Turnout is given as a percentage of the voting-age citizen population.

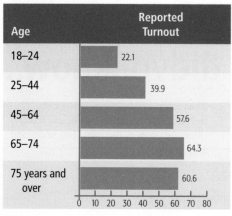

Age	Reported Turnout
18–24	22.1
25–44	39.9
45–64	57.6
65–74	64.3
75 years and over	60.6

Source: U.S. Bureau of the Census, July 1, 2008.

22. Michael P. McDonald and Samuel L. Popkin, "The Myth of the Vanishing Voter," *American Political Science Review,* Vol. 95, No. 4 (December 2001), p. 963.

These statistics reinforce one another. White voters are likely to be wealthier than African American voters, who are also less likely to have obtained a college education.

WHY PEOPLE DO NOT VOTE

For many years, political scientists believed that one reason voter turnout in the United States was so much lower than in other Western nations was that it was very difficult to register to vote. In most states, registration required a special trip to a public office far in advance of elections. During the last decade or so, however, laws have simplified the voter-registration process to a significant degree. Thus, many experts are now proposing other explanations for low U.S. voter turnout.

Uninformative Media Coverage and Negative Campaigning. Several scholars contend that one of the reasons why some people do not vote has to do with media coverage of campaigns. Many researchers have shown that the news media tend to provide much more news about "the horse race," or which candidates are ahead in the polls, than about the actual policy positions of the candidates. According to a 2006 study of voting behavior conducted by the Pew Research Center, lack of information about the candidates was cited by 68 percent of nonvoters as one of their reasons for not voting.[23]

TABLE 9–5: Voting in the 2006 Congressional Elections by Education Level

Turnout is given as a percentage of the voting-age citizen population.

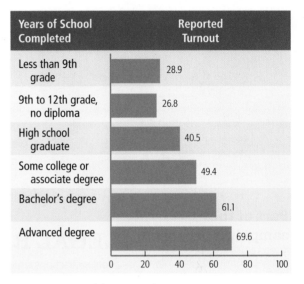

Years of School Completed	Reported Turnout
Less than 9th grade	28.9
9th to 12th grade, no diploma	26.8
High school graduate	40.5
Some college or associate degree	49.4
Bachelor's degree	61.1
Advanced degree	69.6

Source: U.S. Bureau of the Census, July 1, 2008.

Additionally, voters who are asked how a negative ad affects them typically respond that it makes them less likely to vote. Many commentators have concluded, therefore, that the epidemic of negative ads in recent years has depressed turnout. Studies of actual elections, however, suggest that voters subjected to barrages of negative ads vote in *greater* numbers. Political scientist Paul Martin of the University of Virginia contends that seeing negative ads makes people think that there are "more problems facing the country, which encourages people to vote." Stanford University professor Jon Krosnick notes that "turnout goes up when people don't just prefer their candidate, but strongly dislike the other guy."[24]

The Rational Ignorance Effect. Another explanation of low voter turnout suggests that citizens are making a logical choice in not voting. If citizens believe that their votes will not affect the outcome of an election, then they have little incentive to seek the information they need to cast intelligent votes. The lack of incentive to obtain costly (in terms of time, attention, and so on) information about politicians and political issues has been called the **rational ignorance effect.** That term may seem contradictory, but it is not. Rational ignorance is a condition in which people purposely and rationally decide not to obtain information—to remain ignorant.

Why, then, do even one-third to one-half of U.S. citizens bother to show up at the polls? One explanation is that most citizens receive personal satisfaction from the act of voting. It makes them feel that they are fulfilling their duty as citizens and that they are doing something patriotic.[25] Even among voters who are registered and who plan to vote, however, if the cost of voting goes up (in terms of time and inconvenience), the number of voters who actually vote will fall. In particular, bad weather on Election Day means that, on average, a smaller percentage of registered voters will go to the polls.

Rational Ignorance Effect
An effect produced when people purposely and rationally decide not to become informed on an issue because they believe that their vote on the issue is not likely to be a deciding one; a lack of incentive to seek the necessary information to cast an intelligent vote.

23. Pew Research Center for the People and the Press, survey conducted September 21–October 4, 2006, and reported in "Who Votes, Who Doesn't, and Why," released October 28, 2006.
24. Sharon Begley, "Political Scientists Get More Scientific in Studying the Vote," *The Wall Street Journal,* August 18, 2006, p. A11.
25. According to the Pew Research Center study cited in footnote 23, 88 percent of regular voters felt that they had a duty as citizens to always vote, whereas only 39 percent of nonvoters felt that they owed such a duty.

Plans for Improving Voter Turnout. Mail-in voting, Internet voting, registering to vote when you apply for a driver's license, registering to vote on Election Day in all states—these are all ideas that have been either suggested or implemented in the hope of improving voter turnout. Nonetheless, voter turnout remains low.

Two other ideas seemed promising. The first was to allow voters to visit the polls up to three weeks before Election Day. The second was to allow voters to vote by absentee ballot without having to give any particular reason for doing so. In the 2008 general elections, both of these plans were implemented by many states. The 2008 experience and a previous study by Committee for the Study of the American Electorate suggest, however, that states with early voting or unrestricted absentee voting have no better turnout rates than states that require most people to show up at the polls. Apparently, these strategies appeal mostly to people who already intend to vote.

What is left? One possibility is to declare Election Day a national holiday. In this way, more eligible voters will find it easier to go to the polls.

Part of the campaign process
for any candidate is to meet supporters, including children and babies. Why do candidates attempt to connect with "real" people? Do you think such campaigning truly affects the outcome of elections? (AP Photo/Charles Rex Arbogast)

LEGAL RESTRICTIONS ON VOTING

Legal restrictions on voter registration have existed since the founding of our nation. Most groups in the United States have been concerned with the suffrage issue at one time or another.

HISTORICAL RESTRICTIONS

In colonial times, only white males who owned property with a certain minimum value were eligible to vote, leaving a greater number of Americans ineligible than eligible to take part in the democratic process.

Property Requirements. Many government functions concern property rights and the distribution of income and wealth, and some of the founders of our nation believed it was appropriate that only people who had an interest in property should vote on these issues. The idea of extending the vote to all citizens was, according to Charles Pinckney, a South Carolina delegate to the Constitutional Convention, merely "theoretical nonsense."

The logic behind the restriction of voting rights to property owners was questioned seriously by Thomas Paine in his pamphlet *Common Sense*:

> *Here is a man who today owns a jackass, and the jackass is worth $60. Today the man is a voter and goes to the polls and deposits his vote. Tomorrow the jackass dies. The next day the man comes to vote without his jackass and cannot vote at all. Now tell me, which was the voter, the man or the jackass?*[26]

The writers of the Constitution allowed the states to decide who should vote. Thus, women were allowed to vote in Wyoming in 1870 but not in the entire nation until the Nineteenth Amendment was ratified in 1920. By about 1850, most white adult males in virtually all the states could vote without any property qualification. North Carolina was the last state to eliminate its property test for voting—in 1856.

Further Extensions of the Franchise. Extension of the franchise to black males occurred with the passage of the Fifteenth Amendment in 1870. This enfranchisement was short lived, however, as the "redemption" of the South by white racists had rolled back those gains by the end of the century. As discussed in Chapter 5, it was not until the 1960s that African Americans, both male and female, were able to participate in the elec-

---

26. Thomas Paine, *Common Sense* (London: H. D. Symonds, 1792), p. 28.

toral process in all states. Women received full national voting rights with the Nineteenth Amendment in 1920. The most recent extension of the franchise occurred when the voting age was reduced to eighteen by the Twenty-sixth Amendment in 1971. In the years since the amendment was passed, however, young people have traditionally had a low turnout.

Is the Franchise Still Too Restrictive? There continue to be certain classes of people who do not have the right to vote. These include noncitizens and, in most states, convicted felons who have been released from prison. They also include current prison inmates, election law violators, and people who are mentally incompetent. Also, no one under the age of eighteen can vote. A number of political activists have argued that some of these groups should be allowed to vote. Most other democracies do not prevent convicts from voting after they have completed their sentences. In the 1800s, many states let noncitizen immigrants vote.

One discussion concerns the voting rights of convicted felons who are no longer in prison or on parole. Those who oppose letting these people vote contend that voting should be a privilege, not a right, and we should not want the types of people who commit felonies participating in decision making. Others believe that it is wrong to further penalize those who have paid their debt to society. These people argue that barring felons from the polls injures minority groups, because minorities make up a disproportionately large share of former prison inmates.

CURRENT ELIGIBILITY AND REGISTRATION REQUIREMENTS

Voting generally requires **registration,** and to register, a person must satisfy the following voter qualifications, or legal requirements: (1) citizenship, (2) age (eighteen or older), and (3) residency—the duration varies widely from state to state and with types of elections. Since 1972, states cannot impose residency requirements of more than thirty days.

Each state has different qualifications for voting and registration. In 1993, Congress passed the "motor voter" bill, which requires that states provide voter-registration materials when people receive or renew driver's licenses, that all states allow voters to register by mail, and that voter-registration forms be made available at a wider variety of public places and agencies. In general, a person must register well in advance of an election, although voters in Idaho, Maine, Minnesota, Wisconsin, and Wyoming are allowed to register up to, or even on, Election Day. North Dakota has no voter registration at all.

Some argue that registration requirements are responsible for much of the nonparticipation in our political process. Certainly, since their introduction in the late 1800s, registration laws have had the effect of reducing the voting participation of African Americans and immigrants. There also is a partisan dimension to the debate over registration and nonvoting. Republicans generally fear that an expanded electorate would help to elect more Democrats—because more Democrats than Republicans are not registered voters.[27]

The question arises as to whether registration is really necessary. If it decreases participation in the political process, perhaps it should be dropped altogether. Still, as those in favor of registration requirements argue, such requirements may prevent fraudulent voting practices, such as multiple voting or voting by noncitizens.

EXTENSION OF THE VOTING RIGHTS ACT

In the summer of 2006, President Bush signed legislation that extended the Voting Rights Act of 1965 for twenty-five more years. As we discussed in Chapter 5, the Voting Rights Act was enacted to assure that African Americans had equal access to the polls. Any new

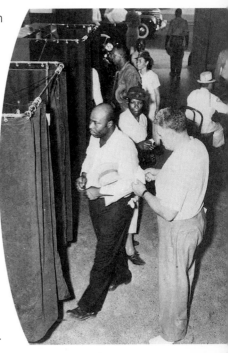

These African American voters are shown in New York City in the mid-1940s. Until the 1965 Voting Rights Act, African Americans and other minorities faced numerous obstacles when trying to exercise their right to vote, especially in the South. If a significant part of the population is not allowed to vote, what effect is that likely to have on the types of legislation passed by Congress or by state legislatures? (Library of Congress/ NAACP Collection)

Registration
The entry of a person's name onto the list of registered voters for elections. To register, a person must meet certain legal requirements of age, citizenship, and residency.

---

27. According to the 2006 Pew study of voting behavior cited earlier in footnote 23, of the approximately one-fifth of the U.S. voting-age population who are not registered to vote, 20 percent are Democrats and 14 percent are Republicans.

voting practices or procedures in jurisdictions with a history of discrimination in voting have to be approved by the U.S. Department of Justice or the federal district court in Washington, D.C., before being implemented. Section 203 of the 2006 act ensures that American citizens with limited proficiency in English can obtain the necessary assistance to enable them to understand and cast a ballot. Further, the act authorizes the U.S. attorney general to appoint federal election observers when there is evidence of attempts to intimidate minority voters at the polls.

THE MEDIA AND POLITICS

The study of people and politics must take into account the role played by the media. Historically, the print media played the most important role in informing public debate. The print media developed, for the most part, our understanding of how news is to be reported. Today, however, more than 90 percent of Americans use television news as their primary source of information. In addition, the Internet has become a source for political communication and fundraising. As Internet use grows, the system of gathering and sharing news and information is changing from one in which the media have a primary role to one in which the individual citizen may play a greater part. With that in mind, it is important to analyze the current relationship between the media and politics.

The mass media perform a number of different functions in any country. In the United States, we can list at least six. Almost all of them can have political implications, and some are essential to the democratic process. These functions are as follows: (1) entertainment, (2) reporting the news, (3) identifying public problems, (4) socializing new generations, (5) providing a political forum, and (6) making profits.

ENTERTAINMENT

By far the greatest number of radio and television hours are dedicated to entertaining the public. The battle for prime-time ratings indicates how important successful entertainment is to the survival of networks and individual stations.

Although there is no direct linkage between entertainment and politics, network dramas often introduce material that may be politically controversial and that may stimulate public discussion. Examples include the TV series *The West Wing* and *Commander in Chief,* which people believe promoted liberal political values. Made-for-TV movies have focused on a number of controversial topics, including AIDS, incest, and wife battering.

REPORTING THE NEWS

A primary function of the mass media in all their forms—newspapers and magazines, radio, television, cable, and online news services—is the reporting of news. The media provide words and pictures about events, facts, personalities, and ideas. The protections of the First Amendment are intended to keep the flow of news as free as possible, because it is an essential part of the democratic process. If citizens cannot obtain unbiased information about the state of their communities and their leaders' actions, how can they make voting decisions? One of the most incisive comments about the importance of the media was made by James Madison, who said, "A people who mean to be their own governors must arm themselves with the power knowledge gives. A popular government without popular information or the means of acquiring it, is but a prologue to a farce or a tragedy or perhaps both."[28]

Many high-profile entertainers, such as actress America Ferrera, engage in charitable appearances to encourage voter registration. What might be the motivation for well-known entertainers to become part of this country's political process? (Photo by Gilbert Carrasquillo/FilmMagic/ Getty Images)

---

28. James Madison, "Letter to W. T. Barry" (August 4, 1822), in Gaillard P. Hunt, ed., *The Writings of James Madison,* Vol. 103 (1910).

IDENTIFYING PUBLIC PROBLEMS

The power of the media is important not only in revealing what the government is doing but also in determining what the government ought to do—in other words, in setting the **public agenda.** The mass media identify public issues, such as convicted sex offenders living in residential neighborhoods on their release from prison. The media then influence the passage of legislation, such as "Megan's Law," which requires police to notify neighbors about the release and/or resettlement of certain offenders. American journalists also work in a long tradition of uncovering public wrongdoing, corruption, and bribery and of bringing such wrongdoing to the public's attention. Closely related to this investigative function is that of presenting policy alternatives.

Public policy is often complex and difficult to make entertaining, but programs devoted to public policy are often scheduled for prime-time television, especially on cable networks. Network shows with a "news magazine" format sometimes include segments on policy issues as well.

SOCIALIZING NEW GENERATIONS

As mentioned in Chapter 6, the media, and particularly television, strongly influence the beliefs and opinions of Americans. Because of this influence, the media play a significant role in the political socialization of the younger generation, as well as immigrants to this country. Through the transmission of historical information (sometimes fictionalized), the presentation of American culture, and the portrayal of the diverse regions and groups in the United States, the media teach young people and immigrants about what it means to be an American. TV talk shows, such as the *Oprah Winfrey Show,* sometimes focus on controversial issues (such as abortion or assisted suicide). Many children's shows are designed not only to entertain young viewers but also to instruct them in the traditional moral values of American society.

As more young Americans turn to the Internet for entertainment, they are also finding an increasing amount of social and political information there. America's youth today are the Internet generation. Young people do not use the Internet just for chat and e-mail. They also participate in political forums, obtain information for writing assignments, and increasingly watch movies and news shows online.

Prior to the January 2008 presidential primary in New Hampshire, Senator John McCain attempted to obtain supporters in a diner in a small town in that state. Why did all of the candidates feel that they had to stop in small eating establishments in New Hampshire before the primary election? (AP Photo/Mary Schwalm)

Public Agenda
Issues that are perceived by the political community as meriting public attention and governmental action.

During the presidential primary campaign season, Oprah Winfrey not only endorsed Barack Obama but also made campaign stops with him and with his wife, Michelle, shown here on the left. How important are endorsements from high-profile TV personalities for the eventual success of a presidential candidate? (Photo by Scott Olson/Getty Images)

PROVIDING A POLITICAL FORUM

As part of their news function, the media also provide a political forum for leaders and the public. Candidates for office use news reporting to sustain interest in their campaigns, while officeholders use the media to gain support for their policies or to present an image of leadership. Presidential trips abroad are an outstanding way for the chief executive to get colorful, positive, and exciting news coverage that makes the president look "presidential." The media also offer ways for citizens to participate in public debate, through letters to the editor, televised editorials, or electronic communications.

MAKING PROFITS

Most of the news media in the United States are private, for-profit corporate enterprises. One of their goals is to make profits for expansion and for dividends to the stockholders who own the companies. In general, profits are made as a result of charging for advertising. Advertising revenues usually are related directly to circulation or to listener/viewer ratings.

For the most part, the media depend on advertisers to obtain revenues to make profits. Media outlets that do not succeed in generating sufficient revenues from advertising either go bankrupt or are sold. Consequently, reporters may feel pressure from media owners and from advertisers. Media owners may take their cues from what advertisers want. If an important advertiser does not like the political bent of a particular reporter, the reporter could be asked to alter his or her "style" of writing. The Project for Excellence in Journalism discovered that 53 percent of local news directors said that advertisers try to tell them what to air and what not to air.[29]

Advertisers have been known to pull ads from newspapers and TV stations whenever they read or view negative publicity about their own companies or products. For example, CBS ran a *60 Minutes* show about Dillard's and other department stores that claimed store security guards used excessive force and racial profiling. In response, Dillard's pulled its ads from CBS. This example can be multiplied many times over.

Several well-known media outlets, in contrast, are publicly owned—public television stations in many communities and National Public Radio. These operate without extensive commercials, are locally supported, and are often subsidized by the government and corporations. A complex relationship exists among the for-profit and nonprofit media, the government, and the public. Throughout the rest of this chapter, we examine some of the many facets of this relationship.

didyouknow...

That the number of people watching the television networks during prime time has declined by almost 25 percent in the last ten years?

THE PRIMACY OF TELEVISION

Television is the most influential medium. It is also big business. National news TV personalities such as Katie Couric and Brian Williams may earn millions of dollars per year from their TV contracts alone. They are paid so much because they command large audiences, and large audiences command high prices for advertising on national news shows. Indeed, news *per se* has become a major factor in the profitability of TV stations.

THE INCREASE IN NEWS-TYPE PROGRAMMING

In 1963, the major networks—ABC, CBS, and NBC—devoted only eleven minutes daily to national news. A twenty-four-hour-a-day news cable channel—CNN—started operating in 1980. With the addition of CNN–Headline News, CNBC, MSNBC, Fox News, and other news-format cable channels since the 1980s, the amount of news-type programming has continued to increase. By 2009, the amount of time the networks devoted to news-type

---

29. Project for Excellence in Journalism, "Gambling with the Future," *Columbia Journalism Review,* November/December 2001.

programming each day had increased to about three hours. In recent years, all of the major networks have also added Internet sites to try to capture that market, but they face thousands of competitors on the Web.

TELEVISION'S INFLUENCE ON THE POLITICAL PROCESS

Television's influence on the political process today is recognized by all who engage in that process. Television news is often criticized for being superficial, particularly compared with the detailed coverage available in newspapers and magazines. In fact, television news is constrained by its technical characteristics, the most important being the limitations of time—stories must be reported in only a few minutes.

"Welcome to 'All About the Media,' where members of the media discuss the role of the media in media coverage of the media."

The Impact of Video. The most interesting aspect of television is, of course, the fact that it relies on pictures rather than words to attract the viewer's attention. Therefore, the video chosen for a particular political story has exaggerated importance. Viewers do not know what other photos may have been taken or what other events may have been recorded—they see only those appearing on their screens. Television news can also be exploited for its drama by well-constructed stories. Some critics suggest that there is pressure to produce television news that has a "story line," like a novel or movie. The story should be short, with exciting pictures and a clear plot. In the extreme case, the news media are satisfied with a **sound bite,** a several-second comment selected or crafted for its immediate impact on the viewer.

It has been suggested that these formatting characteristics—or necessities—of television increase its influence on political events. (Newspapers and news magazines are also limited by their formats, but to a lesser extent.) As you are aware, real life is usually not dramatic, nor do all events have a neat or an easily understood plot. Political campaigns are continuing events, lasting perhaps as long as two years. The significance of their daily turns and twists is only apparent later. The "drama" of Congress, with its 535 players and dozens of important committees and meetings, is also difficult for the media to present. Television requires, instead, dozens of daily three-minute stories.

Cable News Channels. A major change to television from its early days has been the growth in the number and popularity of cable channels. Cable has served to break the control that the three major broadcast networks formerly had on television news. The founding of the twenty-four-hour news channel Cable News Network (CNN) by entrepreneur Ted Turner in 1980 was the first major step in this direction. A second was the establishment of Fox News Channel by Australian-American media magnate Rupert Murdoch in 1996. Fox has become well known for its conservative political positions, although the network itself disputes allegations that it is biased.

Some political scientists have argued that the development of twenty-four-hour news channels, operating internationally, has changed the way that political leaders address crises, such as international incidents, diplomatic initiatives, and natural disasters. Steven Livingston of George Washington University observes that this "CNN effect," by making the public immediately aware of such events, forces leaders to make decisions more rapidly. It can also complicate delicate diplomatic negotiations and compel nations to take positions on controversies they might prefer to avoid.

didyouknow...

That the average length of a quote, or sound bite, for a candidate decreased from forty-nine seconds in 1968 to less than nine seconds today?

Sound Bite
A brief, memorable comment that can easily be fit into news broadcasts.

Many young people obtain information about politics from Jon Stewart on *The Daily Show.* Does this indicate the loss of influence of the major television networks? (Screen capture of the Daily Show)

THE MEDIA AND POLITICAL CAMPAIGNS

All forms of the media—television, newspapers, radio, magazines, the Internet and blogs and podcasts—have a significant political impact on American society. Media influence is most obvious during political campaigns. News coverage of a single event, such as the results of the Iowa caucuses or the New Hampshire primary, may determine whether a candidate is referred to in the media as the front-runner in a presidential campaign. It is not too much of an exaggeration to say that almost all national political figures, starting with the president, plan every public appearance and statement to attract media coverage.

TELEVISION COVERAGE

Because television is still the primary news source for the majority of Americans, candidates and their consultants spend much of their time devising strategies that use television to their benefit. Three types of TV coverage are generally employed in campaigns for the presidency and other offices: political and negative advertising, management of news coverage, and campaign debates.

Political Advertising. Political advertising has become increasingly important for the profitability of television station owners. Hearst-Argyle Television, for example, obtains more than 10 percent of its revenues from political ads during an election year. In addition to typical print ads, online political advertising has been on the rise. Broadcast television still dominates media spending during campaigns, however, and the amounts spent continue to rise. During the 2006 congressional campaigns, the candidates spent $1.6 billion on political advertising. During 2008, total spending on the media by candidates at all levels totaled close to $3 billion.

Negative Advertising. Perhaps one of the most effective political ads of all time was a thirty-second spot created by President Lyndon Johnson's media adviser in 1964. Johnson's opponent in the campaign was Barry Goldwater, a conservative Republican candidate known for his expansive views on the role of the U.S. military. In this ad, a little girl stood in a field of daisies. As she held a daisy, she pulled the petals off and quietly counted to herself. Suddenly, when she reached number ten, a deep bass voice cut in and began a countdown: "10, 9, 8, 7, 6 . . . ." When the voice intoned "zero," the unmistakable mushroom cloud of an atomic bomb began to fill the screen. Then President Johnson's voice was heard: "These are the stakes. To make a world in which all of God's children can live, or to go into the dark. We must either love each other or we must die." At the end of the commercial, the message read, "Vote for President Johnson on November 3."

These images are from television ads for the opposing candidates in the 2008 presidential campaigns. In the top row, ads supporting Democratic candidate Barack Obama sought to link his opponent, John McCain, to policies of the Bush administration. The bottom row reflects McCain's attempts to question Obama's identity and to link Obama with tax increases.
(www.barackobama.com and www.johnmccain.com)

These are stills of a short television advertisement used by presidential candidate Lyndon Johnson in 1964. The "daisy girl" ad contrasted the innocence of childhood with the horror of an atomic bomb. How effective was this negative TV ad? (Doyle, Dane, Bernbach)

Since the daisy girl advertisement, negative advertising has come into its own. In recent elections, an ever-increasing percentage of political ads have been negative in nature. A reporter referred to the 2006 congressional campaigns as "the most toxic midterm campaign environment in memory."[30] In 2008, one study found that two-thirds of the presidential campaign ads were negative, as opposed to one-third in previous presidential election cycles.

The public claims not to like negative advertising, but as one consultant put it, "Negative advertising works."[31] Negative ads can be dangerous, however, when there are three or more candidates in the race, a typical state of affairs in the early presidential primaries. If one candidate attacks another, the attacker as well as the candidate who is attacked may come to be viewed negatively by the public. A candidate who "goes negative" may thus unintentionally boost the chances of a third candidate who is not part of the exchange.

While many complain that negative ads undermine elections and even democracy, some scholars take a different approach. For example, John Geer, a political scientist at Vanderbilt University, argues that attack ads are actually beneficial to the democratic process. Geer claims that this is because negative ads tend to focus on important political issues, unlike positive ads, which are more likely to focus on the candidates' personal characteristics. Thus, negative ads enrich the democratic process by providing the voters with more information than can be gleaned from positive ads.[32]

Many commentators view negative ads as an appeal to the voters' emotions, as opposed to their rational facilities. Indeed, voters' emotional reactions may be more important than their rational judgments, as we see in this chapter's *Politics and Voting* feature on the next page.

---

30. Adam Nagourney, "Campaigns Unified by Toxic Theme," *International Herald Tribune,* September 28, 2006, p. 4.
31. Interestingly, recent brain-imaging research bolsters this view. Studies conducted while subjects watched negative ads on TV indicated that viewers lost empathy for their own candidate once the candidate was attacked in an ad. See Seth Borenstein, "Scientists Track Effects of Negative Ads," *Seattle Post-Intelligencer,* November 3, 2006.
32. John G. Geer, *In Defense of Negativity: Attack Ads in Presidential Campaigns* (Chicago: University of Chicago Press, 2006).

politicsand...voting

ARE VOTER CHOICES RATIONAL?

Quick. Why do you prefer one presidential candidate over another? That is the kind of question you might be asked in an exit poll right after you vote. If you are a typical voter, your answer might be that the candidate you prefer shares your values, or that the candidate has good economic policies, or that the candidate is strong on national security. These are all rational explanations. Voters rarely offer emotionally based reasons for their choices. Nonetheless, political scientists today are starting to believe that whenever it's "head versus heart," the heart wins. Voters' emotional responses to candidates may be more important than rational responses to the candidates' positions in determining how people vote.

VOTERS HAVE WEAK MEMORIES

Most voters cannot (or perhaps will not) learn and remember the positions that a candidate has taken on particular topics or the candidate's record as a member of Congress or as a governor. In the first place, voters may simply choose a candidate based on party affiliation. Researcher Drew Westin of Emory University discovered that voters rely partially or entirely on the party label about 60 percent of the time.

For the remaining 40 percent of their votes, citizens typically use what political scientist Samuel Popkin of the University of California at San Diego calls "gut rationality." Voters tend to evaluate candidates' positions based on how the positions make them feel. Not surprisingly, campaign ads "aim for the heart." Even when candidates take nuanced positions, they try to simplify the presentation and describe their stand as simply as possible, such as "antiwar" or "pro-life." Why? Because

this approach appeals to strong emotional currents within the electorate.

According to political scientist Pippa Morris, voters tend to choose candidates with whom they identify the most—at a "gut level," of course. Perhaps strangely, candidates often obtain votes from voters who believe that the candidates are "just like me."

BRAIN SCANS SUPPORT EMOTION OVER REASON

Political scientists, using information obtained by brain specialists, now have experimental evidence that emotion rules over reason. According to brain scans, the reasoning regions of the brain often do not react when volunteers are asked to analyze written accounts that show that their candidate's deeds did not live up to his or her words. Almost to a person, the volunteers denied the obvious contradictions in their own candidate's behavior but detected such contradictions easily in the opposing candidate. In the brain scan, only the emotional part of the brain was active during this process. The result tells us that partisan beliefs are sufficiently engrained and tied to emotions to be extremely hard to change. This is one reason why Republican George W. Bush was able to win the 2004 presidential elections handily with a strategy of mobilizing his "base," rather than reaching out to voters who had not supported him in the past.

FOR CRITICAL ANALYSIS

Based on the above-outlined research, would you ever expect to see fewer negative campaign ads? Why or why not?

(©Oliver Hammond, Creative Commons/Flicker)

Management of News Coverage. Using political advertising to get a message across to the public is a very expensive tactic. Coverage by the news media, however, is free; it simply demands that the campaign ensure that coverage takes place. In recent years, campaign managers have shown increasing sophistication in creating newsworthy events for journalists to cover.

The campaign staff uses several methods to try to influence the quantity and type of coverage the campaign receives. First, the campaign staff understands the technical aspects of media coverage—camera angles, necessary equipment, timing, and deadlines—and plans political events to accommodate the press. Second, the campaign organization is aware that political reporters and their sponsors—networks, newspapers, or blogs—are in competition for the best stories and can be manipulated through the granting of favors, such as a personal interview with the candidate. Third, the scheduler in the campaign has the important task of planning events that will be photogenic and interesting enough for the evening news. A related goal, although one that is more difficult to attain, is to convince reporters that a particular interpretation of an event is correct.

Today, the art of putting the appropriate **spin** on a story or event is highly developed. Each candidate's or elected official's press advisers, often referred to as **spin doctors,** try to convince the journalists that their interpretations of the political events are correct. For example, George W. Bush's camp repeatedly tried to persuade the media that criticisms of the administration's handling of the Iraq War were inappropriate. The same type of persuasion was used to justify the administration's Middle East policies in general.

Going for the Knockout Punch—Televised Presidential Debates. In presidential elections, perhaps just as important as political advertisements and general news coverage is the performance of the candidate in televised presidential debates. After the first such debate in 1960, in which John Kennedy, the young senator from Massachusetts, took on the vice president of the United States, Richard Nixon, candidates became aware of the great potential of television for changing the momentum of a campaign. In general, challengers have much more to gain from debating than do incumbents. Challengers hope that the incumbent will make a mistake in the debate and undermine the "presidential" image. Incumbent presidents are loath to debate their challengers because it puts their opponents on an equal footing with them, but the debates have become so widely anticipated that it is difficult for an incumbent to refuse.

Debates can affect the outcome of a race. In 2004, John Kerry came close to saving his campaign with a strong debate performance, although in the end George W. Bush won the election. During the debates, Kerry appeared calm and forceful—in a word, presidential. In contrast, Bush seemed somewhat rattled by Kerry's criticisms, especially during the first debate.

In 2008, the three presidential debates may have given Democrat Barack Obama a slight edge over Republican John McCain. Obama received a small positive bump in the polls after each debate, although the effect appeared to be temporary. More important, the debates gave Obama a chance to let the voters become more comfortable with him. His calm demeanor was viewed as a plus. McCain, in contrast, may have hurt himself in the third debate by being too aggressive. The vice-presidential debate was also important because Alaska governor Sarah Palin, the Republican candidate, had not done well in earlier television interviews. Even some Republicans wondered whether she was knowledgeable enough to serve as president should McCain die or become incapacitated. Palin's confident performance in the debates reassured her supporters.

Although debates are justified publicly as an opportunity for the voters to find out how candidates differ on the issues, what the candidates want is to capitalize on the power of television to project an image. They view the debate as a strategic opportunity to improve their own images or to point out the failures of their opponents. Candidates also know that the morning-after interpretation of the debate by the news media may play a crucial role in what the public thinks.

THE INTERNET, BLOGGING, AND PODCASTING

Without a doubt, the Internet has become an important vehicle for campaign advertising and news coverage, as well as for soliciting campaign contributions. This was made clear during the 2004 presidential elections, when 7 percent of all Internet users participated in online campaign activities.

A family watches the 1960 Kennedy-Nixon debates on television. After the debate, TV viewers thought Kennedy had won, whereas radio listeners thought Nixon had won. Why have televised presidential debates become major media events? (Library of Congress)

Spin
An interpretation of campaign events or election results that is favorable to the candidate's campaign strategy.

Spin Doctor
A political campaign adviser who tries to convince journalists of the truth of a particular interpretation of events.

Barack Obama Ad - What If

YouTube

has become the most prominent repository for political video clips, some desired and some undesired by the candidates. Shown here is a clip about Democratic presidential candidate Barack Obama. YouTube has even become the vehicle for presidential candidates' debates during the primary season. Why do candidates spend resources to create video clips for Web sites such as YouTube? What audience are they hoping to reach? (Screen capture from www.YouTube.com)

The Internet became even more important during the 2007–2008 election cycle, when Democrat Barack Obama emerged as the champion of Web-fueled fund-raising. In February 2008, for example, Obama raised a record-setting $55 million, $45 million of it through the Internet. He was able to obtain this financing without holding a single in-person fund-raising party.

One highly effective characteristic of Obama's fund-raising machine was its decentralization, which was powerfully assisted by the nature of the Web. Obama was able to rely on thousands of individual fund-raising activists who solicited their friends and acquaintances, often for relatively small sums. No campaign had ever had so many volunteer fund-raisers or so many donors—1,276,000 through March 2008. Barack's site, MyBarackObama.com, was a major social-networking hub.[33]

Today, the campaign staff of every candidate running for a significant political office includes an Internet campaign strategist—a professional hired to create and maintain the campaign Web site, blogs, and podcasts (blogs and podcasts will be discussed shortly). The work of this strategist includes designing a user-friendly and attractive Web site for the candidate, managing the candidate's e-mail communications, tracking campaign contributions made through the site, hiring bloggers to push the candidate's agenda on the Web, and monitoring Web sites for favorable or unfavorable comments or video clips about the candidate. Additionally, all major interest groups in the United States now use the Internet to promote their causes. Prior to elections, various groups engage in issue advocacy from their Web sites. At little or no cost, they can promote positions taken by favored candidates and solicit contributions.

Blogging. Within the last few years, politicians have also felt obligated to post regular blogs on their Web sites. The word *blog* comes from *Web log,* a regular updating of one's ideas at a specific Web site. Of course, many people besides politicians are also posting blogs. Not all of the millions of blogs posted daily are political in nature. Many are, though, and they can have a dramatic influence on events, giving rise to the term *blogosphere politics.* During the 2004 presidential campaigns, CBS's Dan Rather reported on television that documents showed that President George W. Bush had failed to fulfill his obligations to the National Guard during the 1970s. Within four hours, a blogger on Freerepublic.com pointed out that the documents shown on CBS appeared to have been created in Microsoft Word, even though personal computers and Microsoft Word did not exist in the 1970s. Another blogger, Charles Johnson (Littlegreenfootballs.com), showed that by using Word default settings he could create documents that matched those from CBS. Eleven days later, CBS admitted that an error had been made, and Dan Rather ultimately lost his job as a news anchor.

Blogs are clearly threatening the mainstream media. They can be highly specialized, highly political, and highly entertaining. And they are cheap. The *Washington Post* requires thousands of employees, paper, and ink to generate its offline product and incurs delivery

---

33. Joshua Green, "The Amazing Money Machine," *The Atlantic,* June 2008, p. 52.

elections2008
THE MEDIA AND THE 2008 ELECTIONS

Were the media biased during the 2008 presidential campaigns? Republicans certainly thought so. In a Harris poll, two-thirds of Republicans believed that the press unfairly favored Illinois senator Barack Obama. In another poll, 65 percent of Republicans blamed media coverage for Arizona senator John McCain's loss. Only 29 percent cited the poor state of the economy. Studies by the Project for Excellence in Journalism and the Center for Media and Public Affairs found that after September 15, when bad economic news dominated the headlines, the media were much more critical of McCain than of Obama. This was a new development, however. For the first six weeks of the general election season, Obama was the one to receive negative press. Why the change? A major factor was "horse-race" reporting. For much of the campaign, fully half of all stories focused on who was ahead and who was behind in the polls. Explanations of why a candidate was trailing were inevitably critical. In the last seven weeks of the campaign, McCain was fighting a snowball effect—the economic crisis and Obama's debate performance hurt McCain's polling numbers, and this generated critical news stories. Such coverage cut further into his numbers and produced still more negative press. McCain's attacks on his rival's character, including his attempt to tie Obama to former radical Bill Ayers, did result in a week of bad news for Obama. When McCain and his running mate, Sarah Palin, continued the attacks, however, the story became McCain's negative campaign style. Polls indicated that the aggressive tone, which most Republicans liked, was turning off independent voters.

(Joe Raedle/Getty Images)

costs to get it to readers. A blogging organization such as RealClearPolitics can generate its political commentary with fewer than ten employees. Of course, all of the major newspapers and magazines have their own Web sites and blogs. The problem is how to gain revenue from these projects. Too often, sites operated by the traditional media cost more to maintain than they earn.

Podcasting. Once blogs—written words—became well established, it was only a matter of time before they ended up as spoken words. Enter **podcasting,** so called because the first Internet-communicated spoken blogs were downloaded onto Apple's iPods. Podcasts, though, can be heard on a computer or downloaded onto any portable listening device. Podcasting can also include videos. Hundreds of thousands of podcasts are now generated every day. Basically, anyone who has an idea can easily create a podcast and make it available for downloading. Like blogs, podcasting threatens traditional media sources. Publications that sponsor podcasts find it hard to make them profitable.

Although politicians have been slower to adopt this form of communication, many now are using podcasts to keep in touch with their constituents, and there are currently thousands, if not tens of thousands, of political podcasts. Podcasting played a major part in campaigning during the 2007–2008 election cycle.

Are Candidates Losing Control of Their Campaigns? Blogs and Internet sites such as YouTube are threatening to make it difficult—if not impossible—for candidates to manage the news coverage of their campaigns. It became clear during the 2006 campaigns that short video clips of candidates' bloopers could be propagated with lightning speed over the Internet. All it takes is an onlooker's digital movie camera or smart cell phone and a connection to YouTube.com. A candidate's embarrassing remarks can be downloaded from YouTube by hundreds of thousands of news organizations, campaign opponents, and potential voters within days. A number of candidates discovered, to their peril, that apparent racial slurs and other offensive statements soon found their way onto YouTube. This pattern continued during the 2008 presidential races.

Another problem for candidates is attempting to control their "Netroots" supporters. Online supporters of a candidate may engage in a type of campaigning that is at odds with the candidate's own agenda or campaign ethics. For example, a supporter may post an

Podcasting
A method of distributing multimedia files, such as audio or video files, for downloading onto mobile devices or personal computers.

attack ad against the candidate's opponent that is too harsh or hack into an opponent's Web site to harm the opponent's communications at a crucial moment in the campaign. Given that the Internet has become the source of political news for more than 40 percent of likely voters, candidates are finding themselves in a new battlefield. Indeed, some observers maintain that the Internet today, instead of supplementing campaign efforts as it largely has in the past, has fundamentally altered the political landscape.

GOVERNMENT REGULATION OF THE MEDIA

The United States has one of the freest presses in the world. Nonetheless, regulation of the media, particularly of the electronic media, does exist. We discussed some aspects of this regulation in Chapter 4, when we examined First Amendment rights and the press.

The First Amendment does not mention electronic media, which did not exist when the Bill of Rights was written. For many reasons, the government has much greater control over the electronic media than it does over printed media. Through the Federal Communications Commission (FCC), which regulates communications by radio, television, wire, and cable, the number of radio stations has been controlled for many years, even though technologically we could have many more radio stations than now exist. Also, the FCC created the environment in which for many decades the three major TV networks (NBC, CBS, and ABC) dominated broadcasting.

CONTROLLING OWNERSHIP OF THE MEDIA

Many FCC rules have dealt with ownership of news media, such as how many stations a network can own. In 1996, Congress passed legislation that had far-reaching implications for the communications industry—the Telecommunications Act. The act ended the rule that kept telephone companies from entering the cable business and other communications markets. What this means is that a single corporation—whether Time Warner or Disney—can offer long-distance and local telephone services, cable television, satellite television, Internet services, and, of course, libraries of films and entertainment. The act opened the door to competition and led to more options for consumers, who now can choose among multiple competitors for all of these services delivered to the home. At the same time, it launched a race among competing companies to control media ownership.

Media Conglomerates. Many media outlets are now owned by corporate conglomerates. A single entity may own a television network; the studios that produce shows, news, and movies; and the means to deliver that content to the home via cable, satellite, or the Internet. The question to be faced in the future is how to ensure competition in the delivery of news so that citizens have access to multiple points of view from the media.

All of the prime-time television networks are owned by major American corporations, including such corporate conglomerates as General Electric (owner of NBC) and Disney (owner of ABC). The Turner Broadcasting/CNN network was also purchased by a major corporation, Time Warner. Later, Time Warner was acquired by America Online (AOL), a merger that combined the world's then-largest media company with the world's then-largest online company. Fox Television has always been a part of Rupert Murdoch's publishing and media empire. In addition to taking part in mergers and acquisitions, many of these companies have formed partnerships with computer software makers, such as Microsoft, for joint electronic publishing ventures.

Increased Media Concentration. One measure of a conglomerate's impact is "audience reach," or the percentage of the national viewing public that has access to the conglomerate's outlets. The FCC places an upper limit on audience

Media conglomerates own larger and larger shares of television networks, newspapers, and radio outlets. Shown here is Rupert Murdoch, chairman and chief executive officer of News Corporation. News Corporation has media interests throughout the world. Recently, Murdoch bought Dow Jones & Company, publisher of the *Wall Street Journal*, for around $5 billion. What problems arise when one company owns television, radio, and newspaper companies? (AP Photo/Jason DeCrow)

reach, known as the "audience-reach cap." A few years ago, the FCC raised the national audience-reach cap from 35 percent to 45 percent and also allowed a corporation to own a newspaper and a television station in the same market. Congress rebelled against this new rule, however, and pushed the national audience-reach cap back below 40 percent. Nevertheless, a corporation can still own up to three TV stations in its largest market. The reality today is that there are only a few independent news operations left in the entire country.

This media concentration has led to the disappearance of localism in the news. Obviously, costly locally produced news cannot be shown anywhere except in that local market. In contrast, the costs of producing a similar show for national broadcast can be amortized over millions and millions of viewers and paid for by higher revenues from national advertisers. Another concern, according to former media mogul Ted Turner, is that the rise of media conglomerates may lead to a decline in democratic debate.

The emergence of independent news Web sites, blogs, and podcasts provides an offset to this trend, however. Consequently, the increased concentration of traditional media news organizations may not matter as much as it did in the past. This presumes, of course, that media conglomerates do not use their control over the Internet infrastructure to silence alternative voices. We discuss this issue in this chapter's *Politics and the Cyber Sphere* feature on the following page.

didyouknow...

That a thirty-second television advertisement shown during the Super Bowl costs more than $2.6 million?

GOVERNMENT CONTROL OF CONTENT

On the face of it, the First Amendment would seem to apply to all media. In fact, the United States Supreme Court has often been slow to extend free speech and free press guarantees to new media. For example, in 1915, the Court held that "as a matter of common sense," free speech protections did not apply to cinema. Only in 1952 did the Court find that motion pictures were covered by the First Amendment.[34] In contrast, the Court extended full protection to the Internet almost immediately by striking down provisions of the 1996 Telecommunications Act.[35] Cable TV also received broad protection in 2000.[36]

Control of Broadcasting. While the Court has held that the First Amendment is relevant to radio and television, it has never extended full protection to these media. The Court has used a number of arguments to justify this stand—initially, the scarcity of broadcast frequencies. The Court later held that the government could restrict "indecent" programming based on the "pervasive" presence of broadcasting in the home.[37] On this basis, the FCC has the authority to fine broadcasters for indecency or profanity.

Indecency in broadcasting became a major issue in 2004. In the first three months of that year, the FCC levied fines that exceeded those imposed in the previous nine years combined. Including older fines, radio personality Howard Stern cost his employers almost $2 million. Another triggering episode was singer Janet Jackson's "wardrobe malfunction" during a 2004 Super Bowl halftime performance. As a result, in 2006 Congress increased the maximum fine that the FCC can impose to $325,000 per incident.

The Government's Attempt to Control the Media during the War on Terrorism. Certainly, since the terrorist attacks of September 11, 2001, there has been increased government secrecy, sometimes apparently with the public's acceptance. Senator Patrick Leahy (D., Vt.) has argued that the First Amendment would have trouble winning ratification

---

34. *Joseph Burstyn, Inc. v. Wilson,* 343 U.S. 495 (1952).
35. *Reno v. American Civil Liberties Union,* 521 U.S. 844 (1997).
36. *United States v. Playboy Entertainment Group,* 529 U.S. 803 (2000).
37. *FCC v. Pacifica Foundation,* 438 U.S. 726 (1978). In this case, the Court banned seven swear words (famously used by the late comedian George Carlin) during hours when children could hear them.

POLITICS AND...
the cyber sphere

PRIVATE COMPANIES TRY TO REGULATE THE WEB

What is the freest mode of communication—both literally and figuratively—in this country? Of course, it's the Internet. You can find any opinion on any subject imaginable on the Web. Federal and state governments have generally supported the unfettered dissemination of information on the Internet—with some exceptions, such as child pornography. Two major telecommunications companies—Verizon and AT&T—have gone in a different direction, however.

CONTENT LIMITATIONS ON TEXT-MESSAGING

In the fall of 2007, an organization called Naral Pro-Choice America wanted to send text-message alerts to its supporters. Verizon dropped these messages from its Internet network. It cited its own policy of preventing content that "may be seen as controversial or unsavory." While the company did back down because of a public outcry, it also stated that it reserves the right to deny other such text-messaging programs in the future. Voice messages are different. Under current law, Verizon is not permitted to interfere with anything people say with their voices. Current law, however, does not protect text or data transmissions. Verizon can censor anything it wants that is sent over its broadband network that is not in voice form.

BROADBAND CENSORSHIP MAY CONTINUE

Verizon and AT&T are among the nation's largest Internet service providers. Until relatively recently, AT&T claimed that it had the right to terminate the connection of customers who engaged in "conduct that tended to damage the name or reputation" of the company. Verizon still has this type of language in its terms of service. In view of its behavior in the Naral incident, the company apparently sees no problem in using this right to curtail the expression of political opinions that it does not share.

(Creative Commons)

Some now argue that the Web is too important to entrust to the "shifting whims of a few big companies." So far, however, Congress has seen fit to keep a hands-off approach to this private regulation of the Internet.

FOR CRITICAL ANALYSIS

What problems might arise if Congress began to regulate the behavior of companies engaged in text and data transmissions?

---

today if it were proposed as a constitutional amendment. He based this assertion on a Knight Foundation survey that found that almost 40 percent of 110,000 students believed that newspapers should have to get "government approval" of news articles before they are published.

The charter for the Department of Homeland Security, created soon after the 9/11 terrorist attacks, includes a provision that allows certain groups to stamp "critical infrastructure information" on the top of documents when they submit information to Homeland Security. The public has no right to see this information. Additionally, more and more government documents have been labeled "secret" so that they do not have to be revealed to the public.

Despite such measures, since the war on terror and the second war in Iraq started, there have been numerous intelligence leaks to the press. For example, in 2005, through such a leak, the public first learned of the government's monitoring of domestic phones used in communications with suspected terrorists abroad. The tension between needed intelligence secrecy and the public's "right to know" continues to challenge news editors and publishers.

During the Iraq War, the U.S. military allowed journalists to join military units for the duration of their presence in the Middle East. This program was called "embedding." Here, Chris Tomlinson, right, of the Associated Press, eats a "meal ready to eat" or MRE, at a temporary camp in the desert with U.S. Army soldiers from the A Company 3rd Battalion, 7th Infantry Regiment, about one hundred miles south of Baghdad. How might such close contact between reporters and soldiers affect what the reporters write? (AP Photo/John Moore)

BIAS IN THE MEDIA

For decades, the contention that the mainstream media have a liberal **bias** has been repeated time and again. For example, Bernard Goldberg, a veteran CBS broadcaster, argues that this liberal bias, which "comes naturally to most reporters," has given viewers less reason to trust the big news networks.[38] Conservative journalist William McGowan cites a survey of journalists in which over 80 percent of the respondents said that they were in favor of abortion rights.[39]

In contrast to Goldberg and McGowan, journalist Eric Alterman argues that the media have, on the whole, a conservative bias, especially in their coverage of economic issues. He also observes that the almost complete dominance of talk radio by conservatives has given the political right an outlet that the political left cannot counter. (The rise of such conservative outlets as Fox News reinforces this advantage.) Alterman does find a degree of cultural liberalism among journalists, however, as demonstrated by the resolutely nonreligious nature of mainstream reporting.[40]

The rise of the blogosphere and other online outlets has complicated the picture of media bias considerably. Neither the left nor the right clearly dominates in this arena, although libertarian viewpoints are perhaps overrepresented. The ability of Internet pundits to communicate alternative viewpoints suggests that the problem of media bias, as presented by Goldberg and Alterman, may no longer be as pressing as it was in the past.

didyouknow...

That the average age of CNN viewers is forty-four and that most people who watch the evening network news programs are over age fifty?

Bias
An inclination or preference that interferes with impartial judgment.

38. Bernard Goldberg, *Bias: A CBS Insider Exposes How the Media Distort the News* (Washington, D.C.: Regnery Publishing, 2001).
39. William McGowan, *Coloring the News: How Crusading for Diversity Has Corrupted American Journalism* (San Francisco: Encounter Books, 2001).
40. Eric Alterman, *What Liberal Media? The Truth about Bias and the News* (New York: Basic Books, 2003).

WHY SHOULD YOU CARE ABOUT
themedia?

(©(DeshaCam), 2008. Used under license from Shutterstock.com)

Why should you, as an individual, care about the media? Even if you do not plan to engage in political activism, you have a stake in ensuring that your beliefs are truly your own and that they represent your values and interests. To guarantee this result, you need to obtain accurate information from the media and avoid being swayed by subliminal appeals, loaded terms, or outright bias. If you do not take care, you could find yourself voting for a candidate who is opposed to what you believe in or voting against measures that are in your interest.

THE MEDIA AND YOUR LIFE

Television, newspapers, magazines, and the Internet provide a wide range of choices for Americans who want to stay informed. Still, critics of the media argue that a substantial amount of what we read and see is colored either by the subjectivity of editors and producers or by the demands of profit making. Even when journalists themselves are relatively successful in an attempt to remain objective, they will of necessity give airtime to politicians and interest group representatives who are far from impartial. The ratio of opinion to fact is even greater on the Web than in the traditional media.

It is worth your while to become a critical consumer of the news. You need the ability to determine what motivates the players in the political game and to what extent they are "shading" the news or even propagating outright lies. You also need to determine which news sources are reliable.

HOW YOU CAN MAKE A DIFFERENCE

To become a critical news consumer, you must develop a critical eye and ear. For example, ask yourself what stories are given prominence on the front page of a news-

paper, and which ones merit a photograph. For a contrast to most daily papers, occasionally pick up an explicitly political publication such as the *National Review* or the *New Republic* and take note of the editorial positions.

Watching the evening news can be far more rewarding if you look at how much the news depends on video effects. You will note that stories on the evening news tend to be no more than three minutes long, that stories with excellent videotape get more attention, and that considerable time is taken up with "happy talk" or human interest stories.

Another way to critically evaluate news coverage is to compare how the news is covered by different outlets. For example, you might compare the coverage of events on Fox News with the presentation on NBC, or compare the radio commentary of Rush Limbaugh with that of National Public Radio's *All Things Considered*. When does a show cross the line between news and opinion?

If you wish to obtain more information on the media, you can contact one of the following organizations:

National Association of Broadcasters
1771 N St. N.W.
Washington, DC 20036
202-429-5300
www.nab.org

National Newspaper Association
129 Neff Annex
Columbia, MO 65211
1-800-829-4NNA
www.nna.org

Accuracy in Media (a conservative group)
4455 Connecticut Ave. N.W., Suite 330
Washington, DC 20008
202-364-4401
www.aim.org

People for the American Way (a liberal group)
2000 M St. N.W., Suite 400
Washington, DC 20036
202-467-4999
www.pfaw.org

QUESTIONS FOR
discussion**and**analysis

1. Review the *Which Side Are You On?* feature on page 311. Are voter ID laws of the type recently adopted in Indiana a good idea? Why or why not? What level of identification do you think a voter should have to produce? Should a voter be required to show such identification at every election, or only when the voter registers? Again, why or why not?

2. Some have argued that limits on campaign contributions violate First Amendment guarantees of freedom of speech. How strong is this argument? Can contributions be seen as a form of protected expression? Under what circumstances can contributions be seen instead as a method of bribing elected officials?

3. Many observers believe that holding so many presidential primary elections at such an early point in an election year is a serious problem. How might the problem be resolved? Also, is it fair and appropriate that New Hampshire always holds the first presidential primary and Iowa always conducts the first caucuses? Why or why not?

4. Some people are more likely to vote than others. Older persons vote more frequently than younger people. Wealthy voters make it to the polls more often than poor voters. What might cause older and wealthier individuals to exhibit greater turnout?

5. Conservatives have long accused traditional media outlets of having a liberal bias. Are they correct? If so, to what degree? Regardless of whether this particular accusation is correct, what other kinds of bias might affect the reporting of prominent journalists? To the extent that the press exhibits political bias, what factors might cause this bias?

key**terms**

Australian ballot 308
"beauty contest" 301
bias 331
caucus 302
closed primary 302
coattail effect 309
corrupt practices
  acts 295
credentials
  committee 306
elector 306

focus group 294
front-loading 304
front-runner 304
Hatch Act 295
independent
  expenditures 298
issue advocacy 298
office-block, or
  Massachusetts,
  ballot 308
open primary 303

party-column, or
  Indiana, ballot 308
podcasting 327
political action
  committee (PAC) 296
political consultant 293
presidential
  primary 289
public agenda 319
rational ignorance
  effect 315

registration 317
soft money 297
sound bite 321
spin 325
spin doctor 325
superdelegate 302
tracking poll 293
voter turnout 312

chapter**summary**

1. People may choose to run for political office to further their careers, to carry out specific political programs, or in response to certain issues or events. The legal qualifications for holding political office are minimal at both the state and local levels, but holders of political office still are predominantly white and male and are likely to be from the professional class, especially lawyers.

2. American political campaigns are lengthy and extremely expensive. In the last decade, they have become more candidate centered rather than party centered in response to technological innovations and decreasing party identification.

Candidates have begun to rely on paid professional consultants to perform the various tasks necessary to wage a political campaign. The crucial task of professional political consultants is image building. The campaign organization devises a campaign strategy to maximize the candidate's chances of winning. Candidates use public opinion polls and focus groups to gauge their popularity and to test the mood of the country.

3. The amount of money spent in financing campaigns is increasing steadily. A variety of corrupt practices acts have been passed to regulate campaign finance. The Federal Election Campaign Act of 1971

and its amendments in 1974 and 1976 instituted major reforms by limiting spending and contributions; the acts allowed corporations, labor unions, and interest groups to set up political action committees (PACs) to raise money for candidates. New techniques, including "soft money" contributions to the parties and independent expenditures, were later developed. The Bipartisan Campaign Reform Act of 2002 banned soft money contributions to the national parties and increased the limits on individual contributions. Since then, various kinds of independent, nonparty organizations have become increasingly important.

4. After the Democratic convention of 1968, the McGovern-Fraser Commission formulated new rules for primaries, which were adopted by all Democrats and by Republicans in many states. These reforms opened up the nomination process for the presidency to all voters.

5. A presidential primary is a statewide election to help a political party determine its presidential nominee at the national convention. Some states use the caucus method of choosing convention delegates. The primary campaign recently has been shortened to the first few months of the election year. This "front-loading" of the primaries has caused many to call for a national primary system that would involve rotating regional primaries.

6. The voter technically does not vote directly for president but instead chooses between slates of presidential electors. In most states, the slate that wins the most popular votes throughout the state gets to cast all the electoral votes for the state. The candidate receiving a majority (270) of the electoral votes wins. Both the mechanics and the politics of the Electoral College have been sharply criticized. There have been many proposed reforms, including a proposal that the president be elected on a popular-vote basis.

7. The United States uses the Australian ballot, a secret ballot that is prepared, distributed, and counted by government officials. The office-block ballot groups candidates according to office. The party-column ballot groups candidates according to their party labels and symbols.

8. Voter participation in the United States is low compared with that of other countries. Some view low voter turnout as a threat to representative democracy, whereas others believe it simply indicates greater satisfaction with the status quo. There is an association between voting and a person's age, education, minority status, and income level. Another factor affecting voter turnout is the extent to which elections are competitive within a state. It is also true that the number of eligible voters is smaller than the number of people of voting age because of ineligible felons and immigrants who are not yet citizens.

9. In colonial times, only white males with a certain minimum amount of property were eligible to vote. The suffrage issue has concerned, at one time or another, most groups in the United States. Today, to be eligible to vote, a person must satisfy registration, citizenship, age, and residency requirements. Each state has different qualifications. Some claim that these requirements are responsible for much of the nonparticipation in the political process in the United States.

10. The media are enormously important in American politics today. They perform a number of functions, including (a) entertainment, (b) news reporting, (c) identifying public problems, (d) socializing new generations, (e) providing a political forum, and (f) making profits.

11. The media wield great power during political campaigns and over the affairs of government and government officials by focusing attention on their actions. Political campaigns use political advertising and expert management of news coverage. For presidential candidates, how they appear in presidential debates is of major importance. Internet blogs, podcasts, and Web sites such as YouTube are transforming today's political campaigns and making it difficult for candidates to control their campaigns. According to some observers, the Internet and its uses in political campaigns have fundamentally altered the political landscape.

12. The electronic media are subject to government regulation. Many Federal Communications Commission rules have dealt with ownership of TV and radio stations. Legislation has removed many rules about co-ownership of several forms of media.

selectedprint&mediaresources

SUGGESTED READINGS

Jones, Alex. *Losing the News: The Uncertain Future of the News That Feeds Democracy.* New York: Oxford University Press, 2008. Jones, a Pulitzer Prize-winning journalist at Harvard University, looks at how digital and electronic media are transforming journalism. He warns that the changes may be eroding the "iron core" of fact-based news, replacing it with openly biased opinion.

Martinez, Michael D. *Does Turnout Matter?* Boulder, Colo.: Westview Press, 2009. Scholars have expended much effort in examining why voter turnout is lower in the United States than in many other countries, but the question of whether low turnout actually matters has received less attention. Martinez is a professor of political science at the University of Florida.

Piven, Frances Fox, Lori Minnite, and Margaret Groarke. *Keeping Down the Black Vote: Race and the Demobilization of American Voters.* New York: The New Press, 2009. The authors claim that under the banner of election reform, leading operatives in the Republican Party have sought to affect elections by suppressing the Black vote.

Poundstone, William. *Gaming the Vote: Why Elections Aren't Fair (and What We Can Do About It).* New York: Hill and Wang, 2009. America's first-past-the-post, winner-take-all voting system is not the only one possible, and Poundstone believes that it is actually one of the worst. In this volume, he provides a clear and witty tour of possible voting systems that may better reflect the will of the people.

Simons, Barbara, and Douglas W. Jones. *Who's Minding the Vote?* Sausalito, Calif.: Polipoint Press, 2008. This is a fascinating history of voting machines and technological methods that can be used to rig elections. The authors offer a scathing criticism of certain recently developed electronic voting systems.

Tremayne, Mark, ed. *Blogging, Citizenship, and the Future of Media.* Oxford: Routledge Publishing, 2006. This collection of essays examines the population's growing dependence on blogs for political information. Some of the essays also look at how blog readers differ from the rest of the population. Finally, the book explores the future of traditional media in light of the blogging phenomenon.

MEDIA RESOURCES

All the President's Men—A film, produced by Warner Brothers in 1976, starring Dustin Hoffman and Robert Redford as the two *Washington Post* reporters, Carl Bernstein and Bob Woodward, who broke the story on the Watergate scandal. The film is an excellent portrayal of the *Washington Post* newsroom and the decisions that editors make in such situations.

Bulworth—A 1998 satirical film starring Warren Beatty and Halle Berry. Jay Bulworth, a senator who is fed up with politics and life in general, hires a hit man to carry out his own assassination. He then throws political caution to the wind in campaign appearances by telling the truth and behaving the way he really wants to behave.

The Candidate—A 1972 film, starring the young Robert Redford, that effectively investigates and satirizes the decisions that a candidate for the U.S. Senate must make. A political classic.

Citizen Kane—A 1941 film, based on the life of William Randolph Hearst and directed by Orson Welles, that has been acclaimed as one of the best movies ever made. Welles himself stars as the newspaper tycoon. The film also stars Joseph Cotten and Alan Ladd.

Good Night, and Good Luck—A 2006 film about Edward R. Murrow, directed by George Clooney. Murrow's opposition to the tactics used by Senator Joe McCarthy's witch-hunters in 1953–1954 provides a powerful example of integrity to reporters today.

Hacking Democracy—An HBO production that follows activist Bev Harris of Seattle and others as they take on Diebold, a company that makes electronic voting machines. The documentary argues that security lapses in Diebold's machines are a threat to the democratic process.

Recount—A 2008 film nominated for an Emmy Award that chronicles the disputed 2000 presidential contest in Florida, where a mere 538 ballots separated Republican George W. Bush and Democrat Al Gore. The film makes the victorious Republican operatives out to be much more aggressive than the rather hapless Democrats.

e-mocracy

CAMPAIGNS, ELECTIONS, AND THE MEDIA

Today's voters have a significant advantage over those in past decades. It is now possible to obtain extensive information about candidates and issues simply by going online. Some sites present point-counterpoint articles about the candidates or issues in an upcoming election. Other sites support some candidates and positions and oppose others. The candidates themselves all have Web sites that you can visit if you want to learn more about them and their positions. You can also obtain information online about election results by going to sites such as those listed in the *Logging On* section.

The Internet also offers a great opportunity to those who want to access the news. All of the major news organizations, including radio and television stations and newspapers, are online. Most local newspapers include at least some of their news coverage and features on their Web sites, and all national newspapers are online. Even foreign newspapers can now be accessed online within a few seconds. Also available are purely Web-based news publications, including e-zines (online news magazines) such as *Slate, Salon,* and *Hotwired.* Because it is relatively simple for anyone or any organization to put up a home page or Web site, a wide variety of sites have appeared that critique the news media or give alternative interpretations of the news and the way it is presented.

LOGGING ON

For detailed information about current campaign-financing laws and for the latest filings of finance reports, see the site maintained by the Federal Election Commission at **www.fec.gov**.

To find excellent reports on where campaign money comes from and how it is spent, be sure to view the site maintained by the Center for Responsive Politics at **www.opensecrets.org**.

Another Web site for investigating voting records and campaign-financing information is that of Project Vote Smart. Go to **www.vote-smart.org**.

You can learn about the impact of different voting systems on election strategies and outcomes at the Center for Voting and Democracy, which maintains the following Web site: **www.fairvote.org**.

The Web site of the *American Journalism Review* includes features from the magazine and original content created specifically for online reading. Go to **www.ajr.org**.

To view *Slate,* the e-zine of politics and culture published by Microsoft, go to **www.slate.com**.

Blogs have become a major feature of the Internet. A large number of blogs deal with political topics. For a listing of several hundred political blogs, go to the Blog Search Engine at **www.blogsearchengine.com**.

For an Internet site that provides links to news media around the world, including alternative media, go to **www.mediachannel.org**.

TechPresident.com, which is operated by a team of bloggers who span the political spectrum, tracked how the 2008 presidential candidates were using the Internet, as well as how Internet content affected the 2008 campaigns. Go to **www.techpresident.com**.

10 The Congress

CHAPTER CONTENTS

Foreign leaders often address the U.S. Congress.
Here, the head of the government of Ireland is
shown giving a prepared speech. (NIALL CARSON/
PA Photos/Landov)

what**if**...pork were banned?

BACKGROUND

Through *pork-barrel legislation,* members of Congress "bring home the bacon." Members directly help their constituents by adding into legislation projects that create more jobs and generate more profits locally. The official name for pork is *earmarked spending.* In recent years, from 11,000 to 15,000 earmarks yearly, worth from $15 billion to $69 billion, have passed through Congress. Most earmarks are never discussed on the floor. Many are "air-dropped" at the last minute into nonbinding conference reports that serve as "advice" to federal departments about where to allocate funds. The practice of earmarking is not new, but it has increased significantly over the last few decades. Consider that in 1987, President Ronald Reagan vetoed a bill because it included 157 earmarks valued at $1 billion. By 2006, Congress approved more than 13,000 earmarks worth about $67 billion.

Earmarking is a bipartisan activity. When the Democrats took control of Congress in 2007, they promised to "get tough" on special interest groups and the earmarking that benefits such groups. While the volume of pork did decline slightly, massive quantities of pork continue to be routinely included in legislation.

WHAT IF PORK WERE BANNED?

Without pork, earmarks could not simply be slipped into bills sent to the president as amendments. Because Congress does not have an unlimited amount of time for debate, eliminating pork might reduce federal spending. Realize, though, that the federal budget is about $3.3 trillion, so eliminating pork would not change much.

Banning pork would mean that most spending projects coming before Congress would have to pass through the normal budget process. Ordinarily, the various executive agencies of government receive proposals for spending on various projects. They rank all the requests in order of "need" and choose the ones with the most merit, often within the constraints of formulas that ensure that funds will be spent in all parts of the country. The number of projects is limited by agency funding limits set by the president's Office of Management and Budget (OMB). The OMB submits the resulting budget to Congress.

Before the budget reaches Congress, however, the White House routinely adds its own laundry list of politically desirable projects that were never reviewed by the bureaucracy. The president may actually be the biggest single "porkmeister" in government.

If all pork were really banned, "legitimate pork" would be eliminated, too. After all, members of Congress may at times have a better understanding than does the bureaucracy of local spending needs for hospitals, infrastructure repairs, and the like. If true pork were banned, however, we would not see federal payments for a prison museum near Fort Leavenworth, Kansas. Federal funds would not be spent on the National Mule and Packers Museum in Bishop, California.

THE CHANGING WAYS OF CONGRESS

If pork were eliminated, Congress would have to change the way it goes about its business. Bills get passed in Congress through a process of *logrolling,* or "You scratch my back and I'll scratch yours." In other words, a member who does not favor a bill may be convinced by his colleagues to vote for it if they allow that member to add earmarked spending for his or her constituents. Much legislation gets passed in Congress in this manner. In the absence of pork, it would become harder to convince opposing members to vote in favor of certain legislation. Consequently, the absence of pork might result in less legislation from the halls of Congress.

THE IMPACT ON CAMPAIGNS AND CAMPAIGN CONTRIBUTIONS

Currently, many lobbyist groups are rewarded for their campaign contributions through pork-barrel legislation. Earmarks are a way to show a legislator's appreciation for campaign contributions made by a specific group. For example, management at a defense contractor might make the maximum campaign contributions for the reelection of the local representative. If that representative is reelected, she or he can earmark funds for a weapons system that the contractor manufactures in a local factory, even though the system was never officially requested by the Defense Department.

In the absence of pork, candidates for election or reelection would probably receive fewer campaign contributions from lobbying groups representing local interests. Why? Because those local groups would know they could not easily obtain something in return for their support. We could predict, then, that the number of registered lobbying groups would probably fall.

FOR CRITICAL ANALYSIS

1. In 2006, the Democrats campaigned on an "anti-pork" theme to wrest control of Congress from the Republicans. Nonetheless, pork-barrel legislation continues. Why?
2. If there were less legislation coming out of Congress, would Americans be better off or worse off? Explain your answer.

Most Americans view Congress in a less-than-flattering light. In recent years, Congress has appeared to be deeply split, highly partisan in its conduct, and not very responsive to public needs. Polls show that at times the public has had notably unfavorable opinions about Congress as a whole. Yet individual members of Congress often receive much higher approval ratings from the voters in their districts. This is one of the paradoxes of the relationship between the people and Congress. Members of the public hold the institution in relatively low regard compared with the satisfaction they express with their individual representatives.

Part of the explanation for these seemingly contradictory appraisals is that members of Congress spend considerable time and effort serving their **constituents.** If the federal bureaucracy makes a mistake, the senator's or representative's office tries to resolve the issue. What most Americans see of Congress, therefore, is the work of their own representatives in their home states. Indeed, members of Congress have exceptionally high reelection rates.

Congress, however, was created to work not just for local constituents but also for the nation as a whole; the national interest is sometimes hard to detect in Congress's everyday activities, though, as you learned in the chapter-opening *What If . . .* feature. Understanding the nature of the institution and the process of lawmaking is an important part of understanding how the laws and policies that shape our lives are made. In this chapter, we describe the functions of Congress, including constituent service, representation, lawmaking, and oversight of the government. We review how the members of Congress are elected and how Congress organizes itself when it meets. We also examine how bills pass through the legislative process and become laws.

Constituent
One of the persons represented by a legislator or other elected or appointed official.

The "freshman" class of the 111th Congress gather

on the steps of the Capitol in Washington, D.C. Out of the 535 representatives and senators, what is the percentage of newly elected members? Why is this percentage is so low? (AP Photo/Susan Walsh)

THE NATURE AND FUNCTIONS OF CONGRESS

The founders of the American republic believed that the bulk of the power that would be exercised by a national government should be in the hands of the legislature. The leading role envisioned for Congress in the new government is apparent from its primacy in the Constitution. Article I deals with the structure, the powers, and the operation of Congress.

BICAMERALISM

The **bicameralism** of Congress—its division into two legislative houses—was in part the result of the Connecticut Compromise, which tried to balance the large-state population advantage, reflected in the House, and the small-state demand for equality in policymaking, which was satisfied in the Senate. Beyond that, the two chambers of Congress also reflected the social class biases of the founders. They wished to balance the interests and the numerical superiority of the common citizens with the property interests of the less numerous landowners, bankers, and merchants. They achieved this goal by providing that members of the House of Representatives should be elected directly by "the People," whereas members of the Senate were to be chosen by the elected representatives sitting in state legislatures, who were more likely to be members of the elite. (The latter provision was changed in 1913 by the passage of the Seventeenth Amendment, which provides that senators are also to be elected directly by the people.)

The logic of the bicameral Congress was reinforced by differences in length of tenure. Members of the House are required to face the electorate every two years, whereas senators can serve for a much more secure term of six years—even longer than the four-year term provided for the president. Furthermore, the senators' terms are staggered so that only one-third of the senators face the electorate every two years, along with all of the House members.

The bicameral Congress was designed to perform certain functions for the political system. These functions include lawmaking, representation, service to constituents, oversight, public education, and conflict resolution. Of these, the two most important and the ones that are most often in conflict are lawmaking and representation.

THE LAWMAKING FUNCTION

The principal and most obvious function of any legislature is **lawmaking.** Congress is the highest elected body in the country charged with making binding rules for all Americans. Lawmaking requires decisions about the size of the federal budget, about health-care reform and gun control, and about the long-term prospects for war or peace. This does not mean, however, that Congress initiates most of the ideas for legislation that it eventually considers. A majority of the bills that Congress acts on originate in the executive branch, and many other bills are traceable to interest groups and political party organizations. Through the processes of compromise and **logrolling** (offering to support a fellow member's bill in exchange for that member's promise to support your bill in the future), as well as debate and discussion, backers of legislation attempt to fashion a winning majority coalition. Logrolling often involves agreements to support another member's legislative **earmarks,** also known as *pork.* Earmarks, which were discussed in the opening *What If . . .* feature, are special provisions in legislation to set aside funds for projects that have not passed an impartial evaluation by agencies of the executive branch. (As you will learn at the end of this chapter, normal spending projects pass through such evaluations.)

THE REPRESENTATION FUNCTION

Representation includes both representing the desires and demands of the constituents in the member's home district or state and representing larger national interests, such as the nation's security or the environment. Because the interests of constituents in a

Bicameralism
The division of a legislature into two separate assemblies.

Lawmaking
The process of establishing the legal rules that govern society.

Logrolling
An arrangement in which two or more members of Congress agree in advance to support each other's bills.

Earmarks
Special provisions in legislation to set aside funds for projects that have not passed an impartial evaluation by agencies of the executive branch. Also known as *pork.*

Representation
The function of members of Congress as elected officials representing the views of their constituents.

specific district may be in conflict with the demands of national policy, the representation function is often at variance with the lawmaking function for individual lawmakers—and sometimes for Congress as a whole. For example, although it may be in the interest of the nation to reduce defense spending by closing military bases, such closures are not in the interest of the states and districts that will lose jobs and local spending. Every legislator faces votes that set representational issues against lawmaking realities.

How should the legislators fulfill the representation function? There are several views on how this task should be accomplished.

The Trustee View of Representation. The first approach to the question of how representation should be achieved is that legislators should act as **trustees** of the broad interests of the entire society. They should vote against the narrow interests of their constituents if their conscience and their perception of national needs so dictate. For example, a number of Republican legislators have supported laws regulating the tobacco industry in spite of the views of some of their constituents.

The Instructed-Delegate View of Representation. Directly opposed to the trustee view of representation is the notion that the members of Congress should behave as **instructed delegates;** that is, they should mirror the views of the majority of the constituents who elected them to power in the first place. On the surface, this approach is plausible and rewarding. For it to work, however, we must assume that constituents actually have well-formed views on the issues that are decided in Congress and, further, that they have clear-cut preferences about these issues. Neither condition is likely to be satisfied very often.

Generally, most legislators hold neither a pure trustee view nor a pure instructed-delegate view. Typically, they combine both perspectives in a pragmatic mix that is often called the "politico" style.

SERVICE TO CONSTITUENTS

Individual members of Congress are expected by their constituents to act as brokers between private citizens and the imposing, often faceless federal government. This function of providing service to constituents usually takes the form of **casework.** The legislator and her or his staff spend a considerable portion of their time in casework activities, such as tracking down a missing Social Security check, explaining the meaning of particular bills to people who may be affected by them, promoting a local business interest, or interceding with a regulatory agency on behalf of constituents who disagree with proposed agency regulations.

Legislators and many analysts of congressional behavior regard this **ombudsperson** role as an activity that strongly benefits the members of Congress. A government characterized by a large, confusing bureaucracy and complex public programs offers innumerable opportunities for legislators to come to the assistance of (usually) grateful constituents. Morris P. Fiorina once suggested, somewhat mischievously, that senators and representatives prefer to maintain bureaucratic confusion to maximize their opportunities for performing good deeds on behalf of their constituents:

> Some poor, aggrieved constituent becomes enmeshed in the tentacles of an evil bureaucracy and calls upon Congressman St. George to do battle

Trustee
A legislator who acts according to her or his conscience and the broad interests of the entire society.

Instructed Delegate
A legislator who is an agent of the voters who elected him or her and who votes according to the views of constituents regardless of personal beliefs.

Casework
Personal work for constituents by members of Congress.

Ombudsperson
A person who hears and investigates complaints by private individuals against public officials or agencies.

didyouknow...

That fewer than three in ten people can name the House member from their district, and fewer than half can name even one of the two senators from their state?

Representative Tom Feeney (R., Fla.), who was defeated by Democrat Suzanne Kosmas in the 2008 elections, meets with members of the recording industry in his office. What are the two opposing views of how this member of Congress should deal with this special interest group? (Photo by Gerardo Mora/WireImage for NARAS/Getty Images)

with the dragon. . . . In dealing with the bureaucracy, the congressman is not merely one vote of 435. Rather, he is a nonpartisan power, someone whose phone call snaps an office to attention. He is not kept on hold. The constituent who receives aid believes that his congressman and his congressman alone got results.[1]

THE OVERSIGHT FUNCTION

Oversight of the bureaucracy is essential if the decisions made by Congress are to have any force. **Oversight** is the process by which Congress follows up on the laws it has enacted to ensure that they are being enforced and administered in the way Congress intended. This is done by holding committee hearings and investigations, changing the size of an agency's budget, and cross-examining high-level presidential nominees to head major agencies. Sometimes Congress establishes a special commission to investigate a problem. For example, after Hurricane Katrina devastated New Orleans and parts of surrounding states in 2005, Congress created a commission to determine how and why the federal government, particularly the Federal Emergency Management Agency (FEMA), had mishandled government aid both during and after that natural disaster. Sometimes a commission may take several years to complete its work. One example is the so-called 9/11 Commission, which investigated why the United States was unprepared for the terrorist attacks in 2001.

Senators and representatives traditionally have seen their oversight function as a critically important part of their legislative activities. In part, oversight is related to the concept of constituency service, particularly when Congress investigates alleged arbitrariness or wrongdoing by bureaucratic agencies.

When the Republicans controlled both the executive and legislative branches of government from 2001 to 2007, many claimed that Congress failed to fulfill its oversight function. Serious allegations of wrongdoing by government officials, including some members of Congress, often went uninvestigated. After taking control of Congress in 2007, the Democrats let the nation know that they were taking their oversight function seriously. Within weeks, they had launched a series of investigations into alleged wrongdoing by various government officials.

THE PUBLIC-EDUCATION FUNCTION

Educating the public is a function that is performed whenever Congress holds public hearings, exercises oversight over the bureaucracy, or engages in committee and floor debate on such major issues and topics as immigration, global warming, aging, illegal drugs, and the concerns of small businesses. In so doing, Congress presents a range of viewpoints on pressing national questions. Congress also decides what issues will come up for discussion and decision; this **agenda setting** is a major facet of its public-education function.

THE CONFLICT-RESOLUTION FUNCTION

Congress is commonly seen as an institution for resolving conflicts within American society. Organized interest groups and spokespersons for different racial, religious, economic, and ideological interests look on Congress as an access point for airing their grievances and seeking help. This puts Congress in the position of trying to resolve the differences among competing points of view by passing laws to accommodate as many interested parties as possible. To the extent that Congress meets pluralist expectations in accommodating competing interests, it tends to build support for the entire political process.

Oversight
The process by which Congress follows up on laws it has enacted to ensure that they are being enforced and administered in the way Congress intended.

Agenda Setting
Determining which public-policy questions will be debated or considered.

---

1. Morris P. Fiorina, *Congress: Keystone of the Washington Establishment,* 2d ed. (New Haven, Conn.: Yale University Press, 1989), pp. 44, 47.

THE POWERS OF CONGRESS

The Constitution is both highly specific and extremely vague about the powers that Congress may exercise. The first seventeen clauses of Article I, Section 8, specify most of the **enumerated powers** of Congress—that is, powers expressly given to that body.

ENUMERATED POWERS

The enumerated, or expressed, powers of Congress include the right to impose a variety of taxes, as well as tariffs on imports; borrow funds; regulate interstate commerce and international trade; establish procedures for naturalizing citizens; make laws regulating bankruptcies; coin (and print) money and regulate its value; establish standards of weights and measures; punish counterfeiters; establish post offices and postal routes; regulate copyrights and patents; establish the federal court system; punish illegal acts on the high seas; declare war; raise and regulate an army and a navy; call up and regulate the state militias to enforce laws, to suppress insurrections, and to repel invasions; and govern the District of Columbia.

The most important of the domestic powers of Congress, listed in Article I, Section 8, are the rights to collect taxes, to spend, and to regulate commerce. The most important foreign policy power is the power to declare war. Other sections of the Constitution allow Congress to establish rules for its own members, to regulate the Electoral College, and to override a presidential veto. Congress may also regulate the extent of the Supreme Court's authority to review cases decided by the lower courts, regulate relations among states, and propose amendments to the Constitution.

Powers of the Senate. Some functions are restricted to one chamber. The Senate must advise on, and consent to, the ratification of treaties and must accept or reject presidential nominations of ambassadors, Supreme Court justices, and "all other Officers of the United States." But the Senate may delegate to the president or lesser officials the power to make lower-level appointments.

Constitutional Amendments. Amendments to the Constitution provide for other congressional powers. Congress must certify the election of a president and a vice president or itself choose those officers if no candidate has a majority of the electoral vote (Twelfth Amendment). It may levy an income tax (Sixteenth Amendment) and determine who will be acting president in case of the death or incapacity of the president or vice president (Twentieth Amendment and Twenty-fifth Amendment). In addition, Congress explicitly is given the power to enforce, by appropriate legislation, the provisions of several other amendments.

THE NECESSARY AND PROPER CLAUSE

Beyond these numerous specific powers, Congress enjoys the right under Clause 18 of Article I, Section 8 (the "elastic," or "necessary and proper," clause), "to make all Laws which shall be necessary and proper for carrying into Execution the foregoing Powers [of Article I], and all other Powers vested by this Constitution in the Government of the United States, or in any Department or Officer thereof." As discussed in Chapter 3, this vague statement of congressional responsibilities has provided, over time, the basis for a greatly expanded national government. It also has constituted, at least in theory, a check on the expansion of presidential powers.

One of the expressed powers of Congress is the power to impose and collect taxes. Every year on April 15 (if it falls on a weekday), U.S. residents line up in front of virtually every post office building in America to file their tax returns before the midnight deadline. These New Yorkers have waited until the last minute and are standing in line inside the James A. Farley Post Office building. (Mario Tama/Getty Images)

Rules Committee
A standing committee of the House of Representatives that provides special rules under which specific bills can be debated, amended, and considered by the House.

Filibuster
The use of the Senate's tradition of unlimited debate as a delaying tactic to block a bill.

TABLE 10–1: Differences Between the House and the Senate

House*	Senate*
Members chosen from local districts	Members chosen from an entire state
Two-year term	Six-year term
Originally elected by voters	Originally (until 1913) elected by state legislatures
May impeach (indict) federal officials	May convict federal officials of impeachable offenses
Larger (435 voting members)	Smaller (100 members)
More formal rules	Fewer rules and restrictions
Debate limited	Debate extended
Less prestige and less individual notice	More prestige and more media attention
Originates bills for raising revenues	Has power to advise the president on, and to consent to, presidential appointments and treaties
Local or narrow leadership	National leadership
More partisan	Less party loyalty

*Some of these differences, such as the term of office, are provided for in the Constitution. Others, such as debate rules, are not.

On August 29, 1957, Senator Strom Thurmond (D., S.C.) finished the longest one-man filibuster in the history of the Senate. It lasted for twenty-four hours and nineteen minutes. Thurmond was attempting to prevent the passage of a civil rights bill that nonetheless was later signed into law by the president. (AP Photo)

HOUSE-SENATE DIFFERENCES

Congress is composed of two markedly different—but co-equal—chambers. Although the Senate and the House of Representatives exist within the same legislative institution, each has developed certain distinctive features that clearly distinguish one from the other. A summary of these differences is given in Table 10–1.

SIZE AND RULES

The central difference between the House and the Senate is simply that the House is much larger than the Senate. The House has 435 representatives, plus delegates from the District of Columbia, Puerto Rico, Guam, American Samoa, and the Virgin Islands, compared with just 100 senators. This size difference means that a greater number of formal rules are needed to govern activity in the House, whereas correspondingly looser procedures can be followed in the less crowded Senate.

The effect of the difference in size is most obvious in the rules governing debate on the floors of the two chambers. The Senate normally permits extended debate on all issues that arise before it. In contrast, the House operates with an elaborate system in which its **Rules Committee** normally proposes time limitations on debate for any bill, and a majority of the entire body accepts or modifies those suggested time limits. As a consequence of its stricter time limits on debate, the House, despite its greater size, often is able to act on legislation more quickly than the Senate.

DEBATE AND FILIBUSTERING

The Senate tradition of the **filibuster,** or the use of unlimited debate as a blocking tactic, dates back to 1790. In that year, a proposal to move the U.S. capital from New York to Philadelphia was stalled by such time-wasting maneuvers. This unlimited-debate tradition—which also existed in the House until 1811—is not absolute, however. In 2005, use of the filibuster became the subject of national debate. Senate Democrats had been using the filibuster for some time to block confirmation votes on many of President Bush's most controversial nominees to the federal courts of appeals. Frustrated by this tactic, Republican senators threatened to use what some called the "nuclear option," under which Senate rules would be revised to disallow filibusters against judicial nominees. In the end, though, a bipartisan group engineered a temporary compromise to preserve the filibuster.

Under Senate Rule 22, debate may be ended by invoking *cloture.* Cloture shuts off discussion on a bill. Amended in 1975 and 1979, Rule 22 states that debate may be closed off on a bill if sixteen senators sign a petition requesting it and if, after two days have elapsed, three-fifths of the entire membership (sixty votes, assuming no vacancies) vote for cloture. After cloture is invoked, each senator may speak on a bill for a maximum of one hour before a vote is taken.

In 1979, the Senate refined Rule 22 to ensure that a final vote must take place within one hundred hours of debate after cloture has been imposed. It further limited the use of multiple amendments to stall postcloture final action on a bill.

PRESTIGE

As a consequence of the greater size of the House, representatives generally cannot achieve as much individual recognition and public prestige as can members of the Senate. Senators are better able to gain media exposure and to establish careers as spokespersons for large national constituencies. To obtain recognition for his or her activities, a member of the House generally must do one of two things. He or she might survive in office long enough to join the ranks of the leadership on committees or within the party. Alternatively, the representative could become an expert on some specialized aspect of legislative policy—such as tax laws, the environment, or education.

CONGRESSPERSONS AND THE CITIZENRY: A COMPARISON

Members of the U.S. Senate and the U.S. House of Representatives are not typical American citizens. Members of Congress are older than most Americans, partly because of constitutional age requirements and partly because a good deal of political experience normally is an advantage in running for national office. Members of Congress are also disproportionately white, male, and trained in high-status occupations. Lawyers are by far the largest occupational group among congresspersons, although the proportion

Senate majority leader Harry Reid
(D., Nev.) holds a news conference on Capitol Hill in the spring of 2007. He urged President Bush to sign the war-funding bill just passed by Congress. In spite of the Democrats' taking control of both chambers in Congress, they were unable to make significant legislative changes concerning the war in Iraq during 2007 and 2008. What is the ultimate threat that the president holds over Congress's legislative actions? (AP Photo/Dennis Cook)

TABLE 10–2: Characteristics of the 111th Congress, 2009–2011

Characteristic	U.S. Population (2000)*	House	Senate
Age (median)	36.7	55.9	61.7
Percentage minority	33.6	16.1	5.
Religion			
Percentage church members	61.0	89.9	95.
Percentage Roman Catholic	23.9	30.3	23.
Percentage Protestant	51.3	53.3	54.
Percentage Jewish	1.7	7.1	13.
Percentage female	51.5	17.0	17.
Percentage with advanced degrees	9.7	67.1	78.
Occupation			
Percentage lawyers	0.4	39.3	57.
Percentage blue-collar workers	10.2	1.8	3.
Family income			
Percentage of families earning over $50,000 annually	34.9	100.0	100.
Personal wealth			
Percentage with assets over $1 million	3.0	44.0	58.

*Estimates based on 2000 census.

Sources: *CIA Factbook,* 2008; Census Bureau; and authors' updates.

Speaker of the House Nancy Pelosi (center) and other Democratic congressional leaders are cheering Senator Barack Obama's victory on the night of November 4, 2008. The elections also increased the Democratic majorities in both chambers of Congress. (Brendan Smialowski/Getty Images)

of lawyers in the House is lower now than it was in the past. Compared with the average American citizen, members of Congress are well paid. In 2008, annual congressional salaries were $169,300. Increasingly, members of Congress are also much wealthier than the average citizen. Whereas only about 3 percent of Americans have assets exceeding $1 million, more than one-third of the members of Congress are millionaires. Table 10–2 summarizes selected characteristics of the members of Congress.

Compared with the composition of Congress over the past two hundred years, however, the House and Senate today are significantly more diverse in gender and ethnicity than ever before. There are seventy-four women in the House of Representatives (about 17 percent) and seventeen women in the Senate (17 percent). Minority group members fill over 15 percent of the seats in the House. The 111th Congress has significant numbers of members born in 1946 or later, the so-called Baby Boomers. A majority of House members and a large minority of the Senate belong to this postwar generation. This shift in the character of Congress may prompt consideration of the issues that will affect the Boomers, such as Social Security and Medicare.

CONGRESSIONAL ELECTIONS

The process of electing members of Congress is decentralized. Congressional elections are conducted by the individual state governments. The states, however, must conform to the rules established by the U.S. Constitution and by national statutes. The Constitution states that representatives are to be elected every second year by popular ballot, and the number of seats awarded to each state is to be determined every ten years by the results of the census. Each state has at least one representative, with most congressional districts having about half a million residents. Senators are elected by popular vote (since the passage of the Seventeenth Amendment) every six years; approximately one-third of the seats are chosen every two years. Each state has two senators. Under Article I, Section 4, of the Constitution, state legislatures are given control over "the Times, Places and Manner of holding Elections for Senators and Representatives"; however, "the Congress may at any time by Law make or alter such Regulations."

Only states can elect members of Congress. Therefore, territories such as Puerto Rico and Guam are not represented, though they do elect nonvoting delegates who sit in the House. The District of Columbia is also represented only by a nonvoting delegate.

CANDIDATES FOR CONGRESSIONAL ELECTIONS

Candidates for congressional seats may be self-selected. In districts where one party is very strong, however, there may be a shortage of candidates willing to represent the weaker party. In such circumstances, leaders of the weaker party must often actively recruit candidates. Candidates may resemble the voters of the district in ethnicity or religion, but they are also likely to be very successful individuals who have been active in politics before. House candidates are especially likely to have local ties to their districts. Candidates usually choose to run because they believe they would enjoy the job and its accompanying status. They also may be thinking of a House seat as a stepping-stone to future political office as a senator, governor, or president.

Congressional Campaigns and Elections. Congressional campaigns have changed considerably in the past two decades. Like all other campaigns, they are much more expensive, with the average cost of a winning Senate campaign now $6.5 million and a winning House campaign averaging more than $1.1 million. Campaign funds include direct contributions by individuals, contributions by political action committees (PACs), and "soft money" funneled through state party committees. As you read in Chapter 9, all of these contributions are regulated by laws, including the Federal Election Campaign Act of 1971, as amended, and most recently the Bipartisan Campaign Reform Act of 2002. Once in office, legislators spend time almost every day raising funds for their next campaign.

Most candidates for Congress must win the nomination through a **direct primary,** in which **party identifiers** vote for the candidate who will be on the party ticket in the general election. To win the primary, candidates may take more liberal or more conservative positions to get the votes of party identifiers. In the general election, they may moderate their views to attract the votes of independents and voters from the other party.

Presidential Effects. Congressional candidates are always hopeful that a strong presidential candidate on the ticket will have "coattails" that will sweep in senators and representatives of the same party. In fact, coattail effects have been quite limited and in recent presidential elections have not materialized at all. One way to measure the coattail effect is to look at the subsequent midterm elections, held in the even-numbered years following the presidential contests. In these years, voter turnout falls sharply. The party controlling the White House normally loses seats in Congress in the midterm elections, in part because the coattail effect ceases to apply. Members of Congress who are from contested districts or who are in their first term are more likely not to be reelected. Table 10–3 shows the pattern for midterm elections since 1942. As you can see, the "midterm effect" did not apply to George W. Bush's first term. In his second term, however, his job approval ratings

Direct Primary
An intraparty election in which the voters select the candidates who will run on a party's ticket in the subsequent general election.

Party Identifier
A person who identifies with a political party.

didyouknow...

That 2004 was the first time since 1866 that Republicans increased their majority in the House of Representatives in two consecutive elections?

TABLE 10–3:
Midterm Gains and Losses by the Party of the President, 1942–2006

Seats Gained or Lost by the Party of the President in the House of Representatives	
1942	−45 (D.)
1946	−55 (D.)
1950	−29 (D.)
1954	−18 (R.)
1958	−47 (R.)
1962	−4 (D.)
1966	−47 (D.)
1970	−12 (R.)
1974	−48 (R.)
1978	−15 (D.)
1982	−26 (R.)
1986	−5 (R.)
1990	−8 (R.)
1994	−52 (D.)
1998	+5 (D.)
2002	+5 (R.)
2006	−30 (R.)

TABLE 10–4: The Power of Incumbency

	Election Year													
	1982	1984	1986	1988	1990	1992	1994	1996	1998	2000	2002	2004	2006	2008
House														
Number of incumbent candidates	393	411	394	409	406	368	387	384	402	403	393	404	405	404
Reelected	354	392	385	402	390	325	349	361	395	394	383	397	382	381
Percentage of total	90.1	95.4	97.7	98.3	96.0	88.3	90.2	94.0	98.3	97.8	97.5	98.3	94.3	94.3
Defeated	39	19	9	7	16	43	38	23	7	9	10	7	23	23
In primary	10	3	3	1	1	19	4	2	1	3	3	1	2	5
In general election	29	16	6	6	15	24	34	21	6	6	7	6	21	18
Senate														
Number of incumbent candidates	30	29	28	27	32	28	26	21	29	29	28	26	29	30
Reelected	28	26	21	23	31	23	24	19	26	23	24	25	23	26
Percentage of total	93.3	89.6	75.0	85.2	96.9	82.1	92.3	90.5	89.7	79.3	85.7	96.2	79.3	86.7
Defeated	2	3	7	4	1	5	2	2	3	6	4	1	6	4
In primary	0	0	0	0	0	1	0	1	0	0	1	0	1*	0
In general election	2	3	7	4	1	4	2	1	3	6	3	1	6	3

*Joe Lieberman of Connecticut lost the Democratic primary but won the general election as an independent. He aligned himself with the Senate Democrats for organizational purposes.

Sources: Norman Ornstein, Thomas E. Mann, and Michael J. Malbin, *Vital Statistics on Congress, 2001–2002* (Washington, D.C.: The AEI Press, 2002); and authors' update.

were uncommonly low, often falling below 40 percent. In 2005 and 2006, the Gallup poll consistently found that voters would favor congressional candidates who opposed the president's policies. Not surprisingly, the midterm effect reappeared in 2006 elections.

THE POWER OF INCUMBENCY

The power of incumbency in the outcome of congressional elections cannot be overemphasized. Table 10–4 shows that a sizable majority of representatives and a slightly smaller proportion of senators who decide to run for reelection are successful. This conclusion holds for both presidential-year and midterm elections. A number of scholars contend that the pursuit of reelection is the strongest motivation behind the activities of members of Congress. They pursue the reelection goal in several ways. An incumbent can use the mass media, make personal appearances with constituents, and send newsletters—all to produce a favorable image and to make the incumbent's name a household word. Increasingly, members of Congress are using e-mail, blogs, and podcasts to communicate with constituents. Perhaps because reelection is so easy for incumbents, however, members of Congress are far behind presidential candidates in their use of these media, as we explain in this chapter's *Politics and the Cyber Sphere* feature.

Members of Congress generally try to present themselves as informed, experienced, and responsive to people's needs. Legislators also can point to things that they have done to benefit their constituents—fulfilling the congressional casework function or bringing money for highways or mass transit to the district, for example. Finally, incumbents can demonstrate the positions that they have taken on key issues by referring to their voting records in Congress.

POLITICS AND...
the cyber sphere

MEMBERS OF CONGRESS RESIST THE ONLINE WORLD

No business would ever think about minimizing its online presence. No business would ever think about making it difficult for its customers to send e-mails to complain about a product or to ask a service question. No business would ever pass up an opportunity to obtain funds via the Internet. But the members of Congress are not running a business. The true story of Congress and the Internet is how far behind the technology curve members of Congress remain.

E-MAILING YOUR MEMBER OF CONGRESS

When you have a complaint or a question about a product or service, you often send an e-mail. You might think that the same would hold for your member of Congress. And you are right—you can send an e-mail, for all members of Congress have e-mail addresses. Of course, those members do not see your e-mails themselves; they have staff to read them. The problem is that as e-mail communication became more prevalent, staff members on Capitol Hill quickly realized that they could not handle the volume of e-mails coming in on a daily basis. Consequently, with no sophisticated software to help ferret out the "junk" from the important messages, some congressional staffers have simply turned off their members' public e-mail addresses.

COLLECTING CAMPAIGN CONTRIBUTIONS ONLINE—FOR PRESIDENTIAL CANDIDATES ONLY?

The press has had a field day talking about the importance of small donors during the presidential campaigns in 2008. Hundreds of millions of dollars were raised by all candidates during the primaries and even more after the primaries. Small donations of $200 or less have become the mainstay of presidential races. Not so for members of Congress. Less than 10 percent of all donations for House candidates came in amounts of $200 or less, according to the Federal Election Commission. On average, congressional incumbents received a lower percentage of their campaign funds from small donors than their challengers did.

The reality is that those running for Congress have not yet made full use of the Internet to finance their campaigns. This situation may change, though, because small-donor online vehicles are being developed. They include the Democratic ActBlue and the Republican Slatecard Web sites.

BLOGS OR BLATHER?

Blogging is now a large part of the communications mentality throughout the world. Not so in Congress. Relatively few members of Congress keep blogs. When reading some of these blogs, it seems as if the congresspersons who created them only did so to seem "cool." The few congressional blogs that exist never allow comments. After all, why would they let the public post negative thoughts? Congressional blogs are basically sales devices without much real information.

FOR CRITICAL ANALYSIS

Why do you think that members of Congress avail themselves so little of existing communications technology?

(http://www.slatecard.com)

(http://www.actblue.com)

elections2008

PARTY CONTROL OF CONGRESS AFTER THE 2008 ELECTIONS

(Nicholas Kamm/
AFP/Getty Images)

How many legislators must a party elect before it can control Congress? In 2008, the Democrats added seven senators, by a provisional count, for a total of fifty-eight. In the House, the Democrats gained a provisional twenty-one seats on top of the thirty that they had won in 2006. Shouldn't this be enough for control? Certainly, a party only needs a bare majority to elect the Speaker of the House, committee chairpersons, and other congressional leaders. A simple majority is not always enough to pass legislation in the Senate, however, even when a proposal has the support of the majority caucus. It takes sixty senators to invoke cloture, that is, to shut off debate and end any filibusters. In the 2008 elections, the Senate Democrats set themselves a goal of sixty seats, enough to invoke cloture without

relying on any Republicans. The Democrats were not that successful, however. Does that mean that Republicans in the Senate can block any bill? Not necessarily. The Senate rarely votes on a strict party-line basis. Senate Democrats have a reasonable hope that if they "reach across the aisle" they can win the support of at least a few moderate Republicans. Likewise, the Democratic leadership must make sure that conservative Democrats don't refuse to support the party's legislation. Years ago, the Democratic caucuses in both chambers contained large numbers of very conservative legislators, mostly from the South. In those days, northern Democrats needed a tremendous margin in both chambers to pass legislation. Today, both the Republicans and Democrats are much more ideologically united.

PARTY CONTROL OF CONGRESS AFTER THE 2006 ELECTIONS

In 2006, for the first time since 1994 (when the Republicans took control of Congress for the first time in forty years), the voters returned Democratic majorities to both the Senate and the House of Representatives. Majorities in both chambers meant that the Democrats occupied the leadership positions in Congress. Democrats had little choice but to name loyal and long-serving liberal members to key committee chairs. Clearly, though, the agenda of these more liberal elements in the Democratic Party was tempered to meet the demands of the more moderate Democrats and independents who helped to bring about the Democrats' victory in the elections.

CONGRESSIONAL APPORTIONMENT

Two of the most complicated aspects of congressional elections are apportionment issues—**reapportionment** (the allocation of seats in the House to each state after each census) and **redistricting** (the redrawing of the boundaries of the districts within each state). In a landmark six-to-two vote in 1962, the United States Supreme Court made the apportionment of state legislative districts a **justiciable** (that is, a reviewable) **question.**[2] The Court did so by invoking the Fourteenth Amendment principle that no state can deny to any person "the equal protection of the laws." In 1964, the Court held that *both* chambers of a state legislature must be apportioned so that all districts are equal in population.[3] Later that year, the Court applied this "one person, one vote" principle to U.S. congressional districts on the basis of Article I, Section 2, of the Constitution, which requires that members of the House be chosen "by the People of the several States."[4]

Severe malapportionment of congressional districts before 1964 resulted in some districts containing two or three times the populations of other districts in the same state, thereby diluting the effect of a vote cast in the more populous districts. This system generally benefited the conservative populations of rural areas and small towns and harmed the

Reapportionment
The allocation of seats in the House of Representatives to each state after each census.

Redistricting
The redrawing of the boundaries of the congressional districts within each state.

Justiciable Question
A question that may be raised and reviewed in court.

---

2. *Baker v. Carr*, 369 U.S. 186 (1962). The term *justiciable* is pronounced juhs-*tish*-a-buhl.
3. *Reynolds v. Sims*, 377 U.S. 533 (1964).
4. *Wesberry v. Sanders*, 376 U.S. 1 (1964).

interests of the more heavily populated and liberal cities. In fact, suburban areas have benefited the most from the Court's rulings, as suburbs account for an increasingly larger proportion of the nation's population, while cities include a correspondingly smaller segment of the population.

GERRYMANDERING

Although the general issue of apportionment has been dealt with fairly successfully by the one person, one vote principle, the **gerrymandering** issue has not yet been resolved. This term refers to the legislative-boundary-drawing tactics that were used under Elbridge Gerry, the governor of Massachusetts, in the 1812 elections (see Figure 10–1). A district is said to have been gerrymandered when its shape is altered substantially by the dominant party to maximize its electoral strength at the expense of the minority party.

In 1986, the Supreme Court heard a case that challenged gerrymandered congressional districts in Indiana. The Court ruled for the first time that redistricting for the political benefit of one group could be challenged on constitutional grounds. In this specific case, *Davis v. Bandemer,*[5] however, the Court did not agree that the districts were drawn unfairly, because it could not be proved that a group of voters would consistently be deprived of influence at the polls as a result of the new districts.

REDISTRICTING AFTER THE 2000 CENSUS

In the meantime, political gerrymandering continues. For example, New York Democratic representative Maurice Hinchey's district resembles a soup ladle. Why? That shape guarantees that he will always be able to pick up enough votes in Ithaca and Binghamton to win reelection. Right next to that district is Republican representative Sherwood Boehlert's district, which has been said to resemble a "napping Bugs Bunny."

Congressional and state legislative redistricting decisions are often made by a small group of political leaders within a state legislature. Typically, their goal is to shape voting districts in such a way as to maximize their party's chances of winning state legislative seats, as well as seats in Congress. Two of the techniques they use are called "packing" and "cracking." With the use of powerful computers and software, they *pack* voters supporting the opposing party into as few districts as possible or *crack* the opposing party's supporters into different districts. Consider that in Michigan, the Republicans who dominated redistricting efforts succeeded in packing six Democratic incumbents into only three congressional seats.

Clearly, partisan redistricting aids incumbents. The party that dominates a state's legislature will be making redistricting decisions. Through gerrymandering tactics such as packing and cracking, districts can be redrawn in such a way as to ensure that party's continued strength in the state legislature or Congress. As pointed out on page 350, only a small percentage of the 435 seats in the House of Representatives were open for any real competition in the most recent elections.

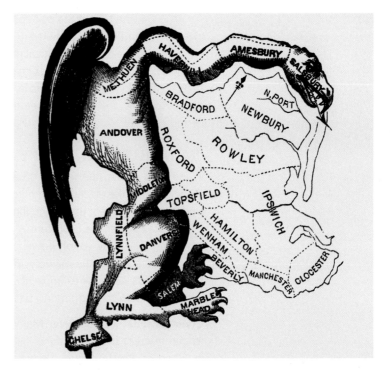

Source: *Congressional Quarterly's Guide to Congress,* 3d ed. (Washington, D.C.: Congressional Quarterly Press, 1982), p. 695.

FIGURE 10–1: The Original Gerrymander

The practice of "gerrymandering"—the excessive manipulation of the shape of a legislative district to benefit a certain incumbent or party—is probably as old as the republic, but the name originated in 1812. In that year, the Massachusetts legislature carved out of Essex County a district that historian John Fiske said had a "dragonlike contour." When the painter Gilbert Stuart saw the misshapen district, he penciled in a head, wings, and claws and exclaimed, "That will do for a salamander!" Editor Benjamin Russell replied, "Better say a Gerrymander" (after Elbridge Gerry, then governor of Massachusetts).

Gerrymandering
The drawing of legislative district boundary lines for the purpose of obtaining partisan or factional advantage. A district is said to be gerrymandered when its shape is manipulated by the dominant party to maximize electoral strength at the expense of the minority party.

---

5. 478 U.S. 109 (1986).

In 2004, the United States Supreme Court reviewed an obviously political redistricting scheme in Pennsylvania. The Court concluded, however, that the federal judiciary would not address purely political gerrymandering claims.[6] Two years later, the Supreme Court reached a similar conclusion with respect to most of the new congressional districts created by the Republicans in the Texas legislature in 2003. Again, except for one district in Texas, the Court refused to intervene in what was clearly a political gerrymandering plan.[7]

"MINORITY-MAJORITY" DISTRICTS

In the early 1990s, the federal government encouraged a type of gerrymandering that made possible the election of a minority representative from a "minority-majority" area. Under the mandate of the Voting Rights Act of 1965, the Justice Department issued directives to states after the 1990 census instructing them to create congressional districts that would maximize the voting power of minority groups—that is, create districts in which minority voters were the majority. The result was a number of creatively drawn congressional districts—see, for example, the depiction of Illinois's Fourth Congressional District in Figure 10–2, which is commonly described as "a pair of earmuffs."

Constitutional Challenges. Many of these "minority-majority" districts were challenged in court by citizens who claimed that creating districts based on race or ethnicity alone violates the equal protection clause of the Constitution. In 1995, the Supreme Court agreed with this argument when it declared that Georgia's new Eleventh District was unconstitutional. The district stretched from Atlanta to the Atlantic, splitting eight counties and five municipalities along the way. The Court referred to the district as a "monstrosity" linking "widely spaced urban centers that have absolutely nothing to do with each other." The Court went on to say that when a state assigns voters on the basis of race, "it engages in the offensive and demeaning assumption that voters of a particular race, because of their race, think alike, share the same political interests, and will prefer the same candidates at the polls." The Court also chastised the Justice Department for concluding that race-based districting was mandated under the Voting Rights Act of 1965: "When the Justice Department's interpretation of the Act compels race-based districting, it by definition raises a serious constitutional question."[8] In subsequent rulings, the Court affirmed its position that when race is the dominant factor in the drawing of congressional district lines, the districts are unconstitutional.

Changing Directions. In the early 2000s, the Supreme Court seemed to take a new direction on racial redistricting challenges. In a 2000 case, the Court limited the federal government's authority to invalidate changes in state and local elections on the basis that the changes were discriminatory. The case involved a proposed school redistricting plan in Louisiana. The Court held that federal approval for the plan could not be withheld simply because the plan was discriminatory. Rather, the test was whether the plan left racial and ethnic minorities worse off than they were before.[9]

FIGURE 10–2: The Fourth Congressional District of Illinois

This district, which is mostly within Chicago's city limits, was drawn to connect two Hispanic neighborhoods separated by an African American majority district.

Districts 1–5 and 7–9

Fourth District

6. *Vieth v. Jubelirer*, 541 U.S. 267 (2004).
7. *League of United Latin American Citizens v. Perry*, 548 U.S. 399 (2006).
8. *Miller v. Johnson*, 515 U.S. 900 (1995).
9. *Reno v. Bossier Parish School Board*, 528 U.S. 320 (2000).

In 2001, the Supreme Court reviewed, for a second time, a case involving North Carolina's Twelfth District. The district was 165 miles long, following Interstate 85 for the most part. According to a local joke, the district was so narrow that a car traveling down the interstate highway with both doors open would kill most of the voters in the district. In 1996, the Supreme Court had held that the district was unconstitutional because race had been the dominant factor in drawing the district's boundaries. Shortly thereafter, the boundaries were redrawn, but the district was again challenged as a racial gerrymander. A federal district court agreed and invalidated the new boundaries as unconstitutional. In 2001, however, the Supreme Court held that there was insufficient evidence for the lower court's conclusion that race had been the dominant factor when the boundaries were redrawn.[10] The Twelfth District's boundaries remained as drawn.

> **Franking**
> A policy that enables members of Congress to send material through the mail by substituting their facsimile signature (frank) for postage.

PERKS AND PRIVILEGES

Legislators have many benefits that are not available to most workers. For example, members of Congress are granted generous **franking** privileges that permit them to mail newsletters, surveys, and other correspondence to their constituents without paying for postage. (The word *franking* derives from the Latin *francus,* which means "free.") The annual cost of congressional mail has risen from $11 million in 1971 to more than $70 million today. Typically, the costs for these mailings rise substantially during election years. Is it fair to allow free mailing privileges to members of Congress? We debate this question in the *Which Side Are You On?* feature on the next page.

didyouknow...

That before the Republicans reorganized House services in 1995, all members had buckets of ice delivered to their offices each day, at an annual cost of $500,000?

PERMANENT PROFESSIONAL STAFFS

More than 30,000 people are employed in the Capitol Hill bureaucracy. About half of them are personal and committee staff members. The personal staff includes office clerks and assistants; professionals who deal with media relations, draft legislation, and satisfy constituency requests for service; and staffers who maintain local offices in the member's home district or state.

The average Senate office on Capitol Hill employs about thirty staff members, and twice that number work on the personal staffs of senators from the most populous states. House office staffs typically are about half as large as those of the Senate. The number of staff members has increased dramatically since 1960. The bulk of those increases has been in assistants to individual members, leading some scholars to question whether staff members are really advising on legislation or are primarily aiding constituents and gaining votes in the next election.

didyouknow...

That the most recently constructed dormitory for Senate pages cost about $8 million, or $264,200 per bed, compared with the median cost of a university dormitory of $22,600 per bed?

Congress also benefits from the expertise of the professional staffs of agencies that were created to produce information for members of the House and Senate. For example, the Congressional Research Service, the Government Accountability Office, and the Congressional Budget Office all provide reports, audits, and policy recommendations for review by members of Congress.

PRIVILEGES AND IMMUNITIES UNDER THE LAW

Members of Congress also benefit from a number of special constitutional protections. Under Article I, Section 6, of the Constitution, they "shall in all Cases, except Treason, Felony and Breach of the Peace, be privileged from Arrest during their Attendance at the Session of their respective Houses, and in going to and returning from the same; and for any Speech or Debate in either House, they shall not be questioned in any other Place." The arrest immunity clause is not really an important provision today. The "speech or

---

10. *Easley v. Cromartie,* 532 U.S. 234 (2001).

whichsideareyouon?

SHOULD FREE CONGRESSIONAL MAILINGS BE ELIMINATED?

The practice of "franking" dates back to the Continental Congress of 1775. *Franking* is the formal word for sending mail postage-free. After the Constitution was adopted, the first U.S. Congress enacted the Franking Law in 1789. This law allows members of Congress to simply sign their names in the upper right-hand corner of official letters and packages instead of using postage.

In a typical year, the House and Senate each spend between $35 million and $40 million by exercising the franking privilege. Members of the House alone send out about 120 million pieces of mail for free every year. This amount of mail is not just in response to constituents' letters. These days, constituents are more likely to send e-mail than letters to their senators and representatives. Modern members of Congress respond to their constituents with e-mail, not letters. The franking privilege is used principally in mass mailings, often of newsletters. Some people ask whether we should eliminate free mailings for members of Congress.

TAXPAYER-FINANCED CONGRESSIONAL MAILINGS MUST STOP

The main purpose of taxpayer-financed mailings by members of Congress is self-promotion. Members use the franking privilege for political reasons that have little to do with benefiting their constituents. Sometimes, members of Congress send free mailings that are worth more than the mail that they purchase with their campaign funds. At least sixty-five House members spend more than $100,000 each year in taxpayer-financed mailing expenses. The newsletters sent out are typically glossy productions with flattering photographs. Often, they list the latest pet projects that the members have brought home to their districts ("bringing home the bacon"). Often, taxpayer-financed mass mailings include obvious advice or information that almost anyone could easily obtain from the Internet. Representative Tim Murphy (R., Pa.) sent out a newsletter suggesting that his constituents "keep your car properly maintained" to increase gasoline mileage. Representative David Dreier (R., Calif.) gave tips on home improvements. It's time to stop the charade—cut off the franking privilege.

MEMBERS OF CONGRESS HAVE THE RIGHT TO KEEP THEIR CONSTITUENTS INFORMED

The reason members of Congress received the franking privilege in the first place was to allow them to more easily keep their constituents informed of the goings-on in Congress. Representative Ginny Brown-Waite (R., Fla.) has pointed out that one of the biggest concerns of her constituents was that her predecessor did not keep them informed of what was happening in Washington. She makes sure that they know now, and she is one of the heaviest users of the franking privilege. Members of Congress should be able to communicate with their constituents without monetary constraints. Free mailings by members of Congress are regulated by a congressional commission that guards against overt political appeals. Franked mail cannot be sent within ninety days of an election. There was a reason that the First Congress created the franking privilege. Now is not the time to change what has worked for more than two hundred years.

(Shutterstock)

debate" clause, however, means that a member may make any allegations or other statements he or she wishes in connection with official duties and normally not be sued for libel or slander or otherwise be subject to legal action. For additional ways in which members of Congress enjoy a working environment that differs dramatically from that of the ordinary citizen, see this chapter's *Politics and Congress* feature.

CONGRESSIONAL CAUCUSES: ANOTHER SOURCE OF SUPPORT

All members of Congress are members of one or more caucuses. The most important caucuses are those established by the parties in each chamber. These Democratic and Republican meetings provide information to the members and devise legislative strategy for the party. Other caucuses have been founded, such as the Democratic Study Group and the Congressional Black Caucus, to support subgroups of members. In 1995, con-

politicsand...congress

A FULL WEEK'S WORK?

(© Cornel Achirerei, 2008. Used under license from Shutterstock.com.)

Making national laws is supposed to be a *deliberative* process. Members of Congress deliberate on which laws to pass, repeal, or change. A deliberative process is supposed to take time. One would think that when Congress is in session, members of Congress would need at least a full workweek, if not longer, to carry out their lawmaking function. Consider, though, what a typical workweek is for an average member of Congress.[a]

A TYPICAL WORKWEEK

While Congress is in session, most members do not come to their offices until early Tuesday morning. A majority of them return to their home districts or states on Thursday night after the last votes are taken. At the latest, they leave Washington, D.C., early Friday morning. This Tuesday-to-Thursday club existed in the past, but only for a select few congressional members. In contrast, today the vast majority of Congress is part of the three-days-a-week club.

SHORT SESSIONS

In 2006, the 109th Congress voted during fewer than one hundred days—fewer days than during the previous sixty years. The number of days in session—voting days plus

---

a. See Thomas E. Mann and Norman J. Ornstein, *The Broken Branch: How Congress Is Failing America and How to Get It Back on Track* (New York: Oxford University Press, 2006).

other days when Congress was officially "open for business"—dropped below 250 per two-year congressional term during the first six years of the Bush administration. In contrast, in the 1960s and 1970s Congress was in session for, on average, 323 days. In 2006, the House spent only 850 hours in session during the year.

Democratic leaders of the 110th Congress claimed that they would have longer workweeks and spend more time in deliberation. Indeed, in 2007, the House spent 1,478 hours in session, as opposed to the 850 hours in 2006. The Democrats had little to show for the increased time in session, however. The number of public laws enacted dropped from 248 in 2006 to 138 in 2007.

WHEN LAWMAKING REALLY GETS DONE

Three-day workweeks and truncated congressional sessions do not lend themselves to much decision making, and certainly not much deliberation. Much of the action takes place behind closed doors, not in the chambers of Congress. A small group of leadership staff, committee staff, industry representatives, and a few important party members put bills together. These bills are then run through subcommittees and committees with minimal debate.

Consider that in the 1960s and 1970s, the average Congress had about 5,400 House committee and subcommittee meetings. By 2006, Congress held barely 2,000 such meetings. Major bills that in the past would have required weeks of hearings and days of markup (rewriting) are often reviewed in a couple of days of hearings. Committees appear to spend little or no visible time on systematic analysis of proposed legislation.

FOR CRITICAL ANALYSIS

Some members of Congress argue that much of their most important work is done in their home districts or states. Do you believe that this is a good enough reason for them to be in Washington, D.C., only three days a week while Congress is in session? Why or why not?

---

cerned with the growth of caucuses supported by public funds, the Republican majority in the House passed a rule that prohibited using free space for caucuses or using public funds to finance them.

The number of caucuses has not declined, however. Instead, the number has increased. There are now more than two hundred caucuses, including small ones (the Albanian Issues Caucus, the Potato Caucus) and large ones (the Sportsmen's Caucus). These organizations, which are now funded by businesses and special interests, provide staff assistance and information for members of Congress and help them build support among specific groups of voters.

Oil In The Outer Continer

21%

79% Available
= 67.7 billion barrels

Rahm Emanuel

(D., Ill.) was the House Democratic Caucus Chairman during the 110th Congress. (In November 2008, President-elect Obama appointed Emanuel as his chief of staff.) Here, he is shown during a news conference that was designed to counter Republican attempts at opening up new offshore oil drilling in 2008 and 2009. The Democratic Caucus countered with proposed legislation that would have required oil and gas companies to develop their existing federal leases under what was called a "use-it-or-lose-it" approach. How important are caucuses within each chamber of Congress? (Photo by Scott J. Ferrell/Congressional Quarterly/Getty Images)

THE COMMITTEE STRUCTURE

Most of the actual work of legislating is performed by the committees and subcommittees within Congress. Thousands of bills are introduced in every session of Congress, and no single member can possibly be adequately informed on all the issues that arise. The committee system is a way to provide for specialization, or a division of the legislative labor. Members of a committee can concentrate on just one area or topic—such as taxation or energy—and develop sufficient expertise to draft appropriate legislation when needed. The flow of legislation through both the House and the Senate is determined largely by the speed with which the members of these committees act on bills and resolutions.

THE POWER OF COMMITTEES

Sometimes called "little legislatures," committees usually have the final say on pieces of legislation.[11] Committee actions may be overturned on the floor by the House or Senate, but this rarely happens. Legislators normally defer to the expertise of the chairperson and other members of the committee who speak on the floor in defense of a committee decision. Chairpersons of committees exercise control over the scheduling of hearings and formal action on a bill. They also decide which subcommittee will act on legislation falling within their committees' jurisdiction.

Committees only very rarely are deprived of control over a bill—although this kind of action is provided for in the rules of each chamber. In the House, if a bill has been considered by a standing committee for thirty days, the signatures of a majority (218) of the House membership on a **discharge petition** can pry a bill out of an uncooperative committee's hands. From 1909 to 2009, however, although more than nine hundred such petitions were initiated, only slightly more than two dozen resulted in successful discharge efforts. Of those, twenty resulted in bills that passed the House.[12]

TYPES OF CONGRESSIONAL COMMITTEES

Over the past two centuries, Congress has created several different types of committees, each of which serves particular needs of the institution.

Standing Committees. By far the most important committees in Congress are the **standing committees**—permanent bodies that are established by the rules of each chamber of Congress and that continue from session to session. A list of the standing committees of the 111th Congress is presented in Table 10–5. In addition, most of the standing committees have created subcommittees to carry out their work. For example, the 111th Congress has 73 subcommittees in the Senate and 104 in the House. Each standing committee is given a specific area of legislative policy jurisdiction, and almost all legislative measures are considered by the appropriate standing committees.

Because of the importance of their work and the traditional influence of their members in Congress, certain committees are considered to be more prestigious than others.

Discharge Petition
A procedure by which a bill in the House of Representatives can be forced (discharged) out of a committee that has refused to report it for consideration by the House. The petition must be signed by an absolute majority (218) of representatives and is used only on rare occasions.

Standing Committee
A permanent committee in the House or Senate that considers bills within a certain subject area.

---

11. The term *little legislatures* is from Woodrow Wilson, *Congressional Government* (New York: Meridian Books, 1956 [first published in 1885]).
12. Congressional Quarterly, Inc., *Guide to Congress,* 5th ed. (Washington, D.C.: CQ Press, 2000); and authors' update.

TABLE 10–5: Standing Committees of the 111th Congress, 2009–2011

House Committees	Senate Committees
Agriculture	Agriculture, Nutrition, and Forestry
Appropriations	Appropriations
Armed Services	Armed Services
Budget	Banking, Housing, and Urban Affairs
Education and Labor	Budget
Energy and Commerce	Commerce, Science, and Transportation
Financial Services	Energy and Natural Resources
Foreign Affairs	Environment and Public Works
Homeland Security	Finance
House Administration	Foreign Relations
Judiciary	Health, Education, Labor, and Pensions
Natural Resources	Homeland Security and Governmental Affairs
Oversight and Government Reform	Judiciary
Rules	Rules and Administration
Science and Technology	Small Business and Entrepreneurship
Small Business	Veterans' Affairs
Standards of Official Conduct	
Transportation and Infrastructure	
Veterans' Affairs	
Ways and Means	

Seats on standing committees that handle spending issues are especially sought after because members can use these positions to benefit their constituents. Committees that control spending include the Appropriations Committee in either chamber and the Ways and Means Committee in the House. Members also normally seek seats on committees that handle matters of special interest to their constituents. A member of the House from an agricultural district, for example, will have an interest in joining the House Agriculture Committee.

Select Committees. In principle, a **select committee** is created for a limited time and for a specific legislative purpose. For example, a select committee may be formed to investigate a public problem, such as child nutrition or aging. In practice, a select committee, such as the Select Committee on Intelligence in each chamber, may continue indefinitely. Select committees rarely create original legislation.

Joint Committees. A **joint committee** is formed by the concurrent action of both chambers of Congress and consists of members from each chamber. Joint committees, which may be permanent or temporary, have dealt with the economy, taxation, and the Library of Congress.

Conference Committees. Special joint committees—**conference committees**—are formed for the purpose of achieving agreement between the House and the Senate on the exact wording of legislative acts when the two chambers pass legislative proposals in different forms. No bill can be sent to the White House to be signed into law unless it first passes both chambers in identical form. Sometimes called the "third house" of Congress,

Select Committee
A temporary legislative committee established for a limited time period and for a special purpose.

Joint Committee
A legislative committee composed of members from both chambers of Congress..

Conference Committee
A special joint committee appointed to reconcile differences when bills pass the two chambers of Congress in different forms.

Senator Patrick Leahy (D., Vt.)

speaks at a hearing before the Senate Judiciary Committee in the late spring of 2008. As committee chairman, Leahy wished to address the high price of oil. To what extent do committee hearings affect proposed and actual legislation? (Photo by Alex Wong/Getty Images)

conference committees are in a position to make significant alterations to legislation and frequently become the focal point of policy debates.

The House Rules Committee. Due to its special "gatekeeping" power over the terms on which legislation will reach the floor of the House of Representatives, the House Rules Committee holds a uniquely powerful position. A special committee rule sets the time limit on debate and determines whether and how a bill may be amended. This practice dates back to 1883. The Rules Committee has the unusual power to meet while the House is in session, to have its resolutions considered immediately on the floor, and to initiate legislation on its own.

THE SELECTION OF COMMITTEE MEMBERS

In both chambers, members are appointed to standing committees by the Steering Committee of their party. The majority-party member with the longest term of continuous service on a standing committee is given preference when the committee selects its chairperson. This is not a law but an informal, traditional process, and it applies to other significant posts in Congress as well. The **seniority system,** although it deliberately treats members unequally, provides a predictable means of assigning positions of power within Congress. The most senior member of the minority party is called the *ranking committee member* for that party.

The general pattern until the 1970s was that members of the House or Senate who represented **safe seats** would be reelected continually and eventually would accumulate enough years of continuous committee service to enable them to become the chairpersons of their committees. In the 1970s, a number of reforms in the chairperson selection process somewhat modified the seniority system. The reforms introduced the use of a secret ballot in electing House committee chairpersons and allowed for the possibility of choosing a chairperson on a basis other than seniority. The Democrats immediately replaced three senior chairpersons who were out of step with the rest of their party. In 1995, under Speaker Newt Gingrich, the Republicans chose relatively junior House members as chairpersons of several key committees, thus ensuring conservative control of the committees. The Republicans also passed a rule limiting the term of a chairperson to six years.

Seniority System

A custom followed in both chambers of Congress specifying that the member of the majority party with the longest term of continuous service will be given preference when a committee chairperson (or a holder of some other significant post) is selected

Safe Seat

A district that returns a legislator with 55 percent of the vote or more.

One important standing committee in the Senate

is the Armed Services Committee. Its chairman is Senator Carl Levin (D., Mich.), who is shown here shaking hands with some decorated Iraq War Army veterans. Chairpersons of congressional committees are almost always from the party that controls each chamber. (AP Photo/Susan Walsh)

THE FORMAL LEADERSHIP

The limited amount of centralized power that exists in Congress is exercised through party-based mechanisms. Congress is organized by party. When the Democratic Party, for example, wins a majority of seats in either the House or the Senate, Democrats control the official positions of power in that chamber, and every important committee has a Democratic chairperson and a majority of Democratic members. The same process holds when Republicans are in the majority.

We next consider the formal leadership positions in the House and Senate separately, but you will note some broad similarities in the way leaders are selected and in the ways they exercise power in the two chambers.

LEADERSHIP IN THE HOUSE

The House leadership is made up of the Speaker, the majority and minority leaders, and the party whips.

The Speaker. The foremost power holder in the House of Representatives is the **Speaker of the House.** The Speaker's position is technically a nonpartisan one, but in fact, for the better part of two centuries, the Speaker has been the official leader of the majority party in the House. When a new Congress convenes in January of odd-numbered years, each party nominates a candidate for Speaker. All Democratic members of the House are expected to vote for their party's nominee, and all Republicans are expected to support their candidate. The vote to organize the House is the one vote in which representatives must vote with their party. In a sense, this vote defines a member's partisan status.

The influence of modern-day Speakers is based primarily on their personal prestige, persuasive ability, and knowledge of the legislative process—plus the acquiescence or active support of other representatives. The major formal powers of the Speaker include the following:

1. Presiding over meetings of the House.
2. Appointing members of joint committees and conference committees.
3. Scheduling legislation for floor action.
4. Deciding points of order and interpreting the rules with the advice of the House parliamentarian.
5. Referring bills and resolutions to the appropriate standing committees of the House.

When the Democrats took control of the House of Representatives after the 2006 midterm elections, they elected Nancy Pelosi (D., Calif.) as Speaker of the House and Steny H. Hoyer (D., Md., center) as House majority leader. John Boehner (R., Ohio) was named House minority leader by the Republicans. These three individuals, as well as the rest of the House leadership, were up for reelection after the 2008 elections. The leadership elections were scheduled for late November 2008. What benefits could a state receive when one of its representatives obtains such a leadership post? (Photos Courtesy of the U.S. Congress)

didyouknow...

That the Constitution does not require that the Speaker of the House of Representatives be an elected member of the House?

Speaker of the House
The presiding officer in the House of Representatives. The Speaker is always a member of the majority party and is the most powerful and influential member of the House.

A Speaker may take part in floor debate and vote, as can any other member of Congress, but recent Speakers usually have voted only to break a tie. Since 1975, the Speaker, when a Democrat, has also had the power to appoint the Democratic Steering Committee, which determines new committee assignments for House party members.

In general, the powers of the Speaker are related to his or her control over information and communications channels in the House. This is a significant power in a large, decentralized institution in which information is a very important resource. With this control, the Speaker attempts to ensure the smooth operation of the chamber and to integrate presidential and congressional policies.

The Majority Leader. The **majority leader of the House** is elected by a caucus of the majority party to foster cohesion among party members and to act as a spokesperson for the party. The majority leader influences the scheduling of debate and acts as the chief supporter of the Speaker. The majority leader cooperates with the Speaker and other party leaders, both inside and outside Congress, to formulate the party's legislative program and to guide that program through the legislative process in the House. The Democrats often recruit future Speakers from those who hold the position of majority leader.

The Minority Leader. The **minority leader of the House** is the candidate nominated for Speaker by a caucus of the minority party. Like the majority leader, the leader of the minority party has as her or his primary responsibility the maintaining of cohesion within the party's ranks. The minority leader works for solidarity among the party's members and speaks on behalf of the president if the minority party controls the White House. In relations with the majority party, the minority leader consults with both the Speaker and the majority leader on recognizing members who wish to speak on the floor, on House rules and procedures, and on the scheduling of legislation. Minority leaders have no actual power in these areas, however.

Whips. The leadership of each party includes assistants to the majority and minority leaders, known as **whips.** The whips are members of Congress who assist the party leaders by passing information down from the leadership to party members and by ensuring that members show up for floor debate and cast their votes on important issues. Whips conduct polls among party members about the members' views on legislation, inform the leaders about whose vote is doubtful and whose is certain, and may exert pressure on members to support the leaders' positions. In the House, serving as a whip is the first step toward positions of higher leadership.

LEADERSHIP IN THE SENATE

The Senate is less than one-fourth the size of the House. This fact alone probably explains why a formal, complex, and centralized leadership structure is not as necessary in the Senate as it is in the House.

The two highest-ranking formal leadership positions in the Senate are essentially ceremonial in nature. Under the Constitution, the vice president of the United States is the president (that is, the presiding officer) of the Senate and may vote to break a tie. The vice president, however, is only rarely present for a meeting of the Senate. The Senate elects instead a **president pro tempore** ("pro tem") to preside over the Senate in the vice president's absence. Ordinarily, the president pro tem is the member of the majority party with the longest continuous term of service in the Senate. The president pro tem is mostly a ceremonial position. Junior senators take turns actually presiding over the sessions of the Senate.

The real leadership power in the Senate rests in the hands of the **Senate majority leader,** the **Senate minority leader,** and their respective whips. The Senate majority and minority leaders have the right to be recognized first in debate on the floor and generally

---

Majority Leader of the House
A legislative position held by an important party member in the House of Representatives. The majority leader is selected by the majority party in caucus or conference to foster cohesion among party members and to act as spokesperson for the majority party in the House.

Minority Leader of the House
The party leader elected by the minority party in the House.

Whip
A member of Congress who aids the majority or minority leader of the House or the Senate.

President Pro Tempore
The temporary presiding officer of the Senate in the absence of the vice president.

Senate Majority Leader
The chief spokesperson of the majority party in the Senate, who directs the legislative program and party strategy.

Senate Minority Leader
The party officer in the Senate who commands the minority party's opposition to the policies of the majority party and directs the legislative program and strategy of his or her party.

exercise the same powers available to the House majority and minority leaders. They control the scheduling of debate on the floor in conjunction with the majority party's Policy Committee, influence the allocation of committee assignments for new members or for senators attempting to transfer to a new committee, influence the selection of other party officials, and participate in selecting members of conference committees. The leaders are expected to mobilize support for partisan legislative or presidential initiatives. The leaders act as liaisons with the White House when the president is of their party, try to obtain the cooperation of committee chairpersons, and seek to facilitate the smooth functioning of the Senate through the senators' unanimous consent. The majority and minority leaders are elected by their respective party caucuses.

Senate party whips, like their House counterparts, maintain communication within the party on platform positions and try to ensure that party colleagues are present for floor debate and important votes. The Senate whip system is far less elaborate than its counterpart in the House, simply because there are fewer members to track.

A list of the formal party leaders of the 110th Congress is presented in Table 10–6 on the next page.

didyouknow...

That in 2004, on the urging of the Alaska congressional delegation, the House approved a $200 million bridge between a town of 7,845 people and an island with 50 residents—the famous "Bridge to Nowhere," which proved to be such a scandal that it had to be canceled?

HOW MEMBERS OF CONGRESS DECIDE

Each member of Congress casts hundreds of votes in each session. Each member compiles a record of votes during the years that he or she spends in the national legislature. There are usually a number of different reasons why any particular vote is cast. Research shows that the best predictor of a member's vote is party affiliation. Obviously, party members do have common opinions on some, if not all, issues facing the nation. In addition, the party leadership in each house works hard to build cohesion and agreement among the members through the activities of the party caucuses and conferences. In recent years, the increase in partisanship in both the House and the Senate has meant that most Republicans vote in opposition to most Democrats.

Conservative Coalition
An alliance of Republicans and southern Democrats that historically formed in the House or the Senate to oppose liberal legislation and support conservative legislation.

TABLE 10–6: Party Leaders in the 110th Congress, 2007–2009*

Position	Incumbent	Party/State	Leader since
HOUSE			
Speaker	Nancy Pelosi	D., Calif.	Jan. 2007
Majority leader	Steny Hoyer	D., Md.	Jan. 2007
Majority whip	James Clyburn	D., S.C.	Jan. 2007
Chair of the Democratic Caucus	Rahm Emanuel	D., Ill.	Jan. 2007
Minority leader	John Boehner	R., Ohio	Jan. 2007
Minority whip	Roy Blunt	R., Mo.	Jan. 2007
Chair of the Republican Conference	Adam Putnam	R., Fla.	Jan. 2007
SENATE			
President pro tempore	Robert Byrd	D., W.Va.	Jan. 2007
Majority leader	Harry Reid	D., Nev.	Jan. 2007
Majority whip	Dick Durbin	D., Ill.	Jan. 2007
Chair of the Democratic Conference	Harry Reid	D., Nev.	Jan. 2007
Minority leader	Mitch McConnell	R., Ky.	Jan. 2007
Minority whip	Jon Kyl	R., Ariz.	Dec. 2007
Chair of the Republican Conference	Lamar Alexander	R., Tenn.	Dec. 2007

*Leaders for the 111th Congress will be elected in late November 2008.

THE CONSERVATIVE COALITION

Political parties are not always unified. In the 1950s and 1960s, the Democrats in Congress were often split between northern liberals and southern conservatives. This division gave rise to the **conservative coalition,** a voting bloc made up of southern Democrats and conservative (which is to say, most) Republicans. This coalition was able to win many votes over the years. Today, however, most southern conservatives are Republicans, so the coalition has almost disappeared.

"CROSSING OVER"

On some votes, individual representatives and senators will vote against their party, "crossing over to the other side," because the interests of their states or districts differ from the interests that prevail within the rest of their party. Additionally, members may vote a certain way because of the influence of regional or national interests, such as public opinion on the Iraq War. Other voting decisions are based on the members' religious or ideological beliefs. Votes on such issues as abortion and gay rights may be motivated by a member's religious views.

There are, however, far too many voting decisions for every member to be fully informed on each issue. Research suggests that many voting decisions are based on cues provide by trusted colleagues or the party leadership. A member who sits on the committee that wrote a law may become a reliable source of information about that law. Alternatively, for cues on voting, a member may turn to a colleague who represents a district in the same state or one who represents a similar district. Cues may also come from fellow committee members, from leaders, and from the administration.

HOW A BILL BECOMES LAW

Each year, Congress and the president propose and approve many laws. Some are budget and appropriations laws that require extensive bargaining but must be passed for the government to continue to function. Other laws are relatively free of controversy and are passed with little dissension. Still other proposed legislation is extremely controversial and reaches to the roots of differences between Democrats and Republicans and between the executive and legislative branches.

As detailed in Figure 10–3 on the next page, each law begins as a bill, which must be introduced in either the House or the Senate. Often, similar bills are introduced in both chambers. A "money bill," however, must start in the House. In each chamber, the bill follows similar steps. It is referred to a committee and its subcommittees for study, discussion, hearings, and rewriting ("markup"). When the bill is reported out to the full chamber, it must be scheduled for debate (by the Rules Committee in the House and by the leadership in the Senate). After the bill has been passed in each chamber, if it contains different provisions, a conference committee is formed to write a compromise bill, which must be approved by both chambers before it is sent to the president to sign or veto.

Another form of congressional action, the *joint resolution,* differs little from a bill in how it is proposed or debated. Once it is approved by both chambers and signed by the president, it has the force of law.[13] A joint resolution to amend the Constitution, however, after it is approved by two-thirds of both chambers, is sent not to the president but to the states for ratification.

> **Executive Budget**
> The budget prepared and submitted by the president to Congress.
>
> **Fiscal Year (FY)**
> A twelve-month period that is used for bookkeeping, or accounting, purposes. Usually, the fiscal year does not coincide with the calendar year. For example, the federal government's fiscal year runs from October 1 through September 30.

HOW MUCH WILL THE GOVERNMENT SPEND?

The Constitution is very clear about where the power of the purse lies in the national government: all taxing or spending bills must originate in the House of Representatives. Today, much of the business of Congress is concerned with approving government expenditures through the budget process and with raising the revenues to pay for government programs.

From 1922, when Congress required the president to prepare and present to the legislature an **executive budget,** until 1974, the congressional budget process was so disjointed that it was difficult to visualize the total picture of government finances. The president presented the executive budget to Congress in January. It was broken down into thirteen or more appropriations bills. Some time later, after all of the bills had been debated, amended, and passed, it was more or less possible to estimate total government spending for the next year.

Frustrated by the president's ability to impound, or withhold, funds and dissatisfied with the entire budget process, Congress passed the Budget and Impoundment Control Act of 1974 to regain some control over the nation's spending. The act required the president to spend the funds that Congress had appropriated, ending the president's ability to kill programs by withholding funds. The other major accomplishment of the act was to force Congress to examine total national taxing and spending at least twice in each budget cycle.

The budget cycle of the federal government is described in the rest of this section. (See Figure 10–4 on page 367 for a graphic illustration of the budget cycle.)

PREPARING THE BUDGET

The federal government operates on a **fiscal year (FY)** cycle. The fiscal year runs from October through September, so that fiscal year 2010, or FY10, runs from October 1, 2009, through September 30, 2010. Eighteen months before a fiscal year starts, the executive branch

"The only solution I can see is to hold a series of long and costly hearings in order to put off finding a solution."

---

13. In contrast, *simple resolutions* and *concurrent resolutions* do not carry the force of law but rather are used by one or both chambers of Congress, respectively, to express facts, principles, or opinions. For example, a concurrent resolution is used to set the time when Congress will adjourn.

FIGURE 10–3: How a Bill Becomes Law

This illustration shows the most typical way in which proposed legislation is enacted into law. Most legislation begins as similar bills introduced into the House and the Senate. The process is illustrated here with two hypothetical bills, House bill No. 100 (HR 100) and Senate bill No. 200 (S 200). The path of HR 100 is shown on the left, and that of S 200, on the right.

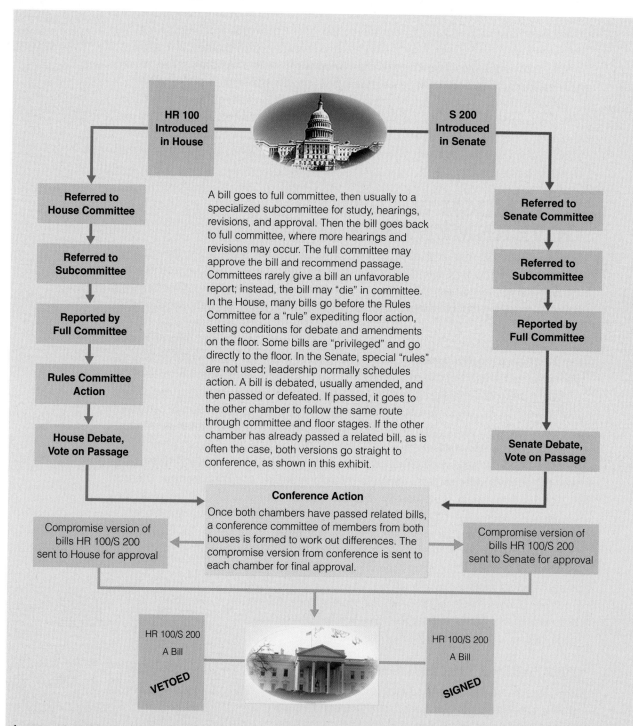

A bill goes to full committee, then usually to a specialized subcommittee for study, hearings, revisions, and approval. Then the bill goes back to full committee, where more hearings and revisions may occur. The full committee may approve the bill and recommend passage. Committees rarely give a bill an unfavorable report; instead, the bill may "die" in committee. In the House, many bills go before the Rules Committee for a "rule" expediting floor action, setting conditions for debate and amendments on the floor. Some bills are "privileged" and go directly to the floor. In the Senate, special "rules" are not used; leadership normally schedules action. A bill is debated, usually amended, and then passed or defeated. If passed, it goes to the other chamber to follow the same route through committee and floor stages. If the other chamber has already passed a related bill, as is often the case, both versions go straight to conference, as shown in this exhibit.

Conference Action

Once both chambers have passed related bills, a conference committee of members from both houses is formed to work out differences. The compromise version from conference is sent to each chamber for final approval.

A compromise bill approved by both houses is sent to the president, who can sign it into law or veto it and return it to Congress. Congress may override a presidential veto by a two-thirds majority in both chambers; the bill then becomes law without the president's signature.

FIGURE 10-4: The Budget Cycle

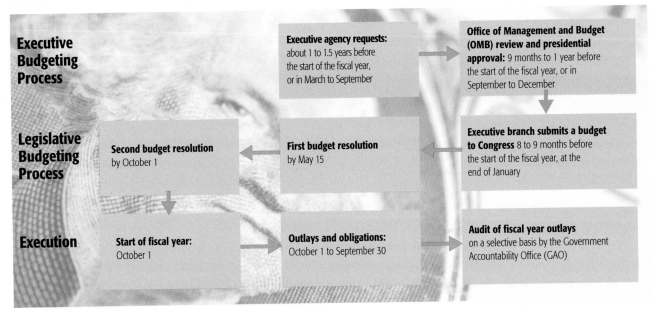

Executive Budgeting Process

Executive agency requests: about 1 to 1.5 years before the start of the fiscal year, or in March to September

Office of Management and Budget (OMB) review and presidential approval: 9 months to 1 year before the start of the fiscal year, or in September to December

Legislative Budgeting Process

Second budget resolution by October 1

First budget resolution by May 15

Executive branch submits a budget to Congress 8 to 9 months before the start of the fiscal year, at the end of January

Execution

Start of fiscal year: October 1

Outlays and obligations: October 1 to September 30

Audit of fiscal year outlays on a selective basis by the Government Accountability Office (GAO)

begins preparing the budget. The Office of Management and Budget (OMB) receives advice from the Council of Economic Advisers and the Treasury Department. The OMB outlines the budget and then sends it to the various departments and agencies. Bargaining follows, in which—to use only two of many examples—the Department of Health and Human Services argues for more welfare spending, and the armed forces argue for more defense spending.

Even though the OMB has fewer than 550 employees, it is one of the most powerful agencies in Washington. It assembles the budget documents and monitors federal agencies throughout each year. Every year, it begins the budget process with a **spring review,** in which it requires all of the agencies to review their programs, activities, and goals. At the beginning of each summer, the OMB sends out a letter instructing agencies to submit their requests for funding for the next fiscal year. By the end of the summer, each agency must submit a formal request to the OMB.

In actuality, the "budget season" begins with the **fall review.** At this time, the OMB looks at budget requests and, in almost all cases, routinely cuts them back. Although the OMB works within guidelines established by the president, specific decisions often are left to the OMB director and the director's associates. By the beginning of November, the director's review begins. The director meets with cabinet secretaries and budget officers. Time becomes crucial. The budget must be completed by January so that it can be included in the *Economic Report of the President.*

CONGRESS FACES THE BUDGET

In January, nine months before the fiscal year starts, the president takes the OMB's proposed budget, approves it, and submits it to Congress. Then the congressional budgeting process takes over. The budgeting process involves two steps. First, Congress must authorize funds to be spent. The **authorization** is a formal declaration by the appropriate congressional committee that a certain amount of funding may be available to an agency. Congressional committees and subcommittees look at the proposals from the executive branch and the Congressional Budget Office in making the decision to authorize funds. After the funds are authorized, they must be appropriated by Congress. The appropriations committees of both the House and the Senate forward spending bills to their respective bodies. The **appropriation** of funds occurs when the final bill is passed.

Spring Review
The annual process in which the Office of Management and Budget requires federal agencies to review their programs, activities, and goals and submit their requests for funding for the next fiscal year.

Fall Review
The annual process in which the Office of Management and Budget, after receiving formal federal agency requests for funding for the next fiscal year, reviews the requests, makes changes, and submits its recommendations to the president.

Authorization
A formal declaration by a legislative committee that a certain amount of funding may be available to an agency. Some authorizations terminate in a year; others are renewable automatically without further congressional action.

Appropriation
The passage, by Congress, of a spending bill specifying the amount of authorized funds that actually will be allocated for an agency's use.

The budget process involves large sums. For example, President George W. Bush's proposed budget for fiscal year 2009 called for expenditures of $3.107 trillion, or $3,107,000,000,000. When forming the budget for a given year, Congress and the president must take into account revenues, primarily in the form of taxes, as well as expenditures to balance the budget. If spending exceeds the amount brought in by taxes, the government runs a budget deficit (and increases the public debt). For example, although President Bush's proposed budget for fiscal year 2009 called for expenditures of $3.107 trillion, projected revenues from taxes amounted to only about $2.700 trillion—leaving a deficit of $407 billion.

With these large sums in play, representatives and senators who chair key committees find it relatively easy to slip spending proposals into a variety of bills. These proposals may have nothing to do with the ostensible purpose of the bill. Such earmarked appropriations are known as "pork," as discussed in the chapter-opening *What If . . .* feature.

BUDGET RESOLUTIONS

The **first budget resolution** by Congress is due in May. It sets overall revenue goals and spending targets. Spending and tax laws that are drawn up over the summer are supposed to be guided by the first budget resolution. By September, Congress is scheduled to pass its **second budget resolution,** one that will set binding limits on taxes and spending for the fiscal year beginning October 1.

In actuality, Congress has finished the budget on time in only three years since 1977. The budget is usually broken up into a series of appropriations bills. If Congress has not passed one of these bills by October 1, it normally passes a **continuing resolution** that allows the affected agencies to keep on doing whatever they were doing the previous year with the same amount of funding. By the 1980s, continuing resolutions had ballooned into massive measures. Budget delays reached a climax in 1995 and 1996, when, in a spending dispute with Democratic president Bill Clinton, the Republican Congress refused to pass any continuing resolutions. As a result, the nonessential functions of the federal government were shut down for twenty-seven days. Since 1987, Congress has generally managed to limit continuing resolutions to their original purpose.

At some point during the beginning of each calendar year, the president submits a budget to Congress. Except for a few years, all such budgets have shown expenditures exceeding revenues. Consequently, most U.S. government budgets have shown deficits. Why would a president submit a budget knowing that expenditures exceed revenues? (AP Photo/Pablo Martinez Monsivais)

WHY SHOULD YOU CARE ABOUT
congress?

Why should you, as an individual, care about Congress? Do you even know the names of your senators and your representative in Congress? A surprising number of Americans do not. Even if you know the names and parties of your elected delegates, there is still much more you could learn about them that would be useful.

CONGRESS AND YOUR LIFE

The legislation that Congress passes can directly affect your life. Consider, for example, the Medicare prescription drug benefit passed in November 2003. Some might think that such a benefit, which only helps persons over the age of sixty-five, would be of no interest to college students. Actually, legislation such as this could affect you long before you reach retirement age. Funding the new benefit may mean that you will have to pay higher taxes when you join the workforce. Also, some students may be affected even sooner than that. Most students are part of a family, and family finances are often important in determining whether a family will help pay for the student's tuition. There are families in which the cost of medicine for the oldest members is a substantial burden.

You can make a difference in our democracy simply by going to the polls on Election Day and voting for the candidates you would like to represent you in Congress. It goes without saying, though, that to cast an informed vote, you need to know how your congressional representatives stand on the issues and, if they are incumbents, how they have voted on bills that are important to you.

HOW YOU CAN MAKE A DIFFERENCE

To contact a member of Congress, start by going to the Web sites of the U.S. House of Representatives (at www.house.gov) and the U.S. Senate (at www.senate.gov). Although you can communicate easily with your representatives by e-mail, using e-mail has some drawbacks. Representatives and senators are now receiving large volumes of e-mail from constituents, and they rarely read it themselves. They have staff members who read and respond to e-mail instead. Many interest groups argue that U.S. mail, or even express mail or a phone call, is more likely to capture the attention of the representative than e-mail. You can contact your representatives using one of the following addresses or phone numbers:

United States House of Representatives
Washington, DC 20515
202-224-3121

United States Senate
Washington, DC 20510
202-224-3121

Interest groups also track the voting records of members of Congress and rate the members on the issues. Project Vote Smart tracks the performance of more than 13,000 political leaders, including their campaign finances, issue positions, and voting records. You can contact Project Vote Smart at:

Project Vote Smart
One Common Ground
Philipsburg, MT 59858
Voter Hotline toll-free:
1-888-VOTE-SMART
(1-888-868-3762)
www.vote-smart.org

Finally, if you want to know how your representatives funded their campaigns, contact the Center for Responsive Politics (CRP), a research group that tracks money in politics, campaign fund-raising, and similar issues. You can contact the CRP at:

The Center for Responsive Politics
1101 14th St. N.W.,
Suite 1030
Washington, DC 20005
202-857-0044
www.opensecrets.org

(Photo credits: www.vote-smart.org and www.opensecrets.org)

QUESTIONS FOR
discussionandanalysis

1. Review the *Which Side Are You On?* feature on page 356. Is it fair to allow the franking privilege to incumbent senators and members of the House? Why or why not? Would it make any sense to offer free mailing privileges to candidates who run against incumbents? Again, why or why not?

2. If nonpartisan panels drew congressional district boundaries, who do you think ought to be appointed to such panels in an attempt to curb gerrymandering? What types of people might be both knowledgeable and fair?

3. The District of Columbia is not represented in the Senate and has a single, nonvoting delegate to the House. Should D.C. be represented in Congress by voting legislators? Why or why not? If it should be represented, how? Would it make sense to admit it as a state? To give it back to Maryland? Explain your reasoning.

4. Identify some advantages to the nation that might follow when one party controls the House, the Senate, and the presidency. Identify some of the disadvantages that might follow from such a state of affairs.

5. When the Senate was first created, Americans were often more loyal to their individual states than they are today. Confederate general Robert E. Lee, for example, believed that his native land was Virginia, not the United States. Given the strong sense of national identity that exists in the country today, is it fair that the Senate gives equal representation to all states regardless of how many people live in each? Why or why not? If not, what (if anything) could be done to address the issue?

keyterms

agenda setting 344
appropriation 367
authorization 367
bicameralism 342
casework 343
conference
   committee 359
conservative
   coalition 364
constituent 341
continuing
   resolution 368
direct primary 349
discharge petition 358
earmarks 342
enumerated power 345

executive budget 365
fall review 367
filibuster 346
first budget
   resolution 368
fiscal year (FY) 365
franking 355
gerrymandering 353
instructed delegate 343
joint committee 359
justiciable question 352
lawmaking 342
logrolling 342
majority leader of the
   House 362

minority leader of the
   House 362
ombudsperson 343
oversight 344
party identifier 349
president pro
   tempore 362
reapportionment 352
redistricting 352
representation 342
Rules Committee 346
safe seat 360
second budget
   resolution 368

select committee 359
Senate majority
   leader 362
Senate minority
   leader 362
seniority system 360
Speaker of the
   House 361
spring review 367
standing
   committee 358
trustee 343
whip 362

chaptersummary

1. The authors of the Constitution believed that the bulk of national power should be in the legislature. The Constitution states that Congress will consist of two chambers. A result of the Connecticut Compromise, this bicameral structure established a balanced legislature, with the membership in the House of Representatives based on population and the membership in the Senate based on the equality of states.

2. The functions of Congress include (a) lawmaking, (b) representation, (c) service to constituents, (d) oversight, (e) public education, and (f) conflict resolution.

3. The first seventeen clauses of Article I, Section 8, of the Constitution specify most of the enumerated, or expressed, powers of Congress, including the right to impose taxes, to borrow funds, to regulate commerce, and to declare war. Besides its enumerated powers, Congress enjoys the right to "make all Laws which shall be necessary and proper for carrying into Execution the foregoing Powers, and all other Powers vested by this Constitution in the Government of the United States, or in any Department or Officer thereof." This is called the elastic, or necessary and proper, clause.

4. There are 435 members in the House of Representatives and 100 members in the Senate. Owing to its larger size, the House has a greater number of formal rules. The Senate tradition of unlimited debate dates back to 1790 and has been used over the years to frustrate the passage of bills. Under Senate Rule 22, cloture can be used to shut off debate on a bill.

5. Members of Congress are not typical American citizens. They are older and wealthier than most Americans, disproportionately white and male, and more likely to be trained in professional occupations.

6. Congressional elections are operated by the individual state governments, which must abide by rules established by the Constitution and national statutes. Most candidates for Congress must win nomination through a direct primary. The overwhelming majority of incumbent representatives and a smaller proportion of senators who run for reelection are successful. A complicated aspect of congressional elections is apportionment—the allocation of legislative seats to constituencies. The Supreme Court's "one person, one vote" rule has been applied to equalize the populations of congressional and state legislative districts.

7. Members of Congress are well paid and enjoy benefits such as free postage. Members of Congress have personal and committee staff members available to them and also enjoy a number of legal privileges and immunities.

8. Most of the actual work of legislating is performed by committees and subcommittees within Congress. Legislation introduced into the House or Senate is assigned to the appropriate standing committees for review. Select committees are created for a limited time for a specific purpose. Joint committees are formed by the concurrent action of both chambers and consist of members from each chamber. Conference committees are special joint committees set up to achieve agreement between the House and the Senate on the exact wording of legislative acts that were passed by both chambers in different forms. The seniority rule, which is usually followed, specifies that the longest-serving member of the majority party will be the chairperson of a committee.

9. The foremost power holder in the House of Representatives is the Speaker of the House. Other leaders are the House majority leader, the House minority leader, and the majority and minority whips. Formally, the vice president is the presiding officer of the Senate, with the most senior member of the majority party serving as the president pro tempore to preside when the vice president is absent. Actual leadership in the Senate rests with the majority leader, the minority leader, and their whips.

10. A bill becomes law by progressing through both chambers of Congress and their appropriate standing and joint committees to the president.

11. The budget process for a fiscal year begins with the preparation of an executive budget by the president. This is reviewed by the Office of Management and Budget and then sent to Congress, which is supposed to pass a final budget by the end of September. Since 1978, Congress generally has not followed its own time rules.

selected**print&media**resources

SUGGESTED READINGS

Just, Ward S. *The Congressman Who Loved Flaubert.* New York: Carrol and Graf Publishers, 1990. This fictional account of a career politician was first published in 1973 and is still a favorite with students of political science. Ward Just is renowned for his political fiction, and particularly for his examination of character and motivation.

Koszczuk, Jackie, and Martha Angle, eds. *CQ's Politics in America 2008: The 110th Congress.* Washington, D.C.: CQ Press, 2007. This "ultimate insider's guide to politics," as it is sometimes described, offers biographical data, voting behavior, ratings by interest groups, campaign-finance sources, and a wealth of information on each of the 535 members of the 110th Congress.

Oleszek, Walter J. *Congressional Procedures and the Policy Process.* Washington, D.C.: CQ Press, 2007. This descriptive book offers a wealth of information for anyone seeking to understand the congressional procedures involved in initiating, debating, and enacting new laws.

Rangel, Charles B., and Leon Wynter. . . . *And I Haven't Had a Bad Day Since: The Memoir of Charles B. Rangel's Journey from the Streets of Harlem to the Halls of Congress.* New York: Scribner, 2007. This biographical account of one of Congress's most flamboyant members tells his story from the streets of Harlem to the halls of Congress. Rangel, a high school dropout, became a lawyer and then a member of Congress. He helped create the earned-income tax credit for working families.

Waxman, Henry. *The Waxman Report: How Congress Really Works.* New York: Twelve, 2009. Waxman has represented the Los Angeles area in Congress for more than three decades and is chairman of the Committee on Oversight and Government Reform. In this work, he shows how important legislation can be crafted even in an environment of gridlock and partisan conflict.

MEDIA RESOURCES

Charlie Wilson's War—One of the best movies of 2007, starring Tom Hanks and Julia Roberts. This hilarious film is based on the true story of how Wilson, a hard-living, hard-drinking representative from Texas, almost single-handedly wins a billion dollars in funding for the Afghans who are fighting a Russian invasion. When equipped with heat-seeking missiles, the Afghans win. Philip Seymour Hoffman steals the show portraying a rogue CIA operative.

The Congress—In one of his earliest efforts (1988), filmmaker Ken Burns profiles the history of Congress. Narration is by David McCullough, and those interviewed include David Broder, Alistair Cooke, and Cokie Roberts. PBS Home Video rereleased this film on DVD in 2003.

Congress: A Day in the Life of a Representative—From political meetings to social functions to campaigning, this 1995 program examines what politicians really do. Featured representatives are Tim Roemer (a Democrat from Indiana) and Sue Myrick (a Republican from North Carolina).

Mr. Smith Goes to Washington—A 1939 film in which Jimmy Stewart plays the naïve congressman who is quickly educated in Washington. A true American political classic.

Porked: Earmarks for Profit—A 2008 release from Fox News Channel that investigates Congressional earmarks. Fox reporters contend that pork wastes tax dollars. Beyond that, the network also claims that some members of Congress have funded projects that benefited the members' own bank accounts.

The Seduction of Joe Tynan—A 1979 film in which Alan Alda plays a young senator who must face serious decisions about his political role and his private life.

e-mocracy

CONGRESS AND THE WEB

Almost all senators and representatives have Web sites that you can find simply by keying in their names in a search engine. As you read in this chapter's *Why Should You Care about Congress?* feature, you can easily learn the names of your congressional representatives by going to the Web site of the House or Senate (see the following *Logging On* section for the URLs for these sites). Once you know the names of your representatives, you can go to their Web sites to learn more about them and their positions on specific issues. You can also check the Web sites of the groups listed in the *Why Should You Care about Congress?* feature to track your representatives' voting records and discover the names of their campaign contributors.

Note that some members of Congress also provide important services to their constituents via their Web sites. Some sites, for example, allow constituents to apply for internships in Washington, D.C., apply for appointments to military academies, order flags, order tours of the Capitol, and register complaints electronically. Other sites may provide forms from certain government agencies, such as the Social Security Administration, that constituents can use to request assistance from those agencies or to register complaints.

LOGGING ON

To find out about the schedule of activities taking place in Congress, use the following Web sites:
www.senate.gov.
www.house.gov.

The Congressional Budget Office is online at
www.cbo.gov.

The URL for the U.S. Government Printing Office is
www.gpoaccess.gov.

For the real inside facts on what's going on in Washington, D.C., you can look at the following resources:

RollCall, the newspaper of the Capitol:
www.rollcall.com.

Congressional Quarterly, a publication that reports on Congress:
www.cq.com.

The Hill, which investigates various activities of Congress:
www.hillnews.com.

11 The President

CHAPTER CONTENTS

President-elect Barack Obama holds a discussion on protecting home ownership. (AP Photo/Chris Carlson)

whatif...there were no executive privilege?

BACKGROUND

When a U.S. president wishes to keep information secret, he or she can invoke *executive privilege*. Although there is no mention of executive privilege in the Constitution, presidents from George Washington to George W. Bush invoked this privilege in response to perceived encroachments on the executive branch by Congress and by the judiciary. For example, in 2006 when two congressional committees were investigating the federal government's response to Hurricane Katrina, the Bush administration cited the need for confidentiality of executive-branch communications as justification for refusing to turn over certain documents, including e-mail correspondence involving White House staff members. The administration had previously refused to release the names of oil company executives who had advised Vice President Cheney on energy policy.

Nonetheless, Congress could try to prohibit the use of executive privilege by passing a law. Alternatively, the Supreme Court could hold that executive privilege is an unconstitutional exercise of executive power.

WHAT IF THERE WERE NO EXECUTIVE PRIVILEGE?

If there were no executive privilege, a president would know that all of his or her words, documents, and actions could be made public. We know from history that when a president does not have full executive privilege to protect information, the results can be devastating.

President Richard Nixon (1969–1974) had tape-recorded hundreds of hours of conversations in the Oval Office. During a scandal involving a cover-up of illegal activities (the Watergate scandal, as you will read later in this chapter), Congress requested those tapes. Nixon invoked executive privilege and refused to turn them over. Ultimately, the Supreme Court ordered him to do so, however, and the tapes provided damning information about Nixon's role in the cover-up. Rather than face impeachment, Nixon resigned the presidency.

Clearly, if executive privilege were eliminated, it is unlikely that conversations between the president and other members of the executive branch would be recorded or otherwise documented. As a result, we would have fewer records of an administration's activities than we do today.

EXECUTIVE PRIVILEGE IN A WORLD FILLED WITH TERRORISM

Following the terrorist attacks on September 11, 2001, Attorney General John Ashcroft advised federal agencies "to lean toward withholding information whenever possible." Often, the Bush administration tried to withhold information from Congress and the courts, not just the public. In one troubling example, a top civil servant was threatened with firing if he told Congress the true projected cost of the administration's Medicare prescription drug bill.

Of course, without executive privilege, the president might experience problems in waging a war on terrorism. While Congress has procedures that can be used to guard sensitive information, it is unaccustomed to keeping secrets and often finds it hard to do so. The very size of the Congress makes it difficult to keep secrets. It increases the number of members—or staff—who might leak information.

PAST, PRESENT, AND FUTURE PRESIDENTIAL PAPERS

The Bush administration attempted to control not only its own records but also those of former presidents, even against their wishes. Soon after September 11, 2001, President Bush signed Executive Order 13233, which provided that former presidents' private papers can be released only with the approval of both the former president in question and the current one. Former president Bill Clinton publicly objected, saying that he wanted all of his papers released to the public. Nevertheless, the Bush administration denied access to documents surrounding the 177 pardons that Clinton granted in the last days of his presidency.

If executive privilege were eliminated, the White House would have a difficult time regulating the flow of past presidential records into the public forum. The behavior of presidents and their administrations would certainly change. They might simply insist that there be no record of sensitive conversations. If so, future Americans would lose much of the historical background for America's domestic and international actions.

FOR CRITICAL ANALYSIS

1. The history of executive privilege dates back to 1796, when President George Washington refused a request by the House for certain documents. Given the changes that have taken place since that time, should executive privilege be eliminated—or is it even more necessary today than it was at that time?

2. What would be the costs to the nation if executive privilege were eliminated?

The writers of the Constitution created the presidency of the United States without any models to follow. Nowhere else in the world was there a democratically selected chief executive. What the founders did not want was a king. In fact, given their previous experience with royal governors in the colonies, many of the delegates to the Constitutional Convention wanted to create a very weak executive who could not veto legislation. Other delegates, especially those who had witnessed the need for a strong leader in the Revolutionary Army, believed a strong executive would be necessary for the new republic. The delegates, after much debate, created a chief executive who had enough powers granted in the Constitution to balance those of Congress.[1]

(©Ted Denson, 2008, Shutterstock.com)

The power exercised by each president who has held the office has been scrutinized and judged by historians, political scientists, the media, and the public. The executive privilege enjoyed by presidents has also been subject to scrutiny and debate, as you learned in the chapter-opening *What If . . .* feature. Indeed, it would seem that Americans are fascinated by presidential power and by the persons who hold the office. In this chapter, after looking at who can become president and at the process involved, we examine closely the nature and extent of the constitutional powers held by the president.

didyouknow...

That George Washington's salary of $25,000 in 1789 was the equivalent of about $600,000 in today's dollars?

WHO CAN BECOME PRESIDENT?

The requirements for becoming president, as outlined in Article II, Section 1, of the Constitution, are not overwhelmingly stringent:

> *No person except a natural born Citizen, or a Citizen of the United States, at the time of the Adoption of this Constitution, shall be eligible to the Office of President; neither shall any Person be eligible to that Office who shall not have attained to the Age of thirty-five Years, and been fourteen Years a Resident within the United States.*

The only question that arises about these qualifications relates to the term *natural born Citizen.* Does that mean only citizens born in the United States and its territories? What about a child born to a U.S. citizen (or to a couple who are U.S. citizens) visiting or living in another country? Although the Supreme Court has never directly addressed the question, it is reasonable to expect that someone would be eligible if her or his parents were Americans. The first presidents, after all, were not even American citizens at birth, and others were born in areas that did not become part of the United States until later.

These questions were debated when George Romney, who was born in Chihuahua, Mexico, made a serious bid for the Republican presidential nomination in the 1960s.[2] The issue also came up when Arizona senator John McCain announced that he was a candidate for president. McCain was born in the Panama Canal Zone. Questions about McCain's eligibility were soon put to rest, however. Not only were McCain's parents both U.S. citizens (his father was an officer in the navy), but at the time McCain was born, the Canal Zone was a U.S. possession.

When Arnold Schwarzenegger became governor of California, many of his supporters suggested that he might be a potential presidential candidate. But Schwarzenegger, who was born in Austria, is a naturalized U.S. citizen and therefore is ineligible to become president under the Constitution. Although a movement sought to amend the Constitution to allow *naturalized* citizens to become president, there has been little support for such an amendment.

The American dream is symbolized by the statement that "anybody can become president of this country." It is true that in modern times, presidents

At times, Governor Arnold Schwarzenegger of California has been popular enough that his supporters have suggested he run for president. Why can't Schwarzenegger become president? (© Ken James/Corbis)

---

1. Forrest McDonald, *The American Presidency: An Intellectual History* (Lawrence, Kans.: University Press of Kansas, 1994), p. 179.
2. George Romney was governor of Michigan from 1963 to 1969. Romney was not nominated for the presidency, and the issue remains unresolved.

**The youngest
president ever**
elected was John F. Kennedy
(1961–1963). (AP Photo)

**The oldest president
ever elected**
was Ronald Reagan (1981–1989).
(AP Photo)

have included a haberdasher (Harry Truman—for a short period of time), a peanut farmer (Jimmy Carter), and an actor (Ronald Reagan). But if you examine the list of presidents in Appendix F at the end of this book, you will see that the most common previous occupational field of presidents in this country has been the law. Out of forty-four presidents, twenty-seven have been lawyers, and many have been wealthy. (There have been fewer lawyers in the last century, however.)

Although the Constitution states that the minimum-age requirement for the presidency is thirty-five years, most presidents have been much older than that when they assumed office. John F. Kennedy, at the age of forty-three, was the youngest elected president, and the oldest was Ronald Reagan, at age sixty-nine. The average age at inauguration has been fifty-four. There has clearly been a demographic bias in the selection of presidents. All have been male, white, and from the Protestant tradition, except for John F. Kennedy, a Roman Catholic, and Barack Obama, an African American. Presidents have been men of great stature, such as George Washington, and men in whom leadership qualities were not so pronounced, such as Warren Harding (1921–1923). A presidential candidate usually has experience as a vice president, senator, or state governor. Former governors have been especially successful at winning the presidency.

THE PROCESS OF BECOMING PRESIDENT

Major and minor political parties nominate candidates for president and vice president at national conventions every four years. As discussed in Chapter 9, the nation's voters do not elect a president and vice president directly but rather cast ballots for presidential electors, who then vote for president and vice president in the Electoral College.

Because victory goes to the candidate with a majority in the Electoral College, it is conceivable that someone could be elected to the office of the presidency without having a plurality of the popular vote cast. Indeed, on four occasions, candidates won elections even though their major opponents received more popular votes. One of those elections occurred in 2000, when George W. Bush won the Electoral College vote and became president even though his opponent, Al Gore, won the popular vote. In elections in which more than two candidates were running for office, many presidential candidates have won with less than 50 percent of the total popular votes cast for all candidates—including

Abraham Lincoln, Woodrow Wilson, Harry Truman, John F. Kennedy, Richard Nixon, and, in 1992, Bill Clinton. Independent candidate Ross Perot garnered a surprising 19 percent of the vote in 1992. Remember from Chapter 9 that no president has won a majority of votes from the entire voting-age population.

On occasion, the Electoral College has failed to give any candidate a majority. At this point, the election is thrown into the House of Representatives. The president is then chosen from among the three candidates having the most Electoral College votes, as noted in Chapter 9. Only two times in our past has the House had to decide on a president. Thomas Jefferson and Aaron Burr tied in the Electoral College in 1800. This happened because the Constitution had not been explicit in indicating which of the two electoral votes was for president and which was for vice president. In 1804, the **Twelfth Amendment** clarified the matter by requiring that the president and vice president be chosen separately. In 1824, the House again had to make a choice, this time among William H. Crawford, Andrew Jackson, and John Quincy Adams. It chose Adams, even though Jackson had more electoral and popular votes.

didyouknow...

That twenty-one presidents have served only one term in office?

THE MANY ROLES OF THE PRESIDENT

The Constitution speaks briefly about the duties and obligations of the president. Based on this brief list of powers and on the precedents of history, the presidency has grown into a very complicated job that requires balancing at least five constitutional roles. These are (1) head of state, (2) chief executive, (3) commander in chief of the armed forces, (4) chief diplomat, and (5) chief legislator of the United States. Here we examine each of these significant presidential functions, or roles. It is worth noting that one person plays all these roles simultaneously and that the needs of these roles may at times come into conflict.

HEAD OF STATE

Every nation has at least one person who is the ceremonial head of state. In most democratic governments, the role of **head of state** is given to someone other than the chief executive, who leads the executive branch of government. In Britain, for example, the head of state is the queen. In much of Europe, the prime minister is the chief executive, and the head of state is a relatively powerless president. (We describe these systems in this chapter's *Beyond Our Borders* feature on the following page.) But in the United States, the president is both chief executive and head of state. According to William Howard Taft, as head of state the president symbolizes the "dignity and majesty" of the American people.

As head of state, the president engages in a number of activities that are largely symbolic or ceremonial, such as the following:

Bill Clinton was elected president twice without having won a majority of votes. Is it necessarily important for a candidate to obtain the majority of the popular vote? (AP Photo/Wirtschafts Blatt/Richard Tanzer)

Twelfth Amendment
An amendment to the Constitution, adopted in 1804, that requires the separate election of the president and vice president by the Electoral College.

Head of State
The role of the president as ceremonial head of the government.

beyondourborders

HEADS OF GOVERNMENT ARE NOT ALWAYS DIRECTLY ELECTED

In the United States, the president is head of state and the head of government. In many democratic countries, however, voters do not directly elect the head of government. This is true of the British parliamentary system and of parliamentary systems around the world. Parliament, the British legislature, chooses the head of government. Canada also uses the British system, and so do Australia, India, Ireland, and many other countries. Japan, Israel, and most nations on the European continent (but not France) have parliamentary systems that differ from the British model only in detail.

THE BRITISH PRIME MINISTER

Under the British system, the head of government is the prime minister. (Originally, *prime minister* meant "the monarch's most important servant.") The prime minister is typically the leader of the party with the most seats in the House of Commons. Parliament also includes the House of Lords, but that body plays little role in the government. Although prime ministers do not necessarily have to be members of Parliament, they usually are. Thus, most prime ministers are elected to a seat in Parliament by a vote of the people who live in a particular district, but the people never vote directly on who should be the head of government.

After an election, the king or queen, as head of state, asks the leader of the largest party in Parliament to "form a government." In doing so, the prime minister

Queen Elizabeth II meets Prime Minister
Gordon Brown at Windsor Castle. What is the official role of the queen?
(Steve Parsons/PA Wire URN: 5998934/Press Association via AP Images)

designates various people, almost always members of Parliament, to cabinet positions. The cabinet members, also called ministers, perform roles that are not too different from those of cabinet secretaries in the United States. All ministers must support the policy of the government, despite any reservations they might hold privately.

Officially, the appointment of the prime minister is a royal prerogative. In reality, the royal naming of the prime minister is purely ceremonial, and the monarch would never designate a prime minister who did not have the support of Parliament. Also note that Britain does not have a written constitution, and the office of prime minister existed long before it was mentioned in state documents. In fact, the first reference to the prime minister in an act of Parliament did not occur until the early twentieth century.

Another major difference between the British and American systems is that in Britain, elections to the House of Commons do not occur at regularly scheduled intervals. The prime minister can call an election, or "go to the country," any time he or she sees fit, with the restriction that no Parliament can sit for more than five years.

SIMILAR SYSTEMS IN CANADA AND ELSEWHERE

As in Britain, the office of prime minister of Canada does not formally exist in the constitution. The office evolved *de facto* into what it is today beginning in the mid-nineteenth century. Also as in Britain, the Canadian prime minister is the leader of the party with the most seats in the Canadian House of Commons. Technically, the prime minister and the rest of the cabinet are appointed by the governor-general, who represents the British monarch (who is also the monarch of Canada).

In parliamentary countries that do not have a king, queen, or emperor, the head of state is typically a president, who may be elected either by the people or by the parliament itself. Like modern European monarchs, these presidents are ceremonial figures who have almost no real power.

FOR CRITICAL ANALYSIS

Would you feel comfortable with a head of government for whom you did not have a chance to vote? Why or why not?

- Decorating war heroes.
- Throwing out the first ball to open the baseball season.
- Dedicating parks and post offices.
- Receiving visiting heads of state at the White House.
- Going on official state visits to other countries.
- Making personal telephone calls to astronauts.
- Representing the nation at times of national mourning, such as after the terrorist attacks of September 11, 2001, after the loss of the space shuttle *Columbia* in 2003, and after the destruction from Hurricane Katrina in 2005.

Some students of the American political system believe that having the president serve as both the chief executive and the head of state drastically limits the time available to do "real" work. Not all presidents have agreed with this conclusion, however—particularly those presidents who have skillfully blended these two roles with their role as politician. Being head of state gives the president tremendous public exposure, which can be an important asset in a campaign for reelection. When that exposure is positive, it helps the president deal with Congress over proposed legislation and increases the chances of being reelected—or getting the candidates of the president's party elected.

President Gerald Ford (1974–1977) throws out the opening pitch of the baseball season. In what capacity does the president serve when he undertakes such ceremonial activities? How important are these activities? (Baseball Hall of Fame photo)

CHIEF EXECUTIVE

According to the Constitution, "The executive Power shall be vested in a President of the United States of America . . . . [H]e may require the Opinion, in writing, of the principal Officer in each of the executive Departments, upon any Subject relating to the Duties of their respective Offices . . . and he shall nominate, and by and with the Advice and Consent of the Senate, shall appoint . . . Officers of the United States. . . . [H]e shall take Care that the Laws be faithfully executed."

As **chief executive,** the president is constitutionally bound to enforce the acts of Congress, the judgments of federal courts, and treaties signed by the United States. The duty to "faithfully execute" the laws has been a source of constitutional power for presidents. Is the president allowed to refuse to enforce certain parts of legislation if he or she believes that they are unconstitutional? This question came to the forefront in recent years because of President George W. Bush's extensive use of signing statements. A **signing statement** is a written declaration that a president may make when signing a bill into law regarding the law's enforcement. Usually, a signing statement points to sections of the law that the president thinks may be unconstitutional.

Presidents have been using such statements for decades, but President Bush used them on more than eight hundred statutes—more than all of the previous presidents combined. Bush also tended to use the statements for a different purpose. When earlier presidents issued signing statements, they were normally used to instruct agencies on how to execute the laws or for similar purposes. In contrast, many, if not most, of Bush's signing statements served notice that he believed parts of bills that he signed were unconstitutional or might be contrary to national security interests. Although some contend that Bush's use of signing statements violated his duty to enforce the laws, others were not so concerned. To date, this issue has not come before any court.

The Powers of Appointment and Removal. To assist in the various tasks of the chief executive, the president has a federal bureaucracy (see Chapter 12), which consists of over 2.7 million federal civilian employees. You might think that the president, as head of the largest bureaucracy in the United States, wields enormous power. The president, however,

didyouknow...

That **Thomas Jefferson** was the first president to be inaugurated in Washington, D.C., where he walked to the Capitol from a boardinghouse, took the oath, made a brief speech in the Senate chamber, and then walked back home?

Chief Executive
The role of the president as head of the executive branch of the government.

Signing Statement
A written declaration that a president may make when signing a bill into law. Usually, such statements point out sections of the law that the president deems unconstitutional.

Civil Service
A collective term for the body of employees working for the government. Generally, *civil service* is understood to apply to all those who gain government employment through a merit system.

Appointment Power
The authority vested in the president to fill a government office or position. Positions filled by presidential appointment include those in the executive branch and the federal judiciary, commissioned officers in the armed forces, and members of the independent regulatory commissions.

only nominally runs the executive bureaucracy. Most government positions are filled by **civil service** employees, who generally gain government employment through a merit system rather than presidential appointment.[3] Therefore, even though the president has important **appointment power,** it is limited to cabinet and subcabinet jobs, federal judgeships, agency heads, and about two thousand lesser jobs. This means that most of the 2.7 million federal employees owe no political allegiance to the president. They are more likely to owe loyalty to congressional committees or to interest groups representing the sector of the society that they serve. Table 11–1 shows what percentage of the total employment in each executive department is available for political appointment by the president.

The president's power to remove from office those officials who are not doing a good job or who do not agree with the president is not explicitly granted by the Constitution and has been limited. In 1926, however, a Supreme Court decision prevented Congress from interfering with the president's ability to fire those executive-branch officials whom the president had appointed with Senate approval.[4] There are ten agencies whose directors the president can remove at any time. These agencies include the Arms Control and Disarmament Agency, the Commission on Civil Rights, the Environmental Protection Agency, the General Services Administration, and the Small Business Administration. In addition, the president can remove all heads of cabinet departments, all individuals in the Executive Office of the President, and all of the 6,280 political appointees listed in Table 11–1.

Harry Truman spoke candidly of the difficulties a president faces in trying to control the executive bureaucracy. On leaving office, he referred to the problems that Dwight Eisenhower, as a former general of the army, was going to have: "He'll sit here and he'll

3. See Chapter 12 for a discussion of the Civil Service Reform Act.
4. *Meyers v. United States,* 272 U.S. 52 (1926).

TABLE 11–1: Total Civilian Employment in Cabinet Departments Available for Political Appointment by the President

Executive Department	Total Number of Employees	Political Appointments Available	Percentage
Agriculture	100,084	384	0.43
Commerce	39,151	324	1.13
Defense	670,568	655	0.06
Education	4,581	260	4.06
Energy	15,689	469	2.75
Health and Human Services	63,323	418	0.61
Homeland Security	165,085	453	0.27
Housing and Urban Development	10,154	152	1.53
Interior	72,982	283	0.32
Justice	126,711	569	0.39
Labor	16,016	219	1.17
State	28,054	1,287	3.79
Transportation	64,131	271	0.42
Treasury	159,274	175	0.14
Veterans Affairs	223,137	361	0.14
TOTAL	1,593,855	6,280	0.39

Source: *Policy and Supporting Positions* (Washington, D.C.: Government Printing Office, 2004). This text, known as "The Plum Book" (see Chapter 12 on page 424), is published after each presidential election. The numbers of employees cited in this table are from 2004. As this book went to press, the post–2008 elections Plum Book had not yet been published.

say do this! do that! and nothing will happen. Poor Ike—it won't be a bit like the Army. He'll find it very frustrating."[5]

The Power to Grant Reprieves and Pardons. Section 2 of Article II of the Constitution gives the president the power to grant **reprieves** and **pardons** for offenses against the United States except in cases of impeachment. All pardons are administered by the Office of the Pardon Attorney in the Department of Justice. In principle, a pardon is granted to remedy a mistake made in a conviction.

The United States Supreme Court upheld the president's power to grant reprieves and pardons in a 1925 case concerning a pardon granted by the president to an individual convicted of contempt of court. The judiciary had contended that only judges had the authority to convict individuals for contempt of court when court orders were violated and that the courts should be free from interference by the executive branch. The Court simply stated that the president could grant reprieves or pardons for all offenses "either before trial, during trial, or after trial, by individuals, or by classes, conditionally or absolutely, and this without modification or regulation by Congress."[6]

In 1974, in a controversial decision, President Gerald Ford pardoned former president Richard Nixon for his role in the Watergate affair before any charges were brought in court. Just before George W. Bush's inauguration in 2001, President Bill Clinton announced pardons for almost two hundred persons. Some of those pardons were controversial. In early 2007, controversy arose over whether President Bush should pardon a member of his own administration. Lewis ("Scooter") Libby, Vice President Dick Cheney's former chief of staff, was convicted in March 2007 of several crimes, including perjury and obstruction of justice, in connection with a leak to the press revealing the identity of a CIA agent. Eventually, Bush commuted Libby's sentence so that he would not have to serve time in prison.

COMMANDER IN CHIEF

The president, according to the Constitution, "shall be Commander in Chief of the Army and Navy of the United States, and of the Militia of the several States, when called into the actual Service of the United States." In other words, the armed forces are under civilian, rather than military, control.

Wartime Powers. Certainly, those who wrote the Constitution had George Washington in mind when they made the president the **commander in chief.** Although we do not expect our president to lead the troops into battle, presidents as commanders in chief have wielded dramatic power. Harry Truman made the awesome decision to drop atomic bombs on Hiroshima and Nagasaki in 1945 to force Japan to surrender and thus bring World War II to an end. Lyndon Johnson ordered bombing missions against North Vietnam in the 1960s, and he personally selected some of the targets. Richard Nixon decided to invade Cambodia in 1970. Ronald Reagan sent troops to Lebanon and Grenada in 1983 and ordered U.S. fighter planes to attack Libya in 1986. George H. W. Bush sent troops to Panama in 1989 and to the Middle East in 1990. Bill Clinton sent troops to Haiti in 1994 and to Bosnia in 1995, ordered missile attacks on alleged terrorist bases in 1998, and sent American planes to bomb Serbia in 1999. Most recently, George W. Bush ordered the invasion of Iraq in 2003.

The president is the ultimate decision maker in military matters. Everywhere the president goes, so too goes the "football"—a briefcase filled with all of the codes necessary to order a nuclear attack. Only the president has the power to order the use of nuclear force.

Presidents have probably exercised more authority in their capacity as commander in chief than in any other role. Constitutionally, Congress has the sole power to declare

Reprieve
A formal postponement of the execution of a sentence imposed by a court of law.

Pardon
A release from the punishment for, or legal consequences of, a crime; a pardon can be granted by the president before or after a conviction.

Commander in Chief
The role of the president as supreme commander of the military forces of the United States and of the state National Guard units when they are called into federal service.

This atomic bomb was dropped on Nagasaki, Japan, instantly killing about 70,000 people. Thousands more died later of radiation poisoning. Was the decision to drop this bomb made by the military or by a civilian? (AP Photo/U.S. Signal Corps)

---

5. Quoted in Richard E. Neustadt, *Presidential Power: The Politics of Leadership* (New York: Wiley, 1960), p. 9. Note that Truman may not have considered the amount of politics involved in decision making in the upper echelon of the army.
6. *Ex parte Grossman,* 267 U.S. 87 (1925).

war, but the president can send the armed forces into a country in situations that are certainly the equivalent of war. Harry Truman dispatched troops to Korea in 1950. Kennedy, Johnson, and Nixon waged an undeclared war in Southeast Asia, where more than 58,000 Americans were killed and 300,000 were wounded. In neither of these situations had Congress declared war.

The War Powers Resolution. In an attempt to gain more control over such military activities, in 1973 Congress passed the **War Powers Resolution**—over President Nixon's veto—requiring that the president consult with Congress when sending American forces into action. Once they are sent, the president must report to Congress within forty-eight hours. Unless Congress approves the use of troops within sixty days or extends the sixty-day time limit, the forces must be withdrawn. The War Powers Resolution was tested in the fall of 1983, when President Reagan requested that troops be left in Lebanon. The resulting compromise was a congressional resolution allowing troops to remain there for eighteen months. Shortly after the resolution was passed, however, more than 240 sailors and Marines were killed in a suicide bombing of a U.S. military housing compound in Beirut. That event provoked a furious congressional debate over the role American troops were playing in the Middle East, and Reagan withdrew all troops shortly thereafter.

Whether Congress had the constitutional power to set conditions on the continuation of the Iraq War was at issue in 2007 and 2008. President Bush threatened to veto any emergency war-funding legislation that conditioned the funds on a time line for the withdrawal or redeployment of the troops in Iraq.

In spite of the War Powers Resolution, the powers of the president as commander in chief are more extensive today than they were in the past. These powers are linked closely to the president's powers as chief diplomat, or chief crafter of foreign policy.

CHIEF DIPLOMAT

The Constitution gives the president the power to recognize foreign governments; to make treaties, with the **advice and consent** of the Senate; and to make special agreements with other heads of state that do not require congressional approval. In addition, the president nominates ambassadors. As **chief diplomat,** the president dominates American foreign policy, a role that has been supported many times by the Supreme Court.

Diplomatic Recognition. An important power of the president as chief diplomat is that of **diplomatic recognition,** or the power to recognize—or refuse to recognize—foreign governments. In the role of ceremonial head of state, the president has always received foreign diplomats. In modern times, the simple act of receiving a foreign diplomat has been equivalent to accrediting the diplomat and officially recognizing his or her government. Such recognition of the legitimacy of another country's government is a prerequisite to diplomatic relations or treaties between that country and the United States.

Deciding when to recognize a foreign power is not always simple. The United States, for example, did not recognize the Soviet Union until 1933—sixteen years after the Russian Revolution of 1917. It was only after all attempts to reverse the effects of that revolution—including military invasion of Russia and diplomatic isolation—had proved futile that Franklin Roosevelt extended recognition to the Soviet government. In December 1978, long after the Communist victory in China in 1949, Jimmy Carter granted official recognition to the People's Republic of China.[7]

A diplomatic recognition issue that faced the Clinton administration involved recognizing a former enemy—the Republic of Vietnam. Many Americans, particularly those who believed that Vietnam had not been forthcoming in the efforts to find the remains of missing American soldiers or to find out about former prisoners of war, opposed any

---

War Powers Resolution
A law passed in 1973 spelling out the conditions under which the president can commit troops without congressional approval.

Advice and Consent
Terms in the Constitution describing the U.S. Senate's power to review and approve treaties and presidential appointments.

Chief Diplomat
The role of the president in recognizing foreign governments, making treaties, and effecting executive agreements.

Diplomatic Recognition
The formal acknowledgment of a foreign government as legitimate.

---

7. The Nixon administration first encouraged new relations with the People's Republic of China by allowing a cultural exchange of table tennis teams.

formal relationship with that nation. After the U.S. government had negotiated with the Vietnamese government for many years over the missing-in-action issue and engaged in limited diplomatic contacts for several years, President Clinton announced on July 11, 1995, that the United States would recognize the government of Vietnam.

At issue today is whether the United States should extend diplomatic recognition to the Iranian government to facilitate diplomatic relations. All official relations with Iran were suspended in 1981 after Iranians took over the U.S. embassy in that nation and held fifty-two Americans hostage for 444 days. The question of whether the president should be willing to open direct talks with the governments of Iran and several other rogue nations became a major issue during the 2008 presidential elections. Democrat Barack Obama argued that such talks could be useful, while Republican John McCain characterized them as a form of surrender. We examine this issue in the *Which Side Are You On?* feature on the following page.

Proposal and Ratification of Treaties. The president has the sole power to negotiate treaties with other nations. These treaties must be presented to the Senate, where they may be modified and must be approved by a two-thirds vote. After ratification, the president can approve the senatorial version of the treaty. Approval poses a problem when the Senate has tacked on substantive amendments or reservations to a treaty, particularly when such changes may require reopening negotiations with the other signatory governments. Sometimes a president may decide to withdraw a treaty if the senatorial changes are too extensive—as Woodrow Wilson did with the Versailles Treaty in 1919. Wilson believed that the senatorial reservations would weaken the treaty so much that it would be ineffective. His refusal to accept the senatorial version of the treaty led to the eventual refusal of the United States to join the League of Nations.

President Jimmy Carter (1977–1981) was successful in lobbying for the treaties that provided for the return of the Panama Canal to Panama by the year 2000 and neutralizing the canal. President Bill Clinton won a major political and legislative victory in 1993 by persuading Congress to ratify the North American Free Trade Agreement (NAFTA). In so doing, he had to overcome opposition from Democrats and most of organized labor. In 2000, President Clinton won another major legislative victory when Congress voted to normalize trade relations with China permanently.

Before September 11, 2001, President George W. Bush indicated his intention to steer the United States in a unilateral direction on foreign policy. He rejected the Kyoto Agreement on global warming and proposed ending the 1972 Anti-Ballistic Missile (ABM) Treaty, which was part of the first Strategic Arms Limitation Treaty (SALT I). After the terrorist attacks of September 11, 2001, however, President Bush sought cooperation from U.S. allies in the war on terrorism. Bush's return to multilateralism was exemplified in the signing of a nuclear weapons reduction treaty with Russia in 2002. Nonetheless, his attempts to gain international support for a war against Iraq to overthrow that country's government were not as successful as he had hoped. During the continuing occupation of Iraq, the Bush administration saw even more erosion in other countries' support of his actions.

On September 7, 1977, President Jimmy Carter signed the Panama Canal Treaty, which gave control of the canal to the government of Panama after December 31, 1999. Here, Carter is shaking hands with King Juan Carlos of Spain, who had joined Latin American heads of state on December 14, 1999, to celebrate the transfer. What limits a U.S. president's ability to negotiate, sign, and put into effect an international treaty? (AP Photo/Greg Bull)

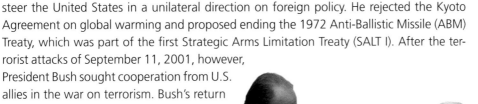

whichsideareYOUon?

SHOULD THE UNITED STATES NEGOTIATE WITH TERRORIST STATES?

The president of the United States is the nation's chief diplomat. Working toward the resolution of conflicts with other nations through diplomacy is an important part of the president's job. *Diplomacy,* broadly defined, is the process by which nations work out their differences peacefully. Normally, war is a last resort—undertaken only when all diplomatic efforts have failed. After the terrorist attacks on September 11, 2001, however, the international diplomatic environment changed. Not only are we now faced with terrorist organizations such as al Qaeda; we are also confronted with nations that we know support and train terrorists and terrorist groups. Iran, for example, supports Hamas in Palestine and Hezbollah in Lebanon. Should the United States negotiate with governments that sponsor such organizations?

JUST SAY NO TO NEGOTIATION

Some people firmly believe that you don't negotiate with evil. You stamp it out. You don't talk to leaders such as Iran's Mahmoud Ahmadinejad, who wants to destroy Israel. Moreover, what could we achieve by negotiating with governments that sponsor terrorism? These governments simply don't play by the same rules as we do. In any such negotiations, the United States would be considered bound by its promises. Can you imagine, however, that a terrorist-friendly government hostile to our values would feel bound by any promises it might make? How could the United States enforce the agreement, anyway? Clearly, the only answer is by military action. But if that is the case, why not use force in the first place instead of attempting negotiation?

Negotiating with an enemy only shows weakness. It amounts to giving in to pressure brought by that enemy against the United States. Britain and France tried negotiating with Adolf Hitler in the late 1930s, in an attempt to curb Hitler's expansionist ambitions and prevent war. Hitler simply ignored what had been negotiated, and the result was World War II.

Finally, negotiation with terrorists and their sponsoring nations tends to give those groups legitimacy. To meet with an enemy that threatens all that we stand for would, in effect, reward the enemy's criminal behavior.

NEGOTIATIONS ARE ALWAYS APPROPRIATE

Negotiating with our enemies is a way to open up lines of communications, and doing so is a sign of strength, not weakness. The more we communicate with a hostile or terrorist-friendly nation, the greater are the chances that we can influence future developments. A refusal to negotiate eliminates any hope of altering the other nation's behavior, short of war.

In 1961, President John F. Kennedy said, "Let us never negotiate out of fear. But let us never fear to negotiate." After World War II, the Soviet Union was the number one enemy of the United States. Its goal was to destroy our way of life and put Communist regimes in place all over the world. Nonetheless, U.S. presidents continually met with Soviet leaders. President Richard Nixon also opened doors to communications with Communist China in the 1970s. In the 1980s, President Ronald Reagan called the Soviet Union "the evil empire," but he also met frequently with the leaders of that country. They negotiated a deceleration in the arms race and in nuclear proliferation.

Often, a dialogue with hostile leaders allows hostile parties to better understand each other's views and needs. Such negotiations are essential if any peaceful resolution of a conflict is to be achieved. Meeting with our enemies requires preparation, but it should not involve preconditions. During the 2008 presidential campaign, Barack Obama pointed out that requiring preconditions is like saying, "I'm not going to talk to you until you agree to do exactly as I want."

Ignoring our enemies accomplishes nothing. It certainly hasn't worked with Cuba, Iran, or Syria. In contrast, the United States did negotiate with Libya. The result was the abandonment by that country of its long-standing support of terrorism and its nuclear weapons program.

President Richard Nixon (left) met with then Chinese premier Zhou Enlai in 1972. President Ronald Reagan (right) met with Soviet leader Mikhail Gorbachev in 1986. Was it appropriate for these U.S. presidents to meet with leaders of countries that had been overtly antagonistic toward the United States and its democratic system? Why or why not? (Left photo: Nixon Library, National Archives; right photo: Courtesy of the Ronald Reagan Presidential Library Foundation)

Executive Agreements. Presidential power in foreign affairs is enhanced greatly by the use of **executive agreements** made between the president and other heads of state. Such agreements do not require Senate approval, although the House and Senate may refuse to appropriate the funds necessary to implement them. Whereas treaties are binding on all succeeding administrations, executive agreements require each new president's consent to remain in effect.

Among the advantages of executive agreements are speed and secrecy. The former is essential during a crisis; the latter is important when the administration fears that open senatorial debate may be detrimental to the best interests of the United States or to the interests of the president.[8] There have been far more executive agreements (about 9,000) than treaties (about 1,300). Many executive agreements contain secret provisions calling for American military assistance or other support. For example, Franklin Roosevelt (1933–1945) used executive agreements to bypass congressional isolationists when he traded American destroyers for British Caribbean naval bases.

(Library of Congress)

CHIEF LEGISLATOR

Constitutionally, presidents must recommend to Congress legislation that they judge necessary and expedient. Not all presidents have wielded their powers as **chief legislator** in the same manner. Some presidents have been almost completely unsuccessful in getting their legislative programs implemented by Congress. Presidents Franklin Roosevelt and Lyndon Johnson, however, saw much of their proposed legislation put into effect.

didyouknow...

That President William Henry Harrison gave the longest inaugural address (8,445 words) of any American president, lasting two hours (the weather was chilly and stormy, and Harrison caught a cold, developed pneumonia and pleurisy, and died a month later)?

Creating the Congressional Agenda. In modern times, the president has played a dominant role in creating the congressional agenda. In the president's annual **State of the Union message,** which is required by the Constitution (Article II, Section 3) and is usually given in late January shortly after Congress reconvenes, the president presents a legislative program. The message gives a broad, comprehensive view of what the president wishes the legislature to accomplish during its session. It is as much a message to the American people and to the world as it is to Congress. Its impact on public opinion can determine the way in which Congress responds to the president's agenda.

Beginning with the presidency of Thomas Jefferson and for a century thereafter, the president's State of the Union message was a written document delivered to Congress and read aloud by a clerk. In 1913, Woodrow Wilson reinstated George Washington's practice of delivering the message himself in a formal address to Congress. Today, this address is one of the great formal ceremonies of American governance.

Many customs have grown up around the address. For example, one cabinet member, the "designated survivor," stays away to ensure that the country will always have a president even if someone manages to blow up the Capitol building. The president is not permitted to enter the House floor without the explicit permission of Congress, and granting that permission is part of the ceremony. Everyone gives the president an initial standing ovation out of respect for the office, but this applause does not necessarily represent support for the individual who holds the office. During the speech, senators and House members either applaud or remain silent to indicate their opinion of the policies that the president announces.

Getting Legislation Passed. The president can propose legislation. Congress, however, is not required to pass—or even introduce—any of the administration's bills. How, then, does the president get those proposals made into law? One way is by exercising the power

Executive Agreement
An international agreement made by the president, without senatorial ratification, with the head of a foreign state.

Chief Legislator
The role of the president in influencing the making of laws.

State of the Union Message
An annual message to Congress in which the president proposes a legislative program. The message is addressed not only to Congress but also to the American people and to the world.

---

8. The Case Act of 1972 requires that all executive agreements be transmitted to Congress within sixty days after the agreement takes effect. Secret agreements are transmitted to the foreign relations committees as classified information.

of persuasion. The president writes to, telephones, and meets with various congressional leaders; makes public announcements to influence public opinion; and, as head of the party, exercises legislative leadership through the congresspersons of that party.

A president whose party holds a majority in both chambers of Congress may have an easier time getting legislation passed than does a president who faces a hostile Congress. Note, though, that even with a Republican-dominated Congress (from 2001 to 2007), President George W. Bush failed to obtain Social Security reform legislation or to make headway with his proposed Federal Marriage Amendment to the Constitution.

Saying No to Legislation. The president has the power to say no to legislation through use of the veto,[9] by which the White House returns a bill unsigned to Congress with a **veto message** attached. Because the Constitution requires that every bill passed by the House and the Senate be sent to the president before it becomes law, the president must act on each bill:

1. If the bill is signed, it becomes law.
2. If the bill is not sent back to Congress after ten congressional working days, it becomes law without the president's signature.
3. The president can reject the bill and send it back to Congress with a veto message setting forth objections. Congress then can change the bill, hoping to secure presidential approval, and repass it. Or Congress can simply reject the president's objections by overriding the veto with a two-thirds roll-call vote of the members present in both the House and the Senate.
4. If the president refuses to sign the bill and Congress adjourns within ten working days after the bill has been submitted to the president, the bill is killed for that session of Congress. This is called a **pocket veto.** If Congress wishes the bill to be reconsidered, the bill must be reintroduced during the following session.

Presidents employed the veto power infrequently until after the Civil War, but it has been used with increasing vigor since then (see Table 11–2). The total number of vetoes from George Washington through August 2008 of George W. Bush's second term in office was 2,562, with about two-thirds of those vetoes being exercised by Grover Cleveland, Franklin Roosevelt, Harry Truman, and Dwight Eisenhower.

George W. Bush was the first president since Martin Van Buren (1837–1841) to serve a full term in office without exercising the veto power. Bush, who had the benefit of a Republican Congress, did not veto any legislation during his first term. Only in the summer of 2006 did Bush finally issue a veto, saying "no" to stem-cell research legislation passed by Congress. Within months of the Democrats taking control of Congress in January 2007, however, the president issued several vetoes—one involving funding for the Iraq war, another again regarding stem-cell research, and one regarding a children's health insurance bill.

The Line-Item Veto. Ronald Reagan lobbied strenuously for Congress to give another tool to the president—the **line-item veto,** which would allow the president to veto *specific* spending provisions of legislation that was passed by Congress. In 1996, Congress passed the Line Item Veto Act, which provided for the line-item veto. Signed by President

---

Veto Message
The president's formal explanation of a veto when legislation is returned to Congress.

Pocket Veto
A special veto exercised by the chief executive after a legislative body has adjourned. Bills not signed by the chief executive die after a specified period of time. If Congress wishes to reconsider such a bill, it must be reintroduced in the following session of Congress.

Line-Item Veto
The power of an executive to veto individual lines or items within a piece of legislation without vetoing the entire bill.

President Lyndon Johnson
(1963–1969) signs the Civil Rights Act of 1964 in the East Room of the White House. If a president does not like a bill, what can he or she do to prevent it from becoming law? (AP Photo)

---

9. *Veto* in Latin means "I forbid."

TABLE 11–2: Presidential Vetoes, 1789 to Present

Years	President	Regular Votes	Vetoes Overrridden	Pocket Vetoes	Total Vetoes
1789–1797	Washington	2	0	0	2
1797–1801	J. Adams	0	0	0	0
1801–1809	Jefferson	0	0	0	0
1809–1817	Madison	5	0	2	7
1817–1825	Monroe	1	0	0	1
1825–1829	J. Q. Adams	0	0	0	0
1829–1837	Jackson	5	0	7	12
1837–1841	Van Buren	0	0	1	1
1841–1841	Harrison	0	0	0	0
1841–1845	Tyler	6	1	4	10
1845–1849	Polk	2	0	1	3
1849–1850	Taylor	0	0	0	0
1850–1853	Fillmore	0	0	0	0
1853–1857	Pierce	9	5	0	9
1857–1861	Buchanan	4	0	3	7
1861–1865	Lincoln	2	0	5	7
1865–1869	A. Johnson	21	15	8	29
1869–1877	Grant	45	4	48	93
1877–1881	Hayes	12	1	1	13
1881–1881	Garfield	0	0	0	0
1881–1885	Arthur	4	1	8	12
1885–1889	Cleveland	304	2	110	414
1889–1893	Harrison	19	1	25	44
1893–1897	Cleveland	42	5	128	170
1897–1901	McKinley	6	0	36	42
1901–1909	T. Roosevelt	42	1	40	82
1909–1913	Taft	30	1	9	39
1913–1921	Wilson	33	6	11	44
1921–1923	Harding	5	0	1	6
1923–1929	Coolidge	20	4	30	50
1929–1933	Hoover	21	3	16	37
1933–1945	F. Roosevelt	372	9	263	635
1945–1953	Truman	180	12	70	250
1953–1961	Eisenhower	73	2	108	181
1961–1963	Kennedy	12	0	9	21
1963–1969	L. Johnson	16	0	14	30
1969–1974	Nixon	26*	7	17	43
1974–1977	Ford	48	12	18	66
1977–1981	Carter	13	2	18	31
1981–1989	Reagan	39	9	39	78
1989–1993	G. H. W. Bush	29	1	15	44
1993–2001	Clinton	36†	2	1	37
2001–	G. W. Bush	11	4	1	12
TOTAL		1,489	110	1,067	2,562

*Two pocket vetoes by President Nixon, overruled in the courts, are counted here as regular vetoes.
†President Clinton's line-item vetoes are not included.
Sources: Office of the Clerk; plus authors' updates through October 2008.

Clinton, the law granted the president the power to rescind any item in an appropriations bill unless Congress passed a resolution of disapproval. Of course, the congressional resolution could be, in turn, vetoed by the president. The law did not take effect until after the 1996 election.

The act was soon challenged in court as an unconstitutional delegation of legislative powers to the executive branch. In 1998, by a six-to-three vote, the United States Supreme

(Library of Congress)

Court agreed and overturned the act. The Court stated that "there is no provision in the Constitution that authorizes the president to enact, to amend or to repeal statutes."[10]

Congress's Power to Override Presidential Vetoes. A veto is a clear-cut indication of the president's dissatisfaction with congressional legislation. Congress, however, can override a presidential veto, although it rarely exercises this power. Consider that two-thirds of the members of each chamber who are present must vote to override the president's veto in a roll-call vote. This means that if only one-third plus one of the members voting in one of the chambers of Congress do not agree to override the veto, the veto holds. It was not until the administration of John Tyler (1841–1845) that Congress overrode a presidential veto. In American history, only about 7 percent of all regular vetoes have been overridden.

OTHER PRESIDENTIAL POWERS

The powers of the president just discussed are called **constitutional powers,** because their basis lies in the Constitution. In addition, Congress has established by law, or statute, numerous other presidential powers—such as the ability to declare national emergencies. These are called **statutory powers.** Both constitutional and statutory powers have been labeled the **expressed powers** of the president, because they are expressly written into the Constitution or into law.

Presidents also have what have come to be known as **inherent powers.** These depend on the statements in the Constitution that "the executive Power shall be vested in a President" and that the president should "take Care that the Laws be faithfully executed." The most common example of inherent powers are those emergency powers invoked by the president during wartime. Franklin Roosevelt, for example, used his inherent powers to move the Japanese and Japanese Americans living in the United States into internment camps for the duration of World War II.

President George W. Bush often justified expanding the powers of his presidency by saying that such powers were necessary to fight the war on terrorism. While the Republicans controlled Congress from 2001 to 2007, Congress did little to counter the president's actions. When the Democrats became a majority in Congress in 2007, however, they let the president know, in Speaker of the House Nancy Pelosi's words, that there was "a new Congress in town."

THE PRESIDENT AS PARTY CHIEF AND SUPERPOLITICIAN

Presidents are by no means above political partisanship, and one of their many roles is that of chief of party. Although the Constitution says nothing about the function of the president within a political party (the mere concept of political parties was abhorrent to most of the authors of the Constitution), today presidents are the actual leaders of their parties.

THE PRESIDENT AS CHIEF OF PARTY

As party leader, the president chooses the national committee chairperson and can try to discipline party members who fail to support presidential policies. One way of exerting political power within the party is through **patronage**—appointing political supporters to government or public jobs. This power was more extensive in the past, before the establishment of the civil service in 1883 (see Chapter 12), but the president retains important patronage power. As we noted earlier, the president can appoint several thousand individuals to jobs in the cabinet, the White House, and the federal regulatory agencies.

Constitutional Power
A power vested in the president by Article II of the Constitution.

Statutory Power
A power created for the president through laws enacted by Congress.

Expressed Power
A power of the president that is expressly written into the Constitution or into statutory law.

Inherent Power
A power of the president derived from the statements in the Constitution that "the executive Power shall be vested in a President" and that the president should "take Care that the Laws be faithfully executed"; defined through practice rather than through law.

Patronage
The practice of rewarding faithful party workers and followers with government employment and contracts.

---

10. *Clinton v. City of New York*, 524 U.S. 417 (1998).

Perhaps the most important partisan role that the president played in the late 1900s and early 2000s was that of fund-raiser. The president is able to raise large amounts for the party through appearances at dinners, speaking engagements, and other social occasions. President Clinton may have raised more than half a billion dollars for the Democratic Party during his two terms. President George W. Bush was even more successful than Clinton during his first term. As his approval ratings dropped in his second term, however, so did his fund-raising opportunities. Indeed, prior to the 2006 and 2008 elections, many Republican candidates tried to distance themselves from the unpopular president and his unpopular policies.

Presidents have a number of other ways of exerting influence as party chief. The president may make it known that a particular congressperson's choice for federal judge will not be appointed unless that member of Congress is more supportive of the president's legislative program.[11] The president may agree to campaign for a particular program or for a particular candidate. Presidents also reward loyal members of Congress with support for the funding of local projects, tax breaks for regional industries, and other forms of "pork."

THE PRESIDENT'S POWER TO PERSUADE

According to political scientist Richard E. Neustadt, without the power to persuade, no president can lead very well. After all, even though the president is in the news virtually every day, the Constitution gives Congress most of the authority in the U.S. political system. Therefore, the president must convince Congress to do what the president wants. As Neustadt argues, "presidential power is the power to persuade."[12] Neustadt argues that one can find a high correlation between effective presidents and those who are best at persuasion. Presidents have to persuade the public, too.

Some scholars, however, have argued that a president's powers extend far beyond the power to persuade. For example, political analysts Kenneth Mayer and William Howell both emphasize that presidents do not need to rely on persuasive powers and normal legislative processes to implement presidential policies. Rather, presidents can take direct action by using other presidential tools, an important one being the *executive order* (executive orders will be discussed shortly).[13] Certainly, President George W. Bush made use of such orders in executing the war on terrorism and, more generally, in expanding presidential powers. For example, Bush created a new cabinet department—the Department of Homeland Security—by presidential order. Later, he used another executive order to give the president greater control over the regulatory decisions of administrative agencies.

President Ronald Reagan

(1981–1989) was often called "the Great Communicator" because of his speech-giving skills. Reagan obviously was at ease when speaking publicly because of his previous career as an actor. How important is the president's ability to speak to the people? (AP Photo)

CONSTITUENCIES AND PUBLIC APPROVAL

All politicians worry about their constituencies, and presidents are no exception. Presidents are also concerned with public approval ratings.

Presidential Constituencies. Presidents have many constituencies. In principle, they are beholden to the entire electorate—the public of the United States—even those who did not vote. They are certainly beholden to their party, because its members helped to put them in office. The president's

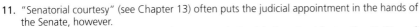

11. "Senatorial courtesy" (see Chapter 13) often puts the judicial appointment in the hands of the Senate, however.

12. Richard E. Neustadt, *Presidential Power and the Modern Presidents: The Politics of Leadership from Roosevelt to Reagan,* rev. ed. (New York: Free Press, 1991).

13. See Kenneth R. Mayer, *With the Stroke of a Pen: Executive Orders and Presidential Power* (Princeton, N.J.: Princeton University Press, 2002); and William G. Howell, *Power without Persuasion: The Politics of Direct Presidential Action* (Princeton, N.J.: Princeton University Press, 2003).

FIGURE 11–1: Public Popularity of Modern Presidents

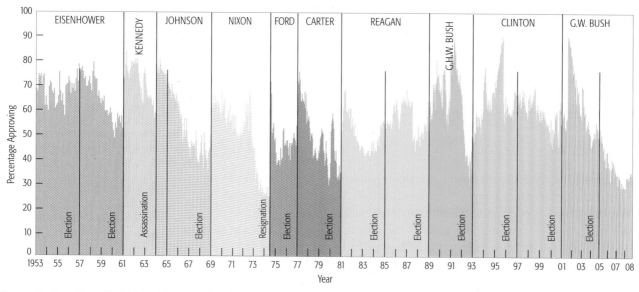

Sources: The Roper Center for Public Opinion Research; Gallup and *USA Today*/CNN polls, March 1992 through September 2008.

President John F. Kennedy reported to the nation on the status of the Cuban crisis on November 2, 1962. He told radio and television listeners that Soviet missile bases "are being destroyed" and that U.S. air surveillance would continue until effective international inspection is arranged. U.S. government conclusions about the missile bases, he said, were based on aerial photographs taken on November 1. (AP Photo)

Washington community
Indiviuals regularly involved with politics in Washington, D.C.

constituencies also include members of the opposing party whose cooperation the president needs. Finally, the president must take into consideration a constituency that has come to be called the **Washington community** (also known as those "inside the beltway"). This community consists of individuals who—whether in or out of political office—are intimately familiar with the workings of government, thrive on gossip, and measure on a daily basis the political power of the president.

Public Approval. All of these constituencies are impressed by presidents who maintain a high level of public approval, partly because doing so is very difficult to accomplish. Presidential popularity, as measured by national polls, gives the president an extra political resource to use in persuading legislators or bureaucrats to pass legislation. After all, refusing to do so might be going against public sentiment. President Bill Clinton showed significant strength in the public opinion polls for a second-term chief executive, as Figure 11–1 indicates.

Notably, President George W. Bush's approval ratings have spanned the gamut of such ratings. Immediately after 9/11, Bush had the highest approval ratings ever recorded. His popularity then entered a steep decline that was interrupted only briefly by high ratings in 2003 during the early phases of the war in Iraq. Such a decline appeared to threaten his reelection. In the end, however, Bush's popularity stabilized at just over 50 percent, reflecting the continued support of his political "base." Bush's support may have come from a narrow majority of the voters, but their support was firm. During his second term, however, Bush's approval ratings reached new lows, falling to 31 percent during May 2006. Later that year, Bush's ratings recovered slightly, but this improvement was temporary. During much of 2008, his ratings were below 30 percent. Few presidents have ever seen their approval ratings stay below 40 percent for such an extended period of time.[14]

"Going Public." Since the early 1900s, presidents have spoken more to the public and less to Congress. In the 1800s, only 7 percent of presidential speeches were addressed to the public; since 1900, 50 percent have been addressed to the public. One scholar, Samuel

---

14. Gallup reports issued April 2007, through September 2008.

politicsand...the presidency

ELECTIONS OF CHANGE

A campaign theme of "change" has long been popular with political candidates. Candidates can always point out the failures of their predecessors. Consequently, candidates can always ask voters to elect them to make a change. Political scientists often talk about "elections of change." They are supposed to be moments of public rebellion. At the federal level, candidates who call for change present themselves as opponents of the insiders who are currently running the government. These candidates say that they offer new directions and a break with the past. Although presidential candidates often articulate this message of change, it can also be used by those running for congressional office.

The French have a saying: "The more it changes, the more it stays the same." In other words, true change is difficult to create. It is not clear that the American electorate is so naïve as to believe that candidates can actually bring about much change in the way business is conducted in Washington, D.C. Voters know that rosy promises are hard to fulfill.

THE REAGAN REVOLUTION—OR WAS IT?

Ronald Reagan was elected president in 1980 on a campaign promise of change. He told the electorate that he would create a smaller, more efficient federal government. The data show otherwise. The U.S. Office of Personnel Management has calculated that during Reagan's tenure as president (1981–1989), the federal civilian payroll grew by more than 40 percent. During that same period, there were frequent allusions to the "Reagan cuts." In reality, while Reagan did cut a few spe-

cific programs, overall he merely slowed the growth of the federal government, rather than actually reducing its size.

THE REPUBLICAN REVOLUTION AND THEN THE DEMOCRATIC REVOLUTION

Consider two relatively modern examples of change in Congress. In 1994, with the so-called Republican revolution, that party won majorities in both chambers of Congress. Having gained control of Congress, the Republicans vowed to change the federal government. There were some major changes, such as welfare reform, but they occurred only when Democratic president Bill Clinton endorsed and helped craft the legislation. Otherwise, not much changed in the way the country was run.

In 2006, the voters returned a Democratic majority to Congress. This Democratic revolution was supposed to make two major changes in the federal government. The first was to end the war in Iraq, and the second was to check the widespread use of pork-barrel legislation. In spite of many congressional hearings, there was little change in the government's Iraq War policy. Indeed, the changes that did take place involved sending more troops, not fewer. And, of course, as you saw in Chapter 10, the Democrats continued to dish up the pork big-time.

FOR CRITICAL ANALYSIS

If newly elected politicians really cannot cause major changes in the federal government, why do candidates nonetheless continue to use the theme of "change"?

Kernell, has proposed that the style of presidential leadership has changed since World War II, owing partly to the influence of television, with a resulting change in the balance of national politics.[15] Presidents frequently go over the heads of Congress and the political elites, taking their cases directly to the people.

This strategy, which Kernell dubbed "going public," gives the president additional power through the ability to persuade and manipulate public opinion. By identifying their own positions so clearly, presidents make compromises with Congress much more difficult and weaken the legislators' positions. Given the increasing importance of the media as the major source of political information for citizens and elites, presidents will continue to use public opinion as part of their arsenal of weapons to gain support from Congress and to achieve their policy goals. Will President Obama—noted for his oratorical skills—be able to use his powers of persuasion to make 2008 a true "election of change"? That is not an easy task, as we point out in this chapter's *Politics and the Presidency* feature.

---

15. Samuel Kernell, *Going Public: New Strategies of Presidential Leadership,* 4th ed. (Washington, D.C.: CQ Press, 2006).

SPECIAL USES OF PRESIDENTIAL POWER

Presidents have at their disposal a variety of special powers and privileges not available in the other branches of the U.S. government. These include (1) emergency powers, (2) executive orders, and (3) executive privilege.

EMERGENCY POWERS

If you read the Constitution, you will find no mention of the additional powers that the executive office may exercise during national emergencies. Indeed, the Supreme Court has indicated that an "emergency does not create power."[16] But it is clear that presidents have made strong use of their inherent powers during times of emergency, particularly in the realm of foreign affairs. The **emergency powers** of the president were first enunciated in the Supreme Court's decision in *United States v. Curtiss-Wright Export Corp.*[17] In that case, President Franklin Roosevelt, without authorization by Congress, ordered an embargo on the shipment of weapons to two warring South American countries. The Court recognized that the president may exercise inherent powers in foreign affairs and that the national government has primacy in these affairs.

Examples of emergency powers are abundant, coinciding with crises in domestic and foreign affairs. Abraham Lincoln suspended civil liberties at the beginning of the Civil War (1861–1865) and called the state militias into national service. These actions and his subsequent governance of conquered areas, and even of areas of northern states, were justified by claims that they were essential to preserve the Union. Franklin Roosevelt declared an "unlimited national emergency" following the fall of France in World War II (1939–1945) and mobilized the federal budget and the economy for war.

President Harry Truman authorized the federal seizure of steel plants and their operation by the national government in 1952 during the Korean War. Truman claimed that he was using his inherent emergency power as chief executive and commander in chief to safeguard the nation's security, as an ongoing strike by steelworkers threatened the supply of weapons to the armed forces. The Supreme Court did not agree, holding that the president had no authority under the Constitution to seize private property or to legislate such action.[18] According to legal scholars, this was the first time a limit was placed on the exercise of the president's emergency powers.

EXECUTIVE ORDERS

As we discussed in Chapter 2, Congress allows the president (as well as administrative agencies) to issue *executive orders* that have the force of law. These executive orders can do the following: (1) enforce legislative statutes, (2) enforce the Constitution or treaties with foreign nations, and (3) establish or modify rules and practices of executive administrative agencies.

An executive order, then, represents the president's legislative power. The only apparent requirement is that under the Administrative Procedure Act of 1946, all executive orders must be published in the ***Federal Register,*** a daily publication of the U.S. government. Some examples of executive orders were given earlier in this chapter. Executive orders have also been used to establish procedures to appoint noncareer administrators, to restructure the White House bureaucracy, to ration consumer goods and to administer wage and price controls under emergency conditions, to classify government information as secret, to regulate the export of restricted items, to establish the Peace Corps, and to establish military tribunals for suspected terrorists.

---

didyouknow...

That the shortest inaugural address was George Washington's second one, at 135 words?

Emergency Power
An inherent power exercised by the president during a period of national crisis.

Federal Register
A publication of the U.S. government that prints executive orders, rules, and regulations.

---

16. *Home Building and Loan Association v. Blaisdell,* 290 U.S. 398 (1934).
17. 299 U.S. 304 (1936).
18. *Youngstown Sheet and Tube Co. v. Sawyer,* 343 U.S. 579 (1952).

EXECUTIVE PRIVILEGE

Another inherent executive power that has been claimed by presidents concerns the ability of the president and the president's executive officials to withhold information from or refuse to appear before Congress or the courts. This is called **executive privilege,** and it relies on the constitutional separation of powers for its basis.

As discussed in this chapter's opening *What If . . .* feature, presidents have frequently invoked executive privilege to avoid having to disclose information to Congress on actions of the executive branch. Executive privilege rests on the assumption that a certain degree of secrecy is essential to the proper functioning of the executive branch. Critics of executive privilege believe that it can be used to shield from public scrutiny actions of the executive branch that should be open to Congress and to the American citizenry.

Limiting Executive Privilege. Limits to executive privilege went untested until the Watergate affair in the early 1970s. Five men had broken into the headquarters of the Democratic National Committee and were caught searching for documents that would damage the candidacy of the Democratic nominee, George McGovern. Later investigation showed that the break-in was planned by members of Richard Nixon's campaign committee and that Nixon and his closest advisers had devised a strategy for impeding the investigation of the crime. After it became known that all of the conversations held in the Oval Office had been tape-recorded on a secret system, Nixon was ordered to turn over the tapes to the special prosecutor.

Nixon refused to do so, claiming executive privilege. He argued that "no president could function if the private papers of his office, prepared by his personal staff, were open to public scrutiny." In 1974, in one of the Supreme Court's most famous cases, *United States v. Nixon,*[19] the justices unanimously ruled that Nixon had to hand over the tapes. The Court held that executive privilege could not be used to prevent evidence from being heard in criminal proceedings.

Clinton's Attempted Use of Executive Privilege. The claim of executive privilege was also raised by the Clinton administration as a defense against the aggressive investigation of Clinton's relationship with Monica Lewinsky by Independent Counsel Kenneth Starr. The Clinton administration claimed executive privilege for several presidential aides who might have discussed the situation with the president. In addition, President Clinton asserted that his White House counsel did not have to testify before the Starr grand jury due to attorney-client privilege. Finally, the Department of Justice claimed that members of the Secret Service who guard the president could not testify about his activities due to a "protective function privilege" inherent in their duties. The federal judge overseeing the case denied the claims of privilege, however, and the decision was upheld on appeal.

Executive Privilege and the Bush Administration. On occasion, President George W. Bush also claimed executive privilege to prevent the disclosure to Congress of confidential communications or materials. For example, in his first term Bush claimed executive privilege to keep his newly appointed homeland security adviser, Tom Ridge, from testifying before Congress. The Bush administration resisted attempts by the congressional Government Accountability Office to obtain information about meetings and documents related to Vice President Dick Cheney's actions as chair of the administration's energy policy task force.

President Bush also asserted executive privilege on several occasions to prevent White House and Justice Department staffers from testifying before Congress about the firing

Executive Privilege
The right of executive officials to withhold information from or to refuse to appear before a legislative committee.

President Richard Nixon says goodbye

outside the White House after his resignation on August 9, 1974, as he prepares to board a helicopter for a flight to nearby Andrews Air Force Base. Nixon addressed members of his staff in the East Room prior to his departure. Was Nixon impeached?

(AP Photo/Bob Daughtery)

19. 318 U.S. 683 (1974).

Impeachment
An action by the House of Representatives to accuse the president, vice president, or other civil officers of the United States of committing "Treason, Bribery, or other high Crimes and Misdemeanors."

of several U.S. attorneys, allegedly for political reasons. In 2007 and 2008, it seemed that this exercise of executive privilege might lead to a major constitutional confrontation between Congress and the White House. In 2007, under presidential orders, current and former Bush staff members Joshua Bolten and Harriet Miers refused even to appear before a House committee. In February 2008, the House voted to hold Bolten and Miers in contempt, and shortly thereafter the House committee sued the two staff members. In July, a federal judge ruled that Bolten and Miers had to appear before the committee. Bolten and Miers appealed the decision, and in September the U.S. Court of Appeals for the District of Columbia temporarily stayed the ruling.

ABUSES OF EXECUTIVE POWER AND IMPEACHMENT

Presidents normally leave office either because their first term has expired and they have not sought (or won) reelection or because, having served two full terms, they are not allowed to be elected for a third term (owing to the Twenty-second Amendment, passed in 1951). Eight presidents have died in office. But there is still another way for a president to leave office—by **impeachment** and conviction. Articles I and II of the Constitution authorize the House and Senate to remove the president, the vice president, or other civil officers of the United States for committing "Treason, Bribery, or other high Crimes and Misdemeanors." According to the Constitution, the impeachment process begins in the House, which impeaches (accuses) the federal officer involved. If the House votes to impeach the officer, it draws up articles of impeachment and submits them to the Senate, which conducts the actual trial.

In the history of the United States, no president has ever actually been impeached and also convicted—and thus removed from office—by means of this process. President Andrew Johnson (1865–1869), who succeeded to the office after the assassination of Abraham Lincoln, was impeached by the House but acquitted by the Senate. More than a century later, the House Judiciary Committee approved articles of impeachment against President Richard Nixon for his involvement in the cover-up of the Watergate break-in of 1972. Informed by members of his own party that he had no hope of surviving the trial in the Senate, Nixon resigned on August 9, 1974, before the full House voted on the articles. Nixon is the only president to have resigned from office.

The second president to be impeached by the House but not convicted by the Senate was President Bill Clinton. In September 1998, Independent Counsel Kenneth Starr sent to Congress the findings of his investigation of the president on the charges of perjury and obstruction of justice. The House approved two charges against Clinton: lying to the grand jury about his affair with Monica Lewinsky and obstruction of justice. The articles of impeachment were then sent to the Senate, which acquitted Clinton.

THE EXECUTIVE ORGANIZATION

Gone are the days when presidents answered their own mail, as George Washington did. It was not until 1857 that Congress authorized a private secretary for the president, to be paid by the federal government. Woodrow Wilson typed most of his correspondence, even though he did have several secretaries. At the beginning of Franklin Roosevelt's long tenure in the White House, the entire staff consisted of thirty-seven employees. With the New Deal and World War II, however, the presidential staff became a sizable organization.

Today, the executive organization includes a White House Office staff of about 600, including some work-

On December 19, 1998, the House of Representatives
voted to impeach President Bill Clinton (1993–2001), shown here with his vice-president, Al Gore, and First Lady Hillary Rodham Clinton. Why was Clinton not forced to leave office because of this impeachment? (AP Photo/Doug Mills)

ers who are part-time employees and others who are borrowed from their departments by the White House. Not all of these employees have equal access to the president, nor are all of them likely to be equally concerned about the administration's political success. The more than 360 employees who work in the White House Office itself are closest to the president. They often include many individuals who worked on the president's campaign. These assistants are most concerned with preserving the president's reputation. Also included in the president's staff are a number of advisory personnel, such as the president's assistant for national security affairs. Although the individuals who hold staff positions in these offices are appointed by the president, they are really more concerned with their own areas than with the president's overall success. The group of appointees who perhaps are least helpful to the president is the cabinet, each member of which is the principal officer of a government department.

THE CABINET

Although the Constitution does not include the word *cabinet,* it does state that the president "may require the Opinion, in writing, of the principal Officer in each of the executive Departments." Since the time of George Washington, these officers have formed an advisory group, or **cabinet,** to which the president turns for counsel.

Members of the Cabinet. Originally, the cabinet consisted of only four officials—the secretaries of state, treasury, and war, and the attorney general. Today, the cabinet numbers fourteen department secretaries and the attorney general. (See Table 11–1 on page 382 for the names of the cabinet departments and Chapter 12 for a detailed discussion of these units.)

The cabinet may include others as well. The president at his or her discretion can, for example, ascribe cabinet rank to the vice president, the head of the Office of Management and Budget, the national security adviser, the ambassador to the United Nations, or additional officials. Under President George W. Bush, the additional members of the cabinet were the following:

- The vice president.
- The White House chief of staff.
- The director, Office of Management and Budget.
- The United States trade representative.
- The director, Environmental Protection Agency.
- The director, Office of National Drug Control Policy.

Often, a president will use a **kitchen cabinet** to replace the formal cabinet as a major source of advice. The term *kitchen cabinet* originated during the presidency of Andrew

Cabinet
An advisory group selected by the president to aid in making decisions. The cabinet includes the heads of fifteen executive departments and others named by the president.

Kitchen Cabinet
The informal advisers to the president.

The first U.S. cabinet
—from left to right, Henry Knox, Thomas Jefferson, Edmund Randolph, and Alexander Hamilton—and the first U.S. president, George Washington.
(National Archives)

President Ronald Reagan and Vice President George H. W. Bush
pose in the oval office with Reagan's first cabinet in February 1981. Are there any constitutional limitations on who may be a member of the president's cabinet? Do the heads of each department necessarily always support the president? (AP Photo/White House)

President George W. Bush

(2001–2009) appointed more minority and female heads of cabinet departments than any previous president had. Here, Secretary of State Condoleezza Rice speaks in the White House briefing room about a free-trade agreement with Colombia in the spring of 2008. Next to her are Secretary of Labor Elaine Chao and Treasury Secretary Henry Paulson. Why do presidents rarely rely on their cabinet members to make important policy decisions? (AP Photo/Ron Edmonds)

Jackson, who relied on the counsel of close friends who allegedly met with him in the kitchen of the White House. A kitchen cabinet is a very informal group of advisers; usually, they are friends with whom the president worked before being elected.

Presidential Use of Cabinets. Because neither the Constitution nor statutory law requires the president to consult with the cabinet, its use is purely discretionary. Some presidents have relied on the counsel of their cabinets more than others. Dwight Eisenhower was used to the team approach to solving problems from his experience as supreme allied commander during World War II, and therefore he frequently turned to his cabinet for advice on a wide range of issues. More often, presidents have solicited the opinions of their cabinets and then have done what they wanted to do anyway. Lincoln supposedly said—after a cabinet meeting in which a vote was seven nays against his one aye—"Seven nays and one aye, the ayes have it." In general, few presidents have relied heavily on the advice of their cabinet members.

It is not surprising that presidents tend to disregard their cabinet members' advice. Often, the departmental heads are more responsive to the wishes of their own staffs or to their own political ambitions than they are to the president. They may be more concerned with obtaining resources for their departments than with achieving the goals of the president. So there is often a strong conflict of interest between presidents and their cabinet members.

THE EXECUTIVE OFFICE OF THE PRESIDENT

When President Franklin Roosevelt appointed a special committee on administrative management, he knew that the committee would conclude that the president needed help. Indeed, the committee proposed a major reorganization of the executive branch. Congress did not approve the entire reorganization, but it did create the **Executive Office of the President (EOP)** to provide staff assistance for the chief executive and to help coordinate the executive bureaucracy. Since that time, a number of agencies have been created within the EOP to supply the president with advice and staff help. These agencies include the following:

- White House Office.
- Office of Administration.
- Council of Economic Advisers.
- Council on Environmental Quality.
- National Security Council.
- Office of Management and Budget.

- Office of National Drug Control Policy.
- Office of Science and Technology Policy.
- Office of the United States Trade Representative.
- President's Foreign Intelligence Advisory Board.

Several of the offices within the EOP are especially important, including the White House Office, the Office of Management and Budget, and the National Security Council. The activities of the Executive Office of the President are featured on the president's own Web site—**www.whitehouse.gov**. The site is an invaluable source of information and also serves to promote the president and the president's initiatives. We consider the tensions between these two contradictory purposes in this chapter's *Politics and the Cyber Sphere* feature.

The White House Office. The **White House Office** includes most of the key personal and political advisers to the president. Among the jobs held by these aides are those of legal counsel to the president, secretary, press secretary, and appointments secretary. Often, the individuals who hold these positions are recruited from the president's campaign staff. Their duties—mainly protecting the president's political interests—are similar

Executive Office of the President (EOP)
An organization established by President Franklin D. Roosevelt to assist the president in carrying out major duties.

White House Office
The personal office of the president, which tends to presidential political needs and manages the media.

POLITICS AND...
the cyber sphere

SCRUBBING THE WHITE HOUSE WEB SITE SQUEAKY CLEAN

Go to **www.whitehouse.gov**. There you will discover a site that purports to provide useful information to all citizens. The president's Web site is indeed the most popular site among those of elected government officials. In fact, it is one of the most popular sites on the Internet.

The site has many useful aspects. It serves as a conduit to more valuable information than do many governmental sites. You can easily find the president's budget. You can also look up all recent press releases and press conferences. The site includes many old press releases and interviews that serve as historical background as well. Especially interesting are old radio interviews.

OLD MAY NOT BE AS GOOD AS NEW

What's left on the White House Web site from years ago may be interesting to some but embarrassing to the president. After all, the real purpose of the site is to promote the president and the president's policies. Those who run the White House Web site feel a strong compulsion to remove old material that is embarrassing today—in the case of President George W. Bush, for example, excessively optimistic assessments of progress in Iraq. The site is so popular, though, that removal of historical interviews, press statements, and the like is easily spotted. And removing this material appears to violate the ostensible purpose of the site—to provide a public record.

Nonetheless, there is frequent "scrubbing" of the White House Web site. In 2007, for example, all of President Bush's radio interviews from 2004 were scrapped. After August 2006, almost no radio interviews were added. Links to members of the president's cabinet often disappeared, too. Former secretary of defense Donald Rumsfeld's April 30, 2004, interview was deleted. Many of the vice president's Web pages were eliminated as well.

At times, even the pull-down menus go dead when a topic within them is considered unpopular, such as Iraq. A famous liberal blog, the Daily Kos (at **www.dailykos.com**), has argued for years that during the Bush administration, the White House "decided to throw obstacles in the path of any journalist or meddlesome citizen who might wish to investigate the administration's past announcements."

ECONOMIC NEWS GETS SCRUBBED, TOO

In the early spring of 2008, the White House Web site did an emergency facelift. Almost all of President Bush's previous positive reflections on the state of the economy were scrubbed. No longer did the site make claims about job creation. Gone were the statements about the need to make the then-temporary tax cuts permanent. In effect, because the economy was slowing down, the president's staff made sure that records of his earlier optimism were no longer easily accessible.

FOR CRITICAL ANALYSIS

Should Congress pass a law requiring each president to leave on the White House Web site links to all interviews and press releases? Why or why not?

(www.whitehouse.gov)

to campaign functions. By 2008, the offices established within the White House Office were the following:

- Domestic Policy Council.
- Homeland Security Council.
- National Economic Council.
- Office of Faith-Based and Community Initiatives.
- Office of the First Lady.
- Office of National AIDS Policy.
- Privacy and Civil Liberties Oversight Board.

- USA Freedom Corps.
- White House Fellows Office.
- White House Military Office.

In all recent administrations, one member of the White House Office has been named **chief of staff.** This person, who is responsible for coordinating the office, is also one of the president's chief advisers.

The president may establish special advisory units within the White House to address topics the president finds especially important. Such units include the long-established Domestic Policy Council and the National Economic Council. Under George W. Bush, these units also included the Office of Faith-Based and Community Initiatives, the USA Freedom Corps, the Office of National AIDS Policy, and the Privacy and Civil Liberties Oversight Board. The White House Office also includes the staff members who support the First Lady.

In addition to civilian advisers, the president is supported by a large number of military personnel, who are organized under the White House Military Office. These members of the military provide communications, transportation, medical care, and food services to the president and the White House staff.

"If I become President, I'm not giving any of my schoolfriends jobs."

(©The New Yorker Collection, 1993. Victoria Roberts, from cartoonbank.com. All Rights Reserved.)

Employees of the White House Office have been both envied and criticized. The White House Office, according to most former staffers, grants its employees access and power. They are able to use the resources of the White House to contact virtually anyone in the world by telephone, cable, fax, or electronic mail, as well as to use the influence of the White House to persuade legislators and citizens. Because of this influence, staffers are often criticized for overstepping the bounds of the office. It is the appointments secretary who is able to grant or deny senators, representatives, and cabinet secretaries access to the president. It is the press secretary who grants to the press and television journalists access to any information about the president.

White House staff members are closest to the president and may have considerable influence over the administration's decisions. Often, when presidents are under fire for their decisions, the staff is accused of keeping the chief executive too isolated from criticism or help. Presidents insist that they will not allow the staff to become too powerful, but, given the difficulty of the office, each president eventually turns to staff members for loyal assistance and protection.

The Office of Management and Budget. The **Office of Management and Budget (OMB)** was originally the Bureau of the Budget, which was created in 1921 within the Department of the Treasury. Recognizing the importance of this agency, Franklin Roosevelt moved it into the White House Office in 1939. Richard Nixon reorganized the Bureau of the Budget in 1970 and changed its name to reflect its new managerial function. It is headed by a director, who makes up the annual federal budget that the president presents to Congress each January for approval. In principle, the director of the OMB has broad fiscal powers in planning and estimating various parts of the federal budget, because all agencies must submit their proposed budget to the OMB for approval. In reality, it is not so clear that the OMB truly can affect the greater scope of the federal budget. Rather, the OMB may be more important as a clearinghouse for legislative proposals initiated in the executive agencies.

The National Security Council. The **National Security Council (NSC)** is a link between the president's key foreign and military advisers and the president. Its members consist of the president, the vice president, and the secretaries of state and defense, plus other

Chief of Staff
The person who is named to direct the White House Office and advise the president.

Office of Management and Budget (OMB)
A division of the Executive Office of the President. The OMB assists the president in preparing the annual budget, clearing and coordinating departmental agency budgets, and supervising the administration of the federal budget.

National Security Council (NSC)
An agency in the Executive Office of the President that advises the president on national security.

informal members. Included in the NSC is the president's special assistant for national security affairs. In 2001, Condoleezza Rice became the first woman to serve as a president's national security adviser, a position that she held until January 2005, when she was appointed secretary of state.

THE VICE PRESIDENCY

The Constitution does not give much power to the vice president. The only formal duty is to preside over the Senate—which is rarely necessary. This obligation is fulfilled when the Senate organizes and adopts its rules and when the vice president is needed to decide a tie vote. In all other cases, the president pro tem manages parliamentary procedures in the Senate. The vice president is expected to participate only informally in senatorial deliberations, if at all.

didyouknow...

That the 2008 presidential elections were the first since 1952 without an incumbent president or vice president running?

THE VICE PRESIDENT'S JOB

Vice presidents have traditionally been chosen by presidential nominees to balance the ticket to attract groups of voters or appease party factions. If a presidential nominee is from the North, it is not a bad idea to have a vice-presidential nominee who is from the South. If the presidential nominee is from a rural state, perhaps someone with an urban background would be most suitable as a running mate. Presidential nominees who are strongly conservative or strongly liberal would do well to have vice-presidential nominees who are more in the middle of the political road.

Strengthening the Ticket. In recent presidential elections, vice presidents have often been selected for other reasons. In 2000, both vice-presidential selections were intended to shore up the respective presidential candidates' perceived weaknesses. Republican George W. Bush, who was subject to criticism for his lack of government experience and his "lightweight" personality, chose Dick Cheney, a former member of Congress who had also served as secretary of defense. Democrat Al Gore chose Senator Joe Lieberman of Connecticut, whose reputation for moral integrity (as an Orthodox Jew) could help counteract the effects of Bill Clinton's sex scandals. In 2004, Democratic presidential candidate John Kerry made a more traditional choice in Senator John Edwards of North Carolina. Edwards provided regional balance and also a degree of socioeconomic balance because, unlike Kerry, he had been born into relatively humble circumstances.

In 2008, after a long, drawn out, and bitter primary season among Democratic candidates, Barack Obama had to decide whether to include Senator Hillary Clinton on his ticket. Many of her supporters argued for this "dream team." In the end, though, Obama chose a long-time senator, Joe Biden, who had extensive foreign affairs experience. For the Republican presidential ticket, John McCain shocked his party and the nation when he chose the governor of Alaska, Sarah Palin. Many criticized his choice of a relatively unknown politician who had previously been mayor of an Alaskan town with only 7,000 people and had been governor of Alaska for less than two years.

Supporting the President. The job of vice president is not extremely demanding, even when the president gives some specific task to the vice president. Typically, vice presidents spend their time supporting the president's activities. During the Clinton administration (1993–2001), however, Vice President Al Gore did much to strengthen the position of vice president by his aggressive support for environmental protection policies on a global basis. He also took a special interest in areas of emerging technology and was instrumental in providing subsidies to public schools for Internet use. Vice President Dick Cheney, as one of President George W. Bush's key advisers, clearly was an influential figure in the Bush administration. Of course, the vice presidency takes on more significance if the president becomes disabled or dies in office—and the vice president becomes president.

Vice-president elect Joe Biden walks on stage during an election night gathering in Grant Park on November 4, 2008, in Chicago, Illinois. Senator Barack Obama (D., Ill.) defeated Republican nominee Senator John McCain (R., Ariz.) by a wide margin in the election to become the first African American U.S. president elect. (Scott Olson/Getty Images)

Only eight presidents have died in office, after which their vice presidents became president. When John F. Kennedy was assassinated in November 1963, then Vice President Lyndon B. Johnson was sworn in as president by a federal judge. Standing alongside Johnson was Kennedy's widow, Jacqueline Kennedy. Who becomes president if both the president and the vice president are killed? (AP Photo/White House, Cecil Stoughton)

Vice presidents sometimes have become elected presidents in their own right. John Adams and Thomas Jefferson were the first to do so. Richard Nixon was elected president in 1968 after he had served as Dwight D. Eisenhower's vice president during 1953–1961. In 1988, George H. W. Bush was elected to the presidency after eight years as Ronald Reagan's vice president.

PRESIDENTIAL SUCCESSION

Eight vice presidents have become president because of the death of the president. John Tyler, the first to do so, took over William Henry Harrison's position after only one month. No one knew whether Tyler should simply be a caretaker until a new president could be elected three and a half years later or whether he actually should be president. Tyler assumed that he was supposed to be the chief executive, and he acted as such—although he was commonly referred to as "His Accidency." Since then, vice presidents taking over the position of the presidency because of the incumbent's death have assumed the presidential powers.

But what should a vice president do if a president becomes incapable of carrying out necessary duties while in office? When James Garfield was shot in 1881, he remained alive for two and a half months. What was Vice President Chester Arthur's role?

This question was not addressed in the original Constitution. Article II, Section 1, says only that "in Case of the Removal of the President from Office, or of his Death, Resignation, or Inability to discharge the Powers and Duties of the said Office, the same shall devolve on [the same powers shall be exercised by] the Vice President." There have been many instances of presidential disability. When Dwight Eisenhower became ill a second time in 1958, he entered into a pact with Richard Nixon specifying that the vice president could determine whether the president was incapable of carrying out his duties if the president could not communicate. John Kennedy and Lyndon Johnson entered into similar agreements with their vice presidents. Finally, in 1967, the **Twenty-fifth Amendment** was passed, establishing procedures in the event of presidential incapacity.

THE TWENTY-FIFTH AMENDMENT

According to the Twenty-fifth Amendment, when a president believes that he or she is incapable of performing the duties of office, the president must inform Congress in writing. Then the vice president serves as acting president until the president can resume

Twenty-fifth Amendment
A 1967 amendment to the Constitution that establishes procedures for filling presidential and vice-presidential vacancies and makes provisions for presidential incapacity.

normal duties. When the president is unable to communicate, a majority of the cabinet, including the vice president, can declare that fact to Congress. Then the vice president serves as acting president until the president resumes normal duties. If a dispute arises over the return of the president's ability, a two-thirds vote of Congress is required to allow the vice president to remain acting president. Otherwise, the president shall resume normal duties.

In 2002, President George W. Bush formally invoked these provisions of the Twenty-fifth Amendment for the first time by officially transferring presidential power to Vice President Dick Cheney while the president underwent a colonoscopy, a twenty-minute procedure. He commented that he undertook this transfer of power "because we're at war," referring to the war on terror. The only other time these provisions of the Twenty-fifth Amendment have been used was during President Reagan's colon surgery in 1985, although Reagan did not formally invoke the amendment.

WHEN THE VICE PRESIDENCY BECOMES VACANT

The Twenty-fifth Amendment also addresses the issue of how the president should fill a vacant vice presidency. Section 2 of the amendment simply states, "Whenever there is a vacancy in the office of the Vice President, the President shall nominate a Vice President who shall take office upon confirmation by a majority vote of both Houses of Congress." This is exactly what occurred when Richard Nixon's first vice president, Spiro Agnew, resigned in 1973 because of his alleged receipt of construction contract kickbacks during his tenure as governor of Maryland. Nixon turned to Gerald Ford as his choice for vice president. After extensive hearings, both chambers of Congress confirmed the appointment. Then, when Nixon resigned on August 9, 1974, Ford automatically became president and nominated as his vice president Nelson Rockefeller. Congress confirmed Ford's choice. For the first time in the history of the country, neither the president nor the vice president had been elected to their positions.

> **didyouknow...**
>
> **That President Richard Nixon** served 56 days without a vice president, and that President Gerald Ford served 132 days without a vice president?

The question of who shall be president if both the president and the vice president die is answered by the Succession Act of 1947. If the president and vice president die, resign, or are disabled, the Speaker of the House will become president, after resigning from Congress. Next in line is the president pro tem of the Senate, followed by the cabinet officers in the order of the creation of their departments (see Table 11–3).

TABLE 11–3: Line of Succession to the Presidency of the United States

1. Vice president	10. Secretary of commerce
2. Speaker of the House of Representatives	11. Secretary of labor
3. Senate president pro tempore	12. Secretary of health and human services
4. Secretary of state	13. Secretary of housing and urban development
5. Secretary of the treasury	14. Secretary of transportation
6. Secretary of defense	15. Secretary of energy
7. Attorney general (head of the Justice Department)	16. Secretary of education
8. Secretary of the interior	17. Secretary of veterans affairs
9. Secretary of agriculture	18. Secretary of homeland security

WHY SHOULD YOU CARE ABOUT
the presidency?

(PhotoDisc by Getty Images)

When it comes to caring about the presidency, most people do not need much encouragement. The president is our most important official. The president serves as the public face of the government, and, indeed, of the nation as a whole. Many people, however, believe the president is such a remote figure that nothing they can do will affect what he or she does. That is not always true. On many issues, your voice—combined, of course, with the voices of many others—can have an impact. Writing to the president is a traditional way for citizens to express their opinions. Every day, the White House receives several thousand letters and other communications.

THE PRESIDENT AND YOUR LIFE

The president can influence many issues that directly affect your life. For example, in 2003 and 2004, in response to the situation in Iraq, a number of Democratic and Republican legislators began raising the idea of reinstating a military draft of young people. Such a measure would probably need the support of the president to succeed. A military draft might affect you or your friends directly. If you have opinions on a topic such as this, you may well want to "cast your vote" by adding your letter to the many others that the president receives on this issue.

Lobbying the president on an issue such as the draft may have an impact, but there may also be issues on which the president refuses to consider popular opinion. President Bush refused to be swayed by the public over the war in Iraq, even after the voters turned Congress over to the Democrats. Bush's determination should remind you of the importance of learning about presidential candidates and their positions on important issues, and then making sure to vote. Once a candidate is elected, it is possible that neither public opinion nor Congress will be able to alter presidential policies to any significant degree.

HOW YOU CAN MAKE A DIFFERENCE

The most traditional form of communication with the White House is, of course, by letter. Letters to the president should be addressed to

The President of the United States
The White House
1600 Pennsylvania Avenue N.W.
Washington, DC 20500

Letters may be sent to the First Lady at the same address. Will you get an answer? Almost certainly. The White House mail room is staffed by volunteers and paid employees who sort the mail for the president and tally the public's concerns. You may receive a standard response to your comments or a more personal, detailed response.

It is possible to call the White House on the telephone and leave a message for the president or First Lady. To call the switchboard, call 202-456-1414, a number publicized by former secretary of state James Baker when he told the Israelis through the media, "When you're serious about peace, call us at . . . ." The switchboard received more than eight thousand calls in the next twenty-four hours.

In most circumstances, a better choice is the round-the-clock comment line, which you can reach at 202-456-1111. When you call that number, an operator will take down your comments and forward them to the president's office.

The home page for the White House is

www.whitehouse.gov.

It is designed to be entertaining and to convey information about the president. You can also send your comments and ideas to the White House using e-mail. Send comments to the president at

comments@whitehouse.gov.

Address e-mail to the vice president at

vice_president@whitehouse.gov.

QUESTIONS FOR
discussionandanalysis

1. Review the *Which Side Are You On?* feature on page 386. Should the president ever meet with the heads of countries that support terror? Why or why not? Should lesser officials be allowed to meet with such leaders? Again, why or why not? If you believe that negotiations are sometimes appropriate, under what conditions should they be undertaken? Under what conditions should they be avoided?

2. What characteristics do you think voters look for when choosing a president? Might these characteristics change as a result of changes in the political environment and the specific problems facing the nation? If you believe voters almost always look for the same characteristics when selecting a president, why is this? If voters seek somewhat different people as president depending on circumstances, which circumstances favor which kinds of leaders?

3. In recent years, many presidents have been lawyers by profession, though George W. Bush was a businessman, Ronald Reagan was an actor, and Jimmy Carter was a naval officer and peanut farmer. What advantages might these three presidents have gained from their career backgrounds? In particular, what benefits might Ronald Reagan have derived from his experience as an actor?

4. Refer to Figure 11–1 on page 392. Note that with a single exception, every eight years since 1953 the presidency has been taken over by the other party. The only exception is Reagan's first term—had Carter been reelected instead, the pattern would have been perfect: eight years of Republican Eisenhower, eight of Democrats Kennedy and Johnson, eight of Republicans Nixon and Ford, eight of Democrat Carter, eight of Republicans Reagan and G. H. W. Bush, eight of Democrat Clinton, eight of Republican G. W. Bush, and finally a Democrat again, Barack Obama. Why might the voters prefer to pick a president from the other party every few years?

5. In 2007, Lewis ("Scooter") Libby, Vice President Dick Cheney's chief of staff, was convicted of four felony counts that included perjury and obstruction of justice. President Bush commuted Libby's sentence so that he would not have to serve time in prison. Was this appropriate, especially given that Libby was a member of Bush's own administration? Why or why not?

keyterms

advice and consent 384

appointment power 382

cabinet 397

chief diplomat 384

chief executive 381

chief legislator 387

chief of staff 400

civil service 382

commander in
chief 383

constitutional
power 390

diplomatic
recognition 384

emergency power 394

executive
agreement 387

Executive Office of the
President (EOP) 398

executive privilege 395

expressed power 390

Federal Register 394

head of state 379

impeachment 396

inherent power 390

kitchen cabinet 397

line-item veto 388

National Security
Council (NSC) 400

Office of Management
and Budget
(OMB) 400

pardon 383

patronage 390

pocket veto 388

reprieve 383

signing statement 381

State of the Union
message 387

statutory power 390

Twelfth
Amendment 379

Twenty-fifth
Amendment 402

veto message 388

War Powers
Resolution 384

Washington
community 392

White House Office 398

chapter**summary**

1. The office of the presidency in the United States, combining as it does the functions of chief of state and chief executive, was unique upon its creation. The framers of the Constitution were divided over whether the president should be a weak or a strong executive.

2. The requirements for the office of the presidency are outlined in Article II, Section 1, of the Constitution. The president's roles include both formal and informal duties. The roles of the president include head of state, chief executive, commander in chief, chief diplomat, chief legislator, and party chief.

3. As head of state, the president is ceremonial leader of the government. As chief executive, the president is bound to enforce the acts of Congress, the judgments of the federal courts, and treaties. The chief executive has the power of appointment and the power to grant reprieves and pardons.

4. As commander in chief, the president is the ultimate decision maker in military matters. As chief diplomat, the president recognizes foreign governments, negotiates treaties, signs agreements, and nominates and receives ambassadors.

5. The role of chief legislator includes recommending legislation to Congress, lobbying for the legislation, approving laws, and exercising the veto power. In addition to constitutional and inherent powers, the president has statutory powers written into law by Congress. Presidents are also leaders of their political parties. Presidents use their power to persuade and their access to the media to fulfill this function.

6. Presidents have a variety of special powers not available in the other branches of the government. These include emergency powers and the power to issue executive orders and invoke executive privilege.

7. Abuses of executive power are dealt with by Articles I and II of the Constitution, which authorize the House and Senate to impeach and remove the president, vice president, or other officers of the federal government for committing "Treason, Bribery, or other high Crimes and Misdemeanors."

8. The president receives assistance from the cabinet and from the Executive Office of the President (including the White House Office).

9. The vice president is the constitutional officer assigned to preside over the Senate and to assume the presidency in the event of the death, resignation, removal, or disability of the president. The Twenty-fifth Amendment, passed in 1967, established procedures to be followed in case of presidential incapacity and when filling a vacant vice presidency.

selected**print&media**resources

SUGGESTED READINGS

Codevilla, Angelo. *Advice to War Presidents: A Remedial Course in Statecraft.* New York: Basic Books, 2009. Since the time of Franklin D. Roosevelt, all of our presidents have been war leaders in one sense or another. Codevilla believes that presidential foreign policy goes wrong when presidents focus too much on the world they would like and not enough on the world as it actually exists.

Eland, Ivan. *Recarving Rushmore: Ranking the Presidents from George Washington to George W. Bush.* Oakland, Calif.: Independent Institute, 2009. Traditionally, attempts to rank the presidents have focused on wartime leadership and the creation of new government programs. Eland, however, takes a more libertarian stand and awards points based on whether a president has protected the people's liberties.

League of Women Voters. *Choosing the President 2008: A Citizen's Guide to the Electoral Process.* Guilford, Conn.: Lyons Press, 2008. This is the latest elections guide by the League of Women Voters, which is perhaps the nation's oldest, and certainly its most famous, nonpartisan voter service and education organization.

Peters, Gerhard, and John T. Woolley, eds. *The Presidency A to Z,* 4th ed. Washington, D.C.: CQ Press, 2007. This book provides a helpful tool for anyone trying to understand the presidency. The book includes biographies of every president and of many presidential assistants; a discussion of presidential powers and presidential relations with other government branches and groups; and many charts, photographs, and cartoons illustrating various topics.

Roberts, Alasdair. *The Collapse of Fortress Bush: The Crisis of Authority in American Government.* New York: New York University Press, 2008. Many believe that George W. Bush expanded presidential power in new and dramatic ways. Roberts, a professor at Syracuse University, has a different view. He portrays a surprisingly weak president, hamstrung by bureaucratic, constitutional, cultural, and economic barriers. Roberts describes how Bush lost key battles with the defense and intelligence communities and was unable to gain effective control of civil agencies after Hurricane Katrina.

Wilentz, Sean. *The Age of Reagan: A History, 1974–2008.* New York: Harper, 2008. Wilentz, a prize-winning Princeton historian, believes that the American Right has defined and shaped the nation's political history since the 1970s. While Wilentz himself is no conservative, he makes the argument that Ronald Reagan was one of our great presidents.

MEDIA RESOURCES

CNN—Election 2000—A politically balanced look at the extraordinarily close presidential elections of 2000, which pitted Republican George W. Bush against Democrat Al Gore. The race was eventually settled by the United States Supreme Court. CNN's Bill Hemmer narrates this 2001 production.

Fahrenheit 9/11—Michael Moore's scathing 2004 critique of the Bush administration has been called "one long political attack ad." It is also the highest-grossing documentary ever made. While the film may be biased, it is—like all of Moore's productions—entertaining.

LBJ: A Biography—An acclaimed biography of Lyndon Johnson that covers his rise to power, his presidency, and the events of the Vietnam War, which ended his presidency; produced in 1991 as part of PBS's *The American Experience* series.

My Life—President Bill Clinton's autobiography, essential source material on a fascinating national leader. Many people consider the print version of this work to be excessively padded, so it is best experienced through the Random House audiobook—the CD and cassette versions of *My Life* are nicely abridged. Clinton's own narration adds considerable flavor to the production.

Nixon—An excellent 1995 film exposing the events of Richard Nixon's troubled presidency. Anthony Hopkins plays the embattled but brilliant chief executive.

Sunrise at Campobello—A classic portrait of one of the greatest presidents, Franklin Delano Roosevelt; produced in 1960 and starring Ralph Bellamy.

e-mocracy

THE PRESIDENCY AND THE INTERNET

Today, the Internet has become such a normal part of most Americans' lives that it is almost hard to imagine what life was like without it. Certainly, accessing the latest press releases from the White House was much more difficult ten years ago than it is today. It was not until the Clinton administration (1993–2001) that access to the White House via the Internet became possible. President Bill Clinton supported making many White House documents available on the White House Web site.

Correspondence with the president and the First Lady quickly moved from ordinary handwritten letters to e-mail. During the Clinton presidency, most agencies of the government, as well as congressional offices, also began to provide access and information on the Internet. Today, you can access the White House Web site (see the following *Logging On* section) to find White House press releases, presidential State of the Union messages and other speeches, historical data on the presidency, and much more.

LOGGING ON

This site offers extensive information on the White House and the presidency:
www.whitehouse.gov.

Inaugural addresses of American presidents from George Washington to George W. Bush can be found at
www.bartleby.com/124.

You can find an excellent collection of data and maps describing all U.S. presidential elections at Dave Leip's Atlas of U.S. Presidential Elections. Go to
uselectionatlas.org.

12 The Bureaucracy

CHAPTER CONTENTS

The Federal Emergency Management Agency (FEMA) is part of the U.S. Department of Homeland Security. Here, members of FEMA and Homeland Security discuss preparations for one of the many serious tropical storms and hurricanes that hit the United States in 2008. (FEMA/Bill Koplitz)

what if...parts of the federal government were privatized?

BACKGROUND

The federal bureaucracy currently includes numerous independent executive agencies, independent regulatory agencies, and so-called government corporations. Many of these federal government agencies, such as the Central Intelligence Agency, provide services that are highly sensitive. Others, such as the National Science Foundation, exist simply to give away funds for specific purposes. Still others, such as the U.S. Postal Service, provide for-fee services that in effect compete with private-sector services.

Agencies such as the U.S. Weather Service provide their services to the U.S. public at no charge. The U.S. Weather Service, nonetheless, is in competition with private weather prediction organizations. The Tennessee Valley Authority (TVA) generates power for a seven-state region at relatively low rates. It is in direct competition with private companies that generate electricity.

WHAT IF PARTS OF THE FEDERAL GOVERNMENT WERE PRIVATIZED?

Throughout the world, governments are selling all or part of government-owned agencies and companies to private investors, including both individuals and existing corporations. Certainly, in the United States, we cannot imagine auctioning off, say, the Central Intelligence Agency to the highest private bidder. Nonetheless, numerous federal government agencies conceivably could be privatized. In particular, it has been proposed that the National Mediation Board, the Smithsonian Institution, and the TVA could be privatized.

There are many methods by which government-owned operations can be privatized. One option would be to issue and sell shares directly to anybody who wishes to buy them. Eventually, a group would control a large enough percentage of shares to elect a board of directors so that the group could steer the newly privatized agency in a particular direction.

Another option would be to offer to sell a government agency to existing corporations that already might be engaged in similar lines of business. The U.S. Postal Service, for example, could be offered for sale to existing delivery companies, such as FedEx. The TVA could be sold in parts to private electric utility companies (which could even be based in other countries). Finally, some of the larger agencies that are spread through-out the United States, such as the Federal Aviation Administration, could be offered for sale in small chunks. For example, each airport control system could be offered for sale to investors in that particular city.

AFTER PRIVATIZATION, THEN WHAT?

It is certain that any federal government agency that became privatized would be subject to a much greater extent to the not-so-tender mercies of the marketplace. If the TVA were privatized, it would be forced to take account of the true costs of all of its operations. Ultimately, to meet its costs, it would have to raise the price of electricity to its customers.

Consider other examples. The U.S. Postal Service probably would be run more like FedEx and UPS. If it were, U.S. postal workers, who are now part of a very strong union, would find privatized postal management much less willing to accept union demands for higher wages. The National Mediation Board would have to bill unions and businesses for its mediation services in labor-management disputes.

CERTAINLY, NOT EVERYONE WOULD BENEFIT FROM INCREASED PRIVATIZATION

If the U.S. Postal Service were purchased by a private company, mail delivery to rural Americans might become much more expensive. In other words, a private postal service might have to charge the true cost of delivering mail to out-of-the-way residents and businesses. Given that an increasing amount of correspondence takes place on the Internet, however, rural Americans might not be overly burdened with higher postal costs. Nonetheless, if mail delivery service became extremely expensive, more people might move to cities.

If the National Mediation Board were privatized and it had to charge the full cost for all of its services, some labor-management disputes might take longer to resolve. Why? Because of the reluctance of the parties to pay more for mediation services.

FOR CRITICAL ANALYSIS

1. Which additional agencies and government operations are likely candidates for privatization? Why?
2. Which government agencies and operations clearly are not candidates for privatization? Why?

Faceless bureaucrats—this image provokes a negative reaction from many, if not most, Americans. Polls consistently report that the majority of Americans support "less government." The same polls, however, report that the majority of Americans support almost every specific program that the government undertakes. The conflict between the desire for small government and the desire for benefits that only a large government can provide has been a constant feature of American politics. For example, the goal of preserving endangered species has widespread support. At the same time, many people believe that restrictions imposed under the Endangered Species Act violate the rights of landowners. Helping the elderly pay their medical bills is a popular objective, but hardly anyone enjoys paying the Medicare tax that supports this effort.

In this chapter, we describe the size, organization, and staffing of the federal bureaucracy. We review modern attempts at bureaucratic reform and the process by which Congress exerts ultimate control over the bureaucracy. We also discuss the bureaucracy's role in making rules and setting policy.

> **Bureaucracy**
> A large organization that is structured hierarchically to carry out specific functions.

THE NATURE OF BUREAUCRACY

Every modern president, at one time or another, has proclaimed that his administration was going to "fix government." All modern presidents also have put forth plans to end government waste and inefficiency (see Table 12–1). Their success has been, in a word, underwhelming. Presidents generally have been powerless to affect the structure and operation of the federal bureaucracy significantly. Could government make better use of the Internet to enhance efficiency? We look at that issue in this chapter's *Politics and the Cyber Sphere* feature on the following page.

A **bureaucracy** is the name given to a large organization that is structured hierarchically to carry out specific functions. Generally, most bureaucracies are characterized by an organization chart. The units of the organization are divided according to the specialization and expertise of the employees.

PUBLIC AND PRIVATE BUREAUCRACIES

We should not think of bureaucracy as unique to government. Any large corporation or university can be considered a bureaucratic organization. The fact is that the handling of complex problems requires a division of labor. Individuals must concentrate their skills on specific, well-defined aspects of a problem and depend on others to solve the rest of it.

Public, or government, bureaucracies differ from private organizations in some important ways, however. A private corporation, such as Microsoft, has a single set of leaders—its board of directors. Public bureaucracies, in contrast, do not have a single set of leaders. Although the president is the chief administrator of the federal system, all bureaucratic

TABLE 12–1: Selected Presidential Plans to End Government Inefficiency

President	Name of Plan
Lyndon Johnson (1963–1969)	Programming, Planning, and Budgeting Systems
Richard Nixon (1969–1974)	Management by Objectives
Jimmy Carter (1977–1981)	Zero-Based Budgeting
Ronald Reagan (1981–1989)	President's Private Sector Survey on Cost Control (the Grace Commission)
George H. W. Bush (1989–1993)	Right-Sizing Government
Bill Clinton (1993–2001)	Reinventing Government
George W. Bush (2001–2009)	Performance-Based Budgeting

POLITICS AND...
the cyber sphere

MOVING GOVERNMENT ONLINE

There is a difference between i-government and e-government. Federal, state, and local governments have done a good job of putting information on the Web. This is *i-government,* where the *i* stands for information. The next step is to use the interactivity and speed of the Internet to provide public services—*e-government,* where the *e* stands for electronic. In the private sector, a good example of interactivity on the Web is the success of Amazon.com, eBay, and other online sellers. This is *e-commerce.* All e-commerce sites work interactively and at the speed of light to benefit their customers. Not so within most government agencies in the United States.

GOVERNMENT INFORMATION ON THE INTERNET—LOTS OF IT

If you are under the age of thirty, you are unlikely to be aware of how hard it was to obtain information on any aspect of government in the past. Getting a government form used to be time consuming and sometimes very difficult. A government printing office sold official documents to cover the costs of printing so many forms, booklets, brochures, and the like. Today, all documents intended for public consumption can be found online. To see this, just go to **usa.gov**. This is probably the best government Web site in the world. It chiefly provides information (although it has about a hundred online services—mainly links to other sites).

E-GOVERNMENT IS NOT AROUND THE CORNER

As mentioned earlier, e-commerce has been very successful. In contrast, e-government, for the most part, has been unsuccessful. One observer has called it a "colossal waste of taxpayers' money on big computer systems, poorly thought out and overpriced." There are rays of hope, nonetheless. City government in Washington, D.C., has put its procurement process online. It offers a Wikipedia-style Web page on which potential bidders and the public can download information about projects, as well as ask questions. Still, many other nations are well ahead of the United States when it comes to e-government—even poor countries such as India, as you will discover in the *Beyond Our Borders* feature later in this chapter on page 430.

THE PERILS OF E-GOVERNMENT

Identity theft has become a serious issue throughout the world. Successful e-government projects may aggravate the problem. Some believe that they will be a pot of gold for fraudsters. After all, e-government requires huge databases on individuals. If these databases are not competently protected, sophisticated identity thieves might be able to obtain valuable information about millions of individuals all at once. As just one example, if all of our nation's medical records were placed in government databases, that information would be valuable to an identity thief. So far, governments have not done very well in verifying who accesses personal information in their data files.

FOR CRITICAL ANALYSIS

Why has i-government grown dramatically, whereas e-government has not?

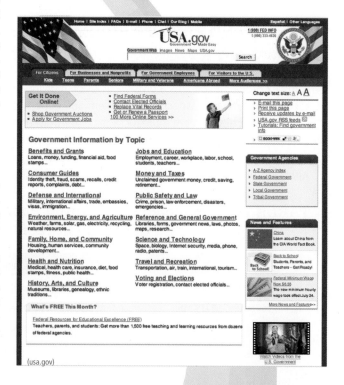

(usa.gov)

agencies are subject to Congress for their funding, staffing, and, indeed, their continued existence. Furthermore, public bureaucracies supposedly serve the citizenry.

One other important difference between private corporations and government bureaucracies is that government bureaucracies are not organized to make a profit. Rather, they are supposed to perform their functions as efficiently as possible to conserve the taxpayers' dollars. Perhaps it is this ideal that makes citizens hostile toward government bureaucracy when they experience inefficiency and red tape.

MODELS OF BUREAUCRACY

Several theories have been offered to help us better understand the ways in which bureaucracies function. Each of these theories focuses on specific features of bureaucracies.

Weberian Model. The classic model, or **Weberian model,** of the modern bureaucracy was proposed by the German sociologist Max Weber.[1] He argued that the increasingly complex nature of modern life, coupled with the steadily growing demands placed on governments by their citizens, made the formation of bureaucracies inevitable. According to Weber, most bureaucracies—whether in the public or private sector—are organized hierarchically and governed by formal procedures. The power in a bureaucracy flows from the top downward. Decision-making processes in bureaucracies are shaped by detailed technical rules that promote similar decisions in similar situations. Bureaucrats are specialists who attempt to resolve problems through logical reasoning and data analysis instead of "gut feelings" and guesswork. Individual advancement in bureaucracies is supposed to be based on merit rather than political connections. Indeed, the modern bureaucracy, according to Weber, should be an apolitical organization.

Acquisitive Model. Other theorists do not view bureaucracies in terms as benign as Weber's. Some believe that bureaucracies are acquisitive in nature. Proponents of the **acquisitive model** argue that top-level bureaucrats will always try to expand, or at least to avoid any reductions in, the size of their budgets. Although government bureaucracies are not-for-profit enterprises, bureaucrats want to maximize the size of their budgets and staffs because these things are the most visible trappings of power in the public sector. These efforts are also prompted by the desire of bureaucrats to "sell" their products— such as national defense, public housing, or agricultural subsidies—to both Congress and the public.

Monopolistic Model. Because government bureaucracies seldom have competitors, some theorists have suggested that these bureaucratic organizations may be explained best by a **monopolistic model.** The analysis is similar to that used by economists to examine the behavior of monopolistic firms. Monopolistic bureaucracies—like monopolistic firms—essentially have no competitors and act accordingly. Because monopolistic bureaucracies usually are not penalized for chronic inefficiency, they have little reason to adopt cost-saving measures or to make more productive use of their resources. Some economists have argued that such problems can be cured only by privatizing certain bureaucratic functions.

BUREAUCRACIES COMPARED

The federal bureaucracy in the United States enjoys a greater degree of autonomy than do federal or national bureaucracies in many other nations. Much of the insularity that is commonly supposed to characterize the bureaucracy in this country may stem from the

German sociologist Max Weber

(1864–1920) created the classic model of the modern bureaucracy. Does the power in the classic bureaucracy flow upward, downward, or horizontally? (Photo Courtesy of Bavarian Academy of Sciences and Humanities)

Weberian Model
A model of bureaucracy developed by the German sociologist Max Weber, who viewed bureaucracies as rational, hierarchical organizations in which decisions are based on logical reasoning.

Acquisitive Model
A model of bureaucracy that views top-level bureaucrats as seeking to expand the size of their budgets and staffs to gain greater power.

Monopolistic Model
A model of bureaucracy that compares bureaucracies to monopolistic business firms. Lack of competition in either circumstance leads to inefficient and costly operations.

---

1. Max Weber, *Theory of Social and Economic Organization,* ed. Talcott Parsons (New York: Oxford University Press, 1974).

The Food and Drug Administration
(FDA) is one of the many agencies within the federal government. These FDA scientists are testing tomatoes suspected of containing salmonella bacteria. Why does this job fall to the FDA and not to local health agencies? (AP Photo/Kevork Djansezian)

sheer size of the government organizations needed to implement an annual budget of over $3 trillion. Because lines of authority often are not well defined, some bureaucracies may be able to operate with a significant degree of autonomy.

The federal nature of the American government also means that national bureaucracies regularly provide financial assistance to their state counterparts. Both the Department of Education and the Department of Housing and Urban Development, for example, distribute funds to their counterparts at the state level. In contrast, most bureaucracies in European countries have a top-down command structure so that national programs may be implemented directly at the lower level. This is due not only to the smaller size of most European countries but also to the fact that public ownership of such businesses as telephone companies, airlines, railroads, and utilities is far more common in Europe than in the United States.

Even though the U.S. government owns relatively few enterprises, this does not mean that its bureaucracies are comparatively powerless. Indeed, there are many **administrative agencies** in the federal bureaucracy—such as the Environmental Protection Agency, the Nuclear Regulatory Commission, and the Securities and Exchange Commission—that regulate private companies.

THE SIZE OF THE BUREAUCRACY

In 1789, the new government's bureaucracy was minuscule. There were three departments—State (with nine employees), War (with two employees), and Treasury (with thirty-nine employees)—and the Office of the Attorney General (which later became the Department of Justice). The bureaucracy was still small in 1798. At that time, the secretary of state had seven clerks and spent a total of $500 (about $9,083 in 2009 dollars) on stationery and printing. In that same year, the Appropriations Act allocated $1.4 million (or $25.4 million in 2009 dollars) to the War Department.[2]

Times have changed, as we can see in Figure 12–1, which shows the various federal agencies and the number of civilian employees in each. Excluding the military, the fed-

Administrative Agency
A federal, state, or local government unit established to perform a specific function. Administrative agencies are created and authorized by legislative bodies to administer and enforce specific laws.

---

2. Leonard D. White, *The Federalists: A Study in Administrative History, 1789–1801* (New York: Free Press, 1948).

FIGURE 12–1: Federal Agencies and Their Respective Numbers of Civilian Employees

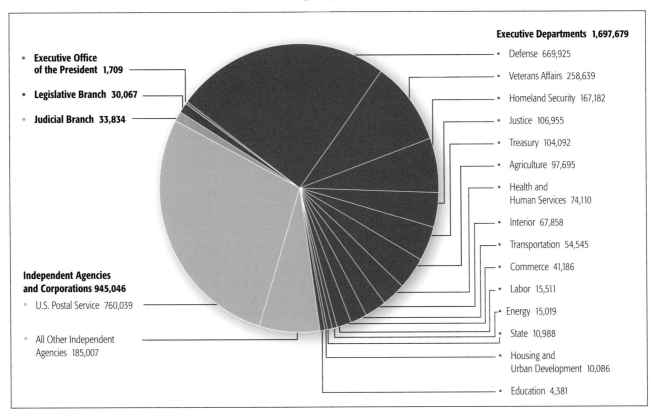

Executive Office of the President 1,709

Legislative Branch 30,067

Judicial Branch 33,834

Independent Agencies and Corporations 945,046

- U.S. Postal Service 760,039

- All Other Independent Agencies 185,007

Executive Departments 1,697,679

- Defense 669,925
- Veterans Affairs 258,639
- Homeland Security 167,182
- Justice 106,955
- Treasury 104,092
- Agriculture 97,695
- Health and Human Services 74,110
- Interior 67,858
- Transportation 54,545
- Commerce 41,186
- Labor 15,511
- Energy 15,019
- State 10,988
- Housing and Urban Development 10,086
- Education 4,381

Source: The U.S. Office of Personnel Management, June 2008.

eral bureaucracy includes approximately 2.7 million government employees. That number has remained relatively stable for the last several decades. It is somewhat deceiving, however, because many other individuals work directly or indirectly for the federal government as subcontractors or consultants and in other capacities, as you will read later in this chapter. In fact, according to some studies, the federal workforce vastly exceeds the number of official federal workers.

The figures for federal government employment are only part of the story. Figure 12–2 shows the growth in government employment at the federal, state, and local levels. Since 1970, this growth has been mainly at the state and, until recently, local levels. If all government employees are included, more than 15 percent of all civilian employment is accounted for by government. The costs of the bureaucracy are commensurately high. The share of the gross domestic product accounted for by all government spending was only about 11 percent in 1929. Today, it exceeds 35 percent. Why is it that government seems to just keep on getting bigger? We look for an answer in this chapter's *Politics and the Bureaucracy* feature.

FIGURE 12–2: Government Employment at the Federal, State, and Local Levels

There are more local government employees than federal and state employees combined.

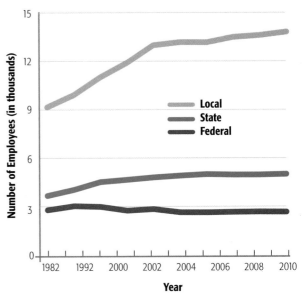

Source: U.S. Census Bureau.

politicsand...the bureaucracy

BIG GOVERNMENT JUST KEEPS GETTING BIGGER

It doesn't really seem to matter who is in the White House or who controls Congress. By whatever measure you wish to use, Big Government is getting bigger and will be bigger yet in the future. More spending, more taxes, and more regulation.

MORE GOVERNMENT REGULATION

As Yale University political scientist Jacob Hacker has argued, "People are more worried about Big Insecurity than Big Government." The recent subprime mortgage market meltdown, coupled with soaring energy prices, has created the impetus for an expansion of government regulation. Federal and state governments are regulating more areas in the economy than ever before—the stock market, banking, mortgage lending, gasoline sales, health care, and the like.

Just consider the number of pages in the *Federal Register,* a government publication that records new and existing government regulations. The size of the *Federal Register,* which reached its peak in 1980, declined during the 1980s while Ronald Reagan was president and then started a gradual creep upward again. It's now almost at its highest level ever—about 80,000 pages per year.

MORE GOVERNMENT SPENDING

In 1983, federal government spending constituted 23.5 percent of total annual output. By 2000, it had dropped to 18.4 percent, the lowest level since 1966. By 2009,

this percentage had gradually crept up to 20.3 percent. During the 2000s, one of the most expensive government programs ever was signed into law—the drug benefit addition to Medicare. At the end of the first decade of the 2000s, the federal government is expanding its investment in public infrastructure—airports, energy delivery systems, broadband access, and bridges. If some members of Congress get their way, attempts at making this nation energy independent will certainly add tens—if not hundreds—of billions of dollars to federal spending.

MORE TAXES ARE A CERTAINTY

In the final analysis, more government spending will have to be paid for by increased taxes. What federal, state, and local governments spend, U.S. residents do not spend. Otherwise stated, the real tax burden on residents of the United States is the percentage of total annual income that is controlled by government. As government spending becomes a larger percentage of total national income, sooner or later the real tax burden for Americans has to rise.

FOR CRITICAL ANALYSIS

How would you personally evaluate whether the increase in government spending and regulation is, on net, beneficial for this nation?

THE ORGANIZATION OF THE FEDERAL BUREAUCRACY

Within the federal bureaucracy are a number of different types of government agencies and organizations. Figure 12–3 outlines the several bodies within the executive branch, as well as the separate organizations that provide services to Congress, to the courts, and directly to the president. In Chapter 11, we discussed those agencies that are considered to be part of the Executive Office of the President.

The executive branch, which employs most of the government's staff, has four major types of structures. They are (1) cabinet departments, (2) independent executive agencies, (3) independent regulatory agencies, and (4) government corporations. Each has a distinctive relationship to the president, and some have unusual internal structures, overall goals, and grants of power.

CABINET DEPARTMENTS

The fifteen **cabinet departments** are the major service organizations of the federal government. They can also be described in management terms as **line organizations.** This means that they are directly accountable to the president and are responsible for perform-

Cabinet Department
One of the fifteen departments of the executive branch (Agriculture, Commerce, Defense, Education, Energy, Health and Human Services, Homeland Security, Housing and Urban Development, Interior, Justice, Labor, State, Transportation, Treasury, and Veterans Affairs).

Line Organization
In the federal government, an administrative unit that is directly accountable to the president.

FIGURE 12–3: Organizational Chart of the Federal Government

THE GOVERNMENT OF THE UNITED STATES

THE CONSTITUTION

LEGISLATIVE BRANCH

THE CONGRESS
SENATE   HOUSE

Architect of the Capitol
United States Botanic Garden
Government Accountability Office
Government Printing Office
Library of Congress
Congressional Budget Office

EXECUTIVE BRANCH

THE PRESIDENT
THE VICE PRESIDENT

Executive Office of the President

White House Office
Council of Economic Advisers
Council on Environmental Quality
National Security Council
Office of Administration

Office of Management and Budget
Office of National Drug Control Policy
Office of Science and Technology Policy
Office of the U.S. Trade Representative
President's Foreign Intelligence
Advisory Board

JUDICIAL BRANCH

The Supreme Court of the United States

United States Courts of Appeals
United States District Courts
Territorial Courts
United States Court of International Trade
United States Court of Federal Claims
United States Court of Appeals
for the Armed Forces
United States Tax Court
United States Court of Appeals for
Veterans Claims
Administrative Office of the
United States Courts
Federal Judicial Center
United States Sentencing Commission

DEPARTMENT OF AGRICULTURE	DEPARTMENT OF COMMERCE	DEPARTMENT OF DEFENSE	DEPARTMENT OF EDUCATION	DEPARTMENT OF ENERGY	DEPARTMENT OF HEALTH AND HUMAN SERVICES	DEPARTMENT OF HOMELAND SECURITY	DEPARTMENT OF HOUSING AND URBAN DEVELOPMENT

DEPARTMENT OF THE INTERIOR	DEPARTMENT OF JUSTICE	DEPARTMENT OF LABOR	DEPARTMENT OF STATE	DEPARTMENT OF TRANSPORTATION	DEPARTMENT OF THE TREASURY	DEPARTMENT OF VETERANS AFFAIRS

INDEPENDENT ESTABLISHMENTS AND GOVERNMENT CORPORATIONS

African Development Foundation
Broadcasting Board of Governors
Central Intelligence Agency
Commodity Futures Trading Commission
Consumer Product Safety Commission
Corporation for National and
  Community Service
Defense Nuclear Facilities Safety Board
Environmental Protection Agency
Equal Employment Opportunity
  Commission
Export-Import Bank of the U.S.
Farm Credit Administration
Federal Communications Commission
Federal Deposit Insurance Corporation
Federal Election Commission
Federal Housing Finance Board

Federal Labor Relations Authority
Federal Maritime Commission
Federal Mediation and Conciliation Service
Federal Mine Safety and Health Review
  Commission
Federal Reserve System
Federal Retirement Thrift Investment Board
Federal Trade Commission
General Services Administration
Inter-American Foundation
Merit Systems Protection Board
National Aeronautics and Space
  Administration
National Archives and Records Administration
National Capital Planning Commission
National Credit Union Administration
National Foundation on the Arts and the
  Humanities

National Labor Relations Board
National Mediation Board
National Railroad Passenger Corporation
  (AMTRAK)
National Science Foundation
National Transportation Safety Board
Nuclear Regulatory Commission
Occupational Safety and Health
  Review Commission
Office of the Director of National
  Intelligence
Office of Government Ethics
Office of Personnel Management
Office of Special Counsel
Overseas Private Investment Corporation
Panama Canal Commission
Peace Corps
Pension Benefit Guaranty Corporation
Postal Rate Commission

Railroad Retirement Board
Securities and Exchange Commission
Selective Service System
Small Business Administration
Social Security Administration
Tennessee Valley Authority
Trade and Development Agency
U.S. Agency for International Development
U.S. Commission on Civil Rights
U.S. International Trade Commission
U.S. Postal Service

Source: *United States Government Manual,* 2007–2008 (Washington, D.C.: U.S. Government Printing Office, 2007).

ing government functions, such as printing money and training troops. These departments were created by Congress when the need for each department arose. The first department to be created was State, and the most recent one was Homeland Security, established in 2003. A president might ask that a new department be created or an old one abolished, but the president has no power to do so without legislative approval from Congress.

didyouknow...

That the government spends about $1 billion every 98 minutes, every day of the year?

Independent Executive Agency
A federal agency that is not part of a cabinet department but reports directly to the president.

Independent Regulatory Agency
An agency outside the major executive departments that is charged with making and implementing rules and regulations.

Each department is headed by a secretary (except for the Justice Department, which is headed by the attorney general). Each department also has several levels of undersecretaries, assistant secretaries, and other personnel.

Presidents theoretically have considerable control over the cabinet departments, because presidents are able to appoint or fire all of the top officials. Even cabinet departments do not always respond to the president's wishes, though. One reason why presidents are frequently unhappy with their departments is that the entire bureaucratic structure below the top political levels is staffed by permanent employees, many of whom are committed to established programs or procedures and who resist change. Table 12–2 shows that each cabinet department employs thousands of individuals, only a handful of whom are under the control of the president. The table also describes some of the functions of each of the departments.

INDEPENDENT EXECUTIVE AGENCIES

Independent executive agencies are bureaucratic organizations that are not located within a department but report directly to the president, who appoints their chief officials. When a new federal agency is created—the Environmental Protection Agency, for example—Congress decides where it will be located in the bureaucracy. In recent decades, presidents often have asked that a new organization be kept separate or independent rather than added to an existing department, particularly if a department may be hostile to the agency's creation. Table 12–3 on page 420 describes the functions of several selected independent executive agencies.

INDEPENDENT REGULATORY AGENCIES

The **independent regulatory agencies** are typically responsible for a specific type of public policy. Their function is to make and implement rules and regulations in a particular sphere of action to protect the public interest. The earliest such agency was the Interstate Commerce Commission (ICC), which was established in 1887 when Americans began to seek some form of government control over the rapidly growing business and industrial sector. This new form of organization, the independent regulatory agency, was supposed to make technical, nonpolitical decisions about rates, profits, and rules that would be for the benefit of all and that did not require congressional legislation. In the years that followed the creation of the ICC, other agencies were formed to regulate such areas as communication (the Federal Communications Commission) and nuclear power (the Nuclear Regulatory Commission). (The ICC was abolished on December 30, 1995.)

The Purpose and Nature of Regulatory Agencies. In practice, the regulatory agencies are administered independently of all three branches of government. They were set up because Congress felt it was unable to handle the complexities and technicalities required to carry out specific laws in the public interest. The regulatory commissions in fact combine some functions of all three branches of government—legislative, executive, and judicial. They are legislative in that they make rules that have the force of law. They are executive in that they provide for the enforcement of those rules. They are judicial in that they decide disputes involving the rules they have made.

Top officials of the
U.S. Department of Homeland Security attend a video teleconference where they receive regional reports on the state of hurricane readiness. What are some other functions of this independent executive agency? (FEMA/Bill Koplitz)

TABLE 12–2: Executive Departments

Department and Year Established	Principal Functions	Selected Subagencies
State (1789) (10,988 employees)	Negotiates treaties; develops foreign policy; protects citizens abroad.	Passport Services Office; Bureau of Diplomatic Security; Foreign Service; Bureau of Human Rights and Humanitarian Affairs; Bureau of Consular Affairs.
Treasury (1789) (104,092 employees)	Pays all federal bills; borrows money; collects federal taxes; mints coins and prints paper currency; supervises national banks.	Internal Revenue Service; U.S. Mint.
Interior (1849) (67,858 employees)	Supervises federally owned lands and parks; supervises Native American affairs.	U.S. Fish and Wildlife Service; National Park Service; Bureau of Indian Affairs; Bureau of Land Management.
Justice (1870)* (106,955 employees)	Furnishes legal advice to the president; enforces federal criminal laws; supervises federal prisons.	Federal Bureau of Investigation; Drug Enforcement Administration; Bureau of Prisons.
Agriculture (1889) (97,695 employees)	Provides assistance to farmers and ranchers; conducts agricultural research; works to protect forests.	Soil Conservation Service; Agricultural Research Service; Food Safety and Inspection Service; Federal Crop Insurance Corporation; Commodity Credit Corporation; Forest Service.
Commerce (1913)† (41,186 employees)	Grants patents and trademarks; conducts a national census; monitors the weather; protects the interests of businesses.	Bureau of the Census; Bureau of Economic Analysis; Patent and Trademark Office; National Oceanic and Atmospheric Administration.
Labor (1913)† (15,511 employees)	Administers federal labor laws; promotes the interests of workers.	Occupational Safety and Health Administration; Bureau of Labor Statistics; Employment Standards Administration; Employment and Training Administration.
Defense (1947)‡ (699,925 employees)	Manages the armed forces (army, navy, air force, and marines); operates military bases; is responsible for civil defense.	National Security Agency; Joint Chiefs of Staff; Departments of the Air Force, Navy, Army; Defense Advanced Research Projects Agency; Defense Intelligence Agency; the service academies.
Housing and Urban Development (1965) (9,593 employees)	Deals with the nation's housing needs; develops and rehabilitates urban communities; oversees resale of mortgages.	Government National Mortgage Association; Office of Community Planning and Development; Office of Fair Housing and Equal Opportunity.
Transportation (1967) (54,545 employees)	Finances improvements in mass transit; develops and administers programs for highways, railroads, and aviation.	Federal Aviation Administration; Federal Highway Administration; National Highway Traffic Safety Administration; Federal Transit Administration.
Energy (1977) (15,019 employees)	Promotes the conservation of energy and resources; analyzes energy data; conducts research and development.	Federal Energy Regulatory Commission; National Nuclear Security Administration.
Health and Human Services (1979)§ (74,110 employees)	Promotes public health; enforces pure food and drug laws; conducts and sponsors health-related research.	Food and Drug Administration; Public Health Service; Centers for Disease Control and Prevention; National Institutes of Health; Centers for Medicare and Medicaid Services.
Education (1979)§ (4,381 employees)	Coordinates federal programs and policies for education; administers aid to education; promotes educational research.	Office of Special Education and Rehabilitation Service; Office of Elementary and Secondary Education; Office of Postsecondary Education; Office of Vocational and Adult Education; Office of Federal Student Aid.
Veterans Affairs (1988) (258,639 employees)	Promotes the welfare of veterans of the U.S. armed forces.	Veterans Health Administration; Veterans Benefits Administration; National Cemetery Systems.
Homeland Security (2003) (167,182 employees)	Attempts to prevent terrorist attacks within the United States, control America's borders, and minimize the damage from natural disasters.	U.S. Customs and Border Protection; U.S. Coast Guard; Secret Service; Federal Emergency Management Agency; U.S. Citizenship and Immigration Services; U.S. Immigration Customs Enforcement.

*Formed from the Office of the Attorney General (created in 1789).
†Formed from the Department of Commerce and Labor (created in 1903).
‡Formed from the Department of War (created in 1789) and the Department of the Navy (created in 1798).
§Formed from the Department of Health, Education, and Welfare (created in 1953).

TABLE 12–3: Selected Independent Executive Agencies

Name	Date Formed	Principal Functions
The Smithsonian Institution (4,910 employees)	1846	Runs the government's museums and the National Zoo.
Central Intelligence Agency (CIA) (number of employees not released)	1947	Gathers and analyzes political and military information about foreign countries; conducts covert operations outside the United States.
General Services Administration (GSA) (12,037 employees)	1949	Purchases and manages property of the federal government; acts as the business arm of the federal government in overseeing federal government spending projects; discovers overcharges in government programs.
National Science Foundation (NSF) (1,415 employees)	1950	Promotes scientific research; provides grants to all levels of schools for instructional programs in the sciences.
Small Business Administration (SBA) (4,240 employees)	1953	Protects the interests of small businesses; provides low-cost loans and management information to small businesses.
National Aeronautics and Space Administration (NASA) (18,548 employees)	1958	Is responsible for the U.S. space program, including the building, testing, and operating of space vehicles.
Environmental Protection Agency (EPA) (18,061 employees)	1970	Undertakes programs aimed at reducing air and water pollution; works with state and local agencies to help fight environmental hazards.
Social Security Administration (SSA)* (64,884 employees)	1995	Manages the government's Social Security programs, including Retirement and Survivors Insurance, Disability Insurance, Supplemental Security Income, and international programs.

*Separated from the Department of Health and Human Services (created in 1979).

didyouknow...

That the Commerce Department's U.S. Travel and Tourism Administration recently gave $440,000 in disaster relief to western ski resort operators because there hadn't been enough snow?

Capture
The act by which an industry being regulated by a government agency gains direct or indirect control over agency personnel and decision makers.

Members of regulatory agency boards or commissions are appointed by the president with the consent of the Senate, although they do not report to the president. By law, the members of regulatory agency boards cannot all be from the same political party. Members may be removed by the president only for causes specified in the law creating the agency. Presidents can influence regulatory agency behavior by appointing people of their own parties or individuals who share their political views when vacancies occur, in particular when the chair is vacant. For example, President George W. Bush placed people on the Federal Communications Commission (FCC) who shared his belief in the need to curb obscene language in the media. Not surprisingly, the FCC soon thereafter started to "crack down" on obscenities on the air. Table 12–4 describes the functions of selected independent regulatory agencies.

Agency Capture. Over the last several decades, some observers have concluded that regulatory agencies, although nominally independent, may in fact not always be so. They contend that many agencies have been **captured** by the very industries and firms that they were supposed to regulate. For example, an agency may consult with leaders of an industry to be regulated and then be influenced by those leaders' suggestions when creating new rules. The results have been less competition rather than more competition, higher prices rather than lower prices, and less choice rather than more choice for consumers.

Deregulation and Reregulation. During the presidency of Ronald Reagan (1981–1989), some significant deregulation (the removal of regulatory restraints—the opposite of regulation) occurred, much of which had started under President Jimmy Carter (1977–1981). For example, President Carter appointed a chairperson of the Civil Aeronautics Board

TABLE 12–4: Selected Independent Regulatory Agencies

Name	Date Formed	Principal Functions
Federal Reserve System Board of Governors (Fed) (1,869 employees)	1913	Determines policy on interest rates, credit availability, and the money supply.
Federal Trade Commission (FTC) (1,112 employees)	1914	Prevents businesses from engaging in unfair trade practices; stops the formation of monopolies in the business sector; protects consumer rights.
Securities and Exchange Commission (SEC) (3,511 employees)	1934	Regulates the nation's stock exchanges, in which shares of stocks are bought and sold; requires full disclosure of the financial profiles of companies that wish to sell stocks and bonds to the public.
Federal Communications Commission (FCC) (1,814 employees)	1934	Regulates all communications by telegraph, cable, telephone, radio, and television.
National Labor Relations Board (NLRB) (1,699 employees)	1935	Protects employees' rights to join unions and bargain collectively with employers; attempts to prevent unfair labor practices by both employers and unions.
Equal Employment Opportunity Commission (EEOC) (2,204 employees)	1964	Works to eliminate discrimination based on religion, gender, race, color, national origin, age, or disability; examines claims of discrimination.
Nuclear Regulatory Commission (NRC) (3,789 employees)	1974	Ensures that electricity-generating nuclear reactors in the United States are built and operated safely; regularly inspects the operations of such reactors.

(CAB) who gradually eliminated regulation of airline fares and routes. Then, under Reagan, the CAB was eliminated on January 1, 1985.

During the administration of George H. W. Bush (1989–1993), calls for reregulation of many businesses increased. Indeed, during that administration, the Americans with Disabilities Act of 1990, the Civil Rights Act of 1991, and the Clean Air Act Amendments of 1991, all of which increased or changed the regulation of many businesses, were passed. Additionally, the Cable Reregulation Act of 1992 was passed.

Under President Bill Clinton (1993–2001), the Interstate Commerce Commission was eliminated, and the banking and telecommunications industries, along with many other sectors of the economy, were deregulated. At the same time, there was extensive regulation to protect the environment, a trend somewhat reversed by the George W. Bush administration.

GOVERNMENT CORPORATIONS

Another form of bureaucratic organization in the United States is the **government corporation.** Although the concept is borrowed from the world of business, distinct differences exist between public and private corporations.

A private corporation has shareholders (stockholders) who elect a board of directors, who in turn choose the corporate officers, such as president and vice president. When a private corporation makes a profit, it must pay taxes (unless it avoids them through various legal loopholes). It then distributes the after-tax profits to shareholders as dividends, plows the profits back into the corporation to make new investments, or both.

A government corporation has a board of directors and managers, but it does not have any stockholders. We cannot buy shares of stock in a government corporation, and if the entity makes a profit, it does not distribute the profit as dividends. Also, if it makes a profit, it does not have to pay taxes; the profits remain in the corporation. Table 12–5 on the next page describes the functions of selected government corporations.

didyouknow...

That the Pentagon and the Central Intelligence Agency once spent more than $11 million on psychics who were supposed to provide special insights regarding various foreign threats?

Government Corporation
An agency of government that administers a quasi-business enterprise. These corporations are used when activities are primarily commercial.

TABLE 12–5: Selected Government Corporations

Name	Date Formed	Principal Functions
Tennessee Valley Authority (TVA) (12,624 employees)	1933	Operates a Tennessee River control system and generates power for a seven-state region and for the U.S. aeronautics and space programs; promotes the economic development of the Tennessee Valley region; controls floods and promotes the navigability of the Tennessee River.
Federal Deposit Insurance Corporation (FDIC) (4,583 employees)	1933	Insures individuals' bank deposits up to $100,000*; oversees the business activities of banks.
Export-Import Bank of the United States (Ex-Im Bank) (358 employees)	1933	Promotes the sale of American-made goods abroad; grants loans to foreign purchasers of American products.
National Railroad Passenger Corporation (AMTRAK) (19,000 employees)	1970	Provides a national and intercity rail passenger service; controls 22,000 miles of track and serves 500 communities.
U.S. Postal Service (USPS)† (760,039 employees)	1970	Delivers mail throughout the United States and its territories; is the largest government corporation.

*This limit was raised to $250,000 in October 2008 as part of a legislative package to bail out the financial industry during the credit crisis.
†Formed from the Post Office Department (an executive department) in 1970.

STAFFING THE BUREAUCRACY

There are two categories of bureaucrats: political appointees and civil servants. As noted earlier, the president is able to make political appointments to most of the top jobs in the federal bureaucracy. The president can also appoint ambassadors to foreign posts. All of the jobs that are considered "political plums" and that usually go to the politically well connected are listed in *Policy and Supporting Positions,* a book published by the Government Printing Office after each presidential election. Informally (and appropriately), this has been called "The Plum Book." The rest of the national government's employees belong to the civil service and obtain their jobs through a much more formal process.

POLITICAL APPOINTEES

To fill the positions listed in "The Plum Book,"[3] the president and the president's advisers solicit suggestions from politicians, businesspersons, and other prominent individuals. Appointments to these positions offer the president a way to pay off outstanding political debts. But the president must also take into consideration such things as the candidate's work experience, intelligence, political affiliations, and personal characteristics. Presidents have differed in the importance they attach to appointing women and minorities to plum positions. Presidents often use ambassadorships, however, to reward individuals for their campaign contributions.

We should note here that just because the president has the power to appoint a government official does not mean that such an appointment will pass muster. Before making any nominations, the administration requires potential appointees to undergo a detailed screening process and answer questions such as the following: What are your accomplishments? Did you ever *not* pay taxes for your nannies or housekeepers? What kinds of investments have you made? What have your past partisan affiliations been?

Such a process takes months, and after completing it, the appointees must be confirmed by the Senate. Even with such a screening process, the Bush administration made some serious errors. For example, the president's appointment of Michael Brown

---

3. See Table 11–1 on page 382 for a list of the number of positions available for presidential appointments in the most recent edition of "The Plum Book."

to head the Federal Emergency Management Agency turned out to be a big mistake because Brown had no experience in emergency planning and relief efforts. As another example, the president's appointee to the National Aeronautics and Space Administration had to resign when officials at Texas A&M University confirmed that he had *not* graduated from that university, contrary to what he stated on his résumé. Indeed, a general criticism of the Bush administration was that the president allowed loyalty to take priority over expertise in the relevant regulatory area as a qualification for holding office.

The Aristocracy of the Federal Government. Political appointees are in some sense the aristocracy of the federal government. But their powers, although appearing formidable on paper, are often exaggerated. Like the president, a political appointee will occupy her or his position for a comparatively brief time. Political appointees often leave office before the president's term actually ends. In fact, the average term of service for political appointees is less than two years. As a result, most appointees have little background for their positions and may be mere figureheads. Often, they only respond to the paperwork that flows up from below. Additionally, the professional civil servants who make up the permanent civil service may not feel compelled to carry out their current boss's directives quickly, because they know that he or she will not be around for very long.

The Difficulty in Firing Civil Servants. This inertia is compounded by the fact that it is very difficult to discharge civil servants. In recent years, fewer than one-tenth of 1 percent of federal employees have been fired for incompetence. Because discharged employees may appeal their dismissals, many months or even years can pass before the issue is resolved conclusively. This occupational rigidity helps to ensure that most political appointees, no matter how competent or driven, will not be able to exert much meaningful influence over their subordinates, let alone implement dramatic changes in the bureaucracy itself.

HISTORY OF THE FEDERAL CIVIL SERVICE

When the federal government was formed in 1789, it had no career public servants but rather consisted of amateurs who were almost all Federalists. When Thomas Jefferson took over as president, few federal administrative jobs were held by members of his party, so he fired more than one hundred officials and replaced them with his own supporters. Then, for the next twenty-five years, a growing body of federal administrators gained experience and expertise, becoming in the process professional public servants. These administrators stayed in office regardless of who was elected president. The bureaucracy had become a self-maintaining, long-term element within government.

To the Victor Belong the Spoils. When Andrew Jackson took over the White House in 1828, he could not believe how many appointed officials (appointed before he became president, that is) were overtly hostile toward him and his Democratic Party. Because the bureaucracy was reluctant to carry out his programs, Jackson did the obvious: he fired federal officials—more than had been fired by all of his predecessors combined. The **spoils system**—an application of the principle that to the victor belong the spoils—became the standard method of filling federal positions. Whenever a new president was elected from a party different from the party of the previous president, there would be an almost complete turnover in the staffing of the federal government.

These former U.S. attorneys, who had been asked to resign by the Bush administration, are sworn in during a House Judiciary Committee hearing. Why might an administration wish to change U.S. attorneys? (Photo by Scott J. Ferrell/Congressional Quarterly/Getty Images)

didyouknow...

That the average federal government civilian worker earns $111,180 a year in total compensation (wages plus health insurance, pension, etc.), whereas the average private-sector worker earns $55,470 a year in total compensation?

Spoils System
The awarding of government jobs to political supporters and friends.

On September 19, 1881, President James A. Garfield was assassinated by a disappointed office seeker, Charles J. Guiteau. The long-term effect of this event was to replace the spoils system with a permanent career civil service. This process began with the passage of the Pendleton Act in 1883, which established the Civil Service Commission. (Library of Congress)

The Civil Service Reform Act of 1883. Jackson's spoils system survived for a number of years, but it became increasingly corrupt. Also, as the size of the bureaucracy increased by 300 percent between 1851 and 1881, the cry for civil service reform became louder. Reformers began to look to the example of several European countries—in particular, Germany, which had established a professional civil service that operated under a **merit system** in which job appointments were based on competitive examinations.

In 1883, the **Pendleton Act**—or **Civil Service Reform Act**—was passed, placing the first limits on the spoils system. The act established the principle of employment on the basis of open, competitive examinations and created the **Civil Service Commission** to administer the personnel service. Only 10 percent of federal employees were covered by the merit system initially. Later laws, amendments, and executive orders, however, increased the coverage to more than 90 percent of federal employees. The effects of these reforms were felt at all levels of government.

The Supreme Court strengthened the civil service system in *Elrod v. Burns*[4] in 1976 and *Branti v. Finkel*[5] in 1980. In those two cases, the Court used the First Amendment to forbid government officials from discharging or threatening to discharge public employees solely for *not* being supporters of the political party in power unless party affiliation is an appropriate requirement for the position. Additional enhancements to the civil service system were added in *Rutan v. Republican Party of Illinois*[6] in 1990. The Court's ruling effectively prevented the use of partisan political considerations as the basis for hiring, promoting, or transferring most public employees. An exception was permitted, however, for senior policymaking positions, which usually go to officials who will support the programs of the elected leaders.

The Civil Service Reform Act of 1978. In 1978, the Civil Service Reform Act abolished the Civil Service Commission and created two new federal agencies to perform its duties. To administer the civil service laws, rules, and regulations, the act created the Office of Personnel Management (OPM). The OPM is empowered to recruit, interview, and test potential government workers and determine who should be hired. The OPM makes recommendations to the individual agencies as to which persons meet the standards (typically, the top three applicants for a position), and the agencies then decide whom to hire. To oversee promotions, employees' rights, and other employment matters, the act created the Merit Systems Protection Board (MSPB). The MSPB evaluates charges of wrongdoing, hears employee appeals from agency decisions, and can order corrective action against agencies and employees.

Federal Employees and Political Campaigns. In 1933, when President Franklin D. Roosevelt set up his New Deal, a virtual army of civil servants was hired to staff the many new agencies that were created. Because the individuals who worked in these agencies owed their jobs to the Democratic Party, it seemed natural for them to campaign for Democratic candidates. The Democrats controlling Congress in the mid-1930s did not object. But in 1938, a coalition of conservative Democrats and Republicans took control of Congress and forced through the Hatch Act—or Political Activities Act—of 1939. The

Merit System
The selection, retention, and promotion of government employees on the basis of competitive examinations.

Pendleton Act (Civil Service Reform Act)
An act that established the principle of employment on the basis of merit and created the Civil Service Commission to administer the personnel service.

Civil Service Commission
The initial central personnel agency of the national government; created in 1883.

---

4. 427 U.S. 347 (1976).
5. 445 U.S. 507 (1980).
6. 497 U.S. 62 (1990).

act prohibited federal employees from actively participating in the political management of campaigns. It also forbade the use of federal authority to influence nominations and elections and outlawed the use of bureaucratic rank to pressure federal employees to make political contributions.

The Hatch Act created a controversy that lasted for decades. Many contended that the act deprived federal employees of their First Amendment freedoms of speech and association. In 1972, a federal district court declared the act unconstitutional. The United States Supreme Court, however, reaffirmed the challenged portion of the act in 1973, stating that the government's interest in preserving a nonpartisan civil service was so great that the prohibitions should remain.[7] Twenty years later, Congress addressed the criticisms of the Hatch Act by passing the Federal Employees Political Activities Act of 1993. This act, which amended the Hatch Act, lessened the harshness of the 1939 act in several ways. Among other things, the 1993 act allowed federal employees to run for office in nonpartisan elections, participate in voter-registration drives, make campaign contributions to political organizations, and campaign for candidates in partisan elections.

MODERN ATTEMPTS AT BUREAUCRATIC REFORM

As long as the federal bureaucracy exists, there will continue to be attempts to make it more open, efficient, and responsive to the needs of U.S. citizens. The most important actual and proposed reforms in the last several decades include sunshine and sunset laws, privatization, incentives for efficiency, and more protection for so-called whistleblowers.

SUNSHINE LAWS BEFORE AND AFTER 9/11

In 1976, Congress enacted the **Government in the Sunshine Act.** It required for the first time that all multiheaded federal agencies—agencies headed by a committee instead of an individual—hold their meetings regularly in public session. The bill defined *meetings* as almost any gathering, formal or informal, of agency members, including a conference telephone call. The only exceptions to this rule of openness are discussions of matters such as court proceedings or personnel problems, and these exceptions are specifically listed in the bill. Sunshine laws now exist at all levels of government.

Information Disclosure. Sunshine laws are consistent with the policy of information disclosure that for decades has been supported by the government for both the public and private sectors. For example, beginning in the 1960s, a number of consumer protection laws have required that certain information be disclosed to consumers when purchasing homes, borrowing funds, and the like. In 1966, the federal government passed the Freedom of Information Act (FOIA), which required federal government agencies, with certain exceptions, to disclose to individuals, on their request, any information about them contained in government files. (You will learn more about this act in the *Why Should You Care . . .* feature at the end of this chapter.)

FOIA requests are not just helpful to individuals. Indeed, the major beneficiaries of the act have been news organizations, which have used it to uncover government

"*Who do I see to get big government off my back?*"

> **Government in the Sunshine Act**
> A law that requires all committee-directed federal agencies to conduct their business regularly in public session.

---

7. *United States Civil Service Commission v. National Association of Letter Carriers,* 413 U.S. 548 (1973).

For years after the 2003 invasion

of Iraq, almost no photos of military personnel who perished in that country were shown to the public. News organizations used the Freedom of Information Act to request a release of over three hundred photographs showing the remains of U.S. service members returning home. Why would the federal government wish to keep such photos out of the public's view? (REUTERS/U.S. Air Force/www.thememoryhole.org/Landov)

waste, scandals, and incompetence. For example, reporters learned that much of the $5 billion allocated to help small businesses recover from the effects of the 9/11 terrorist attacks went to companies that did not need such relief, including a South Dakota country radio station, a dog boutique in Utah, an Oregon winery, and a variety of Dunkin' Donuts and Subway franchises. After studying Veterans Administration records, the *Sacramento Bee* claimed in 2007 that the government was woefully unprepared to care for the flood of veterans returning from Iraq and Afghanistan with post-traumatic stress disorder. A Utah newspaper discovered through FOIA requests that a former air force acquisitions officer pressured a Utah airbase into approving contract changes that improperly benefited the Boeing Corporation. The former acquisitions officer went to prison.

Curbs on Information Disclosure. Since the terrorist attacks of September 11, 2001, the trend toward government in the sunshine and information disclosure has been reversed at both the federal and state levels. Within weeks after September 11, 2001, numerous federal agencies removed hundreds, if not thousands, of documents from Internet sites, public libraries, and the reading rooms found in various federal government departments. Information contained in some of the documents included diagrams of power plants and pipelines, structural details on dams, and safety plans for chemical plants. The military also immediately began restricting information about its current and planned activities, as did the Federal Bureau of Investigation. These agencies were concerned that terrorists could make use of this information to plan attacks. The federal government has also gone back into the archives to remove an increasing quantity of not only sensitive material but also sometimes seemingly unimportant information.

In making official documents inaccessible to the public, the federal government was ahead of state and local governments, but they quickly followed suit. State and local governments control and supervise police forces, dams, electricity sources, and water supplies. Consequently, it is not surprising that many state and local governments followed in the footsteps of the federal government in curbing access to certain public records and information.

Such actions constitute a broad attempt by state and local governments to keep terrorists from learning about local emergency preparedness plans. It is possible, however, that as soon as the public starts to believe that the threat has lessened, some groups will take state and local governments to court in an effort to increase public access to state and local records by reimposing the sunshine laws that were in effect before 9/11.

SUNSET LAWS

Potentially, the size and scope of the federal bureaucracy can be controlled through **sunset legislation,** which places government programs on a definite schedule for congressional consideration. Unless Congress specifically reauthorizes a particular federally operated program at the end of a designated period, the program will be terminated automatically; that is, its sun will set.

The idea of sunset legislation was initially suggested by Franklin D. Roosevelt when he created the host of New Deal agencies in the 1930s. His assistant, William O. Douglas, recommended that each agency's charter should include a provision allowing for its ter-

Sunset Legislation
Laws requiring that existing programs be reviewed regularly for their effectiveness and be terminated unless specifically extended as a result of these reviews.

mination in ten years. Only an act of Congress could revitalize it. The proposal was never adopted. It was not until 1976 that a state legislature—Colorado's—adopted sunset legislation for state regulatory commissions, giving them a life of six years before their suns set. Today, most states have some type of sunset law.

Privatization
The replacement of government services with services provided by private firms.

PRIVATIZATION

Another approach to bureaucratic reform is **privatization,** which occurs when government services are replaced by services from the private sector. For example, the government has contracted with private firms to operate prisons. Supporters of privatization argue that some services could be provided more efficiently by the private sector. Another scheme is to furnish vouchers to "clients" in lieu of services. For example, instead of supplying housing, the government could offer vouchers that recipients could use to "pay" for housing in privately owned buildings.

The privatization, or contracting-out, strategy has been most successful on the local level. Municipalities, for example, can form contracts with private companies for such activities as trash collection. This approach is not a cure-all, however, because many functions, particularly on the national level, cannot be contracted out in any meaningful way. For example, the federal government could not contract out most of the Defense Department's functions to private firms (although the U.S. military has contracted out many services in Iraq and elsewhere).

The increase in the amount of government work being contracted out to the private sector has led to significant controversy in recent years. Some have criticized the lack of competitive bidding for many contracts that the government has awarded to contractors. Another concern is the perceived lack of government oversight over the work done by private contractors. In order to exercise more oversight, in 2007 the government decided to have a study done to evaluate the performance of private contractors. Some reporters noted the irony of the government's decision to have a private contractor undertake this study. For a further discussion of contracting out government work to the private sector, see the *Which Side Are You On?* feature on the following page.

did you know...

That federal officials spent $333,000 building a deluxe, earthquake-proof outhouse for hikers in Pennsylvania's remote Delaware Water Gap recreation area?

INCENTIVES FOR EFFICIENCY AND PRODUCTIVITY

An increasing number of state governments are beginning to experiment with a variety of schemes to run their operations more efficiently and capably. They focus on maximizing the efficiency and productivity of government workers by providing incentives for improved performance. For example, many governors, mayors, and city administrators are considering ways in which government can be made more entrepreneurial. Some of the most promising measures have included such tactics as permitting agencies that do not spend their entire budgets to keep some of the difference and rewarding employees with performance-based bonuses.

Government Performance and Results Act. At the federal level, the Government Performance and Results Act of 1997 was designed to improve efficiency in the federal workforce. The act required that all government agencies (except the Central Intelligence Agency) describe their goals and establish methods for determining whether those goals are met. Goals may be broadly crafted (for example, reducing the time it takes to test a new drug before allowing it to be marketed) or narrowly crafted (for example, reducing the number of times a telephone rings before it is answered).

THE PRIVATIZATION OF THE PENAL SYSTEM

whichsideareyouon?

IS TOO MUCH GOVERNMENT WORK BEING CONTRACTED OUT?

When a job has to be undertaken by the government, those in charge have a choice: they can hire more government workers, or they can *contract out* the job to a private firm. The most recent contracting-out movement had its origins in the Clinton administration's "reinventing government" effort. During the Clinton years, the federal workforce was slashed to its lowest levels since 1960.

More recently, during the George W. Bush administration, the practice of contracting out to private firms exploded. So, too, did the number of scandals associated with these private contractors. After armed guards belonging to the Blackwater security company killed seventeen Iraqi civilians in what the Iraqi government called indiscriminate gunfire, there were widespread calls for an end to the Blackwater contract. Nothing of the sort happened, however. Indeed, in May 2008, Blackwater's contract was renewed for at least another year. "We cannot operate without private security firms in Iraq," said Patrick F. Kennedy, Bush's undersecretary of state for management. "If the contractors were removed, we would have to leave Iraq." In other words, contracting out has become so pervasive that the U.S. military cannot fight a war without it.

CONTRACTING OUT IS THE WAY TO MAKE GOVERNMENT MORE EFFICIENT

Currently, federal contracting out exceeds $450 billion per year. Is this too much? Proponents of even more contracting out argue that government can never be efficient, but the private sector can. They point out that it is almost impossible to fire government employees, no matter how incompetent they are. Also, there is no "bottom line" for any operation undertaken by the government. Consequently, it is a given that when the government does a job, it will do it at a higher cost, and with lower quality, than would a private contractor that did the same job.

The lack of a profit motive for government bureaucrats means that they will spend more time "feathering their own nests" than their counterparts in the private sector. More layers of management will therefore be evident in government bureaucracy than in the private sector doing the same job. Of course, there will be some waste among private contractors, but there is even more when the government undertakes a task. A few scandals among the thousands of private contractors the government is utilizing do not mean that we have contracted out too much government work.

TOO MUCH OF A GOOD THING MEANS WE HAVE GONE TOO FAR IN CONTRACTING OUT

Private contractors have become a virtual fourth branch of government. They now collect income taxes, build ships and satellites, and take down the minutes of policy meetings on the war in Iraq. More people now work under private contracts for the U.S. government than work directly for the government as government employees. Less than half of the private contracts that have been issued by the federal government were the result of competitive bidding. The most successful private contractors do not necessarily do the best job; rather, they have mastered the ability to market themselves to the federal government. In less than ten years, the top twenty private service contractors spent more than $300 million on lobbying and donated more than $25 million to political campaigns.

In 2007, when there was a scandal over the poor treatment of outpatients at Walter Reed Army Medical Center in Washington, D.C., the public learned that the maintenance job at that hospital had been contracted out. The head of Walter Reed, Major General George W. Weightman, testified before Congress that contracting out had "absolutely" contributed to the unsanitary conditions at the hospital. He was relieved of his duties soon thereafter.

WHAT'S YOUR POSITION?

In theory, the private sector can provide more cost-effective services than the government can. In your opinion, why has this not always been true?

GOING ONLINE

You can access a number of articles dealing with this issue by going to **www.govexec.com/outsourcing**.

This is the entrance of the headquarters of Blackwater USA, a private security firm near Moyock, North Carolina. (AP Photo/Karen Tam, file)

The "performance-based budgeting" implemented by President George W. Bush took this results-oriented approach a step further. Performance-based budgeting links agency funding to actual agency performance. Agencies are given specific performance criteria to meet, and the Office of Management and Budget rates each agency to determine how well it has performed. In theory, the amount of funds that each agency will receive in the next annual budget should be determined by the extent to which it has met the performance criteria.

Bureaucracy Has Changed Little. Efforts to improve bureaucratic efficiency are supported by the assertion that although society and industry have changed enormously in the past century, the form of government used in Washington, D.C., and in most states has remained the same. Some observers believe that the nation's diverse economic base cannot be administered competently by traditional bureaucratic organizations. Consequently, government must become more responsive to cope with the increasing demands placed on it. Political scientists Joel Aberbach and Bert Rockman take issue with this contention. They argue that the bureaucracy has changed significantly over time in response to changes desired by various presidential administrations. In their opinion, many of the problems attributed to the bureaucracy are, in fact, a result of the political decision-making process. Therefore, attempts to "reinvent" government by reforming the bureaucracy are misguided.[8]

Other analysts have suggested that the problem lies not so much with traditional bureaucratic organizations as with the people who run them. According to policy specialist Taegan Goddard and journalist Christopher Riback, what needs to be "reinvented" is not the machinery of government but public officials. After each election, new appointees to bureaucratic positions may find themselves managing complex, multimillion-dollar enterprises, yet they often are untrained for their jobs. According to these authors, if we want to reform the bureaucracy, we should focus on preparing newcomers for the task of "doing" government.[9]

Saving Costs through E-Government. Many contend that the communications revolution brought about by the Internet has not only improved the efficiency with which government agencies deliver services to the public but also helped to reduce the cost of government. Agencies can now communicate with members of the public, as well as other agencies, via e-mail. Additionally, every federal agency now has a Web site to which citizens can go to find information about agency services instead of calling or appearing in person at a regional agency office. Since 2003, federal agencies have also been required by the Government Paperwork Elimination Act of 1998 to use electronic commerce whenever it is practical to do so and will save on costs.

Still, government agencies are often not very advanced in how they use the Internet. Some relatively poor countries, such as India, may actually outperform the rich world in their use of e-government, as we show in the *Beyond Our Borders* feature on the next page.

HELPING OUT THE WHISTLEBLOWERS

The term **whistleblower** as applied to the federal bureaucracy has a special meaning: it is someone who blows the whistle on a gross governmental inefficiency or illegal action. Whistleblowers may be clerical workers, managers, or even specialists, such as scientists.

Laws Protecting Whistleblowers. The 1978 Civil Service Reform Act prohibits reprisals against whistleblowers by their superiors, and it set up the Merit Systems Protection Board as part of this protection. Many federal agencies also have toll-free hotlines that

didyouknow...

That a report recently released by the Government Accountability Office (GAO) revealed that the Department of Agriculture sent $1.1 billion in farm payments to more than 170,000 dead people over a seven-year period?

Whistleblower
Someone who brings to public attention gross governmental inefficiency or an illegal action.

---

8. Joel D. Aberbach and Bert A. Rockman, *In the Web of Politics: Three Decades of the U.S. Federal Executive* (Washington, D.C.: Brookings Institution Press, 2000).
9. Taegan D. Goddard and Christopher Riback, *You Won—Now What? How Americans Can Make Democracy Work from City Hall to the White House* (New York: Scribner, 1998).

beyondourborders

INDIA, THE LAND OF BUREAUCRATIC PAPERWORK, GOES ONLINE (AT LEAST IN ONE STATE)

India is known for having one of the world's slowest bureaucracies. Nonetheless, one southern Indian state, Andhra Pradesh, is quickly entering the world of e-government. Hyderabad, the capital of the state, is one of the most important centers of India's rapidly growing high-tech economy. The state government of Andhra Pradesh has developed *e-seva,* a network of public Internet offices where citizens can pay bills online. In the past, citizens had to pay their electricity bills in person, which might have taken an eight-hour wait in a government office. The same was true for water and phone bills, as well as for taxes.

INTERACTING WITH GOVERNMENT ONLINE

Now, all government-provided services in Andhra Pradesh, such as electricity and water,

The speaker at this Asian forum explains the 24/7-type of government available online in the southern Indian state of Andhra Pradesh. (http://www.egovworld.org/egovworld2006/photogallery/Subbarao%20IEG.jpg/view)

can be paid for online. Citizens who have credit cards and computers can go to **e-sevaonline.com** to pay their bills. Those who do not can visit one of the e-seva centers. Today, the number of online transactions exceeds 150,000 per day, and the volume is growing by 25 percent a year. Over 60 percent of all payments for public services are electronic.

EXPANDING THE SYSTEM

Currently, there are about 140 e-seva centers. The government of Andhra Pradesh has plans to extend this number to 4,600, one for every six villages. By the time you read this, residents will be able to use e-seva centers and **e-sevaonline.com** to apply for driver's licenses.

THE MOVE TO MOBILE PHONES

Eventually, all of the services available on e-seva will be available through residents' cell phones. The mobile phone, rather than the computer, will become the main platform for payment. This is important because far more Indians have easy access to cell phones than to computers.

India's bankers have already taken major steps to give cell phone users access to banking services. For example, passengers arriving at the airport in Hyderabad are greeted by advertisements for bank accounts that allow payments to be authorized by a thumbprint—useful in a society in which many people are still illiterate. Some banks already offer e-seva services through a system called *m-banking.* Customers are able to pay for public services by using their cell phones to send a text message and a security code.

FOR CRITICAL ANALYSIS

Why might e-government be more important in rural areas of a country than in major cities?

employees can use anonymously to report bureaucratic waste and inappropriate behavior. About 35 percent of all calls result in agency action or follow-up.

Further protection for whistleblowers was provided in 1989, when Congress passed the Whistle-Blower Protection Act. That act established an independent agency, the Office of Special Counsel (OSC), to investigate complaints brought by government employees who have been demoted, fired, or otherwise sanctioned for reporting government fraud or waste. Congress is currently considering legislation that would extend whistleblower protections to civil servants at national security agencies, employees of government contractors, and federal workers who expose the distortion of scientific data for political reasons.

Some state and federal laws encourage employees to blow the whistle on their employers' wrongful actions by providing monetary incentives to the whistleblowers. At the federal level, the False Claims Act of 1986 allows a whistleblower who has disclosed information about a fraud against the U.S. government to receive a monetary award. If the government chooses to prosecute the case and wins, the whistleblower receives between 15 and 25 percent of the proceeds. If the government declines to intervene, the whistleblower can bring suit on behalf of the government and, if the suit is successful, will receive between 25 and 30 percent of the proceeds.

The Problem Continues. Despite these endeavors to help whistleblowers, there is little evidence that potential whistleblowers truly have received more protection. More than 40 percent of the employees who turned to the OSC for assistance in a recent three-year period stated that they were no longer employees of the government agencies on which they blew the whistle.

Furthermore, during the Bush administration it was widely believed that the OSC was essentially useless in protecting whistleblowers. Allegedly, the agency closed hundreds of cases without bothering to investigate them. In May 2008, agents of the Federal Bureau of Investigation raided the OSC offices and the home of U.S. Special Counsel Scott Bloch. The raid was sparked by accusations that Bloch had destroyed evidence showing that he had retaliated against whistleblowers within the OSC itself.

Additionally, in a significant 2006 decision, the U.S. Supreme Court placed restrictions on lawsuits brought by public workers. The case, *Garcetti v. Ceballos*,[10] involved an assistant district attorney, Richard Ceballos, who wrote a memo asking if a county sheriff's deputy had lied in a search warrant affidavit. Ceballos claimed that he was subsequently demoted and denied a promotion for trying to expose the lie. The outcome of the case turned on an interpretation of an employee's right to freedom of speech—whether it included the right to criticize an employment-related action. In a close (five-to-four) and controversial decision, the Supreme Court held that when public employees make statements relating to their official duties, they are not speaking as citizens for First Amendment purposes. The Court deemed that when he wrote his memo, Ceballos was speaking as an employee, not a citizen, and was thus subject to his employer's disciplinary actions. The ruling will affect millions of governmental employees.

BUREAUCRATS AS POLITICIANS AND POLICYMAKERS

Because Congress is unable to oversee the day-to-day administration of its programs, it must delegate certain powers to administrative agencies. Congress delegates the power to implement legislation to agencies through what is called **enabling legislation.** For example, the Federal Trade Commission was created by the Federal Trade Commission Act of 1914, the Equal Employment Opportunity Commission was created by the Civil Rights Act of 1964, and the Occupational Safety and Health Administration was created by the Occupational Safety and Health Act of 1970. The enabling legislation generally specifies the name, purpose, composition, functions, and powers of the agency.

In theory, the agencies should put into effect laws passed by Congress. Laws are often drafted in such vague and general terms, however, that they provide relatively little guidance to agency administrators as to how the laws should be implemented. This means that the agencies themselves must decide how best to carry out the wishes of Congress.

didyouknow...

That each year, federal administrative agencies produce rules that fill an average of 7,500 pages in the *Code of Federal Regulations* and that the regulations now contained in this code cover 144,000 pages?

Enabling Legislation
A statute enacted by Congress that authorizes the creation of an administrative agency and specifies the name, purpose, composition, functions, and powers of the agency being created.

10. 126 S.Ct. 1951 (2006).

The discretion given to administrative agencies is not accidental. Congress has long realized that it lacks the technical expertise and the resources to monitor the implementation of its laws. Hence, the administrative agency is created to fill the gaps. This gap-filling role requires the agency to formulate administrative rules (regulations) to put flesh on the bones of the law. But it also forces the agency itself to become an unelected policymaker.

THE RULEMAKING ENVIRONMENT

Rulemaking does not occur in a vacuum. Suppose that Congress passes a new air-pollution law. The Environmental Protection Agency (EPA) might decide to implement the new law through a technical regulation on factory emissions. This proposed regulation would be published in the *Federal Register,* a daily government publication, so that interested parties would have an opportunity to comment on it. Individuals and companies that opposed parts or all of the rule might then try to convince the EPA to revise or redraft the regulation. Some parties might try to persuade the agency to withdraw the proposed regulation altogether. In any event, the EPA would consider these comments in drafting the final version of the regulation following the expiration of the comment period.

Waiting Periods and Court Challenges. Once the final regulation has been published in the *Federal Register,* there is a sixty-day waiting period before the rule can be enforced. During that period, businesses, individuals, and state and local governments can ask Congress to overturn the regulation. After that sixty-day period has lapsed, the regulation can still be challenged in court by a party having a direct interest in the rule, such as a company that expects to incur significant costs in complying with it. The company could argue that the rule misinterprets the applicable law or goes beyond the agency's statutory purview. An allegation by the company that the EPA made a mistake in judgment probably would not be enough to convince the court to throw out the rule. The company instead would have to demonstrate that the rule itself was "arbitrary and capricious." To meet this standard, the company would have to show that the rule reflected a serious flaw in the EPA's judgment.

Controversies. How agencies implement, administer, and enforce legislation has resulted in controversy. Decisions made by agencies charged with administering the Endangered Species Act have led to protests from farmers, ranchers, and others whose economic interests have been harmed. For example, the government decided to cut off the flow of irrigation water from Klamath Lake in Oregon in the summer of 2001. That action, which affected irrigation water for more than one thousand farmers in southern Oregon and northern California, was undertaken to save endangered suckerfish and salmon. It was believed that the lake's water level was so low that further use of the water for irrigation would harm these fish. The results of this decision were devastating for many farmers.

At times, a controversy may arise when an agency *refuses* to issue regulations to implement a particular law. Recall from Chapter 3 that when the EPA refused to issue regulations designed to curb the emission of carbon dioxide and other greenhouse gases, state and local governments, as well as a number of environmental groups, sued the agency. The suit was brought to force the EPA to fulfill its obligation to implement the provisions of the Clean Air Act. Ultimately, the Supreme Court held that the EPA had the authority to—and should—regulate such gases.[11]

NEGOTIATED RULEMAKING

Since the end of World War II (1939–1945), companies, environmentalists, and other special interest groups have challenged government regulations in court. In the 1980s, however, the sheer wastefulness of attempting to regulate through litigation became

---

11. *Massachusetts v. EPA,* 127 S.Ct. 1438 (2007).

more and more apparent. Today, a growing number of federal agencies encourage businesses and public-interest groups to become directly involved in drafting regulations. Agencies hope that such participation may help to prevent later courtroom battles over the meaning, applicability, and legal effect of the regulations.

Congress formally approved such a process, which is called *negotiated rulemaking,* in the Negotiated Rulemaking Act of 1990. The act authorizes agencies to allow those who will be affected by a new rule to participate in the rule-drafting process. If an agency chooses to engage in negotiated rulemaking, it must publish in the *Federal Register* the subject and scope of the rule to be developed, the parties affected significantly by the rule, and other information. Representatives of the affected groups and other interested parties then may apply to be members of the negotiating committee. The agency is represented on the committee, but a neutral third party (not the agency) presides over the proceedings. Once the committee members have reached agreement on the terms of the proposed rule, a notice is published in the *Federal Register,* followed by a period for comments by any person or organization interested in the proposed rule. Negotiated rulemaking often is conducted under the condition that the participants promise not to challenge in court the outcome of any agreement to which they were a party.

The internal combustion engines in these cars traveling on the San Diego 405 freeway potentially add to climate change problems. Can the federal government regulate carbon dioxide emissions? (Photo by Evan Hurd Archive/Getty Images)

BUREAUCRATS AS POLICYMAKERS

Theories of public administration once assumed that bureaucrats do not make policy decisions but only implement the laws and policies promulgated by the president and legislative bodies. Many people continue to make this assumption. A more realistic view, which is now held by most bureaucrats and elected officials, is that the agencies and departments of government play important roles in policymaking. As we have seen, many government rules, regulations, and programs are in fact initiated by bureaucrats, based on their expertise and scientific studies. How a law passed by Congress eventually is translated into concrete action—from the forms to be filled out to decisions about who gets the benefits—usually is determined within each agency or department. Even the evaluation of whether a policy has achieved its purpose usually is based on studies that are commissioned and interpreted by the agency administering the program.

The bureaucracy's policymaking role has often been depicted by what traditionally has been called the "iron triangle." Recently, the concept of an "issue network" has been viewed as a more accurate description of the policymaking process.

Iron Triangles. In the past, scholars often described the bureaucracy's role in the policymaking process by using the concept of an **iron triangle**—a three-way alliance among legislators in Congress, bureaucrats, and interest groups. Consider as an example the development of agricultural policy. Congress, as one component of the triangle, includes two major committees concerned with agricultural policy, the House Committee on Agriculture and the Senate Committee on Agriculture, Nutrition, and Forestry. The Department of Agriculture, the second component of the triangle, has almost 100,000 employees, plus thousands of contractors and consultants. Agricultural interest groups, the third component of the iron triangle in agricultural policymaking, include many large and powerful associations, such as the American Farm Bureau Federation, the National Cattleman's Association, and the Corn Growers Association. These three components of the iron triangle work together, formally or informally, to create policy.

For example, the various agricultural interest groups lobby Congress to develop policies that benefit their groups' interests. Members of Congress cannot afford to ignore the wishes

Iron Triangle
The three-way alliance among legislators, bureaucrats, and interest groups to make or preserve policies that benefit their respective interests.

**"I need a farm policy, Murchison.
Something muscular but compassionate."**

of interest groups because those groups are potential sources of voter support and campaign contributions. The legislators in Congress also work closely with the Department of Agriculture, which, in implementing a policy, can develop rules that benefit—or at least do not hurt—certain industries or groups. The Department of Agriculture, in turn, supports policies that enhance the department's budget and powers. In this way, according to theory, agricultural policy is created that benefits all three components of the iron triangle.

Issue Networks. To be sure, the preceding discussion presents a much simplified picture of how the iron triangle works. With the growth in the complexity of government, policymaking also has become more complicated. The bureaucracy is larger, Congress has more committees and subcommittees, and interest groups are more powerful than ever. Although iron triangles still exist, often they are inadequate as descriptions of how policy is actually made. Frequently, different interest groups concerned about a certain area of policy have conflicting demands, making agency decisions difficult. Divided government in some years has meant that departments are sometimes pressured by the president to take one approach and by Congress to take another.

Many scholars now use the term *issue network* to describe the policymaking process. An **issue network** consists of individuals or organizations that support a particular policy position on the environment, taxation, consumer safety, or some other issue. Typically, an issue network includes legislators and/or their staff members, interest groups, bureaucrats, scholars and other experts, and representatives from the media. Members of a particular issue network work together to influence the president, members of Congress, administrative agencies, and the courts to affect public policy on a specific issue. Each policy issue may involve conflicting positions taken by two or more issue networks.[12]

THE BUREAUCRACY AND THE BUSH ADMINISTRATION

One of the aims of the Bush administration was to gain more control over the unwieldy bureaucracy. To this end, President Bush issued an executive order in early 2007 that required each federal agency to establish a Regulatory Policy Office (RPO) to be headed by a political appointee. The job of the RPO is essentially to bring agency rulemaking and interpretation into line with the policies of the administration.

Bush's attempt to gain control over the bureaucracy developed into a major controversy with the firings of several U.S. attorneys. U.S. attorneys, who are appointed by the president and confirmed by the Senate, prosecute criminal cases brought by the federal government and represent the government in civil cases. In 2006, a provision was quietly added to the USA Patriot Act that allowed for the replacement of U.S. attorneys without Senate confirmation. In late 2006, Attorney General Alberto Gonzales fired and replaced eight U.S. attorneys without Senate approval. It was soon alleged that the attorneys were fired for political reasons. One attorney, for example, had refused to indict a Democratic state senator on the eve of the 2006 elections, when the publicity might have benefited Republican candidates. (Delaying such indictments until after the elections had always been governmental policy in the past.) The resulting public furor led to congressional investigations in 2007 and was one factor in Gonzales's eventual resignation.

Issue Network
A group of individuals or organizations—which may consist of legislators and legislative staff members, interest group leaders, bureaucrats, the media, scholars, and other experts—that supports a particular policy position on a given issue.

12. For a landmark work on how the interests and priorities of government agencies, departments, and individuals influence the policymaking process, see Morton H. Halperin and Priscilla A. Clapp, with Arnold Kanter, *Bureaucratic Politics and Foreign Policy,* 2d ed. (Washington, D.C.: The Brookings Institution, 2006). Although the authors focus on foreign policymaking, their insightful analysis has much to say about the policymaking process in general.

CONGRESSIONAL CONTROL OF THE BUREAUCRACY

Many political pundits doubt whether Congress can meaningfully control the federal bureaucracy. Nevertheless, Congress does have some means of exerting control.

WAYS CONGRESS DOES CONTROL THE BUREAUCRACY

These commentators forget that Congress specifies in an agency's "enabling legislation" the powers of the agency and the parameters within which it can operate. Additionally, Congress has the power of the purse and theoretically could refuse to authorize or appropriate funds for a particular agency (see the discussion of the budgeting process in Chapter 10). Whether Congress would actually take such a drastic measure would depend on the circumstances. Certainly, it was one of the options before Congress in 2007, during the standoff between Congress and the Bush administration over the continuation of the war in Iraq. In any event, it is clear that Congress does have the legal authority to decide whether to fund or not to fund administrative agencies. Congress can also exercise oversight over agencies through investigations and hearings.

As discussed earlier in this text, Congress also has investigatory powers. Congressional committees conduct investigations and hold hearings to oversee an agency's actions, reviewing them to ensure compliance with congressional intentions. The agency's officers and employees can be ordered to testify before a committee about the details of an action. Through these oversight activities, especially in the questions and comments of members of the House or Senate during the hearings, Congress indicates its positions on specific programs and issues.

Congress can ask the Government Accountability Office (GAO) to investigate particular agency actions as well. The Congressional Budget Office (CBO) also conducts oversight studies. The results of a GAO or CBO study may encourage Congress to hold further hearings or make changes in the law. Even if a law is not changed explicitly by Congress, however, the views expressed in any investigations and hearings are taken seriously by agency officials, who often act on those views.

In 1996, Congress passed the Congressional Review Act. The act created special procedures that can be employed to express congressional disapproval of particular agency actions. These procedures have rarely been used, however. Since the act's passage, the executive branch has issued more than 15,000 regulations. Yet only eight resolutions of disapproval have been introduced, and none of them were passed by either chamber.

REASONS WHY CONGRESS CANNOT EASILY OVERSEE THE BUREAUCRACY

Despite the powers just described, one theory of congressional control over the bureaucracy suggests that Congress cannot possibly oversee all of the many federal government agencies that exist. Consider two possible approaches to congressional control—(1) the "police patrol" and (2) the "fire alarm" approach. Certain congressional activities, such as annual budget hearings, fall under the police patrol approach. This regular review occasionally catches *some* deficiencies in a bureaucracy's job performance, but it usually fails to detect most problems.

In contrast, the fire alarm approach is more likely to discover gross inadequacies in a bureaucracy's job performance. In this approach, Congress and its committees react to scandal, citizen disappointment, and massive negative publicity by launching a full-scale investigation into whatever agency is suspected of wrongdoing. Clearly, this is what happened when Congress investigated the inadequacies of the Central Intelligence Agency after the 9/11 terrorist attacks. Congress was also responding to an alarm when

WHY SHOULD YOU CARE ABOUT
the bureaucracy?

Why should you, as an individual, care about the bureaucracy? You might consider that the federal government collects billions of pieces of information on tens of millions of Americans each year. These data are stored in files and sometimes are exchanged among agencies. You are probably the subject of several federal records (for example, in the Social Security Administration; the Internal Revenue Service; and, if you are a male, the Selective Service).

THE BUREAUCRACY AND YOUR LIFE

Verifying the information that the government has on you can be important. On several occasions, the records of two people with similar names have become confused. Sometimes innocent persons have had the criminal records of other persons erroneously inserted in their files. Such disasters are not always caused by bureaucratic error. One of the most common crimes in today's world is "identity theft," in which one person makes use of another person's personal identifiers (such as a Social Security number) to commit fraud. In some instances, identity thieves have been arrested and even jailed under someone else's name.

HOW YOU CAN MAKE A DIFFERENCE

The 1966 Freedom of Information Act (FOIA) requires that the federal government release, at your request, any identifiable information it has about you or about any other subject. Ten categories of material are exempted, however (classified material, confidential material on trade secrets, internal personnel rules, personal medical files, and the like). To request material, write directly to the Freedom of Information Act officer at the agency in question (say, the Department of Education). You must have a relatively specific idea about the document or information you want to obtain.

A second law, the Privacy Act of 1974, gives you access specifically to information the government may have collected about you. This law allows you to review records on file with federal agencies and to check those records for possible inaccuracies.

If you want to look at any records or find out if an agency has a record on you, write to the agency head or Privacy Act officer, and address your letter to the specific agency. State that "under the provisions of the Privacy Act of 1974, 5 U.S.C. 522a, I hereby request a copy of (or access to) _____." Then describe the record that you wish to investigate.

The American Civil Liberties Union (ACLU) has published a manual, called *Your Right to Government Information,* that guides you through the steps of obtaining information from the federal government. You can order it online at the following Web site:

www.aclu.org.

Alternatively, you can order the manual from the ACLU at the following address:

ACLU Publications
P.O. Box 4713
Trenton, NJ
08650-4713
1-800-775-ACLU

it investigated the failures of the Federal Emergency Management Agency after Hurricane Katrina. After the Democrats took control of Congress in January 2007, Congress launched a number of investigations into alleged wrongdoing by agency personnel in the Bush administration. Fire alarm investigations will not catch all problems, but they will alert bureaucracies that they need to clean up their procedures before a problem arises in their own agencies.[13]

---

13. Matthew D. McCubbins and Thomas Schwartz, "Congressional Oversight Overlooked: Police Patrols versus Fire Alarms," *American Journal of Political Science,* February 28, 1984, pp. 165–179.

QUESTIONS FOR
discussion**and**analysis

1. Review the *Which Side Are You On?* feature on page 428. Do you think that too much government work is contracted out? Why or why not? What potential difficulties could contracting out present? What are the benefits?

2. Consider the paradox described at the beginning of this chapter: the public believes strongly in "small government" but endorses almost all the activities that government actually performs. Why do you think Americans hold such contradictory beliefs?

3. If Congress tried to make civil servants easier to fire, what political forces might stand in the way?

4. The government's response to the disaster caused by Hurricane Katrina has been widely criticized. Why might the various levels of government have failed in this crisis? What could they have done instead?

5. The U.S. attorney general, head of the Justice Department, is appointed by the president and is frequently the president's close political ally. Should the attorney general and other U.S. attorneys be appointed on a partisan basis? Why or why not?

keyterms

acquisitive model 413
administrative
    agency 414
bureaucracy 411
cabinet department 416
capture 420
Civil Service
    Commission 424
enabling
    legislation 431

government
    corporation 421
Government in the
    Sunshine Act 425
independent executive
    agency 418
independent regulatory
    agency 418
iron triangle 433

issue network 434
line organization 416
merit system 424
monopolistic model 413
Pendleton Act (Civil
    Service Reform
    Act) 424

privatization 427
spoils system 423
sunset legislation 426
Weberian model 413
whistleblower 429

chapter**summary**

1. Bureaucracies are hierarchical organizations characterized by a division of labor and extensive procedural rules. Bureaucracy is the primary form of organization of most major corporations and universities, as well as governments.

2. Several theories have been offered to explain bureaucracies. The Weberian model posits that bureaucracies are rational, hierarchical organizations in which decisions are based on logical reasoning. The acquisitive model views top-level bureaucrats as pressing for ever-larger budgets and staffs to augment their own sense of power and security. The monopolistic model focuses on the environment in which most government bureaucracies operate, stating that bureaucracies are inefficient and excessively costly to operate because they have no competitors.

3. Since the founding of the United States, the federal bureaucracy has grown from 50 to about 2.7 million employees (excluding the military). Federal, state, and local employees together make up more than 15 percent of the nation's civilian labor force. The federal bureaucracy consists of fifteen cabinet departments, as well as a large number of independent executive agencies, independent regulatory agencies, and government corporations. These entities enjoy varying degrees of autonomy, visibility, and political support.

4. A federal bureaucracy of career civil servants was formed during Thomas Jefferson's presidency. Andrew Jackson implemented a spoils system through which he appointed his own political supporters. A civil service based on professionalism and merit was the goal of the Civil Service Reform Act of 1883. Concerns that the civil service be freed from the pressures of politics prompted the passage of the Hatch Act in 1939. Significant changes in the administration of the civil service were made by the Civil Service Reform Act of 1978.

5. There have been many attempts to make the federal bureaucracy more open, efficient, and responsive to the needs of U.S. citizens. The most important reforms have included sunshine and sunset laws, privatization, strategies to provide incentives for increased productivity and efficiency, and protection for whistleblowers.

6. Congress delegates much of its authority to federal agencies when it creates new laws. The bureaucrats who run these agencies may become important policymakers because Congress has neither the time nor the technical expertise to oversee the administration of its laws. In the agency rulemaking process, a proposed regulation is published. A comment period follows, during which interested parties may offer suggestions for changes. Because companies and other organizations have challenged many regulations in court, federal agencies now are authorized to allow parties that will be affected by new regulations to participate in the rule-drafting process.

7. Congress exerts ultimate control over all federal agencies because it controls the federal government's purse strings. It also establishes the general guidelines by which regulatory agencies must abide. The appropriations process may provide a way to send messages of approval or disapproval to particular agencies, as do congressional hearings and investigations of agency actions.

selectedprint&mediaresources

SUGGESTED READINGS

Alexander, David. *The Pentagon: The People, the Building, and the Mission.* Osceola, Wis.: Zenith Press, 2008. Veteran defense writer and novelist David Alexander delivers the inside story on the people who have brought the Pentagon to life, from its initial construction during World War II to its restoration after the terrorist attacks on September 11, 2001.

Burrough, Bryan. *Public Enemies: America's Greatest Crime Wave and the Birth of the F.B.I., 1933–1934.* New York: Penguin Press, 2004. Burroughs strips the myths from such romanticized criminals as John Dillinger while simultaneously showing how incompetent the FBI often was in its initial years.

CQ Press. *Federal Regulatory Directory,* 13th ed. Washington, D.C.: CQ Press, 2007. This book offers a comprehensive overview of federal regulation in the United States. It provides details on numerous federal agencies, lists the various laws administered by each agency, and generally makes it easier to understand the complexity of the bureaucracy.

Freeman, Jody, and Martha Minow. *Government by Contract: Outsourcing and American Democracy.* Cambridge, Mass.: Harvard University Press, 2009. Outsourcing raises questions about costs, quality, and democratic oversight. Harvard law professors Freeman and Minow describe the scope of government contracting and the issues that result.

Haymann, Philip B. *Living the Policy Process.* New York: Oxford University Press, 2008. Haymann uses case studies to examine how policy makers struggle to affect governmental decisions. His detailed accounts range from the cabinet level down to the middle tiers of the federal bureaucracy. Examples include providing support to anti-Soviet Afghan rebels and attempts to restrict smoking.

MEDIA RESOURCES

The Bureaucracy of Government: John Lukacs—A 1988 Bill Moyers special. Historian John Lukacs discusses the common political lament over the giant but invisible mechanism called bureaucracy.

King Corn—A 2007 documentary that demonstrates the impact of corn growing on modern America. Ian Cheney and Curt Ellis learn that corn is in almost everything they eat. They move to Iowa for a year to grow corn and find out what happens to it. Inevitably, they come face-to-face with America's farm policy and its subsidies.

Yes, Minister—A new member of the British cabinet bumps up against the machinations of a top civil servant in a comedy of manners. This popular 1980 BBC comedy is now available on DVD.

When the Levees Broke: A Requiem in Four Acts—A strong treatment of Hurricane Katrina's impact on New Orleans by renowned African American director Spike Lee. We learn about the appalling performance of authorities at every level and the suffering that could have been avoided. Lee's anger at what he sees adds spice to this 2006 production.

e-mocracy

THE PRESIDENCY AND THE INTERNET

All federal government agencies (and nearly all state agencies) have Web pages. Citizens can access these Web sites to find information and forms that, in the past, could normally be obtained only by going to a regional or local branch of the agency. For example, if you or a member of your family wants to learn about Social Security benefits available on retirement, you can simply access the Social Security Administration's Web site to find that information. A number of federal government agencies have also been active in discovering and prosecuting fraud perpetrated on citizens via the Internet.

LOGGING ON

Numerous links to federal agencies and information on the federal government can be found at the U.S. government's official Web site. Go to
www.usa.gov.

You may want to examine two publications available from the federal government to learn more about the federal bureaucracy. The first is the *Federal Register,* which is the official publication for executive-branch documents. You can find it at
www.gpoaccess.gov/fr/index.html.

The second is the *United States Government Manual,* which describes the origins, purposes, and administrators of every federal department and agency. It is available at
www.gpoaccess.gov/gmanual/index.html.

"The Plum Book," which lists the bureaucratic positions that can be filled by presidential appointment, is online at
www.gpoaccess.gov/plumbook/index.html.

To find telephone numbers for government agencies and personnel, you can go to
www.usa.gov/Agencies.shtml.

13

The Courts

This is the east side of the United States
Supreme Court Building in Washington, D.C.
(Jeff Kubina/Creative Commons)

whatif...arguments before the Supreme Court were televised?

BACKGROUND

Since 1955, the United States Supreme Court has created audio recordings of oral arguments before the Court. For cases that generate high public interest, the Court agrees to same-day oral-argument audio releases. During every session of the Supreme Court, a court reporter transcribes every word that is spoken, even with indications when there is laughter. You can find a written transcript of each oral argument at **www.supremecourtus.gov**. At the end of every term, you can obtain all of the audio recordings online at **www.oyez.org**.

Today, many states have gone one step further—they allow appellate court sessions to be televised. The federal appellate courts and the Supreme Court have resisted televising their proceedings, however. Supreme Court justice David H. Souter is on record as saying that "the day you see a camera come into our courtroom, it's going to roll over my dead body." A few years ago, several senators, both Republicans and Democrats, reintroduced a bill to require the Court to televise its proceedings. As Senator Arlen Specter (R., Pa.) has said, "Televising the proceedings of the Supreme Court will allow some light to shine brightly on these proceedings and ensure greater public awareness and scrutiny."

WHAT IF ARGUMENTS BEFORE THE SUPREME COURT WERE TELEVISED?

Presumably, coverage of Supreme Court proceedings would be undertaken in the same way that sessions in the Senate and the House of Representatives are televised by C-SPAN. The C-SPAN coverage includes no commentaries about the proceedings in the chambers of Congress. The television coverage is straightforward, word for word, and often quite boring.

In the Supreme Court, similar television coverage would consist of one or two cameras and their operators discreetly positioned in the courtroom where the nine justices hear oral arguments and question the attorneys. Just as with the C-SPAN coverage of Congress, few individuals would actually watch all of the proceedings each day the Court is in session from October until July.

The Supreme Court could follow the states, which have already developed a wide variety of rules governing television coverage of court proceedings.[a] Most states' rules allow the presiding judge (in the case of the Supreme Court, it would be the chief justice) to limit or preclude coverage. Most states also allow the parties to object to television coverage, and some require the parties' consent.

ENTER THE INTERNET

The two channels of C-SPAN offer a lot more than just coverage of sessions in Congress. A third C-SPAN channel might have to be created to televise Supreme Court proceedings. As an alternative, we could envision Internet video streaming as a low-cost alternative. Indeed, one could imagine that Internet video streaming of the Supreme Court would be available anywhere in the world, thereby allowing the rest of the world to better understand the American judicial system.

GRANDSTANDING—A POSSIBILITY?

Certain sitting judges and others have argued against televising Supreme Court sessions because of the possibility of "grandstanding." In other words, they are worried that justices might ask questions and make comments during the proceedings in the hopes that such comments would become sound bites on the evening news. Justice Anthony M. Kennedy, speaking before the Senate Judiciary Committee, said that televising proceedings would "change our collegial dynamic."

Not everyone agrees. Judge Diarmuid O'Scannlain of the federal Ninth Circuit Court of Appeals believes just the opposite. He has said that the concerns about television coverage leading to grandstanding and politicking in the courtroom are "overstated." Indeed, he argues that televising appellate court proceedings depoliticizes them and improves the public's perception of the appellate legal process.

THE INEVITABLE "SLICING AND DICING"

Specialized channels on cable television would certainly make good use of the televised proceedings of the Supreme Court. These specialized channels would offer highlights from the most important cases heard. Increasingly, there would also be Web sites devoted to dissecting the way Supreme Court cases are decided.

If Supreme Court proceedings were televised, we could expect a media "mini-industry" to follow, particularly on the Internet. There might be new Web sites with portions of Supreme Court proceedings shown in video along with commentary by legal and political experts.

FOR CRITICAL ANALYSIS

1. How wide an audience do you believe the television proceedings of the Supreme Court would have?
2. Do you think that televised proceedings of the Supreme Court would significantly increase public awareness of Supreme Court decisions? Why or why not?

---

a. Radio-Television News Directors' Association, *Cameras in the Court: A State-by-State Guide* (2007).

As Alexis de Tocqueville, a French commentator on American society in the 1800s, noted, "scarcely any political question arises in the United States that is not resolved, sooner or later, into a judicial question."[1] Our judiciary forms part of our political process. The instant that judges interpret the law, they become actors in the political arena—policymakers working within a political institution.

The most important political force within our judiciary is the United States Supreme Court. The justices of the Supreme Court are not elected but rather are appointed by the president and confirmed by the Senate. The same is true for all other federal court judges. Because Supreme Court justices are so important in our governmental system, it has been suggested that arguments before the Court should be televised, as this chapter's opening *What If . . .* feature discussed.

How do courts make policy? Why do the federal courts play such an important role in American government? The answers to these questions lie, in part, in our colonial heritage. Most of American law is based on the English system, particularly the English *common law tradition.* In that tradition, the decisions made by judges constitute an important source of law. We open this chapter with an examination of this tradition and of the various sources of American law. We then look at the federal court system—its organization, how its judges are selected, how these judges affect policy, and how they are restrained by our system of checks and balances.

The Magna Carta
is Latin for "Great Charter." It was issued in England in 1215. It required the king to respect certain legal procedures and accept that his will could be bound by the law. Some argue that the Magna Carta started the historical process that led to our current constitutional law system. (Library of Congress)

THE COMMON LAW TRADITION

In 1066, the Normans conquered England, and William the Conqueror and his successors began the process of unifying the country under their rule. One of the ways in which they did this was to establish king's courts. Before the conquest, disputes had been settled according to local custom. The king's courts sought to establish a common, or uniform, set of rules for the whole country. As the number of courts and cases increased, portions of the most important decisions of each year were gathered together and recorded in *Year Books.* Judges settling disputes similar to ones that had been decided before used the *Year Books* as the basis for their decisions. If a case was unique, judges had to create new laws, but they based their decisions on the general principles suggested by earlier cases. The body of judge-made law that developed under this system is still used today and is known as the **common law.**

The practice of deciding new cases with reference to former decisions—that is, according to **precedent**—became a cornerstone of the English and American judicial systems and is embodied in the doctrine of **stare decisis** (pronounced *ster*-ay dih-*si-ses*), a Latin phrase that means "to stand on decided cases." The doctrine of *stare decisis* obligates judges to follow the precedents set previously by their own courts or by higher courts that have authority over them.

For example, a lower state court in California would be obligated to follow a precedent set by the California Supreme Court. That lower court, however, would not be obligated to follow a precedent set by the supreme court of another state, because each state court system is independent. Of course, when the United States Supreme Court decides an issue, all of the nation's other courts are obligated to abide by the Court's decision—because the Supreme Court is the highest court in the land.

SOURCES OF AMERICAN LAW

The body of American law includes the federal and state constitutions, statutes passed by legislative bodies, administrative law, and case law—the legal principles expressed in court decisions.

Common Law
Judge-made law that originated in England from decisions shaped according to prevailing custom. Decisions were applied to similar situations and gradually became common to the nation.

Precedent
A court rule bearing on subsequent legal decisions in similar cases. Judges rely on precedents in deciding cases.

Stare Decisis
To stand on decided cases; the judicial policy of following precedents established by past decisions.

---

1. Alexis de Tocqueville, *Democracy in America* (New York: Harper & Row, 1966), p. 248.

Case Law
Judicial interpretations of common law principles and doctrines, as well as interpretations of constitutional law, statutory law, and administrative law.

CONSTITUTIONS

The constitutions of the federal government and the states set forth the general organization, powers, and limits of government. The U.S. Constitution is the supreme law of the land. A law in violation of the Constitution, no matter what its source, may be declared unconstitutional and thereafter cannot be enforced. Similarly, the state constitutions are supreme within their respective borders (unless they conflict with the U.S. Constitution or federal laws and treaties made in accordance with it). The Constitution thus defines the political playing field on which state and federal powers are reconciled. The idea that the Constitution should be supreme in certain matters stemmed from widespread dissatisfaction with the weak federal government that had existed previously under the Articles of Confederation adopted in 1781.

STATUTES AND ADMINISTRATIVE REGULATIONS

Although the English common law provides the basis for both our civil and criminal legal systems, statutes (laws enacted by legislatures) have become increasingly important in defining the rights and obligations of individuals. Federal statutes may relate to any subject that is a concern of the federal government and may apply to areas ranging from hazardous waste to federal taxation. State statutes include criminal codes, commercial laws, and laws covering a variety of other matters. Cities, counties, and other local political bodies also pass statutes, which are called *ordinances.* These ordinances may deal with such issues as zoning proposals and public safety. Rules and regulations issued by administrative agencies are another source of law. Today, much of the work of the courts consists of interpreting these laws and regulations and applying them to the specific circumstances of the cases that come before the courts.

CASE LAW

Because we have a common law tradition, in which the doctrine of *stare decisis* (see the discussion of this doctrine on the previous page) plays an important role, the decisions rendered by the courts also form an important body of law, collectively referred to as **case law.** Case law includes judicial interpretations of common law principles and doctrines, as well as interpretations of the types of law just mentioned—constitutional provisions, statutes, and administrative agency regulations. As you learned in previous chapters, it is up to the courts—and ultimately, if necessary, the Supreme Court—to decide what a constitutional provision or a statutory phrase means. In doing so, the courts, in effect, establish law. (We will discuss this policymaking function of the courts in more detail later in the chapter.)

Courts in many of the nations formerly governed or settled by Britain—Australia, Canada, Ireland, the United States, and others—exhibit some broad similarities. All make use of the common law, as well as statutes and administrative regulations. All share the basic judicial requirements that you will learn about shortly. In some lands formerly ruled by Britain, such as India, Nigeria, and Pakistan, the common law is supplemented by local traditional law, including Islamic family law. Islamic family law can have some interesting twists, as we explain in this chapter's *Beyond Our Borders* feature. Nations that do not share the common law tradition typically rely on a statutory code alone, in what is called the civil law system. Judges under the civil law system are not bound by precedent in the way that judges are under the common law system.

Individuals sometimes band together to sue
the federal government for what they believe is a violation of their constitutional rights. The woman on the right is one such individual. She joined together with other immigrants who had waited years to obtain U.S. citizenship. Their attorneys from the American Civil Liberties Union argued in court that their lengthy delays for security checks were not constitutional. Who has the ultimate say on what is or is not constitutional? (AP Photo/ George Nikitin)

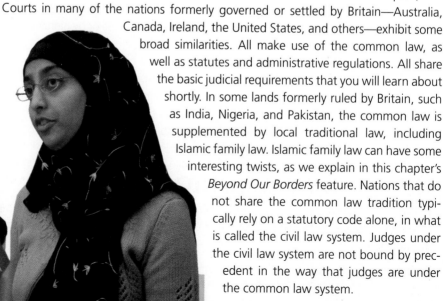

beyondourborders

TECHNOLOGY AND ISLAMIC DIVORCE

Talaq. In Malaysia, this one word translates as "I divorce you." Under current Islamic law—called *sharia*—in Malaysia, if a man states the word *talaq* three times, he is divorced. Since the advent of text messaging, men in some areas of Malaysia can divorce their wives by stating "I divorce you" in their own language three times in a text message.

MALAYSIAN MUSLIM MEN AND MULTIPLE WIVES

Muslim men in Malaysia can take up to four wives. Any Muslim man in that country has the right to divorce. We don't know how many men have sent their wives text messages since the practice started in 2003, but we do know that the text-messaging divorce technique is growing as cell phone use also grows.

Muslim men in Malaysia divorce their wives at a rate five times higher than that of non-Muslims in their country. (Of course, this number is somewhat inflated because not too many non-Muslim men have more than one wife.)

SHARIA COURT RULINGS NOT APPLICABLE IN ALL STATES

As it turns out, the ruling of a *sharia* court in one Malaysian state is not applicable in another. Consequently, a man may divorce one or more of his wives in one state and be required by that *sharia* court to provide child support. He can thereafter move to another Malaysian state and avoid paying child support.

There are other differences in the application of *sharia* among the states in Malaysia. For example, two states give Muslim fathers the right to marry off a daughter without her consent.

FOR CRITICAL ANALYSIS

One government adviser on religious affairs in Malaysia stated that "mobile phone text messaging is just another form of writing." In the situation described in this feature, do you believe that text messaging "I divorce you" should have the same legal effect as stating those words verbally to one's spouse? Why or why not?

In certain areas of the Muslim world, a man can divorce his wife simply by making the statement "I divorce you" in the local language three times. Several Islamic countries have banned this practice, but it still continues in certain areas. In some states in Malaysia, even text-messaging the statement can apparently create a valid divorce. (JIMIN LAI/AFP/Getty Images)

THE FEDERAL COURT SYSTEM

The United States has a dual court system. There are state courts and federal courts. Each of the fifty states, as well as the District of Columbia, has its own independent system of courts. This means that there are fifty-two court systems in total. Here we focus on the federal courts.

BASIC JUDICIAL REQUIREMENTS

Before a case can be brought before a court in any court system, state or federal, certain requirements must be met. Two important requirements are jurisdiction and standing to sue.

Jurisdiction
The authority of a court to decide certain cases. Not all courts have the authority to decide all cases. Where a case arises and what its subject matter is are two jurisdictional issues.

Federal Question
A question that has to do with the U.S. Constitution, acts of Congress, or treaties. A federal question provides a basis for federal jurisdiction.

Diversity of Citizenship
The condition that exists when the parties to a lawsuit are citizens of different states or when the parties are citizens of a U.S. state and citizens or the government of a foreign country. Diversity of citizenship can provide a basis for federal jurisdiction.

Trial Court
The court in which most cases begin.

General Jurisdiction
Exists when a court's authority to hear cases is not significantly restricted. A court of general jurisdiction normally can hear a broad range of cases.

Jurisdiction. A state court can exercise **jurisdiction** (the authority of the court to hear and decide a case) over the residents of a particular geographic area, such as a county or district. A state's highest court, or supreme court, has jurisdictional authority over all residents within the state. Because the Constitution established a federal government with limited powers, federal jurisdiction is also limited.

Article III, Section 1, of the U.S. Constitution limits the jurisdiction of the federal courts to cases that involve either a federal question or diversity of citizenship. A **federal question** arises when a case is based, at least in part, on the U.S. Constitution, a treaty, or a federal law. A person who claims that her or his rights under the Constitution, such as the right to free speech, have been violated could bring a case in a federal court. **Diversity of citizenship** exists when the parties to a lawsuit are from different states or (more rarely) when the suit involves a U.S. citizen and a government or citizen of a foreign country. The amount in controversy must be at least $75,000 before a federal court can take jurisdiction in a diversity case, however.

Standing to Sue. Another basic judicial requirement is standing to sue, or a sufficient "stake" in a matter to justify bringing suit. The party bringing a lawsuit must have suffered a harm, or have been threatened by a harm, as a result of the action that led to the dispute in question. Standing to sue also requires that the controversy at issue be a justiciable controversy. A *justiciable controversy* is a controversy that is real and substantial, as opposed to hypothetical or academic. In other words, a court will not give advisory opinions on hypothetical questions.

TYPES OF FEDERAL COURTS

As you can see in Figure 13–1, the federal court system is basically a three-tiered model consisting of (1) U.S. district courts and various specialized courts of limited jurisdiction (not all of the latter are shown in the figure), (2) intermediate U.S. courts of appeals, and (3) the United States Supreme Court.

U.S. District Courts. The U.S. district courts are trial courts. A **trial court** is what the name implies—a court in which trials are held and testimony is taken. The U.S. district courts are courts of **general jurisdiction,** meaning that they can hear cases involving a

FIGURE 13–1: The Federal Court System

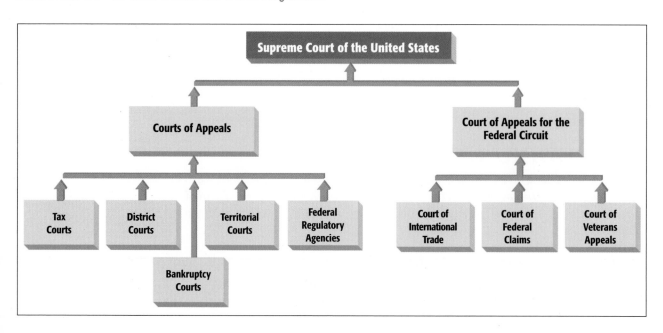

broad array of issues. Federal cases involving most matters typically are heard in district courts. The other courts on the lower tier of the model shown in Figure 13–1 are courts of **limited jurisdiction,** meaning that they can try cases involving only certain types of claims, such as tax claims or bankruptcy petitions.

There is at least one federal district court in every state. The number of judicial districts can vary over time owing to population changes and corresponding caseloads. Currently, there are ninety-four federal judicial districts. A party who is dissatisfied with the decision of a district court can appeal the case to the appropriate U.S. court of appeals, or federal **appellate court.** Figure 13–2 shows the jurisdictional boundaries of the district courts (which are state boundaries, unless otherwise indicated by dotted lines within a state) and of the U.S. courts of appeals.

U.S. Courts of Appeals. There are thirteen U.S. courts of appeals—also referred to as U.S. circuit courts of appeals. Twelve of these courts, including the U.S. Court of Appeals for the District of Columbia, hear appeals from the federal district courts located within their respective judicial circuits (geographic areas over which they exercise jurisdiction). The Court of Appeals for the Thirteenth Circuit, called the Federal Circuit, has national appellate jurisdiction over certain types of cases, such as cases involving patent law and those in which the U.S. government is a defendant.

Note that when an appellate court reviews a case decided in a district court, the appellate court does not conduct another trial. Rather, a panel of three or more judges reviews the record of the case on appeal, which includes a transcript of the trial proceedings, and determines whether the trial court committed an error. Usually, appellate courts

Limited Jurisdiction
Exists when a court's authority to hear cases is restricted to certain types of claims, such as tax claims or bankruptcy petitions.

Appellate Court
A court having jurisdiction to review cases and issues that were originally tried in lower courts.

FIGURE 13–2: Geographic Boundaries of Federal District Courts and U.S. Courts of Appeals

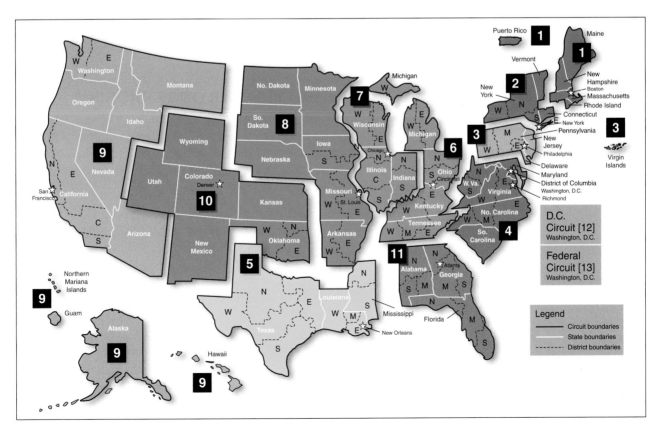

Source: Administrative Office of the United States Courts.

do not look at questions of *fact* (such as whether a party did, in fact, commit a certain action, such as burning a flag) but at questions of *law* (such as whether the act of burning a flag is a form of speech protected by the First Amendment to the Constitution). An appellate court will challenge a trial court's finding of fact only when the finding is clearly contrary to the evidence presented at trial or when there is no evidence to support the finding.

A party can petition the United States Supreme Court to review an appellate court's decision. The likelihood that the Supreme Court will grant the petition is slim, however, because the Court reviews very few of the cases decided by the appellate courts. This means that decisions made by appellate judges usually are final.

The United States Supreme Court. The highest level of the three-tiered model of the federal court system is the United States Supreme Court. When the Supreme Court came into existence in 1789, it had six justices. In the following years, more justices were added. Since 1869 there have been nine justices on the Court. Some have suggested that the number of justices should be increased again. We discuss that idea in this chapter's *Which Side Are You On?* feature.

didyouknow...

That the Supreme Court was not provided with a building of its own until 1935, in the 146th year of its existence?

According to the language of Article III of the U.S. Constitution, there is only one national Supreme Court. All other courts in the federal system are considered "inferior." Congress is empowered to create other inferior courts as it deems necessary. The inferior courts that Congress has created include the district courts, the federal courts of appeals, and the federal courts of limited jurisdiction.

Although the Supreme Court can exercise original jurisdiction (that is, act as a trial court) in certain cases, such as those affecting foreign diplomats and those in which a state is a party, most of its work is as an appellate court. The Court hears appeals not only from the federal appellate courts but also from the highest state courts. Note, though, that the United States Supreme Court can review a state supreme court decision only if a federal question is involved. Because of its importance in the federal court system, we look more closely at the Supreme Court later in this chapter.

FEDERAL COURTS AND THE WAR ON TERRORISM

As noted, the federal court system includes a variety of trial courts of limited jurisdiction, dealing with matters such as tax claims or international trade. The government's attempts to combat terrorism have drawn attention to certain specialized courts that meet in secret. We look next at these courts, as well as at the role of the federal courts with respect to the detainees held at the U.S. Naval Base in Guantánamo Bay, Cuba.

The FISA Court. The federal government created the first secret court in 1978. In that year, Congress passed the Foreign Intelligence Surveillance Act (FISA), which established a court to hear requests for warrants for the surveillance of suspected spies. Officials can request warrants without having to reveal to the suspect or to the public the information used to justify the warrant. The FISA court has approved almost all of the thousands of requests for warrants that the U.S. attorney general's office and other officials have submitted. The seven judges on the FISA court meet in secret, with no published opinions or orders. There is also no public access to the court's proceedings or records. Hence, when the court authorizes surveillance, suspects normally do not even know that they are under scrutiny. During the Clinton administration (1993–2001), the court was given the additional authority to approve physical as well as electronic searches, which means that officials may search a suspect's property without obtaining a warrant in open court and without notifying the subject.

In the aftermath of the terrorist attacks on September 11, 2001, the Bush administration expanded the powers of the FISA court. Previously, the FISA allowed secret

whichsideareyouon?

SHOULD THE NUMBER OF SUPREME COURT JUSTICES BE INCREASED?

The size of the United States Supreme Court is not fixed by the Constitution. It is determined by Congress. The original Judiciary Act of 1789 set the number of justices at six, and that number has changed over time from 1800 to the present. The last and most controversial attempt to change the number of justices occurred in 1937, when President Franklin Roosevelt proposed his famous "Court-packing" scheme. As you learned in Chapter 3, Roosevelt intended to add additional members to the Court who would no longer rule that his New Deal policies were unconstitutional. Publicly, Roosevelt claimed that the justices were too old to keep up with their workload. His plan involved appointing a younger justice to "help out" every justice over the age of seventy. Of course, the new justices would be nominated by the president, as the Constitution provides. At that time, six justices were over the age of seventy. Roosevelt's plan failed.

Some argue that now is the time to add another two justices. Five-person majorities in the nine-justice Court are common—a sign of deep divisions that need to be overcome.

IT'S TIME TO INCREASE THE SIZE OF THE COURT

The Court today is as conservative as at any time in recent history. George W. Bush was able to appoint two more conservative justices, Chief Justice John G. Roberts, Jr., and Samuel Alito, Jr. Consider some of the more recent conservative decisions. In 2005, the Supreme Court ruled that Congress could ban marijuana use even when the state law permitted it. The next year, the conservative majority held that it was not necessary to suppress evidence if the police did not knock and announce their presence before forcibly entering a home. In 2007, the Court upheld a federal law banning partial-birth abortion. The current Supreme Court will stay too far to the right for too long with the current number of justices. Even if liberal-to-moderate justices Ruth Bader Ginsburg, Anthony M. Kennedy, and John Paul Stevens retire and justices with similar ideological views are appointed in their places, the Court will remain dominated by a majority of very conservative figures. Now is the time to add at least two more seats on the Supreme Court to make it again a more neutral arbitrator of legal issues in America. The very small number of cases heard by the Court each year also argues for a larger number of justices.

IF IT'S WORKED FOR DECADES, WHY CHANGE IT?

According to the popular saying, "If it ain't broke, don't fix it." We have had nine justices on the highest court in our federal system for a long time. True, the ideological pendulum has swung back and forth during that period. Nonetheless, history shows that the justices of the Supreme Court have served this country well. They have earned and maintained the respect of the American people by their careful judgments on issues facing the nation.

In 2000, the Supreme Court made a very controversial decision in deciding the presidential election outcome. In that case, the Court essentially said that the state of Florida did not have to manually recount the votes in some counties. The decision paved the way for George W. Bush to become president. Much of the public disagreed with the Court's ruling, which effectively handed the presidency to Bush. Nonetheless, the Court's decision was respected by Americans, and this ruling brought an end to a dangerous electoral controversy.

No one can deny that today's Court is ideologically much further to the right than, say, the very liberal Warren Court (1953–1969). We must remember, however, that in the days of the Warren Court, conservatives complained vocally about the left-leaning nature of the high court. The U.S. Supreme Court will not stay conservative forever, just as the Court did not stay liberal forever after the Warren Court. Leave well enough alone—don't "pack" the Supreme Court.

"IT IS NOT OFTEN IN THE LAW THAT SO FEW HAVE SO QUICKLY CHANGED SO MUCH."
—JUSTICE STEPHEN BREYER

(Nick Anderson, *Houston Chronicle*)

domestic surveillance only if the "purpose" was to combat foreign intelligence gathering. Amendments to the FISA subsequent to the 9/11 terrorist attacks changed this wording to "a significant purpose"—meaning that warrants may now be requested to obtain evidence that can be used in criminal trials.

Alien "Removal Courts." The FISA court is not the only court in which suspects' rights have been reduced. In the wake of the Oklahoma City bombing in 1995, Congress passed the Anti-Terrorism and Effective Death Penalty Act of 1996. The act included a provision creating an alien "removal court" to hear evidence against suspected "alien terrorists." The judges in this court rule on whether there is probable cause for deportation. If so, a public deportation proceeding is held in a U.S. district court. The prosecution does not need to follow procedures that normally apply in criminal cases. In addition, the defendant cannot see the evidence that the prosecution used to secure the hearing.

In the summer of 2008, the House Judiciary Committee held a hearing on the administration's interrogation policies with respect to so-called enemy combatants held in detention. Shown here are three of the former government officials who were involved in creating interrogation policy. They are, from left to right, Chief of Staff David Addington, former legal counsel to Vice President Dick Cheney; John Yoo, a former Department of Justice official; and Christopher Schroeder, former acting assistant attorney general in charge of the Office of Legal Counsel in the Department of Justice. Why did the House committee question these individuals rather than having the Supreme Court deal with the issue? (Photo by Melissa Golden/Getty Images)

The Federal Courts and Enemy Combatants. Subsequent to the 9/11 terrorist attacks, the U.S. military took custody of hundreds of suspected terrorists and held them at the U.S. Naval Base in Guantánamo Bay, Cuba. The detainees include foreigners who were captured during the war in Afghanistan in late 2001 and other suspects who have since been sent to the naval base. The detainees were classified as *enemy combatants,* and, according to the Bush administration, they could be held indefinitely and without the normal legal protections available to U.S. citizens. Additionally, the Bush administration claimed that the detainees, because they had been designated enemy combatants and not prisoners of war, were not protected under international laws governing the treatment of prisoners of war.

Since that time, the treatment of the prisoners at Guantánamo has been a source of ongoing controversy. The U.S. Supreme Court held, first in 2004 and then in 2006, that the Bush administration's treatment of these detainees violated the U.S. Constitution.[2] In response to the 2004 decision, the Republican-led 109th Congress enacted a law establishing special military tribunals to hear the prisoners' cases. In 2006, the Court held that these tribunals did not meet the constitutional demands of due process and other rights of prisoners. A central issue in these decisions concerned the Guantánamo prisoners' right to *habeas corpus*—the right of a detained person to challenge the legality of his or her detention before a judge or other neutral person or entity.

The Military Commissions Act of 2006, passed by Congress in response to the Court's 2006 decision, eliminated federal court jurisdiction over *habeas corpus* challenges by noncitizens held as enemy combatants. Instead, prisoners' challenges to their detention would be reviewed by military commissions, with a limited right of appeal to the federal courts afterward. When the 2006 act was challenged as unconstitutional, a federal appellate court held in favor of the Bush administration. The case was then appealed to the U.S. Supreme Court. In June 2008, the Court ruled that the act's provisions restricting the federal courts' jurisdictional authority over detainees' *habeas corpus* challenges were illegal.[3]

2. *Hamdi v. Rumsfeld,* 542 U.S. 507 (2004); *Hamdan v. Rumsfeld,* 126 S.Ct. 2749 (2006).
3. *Boumediene v. Bush,* 128 S.Ct. 2229 (2008).

The decision gives Guantánamo detainees the right to challenge their detention in federal civil courts. The close (five-to-four) decision dealt a decisive blow to the Bush administration's detention policies.

PARTIES TO LAWSUITS

In most lawsuits, the parties are the plaintiff (the person or organization that initiates the lawsuit) and the defendant (the person or organization against whom the lawsuit is brought). There may be a number of plaintiffs and defendants in a single lawsuit. In the last several decades, many lawsuits have been brought by interest groups (see Chapter 7). Interest groups play an important role in our judicial system, because they **litigate**—bring to trial—or assist in litigating most cases of racial or gender-based discrimination, virtually all civil liberties cases, and more than one-third of the cases involving business matters. Interest groups also file *amicus curiae* (pronounced ah-*mee*-kous *kur*-ee-eye) briefs, or "friend of the court" briefs, in more than 50 percent of these kinds of cases.

Sometimes interest groups or other plaintiffs will bring a **class-action suit,** in which whatever the court decides will affect all members of a class similarly situated (such as users of a particular product manufactured by the defendant in the lawsuit). The strategy of class-action lawsuits was pioneered by such groups as the National Association for the Advancement of Colored People (NAACP), the Legal Defense Fund, and the Sierra Club, whose leaders believed that the courts would offer a more sympathetic forum for their views than would Congress.

PROCEDURAL RULES

Both the federal and the state courts have established procedural rules that shape the litigation process. These rules are designed to protect the rights and interests of the parties, to ensure that the litigation proceeds in a fair and orderly manner, and to identify the issues that must be decided by the court—thus saving court time and costs. Court decisions may also apply to trial procedures. For example, the Supreme Court has held that the parties' attorneys cannot discriminate against prospective jurors on the basis of race or gender. Some lower courts have also held that people cannot be excluded from juries because of their sexual orientation or religion.

The parties must comply with procedural rules and with any orders given by the judge during the course of the litigation. When a party does not follow a court's order, the court can cite him or her for contempt. A party who commits *civil* contempt (failing to comply with a court's order for the benefit of another party to the proceeding) can be taken into custody, fined, or both, until the party complies with the court's order. A party who commits *criminal* contempt (obstructing the administration of justice or bringing the court into disrepute) also can be taken into custody and fined but cannot avoid punishment by complying with a previous order.

Throughout this text, you have read about how technology is affecting all areas of government. The judiciary is no exception. Today's courts post opinions and other information online. Increasingly, lawyers are expected to file court documents electronically. There is little doubt that in the future we will see more court business conducted through use of the Internet.

Litigate
To engage in a legal proceeding or seek relief in a court of law; to carry on a lawsuit.

Amicus Curiae **Brief**
A brief (a document containing a legal argument supporting a desired outcome in a particular case) filed by a third party, or *amicus curiae* (Latin for "friend of the court"), who is not directly involved in the litigation but who has an interest in the outcome of the case.

Class-Action Suit
A lawsuit filed by an individual seeking damages for "all persons similarly situated."

THE SUPREME COURT AT WORK

The Supreme Court begins its regular annual term on the first Monday in October and usually adjourns in late June or early July of the next year. Special sessions may be held after the regular term ends, but only a few cases are decided in this way. More commonly, cases are carried over until the next regular session.

Of the total number of cases that are decided each year in U.S. courts, those reviewed by the Supreme Court represent less than one in four thousand. Included in these, however, are decisions that profoundly affect our lives. In recent years, the United States Supreme Court has decided issues involving capital punishment, the rights of criminal suspects, affirmative action programs, religious freedom, assisted suicide, abortion, property rights, busing, term limits for congresspersons, sexual harassment, pornography, states' rights, limits on federal jurisdiction, and many other matters with significant consequences for the nation.

Because the Supreme Court exercises a great deal of discretion over the types of cases it hears, it can influence the nation's policies by issuing decisions in some types of cases and refusing to hear appeals in others, thereby allowing lower court decisions to stand.

United States Supreme Court

Justice Clarence Thomas is shown with three of his legal clerks in his office at the Supreme Court building in Washington, D.C. What are some of the issues that recent Supreme Courts have tackled? (Photo by David Hume Kennerly/Getty Images)

Indeed, the fact that George W. Bush assumed the presidency in 2001 instead of Al Gore, his Democratic opponent, was largely due to a Supreme Court decision to review a Florida court's ruling. The Supreme Court reversed the Florida court's order to manually recount the votes in selected Florida counties—a decision that effectively handed the presidency to Bush.[4]

WHICH CASES REACH THE SUPREME COURT?

Many people are surprised to learn that in a typical case, there is no absolute right of appeal to the United States Supreme Court. The Court's appellate jurisdiction is almost entirely discretionary—the Court can choose which cases it will decide. The justices never explain their reasons for hearing certain cases and not others, so it is difficult to predict which case or type of case the Court might select.

Factors That Bear on the Decision. Factors that bear on the decision include whether a legal question has been decided differently by various lower courts and needs resolution by the highest court, whether a lower court's decision conflicts with an existing Supreme Court ruling, and whether the issue could have significance beyond the parties to the dispute.

Another factor is whether the solicitor general is pressuring the Court to take a case. The solicitor general, a high-ranking presidential appointee within the Justice Department, represents the national government before the Supreme Court and promotes presidential policies in the federal courts. He or she decides what cases the government should ask the Supreme Court to review and what position the government should take in cases before the Court.

---

4. *Bush v. Gore,* 531 U.S. 98 (2000).

Granting Petitions for Review. If the Court decides to grant a petition for review, it will issue a **writ of *certiorari*** (pronounced sur-shee-uh-*rah*-ree). The writ orders a lower court to send the Supreme Court a record of the case for review. Of the more than eight thousand petitions for review that the Court receives each term, only a small percentage are granted. A denial is not a decision on the merits of a case, nor does it indicate agreement with the lower court's opinion. (The judgment of the lower court remains in force, however.) Therefore, denial of the writ has no value as a precedent. The Court will not issue a writ unless at least four justices approve of it. This is called the **rule of four.**[5]

COURT PROCEDURES

Once the Supreme Court grants *certiorari* in a particular case, the justices do extensive research on the legal issues and facts involved in the case. (Of course, some preliminary research is necessary before deciding to grant the petition for review.) Each justice is entitled to four law clerks, who undertake much of the research and preliminary drafting necessary for the justice to form an opinion.[6]

The Court normally does not hear any evidence, as is true with all appeals courts. The Court's consideration of a case is based on the abstracts, the record, and the briefs. The attorneys are permitted to present **oral arguments.** Unlike the practice in most courts, lawyers addressing the Supreme Court can be (and often are) questioned by the justices at any time during oral argument. All statements and the justices' questions during oral arguments are recorded.

The justices meet to discuss and vote on cases in conferences held throughout the term. In these conferences, in addition to deciding cases already before the Court, the justices determine which new petitions for *certiorari* to grant. These conferences take place in the oak-paneled chamber and are strictly private—no stenographers, audio recorders, or video cameras are allowed. Two pages used to be in attendance to wait on the justices while they were in conference, but fear of information leaks caused the Court to stop this practice.[7]

DECISIONS AND OPINIONS

When the Court has reached a decision, its opinion is written. The **opinion** contains the Court's ruling on the issue or issues presented, the reasons for its decision, the rules of law that apply, and other information. In many cases, the decision of the lower court is **affirmed,** resulting in the enforcement of that court's judgment or decree. If the Supreme Court believes that a reversible error was committed during the trial or that the jury was instructed improperly, however, the decision will be **reversed.** Sometimes the case will be **remanded** (sent back to the court that originally heard the case) for a new trial or other proceeding. For example, a lower court might have held that a party was not entitled to bring a lawsuit under a particular law. If the Supreme Court holds to the contrary, it will remand (send back) the case to the trial court with instructions that the trial go forward.

The Court's written opinion sometimes is unsigned; this is called an opinion *per curiam* ("by the court"). Typically, the Court's opinion is signed by all the justices who agree with it. When in the majority, the chief justice decides who writes the opinion and often writes it personally. When the chief justice is in the minority, the senior justice on the majority side assigns the opinion.

Writ of *Certiorari*
An order issued by a higher court to a lower court to send up the record of a case for review.

Rule of Four
A United States Supreme Court procedure by which four justices must vote to grant a petition for review if a case is to come before the full court.

Oral Arguments
The verbal arguments presented in person by attorneys to an appellate court. Each attorney presents reasons to the court why the court should rule in her or his client's favor.

Opinion
The statement by a judge or a court of the decision reached in a case. The opinion sets forth the applicable law and details the reasoning on which the ruling was based.

Affirm
To declare that a court ruling is valid and must stand.

Reverse
To annul, or make void, a court ruling on account of some error or irregularity.

Remand
To send a case back to the court that originally heard it.

---

5. The "rule of four" is modified when seven or fewer justices participate, which occurs from time to time. When that happens, as few as three justices can grant *certiorari.*

6. For a former Supreme Court law clerk's account of the role these clerks play in the high court's decision-making process, see Edward Lazarus, *Closed Chambers: The First Eyewitness Account of the Epic Struggles inside the Supreme Court* (New York: Times Books, 1998).

7. It turned out that one supposed information leak came from lawyers making educated guesses.

Unanimous Opinion
A court opinion or determination on which all judges agree.

Majority Opinion
A court opinion reflecting the views of the majority of the judges.

Concurring Opinion
A separate opinion prepared by a judge who supports the decision of the majority of the court but who wants to make or clarify a particular point or to voice disapproval of the grounds on which the decision was made.

Dissenting Opinion
A separate opinion in which a judge dissents from (disagrees with) the conclusion reached by the majority on the court and expounds his or her own views about the case.

Types of Opinions. When all justices unanimously agree on an opinion, the opinion is written for the entire Court (all the justices) and can be deemed a **unanimous opinion.** When there is not a unanimous opinion, a **majority opinion** is written, outlining the views of the majority of the justices involved in the case. Often, one or more justices who feel strongly about making or emphasizing a particular point that is not made or emphasized in the unanimous or majority written opinion will write a **concurring opinion.** That means the justice writing the concurring opinion agrees (concurs) with the conclusion given in the majority written opinion, but for different reasons. Finally, in other than unanimous opinions, one or more justices who do not agree with the majority usually will write a **dissenting opinion.** The dissenting opinion is important because it often forms the basis of the arguments used years later if the Court reverses the previous decision and establishes a new precedent.

The Publication of Supreme Court Opinions. Shortly after the opinion is written, the Supreme Court announces its decision from the bench. At that time, the opinion is made available to the public at the office of the clerk of the Court. The clerk also releases the opinion for online publication. Ultimately, the opinion is published in the *United States Reports,* which is the official printed record of the Court's decisions.

The Court's Dwindling Caseload. Some have complained that the Court reviews too few cases each term, thus giving the lower courts less guidance on important issues. Indeed, the number of signed opinions issued by the Court has dwindled notably since the 1980s. For example, in its 1982–1983 term, the Court issued signed opinions in 151 cases. By the early 2000s, this number dropped to between 70 and 80 per term. In the term ending in June 2008, the Court issued 73 written opinions.

Some scholars suggest that one of the reasons the Court hears fewer cases today than in the past is the growing conservatism of the judges sitting on lower courts. More than half of these judges have now been appointed by Republican presidents. As a result, the government loses fewer cases in the lower courts, which lessens the need for the government to appeal the rulings through the solicitor general's office. Some support for this conclusion is given by the fact that the number of petitions filed by that office declined by more than 50 percent during the administration of George W. Bush.

THE SELECTION OF FEDERAL JUDGES

All federal judges are appointed. The Constitution, in Article II, Section 2, states that the president appoints the justices of the Supreme Court with the advice and consent of the Senate. Congress has provided the same procedure for staffing other federal courts. This means that the Senate and the president jointly decide who shall fill every vacant judicial position, no matter what the level.

There are more than 850 federal judgeships in the United States. Once appointed to such a judgeship, a person holds that job for life. Judges serve until they resign, retire voluntarily, or die. Federal judges who engage in blatantly illegal conduct may be removed through impeachment, although such action is rare.

In contrast to federal judges, many state judges—including the judges who sit on state supreme courts—are chosen by the voters in elections. Inevitably, judicial candidates must raise campaign funds. What arguments favor the election of judges? What problems can such a system create? We examine such questions in this chapter's *Politics and the States* feature.

JUDICIAL APPOINTMENTS

Candidates for federal judgeships are suggested to the president by the Department of Justice, senators, other judges, the candidates themselves, and lawyers' associations and other interest groups. In selecting a candidate to nominate for a judgeship, the president

politicsand...the states

JUDICIAL ELECTIONS

All of the judges and justices in the federal court system are appointed by the president and confirmed by the Senate. Federal judges and justices are appointed for life. In thirty-nine states, in contrast, some or all state judges must face election and reelection.

BECOMING A STATE JUDGE CAN BE EXPENSIVE

In a recent election to fill a Wisconsin state supreme court judgeship, the candidates spent more than $5.5 million in all, and more than 12,000 campaign commercials were aired on TV. In the states in which there are state supreme court elections, more than 90 percent involve television campaign commercials. The most expensive of such elections took place in 2004 in the state of Illinois—$9.3 million was spent by rival candidates. The candidates themselves raise funds, mainly from—you guessed it—lawyers. Additional campaign funds are raised by special interest groups that want "their" candidate elected or reelected to the state court in question.

CONDEMNATIONS OF THIS SYSTEM ARE WIDESPREAD

A former Oregon Supreme Court justice, Hans A. Linde, pointed out that "to the rest of the world, American adherence to judicial elections is as incomprehensible as our rejection of the metric system." Former U.S. Supreme Court justice Sandra Day O'Connor also condemned the practice of electing judges: "No other nation in the world does that because they realize you are not going to get fair and impartial judges that way."

Political scientists point out that voters do not have much information, and certainly not enough information, to make sensible choices when they vote for a particular judicial candidate. One study, by researchers Gregory H. Huber and Sanford Gordon, found that in criminal cases, "All judges increased their sentences as reelection nears." In other words, the judges did not want to be labeled as "soft on crime" by their opponents during the campaign.

COMPARING ELECTED JUDGES WITH APPOINTED JUDGES

There is relatively little research on the quality of elected state judges as opposed to nominated state judges. In one study, though, researchers at the University of Chicago

In thirty-nine states, some or all state judges must face election and reelection. Here, Republican judicial candidates, including those lawyers running for various judgeships, appear at a state rally in Harrisburg, Pennsylvania. What are the pros and cons of having judges campaign for election and reelection? (AP Photo/Paul Vathis)

School of Law found that elected judges wrote more opinions than appointed judges, but appointed judges wrote opinions of higher quality. Elections attract and reward politically savvy people. Appointive systems attract more professionally able people. The authors of this study concluded, nonetheless, that "the politically savvy people might give the public what it wants—adequate rather than great opinions, and in greater quantity."

FOR CRITICAL ANALYSIS

Why do you think that attorneys, as a group, contribute more to judicial campaigns than do members of other professions?

Senatorial Courtesy
In federal district court judgeship nominations, a tradition allowing a senator to veto a judicial appointment in his or her state.

TABLE 13–1:
Background of United States Supreme Court Justices to 2009

	Number of Justices (110 = Total)
Occupational Position before Appointment	
Federal judgeship	30
Private legal practice	25
State judgeship	21
Federal executive post	9
U.S. attorney general	7
U.S. senator	6
State governor	3
Deputy or assistant U.S. attorney general	2
U.S. solicitor general	2
U.S. representative	2
Other	3
Religious Background	
Protestant	83
Roman Catholic	13
Unitarian	7
Jewish	6
No religious affiliation	1
Age on Appointment	
Under 40	5
41–50	32
51–60	59
61–70	14
Political Party Affiliation	
Democrat	44
Republican	44
Federalist (to 1835)	13
Jeffersonian Republican (to 1828)	7
Whig (to 1861)	1
Independent	1
Educational Background	
College graduate	94
Not a college graduate	16
Gender	
Male	108
Female	2
Race	
White	108
African American	2

Sources: Congressional Quarterly, *Congressional Quarterly's Guide to the U.S. Supreme Court* (Washington, D.C.: Congressional Quarterly Press, 1996); and authors' update.

considers not only the person's competence but also other factors, including the person's political philosophy (as will be discussed shortly), ethnicity, and gender.

The nomination process—no matter how the nominees are obtained—always works the same way. The president makes the actual nomination, transmitting the name to the Senate. The Senate then either confirms or rejects the nomination. To reach a conclusion, the Senate Judiciary Committee (operating through subcommittees) invites testimony, both written and oral, at its various hearings. A practice used in the Senate, called **senatorial courtesy,** is a constraint on the president's freedom to appoint federal district judges. Senatorial courtesy allows a senator of the president's political party to veto a judicial appointment in her or his state. During much of American history, senators from the "opposition" party (the party to which the president did not belong) also enjoyed the right of senatorial courtesy, although their veto power varied over time.

Federal District Court Judgeship Nominations. Although the president officially nominates federal judges, in the past the nomination of federal district court judges actually originated with a senator or senators of the president's party from the state in which there was a vacancy. In effect, judicial appointments were a form of political patronage. President Jimmy Carter (1977–1981) ended this tradition by establishing independent commissions to oversee the initial nomination process. President Ronald Reagan (1981–1989) abolished Carter's nominating commissions and established complete presidential control of nominations.

In 2000, Orrin Hatch, Republican chair of the Senate Judiciary Committee, announced that the opposition party (at that point, the Democrats) would no longer be allowed to invoke senatorial courtesy. The implementation of the new policy was delayed when Republican senator James Jeffords of Vermont left the Republican Party. Jeffords's departure turned control of the Senate over to the Democrats. After the 2002 elections, however, when the Republicans regained control of the Senate, they put the new policy into effect.

When the Democrats took over the Senate following the elections of 2006, Senator Patrick J. Leahy (D., Vt.), chairman of the Judiciary Committee, let it be known that the old bipartisan system of senatorial courtesy would return. The change had little immediate impact, however. The Republicans, who were now in the minority, were unlikely to object to a nomination submitted by Republican president George W. Bush.

Federal Courts of Appeals Appointments. Appointments to the federal courts of appeals are far less numerous than federal district court appointments, but they are more important. This is because federal appellate judges handle more important matters, at least from the point of view of the president, and therefore presidents take a keener interest in the nomination process for such judgeships. Also, the U.S. courts of appeals have become "stepping-stones" to the Supreme Court.

Supreme Court Appointments. As we have described, the president nominates Supreme Court justices. As you can see in Table 13–1, which summarizes the background of all Supreme Court justices to 2009, the most common occupational background of the justices at the time of their appointment has been private legal practice or state or federal judgeship. Those nine justices who were in federal executive posts at the time of their appointment held the high offices of secretary of state, comptroller of the treasury, secretary of the navy, postmaster general, secretary of the interior, chairman of the Securities and Exchange Commission, and secretary of labor. In the "Other" category under "Occupational Position before Appointment" in Table 13–1 are two justices who were professors of law (including William H. Taft, a former president) and one justice who was a North Carolina state employee with responsibility for organizing and revising the state's statutes.

The Special Role of the Chief Justice. Ideology is always important in judicial appointments, as described next; but when a chief justice is selected for the Supreme Court, other considerations must also be taken into account. The chief justice is not only the head of a group of nine justices who interpret the law. He or she is also in essence the chief executive officer of a large bureaucracy that includes more than one thousand judges with lifetime tenure, hundreds of magistrates and bankruptcy judges with limited tenure, and a staff of about thirty thousand.

The chief justice is also the chair of the Judicial Conference of the United States, a policymaking body that sets priorities for the federal judiciary. That position means that the chief justice indirectly oversees the $6 billion budget of this group.

Finally, the chief justice appoints the director of the Administrative Office of the United States Courts. The chief justice and this director select judges who sit on judicial committees that examine international judicial relations, technology, and a variety of other topics.

This scene took place in a federal courtroom in Concord, New Hampshire. It involves the swearing in of a new federal district court judge. Can anyone become such a judge? Who decides who becomes a federal district court judge? (AP Photo/Jim Cole)

PARTISANSHIP AND JUDICIAL APPOINTMENTS

In most circumstances, the president appoints judges or justices who belong to the president's own political party. Presidents see their federal judiciary appointments as the one sure way to institutionalize their political views long after they have left office. By 1993, for example, Presidents Ronald Reagan and George H. W. Bush together had appointed nearly three-quarters of all federal court judges. This preponderance of Republican-appointed federal judges strengthened the legal moorings of the conservative social agenda on a variety of issues, ranging from abortion to civil rights. President Bill Clinton had the opportunity to appoint about 200 federal judges, thereby shifting the ideological makeup of the federal judiciary. Then, during the first six years of his presidency, George W. Bush appointed more than 250 federal judges, again creating a majority of Republican-appointed judges in the federal courts.

During the first two years of his second term, President Bush also had the opportunity to fill two Supreme Court vacancies—those left by the death of Chief Justice William Rehnquist and by the retirement of Justice Sandra Day O'Connor. Bush appointed two conservatives to these positions—John G. Roberts, Jr., who became chief justice, and Samuel Alito, Jr., who replaced O'Connor. As you will read shortly, these appointments strengthened the rightward movement of the Court that had begun years before, with the appointment of Rehnquist as chief justice.

THE SENATE'S ROLE

Ideology also plays a large role in the Senate's confirmation hearings, and presidential nominees to the Supreme Court have not always been confirmed. In fact, almost 20 percent of presidential nominations to the Supreme Court either have been rejected or not acted on by the Senate. There have been many acrimonious battles over Supreme Court appointments when the Senate and the president have not seen eye to eye about political matters.

The U.S. Senate had a long record of refusing to confirm the president's judicial nominations from the beginning of Andrew Jackson's presidency in 1829 to the end of Ulysses Grant's presidency in 1877. From 1894 until 1968, however, only three nominees were not confirmed. Then, from 1968 through 1987, four presidential nominees to the highest court were rejected. One of the most controversial Supreme Court nominations was that of Clarence Thomas, who underwent an extremely volatile confirmation hearing in 1991, replete with charges against him of sexual harassment. He was ultimately confirmed by the Senate, however.

President Bill Clinton had little trouble gaining approval for both of his nominees to the Supreme Court: Ruth Bader Ginsburg and Stephen G. Breyer. President George W. Bush's nominees faced hostile grilling in their confirmation hearings, and various interest groups mounted intense media ad blitzes against them. Indeed, Bush had to forgo the nomination of Harriet Miers when he realized that he could not win the confirmation battle. Both Clinton and Bush had trouble securing Senate approval for their judicial nominations to the lower courts. In fact, during the late 1990s and early 2000s, the duel between the Senate and the president aroused considerable concern about the consequences of the increasingly partisan and ideological tension over federal judicial appointments.

POLICYMAKING AND THE COURTS

The partisan battles over judicial appointments reflect a significant reality in today's American government: the importance of the judiciary in national politics. Because appointments to the federal bench are for life, the ideology of judicial appointees can affect national policy for years to come. Although the primary function of judges in our system of government is to interpret and apply the laws, inevitably judges make policy when carrying out this task. One of the major policymaking tools of the federal courts is their power of judicial review.

JUDICIAL REVIEW

Remember from Chapter 2 that the power of the courts to determine whether a law or action by the other branches of government is constitutional is known as the power of *judicial review.* This power enables the judicial branch to act as a check on the other two branches of government, in line with the system of checks and balances established by the U.S. Constitution.

The power of judicial review is not mentioned in the Constitution, however. Rather, it was established by the United States Supreme Court's decision in *Marbury v. Madison.*[8] In that case, in which the Court declared that a law passed by Congress violated the Constitution, the Court claimed such a power for the judiciary:

> *It is emphatically the province and duty of the Judicial Department to say what the law is. Those who apply the rule to a particular case must of necessity expound and interpret that rule. If two laws conflict with each other, the courts must decide on the operation of each.*

If a federal court declares that a federal or state law or policy is unconstitutional, the court's decision affects the application of the law or policy only within that court's jurisdiction. For this reason, the higher the level of the court, the greater the impact of the decision on society. Because of the Supreme Court's national jurisdiction, its decisions have the greatest impact. For example, when the Supreme Court held that an Arkansas state constitutional amendment limiting the terms of congresspersons was unconstitutional, laws establishing term limits in twenty-three other states were also invalidated.[9]

Some claim that the power of judicial review gives unelected judges and justices on federal court benches too much influence over national policy. Others argue that the powers exercised by the federal courts, particularly the power of judicial review, are necessary to protect our constitutional rights and liberties. Built into our federal form of government is a system of checks and balances. If the federal courts did not have the power of judicial review, there would be no governmental body to check Congress's lawmaking authority or the unconstitutional use of power by the executive branch.

---

8. 5 U.S. 137 (1803).
9. *U.S. Term Limits v. Thornton,* 514 U.S. 779 (1995).

JUDICIAL ACTIVISM AND JUDICIAL RESTRAINT

Judicial scholars like to characterize different judges and justices as being either "activist" or "restraintist." The doctrine of **judicial activism** rests on the conviction that the federal judiciary should take an active role by using its powers to check the activities of Congress, state legislatures, and administrative agencies when those governmental bodies exceed their authority. One of the Supreme Court's most activist eras was the period from 1953 to 1969, when the Court was headed by Chief Justice Earl Warren. The Warren Court propelled the civil rights movement forward by holding, among other things, that laws permitting racial segregation violated the equal protection clause.

In contrast, the doctrine of **judicial restraint** rests on the assumption that the courts should defer to the decisions made by the legislative and executive branches, because members of Congress and the president are elected by the people whereas members of the federal judiciary are not. Because administrative agency personnel normally have more expertise than the courts do in the areas regulated by the agencies, the courts likewise should defer to agency rules and decisions. In other words, under the doctrine of judicial restraint, the courts should not thwart the implementation of legislative acts and agency rules unless they are clearly unconstitutional.

Judicial activism sometimes is linked with liberalism, and judicial restraint with conservatism. In fact, though, a conservative judge can be activist, just as a liberal judge can be restraintist. In the 1950s and 1960s, the Supreme Court was activist and liberal. Some observers believe that the Rehnquist Court, with its conservative majority, became increasingly activist during the early 2000s. The most conservative members on today's Roberts Court (John Roberts, Antonin Scalia, Clarence Thomas, and Samuel Alito) are regarded by some scholars as restraintist justices because of their deference to laws and regulations reflecting the policy of the Bush administration. These justices may become more activist in their approach to judicial interpretation when they are confronted by a Democratic administration.

STRICT VERSUS BROAD CONSTRUCTION

Other terms that are often used to describe a justice's philosophy are *strict construction* and *broad construction*. Justices who believe in **strict construction** look to the "letter of the law" when they attempt to interpret the Constitution or a particular statute. Those who favor **broad construction** try to determine the context and purpose of the law.

As with the doctrines of judicial restraint and judicial activism, strict construction is often associated with conservative political views, whereas broad construction is often linked with liberalism. These traditional political associations sometimes appear to be reversed, however. Consider the Eleventh Amendment to the Constitution, which rules out lawsuits in federal courts "against one of the United States by Citizens of another State, or by Citizens or Subjects of any Foreign State." Nothing is said about citizens suing their *own* states, and strict construction would therefore find such suits to be constitutional. Conservative justices, however, have construed this amendment broadly to deny citizens the constitutional right to sue their own states in most circumstances. John T. Noonan, Jr., a federal appellate court judge who was appointed by a Republican president, has described these rulings as "adventurous."[10]

Broad construction is often associated with the concept of a "living constitution." Supreme Court justice Antonin Scalia, in contrast, has said that "the Constitution is not a living organism, it is a legal document. It says something and doesn't say other things." Scalia believes that jurists should stick to the plain text of the Constitution "as it was originally written and intended."

didyouknow...

That Constitution Day is celebrated on September 17, the anniversary of the day the framers signed the document?

Judicial Activism
A doctrine holding that the federal judiciary should take an active role by using its powers to check the activities of governmental bodies when those bodies exceed their authority.

Judicial Restraint
A doctrine holding that the courts should defer to the decisions made by the elected representatives of the people in the legislative and executive branches.

Strict Construction
A judicial philosophy that looks to the "letter of the law" when interpreting the Constitution or a particular statute.

Broad Construction
A judicial philosophy that looks to the context and purpose of a law when making an interpretation.

---

10. John T. Noonan, Jr., *Narrowing the Nation's Power: The Supreme Court Sides with the States* (Berkeley: University of California Press, 2002).

THE RIGHTWARD SHIFT OF THE REHNQUIST COURT

William H. Rehnquist became the sixteenth chief justice of the Supreme Court in 1986, after fifteen years as an associate justice. He was known as a strong anchor of the Court's conservative wing until his death in 2005. With Rehnquist's appointment as chief justice, the Court began to take a rightward shift. The Court's rightward movement continued as other conservative appointments to the bench were made during the Reagan and George H. W. Bush administrations.

During the late 1990s and early 2000s, three of the justices (William Rehnquist, Antonin Scalia, and Clarence Thomas) were notably conservative in their views. Four of the justices (John Paul Stevens, David Souter, Ruth Bader Ginsburg, and Stephen Breyer) held liberal-to-moderate views.

Interestingly, to counter the increasingly conservative movement of the Court, some previously conservative justices showed a tendency to "migrate" to a more liberal view of the law. Sandra Day O'Connor, the first female justice and a conservative, gradually shifted to the left on a number of issues, including abortion. Justice Anthony Kennedy also migrated to the left on occasion. Generally, O'Connor and Kennedy provided the "swing votes" on the Rehnquist Court.

Although the Court moved to the right during the Rehnquist era, its decisions were not always in line with conservative ideology. The Court was closely divided in many cases, making it difficult to predict how the Court might rule on any particular issue. Consider the Court's rulings with respect to states' rights. In 1995, the Court held, for the first time in sixty years, that Congress had overreached its powers under the commerce clause when it attempted to regulate the possession of guns in school zones. According to the Court, the possession of guns in school zones had nothing to do with the commerce clause.[11] Yet in a 2005 case, the Court ruled that Congress's power to regulate commerce allowed it to ban marijuana use even when a state's law permitted such use and the growing and use of the drug were strictly local in nature.[12]

THE ROBERTS COURT

During its first term, which ended on June 30, 2006, the Roberts Court (see Figure 13–3) accepted few controversial cases for review. Thus, many claimed that it was premature at that point to make predictions about the ideology of the Roberts Court. Other scholars, however, believe that the Court's first term revealed that the two new justices, Chief Justice Roberts and Justice Alito, were far from the mainstream jurists that many liberals and moderates had hoped they would be.

Chief Justice Roberts Aligns with the Right. After Roberts was appointed as chief justice, he voted most of the time with the Court's most conservative justices, Antonin Scalia and Clarence Thomas. Furthermore, in the sixteen decisions that were decided by a five-to-four vote, Alito also aligned with this conservative group of justices.

In *Hudson v. Michigan,*[13] Roberts wrote the majority opinion in a five-to-four decision holding that it was not necessary to suppress evidence if the police did not knock and announce their presence before forcibly entering a home. This decision effectively removed the protections of the "knock and announce" rule for criminal suspects. Also, Roberts's dissenting opinions reveal a strongly conservative ideology. Consider just a few examples of what would have resulted if Roberts's views had prevailed in some of the cases heard by the Roberts Court: the scope of the Clean Water Act would have been dramatically reduced,[14] Oregon's law allowing physician-assisted suicide would have been

didyouknow...

That a proclamation by President George Washington and a congressional resolution established the first national Thanksgiving Day on November 26, 1789? The reason for the holiday was to give thanks for the new Constitution.

---

11. *United States v. Lopez,* 514 U.S. 549 (1995).
12. *Gonzales v. Raich,* 545 U.S. 1 (2005).
13. 547 U.S. 586 (2006).
14. *Rapanos v. United States,* 547 U.S. 715 (2006).

FIGURE 13–3: The Roberts Court

The members of the United States Supreme Court as of 2009.

Stephen Breyer

Ruth Bader Ginsburg

Samuel Alito, Jr.

Anthony Kennedy

John Roberts, Jr.

Antonin Scalia

Clarence Thomas

David Souter

John Paul Stevens

(The U.S. Supreme Court)

struck down,[15] and a death row inmate would not be entitled to present possible DNA evidence of his or her innocence.[16] In the close (five-to-four) decisions, Justice Kennedy provided the decisive vote.

The Roberts Court's Second Term. In the second term of the Roberts Court (2006–2007), Chief Justice Roberts and associate justices Scalia, Thomas, and Alito continued in their attempts to move the Court to the right. The liberal-to-moderate side did score one notable victory, however: in an important decision challenging the Bush administration's contention that the Environmental Protection Agency (EPA) did not have the authority under the Clean Air Act to regulate emissions of greenhouse gases, the majority on the Court held that the EPA *did* have this authority and should exercise it. Roberts, Scalia, Thomas, and Alito, however, dissented from the majority's opinion.[17] Again, Justice Kennedy provided the swing vote.

In another 2007 case, the Court upheld a 2003 federal law banning partial-birth abortion, again by a close (five-to-four) vote.[18] This time, Justice Kennedy sided with the conservatives on the Court, giving them a majority. (See Chapter 4 on pages 132 and 133 for

---

15. *Gonzales v. Oregon,* 546 U.S. 243 (2006).
16. *House v. Bell,* 126 S.Ct. 2064 (2006).
17. *Massachusetts v. E.P.A.,* 127 S.Ct. 1438 (2007).
18. *Gonzales v. Carhart,* 127 S.Ct. 1610 (2007).

"It's from the government—we'll have to file an environmental-impact statement before we can evolve."

more details on this issue.) Ruth Bader Ginsburg, in a dissenting opinion signed by the four liberal-to-moderate justices, stated that the majority opinion "cannot be understood as anything other than an effort to chip away at a right declared again and again by this court."

In a five-to-four decision at the end of its 2006–2007 term, the Court issued another conservative opinion. This case involved two school districts' admissions policies that included race as a determining factor in certain limited situations. The policies were ruled unconstitutional by the Court on the ground that they violated the equal protection clause.[19]

Other major cases that displayed the Court's rightward course included *FEC v. Wisconsin Right to Life,*[20] which you learned about in Chapter 9 on page 299. In this case, the Court struck down restrictions on preelection issue advertisements that were imposed by the Bipartisan Campaign Reform Act of 2002. In *Morse v. Frederick,*[21] the "Bong Hits 4 Jesus" case described on page 126 of Chapter 4, the Court significantly restricted the First Amendment rights of high school students. In one notable case, a convicted murderer was late in filing an appeal because he relied on an incorrect date provided by a district court judge. The Supreme Court nevertheless denied the appeal.[22]

The rightward drift of the Roberts Court resulted in some harsh criticisms, not all of which came from liberals. For example, Richard Posner, a well-known and relatively conservative federal appeals court judge in Chicago, has noted that what Roberts said during his confirmation hearings is often at odds with Roberts's actions as chief justice.[23] The case that drew the most negative public response may have been *Ledbetter v. Goodyear Tire & Rubber Co.,*[24] another case in which the Court imposed inflexible deadlines. The Court held, in a five-to-four decision, that employers are protected from lawsuits over race or gender pay discrimination if the claims are based on decisions made by the employer more than 180 days before the claims are filed. Many observers argued that this verdict would make pay discrimination suits almost impossible to win. The *Ledbetter* case was only the most conspicuous of a series of cases in which the Court sided with business interests. The U.S. Chamber of Commerce was successful in thirteen of the fifteen cases in which it filed *amicus curiae* (friend-of-the-court) briefs, an all-time high.

The Court Backpedals Slightly. The justices continued to chart a conservative course in the Roberts Court's third term, from 2007 to 2008. They drew back, however, from the strong pro-employer stance they had taken previously. In two cases, the Court held that workers who complain about racial or age-based bias may sue for damages if they face retaliation from their employers.[25] The Court also decided three other discrimination cases in favor of the employees. Still, it was not a bad term for business interests—several rulings restricted the extent to which corporations are exposed to lawsuits. Notably, the Court cut a $2.5 billion punitive damages award against Exxon Mobil resulting from the *Exxon Valdez* supertanker oil spill in Alaska to about $500 million.[26]

19. *Parents Involved in Community Schools v. Seattle School District No. 1,* 127 S.Ct. 2738 (2007).
20. 127 S.Ct. 2652 (2007).
21. 127 S.Ct. 2618 (2007).
22. *Bowles v. Russell,* 127 S.Ct. 2360 (2007).
23. Richard A. Posner, *How Judges Think* (Cambridge, Mass.: Harvard University Press, 2008).
24. 127 S.Ct. 2162 (2007).
25. *CBOCS West, Inc. v. Humphries,* 128 S.Ct. 1951 (2008); and *Gomez-Perez v. Potter,* 128 S.Ct. 1931 (2008).
26. *Exxon Shipping Co. v. Baker,* 128 S.Ct. 2605 (2008).

Probably the most significant of the Court's right-of-center rulings came in *District of Columbia v. Heller,* when it overturned the District of Columbia's ban on handguns.[27] For the first time, the Court established the right of individuals to own guns for private use, not only as members of a militia. The five-to-four majority left considerable room for the states to regulate gun ownership, however. The Court also upheld Kentucky's method of execution by lethal injection,[28] Indiana's law requiring photo identification at the polls,[29] and a recent federal law that criminalizes offers to sell child pornography even if the pornography does not actually exist.[30]

The Court also took a strong line in defense of civil liberties in a five-to-four ruling that affected alleged terrorists held at the Guantánamo Bay naval base in Cuba. The Court reaffirmed that these prisoners have *habeas corpus* rights, that is, the right to challenge the legitimacy of their detention in federal court. The Bush administration had established the prison at Guantánamo Bay precisely because it would then be outside the reach of U.S. law.

Often, the Court's opinions were narrowly enough drawn to prevent the five-to-four splits that had characterized the Court in its previous term. When the Court was narrowly divided, Justice Kennedy continued to provide the swing vote.

WHAT CHECKS OUR COURTS?

Our judicial system is one of the most independent in the world. But the courts do not have absolute independence, for they are part of the political process. Political checks limit the extent to which courts can exercise judicial review and engage in an activist policy. These checks are exercised by the executive branch, the legislature, the public, and, finally, the judiciary itself.

EXECUTIVE CHECKS

President Andrew Jackson was once supposed to have said, after Chief Justice John Marshall made an unpopular decision, "John Marshall has made his decision; now let him enforce it."[31] This purported remark goes to the heart of **judicial implementation**—the enforcement of judicial decisions in such a way that those decisions are translated into policy. The Supreme Court simply does not have any enforcement powers, and whether a decision will be implemented depends on the cooperation of the other two branches of government. Rarely, though, will a president refuse to enforce a Supreme Court decision, as President Jackson did. To take such an action could mean a significant loss of public support because of the Supreme Court's stature in the eyes of the nation.

More commonly, presidents exercise influence over the judiciary by appointing new judges and justices as federal judicial seats become vacant. Additionally, as mentioned earlier, the U.S. solicitor general plays a significant role in the federal court system, and the person holding that office is a presidential appointee.

Executives at the state level may also refuse to implement court decisions with which they disagree. A notable example of such a refusal occurred in Arkansas after the U.S.

Lilly Ledbetter discovered that she had been paid less than male employees in her same position at Goodyear Tire and Rubber Company. She sued, taking the case all the way to the Supreme Court, where she lost. Later, she lobbied to have Congress pass a new law that would make it easier for women to sue their employers for pay discrimination. What normally happens after a party loses his or her case before the Supreme Court? (Scott J. Ferrell/Congressional Quarterly/Getty Images)

Judicial Implementation
The way in which court decisions are translated into action.

27. 128 S.Ct. 2783 (2008).
28. *Baze and Bowling v. Rees,* 128 S.Ct. 152 (2008).
29. *Crawford v. Marion County Election Board,* 553 U.S. __ (2008). Also see the *Which Side Are You On?* feature in Chapter 9 on page 311.
30. *United States v. Williams,* 128 S.Ct. 1830 (2008).
31. The decision referred to was *Cherokee Nation v. Georgia,* 30 U.S. 1 (1831).

Supreme Court ordered schools to desegregate "with all deliberate speed" in 1955.[32] Arkansas governor Orval Faubus refused to cooperate with the decision and used the state's National Guard to block the integration of Central High School in Little Rock. Ultimately, President Dwight Eisenhower had to federalize the Arkansas National Guard and send federal troops to Little Rock to quell the violence that had erupted.

LEGISLATIVE CHECKS

Courts may make rulings, but often the legislatures at local, state, and federal levels are required to appropriate funds to carry out the courts' rulings. A court, for example, may decide that prison conditions must be improved, but it is up to the legislature to authorize the funds necessary to carry out the ruling. When such funds are not appropriated, the court that made the ruling, in effect, has been checked.

Constitutional Amendments. Courts' rulings can be overturned by constitutional amendments at both the federal and state levels. Many of the amendments to the U.S. Constitution (such as the Fourteenth, Fifteenth, and Twenty-sixth Amendments) check the state courts' ability to allow discrimination, for example. Proposed constitutional amendments that were created in an effort to reverse courts' decisions on school prayer, abortion, and same-sex marriage have failed.

Rewriting Laws. Finally, Congress or a state legislature can rewrite (amend) old laws or enact new ones to overturn a court's rulings if the legislature concludes that the court is interpreting laws or legislative intentions erroneously. For example, Congress passed the Civil Rights Act of 1991 in part to overturn a series of conservative rulings in employment-discrimination cases. In 1993, Congress enacted the Religious Freedom Restoration Act (RFRA), which broadened religious liberties, after Congress concluded that a 1990 Supreme Court ruling restricted religious freedom to an unacceptable extent.[33]

According to political scientist Walter Murphy, "A permanent feature of our constitutional landscape is the ongoing tug and pull between elected government and the courts."[34] Certainly, over the last few decades the Supreme Court has been in conflict with the other two branches of government. Congress at various times has passed laws that, among other things, made it illegal to burn the American flag and attempted to curb pornography on the Internet. In each instance, the Supreme Court ruled that those laws were unconstitutional. The Court also invalidated the RFRA, described above. More recently, the Supreme Court and the Bush administration, backed by the Republican-led 109th Congress, engaged in a political tug-of-war over the rights of the prisoners held at Guantánamo Bay, Cuba, as discussed earlier in this chapter.

The states can also negate or alter the effects of Supreme Court rulings, when such decisions allow it. A good case in point is *Kelo v. City of New London*.[35] In that case, the Supreme Court allowed a city to take private property for redevelopment by private businesses. Since that case was decided, a majority of states have passed legislation limiting or prohibiting such takings.

didyouknow...

That Justice Byron ("Whizzer") White (1962–1993) is the only justice to be in the College Football Hall of Fame?

PUBLIC OPINION

Public opinion plays a significant role in shaping government policy, and certainly the judiciary is not excepted from this rule. For one thing, persons affected by a Supreme Court decision that is noticeably at odds with their views may simply ignore it. Officially sponsored prayers were banned in public schools in 1962, yet it was widely known that

---

32. *Brown v. Board of Education,* 349 U.S. 294 (1955)—the second *Brown* decision.
33. *Employment Division, Department of Human Resources of Oregon v. Smith,* 494 U.S. 872 (1990).
34. As quoted in Neal Devins, "The Last Word Debate: How Social and Political Forces Shape Constitutional Values," *American Bar Association Journal,* October 1997, p. 48.
35. 545 U.S. 469 (2005).

the ban was (and still is) ignored in many southern and rural districts. What can the courts do in this situation? Unless someone complains about the prayers and initiates a lawsuit, the courts can do nothing.

The public can also pressure state and local government officials to refuse to enforce a certain decision. As already mentioned, judicial implementation requires the cooperation of government officials at all levels, and public opinion in various regions of the country will influence whether such cooperation is forthcoming.

Additionally, the courts themselves necessarily are influenced by public opinion to some extent. After all, judges are not "islands" in our society; their attitudes are influenced by social trends, just as the attitudes and beliefs of all persons are. Courts generally tend to avoid issuing decisions that they know will be noticeably at odds with public opinion.[36] In part, this is because the judiciary, as a branch of the government, prefers to avoid creating divisiveness among the public. Also, a court—particularly the Supreme Court—may lose stature if it decides a case in a way that markedly diverges from public opinion. For example, in 2002 the Supreme Court ruled that the execution of mentally retarded criminals violates the Eighth Amendment's ban on cruel and unusual punishment. In its ruling, the Court indicated that the standards of what constitutes cruel and unusual punishment are influenced by public opinion and that there is "powerful evidence that today our society views mentally retarded offenders as categorically less culpable than the average criminal."[37]

JUDICIAL TRADITIONS AND DOCTRINES

Supreme Court justices (and other federal judges) typically exercise self-restraint in fashioning their decisions. In part, this restraint stems from their knowledge that the other two branches of government and the public can exercise checks on the judiciary, as previously discussed. To a large extent, however, this restraint is mandated by various judicially established traditions and doctrines. For example, in exercising its discretion to hear appeals, the Supreme Court will not hear a meritless appeal just so it can rule on the issue. Also, when reviewing a case, the Supreme Court typically narrows its focus to just one issue or one aspect of an issue involved in the case. The Court rarely makes broad, sweeping decisions on issues. Furthermore, the doctrine of *stare decisis* acts as a restraint because it obligates the courts, including the Supreme Court, to follow established precedents when deciding cases. Only rarely will courts overrule a precedent.

Hypothetical and Political Questions. Other judicial doctrines and practices also act as restraints. As already mentioned, the courts will hear only what are called justiciable disputes—disputes that arise out of actual cases. In other words, a court will not hear a case that involves a merely hypothetical issue. Additionally, if a political question is involved, the Supreme Court often will exercise judicial restraint and refuse to rule on the matter. A **political question** is one that the Supreme Court declares should be decided by the elected branches of government—the executive branch, the legislative branch, or those two branches acting together. For example, the Supreme Court has refused to rule on the controversy regarding the rights of gay men and lesbians in the military, preferring instead to defer to the executive branch's decisions on the matter. Generally, though, fewer questions are deemed political questions by the Supreme Court today than in the past.

Senator Christopher J. Dodd (D., Conn.) discusses legislation concerning amendments to the Foreign Intelligence Surveillance Act (FISA). At issue was whether telecommunications companies would receive immunity for turning over records requested by the federal government. If an aggrieved party, such as an individual, wants to bring suit against a phone company for violating that person's right to privacy, whom would he or she sue and in what court? (Scott J. Ferrell/Congressional Quarterly/Getty Images)

Political Question
An issue that a court believes should be decided by the executive or legislative branch—or these two branches acting together.

---

36. One striking counterexample is the *Kelo v. City of New London* decision mentioned earlier.
37. *Atkins v. Virginia*, 536 U.S. 304 (2002).

The Impact of the Lower Courts. Higher courts can reverse the decisions of lower courts. Lower courts can act as a check on higher courts, too. Lower courts can ignore—and have ignored—Supreme Court decisions. Usually, this is done indirectly. A lower court might conclude, for example, that the precedent set by the Supreme Court does not apply to the exact circumstances in the case before the court; or the lower court may decide that the Supreme Court's decision was ambiguous with respect to the issue before the lower court. The fact that the Supreme Court rarely makes broad and clear-cut statements on any issue makes it easier for the lower courts to interpret the Supreme Court's decisions in different ways.

WHY SHOULD YOU CARE ABOUT
thecourts?

Why should you, as an individual, care about the courts? The U.S. legal system may seem too complex to be influenced by one individual, but its power nonetheless depends on the support of individuals. The public has many ways of resisting, modifying, or overturning statutes and rulings of the courts.

THE COURTS AND YOUR LIFE

Legislative bodies may make laws and ordinances, but legislation is given its practical form by court rulings. Therefore, if you care about the effects of a particular law, you may have to pay attention to how the courts are interpreting it. For example, do you believe that sentences handed down for certain crimes are too lenient—or too strict? Legislative bodies can attempt to establish sentences for various offenses, but the courts inevitably retain considerable flexibility in determining what happens in any particular case.

HOW YOU CAN MAKE A DIFFERENCE

Public opinion can have an effect on judicial policies. One example of the kind of pressure that can be exerted on the legal system began with a tragedy. In 1980, thirteen-year-old Cari Lightner was hit from behind and killed by a drunk driver while she was walking in a bicycle lane. The driver was a forty-seven-year-old man with two prior drunk-driving convictions. He was at that time out on bail after a third arrest. Cari's mother, Candy, quit her job as a real estate agent to form Mothers Against Drunk Driving (MADD) and launched a campaign to stiffen penalties for drunk-driving convictions.

The organization now has 3 million members and supporters. Outraged by the thousands of lives lost every year because of drunk driving, the group seeks stiff penalties against drunk drivers. MADD, by becoming involved, has gotten results. Owing to the efforts of MADD and other citizen-activist groups, many states have responded with stiffer penalties and deterrents. If you feel strongly about this issue and want to get involved, contact:

MADD
P.O. Box 541688
Dallas, TX 75354-1688
1-800-GET-MADD
www.madd.org.

If you want information about the Supreme Court, contact the following by telephone or letter:

Clerk of the Court
The Supreme Court of the United States
1 First St., N.E.
Washington, DC 20543
202-479-3000

You can access online information about the Supreme Court at the following site:
www.oyez.org.

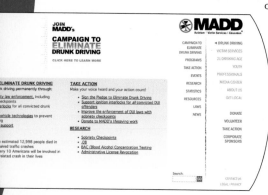

QUESTIONS FOR
discussion**and**analysis

1. Review the *Which Side Are You On?* feature on page 449. Would it be a good idea to increase the number of Supreme Court justices? Why or why not? What impact would such a change have on the Court's workload? How might the change affect the Court's political makeup?

2. What are the benefits of having lifetime appointments to the United States Supreme Court? What problems might such appointments cause? What would be the likely result if Supreme Court justices faced term limits?

3. Under both presidents Bill Clinton and George W. Bush, members of the opposition party in the Senate often blocked the president's nominations to district and circuit courts. Under what circumstances are such blocking actions a legitimate exercise of the Senate's power? Under what circumstances can they rightly be described as inappropriate political maneuvers?

4. On page 460, we described how the Rehnquist Court ruled in favor of states' rights in a gun-control case and against states' rights on a matter concerning marijuana. Why do you think the justices might have come to different conclusions in these two cases?

5. Should Congress ever limit the jurisdiction of the federal courts for political reasons? Should Congress block the Court's ability to rule on cases raised by the prisoners at Guantánamo Bay? Why or why not?

key**terms**

affirm 453
amicus curiae brief 451
appellate court 447
broad construction 459
case law 444
class-action suit 451
common law 443
concurring opinion 454
dissenting opinion 454

diversity of
   citizenship 446
federal question 446
general
   jurisdiction 446
judicial activism 459
judicial
   implementation 463
judicial restraint 459

jurisdiction 446
limited jurisdiction 447
litigate 451
majority opinion 454
opinion 453
oral arguments 453
political question 465
precedent 443
remand 453

reverse 453
rule of four 453
senatorial courtesy 456
stare decisis 443
strict construction 459
trial court 446
unanimous opinion 454
writ of *certiorari* 453

chapter**summary**

1. American law is rooted in the common law tradition, which is part of our heritage from England. The common law doctrine of *stare decisis* (which means "to stand on decided cases") obligates judges to follow precedents established previously by their own courts or by higher courts that have authority over them. Precedents established by the United States Supreme Court, the highest court in the land, are binding on all lower courts. Fundamental sources of American law include the U.S. Constitution and state constitutions, statutes enacted by legislative bodies, regulations issued by administrative agencies, and case law.

2. Article III, Section 1, of the U.S. Constitution limits the jurisdiction of the federal courts to cases involving (a) a federal question, which is a question based, at least in part, on the U.S. Constitution, a treaty, or a federal law; or (b) diversity of citizenship—which arises when parties to a lawsuit are from different states or when the lawsuit involves a foreign citizen or foreign government. The federal court system is a three-tiered model consisting of (a) U.S. district (trial) courts and various lower courts of limited jurisdiction; (b) U.S. courts of appeals; and (c) the United States Supreme Court. Cases may be appealed from the district courts to the appellate courts. In most cases, the decisions of the federal appellate courts are final because the Supreme Court hears relatively few cases.

3. The Supreme Court's decision to review a case is influenced by many factors, including the significance of the issues involved and whether the

solicitor general is pressing the Court to take the case. After a case is accepted, the justices (with the help of their law clerks) undertake research on the issues involved in the case, hear oral arguments from the parties, meet in conference to discuss and vote on the issue, and announce the opinion, which is then released for publication.

4. Federal judges are nominated by the president and confirmed by the Senate. Once appointed, they hold office for life, barring gross misconduct. The nomination and confirmation process, particularly for Supreme Court justices, is often extremely politicized. Democrats and Republicans alike realize that justices may occupy seats on the Court for decades and naturally want to have persons appointed who share their basic views. Nearly 20 percent of all Supreme Court appointments have either been rejected or not acted on by the Senate.

5. In interpreting and applying the law, judges inevitably become policymakers. The most important policymaking tool of the federal courts is the power of judicial review. This power was not mentioned specifically in the Constitution, but the Supreme Court claimed the power for the federal courts in its 1803 decision in *Marbury v. Madison*.

6. Judges who take an active role in checking the activities of the other branches of government sometimes are characterized as "activist" judges, and judges who defer to the other branches' decisions sometimes are regarded as "restraintist" judges. The Warren Court of the 1950s and 1960s was activist in a liberal direction, whereas the Rehnquist and Roberts Courts became increasingly activist in a conservative direction.

7. When William Rehnquist was appointed chief justice in 1986, the Supreme Court began a rightward shift and over time issued a number of conservative opinions. To date, the Roberts Court appears to be continuing the rightward movement of the Court. The Court, however, is fairly evenly divided between strongly conservative justices and liberal-to-moderate justices, with Justice Kennedy often providing swing votes in key cases before the Court.

8. Checks on the powers of the federal courts include executive checks, legislative checks, public opinion, and judicial traditions and doctrines.

selected print&media resources

SUGGESTED READINGS

Bach, Amy. *Ordinary Injustice: How America Holds Court.* New York: Metropolitan Books, 2009. In an investigation that moves from small-town Georgia to upstate New York, from Chicago to Mississippi, lawyer Amy Bach uncovers the chronic injustice meted out daily to ordinary Americans by a legal system so underfunded and understaffed that it is a menace to the people it is designed to serve.

Greenburg, Jan Crawford. *Supreme Conflict: The Inside Story of the Struggle for Control of the United States Supreme Court.* New York: Penguin Press, 2007. Greenburg, a reporter who has covered the Supreme Court for many years, presents a very readable account of the inner workings of the Court, the justices' personalities, and the various persuasive strategies used by the justices in building coalitions.

Roosevelt, Kermit. *The Myth of Judicial Activism: Making Sense of Supreme Court Decisions.* New Haven, Conn.: Yale University Press, 2008. Roosevelt, a University of Pennsylvania professor, defends the Court against charges of undue judicial activism. Roosevelt finds the Court's decisions to be reasonable, although he disagrees with some of them.

Rosen, Jeffrey. *The Supreme Court: The Personalities and Rivalries That Defined America.* New York: Times Books, 2007. Rosen, a longtime scholar of the Supreme Court, describes how the ideologies, personalities, and personal styles of the justices on the Court affect their decision making.

MEDIA RESOURCES

Amistad—A 1997 movie, starring Anthony Hopkins, about a slave ship mutiny in 1839. Much of the story revolves around the prosecution, ending at the Supreme Court, of the slave who led the revolt.

Gideon's Trumpet—A 1980 film, starring Henry Fonda as the small-time criminal James Earl Gideon, which makes clear the path a case takes to the Supreme Court and the importance of cases decided there.

Justice Sandra Day O'Connor—In a 1994 program, Bill Moyers conducts Justice O'Connor's first television interview. Topics include women's rights, O'Connor's role as the Supreme Court's first female justice, and her difficulties breaking into the male-dominated legal profession. O'Connor defends her positions on affirmative action and abortion.

The Magnificent Yankee—A 1950 movie, starring Louis Calhern and Ann Harding, that traces the life and philosophy of Oliver Wendell Holmes, Jr., one of the Supreme Court's most brilliant justices.

Marbury v. Madison—A 1987 video on the famous 1803 case that established the principle of judicial review.

The Supreme Court—A four-part PBS series that won a 2008 Parents' Choice Gold Award. The series fol-lows the history of the Supreme Court from the first chief justice, John Marshall, to the earliest days of the Roberts Court. Some of the many top-ics are the Court's dismal performance in the Civil War era, its conflicts with President Franklin D. Roosevelt, its role in banning the segregation of African Americans, and the abortion controversy.

e-mocracy

COURTS ON THE WEB

Most courts in the United States have sites on the Web. These sites vary in what they include. Some courts simply display contact information for court personnel. Others include recent judicial decisions along with court rules and forms. Many federal courts permit attorneys to file documents electronically. The information available on these sites continues to grow as courts try to avoid being left behind in the information age. One day, courts may decide to implement *virtual courtrooms,* in which judi-cial proceedings take place totally via the Internet. The Internet may ultimately provide at least a partial solution to the twin problems of overloaded dockets and the high time and financial costs of litigation.

LOGGING ON

The home page of the federal courts is a good starting point for learning about the federal court system in gen-eral. At this site, you can even follow the path of a case as it moves through the federal court system. Go to **www.uscourts.gov**.

To access the Supreme Court's official Web site, on which Supreme Court decisions are made available within hours of their release, go to **www.supremecourtus.gov**.

Several Web sites offer searchable databases of Supreme Court decisions. You can access Supreme Court cases since 1970 at FindLaw's site: **www.findlaw.com**.

The following Web site also offers an easily searchable index to Supreme Court opinions, including some impor-tant historic decisions: **www.law.cornell.edu/supct**.

You can find information on the justices of the Supreme Court, as well as their decisions, at **www.oyez.org**.

14

Domestic and Economic Policy

Traders on the floor of the New York Stock Exchange in October 2008, during a period known at the Crash of 2008, when stock prices experienced huge swings over several weeks. (AP Photo/Richard Drew)

what**if**...we had universal health care?

BACKGROUND

Currently, more than 40 million Americans do not have health insurance. Some of those uninsured are between jobs; others are young people who are single and healthy and have chosen *not* to purchase health insurance. Others are unable to purchase health insurance because they are homeless; have preexisting conditions, such as diabetes, AIDS, or cancer; or simply cannot afford it. In the United States, those without such insurance often seek primary care in hospital emergency rooms. According to two Pulitzer Prize–winning journalists, "U.S. health care is second rate at the start of the twenty-first century and destined to get a lot worse and more expensive."[a]

As noted in Chapter 6, the public has frequently ranked health care as one of the most important problems facing the nation. The 2008 presidential candidates proposed a variety of health care reforms in response to this public concern. Some of the plans would have the effect of providing universal health care.

WHAT IF WE HAD UNIVERSAL HEALTH CARE?

With universal health care, everyone in need of basic medical care would have access to physicians, clinics, hospitals, and the like. Note that when we refer to universal health care, we are not specifying how such a service would be funded—a major political issue. Most wealthy nations other than the United States have universal, government-administered health insurance systems, but other models are certainly possible.

THE SAN FRANCISCO EXPERIMENT

To look at one way that universal health care might work, we can go to San Francisco, where a universal health-care plan was approved in the summer of 2006. The San Francisco Health Access Plan, as it is called, is financed by local government, mandatory contributions from employers, and income-adjusted premiums from users.

Enrollment fees range from $3 to $201, and most participants pay $35 a month. Uninsured San Franciscans can then seek comprehensive primary care in the city's public and private clinics and hospitals. San Francisco mayor Gavin Newsom described the city's historic undertaking as a "moral obligation."

Not everybody in the city is happy about the new plan, however. To offset the estimated annual price tag of more than $200 million, firms with twenty or more workers have to contribute about a dollar per hour worked by any employee. Firms with more than a hundred workers have to pay $1.60 per hour, up to a monthly maximum of $180 per worker.

Many contend that these added costs are making it difficult for new businesses to locate in San Francisco. They also argue that goods and services within the city will become increasingly more expensive as employers pass on the added health-care costs to customers.

THE RELATIONSHIP BETWEEN UNIVERSAL HEALTH-CARE ACCESS AND THE NUMBER OF UNINSURED

Economic analysis yields a simple relationship between price and quantity demanded—the lower the price, the higher the quantity demanded. Medical care is a service like any other. If medical care is provided at a lower price to those who desire it, more medical care will be demanded.

We can predict that if a universal health-care plan like the one in San Francisco were implemented, the number of people without health insurance would increase. To understand this, consider how people would behave if universal health-care access became a reality. Over time, some individuals and families would choose not to renew their health insurance because they would know that they could rely on universal health-care access. Consequently, the existence of universal health care would actually increase the number of those who do not have health insurance.

THE RELATIONSHIP BETWEEN UNIVERSAL HEALTH CARE AND THE BURDEN ON CLINICS AND HOSPITALS

It is likely that, as more individuals and families took advantage of universal health-care access, the burden on existing clinics and hospitals would increase. Health-insurance companies have the data. Those individuals who have health-insurance policies with zero or small deductibles utilize the services of the health-care sector much more than those who have a high deductible. In essence, universal health-care coverage is the equivalent of having a zero deductible for primary care. Additionally, the health-care system would require more general practitioners and fewer emergency-room physicians. Under current conditions, emergency rooms are a major source of health care for the uninsured.

FOR CRITICAL ANALYSIS

1. Administratively, what is the difference between setting up San Francisco–style universal health care and providing universal health insurance?
2. If universal health-care access became a reality, how would physicians have to alter their practices?

---

a. Donald Barlett and James Steele, *Critical Condition* (New York: Broadway Books, 2006).

Frequently, when a policy decision is made, some groups are better off and some groups are hurt. Policymaking typically involves such a dilemma.

Part of the public-policy debate in our nation involves domestic problems. **Domestic policy** can be defined as all of the laws, government planning, and government actions that concern internal issues of national importance. Consequently, the span of such policies is enormous. Domestic policies range from relatively simple issues, such as what the speed limit should be on interstate highways, to more complex ones, such as how best to protect our environment or whether we should have universal health-care access, as discussed in this chapter's opening *What If . . .* feature. Many of our domestic policies are formulated and implemented by the federal government, but a number of others are the result of the combined efforts of federal, state, and local governments.

It is possible to define several types of domestic policy. *Regulatory policy* seeks to define what is and is not legal. Setting speed limits is obviously regulatory policy. *Redistributive policy* transfers income from certain individuals or groups to others, often based on the belief that these transfers enhance fairness. Social Security is an example. *Promotional policy* seeks to foster or discourage various economic or social activities, typically through subsidies and tax breaks. The farm bill, which we describe shortly, is an example, although the bill's large food stamp component is more properly considered to be redistributive policy.

In this chapter, we look at domestic policy issues involving health care, poverty and welfare, immigration, crime, and the environment. We also examine national economic policies undertaken by the federal government. Before we start our analysis, though, we must look at how public policies are made.

> **Domestic Policy**
> All government laws, planning, and actions that concern internal issues of national importance, such as poverty, crime, and the environment.

THE POLICYMAKING PROCESS

How does any issue get resolved? First, of course, the issue must be identified as a problem. Often, policymakers have only to open their local newspapers—or letters from their constituents—to discover that a problem is brewing. On rare occasions, a crisis, such as that brought about by the terrorist attacks of September 11, 2001, creates the need to formulate policy. Like most Americans, however, policymakers receive much of their information from the national media. Finally, various lobbying groups provide information to members of Congress.

As an example of policymaking, consider the $307 billion farm bill that became law over President George W. Bush's veto in 2008. The new farm bill provided for a continuation of all payments to farmers for at least another five years. Since 1970, farm subsidies have exceeded $650 billion. The origin of our current farm legislation is the Agricultural Adjustment Act, a bill signed into law by President Franklin D. Roosevelt on May 12, 1933. This original farming legislation allowed the government to control crop production and to pay farmers to limit plantings. Stabilizing farmers' incomes became a political matter in 1933 and has continued to be one ever since. When the first subsidies were given to farmers during the Great Depression, their per capita income was a third lower than nonfarm incomes. Today, in contrast, per capita farm income is about a third higher than the U.S. average income.

No matter how simple or how complex the problems, those who make policy follow a number of steps. We can divide

These senators were conferring during a House-Senate conference on the 2008 farm bill. There were many issues to work out. Nonetheless, a compromise bill was hammered out that gave "something to everybody." Who benefits from subsidizing farm production? Who pays for subsidizing farm production? (Scott J. Ferrell/Congressional Quarterly/Getty Images)

the process of policymaking into at least five steps: agenda building, policy formulation, policy adoption, policy implementation, and policy evaluation. We look next at each of these steps, particularly with reference to the passage of the 2008 farm bill.

AGENDA BUILDING

First of all, issues must get on the agenda. In other words, Congress must become aware that an issue requires congressional action. Agenda building may occur as the result of a crisis, technological change, or mass media campaign, as well as through the efforts of strong political personalities and effective lobbying groups.

The new farm bill became part of the agenda in a much more mundane way. The old farm bill was expiring in the fall of 2007. The American Farm Bureau Federation and other agricultural organizations started putting out their "feelers" in Congress in 2005. Over the next two years, lobbying groups for the commercial crops of corn, cotton, rice, soybeans, and wheat intensified their work in the halls of Congress. Additionally, lobbyists for sugar, honey, and dairy producers argued for an expansion of their price supports.

Not to be outdone, lobbyists for fruit, vegetable, and nut growers pitched in hard to get something added to the new farm bill. California asparagus growers wanted a piece of the action, as did Idaho chickpea producers. Lobbyists for North Dakota and Washington producers of dried peas and lentils also walked the halls of Congress during this period, attempting to add subsidies for these agricultural products. Georgia peanut farmers lobbied hard for additional aid each year in the future.

For decades, dairy farmers have received subsidies from the federal government. Their lobbyists plied the halls of Congress starting in 2005 all the way up to the signing of the new farm bill in 2008. They argued for an expansion of their price supports. What kind of arguments would you use if you were a lobbyist for the dairy farmers in order to convince members of Congress to increase dairy price supports? (©Peter Clark, 2008. Used under license from Shutterstock.com)

POLICY FORMULATION

During the next step in the policymaking process, various policy proposals are discussed among government officials and the public. Such discussions may take place in the printed media, on television, on the Internet, and in the halls of Congress. Congress holds hearings, the president voices the administration's views, and the topic may even become a campaign issue.

During the policy formation phase surrounding the new farm bill, there was relatively little discussion of the bill on television or radio news shows. The printed media, though, did start voicing concerns that the new farm bill would increase subsidies to farmers during a period of rising food prices. Throughout 2007 and 2008, food prices rose faster than at any time in the previous eighteen years. By the end of 2007, for example, corn prices were twice as high as they had been at the beginning of 2006. In 2007 alone, farming incomes climbed by 44 percent.

The Bush administration indicated in 2007 that the president would veto any farm bill that increased subsidies to already-rich farmers. Many conservative members of Congress raised their voices against such "wasteful" spending for a group of Americans who are far from poor. Both Republicans and Democrats in Congress voiced concerns about the excessive subsidies during a time of rising food prices.

POLICY ADOPTION

The third step in the policymaking process involves choosing a specific policy from among the proposals that have been discussed. Because members of Congress had been warned that President Bush would veto the farm bill, they had to come up with enough supporters to override any presidential veto. (Remember from Chapter 11 that a two-thirds majority vote in each chamber of Congress is required to override a presidential veto.) To obtain that support, many additions to the new farm bill were created to make sure that members of Congress from farming regions and big cities alike would vote for the bill. So, the final bill included a $93 million tax benefit to thoroughbred racehorse owners, as well as increased payments to food stamp recipients. Organic farmers got funds for research, data collection, and certification help for small growers. Environmentalists obtained $4 billion of new funding for their programs. Not surprisingly, members of the House who created the bill, who constituted only one-tenth of the members of that chamber, obtained for their districts 45 percent of the benefits of the commercial crop subsidies.

Notably, partisanship played an insignificant role with respect to the new farm legislation. Both Democrats and Republicans worked together to create the largest farm bill ever.

POLICY IMPLEMENTATION

The fourth step in the policymaking process involves the implementation of the policy alternative chosen by government. Government policies must be implemented by bureaucrats, the courts, the police, and individual citizens. With respect to the new farm bill, most of it went into effect almost immediately after its passage in 2008. The federal funds started flowing to designated individuals and groups who were meant to receive direct and indirect payments. These payments will continue through 2012, when the process of creating yet another farm bill will start again (if not several years before).

POLICY EVALUATION

After a policy has been implemented, it is evaluated. Groups inside and outside the government conduct studies to determine what actually happens after a policy has been in place for a given period of time. Based on this feedback and the perceived success or failure of the policy, a new round of policymaking initiatives might be undertaken to improve on the effort. Because the new farm bill is just a continuation of previous farm legislation, we already have numerous studies that demonstrate the effectiveness of such legislation. We know that the majority of direct subsidies—as much as 90 percent—are paid to the top 10 percent of farm income earners. We know that past farm legislation has raised America's food expenditures by at least $12 billion a year. In other words, we have a lot of analyses of past farm legislation that will be re-created when examining the now-current farm legislation.

Food prices rose
rather dramatically in 2007 and 2008. Why do you believe that agricultural producers, nonetheless, obtained a big increase in subsidies from the federal government? (©Jyn Meyer, 2008. Used under license from Shutterstock.com)

Gross Domestic Product (GDP)
The dollar value of all final goods and services produced in a one-year period.

HEALTH CARE

Spending for health care is estimated to account for about 16 percent of the total U.S. economy. In 1965, about 6 percent of our income was spent on health care (as shown in Figure 14–1), but that percentage has been increasing ever since. Per capita spending on health care is greater in the United States than almost anywhere else in the world. Measured by the percentage of the **gross domestic product (GDP)** devoted to health care, America spends almost twice as much as Britain or Spain—see Figure 14–2 on the next page. (The GDP is the dollar value of all final goods and services produced in a one-year period.)

THE RISING COST OF HEALTH CARE

Numerous explanations exist for why health-care costs have risen so much. At least one has to do with changing demographics—the U.S. population is getting older. Life expectancy has gone up, as shown

FIGURE 14–1: Percentage of Total National Income Spent on Health Care in the United States

The portion of total national income spent on health care has risen steadily since 1965.

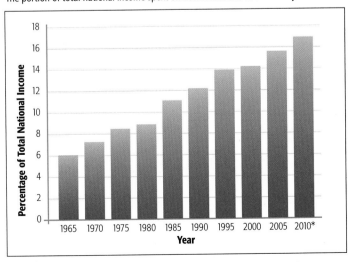

*Estimate

Sources: U.S. Department of Commerce; U.S. Department of Health and Human Services; Deloitte and Touche LLP; and VHA, Inc.

FIGURE 14–2: Cost of Health Care in Economically Advanced Nations

Cost is given as a percentage of total gross domestic product (GDP).

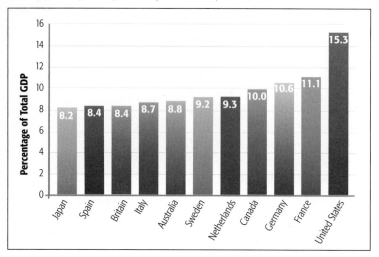

Source: Organization for Economic Cooperation and Development, *OECD Health Data,* 2008.

Medicare
A federal health-insurance program that covers U.S. residents over the age of sixty-five. The costs are met by a tax on wages and salaries.

Medicaid
A joint state-federal program that provides medical care to the poor (including indigent elderly persons in nursing homes). The program is funded out of general government revenues.

FIGURE 14–3: Life Expectancy in the United States

Along with health-care spending, life expectancy has gone up. Therefore, we are presumably getting some return for our spending.

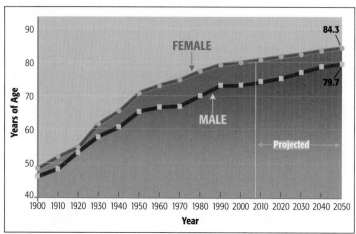

Source: Social Security Administration, Office of the Chief Actuary.

in Figure 14–3. The top 5 percent of those using health care incur over 50 percent of all health-care costs. The bottom 70 percent of health-care users account for only 10 percent of health-care expenditures. Not surprisingly, the elderly make up most of the top users of health-care services. Nursing home expenditures are generally made by people older than age seventy. The use of hospitals is also dominated by the aged.

Advanced Technology. Another reason why health-care costs have risen so dramatically is advancing technology. A CT (computerized tomography) scanner costs more than $1 million. An MRI (magnetic resonance imaging) scanner can cost more than $2 million. A PET (positron-emission tomography) scanner can cost up to $4 million. All of these machines have become increasingly available in recent decades and are in demand around the country. Procedures using these scanners are also costly. For example, CT scans can cost $1,000 and up. Typically, fees for PET scans are two or three times that amount. The development of new technologies that help physicians and hospitals prolong human life is an ongoing process in an ever-advancing industry. New procedures that involve even greater costs can be expected in the future.

The Government's Role in Financing Health Care. Currently, government spending on health care constitutes more than 45 percent of total health-care spending. Private insurance accounts for just under 35 percent of payments for health care. The remainder—less than 20 percent—is paid directly by individuals or by philanthropy. Medicare and Medicaid are the main sources of hospital and other medical benefits for 40 million U.S. residents, most of whom are over the age of sixty-five.

Medicare is specifically designed to support the elderly, regardless of income. **Medicaid,** a joint state-federal program, is in principle a program to subsidize health care for the poor. In practice, it often provides long-term health care to persons living in nursing homes. (To become eligible for Medicaid, these individuals must first exhaust their financial assets.) Medicare, Medicaid, and private insurance companies are called *third parties.* Caregivers and patients are the two primary parties. When third parties pay for medical care, the quantity demanded of such services increases; health-care recipients have no incentive to restrain their use of health care. One result is some degree of wasted resources.

MEDICARE

The Medicare program, which was created in 1965 under President Lyndon Johnson (1963–1969), pays hospital and physicians' bills for U.S. residents over the age of sixty-five. Since 2006,

Medicare has also paid for at least part of the prescription drug expenses of the elderly. In return for paying a tax on their earnings (currently set at 2.9 percent of wages and salaries) while in the workforce, retirees are assured that the majority of their hospital and physicians' bills will be paid for with public funds.

Medicare is now the second-largest domestic spending program, after Social Security. One response by the federal government to soaring Medicare costs has been to impose arbitrary reimbursement caps on specific procedures. To avoid going over Medicare's reimbursement caps, however, hospitals have sometimes discharged patients too soon or in an unstable condition. The government has also cut rates of reimbursement to individual physicians and physician groups, such as health maintenance organizations (HMOs). One consequence has been a nearly 15 percent reduction in the amount the government pays for Medicare services provided by physicians. As a result, physicians and HMOs have become reluctant to accept Medicare patients. Several of the nation's largest HMOs have withdrawn from certain Medicare programs. A growing number of physicians now refuse to treat Medicare patients.

MEDICAID

Within a few short years, the joint federal-state taxpayer-funded Medicaid program for the "working poor" has generated one of the biggest expansions of government entitlements in the last fifty years. In 1997, federal Medicaid spending was around $150 billion. Ten years later, it easily exceeded $300 billion. At the end of the last decade, 34 million people were enrolled in the program. Today, there are more than 50 million. When you add Medicaid coverage to Medicare and the military and federal employee health plans, the government has clearly become the nation's primary health insurer. More than 100 million people—one in three—in the United States have government coverage.

Why Has Medicaid Spending Exploded? One of the reasons Medicaid has become such an important health-insurance program is that the income ceiling for eligibility has increased to twice the "poverty level" of income in most states, which is currently about $20,000 for a family of four. In other words, a family of four can earn up to $40,000 and still obtain health insurance through Medicaid for its children. Indeed, many low-income workers choose Medicaid over health insurance offered by employers. Why? The reason is that Medicaid is less costly and sometimes covers more medical expenses. Indeed, to most recipients, Medicaid is either free or almost free.

Medicaid and the States. On average, the federal government pays almost 60 percent of Medicaid's cost—the states pay the rest. Certain states, particularly in the South, receive even higher reimbursements. In general, such states are not complaining about the expansion of Medicaid. Other states, however, such as New York, have been overwhelmed by the rate of increase in Medicaid spending. Even with the federal government's partial reimbursement, the portion paid by the states has increased so rapidly that the states are finding themselves financially strapped. Florida, for example, had to drastically revise its Medicaid eligibility rules to reduce the number of families using Medicaid. Otherwise, the state projected a budget deficit that it would not be able to handle.

THE UNINSURED

More than 40 million Americans—about 16 percent of the population—do not have health insurance. The proportion of the population that is uninsured varies from one part of the country to another. In Hawaii and Minnesota, only 7 percent of working adults lack coverage. In Texas, however, the figure is 27 percent. According to the Congressional Black Caucus Foundation, African Americans, Hispanics, and Asian/Pacific Islanders make up more than half of the year-round uninsured, even though they constitute only 29 percent of the total U.S. population. Hispanic Americans are the most likely to be uninsured, with only 35 percent of working Hispanic adults having coverage.

These members of the Mississippi state senate are attempting to pass legislation that will ease that state's Medicare deficit. How does a state, even one that obtains a 60 percent federal reimbursement for Medicare expenditures, end up with a budgetary problem? (AP Photo/Rogelio V. Solis)

According to surveys, being uninsured has negative health consequences. People without coverage are less likely to get basic preventive care, such as mammograms; less likely to have a personal physician; and more likely to rate their own health as only poor or fair.

The uninsured population is relatively young, in part due to Medicare, which covers almost everyone over the age of sixty-five. Also, younger workers are more likely to be employed in entry-level jobs that do not offer health-insurance benefits. The current system of health care in the United States assumes that employers will provide health insurance to working-age persons. Many small businesses, however, simply cannot afford to offer their workers health insurance. Average insurance benefits now cost more than $20,000 per year for each covered employee, according to the U.S. Chamber of Commerce.

A further problem faced by the uninsured is that when they do seek medical care, they must usually pay much higher fees than would be paid on their behalf if they had insurance coverage. Large third-party insurers, private or public, normally strike hard bargains with hospitals and physicians over how much they will pay for procedures and services. The uninsured have less bargaining power. As a result, hospitals attempt to recover from the uninsured the revenues they lose from underpaying third-party insurers. One result is that individual health-insurance policies (those not obtained through an employer) are extremely costly, and for persons with preexisting health conditions this coverage may be impossible to obtain at any price.

One benefit of insurance coverage is that it protects the insured against catastrophic costs resulting from unusual events. Medical care for life-threatening accidents or diseases can run into tens or even hundreds of thousands of dollars. An uninsured person who requires this kind of medical care may be forced into bankruptcy.

THE ISSUE OF UNIVERSAL COVERAGE

The United States is the only advanced industrial country with a large pool of citizens who lack health insurance. Australia, Canada, Japan, and Western Europe all provide systems of universal coverage. Such coverage is typically provided through **national health insurance.** In effect, the government takes over the economic function of providing basic health-care coverage. Private insurers are excluded from this market (though they may be able to offer supplementary plans). The government collects premiums from employers and employees on the basis of their ability to pay and then provides basic services to the entire population.

Because the government provides all basic insurance coverage, national health insurance systems are often called *single-payer plans.* Such plans can significantly reduce administrative overhead, because physicians need deal with only a single set of forms and requirements. The number of employees required to process claims is also lowered. In France, for example, which has national health insurance, administrative overhead is 5 percent of total costs, compared with 14 percent in the United States. The French experience suggests that containing unnecessary procedures may be more difficult with a single-payer plan, however.

The Clinton Health Care Proposal. Since the time of President Harry Truman (1945–1953), some liberals have sought to establish a national health-insurance system in this

National Health Insurance
Programs offered in most advanced countries under which the central government provides basic health insurance to all citizens. In most such plans, the program is funded by taxes on wages or salaries.

country. During his first two years in office, President Bill Clinton (1993–2001) attempted to steer such a proposal through Congress. Clinton's plan, developed by a panel chaired by his wife, Hillary Clinton, was dauntingly complex, and the Clintons failed to build the political groundwork necessary for such a major change. Lobbyists for private insurance companies knew the Clinton program would deprive them of a major line of business and naturally did everything in their power to stop the bill. In the end, the proposal was defeated. Indeed, the proposal may have been an important reason why the Republicans gained control of Congress in the 1994 elections.

A Republican Alternative: The Health Savings Account. In 2003, President Bush and the Republican-led Congress created the health savings account (HSA) program as an alternative to completely changing the U.S. health-care industry. Most taxpayers can set up a tax-free HSA, which must be combined with a high-deductible health-insurance policy. As of 2008, eligible individuals or families could make an annual tax-deductible contribution to an HSA up to a limit of $2,900 per individual or $5,800 per family. Funds in the HSA accumulate tax free, and distributions of HSA funds for medical expenses are also exempt. Any funds remaining in an HSA after an individual reaches age sixty-five can be withdrawn tax free. The benefits can be impressive—a single person depositing around $1,500 each year with no withdrawals will have hundreds of thousands of dollars in the account after forty years. Plans may be sponsored by employers.

For individuals using an HSA, the physician-patient relationship remains intact because third-party payers do not intervene in paying or monitoring medical expenses. The patients, rather than third parties, have an incentive to discourage their physicians from ordering expensive tests for every minor ache and pain because they are allowed to keep any funds saved in the HSA. Some critics argue that HSA participants might also forgo necessary medical attention and develop more serious medical problems as a consequence. Also, HSAs do not address the issue of universal access to health care. After all, even if HSAs became common, not everyone would be willing or able to participate. In January 2008, about 4.5 million Americans were covered by HSA plans, up from 3.2 million in 2006.

Recent Proposals. In the first decade of the twenty-first century, universal health insurance began to revive as a political issue. Unlike national health insurance plans, **universal health insurance** does not provide for a federal monopoly on basic heath insurance.

Universal Health Insurance
Any of several possible programs to provide health insurance to everyone in the country. The central government does not necessarily provide the insurance itself, but may subsidize the purchase of insurance from private insurance companies.

These New York City health-care workers support universal health care. What is the difference between universal health care and universal health insurance? (AP Photo/Jennifer Graylock)

Instead, universal coverage results from a mandate that all citizens must buy health insurance from some source—through an employer, Medicare or Medicaid, private coverage, or a new plan sponsored by the federal or state government. Low-income families would receive a subsidy to help them pay their insurance premiums. Insurers could not reject applicants.

The first program of this nature was adopted by the state of Massachusetts in 2006 in response to a proposal by Republican governor Mitt Romney. The plan actually adopted was more generous than Romney's initial proposal. In 2007, Arnold Schwarzenegger, Republican governor of California, suggested a similar plan for his state, but lawmakers balked at the cost.

In their campaigns for the 2008 Democratic presidential nomination, former senator John Edwards (D., N.C.) and Senator Hillary Clinton (D., N.Y.) called for universal coverage plans. Although both plans relied on private insurers, each would offer much more extensive coverage than the Massachusetts plan. Senator Barack Obama (D., Ill.), the eventual winner of the presidential race, proposed a plan that limited universal coverage to children. Parents would be required to purchase insurance for their children, which presumably would be relatively inexpensive because most children are healthy. Obama's plan also sought to make insurance coverage for adults universally available and affordable, but it would not require adults to actually buy coverage.

While Republican candidates offered a variety of health-care proposals, all of the Republicans opposed any move to universal national coverage—this was true even of Romney, who had supported a universal coverage plan for his own state. Senator John McCain (R., Ariz.), the Republican nominee, proposed a plan that expanded on the HSA concept. McCain's plan would subsidize private insurance for families not participating in employer-provided insurance plans. Resolving the issue of persons who cannot purchase private plans because of preexisting conditions would be left largely to the states, however. Clearly, under President Obama, health-care reform is poised to become one of the most important issues facing the 111th Congress.

POVERTY AND WELFARE

Throughout the world, poverty has historically been accepted as inevitable. The United States and other industrialized nations, however, have sustained enough economic growth in the past several hundred years to eliminate mass poverty. In fact, considering the wealth and high standard of living in the United States, the persistence of poverty here appears bizarre and anomalous. How can there still be so much poverty in a nation of so much abundance? And what can be done about it?

A traditional solution has been **income transfers.** These are methods of transferring income from relatively well-to-do to relatively poor groups in society, and as a nation, we have been using such transfers for a long time. Before we examine these efforts, let us look at the concept of poverty in more detail and at the characteristics of the poor.

Income Transfer
A transfer of income from some individuals in the economy to other individuals. This is generally done by government action.

THE LOW-INCOME POPULATION

We can see in Figure 14–4 that the number of people classified as poor fell steadily from 1961 to 1968—that is, during the presidencies of John Kennedy and Lyndon Johnson. The number remained level until the recession of 1981–1982, under Ronald Reagan, when it increased substantially. The number fell during the "Internet boom" of 1994–2000, but then it started to rise again. For 2008, the official poverty level for a family of four was $21,200. The official poverty level is based on pre-tax income, including cash but not **in-kind subsidies**—food stamps, housing vouchers, and the like. If we correct poverty levels for such benefits, the percentage of the population that is below the poverty line drops dramatically.

FIGURE 14–4: The Official Number of Poor in the United States

The number of individuals classified as poor fell steadily from 1961 through 1968. It then increased during the 1981–1982 recession. After 1994, the number fell steadily until 2000, when it started to rise again.

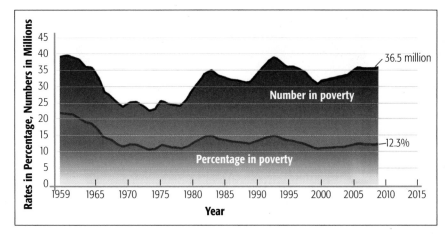

Source: U.S. Department of Labor.

THE ANTIPOVERTY BUDGET

It is not always easy to determine how much the government spends to combat poverty. In part, this is because it can be difficult to decide whether a particular program is an antipoverty program. Are grants to foster parents an antipoverty measure? What about job-training programs? Are college scholarships for low-income students an antipoverty measure? President George W. Bush's federal budget for 2009 allocated $19 billion for such scholarships.

In 2008, the federal government spent $445.5 billion on antipoverty programs, or about 3 percent of the nation's total gross domestic product. (This sum does not include the earned-income tax credit program, which we describe shortly.) Of this amount, $203.8 billion was for Medicaid, which funds medical services for the poor, as discussed earlier. The states were expected to contribute about an additional $150 billion to Medicaid. Medical care is by far the largest portion of the antipoverty budget. One reason medical spending is high is the widespread belief that everyone should receive medical care that at least approximates the care received by an average person. No such belief supports spending for other purposes, such as shelter or transportation. Elderly people receive 70 percent of Medicaid spending.

BASIC WELFARE

Only a small share of the funds involved in the government's antipoverty spending is paid directly to individuals. The program that most people think of when they hear the word *welfare* is called **Temporary Assistance to Needy Families (TANF).** With the passage in 1996 of the Personal Responsibility and Work Opportunity Reconciliation Act, popularly known as the Welfare Reform Act, the government created TANF to replace an earlier program known as Aid to Families with Dependent Children (AFDC). The AFDC program provided "cash support for low-income families with dependent children who have been deprived of parental support due to death, disability, continued absence of a parent, or unemployment." Unlike AFDC, TANF consists of block grants to the states.

One of the aims of the Welfare Reform Act was to reduce welfare spending. To do this, the act made two significant changes in the basic welfare program. One change

didyouknow...

That the **Greenville County** Department of Social Services in South Carolina wrote to a food stamp recipient, "Your food stamps will be stopped . . . because we received notice that you passed away. May God bless you. You may reapply if there is a change in your circumstances."?

In-Kind Subsidy
A good or service—such as food stamps, housing, or medical care—provided by the government to low-income groups.

Temporary Assistance to Needy Families (TANF)
A state-administered program in which grants from the national government are used to provide welfare benefits. The TANF program replaced the Aid to Families with Dependent Children (AFDC) program.

This single parent benefited from the Access Project, a program that offers a free college education to welfare-eligible parents in central New York. (AP Photo/Kevin Rivoli)

was to limit most welfare recipients to only two years of assistance at a time. The second change was to impose a lifetime limit on welfare assistance of five years. The Welfare Reform Act has largely met its objectives. During the first five years after the act was passed, the number of families receiving welfare payments was cut in half. As a result, welfare spending is no longer the burning political issue that it was until 1996. The 2009 federal buget allocated $16.9 billion to TANF block grants.

Whether known as AFDC or TANF, however, the basic welfare program has always been controversial. Conservative and libertarian voters often object to welfare spending as a matter of principle, believing that it reduces the incentive to find paid employment. Because AFDC and TANF have largely supported single-parent households, some also believe that such programs are antimarriage. Finally, certain people object to welfare spending out of a belief that welfare recipients are "not like us." In fact, non-Hispanic whites made up only 30 percent of TANF recipients in the early 2000s. As a result of all these factors, basic welfare payments in the United States are relatively low compared with similar payments in other industrialized nations. In 2008, the average monthly TANF payment nationwide was about $435 per family.

OTHER FORMS OF GOVERNMENT ASSISTANCE

The **Supplemental Security Income (SSI)** program was established in 1974 to provide a nationwide minimum income for elderly persons and persons with disabilities who do not qualify for Social Security benefits. The 2009 budget allocated $43.2 billion to this program.

The government also issues **food stamps,** benefits that can be used to purchase food; they are usually provided electronically through a card similar to a debit card. Food stamps are available to low-income individuals and families. Recipients must prove that they qualify by showing that they have a low income (or no income at all). Food stamps go to a much larger group of people than TANF payments. The food stamp program has become a major part of the welfare system in the United States, although it was started in 1964 mainly to benefit farmers by distributing surplus food through retail channels.

The 2008 farm bill, which was passed over President Bush's veto, allocated $209 billion to food stamps and related nutrition spending. The bill also renamed the food stamp program to be the Supplemental Nutrition Assistance Program, or SNAP.

The **earned-income tax credit (EITC) program** was created in 1975 to help low-income workers by giving back part or all of their Social Security and Medicare payroll taxes. Currently, about 17 percent of all taxpayers claim an EITC, and more than $46 billion a year is rebated to taxpayers through the program.

IMMIGRATION

Today, immigration rates for the United States are among the highest they have been since their peak in the early twentieth century. Every year, more than one million people immigrate to this country legally, a figure that does not include the large number of unauthorized immigrants. People who were born on foreign soil now constitute about 13 percent of the U.S. population—more than twice the percentage of thirty years ago.

Since 1977, four out of five immigrants have come from Latin America or Asia. Hispanics have overtaken African Americans as the nation's largest minority. As you

Supplemental Security Income (SSI)
A federal program established to provide assistance to elderly persons and persons with disabilities.

Food Stamps
Benefits issued by the federal government to low-income individuals to be used for the purchase of food; originally provided as coupons but now typically provided electronically through a card similar to a debit card.

Earned-Income Tax Credit (EITC) Program
A government program that helps low-income workers by giving back part or all of their Social Security taxes.

learned in Chapter 5, if current immigration rates continue, by the year 2042, minority groups collectively will constitute the "majority" of Americans. If Hispanics, African Americans, and perhaps Asians were to form coalitions, they could increase their political power dramatically and would have the numerical strength to make significant changes. According to Ben Wattenberg of the American Enterprise Institute, in the future the "old guard" white majority will no longer dominate American politics.

Some regard the high rate of immigration as a plus for America because it offsets the low birthrate and aging population, which we also discussed in Chapter 5. Immigrants expand the workforce and help to support, through their taxes, government programs that benefit older Americans, such as Medicare and Social Security. If it were not for immigration, contend these observers, the United States would be facing even more serious problems than it already does with funding these programs (see the discussion of Social Security later in this chapter). In contrast, nations that do not have high immigration rates, such as Japan, are experiencing serious fiscal challenges due to their aging populations.

A significant number of U.S. citizens, however, believe that immigration—both legal and illegal—negatively affects America. They argue, among other things, that the large number of immigrants seeking work results in lower wages for Americans, especially those with few skills. They also worry about the cost of providing immigrants with services such as schools and medical care.

One result of the public's concern about the effects of even legal immigration has been a series of laws that seriously restrict the rights of immigrants. In 1996, the Antiterrorism and Effective Death Penalty Act (AEDPA) and Illegal Immigration Reform and Immigrant Responsibility Act (IIRIRA) greatly increased the types of criminal activity for which immigrants, including permanent residents, can be deported. More than one million people have been deported since the two acts went into effect. We detailed some of the effects of these laws in Chapter 5.

THE ISSUE OF UNAUTHORIZED IMMIGRATION

Illegal immigration—or unauthorized immigration, to use the terminology of the Department of Homeland Security—has become a major national issue. Latin Americans, especially those migrating from Mexico, constitute the majority of individuals entering the United States without permission. In addition, many unauthorized immigrants enter the country legally, often as tourists or students, and then fail to return home when their visa status expires.

In the southwestern states bordering Mexico, Hispanic populations have surged dramatically, in part because of unauthorized immigration. The immigrants typically come to the United States to work, and in recent years their labor has been in high demand. The housing boom, which came to an abrupt end in the fall of 2007, was partially fueled by the steady stream of unauthorized immigrants seeking jobs. Until the Immigration Reform and Control Act of 1986, there was no law against hiring foreign citizens who lacked proper papers. Until recently, laws penalizing employers were infrequently enforced. In 2007, however, Arizona adopted a state law that imposed severe sanctions on businesses that employ unauthorized workers. As a result, many Arizona businesses have begun to report labor shortages. In 2007 and 2008, the federal government launched a series of major crackdowns on unauthorized immigrant employees. Is the government treating these people too harshly? We examine that question in the *Which Side Are You On?* feature on the next page.

Characteristics of the Undocumented Population. Studies of unauthorized immigrants have revealed that a large share of them eventually

Customs agents
have aggressively pursued unauthorized immigrants in the last few years. Here is a photo of some of those who are awaiting deportation at the San Ysidro Customs Port in Tijuana, Mexico. According to data compiled by the Mexican government, over seven hundred Mexicans are expelled from the United States each day through this facility alone. Have there been periods in U.S. history when the federal and state governments made few attempts to deport unauthorized immigrants? (AP Photo/Guillermo Arias)

whichsideareyouon?

DO WE TREAT IMMIGRANTS TOO HARSHLY?

America is a land of immigrants. Except for Native Americans, everyone who lives in the United States is either an immigrant or a descendant of immigrants. There have been various waves of immigrants into the United States, usually followed by complaints about too many immigrants from those who already live in this country. How we treat immigrants, including unauthorized immigrants, is a reflection of the character of this nation. Some believe that we treat them too harshly, and some believe that we don't treat them firmly enough.

WE HAVE TO REDUCE THE FLOW OF IMMIGRANTS TO THIS COUNTRY

Those who believe that we do not treat immigrants too harshly contend that immigrants take American jobs. These people also believe that immigrants place a bur-

These immigrants are shown on the steerage deck of a ship coming to America in 1907.
(Photo by Alfred Steiglitz, Library of Congress)

den on taxpayers because of increased costs for education, health care, and welfare benefits. When the issue involves unauthorized immigrants (often referred to as *illegal immigrants* or *undocumented workers*), the anti-immigration camp points out that unauthorized immigrants have violated our laws by entering this country. If we do anything to accommodate these undocumented immigrants, it will be unfair to those who follow the law. Another issue is that immigration leads to overcrowding in our schools and congested highways, particularly in California and other states where the inflow is large. Those on this side of the debate would have us "seal our borders" in an attempt not only to stop more unauthorized immigrants from entering the country but also to curb population growth in general.

THE WAY WE TREAT IMMIGRANTS IS A NATIONAL SCANDAL

There are those in America who believe that we are facing a false immigration panic. A nation of immigrants is holding another "nation" of immigrants in bondage—those who are here illegally but are being exploited in the labor market. Americans sympathetic to the immigrants contend that we have prevented 12 million otherwise law-abiding, hardworking U.S. residents from following a path toward living lawfully in this country. The escalating number of raids on workplaces and homes to ferret out illegal immigrants has nothing to do with securing our borders against terrorists, as is sometimes claimed. Arresting hundreds of workers at a kosher meat-packing plant in Iowa does nothing to keep this country safer—it is simply a way to show that the government is "doing something." Immigrants rounded up in these raids languish without lawyers and decent medical care in substandard "holding pens." The government has actually ordered prison jumpsuits in children's sizes to facilitate the imprisonment of small children. Illegality is not an identity. Rather, it is a status that can be repaired by Congress. We have discriminated against immigrants in the past—the Chinese, the Irish, Catholics, and Japanese Americans. We are a better country than that today, aren't we?

return to their home countries, where they frequently set up small businesses or retire. Many send remittances back to relatives in their homeland. In 2008, Mexico received $20.2 billion in such remittances. Vicente Fox, who was then president of Mexico, stated that remittances "are our biggest source of foreign income, bigger than oil, tourism, or foreign investment." In these ways, unauthorized immigrants are acting as immigrants to the United States always have. Throughout American history, immigrants frequently returned home or sent funds to relatives in the "old country."

Unauthorized immigrants very often live in mixed households, in which one or more members of a family have lawful resident status, but others do not. A woman from Guatemala with permanent resident status, for example, might be married to a Guatemalan man who is in the country illegally. A common circumstance is for the parents in a family to be unauthorized, whereas the children, who were born in the United States, possess American citizenship. Mixed families mean that deporting the unauthorized immigrant will either break up a family or force one or more American citizens into exile.

Concerns about Unauthorized Immigration. The number-one popular complaint about unauthorized immigrants is that they are breaking the law and "not playing by the rules." U.S. voters often have other concerns as well, some of which involve crime. "Coyotes," or smugglers who help such persons cross the border, may exploit or abuse their clients. Smugglers have raped Mexican women trying to enter the United States. Others crossing the border have found themselves abandoned in desert areas without sufficient water and have died of thirst or exposure. Illegal immigration may also contribute to the drug trade along the U.S.-Mexican border. In 2005, federal agents discovered an extensive underground tunnel that was used as a pipeline for a lucrative drug-trafficking scheme.

ATTEMPTS AT IMMIGRATION REFORM

In polls by Gallup and other organizations, Americans express opinions about illegal immigration (the term used in the questions) that are highly contradictory. A majority of respondents express sympathy toward the immigrants and believe that a way should be found to normalize their status. Only about a fifth favor immediate, permanent deportation. In the very same polls, however, four-fifths agree that illegal immigration is out of control, three-fifths believe that illegal immigration should be a crime, and half believe it should be a crime to assist illegal immigrants. While a majority of Americans believe that the illegal immigration problem is serious, most do not consider it a priority issue for the government. Those who do consider it a priority, however, have very strong feelings on the topic—and in American politics, a minority with strong feelings can often outbid a largely indifferent majority.

These crosses show the names of Mexicans who died trying to cross the border to the United States. This fence is located in the Colonia Libertad neighborhood in Tijuana, Mexico. Is it possible to erect an effective fence along the entire multi-thousand-mile border with Mexico? Why or why not? *(AP Photo/ Dario Lopez-Mills)*

A First Attempt to Deal with Unauthorized Immigration. In addition to making it illegal to hire undocumented workers, the Immigration Reform and Control Act of 1986, passed under President Ronald Reagan, also provided an amnesty for about 2.7 million unauthorized immigrants and strengthened the Border Patrol in hopes of deterring additional unauthorized crossings. The measure has since been strongly criticized because it was almost completely ineffective in reducing unauthorized immigration. Indeed, by holding out the possibility of forgiveness, it may even have encouraged border crossing.

Failure of Immigration Reform in 2005 and 2006. In May 2005, Senators Ted Kennedy (D., Mass.) and John McCain introduced the Secure America and Orderly Immigration Act in the Senate. The measure, also known as the McCain-Kennedy bill, would have enhanced border enforcement, created a "guest worker" program, and provided a path to legalization for unauthorized immigrants. The bill never came to a vote, however. President George W. Bush favored a similar approach. In his 2006 State of the Union Address, he advocated a program to curb the flow of additional unauthorized immigrants by stepped-up border security and the creation of a guest worker program that would ease the demand for low-wage foreign labor.

The U.S. House had other ideas. In December 2005, it passed the Border Protection, Antiterrorism, and Illegal Immigration Control Act, a bill that would have made unauthorized status a felony, criminalized attempts to assist unauthorized immigrants, and funded up to 700 miles of new fencing along the Mexican border. The measure passed on a near-party-line vote, with 92 percent of Republicans in support and 82 percent of Democrats in opposition. The House measure resulted in a series of ever-larger demonstrations across the country in favor of immigrant rights. Initially, some demonstrators carried Mexican flags, which led to denunciations by anti-immigrant advocates on talk radio and the Internet. Organizers of later protests made sure that the U.S. flag was visible in all images of the crowds.

In April 2006, the Comprehensive Immigration Reform Act was introduced in the U.S. Senate. This act was a substantially revised version of the 2005 McCain-Kennedy bill. President Bush endorsed the measure and spoke in its favor. It passed the Senate with bipartisan support in May. The House and Senate, however, were unable to bridge their differences in conference committee, and no comprehensive bill passed Congress as a whole. In October, however, Congress did pass a measure to build 700 miles of fencing.

Failure in 2007. Reform bills based on the Comprehensive Immigration Reform Act of 2006 were introduced into the Senate and House in 2007. Because the Democrats were now in control of both chambers of Congress, many observers thought that the legislation would finally pass. It did not, however. The Secure Borders, Economic Opportunity and Immigration Reform Act of 2007, as the Senate measure was officially called, failed to win the votes needed to end debate. With the Senate version dead, the House ceased work on its edition of the bill. The 2007 measure contained a variety of added provisions that drew criticism from the left as well as the right, including limits on family reunification and the abolition of a program that allowed high-tech industry to recruit skilled employees. Many experts considered the act as a whole unworkable, even if it contained various elements that they could support. A major factor in the bill's defeat in the Senate was an exceptionally vehement campaign against the measure by right-wing opponents. So many of the bill's foes contacted senators that both the Senate's Internet server and phone system crashed at different times.

By 2008, however, immigration was overshadowed in the public mind by economic problems. The issue played little role in the presidential campaigns, in part because the differences between Republican candidate McCain and Democratic candidate Obama were not great. The Republicans who had taken a hard line on immigration, including former New York City mayor Rudy Giuliani and former Massachusetts governor Mitt Romney, were forced out of the race early on. The remaining Republican candidates, McCain and former Arkansas governor Mike Huckabee, took a more conciliatory stand.

CRIME IN THE TWENTY-FIRST CENTURY

Virtually all polls taken in the United States in the last ten years have shown that crime remains one of the major concerns of the public. A related issue that has been on the domestic policy agenda for decades is controlling the use and sale of illegal drugs—activities that are often associated with crimes of violence. More recently, finding ways to deal with terrorism has become a priority for the nation's policymakers.

CRIME IN AMERICAN HISTORY

In every period in the history of this nation, people have voiced apprehension about crime. During the Civil War, mob violence and riots erupted in several cities. After the Civil War, people in San Francisco were told that "no decent man is in safety to walk the streets after dark; while at all hours, both night and day, his property is jeopardized by incendiarism [arson] and burglary."[1] In 1886, *Leslie's Weekly* reported, "Each day we see ghastly records of crime . . . murder seems to have run riot and each citizen asks . . . 'who is safe?'"

---

1. President's Commission on Law Enforcement and Administration of Justice, *Challenge of Crime in a Free Society* (Washington, D.C.: Government Printing Office, 1967), p. 19.

In fact, studies by historians have shown that preindustrial agricultural communities had very high levels of interpersonal violence, and that crime rates in the United States and other Western countries fell steadily from the second quarter of the nineteenth century into the twentieth century. Some historians suggest that this century-long decline came about because industrialization, urbanization, and the growth of bureaucratic institutions such as factories and schools socialized the lower classes into patterns of conformity and rule observance. It is notable that newly settled communities in the American West, where such socialization had yet to take hold, had much higher rates of crime—the "Wild West" was not entirely a myth.

The United States then experienced a substantial crime wave in the 1920s and the first half of the 1930s. This was the period of Prohibition, when the production and sale of alcoholic beverages was illegal. Criminals such as the famous Al Capone organized gangs to provide illicit alcohol to the public. After the end of Prohibition, crime rates dropped until after World War II (1939–1945).

The Great Crime Wave of the Late Twentieth Century. Crime rates in Western countries began to rise in the 1950s. The United States, in particular, experienced an explosive growth in violent crime that began in the 1960s. The murder rate per 100,000 people in 1964 was 4.9, whereas in 1994 it was estimated at 9.3, an increase of almost 100 percent. Between 1995 and 2004, however, violent crime rates declined. Some argue that this decline was due to the growing economy the United States had generally enjoyed since about 1993. Others claim that the $3 billion of additional funds the federal government spent to curb crime in the last few ye??ease to less crime. Still others claim th??ailed or in the number of persons ?? reduction. imprisoned is responsib?? egalized abortion that is likely Some have even arg?? event, the violent tion has reduced?? have leveled off. Since to commit cr?? fluctuations in the rate crime rate. You can see changes in the 2002, ??cides, violent crimes, and thefts ha??4–5, 14–6, and 14–7, respectively.

FIGURE 14–5: Homicide Rates

Homicide rates recently declined to levels last seen in the late 1960s. (The 2001 rate does *not* include deaths attributed to the 9/11 terrorist attacks.)

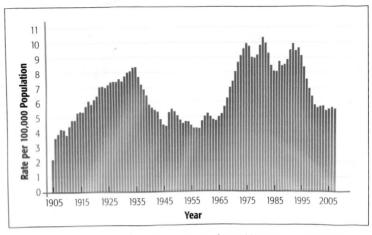

Sources: U.S. Department of Justice; National Center for Health Statistics, *Vital Statistics.*

FIGURE 14–6: Violent Crime Rates

Violent crime rates began a steep decline in 1994, reaching the lowest level ever recorded in 2002, after which they leveled off. The crimes included in this chart are rape, robbery, aggravated and simple assault, and homicide.

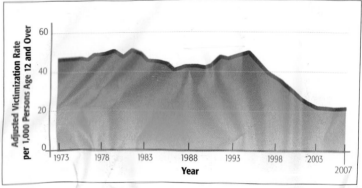

Sources: U.S. Department of Justice; rape, robbery, and assault data are from the *National Crime Victimization Survey;* the homicide data are from the Federal Bureau of Investigation's *Uniform Crime Reports.*

FIGURE 14–7: Theft Rates

Theft rates have declined significantly since the 1970s. *Theft* is defined as completed or attempted theft of property or cash without personal contact.

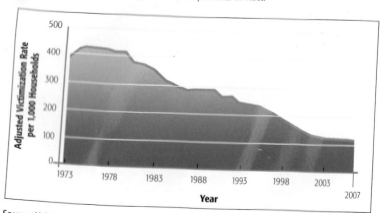

Source: U.S. Department of Justice, *National Crime Victimization Survey.*

The United States Compared with Other Countries. Many people have heard that the United States has the highest crime rates in the world. This is not actually true. Total crime rates are higher in some other countries, including Britain, Denmark, and Sweden, than in the United States. You are much more likely to be robbed in London than in New York City. What the United States has is not a high total crime rate, but a *murder* rate that is unusually high for an advanced industrialized nation. Explanations for this fact vary from easy access to firearms to a cultural predisposition for settling disputes with violence. It is worth noting, however, that many countries in Asia, Africa, and Latin America have much higher homicide rates than the United States.

CRIMES COMMITTED BY JUVENILES

A disturbing aspect of crime is the number of serious crimes committed by juveniles, although the number of such crimes has dropped significantly from what it was in the mid-1990s, as shown in Figure 14–8. The political response to serious juvenile crimes has been varied. Some cities have established juvenile curfews. Several states have begun to try more juveniles as adults, particularly juveniles who have been charged with homicides. Still other states are operating "boot camps" to try to "shape up" less violent juvenile criminals. Additionally, victims of juvenile crime and victims' relatives are attempting to pry open the traditionally secret juvenile court system.[2]

SCHOOL SHOOTINGS

School shootings are a form of violent crime that, for most people, is particularly shocking and difficult to understand. Perhaps the most widely publicized of all school shootings in the United States occurred in 1999 in Littleton, Colorado. In what has become known as the Columbine High School massacre, two teenaged students went on a shooting rampage, killing twelve students and a teacher, and wounding twenty-four others, before committing suicide.

School shootings occur not only in secondary schools but also in elementary schools and on college campuses. Even a one-room elementary school in Lancaster County, Pennsylvania, was not immune from such violence: in October 2006, a milk-truck driver held ten Amish girls hostage before shooting five of them and then himself at the small schoolhouse. The deadliest school shooting to date, however, occurred on a college campus. On April 16, 2007, the nation was stunned to learn that a South Korean student at Virginia Polytechnic Institute and State University (Virginia Tech), in Blacksburg, Virginia, had killed thirty-two students and wounded some twenty-nine others before killing himself.

The perception of school shootings as a growing form of violence is reinforced, to some extent, by the extraordinary media attention that such killings receive. Even while homicide rates in the ... were declining from 1993 to 2002, this per... not change. Although the rates have ... since 2003, especially in 2007 due ... ber of victims at the Virginia Tech ...continue to face less risk of ... violent crimes while at ...hool.[3]

These local police personnel take one teenager into custody after breaking up a gang fight. How can communities lower the juvenile crime rate? (© Aristide Economopoulos/Star Ledger/Corbis)

2. See Chapter 5 for details ... our legal system.
3. National School Safety Cent... Crime and Safety, 2006 (Washi...of juveniles in Justice Statistics, 2006).

THE PRISON POPULATION BOMB

Many Americans believe that the best solution to the nation's crime problem is to impose stiff prison sentences on offenders. Such sentences, in fact, have become national policy. By 2008, U.S. prisons and jails held 2.3 million people. About two-thirds of the incarcerated population were in state or federal prisons, with the remainder held in local jails. About 60 percent of the persons held in local jails were awaiting court action. The other 40 percent were serving sentences.

The number of incarcerated persons has grown rapidly in recent years. In 1990, for example, the total number of persons held in U.S. jails or prisons was still only 1.1 million. From 1995 to 2002, the incarcerated population grew at an average of 3.8 percent annually. The rate of growth has slowed since 2002, however.

The Incarceration Rate. Some groups of people are much more likely to find themselves behind bars than others. Men are more than ten times more likely to be incarcerated than women. Prisoners are also disproportionately African American. To measure how frequently members of particular groups are imprisoned, the standard statistic is the **incarceration rate.** This rate is the number of people incarcerated for every 100,000 persons in a particular population group. To put it another way, an incarceration rate of 1,000 means that 1 percent of a particular group is in custody. Using this statistic, we can say that U.S. men have an incarceration rate of 1,384, compared with a rate of 134 for U.S. women. This figure, an all-time high, means that more than 1 male out of every 100 is in jail or prison in this country. Figure 14–9 shows selected incarceration rates by gender, race, and age. Note the very high incarceration rate for African Americans between the ages of twenty-five and twenty-nine—at any given time, almost 12 percent of this group is in jail or prison.

International Comparisons. The United States has more people in jail or prison than any other country in the world. That fact is not necessarily surprising, because the United States also has one of the world's largest total populations. More to the point, the United States has the highest reported incarceration rate of any country on earth.[4] Figure 14–10 on the following page compares U.S. incarceration rates, measured by the number of prisoners per 100,000 residents, with incarceration rates in other major countries.

Prison Construction and Conditions. To house a growing number of inmates, prison construction and management have become sizable industries in the United States. Ten

FIGURE 14–8: Serious Violent Crime by Perceived Age of Offender

The number of serious violent crimes committed by juveniles has generally declined since 1993. The crimes included are rape, robbery, aggravated assault, and homicide.

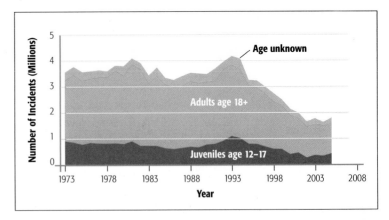

Sources: U.S. Department of Justice; rape, robbery, and assault data are from the *National Crime Victimization Survey.* The homicide data are from the FBI's *Uniform Crime Reports.*

FIGURE 14–9: Incarceration Rates per 100,000 Persons for Selected U.S. Population Groups

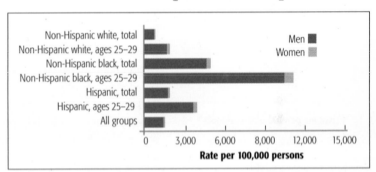

Source: "Prison and Jail Inmates at Midyear 2007," *Bureau of Justice Statistics Bulletin,* U.S. Department of Justice (2008).

Incarceration Rate
The number of persons held in jail or prison for every 100,000 persons in a particular population group.

---

4. North Korea almost certainly has a higher incarceration rate than the United States, but that nation does not report its incarceration statistics.

FIGURE 14–10:
Incarceration Rates around the World

Incarceration rates of major nations measured by the number of prisoners per 100,000 residents. Some authorities believe that the estimate for China is too low.

Prisoners per 100,000 Residents

Source: Roy Walmsley, *World Prison Population List,* 7th ed. (London: King's College, International Centre for Prison Studies, 2007).

didyouknow...

That the odds are one in twenty that an American born today will wind up in jail or prison at some point during his or her lifetime?

years ago, prison overcrowding was a major issue. In 1994, for example, state prisons had a rated capacity of about 500,000 inmates but actually held 900,000 people. The prisons were therefore operating at 80 percent above capacity. Today, after a major prison construction program, many state prisons are operating within their capacity, but some state systems are still at 20 percent above capacity or more. The federal prison system is still 37 percent above capacity. Since 1980, Texas has built 120 new prisons, Florida has built 84, and California has built 83. In 1923, there were only 61 prisons in the entire United States.

Nationwide, local jails are operating at 93 percent of capacity. That figure conceals major differences among jurisdictions, however. Seventeen of the fifty largest jail jurisdictions are operating at more than 100 percent of their rated capacity. Clark County, Nevada (Las Vegas), is 66 percent above capacity and Maricopa County, Arizona (Phoenix), is 52 percent above capacity.

For all of the prison building, American prisons are dangerously overcrowded, according to a national commission established by the Vera Institute of Justice, a New York policy institute, to study prison conditions.[5] The commissioners' report also stated that the nation's prisons are characterized by unnecessary violence, the lack of any meaningful programs for inmates, an underpaid and undertrained staff, and, generally, a culture of abuse. Additionally, today's prisons are breeding grounds for infectious diseases and house a large number of people with mental illnesses (those with mental illnesses constitute about 16 percent of the prison population). The authors note that while the prisons at Guantánamo Bay in Cuba and Abu Ghraib in Iraq have received wide publicity, little is written on the prison conditions in the United States, even though these conditions affect millions of people.

Effects of Incarceration. When imprisonment keeps truly violent felons behind bars longer, it prevents them from committing additional crimes. The average predatory street criminal commits fifteen or more crimes each year when not behind bars. But most prisoners are in for a relatively short time and are released on parole early, often because of prison overcrowding. Then many find themselves back in prison because they have violated parole, typically by using illegal drugs. Indeed, of the 1.5 million people who are arrested each year, the majority are arrested for drug offenses. Given that from 20 million to 40 million Americans violate one or more drug laws each year, the potential "supply" of prisoners seems virtually limitless. Consequently, it may not matter how many prisons are built; there will still be overcrowding as long as we maintain the same legislation on illegal drugs (federal drug policy will be discussed in the next section).

In his recent study of prisons, Princeton sociologist Bruce Western looked at the effects of incarceration not only on released prisoners but also on their families and communities. According to Western, most incarcerated men have children, and thus the prison boom has been a growing source of disadvantage for young people. This is particularly notable among blacks because of the higher incarceration rate for blacks, which Western points out is twelve times the incarceration rate for whites. Whereas just over 1 percent of white children have fathers behind bars, in the black community, this figure climbs to 10 percent. Additionally, states Western, a prison record reduces a man's earnings by 30 to 40 percent because of the lower availability of work and lower pay.[6]

---

5. John J. Gibbons and Nicholas de B. Katzenbach, *Confronting Confinement: A Report of the Commission on Safety and Abuse in America's Prisons* (New York: Vera Institute of Justice, 2006).
6. Bruce Western, *Punishment and Inequality in America* (New York: Russell Sage Foundation, 2006).

FEDERAL DRUG POLICY

Illegal drugs are a major cause of crime in America. A rising percentage of arrests are for illegal drug trafficking. The latest major illegal drug has contributed to an increase in the number of drug arrests. That drug is methamphetamine, sometimes known as meth or speed. Methamphetamine is often made in small home laboratories using toxic household chemicals. Raids on meth labs around the country have become common news stories. The violence that often accompanies the illegal drug trade occurs for several reasons. One is that drug dealers engage in "turf wars" over the territories in which drugs can be sold. Another is that when drug deals go bad, drug dealers cannot turn to the legal system for help, so they resort to violence. Finally, drug addicts who do not have the income to finance their habits often engage in crime—assault, robbery, and sometimes murder.

The war on drugs and the increased spending on drug interdiction over the years have had virtually no effect on overall illegal drug consumption in the United States. Mandatory sentences, which have been imposed by the federal government since the late 1980s for all federal offenses, including the sale or possession of illegal drugs, are also not an ideal solution. Mandatory sentences lead to a further problem—overcrowded prisons. Furthermore, almost half of the 1.5 million people arrested each year in the United States on drug charges are arrested for marijuana offenses—and of these, almost 90 percent are charged with possession only.

While the federal government has done little to modify its drug policy, state and local governments have been experimenting with new approaches to the problem. Many states now have special "drug courts" for those arrested for illegal drug use. In these courts, offenders typically are "sentenced" to a rehabilitation program.

CONFRONTING TERRORISM

Of all of the different types of crimes, terrorism can be the most devastating. The victims of terrorist attacks can number in the hundreds—or even in the thousands, as was the case when hijacked airplanes crashed into the Pentagon and the World Trade Centers on September 11, 2001. Additionally, locating the perpetrators is often extremely difficult. In a suicide bombing, the perpetrators have themselves been killed, so the search is not for the perpetrators but for others who might have conspired with them in planning the attack.

Terrorism is definitely not a new phenomenon in the world, but it is a relatively new occurrence on U.S. soil. And certainly, the 9/11 attacks made many Americans aware for the first time of the hatred of America harbored by some foreigners—in this case, a network of religious extremists in foreign countries. As you have read elsewhere in this text, immediately after 9/11 the U.S. government took many actions, including launching a war in Afghanistan, as part of a "war on terror." Congress quickly passed new legislation to fund these efforts, as well as a number of other acts, such as the Aviation Security Act.

Some of the actions taken in the wake of 9/11, such as the war in Afghanistan, were widely supported by the public. Others, such as the enactment of the USA Patriot Act and President George W. Bush's executive order establishing military tribunals, have been criticized for infringing

Jim Robinson, shown here on the right, is a former U.S. assistant attorney general in charge of the Criminal Division of the U.S. Department of Justice. He is shown here speaking at a news conference held by the American Civil Liberties Union to mark the one millionth addition to the Transportation Security Administration's terrorist watch list. How has the war against terrorism affected travel in the United States and elsewhere? (Patrick D. McDermott/UPI /Landov)

Environmental Impact Statement (EIS)
A report that must show the costs and benefits of major federal actions that could significantly affect the quality of the environment.

too much on Americans' civil liberties. In some situations, the Bush administration had to modify its policies in response to public pressure.

Of course, one of the most serious policy actions taken in response to 9/11 was the decision to invade Iraq. By 2006, the Bush administration's Iraq War policy had come under particularly heavy fire. Nonetheless, President Bush continued to regard the war effort in Iraq as essential to success in the war on terrorism. We will examine the clash between the president and Congress over the Iraq War in Chapter 15, in the context of foreign policy.

ENVIRONMENTAL POLICY

Americans have paid increasing attention to environmental issues in the last three decades. A major source of concern for the general public has been the emission of pollutants into the air and water. Each year, the world atmosphere receives 150 million metric tons of sulfur dioxide, 125 million metric tons of nitrogen oxides, and more than a billion metric tons of carbon monoxide.

CLEANING UP THE AIR AND WATER

The government has been responding to pollution problems since before the American Revolution, when the Massachusetts Bay Colony issued regulations to try to stop the pollution of Boston Harbor. In the 1800s, states passed laws controlling water pollution after scientists and medical researchers convinced most policymakers that dumping sewage into drinking and bathing water caused disease. At the national level, the Federal Water Pollution Control Act of 1948 provided research and assistance to the states for pollution-control efforts, but little was done.

The National Environmental Policy Act. The year 1969 marked the start of the most concerted national government involvement in solving pollution problems. In that year, the conflict between oil-exploration interests and environmental interests literally erupted when an oil well six miles off the coast of Santa Barbara, California, exploded, releasing 235,000 gallons of crude oil. The result was an oil slick, covering an area of eight hundred square miles, that washed up on the city's beaches and killed plant life, birds, and fish. Hearings in Congress revealed that the Interior Department had no guidance in the energy-environment trade-off. Congress soon passed the National Environmental Policy Act of 1969. This landmark legislation established, among other things, the Council on Environmental Quality. It also mandated that an **environmental impact statement (EIS)** be prepared for all major federal actions that could significantly affect the quality of the environment. The act gave citizens and public-interest groups concerned with the environ-

This family of polar bears finds itself on a shaky ice floe.
Some experts on polar bears in the Arctic claim that if the warming trend in that part of the world continues, these majestic animals will have a hard time surviving into the second half of this century. (Johnny Johnson/Getty Images)

ment a weapon against the unnecessary and inappropriate use of natural resources by the government.

Curbing Air Pollution. Beginning in 1975, the government began regulating tailpipe emissions from cars and light trucks in an attempt to curb air pollution. In 1990, after years of lobbying by environmentalists, Congress passed the Clean Air Act of 1990. The act established tighter standards for emissions of nitrogen dioxide (NO_2) and other pollutants by newly built cars and light trucks. California was allowed to establish its own, stricter standards. By 1994, the maximum allowable NO_2 emissions (averaged over each manufacturer's "fleet" of vehicles) were about a fifth of the 1975 standard. The "Tier 2" system, phased in between 2004 and 2007, reduced maximum fleet emissions by cars and light trucks to just over 2 percent of the 1975 standard. In 2008–2009, the standards were extended to trucks weighing between 6,000 and 8,500 pounds.

Stationary sources of air pollution were also made subject to more regulation under the 1990 act. The act required 110 of the oldest coal-burning power plants in the United States to cut their emissions 40 percent by 2001. Controls were placed on other factories and businesses in an attempt to reduce ground-level ozone pollution in ninety-six cities to healthful levels by 2005 (except in Los Angeles, which was given until 2010 to meet the standards). The act also required that the production of chlorofluorocarbons (CFCs) be stopped completely by 2002. CFCs are thought to deplete the ozone layer in the upper atmosphere and increase the levels of harmful radiation reaching the earth's surface. CFCs were formerly used in air-conditioning and other refrigeration units.

In 1997, in light of evidence that very small particles (2.5 microns, or millionths of a meter) of soot might be dangerous to our health, the Environmental Protection Agency (EPA) issued new particulate standards for motor vehicle exhaust systems and other sources of pollution. The EPA also established a more rigorous standard for ground-level ozone, which is formed when sunlight combines with pollutants from cars and other sources. Ozone is a major component of smog.

Regulating Water Pollution. One of the most important acts regulating water pollution is the Clean Water Act of 1972, which amended the Federal Water Pollution Control Act of 1948. The Clean Water Act established the following goals: (1) make waters safe for swimming, (2) protect fish and wildlife, and (3) eliminate the discharge of pollutants into the water. The act set specific time schedules, which were subsequently extended by further legislation. Under these schedules, the EPA establishes limits on discharges of types of pollutants based on the technology available for controlling them. The 1972 act also required municipal and industrial polluters to apply for permits before discharging wastes into navigable waters.

The Clean Water Act also prohibits the filling or dredging of wetlands unless a permit is obtained from the Army Corps of Engineers. The EPA defines *wetlands* as "those areas that are inundated or saturated by surface or ground water at a frequency and duration sufficient to support, and that under normal circumstances do support, a prevalence of vegetation typically adapted for life in saturated soil conditions." In recent years, the broad interpretation of what constitutes a wetland subject to the regulatory authority of the federal government has generated substantial controversy.

Perhaps one of the most controversial regulations concerning wetlands was the "migratory-bird rule" issued by the Army Corps of Engineers. Under this rule, any bodies of water that could affect interstate commerce, including seasonal ponds or waters "used or suitable for use by migratory birds" that fly over state borders, were "navigable waters" subject to federal regulation under the Clean Water Act as wetlands. In 2001, after years of controversy, the United States Supreme Court struck down the rule. The Court stated that it was not prepared to hold that isolated and seasonal ponds, puddles, and "prairie

Former U.S. vice president Al Gore won a Nobel Peace Prize for his work related to global warming. He also produced an Oscar-winning film called *An Inconvenient Truth.* He is shown here at the 2007 Cannes Film Festival, where the film won another prize. While there is little disagreement about the reality of global warming, there is much disagreement about its size and timing. What kind of trade-offs are involved in spending resources today in an attempt to prevent global warming? (Valery Hache/AFP/Getty Images)

potholes" become "navigable waters of the United States" simply because they serve as a habitat for migratory birds.[7]

GLOBAL WARMING

In the 1990s, scientists working on climate change began to conclude that average world temperatures will rise significantly in the twenty-first century. Gases released by human activity, principally carbon dioxide, are producing a "greenhouse effect," trapping the sun's heat and slowing its release into outer space. In fact, many studies have shown that global warming has already begun. Christine Todd Whitman, who headed the Environmental Protection Agency from 2001 to 2003, called global warming "one of the greatest environmental challenges we face, if not the greatest."

The Kyoto Protocol. In 1997, delegates from around the world gathered in Kyoto, Japan, for a global climate conference sponsored by the United Nations. The conference issued a proposed treaty aimed at reducing emissions of greenhouse gases to 5.2 percent below 1990 levels by 2012. Just thirty-five developed nations were mandated to reduce their emissions, however—developing nations faced only voluntary limits. The U.S. Senate voted unanimously in 1997 that it would not accept a treaty that exempted developing countries, and in 2001 President Bush announced that he would not submit the Kyoto protocol to the Senate for ratification. By 2008, the protocol had 178 member parties. Its rejection by the United States, however, raised the question of whether it could ever be effective.

Even in those European countries that most enthusiastically supported the Kyoto protocol and signed it, the results have not been overly positive. Thirteen of the fifteen original European Union signatories will miss their 2010 emission targets. For example, Spain will miss its target by 33 percentage points. Denmark had agreed to reduce its levels of greenhouse gas emissions by 21 percent, but so far its emissions have *increased* by more than 6 percent since 1990. Greece has seen its greenhouse gas emissions increase by 23 percent since 1990. Closer to home, in 2005 Prime Minister Paul Martin of Canada lambasted the United States for its lack of a "global conscience." But since 1990, Canada's emissions have risen by 24 percent, much faster than the U.S. rate.

The Global Warming Debate. While almost all scientists who perform research on the world's climate believe that global warming will be significant, there is considerable disagreement as to how much warming will actually occur. It is generally accepted that world temperatures have already increased by at least 0.6 degree Celsius over the last century. Scenarios by the United Nations Intergovernmental Panel on Climate Change predict increases ranging from 2.0 to 4.5 degrees Celsius by the year 2100. More conservative estimates, such as those by climate experts James Hansen and Patrick Michaels, average around 0.75 degree Celsius.[8]

Global warming has become a major political football to be kicked back and forth by conservatives and liberals. Former vice president Al Gore's Oscar-winning and widely viewed documentary on global warming, released in 2006, further fueled the debate. Titled *An Inconvenient Truth,* the film stressed that actions to mitigate global warming must be taken now if we are to avert a planet-threatening crisis. Environmental groups and others have

7. *Solid Waste Agency of Northern Cook County v. U.S. Army Corps of Engineers,* 531 U.S. 159 (2001).
8. J. E. Hansen, "Defusing the Global Warming Time Bomb," *Scientific American,* March 2004, pp. 69–77.

been pressing the federal government to do just that. Indeed, as mentioned earlier in this text, discouraged by the refusal of the EPA to regulate emissions of carbon dioxide and other greenhouse gases, a group of state and local governments, joined by several environmental groups, sued the EPA to force the agency to take action. When the case reached the United States Supreme Court, the Court held that the EPA had the authority to regulate such emissions in an attempt to curb global warming and should do so.[9]

Some conservatives have seized on the work of scientists who believe that global warming does not exist at all. (Some of these researchers work for oil companies.) If this were true, there would be no reason to limit emissions of carbon dioxide and other greenhouse gases. A more sophisticated argument by conservatives is that major steps to limit emissions in the near future would not be cost-effective. Bjørn Lomborg, a critic of the environmental movement, suggests that it would be more practical to take action against global warming later in the century, when the world will be (presumably) richer and when renewable energy sources will have become more competitive in price.[10]

Bjørn Lomborg, the director of the Copenhagen Consensus Center at the Copenhagen Business School, argues that limiting emissions of carbon dioxide and other greenhouse gases is not a cost-effective policy today. He also argues that global warming, while a significant issue, is not as serious as other problems facing the world. What are some of the other problems in the world that might take priority over the issue of global warming? (Suzanne Plunkett/Bloomberg News/Landov)

THE POLITICS OF ECONOMIC DECISION MAKING

Nowhere are the principles of public policymaking more obvious than in the economic decisions made by the federal government. The president and Congress (and to a growing extent, the judiciary) are constantly faced with questions of economic policy. Such issues become especially important in periods of economic difficulty. One such period began in late 2007 with the collapse in the housing market and turmoil in the financial world.

FISCAL POLICY

To smooth out the ups and downs of the national economy, the government has several policy options. One is to change the level of taxes or government spending. The other possibility involves influencing interest rates and the monetary side of the economy. We will examine taxing and spending, or **fiscal policy**, first. Fiscal policy is the domain of Congress. A fiscal policy approach to stabilizing the economy is often associated with a twentieth-century British economist named John Maynard Keynes.

Keynes (1883–1946) originated the school of thought called **Keynesian economics**, which supports the use of government spending and taxing to help stabilize the economy. (*Keynesian* is pronounced *kayn*-zee-un.) Keynes believed that there was a need for government intervention in the economy, in part because after falling into a **recession** or depression, a modern economy may become trapped in an ongoing state of less than full employment.

Government Spending and Borrowing. Keynes developed his fiscal policy theories during the Great Depression. He believed that the forces of supply and demand operated too slowly on their own in such a serious recession. Unemployment meant people had less to spend, and because they could not buy things, more businesses failed, creating additional unemployment. It was a vicious cycle. Keynes's idea was simple: in such circumstances, the *government* should step in and undertake the spending that is needed to return the economy to a more normal state.[11]

Government spending can be financed in a number of ways, including increasing taxes and borrowing. For government spending to have the effect Keynes wanted,

Fiscal Policy
The federal government's use of taxation and spending policies to affect overall business activity.

Keynesian Economics
A school of economic thought that tends to favor active federal government policymaking to stabilize economy-wide fluctuations, usually by implementing discretionary fiscal policy.

Recession
Two or more successive quarters in which the economy shrinks instead of grows.

9. *Massachusetts v. EPA*, 127 S.Ct. 1438 (2007).
10. Bjørn Lomborg, *Cool It: The Skeptical Environmentalist's Guide to Global Warming* (New York: Knopf, 2008).
11. Robert Skidelsky, *John Maynard Keynes: The Economist as Savior, 1920–1937: A Biography* (New York: Penguin USA, 1994).

Budget Deficit
Government expenditures that exceed receipts.

U.S. Treasury Bond
Debt issued by the federal government.

however, it was essential that the spending be financed by borrowing, and not by taxes. In other words, the government should run a **budget deficit**—it should spend more than it receives. If the government financed its spending during a recession by taxation, the government would be spending funds that would, for the most part, otherwise have been spent by taxpayers.

Discretionary Fiscal Policy. Keynes originally developed his fiscal theories as a way of lifting an economy out of a major disaster such as the Great Depression. Beginning with the presidency of John F. Kennedy (1961–1963), however, policymakers have attempted to use Keynesian methods to "fine-tune" the economy. This is discretionary fiscal policy—*discretionary* meaning left to the judgment or discretion of a policymaker. For example, President George W. Bush advertised his tax cuts of 2001 and 2003 as a method of stimulating the economy to halt the economic slowdown of those years. In 2008, the economy slowed again. Falling housing prices and a wave of defaults and foreclosures shook the financial markets and contributed to a growing financial crisis. President Bush and the Democratic Congress quickly united, first to create a stimulus package that, among other things, provided income tax rebates to most taxpayers, and later to provide a $700 billion "bailout" or "rescue" plan to ease the crisis in the financial markets.

Attempts to fine-tune the economy face a timing problem. It takes a while to collect and assimilate economic data. Time may go by before an economic problem can be identified. After an economic problem is recognized, a solution must be formulated. There will be an action time lag between the recognition of a problem and the implementation of policy to solve it. Getting Congress to act can easily take a year or two. Finally, after fiscal policy is enacted, it takes time for the policy to act on the economy. Because fiscal policy time lags are long and variable, a policy designed to combat a recession may not produce results until the economy is already out of the recession.

DEFICIT SPENDING AND THE PUBLIC DEBT

The federal government typically borrows by selling **U.S. Treasury bonds.** The sale of these federal government bonds to corporations, private individuals, pension plans, foreign governments, foreign businesses, and foreign individuals adds to this nation's *public debt*. In the last few years, foreign governments, especially those of China and Japan, have come to own about 50 percent of the net U.S. public debt. Thirty years ago, the share of the U.S. public debt held by foreigners was only 15 percent.

Deficit Spending. When a household spends more than it earns, it must either borrow, receive gifts from family and friends, or sell off assets. When the federal government spends more than it receives in revenues, it typically borrows by selling U.S. Treasury bonds. Individuals, businesses, and foreigners buy U.S. Treasury bonds. Every time the federal government engages in deficit spending, it increases the size of its total debt.

Can deficit spending go on forever? Certainly not for a household, but for quite a long time for the U.S. government. After all, as long as individuals, businesses, and foreigners (especially foreign governments) are willing to purchase U.S. Treasury bonds, the government can continue to engage in deficit spending. Just as deficit spending is not

Representative John M. Spratt, Jr.
(D., S.C.), Chair of the House Budget Committee, held a news conference to discuss the Office of Management and Budget's new federal budget deficit projections. At the time, he did not have any of the projections based on the massive 2008 Treasury bailout of financial institutions throughout the United States. The ultimate cost of that bailout to the federal government (that is, to U.S. taxpayers) could be in the hundreds of billions of dollars.
(Ryan Kelly/Congressional Quarterly/Getty Images)

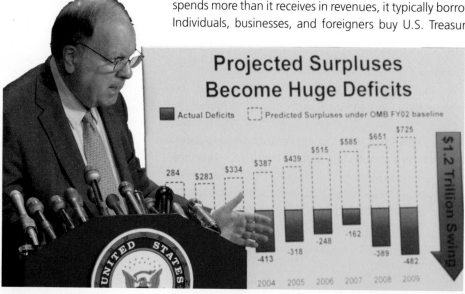

Projected Surpluses Become Huge Deficits

■ Actual Deficits   ⬚ Predicted Surpluses under OMB FY02 baseline

$1.2 Trillion Swing

	284	$283	$334	$387	$439	$515	$585	$651	$725
					-248	-162		-389	-482
				-318					
		-413							
	2004	2005	2006	2007	2008	2009			

a good way to run a household, however, it is also not a great way to run a government. If deficit spending goes on long enough, the rest of the world—which owns about 50 percent of all U.S. Treasury bonds—may lose faith in our government. Consequently, U.S. government borrowing might become more expensive. We, as taxpayers, are responsible for the interest that the federal government pays when it issues U.S. Treasury bonds. A vicious cycle might occur—more deficit spending could lead to higher interest rate costs on the U.S. debt, leading in turn to even larger deficits.

The Public Debt in Perspective. Did you know that the federal government has accumulated trillions of dollars in debt? Does that scare you? It certainly would if you thought that we had to pay it back tomorrow. But we do not.

There are two types of public debt—gross and net. The **gross public debt** includes all federal government interagency borrowings, which really do not matter. This is similar to your taking an IOU ("I owe you") out of your left pocket and putting it into your right pocket. Today, federal interagency borrowings account for about $4.3 trillion of the gross public debt. What is important is the **net public debt**—the public debt that does not include interagency borrowing. Figure 14–11 shows the net public debt of the federal government since 1940.

This figure does not take into account two very important variables: inflation (a sustained rise in the general price level of goods and services) and increases in population. A better way to examine the relative importance of the public debt is to compare it with the *gross domestic product (GDP)*, as is done in Figure 14–12. (Remember from earlier in this chapter that the gross domestic product is the dollar value of all final goods and services produced in a one-year period.) There you see that the public debt reached its peak during World War II and fell thereafter. Since about 1960, the net public debt as a percentage of GDP has ranged between 30 and 50 percent.

Are We Always in Debt? From 1960 until the last few years of the twentieth century, the federal government spent more than it received in all but two years. Some observers consider these ongoing budget deficits to be the negative result of Keynesian policies. Others argue that the deficits actually result from the abuse of Keynesianism. Politicians have been more than happy to run budget deficits in recessions, but they have often refused to implement the other side of Keynes's recommendations—to run a *budget surplus* during boom times.

In 1993, however, President Bill Clinton (1993–2001) obtained a tax increase as the nation emerged from a mild recession. For the first time, the federal government implemented the more painful side of Keynesianism. In any event, between the tax increase and the "dot-com boom," the United States had a budget surplus each year from 1998

FIGURE 14–11:
Net Public Debt of the Federal Government

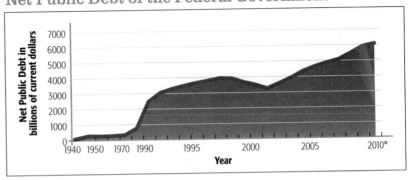

*Figures for 2007 through 2010 are estimates.

Source: U.S. Office of Management and Budget.

FIGURE 14–12: Net Public Debt as a Percentage of the Gross Domestic Product

During World War II, the net public debt as a percentage of GDP grew dramatically. It fell thereafter but rose again from 1975 to 1995. The percentage fell after 1995 and recently has been increasing again.

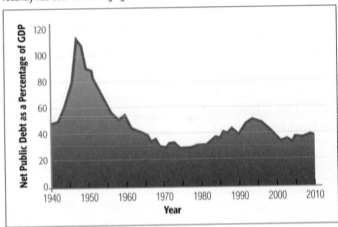

Source: U.S. Department of the Treasury.

Gross Public Debt
The net public debt plus interagency borrowings within the government.

Net Public Debt
The accumulation of all past federal government deficits; the total amount owed by the federal government to individuals, businesses, and foreigners.

Federal Reserve System (the Fed)
The agency created by Congress in 1913 to serve as the nation's central banking organization.

Federal Open Market Committee
The most important body within the Federal Reserve System. The Federal Open Market Committee decides how monetary policy should be carried out.

to 2002. Some commentators predicted that we would be running federal government surpluses for years to come. All of those projections went by the wayside because of several events.

One event was the "dot-com bust" followed by the 2001–2002 recession, which lowered the rate of growth of not only the economy but also the federal government's tax receipts. Another event was a series of large tax cuts passed by Congress in 2001 and 2003 at the urging of President George W. Bush.

A major event took place on September 11, 2001. Basically, as a result of the terrorist attacks, the federal government spent much more than it had planned to spend on security against terrorism. Finally, the government had to pay for the war in Iraq in 2003 and the occupation of that country thereafter. The federal budget deficit for 2007 was $162 billion. For 2008, the estimated deficit rose to $439 billion due to the economic slowdown. In 2009, it may become much larger because of the banking bailout bill.

MONETARY POLICY

Controlling the rate of growth of the money supply is called *monetary policy*. This policy is the domain of the **Federal Reserve System,** also known simply as the **Fed.** The Fed is the most important regulatory agency in the U.S. monetary system.

The Fed performs a number of important functions. Perhaps the Fed's most important ability is that it is able to regulate the amount of money in circulation, which can be defined loosely as checkable account balances and currency. The Fed also provides a system for transferring checks from one bank to another. In addition, it holds reserves deposited by most of the nation's banks, savings and loan associations, savings banks, and credit unions, and it plays a role in supervising the banking industry.

Organization of the Federal Reserve System. A board of governors manages the Fed. This board consists of seven full-time members appointed by the president with the approval of the Senate. The twelve Federal Reserve district banks have twenty-five branches. The most important unit within the Fed is the **Federal Open Market Committee.** This is the body that actually determines the future growth of the money supply and other important economy-wide financial variables. This committee is composed of the members of the Board of Governors, the president of the New York Federal Reserve Bank, and presidents of four other Federal Reserve banks, rotated periodically.

The Board of Governors of the Federal Reserve System is independent. The president can attempt to influence the board, and Congress can threaten to merge the Fed into the Treasury Department, but as long as the Fed retains its independence, its chairperson and governors can do what they please. Hence, any talk about "the president's monetary policy" or "Congress's monetary policy" is inaccurate. To be sure, the Fed has, on occasion, yielded to presidential pressure, and for a while the Fed's chairperson had to observe a congressional resolution requiring him to report monetary targets over each six-month period. But now, more than ever before, the Fed remains one of the truly independent sources of economic power in the government.

The current Federal Reserve Chairman is Ben Bernanke, shown on the left in this photo. At this hearing on Capitol Hill, Bernanke was justifying the Federal Reserve's financial assistance for an investment banking firm. Why would the Federal Reserve want to help any private company? (Photo by Mark Wilson/Getty Images)

HON. BEN S. BERNANKE

Loose and Tight Monetary Policies. The Federal Reserve System seeks to stabilize nationwide economic activity by controlling the amount of money in circulation. Changing the amount of money in circulation is a major aspect of **monetary policy.** You may have read a news report in which a business executive complained that money is "too tight." You may have run across a story about an economist who has warned that money is "too loose." In these instances, the terms *tight* and *loose* refer to the monetary policy of the Fed.

Credit, like any good or service, has a cost. The cost of borrowing—the interest rate—is similar to the cost of any other aspect of doing business. When the cost of borrowing falls, businesspersons can undertake more investment projects. When it rises, businesspersons will undertake fewer projects. Consumers also react to interest rates when deciding whether to borrow funds to buy houses, cars, or other "big-ticket" items.

If the Fed implements a **loose monetary policy** (often called an "expansionary" policy), the supply of credit increases and its cost falls. If the Fed implements a **tight monetary policy** (often called a "contractionary" policy), the supply of credit falls and its cost increases. A loose money policy is often implemented as an attempt to encourage economic growth. You may be wondering why any nation would want a tight money policy. The answer is to control inflation. If money becomes too plentiful too quickly, prices (and ultimately the price level) increase and the purchasing power of the dollar decreases.

Time Lags for Monetary Policy. You learned earlier that policymakers who implement fiscal policy—the manipulation of budget deficits and the tax system—experience problems with time lags. The Fed faces similar problems when it implements monetary policy.

Sometimes accurate information about the economy is not available for months. Once the state of the economy is known, time may elapse before any policy can be put into effect. Still, the time lag in implementing monetary policy is usually much shorter than the lag involved in fiscal policy. The Federal Open Market Committee meets eight times a year and can put a policy into effect relatively quickly. Nevertheless, a change in the money supply may not have an effect for several months.

Regulating Banks. In addition to managing the money supply, the Federal Reserve has a variety of responsibilities in the area of bank regulation. The Fed ensures that banks have a large enough quantity of reserve capital to back up the loans they are making. It also administers various regulations that protect consumers. In the past, not all banks fell under the regulatory oversight of the Fed. For example, the Fed did not supervise investment banks that do not take deposits from customers. This exemption came to an end in 2008 when the collapse of Bear Stearns, an investment bank, threatened to bring down large numbers of other institutions that had financial ties to the ailing firm. The Fed stepped in to extend Bear Stearns an emergency loan and to force it to sell out to JPMorgan, a much stronger institution, for a nominal price. Subsequently, the president and Congress took action to provide $700 billion to "rescue" other financial firms facing collapse.

THE POLITICS OF TAXES

Taxes are enacted by members of Congress. Today, the Internal Revenue Code encompasses tens of thousands of pages, thousands of sections, and thousands of subsections—our tax system is very complex.

Americans pay a variety of different taxes. At the federal level, the income tax is levied on most sources of income. Social Security and Medicare taxes are assessed on wages and salaries. There is an income tax for corporations, which has an indirect effect on many individuals. The estate tax is collected from property left behind by those who have died. State and local governments also assess taxes on income, sales, and land. Altogether, the value

---

Monetary Policy
The utilization of changes in the amount of money in circulation to alter credit markets, employment, and the rate of inflation.

Loose Monetary Policy
Monetary policy that makes credit inexpensive and abundant, possibly leading to inflation.

Tight Monetary Policy
Monetary policy that makes credit expensive in an effort to slow the economy.

---

didyouknow...

That it costs the U.S. Mint 1.4 cents to make a penny and 7.8 cents to make a nickel?

FIGURE 14–13: Total Amount of Taxes Collected as a Percentage of Gross Domestic Product (GDP) in Major Industrialized Nations

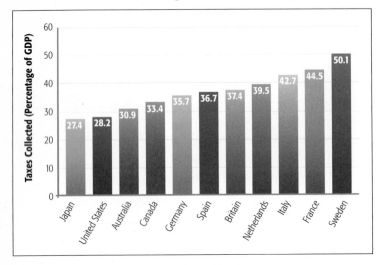

Source: Organization for Economic Cooperation and Development.

of all taxes collected by the federal government and by state and local governments approaches 30 percent of the GDP. This is a substantial sum, but it is less than what many other countries collect, as you can see in Figure 14–13.

FEDERAL INCOME TAX RATES

Individuals and businesses pay taxes based on tax rates. Not all of your income is taxed at the same rate. The first few dollars you make are not taxed at all. The highest rate is imposed on the "last" dollar you make. This highest rate is the *marginal tax rate*. Table 14–1 shows the 2008 marginal tax rates for individuals and married couples (tax forms filed in 2009). The higher the tax rate—the action on the part of the government—the greater the public's reaction to that tax rate. If the highest tax rate you pay on the income you make is 15 percent, then any method you can use to reduce your taxable income by one dollar saves you fifteen cents in tax liabilities that you owe the federal government. Individuals paying a 15 percent rate have a relatively small incentive to avoid paying taxes, but consider the individuals who faced a marginal tax rate of 94 percent in the 1940s. They had a tremendous incentive to find legal ways to reduce their taxable incomes. For every dollar of income that was somehow deemed nontaxable, these taxpayers would reduce tax liabilities by ninety-four cents.

LOOPHOLES AND LOWERED TAXES

Individuals and corporations facing high tax rates will adjust their earning and spending behavior to reduce their taxes. They will also make concerted attempts to get Congress to add **loopholes** to the tax law that allow them to reduce their taxable incomes. When Congress imposed very high tax rates on high incomes, it also provided for more loopholes than it does today. For example, special provisions enabled investors in oil and gas wells to reduce their taxable incomes.

In 2001, President George W. Bush fulfilled a campaign pledge by persuading Congress to enact new legislation lowering tax rates for a period of several years. In 2003, rates were lowered again, retroactive to January 2003; these rates are reflected in Table 14–1.

Loophole
A legal method by which individuals and businesses are allowed to reduce the tax liabilities owed to the government.

TABLE 14–1: Marginal Tax Rates for Single Persons and Married Couples (2008)

Single Persons		Married Filing Jointly	
Marginal Tax Bracket	Marginal Tax Rate	Marginal Tax Bracket	Marginal Tax Rate
$ 0–$ 8,025	10%	$ 0–$ 16,050	10%
$ 8,025–$ 32,550	15%	$ 16,050–$ 65,100	15%
$ 32,550–$ 78,850	25%	$ 65,100–$131,450	25%
$ 78,850–$164,550	28%	$131,450–$200,300	28%
$164,550–$357,700	33%	$200,300–$357,700	33%
$357,700 and higher	35%	$357,700 and higher	35%

As a result of other changes contained in the new tax laws, the U.S. tax code became even more complicated than it was before.

Progressive and Regressive Taxation. As Table 14–1 shows, the greater your income, the higher the marginal tax rate. Persons with large incomes pay a larger share of their income in income tax. A tax system in which rates go up with income is called a **progressive tax** system. The federal income tax is clearly progressive.

The income tax is not the only tax you must pay. For example, the federal Social Security tax is levied on wage and salary income at a flat rate of 6.2 percent. (Employers pay another 6.2 percent, making the total effective rate 12.4 percent.) In 2008, however, there was no Social Security tax on wages and salaries in excess of $102,000. (This threshold changes from year to year.) Persons with very high salaries therefore pay no Social Security tax on much of their wages. In addition, the tax is not levied on investment income (including capital gains, rents, royalties, interest, dividends, or profits from a business). The wealthy receive a much greater share of their income from these sources than do the poor. As a result, the wealthy pay a much smaller portion of their income in Social Security taxes than do the working poor. The Social Security tax is therefore a **regressive tax.** Note that three-quarters of all taxpayers owe more in payroll taxes, such as Social Security and Medicare taxes, than they do in income taxes.

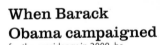

Who Pays? The question of whether the tax system should be progressive—and if so, to what degree—is subject to vigorous political debate. Democrats in general and liberals in particular favor a tax system that is significantly progressive. Republicans and conservatives are more likely to prefer a tax system that is proportional or even regressive. For example, President Bush's tax cuts made the federal system somewhat less progressive, largely because they significantly reduced taxes on nonsalary income.

Overall, what kind of tax system do we have? The various taxes Americans pay pull in different directions. The 1.45 percent Medicare tax, as applied to wages and salaries, is entirely flat—that is, neither progressive nor regressive. Because it is not levied on investment income, however, it is regressive overall. Sales taxes are regressive because the wealthy spend a relatively smaller portion of their income on items subject to the sales tax. Table 14–2 lists the characteristics of major taxes. Add everything up, and the tax system as a whole is probably slightly progressive. Given all this, who pays the lion's share of taxes? We look at that question in the *Politics and Taxes* feature on the next page.

THE SOCIAL SECURITY PROBLEM

Closely related to the question of taxes in the United States is the viability of the Social Security system. Social Security taxes came into existence when the Federal Insurance Contribution Act (FICA) was passed in 1935. Social Security was established as a means of guaranteeing a minimum level of pension benefits to all persons. Today, many people regard Social Security as a kind of "social compact"—a national promise to successive generations that they will receive support in their old age.

To pay for Social Security, as of 2008, a 6.2 percent rate is imposed on each employee's wages up to a maximum of $102,000. Employers must pay in ("contribute") an equal percentage. In addition, a combined employer/employee 2.9 percent tax rate is assessed

Progressive Tax
A tax that rises in percentage terms as incomes rise.

Regressive Tax
A tax that falls in percentage terms as incomes rise.

When Barack Obama campaigned for the presidency in 2008, he promised that there would be tax relief for the middle class. Why do most candidates favor some tax reductions while at the same time also favor increased government spending on many new programs? (Photo by Darren McCollester/Getty Images)

TABLE 14–2:
Progressive versus Regressive Taxes

Progressive Taxes
Federal income tax
State income taxes
Federal corporate income tax
Estate tax

Regressive Taxes
Social Security tax
Medicare tax
State sales taxes
Local real estate taxes

politicsand...taxes

WHO PAYS THE LION'S SHARE OF TAXES?

There hasn't been a presidential primary season in decades without at least one candidate claiming that we have to change the tax system so that "the rich pay their fair share." Some would argue, however, that the rich—and, increasingly, the not-so-rich—actually pay more than their fair share of taxes already.

WHAT THE RICH AND THE POOR PAY IN INCOME TAX

Let's look at the federal income tax, the most important tax in the U.S. tax system. Obviously, even if lower-income individuals faced the same income tax rates as higher-income individuals, the former group would pay a smaller share of total income taxes because they earn lower incomes. We have a *progressive* federal income tax system, though. As a result, lower-income individuals also pay lower tax *rates* than those assessed against incomes of higher earners. Under our progressive federal income tax system, lower-income individuals pay a very small share of total tax payments.

Look at Figure 14–14. Taxpayers among the bottom 50 percent of income earners—those who earn about 14 percent of all income—account for less than 4 percent of federal income taxes paid. As a result, the share of income taxes paid by the lowest-income individuals is considerably less than their share of total income.

Figure 14–14 also shows that the bulk of income tax payments in America is concentrated among the highest-income taxpayers. Consider the numbers: The top 10 percent of income earners—those that earn just over 46 percent of all income—pay about 70 percent of federal income taxes. The top 5 percent—those with incomes of $145,300 or more—pay 59.7 percent of all federal income

taxes, but earn only 30 percent of all total adjusted gross income. Those among the top 1 percent earn about 21 percent of all income, but account for more than 39.4 percent of the government's total receipts. The richest 1.3 million taxpayers—those who earn $365,000 or more—pay more income taxes than all of the 66 million American tax filers below the medium in income. Ten times more, in fact.

THE EFFECTS OF THE INCOME TAX

No matter what politicians say about the rich not paying their fair share of taxes, the income tax figures say something else. The highest-income earners in the United States pay a considerably larger share of the nation's overall income tax bill than lower-income taxpayers. The highest-income taxpayers also pay proportionately higher shares of taxes than their own shares of total income. Because of the income tax, the United States does indeed have a progressive tax system.

AND THERE ARE THOSE WITH NEGATIVE INCOME TAX RATES

One major aspect of the tax system is the earned-income tax credit (EITC), which we mentioned earlier in this chapter. If you earn a relatively small amount of income, you are often eligible for this credit, under which the government rebates part of your Social Security and Medicare payroll taxes. In recent years, 17 percent of taxpayers received an EITC refund on their payroll taxes. For many who receive the EITC, the refund is larger than their entire income tax obligation. The income tax rate of these taxpayers, in other words, is negative. If you adjust income tax rates for the effects of the EITC, the top 50 percent of income earners in the United States provide 97 percent of the U.S. Treasury's total income tax revenues.

So, when politicians talk about how much the rich benefit from tax cuts, they are right. The rich are the ones who pay most of the federal income taxes in the United States. Naturally, tax cuts help them more.

FOR CRITICAL ANALYSIS

Even though the data presented alongside suggest that the rich pay more than their fair share of taxes, some politicians continue to campaign on the theme of "taxing the rich more." Why?

FIGURE 14–14:
Shares of Income Taxes and Income

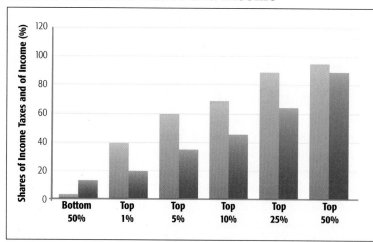

for Medicare on all wage income, with no upper limit. Medicare is a federal program, begun in 1965, that pays hospital and physicians' bills for persons over the age of sixty-five.

SOCIAL SECURITY IS NOT A PENSION FUND

One of the problems with the Social Security system is that people who pay into Social Security think that they are actually paying into a fund, perhaps with their name on it. This is what you do when you pay into a private pension plan. It is not the case, however, with the federal Social Security system, which is basically a pay-as-you-go transfer system in which those who are working are paying benefits to those who are retired.

Currently, the number of people who are working relative to the number of people who are retiring is declining. Therefore, those who continue to work will have to pay more in Social Security taxes to fund the benefits of those who retire. In 2025, when the retirement of the Baby Boomer generation is complete, benefits are projected to cost almost 25 percent of taxable payroll income in the economy, compared with the current rate of 16 percent. In today's dollars, that amounts to more than $1 trillion of additional taxes annually.

WORKERS PER RETIREE

Consider the number of workers available to support each retiree in greater detail. As you can see in Figure 14–15, just over three workers now provide for each retiree's Social Security, plus his or her Medicare benefits. Unless the current system is changed, by 2030 only two workers will be available to pay the Social Security and Medicare benefits due each recipient.

The growing number of people claiming the Social Security retirement benefit may actually pose less of a problem than the ballooning cost of Medicare. In the first place, an older population will require greater expenditures on medical care. In addition, medical expenditures *per person* are increasing rapidly. Given continuing advances in medical science, Americans may logically wish to devote an ever-greater share of the national income to medical care. This choice puts serious pressure on federal and state budgets, however, because a large part of the nation's medical bill is funded by the government.

FIGURE 14–15:

Workers per Social Security Retiree

The average number of workers per Social Security retiree has declined dramatically since the program began.

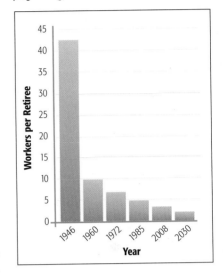

Sources: Social Security Administration; authors' estimates.

Senator Max Baucus (D., Mont.) discusses the inclusion of senior citizens who live on Social Security in Congress's proposed economic stimulus package in late 2008. Why would this senator be so concerned about senior citizens? (Alex Wong/Getty Images)

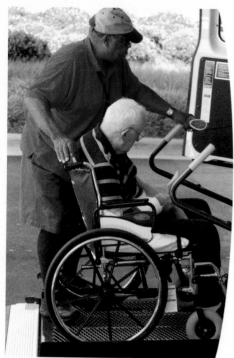

As the percentage of Americans over the age of sixty-five increases, Social Security payments and Medicare payments will also increase. How are these two benefit programs for seniors financed? (©Andrew Gentry, 2008. Used under license from Shutterstock.com)

WHAT WILL IT TAKE TO SALVAGE SOCIAL SECURITY?

The facts just discussed illustrate why efforts to reform Social Security and Medicare have begun to dominate the nation's public agenda. What remains to be seen is how the government ultimately will resolve the problem. What, if anything, might be done?

Raise Taxes. One option is to raise the combined Social Security and Medicare payroll tax rate. A 2.2 percentage point hike in the payroll tax rate, to an overall rate of 17.5 percent, would yield an $80 billion annual increase in contributions. Such a tax increase would keep current taxes above current benefits until 2020, after which the system would again technically be in "deficit." Another option is to eliminate the current cap on the level of wages to which the Social Security payroll tax is applied; this measure would also generate about $80 billion per year in additional tax revenues. Nevertheless, even a combined policy of eliminating the wage cap and implementing a 2.2 percentage point tax increase would not keep tax collections above benefit payments forever.

Other Options. Proposals are also on the table to increase the age of full benefit eligibility, perhaps to as high as seventy. In addition, many experts believe that increases in immigration offer the best hope of dealing with the tax burdens and workforce shrinkage of the future. Unless Congress changes the existing immigration system to permit the admission of a much larger number of working-age immigrants with useful skills, however, immigration is unlikely to relieve fully the pressure building due to our aging population.

Still another proposal calls for partially privatizing the Social Security system in the hope of increasing the rate of return on individuals' retirement contributions. After his reelection in 2004, President Bush proposed a partial privatization of Social Security. The plan called for workers to invest a specified portion of their Social Security payroll taxes in the stock market and possibly in other investment options. Although Bush's plan received some initial support, many older Americans were strongly opposed to the idea. One group in particular, AARP (formerly known as the American Association of Retired Persons), led a massive—and successful—lobbying and advertising campaign to change public opinion. By the summer of 2005, a majority of Americans opposed partial privatization of Social Security, and Bush backed away from his plan, which at that point had become a political liability. Sooner or later, however, the government will be forced to address the problem of retirement spending. The financial crash of 2008 described in this chapter's *Politics and Economics* feature means that the government is unlikely to face this problem immediately.

WORLD TRADE

Most of the consumer electronic goods you purchase—flat-screen television sets and digital cameras—are made in other countries. Many of the raw materials used in manufacturing in this country are also purchased abroad. For example, more than 90 percent of bauxite, from which aluminum is made, is brought in from other nations.

World trade, however, is a controversial topic. Since 1999, meetings of major trade bodies such as the World Trade Organization have been marked by large and sometimes violent demonstrations against "globalization." Opponents of globalization often refer to "slave" wages in developing countries as a reason to restrict imports from those nations. Others argue that we should restrict imports from countries that do not follow the same environmental standards as the United States.

Although economists of all political persuasions are strong believers in the value of international trade, this is not true of the general public. A recent Gallup poll asked a sam-

politicsand...economics

THE FEDERAL GOVERNMENT'S RESPONSE TO THE FINANCIAL CRASH OF 2008

In late 2007, housing prices started to fall. By 2008, the housing market was in crisis. So, too, was the economy.

THE SUB-PRIME MESS

At first, Americans thought of this financial problem simply as the "sub-prime mess." Sub-prime real estate loans are designed for individuals with poor credit ratings. Starting in 1995, the federal government pushed mortgage lenders, as well as two government-sponsored enterprises (quaintly called Freddie Mac and Fannie Mae), to give more mortgages to low-income individuals with risky credit ratings. After the housing bubble burst, many of these people defaulted on their mortgages. Commercial and investment banks, pension plans, and individuals had invested in packages of sub-prime mortgages and in other investment devices based on them. Suddenly, the market values of all these investments fell dramatically, causing a great financial panic.

UNCLE SAM COMES TO THE RESCUE

In March 2008, the federal government rescued Bear Stearns, a big Wall Street investment bank. It took over Freddie Mac and Fannie Mae in September, and that month it also lent $120 billion to one of the world's largest insurance companies, American International Group (AIG). These rescues may ultimately cost taxpayers in the hundreds of billions of dollars (if not more!). Also in September, however, the government let two big banks fail—Lehman Brothers and Washington Mutual—wiping out investors. By this time, banks had stopped making loans to each other because they were afraid they would not get the funds back. The money market, which provides short-term corporate finance, froze up. In response, the government guaranteed existing money market mutual funds.

OH YES, A $700 BILLION BAILOUT FROM CONGRESS, TOO

On September 20, Treasury Secretary Henry Paulson demanded that Congress pass a $700 billion bill to bail out financial enterprises. After one false start, Congress did so. The bill, passed on October 3, allowed the Treasury

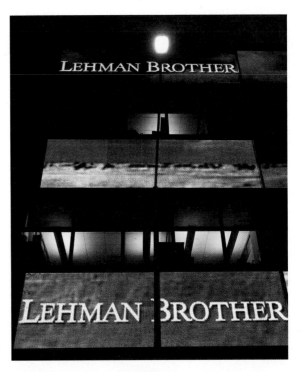

At the heart of the financial meltdown in the United States and the rest of the world was the failure in September 2008 of one of Wall Street's oldest investment institutions— Lehman Brothers. Its management tried in vain to obtain a bailout from the federal government. Because Lehman had sold so many investments throughout the world, its bankruptcy created a domino effect. The world financial crisis really became serious thereafter. (Mario Tama/Getty Images)

to actually buy shares in banks throughout the United States—partially nationalizing many of them. It included a $25 billion loan guarantee to American auto makers (which turned out to be inadequate). The federal guarantee on bank deposits was increased from $100,000 to $250,000. Where did all these funds come from? As of late 2008, nobody really knew. The government was doing so much so fast that it was impossible to estimate the total cost to taxpayers. For sure, the federal deficit in 2009 would rise by another $500 billion. Some argued that ultimately taxpayers would cough up from $1 trillion to $2 trillion for bailing out the financial system.

FOR CRITICAL ANALYSIS

By the time Barack Obama won the elections, some commentators argued that he would be unable to deal with health care, long-run retirement problems, and other pressing issues. Why did they draw this conclusion?

pling of Americans whether they believed that increased trade between the United States and other countries helped or hurt U.S. workers. Nearly two-thirds of the respondents said that they thought international trade hurt the workers. About half of the respondents said that increased international trade also hurt U.S. companies.

Imports
Goods and services produced outside a country but sold within its borders.

Exports
Goods and services produced domestically for sale abroad.

IMPORTS AND EXPORTS

Imports are those goods (and services) that we purchase from outside the United States. Today, imports make up about 17 percent of the U.S. GDP. This is a significant share of the U.S. economy, but actually it is quite small in comparison with many other countries.

We not only import goods and services from abroad; we also sell goods and services abroad, called **exports.** In 2008, we exported about $1.23 trillion of goods. In addition, we exported $460 billion of services. The United States exports about 11 percent of its GDP. Like our imports, our exports are a relatively small part of our economy compared with those of many other countries.

FIGURE 14–16: World Trade Keeps Growing

In this chart, the volume of world trade and world GDP are both represented by indexes. The base year is 1950, which means that the index is set to equal 100 for that year. While world output has increased by about eight times since 1950, world trade has increased by more than twenty-six times.

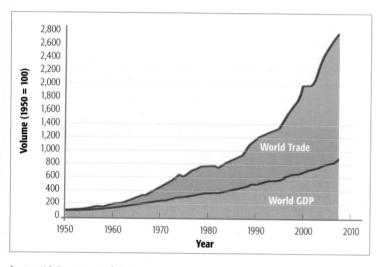

Source: U.S. Department of Commerce.

Back in the 1950s, imports and exports made up only about 4 percent of the U.S. GDP. In other words, international trade has become more important for the United States. This is also true for the world as a whole. Consider Figure 14–16. There, you see that since the 1950s, world trade has increased by more than twenty-eight times. The trade in services can include some unusual things, as you will see in this chapter's *Politics and the Cyber Sphere* feature on the facing page.

FREE TRADE AREAS AND COMMON MARKETS

To lower or even eliminate restrictions on free trade among nations, some nations and groups of nations have created free trade areas, sometimes called common markets. The oldest and best-known common market is today called the European Union (EU). As of 2009, the EU consisted of twenty-seven member nations. These countries have eliminated almost all restrictions on trade in both goods and services among themselves.

On our side of the Atlantic, the best-known free trade zone consists of Canada, the United States, and Mexico. This free trade zone was created by the North American Free Trade Agreement (NAFTA), approved by Congress in 1993. A more recent trade agreement is the Central America–Dominican Republic–United States Free Trade Agreement (CAFTA-DR),

These assembly-line workers are putting together dolls in Guangzhou, China. After some Chinese-made toys were found to contain traces of lead, China opened a toy-testing lab. Does the United States ultimately benefit or lose from its international trade with China? Why? (AP Photo/ Eugene Hoshiko)

POLITICS AND...
the cyber sphere

ONLINE GAMBLING AND FREE TRADE

The future of online gambling appears to be linked to the future of free trade around the world. Gambling is, at a minimum, a $30 billion-a-year industry in the United States. Some of that gambling takes place online. Both the federal government and many state governments have declared that most online gambling is illegal, however. The problem the United States faces is that online gambling is not illegal in Europe or on many Caribbean islands.

ANTIGUA AND BARBUDA

The Caribbean island nation of Antigua and Barbuda legalized Internet gambling years ago, before it became popular. Subsequently, Internet gambling operations were a major source of jobs for that nation's people. In 2003, Antigua and Barbuda complained to the World Trade Organization (WTO) that U.S. laws that restrict gambling were in violation of the free trade principles underlying the WTO.

Realizing that it was unlikely to win this dispute, the United States took the unprecedented step of unilaterally excluding Internet gambling from its list of services covered by the WTO. In so doing, the United States made use of a big loophole in the WTO that allows a country to modify or withdraw any commitment to provide open access to services.

The downside of using this WTO escape clause is that the United States is supposed to compensate the injured country for lost revenues. Antigua has demanded

$3.4 billion. In addition, Australia, Canada, Costa Rica, the European Union, India, Japan, and Macao are also seeking damages because of the U.S. interdiction against Internet gambling. American officials claim that the United States owes nothing. Why? Because when it signed the free trade agreement in 1994, online betting did not yet exist.

THE EUROPEAN UNION LAUNCHES AN INVESTIGATION

In 2008, the European Union officially launched an investigation into whether the U.S. Department of Justice selectively enforces its antigambling laws against European online firms. European officials point out that in the United States, it is legal to engage in Internet horse-race betting, although all other types of sports betting are illegal. In a countermove, the United States has begun threatening criminal charges against foreign online gaming operations and, in some instances, has actually issued indictments. Consequently, many executives of European online gambling operations no longer visit the United States. They are afraid of being arrested.

FOR CRITICAL ANALYSIS

Which businesses in the United States might oppose online gambling, and why?

---

which was signed into law by President George W. Bush in 2005. This agreement was formed by Costa Rica, the Dominican Republic, El Salvador, Guatemala, Honduras, Nicaragua, and the United States. As of 2008, legislatures from all seven countries had approved CAFTA-DR, despite significant opposition in certain nations, including Costa Rica.

THE WORLD TRADE ORGANIZATION

Since 1997, the principal institution overseeing **tariffs** throughout the world has been the World Trade Organization (WTO). The goal of the nations that created the WTO was to lessen trade barriers throughout the world so that all nations can benefit from freer international trade. The WTO's many tasks include administering trade agreements, acting as a forum for trade negotiations, settling trade disputes, and reviewing national trade policies. Today, the WTO has 152 members, which account for more than 97 percent of

Tariff
A tax on imports.

world trade. Another thirty countries are negotiating to obtain membership. Since the WTO came into being, it has settled many trade disputes between countries—disputes sometimes involving the United States.

Opponents of globalization have settled on the WTO as the embodiment of their fears. WTO meetings in recent years have been the occasion for widespread and sometimes violent demonstrations. Indeed, the WTO raises serious political questions for many Americans. Although the WTO has arbitration boards to settle trade disputes, no country has veto power. Some people claim that a "vetoless" America will be repeatedly outvoted by the countries of Western Europe and East Asia. Some citizens' groups have warned that the unelected WTO bureaucrats based in Geneva, Switzerland, might be able to weaken environmental, health, and consumer safety laws if such laws affect international trade flows. Investments by foreign governments in U.S. companies have been another source of concern, as we point out in this chapter's *Beyond Our Borders* feature.

beyondourborders

SHOULD WE BE WORRIED ABOUT FOREIGN GOVERNMENTS INVESTING IN AMERICA?

Periodically, Americans have debated the issue of foreign corporations investing in this country. Not that many years ago, people were worried that Japanese investors were buying up too much prime American real estate in New York and California. The current debate about investment is quite different. It no longer involves private foreign companies and individuals wanting "a piece of the action" in the United States. Rather, foreign governments, through so-called sovereign funds, have begun buying shares in major American businesses.

THE ORIGIN OF SOVEREIGN FUNDS

Oil-rich countries, such as Saudi Arabia and Russia, have amassed large pools of wealth in the last ten years. Some of that wealth has gone into what we now call sovereign funds. These are investment operations owned by foreign governments. The managers of these funds seek to locate good investments. In the past, the funds usually bought U.S. Treasury bonds and similar bonds issued by other countries. Recently, however, sovereign funds have invested tens of billions of dollars in some of the most important names on Wall Street, such as Citigroup and Goldman Sachs.

CONGRESSIONAL CONCERNS

Sovereign funds are estimated to possess as much as $3 trillion in assets. Some members of Congress are worried that foreign governments could use their investments in the United States for political ends. One such goal would be to gain access to technology secrets. U.S. lawmakers are particularly concerned about the aggressive investments made by both China and Russia—not our greatest friends. According to Senator Evan Bayh (D., Ind.), "Sovereign nations have interests other than maximizing profits and can be expected to pursue them with every tool at their disposal, including financial power." For this reason, Bayh wants Congress to impose new standards of transparency and behavior on sovereign funds investing in the United States.

FOR CRITICAL ANALYSIS

Why is a sovereign fund different from a *private* foreign organization wishing to invest in the United States?

Funds owned by sovereign nations have been invested in major U.S. businesses, such as Citigroup. What are the dangers of such actions by investing entities owned by foreign governments? (AP Photo/Mary Altaffer, file)

WHY SHOULD YOU CARE ABOUT
domesticpolicy?

It should be relatively easy to see why you, as an individual, should care about domestic policy. Countless domestic policy decisions have a direct impact on your purse or wallet. For example, the growing number of elderly people and increases in the cost of medical care will force changes in the Social Security and Medicare programs in years to come. The nature of these changes is still an open question.

DOMESTIC POLICY AND YOUR LIFE

Unless you die before your time, you will grow old. Paying for your retirement will become an important issue. Even while you are still young, you may consider the cost of Social Security taxes on your wages or salary. What should the trade-off be between the interests of the elderly and the interests of younger persons who are members of the workforce? Few questions will have a greater impact on your pocketbook, today and in the future.

HOW YOU CAN MAKE A DIFFERENCE

Should Social Security and Medicare be changed as little as possible, to keep the system at least close to what now exists? Or should we make more radical changes, such as replacing the existing programs with a system of private pensions? You can develop your own opinions by learning more about the Social Security issue.

There are a variety of proposals for privatizing Social Security. Some call for a complete replacement of the existing system. Others call for combining a market-based plan with parts of the existing program. In general, advocates of privatization believe that the government should not be in the business of providing pensions and that pensions and health insurance are best left to the private sector. The following organizations advocate privatization:

National Center for Policy Analysis
12655 N. Central Expy., Suite 720
Dallas, TX 75243–1739
972-386-6272
www.ncpa.org
www.teamncpa.org

Institute for Policy Innovation
250 S. Stemmons Freeway, Suite 215
Lewisville, TX 75067
972-874-5139
www.ipi.org.

A variety of organizations oppose privatization in the belief that it will lead to reduced benefits for some or all older people. Opponents of privatization believe that privatization plans are motivated more by ideology than by practical considerations. Organizations opposing privatization include the following:

AARP
601 E Street N.W.
Washington, DC 20049
1-800-424-3410
www.aarp.org/bulletin/socialsec/sssaveit.html

National Committee to Preserve Social Security
    and Medicare
10 G Street N.E., Suite 600
Washington, DC 20002
202-216-0420
www.ncpssm.org.

QUESTIONS FOR
discussionandanalysis

1. Review the *Which Side Are You On?* feature on page 484. Are the recent sweeps that have resulted in the arrest of large numbers of unauthorized immigrant workers unfair? Why or why not? How should we balance the human rights of unauthorized immigrants against our desire to gain control over immigration into this country? Should the problem of illegal immigration be addressed by making legal immigration easier? Why or why not?

2. Throughout modern American history, Congress has opposed the establishment of a universal health insurance system for the United States. What could be the reasons for this stance? Are those reasons compelling? What political interests might oppose a universal system, and why?

3. If a universal health insurance system were established, we would face the question of whether

unauthorized immigrants would be covered. (They do, after all, make up a major part of the uninsured population.) What complications could arise as a result?

4. Do Bjørn Lomborg's arguments against taking immediate action on global warming represent good sense or dangerous nonsense? In either case, why? What about the requirements spelled out in the Kyoto treaty: Do they reflect good sense or dangerous nonsense? Again, explain your reasoning.

5. The federal income tax system collects a greater percentage of the income of wealthier persons than of poorer ones. The Social Security tax, in contrast, is a flat rate on all incomes—and it is not collected at all on income above a certain threshold. Are the higher income-tax rates for wealthy people fair? Why or why not? Is the method of calculating the Social Security tax fair? Why or why not?

key**terms**

budget deficit 496

domestic policy 473

earned-income tax
    credit (EITC)
    program 482

environmental impact
    statement (EIS) 492

exports 506

Federal Open Market
    Committee 498

Federal Reserve System
    (the Fed) 498

fiscal policy 495

food stamps 482

gross domestic
    product (GDP) 475

gross public debt 497

imports 506

incarceration rate 489

income transfer 480

in-kind subsidy 481

Keynesian
    economics 495

loophole 500

loose monetary
    policy 499

Medicaid 476

Medicare 476

monetary policy 499

national health
    insurance 478

net public debt 497

progressive tax 501

recession 495

regressive tax 501

Supplemental Security
    Income (SSI) 482

tariff 507

Temporary Assistance
    to Needy Families
    (TANF) 481

tight monetary
    policy 499

universal health
    insurance 479

U.S. Treasury bond 496

chapter**summary**

1. Domestic policy consists of all of the laws, government planning, and government actions that concern internal issues of national importance. Policies are created in response to public problems or public demand for government action. The policymaking process is initiated when policymakers become aware—through the media or from their constituents—of a problem that needs to be addressed by the legislature and the president. The process of policymaking includes five steps: agenda building, policy formulation, policy adoption, policy implementation, and policy evaluation. All policy actions necessarily result in both costs and benefits for society.

2. Health-care spending is more than 16 percent of the U.S. economy and is growing. Reasons for this growth include the increasing number of elderly persons, advancing technology, and higher demand because costs are picked up by third-party insurers. A major third party is Medicare, the federal program that pays health-care expenses of U.S. residents over the age of sixty-five. The federal government has tried to restrain the growth in Medicare spending, but it has also expanded the program to cover prescription drugs. About 16 percent of the population does not have health insurance—a major political issue. In the 2008 presidential elections, Democratic candidates advocated universal health insurance as a solution to this problem.

3. In spite of the wealth of the United States, a significant number of Americans live in poverty. The official poverty level is based on pretax income, including cash, and does not take into consideration in-kind subsidies (food stamps, housing vouchers, and so on). The 1996 Welfare Reform Act transferred more control over welfare programs to the states and limited the number of years people can receive welfare assistance. The reform act succeeded in reducing the number of welfare recipients in the United States by at least 50 percent.

4. Today, more than one million immigrants from other nations enter the United States each year, and about 13 percent of the U.S. population consists of foreign-born persons. Illegal immigration, or unauthorized immigration (the Department of Homeland Security term), is a major political issue. Until 1986, it was legal to employ unauthorized workers, and

until recently the laws against doing so were infrequently enforced. From 2005 to 2007, President George W. Bush and Congress tried to reform the immigration system, but they failed. Questions include how to improve border control and whether the existing unauthorized population should be allowed to seek citizenship.

5. There is widespread concern in this country about violent crime, particularly the large number of crimes that are committed by juveniles. The overall rate of violent crime, including crimes committed by juveniles, declined between 1995 and 2004, and has leveled off since. In response to crime concerns, the United States has incarcerated an unusually large number of persons. Crimes associated with illegal drug sales and use have also challenged policymakers. A pressing issue facing Americans and their government today, of course, is terrorism—one of the most devastating forms of crime.

6. Pollution problems continue to plague the United States and the world. Since the 1800s, a number of significant federal acts have been passed in an attempt to curb the pollution of our environment. The National Environmental Policy Act of 1969 established the Council on Environmental Quality. That act also mandated that environmental impact statements be prepared for all legislation or major federal actions that might significantly affect the quality of the environment. The Clean Water Act of 1972 and the Clean Air Act amendments of 1990 constituted the most significant government attempts at cleaning up our environment. Recent environmental controversies have centered on climate change and global warming.

7. Fiscal policy is the use of taxes and spending to affect the overall economy. Time lags in implementing fiscal policy can create serious difficulties. The federal government has experienced ongoing budget deficits. A budget deficit is met by U.S. Treasury borrowing. This adds to the public debt of the U.S. government. Although the budget was temporarily in surplus from 1998 to 2002, deficits now seem likely for many years to come.

8. Monetary policy is controlled by the Federal Reserve System, or the Fed. Monetary policy involves changing the rate of growth of the money supply in an attempt to either stimulate or cool the economy. A loose monetary policy, in which more money is created, encourages economic growth. A tight monetary policy, in which less money is created, may be necessary to control inflation.

9. U.S. taxes approach 30 percent of the gross domestic product, a percentage that is not particularly high by international standards. Individuals and corporations that pay taxes at the highest rates try to pressure Congress into creating exemptions and tax loopholes. Loopholes allow high-income earners to reduce their taxable incomes. The federal income tax is progressive; that is, tax rates increase as income increases. Some other taxes, such as the Social Security tax and state sales taxes, are regressive—they take a larger share of the income of poorer people. As a whole, the tax system is probably slightly progressive.

10. Closely related to the question of taxes is the viability of the Social Security and Medicare systems. As the number of people who are retired increases relative to the number of people who are working, those who are working may have to pay more for the benefits of those who retire. Proposed solutions to the problem include raising taxes, reducing benefits, allowing more immigration, and partially privatizing the Social Security system in hopes of obtaining higher rates of return on contributions.

11. World trade has grown rapidly since 1950. The United States imports and exports not only goods but services as well. Groups of nations have established free trade blocs to encourage trade among themselves. Examples include the European Union and the North American Free Trade Agreement. The World Trade Organization (WTO) is an international organization set up to oversee trade disputes and provide a forum for negotiations to reduce trade restrictions. The WTO has been a source of controversy in American politics.

selected print&media resources

SUGGESTED READINGS

CQ Press. *Social Security: A Documentary History.* Washington, D.C.: CQ Press, 2007. This book is filled with primary sources, each of which is introduced with an explanation of the document and its importance, and it provides a chronological, easy-to-understand history of Social Security from its origins in 1935 to present-day controversies.

Grewal, David Singh. *Network Power: The Social Dynamics of Globalization.* New Haven, Conn.:

Yale University Press, 2008. Singh, a lawyer, seeks to explain globalization as a growth in the density of social relations and the increased adoption of worldwide standards. Examples include the spread of English and the success of Microsoft's computing standards.

Laufer, Peter, and Markos Kounalakis. *Calexico: Hope and Hysteria in the California Borderlands.* Sausalito, Calif.: PoliPointPress, 2009. *Calexico* is a news-gathering travelogue that explores the California–Mexico border region, a land of its own inhabited by people who experience the immigration crisis in all its dimensions, every day. Laufer is a foreign affairs journalist and radio commentator; Kounalakis is the editor of the *Washington Monthly*.

Miller, Roger LeRoy, *et al. The Economics of Public Issues*, 15th ed. Reading, Mass.: Addison-Wesley, 2007. Chapters 4, 8, 11, 13, 19, 20, 22, 24, and 27 are especially useful. The authors use short essays of three to seven pages to explain the purely economic aspects of numerous social problems, including health care, the environment, and poverty.

Morris, Charles R. *The Trillion Dollar Meltdown: Easy Money, High Rollers, and the Great Credit Crash*. New York: PublicAffairs, 2008. Written just as the housing market came crashing down, this book describes the immense financial leverage and arcane instruments that brought on the crisis. A banker himself, Morris briefly runs through financial history from the 1960s on, ending with the reckless lending practices that caused our current troubles.

Venkatesh, Sudhir. *Gang Leader for a Day: A Rogue Sociologist Takes to the Streets*. New York: Penguin Press, 2008. Columbia University professor Venkatesh spent seven years following and befriending a Chicago crack-dealing gang. He came away with insights into criminal behavior that could have been gained in no other way.

Walsh, Carl, and Mary Lesser. *Understanding the Fed and Monetary Policy*. New York: Palgrave Macmillan, 2008. Two economics professors, Walsh and Lesser, provide a succinct and lively guide to the Federal Reserve Bank and monetary policy. They place the Fed in its political context by examining its independent role and historical development. They also explore the way the Fed develops monetary policy, how it collects data, and the work of the Open Market Committee.

MEDIA RESOURCES

A Day's Work, A Day's Pay—This 2002 documentary by Jonathan Skurnik and Kathy Leichter follows three welfare recipients in New York City from 1997 to 2000. When forced to work at city jobs for well below the prevailing wage and not allowed to go to school, the three fight for programs that will help them get better jobs.

The Age of Terror: A Survey of Modern Terrorism—A four-part series, released in 2002, that contains unprecedented interviews with bombers, gunmen, hijackers, and kidnappers. The interviews are combined with photos from police and news archives. The four tapes are *In the Name of Liberation, In the Name of Revolution, In the Name of God*, and *In the Name of the State*.

America's Promise: Who's Entitled to What?—A four-part series that examines the current state of welfare reform and its impact on immigrant and other populations.

An Inconvenient Truth—A 2006 Paramount Classics production of former vice president Al Gore's Oscar-winning documentary on global warming and actions that can be taken in response to this challenge.

LaLee's Kin: The Legacy of Cotton—A documentary on poverty that was nominated for an Academy Award in 2002. The film tells of LaLee Wallace and her many descendents. LaLee, an illiterate sixty-two-year-old woman, lives in one of the nation's poorest counties. A second story line features Reggie Barnes, superintendent of the local schools, who faces enormous difficulties in teaching the children of illiterate parents.

Sicko—Michael Moore's 2007 effort, which takes on the U.S. health care industry. Rather than focusing on the plight of the uninsured, Moore addresses the troubles of those who have been denied coverage by their insurance companies. In his most outrageous stunt ever, Moore assembles a group of 9/11 rescue workers who have been denied proper care and takes them to Cuba, where the government, perfectly aware of the propaganda implications, is more than happy to arrange for their treatment.

Traffic—A 2001 film, starring Michael Douglas and Benicio Del Toro, that offers compelling insights into the consequences of failed drug policies. (Authors' note: Be aware that this film contains material of a violent and sexual nature that may be offensive.)

Young Criminals, Adult Punishment—An ABC program that examines the issue of whether the harsh sentences given out to adult criminals, including capital punishment, should also be applied to young violent offenders.

e-mocracy

PUBLIC POLICY

Today, the World Wide Web offers opportunities for you to easily access information about any domestic policy issue. The *Logging On* section that follows lists a variety of Web sites where you can learn more about domestic policy issues and how they affect you. Many other sites are available as well. For example, would you like to learn more about prisons and imprisonment rates in different countries? The Web site of the International Center for Prison Studies (ICPS) can help. A URL for the ICPS is **www.kcl.ac.uk/depsta/rel/icps/worldbrief/world_brief.html**. Would you like to take a turn at proposing a federal budget and allocating spending among different programs, domestic or otherwise? You can find a budget simulation game at **www.kowaldesign.com/budget**. Of course, most news media outlets have their own Web sites, which are useful for keeping up to date on the latest domestic policy developments.

LOGGING ON

For current statistics on poverty in the United States, go to
www.census.gov/hhes/www/poverty/poverty.html.

The National Governors Association offers information on the current status of Medicaid and other topics at
www.nga.org.

The Federal Bureau of Investigation offers information about crime rates on its Web site at
www.fbi.gov/ucr/ucr.htm.

You can keep up with actions taken by the Federal Reserve by checking the home page of the Federal Reserve Bank of San Francisco at
www.frbsf.org.

For further information on Social Security, access the Social Security Administration's home page at
www.ssa.gov.

For information on the 2009 budget of the U.S. government, go to
www.whitehouse.gov/omb/budget/fy2009.

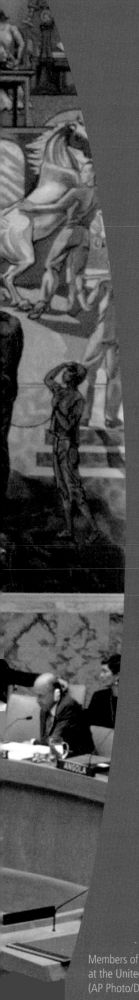

15

Foreign Policy

CHAPTER CONTENTS

Members of the United Nations Security Council meet
at the United Nations headquarters in New York City.
(AP Photo/David Karp)

whatif...we brought back the draft?

BACKGROUND

Young people today have no direct memory of the draft—forced military conscription—because military service became voluntary in 1973. From 1948 to 1973, however, all American males were subject to the draft. Draftees filled the ranks of the armed forces during war and peace. In this country, the military draft was first introduced in the Union Army during the Civil War. At that time, draftees could pay substitutes to fight in their place. The United States didn't see a military draft again until 1917, during World War I. Required military service ended in 1947 after World War II, but it resumed in 1948 to provide large military forces to confront the Soviet Union during the Cold War (a period you will read about in this chapter). The military draft was used during the war in Vietnam (1964–1975), when it became a heated issue. In recent years, the idea of bringing back the draft has reappeared in public debate. In 2006, Representative Charles Rangel (D., N.Y.) called for the reinstatement of the draft. In 2006 and 2007, members of the Bush administration also suggested that we bring back the draft.

WHAT IF WE BROUGHT BACK THE DRAFT?

The first thing that would happen if we brought back the draft is that the U.S. Selective Service would once again become an important and powerful bureaucratic organization. At the height of the Vietnam War, young men over the age of eighteen focused much of their attention on avoiding the draft. They studied how the Selective Service operated. They spent time networking with other young men to figure out how to be rejected by local draft boards. The same would certainly be true if we brought the draft back today.

The reality today is that the pool of draft-eligible men (and women if they are included) is much larger than required by the U.S. military. Even though the military has recently been stretched thin, "boots on the ground" are becoming less important as the military continues to evolve toward technological warfare. At the peak of the Vietnam War, there were more than 500,000 U.S. troops in Southeast Asia. Currently, there are about 160,000 in Iraq. Consequently, the Selective Service might have to create many more deferments than were available during the Vietnam War.

TOWARD A FAIRER SYSTEM

If we brought the draft back, the U.S. military would also contain children of wealthy families, unlike the situation today. In principle, therefore, service to one's country would become more evenly distributed across social and economic classes, thereby promoting fairness. Because not all who are eligible for the draft could be used by the military services, there would probably have to be an alternative civilian service. Persons who opted for such a program might be called upon to provide care for the elderly or government services in the inner cities.

NO MORE TROOP SHORTAGES

At various times during our military actions in Afghanistan and Iraq, U.S. forces have been overburdened. The Department of Defense has been forced to extend tours of duty for units that were about to be brought home. This also meant extending the service of National Guard units. A draft would prevent these kinds of troop shortages. In particular, a draft could eliminate the unfairness involved in stationing National Guard troops abroad for long periods of time.

A DRAFT WOULD LOWER THE EXPLICIT COST OF THE MILITARY

Typically, draftees are paid nominal amounts—less than they could earn in the civilian sector. It is not necessary to pay draftees the relatively high salaries and benefits required to induce young Americans to volunteer for military service. As a result, with a draft, federal expenditures for the military would decline. The financial burden of staging military actions in countries such as Afghanistan and Iraq would fall in part on the draftees themselves. They would effectively be paying the difference between what they could earn outside the U.S. military and what they were paid by the services.

WITH A DRAFT, THE GOVERNMENT MIGHT BE LESS EAGER TO GO TO WAR

Some argue that a draft would cause Congress and the president to think differently about military operations. If the children of senators and representatives were drafted and sent to dangerous regions, such as areas in the Middle East, those leaders probably would be more cautious about military operations. If the sons and daughters of members of Congress were better represented on the battlefield, Congress would probably pay more attention to the problem of old and ineffective equipment for our combat troops.

FOR CRITICAL ANALYSIS

1. Some argue that the volunteer nature of our U.S. military is responsible for the relatively small antiwar movement in this country today. Why might that be so?
2. What alternatives to military service might be possible?

On September 11, 2001, Americans were forced to change their view of national security and of our relations with the rest of the world—literally overnight. No longer could citizens of the United States believe that national security issues involved only threats overseas or that the American homeland could not be attacked. No longer could Americans believe that regional conflicts in other parts of the world had no direct impact on the United States.

Within a few days, it became known that the 9/11 attacks on the World Trade Center and on the Pentagon had been planned and carried out by a terrorist network named al Qaeda that was funded and directed by the radical Islamist leader Osama bin Laden. The network was closely linked to the Taliban government of Afghanistan, which had ruled that nation since 1996.

Americans were shocked by the complexity and the success of the attacks. They wondered how our airport security systems could have failed so drastically. How could the Pentagon, the heart of the nation's defense, have been successfully attacked? Shouldn't our intelligence community have known about and defended against this network? And, finally, how could our foreign policy have been so deaf to the anger voiced by Islamist groups throughout the world?

In this chapter, we examine the tools of foreign policy and national security policy in light of the many challenges facing the United States today. One of the major challenges for U.S. foreign policymakers is how best to respond to the threat of terrorism. One question raised by the resulting U.S. military commitments in Iraq and elsewhere is whether we need to bring back the draft, as we discussed in the chapter-opening *What If . . .* feature. The chapter concludes with a look at major themes in the history of American foreign policy.

FACING THE WORLD: FOREIGN AND DEFENSE POLICY

The United States is only one nation in a world with almost two hundred independent countries, many located in regions where armed conflict is ongoing. What tools does our nation have to deal with the many challenges to its peace and prosperity? One tool is **foreign policy.** By this term, we mean both the goals the government wants to achieve in the world and the techniques and strategies to achieve them. For example, if one national goal is to achieve stability in the Middle East and to encourage the formation of pro-American governments there, U.S. foreign policy in that area may be carried out through **diplomacy, economic aid, technical assistance,** or military intervention. Sometimes foreign policies are restricted to statements of goals or ideas, such as helping to end world poverty, whereas at other times foreign policies are comprehensive efforts to achieve particular objectives, such as changing the regime in Iraq.

As you will read later in this chapter, in the United States, the **foreign policy process** usually originates with the president and those agencies that provide advice on foreign policy matters. Congressional action and national public debate often affect foreign policy formulation as well.

NATIONAL SECURITY POLICY

As one aspect of overall foreign policy, **national security policy** is designed primarily to protect the independence and the political integrity of the United States. It concerns itself with the defense of the United States against actual or potential (real or imagined) enemies, domestic or foreign.

U.S. national security policy is based on determinations made by the Department of Defense, the Department of State, and a number of other federal agencies, including the National Security Council (NSC). The NSC acts as an advisory body to the president, but it

An American flag is posted in the rubble of the World Trade Center towers two days after the September 11, 2001, terrorist attacks. In what ways did the events of 9/11 change U.S. foreign policy? (Beth A. Keiser/AFP/Getty Images)

Foreign Policy
A nation's external goals and the techniques and strategies used to achieve them.

Diplomacy
The process by which states carry on political relations with each other; settling conflicts among nations by peaceful means.

Economic Aid
Assistance to other nations in the form of grants, loans, or credits to buy the assisting nation's products.

Technical Assistance
The practice of sending experts in such areas as agriculture, engineering, or business to aid other nations.

Foreign Policy Process
The steps by which foreign policy goals are decided and acted on.

National Security Policy
Foreign and domestic policy designed to protect the nation's independence and political and economic integrity; policy that is concerned with the safety and defense of the nation.

Defense Policy
A subset of national security policies having to do with the U.S. armed forces.

Moral Idealism
A philosophy that sees nations as normally willing to cooperate and agree on moral standards for conduct.

has increasingly become a rival to the State Department in influencing the foreign policy process.

Defense policy is a subset of national security policy. Generally, defense policy refers to the set of policies that direct the scale and size of the U.S. armed forces. Among the questions defense policymakers must consider is the number of major wars the United States should be prepared to fight simultaneously. Defense policy also considers the types of armed forces units we need to have, such as Rapid Defense Forces or Marine Expeditionary Forces, and the types of weaponry that should be developed and maintained for the nation's security. Defense policies are proposed by the leaders of the nation's military forces and the secretary of defense, and these policies are greatly influenced by congressional decision makers.

DIPLOMACY

Diplomacy is another aspect of foreign policy. Diplomacy includes all of a nation's external relationships, from routine diplomatic communications to summit meetings among heads of state. More specifically, diplomacy refers to the settling of disputes and conflicts among nations by peaceful methods. Diplomacy is the set of negotiating techniques by which a nation attempts to carry out its foreign policy.

The United Nations often spearheads diplomatic actions in the interests of maintaining peace in certain areas. For example, in 2006 several incidents set off an ever-escalating war between Israel and Hezbollah, a militant Shiite Islamist group based in Lebanon. While Israeli aircraft bombed Hezbollah's positions inside Lebanon and Hezbollah shelled Israeli cities with rockets, diplomatic efforts persisted at the United Nations. The diplomatic goal of establishing a cease-fire was eventually realized, but not until after many Israelis and Lebanese had died.

Of course, diplomacy can be successful only if the parties are willing to negotiate. The question of whether to negotiate with leaders such as Mahmoud Ahmadinejad, the president of Iran, became an issue in the 2008 U.S. presidential campaigns. Illinois senator Barack Obama, the Democrat, favored negotiating with Ahmadinejad without preconditions. Arizona senator John McCain, the Republican, denounced the idea of negotiating with him at all.

A Peace Corps volunteer helps
children in Cameroon paint a mural about water sanitation in Madouma, East Province. How do such actions by Americans constitute part of a foreign policy rooted in moral idealism?
(Amcaja/Wikimedia)

MORALITY VERSUS REALITY IN FOREIGN POLICY

From the earliest years of the republic, Americans have felt that their nation had a special destiny. The American experiment in democratic government and capitalism, it was thought, would provide the best possible life for men and women and be a model for other nations. As the United States assumed greater status as a power in world politics, Americans came to believe that the nation's actions on the world stage should be guided by American political and moral principles. As Harry Truman stated, "The United States should take the lead in running the world in the way that it ought to be run."

MORAL IDEALISM

This view of America's mission has led to the adoption of many foreign policy initiatives that are rooted in **moral idealism.** This philosophy sees the world as fundamentally benign and assumes that most nations can be persuaded to take moral considerations into account when setting their policies.[1] In this perspective, nations

---

1. Eugene R. Wittkopf, Charles W. Kegley, and James M. Scott, *American Foreign Policy,* 7th ed. (Belmont, Calif.: Wadsworth Publishing, 2007).

should come together and agree to keep the peace, as President Woodrow Wilson (1913–1921) proposed for the League of Nations. Many of the foreign policy initiatives taken by the United States have been based on this idealistic view of the world. The Peace Corps, which was created by President John Kennedy in 1961, is one example of an effort to spread American goodwill and the technology that the country has developed to achieve some of its goals.

Political Realism
A philosophy that sees each nation acting principally in its own interest.

POLITICAL REALISM

In opposition to the moral perspective is **political realism,** often called *realpolitik* (a German word meaning "realistic politics"). Realists see the world as a dangerous place in which each nation strives for its own survival and interests regardless of moral considerations. The United States must also base its foreign policy decisions on cold calculations without regard for morality. Realists believe that the United States must be prepared militarily to defend itself, because all other nations are, by definition, dangerous. A strong defense will show the world that the United States is willing to protect its interests. The practice of political realism in foreign policy allows the United States to sell weapons to military dictators who will support its policies, to support American business around the globe, and to repel terrorism through the use of force.

AMERICAN FOREIGN POLICY—A MIXTURE OF BOTH

It is important to note that the United States has never been guided by only one of these principles. Instead, both moral idealism and political realism affect foreign policymaking. President George W. Bush drew on the tradition of morality in foreign policy when he declared that the al Qaeda network of Osama bin Laden was "evil" and that fighting terrorism was fighting evil. The war against the Taliban government in Afghanistan, which had sheltered al Qaeda terrorists, was dubbed "Operation Enduring Freedom," a title that reflected the moral ideal of spreading democracy.

To actually wage war on the Taliban in Afghanistan, however, U.S. forces needed the right to use the airspace of India and Pakistan, neighbors of Afghanistan. The United States had previously criticized both of these South Asian nations because they had developed and tested nuclear weapons. In addition, the United States had taken the moral stand that it would not deliver certain fighter aircraft to Pakistan as long as that nation continued its weapons program. When it became absolutely necessary to work with India and Pakistan, the United States switched to a realist policy, promising aid and support to both regimes in return for their assistance in the war on terrorism.

The Iraq War that began in 2003 also revealed a mixture of idealism and realism. While the primary motive for invading Iraq was realistic (the interests of U.S. security), another goal of the war reflected idealism—the liberation of the Iraqi people from an oppressive regime and the establishment of a democratic model in the Middle East. The reference to the war effort as "Operation Iraqi Freedom" emphasized this idealistic goal.

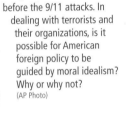

This photo of Osama bin Laden was taken in a secret hiding place somewhere in the mountains of Pakistan. Bin Laden has led the terrorist network called al Qaeda since sometime before the 9/11 attacks. In dealing with terrorists and their organizations, is it possible for American foreign policy to be guided by moral idealism? Why or why not? (AP Photo)

CHALLENGES IN WORLD POLITICS

The foreign policy of the United States, whether moralistic, realistic, or both, must be formulated to deal with world conditions. Early in its history, the United States was a weak, new nation facing older nations well equipped for world domination. In the twenty-first century, the United States faces different challenges. Now it must devise foreign and defense policies that will enhance its security in a world in which it is the global superpower and has no equal.

THE EMERGENCE OF TERRORISM

Dissident groups, rebels, and other revolutionaries have long engaged in terrorism to gain attention and to force their enemies to the bargaining table. Over the last two decades, however, terrorism has increasingly threatened world peace and the lives of ordinary citizens. A potential form of terrorism that the government must concern itself with involves cyber attacks—see this chapter's *Politics and the Cyber Sphere* feature for a discussion of this threat.

Terrorism and Regional Strife. Terrorism can be a weapon of choice in regional or domestic strife. The conflict in the Middle East between Israel and the Arab states is an example. Until recently, the conflict had been lessened by a series of painfully negotiated agreements between Israel and some of the Arab states. Those opposed to the peace process, however, have continued to disrupt the negotiations through assassinations, mass murders, and bomb blasts in the streets of Israeli cities. Other regions have also experienced terrorism. In September 2004, terrorists acting on behalf of Chechnya, a breakaway republic of Russia, seized a school at Besian in the nearby Russian republic of North Ossetia. In the end, at least 330 people—most of them children—were dead.

September 11. In 2001, terrorism came home to the United States in ways that few Americans could have imagined. In a well-coordinated attack, nineteen terrorists hijacked four airplanes and crashed three of them into buildings—two into the World Trade Center towers in New York City and one into the Pentagon in Washington, D.C. The fourth airplane crashed in a field in Pennsylvania, after the passengers fought the hijackers. Why did the al Qaeda network plan and launch attacks on the United States? Apparently, the leaders of the network, including Osama bin Laden, were angered by the presence of U.S. troops on the soil of Saudi Arabia, which they regard as sacred. They also saw the United States as the primary defender of Israel against the Palestinians and as the defender of the royal family that governs Saudi Arabia. The attacks were intended to so frighten and demoralize the American people that they would convince their leaders to withdraw American troops from the Middle East.

Bombings in Madrid and London. On March 11, 2004, ten coordinated train bombings in Madrid killed 191 people and wounded more than 2,000 others. The subsequent investigation revealed that the attacks were carried out by Islamist extremists.

On July 7, 2005, terrorists carried out synchronized bombings of the London Underground (subway) and bus network. Four suicide bombers, British citizens of Middle Eastern descent, claimed the lives of fifty-two other people and wounded hundreds more in the attacks.

In August 2006, British authorities foiled a plot to bring down ten planes scheduled to leave London's Heathrow Airport for the United States. If successful, it would have been the biggest terrorist attack since September 11. The alleged bombers planned to blow

Acts of terrorism can occur anywhere, as the Spanish found out when ten coordinated train bombings occurred in Madrid on March 11, 2004. On that bloody day, 191 people were killed and more than 2,000 were wounded. Why would Islamic extremists be interested in killing Spaniards? (AP Photo/Alvaro Hernandez)

POLITICS AND...
the cyber sphere

CYBER ATTACKS ON OUR NATIONAL SECURITY

As you read this text, various branches of the U.S. government are fending off sophisticated attempts to obtain sensitive data about our military. The same is true for private contractors who perform services for the U.S. military. In the last few years, both the U.S. government and its defense contractors have faced attempted espionage on a massive scale. Seemingly innocuous e-mails sent to the Pentagon and defense contractors have contained sophisticated embedded programs that can track the recipient's every keystroke if the recipient opens up an attachment to the e-mail. In any one year, there are at least 13,000 cyber-security incidents at the Homeland Security Department alone. Military networks in the United States fend off thousands of attempted incursions each year.

ENTER OPERATION BYZANTINE FOOTHOLD

In response to the increasing number of cyber attacks, the U.S. Defense Department has launched a classified operation called Byzantine Foothold. Its goal is to detect, track, and disarm the thousands of intrusions into the government's most critical networks. In 2008, the president issued an executive order known as the Cyber Initiative. The goal of this initiative is to overhaul U.S. cyber defenses. The initiative will cost U.S. taxpayers tens of billions of dollars.

FOREIGN GOVERNMENTS AND TRAINED CYBER ATTACKERS

While many of the cyber attacks on U.S. government networks are simply done for fun by amateur hackers, the most serious ones are carried out by trained professionals backed by foreign governments. According to military intelligence communities, for the moment the main culprit is the People's Republic of China. Officials in China deny this charge.

REALITY MIMICS FICTION

Cyber attacks are at the center of the plot of *Live Free or Die Hard*, the latest *Die Hard* movie starring Bruce Willis. Cyber terrorists reach the Federal Bureau of Investigation's networks, obtain financial data, and also bring car traffic to a halt in Washington, D.C. According to Senator Christopher Bond (R., Miss.), this fictional movie is not that much of an exaggeration: "The movie illustrates the potential impact of a cyber conflict. Except for a few things, let me just tell you: it's credible."

According to some government sources, cyber intruders were able to penetrate a network belonging to the State Department's highly sensitive Bureau of Intelligence and Research. This security breach put operatives of the Central Intelligence Agency and worldwide embassies at risk. The breach occurred when an employee of the State Department clicked on an attachment of what appeared to be an authentic e-mail. In the process, a Trojan "backdoor" got to look inside the State Department's networks. For a time, professional antihacker teams at the State Department watched helplessly as streams of data slipped through this backdoor and onto the Internet.

FOR CRITICAL ANALYSIS

What is fundamentally different between cyber attacks and traditional military attacks?

(© 2008, Phecsone. Used under license from Shutterstock.com.)

up the airplanes with liquid chemicals that could be combined to make a bomb. After the suspects were arrested, the London airport was shut down, flights to the United States were canceled, and travel by air was extremely difficult in England for a few days. Since then, airline passengers have faced limits on the amount of shampoo and other liquids that they can carry onto aircraft.

Airline passengers have wondered for years whether the antiterrorism rules that they face are truly worth the cost and inconvenience that is involved. For another example of

antiterrorism actions that may not be cost-effective, see this chapter's *Politics and the States* feature on the facing page.

THE WAR ON TERRORISM

After 9/11, President George W. Bush implemented stronger security measures to help ensure homeland security and protect U.S. facilities and personnel abroad. The president sought and received congressional support for heightened airport security, new laws allowing greater domestic surveillance of potential terrorists, and new funding for the military. The Bush administration also conducted two military efforts as part of the war on terrorism.

Military Responses. The first military effort was directed against al Qaeda camps in Afghanistan and the Taliban regime, which had ruled that country since 1996. In late 2001, after building a coalition of international allies and anti-Taliban rebels within Afghanistan, the United States defeated the Taliban and fostered the creation of an interim government that did not support terrorism.

Then, during 2002 and early 2003, the U.S. government turned its attention to the threat posed by Saddam Hussein's government in Iraq. (The war in Iraq and the subsequent occupation of that country will be discussed in detail shortly.)

A New Kind of War. Terrorism posed a unique challenge for U.S. foreign policymakers. The Bush administration's response also was unique. In September 2002, President Bush enunciated what has since become known as the "Bush doctrine," or the doctrine of preemption:

> We will . . . [defend] the United States, the American people, and our interests at home and abroad by identifying and destroying the threat before it reaches our borders. While the United States will constantly strive to enlist the support of the international community, we will not hesitate to act alone, if necessary to exercise our right of self-defense by acting preemptively against such terrorists, to prevent them from doing harm against our people and our country.[2]

The concept of "preemptive war" as a defense strategy is a new element in U.S. foreign policy. The concept is based on the assumption that in the war on terrorism, self-defense must be *anticipatory.* As President Bush stated on March 17, 2003, just before launching the invasion of Iraq, "Responding to such enemies only after they have struck first is not self-defense, it is suicide."

The Bush doctrine has been much criticized. Some point out that preemptive wars against other nations have traditionally been waged by dictators and rogue states—not democratic nations. By employing such tactics, the United States would seem to be contradicting its basic values. Others claim that launching preemptive wars will make it difficult for the United States to further world peace in the future. By endorsing such a policy itself, the United States could hardly argue against the decisions of other nations to do likewise when they feel threatened.

WARS IN IRAQ

On August 2, 1990, the Persian Gulf became the setting for a major challenge to the international system set up after World War II (1939–1945). President Saddam Hussein of Iraq sent troops into the neighboring oil sheikdom of Kuwait, occupying that country.

This London bus was destroyed by a bomb, as were several other buses and subway cars in that city. Four suicide bombers, all British citizens of Middle Eastern descent, ultimately killed fifty-two other people and wounded hundreds more. How might a city government prevent such terrorist actions? (AP Photo/Peter Macdiarmid, Pool)

---

2. George W. Bush, September 17, 2002. The full text of the document from which this statement is taken can be accessed at **www.whitehouse.gov/nsc/nssall.html**.

politicsand...the states

FEDERAL ANTI-TERRORISM FINANCING VERSUS STATE PRIORITIES

Since the terrorist attacks on September 11, 2001, the federal government has meted out about $25 billion to the states with the goal of ensuring domestic security. Many of these funds, given out in the form of federal grants, have been used to improve communications and coordination among federal, state, and local law enforcement personnel. Billions of dollars have been spent to link federal law enforcement and intelligence agencies to the hundreds of thousands of highway patrol officers, police officers, and sheriffs throughout the nation.

PERHAPS THE FOCUS IS MISGUIDED

If you ask Massachusetts homeland security advisor Juliette Kayyem about obtaining federal security funds, however, you'll get an earful. She discovered that Massachusetts had to do something special to qualify for its full federal grant—it had to come up with a plan to protect the state against improvised explosive devices (IEDs). These are the same nefarious bombs used against American troops in Iraq. As Kayyem points out, there was no new intelligence to justify the requirement. It just came out of nowhere. Other state and local officials argue that federal officials are pushing them to spend funds on terrorism threats that are too remote or too vague.

State and local officials face another problem as well—insufficient funding. Local governments are being forced to spend scarce resources on antiterrorism and intelligence programs, but the Department of Homeland Security has not been paying all of the costs. As a response, some local governments have put counterterrorism programs low on their priority lists.

THE MONEY'S TOO GOOD— STATES END UP COMPLYING

In the Massachusetts example, Kayyem couldn't pass up the $20 million federal antiterrorism grant. Technically, one quarter of the funds had to be spent planning for protection against IEDs or the state would not be eligible for the funds. Massachusetts officials therefore pledged that they would upgrade bomb squads in the state's 351 cities and towns. They pledged further that they would buy more hazardous-material suits, as well as radios for communication.

FOR CRITICAL ANALYSIS

Why does the federal government institute uniform anti-terrorism requirements for all states, even though some states face much lower threats from terrorism than others do?

These Taliban militants were photographed in the late summer of 2008 in an undisclosed location in Ghazni Province in Afghanistan. Many political analysts believe that the Taliban are regaining a foothold in Afghanistan and that additional troops will be needed to keep that country free of their radical influence. Is the United States capable of pursuing antiterrorist "wars" in several countries simultaneously? (AP Photo/Rahmatullah Naikzad)

U.S. marines were
a major part of the first and second wars in Iraq. These marines are preparing to board a Chinook CH-46 helicopter during a deployment exercise in the Saudi Arabian desert. Why were there two wars in Iraq in the last two decades? (AP Photo/ Sadayuki Mikami)

This was the most clear-cut case of aggression against an independent nation in half a century.

The Persian Gulf—The First Gulf War. At the formal request of the king of Saudi Arabia, American troops were dispatched to set up a defensive line at the Kuwaiti border. After the United Nations (UN) approved a resolution authorizing the use of force if Saddam Hussein did not respond to sanctions, the U.S. Congress also granted such an authorization. On January 17, 1991, two days after a deadline for Hussein to withdraw, U.S.-led coalition forces launched a massive air attack on Iraq. After several weeks, the ground offensive began. Iraqi troops retreated from Kuwait a few days later, and the First Gulf War ended. Many Americans, however, criticized President George H. W. Bush for not sending troops to Baghdad to depose Saddam Hussein.

As part of the cease-fire that ended the First Gulf War, Iraq agreed to abide by all UN resolutions and to allow UN weapons inspectors to search for, and oversee the destruction of, its medium-range missiles and all weapons of mass destruction, including any chemical and nuclear weapons, and related research facilities. Economic sanctions were to be imposed on Iraq until the weapons inspectors finished their work. In 1999, however, Iraq placed so many obstacles in the path of the UN inspectors that they withdrew from the country.

The Persian Gulf—The Second Gulf War. After the terrorist attacks on the United States on September 11, 2001, President George W. Bush called Iraq and Saddam Hussein part of an "axis of evil" that threatened world peace. In 2002 and early 2003, Bush called for "regime change" in Iraq and began assembling an international coalition that might support further military action in Iraq.

Having tried and failed to convince the UN Security Council that the UN should take action to enforce its resolutions, Bush decided to take unilateral action against Iraq. In March 2003, supported by a coalition of thirty-five other nations, including Britain, the United States invaded Iraq. Within three weeks, the coalition forces had toppled Hussein's decades-old dictatorship and were in control of Baghdad and most of the other major Iraqi cities.

The process of establishing order and creating a new government in Iraq turned out to be extraordinarily difficult, however. In the course of the fighting, the Iraqi army, rather than surrendering, disbanded itself. Soldiers simply took off their uniforms and made their way home. As a result, the task of maintaining law and order fell on the shoulders of a remarkably small coalition expeditionary force. Coalition troops were unable to put an immediate halt to the wave of looting and disorder that spread across Iraq in the wake of the invasion.

Occupied Iraq. The people of Iraq are divided into three principal groups by ethnicity and religion. The Kurdish-speaking people of the north, who had in practice been functioning as an American-sponsored independent state since the First Gulf War, were overjoyed by the invasion. The Arabs adhering to the Shiite branch of Islam live principally in the south and constitute a majority of the population. The Shiites were glad that Saddam Hussein, who had murdered many thousands of Shiites, was gone. They were deeply skeptical of U.S. intentions, however. The Arabs belonging to the Sunni branch of Islam live mainly in the center of the country, west of Baghdad. Although the Sunnis constituted only a minority of the population, they had controlled the government under Hussein. Many of them considered the occupation to be a disaster. Figure 15–1 shows the distribution of major ethnic and religious groups in Iraq.

The Insurgency. An American-led Coalition Provisional Authority (CPA) governed Iraq until the establishment of an Iraqi interim government in 2004. One of the first acts of the CPA was to formally disband the Iraqi army, which in any event was in a serious state of disarray. In retrospect, this decision has been widely viewed as a disaster. It released hundreds of thousands of well-armed young men, largely Sunnis, who no longer had jobs but did possess a great resentment toward the American invaders. In short order, a guerrilla insurgency arose and launched attacks against the coalition forces. U.S. and British troops faced sniper attacks and improvised explosive devices (IEDs) placed on roadways. The occupation forces also came under attack by Shiite forces loyal to Muqtada

FIGURE 15–1: Ethnic/Religious Groups in Iraq

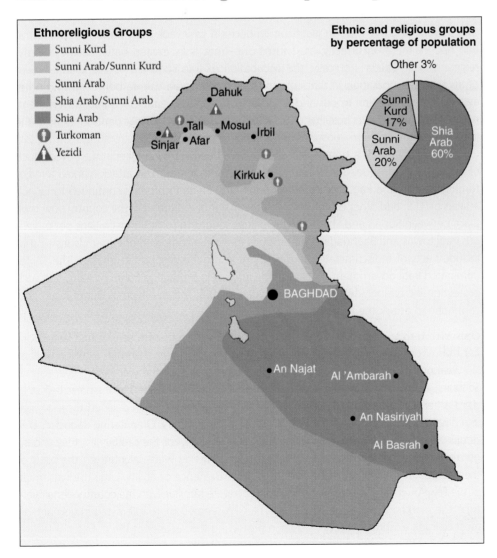

Source: The Central Intelligence Agency, as adapted by www.globalsecurity.org.

"Let's change 'brink of chaos' to 'Everything is wonderful.'"

al Sadr, a radical cleric who was the son of a famous Shiite martyr. Counterattacks by the coalition forces inevitably resulted in civilian casualties.

Public opinion polls in Iraq revealed that hostility toward the occupation forces had grown dramatically. To make matters worse, in May 2004, graphic photographs were published showing that U.S. guards at Abu Ghraib prison in Baghdad had subjected prisoners to physical and sexual abuse.

While coalition forces were able to maintain control of the country, they were now suffering monthly casualties comparable to those experienced during the initial invasion. Iraq had begun to be a serious political problem for President Bush. By May 2004, a majority of Americans no longer believed that going to war had been the right thing to do, and Bush's overall job-approval rating had fallen significantly.

The Threat of Civil War. In justifying its decision to invade Iraq, the Bush administration had claimed—incorrectly, as it turns out—that links existed between the Hussein regime and al Qaeda. Ironically, the occupation of Iraq soon led to the establishment of an al Qaeda operation in that country, which sponsored suicide bombings and other attacks against coalition troops and the forces of the newly established Iraqi government. Al Qaeda did not limit its hostility to the Americans but issued vitriolic denunciations of the Iraqi Shiites, calling them apostates and traitors to the Arab cause.

In February 2006, a bomb, believed to have been set by al Qaeda, destroyed much of the al Askari mosque, one of the holiest Shiite sites in Iraq. This attack marked a major turning point in the Iraq conflict. While Sunni and Shiite insurgents continued to launch attacks on U.S. and other coalition forces, the major bloodletting in the country now took place between Sunnis and Shiites. Shiite militias sought to force Sunni civilians out of various Iraqi towns and Baghdad neighborhoods through a campaign of ethnic cleansing that included acts of indiscriminate murder. Sunni insurgents responded in kind. The Shiite-dominated Iraqi government displayed little interest in protecting Sunni civilians, and such protection increasingly fell onto the shoulders of U.S. forces—even as Sunni insurgents continued to attack the Americans.

Opposition to the War. By 2008, the war in Iraq was in its fifth year. It had lasted longer than World War II (1941–1945) and cost the nation more than half a trillion dollars. No weapons of mass destruction—the ostensible reason for the war—were ever found. Scholars, journalists, and even intelligence reports that were leaked to the press began to paint a harsh picture both of the way in which the administration decided to go to war and how it handled the aftermath of the initial military victory. On entering Baghdad, U.S. troops were ordered *not* to act against the looting that swept the capital, lest they endanger themselves. Members of the CPA that governed Iraq were selected on the basis of their conservative ideology rather than for their experience or ability. Little use was made of the few Americans who spoke Arabic or who were familiar with the country—their very expertise marked them as security risks. The CPA seemed more interested in dismantling most of Iraq's existing institutions than in protecting the security of the public.

By late 2006, polls indicated that about two-thirds of Americans wanted to see an end to the Iraq War—a sentiment clearly expressed in the 2006 elections, which were seen largely as a referendum on the Iraq War policy of President Bush and the Republican-led

Congress. One immediate result of the elections was that Bush dismissed his secretary of defense, Donald Rumsfeld, who was closely associated with Iraq policy failures.

Shortly after the elections, the Iraq Study Group, a bipartisan commission of prominent individuals established by Congress, issued its report. The group recommended that the United States launch a diplomatic offensive to involve Iraq's neighbors, including Syria and Iran, in the stability of the country. U.S. forces in Iraq should also be drawn down. President Bush, however, accepted neither of these recommendations. Instead, in January 2007, Bush announced a major increase, or "surge," in U.S. troop strength.

Small Signs of Progress. Bush placed General David Petraeus, the U.S. Army's leading counterinsurgency expert, in charge of all forces in Iraq. Petraeus was unanimously confirmed by the Senate, and many observers thought that he was the first leader of the American war effort to demonstrate true ability. Nevertheless, skeptics doubted that Petraeus's competence and the increased number of troops would have much effect on the outcome.

In April 2007, however, a new development transformed the situation in Iraq once again. Beginning in the western Sunni heartland of Anbar Province, tribal leaders rose up against al Qaeda in Iraq and called in U.S. troops to help them. The new movement, called the Awakening, spread rapidly through most Sunni districts and Baghdad neighborhoods. Al Qaeda, it seems, had badly overplayed its hand by terrorizing the Sunni population. Anbar Province, once the most dangerous part of Iraq, was soon one of the safest. The Awakening did not solve Iraq's political problems, however. The Shiite-dominated central government resisted cooperation with the Awakening, fearing that the new movement might turn its U.S.-supplied weapons against the government. Attempts to bring Sunnis and Shiites into a national coalition of reconciliation broke down repeatedly.

An additional positive development in 2007 was the announcement by radical cleric Muqtada al Sadr that his militia, known as the Mahdi Army, would begin observing a cease-fire. A number of Mahdi Army units had degenerated into criminal organizations, however, and these rogue bodies continued to spread violence in Baghdad and elsewhere. The U.S. government accused Iran of supplying explosives and other equipment to Mahdi Army factions. In March 2008, al Sadr suspended the cease-fire; and on March 25, the Iraqi government launched an operation to drive the Mahdi Army out of the southern city of Basra—without bothering to fully inform the Americans and the British of its plans. The government forces ran into trouble and were forced to call on the Americans and British for support, but ultimately they prevailed. The very fact that the Iraqi government was willing to launch such an effort was a sign of its growing self-confidence.

Continued Antiwar Sentiment in the United States. These positive developments in Iraq seemed to have little impact on American attitudes toward the war. Republican presidential candidate John McCain gained little traction with his strong pro-war stand. Many voters apparently recalled the Bush administration's many false claims of success, and now that progress had actually occurred, they no longer gave such claims much credence—the administration had

General David Petraeus

was the U.S. Army's leading counterinsurgency expert when he was put in charge of all forces in Iraq in 2007. With the help of twenty thousand additional American troops, Petraeus appeared to have succeeded in stabilizing the insurgency in Iraq. What are some of the characteristics of the current war in Iraq? (AP Photo/Maya Alleruzzo)

Cold War
The ideological, political, and economic confrontation between the United States and the Soviet Union following World War II.

become like the little boy who cried "wolf" once too often. In addition, many Americans who did believe that conditions in Iraq were improving saw this progress as grounds for pulling U.S. troops out sooner, rather than later.

NUCLEAR WEAPONS

In 1945, the United States was the only nation to possess nuclear weapons. Several nations quickly joined the "nuclear club," however, including the Soviet Union in 1949, Britain in 1952, France in 1960, and China in 1964. Few nations have made public their nuclear weapons programs since China's successful test of nuclear weapons in 1964. India and Pakistan, however, detonated nuclear devices within a few weeks of each other in 1998, and North Korea conducted an underground nuclear explosive test in October 2006. Several other nations are suspected of possessing nuclear weapons or the capability to produce them in a short time. South Africa developed six nuclear warheads in the 1980s but dismantled them in 1990. In 2003, Libya announced that it was abandoning a secret nuclear weapons program.

With nuclear weapons, materials, and technology available worldwide, it is conceivable that terrorists could develop a nuclear device and use it in a terrorist act. In fact, a U.S. federal indictment filed in 1998, after the attack on the American embassies in Kenya and Tanzania, charged Osama bin Laden and his associates with trying to buy components for a nuclear bomb "at various times" since 1992.

Nuclear Stockpiles. More than 32,000 nuclear warheads are known to be stocked worldwide, although the exact number is uncertain because some countries do not reveal the extent of their nuclear stockpiles. Although the United States and Russia have dismantled some of their nuclear weapons systems since the end of the **Cold War** (discussed later in this chapter), both still retain sizable nuclear arsenals. Also, since the dissolution of the Soviet Union in 1991, the security of its nuclear arsenal has declined. There have been reported thefts, smugglings, and illicit sales of nuclear material from the former Soviet Union in the past fifteen years. In addition, Israel is known to possess more than one hundred nuclear warheads.

This nuclear reactor was destroyed by the North Korean government in 2008 as part of its compliance with agreements reached between the United States and other countries to halt its nuclear weapons activities. In the fall of that year, however, it refused to allow further inspection of its nuclear activities and claimed to have started rebuilding its uranium enrichment capabilities. How does a North Korea equipped with nuclear weapons pose a threat to the United States? (AP Photo/S. S. Hecker, HO, File)

Attempts to Curb Nuclear Proliferation. The United States has attempted to influence late arrivals to the "nuclear club" through a combination of rewards and punishments. In some cases, the United States has promised aid to a nation to gain cooperation. In other cases, such as those of India and Pakistan, it has imposed economic sanctions as a punishment for carrying out nuclear tests. In spite of the United States' disagreement with these countries, President Bush signed a new nuclear pact with India in March 2006.

In 1999, President Bill Clinton presented the Comprehensive Nuclear Test Ban Treaty to the Senate for ratification. The treaty, formed in 1996, prohibits all nuclear test explosions worldwide and provides for the establishment of a global network of monitoring stations. Ninety-three nations have ratified the treaty. Among those that have not are China, India, Israel, and Pakistan. In a defeat for the Clinton administration, the U.S. Senate rejected the treaty in 1999.

The Nuclear Ambitions of Iran and North Korea. For years, the United States, the European Union, and the United Nations (UN) have tried to prevent Iran from becoming a nuclear power. In spite of these efforts, many observers believe that Iran is now in the process of developing a nuclear weapon—although Iran maintains that it is interested in developing nuclear power only for peaceful purposes. Continued diplomatic attempts to at least slow down Iran's quest for a nuclear bomb have proved ineffectual at best, and it is unclear whether recently imposed UN sanctions will be an effective deterrent.

Early in his presidency, George W. Bush described both Iran and North Korea as members of an "axis of evil." Since then, Bush has been largely unwilling to engage in direct negotiations with Iran. The Bush administration has participated in multilateral negotiations with North Korea, however, and an agreement with North Korea was reached in February 2007. The agreement provided that North Korea would start disabling its nuclear facilities and allow UN inspectors into the country. In return, China, Japan, Russia, South Korea, and the United States agreed to provide $400 million in various kinds of aid to North Korea. North Korea, however, was allowed to keep for now a nuclear arsenal, which American intelligence officials believe may include as many as six nuclear bombs or the fuel to make them. Whether North Korea would actually abandon its nuclear program was at issue for a time, but by July 2007 North Korea had dismantled one of its nuclear reactors and had admitted UN inspectors into that country.

Is a nuclear-free world possible? We look at that question in the *Which Side Are You On?* feature on the following page.

THE NEW POWER: CHINA

Since Richard Nixon's visit to China in 1972, American policy has been to engage gradually the Chinese in diplomatic and economic relationships in the hope of turning the nation in a more pro-Western direction. In 1989, however, when Chinese students engaged in extraordinary pro-democracy demonstrations that were centered in Tiananmen Square in Beijing, the Chinese government crushed the demonstrations, killing a number of students and protesters and imprisoning others. The result was a distinct chill in Chinese-American relations.

Chinese-American Trade Ties. An important factor in U.S.-Chinese relations has been the large and growing trade ties between the two countries. In 1980, China was granted *most-favored-nation status* for tariffs and trade policy on a year-to-year basis. To prevent confusion, in 1998 the status was renamed **normal trade relations (NTR) status.** In 2000, over objections from organized labor and human rights groups, Congress approved a permanent grant of NTR status to China. In 2001, Congress endorsed China's application to join the World Trade Organization (WTO), thereby effectively guaranteeing China's admission to that body. For a country that is officially Communist, China already permits a striking degree of free enterprise, and the rules China must follow as a WTO member will further increase the role of the private sector in China's economy.

China's Explosive Economic Growth. The growth of the Chinese economy during the last thirty-five years is one of the most important developments in world history. For the past several decades, the Chinese economy has grown at a rate of about 10 percent annually, a long-term growth rate previously unknown in human history. Never have so many escaped poverty so quickly.

China now produces more steel than America and Japan combined. It generates more than 40 percent of the world's output of cement. The new electrical generating capacity that China adds each year exceeds the entire installed capacity of Britain. (The new plants, which are usually coal fired, promote global warming and also generate some of the world's worst air pollution.) Skyscrapers fill the skyline of every major Chinese city.

In 2007, for the first time, China actually manufactured more passenger automobiles than the United States. China is building a limited-access highway system that, when complete, will be longer than the U.S. interstate highway system. Chinese demand for

Normal Trade Relations (NTR) Status
A status granted through an international treaty by which each member nation must treat other members at least as well as it treats the country that receives its most favorable treatment. This status was formerly known as *most-favored-nation status.*

whichsideareYOUon?

IS A NUCLEAR-FREE WORLD POSSIBLE?

The destructive capability of the atom bomb was obvious after the United States dropped one each on the Japanese cities of Hiroshima and Nagasaki in 1945. Since then, there have been no more nuclear bombs detonated over populated areas. At the same time, there has been an accelerating spread of nuclear weapons, nuclear know-how, and nuclear material. The biggest threat facing America and the world appears to be the possibility that the deadliest weapons ever invented could fall into the wrong hands.

A nuclear Minuteman missile.
(Creative Commons)

When the United States and Western Europe were engaged in the Cold War against the Soviet Union and its Communist allies, it was the conflict between two ideologically opposed political systems that created the threat of nuclear war. Then the Cold War ended. Nuclear forces no longer seemed central to America's security strategy. Not surprisingly, today some politicians and concerned citizens would like to make the complete elimination of nuclear weapons a major principle of U.S. foreign policy. Should we attempt to create a nuclear-free world?

OUR GOAL SHOULD BE NO MORE NUCLEAR WEAPONS ANYWHERE

The former head of the Soviet Union, Mikhail Gorbachev, wrote in 2007, "It is becoming clearer that nuclear weapons are no longer a means of achieving security; in fact, with every passing year, they make our security more precarious." He joined an expanding list of past and present U.S. officials who argue that we must move toward a nuclear-free world. These individuals argue that we should discard any existing operational plans for massive nuclear attacks—plans that are leftovers from the Cold War days. On our road to a nuclear-free world, we must dramatically accelerate work to provide the highest possible standards of security for all nuclear weapons.

Men and women make mistakes. Consider that on August 29, 2007, six cruise missiles armed with nuclear warheads were mistakenly loaded onto a U.S. Air Force plane and flown across the country. For more than a day, no one knew that these warheads were missing or where they were. Today, the United States and Russia still possess 95 percent of all known nuclear weapons. We should undertake additional agreements to reduce the nuclear forces of these two countries. Our ultimate goal should be no more nuclear weapons. We will also have to monitor secret attempts by countries to break out of any agreements reached to eliminate nuclear weapons.

NUCLEAR DISARMAMENT IS NOT POSSIBLE

Even if the United States declared that it would eliminate nuclear weapons in the distant future, such a declaration would have no direct effect on those countries attempting to "go nuclear." There are nations that believe that the acquisition of nuclear weapons will improve their security. What the United States does really doesn't matter to them. Certainly, what the United States does will have no impact on attempts by terrorist groups to gain nuclear materials. The United States—even with the help of Russia—cannot eliminate the scientific knowledge and know-how that already exist about the making of nuclear weapons. Moreover, even if all nations that have nuclear weapons agreed to get rid of them, many would probably keep a few clandestinely, "just to be sure."

Given that nuclear weapons exist elsewhere, the United States cannot "go naked." It must maintain its own nuclear weapons to deter potential opponents and to avoid being intimidated by nuclear-armed nations. To be sure, given the capability of conventional U.S. weapons, the United States can reduce the number of nuclear warheads that it has, but they should not be reduced to zero. The United States has entered, and should continue to enter, into direct negotiations with countries that have—or seek to have—nuclear weapons. We did this with Argentina, Brazil, South Korea, and Taiwan. Most recently, we did it with Libya. We should continue such actions. But we should always remember that for the United States, nuclear weapons play an important deterrent role—they must not be eliminated.

raw materials, notably petroleum, has led, in part, to dramatic increases in the price of oil and other commodities. Its people have begun to eat large quantities of meat, which adds to the strain on world food production. By 2050, if not before, the economy of China is expected to be larger than that of the United States. China, in short, will become the world's second superpower.

The Issue of Taiwan. Inevitably, economic power translates into military potential. Is this a problem? It could be if China had territorial ambitions. Currently, China does not appear to have an appetite for non-Chinese territory, and it does not seem likely to develop one. But China has always considered the island of Taiwan to be Chinese territory. In principle, Taiwan agrees. Taiwan calls itself the "Republic of China" and officially considers its government to be the legitimate ruler of the entire country. This diplomatic fiction has remained in effect since 1949, when the Chinese Communist Party won a civil war and drove the anti-Communist forces off the mainland.

China's position is that sooner or later, Taiwan must rejoin the rest of China. The position of the United States is that this reunification must not come about by force. Is peaceful reunification possible? China holds up Hong Kong as an example. Hong Kong came under Chinese sovereignty peacefully in 1997. The people of Taiwan, however, are far from considering Hong Kong to be an acceptable precedent.

Chinese Nationalism. A disturbing recent development—the growth in public expressions of Chinese nationalism—could have an impact on the Taiwan question. This increased expression has taken the form of heated rhetoric on the Web, cyber attacks against computers of other nations, and even violent demonstrations. The United States was the target in 1999, after U.S. forces accidentally bombed the Chinese Embassy in Serbia and again in 2001 after a collision between U.S. and Chinese military aircraft. In 2005, anti-Japanese riots broke out after that country's government approved history textbooks that seemed to deny Japanese atrocities in China during World War II. In 2008, following anti-Chinese riots in Tibet, China condemned France for not adequately protecting the Olympic torch from pro-Tibet demonstrators while the torch was en route to the Beijing Olympics. The Chinese government has sometimes appeared to support nationalist agitation because it benefits politically from it. When nationalism has seemed to be getting out of hand, however, the government has cracked down.

The growth of Chinese economic power is not the only long-term development that is changing the shape of our world. We discuss the impact of population growth on world affairs in this chapter's *Beyond Our Borders* feature on the next page.

Protesters demanding more rights for ethnic minorities in China, including Tibetans, Mongolians and Uighurs, demonstrate with Tibetan flags outside the Chinese embassy in Berlin, Germany, a day before the opening ceremony of the 2008 Olympic Games in Beijing. (Junko Kimura/Getty Images)

REGIONAL CONFLICTS

The United States has played a role—sometimes alone, sometimes with other powers—in many regional conflicts during the 1990s and 2000s.

Cuba. Tensions between the United States and Cuba have been frequent since Fidel Castro took power in Cuba in 1959. Relations with Cuba continue to be politically important in the United States because the Cuban American population can influence election outcomes in Florida, a state that all presidential candidates try to win. When Fidel Castro became seriously ill and underwent surgery in the summer of 2006, his brother, Raul, assumed power. No one believes that if Castro dies, his brother will be any more amenable to normal relations with the United States.

Israel and the Palestinians. As a longtime supporter of Israel, the United States has undertaken to persuade the Israelis to negotiate with the Palestinian Arabs who live in the territories occupied by the state of Israel. The conflict, which began in 1948, has been extremely hard to resolve. The internationally suggested solution is for Israel to yield the West Bank and the Gaza Strip to the Palestinians in return for effective security

beyondourborders

THE IMPACT OF POPULATION GROWTH ON AMERICA'S FUTURE ROLE IN THE WORLD

Do numbers matter? Apparently so, at least when it comes to population numbers and world power. After World War II, the United States faced an adversary—the Union of Soviet Socialist Republics (U.S.S.R.)—which was alleged to have the second-largest economy in the world, half the size of ours. Its military was definitely much larger than ours. When World War II ended, many believed that the Soviet army had defeated Hitler by the force of numbers alone. By 1990, the Soviet population was 289 million, compared with America's 256 million. A year later, when the Soviet Union disintegrated,

Russia was down to fewer than 149 million people. For a time, Russia's economy didn't even appear on lists of the world's ten largest. The United States was now the world's third most populous nation, with U.S. military spending approaching that of all other nations combined.

POPULATION CHANGES THAT WILL AFFECT WORLD POWER RELATIONSHIPS

The United Nations projects that in forty years, both India and China will have around 1.5 billion residents each, compared with 400 million residents in the United States. Populations in Arab and Pashtun nations are all growing. Pakistan's population, for example, will increase from 144 million to almost 300 million in the next forty years. China's population is stabilizing. Not so the population of Africa. The continent's population was only 224 million in 1950, reached 821 million in 2000, and by 2050 will be almost 2 billion. Africa's economy is growing, albeit slowly, on a per capita basis. We can predict, therefore, that over time, African nations might become more important in world affairs. Russia is another story, as is Japan. By 2050, these two nations won't even be among the top ten nations in the world with respect to population.

AND WHAT ABOUT THE UNITED STATES?

Currently, the United States is the only major power that is experiencing significant population growth. By 2050, the United States will have an estimated 4.37 percent of the world's population, down somewhat from 4.65 percent in 2000. Russia's population is dwindling, sometimes at a shocking rate, because of poor diet and health care, alcoholism, and AIDS. Many Western European countries are predicted to fall in population as well. It is possible that Russia may dwindle into insignificance and that Western Europe and Japan will lose clout. The United States should remain one of the world's superpowers for a long time to come, but it is likely to be joined by China and, later on, India as well.

This crowded scene in the old section of New Delhi is a common sight. The population of India, as with China, is expected to exceed 1.5 billion within four decades. Does population matter in terms of projecting world power? Why or why not? (AP Photo/Manish Swarup)

FOR CRITICAL ANALYSIS

Does it really matter whether the United States remains a superpower? Why or why not?

commitments and abandonment by the Palestinians of any right of return to Israel proper. The Palestinians, however, have been unwilling to stop terrorist attacks on Israel, and Israel has been unwilling to dismantle its settlements in the occupied territories. Further, the two parties have been unable to come to an agreement on how much of the West Bank should go to the Palestinians and on what compensation (if any) the Palestinians should receive for abandoning all claims to settlement in Israel proper.

In December 1988, the United States began talking directly to the Palestine Liberation Organization (PLO), and in 1991, under great pressure from the United States, the Israelis opened talks with representatives of the Palestinians and other Arab states. In 1993, both parties agreed to set up Palestinian self-government in the West Bank and the Gaza Strip. The historic agreement, signed in Cairo on May 4, 1994, put in place a process by which the Palestinians would assume self-rule in the Gaza Strip and in the town of Jericho. In the months that followed, Israeli troops withdrew from much of the occupied territory, the new Palestinian Authority assumed police duties, and many Palestinian prisoners were freed by the Israelis.

These Palestinian children scavenge around the rubble of a five-story apartment building that was destroyed in their neighborhood. Violence became commonplace after Palestinian radicals rejected the so-called Oslo Peace Agreement signed in 2000. The Palestinian-Israeli conflict has created tension between the United States and much of the Arab world. What are some possible solutions to this ongoing conflict? (AP Photo/Jacqueline Larma)

The Collapse of the Israeli-Palestinian Peace Process. Although negotiations between the Israelis and the Palestinians resulted in more agreements in Oslo, Norway, in 2000, the agreements were rejected by Palestinian radicals, who began a campaign of suicide bombings in Israeli cities. In 2002, the Israeli government responded by moving tanks and troops into Palestinian towns to kill or capture the terrorists. One result of the Israeli reoccupation was an almost complete collapse of the Palestinian Authority. Groups such as Hamas (the Islamic Resistance Movement), which did not accept the concept of peace with Israel even in principle, moved into the power vacuum.

In 2003, President Bush attempted to renew Israeli-Palestinian negotiations by sponsoring a "road map" for peace. In its weakened condition, however, the Palestinian Authority was unable to make any commitments, and the road map process ground to a halt. In February 2004, Israeli prime minister Ariel Sharon announced a plan under which Israel would withdraw from the Gaza Strip regardless of whether a deal could be reached with the Palestinians. Sharon's plan met with strong opposition, but ultimately the withdrawal took place.

In January 2006, the militant group Hamas won a majority of the seats in the Palestinian legislature. American and European politicians refused to talk to Hamas until it agreed to rescind its avowed desire to destroy Israel, but so far, it has not done so. In June 2007, the uneasy balance between the Palestinian Hamas-dominated legislature and the PLO president broke down. After open fighting between the two parties, Hamas wound up in complete control of the Gaza Strip, and the PLO retained exclusive power in the West Bank. Western leaders speculated that it might be possible to negotiate exclusively with the PLO government on the West Bank, freezing out Hamas and the Gaza Strip.

The Israeli-Hezbollah (Lebanon) War. In the summer of 2006, Israel went to war with the militant group Hezbollah in Lebanon. The conflict started after Hezbollah captured several Israeli soldiers and commenced firing rockets into Israel. The United States at first did nothing, agreeing with Israel that Hezbollah had to be disarmed and weakened for there

didyouknow...

That the United States invaded and occupied part of Russia in 1919?

to be viable peace in the region. Eventually, though, as more lives were lost on both sides, the United States endorsed a UN-brokered cease-fire.

AIDS in Southern Africa. During the early 2000s, the disease AIDS (acquired immune deficiency syndrome) continued to spread throughout southern Africa. This disease infects one-fourth of the populations of Botswana and Zimbabwe and is endemic in most other nations in the southernmost part of the continent. Millions of adults are dying from AIDS, leaving orphaned children. The epidemic is taking a huge economic toll on the affected countries because of the cost of caring for patients and the loss of skilled workers. The disease may be the greatest single threat to world stability emanating from Africa. The Bush administration put in place a special aid package directed at this problem amounting to $15 billion over five years.

The Crisis in Darfur. In 2004, the world woke up to a growing disaster in Darfur, a western province of Sudan. In the spring of 2004, Sudan had reached a tenuous agreement with rebels in the southern part of the country, but the agreement did not cover a separate rebellion in Darfur. Government-sponsored militias drove more than one million inhabitants of Darfur from their homes and into refugee camps, where they faced starvation. In spite of a cease-fire, fighting renewed during the summer of 2006 and continued to plague the region. Today, at least 200,000 (some put the number as high as 450,000) have died, and more than 2.5 million have been made homeless by the militia attacks.

Until 2007, the president of Sudan repeatedly denied UN requests to intervene in Darfur, claiming that such intervention would violate his country's sovereignty. In April 2007, the Sudanese president finally agreed to accept large-scale UN assistance. In the subsequent months, however, the Sudanese president backed away from this commitment.

WHO MAKES FOREIGN POLICY?

Given the vast array of challenges in the world, developing a comprehensive U.S. foreign policy is a demanding task. Does this responsibility fall to the president, to Congress, or to both acting jointly? There is no easy answer to this question, because, as constitutional authority Edwin S. Corwin once observed, the U.S. Constitution created an "invitation to struggle" between the president and Congress for control over the foreign policy process. Let us look first at the powers given to the president by the Constitution.

These displaced Sudanese women were part of a group of over two million people who became homeless because of militia attacks in Darfur. What role, if any, should the United States play in resolving such a crisis?
(AP Photo/James Nachtwey/VII)

CONSTITUTIONAL POWERS OF THE PRESIDENT

The Constitution confers on the president broad powers that are either explicit or implied in key constitutional provisions. Article II vests the executive power of the government in the president. The presidential oath of office given in Article II, Section 1, requires that the president "solemnly swear" to "preserve, protect and defend the Constitution of the United States."

War Powers. In addition, and perhaps more important, Article II, Section 2, designates the president as "Commander in Chief of the Army and Navy of the United States." Starting with Abraham Lincoln, all presidents have interpreted this authority dynamically and broadly. Indeed, since George Washington's administration, the United States has been involved in at least 125 undeclared wars that were conducted under presidential authority. For example, in 1950 Harry Truman ordered U.S. armed forces in the Pacific to counter North Korea's invasion of South Korea. Bill Clinton sent troops to Haiti and Bosnia. In 2001, George W. Bush authorized an attack against the al Qaeda terrorist network and the Taliban government in Afghanistan. As described earlier, in 2003 Bush sent military forces to Iraq to destroy Saddam Hussein's government.

didyouknow...

That it is estimated that the Central Intelligence Agency has more than 16,000 employees, with about 5,000 in the clandestine services?

Treaties and Executive Agreements. Article II, Section 2, of the Constitution also gives the president the power to make treaties, provided that two-thirds of the senators present concur. Presidents usually have been successful in getting treaties through the Senate. In addition to this formal treaty-making power, the president makes use of executive agreements (discussed in Chapter 11). Since World War II (1939–1945), executive agreements have accounted for almost 95 percent of the understandings reached between the United States and other nations.

Executive agreements have a long and important history. During World War II, Franklin Roosevelt reached several agreements with Britain, the Soviet Union, and other countries. In other important agreements, Presidents Eisenhower, Kennedy, and Johnson all promised support to the government of South Vietnam. In all, since 1946 more than eight thousand executive agreements with foreign countries have been made. There is no way to obtain an accurate count, because perhaps as many as several hundred of these agreements have been secret.

Other Constitutional Powers. An additional power conferred on the president in Article II, Section 2, is the right to appoint ambassadors, other public ministers, and consuls. In Section 3 of that article, the president is given the power to recognize foreign governments by receiving their ambassadors.

INFORMAL TECHNIQUES OF PRESIDENTIAL LEADERSHIP

Other broad sources of presidential power in the U.S. foreign policy process are tradition, precedent, and the president's personality. The president can employ a host of informal techniques that give the White House overwhelming superiority within the government in foreign policy leadership.

First, the president has access to information. The Central Intelligence Agency (CIA), the State Department, and the Defense Department make more information available to the president than to any other governmental official. This information carries with it the ability to make quick decisions—and the president uses that ability often. Second, the president is a legislative leader who can influence the funds that are allocated for different programs. Third, the president can influence public opinion. President Theodore Roosevelt once made the following statement:

People used to say to me that I was an astonishingly good politician and divined what the people are going to think. . . . I did not "divine" how the people were going to think; I simply

President Bill Clinton shakes hands with U.S. soldiers who were stationed in Bosnia after "peacekeeping efforts" in 1995. Why would the United States send troops to a country so close to its European allies? Shouldn't those allies have undertaken this peacekeeping effort? Why or why not? (AP Photo/J Scott Applewhite)

made up my mind what they ought to think and then did my best to get them to think it.[3]

Presidents are without equal with respect to influencing public opinion, partly because of their ability to command the media. Depending on their skill in appealing to patriotic sentiment (and sometimes fear), they can make people believe that their course in foreign affairs is right and necessary. Public opinion often seems to be impressed by the president's decision to make a national commitment abroad. President George W. Bush's speech to Congress shortly after the 9/11 attacks rallied the nation and brought new respect for his leadership. It is worth noting that presidents normally, although certainly not always, receive the immediate support of the American people in a foreign policy crisis.

Finally, the president can commit the nation morally to a course of action in foreign affairs. Because the president is the head of state and the leader of one of the most powerful nations on earth, once the president has made a commitment for the United States, it is difficult for Congress or anyone else to back down on that commitment.

OTHER SOURCES OF FOREIGN POLICYMAKING

In addition to the president, there are at least four foreign policymaking sources within the executive branch. These are (1) the Department of State, (2) the National Security Council, (3) the intelligence community, and (4) the Department of Defense.

The Department of State. In principle, the State Department is the executive agency that has primary authority over foreign affairs. It supervises U.S. relations with the nearly two hundred independent nations around the world and with the United Nations and other multinational groups, such as the Organization of American States. It staffs embassies and consulates throughout the world. It does all this with one of the smallest budgets of the cabinet departments.

Newly elected presidents usually tell the American public that the new secretary of state is the nation's chief foreign policy adviser. Nonetheless, the State Department's preeminence in foreign policy has declined since World War II. The State Department's image within the White House Executive Office and Congress (and even with foreign governments) is quite poor—a slow, plodding, bureaucratic maze of inefficient, indecisive individuals. Reportedly, Premier Nikita Khrushchev of the Soviet Union urged President John Kennedy to formulate his own views rather than rely on State Department officials who, according to Khrushchev, "specialized in why something had not worked forty years ago."[4] In any event, since the days of Franklin Roosevelt, the State Department has often been bypassed or ignored when crucial decisions are made.

It is not surprising that the State Department has been overshadowed in foreign policy. It has no natural domestic constituency as does, for example, the Department of Defense, which can call on defense contractors for support. Instead, the State Department has what might be called **negative constituents**—U.S. citizens who openly oppose the government's policies.

President Richard Nixon (right) is shown congratulating Secretary of State Henry Kissinger in the fall of 1973 when Kissinger was awarded the Nobel Peace Prize. Kissinger's co-recipient was diplomat Lo Duc Tho from North Vietnam. They worked together to end the war in Vietnam. Is the secretary of state the principal architect of foreign policy for the United States? (AP Photo)

Negative Constituents
Citizens who openly oppose the government's policies.

---

3. Sidney Warren, *The President as World Leader* (New York: McGraw-Hill, 1964), p. 23.
4. Theodore C. Sorensen, *Kennedy* (New York: Harper & Row, 1965), pp. 554–555.

The National Security Council. The job of the National Security Council (NSC), created by the National Security Act of 1947, is to advise the president on the integration of "domestic, foreign, and military policies relating to the national security." Its larger purpose is to provide policy continuity from one administration to the next. As it has turned out, the NSC—consisting of the president, the vice president, the secretaries of state and defense, the director of emergency planning, and often the chairperson of the joint chiefs of staff and the director of the CIA—is used in just about any way the president wants to use it.

The role of national security adviser to the president seems to adjust to fit the player. Some advisers have come into conflict with heads of the State Department. Henry A. Kissinger, Richard Nixon's flamboyant and aggressive national security adviser, rapidly gained ascendancy over William Rogers, the secretary of state. More recently, Condoleezza Rice played an important role as national security adviser during George W. Bush's first term. Like Kissinger, Rice eventually became secretary of state.

The Intelligence Community. No discussion of foreign policy would be complete without some mention of the **intelligence community.** This consists of the forty or more government agencies or bureaus that are involved in intelligence activities. They include the following:

1. Central Intelligence Agency (CIA).
2. National Security Agency (NSA).
3. Defense Intelligence Agency (DIA).
4. Offices within the Department of Defense.
5. Bureau of Intelligence and Research in the Department of State.
6. Federal Bureau of Investigation (FBI).
7. Army intelligence.
8. Air Force intelligence.
9. Drug Enforcement Administration (DEA).
10. Department of Energy.
11. Directorate of Information Analysis and Infrastructure Protection in the Department of Homeland Security.
12. Office of the Director of National Intelligence.

Intelligence Community
The government agencies that gather information about the capabilities and intentions of foreign governments or that engage in covert actions.

didyouknow...

That in the name of national security, the United States spends at least $5.6 billion annually to keep information classified?

President Bush is shown with his National Security Council (NSC) the day after the terrorist attacks on September 11, 2001. At that time, the NSC consisted of the director of the Central Intelligence Agency, the secretary of defense, the secretary of state, the vice president, the chairman of the joint chiefs of staff, and, of course, the national security adviser. How important is the NSC's role in determining U.S. foreign policy? (AP Photo/Doug Mills)

The CIA, created as part of the National Security Act of 1947, is the key official member of the intelligence community.

Covert Actions. Intelligence activities consist mostly of overt information gathering, but covert actions also are undertaken. Covert actions, as the name implies, are carried out in secret, and the American public rarely finds out about them. The CIA covertly aided in the overthrow of the Mossadegh regime in Iran in 1953 and the Arbenz government of Guatemala in 1954. The agency was instrumental in destabilizing the Allende government in Chile from 1970 to 1973.

During the mid-1970s, the "dark side" of the CIA was partly uncovered when the Senate undertook an investigation of its activities. One of the major findings of the Senate Select Committee on Intelligence was that the CIA had routinely spied on American citizens domestically, which was supposedly a prohibited activity. Consequently, the CIA came under the scrutiny of oversight committees within Congress, which restricted the scope of its operations. By 1980, however, the CIA had regained much of its lost power to engage in covert activities.

Criticisms of the Intelligence Community. By 2001, the CIA had come under fire for a number of lapses, including the discovery that one of its agents had been spying on behalf of a foreign power, the failure to detect the nuclear arsenals of India and Pakistan, and, above all, the failure to obtain advance knowledge about the 9/11 terrorist attacks. With the rise of terrorism as a threat, the intelligence agencies have received more funding and enhanced surveillance powers, but these moves have also provoked fears of civil liberties violations.

In 2004, the bipartisan 9/11 commission called for a new intelligence czar to oversee the entire intelligence community, with full control of all agency budgets. After initially balking at this recommendation, President Bush eventually called for a partial implementation of the commission's report. Legislation enacted in 2004 established the Office of the Director of National Intelligence to oversee the intelligence community. In 2005, Bush appointed John Negroponte to be the first director.

Given the ease with which information can now be collected using the Internet, how useful are old-fashioned spies? We look at that issue in this chapter's *Politics and Foreign Policy* feature.

The Department of Defense. The Department of Defense (DOD) was created in 1947 to bring all of the various activities of the American military establishment under the jurisdiction of a single department headed by a civilian secretary of defense. At the same time, the joint chiefs of staff, consisting of the commanders of the various military branches and a chairperson, was created to formulate a unified military strategy.

Although the Department of Defense is larger than any other federal department, it declined in size after the fall of the Soviet Union in 1991. In the subsequent ten years, the total number of civilian employees was reduced by nearly 400,000, to about 665,000. Military personnel were also reduced in number. The defense budget remained relatively flat for several years, but with the advent of the war on terrorism and the use of military forces in Afghanistan and Iraq, funding has again been increased.

didyouknow...

That the Pentagon's stockpile of strategic materials includes 1.5 million pounds of quartz crystals used in pre–Great Depression radios and 150,000 tons of tannin used in tanning cavalry saddles?

This aerial view of the five-sided Pentagon building shows where many of the defense personnel work in Arlington, Virginia. The Pentagon covers an area of twenty-nine acres. When was the Department of Defense created? *(AP Photo)*

politicsand...foreign policy

DO WE STILL NEED SPIES?

Stories about spies have filled endless numbers of novels and have been the subject matter of numerous films. For the past four decades, every U.S. president has begun each day with a top-secret, personal briefing on security threats and global affairs. Much of this information has been obtained through covert spy missions, as well as from other highly classified intelligence sources. Increasingly, though, this information comes from the Internet.

OPEN SOURCES ARE INDEED OPEN TO EVERYONE

It's hard to stop anyone from accessing much on the Internet these days. Hence, much of the content of the President's Daily Brief can be accessed from the Internet rather than from secrets obtained by risky espionage missions. The Central Intelligence Agency (CIA) has set up open-source centers. Every day, CIA operatives examine al Qaeda Web sites. They also look at everything that high-level Russian officials say and that is recorded on the Internet.

Instead of sending potential spies to expensive training camps, the Defense Intelligence Agency is training analysts to mine open sources on the Internet. They learn to vet (scrutinize) information to make sure that it is not misinformation from terrorist groups and from not-so-friendly governments in China and Russia.

GOOGLE SEARCH WORKS FINE, TOO

When the U.S. State Department wanted to find out the names of Iranians who could be sanctioned for their involvement in the clandestine nuclear weapons program, it could not get that information from the CIA. The second-best solution was to assign a junior Foreign Service officer to find the names by doing a Google search. The junior officer entered a number of search

(© 2008, Tomasz Trojanowski. Used under license from Shutterstock.com.)

terms, including "Iran and nuclear." The names of Iranians with the most hits became suspicious targets for international rebuke. Eventually, the CIA vetted the list of names that the junior officer from the Foreign Service had prepared. The result was thinned down to a handful of names. These names were given to the United Nations for censure. The beauty of this method is that the U.S. intelligence services do not have to justify using sensitive information from intelligence programs that might contain these names. After all, the initial list of names was merely the result of a Google search!

FOR CRITICAL ANALYSIS

U.S. government officials now claim that Russia is attempting to obtain information on U.S. domestic, foreign, and military policy via an intensive intelligence offensive. What does the information presented above tell you about how Russian secret agents might be accomplishing this task?

CONGRESS BALANCES THE PRESIDENCY

A new interest in the balance of power between Congress and the president on foreign policy questions developed during the Vietnam War (1964–1975). Sensitive to public frustration over the long and costly war and angry at Richard Nixon for some of his other actions as president, Congress attempted to establish limits on the power of the president in setting foreign and defense policy.

THE WAR POWERS RESOLUTION OF 1973

In 1973, Congress passed the War Powers Resolution over President Nixon's veto. The act limited the president's use of troops in military action without congressional approval (see Chapter 11). Most presidents, however, have not interpreted the "consultation" provisions of the act as meaning that Congress should be consulted before military action is taken. Instead, Presidents Ford, Carter, Reagan, George H. W. Bush, and Clinton ordered troop movements and then informed congressional leaders. Critics note that it is quite possible for a president to commit troops to a situation from which the nation could not withdraw without incurring heavy losses, whether or not Congress is consulted.

THE POWER OF THE PURSE

One of Congress's most significant constitutional powers is the so-called power of the purse. In other words, the president may order that a certain action be taken, but that decision cannot be executed unless it is funded by Congress. When the Democrats assumed control of Congress in January 2007, many expected that the new Congress would use its power of the purse to bring an end to the Iraq War, in view of the strong public opinion against the war. After all, Congress had exerted its authority in the past by limiting or denying presidential funding requests for military assistance to various groups (such as Angolan rebels and the government of El Salvador).

Because the Democratic majority in Congress was so slim, however, Congress could not gain enough votes to ensure an override of President Bush's veto of any legislation forcing him to change his war policy. (Recall from Chapter 11 that to override a presidential veto requires a two-thirds majority in each chamber.)

THE MAJOR FOREIGN POLICY THEMES

Although some observers might suggest that U.S. foreign policy is inconsistent and changes with the current occupant of the White House, the long view of American diplomatic ventures reveals some major themes underlying foreign policy. In the early years of the nation, presidents and the people generally agreed that the United States should avoid foreign entanglements and concentrate instead on its own development. From the beginning of the twentieth century until the present, however, a major theme has been increasing global involvement. The theme of the post–World War II years was the containment of communism. The theme for at least the first part of the twenty-first century may be the containment of terrorism.

THE FORMATIVE YEARS: AVOIDING ENTANGLEMENTS

Foreign policy was largely nonexistent during the formative years of the United States. Remember that the new nation was operating under the Articles of Confederation. The national government had no right to levy or collect taxes, no control over commerce, no right to make commercial treaties, and no power to raise an army (the Revolutionary army was disbanded in 1783). The government's lack of international power was made clear when Barbary pirates seized American hostages in the Mediterranean. The United States was unable to rescue the hostages and ignominiously had to purchase them in a treaty with Morocco.

The founders of this nation had a basic mistrust of European governments. This was a logical position at a time when the United States was so weak militarily that it could not influence European development directly. Moreover, being protected by oceans that took weeks to traverse certainly allowed the nation to avoid entangling alliances. During the 1800s, therefore, the United States generally stayed out of European conflicts and

President James Monroe is associated most commonly with what foreign policy doctrine? (AP Photo)

politics. In this hemisphere, however, the United States pursued an actively expansionist policy. The nation purchased Louisiana in 1803, annexed Texas in 1845, gained substantial territory from Mexico in 1848, purchased Alaska in 1867, and annexed Hawaii in 1898.

The Monroe Doctrine. President James Monroe, in his message to Congress on December 2, 1823, stated that the United States would not accept foreign intervention in the Western Hemisphere. In return, the United States would not meddle in European affairs. The **Monroe Doctrine** was the underpinning of the U.S. **isolationist foreign policy** toward Europe, which continued throughout the 1800s.

The Spanish-American War and World War I. The end of the isolationist policy started with the Spanish-American War in 1898. Winning the war gave the United States possession of Guam, Puerto Rico, and the Philippines (which gained independence in 1946). On the heels of that war came World War I (1914–1918). The United States declared war on Germany on April 6, 1917, because that country refused to give up its campaign of sinking all ships headed for Britain, including passenger ships from America. (Large passenger ships of that time commonly held over a thousand people, so the sinking of such a ship was a disaster comparable to the attack on the World Trade Center.)

In the 1920s, the United States went "back to normalcy," as President Warren G. Harding urged it to do. U.S. military forces were largely disbanded, defense spending dropped to about 1 percent of total annual national income, and the nation returned to a period of isolationism.

THE ERA OF INTERNATIONALISM

Isolationism was permanently shattered by the bombing of the U.S. naval base at Pearl Harbor, Hawaii, on December 7, 1941. The surprise attack by the Japanese caused the deaths of 2,403 American servicemen and wounded 1,143 others. Eighteen warships were sunk or seriously damaged, and 188 planes were destroyed at the airfields. President Franklin Roosevelt asked Congress to declare war on Japan immediately, and the United States entered World War II.

The United States was the only major participating country to emerge from World War II with its economy intact, and even strengthened. The United States was also the only country to have control over operational nuclear weapons. President Harry Truman had made the decision to use two atomic bombs, on August 6 and August 9, 1945, to end the war with Japan. (Historians still argue over the necessity of this action, which ultimately killed more than 100,000 Japanese and left an equal number permanently injured.) The United States truly had become the world's superpower.

The Cold War. The United States had become an uncomfortable ally of the Soviet Union after Adolf Hitler's invasion of that country. Soon after World War II ended, relations between the Soviet Union and the West deteriorated. The Soviet Union wanted a weakened Germany, and to achieve this, it insisted that Germany be divided in two, with East Germany becoming a buffer against the West. Little by little, the Soviet Union helped

Monroe Doctrine
A policy statement made by President James Monroe in 1823, which set out three principles: (1) European nations should not establish new colonies in the Western Hemisphere, (2) European nations should not intervene in the affairs of independent nations of the Western Hemisphere, and (3) the United States would not interfere in the affairs of European nations.

Isolationist Foreign Policy
A policy of abstaining from an active role in international affairs or alliances, which characterized U.S. foreign policy toward Europe during most of the 1800s.

In a famous meeting in Yalta in February 1945, British prime minister Winston Churchill (left), U.S. president Franklin Roosevelt (center), and Soviet leader Joseph Stalin (right) decided on the fate of several nations in Europe, including Germany. What happened to Germany immediately after World War II? (Library of Congress)

to install Communist governments in Eastern European countries, which began to be referred to collectively as the **Soviet bloc.** In response, the United States encouraged the rearming of Western Europe. The Cold War had begun.[5]

Containment Policy. In 1947, a remarkable article was published in *Foreign Affairs.* The article was signed by "X." The actual author was George F. Kennan, chief of the policy-planning staff for the State Department. The doctrine of **containment** set forth in the article became—according to many—the bible of Western foreign policy. "X" argued that whenever and wherever the Soviet Union could successfully challenge the West, it would do so. He recommended that our policy toward the Soviet Union be "firm and vigilant containment of Russian expansive tendencies."[6]

The containment theory was expressed clearly in the **Truman Doctrine,** which was enunciated by President Harry Truman in 1947. Truman held that the United States must help countries in which a Communist takeover seemed likely. Later that year, he backed the Marshall Plan, an economic assistance plan for Europe that was intended to prevent the expansion of Communist influence there. In 1950, the United States entered into a military alliance with European nations commonly called the North Atlantic Treaty Organization, or NATO, to maintain a credible response to any Soviet military attack. Figure 15–2 shows the face-off between the U.S.-led NATO alliance and the Soviet-led Warsaw Pact—an agreement formed by Communist nations to counter the NATO alliance.

SUPERPOWER RELATIONS

During the Cold War, there was never any direct military conflict between the United States and the Soviet Union. Only on occasion did the United States enter a conflict with any Communist country. Two such occasions were in Korea and in Vietnam.

After the end of World War II, northern Korea was occupied by the Soviet Union, and southern Korea was occupied by the United States. The result was two rival Korean governments. In 1950, North Korea invaded South Korea. Under UN authority, the United States entered the war, which prevented an almost certain South Korean defeat. When

Soviet Bloc
The Soviet Union and the Eastern European countries that installed Communist regimes after World War II and were dominated by the Soviet Union.

Containment
A U.S. diplomatic policy adopted by the Truman administration to contain Communist power within its existing boundaries.

Truman Doctrine
The policy adopted by President Harry Truman in 1947 to halt Communist expansion in southeastern Europe.

---

5. See John Lewis Gaddis, *The United Nations and the Origins of the Cold War* (New York: Columbia University Press, 1972).
6. X, "The Sources of Soviet Conduct," *Foreign Affairs,* July 1947, p. 575.

FIGURE 15–2: Europe during the Cold War

This map shows the face-off between NATO (led by the United States) and the Soviet bloc (the Warsaw Pact). Note that West Germany did not join NATO until 1955, and Albania suspended participation in the Warsaw Pact in 1960. France was out of NATO from 1966 to 1996, and Spain did not join until 1982.

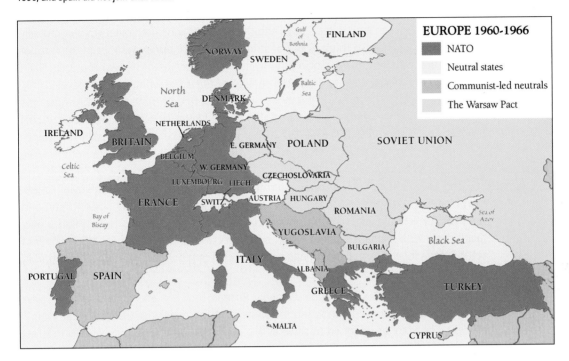

EUROPE 1960-1966
- NATO
- Neutral states
- Communist-led neutrals
- The Warsaw Pact

U.S. forces were on the brink of conquering North Korea, however, China joined the war on the side of the North, resulting in a stalemate. An armistice signed in 1953 led to the two Koreas that exist today. U.S. forces have remained in South Korea since that time.

The Vietnam War (1964–1975) also involved the United States in a civil war between a Communist North Vietnam and pro-Western South Vietnam. When the French army in Indochina was defeated by the Communist forces of Ho Chi Minh and the two Vietnams were created in 1954, the United States assumed the role of supporting the South Vietnamese government against North Vietnam. President John Kennedy sent 16,000 "advisers" to help South Vietnam, and after Kennedy's death in 1963, President Lyndon Johnson greatly increased the scope of that support. About 500,000 American troops were in Vietnam at the height of the U.S. involvement. More than 58,000 Americans were killed and 300,000 were wounded in the conflict. A peace agreement in 1973 allowed U.S. troops to leave the country, and in 1975 North Vietnam easily occupied Saigon (the South Vietnamese capital) and unified the nation.

Over the course of the Vietnam War, the debate over U.S. involvement became extremely heated and, as mentioned previously, spurred congressional efforts to limit the ability of the president to commit forces to armed combat. The military draft was also a major source of contention during the Vietnam War. Do events in Iraq justify bringing back the draft? We examined this question in this chapter's opening *What If . . .* feature.

The Cuban Missile Crisis. Perhaps the closest the two superpowers came to a nuclear confrontation was the Cuban missile crisis in 1962. The Soviets installed missiles in Cuba, ninety miles off the U.S. coast, in response to Cuban fears of an American invasion and to try to balance an American nuclear advantage. President Kennedy and his advisers rejected the option of invading Cuba and set up a naval blockade around the island instead. When Soviet vessels appeared near Cuban waters, the tension reached its height. After intense negotiations between Washington and Moscow, the Soviet ships turned around on October 25, and on October 28 the Soviet Union announced the withdrawal

Détente
A French word meaning a relaxation of tensions. The term characterized U.S.-Soviet relations as they developed under President Richard Nixon and Secretary of State Henry Kissinger.

Strategic Arms Limitation Treaty (SALT I)
A treaty between the United States and the Soviet Union to stabilize the nuclear arms competition between the two countries. SALT I talks began in 1969, and agreements were signed on May 26, 1972.

of its missile operations from Cuba. In exchange, the United States agreed not to invade Cuba in the future and to remove some of its own missiles that were located near the Soviet border in Turkey.

A Period of Détente. The French word **détente** means a relaxation of tensions. By the end of the 1960s, it was clear that some efforts had to be made to reduce the threat of nuclear war between the United States and the Soviet Union. The Soviet Union gradually had begun to catch up in the building of strategic nuclear delivery vehicles in the form of bombers and missiles, thus balancing the nuclear scales between the two countries. Each nation had acquired the military capacity to destroy the other with nuclear weapons.

As the result of lengthy negotiations under Secretary of State Henry Kissinger and President Nixon, the United States and the Soviet Union signed the **Strategic Arms Limitation Treaty (SALT I)** in May 1972. That treaty "permanently" limited the development and deployment of antiballistic missiles (ABMs) and limited the number of offensive missiles each country could deploy.

The policy of détente was not limited to the U.S. relationship with the Soviet Union. Seeing an opportunity to capitalize on increasing friction between the Soviet Union and the People's Republic of China, Kissinger secretly began negotiations to establish a new relationship with China. President Nixon eventually visited that nation in 1972. The visit set the stage for the formal diplomatic recognition of that country, which occurred during the Carter administration (1977–1981).

The Reagan-Bush Years. President Ronald Reagan took a hard line against the Soviet Union during his first term, proposing the strategic defense initiative (SDI), or "Star Wars," in 1983. The SDI was designed to serve as a space-based defense against enemy missiles. Reagan and others in his administration argued that the program would deter nuclear war by shifting the emphasis of defense strategy from offensive to defensive weapons systems.

In November 1985, however, President Reagan and Mikhail Gorbachev, the Soviet leader, began to work on an arms reduction compact. In 1987, the negotiations resulted in the Intermediate-Range Nuclear Force (INF) Treaty, which required the superpowers to dismantle a total of four thousand intermediate-range missiles within the first three years of the agreement.

Beginning in 1989, President George H. W. Bush continued the negotiations with the Soviet Union to reduce the number of nuclear weapons and the number of armed troops in Europe. Subsequent events, including the dissolution of the Soviet Union (in December 1991), made the process much more complex. American strategists worried as much about who now controlled the Soviet nuclear arsenal as about completing the treaty process. In 1992, the United States signed the Strategic Arms Reduction Treaty (START) with four former Soviet republics—Russia, Ukraine, Belarus, and Kazakhstan—to reduce the number of long-range nuclear weapons.

President George W. Bush changed directions in 2001, announcing that the United States was withdrawing from the 1972 ABM treaty (SALT I). Six months later, however, Bush and Russian president Vladimir Putin signed an agreement greatly reducing the number of nuclear weapons on each side over the next few years.

The Dissolution of the Soviet Union. After the fall of the Berlin Wall in 1989, it was clear that the Soviet Union had relinquished much of its political and military control over the states of Eastern Europe that formerly had been part of the Soviet bloc. No one expected the Soviet Union to dissolve into separate states as quickly as it did, however. Although Gorbachev tried to adjust the Soviet constitution and political system to allow greater autonomy for the republics within the union, demands for political,

This is a picture of a "fat man" nuclear bomb
of the type tested in New Mexico and eventually dropped on Nagasaki, Japan, in August 1945, ending the war in Japan. Has there been a nuclear bomb blast over a populated area since World War II? (AP Photo)

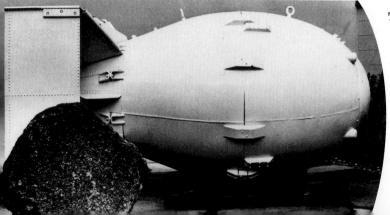

ethnic, and religious autonomy grew. In August 1991, anti-reformist conspirators launched an attempt to overthrow the Soviet government and to depose Gorbachev. These efforts were thwarted by the Russian people and parliament under the leadership of Boris Yeltsin, then president of Russia.

Instead of restoring the Soviet state, the attempted *coup d'état* hastened the process of creating an independent Russian state led by Yeltsin. On the day after Christmas in 1991, the Soviet Union was officially dissolved. Another uprising in Russia, this time led by anti-Yeltsin members of the new parliament who wanted to restore the Soviet Union immediately, failed in 1993. Figure 15–3 shows the situation in Europe today.

In 2000, Yeltsin resigned due to poor health. He named Vladimir Putin, architect of the Russian military effort against the independence movement in the province of Chechnya, as acting president. A few months later, Putin won the presidency in a national election. Putin was a former official of the KGB, the Soviet secret police and espionage agency, and his experiences may have shaped his actions as president. By 2004, international observers were alarmed at the degree to which Putin had enhanced the power of the presidency by gaining control over parliament, civil society, and regional officeholders. Putin slowly but surely limited freedom of the press and of speech, and he effectively destroyed the ability of opposition parties to challenge his authority.

Still, Putin was enormously popular among ordinary Russians, in part because his presidency was marked by a return to order after the chaos that had preceded him. It did not hurt that Russia's economy grew rapidly on his watch, in part due to ample revenues from oil production. In 2008, Putin's second term as president expired, and he was not eligible to run again. He managed to retain power, however, through a simple expedient. He oversaw the election as president of Dmitry Medvedev, one of his close supporters. Medvedev then appointed Putin as prime minister. Thereafter, the prime minister, rather than the president, was the top Russian leader.

didyouknow...

That Russia has suffered more battle deaths in putting down the rebellion in Chechnya than the Soviet Union experienced in its decades-long attempt to subdue Afghanistan?

FIGURE 15–3: Europe after the Fall of the Soviet Union

This map shows the growth in European unity as marked by participation in transnational organizations. The United States continues to lead NATO (and would be orange if it were on the map). Note the reunification of Germany and the creation of new states from the former Yugoslavia and the former Soviet Union. Croatia and Albania are expected to join NATO during 2009.

In August 2008, the former Soviet republic of Georgia, on Russia's border, attempted to reoccupy a breakaway region known as South Ossetia. This region had established a de facto independence from Georgia under Russian protection. Prime Minister Putin ordered the Russian armed forces to retake South Ossetia and also to occupy positions in Georgia proper. Despite international calls for Russia to withdraw, its troops remained.

The war in South Ossetia led to a major freeze in relations between Russia and the West. NATO ended its regular consultations with that country, and Russia also forfeited its chance of joining the World Trade Organization. Russia's leaders responded to international condemnation with harsh language. Putin blamed America for encouraging the initial Georgian attack. The United States, and the world, now faced a new major issue—Russia's willingness to intimidate its immediate neighbors.

WHY SHOULD YOU CARE ABOUT
foreignpolicy?

One foreign policy issue worth caring about is human rights. In many countries throughout the world, human rights are not protected. In some nations, people are imprisoned, tortured, or killed because they oppose the current regime. In other nations, certain ethnic or racial groups are oppressed by the majority population.

FOREIGN POLICY AND YOUR LIFE

The strongest reason for involving yourself with human rights issues in other countries is simple moral altruism—unselfish regard for the welfare of others. The defense of human rights is unlikely to put a single dollar in your pocket.

A broader consideration, however, is that human rights abuses are often associated with the kind of dictatorial regimes that are likely to provoke wars. To the extent that the people of the world can create a climate in which human rights abuses are unacceptable, they may also create an atmosphere in which national leaders believe that they must display peaceful conduct generally. This, in turn, might reduce the frequency of wars, some of which could involve the United States. Less war would mean preserving peace and human life, not to mention reducing the financial burden.

HOW YOU CAN MAKE A DIFFERENCE

What can you do to work for the improvement of human rights in other nations? One way is to join an organization that attempts to keep watch over human rights violations. (Two such organizations are listed at the end of this feature.) By publicizing human rights violations, such organizations try to pressure nations into changing their practices. Sometimes, these organizations are able to apply enough pressure and cause enough embarrassment that victims may be freed from prison or allowed to emigrate.

Another way to work for human rights is to keep informed about the state of affairs in other nations and to write personally to governments that violate human rights or to their embassies, asking them to cease these violations.

If you want to receive general information about the position of the United States on human rights violations, you can contact the State Department:

U.S. Department of State Bureau of Democracy, Human Rights, and Labor
2201 C St. N.W.
Washington, DC 20520
202-647-4000
www.state.gov/g/drl/hr

The following organizations are well known for their watchdog efforts in countries that violate human rights for political reasons:

Amnesty International U.S.A.
322 Eighth Ave., Floor 10
New York, NY 10001
212-807-8400
www.amnestyusa.org

American Friends Service Committee
1501 Cherry St.
Philadelphia, PA 19102
215-241-7000
www.afsc.org

QUESTIONS FOR
discussion**and**analysis

1. Review the *Which Side Are You On?* feature on page 530. Is a world free of nuclear weapons even possible? Why or why not? In what ways might the world be different if no nation had such weapons?

2. Why do you think that North Korea and Iran might want to possess nuclear weapons, even though they can never hope to match the nuclear arsenals of the original five nuclear powers?

3. Some people believe that if no U.S. military personnel were stationed abroad, terrorists would have less desire to harm Americans or the United States. Do you agree? Why or why not?

4. As of late 2008, no terrorist act remotely comparable to the attacks of 9/11 had taken place on U.S. soil. Why do you think that is so? How much credit can the government take? To what extent might terrorists experience practical difficulties in accomplishing anything like the damage inflicted on 9/11?

5. It is widely believed that the result of an immediate withdrawal of American forces from Iraq would be a full-blown civil war between Sunni and Shiite factions, probably drawing in the Kurds as well, and possibly even foreign nations. Do U.S forces have a chance of permanently heading off such a conflict by remaining in Iraq? Why or why not?

key**terms**

Cold War 528
containment 542
defense policy 518
détente 544
diplomacy 517
economic aid 517
foreign policy 517

foreign policy
  process 517
intelligence
  community 537
isolationist foreign
  policy 541
Monroe Doctrine 541
moral idealism 518

national security
  policy 517
negative
  constituents 536
normal trade relations
  (NTR) status 529
political realism 519

Soviet bloc 542
Strategic Arms
  Limitation Treaty
  (SALT I) 542
technical assistance 517
Truman Doctrine 542

chapter**summary**

1. Foreign policy includes the nation's external goals and the techniques used to achieve them. National security policy, which is one aspect of foreign policy, is designed to protect the independence and the political and economic integrity of the United States. Diplomacy involves the nation's external relationships and is an attempt to resolve conflict without resort to arms. U.S. foreign policy is sometimes based on moral idealism and sometimes on political realism.

2. Terrorism has become a major challenge facing the United States and other nations. The United States waged war on terrorism after the attacks of September 11, 2001. U.S. armed forces occupied Afghanistan in 2001 and Iraq in 2003.

3. Nuclear proliferation continues to be an issue due to the breakup of the Soviet Union and loss of control over its nuclear arsenal, along with the continued efforts of other nations to gain nuclear warheads. More than 32,000 nuclear warheads are known to exist worldwide. A current challenge for world leaders is how to contain the nuclear ambitions of Iran and North Korea.

4. Ethnic tensions and political instability in many regions of the world provide challenges to the United States. In the Caribbean, Cuba requires American attention because of its proximity. The Middle East continues to be a hotbed of conflict despite efforts to continue the peace process. In 1991 and again in 2003, the United States sent combat troops to Iraq. The second war in Iraq, begun in 2003, succeeded in toppling that nation's decades-long dictatorship. The war is still being waged, and the Bush administration has been strongly criticized both for launching the war under false pretenses and for mismanaging the conflict thereafter.

5. The formal power of the president to make foreign policy derives from the U.S. Constitution, which designates the president as commander in chief of the army and navy. Presidents have interpreted this authority broadly. They also have the power to make treaties and executive agreements. In principle, the State Department is the executive agency with primary authority over foreign affairs. The National Security Council also plays a major role. The intelligence community consists of government agencies

engaged in activities varying from information gathering to covert operations. In response to presidential actions in the Vietnam War, Congress attempted to establish some limits on the power of the president to intervene abroad by passing the War Powers Resolution in 1973.

6. Three major themes have guided U.S. foreign policy. In the early years of the nation, isolationism was the primary strategy. With the start of the twentieth century, isolationism gave way to global involvement. From the end of World War II through the 1980s, the major goal was to contain communism and the influence of the Soviet Union.

7. During the 1800s, the United States had little international power and generally stayed out of European conflicts and politics, so these years have been called the period of isolationism. The Monroe Doctrine of 1823 stated that the United States would not accept foreign intervention in the Western Hemisphere and would not meddle in European affairs. The United States pursued an actively expansionist policy in the Americas and the Pacific area, however.

8. The end of the policy of isolationism toward Europe started with the Spanish-American War of 1898. U.S. involvement in European politics became more extensive when the United States entered World

War I on April 6, 1917. World War II marked a lasting change in American foreign policy. The United States was the only major country to emerge from the war with its economy intact and the only country with operating nuclear weapons.

9. Soon after the close of World War II, the uncomfortable alliance between the United States and the Soviet Union ended, and the Cold War began. A policy of containment, which assumed an expansionist Soviet Union, was enunciated in the Truman Doctrine. Following the frustrations of the Vietnam War and the apparent arms equality of the United States and the Soviet Union, the United States adopted a policy of détente, or loosening of tensions.

10. Although President Reagan took a tough stance toward the Soviet Union during his first term, his second term saw serious negotiations toward arms reduction, culminating in the signing of the Intermediate-Range Nuclear Force Treaty in 1987. After the fall of the Soviet Union, Russia emerged as a less threatening state and signed the Strategic Arms Reduction Treaty with the United States in 1992. Under President Vladimir Putin, Russia has moved away from democracy and has in part returned to its old autocratic traditions.

selected**print&media**resources

SUGGESTED READINGS

Human Rights Watch. *World Report 2009.* New York: Seven Stories Press, 2009. This volume is one of the most probing reviews of human rights developments available. It contains concise overviews of pressing human rights concerns in countries ranging from Afghanistan to Zimbabwe.

Power, Samantha. *A Problem from Hell: America and the Age of Genocide.* New York: HarperCollins, 2007. This well-known former journalist, who is now the executive director of Harvard's Carr Center for Human Rights, looks at U.S. responses to genocide in Rwanda, Darfur, and other areas of the world during the last century. She argues that U.S. intervention has been woefully inadequate.

Ricks, Thomas E. *The Gamble: General David Petraeus and the American Military Adventure in Iraq, 2006–2008.* New York: Penguin Press, 2009. In 2007, Ricks released *Fiasco: The American Military Adventure in Iraq, 2003 to 2005.* This was one of the most well received and scathing accounts of disastrous U.S. policies and practices in that country and became a number-one *New York Times* bestseller. In *The Gamble,* Ricks returns to Iraq to find out whether America's new counter-insurgency strategy can rescue a seemingly impossible situation.

Ritter, Scott. *Dangerous Ground: On the Trail of America's Failed Arms Control Policy.* New York: Nation Books, 2009. Ritter, the chief weapons inspector for the United Nations Special Commission in Iraq from 1991 to 1998, believes that the Bush administration misidentified the true dangers of nuclear proliferation. He presents a blueprint for addressing what he believes are the real dangers.

Woodward, Bob. *State of Denial.* New York: Simon and Schuster, 2006. This is the third of Woodward's masterful inside accounts of policymaking in George W. Bush's administration. *Bush at War* (2002) dealt with 9/11 and the war in Afghanistan. *Plan of Attack* (2004) covered the war in Iraq and its aftermath. *State of Denial* provides the fullest, and most critical, account of the development and implementation of the Bush administration's Iraq policy.

Zakaria, Fareed. *The Post-American World.* New York: W. W. Norton, 2008. Zakaria, a *Newsweek* editor and television commentator, does not write about the decline of America, but about the rise of other nations, especially China and India. An optimist despite the current terror crisis, Zakaria contends that the world is richer and more peaceful than it has ever been and that these trends are likely to continue. He concludes with a critique of the U.S. foreign policy process, which he believes is designed for partisan battles rather than problem solving.

MEDIA RESOURCES

Black Hawk Down—A 2002 film that recounts the events in Mogadishu, Somalia, in October 1993, during which two U.S. Black Hawk helicopters were shot down. The film, which is based on reporter Mark Bowden's best-selling book by the same name, contains graphic scenes of terrifying urban warfare.

The Fall of Milošević—A highly acclaimed 2003 documentary by Norma Percy and Brian Lapping. This film covers the final years of the crisis in former Yugoslavia, including the war in Kosovo and the fall of Slobodan Milošević, Serb nationalist leader and alleged war criminal. Except for Milošević himself, almost all top Serb and Albanian leaders are interviewed, as are President Bill Clinton and British prime minister Tony Blair.

The 50 Years War—Israel and the Arabs—A two-volume PBS Home Video released in 2000. More balanced than some accounts, this film includes interviews with many leaders involved in the struggle, including the following: from Israel, Yitzhak Rabin, Shimon Peres, Benjamin Netanyahu, and Ariel Sharon; from the Arab world, Egypt's Anwar al-Sadat, Jordan's King Hussein, and Yasir Arafat; and from the United States, Presidents Jimmy Carter, George H. W. Bush, and Bill Clinton.

No End in Sight: Iraq's Descent into Chaos—Packed with interviews of officials, generals, and soldiers, this 2007 film argues that insufficient troop levels, the disbanding of Iraq's army, and the dismantling of the Iraqi government led to the insurgency and chaos that have bedeviled the country. *No End in Sight* is a shocking portrait of arrogance and incompetence, laced with terrifying war footage.

Senator Obama Goes to Africa—A documentary of Barack Obama's 2006 trip to Kenya, South Africa, and Chad. Despite the many questions Americans have had about Barack Obama, he has been more open about his unusual past than most politicians. One source of information is this film, which shows some of the advantages and disadvantages of Obama's international fame. In the end, he can do little about the suffering that he sees.

United 93—A 2006 documentary about the fourth airplane hijacked on 9/11. When they learned the fate of the other three planes through cell phones, the passengers decided to fight back, with the result that the flight crashed in a Pennsylvania field, far from its intended target. *United 93* takes place in real time and is almost unbearably moving. Several critics named it the best film of the year.

e-mocracy

INTERNATIONAL ORGANIZATIONS

For years, international organizations have played a key role in world affairs, and these organizations are likely to become even more important in years to come. In the United States, the incoming administration has promised to place greater reliance on multilateral approaches when addressing problems abroad—in contrast to the Bush administration's "go it alone" approach.

International organizations do not only dispense aid, loans, and advice. Several of them field troops supplied by member nations. The "blue helmets" of the United Nations (UN) take part in seventeen missions, many in the Middle East or Africa. American forces in Afghanistan cooperate with those of other nations through the North Atlantic Treaty Organization (NATO). The UN, NATO, and other multinational organizations all have Web sites where you can learn about the history and status of current international conflicts.

LOGGING ON

In addition to materials on international crises, the United Nations Web site contains a treasure trove of international statistics. To access this site, go to **www.un.org/english.**

For news about NATO, visit **www.nato.int.**

The European Union, a confederation of twenty-seven nations, is one of the most important international bodies in existence. You can learn more about it at **www.europa.eu/index_en.htm.**

The Organisation for Economic Cooperation and Development (OECD) provides another major source of international statistics and economic analysis. You can access the OECD's Web site at **www.oecd.org.**

APPENDIX A

THE DECLARATION OF INDEPENDENCE

In Congress, July 4, 1776

A Declaration by the Representatives of the United States of America, in General Congress assembled. When in the Course of human Events, it becomes necessary for one People to dissolve the Political Bands which have connected them with another, and to assume among the Powers of the Earth, the separate and equal Station to which the Laws of Nature and of Nature's God entitle them, a decent Respect to the Opinions of Mankind requires that they should declare the causes which impel them to the Separation.

We hold these Truths to be self-evident, that all Men are created equal, that they are endowed by their Creator with certain unalienable Rights, that among these are Life, Liberty, and the Pursuit of Happiness—That to secure these Rights, Governments are instituted among Men, deriving their just Powers from the Consent of the Governed, that whenever any Form of Government becomes destructive of these Ends, it is the Right of the People to alter or to abolish it, and to institute new Government, laying its Foundation on such Principles, and organizing its Powers in such Forms, as to them shall seem most likely to effect their Safety and Happiness. Prudence, indeed, will dictate that Governments long established should not be changed for light and transient Causes; and accordingly all Experience hath shewn, that Mankind are more disposed to suffer, while Evils are sufferable, than to right themselves by abolishing the Forms to which they are accustomed. But when a long Train of Abuses and Usurpations, pursuing invariably the same Object, evinces a Design to reduce them under absolute Despotism, it is their Right, it is their Duty, to throw off such Government, and to provide new Guards for their future Security. Such has been the patient Sufferance of these Colonies; and such is now the Necessity which constrains them to alter their former Systems of Government. The History of the present King of Great-Britain is a History of repeated Injuries and Usurpations, all having in direct Object the Establishment of an absolute Tyranny over these States. To prove this, let Facts be submitted to a candid World.

He has refused his Assent to Laws, the most wholesome and necessary for the public Good.

He has forbidden his Governors to pass Laws of immediate and pressing Importance, unless suspended in their Operation till his Assent should be obtained; and when so suspended, he has utterly neglected to attend to them.

He has refused to pass other Laws for the Accommodation of large Districts of People, unless those People would relinquish the Right of Representation in the Legislature, a Right inestimable to them, and formidable to Tyrants only.

He has called together Legislative Bodies at Places unusual, uncomfortable, and distant from the Depository of their Public Records, for the sole Purpose of fatiguing them into Compliance with his Measures.

He has dissolved Representative Houses repeatedly, for opposing with manly Firmness his Invasions on the Rights of the People.

He has refused for a long Time, after such Dissolutions, to cause others to be elected; whereby the Legislative Powers, incapable of Annihilation, have returned to the People at large for their exercise; the State remaining in the mean time exposed to all the Dangers of Invasion from without, and Convulsions within.

He has endeavoured to prevent the Population of these States; for that Purpose obstructing the Laws for Naturalization of Foreigners; refusing to pass others to encourage their Migrations hither, and raising the Conditions of new Appropriations of Lands.

He has obstructed the Administration of Justice, by refusing his Assent to Laws for establishing Judiciary Powers.

He has made Judges dependent on his Will alone, for the Tenure of their offices, and the Amount and payment of their Salaries.

He has erected a Multitude of new Offices, and sent hither Swarms of Officers to harass our People, and eat out their Substance.

He has kept among us, in Times of Peace, Standing Armies, without the consent of our Legislatures.

He has affected to render the Military independent of, and superior to the Civil Power.

He has combined with others to subject us to a Jurisdiction foreign to our Constitution, and unacknowledged by our Laws; giving his Assent to their Acts of pretended Legislation:

For quartering large Bodies of Armed Troops among us:

For protecting them, by a mock Trial, from Punishment for any Murders which they should commit on the Inhabitants of these States:

For cutting off our Trade with all Parts of the World:

For imposing Taxes on us without our Consent:

For depriving us, in many cases, of the Benefits of Trial by Jury:

For transporting us beyond Seas to be tried for pretended Offences:

For abolishing the free System of English Laws in a neighbouring Province, establishing therein an arbitrary Government, and enlarging its Boundaries, so as to render it at once an Example and fit Instrument for introducing the same absolute Rule into these Colonies:

For taking away our Charters, abolishing our most valuable Laws, and altering fundamentally the Forms of our Governments:

For suspending our own Legislatures, and declaring themselves invested with Power to legislate for us in all Cases whatsoever.

He has abdicated Government here, by declaring us out of his Protection and waging War against us.

He has plundered our Seas, ravaged our Coasts, burnt our towns, and destroyed the Lives of our People.

He is, at this Time, transporting large Armies of foreign Mercenaries to compleat the works of Death, Desolation, and Tyranny, already begun with circumstances of Cruelty and Perfidy, scarcely paralleled in the most barbarous Ages, and totally unworthy the Head of a civilized Nation.

He has constrained our fellow Citizens taken Captive on the high Seas to bear Arms against their Country, to become the Executioners of their Friends and Brethren, or to fall themselves by their Hands.

He has excited domestic Insurrections amongst us, and has endeavoured to bring on the Inhabitants of our Frontiers, the merciless Indian Savages, whose known Rule of Warfare, is an undistinguished Destruction, of all Ages, Sexes and Conditions.

In every state of these Oppressions we have Petitioned for Redress in the most humble Terms: Our repeated Petitions have been answered only by repeated Injury. A Prince, whose Character is thus marked by every act which may define a Tyrant, is unfit to be the Ruler of a free People.

Nor have we been wanting in Attentions to our British Brethren. We have warned them from Time to Time of Attempts by their Legislature to extend an unwarrantable Jurisdiction over us. We have reminded them of the Circumstances of our Emigration and Settlement here. We have appealed to their native Justice and Magnanimity, and we have conjured them by the Ties of our common Kindred to disavow these Usurpations, which, would inevitably interrupt our Connections and Correspondence. They too have been deaf to the Voice of Justice and of Consanguinity. We must, therefore, acquiesce in the Necessity, which denounces our Separation, and hold them, as we hold the rest of Mankind, Enemies in War, in Peace, Friends.

We, therefore, the Representatives of the UNITED STATES OF AMERICA, in General Congress Assembled, appealing to the Supreme Judge of the World for the Rectitude of our Intentions, do, in the Name, and by the Authority of the good People of these Colonies, solemnly Publish and Declare, That these United Colonies are, and of Right ought to be, Free and Independent States; that they are absolved from all Allegiance to the British Crown, and that all political Connection between them and the State of Great-Britain, is and ought to be totally dissolved; and that as Free and Independent States, they have full Power to levy War, conclude Peace, contract Alliances, establish Commerce, and to do all other Acts and Things which Independent States may of right do. And for the support of this declaration, with a firm Reliance on the Protection of divine Providence, we mutually pledge to each other our lives, our Fortunes, and our sacred Honor.

APPENDIX B

HOW TO READ CASE CITATIONS AND FIND COURT DECISIONS

Many important court cases are discussed in references in footnotes throughout this book. Court decisions are recorded and published. When a court case is mentioned, the notation that is used to refer to, or to cite, the case denotes where the published decision can be found.

State courts of appeals decisions are usually published in two places, the state reports of that particular state and the more widely used *National Reporter System* published by West Publishing Company. Some states no longer publish their own reports. The National Reporter System divides the states into the following geographic areas: Atlantic (A. or A.2d, where *2d* refers to *Second Series*), South Eastern (S.E. or S.E.2d), South Western (S.W., S.W.2d, or S.W.3d), North Western (N.W. or N.W.2d), North Eastern (N.E. or N.E.2d), Southern (So. or So.2d), and Pacific (P., P.2d, or P.3d).

Federal trial court decisions are published unofficially in West's *Federal Supplement* (F.Supp. or F.Supp.2d), and opinions from the circuit courts of appeals are reported unofficially in West's *Federal Reporter* (F., F.2d, or F.3d). Opinions from the United States Supreme Court are reported in the *United States Reports* (U.S.), the *Lawyers' Edition of the Supreme Court Reports* (L.Ed. or L.Ed.2d), West's *Supreme Court Reporter* (S.Ct.), and other publications. The *United States Reports* is the official publication of United States Supreme Court decisions. It is published by the federal government. Many early decisions are missing from these volumes. The citations of the early volumes of the *United States Reports* include the names of the actual reporters, such as Dallas, Cranch, or Wheaton. *McCulloch v. Maryland,* for example, is cited as 17 U.S.

(4 Wheat.) 316. Only after 1874 did the present citation system, in which cases are cited based solely on their volume and page numbers in the *United States Reports,* come into being. The *Lawyers' Edition of the Supreme Court Reports* is an unofficial and more complete edition of Supreme Court decisions. West's *Supreme Court Reporter* is an unofficial edition of decisions dating from October 1882. These volumes contain headnotes and numerous brief editorial statements of the law involved in each case.

State courts of appeals decisions are cited by giving the name of the case; the volume, name, and page number of the state's official report (if the state publishes its own reports); the volume, unit, and page number of the *National Reporter;* and the volume, name, and page number of any other selected reporter. Federal court citations are also listed by giving the name of the case and the volume, name, and page number of the reports. In addition to the citation, this textbook lists the year of the decision in parentheses. Consider, for example, the case *Massachusetts v. EPA,* 127 S.Ct. 1438 (2007). The Supreme Court's decision of this case may be found in volume 127 of the *Supreme Court Reporter* on page 1438. The case was decided in 2007.

Today, many courts, including the United States Supreme Court, publish their opinions online. This makes it much easier for students to find and read cases, or summaries of cases, that have significant consequences for American government and politics. To access cases via the Internet, use the URLs given in the *Logging On* section at the end of Chapter 13.

APPENDIX C

FEDERALIST PAPERS NOS. 10, 51, AND 78

In 1787, after the newly drafted U.S. Constitution was submitted to the thirteen states for ratification, a major political debate ensued between the Federalists (who favored ratification) and the Anti-Federalists (who opposed ratification). Anti-Federalists in New York were particularly critical of the Constitution, and in response to their objections, Federalists Alexander Hamilton, James Madison, and John Jay wrote a series of eighty-five essays in defense of the Constitution. The essays were published in New York newspapers and reprinted in other newspapers throughout the country.

For students of American government, the essays, collectively known as the Federalist Papers, are particularly important because they provide a glimpse of the founders' political philosophy and intentions in designing the Constitution—and, consequently, in shaping the American philosophy of government.

We have included in this appendix three of these essays: Federalist Papers Nos. 10, 51, and 78. Each essay has been annotated by the authors to indicate its importance in American political thought and to clarify the meaning of particular passages.

Federalist Paper No. 10

Federalist Paper No. 10, penned by James Madison, has often been singled out as a key document in American political thought. In this essay, Madison attacks the Anti-Federalists' fear that a republican form of government will inevitably give rise to "factions"—small political parties or groups united by a common interest—that will control the government. Factions will be harmful to the country because they will implement policies beneficial to their own interests but adverse to other people's rights and to the public good. In this essay, Madison attempts to lay to rest this fear by explaining how, in a large republic such as the United States, there will be so many different factions, held together by regional or local interests, that no single one of them will dominate national politics.

Madison opens his essay with a paragraph discussing how important it is to devise a plan of government that can control the "instability, injustice, and confusion" brought about by factions.

Among the numerous advantages promised by a well-constructed Union, none deserves to be more accurately developed than its tendency to break and control the violence of faction. The friend of popular governments never finds himself so much alarmed for their character and fate as when he contemplates their propensity to this dangerous vice. He will not fail, therefore, to set a due value on any plan which, without violating the principles to which he is attached, provides a proper cure for it. The instability, injustice, and confusion introduced into the public councils have, in truth, been the mortal diseases under which popular governments have everywhere perished, as they continue to be the favorite and fruitful topics from which the adversaries to liberty derive their most specious declamations. The valuable improvements made by the American constitutions on the popular models, both ancient and modern, cannot certainly be too much admired; but it would be an unwarrantable partiality to contend that they have as effectually obviated the danger on this side, as was wished and expected. Complaints are everywhere heard from our most considerate and virtuous citizens, equally the friends of public and private faith and of public and personal liberty, that our governments are too unstable, that the public good is disregarded in the conflicts of rival parties, and that measures are too often decided, not according to the rules of justice and the rights of the minor party, but by the superior force of an interested and overbearing majority. However anxiously we may wish that these complaints had no foundation, the evidence of known facts will not permit us to deny that they are in some degree true. It will be found, indeed, on a candid review of our situation, that some of the distresses under which we labor have been erroneously charged on the operation of our governments; but it will be found, at the same time, that other causes will not alone account for many of our heaviest misfortunes; and, particularly, for that prevailing and increasing distrust of public engagements and alarm for private rights which are echoed from one end of the continent to the other. These must be chiefly, if not wholly, effects of the unsteadiness and injustice with which a factious spirit has tainted our public administration.

Madison now defines what he means by the term faction.

By a faction I understand a number of citizens, whether amounting to a majority or minority of the whole, who are united and actuated by some common impulse of passion, or of interest, adverse to the rights of other citizens, or the permanent and aggregate interests of the community.

Madison next contends that there are two methods by which the "mischiefs of faction" can be cured: by removing the causes of faction or by controlling their effects. In the following paragraphs, Madison explains how liberty itself nourishes factions. Therefore, to abolish factions would involve abolishing liberty—a cure "worse than the disease."

There are two methods of curing the mischiefs of faction: the one, by removing its causes; the other, by controlling its effects.

There are again two methods of removing the causes of faction: the one, by destroying the liberty which is essential to its existence; the other, by giving to every citizen the same opinions, the same passions, and the same interests.

It could never be more truly said than of the first remedy that it was worse than the disease. Liberty is to faction what air is to fire, an aliment without which it instantly expires. But it could not be a less folly to abolish liberty, which is essential to political life, because it nourishes faction than it would be to wish the annihilation of air, which is essential to animal life, because it imparts to fire its destructive agency.

The second expedient is as impracticable as the first would be unwise. As long as the reason of man continues fallible, and he is at liberty to exercise it, different opinions will be formed. As long as the connection subsists between his reason and his self-love, his opinions and his passions will have a reciprocal influence on each other; and the former will be objects to which the latter will attach themselves. The diversity in the faculties of men, from which the rights of property originate, is not less an insuperable obstacle to a uniformity of interests. The protection of these faculties is the first object of government. From the protection of different and unequal faculties of acquiring property, the possession of different degrees and kinds of property immediately results; and from the influence of these on the sentiments and views of the respective proprietors ensues a division of the society into different interests and parties.

The latent causes of faction are thus sown in the nature of man; and we see them everywhere brought into different degrees of activity, according to the different circumstances of civil society. A zeal for different opinions concerning religion, concerning government, and many other points, as well of speculation as of practice; an attachment to different leaders ambitiously contending for pre-eminence and power; or to persons of other descriptions whose fortunes have been interesting to the human passions, have, in turn, divided mankind into parties, inflamed them with mutual animosity, and rendered them much more disposed to vex and oppress each other than to co-operate for their common good. So strong is this propensity of mankind to fall into mutual animosities that where no substantial occasion presents itself the most frivolous and fanciful distinctions have been sufficient to kindle their unfriendly passions and excite their most violent conflicts. But the most common and durable source of factions has been the various and unequal distribution of property. Those who hold and those who are without property have ever formed distinct interests in society. Those who are creditors, and those who are debtors, fall under a like discrimination. A landed interest, a manufacturing interest, a mercantile interest, a moneyed interest, with many lesser interests, grow up of necessity in civilized nations, and divide them into different classes, actuated by different sentiments and views. The regulation of these various and interfering interests forms the principal task of modern legislation and involves the spirit of party and faction in the necessary and ordinary operations of government.

No man is allowed to be a judge in his own cause, because his interest would certainly bias his judgment, and, not improbably, corrupt his integrity. With equal, nay with greater reason, a body of men are unfit to be both judges and parties at the same time; yet what are many of the most important acts of legislation but so many judicial determinations, not indeed concerning the rights of single persons, but concerning the rights of large bodies of citizens? And what are the different classes of legislators but advocates and parties to the causes which they determine? Is a law proposed concerning private debts? It is a question to which the creditors are parties on one side and the debtors on the other. Justice ought to hold the balance between them. Yet the parties are, and must be, themselves the judges; and the most numerous party, or in other words, the most powerful faction must be expected to prevail. Shall domestic manufacturers be encouraged, and in what degree, by restrictions on foreign manufacturers? [These] are questions which would be differently decided by the landed and the manufacturing classes, and probably by neither with a sole regard to justice and the public good. The apportionment of taxes on the various descriptions of property is an act which seems to require the most exact impartiality; yet there is, perhaps, no legislative act in which greater opportunity and temptation are given to a predominant party to trample on the rules of justice. Every shilling with which they overburden the inferior number is a shilling saved to their own pockets.

It is in vain to say that enlightened statesmen will be able to adjust these clashing interests and render them all subservient to the public good. Enlightened statesmen will not always be at the helm. Nor, in many cases, can such an adjustment be made at all without taking into view indirect and remote considerations, which will rarely prevail over the immediate interest which one party may find in disregarding the rights of another or the good of the whole.

The inference to which we are brought is that the *causes* of faction cannot be removed and that relief is only to be sought in the means of controlling its *effects*.

Having concluded that "the causes of faction cannot be removed," Madison now looks in some detail at the other method by which factions can be cured—by controlling their effects. This is the heart of his essay. He begins by positing a significant question: How can you have self-government without risking the possibility that a ruling faction, particularly a majority faction, might tyrannize over the rights of others?

If a faction consists of less than a majority, relief is supplied by the republican principle, which enables the majority to defeat its sinister views by regular vote. It may clog the administration, it may convulse the society; but it will be unable to execute and mask its violence under the forms of the Constitution. When a majority is included in a faction, the form of popular government, on the other hand, enables it to sacrifice to its ruling passion or interest both the public good and the rights of other citizens. To secure the public good and private rights against the danger of such a faction, and at the same time to preserve the spirit and the form of popular government, is then the great object to which our inquiries are directed. Let me add that it is the great desideratum by which alone this form of government can be rescued from the opprobrium under which it has so long labored and be recommended to the esteem and adoption of mankind.

Madison now sets forth the idea that one way to control the effects of factions is to ensure that the majority is rendered incapable of acting in concert in order to "carry into effect schemes of oppression." He goes on to state that in a democracy, in which all citizens participate personally in government decision making, there is no way to prevent the majority from communicating with each other and, as a result, acting in concert.

By what means is this object attainable? Evidently by one of two only. Either the existence of the same passion or interest in a majority at the same time must be prevented, or the majority, having such coexistent passion or interest, must be rendered, by their number and local situation, unable to concert and carry into effect schemes of oppression. If the impulse and the opportunity be suffered to coincide, we well know that neither moral nor religious motives can be relied on as an adequate control. They are not found to be such on the injustice and violence of individuals, and lose their efficacy in proportion to the number combined together, that is, in proportion as their efficacy becomes needful.

From this view of the subject it may be concluded that a pure democracy, by which I mean a society consisting of a small number of citizens, who assemble and administer the government in person, can admit of no cure for the mischiefs of faction. A common passion or interest will, in almost every case, be felt by a majority of the whole; a communication and concert results from the form of government itself; and there is nothing to check the inducements to sacrifice the weaker party or an obnoxious individual. Hence it is that such democracies have ever been spectacles of turbulence and contention; have ever been found incompatible with personal security or the rights of property; and have in general been as short in their lives as they have been violent in their deaths. Theoretic politicians, who have patronized this species of government, have erroneously supposed that by reducing mankind to a perfect equality in their political rights, they would at the same time be perfectly equalized and assimilated in their possessions, their opinions, and their passions.

Madison now moves on to discuss the benefits of a republic with respect to controlling the effects of factions. He begins by defining a republic and then pointing out the "two great points of difference" between a republic and a democracy: a republic is governed by a small body of elected representatives, not by the people directly; and a republic can extend over a much larger territory and embrace more citizens than a democracy can.

A republic, by which I mean a government in which the scheme of representation takes place, opens a different prospect and promises the cure for which we are seeking. Let us examine the points in which it varies from pure democracy, and we shall comprehend both the nature of the cure and the efficacy which it must derive from the Union.

The two great points of difference between a democracy and a republic are: first, the delegation of the government, in the latter, to a small number of citizens elected by the rest; secondly, the greater number of citizens and greater sphere of country over which the latter may be extended.

In the following four paragraphs, Madison explains how in a republic, particularly a large republic, the delegation of authority to elected representatives will increase the likelihood that those who govern will be "fit" for their positions and that a proper balance will be achieved between local (factional) interests and national interests. Note how he stresses that the new federal Constitution, by dividing powers between state governments and the national government, provides a "happy combination in this respect."

The effect of the first difference is, on the one hand, to refine and enlarge the public views by passing them through the medium of a chosen body of citizens, whose wisdom may best discern the true interest of their country and whose patriotism and love of justice will be least likely to sacrifice it to temporary or partial considerations. Under such a regulation it may well happen that the public voice, pronounced by the representatives of the people, will be more consonant to the public good than if pronounced by the people themselves, convened for the purpose. On the other hand, the effect may be inverted. Men of factious tempers, of local prejudices, or of sinister designs, may, by intrigue, by corruption, or by other means, first obtain the suffrages, and then betray the interests of the people. The question resulting is, whether small or extensive republics are most favorable to the election of proper guardians of the public weal; and it is clearly decided in favor of the latter by two obvious considerations.

In the first place, it is to be remarked that however small the republic may be the representatives must be raised to a certain number in order to guard against the cabals of a few; and that however large it may be, they must be limited to a certain number in order to guard against the confusion of a multitude. Hence, the number of representatives in the two cases not being in proportion to that of the constituents, and being proportionally greater in the small republic, it follows that if the proportion of fit characters be not less in the large than in the small republic, the former will present a greater option, and consequently a greater probability of a fit choice.

In the next place, as each representative will be chosen by a greater number of citizens in the large than in the small republic, it will be more difficult for unworthy candidates to practice with success the vicious arts by which elections are too often carried; and the suffrages of the people being more free, will be more likely to center on men who possess the most attractive merit and the most diffusive and established characters.

It must be confessed that in this, as in most other cases, there is a mean, on both sides of which inconveniencies will be found to lie. By enlarging too much the number of electors, you render the representative too little acquainted with all their local circumstances and lesser interests; as by reducing it too much, you render him unduly attached to these, and too little fit to comprehend and pursue great and national objects. The federal Constitution forms a happy combination in this respect; the great and aggregate interests being referred to the national, the local and particular to the State legislatures.

Madison now looks more closely at the other difference between a republic and a democracy—namely, that a republic can encompass a larger territory and more citizens than a democracy can. In the remaining paragraphs of his essay, Madison concludes that in a large republic, it will be difficult for factions to act in concert. Although a factious group—religious, political, economic, or otherwise—may control a local or regional government, it will have little chance of gathering a national following. This is because in a large republic, there will be numerous factions whose work will offset the work of any one particular faction ("sect"). As Madison phrases it, these numerous factions will "secure the national councils against any danger from that source."

The other point of difference is the greater number of citizens and extent of territory which may be brought within the compass of republican than of democratic government; and it is this circumstance principally which renders factious combinations less to be dreaded in the former than in the latter. The smaller the society, the fewer probably will be the distinct parties and interests composing it; the fewer the distinct parties and interests, the more frequently will a majority be found of the same party; and the smaller the number of individuals composing a majority, and the smaller the compass within which they are placed, the more easily will they concert and execute their plans of oppression. Extend the sphere and you take in a greater variety of parties and interests; you make it less probable that a majority of the whole will have a common motive to invade the rights of other citizens; or if such a common motive exists, it will be more difficult for all who feel it to discover their own strength and to act in unison with each other. Besides other impediments, it may be remarked that, where there is a consciousness of unjust or dishonorable purposes, communication is always checked by distrust in proportion to the number whose concurrence is necessary.

Hence, it clearly appears that the same advantage which a republic has over a democracy in controlling the effects of faction is enjoyed by a large over a small republic—is enjoyed by the Union over the States composing it. Does this advantage consist in the substitution of representatives whose enlightened views and virtuous sentiments render them superior to local prejudices and to schemes of injustice? It will not be denied that the representation of the Union will be most likely to possess these requisite endowments. Does it consist in the greater security afforded by a greater variety of parties, against the event of any one party being able to outnumber and oppress the rest? In an equal degree does the increased variety of parties comprised within the Union increase this security. Does it, in fine, consist in the greater obstacles opposed to the concert and accomplishment of the secret wishes of an unjust and interested majority? Here

again the extent of the Union gives it the most palpable advantage.

The influence of factious leaders may kindle a flame within their particular States but will be unable to spread a general conflagration through the other States. A religious sect may degenerate into a political faction in a part of the Confederacy; but the variety of sects dispersed over the entire face of it must secure the national councils against any danger from that source. A rage for paper money, for an abolition of debts, for an equal division of property, or for any other improper or wicked project, will be less apt to pervade the whole body of the Union than a particular member of it, in the same proportion as such a malady is more likely to taint a particular county or district than an entire State.

In the extent and proper structure of the Union, therefore, we behold a republican remedy for the diseases most incident to republican government. And according to the degree of pleasure and pride we feel in being republicans ought to be our zeal in cherishing the spirit and supporting the character of federalists.

Publius
(James Madison)

Federalist Paper No. 51

Federalist Paper No. 51, also authored by James Madison, is another classic in American political theory. Although the Federalists wanted a strong national government, they had not abandoned the traditional American view, particularly notable during the revolutionary era, that those holding powerful government positions could not be trusted to put national interests and the common good above their own personal inter-ests. In this essay, Madison explains why the separation of the national government's powers into three branches—executive, legislative, and judicial—and a federal structure of government offer the best protection against tyranny.

To what expedient, then, shall we finally resort, for maintaining in practice the necessary partition of power among the several departments as laid down in the Constitution? The only answer that can be given is that as all these exterior provisions are found to be inadequate the defect must be supplied, by so contriving the interior structure of the government as that its several constituent parts may, by their mutual relations, be the means of keeping each other in their proper places. Without presuming to undertake a full development of this important idea I will hazard a few general observations which may perhaps place it in a clearer light, and enable us to form a more correct judgment of the principles and structure of the government planned by the convention.

In the next two paragraphs, Madison stresses that for the powers of the different branches (departments) of government to be truly separated, the personnel in one branch should not be dependent on another branch for their appointment or for the "emoluments" (compensation) attached to their offices.

In order to lay a due foundation for that separate and distinct exercise of the different powers of government, which to a certain extent is admitted on all hands to be essential to the preservation of liberty, it is evident that each department should have a will of its own; and consequently should be so constituted that the members of each should have as little agency as possible in the appointment of the members of the others. Were this principle rigorously adhered to, it would require that all the appointments for the supreme executive, legislative, and judiciary magistracies should be drawn from the same fountain of authority, the people, through channels having no communication whatever with one another. Perhaps such a plan of constructing the several departments would be less difficult in practice than it may in contemplation appear. Some difficulties, however, and some additional expense would attend the execution of it. Some deviations, therefore, from the principle must be admitted. In the constitution of the judiciary department in particular, it might be inexpedient to insist rigorously on the principle: first, because peculiar qualifications being essential in the members, the primary consideration ought to be to select that mode of choice which best secures these qualifications; second, because the permanent tenure by which the appointments are held in that department must soon destroy all sense of dependence on the authority conferring them.

It is equally evident that the members of each department should be as little dependent as possible on those of the others for the emoluments annexed to their offices. Were the executive magistrate, or the judges, not independent of the legislature in this particular, their independence in every other would be merely nominal.

In the following passages, which are among the most widely quoted of Madison's writings, he explains how the separation of the powers of government into three branches helps to counter the effects of personal ambition on government. The separation of powers allows personal motives to be linked to the constitutional rights of a branch of government. In effect, competing personal interests in each branch will help to keep the powers of the three government branches separate and, in so doing, will help to guard the public interest.

But the great security against a gradual concentration of the several powers in the same department consists in giving to those who administer each department the necessary constitutional means and personal motives to resist encroachments of the others. The provision for defense must in this, as in all other cases, be made commensurate to the danger of attack. Ambition must be made to counteract ambition. The interest of the man must be connected with the constitutional rights of the place. It may be a reflection on human nature that such devices should be necessary to control the abuses of government. But what is government itself but the greatest of all reflections on human nature? If men were angels, no government would be necessary. If angels were to govern men, neither external nor internal controls on government would be necessary. In framing a government which is to be administered by men over men, the great difficulty lies in this: you must first enable the government to control the governed; and in

the next place oblige it to control itself. A dependence on the people is, no doubt, the primary control on the government; but experience has taught mankind the necessity of auxiliary precautions.

This policy of supplying, by opposite and rival interests, the defect of better motives, might be traced through the whole system of human affairs, private as well as public. We see it particularly displayed in all the subordinate distributions of power, where the constant aim is to divide and arrange the several offices in such a manner as that each may be a check on the other—that the private interest of every individual may be a sentinel over the public rights. These inventions of prudence cannot be less requisite in the distribution of the supreme powers of the State.

Madison now addresses the issue of equality between the branches of government. The legislature will necessarily predominate, but if the executive is given an "absolute negative" (absolute veto power) over legislative actions, this also could lead to an abuse of power. Madison concludes that the division of the legislature into two "branches" (parts, or chambers) will act as a check on the legislature's powers.

But it is not possible to give to each department an equal power of self-defense. In republican government, the legislative authority necessarily predominates. The remedy for this inconveniency is to divide the legislature into different branches; and to render them, by different modes of election and different principles of action, as little connected with each other as the nature of their common functions and their common dependence on the society will admit. It may even be necessary to guard against dangerous encroachments by still further precautions. As the weight of the legislative authority requires that it should be thus divided, the weakness of the executive may require, on the other hand, that it should be fortified. An absolute negative on the legislature appears, at first view, to be the natural defense with which the executive magistrate should be armed. But perhaps it would be neither altogether safe nor alone sufficient. On ordinary occasions it might not be exerted with the requisite firmness, and on extraordinary occasions it might be perfidiously abused. May not this defect of an absolute negative be supplied by some qualified connection between this weaker department and the weaker branch of the stronger department, by which the latter may be led to support the constitutional rights of the former, without being too much detached from the rights of its own department?

If the principles on which these observations are founded be just, as I persuade myself they are, and they be applied as a criterion to the several State constitutions, and to the federal Constitution, it will be found that if the latter does not perfectly correspond with them, the former are infinitely less able to bear such a test.

In the remainder of the essay, Madison discusses how a federal system of government, in which powers are divided between the states and the national government, offers "double security" against tyranny.

There are, moreover, two considerations particularly applicable to the federal system of America, which place that system in a very interesting point of view.

First. In a single republic, all the power surrendered by the people is submitted to the administration of a single government; and the usurpations are guarded against by a division of the government into distinct and separate departments. In the compound republic of America, the power surrendered by the people is first divided between two distinct governments, and then the portion allotted to each subdivided among distinct and separate departments. Hence a double security arises to the rights of the people. The different governments will control each other, at the same time that each will be controlled by itself.

Second. It is of great importance in a republic not only to guard the society against the oppression of its rulers, but to guard one part of the society against the injustice of the other part. Different interests necessarily exist in different classes of citizens. If a majority be united by a common interest, the rights of the minority will be insecure. There are but two methods of providing against this evil: the one by creating a will in the community independent of the majority—that is, of the society itself; the other, by comprehending in the society so many separate descriptions of citizens as will render an unjust combination of a majority of the whole very improbable, if not impracticable. The first method prevails in all governments possessing an hereditary or self-appointed authority. This, at best, is but a precarious security; because a power independent of the society may as well espouse the unjust views of the major as the rightful interests of the minor party, and may possibly be turned against both parties. The second method will be exemplified in the federal republic of the United States. Whilst all authority in it will be derived from and dependent on the society, the society itself will be broken into so many parts, interests and classes of citizens, that the rights of individuals, or of the minority, will be in little danger from interested combinations of the majority.

In a free government the security for civil rights must be the same as that for religious rights. It consists in the one case in the multiplicity of interests, and in the other in the multiplicity of sects. The degree of security in both cases will depend on the number of interests and sects; and this may be presumed to depend on the extent of country and number of people comprehended under the same government. This view of the subject must particularly recommend a proper federal system to all the sincere and considerate friends of republican government, since it shows that in exact proportion as the territory of the Union may be formed into more circumscribed Confederacies, or States, oppressive combinations of a majority will be facilitated; the best security, under the republican forms, for the rights of every class of citizen, will be diminished; and consequently the stability and independence of some member of the government, the only other security, must be proportionally increased. Justice is the end of government. It is the end of civil society. It ever has been and ever will be pursued until it be obtained, or until liberty be lost in the pursuit. In a society under the forms of which the stronger faction can readily unite and oppress the weaker, anarchy may as truly be said to reign as in a state of nature, where the weaker individual is not secured against the violence of the stronger; and as, in the latter state, even the stronger individuals are prompted, by the uncertainty of their condition, to submit to a government which may protect the weak as well as themselves; so, in the former state, will the more powerful factions or parties be gradually induced, by a like motive, to wish for a government which will protect all parties, the weaker as well as the more powerful.

It can be little doubted that if the State of Rhode Island was separated from the Confederacy and left to itself, the insecurity of rights under the popular form of government within such narrow limits would be displayed by such reiterated oppressions of factious majorities that some power altogether independent of the people would soon be called for by the voice of the very factions whose misrule had proved the necessity of it. In the extended republic of the United States, and among the great variety of interests, parties, and sects which it embraces, a coalition of a majority of the whole society could seldom take place on any other principles than those of justice and the general good; whilst there being thus less danger to a minor from the will of a major party, there must be less pretext, also, to provide for the security of the former, by introducing into the government a will not dependent on the latter, or, in other words, a will independent of the society itself. It is no less certain than it is important, notwithstanding the contrary opinions which have been entertained, that the larger the society, provided it lie within a practicable sphere, the more duly capable it will be of self-government. And happily for the republican cause, the practicable sphere may be carried to a very great extent by a judicious modification and mixture of the *federal principle.*

Publius
(James Madison)

Federalist Paper No. 78

In this essay, Alexander Hamilton looks at the role of the judicial branch (the courts) in the new government fashioned by the Constitution's framers. The essay is historically significant because, among other things, it provides a basis for the courts' power of judicial review, which was not explicitly set forth in the Constitution (see Chapters 2 and 13).

After some brief introductory remarks, Hamilton explains why the founders decided that federal judges should be appointed and given lifetime tenure. Note how he describes the judiciary as the "weakest" and "least dangerous" branch of government. Because of this, claims Hamilton, "all possible care" is required to enable the judiciary to defend itself against attacks by the other two branches of government. Above all, the independence of the judicial branch should be secured, because if judicial powers were combined with legislative or executive powers, there would be no liberty.

We proceed now to an examination of the judiciary department of the proposed government.

In unfolding the defects of the existing Confederation, the utility and necessity of a federal judicature have been clearly pointed out. It is the less necessary to recapitulate the considerations there urged, as the propriety of the institution in the abstract is not disputed; the only questions which have been raised being relative to the manner of constituting it, and to its extent. To these points, therefore, our observations shall be confined.

The manner of constituting it seems to embrace these several objects: 1st. The mode of appointing the judges. 2d. The tenure by which they are to hold their places. 3d. The partition of the judiciary authority between different courts, and their relations to each other.

First. As to the mode of appointing the judges; this is the same with that of appointing the officers of the Union in general, and has been so fully discussed in the last two numbers, that nothing can be said here which would not be useless repetition.

Second. As to the tenure by which the judges are to hold their places; this chiefly concerns their duration in office; the provisions for their support; the precautions for their responsibility.

According to the plan of the convention, all judges who may be appointed by the United States are to hold their offices during good behavior; which is conformable to the most approved of the State constitutions and among the rest, to that of this State. Its propriety having been drawn into question by the adversaries of that plan, is no light symptom of the rage for objection, which disorders their imaginations and judgments. The standard of good behavior for the continuance in office of the judicial magistracy, is certainly one of the most valuable of the modern improvements in the practice of government. In a monarchy it is an excellent barrier to the despotism of the prince; in a republic it is a no less excellent barrier to the encroachments and oppressions of the representative body. And it is the best expedient which can be devised in any government, to secure a steady, upright, and impartial administration of the laws.

Whoever attentively considers the different departments of power must perceive, that, in a government in which they are separated from each other, the judiciary, from the nature of its functions, will always be the least dangerous to the political rights of the Constitution; because it will be least in a capacity to annoy or injure them. The Executive not only dispenses the honors, but holds the sword of the community. The legislature not only commands the purse, but prescribes the rules by which the duties and rights of every citizen are to be regulated. The judiciary, on the contrary, has no influence over either the sword or the purse; no direction either of the strength or of the wealth of the society; and can take no active resolution whatever. It may truly be said to have neither force nor will, but merely judgment; and must ultimately depend upon the aid of the executive arm even for the efficacy of its judgments.

This simple view of the matter suggests several important consequences. It proves incontestably, that the judiciary is beyond comparison the weakest of the three departments of power; that it can never attack with success either of the other two; and that all possible care is requisite to enable it to defend itself against their attacks. It equally proves, that though individual oppression may now and then proceed from the courts of justice, the general liberty of the people can never be endangered from that quarter; I mean so long as the judiciary remains truly distinct from both the legislature and the Executive. For I agree, that "there is no liberty, if the power of judging is not separated from the legislative and executive powers." And it proves, in the last place, that as liberty can have nothing to fear from the judiciary alone, but would have everything to fear from its union with either of the other departments; that as all the effects of such a union must ensue from a dependence of the former on the latter, notwithstanding a nominal and apparent separation; that as, from the natural feebleness of the judiciary, it is in continual jeopardy of being overpowered, awed, or influenced by its co-ordinate branches; and that as nothing can contribute so much to its firmness and independence as permanency in office, this quality may therefore be justly regarded as an indispensable ingredient in its constitution, and, in a great measure, as the citadel of the public justice and the public security.

Hamilton now stresses that the "complete independence of the courts" is essential in a limited government, because it is up to the courts to interpret the laws. Just as a federal court can decide which of two conflicting statutes should take priority, so can that court decide whether a statute conflicts with the Constitution. Essentially, Hamilton sets forth here the theory of judicial review—the power of the courts to decide whether actions of the other branches of government are (or are not) consistent with the Constitution. Hamilton points out that this "exercise of judicial discretion, in determining between two contradictory laws," does not mean that the judicial branch is superior to the legislative branch. Rather, it "supposes" that the power of the people (as declared in the Constitution) is superior to both the judiciary and the legislature.

The complete independence of the courts of justice is peculiarly essential in a limited Constitution. By a limited Constitution, I understand one which contains certain specified exceptions to the legislative authority; such, for instance, as that it shall pass no bills of attainder, no ex-post-facto laws, and the like. Limitations of this kind can be preserved in practice no other way than through the medium of courts of justice, whose duty it must be to declare all acts contrary to the manifest tenor of the Constitution void. Without this, all the reservations of particular rights or privileges would amount to nothing. Some perplexity respecting the rights of the courts to pronounce legislative acts void, because contrary to the Constitution, has arisen from an imagination that the doctrine would imply a superiority of the judiciary to the legislative power. It is urged that the authority which can declare the acts of another void, must necessarily be superior to the one whose acts may be declared void. As this doctrine is of great importance in all the American constitutions, a brief discussion of the ground on which it rests cannot be unacceptable.

There is no position which depends on clearer principles, than that every act of a delegated authority, contrary to the tenor of the commission under which it is exercised, is void. No legislative act, therefore, contrary to the Constitution, can be valid. To deny this, would be to affirm, that the deputy is greater than his principal; that the servant is above his master; that the representatives of the people are superior to the people themselves; that men acting by virtue of powers, may do not only what their powers do not authorize, but what they forbid.

If it be said that the legislative body are themselves the constitutional judges of their own powers, and that the construction they put upon them is conclusive upon the other departments, it may be answered, that this cannot be the natural presumption, where it is not to be collected from any particular provisions in the Constitution. It is not otherwise to be supposed, that the Constitution could intend to enable the representatives of the people to substitute their will to that of their constituents. It is far more rational to suppose, that the courts were designed to be an intermediate body between the people and the legislature, in order, among other things, to keep the latter within the limits assigned to their authority. The interpretation of the laws is the proper and peculiar province of the courts. A constitution is, in fact, and must be regarded by the judges, as a fundamental law. It therefore belongs to them to ascertain its meaning, as well as the meaning of any particular act proceeding from the legisla-tive body. If there should happen to be an irreconcilable variance between the two, that which has the superior obligation and validity ought, of course, to be preferred; or, in other words, the Constitution ought to be preferred to the statute, the intention of the people to the intention of their agents.

Nor does this conclusion by any means suppose a superiority of the judicial to the legislative power. It only supposes that the power of the people is superior to both; and that where the will of the legislature, declared in its statutes, stands in opposition to that of the people, declared in the Constitution, the judges ought to be governed by the latter rather than the former. They ought to regulate their decisions by the fundamental laws, rather than by those which are not fundamental.

This exercise of judicial discretion, in determining between two contradictory laws, is exemplified in a familiar instance. It not uncommonly happens, that there are two statutes existing at one time, clashing in whole or in part with each other, and neither of them containing any repealing clause or expression. In such a case, it is the province of the courts to liquidate and fix their meaning and operation. So far as they can, by any fair construction, be reconciled to each other, reason and law conspire to dictate that this should be done; where this is impracticable, it becomes a matter of necessity to give effect to one, in exclusion of the other. The rule which has obtained in the courts for determining their relative validity is, that the last in order of time shall be preferred to the first. But this is a mere rule of construction, not derived from any positive law, but from the nature and reason of the thing. It is a rule not enjoined upon the courts by legislative provision, but adopted by themselves, as consonant to truth the propriety, for the direction of their conduct as interpreters of the law. They thought it reasonable, that between the interfering acts of an equal authority, that which was the last indication of its will should have the preference.

But in regard to the interfering acts of a superior and subordinate authority, of an original and derivative power, the nature and reason of the thing indicate the converse of that rule as proper to be followed. They teach us that the prior act of a superior ought to be preferred to the subsequent act of an inferior and subordinate authority; and that accordingly, whenever a particular statute contravenes the Constitution, it will be the duty of the judicial tribunals to adhere to the latter and disregard the former.

It can be of no weight to say that the courts, on the pretense of a repugnancy, may substitute their own pleasure to the constitutional intentions of the legislature. This might as well happen in the case of two contradictory statutes; or it might as well happen in every adjudication upon any single statute. The courts must declare the sense of the law; and if they should be disposed to exercise will instead of judgment, the consequence would equally be the substitution of their pleasure to that of the legislative body. The observation, if it prove anything, would prove that there ought to be no judges distinct from that body.

If, then, the courts of justice are to be considered as the bulwarks of a limited Constitution against legislative encroachments, this consideration will afford a strong argument for the permanent tenure of judicial offices, since nothing will contribute so much as this to that independent spirit in the judges which must be essential to the faithful performance of so arduous a duty.

The independence of the judges is equally requisite to guard the Constitution and the rights of individuals from the effects of those ill humors, which the arts of designing men, or the influence of particular conjunctures, sometimes disseminate among the people themselves, and which, though they speedily give place to better information, and more deliberate reflection, have a tendency, in the meantime, to occasion dangerous innovations in the government, and serious oppressions of the minor party in the community. Though I trust the friends of the proposed Constitution will never concur with its enemies, in questioning that fundamental principle of republican government, which admits the right of the people to alter or abolish the established Constitution, whenever they find it inconsistent with their happiness, yet it is not to be inferred from this principle, that the representatives of the people, whenever a momentary inclination happens to lay hold of a majority of their constituents, incompatible with the provisions of the existing Constitution, would, on that account, be justifiable in a violation of those provisions; or that the courts would be under a greater obligation to connive at infractions in this shape, than when they had proceeded wholly from the cabals of the representative body. Until the people have, by some solemn and authoritative act, annulled or changed the established form, it is binding upon themselves collectively, as well as individually; and no presumption, or even knowledge, of their sentiments, can warrant their representatives in a departure from it, prior to such an act. But it is easy to see, that it would require an uncommon portion of fortitude in the judges to do their duty as faithful guardians of the Constitution, where legislative invasions of it had been instigated by the major voice of the community.

But it is not with a view to infractions of the Constitution only, that the independence of the judges may be an essential safeguard against the effects of occasional ill humors in the society. These sometimes extend no farther than to the injury of the private rights of particular classes of citizens, by unjust and partial laws. Here also the firmness of the judicial magistracy is of vast importance in mitigating the severity and confining the operation of such laws. It not only serves to moderate the immediate mischiefs of those which may have been passed, but it operates as a check upon the legislative body in passing them; who, perceiving that obstacles to the success of iniquitous intention are to be expected from the scruples of the courts, are in a manner compelled, by the very motives of the injustice they meditate, to qualify their attempts. This is a circumstance calculated to have more influence upon the character of our governments, than but few may be aware of. The benefits of the integrity and moderation of the judiciary have already been felt in more States than one; and though they may have displeased those whose sinister expectations they may have disappointed, they must have commanded the esteem and applause of all the virtuous and disinterested. Considerate men, of every description, ought to prize whatever will tend to beget or fortify that temper in the courts; as no man can be sure that he may not be tomorrow the victim of a spirit of injustice, by which he may be a gainer today. And every man must now feel, that the inevitable tendency of such a spirit is to sap the foundations of public and private confidence, and to introduce in its stead universal distrust and distress.

That inflexible and uniform adherence to the rights of the Constitution, and of individuals, which we perceive to be indispensable in the courts of justice, can certainly not be expected from judges who hold their offices by a temporary commission. Periodical appointments, however regulated, or by whomsoever made, would, in some way or other, be fatal to their necessary independence. If the power of making them was committed either to the Executive or legislature, there would be danger of an improper complaisance to the branch which possessed it; if to both, there would be an unwillingness to hazard the displeasure of either; if to the people, or to persons chosen by them for the special purpose, there would be too great a disposition to consult popularity, to justify a reliance that nothing would be consulted but the Constitution and the laws.

Hamilton points to yet another reason why lifetime tenure for federal judges will benefit the public: effective judgments rest on a knowledge of judicial precedents and the law, and such knowledge can only be obtained through experience on the bench. A "temporary duration of office," according to Hamilton, would "discourage individuals [of 'fit character'] from quitting a lucrative practice to serve on the bench" and ultimately would "throw the administration of justice into the hands of the less able, and less well qualified."

There is yet a further and a weightier reason for the permanency of the judicial offices, which is deducible from the nature of the qualifications they require. It has been frequently remarked, with great propriety, that a voluminous code of laws is one of the inconveniences necessarily connected with the advantages of a free government. To avoid an arbitrary discretion in the courts, it is indispensable that they should be bound down by strict rules and precedents, which serve to define and point out their duty in every particular case that comes before them; and it will readily be conceived from the variety of controversies which grow out of the folly and wickedness of mankind, that the records of those precedents must unavoidably swell to a very considerable bulk, and must demand long and laborious study to acquire a competent knowledge of them. Hence it is, that there can be but few men in the society who will have sufficient skill in the laws to qualify them for the stations of judges. And making the proper deductions for the ordinary depravity of human nature, the number must be still smaller of those who unite the requisite integrity with the requisite knowledge. These considerations apprise us, that the government can have no great option between fit character; and that a temporary duration in office, which would naturally discourage such characters from quitting a lucrative line of practice to accept a seat on the bench, would have a tendency to throw the administration of justice into hands less able, and less well qualified, to conduct it with utility and dignity. In the present circumstances of this country, and in those in which it is likely to be for a long time to come, the disadvantages on this score would be greater than they may at first sight appear; but it must be confessed, that they are far inferior to those which present themselves under other aspects of the subject.

Upon the whole, there can be no room to doubt that the convention acted wisely in copying from the models of those constitutions which have established good behavior as the tenure of their judicial offices, in point of duration; and that so far from being blamable on this account, their plan would have been inexcusably defective, if it had wanted this important feature of good government. The experience of Great Britain affords an illustrious comment on the excellence of the institution.

Publius
(Alexander Hamilton)

APPENDIX D

JUSTICES OF THE UNITED STATES SUPREME COURT SINCE 1900

Chief Justices

Name	Years of Service	State App't from	Appointing President	Age at App't	Political Affiliation	Educational Background*
Fuller, Melville Weston	1888–1910	Illinois	Cleveland	55	Democrat	Bowdoin College; studied at Harvard Law School
White, Edward Douglass	1910–1921	Louisiana	Taft	65	Democrat	Mount St. Mary's College; Georgetown College (now University)
Taft, William Howard	1921–1930	Connecticut	Harding	64	Republican	Yale; Cincinnati Law School
Hughes, Charles Evans	1930–1941	New York	Hoover	68	Republican	Colgate University; Brown; Columbia Law School
Stone, Harlan Fiske	1941–1946	New York	Roosevelt, F.	69	Republican	Amherst College; Columbia
Vinson, Frederick Moore	1946–1953	Kentucky	Truman	56	Democrat	Centre College
Warren, Earl	1953–1969	California	Eisenhower	62	Republican	University of California, Berkeley
Burger, Warren Earl	1969–1986	Virginia	Nixon	62	Republican	University of Minnesota; St. Paul College of Law (Mitchell College)
Rehnquist, William Hubbs	1986–2005	Virginia	Reagan	62	Republican	Stanford; Harvard; Stanford University Law School
Roberts, John G., Jr.	2005–present	District of Columbia	G. W. Bush	50	Republican	Harvard; Harvard Law School

Associate Justices

Name	Years of Service	State App't from	Appointing President	Age at App't	Political Affiliation	Educational Background*
Harlan, John Marshall	1877–1911	Kentucky	Hayes	61	Republican	Centre College; studied law at Transylvania University
Gray, Horace	1882–1902	Massachusetts	Arthur	54	Republican	Harvard College; Harvard Law School
Brewer, David Josiah	1890–1910	Kansas	Harrison	53	Republican	Wesleyan University; Yale; Albany Law School
Brown, Henry Billings	1891–1906	Michigan	Harrison	55	Republican	Yale; studied at Yale Law School and Harvard Law School
Shiras, George, Jr.	1892–1903	Pennsylvania	Harrison	61	Republican	Ohio University; Yale; studied law at Yale and privately
White, Edward Douglass	1894–1910	Louisiana	Cleveland	49	Democrat	Mount St. Mary's College; Georgetown College (now University)
Peckham, Rufus Wheeler	1896–1909	New York	Cleveland	58	Democrat	Read law in father's firm
McKenna, Joseph	1898–1925	California	McKinley	55	Republican	Benicia Collegiate Institute, Law Department
Holmes, Oliver Wendell, Jr.	1902–1932	Massachusetts	Roosevelt, T.	61	Republican	Harvard College; studied law at Harvard Law School

*Sources: Educational background information derived from Elder Witt, *Guide to the U.S. Supreme Court,* 2d ed. (Washington, D.C.: Congressional Quarterly Press, Inc., 1990). Reprinted with the permission of the publisher. Plus authors' update.

(Continued)

Associate Justices (Continued)

Name	Years of Service	State App't from	Appointing President	Age at App't	Political Affiliation	Educational Background
Day, William Rufus	1903–1922	Ohio	Roosevelt, T.	54	Republican	University of Michigan; University of Michigan Law School
Moody, William Henry	1906–1910	Massachusetts	Roosevelt, T.	53	Republican	Harvard; Harvard Law School
Lurton, Horace Harmon	1910–1914	Tennessee	Taft	66	Democrat	University of Chicago; Cumberland Law School
Hughes, Charles Evans	1910–1916	New York	Taft	48	Republican	Colgate University; Brown University; Columbia Law School
Van Devanter, Willis	1911–1937	Wyoming	Taft	52	Republican	Indiana Asbury University; University of Cincinnati Law School
Lamar, Joseph Rucker	1911–1916	Georgia	Taft	54	Democrat	University of Georgia; Bethany College; Washington and Lee University
Pitney, Mahlon	1912–1922	New Jersey	Taft	54	Republican	College of New Jersey (Princeton); read law under father
McReynolds, James Clark	1914–1941	Tennessee	Wilson	52	Democrat	Vanderbilt University; University of Virginia
Brandeis, Louis Dembitz	1916–1939	Massachusetts	Wilson	60	Democrat	Harvard Law School
Clarke, John Hessin	1916–1922	Ohio	Wilson	59	Democrat	Western Reserve University; read law under father
Sutherland, George	1922–1938	Utah	Harding	60	Republican	Brigham Young Academy; one year at University of Michigan Law School
Butler, Pierce	1923–1939	Minnesota	Harding	57	Democrat	Carleton College
Sanford, Edward Terry	1923–1930	Tennessee	Harding	58	Republican	University of Tennessee; Harvard; Harvard Law School
Stone, Harlan Fiske	1925–1941	New York	Coolidge	53	Republican	Amherst College; Columbia University Law School
Roberts, Owen Josephus	1930–1945	Pennsylvania	Hoover	55	Republican	University of Pennsylvania; University of Pennsylvania Law School
Cardozo, Benjamin Nathan	1932–1938	New York	Hoover	62	Democrat	Columbia University; two years at Columbia Law School
Black, Hugo Lafayette	1937–1971	Alabama	Roosevelt, F.	51	Democrat	Birmingham Medical College; University of Alabama Law School
Reed, Stanley Forman	1938–1957	Kentucky	Roosevelt, F.	54	Democrat	Kentucky Wesleyan University; Foreman Yale; studied law at University of Virginia and Columbia University; University of Paris
Frankfurter, Felix	1939–1962	Massachusetts	Roosevelt, F.	57	Independent	College of the City of New York; Harvard Law School
Douglas, William Orville	1939–1975	Connecticut	Roosevelt, F.	41	Democrat	Whitman College; Columbia University Law School
Murphy, Frank	1940–1949	Michigan	Roosevelt, F.	50	Democrat	University of Michigan; Lincoln's Inn, London; Trinity College
Byrnes, James Francis	1941–1942	South Carolina	Roosevelt, F.	62	Democrat	Read law privately
Jackson, Robert Houghwout	1941–1954	New York	Roosevelt, F.	49	Democrat	Albany Law School
Rutledge, Wiley Blount	1943–1949	Iowa	Roosevelt, F.	49	Democrat	University of Wisconsin; University of Colorado

Associate Justices (Continued)

Name	Years of Service	State App't from	Appointing President	Age at App't	Political Affiliation	Educational Background
Burton, Harold Hitz	1945–1958	Ohio	Truman	57	Republican	Bowdoin College; Harvard Law School
Clark, Thomas Campbell	1949–1967	Texas	Truman	50	Democrat	University of Texas
Minton, Sherman	1949–1956	Indiana	Truman	59	Democrat	Indiana University College of Law; Yale Law School
Harlan, John Marshall	1955–1971	New York	Eisenhower	56	Republican	Princeton; Oxford University; New York Law School
Brennan, William J., Jr.	1956–1990	New Jersey	Eisenhower	50	Democrat	University of Pennsylvania; Harvard Law School
Whittaker, Charles Evans	1957–1962	Missouri	Eisenhower	56	Republican	University of Kansas City Law School
Stewart, Potter	1958–1981	Ohio	Eisenhower	43	Republican	Yale; Yale Law School
White, Byron Raymond	1962–1993	Colorado	Kennedy	45	Democrat	University of Colorado; Oxford University; Yale Law School
Goldberg, Arthur Joseph	1962–1965	Illinois	Kennedy	54	Democrat	Northwestern University
Fortas, Abe	1965–1969	Tennessee	Johnson, L.	55	Democrat	Southwestern College; Yale Law School
Marshall, Thurgood	1967–1991	New York	Johnson, L.	59	Democrat	Lincoln University; Howard University Law School
Blackmun, Harry A.	1970–1994	Minnesota	Nixon	62	Republican	Harvard; Harvard Law School
Powell, Lewis F., Jr.	1972–1987	Virginia	Nixon	65	Democrat	Washington and Lee University; Washington and Lee University Law School; Harvard Law School
Rehnquist, William H.	1972–1986	Arizona	Nixon	48	Republican	Stanford; Harvard; Stanford University Law School
Stevens, John Paul	1975–present	Illinois	Ford	55	Republican	University of Colorado; Northwestern University Law School
O'Connor, Sandra Day	1981–2006	Arizona	Reagan	51	Republican	Stanford; Stanford University Law School
Scalia, Antonin	1986–present	Virginia	Reagan	50	Republican	Georgetown University; Harvard Law School
Kennedy, Anthony M.	1988–present	California	Reagan	52	Republican	Stanford; London School of Economics; Harvard Law School
Souter, David Hackett	1990–present	New Hampshire	G. H. W. Bush	51	Republican	Harvard; Oxford University
Thomas, Clarence	1991–present	District of Columbia	G. H. W. Bush	43	Republican	Holy Cross College; Yale Law School
Ginsburg, Ruth Bader	1993–present	District of Columbia	Clinton	60	Democrat	Cornell University; Columbia Law School
Breyer, Stephen G.	1994–present	Massachusetts	Clinton	55	Democrat	Stanford University; Oxford University; Harvard Law School
Alito, Samuel Anthony, Jr.	2006–present	New Jersey	G. W. Bush	55	Republican	Princeton University; Yale Law School

APPENDIX E

PARTY CONTROL OF CONGRESS SINCE 1900

Congress	Years	President	Majority Party in House	Majority Party in Senate
57th	1901–1903	McKinley/T. Roosevelt	Republican	Republican
58th	1903–1905	T. Roosevelt	Republican	Republican
59th	1905–1907	T. Roosevelt	Republican	Republican
60th	1907–1909	T. Roosevelt	Republican	Republican
61st	1909–1911	Taft	Republican	Republican
62d	1911–1913	Taft	Democratic	Republican
63d	1913–1915	Wilson	Democratic	Democratic
64th	1915–1917	Wilson	Democratic	Democratic
65th	1917–1919	Wilson	Democratic	Democratic
66th	1919–1921	Wilson	Republican	Republican
67th	1921–1923	Harding	Republican	Republican
68th	1923–1925	Harding/Coolidge	Republican	Republican
69th	1925–1927	Coolidge	Republican	Republican
70th	1927–1929	Coolidge	Republican	Republican
71st	1929–1931	Hoover	Republican	Republican
72d	1931–1933	Hoover	Democratic	Republican
73d	1933–1935	F. Roosevelt	Democratic	Democratic
74th	1935–1937	F. Roosevelt	Democratic	Democratic
75th	1937–1939	F. Roosevelt	Democratic	Democratic
76th	1939–1941	F. Roosevelt	Democratic	Democratic
77th	1941–1943	F. Roosevelt	Democratic	Democratic
78th	1943–1945	F. Roosevelt	Democratic	Democratic
79th	1945–1947	F. Roosevelt/Truman	Democratic	Democratic
80th	1947–1949	Truman	Republican	Democratic
81st	1949–1951	Truman	Democratic	Democratic
82d	1951–1953	Truman	Democratic	Democratic
83d	1953–1955	Eisenhower	Republican	Republican
84th	1955–1957	Eisenhower	Democratic	Democratic
85th	1957–1959	Eisenhower	Democratic	Democratic
86th	1959–1961	Eisenhower	Democratic	Democratic
87th	1961–1963	Kennedy	Democratic	Democratic
88th	1963–1965	Kennedy/Johnson	Democratic	Democratic
89th	1965–1967	Johnson	Democratic	Democratic
90th	1967–1969	Johnson	Democratic	Democratic
91st	1969–1971	Nixon	Democratic	Democratic
92d	1971–1973	Nixon	Democratic	Democratic
93d	1973–1975	Nixon/Ford	Democratic	Democratic
94th	1975–1977	Ford	Democratic	Democratic
95th	1977–1979	Carter	Democratic	Democratic
96th	1979–1981	Carter	Democratic	Democratic
97th	1981–1983	Reagan	Democratic	Republican
98th	1983–1985	Reagan	Democratic	Republican
99th	1985–1987	Reagan	Democratic	Republican
100th	1987–1989	Reagan	Democratic	Democratic
101st	1989–1991	G. H. W. Bush	Democratic	Democratic
102d	1991–1993	G. H. W. Bush	Democratic	Democratic
103d	1993–1995	Clinton	Democratic	Democratic
104th	1995–1997	Clinton	Republican	Republican
105th	1997–1999	Clinton	Republican	Republican
106th	1999–2001	Clinton	Republican	Republican
107th	2001–2003	G. W. Bush	Republican	Democratic
108th	2003–2005	G. W. Bush	Republican	Republican
109th	2005–2007	G. W. Bush	Republican	Republican
110th	2007–2009	G. W. Bush	Democratic	Democratic
111th	2009–2011	Obama	Democratic	Democratic

APPENDIX F

SPANISH EQUIVALENTS FOR IMPORTANT TERMS IN AMERICAN GOVERNMENT

Acid Rain: Lluvia Acida
Acquisitive Model: Modelo Adquisitivo
Actionable: Procesable, Enjuiciable
Action-Reaction Syndrome: Sídrome de Acción y Reacción
Actual Malice: Malicia Expresa
Administrative Agency: Agencia Administrativa
Advice and Consent: Consejo y Consentimiento
Affirm: Afirmar
Affirmative Action: Acción Afirmativa
Agenda Setting: Agenda Establecida
Aid to Families with Dependent Children (AFDC): Ayuda para Familias con Niños Dependientes
***Amicus Curiae* Brief:** Tercer persona o grupo no involucrado en el caso, admitido en un juicio para hacer valer el intéres público o el de un grupo social importante.
Anarchy: Anarquía
Anti-Federalists: Anti-Federalistas
Appellate Court: Corte de Apelación
Appointment Power: Poder de Apuntamiento
Appropriation: Apropiación
Aristocracy: Aristocracia
Attentive Public: Público Atento
Australian Ballot: Voto Australiano
Authority: Autoridad
Authorization: Autorización

Bad-Tendency Rule: Regla de Tendencia-mala
"Beauty Contest": Concurso de Belleza
Bicameralism: Bicameralismo
Bicameral Legislature: Legislatura Bicameral
Bill of Rights: Declaración de Derechos
Blanket Primary: Primaria Comprensiva
Block Grants: Concesiones de Bloque
Bureaucracy: Burocracia
Busing: Transporte Público

Cabinet: Gabinete, Consejo de Ministros
Cabinet Department: Departamento del Gabinete
Cadre: El núcleo de activistas de partidos políticos encargados de cumplir las funciones importantes de los partidos políticos americanos.

Canvassing Board: Consejo encargado con la encuesta de una violación.
Capture: Captura, toma
Casework: Trabajo de Caso
Categorical Grants-in-Aid: Concesiones Categóricas de Ayuda
Caucus: Reunión de Dirigentes
Challenge: Reto
Checks and Balances: Chequeos y Equilibrio
Chief Diplomat: Jefe Diplomático
Chief Executive: Jefe Ejecutivo
Chief Legislator: Jefe Legislador
Chief of Staff: Jefe de Personal
Chief of State: Jefe de Estado
Civil Law: Derecho Civil
Civil Liberties: Libertades Civiles
Civil Rights: Derechos Civiles
Civil Service: Servicio Civil
Civil Service Commission: Comisión de Servicio Civil
Class-Action Suit: Demanda en representación de un grupo o clase.
Class Politics: Política de Clase
Clear and Present Danger Test: Prueba de Peligro Claro y Presente
Climate Control: Control de Clima
Closed Primary: Primaria Cerrada
Cloture: Cierre al voto
Coattail Effect: Effecto de Cola de Chaqueta
Cold War: Guerra Fría
Commander in Chief: Comandante en Jefe
Commerce Clause: Clausula de Comercio
Commercial Speech: Discurso Comercial
Common Law: Ley Común, Derecho Consuetudinario
Comparable Worth: Valor Comparable
Compliance: De acuerdo
Concurrent Majority: Mayoría Concurrente
Concurring Opinion: Opinión Concurrente
Confederal System: Sistema Confederal
Confederation: Confederación
Conference Committee: Comité de Conferencia
Consensus: Concenso
Consent of the People: Consentimiento de la Gente
Conservatism: Calidad de Conservador

Conservative Coalition: Coalición Conservadora
Consolidation: Consolidación
Constant Dollars: Dólares Constantes
Constitutional Initiative: Iniciativa Constitucional
Constitutional Power: Poder Constitucional
Containment: Contenimiento
Continuing Resolution: Resolució Contínua
Cooley's Rule: Régla de Cooley
Cooperative Federalism: Federalismo Cooperativo
Corrupt Practices Acts: Leyes Contra Acciones Corruptas
Council of Economic Advisers (CEA): Consejo de Asesores Económicos
Council of Government (COG): Consejo de Gobierno
County: Condado
Credentials Committee: Comité de Credenciales
Criminal Law: Ley Criminal

***De Facto* Segregation:** Segregación de Hecho
***De Jure* Segregation:** Segregación Cotidiana
Defamation of Character: Defamación de Carácter
Democracy: Democracia
Democratic Party: Partido Democratico
Dillon's Rule: Régla de Dillon
Diplomacy: Diplomácia
Direct Democracy: Democracia Directa
Direct Primary: Primaria Directa
Direct Technique: Técnica Directa
Discharge Petition: Petición de Descargo
Dissenting Opinion: Opinión Disidente
Divisive Opinion: Opinión Divisiva
Domestic Policy: Principio Político Doméstico
Dual Citizenship: Ciudadanía Dual
Dual Federalism: Federalismo Dual
Détente: No Spanish equivalent

Economic Aid: Ayuda Económica
Economic Regulation: Regulación Económica
Elastic Clause, or Necessary and Proper Clause: Cláusula Flexible o Cláusula Propia Necesaria

Elector: Elector
Electoral College: Colegio Electoral
Electronic Media: Media Electronica
Elite: Elite (el selecto)
Elite Theory: Teoría Elitista (de lo selecto)
Emergency Power: Poder de Emergencia
Enumerated Power: Poder Enumerado
Environmental Impact Statement (EIS): Afirmación de Impacto Ambiental
Equality: Igualdad
Equalization: Igualación
Equal Employment Opportunity Commission (EEOC): Comisión de Igualdad de Oportunidad en el Empleo
Era of Good Feeling: Era de Buen Sentimiento
Era of Personal Politics: Era de Política Personal
Establishment Clause: Cláusula de Establecimiento
Euthanasia: Eutanasia
Exclusionary Rule: Regla de Exclusión
Executive Agreement: Acuerdo Ejecutivo
Executive Budget: Presupuesto Ejecutivo
Executive Office of the President (EOP): Oficina Ejecutiva del Presidente
Executive Order: Orden Ejecutivo
Executive Privilege: Privilegio Ejecutivo
Expressed Power: Poder Expresado
Extradite: Entregar por Extradición

Faction: Facción
Fairness Doctrine: Doctrina de Justicia
Fall Review: Revision de Otoño
Federalists: Federalistas
Federal Mandate: Mandato Federal
Federal Open Market Committee (FOMC): Comité Federal de Libre Mercado
Federal Register: Registro Federal
Federal System: Sistema Federal
Fighting Words: Palabras de Provocación
Filibuster: Obstrucción de iniciativas de ley
Fireside Chat: Charla de Hogar
First Budget Resolution: Resolució Primera Presupuesta
First Continental Congress: Primér Congreso Continental
Fiscal Policy: Politico Fiscal
Fiscal Year (FY): Año Fiscal
Fluidity: Fluidez
Food Stamps: Estampillas para Comida
Foreign Policy: Politica Extranjera
Foreign Policy Process: Proceso de Politica Extranjera

Franking: Franqueando
Fraternity: Fraternidad
Free Exercise Clause: Cláusula de Ejercicio Libre
Full Faith and Credit Clause: Cláusula de Completa Fé y Crédito
Functional Consolidation: Consolidación Funcional

Gag Order: Orden de Silencio
Garbage Can Model: Modelo Bote de Basura
Gender Gap: Brecha de Género
General Law City: Regla General Urbana
General Sales Tax: Impuesto General de Ventas
Generational Effect: Efecto Generacional
Gerrymandering: División arbitraria de los distritos electorales con fines políticos.
Government: Gobierno
Government Corporation: Corporación Gubernamental
Government in the Sunshine Act: Gobierno en la acta: Luz del Sol
Grandfather Clause: Clausula del Abuelo
Grand Jury: Gran Jurado
Great Compromise: Grán Acuerdo de Negociación

Hatch Act (Political Activities Act): Acta Hatch (acta de actividades politicas)
Hecklers' Veto: Veto de Abuchamiento
Home Rule City: Regla Urbana
Horizontal Federalism: Federalismo Horizontal
Hyperpluralism: Hiperpluralismo

Ideologue: Ideólogo
Ideology: Ideología
Image Building: Construcción de Imágen
Impeachment: Acción Penal Contra un Funcionario Público
Inalienable Rights: Derechos Inalienables
Income Transfer: Transferencia de Ingresos
Incorporation Theory: Teoría de Incorporación
Independent: Independiente
Independent Candidate: Candidato Independiente
Independent Executive Agency: Agencia Ejecutiva Independiente
Independent Regulatory Agency: Agencia Regulatoria Independiente
Indirect Technique: Técnica Indirecta

Inherent Power: Poder Inherente
Initiative: Iniciativa
Injunction: Injunción, Prohibición Judicial
In-Kind Subsidy: Subsidio de Clase
Institution: Institución
Instructed Delegate: Delegado con Instrucciones
Intelligence Community: Comunidad de Inteligencia
Intensity: Intensidad
Interest Group: Grupo de Interés
Interposition: Interposición
Interstate Compact: Compacto Interestatal
Iron Curtain: Cortina de Acero
Iron Triangle: Triágulo de Acero
Isolationist Foreign Policy: Politica Extranjera de Aislamiento
Issue Voting: Voto Temático
Item Veto: Artículo de Veto

Jim Crow Laws: No Spanish equivalent.
Joint Committee: Comité Mancomunado
Judicial Activism: Activismo Judicial Judicial
Implementation: Implementacion Judicial
Judicial Restraint: Restricción Judicial
Judicial Review: Revisión Judicial
Jurisdiction: Jurisdicción
Justiciable Dispute: Disputa Judiciaria
Justiciable Question: Pregunta Justiciable

Keynesian Economics: Economía Keynesiana
Kitchen Cabinet: Gabinete de Cocina

Labor Movement: Movimiento Laboral
Latent Public Opinion: Opinión Pública Latente
Lawmaking: Hacedores de Ley
Legislative History: Historia Legislativa
Legislative Initiative: Iniciativa de legislación
Legislative Veto: Veto Legislativo
Legislature: Legislatura
Legitimacy: Legitimidad
Libel: Libelo, Difamación Escrita
Liberalism: Liberalismo
Liberty: Libertad
Limited Government: Gobierno Limitado
Line Organization: Organización de Linea
Literacy Test: Exámen de alfabetización
Litigate: Litigar
Lobbying: Cabildeo

Logrolling: Práctica legislativa que consiste en incluir en un mismo proyecto de ley temas de diversa ídole.
Loophole: Hueco Legal, Escapatoria

Madisonian Model: Modelo Madisónico
Majority: Mayoría
Majority Floor Leader: Líder Mayoritario de Piso
Majority Leader of the House: Líder Mayoritario de la Casa
Majority Opinion: Opinión Mayoritaria
Majority Rule: Regla de Mayoría
Managed News: Noticias Manipuladas
Mandatory Retirement: Retiro Mandatorio
Matching Funds: Fondos Combinados
Material Incentive: Incentivo Material
Media: Media
Media Access: Acceso de Media
Merit System: Sistema de Mérito
Military-Industrial Complex: Complejo Industriomilitar
Minority Floor Leader: Líder Minoritario de Piso
Minority Leader of the House: Líder Minorial del Cuerpo Legislativo
Monetary Policy: Politica Monetaria
Monopolistic Model: Modelo Monopólico
Monroe Doctrine: Doctrina Monroe
Moral Idealism: Idealismo Moral
Municipal Home Rule: Regla Municipal

Narrowcasting: Mensaje Dirigído
National Committee: Comité Nacional
National Convention: Convención Nacional
National Politics: Politica Nacional
National Security Council (NSC): Concilio de Seguridad Nacional
National Security Policy: Politica de Seguridad Nacional
Natural Aristocracy: Aristocracia Natural
Natural Rights: Derechos Naturales
Necessaries: Necesidades
Negative Constituents: Constituyentes Negativos
New England Town: Pueblo de Nueva Inglaterra
New Federalism: Federalismo Nuevo
Nullification: Nulidad, Anulación

Office-Block, or Massachusetts, Ballot: Cuadro-Oficina, o Massachusetts, Voto
Office of Management and Budget (OMB): Oficina de Administració y Presupuesto
Oligarchy: Oligarquía

Ombudsman: Funcionario que representa al ciudadano ante el gobierno.
Open Primary: Primaria Abierta
Opinion: Opinión
Opinion Leader: Líder de Opinión
Opinion Poll: Encuesta, Conjunto de Opinión
Oral Arguments: Argumentos Orales
Oversight: Inadvertencia, Omisión

Paid-for Political Announcement: Anuncios Politicos Pagados
Pardon: Perdón
Party-Column, or Indiana, Ballot: Partido-Columna, o Indiana, Voto
Party Identification: Identificación de Partido
Party Identifier: Identificador de Partido
Party-in-Electorate: Partido Electoral
Party-in-Government: Partido en Gobierno
Party Organization: Organización de Partido
Party Platform: Plataforma de Partido
Patronage: Patrocinio
Peer Group: Grupo de Contemporáneos
Pendleton Act (Civil Service Reform Act): Acta Pendleton (Acta de Reforma al Servicio Civil)
Personal Attack Rule: Regla de Ataque Personal
Petit Jury: Jurado Ordinario
Pluralism: Pluralismo
Plurality: Pluralidad
Pocket Veto: Veto de Bolsillo
Police Power: Poder Policiaco
Policy Trade-offs: Intercambio de Politicas
Political Action Committee (PAC): Comité de Acción Política
Political Consultant: Consultante Político
Political Culture: Cultura Politica
Political Party: Partido Político
Political Question: Pregunta Politica
Political Realism: Realismo Político
Political Socialization: Socialización Politica
Political Tolerance: Tolerancia Política
Political Trust: Confianza Política
Politico: Político
Politics: Politica
Poll Tax: Impuesto sobre el sufragio
Poll Watcher: Observador de Encuesta
Popular Sovereignty: Soberanía Popular
Power: Poder
Precedent: Precedente

Preferred-Position Test: Prueba de Posición Preferida
Presidential Primary: Primaria Presidencial
President Pro Tempore: Presidente Provisoriamente
Press Secretary: Secretaría de Prensa
Prior Restraint: Restricción Anterior
Privileges and Immunities: Privilégios e Imunidades
Privitization, or Contracting Out: Privatización
Property: Propiedad
Property Tax: Impuesto de Propiedad
Public Agenda: Agenda Pública
Public Debt Financing: Financiamiento de Deuda Pública
Public Debt, or National Debt: Deuda Pública o Nacional
Public Interest: Interes Público
Public Opinion: Opinión Pública
Purposive Incentive: Incentivo de Propósito

Ratification: Ratificación
Rational Ignorance Effect: Effecto de Ignorancia Racional
Reapportionment: Redistribución
Recall: Suspender
Recognition Power: Poder de Reconocimiento
Recycling: Reciclaje
Redistricting: Redistrictificación
Referendum: Referédum
Registration: Registración
Regressive Tax: Impuestos Regresivos
Relevance: Pertinencia
Remand: Reenviar
Representation: Representación
Representative Assembly: Asamblea Representativa
Representative Democracy: Democracia Representativa
Reprieve: Trequa, Suspensión
Republic: República
Republican Party: Partido Republicano
Resulting Powers: Poderes Resultados
Reverse: Cambiarse a lo contrario
Reverse Discrimination: Discriminación Reversiva
Rule of Four: Regla de Cuatro
Rules Committee: Comité Regulador
Run-off Primary: Primaria Residual

Safe Seat: Asiento Seguro
Sampling Error: Error de Encuesta
Secession: Secesión
Second Budget Resolution: Resolución Segunda Presupuestal
Second Continental Congress: Segundo Congreso Continental

Sectional Politics: Política Seccional
Segregation: Segregación
Select Committee: Comité Selecto
Selectperson: Persona Selecta
Senatorial Courtesy: Cortesia Senatorial
Seniority System: Sistema Señiorial
Separate-but-Equal Doctrine: Separados pero iguales
Separation of Powers: Separación de Poderes
Service Sector: Sector de Servicio
Sexual Harassment: Acosamiento Sexual
Sex Discrimination: Discriminacion Sexual
Slander: Difamación Oral, Calumnia
Sliding-Scale Test: Prueba Escalonada
Social Movement: Movimiento Social
Social Security: Seguridad Social
Socioeconomic Status: Estado Socioeconómico
Solidary Incentive: Incentivo de Solideridad
Solid South: Súr Sólido
Sound Bite: Mordida de Sonido
Soviet Bloc: Bloque Soviético
Speaker of the House: Vocero de la Casa
Spin: Girar/Giro
Spin Doctor: Doctor en Giro
Spin-off Party: Partido Estático
Spoils System: Sistema de Despojos
Spring Review: Revisión de Primavera
Stability: Estabilidad
Standing Committee: Comité de Sostenimiento
Stare Decisis: El principio característico del ley comú por el cual los precedentes jurisprenciales tienen fuerza obligatoria, no sólo entre las partes, sino tambien para casos sucesivos análogos.
State: Estado
State Central Committee: Comité Central del Estado

State of the Union Message: Mensaje Sobre el Estado de la Unión
Statutory Power: Poder Estatorial
Strategic Arms Limitation Treaty (SALT I): Tratado de Limitación de Armas Estratégicas
Subpoena: Orden de Testificación
Subsidy: Subsidio
Suffrage: Sufrágio
Sunset Legislation: Legislación Sunset
Superdelegate: Líder de partido o oficial elegido quien tiene el derecho de votar.
Supplemental Security Income (SSI): Ingresos de Seguridad Suplementaria
Supremacy Clause: Cláusula de Supremacia
Supremacy Doctrine: Doctrina de Supremacia
Symbolic Speech: Discurso Simbólico

Technical Assistance: Asistencia Técnica
Third Party: Tercer Partido
Third-Party Candidate: Candidato de Tercer Partido
Ticket Splitting: División de Boletos
Totalitarian Regime: Régimen Totalitario
Town Manager System: Sistema de Administrador Municipal
Town Meeting: Junta Municipal
Township: Municipio
Tracking Poll: Seguimiento de Encuesta
Trial Court: Tribunal de Primera
Truman Doctrine: Doctrina Truman
Trustee: Depositario
Twelfth Amendment: Doceava Enmienda
Twenty-fifth Amendment: Veinticincoava Enmienda
Two-Party System: Sistema de Dos Partidos

Unanimous Opinion: Opinión Unánime
Underground Economy: Economía Subterráea
Unicameral Legislature: Legislatura Unicameral
Unincorporated Area: Area no Incorporada
Unitary System: Sistema Unitario
Unit Rule: Regla de Unidad
Universal Suffrage: Sufragio Universal
U.S. Treasury Bond: Bono de la Tesoreria de E.U.A.

Veto Message: Comunicado de Veto
Voter Turnout: Renaimiento de Votantes

War Powers Act: Acta de Poderes de Guerra
Washington Community: Comunidad de Washington
Weberian Model: Modelo Weberiano
Whip: Látigo
Whistleblower: Privatización o Contratista
White House Office: Oficina de la Casa Blanca
White House Press Corps: Cuerpo de Prensa de la Casa Blanca
White Primary: Sufragio en Elección Primaria/Blancos Solamente
Writ of *Certiorari:* Prueba de certeza; orden emitida por el tribunal de apelaciones para que el tribunal inferior dé lugar a la apelación.
Writ of *Habeas Corpus:* Prueba de Evidencia Concreta
Writ of *Mandamus:* Un mandato por la corte para que un acto se lleve a cabo.

Yellow Journalism: Amarillismo Periodístico

GLOSSARY

A

Acquisitive Model A model of bureaucracy that views top-level bureaucrats as seeking to expand the size of their budgets and staffs to gain greater power.

Actual Malice Either knowledge of a defamatory statement's falsity or a reckless disregard for the truth.

Administrative Agency A federal, state, or local government unit established to perform a specific function. Administrative agencies are created and authorized by legislative bodies to administer and enforce specific laws.

Advice and Consent Terms in the Constitution describing the U.S. Senate's power to review and approve treaties and presidential appointments.

Affirm To declare that a court ruling is valid and must stand.

Affirmative Action A policy in educational admissions or job hiring that gives special attention or compensatory treatment to traditionally disadvantaged groups in an effort to overcome present effects of past discrimination.

Agenda Setting Determining which public-policy questions will be debated or considered.

Amicus Curiae **Brief** A brief (a document containing a legal argument supporting a desired outcome in a particular case) filed by a third party, or *amicus curiae* (Latin for "friend of the court"), who is not directly involved in the litigation but who has an interest in the outcome of the case.

Anarchy The condition of no government.

Anti-Federalist An individual who opposed the ratification of the new Constitution in 1787. The Anti-Federalists were opposed to a strong central government.

Appellate Court A court having jurisdiction to review cases and issues that were originally tried in lower courts.

Appointment Power The authority vested in the president to fill a government office or position. Positions filled by presidential appointment include those in the executive branch and the federal judiciary, commissioned officers in the armed forces, and members of the independent regulatory commissions.

Appropriation The passage, by Congress, of a spending bill specifying the amount of authorized funds that actually will be allocated for an agency's use.

Aristocracy Rule by the "best"; in reality, rule by an upper class.

Arraignment The first act in a criminal proceeding, in which the defendant is brought before a court to hear the charges against him or her and enter a plea of guilty or not guilty.

Australian Ballot A secret ballot prepared, distributed, and tabulated by government officials at public expense. Since 1888, all states have used the Australian ballot rather than an open, public ballot.

Authoritarianism A type of regime in which only the government itself is fully controlled by the ruler. Social and economic institutions exist that are not under the government's control.

Authority The right and power of a government or other entity to enforce its decisions and compel obedience.

Authorization A formal declaration by a legislative committee that a certain amount of funding may be available to an agency. Some authorizations terminate in a year; others are renewable automatically without further congressional action.

B

"Beauty Contest" A presidential primary in which contending candidates compete for popular votes but the results do not control the selection of delegates to the national convention.

Bias An inclination or preference that interferes with impartial judgment.

Bicameral Legislature A legislature made up of two parts, called chambers. The U.S. Congress, composed of the House of Representatives and the Senate, is a bicameral legislature.

Bicameralism The division of a legislature into two separate assemblies.

Bill of Rights The first ten amendments to the U.S. Constitution.

Block Grants Federal programs that provide funds to state and local governments for broad functional areas, such as criminal justice or mental-health programs.

Boycott A form of pressure or protest—an organized refusal to purchase a particular product or deal with a particular business.

Broad Construction A judicial philosophy that looks to the context and purpose of a law when making an interpretation.

Budget Deficit Government expenditures that exceed receipts.

Bureaucracy A large organization that is structured hierarchically to carry out specific functions.

Busing In the context of civil rights, the transportation of public school students from areas where they live to schools in other areas to eliminate school segregation based on residential patterns.

C

Cabinet An advisory group selected by the president to aid in making decisions. The cabinet includes the heads of fifteen executive departments and others named by the president.

Cabinet Department One of the fifteen departments of the executive branch (Agriculture, Commerce, Defense, Education, Energy, Health and Human Services, Homeland Security, Housing and Urban Development, Interior, Justice, Labor, State, Transportation, Treasury, and Veterans Affairs).

Capitalism An economic system character-ized by the private ownership of wealth-creating assets, free markets, and freedom of contract.

Capture The act by which an industry being regulated by a government agency gains direct or indirect control over agency personnel and decision makers.

Case Law Judicial interpretations of common law principles and doctrines, as well as interpretations of constitutional law, statutory law, and administrative law.

Casework Personal work for constituents by members of Congress.

Categorical Grants Federal grants to states or local governments that are for specific programs or projects.

Caucus A meeting of party members designed to select candidates and propose policies.

Checks and Balances A major principle of the American system of government whereby each branch of the government can check the actions of the others.

Chief Diplomat The role of the president in recognizing foreign governments, making treaties, and effecting executive agreements.

Chief Executive The role of the president as head of the executive branch of the government.

Chief Legislator The role of the president in influencing the making of laws.

Chief of Staff The person who is named to direct the White House Office and advise the president.

Civil Disobedience A nonviolent, public refusal to obey allegedly unjust laws.

Civil Law The law regulating conduct between private persons over noncriminal matters, including contracts, domestic relations, and business interactions.

Civil Liberties Those personal freedoms, including freedom of religion and freedom of speech, that are protected for all individuals. The civil liberties set forth in the U.S. Constitution, as amended, restrain the government from taking certain actions against individuals.

Civil Rights Generally, all rights rooted in the Fourteenth Amendment's guarantee of equal protection under the law.

Civil Service A collective term for the body of employees working for the government. Generally, *civil service* is understood to apply to all those who gain government employment through a merit system.

Civil Service Commission The initial central personnel agency of the national government; created in 1883.

Class-Action Suit A lawsuit filed by an individual seeking damages for "all persons similarly situated."

Clear and Present Danger Test The test proposed by Justice Oliver Wendell Holmes for determining when government may restrict free speech. Restrictions are permissible, he argued, only when speech creates a *clear and present danger* to the public order.

Climate Control The use of public relations techniques to create favorable public opinion toward an interest group, industry, or corporation.

Closed Primary A type of primary in which the voter is limited to choosing candidates of the party of which he or she is a member.

Coattail Effect The influence of a popular candidate on the electoral success of other candidates on the same party ticket. The effect is increased by the party-column ballot, which encourages straight-ticket voting.

Cold War The ideological, political, and economic confrontation between the United States and the Soviet Union following World War II.

Commander in Chief The role of the president as supreme commander of the military forces of the United States and of the state National Guard units when they are called into federal service.

Commerce Clause The section of the U.S. Constitution in which Congress is given the power to regulate trade among the states and with foreign countries.

Commercial Speech Advertising statements, which increasingly have been given First Amendment protection.

Common Law Judge-made law that originated in England from decisions shaped according to prevailing customs. Decisions were applied to similar situations and thus gradually became common to the nation.

Common Law Judge-made law that originated in England from decisions shaped according to prevailing custom. Decisions were applied to similar situations and gradually became common to the nation.

Communism A variant of socialism that favors a partisan (and often totalitarian) dictatorship, government control of all enterprises, and the replacement of free markets with central planning.

Concurrent Powers Powers held jointly by the national and state governments.

Concurring Opinion A separate opinion prepared by a judge who supports the decision of the majority of the court but who wants to make or clarify a particular point or to voice disapproval of the grounds on which the decision was made.

Confederal System A system consisting of a league of independent states, each having essentially sovereign powers. The central government created by such a league has only limited powers over the states.

Confederation A political system in which states or regional governments retain ultimate authority except for those powers they expressly delegate to a central government; a voluntary association of independent states, in which the member states agree to limited restraints on their freedom of action.

Conference Committee A special joint committee appointed to reconcile differences when bills pass the two chambers of Congress in different forms.

Consensus General agreement among the citizenry on an issue.

Consent of the People The idea that governments and laws derive their legitimacy from the consent of the governed.

Conservatism A set of beliefs that includes a limited role for the national government in helping individuals, support for traditional values and lifestyles, and a cautious response to change.

Conservative Coalition An alliance of Republicans and southern Democrats that historically formed in the House or the Senate to oppose liberal legislation and support conservative legislation.

Constituent One of the persons represented by a legislator or other elected or appointed official.

Constitutional Power A power vested in the president by Article II of the Constitution.

Containment A U.S. diplomatic policy adopted by the Truman administration to contain Communist power within its existing boundaries.

Continuing Resolution A temporary funding law that Congress passes when an appropriations bill has not been decided by the beginning of the new fiscal year on October 1.

Cooperative Federalism A model of federalism in which the states and the national government cooperate in solving problems.

Corrupt Practices Acts A series of acts passed by Congress in an attempt to limit and regulate the size and sources of contributions and expenditures in political campaigns.

Credentials Committee A committee used by political parties at their national conventions to determine which delegates may participate. The committee inspects the claim of each prospective delegate to be seated as a legitimate representative of his or her state.

Criminal Law The law that defines crimes and provides punishment for violations. In criminal cases, the government is the prosecutor.

D

***De Facto* Segregation** Racial segregation that occurs because of past social and economic conditions and residential racial patterns.

***De Jure* Segregation** Racial segregation that occurs because of laws or administrative decisions by public agencies.

Dealignment A decline in party loyalties that reduces long-term party commitment.

Defamation of Character Wrongfully hurting a person's good reputation. The law imposes a general duty on all persons to refrain from making false, defamatory statements about others.

Defense Policy A subset of national security policies having to do with the U.S. armed forces.

Democracy A system of government in which political authority is vested in the people. The term is derived from the Greek words *demos* ("the people") and *kratos* ("authority").

Democratic Party One of the two major American political parties evolving out of the Republican Party of Thomas Jefferson.

Democratic Republic A republic in which representatives elected by the people make and enforce laws and policies.

Détente A French word meaning a relaxation of tensions. The term characterized U.S.-Soviet relations as they developed under President Richard Nixon and Secretary of State Henry Kissinger.

Devolution The transfer of powers from a national or central government to a state or local government.

Diplomacy The process by which states carry on political relations with each other; settling conflicts among nations by peaceful means.

Diplomatic Recognition The formal acknowledgment of a foreign government as legitimate.

Direct Democracy A system of government in which political decisions are made by the people directly, rather than by their elected representatives; probably attained most easily in small political communities.

Direct Primary An intraparty election in which the voters select the candidates who will run on a party's ticket in the subsequent general election.

Direct Technique An interest group activity that involves interaction with government officials to further the group's goals.

Discharge Petition A procedure by which a bill in the House of Representatives can be forced (discharged) out of a committee that has refused to report it for consideration by the House. The petition must be signed by an absolute majority (218) of representatives and is used only on rare occasions.

Dissenting Opinion A separate opinion in which a judge dissents from (disagrees with) the conclusion reached by the majority on the court and expounds his or her own views about the case.

Diversity of Citizenship The condition that exists when the parties to a lawsuit are citizens of different states or when the parties are citizens of a U.S. state and citizens or the government of a foreign country. Diversity of citizenship can provide a basis for federal jurisdiction.

Divided Government A situation in which one major political party controls the presidency and the other controls the chambers of Congress, or in which one party controls a state governorship and the other controls the state legislature.

Divided Opinion Public opinion that is polarized between two quite different positions.

Domestic Policy All government laws, planning, and actions that concern internal issues of national importance, such as poverty, crime, and the environment.

Dominant Culture The values, customs, and language established by the group or groups that traditionally have controlled politics and government in a society.

Dual Federalism A model of federalism in which the states and the national government each remain supreme within their own spheres. The doctrine looks on nation and state as co-equal sovereign powers. Neither the state government nor the national government should interfere in the other's sphere.

E

Earmarks Special provisions in legislation to set aside funds for projects that have not passed an impartial evaluation by agencies of the executive branch. Also known as "pork."

Earned-Income Tax Credit (EITC) Program A government program that helps low-income workers by giving back part or all of their Social Security taxes.

Economic Aid Assistance to other nations in the form of grants, loans, or credits to buy the assisting nation's products.

Elastic Clause, or Necessary and Proper Clause The clause in Article I, Section 8, that grants Congress the power to do whatever is necessary to execute its specifically delegated powers.

Elector A member of the electoral college, which selects the president and vice president. Each state's electors are chosen in each presidential election year according to state laws.

Electoral College A group of persons, called electors, who are selected by the voters in each state. This group officially elects the president and the vice president of the United States.

Elite Theory A perspective holding that society is ruled by a small number of people who exercise power to further their self-interest.

Emergency Power An inherent power exercised by the president during a period of national crisis.

Enabling Legislation A statute enacted by Congress that authorizes the creation of an administrative agency and specifies the name, purpose, composition, functions, and powers of the agency being created.

Enumerated Power A power specifically granted to the national government by the Constitution. The first seventeen clauses of Article I, Section 8, specify most of the enumerated powers of Congress.

Environmental Impact Statement (EIS) A report that must show the costs and benefits of major federal actions that could significantly affect the quality of the environment.

Equality As a political value, the idea that all people are of equal worth.

Era of Good Feelings The years from 1817 to 1825, when James Monroe was president and there was, in effect, no political opposition.

Establishment Clause The part of the First Amendment prohibiting the establishment of a church officially supported by the national government. It is applied to questions of the legality of giving state and local government aid to religious organizations and schools, allowing or requiring school prayers, and teaching evolution versus intelligent design.

Exclusionary Rule A judicial policy prohibiting the admission at trial of illegally seized evidence.

Executive Agreement An international agreement between chiefs of state that does not require legislative approval.

Executive Agreement An international agreement made by the president, without senatorial ratification, with the head of a foreign state.

Executive Budget The budget prepared and submitted by the president to Congress.

Executive Office of the President (EOP) An organization established by President Franklin D. Roosevelt to assist the president in carrying out major duties.

Executive Order A rule or regulation issued by the president that has the effect of law. Executive orders can implement and give administrative effect to provisions in the U.S. Constitution, treaties, or statutes.

Executive Privilege The right of executive officials to withhold information from or to refuse to appear before a legislative committee.

Exports Goods and services produced domestically for sale abroad.

Expressed Power A power of the president that is expressly written into the Constitution or into statutory law.

F

Faction A group or bloc in a legislature or political party that is trying to obtain power or benefits.

Fall Review The annual process in which the Office of Management and Budget, after receiving formal federal agency requests for funding for the next fiscal year, reviews the requests, makes changes, and submits its recommendations to the president.

Fascism A twentieth-century ideology—often totalitarian—that exalts the national collective united behind an absolute ruler. Fascism rejects liberal individualism, values action over rational deliberation, and glorifies war.

Federal Mandate A requirement in federal legislation that forces states and municipalities to comply with certain rules.

Federal Open Market Committee The most important body within the Federal Reserve System. The Federal Open Market Committee decides how monetary policy should be carried out.

Federal Question A question that has to do with the U.S. Constitution, acts of Congress, or treaties. A federal question provides a basis for federal jurisdiction.

Federal Register A publication of the U.S. government that prints executive orders, rules, and regulations.

Federal Reserve System (the Fed) The agency created by Congress in 1913 to serve as the nation's central banking organization.

Federal System A system of government in which power is divided between a central government and regional, or subdivisional, governments. Each level must have some domain in which its policies are dominant and some genuine political or constitutional guarantee of its authority.

Federalist The name given to one who was in favor of the adoption of the U.S. Constitution and the creation of a federal union with a strong central government.

Feminism The movement that supports political, economic, and social equality for women.

Fertility Rate A statistic that measures the average number of children that women in a given group are expected to have over the course of a lifetime.

Filibuster The use of the Senate's tradition of unlimited debate as a delaying tactic to block a bill.

First Budget Resolution A resolution passed by Congress in May that sets overall revenue and spending goals for the following fiscal year.

Fiscal Policy The federal government's use of taxation and spending policies to affect overall business activity.

Fiscal Year (FY) A twelve-month period that is used for bookkeeping, or accounting, purposes. Usually, the fiscal year does not coincide with the calendar year. For example, the federal government's fiscal year runs from October 1 through September 30.

Focus Group A small group of individuals who are led in discussion by a professional consultant in order to gather opinions on and responses to candidates and issues.

Food Stamps Benefits issued by the federal government to low-income individuals to be used for the purchase of food; originally provided as coupons but now typically provided electronically through a card similar to a debit card.

Foreign Policy A nation's external goals and the techniques and strategies used to achieve them.

Foreign Policy Process The steps by which foreign policy goals are decided and acted on.

Franking A policy that enables members of Congress to send material through the mail by substituting their facsimile signature (frank) for postage.

Free Exercise Clause The provision of the First Amendment guaranteeing the free exercise of religion. The provision constrains the national government from prohibiting individuals from practicing the religion of their choice.

Free Rider Problem The difficulty interest groups face in recruiting members when the benefits they achieve can be gained without joining the group.

Front-Loading The practice of moving presidential primary elections to the early part of the campaign to maximize the impact of these primaries on the nomination.

Front-Runner The presidential candidate who appears to be ahead at a given time in the primary season.

G

Gag Order An order issued by a judge restricting the publication of news about a trial or a pretrial hearing to protect the accused's right to a fair trial.

Gender Discrimination Any practice, policy, or procedure that denies equality of treatment to an individual or to a group because of gender.

Gender Gap The difference between the percentage of women who vote for a particular candidate and the percentage of men who vote for the candidate.

General Jurisdiction Exists when a court's authority to hear cases is not significantly restricted. A court of general jurisdiction normally can hear a broad range of cases.

Generational Effect A long-lasting effect of the events of a particular time on the political opinions of those who came of political age at that time.

Gerrymandering The drawing of legislative district boundary lines for the purpose of obtaining partisan or factional advantage. A district is said to be gerrymandered when its shape is manipulated by the dominant party to maximize electoral strength at the expense of the minority party.

Government The preeminent institution within society in which decisions are made that resolve conflicts or allocate benefits and privileges. It is unique because it has the ultimate authority for making decisions and establishing political values.

Government Corporation An agency of government that administers a quasi-business enterprise. These corporations are used when activities are primarily commercial.

Government in the Sunshine Act A law that requires all committee-directed federal agencies to conduct their business regularly in public session.

Grandfather Clause A device used by southern states to disenfranchise African Americans. It restricted voting to those whose grandfathers had voted before 1867.

Great Compromise The compromise between the New Jersey and Virginia plans that created one chamber of the Congress based on population and one chamber representing each state equally; also called the Connecticut Compromise.

Gross Domestic Product (GDP) The dollar value of all final goods and services produced in a one-year period.

Gross Public Debt The net public debt plus interagency borrowings within the government.

H

Hatch Act An act passed in 1939 that restricted the political activities of government employees. It also prohibited a political group from spending more than $3 million in any campaign and limited individual contributions to a campaign committee to $5,000.

Head of State The role of the president as ceremonial head of the government.

Hispanic Someone who can claim a heritage from a Spanish-speaking country (other than Spain). The term is used only in the United States or other countries that receive immigrants—Spanish-speaking persons living in Spanish-speaking countries do not normally apply the term to themselves.

I

Ideology A comprehensive set of beliefs about the nature of people and about the role of an institution or government.

Impeachment An action by the House of Representatives to accuse the president, vice president, or other civil officers of the United States of committing "Treason, Bribery, or other high Crimes and Misdemeanors."

Imports Goods and services produced outside a country but sold within its borders.

Incarceration Rate The number of persons held in jail or prison for every 100,000 persons in a particular population group.

Income Transfer A transfer of income from some individuals in the economy to other individuals. This is generally done by government action.

Incorporation Theory The view that most of the protections of the Bill of Rights apply to state governments through the Fourteenth Amendment's due process clause.

Independent A voter or candidate who does not identify with a political party.

Independent Executive Agency A federal agency that is not part of a cabinet department but reports directly to the president.

Independent Expenditures Nonregulated contributions from PACs, organizations, and individuals. The funds may be spent on advertising or other campaign activities so long as those expenditures are not coordinated with those of a candidate.

Independent Regulatory Agency An agency outside the major executive departments charged with making and implementing rules and regulations.

Indirect Technique A strategy employed by interest groups that uses third parties to influence government officials.

Inherent Power A power of the president derived from the statements in the Constitution that "the executive Power shall be vested in a President" and that the president should "take Care that the Laws be faithfully executed"; defined through practice rather than through law.

Initiative A procedure by which voters can propose a law or a constitutional amendment.

In-Kind Subsidy A good or service—such as food stamps, housing, or medical care—provided by the government to low-income groups.

Institution An ongoing organization that performs certain functions for society.

Instructed Delegate A legislator who is an agent of the voters who elected him or her and who votes according to the views of constituents regardless of personal beliefs.

Intelligence Community The government agencies that gather information about the capabilities and intentions of foreign governments or that engage in covert actions.

Interest Group An organized group of individuals sharing common objectives who actively attempt to influence policymakers.

Interstate Compact An agreement between two or more states. Agreements on minor matters are made without congressional consent, but any compact that tends to increase the power of the contracting states relative to other states or relative to the national government generally requires the consent of Congress.

Iron Triangle The three-way alliance among legislators, bureaucrats, and interest groups to make or preserve policies that benefit their respective interests.

Islamism A political ideology based on a radical and fundamentalist interpretation of Islam. Islamists reject all Western democratic values and often call for a worldwide Islamist political order. Radical Islamists have provided the membership of many recent terrorist groups.

Isolationist Foreign Policy A policy of abstaining from an active role in international affairs or alliances, which characterized U.S. foreign policy toward Europe during most of the 1800s.

Issue Advocacy Advertising paid for by interest groups that support or oppose a candidate or a candidate's position on an issue without mentioning voting or elections.

Issue Network A group of individuals or organizations—which may consist of legislators and legislative staff members, interest group leaders, bureaucrats, the media, scholars, and other experts—that supports a particular policy position on a given issue.

J

Joint Committee A legislative committee composed of members from both chambers of Congress.

Judicial Activism A doctrine holding that the federal judiciary should take an active role by using its powers to check the activities of governmental bodies when those bodies exceed their authority.

Judicial Implementation The way in which court decisions are translated into action.

Judicial Restraint A doctrine holding that the courts should defer to the decisions made by the elected representatives of the people in the legislative and executive branches.

Judicial Review The power of the Supreme Court and other courts to declare unconstitutional federal or state laws and other acts of government.

Jurisdiction The authority of a court to decide certain cases. Not all courts have the authority to decide all cases. Where a case arises and what its subject matter is are two jurisdictional issues.

Justiciable Question A question that may be raised and reviewed in court.

K

Keynesian Economics A school of economic thought that tends to favor active federal government policymaking to stabilize economy-wide fluctuations, usually by implementing discretionary fiscal policy.

Kitchen Cabinet The informal advisers to the president.

L

Labor Movement Generally, the economic and political expression of working-class interests; politically, the organization of working-class interests.

Latent Interests Public-policy interests that are not recognized or addressed by a group at a particular time.

Latino An alternative to the term Hispanic that is preferred by many.

Lawmaking The process of establishing the legal rules that govern society.

Legislature A governmental body primarily responsible for the making of laws.

Legitimacy Popular acceptance of the right and power of a government or other entity to exercise authority.

Libel A written defamation of a person's character, reputation, business, or property rights.

Liberalism A set of beliefs that includes the advocacy of positive government action to improve the welfare of individuals, support for civil rights, and tolerance for political and social change.

Libertarianism A political ideology based on skepticism or opposition toward most government activities.

Liberty The greatest freedom of the individual that is consistent with the freedom of other individuals in the society.

Lifestyle Effect A phenomenon in which certain attitudes occur at certain chronological ages.

Limited Government A government with powers that are limited either through a written document or through widely shared beliefs.

Limited Jurisdiction Exists when a court's authority to hear cases is restricted to certain types of claims, such as tax claims or bankruptcy petitions.

Line Organization In the federal government, an administrative unit that is directly accountable to the president.

Line-Item Veto The power of an executive to veto individual lines or items within a piece of legislation without vetoing the entire bill.

Literacy Test A test administered as a precondition for voting, often used to prevent African Americans from exercising their right to vote.

Litigate To engage in a legal proceeding or seek relief in a court of law; to carry on a lawsuit.

Lobbyist An organization or individual who attempts to influence legislation and the administrative decisions of government.

Logrolling An arrangement in which two or more members of Congress agree in advance to support each other's bills.

Loophole A legal method by which individuals and businesses are allowed to reduce the tax liabilities owed to the government.

Loose Monetary Policy Monetary policy that makes credit inexpensive and abundant, possibly leading to inflation.

M

Madisonian Model A structure of government proposed by James Madison in which the powers of the government are separated into three branches: executive, legislative, and judicial.

Majoritarianism A political theory holding that in a democracy, the government ought to do what the majority of the people want.

Majority The age at which a person is entitled by law to the right to manage her or his own affairs and to the full enjoyment of civil rights. Or more than 50 percent.

Majority Leader of the House A legislative position held by an important party member in the House of Representatives. The majority leader is selected by the majority party in caucus or conference to foster cohesion among party members and to act as spokesperson for the majority party in the House.

Majority Opinion A court opinion reflecting the views of the majority of the judges.

Majority Rule A basic principle of democracy asserting that the greatest number of citizens in any political unit should select officials and determine policies.

Mandatory Retirement Forced retirement when a person reaches a certain age.

Material Incentive A reason or motive based on the desire to enjoy certain economic benefits or opportunities.

Media The channels of mass communication.

Medicaid A joint state-federal program that provides medical care to the poor (including indigent elderly persons in nursing homes). The program is funded out of general government revenues.

Medicare A federal health-insurance program that covers U.S. residents over the age of sixty-five. The costs are met by a tax on wages and salaries.

Merit System The selection, retention, and promotion of government employees on the basis of competitive examinations.

Minority Leader of the House The party leader elected by the minority party in the House.

Monetary Policy The utilization of changes in the amount of money in circulation to alter credit markets, employment, and the rate of inflation.

Monopolistic Model A model of bureaucracy that compares bureaucracies to monopolistic business firms. Lack of competition in either circumstance leads to inefficient and costly operations.

Monroe Doctrine A policy statement made by President James Monroe in 1823, which set out three principles: (1) European nations should not establish new colonies in the Western Hemisphere, (2) European nations should not intervene in the affairs of independent nations of the Western Hemisphere, and (3) the United States would not interfere in the affairs of European nations.

Moral Idealism A philosophy that sees nations as normally willing to cooperate and agree on moral standards for conduct.

N

National Committee A standing committee of a national political party established to direct and coordinate party activities between national party conventions.

National Convention The meeting held every four years by each major party to select presidential and vice-presidential candidates, write a platform, choose a national committee, and conduct party business.

National Health Insurance Programs offered in most advanced countries under which the central government provides basic health insurance to all citizens. In most such plans, the program is funded by taxes on wages or salaries.

National Security Council (NSC) An agency in the Executive Office of the President that advises the president on national security.

National Security Policy Foreign and domestic policy designed to protect the nation's independence and political and economic integrity; policy that is concerned with the safety and defense of the nation.

Natural Rights Rights held to be inherent in natural law, not dependent on governments. John Locke stated that natural law, being superior to human law, specifies certain rights of "life, liberty, and property." These rights, altered to become "life, liberty, and the pursuit of happiness," are asserted in the Declaration of Independence.

Necessaries Things necessary for existence. In contract law, necessaries include whatever is reasonably necessary for suitable subsistence as measured by age, state, condition in life, and the like.

Negative Constituents Citizens who openly oppose the government's policies.

Net Public Debt The accumulation of all past federal government deficits; the total amount owed by the federal government to individuals, businesses, and foreigners.

Normal Trade Relations (NTR) Status A status granted through an international treaty by which each member nation must treat other members at least as well as it treats the country that receives its most favorable treatment. This status was formerly known as *most-favored-nation status*.

O

Office of Management and Budget (OMB) A division of the Executive Office of the President. The OMB assists the president in preparing the annual budget, clearing and coordinating departmental agency budgets, and supervising the administration of the federal budget.

Office-Block, or Massachusetts, Ballot A form of general election ballot in which candidates for elective office are grouped together under the title of each office. It emphasizes voting for the office and the individual candidate, rather than for the party.

Oligarchy Rule by a few.

Ombudsperson A person who hears and investigates complaints by private individuals against public officials or agencies.

Open Primary A primary in which any registered voter can vote (but must vote for candidates of only one party).

Opinion The statement by a judge or a court of the decision reached in a case. The opinion sets forth the applicable law and details the reasoning on which the ruling was based.

Opinion Leader One who is able to influence the opinions of others because of position, expertise, or personality.

Opinion Poll A method of systematically questioning a small, selected sample of respondents who are deemed representative of the total population.

Oral Arguments The verbal arguments presented in person by attorneys to an appellate court. Each attorney presents reasons to the court why the court should rule in her or his client's favor.

Order A state of peace and security. Maintaining order by protecting members of society from violence and criminal activity is the oldest purpose of government.

Oversight The process by which Congress follows up on laws it has enacted to ensure that they are being enforced and administered in the way Congress intended.

P

Pardon A release from the punishment for, or legal consequences of, a crime; a pardon can be granted by the president before or after a conviction.

Party Identification Linking oneself to a particular political party.

Party Identifier A person who identifies with a political party.

Party Organization The formal structure and leadership of a political party, including election committees; local, state, and national executives; and paid professional staff.

Party Platform A document drawn up at each national convention, outlining the policies, positions, and principles of the party.

Party-Column, or Indiana, Ballot A form of general-election ballot in which all of a party's candidates for elective office are arranged in one column under the party's label and symbol. It emphasizes voting for the party, rather than for the office or individual.

Party-in-Government All of the elected and appointed officials who identify with a political party.

Party-in-the-Electorate Those members of the general public who identify with a political party or who express a preference for one party over another.

Patronage The practice of rewarding faithful party workers and followers with government employment and contracts.

Peer Group A group consisting of members sharing common social characteristics. These groups play an important part in the socialization process, helping to shape attitudes and beliefs.

Pendleton Act (Civil Service Reform Act) An act that established the principle of employment on the basis of merit and created the Civil Service Commission to administer the personnel service.

Picket-Fence Federalism A model of federalism in which specific programs and policies (depicted as vertical pickets in a picket fence) involve all levels of government—national, state, and local (depicted by the horizontal boards in a picket fence).

Pluralism A theory that views politics as a conflict among interest groups. Political decision making is characterized by compromise and accommodation.

Plurality A number of votes cast for a candidate that is greater than the number of votes for any other candidate but not necessarily a majority.

Pocket Veto A special veto exercised by the chief executive after a legislative body has adjourned. Bills not signed by the chief executive die after a specified period of time. If Congress wishes to reconsider such a bill, it must be reintroduced in the following session of Congress.

Podcasting A method of distributing multimedia files, such as audio or video files, for downloading onto mobile devices or personal computers.

Police Power The authority to legislate for the protection of the health, morals, safety, and welfare of the people. In the United States, most police power is reserved to the states.

Political Action Committee (PAC) A committee set up by and representing a corporation, labor union, or special interest group. PACs raise and give campaign donations.

Political Consultant A paid professional hired to devise a campaign strategy and manage a campaign.

Political Culture A patterned set of ideas, values, and ways of thinking about government and politics.

Political Party A group of political activists who organize to win elections, operate the government, and determine public policy.

Political Question An issue that a court believes should be decided by the executive or legislative branch.

Political Realism A philosophy that sees each nation acting principally in its own interest.

Political Socialization The process by which people acquire political beliefs and values.

Political Trust The degree to which individuals express trust in the government and political institutions, usually measured through a specific series of survey questions.

Politics The process of resolving conflicts and deciding "who gets what, when, and how." More specifically, politics is the struggle over power or influence within organizations or informal groups that can grant or withhold benefits or privileges.

Poll Tax A special tax that must be paid as a qualification for voting. In 1964, the Twenty-fourth Amendment to the Constitution outlawed the poll tax in national elections, and in 1966 the Supreme Court declared it unconstitutional in all elections.

Popular Sovereignty The concept that ultimate political authority is based on the will of the people.

Precedent A court rule bearing on subsequent legal decisions in similar cases. Judges rely on precedents in deciding cases.

President Pro Tempore The temporary presiding officer of the Senate in the absence of the vice president.

Presidential Primary A statewide primary election of delegates to a political party's national convention, held to determine a party's presidential nominee.

Prior Restraint Restraining an activity before it has actually occurred. When expression is involved, this means censorship.

Privatization   The replacement of government services with services provided by private firms.

Progressive Tax   A tax that rises in percentage terms as incomes rise.

Property   Anything that is or may be subject to ownership. As conceived by the political philosopher John Locke, the right to property is a natural right superior to human law (laws made by government).

Public Agenda   Issues that are perceived by the political community as meriting public attention and governmental action.

Public Figure   A public official, a public employee who exercises substantial governmental power, or any other person, such as a movie star, known to the public because of his or her position or activities.

Public Interest   The best interests of the overall community; the national good, rather than the narrow interests of a particular group.

Public Opinion   The aggregate of individual attitudes or beliefs shared by some portion of the adult population.

Purposive Incentive   A reason for supporting or participating in the activities of a group that is based on agreement with the goals of the group. For example, someone with a strong interest in human rights might have a purposive incentive to join Amnesty International.

R

Ratification   Formal approval.

Rational Ignorance Effect   An effect produced when people purposely and rationally decide not to become informed on an issue because they believe that their vote on the issue is not likely to be a deciding one; a lack of incentive to seek the necessary information to cast an intelligent vote.

Realignment   A process in which a substantial group of voters switches party allegiance, producing a long-term change in the political landscape.

Reapportionment   The allocation of seats in the House of Representatives to each state after each census.

Recall   A procedure allowing the people to vote to dismiss an elected official from state office before his or her term has expired.

Recession   Two or more successive quarters in which the economy shrinks instead of grows.

Redistricting   The redrawing of the boundaries of the congressional districts within each state.

Referendum   An electoral device whereby legislative or constitutional measures are referred by the legislature to the voters for approval or disapproval.

Registration   The entry of a person's name onto the list of registered voters for elections. To register, a person must meet certain legal requirements of age, citizenship, and residency.

Regressive Tax   A tax that falls in percentage terms as incomes rise.

Remand   To send a case back to the court that originally heard it.

Representation   The function of members of Congress as elected officials representing the views of their constituents.

Representative Assembly   A legislature composed of individuals who represent the population.

Representative Democracy   A form of government in which representatives elected by the people make and enforce laws and policies; may retain the monarchy in a ceremonial role.

Reprieve   A formal postponement of the execution of a sentence imposed by a court of law.

Republic   A form of government in which sovereign power rests with the people, rather than with a king or a monarch.

Republican Party   One of the two major American political parties. It emerged in the 1850s as an antislavery party and consisted of former northern Whigs and antislavery Democrats.

Reverse   To annul, or make void, a court ruling on account of some error or irregularity.

Reverse Discrimination   The situation in which an affirmative action program discriminates against those who do not have minority status.

Reverse-Income Effect   A tendency for wealthier states or regions to favor the Democrats and for less wealthy states or regions to favor the Republicans. The effect appears paradoxical because it reverses traditional patterns of support.

Rule of Four   A United States Supreme Court procedure by which four justices must vote to grant a petition for review if a case is to come before the full court.

Rules Committee   A standing committee of the House of Representatives that provides special rules under which specific bills can be debated, amended, and considered by the House.

S

Safe Seat   A district that returns a legislator with 55 percent of the vote or more.

Sampling Error   The difference between a sample's results and the true result if the entire population had been interviewed.

Second Budget Resolution   A resolution passed by Congress in September that sets "binding" limits on taxes and spending for the following fiscal year.

Select Committee   A temporary legislative committee established for a limited time period and for a special purpose.

Senate Majority Leader   The chief spokesperson of the majority party in the Senate, who directs the legislative program and party strategy.

Senate Minority Leader   The party officer in the Senate who commands the minority party's opposition to the policies of the majority party and directs the legislative program and strategy of his or her party.

Senatorial Courtesy   In federal district court judgeship nominations, a tradition allowing a senator to veto a judicial appointment in his or her state.

Seniority System   A custom followed in both chambers of Congress specifying that the member of the majority party with the longest term of continuous service will be given preference when a committee chairperson (or a holder of some other significant post) is selected.

Separate-but-Equal Doctrine   The doctrine holding that separate-but-equal facilities do not violate the equal protection clause of the Fourteenth Amendment to the U.S. Constitution.

Separation of Powers   The principle of dividing governmental powers among different branches of government.

Service Sector   The sector of the economy that provides services—such as health care, banking, and education—in contrast to the sector that produces goods.

Sexual Harassment   Unwanted physical or verbal conduct or abuse of a sexual nature that interferes with a recipient's job performance, creates a hostile work environment, or carries with it an implicit or explicit threat of adverse employment consequences.

Signing Statement   A written declaration that a president may make when signing a bill into law. Usually, such statements point out sections of the law that the president deems unconstitutional.

Slander   The public uttering of a false statement that harms the good reputation of another. The statement must be made to, or within the hearing of, persons other than the defamed party.

Social Contract A voluntary agreement among individuals to secure their rights and welfare by creating a government and abiding by its rules.

Social Movement A movement that represents the demands of a large segment of the public for political, economic, or social change.

Socialism A political ideology based on strong support for economic and social equality. Socialists traditionally envisioned a society in which major businesses were taken over by the government or by employee cooperatives.

Socioeconomic Status The value assigned to a person due to occupation or income. An upper-class person, for example, has high socioeconomic status.

Soft Money Campaign contributions unregulated by federal or state law, usually given to parties and party committees to help fund general party activities.

Solidary Incentive A reason or motive that follows from the desire to associate with others and to share with others a particular interest or hobby.

Sound Bite A brief, memorable comment that can easily be fit into news broadcasts.

Soviet Bloc The Soviet Union and the Eastern European countries that installed Communist regimes after World War II and were dominated by the Soviet Union.

Speaker of the House The presiding officer in the House of Representatives. The Speaker is always a member of the majority party and is the most powerful and influential member of the House.

Spin An interpretation of campaign events or election results that is favorable to the candidate's campaign strategy.

Spin Doctor A political campaign adviser who tries to convince journalists of the truth of a particular interpretation of events.

Splinter Party A new party formed by a dissident faction within a major political party. Often, splinter parties have emerged when a particular personality was at odds with the major party.

Split-Ticket Voting Voting for candidates of two or more parties for different offices, such as voting for a Republican presidential candidate and a Democratic congressional candidate.

Spoils System The awarding of government jobs to political supporters and friends.

Spring Review The annual process in which the Office of Management and Budget requires federal agencies to review their programs, activities, and goals and submit their requests for funding for the next fiscal year.

Standing Committee A permanent committee in the House or Senate that considers bills within a certain subject area.

Stare Decisis To stand on decided cases; the judicial policy of following precedents established by past decisions.

State A group of people occupying a specific area and organized under one government; may be either a nation or a subunit of a nation.

State Central Committee The principal organized structure of each political party within each state. This committee is responsible for carrying out policy decisions of the party's state convention.

State of the Union Message An annual message to Congress in which the president proposes a legislative program. The message is addressed not only to Congress but also to the American people and to the world.

Statutory Power A power created for the president through laws enacted by Congress.

Straight-Ticket Voting Voting exclusively for the candidates of one party.

Strategic Arms Limitation Treaty (SALT I) A treaty between the United States and the Soviet Union to stabilize the nuclear arms competition between the two countries. SALT I talks began in 1969, and agreements were signed on May 26, 1972.

Strict Construction A judicial philosophy that looks to the "letter of the law" when interpreting the Constitution or a particular statute.

Subpoena A legal writ requiring a person's appearance in court to give testimony.

Suffrage The right to vote; the franchise.

Sunset Legislation Laws requiring that existing programs be reviewed regularly for their effectiveness and be terminated unless specifically extended as a result of these reviews.

Superdelegate A party leader or elected official who is given the right to vote at the party's national convention. Superdelegates are not elected at the state level.

Supplemental Security Income (SSI) A federal program established to provide assistance to elderly persons and persons with disabilities.

Supremacy Clause The constitutional provision that makes the Constitution and federal laws superior to all conflicting state and local laws.

Supremacy Doctrine A doctrine that asserts the priority of national law over state laws. This principle is rooted in Article VI of the Constitution, which provides that the Constitution, the laws passed by the national government under its constitutional powers, and all treaties constitute the supreme law of the land.

Swing Voters Voters who frequently swing their support from one party to another.

Symbolic Speech Expression made through articles of clothing, gestures, movements, and other forms of nonverbal conduct. Symbolic speech is given substantial protection by the courts.

T

Tariff A tax on imports.

Technical Assistance The practice of sending experts in such areas as agriculture, engineering, or business to aid other nations.

Temporary Assistance to Needy Families (TANF) A state-administered program in which grants from the national government are used to provide welfare benefits. The TANF program replaced the Aid to Families with Dependent Children (AFDC) program.

Theocracy Literally, rule by God or the gods; in practice, rule by religious leaders, typically self-appointed.

Third Party A political party other than the two major political parties (Republican and Democratic).

Tight Monetary Policy Monetary policy that makes credit expensive in an effort to slow the economy.

Tipping A phenomenon that occurs when a group that is becoming more numerous over time grows large enough to change the political balance in a district, state, or country.

Totalitarian Regime A form of government that controls all aspects of the political and social life of a nation.

Tracking Poll A poll taken for the candidate on a nearly daily basis as election day approaches.

Trial Court The court in which most cases begin.

Truman Doctrine The policy adopted by President Harry Truman in 1947 to halt Communist expansion in southeastern Europe.

Trustee A legislator who acts according to her or his conscience and the broad interests of the entire society.

Twelfth Amendment Adopted in 1804, an amendment to the Constitution that requires the separate election of the president and vice president by the electoral college.

Twenty-fifth Amendment A 1967 amendment to the Constitution that establishes procedures for filling presidential and vice-presidential vacancies and makes provisions for presidential incapacity.

Two-Party System A political system in which only two parties have a reasonable chance of winning.

U

U.S. Treasury Bond Debt issued by the federal government.

Unanimous Opinion A court opinion or determination on which all judges agree.

Unicameral Legislature A legislature with only one legislative chamber, as opposed to a bicameral (two-chamber) legislature, such as the U.S. Congress. Today, Nebraska is the only state in the Union with a unicameral legislature.

Unit Rule A rule by which all of a state's electoral votes are cast for the presidential candidate receiving a plurality of the popular vote in that state.

Unitary System A centralized governmental system in which ultimate governmental authority rests in the hands of the national, or central, government.

Universal Health Insurance Any of several possible programs to provide health insurance to everyone in the country. The central government does not necessarily provide the insurance itself, but may subsidize the purchase of insurance from private insurance companies.

Universal Suffrage The right of all adults to vote for their representatives.

V

Veto Message The president's formal explanation of a veto when legislation is returned to Congress.

Voter Turnout The percentage of citizens taking part in the election process; the number of eligible voters that actually "turn out" on election day to cast their ballots.

W

War Powers Resolution A law passed in 1973 spelling out the conditions under which the president can commit troops without congressional approval.

Washington Community Indiviuals regularly involved with politics in Washington, D.C.

Watergate Break-In The 1972 illegal entry into the Democratic National Committee offices by participants in President Richard Nixon's reelection campaign.

Weberian Model A model of bureaucracy developed by the German sociologist Max Weber, who viewed bureaucracies as rational, hierarchical organizations in which decisions are based on logical reasoning.

Whig Party A major party in the United States during the first half of the nineteenth century, formally established in 1836. The Whig Party was anti-Jackson and represented a variety of regional interests.

Whip A member of Congress who aids the majority or minority leader of the House or the Senate.

Whistleblower Someone who brings to public attention gross governmental inefficiency or an illegal action.

White House Office The personal office of the president, which tends to presidential political needs and manages the media.

White Primary A state primary election that restricts voting to whites only; outlawed by the Supreme Court in 1944.

Writ of *Certiorari* An order issued by a higher court to a lower court to send up the record of a case for review.

Writ of *Habeas Corpus* *Habeas corpus* means, literally, "you have the body." A writ of *habeas corpus* is an order that requires jailers to bring a prisoner before a court or a judge and explain why the person is being held.

INDEX

A

AARP
  accomplishments of, 235
  budget of, 235
  contacting, 509
  large membership of, 227, 235–236, 237, 245
  material incentives to join, 227
  power of, 227, 235–236, 237, 245
  on privatization of Social Security, 504
ABA (American Bar Association), 232
ABC TV, 320, 328
Aberbach, Joel, 429
Abington School District v. Schempp, 117
ABM (Anti-Ballistic Missile) Treaty (1972), 385
Abortion(s)
  clinic protests against, 132
  Democrats versus Republicans on, 264
  as major issue, 58
  O'Connor's view shift on, 460
  partial-birth, 132–133, 449, 461–462
  privacy rights and, 14, 131–133
  proposed constitutional amendment on, 464
  public opinion regarding, 215
  Religious Right on, 266
  Roe v. Wade and, 14n, 131–132, 133
  special interest groups and, 58, 235
Abramoff, Jack, 236, 243
Absentee ballots, 309, 314, 316
Abu Ghraib prison, 490, 526
Accuracy, of opinion polls, 206
Accuracy in Media, 332
Accused, rights of. *See also* Crime(s)
  extending, 137–138
  knock and announce rule and, 449, 460
  rights of society versus, 136–139
ACLU. *See* American Civil Liberties Union
Acquisitive model of bureaucracy, 413
ActBlue (Democratic Party) Web site, 351
Actual malice, 128
ADA (Americans with Disabilities Act, 1990), 176–177
Adams, John, 13, 255, 402
Adams, John Quincy, 13, 256, 273, 307, 379
Adams, Samuel, 47
Adarand Constructors, Inc. v. Peña, 174
Addams, Jane, 259
Addington, David, 450
ADEA (Age Discrimination in Employment Act, 1967), 175–176
Administrative agencies, 414
  capture and, 420
  deregulation and reregulation of, 420–421
  federal, number of civilian employees of, 415
  independent executive, 418
    selected, listed, 420
  independent regulatory (*See* Independent regulatory agencies)
  regulations of (*See* Government regulation(s))
Administrative Office of the United States Courts, 457
Administrative Procedure Act (1946), 394
Adoption, gay males and lesbians and, 181
Advertising
  "daisy girl," 322–323
  FECA limits on, 295
  First Amendment protection of, 123
  by interest groups, 234–235, 240–241
  media influences and, 198

  microtargeting, 199
  National Organization for Women formation and, 226
  political, 199, 289, 292, 293, 294, 298, 322
  for private lotteries, 80
  shaping public opinion through, 192
  during Super Bowl, 329
  swing voters and, 281
  television, 322–323
Advice and consent, 345, 384, 457–458
AEDPA (Antiterrorism and Effective Death Penalty Act, 1996), 483
AFDC (Aid to Families with Dependent Children), 95, 97, 481
Affirmation of judgment, 453
Affirmative action
  on campus, 127
  defined, 172
  further limits on, 174
  future of, 174–175
  in India, 173
Afghanistan
  American attacks on al Qaeda camps and Taliban regime in, 522, 535
  enemy combatants captured in, 450
  poll of service members returning from, 180
  Taliban government in, 517
  Taliban militants in, 523
  U.S. and war in, 491
AFL (American Federation of Labor), 230
AFL-CIO, 230–231
  Committee on Political Education of, 230
  Public Employee Department of, 232
Africa
  America's world role and population growth in, 532
  homicide rates in U.S. versus, 488
  southern, AIDS epidemic in, 534
  terrorist bombings of American embassies in, 527
African Americans. *See also* Segregation; Slaves, slavery
  Black Muslims and, 155
  Black power and, 155
  citizenship for, 92
  civil rights for, 15, 98, 149–160
  consequences of slavery and, 149–154
  equal treatment under the law for, 98
  equality and, 149
  extralegal methods of enforcing white supremacy and, 152
  Freedmen's Villages for, 93
  Hispanics and, 159
  incarceration effects on, 490
  incarceration rate for, 489
  Internet use by, 211
  lingering social and economic disparities and, 159–160
  lynching and, 152
  mistakes by election officials and, 310
  New Deal programs, Democratic Party and, 258, 259
  nonviolent demonstrations by, 154–155
  party identification among, 201, 202
  political participation by, 158
  in population, 149, 170
  as presidential candidates, 378
  public officials, 291
  race riots and, 152, 157
  school integration and, 153–154
  schools with 90% minority enrollment and, 154

  separate-but-equal doctrine and, 56, 151, 152–153
  states' rights after Civil War and, 93
  support for Democratic Party by, 260
  uninsured, 477
  voter turnout by, 314, 315
  voting rights for, 10, 93, 150, 151–152, 156–157, 316–317
  Wilson administration and, 258
Age
  discrimination on basis of, 175–176, 185, 462
  health care costs and, 475–476
  of majority, 183
  right to vote and, 182, 234, 317
  of Social Security benefit eligibility, 504
  uninsured and, 478
  voter registration and, 317
  voter turnout and, 182, 314
Age Discrimination in Employment Act (ADEA, 1967), 175–176
Agenda building, 474
Agenda setting
  by Congress, 340
  defined, 197, 344
  by media, 197, 198, 214, 319
Agnew, Spiro, 403
Agricultural Adjustment Act
  of 1933, 95, 230n, 473
  of 1938, 230n
Agricultural interest groups, 227, 433–434
Ahmadinejad, Mahmoud, 7, 386, 518
Aid to Families with Dependent Children (AFDC), 95, 97, 481
AIDS (acquired immune deficiency syndrome), 176, 534
AIPAC (American Israel Public Affairs Committee), 235, 237
Air pollution. *See also* Pollution
  federalism and control of, 99
  national policy on, 492
  state initiatives on, 83
Air travelers
  on effectiveness of antiterrorism rules, 521–522
  Transportation Security Administration screening luggage of, 78–79
al Qaeda. *See also* Terrorism, terrorists
  attempts to buy components for nuclear bomb by, 527
  defined, 22n
  ideology of, 22
  in Iraq, 526
  September 11, 2001 terrorist attacks and, 22, 517
  United Arab Emirates and, 236
al Sadr, Muqtada, 22, 525–526, 527
Albanian Issues Caucus, 357
Albright, Madeleine, 165
Alden v. Maine, 101n
Alien "removal courts," 450
Alito, Samuel, 57, 457, 459, 460, 461
All Things Considered, 332
Allende, Salvador, 538
Alliance of Motion Picture and Television Producers, 232
Alterman, Eric, 331
AMA (American Medical Association), 232
Amazon.com, 412
America Online (AOL), 328
American Association of Community Colleges, 227

PRESIDENTS OF THE UNITED STATES

	Term of Service	Age at Inauguration	Political Party	College or University	Occupation or Profession
1. George Washington	1789–1797	57	None	Planter	
2. John Adams	1797–1801	61	Federalist	Harvard	Lawyer
3. Thomas Jefferson	1801–1809	57	Jeffersonian Republican	William and Mary	Planter, Lawyer
4. James Madison	1809–1817	57	Jeffersonian Republican	Princeton	Lawyer
5. James Monroe	1817–1825	58	Jeffersonian Republican	William and Mary	Lawyer
6. John Quincy Adams	1825–1829	57	Jeffersonian Republican	Harvard	Lawyer
7. Andrew Jackson	1829–1837	61	Democrat		Lawyer
8. Martin Van Buren	1837–1841	54	Democrat		Lawyer
9. William H. Harrison	1841	68	Whig	Hampden-Sydney	Soldier
10. John Tyler	1841–1845	51	Whig	William and Mary	Lawyer
11. James K. Polk	1845–1849	49	Democrat	U. of N. Carolina	Lawyer
12. Zachary Taylor	1849–1850	64	Whig		Soldier
13. Millard Fillmore	1850–1853	50	Whig		Lawyer
14. Franklin Pierce	1853–1857	48	Democrat	Bowdoin	Lawyer
15. James Buchanan	1857–1861	65	Democrat	Dickinson	Lawyer
16. Abraham Lincoln	1861–1865	52	Republican		Lawyer
17. Andrew Johnson	1865–1869	56	National Union†		Tailor
18. Ulysses S. Grant	1869–1877	46	Republican	U.S. Mil. Academy	Soldier
19. Rutherford B. Hayes	1877–1881	54	Republican	Kenyon	Lawyer
20. James A. Garfield	1881	49	Republican	Williams	Lawyer
21. Chester A. Arthur	1881–1885	51	Republican	Union	Lawyer
22. Grover Cleveland	1885–1889	47	Democrat		Lawyer
23. Benjamin Harrison	1889–1893	55	Republican	Miami	Lawyer
24. Grover Cleveland	1893–1897	55	Democrat		Lawyer
25. William McKinley	1897–1901	54	Republican	Allegheny College	Lawyer
26. Theodore Roosevelt	1901–1909	42	Republican	Harvard	Author
27. William H. Taft	1909–1913	51	Republican	Yale	Lawyer
28. Woodrow Wilson	1913–1921	56	Democrat	Princeton	Educator
29. Warren G. Harding	1921–1923	55	Republican		Editor
30. Calvin Coolidge	1923–1929	51	Republican	Amherst	Lawyer
31. Herbert C. Hoover	1929–1933	54	Republican	Stanford	Engineer
32. Franklin D. Roosevelt	1933–1945	51	Democrat	Harvard	Lawyer
33. Harry S. Truman	1945–1953	60	Democrat		Businessman
34. Dwight D. Eisenhower	1953–1961	62	Republican	U.S. Mil. Academy	Soldier
35. John F. Kennedy	1961–1963	43	Democrat	Harvard	Author
36. Lyndon B. Johnson	1963–1969	55	Democrat	Southwest Texas State	Teacher
37. Richard M. Nixon	1969–1974	56	Republican	Whittier	Lawyer
38. Gerald R. Ford‡	1974–1977	61	Republican	Michigan	Lawyer
39. James E. Carter, Jr.	1977–1981	52	Democrat	U.S. Naval Academy	Businessman
40. Ronald W. Reagan	1981–1989	69	Republican	Eureka College	Actor
41. George H. W. Bush	1989–1993	64	Republican	Yale	Businessman
42. Bill Clinton	1993–2001	46	Democrat	Georgetown	Lawyer
43. George W. Bush	2001–	54	Republican	Yale	Businessman
44. Barack Obama	2009–	47	Democrat	Harvard	Lawyer

*Church preference; never joined any church.
†The National Union Party consisted of Republicans and War Democrats. Johnson was a Democrat.
**Inaugurated Dec. 6, 1973, to replace Agnew, who resigned Oct. 10, 1973.